INTELLECTUAL PROPERTY LAW

INTELLECTUAL PROPERTY LAW

Text, Cases, and Materials

THIRD EDITION

Tanya Aplin and Jennifer Davis

OXFORD
UNIVERSITY PRESS

OXFORD
UNIVERSITY PRESS

Great Clarendon Street, Oxford, OX2 6DP,
United Kingdom

Oxford University Press is a department of the University of Oxford.
It furthers the University's objective of excellence in research, scholarship,
and education by publishing worldwide. Oxford is a registered trade mark of
Oxford University Press in the UK and in certain other countries

First edition 2009
Second edition 2013
Impression: 1

Published in the United States of America by Oxford University Press
198 Madison Avenue, New York, NY 10016, United States of America

British Library Cataloguing in Publication Data
Data available

Library of Congress Control Number: 2016950470

ISBN 978-0-19-874354-5

Printed in Great Britain by
Bell & Bain Ltd., Glasgow

PREFACE

Since the first edition of this text was published in 2009, intellectual property law has continued to evolve and its reach to expand. It has done so, not least to meet the challenges posed by new technology, novel methods of commerce, and greater expectations of privacy, to name but a few areas of considerable change. In preparing successive editions, we have sought to incorporate these changes in a way that does not vastly increase the weight of the book but does ensure its adequate coverage of this field of law. Thus, as with previous volumes, we have again sought to expose readers to the core legal concepts and debates within intellectual property law in a way that we hope readers will find both manageable and complete. It has also meant that while, in this edition, there is a general, introductory section on remedies, a full chapter detailing intellectual property law in action is now provided on the Online Resource Centre.

The book is configured so that it reflects what we see as important long-term developments in the evolution of intellectual property law. We have chosen to excerpt cases which are either authoritative, add something new to the existing legal corpus, or point the way to future developments. In recognition of the pervasive influence of the EU on UK intellectual property law, the book inevitably includes substantial extracts from Court of Justice rulings. We have also, as in the past, included coverage of major new developments in EU intellectual property legislation such as the introduction of a new Trade Mark Directive and Regulations and the new Trade Secrets Directive. (The Digital Single Market proposed directive and regulations were published too late, however, to be included.) Domestic legislative initiatives are also included such as key changes to the law of copyright and designs.

However, it is clearly the case that this edition appears at a time of some uncertainty. The UK is committed to negotiations which will ultimately lead to its exit from the European Union. Until that occurs, and the best estimate is that it will take a minimum of two years, a large amount of intellectual property law in the UK will continue to be derived from the EU as it has in the past. Indeed, even once the UK's withdrawal is complete, it will almost certainly take a number of years before its domestic law begins to diverge from EU intellectual property law in any substantial way. In this spirit, the third edition of *Intellectual Property Law: Text, Cases, and Materials*, like previous ones, will continue to recognize EU intellectual property law as a central component of UK intellectual property law and to treat it as such.

In preparing this new edition, we are grateful to the editorial team at OUP, especially Carol Barber, Sarah Stephenson, Joy Ruskin-Tompkins and Jonathon Price for their support. Thanks also to Graeme Dinwoodie, Matthew Fisher, Dev Gangjee, and Justin Koo for commenting on sections of the book. And thanks to Birgit Lintner and Gillian Sanders at Wolfson College for their willing assistance. Finally, special thanks must go to our family, loved ones, and friends for their good humour and patience.

We have sought to set out the law as at 30 June 2016.

Tanya Aplin and Jennifer Davis

ACKNOWLEDGEMENTS

We are grateful to the following for permission to reproduce copyright material and commercial documents:

Boyle, James: extract from James Boyle, 'The second enclosure movement and the construction of the public domain' (Winter/Spring 2003) 66(33) *Law and Contemporary Problems*, 58–62.

Buffalo Law Review: extract from R. Gutowski, 'The marriage of intellectual property and international trade in the TRIPs agreement: Strange bedfellows or a match made in heaven?' (1999) 47 *Buffalo Law Review* 754, 754–60.

Cambridge University Press: extracts from Huw Beverley-Smith, *The Commercial Appropriation of Personality* (CUP Cambridge, 2002), pp. 181–183; Donald S. Chisum, 'Common law and civil law approaches to patent claim interpretation: "Fence posts" and "sign posts" ' in David Vaver and Lionel Bently (eds), *Intellectual Property in the New Millennium: Essays in Honour of William R. Cornish* (CUP Cambridge, 2004), at p. 97; and Fritz Machlup and Edith Penrose, 'The patent controversy in the nineteenth century' (1950) 10 *The Journal of Economic History* 1, 9–26.

Edward Elgar: N. Lee, 'Public domain at the interface of trade mark and unfair competition law: The case of referential use of trade marks' in N. Lee, G. Westkamp, A. Kur and A. Ohly (eds), *Intellectual Property, Unfair Competition and Publicity: Convergences and Development* (Cheltenham; Edward Elgar, 2014), p.334. By permission of the publisher, the author and the editors.

Fordham Intellectual Property and Media Law Journal and Gervais, D.J.: extract from D. J. Gervais, 'The internationalization of intellectual property: New challenges from the very old and the very new' (2001–2) 12 *Fordham Intellectual Property Media and Entertainment Law Journal* 929, 955–65.

Georgetown University Law Center: extract from Justin Hughes, 'The Philosophy of Intellectual Property' 77 *Georgetown Law Journal* 287 (1988–9) 330, 337–338. Reprinted with permission of the publisher, Georgetown Law Journal © 1988.

Hackett Publishing Company, Inc.: extract from J. Locke, *The Second Treatise on Government, 1690* (Indianapolis, IN: Hackett Publishing, 1980), p. 19–21. Reprinted with permission of Hackett Publishing Company, Inc., All rights reserved.

Hart Publishing Limited: extract from Tanya Aplin, *Copyright Law in the Digital Society: The Challenges of Multimedia* (Hart Oxford, 2005), pp. 179–80. Used by permission of Bloomsbury Publishing Plc.

Harvard University Press: extract from *The Economic Structure of Intellectual Property Law* by William M. Landes and Richard A. Posner, Cambridge, Mass.: The Belknap Press of Harvard University Press, Copyright © 2003 by the President and Fellows of Harvard College.

Incorporated Council of Law Reporting for England and Wales: extracts from the Law Reports: Appeal Cases (AC), Business Law Reports (Bus LR), Chancery Division (Ch), Queen's Bench Division (QB), and Weekly Law Reports (WLR).

Kur, Annette: extract from 'Too common, too splendid, or "just right"?: Trade mark protection for product shapes', Max Planck Institute for Innovation and Competition Research Paper No. 14–17, 201, pp. 1–2.

Oxford University Press: extracts from Judith McNamara and Lucy Cradduck, 'Can we protect how we do what we do? A consideration of business method patents in Australia and Europe' (2008) *International Journal of Law and Information Technology* 96, 113–16 and Jennifer Davis, 'The Need to Leave Free for Others to Use and the Trade Mark Common' from *Trade Mark Use* edited by Jeremy Phillips & Ilanah Simon (2005), pp. 39–45. By permission of Oxford University Press.

Ridinghouse and Spence, Michael: extract from Michael Spence, 'Justifying copyright' in Daniel McClean and Karsten Schubert (eds), *Dear Images: Art, Copyright and Culture* (Ridinghouse Manchester, 2002), pp. 389–403.

Springer: extract from Huaiwen He, 'The development of free trade agreements and international protection of intellectual property rights in the WTO era—new bilateralism and its future' (2010) *IIC* 254, 257.

Sweet & Maxwell Ltd: extracts from Entertainment Law Review: J. Ginsburg, 'Moral rights in the common law system' [1990] *Ent LR* 121, 122; from European Intellectual Property Review: G. Black, 'Exploiting Image: Making a case for the legal regulation of publicity rights in the UK' [2011] *EIPR* 413, 415–16; L. Bently, 'The Return of Industrial Copyright' [2012] *EIPR* 654; from Intellectual Property Quarterly: J. Griffiths, 'Copyright law after Ashdown: Time to deal fairly with the public' [2002] *IPQ* 240, 257–59; H. Carty, 'Advertising, Publicity Rights and English Law' [2004] *IPQ* 209, 249–50; I. Stamatoudi, 'Moral rights of authors in England: The missing emphasis on the role of creators' [1997] *IPQ* 478, 498–500; H. Carty, 'Passing off: frameworks for liability debated' [2012] *IPQ* 106, 10; and extracts from Common Market Law Reports, Entertainment and Media Law Reports, European Copyright and Design Reports, European Patent Office Reports, European Trade Mark Reports, and Fleet Street Reports reproduced with permission of THOMSON REUTERS (PROFESSIONAL) UK LIMITED via PLSclear.

Taylor & Francis Group: extract from P. Drahos and J. Braithwaite, *Information Feudalism: Who Owns the Knowledge Economy?* (Earthscan London 2002), pp. 10–13. Reproduced with permission of Taylor & Francis Books UK.

University of Chicago Press: extracts from W. Landes and R. Posner, 'Trademark law: An economic perspective' (1987) 30(2) *Journal of Law and Economics* 265–309; and Mark A. Lemley, 'Ex Ante versus Ex Post Justifications for Intellectual Property' 71 *University of Chicago Law Review* [2004] 129, at 130–31.

John Wiley & Sons, Inc: extracts from D. Gangjee and R. Burrell, 'Because you're worth it: L'Oreal and the prohibition on free riding' (2010) 73(2) *Modern Law Review* 282–301; and E. C. Hettinger, 'Justifying intellectual property' (1989) 18 *Philosophy and Public Affairs* 31, 47–51. Permission conveyed through Copyright Clearence Center.

World Trade Organization: for extracts from the TRIPS Agreement. © World Trade Organization (WTO) 2016: <https://www.wto.org/english/tratop_e/trips_e/intel2_e.htm>.

Yale Law Journal: J. Litman, 'Breakfast with Batman: The public interest in the advertising age' (1999) 108 *Yale LJ* 1717, 1728–30.

Zed Books: extract from Vandana Shiva, *Protect or Plunder? Understanding Intellectual Property Rights* (Zed Books London, 2001) pp. 21–3, 26.

Every effort has been made to trace and contact the copyright holders but this has not been possible in all cases. If notified, the publisher will undertake to rectify any errors or omissions at the earliest opportunity.

OUTLINE TABLE OF CONTENTS

CONTENTS

TABLE OF CASES

Where cases are dealt with in detail the relevant page numbers are shown in **bold**.

TABLE OF LEGISLATION

Page references in **bold** indicate that the section is reproduced in the text

TABLE OF SECONDARY LEGISLATION

United Kingdom Statutory Instruments

EU Directives

TABLE OF INTERNATIONAL TREATIES AND CONVENTIONS

1

AN INTRODUCTION
TO INTELLECTUAL PROPERTY

1.1 INTRODUCTION

What is intellectual property law? In 2012, the Supreme Court of the United Kingdom declared that 'there is a general consensus as to its core content (patents for inventions, literary, dramatic, musical and artistic copyright, copyright in recordings, films and broadcasts, registered and unregistered design rights and trade marks ...), but no general consensus as to its limits.'[1] All of the rights identified by the Supreme Court will be considered in this book. Conventionally, intellectual property law textbooks have also encompassed other areas of the law, in particular those relating to confidential information, privacy, and databases. These too will be considered in later chapters.

It is not always obvious what unites these various areas of the law. The rights under the umbrella term, intellectual property, will apply to various types of subject matter to a differing extent. They may derive from either statute or common law and be acquired by formal registration or not, as the case may be. For example, copyright is a set of exclusive rights granted by statute in relation to literary and artistic creations (in a broad sense) that generally lasts for 70 years after the death of the author. A copyright arises through the act of creation and does not need to be registered. A patent is a monopoly right granted by statute for the commercial exploitation of an invention for a limited time, usually 20 years. Patents may only be acquired through registration. Trade marks indicate the origin of goods and services, and may be protected from misuse by third parties, either by rights acquired via registration or through evidence of use. The protection granted to a trade mark will last as long as it fulfils its role as an indicator of origin. Designs may be protected through the act of creation or by registration and there is a plurality of design rights available. They may extend to the aesthetic or functional aspects of the designs of industrial articles; protect against the copying or misuse of designs; and last between three and 25 years. Confidential information (which covers but is not limited to commercial secrets) is granted protection

[1] *Phillips v News Group Newspapers Ltd* [2012] UKSC 28, [2013] 1 AC 1, [20].

through the common law so long as it maintains its confidentiality. There is now also an action for misuse of private information, which has developed from the protection of confidential information, and offers a narrow privacy right. Finally, there is a statutory right for databases which is based on the substantial investment made in them. The right protects against extraction and reuse of data for at least 15 years.

What unites all of the different rights covered in this book, which are generally held to fall under the rubric 'intellectual property', is that the subject matter of protection is *intangible*, whether an intellectual creation, innovation, or information per se. This has two main consequences. First, in any litigation about infringement of intellectual property rights (IPRs), the courts must identify the boundaries of the subject matter being protected. Second, there is a difficulty in drawing the boundary between two intangible subject matters, when one is alleged to have infringed the other. Indeed, it may only be in the context of intellectual property litigation that the boundaries of the intangible subject matter will be delineated at all. This may perhaps appear to be more true for some IPRs than others. Thus, in the case of patents, the patent specification exists. It is a document that attempts to describe and define the invention that is protected. Similarly, UK trade marks must be capable of graphical representation to be registered. We will explore in later chapters the extent to which patent registration or trade mark registration can actually overcome the uncertainty as to the definition of intangible subject matter.

However one defines intellectual property, it is certainly true that over the past decades its exploitation has played an increasingly important role in the global economy. This is particularly so for the UK. As was pointed out in the Hargreaves Report of 2011: 'Every year in the last decade, investment by UK business in intangible assets has outstripped investment in tangible assets: by £137 billion to £104 billion in 2008.' Further, according to Hargreaves, 'Global trade in IP licences alone is worth more than £600 billion a year: five per cent of world trade and rising.' Another way of looking at the value of intellectual property is to recognize its importance to individual companies. Apple is now the most valuable company in the world. In large measure, its $700 billion worth derives from its powerful trade marks (the Apple brand alone is valued at $170.3 billion), from its innovative designs, and from the sophisticated functionality of its products rather than from its investment in manufacture of the physical items. Similarly, the immense value of Pfizer, like other pharmaceutical companies, derives from its patent portfolio rather than the cost of manufacturing the pharmaceuticals themselves. Given the value of intellectual property in global trade, it is not surprising that the scope and enforcement of IPRs has become an important political concern, addressed in international fora and by individual governments.

In this introductory chapter, we will consider the philosophical and justificatory context in which IPRs have developed and the international and regional frameworks which have emerged for their protection. In the process, we will examine some of the important contemporary debates surrounding IPRs and we will also consider the remedies for IP infringement. In succeeding chapters, these topics will be re-examined in relation to each of the individual IPRs.

1.2 JUSTIFICATIONS

IPRs grant to owners exclusive rights to do certain acts and prohibit others from doing these same acts. Such exclusive rights allow owners, for example, to charge higher prices for their intellectual products than they would otherwise be able to do and to restrict others from using them. Thus, the owner of a pharmaceutical patent will be able to charge more for the pharmaceutical than would otherwise be the case were it merely valued on its physical composition. To the extent that IPRs confer a monopoly, it has generally been thought necessary to justify this privilege. What follows is a general introduction to the justifications for IPRs. It is important to remember that some of these justifications are more apt for some IPRs than for others.

1.2.1 UNJUST ENRICHMENT

There is a significant amount of literature about the justifications for granting IPRs. The literature reveals a number of justificatory bases for intellectual property law of which the most important are the natural-rights, utilitarian, and economic justifications. But before we address these, it is worthwhile looking at a fairly simple justification, which is frequently invoked because of its common sense attraction. This is the argument from 'unjust enrichment', sometimes described as 'reaping without sowing'. Michael Spence discusses this argument and its limitations in the following extract.

M. Spence, 'Justifying copyright' in D. McClean and K. Schubert (eds),
Dear Images: Art, Copyright and Culture (Manchester: Ridinghouse, 2002),
pp. 389–403 at pp. 395–6

b. The Argument from Unjust Enrichment

The argument from unjust enrichment is that the unauthorised user of a work receives a benefit from its use and thereby 'reaps where she has not sown'. This behaviour of 'reaping without sowing' is assumed to be morally reprehensible. The phrase is biblical and assumes much of its rhetorical power from that resonance, although its equivalent biblical usage occurs in a New Testament parable in which the behaviour is neither condoned nor condemned. This principle, and the corresponding argument from unjust enrichment, are even more problematic than the argument from harm to the creator.

First, it is clear that the principle against reaping without sowing is not absolute. We all reap without sowing, and regard ourselves as justified in doing so, even without the consent, implicit or explicit, of those upon whose efforts we build. For example, the pioneer of a new style or technique in the visual arts might establish an artistic language and educate a public to understand it. The pioneer may wish to preserve the style or technique she develops for her own use, or for the use of those within her circle. But subsequent creators will imitate, adapt and expand that style or technique. Imitation—authorised and unauthorised—is a vital part of ongoing artistic discourse. To condemn all reaping without sowing would be to condemn all imitation and to stifle the development of artistic traditions. It would be to condemn us to live in a world of self-sufficiency mitigated only by agreement, a world in which few of us either could, or would want to, live.

Second, the principle against reaping without sowing is not an independent principle that can be used to justify entitlements to the exclusive use of a work. It is relevant, if at all, only once such an entitlement has been established. Given that the principle is not absolute, the question upon which its application depends is precisely when, if ever, it is wrong to reap without sowing. The answer implicit in the principle is that it is wrong to reap without sowing if someone else, and in particular the sower, has a stronger claim to that which is reaped. But this, of course, assumes that the sower does have a claim to that which is reaped and that its strength can be assessed. This assumption cannot be justified on the basis of the principle itself. In the copyright context, whether a particular unauthorised use constitutes an *unjust* enrichment depends upon whether, and how strongly a creator's claim to exclude others from its use can be justified. But that is exactly what the various justifications for copyright are seeking to determine. So the principle against reaping without sowing turns out to be one that can only apply once it has been determined on other grounds that a creator ought to be able to exclude others from the use of her work. It adds nothing to the substantive justification of the law of copyright.

Spence demonstrates that although the argument from unjust enrichment may be intuitively appealing, it is not entirely persuasive. This is because it does not assist us with determining when enrichment at another's expense is *unjust*. In other words, it does not establish why the creator has a stronger claim to his or her work than other persons. A stronger claim might be based on the fact that the creator has *laboured* to produce a work or because the work that has been produced is a *valuable contribution* to society. However, these reasons do not form part of the 'unjust enrichment' justification. Rather, they represent a natural-rights justification stemming from the work of John Locke to which we now turn.

1.2.2 NATURAL RIGHTS

It is important to note that John Locke's writing supports a theory of *property*, as opposed to *intellectual property*. Nonetheless, scholars have utilized Locke's theory of property to justify the existence of IPRs, arguably because of its rhetorical force and because Locke's arguments, at least superficially, translate effectively. The following passage from Locke's writing has been relied upon by legal scholars to support property rights and, by extension, IPRs.

J. Locke, *The Second Treatise on Government*, 1690 (Indianapolis, IN: Hackett Publishing, 1980)

Chapter V: Of Property

25. God, who hath given the world to man in common, hath also given them reason to make use of it to the best advantage of life and convenience. The earth and all that is therein is given to man for the support and comfort of their being. And though all the fruits it naturally produces, and beasts it feeds, belong to mankind in common, as they are produced by the spontaneous hand of Nature, and nobody has originally a private dominion exclusive of the rest of mankind in any of them, as they are thus in their natural state, yet being given for the use of men, there must of necessity be a means to appropriate them some way or other before they can be of any use, or at all beneficial, to any particular men. The fruit or venison which nourishes the wild Indian, who knows no enclosure, and is still a tenant in common, must be his, and so his—i.e., a part of him, that another can no longer have any right to it before it can do him any good for the support of his life.

26. Though the earth and all inferior creatures be common to all men, yet every man has a 'property' in his own 'person'. This nobody has any right to but himself. The 'labour' of his body and the 'work' of his hands, we may say are properly his. Whatsoever, then, he removed out of the state that Nature has provided and left it in, he hath mixed his labour with

it, and joined to it something that is his own, and thereby makes it his property. It being by him removed from the common state Nature hath placed it in, it hath by this labour something annexed to it that excludes the common right of other men. For this 'labour' being the unquestionable property of the labourer, no man but he can have a right to what that is once joined to, at least where there is enough, and as good left in the common for others.

27. He that is nourished by the acorns he picked up under an oak, or the apples he gathered from the trees in the wood, has certainly appropriated them to himself. Nobody can deny but the nourishment is his. I ask, then, when did they begin to be his? When he digested? Or when he ate? Or when he boiled? Or when he brought them home? Or when he picked them up? And it is plain, if the first gathering made them not his, nothing else could. The labour put a distinction between them and common. That added something to them more than Nature, the common mother of all, had done, and so they became his private right. And will any one say he had no right to those acorns or apples he thus appropriated because he had not the consent of all mankind to make them his? Was it a robbery thus to assume to himself what belonged to all in common? If such a consent as that was necessary, man had starved, notwithstanding the plenty God had given him. We see in commons, which remain so by compact, that it is the taking any part of what is common, and removing it out of the state Nature leaves it in, which begins the property, without which the common is of no use. And the taking of this or that part does not depend on the express consent of all the commoners... The labour that was mine, removing them out of the common state they were in, hath fixed my property in them.
...

30. It will perhaps be objected to this, that if gathering the acorns or other fruits of the earth, etc., makes a right to them, then any one may engross as much as he will. To which I answer, Not so. The same law of Nature that does by this means give us property does also bound that property too. 'God has given us all things richly.' Is the voice of reason confirmed by inspiration? But how far has He given it us—'to enjoy'? As much as any one can make use of any advantage of life before it spoils, so much he may by his labour fix a property in. Whatever is beyond this is more than his share, and belongs to others...

31. ...As much land as a man tills, plants, improves, cultivates, and can use the product of, so much is his property. He by his labour does, as it were, enclose it from the common. Nor will it invalidate his right to say everybody else has an equal title to it, and therefore he cannot appropriate, he cannot enclose, without the consent of all his fellow-commoners all mankind. God, when He gave the world in common to all mankind, commanded man also to labour, and the penury of his condition required it of him. God and his reason commanded him to subdue the earth—i.e., improve it for the benefit of life and there in lay out something upon it that was his own, his labour. He that, in obedience to this command of God, subdued tilled, and sowed any part of it, thereby annexed to it something that was his property, which another had no title to, nor could without injury take from him.

32. Nor was this appropriation of any parcel of land, by improving it, any prejudice to any other man, since there was still enough and as good left, and more than the yet unprovided could use. So that, in effect, there was never the less left for others because of his enclosure for himself. For he that leaves as much as another can make use of does as good as take nothing at all. Nobody could think himself injured by the drinking of another man, though he took a good draught, who had a whole river of the same water left him to quench his thirst. And the case of land and water, where there is enough of both, is perfectly the same.

33. God gave the world to men in common, but since He gave it them for their benefit and the greatest conveniences of life they were capable to draw from it, it cannot be supposed He meant it should always remain common and uncultivated. He gave it to the use of the

industrious and rational (and labour was to be his title to it); not to the fancy or covetous-ness of the quarrelsome and contentious. He that had as good left for his improvement as was already taken up needed not to complain, ought not to meddle with what was already improved by another's labour; if he did it is plain he desired the benefit of another's pains, which he had no right to, and not the ground which God had given him, in common with oth-ers to labour on, and whereof there was as good left as that already possessed, and more than he knew what to do with, or his industry could reach to.

Applying Locke's theory of property to intangible or intellectual property, it can be said that every person has property in their *intellectual labour*, so that whenever a person mixes their intellectual labour with something from the commons (of ideas, theories, or raw material), they thereby make it their property. Property rights in intangible creations operate as a *reward* for the author's intellectual *labour*. Alternatively, they are a reward for the *contri-bution* that the intangible creation makes to society.[2] In both cases, the argument is that a person's labour or contribution *should* be rewarded per se. In other words, it is a natural-rights justification. The argument is not that a reward is given in order to encourage labour or contributions to society. This type of reasoning is utilitarian in nature and, although Locke's theory of property could be used in this way, it has primarily been used to support a natural-rights justification of intellectual property.

Probably the most serious objection to Locke's theory of property (and thus to its useful-ness for justifying intellectual property) concerns the role of labour. First, it is not clear that the total value of an intellectual creation is entirely attributable to the labour of an individual, given that intellectual creations may be considered as social products, i.e. influenced by a range of previous creators and works. Second, it is unclear why labour should entitle an individual to ownership over the whole work when a person's labour may only explain the added value within the intellectual creation and not its entire value. Finally, labour is an imprecise tool for designating the boundaries of intangible objects. For example, if an author takes a stock-in-trade plot of two lovers who, because of their different backgrounds, are prevented from being together and whose thwarted love reaches a tragic climax, and develops this into a detailed narrative, are we to conclude that every aspect of the story should be owned by the author?

Another objection to the Lockean theory of property is that alternative mechanisms could be used to reward creators instead of property rights. It might be possible, for exam-ple, to rely on 'fees, awards, acknowledgement, gratitude, praise, security, power, status, and public financial support' to reward a creator of intangible works.[3]

Other difficulties with the Lockean theory arise. If the justification for property rights is taking something from the 'commons' and mixing one's labour with it, this begs the ques-tion what exactly constitutes the (intellectual) commons? Is it facts, languages, cultural her-itage, ideas (existing or potential), or all of these?[4] As well, Locke speaks of the labourer being obliged to leave 'as much and as good' for others in the commons, which is known as the 'sufficiency' proviso. How constraining is this proviso? Is it satisfied by virtue of IPRs

---

[2] This is described by Shiffrin as the 'standard account': see S. V. Shiffrin, 'Lockean arguments for pri-vate intellectual property' in S. R. Munzer (ed.), *New Essays in the Legal and Political Theory of Property* (Cambridge: Cambridge University Press, 2001), p. 148. Shiffrin, however, adopts a different account of Locke's theory which places more emphasis on the notion that the world is initially owned in common and argues that labour plays a subsidiary role.

[3] E. C. Hettinger, 'Justifying intellectual property' (1989) 18 Philosophy & Public Affairs 31, 41.

[4] W. Fisher, 'Theories of intellectual property' in S. R. Munzer (ed.), *New Essays in the Legal and Political Theory of Property* (Cambridge: Cambridge University Press, 2001), p. 186.

incentivizing innovations and creativity which in turn enlarges the available set of ideas? Or is the fact that certain intellectual products are monopolized (e.g. the word 'Olympics') actually depleting the commons?[5]

While the Lockean theory for IPRs may seem intuitively appealing, on closer scrutiny it has numerous contentious features. Therefore, and perhaps unsurprisingly, we see supporters of IPRs frequently invoke an alternative natural-rights justification, namely the Hegelian personality theory. We turn to discuss this in the following section.

FURTHER READING

J. Hughes, 'The philosophy of intellectual property' (1988–9) 77 Geo. L. J. 287.

S. V. Shiffrin, 'Lockean arguments for private intellectual property' in S. R. Munzer (ed.), *New Essays in the Legal and Political Theory of Property* (Cambridge: Cambridge University Press, 2001), pp. 138–67.

1.2.3 PERSONALITY THEORY

As the following extract illustrates, a personality justification for IPRs has an obvious appeal and perhaps for that reason has gained supporters. Both Hegel and Kant have been relied upon for a personality justification for IPRs; however, the Hegelian version has attracted greater attention and thus is the focus of this section.

J. Hughes, 'The philosophy of intellectual property' (1988–9) 77 Geo. L. J. 287 at 330, 337–8

The most powerful alternative to a Lockean model of property is a personality justification. Such a justification posits that property provides a unique or especially suitable mechanism for self-actualization, for personal expression, and for dignity and recognition as an individual person. Professor Margaret Radin describes this as the 'personhood perspective' and identifies as its central tenet the proposition that, 'to achieve proper self-development—to be a *person*—an individual needs some control over resources in the external environment.' According to this personality theory, the kind of control needed is best fulfilled by the set of rights we call property rights.

Like the labor theory, the personality theory has an intuitive appeal when applied to intellectual property: an idea belongs to its creator because the idea is a manifestation of the creator's personality or self. The best known personality theory is Hegel's theory of property.

...

For Hegel, intellectual property need not be justified by analogy to physical property. In fact, the analogy to physical property may distort the status Hegel ascribes to personality and mental traits in relation to the will. Hegel writes:

Mental aptitudes, erudition, artistic skill, even things ecclesiastical (like sermons, masses, prayers, consecration of votive objects), inventions, and so forth, become subjects of a contract, brought on to a parity, through being bought and sold, with things recognized as things.

[5] Fisher, 'Theories of intellectual property', p. 188.

It may be asked whether the artist, scholar, &c., is from the legal point of view in possession of his art, erudition, ability to preach a sermon, sing a mass, &c., that is, whether such attainments are 'things'. We may hesitate to call such abilities, attainments, aptitudes, &c., 'things', for while possession of these may be the subject of business dealings and contracts, as if they were things, there is also something inward and mental about it, and for this reason the Understanding may be in perplexity about how to describe such possession in legal terms…

Intellectual property provides a way out of this problem, by 'materializing' these personal traits. Hegel goes on to say that '[a]ttainments, eruditions, talents, and so forth, are, of course, owned by free mind and are something internal and not external to it, but even so, by expressing them it may embody them in something external and alienate them.'

Hegel takes the position that one cannot alienate or surrender any universal element of one's self. Hence slavery is not permissible because by 'alienating the whole of my time, as crystallized in my work, I would be making into another's property the substance of my being, my universal activity and actuality, my personality.' Similarly, there is no right to sacrifice one's life because that is the surrender of the 'comprehensive sum of external activity'. This doctrine supplies at least a framework to answer the question of intellectual property that most concerns Hegel. It is a question we ignore today, but one that is not easy to answer: what justified the author in alienating copies of his work while retaining the exclusive right to reproduce further copies of that work?

…

In resolving this dilemma, Hegel says that the alienation of a single copy of a work need not entail the right to produce facsimiles because such reproduction is one of the 'universal ways and means of expression… which belong to [the author].' Just as he does not sell himself into slavery, the author keeps the universal aspect of expression as his own. The copy sold is for the buyer's own consumption; its only purpose is to allow the buyer to incorporate these ideas into his 'self'.

A key difficulty with the Hegelian personality justification is what is meant by 'personality'. Michael Spence has suggested that personality differs from reputation and instead means self-presentation, including self-expression.[6] Even if it is possible to agree on the nature of 'personality', some commentators express doubts about whether personality can be discerned in a creator's work. Hughes argues, for example, that some works are better suited to displaying a creator's personality than others. Creations such as novels, poems, music, and fine art are 'clearly receptacles for personality' whereas computer software and other technological creations, such as inventions, microchips, and trade secrets are not generally regarded 'as manifesting the personality of an individual, but rather as manifesting a raw, almost generic insight' because considerations of economic efficiency and physical limitations constrain the range of expression.[7]

FURTHER READING

P. Drahos, *A Philosophy of Intellectual Property* (Aldershot: Dartmouth, 1997).

J. Hughes, 'The philosophy of intellectual property' (1988–9) 77 Geo. L. J. 287.

M. J. Radin, 'Property and personhood' (1982) 34 Stanford L. Rev. 957.

---

[6] M. Spence, 'Justifying copyright' in D. McClean and K. Schubert (eds), *Dear Images: Art, Copyright and Culture* (Manchester: Ridinghouse, 2002), p. 399.

[7] J. Hughes, 'The philosophy of intellectual property' (1988–9) 77 Geo. L. J. 287, 340, 341.

1.2.4 HUMAN RIGHTS

The linking of IPRs and human rights is a fairly recent development. Broadly speaking, the literature shows a preoccupation with either intellectual property *as* human rights or the human rights implications of intellectual property protection. The latter concern came to the fore particularly because of the neglected protection of indigenous peoples' cultural knowledge and also with the coupling of trade and IPRs through the Agreement on Trade Related Aspects of Intellectual Property Rights (TRIPS) and Free Trade Agreements.[8] Both of these developments are discussed later in this chapter. Our concern here, however, is with the conceptualization of IPRs *as* human rights.

The basis for treating IPRs as human rights emerges from international conventions and, most recently, the Charter of Fundamental Rights of the EU.[9] For example, the Universal Declaration of Human Rights, Article 27 states that: 'Everyone has the right to the protection of the moral and material interests resulting from any scientific, literary, or artistic production of which he is the author.' Article 1, Protocol 1 of the European Convention on Human Rights (ECHR) stipulates that: 'Every natural or legal person is entitled to the peaceful enjoyment of his possessions' and 'possessions' has been interpreted by the European Commission on Human Rights[10] and the European Court of Human Rights to include patents,[11] copyright,[12] and trade marks.[13] The Charter on Fundamental Rights of the EU, Article 17 is similar to that of Article 1, Protocol 1 ECHR, but importantly Article 17(2) of the Charter explicitly recognizes that intellectual property falls within the scope of the 'right to own, use, dispose of and bequeath his or her lawfully acquired possessions' (Article 17(1)). Already we have seen the Court of Justice of the EU (CJEU) invoke the fundamental right to property in aid of intellectual property protection.[14]

For some, it may seem surprising to characterize IPRs as human rights, particularly when compared with fundamental human rights such as the rights to freedom of expression and religion, the rights to prohibit slavery and torture, and the right to a fair trial. As Peter Yu observes:

> the inclusion in the human rights debate of a relatively trivial item like intellectual property protection would undermine the claim that human rights are of fundamental importance to humanity. Such inclusion may also revive the old, and somewhat lingering, debate about whether economic, social, and cultural rights should be considered as significant as civil and political rights, or the so-called 'first generation' human rights.[15]

---

[8] L. R. Helfer, 'Toward a human rights framework for intellectual property' (2007) 40 U. C. Davis L. Rev. 971, 982.

[9] 2000/C 364/01.

[10] Which was abolished after Protocol 11 was added to the ECHR, thus allowing individuals to bring claims directly to the European Court of Human Rights.

[11] *Smith Kline and French Laboratories Ltd v The Netherlands* App. No. 12633/87, 4 October 1990, Decisions and Reports (DR) 66; *Lenzing AG v United Kingdom* App. No. 38817/97, 9 September 1998 (unreported).

[12] *Aral, Tekin and Aral v Turkey* App. No. 24563/94, 14 January 1998; *Balan v Moldova* App. No. 19247/03, 29 January 2008 (Court, Fourth Section); *Dima v Romania* App. No. 58472/00.

[13] *Anheuser-Busch Inc. v Portugal* App. No. 73049/01, 11 January 2007 (Grand Chamber).

[14] *Luksan v Van der Let* Case C-277/10 [2013] ECDR 5 where the CJEU (Third Chamber) held that a provision of Austrian law concerning entitlement to copyright in cinematographic works contravened the fundamental right to property in Art. 17(2) of the Charter.

[15] P. K. Yu, 'Ten common questions about intellectual property and human rights' (2006–7) 23 Ga. St U. L. Rev. 709, 713–14.

But, as Peter Yu explains in the following extract, the major concern—at least for intellectual property scholars—about characterizing IPRs as human rights is whether this will lead to an inevitable and continuing expansion of protection.

P. K. Yu, 'Ten common questions about intellectual property and human rights' (2006–7) 23 Ga. St. U. L. Rev. 709 at 738–40

One of the most predominant concerns about developing a human rights framework for intellectual property is the ratcheting up of the already very high protection under the existing international intellectual property system…

Some public interest advocates may remain concerned about the 'marriage' of human rights and intellectual property rights by pointing out that, in a human rights framework, the status of all intellectual property rights, regardless of their basis, will be elevated to that of human rights in rhetoric even if that status will not be elevated in practice. Indeed, intellectual property rights holders have widely used the rhetoric of private property to support their lobby efforts and litigation, despite the many limitations, safeguards, and obligations in the property system. The property gloss over intellectual property rights has also confused policymakers, judges, jurors, and commentators, even though there are significant differences between the attributes of real property and those of intellectual property.

Yu notes that 'the concerns over rhetorical effects are valid and important' but he is optimistic about the ways in which the concerns may be alleviated, arguing that a nuanced assessment is required whereby one identifies which attributes of IPRs qualify as human rights, and which do not.

The concerns raised by Yu regarding the complicated relationship between IPRs and human rights have come to the fore as a number of countries have sought to introduce plain packaging for cigarettes. These countries have taken the view, which they argue is supported by considerable research, that the attractive packaging of cigarettes encourages young people to take up smoking and discourages those already smoking from quitting the habit. Considerable opposition to plain packaging has come, perhaps not surprisingly, from the tobacco industry. As well as contesting the research findings, a key plank of the tobacco companies' opposition is that plain packaging interferes with their right to the peaceful enjoyment of their property, in this case their trade marks. Thus, although the move to plain packaging for the most part allows for the placing of the relevant trade mark, in its simplest form, on the packaging, it will almost certainly be against a plain background or one which visually highlights the dangers of smoking. As a result, its opponents argue, any attractive qualities or goodwill that the trade mark may have acquired would be undercut or entirely cancelled out and its commercial value diminished.

The first major action in which tobacco companies sought to prevent the introduction of plain packaging was in Australia. Their argument, which was ultimately unsuccessful, was that the Australian Tobacco Plain Packaging Act 2011 (Cth) was a breach of their constitutional rights in that it allowed the state to acquire their intellectual property without adequate compensation. However, the court held that the Act, which dictated the manner in which trade marks could be deployed on cigarette packets, did not amount to the acquisition of property by the state.[16] More recently, a number of tobacco companies sought judicial

---

[16] The reference was to section 51(xxxi) of the Australian Constitution. The tobacco companies lost a subsequent action based on the argument that the Tobacco Plain Packaging Act 2011 (Cth) breached the

review of the Standardised Packaging of Tobacco Products Regulations 2015,[17] which similarly introduced plain packaging into the UK. The request for judicial review was founded on a number of grounds, one of which was the claimants' right to property. The argument of the tobacco companies, on this point, and the court's response was summarized at the start of Mr Justice Green's lengthy judgment.

R. (on the application of British American Tobacco UK Ltd) v Secretary of State for Health [2016] EWHC 1169 (Admin)

Mr Justice Green:

(8) Violation of property rights

38. The Claimants contend that under A1P1 (Ground 6), under the Fundamental Charter (Ground 7) and under domestic common law (Ground 8) they have a property right (their intellectual property and goodwill) which has been unlawfully expropriated from them by the Regulations without compensation. I accept that their trade marks and other relevant intellectual property amount to '*possessions*' or '*property*' which in principle are capable of falling with the protective principles involved. I also accept that in principle certain types of goodwill can also amount to a protectable interest (though on the facts of the case it is not possible to form a concluded view as to the extent to which there are goodwill related rights arising). I reject the submission however that the rights have been expropriated. Title to the rights in issue remains in the hands of the tobacco companies; the Regulations curtail the *use* that can be made of those rights but they are not expropriated. Indeed, the rights remain important in the hands of the tobacco companies because the word marks can still be used on packaging and will serve their traditional function as an identifier of origin. I accept that the figurative marks cannot be used in this manner but they still have certain, admittedly very limited, vestigial uses, which the Regulations do not curtail. Further the restrictions imposed pursue a legitimate public health based interest; a conclusion not challenged by the Claimants. These two factors (retention of title and measures imposed for legitimate public interest reasons) are in large measure sufficient to defeat in law the submission that the rights have been expropriated. But if I am wrong in this and the Claimants' rights have been expropriated I have then to decide whether compensation should be paid. The law indicates that in cases of true expropriation full compensation is payable save in 'exceptional' circumstances. In my judgment it is quite obvious that the circumstances are exceptional. Tobacco usage is classified as a health evil, albeit that it remains lawful. There is no precedent where the law has provided compensation for the suppression of a property right which facilitates and furthers, quite deliberately, a health epidemic. And moreover, a health epidemic which imposes vast negative health and other costs upon the very State that is then being expected to compensate the property right holder for ceasing to facilitate the epidemic.

39. In my judgment this is not a case of expropriation but a case of curtailment of use. Where that occurs the obligation upon the State to pay compensation is governed by a '*fair balance*' test. This is, in essence, the same analysis as occurs under the component of the

---

foreign investment provisions of Australia's 1993 Investment Promotion and Protection Agreement with Hong Kong.

[17] SI 2015/829.

> proportionality test which I have addressed under Ground 5. I reject the claim for compensa-
> tion. It is 'fair' not to compensate the tobacco companies for requiring them to cease using
> their property rights to facilitate a health epidemic. In my judgment it would not be right to
> expect the State to pay any compensation for the restrictions imposed upon the use of the
> rights in question.

After this decision, which denied the request for judicial review, the claimants' sought
to appeal. However, the omens for a different outcome are surely not encouraging. Not
only did Green J take a similar approach to that taken by the Australian High Court, but
almost simultaneously the CJEU held that the EU Directive on Plain Packaging, which
similarly delimited the use of trade marks on cigarette packets, could be implemented
in the UK.[18]

The controversy over plain packaging and its effect on trade marks understood as property shows clearly that human rights considerations in relation to IPRs are not going to
disappear, especially in the EU where they have been entrenched by the Charter and also
Article 6(3) of the revised Treaty of the European Union.[19] The challenge for the CJEU and
national courts will be to assess and weigh competing rights and interests, such as the right
to property against the right to freedom of expression or of the state to protect the health of
its citizens.

FURTHER READING

K. D. Beiter, 'The right to property and the protection of interests in intellectual
property—a human rights perspective on the European Court of Human Rights'
decision in *Anheuser-Busch Inc v Portugal*' (2008) 39 IIC 714.

C. Geiger (ed.), *Research Handbook on Human Rights and Intellectual Property*
(Cheltenham: Edward Elgar, 2015).

J. Griffiths, ' "On the back of a cigarette packet": standardised packaging legislation
and the tobacco industry's fundamental right to (intellectual) property' [2015]
IPQ 343.

L. R. Helfer, 'Toward a human rights framework for intellectual property' (2007) 40
U. C. Davis L. Rev. 971.

L. R. Helfer and G. W. Austin, *Human Rights and Intellectual Property* (Cambridge:
Cambridge University Press, 2011).

P. L. C. Torremans (ed.), *Intellectual Property and Human Rights* (3rd edn, Alphen aan
den Rijn: Wolters Kluwer, 2015).

P. K. Yu, 'Ten common questions about intellectual property and human rights' (2006–7)
23 Ga. St. U. L. Rev. 709.

---

[18] *Philip Morris (et al.) v Secretary of State for Health* Case C-547/14, 4 May 2016. Directive 2014/40/EU of
the European Parliament and of the Council of 3 April 2014 on the approximation of the laws, regulations
and administrative provisions of the Member States concerning the manufacture, presentation and sale of
tobacco and related products and repealing Directive 2001/37/EC [2014] OJ L127/1.

[19] Which states: 'Fundamental rights, as guaranteed by the European Convention for the Protection of
Human Rights and Fundamental Freedoms and as they result from the constitutional traditions common to
the Member States, shall constitute general principles of the Union's law.'

1.2.5 THE UTILITARIAN JUSTIFICATION

Though Locke's work is generally used to support a natural-rights theory of intellectual property, we have noted that his theory of property can also be used to support a utilitarian justification. However, it is Jeremy Bentham, rather than John Locke, who tends to be cited in support of utilitarianism. Bentham rejected the idea that laws derive from natural rights. Rather, he argued that laws were socially justified if they brought the greatest happiness, or benefit, to the greatest number of people. The utilitarian approach to law making, and in particular to intellectual property protection, has traditionally found favour in the US. Perhaps the most prominent example of the influence of utilitarian ideas on intellectual property law is to be found in the Copyright and Patents clause of the US Constitution itself, which gives Congress power to:

> promote the progress of science and useful arts, by securing for limited times to authors and inventors the exclusive right to their respective writings and discoveries.[20]

According to the US Supreme Court, this clause is:

> intended definitely to grant valuable, enforceable rights to authors, publishers, etc, without burdensome requirements to afford greater encouragement to the production of literary [or artistic] works of lasting benefit to the world.[21]

A general account of the way utilitarian ideas might justify IPRs is provided by Hettinger.

E. C. Hettinger, 'Justifying intellectual property' (1989) 18 Philosophy & Public Affairs 31 at 47–51

The strongest and most widely appealed to justification for intellectual property is a utilitarian argument based on providing incentives. The constitutional justification for patents and copyrights—'to promote the progress of science and the useful arts'—is itself utilitarian. Given the shortcomings of the other arguments for intellectual property, the justifiability of copyrights, patents, and trade secrets depends, in the final analysis, on this utilitarian defense.

According to this argument, promoting the creation of valuable intellectual works requires that intellectual laborers be granted property rights in those works. Without the copyright, patent, and trade secret property protections, adequate incentives for the creation of a socially optimal output of intellectual products would not exist. If competitors could simply copy books, movies, and records, and take one another's inventions and business techniques, there would be no incentive to spend the vast amounts of time, energy, and money necessary to develop these products and techniques. It would be in each firm's self-interest to let others develop products, and then mimic the result. No one would engage in original development, and consequently no new writings, inventions, or business techniques would be developed. To avoid this disastrous result, the argument claims, we must continue to grant intellectual property rights.

Notice that this argument focuses on the users of intellectual products, rather than on the producers. Granting property rights to producers is here seen as necessary to ensure that

---

[20] Art. 1, s. 8.   [21] *Washington Pub. Co. v Pearson*, 59 S Ct 397, 400 (1939), para. 36.

enough intellectual products (and the countless other goods based on these products) are available to users. The grant of property rights to the producers is a mere means to this end.

This approach is paradoxical. It establishes a right to restrict the current availability and use of intellectual products for the purpose of increasing the production and thus future availability and use of new intellectual products. As economist Joan Robinson says of patents: 'A patent is a device to prevent the diffusion of new methods before the original investor has recovered profit adequate to induce the requisite investment. The justification of the patent system is that by slowing down the diffusion of technical progress it ensures that there will be more progress to diffuse…Since it is rooted in a contradiction, there can be no such thing as an ideally beneficial patent system, and it is bound to produce negative results in particular instances, impeding progress unnecessarily even if its general effect is favourable on balance.' Although this strategy may work, it is to a certain extent self-defeating. If the justification for intellectual property is utilitarian in this sense, then the search for alternative incentives for the production of intellectual products takes on a good deal of importance. It would be better to employ equally powerful ways to stimulate the production and thus use of intellectual products which did not also restrict their use and availability.

Government support of intellectual work and public ownership of the result may be one such alternative. Governments already fund a great deal of basic research and development, and the results of this research often become public property. Unlike private property rights in the results of intellectual labor, government funding of this labor and public ownership of the result stimulate new inventions and writings without restricting their dissemination and use. Increased government funding of intellectual labor should thus be seriously considered.

This proposal need not involve government control over which research projects are to be pursued. Government funding of intellectual labor can be divorced from government control over what is funded. University research is an example. Most of this is supported by public funds, but government control over its content is minor and indirect. Agencies at different governmental levels could distribute funding for intellectual labor with only the most general guidance over content, leaving businesses, universities, and private individuals to decide which projects to pursue.

If the goal of private intellectual property institutions is to maximize the dissemination and use of information, to the extent that they do not achieve this result, these institutions should be modified. The question is not whether copyrights, patents, and trade secrets provide incentives for the production of original works of authorship, inventions, and innovative business techniques. Of course they do. Rather, we should ask the following questions: Do copyrights, patents, and trade secrets increase the availability and use of intellectual products more than they restrict this availability and use? If they do, we must then ask whether they increase the availability and use of intellectual products more than any alternative mechanism would. For example, could better overall results be achieved by shortening the length of copyright and patent grants, or by putting a time limit on trade secrets (and on the restrictions on future employment employers are allowed to demand of employees)? Would eliminating most types of trade secrets entirely and letting patents carry a heavier load produce improved results? Additionally, we must determine whether and to what extent public funding and ownership of intellectual products might be a more efficient means to these results.

We should not expect an across-the-board answer to these questions. For example, the production of movies is more dependent on copyright than is academic writing. Also, patent protection for individual inventors and small beginning firms makes more sense than patent protection for large corporations (which own the majority of patents). It has been argued that patents are not important incentives for the research and innovative activity of large corporations in competitive markets. The short-term advantage a company gets from developing a new product and being the first to put it on the market may be incentive enough.

> That patents are conducive to a strong competitive economy is also open to question. Our patent system, originally designed to reward the individual inventor and thereby stimulate invention, may today be used as a device to monopolize industries. It has been suggested that in some cases 'the patent position of the big firms makes it almost impossible for new firms to enter the industry' and that patents are frequently bought up in order to suppress competition.
>
> Trade secrets as well can stifle competition, rather than encourage it. If a company can rely on a secret advantage over a competitor, it has no need to develop new technologies to stay ahead. Greater disclosure of certain trade secrets—such as costs and profits of particular product lines—would actually increase competition, rather than decrease it, since with this knowledge firms would then concentrate on one another's most profitable products. Furthermore, as one critic notes, trade secret laws often prevent a former employee 'from doing work in just that field for which his training and experience have best prepared him. Indeed, the mobility of engineers and scientists is often severely limited by the reluctance of new firms to hire them for fear of exposing themselves to a lawsuit.' Since the movement of skilled workers between companies is a vital mechanism in the growth and spread of technology, in this important respect trade secrets actually slow the dissemination and use of innovative techniques.
>
> These remarks suggest that the justifiability of our intellectual property institutions is not settled by the facile assertion that our system of patents, copyrights, and trade secrets provides necessary incentives for innovation and ensures maximally healthy competitive enterprise. This argument is not as easy to construct as one might at first think; substantial empirical evidence is needed. The above considerations suggest that evidence might not support this position.

In the above extract, Hettinger claims that the utilitarian argument is the 'strongest and most widely appealed to justification for intellectual property'. In considering this statement, it is important to remember that Hettinger's focus is on the US and that the constitutional justification which he relies upon is not mirrored in other jurisdictions such as the UK. Thus, while the utilitarian justification tends to be more closely associated with common law rather than civil law jurisdictions, we should be wary of assuming that the utilitarian argument is the definitive basis for intellectual property laws in the UK.

As Hettinger points out, the essence of the utilitarian justification is that IPRs provide the incentives needed for the creation of intangible works. However, his discussion raises three key difficulties with this rationale. First, there is an absence of empirical evidence that authors or inventors would not create in the absence of IPRs. Second, since IPRs restrict the use and dissemination of intangible creations, we should expect to see laws calibrated in a manner which provides an optimal amount of protection, i.e. only as much protection as is needed to stimulate creation. Finally, there may exist alternative ways of providing incentives to create which do not restrict the use and availability of works: an example of this is government funding of university research.

The case of computer software is useful in illustrating the above difficulties.[22] In the early to mid-1980s, courts and legislatures in countries such as the UK, US, and Australia came under pressure to clarify whether computer software was protected by copyright law. However, in countries such as the US, this lack of clarity did not apparently inhibit the growth of the software industry. Nonetheless, in various jurisdictions, copyright laws were amended explicitly to protect computer programs as literary works and, as such, they

[22] For further discussion see 2.5.1.2.2.

obtained protection for at least 50 years after the death of the author. Yet it may be queried whether software, which has a relatively short life cycle, really warrants such a lengthy term of protection. Further, the investment of software producers can be protected by means other than intellectual property law. In particular, the use of software can be regulated via contract, and the ease of entering into contracts with purchasers of software has been facilitated by so-called 'shrink-wrap' licences and, in an online context, 'click-wrap' licences. In addition to these licences, technological protection measures can be used to restrict access to, and the use of, software.

1.2.6 LAW AND ECONOMICS

The law and economics approach also addresses the question of what incentives are needed to create intellectual property and the optimal amount of protection that should be afforded to it. However, proponents of law and economics do so from the perspective of what is best for the functioning of the market. In general, the law and economics approach looks to the allocative efficiency of a market where intellectual property is privately owned. Private ownership provides incentives for the production of intellectual goods for which there is a market. If intellectual property were not protected then the needs of the market would not be met. For many adherents of law and economics theory, a natural corollary is that intellectual property should have strong protection since the ability to 'free-ride' on another's intellectual property would undermine allocative efficiency. However, the more sophisticated advocates of the law and economics approach, such as William M. Landes and Richard A. Posner, recognize that strong intellectual property protection can bring both costs and benefits. In the following extract they begin by comparing the benefits of rights in intellectual property to the enclosure of common agricultural land, which gave exclusive ownership in the products of that land to the landowner. They suggest that the benefit of such property rights can be static, enabling the owner to exclude others from use of the property and to transfer that property to another, as well as dynamic.

W. M. Landes and R. A. Posner, *The Economic Structure of Intellectual Property Law* (Cambridge, MA: Harvard University Press, 2003), pp. 13–14

The dynamic benefit of a property right is the incentive that possession of such a right imparts to invest in the creation or improvement of a resource in period 1 (for example, planting a crop), given that no one else can appropriate the resource in period 2 (harvest time). It enables people to reap where they have sown. Without that prospect the incentive to sow is diminished. To take an example from intellectual property, a firm is less likely to expend resources on developing a new product if competing firms that have not borne the expense of development can duplicate the product and produce it at the same marginal cost as the innovator; competition will drive price down to marginal cost and the sunk costs of invention will not be recouped. This prospect provides the traditional economic rationale for intellectual property rights, though it involves as we shall see a significant degree of oversimplification. The possibility that such rights might also confer static benefits, eliminating congestion externalities comparable to those of the common pasture with which we began, has been neglected because of the widely held belief that intellectual property, not being physical, cannot be worn out, crowded, or otherwise impaired by additional uses.

> It is a 'public good' in the economist's sense that consumption of it by one person does not reduce its consumption by another. More accurately, it has public good characteristics, for we shall show that in some circumstances propertizing intellectual property can prevent overuse or congestion in economically meaningful senses of these terms.

Landes and Posner then consider the costs involved in propertizing intellectual output. Among these costs, they identify: transaction costs (or the costs of transferring IPRs); rent seeking (the opportunity to charge monopoly prices); and the cost of protection, which they see as likely to be high in relation to intellectual property because of its nature as a public good. They continue at pp. 19–21:

> The public-good character of intellectual property is pronounced. In the case of farmland, whether cultivated or uncultivated, adding a user will ... impose costs on the existing user(s). So the fact that a fence keeps additional users out need not impose a net cost on users as a group, and if not, the only cost of the property right will be the fence.
>
> ...
>
> Often and not merely exceptionally, adding users will impose no costs on previous users of intellectual property. One farmer's using the idea of crop rotation does not prevent any other farmer from using the same idea. It is true that when more farmers use crop rotation, output will rise and prices will fall, hurting farmers already using crop rotation. But the price effects of the diffusion of the idea are purely pecuniary externalities because the losses to the farmers are completely offset by the gains to consumers; there is no reduction in the aggregate value of the society's economic resources. However, when the marginal cost of using a resource is zero, excluding someone (the marginal purchaser) from using it by charging a positive price for its use creates a deadweight loss, in addition to the out-of-pocket cost of enforcing exclusion by fences, security guards, police, lawyers and registries of title deeds, because the price deflects some users to substitute goods that have a positive marginal cost. This loss is rarely significant in the case of physical property because, as we said, it brings with it a benefit; it avoids crowding in the pasture and shopping center cases, and worse when joint consumption is not possible. More broadly, it allocates scarce resources to their highest-valued uses. Two people cannot eat the same radish or wear the same pair of shoes at the same time. There must be a mechanism for allocation, and normally the most efficient is the price system. Hence, Plant's point that intellectual property rights create scarcity whereas property rights in physical goods manage scarcity.
>
> But the point is incomplete. Unless there is power to exclude, the incentive to create intellectual property in the first place may be impaired. Socially desirable investments (investments that yield social benefits in excess of their social costs) may be deterred if the creators of intellectual property cannot recoup their sunk costs. That is the *dynamic* benefit of property rights, and the result is the 'access versus incentives' tradeoff; charging a price for a public good reduces access to it (a social cost), making it artificially scarce (Plant's point), but increases the incentive to create it in the first place, which is a possibly offsetting social benefit.

In relying on an incentive to create or produce argument, we would expect IPRs to be granted only to the extent that they *do* provide incentives. To grant more extensive protection than is needed would result in the social costs exceeding any dynamic benefit. For example, Mark Lemley draws a distinction between *ex ante* and *ex post* justifications for intellectual property. He argues that providing extensive intellectual property protection would almost certainly provide an incentive to create, but that it would have a less beneficial effect once the intellectual property had been created.

M. A. Lemley, 'Ex ante versus ex post justifications for intellectual property' (2004) 71 U. Chi. L. Rev. 129 at 130–1

Of late, commentators and courts have invoked new justifications for intellectual property protection. These arguments focus not on the incentive to create new ideas, but on what happens to those ideas after they have been developed. One form of the new justifications argues that intellectual property protection is necessary to encourage the intellectual property owner to make some further investment in the improvement, maintenance, or commercialization of a product. Another strand argues that such protection is necessary to prevent a sort of 'tragedy of the commons' in which the new idea will be overused. I refer to both of these new arguments as ex post justifications for intellectual property because they defend intellectual property rights, not on the basis of the incentives they give to create new works, but on the basis of the incentives the right gives its owner to manage works that have already been created.

Distinguishing between ex ante and ex post justifications for intellectual property is more than just a philosophical exercise. The different explanations entail very different consequences for the scope, duration, and enforcement of intellectual property rights. Under the classic incentive story, intellectual property is a necessary evil. We grant creators exclusive rights in their works—permitting them to charge a supracompetitive price—to encourage them to make such works in the first place. This supracompetitive price in turn artificially depresses the consumption of the newly created work; some people who would be willing to pay more than the marginal cost of a copy of the idea will not be able to access it. Further, the exclusive control intellectual property rights grant to pioneers may stifle the invention of improvers. As a result, the incentive theory of intellectual property dictates that intellectual property rights should be granted only where necessary.

The new ex post justifications, by contrast, endorse a greater and perhaps unlimited duration and scope of intellectual property rights. If the reason for granting intellectual property rights is to ensure that an invention, a movie, or a person name is managed efficiently, there seems little reason to terminate that right after a period of years. Similarly, if intellectual property rights are designed to prevent overuse of an information resource, permitting significant unauthorized 'fair use' by third parties would seem to undermine that goal. The ex post justifications seem to provide economic support for the legions of new intellectual property owners who claim a moral entitlement to capture all possible value from 'their' information—a view that scholars have derided as 'if value, then right.' Because the optimal intellectual property regime may look very different under an ex post approach than under an ex ante approach, we should critically evaluate the claimed ex post justifications for intellectual property.

Lemley then looks at the possible consequences of assuming that the rightsholder will be best placed to exploit intellectual property once it has been created. In particular, in the following extract, he addresses those who were arguing for the passage of the Copyright Term Extension Act 1998 (CTEA) which increased copyright protection in the US by an additional 20 years to 70 years plus the life of the author. Lemley goes on to argue that a number of companies operating in a market economy will make better use of an idea than a single company, which has been able to nurture that idea through copyright or patent protection, once that protection has expired. He uses the example of 'paper clips' to argue that, if a single company were given a monopoly on the production of paper clips, neither their price nor their levels of production would find an optimal level. He then returns to the CTEA and asserts that 'old books', such as James Joyce's *Ulysses* are no different from paper clips. If they are given excessive copyright protection, they will inevitably be sold at a higher price than that which might be dictated by the market.

Lemley is clearly a strong believer in the efficiency of the market to produce the optimal level of goods (or in this case, goods embodying IPRs) for consumers at the optimal price. He rejects the argument put by supporters of a longer copyright term that the public goods problem differentiates intellectual property from other sorts of goods and that, as a consequence, they need protection from the market. He writes:

> Why then does the argument seem to have resonance? The answer lies in a sort of intellectual free riding by supporters of the CTEA. They have taken the logic of intellectual property law as a solution to the public goods problem and applied it where there is no public goods problem. We need to give creators of patented and copyrighted works power over price because the act of creation imposes a cost that imitators do not share. There is no similar cost imbalance when it comes to the distribution of work that has already been created. Some companies may be more efficient manufacturers and distributors than others, but we need not worry that no one will distribute a work without a monopoly incentive. If people are willing to pay enough to justify printing copies of *Ulysses*, copies of *Ulysses* will be printed. And if people are not willing to pay even the marginal cost of printing, granting exclusive rights over *Ulysses* would not solve the problem. Indeed, it will make it worse—people who are not willing to pay the marginal cost surely will not pay the supracompetitive price sole owners can command.[23]

Lemley then turns to the related argument of whether monopoly rights are necessary to ensure a creator will improve on an existing work. He questions whether it is always the case that the creator is best placed to improve on his work and suggests that once again the market may be trusted to ensure such improvements will occur should there be demand. Finally, Lemley addresses the argument that IPRs are necessary post-creation in order to ensure that the intellectual property is not 'overused' and hence loses its value: what has been termed the 'tragedy of the information commons'. Once again he is not convinced:

> The idea that granting exclusive rights over information will reduce the use and distribution of that information compared with an open market makes perfect sense. It is consistent with everything we know about basic economics. The question here is why we should want to reduce the use and distribution of information when there is no public goods problem for intellectual property to solve. Reducing the distribution of information is a good thing if but only if, such information is in fact overproduced or over distributed. In other words, this justification for intellectual property depends upon proof that there is in fact a tragedy of the commons in information.
>
> The idea of a tragedy of the information commons, however, is fundamentally flawed because it misunderstands the nature of information. A tragedy of the commons occurs when a finite natural resource is depleted by overuse. Information cannot be depleted, however; in economic terms, its consumption is nonrivalrous. It simply cannot be 'used up'. Indeed, copying information actually multiplies the available resources, not only by making a new physical copy but by spreading the idea and therefore permitting others to use and enjoy it. The result is that rather than a tragedy, an information commons is a 'comedy' in which everyone benefits. The notion that information will be depleted by overuse simply ignores basic economics.[24]

---

23 At 138.   24 At 142–3.

At least in relation to copyright works, Lemley's argument that the market not the creator may be more efficient at determining whether it is worthwhile to distribute intellectual property once it has been created appears to be strengthened by the low costs involved in digital copying and distribution. After all, in the unlikely event that only a very small number of people now want to read *Ulysses*, the ability to distribute the book digitally rather than as a printed edition would almost certainly make such distribution profitable. There may, however, be stronger arguments that it is possible to deplete an information commons. Perhaps the question should be not whether the commons, or as it is more commonly termed the 'public domain', would be better preserved either by giving stronger protection to rightsholders or by leaving its fate to the market, but rather whether the public domain itself should be given legal protection. This is the question to which we now turn.

1.2.7 THE PUBLIC DOMAIN

A common feature of the main justifications for IPRs is that each recognizes the need for the protection of what is often referred to as a 'public domain' (or less frequently, a 'commons') where intellectual property laws should not operate. Thus, the Lockean theory emphasizes the need to preserve an intellectual commons where 'enough and as good' is left for others to access once intellectual creations have been removed. The utilitarian justification also recognizes the need to limit intellectual property protection. In this instance, this aim is achieved by limiting the period of protection which is given to intellectual property, so that when the relevant IPRs expire the intellectual creations will return to a public domain and be available for others to use in their own creative endeavours. The law and economics approach also recognizes the economic efficiency of refreshing the public domain with works whose protection has expired. We shall see when we consider the individual IPRs later in this book that each sets limits as to what will be legally protected. Thus, copyright does not extend to ideas and discoveries are not patentable.

While there is wide recognition of the need to preserve a public domain, there is less agreement on how its boundaries should be mapped. For example, should the public domain encompass only intellectual products for which the period of protection has expired or which are not suitable subject matter for protection, such as ideas? Or should the public domain also contain intellectual products that are, in principle, protectable but for which, nonetheless, there is a public interest in leaving them free?

The various ways one might constitute a public domain are examined by James Boyle.

J. Boyle, 'The second enclosure movement and the construction of the public domain' (Winter/Spring 2003) 66 Law and Contemporary Problems 33 at 58–62

By defense of the public domain, I do not mean mere usage of the word. Though 'public domain' was a term widely used to describe public lands in the United States, the intellectual property usage of the term comes to us from the French *domaine public* which made its way into American law in the late nineteenth century via the language of the Berne Convention. But at what point do we find a defense of the public domain, rather than merely a criticism of the costs of intellectual property?

. . .

... [T]here are a number of possible places where one could say, 'the defense of the public domain begins here'. But, like most people, I attribute central importance to the writing of my friend and colleague David Lange, whose article *Recognizing the Public Domain* really initiated contemporary study of the subject. Lange's article was driven by indignation about, indeed eloquently sarcastic ridicule of, expansions of intellectual property protection in the 1960s and 1970s. Lange claims that one major cause of this expansion was that intellectual property rights are intangible, abstract, and thus, imprecise. He argues, in a way that would have been familiar to Macaulay or Jefferson, that we should cease the reckless expansion. But he also argues that 'recognition of new intellectual property interests should be offset today by equally deliberate recognition of individual rights in the public domain'.

Lange is not arguing:

that intellectual property is undeserving of protection, but rather that such protection as it gets ought to reflect its unique susceptibility to conceptual imprecision and to infinite replication. These attributes seem to me to require the recognition of two fundamental principles. One is that intellectual property theory must always accept something akin to a 'no-man's land' at the boundaries; doubtful cases of infringement ought always to be resolved in favour of the defendant. The other is that no exclusive interest should ever have affirmative recognition unless its conceptual opposite is also recognized. Each right ought to be marked off clearly against the public domain.

But what does this *mean*? What is the nature of these 'individual rights in the public domain'? Who holds them? Indeed, what *is* the public domain? Does it consist only of works that are completely unprotected, say books whose copyright term has lapsed? Does it include *aspects* of works that are unprotectable, such as the ideas or the facts on which an argument is based, even if the expression of that argument is protected? What about limitations on exclusive rights, privileges of users, or affirmative defenses, are those part of the public domain too? Is the parody-able aspect of your novel in the public domain? What about the short quote on which a critical argument is mounted? Earlier in this article, I discussed the 'commons of the mind'. What is the relationship between the public domain—however defined—and the commons? If the public domain is so great, why? What does it do for us? What is its role? These questions can be reduced to two: (1) What is the public domain? (2) Why should we focus on it? In the following pages, I will argue that the answer to the first question depends on the answer to the second.

Work that followed Lange's article offered various answers to the questions posed. For example, Lindberg and Patterson's book *The Nature of Copyright* (L. R. Patterson and Stanley W. Lindberg, *The Nature of Copyright: A Law of Users' Rights* (1991)) reverses the polarity from the normal depiction, and portrays copyright as a law of users' rights. The public domain is the figure and copyright the ground. The various privileges and defenses are not exceptions, they are at the heart of copyright, correctly understood. Copyright is, in fact, a system designed to feed the public domain providing temporary and narrowly limited rights, themselves subject to considerable restrictions even during their existence—all with the ultimate goal of promoting free access.

Jessica Litman's fine 1990 article, *The Public Domain*, portrays the public domain's primary function as allowing copyright law to continue to work notwithstanding the unrealistic, individualistic idea of creativity it depends on:

The public domain rescues us from this dilemma. It permits us to continue to exhort originality without acknowledging that our claims to take originality seriously are mostly pretense. It furnishes a crucial device to an otherwise unworkable system by reserving the raw material of authorship to the commons, thus leaving that raw material available for other authors to use. The public domain thus permits the law of copyright to avoid a confrontation with the poverty of some of the assumptions on which it is based.

Litman's definition of the public domain is both clear and terse: '[A] commons that includes those aspects of copyrighted works which copyright does not protect.' Precisely because she sees the function of the public domain as allowing the kinds of additive and interstitial creation that the language of individual originality fails to capture, her *definition* of the public domain includes the recyclable, unprotected elements in existing copyrighted works as well as those works that are not protected at all. Form follows function.

Yochai Benkler takes a slightly different approach. He follows Litman in rejecting the traditional, absolutist conception of the public domain, a conception which included only those things which are totally unprotected by copyright:

> The particular weakness of the traditional definition of the public domain is that it evokes an intuition about the baseline, while not in fact completely describing it. When one calls certain information 'in the public domain', one means that it is information whose use, absent special reasons to think otherwise, is permissible to anyone. When information is properly subject to copyright, the assumption (again absent specific factors to the contrary) is that its use is *not* similarly allowed to anyone but the owner and his or her licensees. The limited, term-of-art (public domain) does not include some important instances that, as a descriptive matter, are assumed generally to be permissible. For example, the traditional definition of public domain would treat short quotes for purposes of critical review as a fair use—hence as an affirmative defense—and not as a use in the public domain. It would be odd, however, to describe our system of copyright law as one in which users assume that they may not include a brief quotation in a critical review of its source. I venture that the opposite is true: such use generally is considered permissible, absent peculiar facts to the cont[r]ary.

Benkler's alternative definition, however, does not include every privileged use—such as, for example, the fair use privilege that I am able to vindicate only after litigating an intensely complicated case that involves highly specific factual inquiries.

> The functional definition therefore would be: The public domain is a range of uses of information that any person is privileged to make absent individualized facts that make a particular use by a particular person unprivileged. Conversely, the enclosed domain is the range of uses of information as to which someone has an exclusive right, and that no other person may make absent individualized facts that indicated permission from the holder of the right or otherwise privilege the specific use under the stated facts. These definitions add to the legal rules additionally thought of as the public domain, the range of privileged uses that are 'easy cases'.

The key to Benkler's analysis is his focus on the public domain's role in information production and use by all of us in our roles as consumers, citizens and future creators. We need to focus on those works, and aspects of works, that the public can notably free without having to go through a highly individualized factual inquiry. 'Free' meaning what? Earlier in this essay I asked what we mean when we speak of the freedom that the public domain will allow. Free trade in expression and innovation, as opposed to monopoly? Free access to expression and innovation, as opposed to access for pay? Or free access to innovation and expression, in the sense of not being subject to the right of another person to pick and choose who is given access, even if all have to pay some flat fee? Or is it common ownership or control that we seek, including the communal right to forbid certain kinds of uses of the shared resources? I *think* Benkler is arguing that the most important question here is whether lay people would know that a particular piece or aspect of information is free—in the sense of being *both* uncontrolled by anyone else and costless.

In this extract, the focus is on the importance of the public domain as it relates to the protection of copyright works. However, it is certainly the case that all the rights covered in this book raise questions regarding the public domain. As an example, while the colour orange might in principle function as a trade mark, given the limited number of colours available, it might also be a mark which many traders would wish to use. Similarly, in the case of patents, it is not possible to patent substances found in nature, such as a gene sequence, even though its discovery may have entailed considerable investment and skill. On the other hand, isolating a gene sequence through a technical process is characterized as a patentable 'invention'. Interestingly, there may be little difference between the two processes, suggesting the difficulties of mapping the boundaries of the public domain.

Another area where what belongs in the public domain is contested relates to intellectual creations (often biological, genetic, or cultural) that are generated communally and over time. The general term used to characterize these intangible creations is 'traditional knowledge'. At present, much of this 'traditional knowledge' is deemed to belong in the public domain because it does not fall within any of the obvious categories of intellectual property. As we shall see in the extract below, it is developing countries, many of which are rich in traditional knowledge, which are seeking the introduction of new forms of IPRs to protect traditional knowledge from misappropriation by those who were not responsible for producing it.

D. J. Gervais, 'The internationalization of intellectual property: new challenges from the very old and the very new' (2001–2) 12 Fordham Intellectual Property Media and Entertainment L. J. 929 at 955–65

i. The Importance of Traditional Knowledge

The expression 'traditional knowledge' is a shorter form of 'traditional knowledge, innovations and practices'. It includes a broad range of subject matters, for example traditional agricultural, biodiversity-related and medicinal knowledge and folklore. In the Model Provisions for National Laws on the Protection of Expressions of Folklore Against Illicit Exploitation and Other Prejudicial Actions, the WIPO and UNESCO define folklore as 'production consisting of characteristic elements of the traditional individuals reflecting the traditional artistic expectations of such a community ...' The protection of traditional knowledge is progressively taking center stage in global discussions concerning intellectual property and trade.

There are several reasons for the issue's sudden move to the forefront. First, a large number of countries believe that up to now they have not derived great benefits from 'traditional' forms of intellectual property, yet find themselves rich with traditional knowledge, especially genetic resources and folklore. They would like to exploit these resources, and several major companies share this interest. The second reason is the growing political importance of aboriginal communities in several countries.

...

ii. The Nature of the Challenge

Why is traditional knowledge such a challenge for the intellectual property framework? Expressions of folklore and several other forms of traditional knowledge do not qualify for protection because they are too old and are, therefore, in the public domain. Providing exclusive rights of any kind for an unlimited period of time would seem to go against the principle that intellectual property can be awarded only for a limited period of time, thus ensuring the return of intellectual property to the public domain for others to use. That way, it promotes the constitutional objective of progress in science and the useful arts. In other cases, the author of the material is not identifiable and there is thus no 'rightsholder' in the usual sense of the term. In fact, the author or inventor is often a large and diffuse group of people and the same 'work' or invention may have several versions and incarnations. Textile patterns, musical rhythms and dances are good examples of this kind of material. Additionally, expressions of folklore are refined and evolve over time.

Apart from the above-mentioned reasons for excluding some forms of traditional knowledge, there is clearly a lot of traditional material that is unfit for protection as intellectual property in any form. Examples include spiritual beliefs, methods of governance, languages, human remains and biological and genetic resources in their natural state, i.e. without any knowledge concerning their medicinal use. With the exception of these types of material not proper subject matter for protection per se, however, most other forms of traditional knowledge *could* qualify for copyright or patent protection if they had been created or invented in the usual sense. In response, holders of traditional knowledge argue that the current intellectual property regime was designed by Western countries for Western countries. It is certainly true that the main intellectual property agreements, including the Berne Convention, the Paris Convention and the more recent TRIPS Agreement were negotiated among mostly industrialized countries.

[After considering the difficulties of incorporating traditional knowledge within the subject matter protected by copyright and patents, Gervais continues:]

Property rights, as they are understood in Western legal systems, often do not exist in indigenous and local communities that hold traditional knowledge. In fact, because of its exclusionary effect, they now tend to see the attempt to obtain property rights on derivatives of their traditional knowledge as 'piracy'. Regarding the pharmaceutical, seed and agrochemical industries, they coined the term 'biopiracy' to denote the extraction and utilization of traditional knowledge, associated biological and genetic resources, and the acquisition of intellectual property rights on inventions derived from such knowledge or resources without providing for benefit-sharing with the individuals or community that provided the knowledge or resources.

iii. Assessing the Criticism

Some of the criticism leveled at the current intellectual system concerning its exclusionary effect is fair, but may be dealt with by relatively minor changes to current practices. For example, for applications for patents concerning drugs or other products that are derived from traditional knowledge sources, prior art searches could include traditional knowledge sources to ensure that the invention is indeed novel and non-obvious as required by patent laws worldwide. That said, cases in which patents should not have been granted are examples of bad patents, not of a bad patent system. Clearly, in that respect a dialogue has to be established among holders of traditional knowledge, the private sector and governments. 'Greater awareness-raising may assist to dispel certain misconceptions concerning intellectual property and result in more technical, finely-calibrated and nuanced assessments of the traditional knowledge/intellectual property nexus.'

Arguments used to show that the current intellectual property system cannot protect traditional knowledge are not all convincing either. The fact that a community owns traditional knowledge does not in itself exclude all forms of intellectual property protection. The example of collective marks and geographical indications show that in certain cases, rights can be granted to 'representatives' of a group or a community. There are also real property law concepts that would most closely match the needs of the traditional knowledge community and could perhaps be applied to intellectual property. The best example is probably the concept of 'communal property'.

[Gervais then goes on to ask how nonetheless traditional knowledge can be protected. He concludes that there is a second question which needs answering, that is on what basis intellectual property, itself, should be protected, as a way to answering the first.]

The challenge of protecting traditional knowledge forces one to think about what intellectual property actually is. An 'intellectual property-like' system could be adopted but this would beg the question of *what it is*, if *not* intellectual property. In other words, *why is it not intellectual property?* If we look at the constitutional 'requirement' that intellectual property promote the progress of science and useful arts, why would certain forms of traditional knowledge not be protected by intellectual property? Put differently, in the absence of a statutory exception, should intellectual property be defined by the common characteristics of current forms of intellectual property, namely (a) identifiable authors or inventors, (b) an identifiable work or invention or other object, and (c) defined restricted acts in relation to the said object without the authorization of the rightsholders? Or are these historical accidents, as it were, of the nineteenth century world in which these forms of intellectual property emerged? And yet, even if that is the case, how can one protect amorphous objects or categories of objects and grant exclusive rights to an ill-defined (and ill-definable) community or group of people?

These are the questions coming from traditional knowledge holders.

Gervais concludes his discussion of traditional knowledge by asking whether our current conceptions of intellectual property, particularly in relation to whom we identify as creators of intellectual property and what we deem to be appropriate subject matter for intellectual property protection, should be rethought.

FURTHER READING

J. Curci, *The Protection of Biodiversity and Traditional Knowledge in International Law of Intellectual Property* (Cambridge: Cambridge University Press, 2009).

H. Dagan, 'Property and the public domain' (2006) 18 Yale J. L. & Humanities 84.

A. Di Blasé, 'Traditional knowledge: cultural heritage or intellectual property right?' in V. Vadi and B. de Witte (eds), *Culture and International Economic Law* (London: Routledge, 2015).

P. Drahos, *Intellectual Property, Indigenous People and Their Knowledge* (Cambridge: Cambridge University Press, 2014).

G. Dutfield, 'Traditional knowledge, intellectual property and pharmaceutical innovation: what's left to discuss?' in M. M. David and D. J. Halbert (eds), *The SAGE Handbook of Intellectual Property* (London: SAGE, 2014).

D. Lametti, 'The concept of the anticommons' in H. Howe and J. Griffiths (eds), *Concepts of Property in Intellectual Property Law* (Cambridge: Cambridge University Press, 2013), ch. 10.

B. Vezina, 'Are they in or are they out? Traditional cultural expressions and the public domain: implications for trade' in C. B. Graber, K. Kuprecht, and J. C. Lai (eds), *International Trade in Indigenous Culture Heritage: Legal and Policy Issues* (Cheltenham: Edward Elgar, 2012).

J. Wilson, 'On the value of intellectual commons' in A. Lever (ed.), *New Frontiers in the Philosophy of Intellectual Property* (Cambridge: Cambridge University Press, 2012).

D. Zografos, *Intellectual Property and Traditional Cultural Expressions* (London: Edward Elgar, 2010).

1.2.8 CONCLUSION

The above discussion shows that each of the key justifications—natural rights, utilitarian, and economic—for IPRs, like the notion of the public domain, has contentious aspects. As such, you may feel that one justification is no more persuasive than any other. Indeed, attempting to explain IPRs according to one particular justification, apart from anything else, oversimplifies the ways in which laws are generated. That being said, it is still useful to be aware of the key features and limitations of the justifications usually propounded for IPRs, not least because these arguments tend to be utilized, either separately or cumulatively, in the context of law reform. As one commentator has observed, 'The other reason intellectual property theory retains value is that it can catalyze useful conversations among the various people and institutions responsible for the shaping of the law.'[25]

FURTHER READING

G. S. Alexander and E. M. Peñalver, *An Introduction to Property Theory* (Cambridge: Cambridge University Press, 2012), ch. 9, 'Intellectual property'.

W. Fisher, 'Theories of intellectual property' in S. R. Munzer (ed.), *New Essays in the Legal and Political Theory of Property* (Cambridge: Cambridge University Press, 2001), pp. 168–99.

R. P. Merges, *Justifying Intellectual Property* (Cambridge, MA: Harvard University Press, 2011).

1.3 INTERNATIONAL AND REGIONAL FRAMEWORK

1.3.1 THE INTERNATIONAL CONTEXT

1.3.1.1 Introduction and WIPO

As early as the middle of the 19th century, countries were entering into bilateral agreements with the aim of protecting their intellectual property. And it was at this time that a coherent intellectual property regime first began to emerge. These developments coincided with, and arguably were in part a consequence of, a period of growth in international trade. Individual countries were concerned that the interests of their traders should be protected when they

---

[25] Fisher, 'Theories of intellectual property', pp. 168–99.

ventured into foreign markets. Indeed, by the end of that century, again as a reaction to this increase in international commerce, international multilateral agreements also came into being. Of these, the most important are the Berne Convention and the Paris Convention because they were the first multilateral treaties dealing with, in the case of the former, copyrights and, in the case of the latter, patents, trade marks, and designs. Indeed, these conventions continue to have relevance to the present day and will be discussed in more detail in later chapters.[26] Another product of this period was the United International Bureaux for the Protection of Intellectual Property (BIRPI), which became the predecessor to the World Intellectual Property Organization (WIPO). The climax of this internationalism or multilateralism was perhaps the establishment of the World Trade Organization (WTO) in the second half of the 20th century and the later Agreement on Trade Related Aspects of Intellectual Property Rights (TRIPS). Finally, it has been argued that, most recently, we are in a new phase of bilateralism (reflected in the growth of free trade agreements) and plurilateralism (as manifested in the push for a number of countries to agree the Anti-Counterfeiting Trade Agreement (ACTA)), a trend that we will examine in the conclusion of this section.

As we have seen, the predecessor to WIPO was BIRPI, which was established in 1893 to administer the Paris and Berne Conventions. Today that role is handled by WIPO, an agency of the United Nations established in 1970 following the entry into force of the WIPO Convention 1967 and based in Geneva.

According to Article 3 of the Convention, one of the central aims of WIPO is:

> to promote the protection of intellectual property throughout the world through cooperation among States and, where appropriate, in collaboration with any other international organization.

WIPO fulfils this aim by, inter alia, administering a host of international intellectual property conventions. Some of the most important of these include: the Berne Convention[27] (which is concerned with the protection of authors in relation to literary and artistic works); the Paris Convention[28] (dealing with patents, trade marks, and designs); the Rome Convention[29] (concerning the protection of performers, sound recordings, and broadcasts); the WIPO Copyright Treaty and the WIPO Performances and Phonograms Treaty;[30] the Madrid Protocol[31] (which facilitates filing trade marks in multiple countries); and the Patent Cooperation Treaty[32] (which facilitates the filing of patents). Each of these treaties will be considered in more detail in the relevant chapters).

WIPO also provides a number of important services. Among these is its role as a domain name dispute resolution provider. As well, WIPO provides the necessary infrastructure for the Madrid Protocol and the Patent Cooperation Treaty. Because of its international membership, WIPO also provides a useful forum for the discussion of new initiatives in

---

[26] See Chapters 2 and 9.

[27] Berne Convention for the Protection of Literary and Artistic Works 1886 (revised, Paris 1971).

[28] Paris Convention for the Protection of Industrial Property 1883 (revised, Stockholm 1967).

[29] Rome Convention for the Protection of Performers, Producers of Phonograms and Broadcasting Organizations 1961.

[30] WIPO Copyright Treaty 1996 and WIPO Performances and Phonograms Treaty 1996.

[31] Protocol Relating to the Madrid Agreement Concerning the International Registration of Marks 1989 (last amended 2007).

[32] Patent Cooperation Treaty 1970.

intellectual property regulation. For example, WIPO regularly hosts meetings on the issue of the protection of traditional knowledge and cultural expression and, in 2012, a Diplomatic Conference at which the Beijing Treaty on Audiovisual Performances was adopted.

1.3.1.2 WTO and the TRIPS Agreement

In the 1980s and 1990s, developed countries became increasingly frustrated with WIPO. This was for two main reasons. First, numerous developing countries were now signatories to conventions administered by WIPO and attempts to revise those conventions inevitably gave rise to complex and highly politicized negotiations, which a number of countries concluded could not be resolved within a specialist organization such as WIPO. Second, and importantly for countries which were net exporters of intellectual property, there were no real international enforcement mechanisms available if signatories did not comply with their convention obligations. The answer to both these problems for these latter countries was to seek to bring the international regulation of intellectual property within the jurisdiction of the WTO. This organization was established on 1 January 1995, following the Uruguay round of trade negotiations. Unlike WIPO, the WTO, which is also based in Geneva, is concerned with the regulation of world trade more generally and, as of 2015, had a membership of 162 countries. The WTO administers the TRIPS Agreement, which was also a product of the Uruguay round. It is to this agreement that we now turn.

According to the WTO, the TRIPS Agreement has as its aim the provision of adequate IPRs, the provision of effective enforcement measures for those rights, and a forum for the settlement of multilateral disputes. A summary of the main features of the TRIPS Agreement is provided on the WTO website[33] and is extracted below:

> The areas of intellectual property that it covers are: copyright and related rights (i.e. the rights of performers, producers of sound recordings and broadcasting organizations); trademarks including service marks; geographical indications including appellations of origin; industrial designs; patents including the protection of new varieties of plants; the layout-designs of integrated circuits; and undisclosed information including trade secrets and test data.
>
> The three main features of the Agreement are:
>
> * Standards. In respect of each of the main areas of intellectual property covered by the TRIPS Agreement, the Agreement sets out the minimum standards of protection to be provided by each Member. Each of the main elements of protection is defined, namely the subject-matter to be protected, the rights to be conferred and permissible exceptions to those rights, and the minimum duration of protection. The Agreement sets these standards by requiring, first, that the substantive obligations of the main conventions of the WIPO, the Paris Convention for the Protection of Industrial Property (Paris Convention) and the Berne Convention for the Protection of Literary and Artistic Works (Berne Convention) in their most recent versions, must be complied with. With the exception of the provisions of the Berne Convention on moral rights, all the main substantive provisions of these conventions are incorporated by reference and thus become obligations under the TRIPS Agreement between TRIPS Member countries. The relevant provisions are to be found in Articles 2.1 and 9.1 of the TRIPS Agreement, which relate, respectively, to the Paris Convention and to the Berne Convention. Secondly, the TRIPS Agreement adds a substantial number of additional obligations

---

[33] <www.wto.org/english/tratop_e/trips_e/intel2_e.htm>.

on matters where the pre-existing conventions are silent or were seen as being inadequate. The TRIPS Agreement is thus sometimes referred to as a Berne and Paris-plus agreement.

- Enforcement. The second main set of provisions deals with domestic procedures and remedies for the enforcement of intellectual property rights. The Agreement lays down certain general principles applicable to all IPR enforcement procedures. In addition, it contains provisions on civil and administrative procedures and remedies, provisional measures, special requirements related to border measures and criminal procedures, which specify, in a certain amount of detail, the procedures and remedies that must be available so that right holders can effectively enforce their rights.

- Dispute settlement. The Agreement makes disputes between WTO Members about the respect of the TRIPS obligations subject to the WTO's dispute settlement procedures.

In addition the Agreement provides for certain basic principles, such as national and most-favoured-nation treatment, and some general rules to ensure that procedural difficulties in acquiring or maintaining IPRs do not nullify the substantive benefits that should flow from the Agreement. The obligations under the Agreement will apply equally to all Member countries, but developing countries will have a longer period to phase them in. Special transition arrangements operate in the situation where a developing country does not presently provide product patent protection in the area of pharmaceuticals.

The TRIPS Agreement is a minimum standards agreement, which allows Members to provide more extensive protection of intellectual property if they so wish. Members are left free to determine the appropriate method of implementing the provisions of the Agreement within their own legal system and practice.

It is clear from this description that the TRIPS provisions have an inevitable impact on each of the IPRs. The details of this impact will be looked at in the individual chapters concerning those rights. For now, it is worth mentioning the WTO Dispute Settlement mechanism that is available where there is a dispute concerning TRIPS. A complaint by a WTO member that another member is violating the TRIPS Agreement will first trigger a consultation, which if it does not settle the dispute may lead to the establishment of an expert panel which will issue a report, with the possibility of review by an appellate panel. Since the TRIPS Agreement came into effect, there have been 34 requests for consultation, which have ranged across the areas of copyright, trade marks, geographical indications, patents, and enforcement. Initially, by far the largest number of complaints emanated from the US and the EU. More recently, not only have the number of complaints declined but those initiating them have tended to be developing countries. Indeed, the last time either the US or EU brought a complaint was in 2010. It is difficult to draw firm conclusions from these figures, but one might speculate that the TRIPS Agreement has failed to be the efficient mechanism for dispute settlements as had been hoped for by its signatories.

As we have just seen, one goal of the TRIPS Agreement was to provide an enforcement mechanism where there are disputes concerning intellectual property between WTO members. However, for its original signatories it had another important purpose, which was to harmonize IPRs internationally. At the time, the high level of harmonization in relation to various IPRs, together with the coercive effect of the WTO Dispute Resolution Procedure, created an enormous pressure on developing countries to raise their standards of intellectual property protection. Although they were given some leeway in the time frame for compliance (developing countries by 1999, and least developed countries by 2005), nonetheless, it proved difficult and some would argue counterproductive for developing countries to meet these standards. Indeed, much of the criticism of TRIPS has revolved around the relative disadvantages that it is supposed to create for developing countries. This is a view taken by Peter Drahos and John Braithwaite.

P. Drahos and J. Braithwaite, *Information Feudalism: Who Owns the Knowledge Economy?* (London: Earthscan, 2002), pp. 10–13

Why sign TRIPS?

During the course of an interview in 1994 with a senior US trade negotiator he remarked to us that 'probably less than 50 people were responsible for TRIPS'. TRIPS is the most important agreement on intellectual property of the 20th century. More than one hundred signed it on behalf of their nations in the splendid Salle Royale of the Palais des Congres in Marrakesh on 15th April 1994.

TRIPS is one of 28 agreements that make up the Final Act of the Uruguay Round of MultiLateral Trade Negotiations, the negotiations that had begun in Punta del Este in 1986. Another of those agreements established the WTO, and it is the WTO that administers TRIPS. In the US, high technology multinationals greeted the signing of TRIPS with considerable satisfaction. TRIPS was the first stage in the global recognition of an investment morality that sees knowledge as a private, rather than public, good. The intellectual property standards contained in TRIPS, obligatory on all members of the WTO, would help them to enforce that morality around the world. In India, after the signing of TRIPS, hundreds of thousands of farmers gathered to protest the intrusion of patents on the seeds of their agricultural futures. The Indian generics industry warned of dramatic price increases in essential medicines that would follow from the obligation in TRIPS to grant 20-year patents on pharmaceutical products. In Africa, there was little discussion of TRIPS.

TRIPs is about more than patents. It sets minimum standards in copyright, trade marks, geographical indications, industrial designs and layout designs of integrated circuits. TRIPS effectively globalizes the set of intellectual property principles it contains, because most states of the world are members of, or are seeking membership of, the WTO. It also has a crucial harmonizing impact on intellectual property regulation because it sets, in some cases, quite detailed standards of intellectual property law. Every member, for example, has to have a copyright law that protects computer programs as a literary work, as well as a patent law that does not exclude micro-organisms and microbiological processes from patentability. The standards in TRIPS will profoundly affect the ownership of the 21st century's two great technologies—digital technology and biotechnology. Copyright, patents and protection for layout-designs are all used to protect digital technology, whereas patents and trade secrets are the principal means by which biotechnological knowledge is being enclosed. TRIPS also obliges states to provide effective enforcement procedures against the infringement of intellectual property rights.

One of the puzzles this book sets out to solve is why states should give up sovereignty over something as fundamental as the property laws that determine the ownership of information and the technologies that so profoundly affect the basic rights of their citizens. The puzzle deepens when it is realized that in immediate trade terms the globalization of intellectual property really only benefitted the US and to a lesser extent the European Community. No one disagrees that TRIPS has conferred massive benefits on the US economy, the world's biggest net intellectual property exporter or that it has strengthened the hand of those corporations with large intellectual property portfolios. It was the US and the European Community that between them had the world's dominant software, pharmaceutical, chemical and entertainment industries, as well as the world's most important trade marks. The rest of the developed countries and all developing countries were in the position of being importers with nothing really to gain by agreeing to terms of trade for intellectual property that would offer so much protection to the comparative advantage the US enjoyed in intellectual property-related goods.

...

One standard reply we received in our interviews when we put this puzzle to policy-makers was that 'TRIPS was part of a package in which we got agriculture'. The WTO Agreement on Agriculture, however, does not confer anything like the benefits on developing countries that TRIPS does on the US and the European Community. There is also another irony here. Increasingly, agricultural goods are the subject of intellectual property rights as patents are extended to seeds and plants. Agricultural countries will find that they have to pay more for the patented agricultural inputs that they purchase from the world's agro-chemical companies. In addition they will have to compete with the cost-advantages that biotechnology brings to US farmers (not to mention the subsidies that US and EU farmers continue to receive). By signing TRIPS, agricultural exporters have signed away at least some of their comparative advantage in agriculture.

Sometimes we were told that 'we will be eventual winners from intellectual property'. While it is good to be optimistic about one's distant destiny, it does explain why normally hard-nosed trade negotiators would take the highly dangerous route of agreeing to the globalization of property rules over knowledge that had brought their countries so few gains in the past. Of the 3.5 million patents in existence in the 1970s, the decade before the TRIPS negotiations, nationals of developing countries held about 1 percent. Developing countries such as South Korea, Singapore, Brazil and India, that were industrializing, were doing so in the absence of a globalized intellectual property regime.

More disturbing for developing countries is the development cost of an intellectual property regime. The basis of competition lies in the development of skills. The acquisition of skills by newcomers disturbs roles and hierarchies. After India built a national drug industry, it began exporting bulk drugs and formulations to places such as Canada. A developing country which had acquired skills threatened those at the top of the international hierarchy of pharmaceutical production—the US, Japan, Germany and the UK.

...

The answer to our question about why developing countries signed TRIPS has much to do with democracy—or rather, its failure...Put starkly, the intellectual property rights regime we have today largely represents the failure of democratic processes both nationally and internationally. A small number of US companies, which were established players in the knowledge game...captured the US trade-agenda-setting process and then, in partnership with European and Japanese multinationals, drafted intellectual property principles that became the blueprint for TRIPS...The resistance of developing countries was crushed through trade power...

One retort to this might be that corporations are entitled to lobby, and, in any case, developing countries agreed to TRIPS through a process of bargaining amongst sovereigns. It is indeed true that corporations are entitled to lobby. It is important that big business makes its views and policy preferences known to government since around the globe it represents hundreds of millions of jobs and investors. However, that lobbying in relation to property rights should take place under conditions of democratic bargaining. Democratic bargaining matters crucially to the definition of property rights because of the consequences of property rules for all individuals within a society. Property rights confer authority over resources. When authority is granted to the few over resources on which the many depend, the few gain power over the goals of the many. This has consequences for both political and economic freedom within a society.

The stakes are high in the case of intellectual property rights. Intellectual property rights are a source of authority and power over informational resources on which the many depend—information in the form of chemical formulae, the DNA in plants and animals, the algorithms that underpin digital technology and the knowledge in books and electronic databases. These resources matter to communities, regions and to the development of states.

Drahos and Braithwaite argue that adherence to the TRIPS Agreement has come at a cost to developing and the least developed countries. By way of contrast, Gutowski suggests that such a view is too simplistic. In particular, it fails to recognize that the TRIPS Agreement is based on economic rather than moral principles.

R. Gutowski, 'The marriage of intellectual property and international trade in the TRIPs agreement: strange bedfellows or a match made in heaven' (1999) 47 Buff. L. R. 713 at 754–60

Indeed, outside the ballyhooed rhetoric of politicians and industry lobbyists, IP protection is generally recognized as an economic, not a moral issue. The fact that an ever-increasing percentage of international trade involves IP corroborates this observation. The WTO is thus the appropriate forum to address the international impacts of IP. At another time IP may have more properly been left to bilateral arrangements; however, today's truly global economy and the paramount importance of technology and information point to the strong link between trade and IP. Even concerns about ideological imperialism and insensitivity to cultural differences are less than compelling today given the global movement towards market economies and free trade. This shift is consistent with inclusion of IP in trade negotiations. The fact that most nations have actively selected this course makes it difficult to point a finger at the West for stamping out indigenous beliefs or alternate notions of property. Local governments are complicit. They have accepted the market paradigm, for better or worse, of which IP is an increasingly important component. Indeed, one author who contends that 'the culture and heritage of developing countries [are] on a collision course with the global consumer culture of the more powerful developed countries,' nonetheless urges that an IP regime can and should be used as a 'cultural shield' to protect native and indigenous culture. Sound development strategies must therefore recognize local and foreign IPRs. In this context IP concerns cannot and should not escape the auspices of the WTO, as the fortunes of the developing countries and the world trading system are closely intertwined.

Developing countries ultimately accepted the TRIPs Agreement in a bargained-for exchange which included concessions on agricultural export subsidies by the European Community, increased market access for tropical products, generous transitional arrangements, and protection against unilateral measures primarily by the United States and other powerful, Western industrialized nations. Certainly the dispute resolution procedures of the WTO make developing countries less vulnerable to bilateral confrontation with the United States and the European Community. Moreover, developing nations also realized that IP protection is increasingly important in order to attract multinational capital and investment. For certain large developing countries such as India and Brazil, it is likely that they recognized IP protection was in their own best interests in benefiting local inventors. Some analysts have found that in newly industrializing economies, recognition of IPRs correlates with the level of economic development. That is, once a country reaches a certain 'development threshold,' then protection of IPRs will generate economic activity sufficient for the political structure to favour innovation over imitation.

The result of increased global IP protection is a balance between gains and concessions. While the effect of protecting foreign IP will likely increase the short-term cost of knowledge-intensive goods to developing countries as importers, this loss is set against concessions on important exports, such as textiles and agriculture, from developing nations. Additionally developing countries will benefit from the advantages of a multilateral agreement over the likely stricter consequences of unilateral accords. At a minimum, for developing countries inclusion of IP protection into GATT was a lesser evil than assured pressure and likely sanctions from developed-world trading partners.

Ultimately, recognition and protection of IPRs is important not simply because Madonna or Nike or Microsoft has a 'right' to stop international piracy and copying of their intellectual property. More importantly, there are compelling arguments that IP protection will indeed benefit the developing world in the long-run—particularly in creating incentives for domestic and foreign researchers and entrepreneurs to invest resources in innovative technologies and solutions to problems indigenous to their countries.

The impact of IP on diverse fields ranging from scientific research to creative authorship to commercial development highlights its pervasive importance to industrial progress. Furthermore, protection of IP in developing nations will reduce the 'brain drain' of talented individuals who leave poor countries in order to make a better living elsewhere. Recognition of IPRs will make it possible for these professionals to profit from their creativity and inventiveness in their home country.

We must disabuse ourselves of the image that all technology comes from developed countries. Incremental innovation rather than media-hyped technological 'break-throughs' can be of immense value to a developing nation. Developing nations recognized this potential in signing on to TRIPs. IP protection is not a singular prescription for development, but it is one important aspect to a development plan. Although the origins of IPRs may hearken back to a brute egoist carving out exclusive proprietorship of ideas, utilized appropriately they can and often have transcended their raw foundation to advance economic development.

Gutowski characterizes the TRIPS Agreement as a balance of gains and concessions for both developed and developing countries. Others have seen the TRIPS Agreement as imbalanced, with its advantages accruing largely to the developed countries. Recently, it has been suggested that we are now entering a period of what has been termed the 'new bilateralism' characterized, inter alia, by the proliferation of free trade agreements (FTAs). According to this view, these bilateral agreements are a consequence of a failure of TRIPS to evolve to meet new challenges arising from the interaction between intellectual property and global commerce.

H. He, 'The development of free trade agreements and international protection of intellectual property rights in the WTO era—new bilateralism and its future' (2010) 41 IIC 254 at 257, 262–3, 264, 283

B. Seeking Non-Tariff Benefits

In general, WTO members enter into FTAs for preferential treatment. The WTO erases significant trade barriers throughout the world. At the same time, it intensifies global competition, especially among developing countries. FTAs, however, can provide the parties trade protection from global competition, giving them a competitive advantage. By definition, an FTA eliminates barriers to trade in goods (and increasingly services) among its parties, but each party remains free to pursue its own trade policy with regard to third parties. In short, FTAs are a legal vehicle to provide preferential treatment to the parties to the exclusion of other WTO members.

But developed and developing countries have different interests in preferential treatment. Developing countries enter FTAs for tariff benefits, seeking a better position in world major markets. To some extent, developing countries are compelled to enter FTAs. The cost of non-participation mounts as more countries enter FTAs. Bolivia, India, Mongolia, Pakistan and Sri Lanka do not enjoy the same access to the United States or the EU markets as Chile, Jordan or Mexico, and they have already seen their trade diminish since bilateral trade agreements were signed. In contrast, developed countries, such as the United States, enter FTAs primarily for non-tariff benefits.

[By non-tariff benefits, he is referring to what is termed the 'TRIPS plus nature' of many FTAs, in that they confer greater protection on IPRs in the contracting countries than is demanded by TRIPS.]

...

Non-tariff benefits are not the entire reason for developed countries to pursue a new bilateralism. Economically, the WTO, as a global trade system, is superior to bilateral, even regional, trade systems. Institutionally, however, negotiations on global trade agreements involve huge transaction costs relative to bilateral agreements.

...

Consequently, if IPR protection is to be upgraded within the WTO forum, tremendous difficulties must be surmounted. In establishing the WTO Agreements, the security and predictability of the multilateral trading system took high priority. The TRIPS Agreement has proved to be almost unchangeable. The WTO consensus-based decision-making process, the Council for TRIPS and the Dispute Settlement Body are all accountable.

...

[He then goes on to examine the relationship between FTAs and the most favoured nation treatment obligation under the TRIPS Agreement. He argues that although FTAs are bilateral, once the parties have raised the level of protection afforded to IPRs within their borders beyond the minimum standards demanded by TRIPS, they are obligated by Article 4 to accord the same heightened protection to the IPRs of any nationals of any other country which is a party to TRIPs. He continues at 283:]

... [T]he new bilateralism produces TRIPS-plus provisions that are global in nature due to the MFN [most favoured nation] treatment obligation under the TRIPS Agreement, even though these provisions are in bilateral FTAs. These TRIPS-plus provisions are shaping international IPR protection and enforcement. On the other hand, in contrast to the old bilateralism, the traditional wisdom can lead the new bilateralism nowhere. It is not true in the WTO era that a party to an FTA, enjoying preferential treatment under the FTA, must favour further multilateral trade liberalization, and thus it is always wise to tie IPR issues to trade negotiations. To the extent that the vested interest in existing preferential treatment under FTAs is greater than that in advancing plurilateral or multilateral trade agreements, existing parties to FTAs tend to avert further trade liberalization.

In his article, He notes that it has proved difficult to amend TRIPS and this is one reason for the rise in bilateral agreements. This difficulty has also manifested itself in failed attempts by developed countries to negotiate stronger enforcement mechanisms within the context of the WTO and the TRIPS Agreement commensurate with the TRIPS plus measures incorporated into the FTAs. In part, this is because developing countries within the WTO see no particular benefit to themselves in such changes. The result, according to He, has been the rise of a new multilateralism.

One example of this new multilateralism has been the attempt by the developed countries to negotiate a new agreement, ACTA. The aim of ACTA is to raise the levels of enforcement for IPRs (particularly through cross-border measures and criminal penalties) and it would be administered outside existing international fora such as the WTO and WIPO. The first negotiations took place between a small group of countries—Japan, the US, and the EU—and later extended to several more. By January 2012, it had been signed by Australia, Canada, Japan, Korea, Morocco, New Zealand, Singapore, and the US and by the EU and 22 of its Member States. As such, some commentators have described it as a plurilateral treaty. The possible future effects of ACTA will depend on how many countries ratify the agreement.[34] Interestingly, as of January 2016, only one signatory, Japan, has ratified ACTA. Indeed, in June 2013, the EU Parliament voted to reject the agreement, not least because of the secrecy of the surrounding negotiations and a consequent concern amongst some Member States that it would be overly protective of IPRs.

Similar concerns have been raised about two trade and investment treaties, the EU–US Transatlantic Trade and Investment Partnership (TTIP) and the Trans-Pacific Partnership (TPP). TTIP is currently under negotiation and TPP was signed on 4 February 2016 but has not yet come into force. The purpose of these treaties is to promote free trade amongst its signatories and intellectual property is one of their concerns. Amongst the issues raised in relation to intellectual property in TTIP is the need for appropriate and uniform levels of protection for geographical indications and trade secrets. TPP has extensive provisions dealing with various aspects of intellectual property which again are aimed at creating mutually agreed levels of protection and enforcement. For example, copyright protection is set at a minimum of the life of the author plus 70 years. And, in the case of trade secrets, criminal procedures and penalties will need to be introduced. It is notable, however, that the parties were unable to agree on the type of protection to be offered to geographical indications. It will be interesting to see if the negotiations on TTIP will be any more successful.

FURTHER READING

M. Blakeney, 'International proposals for the criminal enforcement of intellectual property rights: international concern with counterfeiting and piracy' [2009] IPQ 1.

C. M. Correa, *Trade Related Aspects of Intellectual Property Rights: A Commentary on the TRIPS Agreement* (Oxford: Oxford University Press, 2007).

G. B. Dinwoodie and R. C. Dreyfuss, *A Neofederalist Vision of TRIPS: The Resilience of the International Intellectual Property Regime* (Oxford: Oxford University Press, 2012).

C. Geiger, 'Weakening multilateralism in intellectual property lawmaking: a European perspective on ACTA' [2012] WIPO J 166.

A. Kur and M. Levin, *Intellectual Property Rights in a Fair World Trade System: Proposals for Reform of TRIPS* (Cheltenham: Edward Elgar, 2011).

---

[34] Six ratifications are necessary for ACTA to come into force.

D. Matthews and P. Zikovska, 'The rise and fall of the anti-counterfeiting trade agreement (ACTA): lessons for the European Union' [2013] IIC 626.

C. May, *A Global Political Economy of Intellectual Property Rights* (London: Routledge, 2000), ch. 3, 'TRIPS as a watershed'.

S. Sell, *Private Power, Public Law: The Globalization of Intellectual Property Rights* (Cambridge: Cambridge University Press, 2003).

K. Weatherall, 'ACTA as a new kind of international IP lawmaking' (2011) 26 American University International Law Review 839.

K. Weatherall, 'Politics, compromise, text, and the failures of the Anti-Counterfeiting Trade Agreement' (2011) 33 Sydney Law Review 229–63.

P. K. Yu, 'The non-multilateral approach to international intellectual property norm-setting' in D. J. Gervais (ed.), *International Intellectual Property: A Handbook of Contemporary Research* (Cheltenham: Edward Elgar, 2015), ch. 3, pp. 83–120.

1.3.2 THE EUROPEAN CONTEXT

Another influence on the shape of UK intellectual property law has been EU law. As long as it is a Member State of the European Union, the UK is bound by the Treaty on the Functioning of the European Union (TFEU)[35] and related legislation. The TFEU now explicitly refers to intellectual property,[36] highlighting how over the past few decades (and coinciding with the increased importance of intellectual property to global economies), the European Union has become increasingly preoccupied with the protection of intellectual property and with its implications for the single European market and the promotion of undistorted competition between Member States. This preoccupation has manifested itself in three key areas: free movement of goods and the exhaustion doctrine; the harmonization of IPRs and the introduction of EU-wide IPRs; and the relationship between IPRs and competition law. The common thread between these three areas is that they all, at some level, concern the relationship between the internal market and competition.

1.3.2.1 Free movement of goods and exhaustion of rights

One of the key goals of the TFEU is to create a single market. Articles 34 and 35 TFEU (ex Articles 28 and 29 TEC) prohibit the quantitative restrictions on the import and export of goods, and all measures having equivalent effect. Article 36 TFEU (ex Article 30 TEC) creates an exception to this prohibition, in that it does not preclude prohibitions or restrictions in relation to, inter alia, the protection of industrial and commercial property, which

---

[35] Previously known as the Treaty establishing the European Economic Community 1957, renamed as the Treaty establishing the European Community (TEC) by the Treaty of the European Union 1992 (TEU), and subsequently renamed again as the Treaty on the Functioning of the European Union (TFEU) as a result of the Treaty of Lisbon 2007.

[36] See in particular Art. 118 TFEU: 'In the context of the establishment and functioning of the internal market, the European Parliament and the Council, acting in accordance with the ordinary legislative procedure, shall establish measures for the creation of European intellectual property rights to provide uniform protection of intellectual property rights throughout the Union and for the setting up of centralised Union-wide authorisation, coordination and supervision arrangements.' See also Arts 207 and 262 TFEU.

has been interpreted by the CJEU to include IPRs. However, Article 36 TFEU also states that such prohibitions or restrictions shall not constitute a means of arbitrary discrimination or a disguised restriction on trade between Member States. Such a problem might arise because IPRs are territorial in nature. As a result, an IPR owner in one Member State might seek to prevent the importation of goods embodying their IPR and legitimately placed on the market in other Member States. So, for example, Dior, which has trade marks for Dior perfume in both France and the Netherlands, may seek to prevent perfumes legitimately purchased under their trade mark in France from being imported and resold in the Netherlands. Obviously, if IPRs are used in this way to control the import or export of goods this could be seen as a means of arbitrary discrimination or a disguised restriction on trade between Member States.

The apparent contradiction within Article 36 TFEU between the aim of establishing free movement of goods and the protection of IPRs is one that the CJEU has sought to reconcile via the doctrine of exhaustion of rights. Put briefly, this doctrine is that, where goods have been first placed on the market in one Member State by an IPR owner or with his consent, the IPR owner cannot rely on his IPRs to oppose further dealings in those particular goods in that or other Member States. In more positive terms, Keeling has described the doctrine of exhaustion as meaning: 'simply that the lawful owner of specific products that have been placed on the market by, or with the consent of the right-owner may use, sell, or otherwise dispose of those products'.[37] The doctrine was first established in *Deutsche Grammophon v Metro*.

Deutsche Grammophon v Metro Case 78/70 [1971] CMLR 631

A subsidiary of Deutsche Grammophon had marketed sound recordings in France. These sound recordings were purchased by Metro who sought to import them into Germany. Deutsche Grammophon objected that this was an infringement of its distribution right under German copyright law and obtained an injunction from the German regional court (Landgericht), Hamburg, prohibiting Metro from selling or otherwise distributing the sound recordings. On appeal to the Main regional court (Oberlandesgericht), proceedings were stayed and questions referred to the CJEU. In delivering its preliminary ruling, the Court clarified the scope of Article 36 of the then EEC Treaty, which is now Article 36 TFEU.

[11] Article 36 mentions among the prohibitions or restrictions on the free movement of goods permitted by it those that are justified for the protection of industrial and commercial property. If it be assumed that a right analogous to copyright can be covered by these provisions it follows, however, from this Article that although the Treaty does not affect the existence of the industrial property rights conferred by the national legislation of a member-State, the exercise of these rights may come within the prohibitions of the Treaty. Although Article 36 permits prohibitions or restrictions on the free movement of goods that are justified for the protection of industrial and commercial property, it only allows such restrictions on the freedom of trade to the extent that they are justified for the protection of the rights that form the specific object of this property.

---

[37] D. T. Keeling, *Intellectual Property Rights in EU Law*, vol. 1 (Oxford: Oxford University Press, 2003), p. 76.

[12] If a protection right analogous to copyright is used in order to prohibit in one member-State the marketing of goods that have been brought onto the market by the holder of the right or with his consent in the territory of another member-State solely because this marketing has not occurred in the domestic market, such a prohibition maintaining the isolation of the national markets conflicts with the essential aim of the Treaty, the integration of the national markets into one uniform market. This aim could not be achieved if by virtue of the various legal systems of the member-States private persons were able to divide the market and cause arbitrary discriminations or disguised restrictions in trade between the member-States.

[13] Accordingly, it would conflict with the provisions regarding the free movement of goods in the Common Market if a manufacturer of recordings exercised the exclusive right granted to him by the legislation of a member-State to market the protected articles in order to prohibit the marketing in that member-State of products that had been sold by him himself or with his consent in another member-State solely because this marketing had not occurred in the territory of the first member-State.

In *Deutsche Grammophon*, the CJEU sought to justify the exhaustion of rights doctrine in the context of Article 36 of the EEC Treaty (now Article 36 TFEU) by drawing a distinction between the existence and exercise of the IPR. The doctrine was meant to impact only upon the exercise of the IPR and not its existence. The existence/exercise dichotomy held sway for much of the 1970s, but it came to be seen as a vague and artificial distinction[38] and eventually gave way to the idea first canvassed in *Deutsche Grammophon* that the Article 36 exception is only relevant where it is being used to protect the specific subject matter of the IPR.

An early attempt to define the somewhat 'esoteric concept' of the 'specific subject matter' of the IPR,[39] at least in relation to patents and trade marks, occurred in *Centrafarm v Sterling Drug*.

Centrafarm v Sterling Drug Case 15/74 [1974] ECR 1147

A patented drug had been marketed under the trade mark 'Negram' by a subsidiary of the patent owner (Sterling Drug) in both Germany and the UK. Centrafarm purchased quantities of this drug placed on the market in the UK and sought to import it into the Netherlands and to sell it under the name 'Negram'. Sterling Drug brought proceedings in the Dutch court for both patent and trade mark infringement. The Hoge Raad referred a number of interrelated questions concerning free movement of goods to the CJEU. In its judgment, the CJEU first considered the relationship between the free movement of goods and patent protection.

As regards question I (a)

4. This question requires the court to state whether, under the conditions postulated, the rules in the EEC Treaty concerning the free movement of goods prevent the patentee from ensuring that the product protected by the patent is not marketed by others.

---

[38] Keeling, *Intellectual Property Rights in EU Law*, pp. 54–5.
[39] Keeling, *Intellectual Property Rights in EU Law*, p. 61.

5. As a result of the provisions in the Treaty relating to the free movement of goods and in particular of Article 30 [now Article 34 TFEU], quantitative restrictions on imports and all measures having equivalent effect are prohibited between Member States.

6. By Article 36 [now Article 36 TFEU] these provisions shall nevertheless not include prohibitions or restrictions on imports justified on grounds of the protection of industrial or commercial property.

7. Nevertheless, it is clear from this same Article, in particular its second sentence, as well as from the context, that whilst the Treaty does not affect the existence of rights recognized by the legislation of a Member State in matters of industrial and commercial property, yet the exercise of these rights may nevertheless, depending on the circumstances, be affected by the prohibitions in the Treaty.

8. Inasmuch as it provides an exception to one of the fundamental principles of the common market, Article 36 [now Article 36 TFEU] in fact only admits of derogations from the free movement of goods where such derogations are justified for the purpose of safeguarding rights which constitute the specific subject matter of this property.

9. In relation to patents, the specific subject matter of the industrial property is the guarantee that the patentee, to reward the creative effort of the inventor, has the exclusive right to use an invention with a view to manufacturing industrial products and putting them into circulation for the first time, either directly or by the grant of licences to third parties, as well as the right to oppose infringements.

10. An obstacle to the free movement of goods may arise out of the existence, within a national legislation concerning industrial and commercial property, of provisions laying down that a patentee's right is not exhausted when the product protected by the patent is marketed in another Member State, with the result that the patentee can prevent importation of the product into his own Member State when it has been marketed in another state.

11. Whereas an obstacle to the free movement of goods of this kind may be justified on the ground of protection of industrial property where such protection is invoked against a product coming from a Member State where it is not patentable and has been manufactured by third parties without the consent of the patentee and in cases where there exist patents, the original proprietors of which are legally and economically independent, a derogation from the principle of the free movement of goods is not, however, justified where the product has been put onto the market in a legal manner, by the patentee himself or with his consent, in the Member State from which it has been imported, in particular in the case of a proprietor of parallel patents.

12. In fact, if a patentee could prevent the import of protected products marketed by him or with his consent in another Member State, he would be able to partition off national markets and thereby restrict trade between Member States, in a situation where no such restriction was necessary to guarantee the essence of the exclusive rights flowing from the parallel patents.

13. The plaintiff in the main action claims, in this connection, that by reason of divergences between national legislations and practice, truly identical or parallel patents can hardly be said to exist.

14. It should be noted here that, in spite of the divergences which remain in the absence of any unification of national rules concerning industrial property, the identity of the protected invention is clearly the essential element of the concept of parallel patents which it is for the courts to assess.

> 15. The question referred should therefore be answered to the effect that the exercise, by a patentee, of the right which he enjoys under the legislation of a Member State to prohibit the sale, in that state, of a product protected by the patent which has been marketed in another Member State by the patentee or with his consent is incompatible with the rules of the EEC Treaty concerning the free movement of goods within the common market.

In *Centrafarm*, the CJEU explained that Article 36 of the EEC Treaty (now Article 36 TFEU) allowed derogations from the prohibitions set out in previous Articles 30 and 31 of the EEC Treaty (now Articles 34 and 35 TFEU) where those derogations were necessary to protect the specific subject matter of the IPR. In other words, the exhaustion of rights doctrine was justified on the basis that it does not derogate from the specific subject matter of an IPR. We have seen, in the above passage, the definition of specific subject matter in relation to patents. While the CJEU has been willing also to define the specific subject matter of trade marks,[40] they have been less keen to do so in the context of copyright and related rights, along with design rights.[41]

A key issue has been in what circumstances does an IPR owner consent to goods being first marketed in a Member State?[42] This has been a particularly urgent question in relation to trade marks and it is here that rulings of the CJEU have been largely concentrated.[43]

Another key issue is whether international, as opposed to EU-wide, exhaustion is recognized. The type of exhaustion that was established in *Deutsche Grammophon* and which has been discussed so far is EU-wide exhaustion. According to this doctrine, first marketing of goods *in any Member State* by an IPR owner exhausts the right of distribution in those particular goods in the European Union. Thus, the IPR owner would be precluded from invoking the right to prevent importation of the goods into any other Member State. At this point, it is worth noting that the Agreement on the European Economic Area of 17 March 1993 (EEA Agreement), which entered into force on 1 January 1994, widened the principle of EU-wide exhaustion to include the EU Member States and the three EEA EFTA states, Iceland, Liechtenstein, and Norway.[44] This is known as the European Economic Area (EEA) and, as such, cases discuss whether the goods have been put on the market in the EEA (and not simply the EU). In contrast, a doctrine of international exhaustion occurs where first marketing of goods *outside the EEA* by the IPR owner exhausts the right of distribution in those goods within the EEA.

The provisions of the TFEU do not preclude a doctrine of international exhaustion as part of the domestic law of Member States. Thus, it is left up to individual Member States as to whether they apply this doctrine or not. However, and very importantly, this is subject to the EU legislature not having intervened to provide otherwise. The EU legislature has intervened in the case of trade marks, designs, and copyright[45] but for now this point

---

[40] See e.g. *IHT International Heiztechnik v Ideal Standard* Case C-9/93 [1994] ECR I-2789.

[41] Keeling, *Intellectual Property Rights in EU Law*, pp. 66–7.

[42] A detailed analysis of the jurisprudence on this issue is available in Keeling, *Intellectual Property Rights in EU Law*, pp. 82–95.

[43] For further discussion see Chapter 8.

[44] See <www.efta.int/eea/eea-agreement> for further details.

[45] See Directive 89/104/EEC of 21 December 1988 to approximate the laws of the Member States relating to trade marks, now codified as 2008/95/EC of 22 October 2008, Art. 7(1); Council Regulation (EC)

will be illustrated through the example of trade marks. Article 7(1) of the Trade Marks Directive[46] states:

> The trade mark shall not entitle the proprietor to prohibit its use in relation to goods which have been put on the market in the Community under that trade mark by the proprietor or with his consent.

Article 7(1) has been interpreted by the CJEU in *Silhouette v Hartlauer*,[47] to mean that Member States are not permitted to apply a doctrine of international exhaustion in the area of trade marks. Thus, in the trade mark field, only EEA-wide exhaustion applies.[48] Whether a doctrine of international exhaustion should be adopted is now a political, rather than legal, question.[49]

So far in this discussion, there has been emphasis on the free movement of goods and the extent to which the IPRs are exhausted; however, in the copyright sphere in particular, the emphasis is beginning to shift towards free movement of services.[50] This is because increasingly in an internet environment copyright works (such as films, music, and books) are distributed in a digital, online format as well as in material form. When such works are distributed online they more closely resemble services (e.g. the streaming of live football matches or the ability to download music and film via iTunes) and, as such, raise questions about the free movement of *services*, as opposed to goods. The jurisprudence on free movement of services as it relates to intellectual property is relatively underdeveloped,[51] but we have seen this issue arise in relation to copyright in *FAPL v QC Leisure* where a key question was *when* exhaustion occurred.[52] Although the case was confined to broadcasting of live football matches, it raises the wider issue of whether online delivery of *any* copyright work will suffice to exhaust the rights that the owner has in that work. Recent CJEU jurisprudence suggests that such exhaustion will not occur and that exhaustion is limited to tangible objects.[53]

No. 40/94 of 20 December 1993 on the Community Trade Mark, now codified as Council Regulation (EC) No. 207/2009 of 26 February 2009, Art. 13; Directive 98/71/EC of 13 October 1998 on the legal protection of designs, Art. 15; Council Regulation (EC) No. 6/2002 of 12 December 2001, Art. 21; and Directive 2001/29/EC of 22 May 2001 on the harmonization of certain aspects of copyright and related rights in the information society, Art. 4. See also Keeling, *Intellectual Property Rights in EU Law*, pp. 130–46 for further discussion.

[46] Directive 89/104/EEC of 21 December 1988 to approximate the laws of the Member States relating to trade marks, now codified as 2008/95/EC of 22 October 2008. The relationship between trade marks and exhaustion of rights is considered at 1.3.2.1.

[47] Case C-355/96 [1998] ECR I-6. See 8.4.1.1.

[48] The same conclusion was reached for copyright: see *Laserdisken v Kulturministeriet* Case C-479/04, Judgment of the Court (Grand Chamber), 12 September 2006. Although there is no ruling on designs, the conclusion is likely to be the same given the language of the relevant statutory provisions.

[49] See C. Stothers, *Parallel Trade in Europe: Intellectual Property, Competition and Regulatory Law* (Oxford: Hart, 2007), pp. 347–54 for a discussion.

[50] Note that Art. 56 TFEU prohibits the restriction of the freedom to provide services within the EU.

[51] See e.g. *Coditel v Ciné Vog Films SA* Case 62/79 ('*Coditel I*') [1980] ECR 881; *Coditel v Ciné Vog Films SA* Case 262/81 ('*Coditel II*') [1982] ECR 3381.

[52] *Football Association Premier League v QC Leisure* Case C-403/08, Judgment of the Court (Grand Chamber), 4 October 2011 [2012] 1 CMLR 29, [2012] FSR 1, [84] et seq.

[53] *Art & Allposters International BV v Stichting Pictoright* Case C-419/13 [2016] FSR 6, [40].

FURTHER READING

S. Karapapa, 'Reconstructing copyright exhaustion in the online world' [2014] IPQ 307.

D. T. Keeling, *Intellectual Property Rights in EU Law*, vol. 1 (Oxford: Oxford University Press, 2004).

P. Oliver (ed.), *Oliver on Free Movement of Goods in the European Union* (5th edn, Oxford: Oxford University Press, 2010).

C. Stothers, *Parallel Trade in Europe: Intellectual Property, Competition and Regulatory Law* (Oxford: Hart, 2007).

1.3.2.2 Harmonization and unitary rights

Harmonization of Member States' national laws on intellectual property is another means of addressing the conflict between free movement and IPRs. For example, if a musical work is protected for the life of the author plus 70 years in Germany and for the life of the author plus 50 years in the UK, this would mean the musical work entered the public domain in the UK 20 years before it did so in Germany. In other words, copyright in the musical work would be enforceable in Germany for an additional 20 years and the rightsholder in Germany would be able to restrain the importation of copies of the musical work that had lawfully been put on the market in the UK at the expiration of the copyright period in the UK. This, in turn, would give rise to an impediment to the free movement of goods. Obviously, then, a way of removing this impediment would be to harmonize the term of copyright protection throughout the European Union. In fact, in the field of copyright and related rights, we have seen harmonization of the term of protection by virtue of the Term Directive.[54]

Thus, harmonization of intellectual property laws in the European Union, by ironing out discrepancies between Member States, helps minimize obstacles to the free movement of goods. Unsurprisingly, therefore, the EU legislature has been active in the field of harmonization. Significant harmonization has occurred in the field of trade mark law (Trade Marks Directive[55]) and in the law relating to registered designs (Designs Directive[56]). In the field of copyright law, there have been several harmonizing directives, most of which have focused on either particular subject matter (Software[57] and Database[58] Directives), particular rights (Cable and Satellite Directive,[59] Rental Rights Directive,[60] Resale Royalty

---

[54] Directive 93/98/EEC, which was subsequently codified by Directive 2006/116/EC of 12 December 2006 on the term of protection of copyright and certain related rights and amended by Directive 2011/77/EU of the European Parliament and of the Council of 27 September 2011 amending Directive 2006/116/EC on the term of protection of copyright and certain related rights.

[55] Directive 89/104/EEC of 21 December 1988 to approximate the laws of the Member States relating to trade marks, now codified as 2008/95/EC of 22 October 2008. Now Directive 2015/2436.

[56] Directive 98/71/EC of the European Parliament and of the Council of 13 October 1998 on the legal protection of designs.

[57] Directive 2009/24/EC of 23 April 2009 on the legal protection of computer programs [2009] OJ L111/16.

[58] Directive 96/9/EC of the European Parliament and of the Council of 11 March 1996 on the legal protection of databases [1996] OJ L77/20.

[59] Directive 93/83/EEC of 27 September 1993 on the coordination of certain rules concerning copyright and rights related to copyright applicable to satellite broadcasting and cable retransmission [1993] OJ L248/15.

[60] Directive 92/100/EEC of 19 November 1992 on rental and lending rights and on certain rights related to copyright in the field of intellectual property [1992] OJ L346/61, codified in Directive 2006/115/EC of the European Parliament and of the Council of 12 December 2006 on rental right and lending right and on certain rights related to copyright in the field of intellectual property.

Right Directive[61]), or particular issues (Term Directive[62]). The most far-reaching harmonization of copyright law to date has occurred through the Information Society Directive,[63] which harmonizes aspects of copyright and related rights, in particular in relation to the digital environment. In addition, the way in which the CJEU has recently interpreted the harmonizing directives in copyright law has led, according to some, to harmonization via the back door. More specifically, the CJEU has articulated principles which go beyond those stated in the directives.[64] In the field of patent law, however, harmonization has been limited to biotechnological inventions (Biotechnology Directive[65]). Finally, across the different regimes of IPRs, there has been harmonization of enforcement measures via the Enforcement Directive.[66] The details, and impact, of these directives will be discussed in more detail in later chapters.

While harmonization can reduce the discrepancies between national laws and thus minimize obstacles to the free movement of goods, it cannot address the problems that flow from the territoriality of IPRs. For example, even if musical works are protected for the same amount of time, i.e. the life of the author plus 70 years, the owner of copyright in a musical work, A, who puts copies on the market in the UK could still try and prohibit the importation of those copies into another Member State, such as France. Of course, as was discussed in the previous section, the doctrine of exhaustion of rights was developed to remove this type of obstacle to the free movement of goods. However, it is also possible to alleviate this sort of problem by creating unitary, EU-wide IPRs. In other words, to create IPRs which are valid and enforceable throughout the entire EU (i.e. supranational), as one single territory, as opposed to within each individual Member State (national), which is the extent of national IPRs.

The EU has introduced two unitary rights: the EU trade mark (introduced by the Community Trade Mark Regulation[67]) and the EU design right (introduced by the Community Design Right Regulation[68]). Attempts have been made on several occasions to introduce an EU-wide patent, but they have proved unsuccessful—at least until recently.[69] In later chapters of the book, the harmonizing directives and unitary rights will be discussed in detail. For the moment it suffices to note two things about the EU trade mark and EU design rights.[70] First, these unitary rights are alternatives to, rather than replacements of, national trade marks and national design rights. Second, centralization of the granting procedure (i.e. registration) represents a key feature and benefit of these rights. It provides benefits to applicants in terms of lower transaction costs for the acquisition and maintenance of IPRs within the European Union.

[61] Directive 2001/84/EC of the European Parliament and of the Council of 27 September 2001 on the resale right for the benefit of the author of an original work of art [2001] OJ L272/32.

[62] Directive 93/98/EEC, which was subsequently codified by Directive 2006/116/EC of 12 December 2006 on the term of protection of copyright and certain related rights.

[63] Directive 2001/29/EC on the harmonization of certain aspects of copyright and related rights in the information society [2001] OJ L167/10.

[64] J. Griffiths, 'Constitutionalising or harmonising? The Court of Justice, the right to property and European copyright law' (2013) 38 E. L. Rev. 65.

[65] Directive 98/44/EC of the European Parliament and of the Council of 6 July 1998 on the legal protection of biotechnological inventions.

[66] Directive 2004/48/EC of the European Parliament and of the Council of 29 April 2004 on the enforcement of intellectual property rights [2004] OJ L195/16.

[67] Council Regulation (EC) No. 207/2009 of 26 February 2009 on the Community Trade Mark [2009] OJ L78/1. Now EU Regulation No. 2015/2424.

[68] Council Regulation (EC) No. 6/2002 of 12 December 2001 on Community designs [2002] OJ L3/1.

[69] See 11.4.2.6.

[70] See Ullrich, 'Harmony and unity of European intellectual property protection', pp. 39–41.

FURTHER READING

M. van Eechoud, P. B. Hugenholtz, S. van Gompel, L. Guibault, and N. Helberger, *Harmonizing European Copyright Law: The Challenges of Better Lawmaking* (Alphen aan den Rijn: Kluwer Law International, 2009).

H. Ullrich, 'Harmony and unity of European intellectual property protection' in D. Vaver and L. Bently (eds), *Intellectual Property in the New Millennium* (Cambridge: Cambridge University Press, 2004), pp. 20–46.

1.3.2.3 Competition law and IPRs

As we have seen from our discussion in previous sections, Article 36 TFEU and the doctrine of EEA-wide exhaustion address the way in which the territorial nature of IPRs can create barriers to trade within the internal market. Articles 101 and 102 TFEU (previously Articles 81 and 82 TEC), on the other hand, relate to a different aspect of IPRs, namely, the fact that owners of IPRs are granted a monopoly right (i.e. an exclusive right) to do certain acts. As such, these monopoly rights may be misused or abused in ways that restrict competition. Article 101 is concerned with anti-competitive agreements and Article 102 targets abuse of a dominant position.

Article 101 provides:

1. The following shall be prohibited as incompatible with the common market: all agreements between undertakings, decisions by associations of undertakings and concerted practices which may affect trade between Member States and which have as their object or effect the prevention, restriction or distortion of competition within the common market, and in particular those which:

   (a) directly or indirectly fix purchase or selling prices or any other trading conditions;

   (b) limit or control production, markets, technical development, or investment;

   (c) share markets or sources of supply;

   (d) apply dissimilar conditions to equivalent transactions with other trading parties, thereby placing them at a competitive disadvantage;

   (e) make the conclusion of contracts subject to acceptance by the other parties of supplementary obligations which, by their nature or according to commercial usage, have no connection with the subject of such contracts.

2. Any agreements or decisions prohibited pursuant to this Article shall be automatically void.

3. The provisions of paragraph 1 may, however, be declared inapplicable in the case of:

   – any agreement or category of agreements between undertakings;

   – any decision or category of decisions by associations of undertakings;

   – any concerted practice or category of concerted practices;

   which contributes to improving the production or distribution of goods or to promoting technical or economic progress, while allowing consumers a fair share of the resulting benefit, and which does not:

   (a) impose on the undertakings concerned restrictions which are not indispensable to the attainment of these objectives;

   (b) afford such undertakings the possibility of eliminating competition in respect of a substantial part of the products in question.

The purpose of Article 101 TFEU is to prevent collusion (through agreements, decisions, or concerted practices) between competitors, which would undermine the workings of a healthy market economy. Article 101(1) prohibits collusion of this nature and indicates the sorts of agreements, decisions, or concerted practices that may have an anti-competitive effect, one such example being 'price-fixing'.[71] Article 101(2) declares agreements or decisions of this kind null and void.

Article 101(1) may apply to assignments or licences of IPRs. For example, it would forbid a patent licence from including a price-fixing or tie-in clause. An example of a tie-in clause would be where, in exchange for granting a licence to manufacture a patented good, the licence required the licensee to purchase the components necessary for manufacturing that good from the licensor.

Article 101(3), however, exempts certain agreements, decisions, or concerted practices which are beneficial to technical or economic progress, i.e. which are pro-competitive. In the field of intellectual property, this provision empowered the Commission to introduce the Technology Transfer Agreement Regulation No. 772/2004.[72] The regulation creates a 'block' exemption for technology transfer agreements, which are defined in Article 1(b) as patent licensing agreements, know-how licensing agreements, software copyright licensing agreements, and mixed patent, know-how, and software copyright licensing agreements. Article 101(1) is declared not to apply to technology transfer agreements between competing undertakings (on the relevant technology or product market) where the combined market share of the parties does not exceed 20 per cent of the relevant market.[73] The exemption also applies to non-competing undertakings where the combined market share of the parties does not exceed 30 per cent of the relevant market.[74] Agreements containing restrictions that are severely anti-competitive are excluded from the benefit of the block exemption, one such example being price-fixing.[75] Certain restrictions (as opposed to the whole agreement) are also excluded from the benefit of the block exemption, such as a direct or indirect obligation on the licensee to assign or grant an exclusive licence to the licensor in respect of its own severable improvements to it or its own new applications of the licensed technology.[76] Finally, the Commission may withdraw the benefit of the exemption where it finds in any particular case that a technology transfer agreement nevertheless has effects which are incompatible with Article 101(3) TFEU.

Where the Technology Transfer Regulation does not apply (e.g. because there is a trade mark licensing agreement), persons would then fall back on general principles, as established by Council Regulation (EC) No. 1/2003 of 16 December 2002 on the implementation of the rules on competition laid down in Articles 81 and 82 of the Treaty.[77] Article 1 of the regulation makes clear that if agreements satisfy the requirements of Article 101(3) TFEU (ex Article 81(3) TEU) they will not be considered prohibited by Article 101(1) and this will be the case without the need for a prior decision to that effect by either the European Commission or a national competition authority. This does not, however, prevent the European Commission or national competition authority from acting on a complaint, or on its own initiative, to determine whether an infringement of Article 101 (ex Article 81(3) TEU) has occurred.

---

[71] Art. 101(1)(a) TFEU.

[72] Commission Regulation (EC) No. 772/2004 of 27 April 2004 on the application of Article 81(3) of the Treaty to categories of technology transfer agreements.

[73] Technology Transfer Regulation, Art. 3(1).   [74] Technology Transfer Regulation, Art 3(2).

[75] Technology Transfer Regulation, Art. 4(1)–(2).   [76] Technology Transfer Regulation, Art 5.

[77] [2003] OJ L1/1. The relevant provisions are now, of course, Arts 101 and 102 TFEU.

Whereas Article 101 is concerned with anti-competitive agreements, Article 102 TFEU targets situations where persons having exceptional market power abuse their dominance. Article 102 provides:

> Any abuse by one or more undertakings of a dominant position within the common market or in a substantial part of it shall be prohibited as incompatible with the common market insofar as it may affect trade between Member States:
>
> Such abuse may, in particular, consist in:
>
> a. directly or indirectly imposing unfair purchase or selling prices or other unfair trading conditions;
>
> b. limiting production, markets or technical development to the prejudice of consumers;
>
> c. applying dissimilar conditions to equivalent transactions with other trading parties, thereby placing them at a competitive disadvantage;
>
> d. making the conclusion of contracts subject to acceptance by the other parties of supplementary obligations which, by their nature or according to commercial usage, have no connection with the subject of such contracts.

As mentioned earlier, intellectual property law grants exclusive rights to owners and, as such, this may cause the intellectual property owner to occupy a dominant position in the market. For example, as Keeling (2003) describes:

> Suppose someone patents, throughout Europe, a pharmaceutical that is capable of curing AIDS. If no other pharmaceutical capable of curing AIDS exists, the proprietor of the patent will inevitably hold a dominant position. The relevant product market can only be defined as the market in pharmaceuticals for successfully treating AIDS, since no other product could be substituted for the patented pharmaceutical. The patentee would enjoy a legal monopoly on the relevant market throughout Europe and the entry barrier would be insuperable during the life of the patent (unless, of course, someone else developed a non-infringing drug also capable of curing AIDS).[78]

However, the fact that an intellectual property owner occupies a dominant position is not enough to infringe Article 102—there must be an *abuse* of that dominant position. As discussed by Keeling, this is somewhat problematic—how can it be said that the exercise of an IPR, which right is intended to confer a limited monopoly on an owner, constitutes an abuse?

D. T. Keeling, *Intellectual Property Rights in EU Law*, vol. 1 (Oxford: Oxford University Press, 2003), pp. 376–8

> The idea that an undertaking may commit an unlawful abuse of its dominant position by exercising its intellectual property rights is problematical. The very essence of an intellectual property right is that the State grants a limited monopoly to someone for a specific purpose, e.g. to reward inventiveness, creativity, investment in research, or to help firms to protect their goodwill. The laws governing the grant of intellectual property rights generally involve a

---

[78] At p. 371.

balancing exercise. Patent laws, for example, balance the need to reward and stimulate innovation against the need to grant public access to knowledge and to encourage competition in the production of goods. Similar considerations apply to design rights and to copyright. In all these cases the law, as an act of policy, places the intellectual property owner in a privileged position, partially exempting him from competition. It does so with the deliberate intention of allowing him to exploit his statutory monopoly and thereby obtain his just reward.

...

It is legitimate, then, to ask whether competition law should be allowed to censure the exploitation of intellectual property rights when intellectual property law itself attempted to strike a balance between public and private interests.

...

The point is that intellectual property rights are a fairly crude method of rewarding innovation and excellence in the market-place. They are granted on the basis of general criteria, no account being taken of the particular circumstances of each case. Intellectual property legislation cannot address all of the concerns that fall within the province of competition law. Above all, intellectual property legislation cannot examine whether effective competition in a particular market is being damaged as a result of the manner in which a dominant undertaking is exercising its intellectual property rights.

It follows that there is a legitimate role for Article 82 [now Article 102 TFEU] in relation to the exercise of intellectual property rights by dominant undertakings. The problem is to determine precisely what that role should be. Not surprisingly, the Court of Justice has generally taken a cautious approach. It has been reluctant to accept that mere exercise of an intellectual property right can constitute an abuse of dominant position, except in very specific circumstances.

As Keeling notes, there have been very few instances where the CJEU has held that exercise of an IPR infringes Article 102 TFEU. A famous example is the *Magill* decision[79] where the CJEU held that the refusal by certain broadcasting organizations to license the reproduction of their advance weekly programme listings (which were protected as copyright works) was an abuse of dominant position. The CJEU stressed that ownership of an IPR will not always result in a dominant position. However, it did so on the facts of the case because the broadcasting organizations enjoyed a de facto monopoly over the data used to compile listings for television programmes and thus were in a position to prevent effective competition on the market in weekly television guides. The Court also emphasized that exercise of an IPR may, in exceptional circumstances, involve abusive conduct. Such exceptional circumstances existed in *Magill* because there was no actual or potential substitute for a weekly television guide and yet there was a specific, constant, and regular demand on the part of consumers for such a guide. Thus, the refusal to license the copyright work (i.e. the listings data), which was indispensable to Magill's business, prevented the appearance of a new product on the market. Further, there was no objective justification for such a refusal and, finally, by their conduct, the broadcasting organizations had reserved to themselves the secondary market of weekly television guides by excluding all competition in that market by denying access to the basic listings data.

It is fair to say that the issue of when the exercise of IPRs will amount to an abuse of Article 102 remains an important question, which seems to be raised with greater frequency

[79] *Radio Telefis Eireann and Independent Television Publications Ltd (Intellectual Property Owners Inc. intervening) v EC Commission (Magill TV Guide Ltd intervening)* Joined Cases C-241 and 242/91 P [1995] 4 CMLR 718.

in the courts.[80] However, it must also be remembered that aside from the external controls of competition law represented by Articles 101 and 102 TFEU, there are internal mechanisms *within* the various intellectual property regimes that seek to lessen the anti-competitive impact that IPRs may have on the market, by virtue of granting exclusive rights. These mechanisms are either judicially developed doctrines or legislative interventions, and some of these will be explored in greater detail in later chapters.[81]

FURTHER READING

S. Anderman (ed.), *The Interface between Intellectual Property and Competition Policy* (Cambridge: Cambridge University Press, 2009).

S. Anderman and A. Ezrachi (eds), *Intellectual Property and Competition Law: New Frontiers* (Oxford: Oxford University Press, 2011).

T. Käseberg, *Intellectual Property, Antitrust and Cumulative Innovation in the EU and US* (Oxford: Hart, 2012).

V. Korah, *Intellectual Property Rights and the EC Competition Rules* (Oxford: Hart, 2006).

1.4 REMEDIES

In this section we give a general overview of the procedural law relating to intellectual property disputes, including the appropriate fora and the available remedies.[82] We begin by identifying the international and regional agreements that govern UK law in this area. These are the TRIPS Agreement and the EU Enforcement Directive. We then turn to examine the interim and final remedies available in civil proceedings. We conclude by briefly considering criminal penalties.

1.4.1 INTERNATIONAL AND REGIONAL FRAMEWORK

The TRIPS Agreement includes specific mechanisms for enforcing a failure to comply with TRIPS obligations.[83] It also imposes minimum standards for enforcement of IPRs on WTO members. Signatories must provide a range of procedures and remedies relevant to the enforcement of rights, including interim measures such as pre-trial injunctions, as well as

---

[80] In the UK, see e.g. *BHB Enterprises plc v Victor Chandler (International) Ltd* [2005] EWHC 1074 (Ch), [2005] ECC 40; *Attheraces Ltd v British Horseracing Ltd* [2007] EWCA Civ 38, [2007] ECC 7; *Intel Corp. v Via Technologies Inc.* [2003] EWCA Civ 1905, [2003] ECC 16; *Oracle America Inc. (formerly Sun Microsystems Inc.) v M-Tech Data Ltd* [2012] UKSC 27. In the CJEU, see e.g. *IMS Health GmbH & Co. OHG v NDC Health GmbH & Co. KG* Case C-418/01 [2004] ECR I-5039, [2004] 4 CMLR 28; *Microsoft Corp. v Commission of the European Communities* Case T-201/04 [2007] ECR II-3601, [2007] 5 CMLR 11; *Astrazeneca AB and Astrazeneca plc v European Commission* Case C-457/10 P [2013] 4 CMLR 7; and *Huawei Technologies Co. Ltd v ZTE Corp.* 9 Case C-170/13 [2015] 5 CMLR 14.

[81] See e.g. the idea/expression dichotomy and the 'must fit' and 'must match' exceptions discussed in Chapters 4 and 14 respectively.

[82] There is a more detailed discussion of remedies in Chapter 15 which is to be found on the Online Resource Centre.

[83] See 1.3.1.2.

awards of damages and final injunctions and, in relation to trade marks and copyright, criminal sanctions where infringement is on a commercial scale. Finally, signatories must take measures to ensure that their borders are secured against the importation or exportation of infringing and counterfeit goods.

At the European level, Member States have implemented the EU Enforcement Directive.[84] The object of the directive, according to recital 10, is to 'approximate legislative systems so as to ensure a high, equivalent and homogeneous level of protection in the Internal Market'. IPRs are undefined in the directive, but the Commission has clarified that 'at least the following intellectual property rights are covered by the scope of the Directive: copyright, rights related to copyright, *sui generis* right of a database maker, rights of the creator of the topographies of a semiconductor product, trade mark rights, design rights, patent rights, including rights derived from supplementary protection certificates, geographical indications, utility model rights, plant variety rights, trade names, in so far as these are protected as exclusive property in the national law concerned'.[85] Trade secrets and other confidential information are omitted from this list and the recent adoption of the Trade Secrets Directive seems to confirm this view.[86] However, in *Vestergaard v Bestnet* the Court of Appeal assumed that the directive was applicable.[87] The Enforcement Directive is limited to civil measures and, aside from some aspects of financial remedies, it is generally accepted that, in the case of the UK, its implementation has entailed minimal change to the existing law relating both to enforcement and to remedies.[88]

1.4.2 CIVIL PROCEEDINGS

Despite the recent moves to harmonize certain aspects of IPR enforcement across the EU, intellectual property disputes are almost exclusively a matter for domestic courts. In the case of EU IPRs (most notably EU trade marks and designs), certain UK courts have been designated EU courts for the purposes of hearing infringement and invalidity proceedings in relation to these rights.

Intellectual property disputes may be heard in the Chancery Division of the High Court and in any county court which has a Chancery District Registry.[89] In the case of patents, disputes may be heard at the Patents Court or before the Comptroller of Patents,[90] as may

---

[84] Directive 2004/48/EC of the European Parliament and of the Council of 29 April 2004 on the enforcement of intellectual property rights [2004] OJ L195/16. There is also a regulation intended to protect IPRs using border controls: see Regulation (EU) No. 608/2013 of the European Parliament and of the Council of 12 June 2013 concerning customs enforcement of intellectual property rights and repealing Council Regulation (EC) No. 1383/2003.

[85] Statement by the Commission concerning Article 2 of Directive 2004/48/EC of the European Parliament and of the Council on the enforcement of intellectual property rights (2005/295/EC) [2005] OJ L94/37.

[86] Directive (EU) 2016/943 of 8 June 2016 on the protection of undisclosed know-how and business information (trade secrets) against their unlawful acquisition, use and disclosure [2016] OJ L157/1.

[87] *Vestergaard Frandsen S/A and Ors v Bestnet Europe Ltd* [2011] EWCA Civ 424, [56]. Whether this is the right assumption has been doubted: see T. Aplin, L. Bently, P. Johnson, and S. Malynicz, *Gurry on Confidence: The Protection of Confidential Information* (Oxford: Oxford University Press, 2012), para. 17.05.

[88] See the Intellectual Property (Enforcement, etc.) Regulations 2006 (SI 2006/1028) and the Civil Procedure (Amendment No. 4) Rules 2005 (SI 2005/3515).

[89] Practice Direction, supplementary CPR, Part 63, Section II, Allocation (r. 63.13) 2007.

[90] This will change once the Unitary Patent Package has been adopted—see 11.4.2.6.

UK registered design disputes and EU design cases. There is also an Intellectual Property Enterprise Court (IPEC)[91] which hears cases involving all IPRs and is designed to offer a speedier and cheaper forum than the High Court. Thus, at the IPEC damages are limited to £500,000 and costs to £50,000.[92]

When an action is threatened or indeed taken, in relation to patents, trade marks, and designs, it is possible for the alleged defendant to bring an action against the claimant on the basis that the allegations are based on groundless threats.[93] An action against groundless threats marks a recognition that a threat by one party to issue proceedings against another for the infringement of an IPR may have serious economic consequences for the latter. A shopkeeper who is threatened with legal proceedings for selling goods which carry an allegedly infringing trade mark may feel he has no choice but to withdraw the goods from sale even if the threats are groundless. The English Law Commission recently reviewed the current provisions relating to groundless threats and a Bill was introduced on 19 May 2016.[94] The Bill would ensure that the same approach is taken for trade marks, designs, and patents with regard to groundless threats. It also seeks to provide a clearer framework for what constitutes unjustified threats with a view to resolving disputes and avoiding litigation. Finally, the Bill would extend unjustified threats to European patents which fall within the jurisdiction of the Unified Patent Court.

1.4.3 PRE-TRIAL RELIEF

Most disputes involving intellectual property begin with a letter before action from the rightsholder to the alleged wrongdoer. The exceptions are disputes which are initiated by an *ex parte* order, such as a search order.[95] In fact, actions involving IPRs infrequently come to trial. This is because rightsholders are usually most interested in preventing the offending behaviour in a timely fashion, with remedies of only secondary concern. There are three key orders which may be obtained pre-trial. They are the search order, the freezing order (also known as a Mareva injunction), and the Norwich Pharmacal order. In addition, a rightsholder may succeed in obtaining an interim injunction to prevent the allegedly infringing behaviour of the third party until trial. Each is considered below.

1.4.3.1 The search order

The search order is granted in the High Court and obtained *ex parte*.[96] Its first appearance was in *Anton Piller KG v Manufacturing Processes Ltd*, a Court of Appeal decision concerning passing off and confidential information.[97] In his judgment, Ormrod LJ set out the three criteria for granting the order, which still pertain today. The claimant must have a strong prima facie case. Second, there must be clear evidence that the defendants have in their possession incriminating goods or documents and that, if put on notice, there is a genuine risk that they might destroy them. Third, the potential damage to the claimant must be very

---

[91] Until 2013 called the Patents County Court.
[92] Registered trade mark actions may also be heard in the IPEC.
[93] See Patents Act 1977 (PA 77), s. 70, Trade Marks Act 1994 (TMA), s. 21, Registered Designs Act 1949 (RDA), s. 26, and Copyright, Designs and Patents Act 1988 (CDPA), s. 21.
[94] See <www.lawcom.gov.uk/government-introduces-the-intellectual-property-unjustified-threats-bill-into-parliament/> and the Intellectual Property (Unjustified Threats) Bill 2016.
[95] The UK Intellectual Property Office also offers a mediation service.
[96] Civil Procedure Act 1997, s. 7.   [97] [1976] Ch 55.

serious. The 'Anton Piller order', as it was known, attracted a strong measure of judicial criticism. A key concern was the difficulty faced by many defendants of obtaining expert and urgent legal advice upon the service of an order, particularly if it occurred outside business hours. This was a point taken up by the Vice-Chancellor in *Universal Thermosensors Ltd v Hibben* which concerned confidential information.[98] He set down a number of guidelines which must be followed when executing a search order which are incorporated into a standard form of the order set out in a 1996 Practice Direction. Most importantly, the order must be served and its execution overseen by an independent Supervising Solicitor. In addition, the order should be executed during business hours and on a weekday to ensure that the defendant is able to obtain legal advice.

Search orders frequently require defendants to provide self-incriminating information. For instance, a defendant may be ordered to disclose the whereabouts of allegedly infringing material. Following a number of successful legal challenges, including one which went to the House of Lords (*Rank Film Distributors Ltd v Video Information Centre*),[99] the privilege against self-incrimination in civil proceedings was set aside by section 72 of the Supreme Court Act 1991. However, it continues to apply in criminal proceedings which might be brought as a result of complying with the order. A challenge to the search order was also mounted in the European Court of Human Rights (*Chappell v United Kingdom*)[100] based on the right to privacy guaranteed by Article 8 of the ECHR. The Court rejected the challenge, holding that the order, as it had been developed by the UK courts, did not violate the claimant's rights. Nonetheless, it is submitted that a search order may still be open to criticism.

1.4.3.2 Freezing orders

These orders, otherwise known as Mareva injunctions,[101] are intended to restrain defendants from dissipating their assets before trial. The order does not attach to the defendant's assets as such, but rather to the defendant *in personam*. It is frequently deployed in intellectual property disputes, often in conjunction with a search order. Freezing orders only apply at an interlocutory stage and there must be a substantive cause of action.[102] Indeed, the claimant must establish a 'good arguable case'.[103] There is no doubt that a freezing order has the potential to be oppressive. As a result, a series of safeguards has been developed by the courts. These include allowing the defendant sufficient funds to carry on business and for living expenses. Furthermore, a freezing order has to be revoked within 31 calendar days after it has been executed if no proceedings have begun.[104]

1.4.3.3 Norwich Pharmacal orders

A Norwich Pharmacal order is designed to obtain information which is necessary to identify a wrongdoer.[105] The order places an individual, who becomes involved in another's wrongdoing whether or not innocently, under a duty to disclose information which might identify

---

[98] [1992] FSR 361.   [99] [1982] AC 380.   [100] (1990) 12 EHRR 1.

[101] *Mareva Compania Naviera SA v International Bulkcarriers SA* [1975] 2 Lloyd's Rep 509.

[102] *Siskina v Distos Compania Naviera SA* [1979] AC 210.

[103] *Rasu Maritima SA v Perusahaan Pertambangan Minyak Dan Gas Bumi Negara (Government of the Republic of Indonesia intervening) (Pertamina)* [1978] 1 QB 644.

[104] There is a standard form for use by the courts. Practice Direction [1996] 1 WLR 1552 amending Practice Direction [1994] 1 WLR 1233.

[105] See *Norwich Pharmacal v Customs and Excise* [1974] AC 133 (a patent action).

the alleged wrongdoer to the person who is injured by the wrongful acts. The jurisdiction to make a Norwich Pharmacal order was first established in an action for patent infringement, *Norwich Pharmacal v Customs and Excise*. In *Productores de Música de España (Promusicae) v Telefónica de España SAU* (2008),[106] the CJEU held that while it is appropriate to use such orders in intellectual property cases, in doing so courts must ensure that a fair balance with the fundamental rights of the individual concerned is maintained. Following *Promusicae*, the Supreme Court considered the balancing of fundamental rights in *Rugby Football Union v Viagogo Ltd* and held that *Promusicae* required national courts to weigh the potential value of the claim to the claimant against the interests of the data subject.[107]

1.4.3.4 Interim injunctions

The granting of an interim (previously known as an interlocutory) injunction is designed to ensure that a claimant will not be irrevocably harmed by the defendant's actions in the period between the issuing of proceedings and trial. In essence, it is intended to preserve the status quo until the matter can be determined at trial. As with the search order, there is now a standard form for use by the courts.[108] Recently, there has also been the growth in use of the so-called super-injunctions, particularly in cases involving issues of privacy.

In *American Cyanamid v Ethicon*,[109] the House of Lords set out the conditions for the granting of an interim injunction. These are: (1) there is a serious issue to be tried; (2) damages would not be an adequate remedy at trial; (3) that were the defendant to succeed at trial damages would be an adequate compensation; and (4) the balance of convenience must be taken into account.

Following the passage of the Human Rights Act 1998 (HRA), in the particular situation where the defendant seeks to justify disclosure by reference to freedom of expression, the *American Cyanamid* approach is no longer followed. Rather, according to section 12(3) of the HRA, interim relief is not to be granted 'unless the court is satisfied that the applicant is likely to establish that publication should not be allowed'. In *Cream Holdings v Banerjee*,[110] the House of Lords held that the threshold of 'likely' referred to in section 12(3) usually means 'more likely that not', which is higher than the threshold of 'serious question to be tried'.

As with other forms of interim relief, where a claimant obtains an interim injunction, this may bring an immediate end to the proceedings. Thus, a trader who has introduced a new product which allegedly carries an infringing trade mark may prefer to rebrand their product rather than withdraw it from the market until after trial, whether or not the trader believes in the merits of the rightsholder's claims. It follows that the granting of pre-trial orders or interim injunctions will very frequently determine the outcome of a case in favour of the claimant. Yet failure to grant such orders might result in a claimant suffering long-term damage to its IPRs in the period before trial, for which there will be no adequate compensation once the trial is concluded. It is thus important to ask whether the courts have found the correct balance between the interests of the claimants and the defendants when granting these orders.

---

[106] Case C-275/06 [2008] ECR I-271.

[107] [2012] UKSC 55, [2013] FSR 23. See also *Golden Eye (International) Ltd v Telefonica UK Ltd* [2012] EWCA Civ 1740, [2013] 2 CMLR 27.

[108] Practice Direction [1996] 1 WLR 1552 amending Practice Direction [1994] 1 WLR 1233.

[109] [1975] AC 396.   [110] [2005] 1 AC 253.

1.4.4 FINAL REMEDIES

Where an intellectual dispute does not settle at the pre-trial stage, the most likely post-trial remedy is a final injunction. As well as a final injunction, financial remedies may also be available: damages or an account of profits. We look at each of these in turn.

1.4.4.1 Injunction

In general, once liability has been established in an intellectual property action, the claimant may expect to be awarded a final injunction. These are designed to restrain further breaches of the claimant's rights. In *Cantor Gaming v Gameaccount*,[111] Daniel Alexander QC sitting as a Deputy High Court Judge offered a useful summary of the circumstances in which a final injunction will be granted in intellectual property disputes.[112]

> **Summary of principles**
>
> 113. I therefore summarise the applicable principles as follows. First, an injunction may be granted pursuant to s. 37(1) of the Supreme Court Act 1981 whenever it is just and convenient to do so. Secondly, the grant of an injunction involves the exercise of the court's discretion, and the court should, in so doing, take account of all of the circumstances, one factor of which is the importance or triviality of the breach. Thirdly, there are certain kinds of case, of which intellectual property cases are examples, in which an injunction will normally be granted if a claimant has established infringement of its rights and there is a threat to continue (or at least no clear and unequivocal undertaking not to continue). Fourthly, where there is no threat to continue acts which have been held to be unlawful, because the defendant has clearly and unequivocally agreed not to do them before the action was brought, it is not right in principle to grant an injunction. Fifthly, there may, however, be situations where, even though a defendant may have agreed not to undertake the acts in question, an injunction may be just and convenient, having regard to all the circumstances. This may be, for example, because of the greater incentive for respect of a claimant's rights that an injunction would provide, and which, in particular cases, it may appear just to grant. Sixthly, the court may, in appropriate cases, take proportionality into account in granting or refusing injunctive relief.

Article 11 of the EU Enforcement Directive provides that Member States must ensure that where there has been a finding of infringement of an IPR, the court may issue an injunction to prevent the continuation of the infringement. In addition, Member States should ensure that rightsholders can apply for injunctions against intermediaries whose services are used by third parties to infringe IPRs. Further, the CJEU has ruled that any injunction must be proportionate.[113] It is generally accepted that UK law in relation to injunctions will comply with the terms of the Enforcement Directive.

---

[111] [2008] FSR 4.

[112] Contrast the position taken by the US Supreme Court in *eBay Inc. v MercExchange LLC*, 547 US 388 (2006). For a discussion see S. Subramanian, 'eBay ruling and US obligation to the TRIPs Agreement' [2008] EIPR 444, 449–50.

[113] *L'Oreal SA v eBay UK Ltd* Case C-324/09 [2011] RPC 27.

1.4.4.2 Damages

An award of damages seeks to compensate for the loss or injury caused by an infringement. The key principles for assessment of damages were set out in *General Tire and Rubber Co v Firestone Tyre and Rubber Co. Ltd*.[114] The measure of damages is the sum of money that would restore the injured party to the same position as if the wrong had not occurred. According to *General Tire*, the measure of damages may be assessed according to lost sales, lost royalties, or a lost licence fee. It is for the claimant to prove to the court the extent of the loss resulting from the defendant's infringing acts. In relation to consequential loss, general tort principles of foreseeability apply.[115]

In relation to some IPRs, 'innocent' infringers are exempt from paying damages subject to certain conditions being met. This is true in relation to copyright, the *sui generis* database right, UK unregistered design, UK registered design, and patent infringements. No such exemption is available for infringement of the EU design rights or for trade mark infringement or passing off. In cases of copyright and the UK unregistered design right, the CDPA[116] provides that courts may award additional damages as the justice of the case may require. The court must have regard to all the circumstances and, in particular, the flagrancy of the infringement and any benefit accruing to the defendant by reason of the infringement. Finally, an award of exemplary damages may be available as part of the court's inherent jurisdiction, although it is not currently available in privacy actions.[117]

The Intellectual Property (Enforcement, etc.) Regulations 2006,[118] implementing Article 14 of the Enforcement Directive, introduced regulation 3 concerning damages. This provision states:

(1) Where in an action for infringement of an intellectual property right the defendant knew, or had reasonable grounds to know, that he engaged in infringing activity, the damages awarded to the claimant shall be appropriate to the actual prejudice he suffered as a result of the infringement.

(2) When awarding such damages—

    (a) all appropriate aspects shall be taken into account, including in particular—

        (i) the negative economic consequences, including any lost profits, which the claimant has suffered, and any unfair profits made by the defendant; and

        (ii) elements other than economic factors, including the moral prejudice caused to the claimant by the infringement; or

    (b) where appropriate, they may be awarded on the basis of the royalties or fees which would have been due had the defendant obtained a licence.

However, regulation 3 gives rise to some uncertainties, in particular, the phrase 'any unfair profits made by the defendant' in paragraph (2)(a) is at odds with the statement in paragraph (1) that the award of damages shall be appropriate to the actual prejudice suffered as a result

---

[114] [1976] RPC 197 (HL).

[115] *Gerber Garment Technology Inc. v Lectra Systems Ltd* [1997] RPC 443 (CA).

[116] CDPA, s. 97(1) for copyright, and s. 229(3) for UK unregistered design right.

[117] *Kuddus v Chief Constable of Leicestershire Constabulary* [2002] 2 AC 122, 130, and 134 (Lord Slynn), 138 and 140 (Lord Mackay), 145 (Lord Nicholls), 150 (Lord Hutton).

[118] SI 2006/1028.

of the infringement and the compensatory purpose of damages.[119] The case of *Henderson v All Around the World Recordings Ltd*[120] suggests that damages cannot be calculated on the basis of lost profits to the claimant *and* unfair profits made by the defendant since this would risk imposing punitive damages. In addition, it is unclear what is meant by unfair profits. English courts have not treated these as synonymous with an account of profits. A further uncertainty is what constitutes moral prejudice. The Enforcement Directive suggests this may encompass loss of reputation and exclusive image, but English courts have doubted whether this constitutes non-economic loss of the relevant kind. In *Henderson*, it was held that damages for moral prejudice would only be available in unusual circumstances where moral prejudice is significant and damages for economic loss alone would not be proportionate to the overall prejudice suffered by the claimant.[121]

1.4.4.3 Account of profits

An account of profits is an equitable remedy and thus it is within the court's discretion whether to order it or not. It differs from damages in that it calculates the gain made by the defendant as a result of the infringing behaviour, as opposed to the loss caused to the claimant. According to Laddie J in *Celanese International Corp. v BP Chemicals Ltd*:[122] 'The defendant is treated as if he conducted his business and made profits on behalf of the plaintiff.' Also in *Celanese*, Laddie J stressed 'there should be no answer to an account that the defendant could have made the same profits by following an alternative non-infringing course'.[123] Nor can the claimant argue that the defendant could and should have made higher profits. The question is what profits were made because of the actual infringing activity. This can be a complex and uncertain assessment and hence it is relatively unusual for a claimant to opt for an account of profits. Importantly, a claimant may not seek both an award of damages *and* an order for an account of profits, but must choose between them.[124] To assist in making an informed choice, the claimant is entitled to the disclosure of relevant information by the defendants, such as financial records.[125]

1.4.4.4 Delivery up and disposal

A statutory remedy exists for the delivery up of articles which infringe copyright,[126] UK unregistered design right,[127] UK registered design right,[128] EU design rights,[129] patents,[130] and trade marks,[131] although the circumstances in which delivery up will be ordered differ between the various rights. Normally, an order for delivery up requires the delivery up of those goods which are in the UK and within the defendant's possession, custody, power, or control on the day that the order is made.[132] In the case of copyright and designs, an order might also include articles designed to make copies of a copyright work or a registered or unregistered design as well as the articles embodying the infringing copies. Where infringing goods or articles have been delivered up, an application may be made to the court for an

---

[119] See recital 26 of the Enforcement Directive.
[120] [2014] EWHC 3087 (IPEC).   [121] [94]–[95].   [122] [1999] RPC 203, [36].   [123] [39].
[124] *Island Records Ltd v Tring International Plc* [1996] 1 WLR 1256.   [125] *Island Records v Tring*.
[126] CDPA, s. 99.   [127] CDPA, s. 230(1).   [128] RDA, s. 24C.
[129] Community Design Regulations 2005 (SI 2005/2339) (CDRs), reg. 1B.   [130] PA 77, s. 61(1)(b).
[131] TMA, s. 16.   [132] *Mayne Pharma v Pharmacia Italia* [2005] EWCA Civ 294.

order for disposal. The court may order that the articles be destroyed or otherwise dealt with as it thinks fit or forfeited to the owner of the relevant IPR.[133] Again, the circumstances in which an order for disposal is made may differ depending upon the right.

1.5 CRIMINAL PENALTIES

Article 61 of the TRIPS Agreement stipulates that:

> Members shall provide for criminal procedures and penalties to be applied at least in cases of willful trademark counterfeiting or copyright piracy on a commercial scale.

This article creates a fairly restricted obligation to criminalize certain trade mark and copyright infringements. That said, controversy surrounds the scope of this provision, in particular what constitutes counterfeiting or piracy *on a commercial scale*. In the dispute between China and the US before the WTO,[134] the WTO Panel Report concluded that[135] 'commercial scale' is a relative and flexible standard and, as such, leaves significant room to national legislators when it comes to setting thresholds for criminal liability.[136] Attempts to harmonize criminal penalties for intellectual property infringement across the EU have so far been unsuccessful.

In certain cases, copyright, registered designs, and trade mark actions may also be brought in criminal courts. As we have seen, use of the criminal law has been largely aimed at infringing activities which are carried out on a commercial scale, such as the unauthorized streaming of movies and music or the use of trade marks on counterfeit goods. Criminal actions may not be as costly as civil actions and they can have a deterrent effect. They give the rightsholder the assistance, where necessary, of state agencies such as the Trading Standards Office to ensure enforcement. However, criminal actions also carry disadvantages. They can take time to initiate and they will not carry the range of remedies both pre- and post-trial which are available in civil actions (see, e.g., the case of *R v Crown Court at Harrow, ex p Unic Centre Sarl* concerning forfeiture[137]).

FURTHER READING

C. Geiger (ed.), *Criminal Enforcement of Intellectual Property: A Handbook of Contemporary Research* (Cheltenham: Edward Elgar, 2012).

R. Garcia Perez, 'Injunctions in intellectual property cases: what is the power of the courts?' [2016] IPQ 87.

---

[133] TMA, s. 19 (trade marks); CDPA, s. 231 (UK unregistered design right); CDPA, s. 114, (copyright); RDA, s. 24D (UK registered designs); CDRs, reg. 1C (Community unregistered and registered designs).

[134] See Panel Report, 'China—Measures affecting the protection and enforcement of intellectual property rights', DS 362, 26 January 2009, paras 7.516–7.669.

[135] Panel Report, para. 7.577.

[136] H. Grosse Ruse-Khan, 'Criminal enforcement and international IP law' in C. Geiger (ed.), *Criminal Enforcement of Intellectual Property: A Handbook of Contemporary Research* (Cheltenham: Edward Elgar, 2012), p. 181.

[137] [2000] 1 WLR 2112.

G. Mei, 'Interlocutory injunctions in IP infringement actions in England and Wales and in Ireland—*American Cyanamid* revisited' (2015) 46 IIC 175.

C. Scott, 'Damages inquires and accounts of profits in the IPEC' [2016] EIPR 273.

X. Seuba, 'The economics of intellectual property enforcement' [2015] WIPO J 133.

P. Sugden, 'The power of one! The failure of criminal copyright laws (piracy) to blend into greater cultural consciousness!' [2014] EIPR 263.

1.6 CONCLUSION

In this chapter we have looked at both the justifications for intellectual property protection and also the international and regional frameworks that have emerged to regulate intellectual property. What our discussion reveals is that there are numerous and sometimes conflicting interests that need to be accounted for when deciding on the optimal level of intellectual property protection. In relation to justifications, we have seen that a law and economics approach will emphasize the interests of rightsholders and consumers, while discussions of the public domain will frequently draw a distinction between the interests of creators and the public. Turning to international protection, we can see that the interests of different countries may vary depending on whether the country is developed or developing, rich in intellectual property or traditional knowledge. While, in relation to remedies, it would appear that pre-trial orders might at times be oppressive for the defendant, there is also the need to ensure that the claimant's own position is not damaged irreparably before trial. It is important to remember when you read the following chapters that a crucial feature of any IPR is the need to reconcile these different, and sometimes conflicting, interests.

2

COPYRIGHT I:

HISTORY, JUSTIFICATIONS, SOURCES OF LAW, AND SUBSISTENCE

2.1 INTRODUCTION

Copyright may be described as a set of exclusive rights in relation to, broadly speaking, cultural creations. As such, it underpins an array of cultural works, such as literature, newspapers, photographs, drawings, artworks, films, music, and plays. It also extends to less obviously aesthetic creations, such as computer programs and databases. In our daily lives these are creations that we regularly enjoy, consume, and use and they may be a source of entertainment, education, pleasure, or profit. The importance, therefore, of copyright law cannot be underestimated. Indeed, one needs only to mention Hollywood, Bollywood, and the US record industry, to be reminded of how much may be at stake when it comes to copyright-protected material. Copyright, therefore, has a global significance, but its nature is territorial (i.e. the exclusive rights that it grants are limited to a particular territory, such as the UK). This has led to international and regional attempts at harmonization in order to ensure some basic uniformity of approach. The focus of this chapter will be on situating UK copyright law within a historical, normative, and legislative framework. We will then turn to examine the principles of UK copyright law, beginning with the requirements for copyright to subsist in a work. Chapter 3 will examine the important principles relating to authorship, ownership, term of protection, and exclusive rights, while Chapter 4 will deal with infringement, exceptions, and database right.

2.2 HISTORY

In order to better understand UK copyright law, this section will attempt briefly to place it in historical context. The origin of copyright law is linked to one particularly important technological development—the printing press—and its later development has also been significantly shaped by technological change. In the 15th and 16th centuries, many European states were in the habit of granting printing privileges to printers. In England, printing privileges first appeared in 1518 and were granted via royal prerogative. Also in existence in the 16th century was a guild system for the printing of books, which was run by the Stationers' Company. The Stationers' Company derived its authority from a Royal Charter of 1557, which granted the guild a monopoly on the printing of books. The right to print a book was obtained by entering it in the company's register and only members of the company might own 'copies' of books. The guild was self-regulating and also had powers to enforce claims of infringement against unlicensed printers. In return for this monopoly, the Stationers' Company was expected to implement the Crown's censorship policies to prevent the publication of seditious and heretical books. The monopoly of the Stationers' Company over the book trade and its censorship role was cemented by the Licensing Act 1662. Thus, early copyright law was very much a mixture of trade regulation and censorship.

A crucial turning point, however, came in 1695 when the Licensing Act 1662 lapsed and with it the privileges and powers of the Stationers' Company. Attempts by the guild to persuade Parliament to restore the powers under the Act were unsuccessful, largely because of concerns about the damaging effects of monopolies. But renewed lobbying efforts on the part of the Stationers' Company led to the first copyright Act, the Statute of Anne 1710, which was entitled, 'An Act for the Encouragement of Learning, by vesting the Copies of Printed Books in the Authors or Purchasers of such Copies, during the Times therein mentioned'. Anyone, i.e. printer or author, was eligible for protection under the Act by enrolling their book in the register of the Stationers' Company. The Act gave authors of books not yet printed or published the sole liberty of printing and reprinting their books for 14 years, with the possibility of renewal for a further 14 years if the author was still alive at the end of the first 14-year period. It also gave authors and proprietors of 'copies' of books that were already in print the sole liberty of printing these books for a single term of 21 years.

Much has been written about the Statute of Anne and its significance for copyright law. Some commentators argue that it was a way of securing the interests of printers and booksellers (albeit through using the rhetorical device of 'author'), while others have characterized it as a device for breaking the printing monopolies. Others suggest that the statute in fact brokered a deal between authors, booksellers, *and* the reading public. Certainly, it can be said that with the introduction of the Act, the roles of censorship and printing were decoupled.

The Statute of Anne was also a source of considerable controversy during its existence. Once the first copyrights under the Act began to expire and attempts to extend the term of protection failed, the London publishers argued that perpetual copyright existed at common law. The issue became whether or not the Statute of Anne was exhaustive of protection, or whether it merely supplemented a common law right to property that was perpetual. Legal disputes, as well as much public debate, ensued and this became known as the 'Literary Property Debate'. The culmination of the debate was the case of *Donaldson v Becket* (1774), in which the House of Lords had to decide whether Donaldson (a Scottish bookseller) had infringed any (common law) rights that existed in the poem *The Seasons*. What exactly was decided in *Donaldson* has itself been the subject of some confusion, caused partly by the misreporting of some of the lords' opinions and partly by the fact that the common law judges gave their opinion to the House of Lords but the entirety of the House voted, it seems, contrary to the opinion of the judges. One view of *Donaldson* is that the House of Lords held that the Statute of Anne took away any common law rights that existed in published works. Another view is that the House in fact denied the existence of common law copyright. Whichever view is taken, it is fair to say that the decision at least quelled the Literary Property Debate.

The early 19th century saw the Statute of Anne replaced by the Copyright Act 1814. The Act extended copyright in literary works to 28 years after publication and, if the author was still alive at the end of this period, for the remainder of his life. This extension of term was relatively uncontroversial, in stark contrast to later proposals put forward by Thomas Noon Talfourd in 1837. Talfourd proposed a term of life of the author plus 60 years, which met with intense opposition from publishers, printers, and radical politicians. Eventually, a compromise was reached and the Copyright Amendment Act 1842 provided for a term of either the life of the author plus seven years or 42 years from the first publication (whichever was longer). This was the first time that term of protection had been calculated on a post-mortem basis.

What of creative works other than literary ones, such as plays, music, and art works? The 18th and 19th centuries saw other types of creations being protected on a subject-specific basis. For example, the Engravers' Act 1735 gave persons who invented and designed engravings and etchings, 'the sole right and liberty of printing and reprinting their work' for a term of 14 years from first publication. This was the first time copyright extended to matter other than literary works. The Models and Busts Act 1798 granted exclusive rights to persons who created new models or casts of humans or animal figures for a period of 14 years. The Dramatic Literary Property Act 1833 was the first time in which authors of dramatic manuscripts were granted rights of reproduction and public performance and this protection lasted for 28 years from the day of first publication. Paintings, drawings, and photographs did not attract copyright protection until the passing of the Fine Arts Copyright Act 1862. This Act gave authors of 'original' paintings, drawings, and photographs the sole and exclusive right of 'copying, engraving, reproducing, and multiplying' their work 'by any means and of any size'. This was the first occasion on which the requirement of 'originality' was introduced (a requirement discussed at length later).

Thus, by the end of the 19th century it is fair to say that copyright was a chaotic collection of subject-specific statutes. Attempts to codify this legislation (in 1837 and in 1857) failed. It was not until the beginning of the 20th century that codification successfully occurred in the form of the Copyright Act 1911. The 1911 Act conferred copyright protection on several works, including some that had previously been unprotected (works of architecture, sound recordings, and films). Protection was granted to unpublished *and* published works and, as such, common law copyright in unpublished works was abolished. The term of protection was for the life of the author plus 50 years and all formalities, in particular the requirement of registration with the Stationers' Company, were abolished. The 1911 Act was exported to numerous Commonwealth states. As such, it had an enormous influence in shaping the copyright laws of many common law countries.

Following a review of the 1911 Act by the Gregory Committee, the Copyright Act 1956 was introduced. Protection was extended to sound and television broadcasts, along with typographical arrangements of published editions. These new rights were grouped together with rights in relation to sound recordings and films and were classified as 'subject matter'. This was in contrast to 'works' (i.e. literary, dramatic, musical, and artistic works). The 1956 Act was later amended to provide protection for cable transmissions and software.

A review of the 1956 Act by the Whitford Committee resulted in the Copyright, Designs and Patents Act 1988 (CDPA). Importantly, the CDPA removed the distinction between 'works' and 'subject matter' and classified all creations as 'works'. The protection given to copyright owners was extended significantly, to include distribution and rental rights, and authors were granted for the first time 'moral rights' in their works. Performers rights were also included in the CDPA, along with a new unregistered design right. The CDPA has been amended on numerous occasions since its enactment, largely to implement the plethora of EU directives concerning copyright law. The CDPA, as most recently amended, is the law currently governing copyright in the UK.

FURTHER READING

AHRC, Primary Sources on Copyright (1450–1900) <http://www.copyrighthistory.org/cam/index.php>.

I. Alexander, *Copyright Law and the Public Interest in the Nineteenth Century* (Oxford: Hart, 2010).

W. R. Cornish et al., *Oxford History of the Laws of England*, vols XI–XIII (1820–1914) (Oxford: Oxford University Press, 2010), vol. XIII, Part Five, ch. II, 'Copyright'.

R. Deazley, *On the Origin of the Right to Copy: Charting the Movement of Copyright Law in Eighteenth-Century Britain (1695–1775)* (Oxford: Hart, 2004).

J. C. Ginsburg, 'A tale of two copyrights: literary property in revolutionary France and America' (1991) 147 RIDA 125 (also published in (1990) 64 Tul. L. Rev. 991).

M. F. Makeen, *Copyright in a Global Information Society: The Scope of Copyright Protection under International, US, UK and French Law* (London: Kluwer, 2000), pp. 1–12, 23–4.

L. R. Patterson, *Copyright in Historical Perspective* (Nashville, TN: Vanderbilt University Press, 1968).

C. Seville, *Literary Copyright Reform in Early Victorian England* (Cambridge: Cambridge University Press, 1999).

C. Seville, *The Internationalisation of Copyright Law: Books, Buccaneers and the Black Flag in the Nineteenth Century* (Cambridge: Cambridge University Press, 2006).

C. Seville, 'The Statute of Anne: rhetoric and reception in the nineteenth century' (2010) 47 Houston L. Rev. 819.

B. Sherman and L. Bently, *The Making of Modern Intellectual Property Law* (Cambridge: Cambridge University Press, 1999).

B. Sherman and L. Wiseman (eds), *Copyright and the Challenge of the New* (Alphen aan den Rijn: Kluwer, 2012).

2.3 JUSTIFICATIONS

In Chapter 1 at 1.2 we explored the justifications for intellectual property law generally, including natural-rights, utilitarian, and economic rationales. At this point, it may be useful to turn back and revisit this discussion. When it comes to copyright, economic and natural-rights justifications are frequently invoked. The applicability of these justifications to copyright in particular is discussed by Spence in the following extract.

M. Spence, 'Justifying copyright' in D. McClean and K. Schubert (eds), *Dear Images: Art, Copyright and Culture* (Manchester: Ridinghouse, 2002), pp. 389–403

Economic Justifications for Copyright

The economic justifications for copyright focus on the need to provide incentives for the creation and dissemination of creative works. For economic theorists the intended beneficiary of the copyright system is the community as a whole, which demands the production of, and access to, as many creative works as possible. It is assumed that, in perfect conditions, the market will ensure the production of goods and those goods will be allocated to the party who values them the most. There will be incentive to produce goods because their selling price will allow a producer to recoup both the costs of production and the benefit of the goods to a purchaser. But creative works are said to be 'public goods' in that it is difficult to exclude non-purchasers from their enjoyment. Because of the difficulty of excluding non-purchasers, there will be no incentive to create and to disseminate works. They will be under-produced unless the law intervenes to cure this 'market failure'. Even assuming that the rights given to the copyright owner constitute some type of 'monopoly' and entail the dead-weight loss associated with all monopolies, the advantages of the copyright system in curing this market failure are said to outweigh those losses. Other potential methods of curing the relevant market failure, such as systems of state or private patronage, are seen as less desirable in that they involve the centralization of decisions about which types of works will be produced.

...

The problem with the economic justification of copyright is that: (i) there is much which copyright protects that would be produced and disseminated even without the incentive effects of the copyright regime, and (ii) it is difficult to structure copyright such that the monopoly losses associated with the regime are no greater than those required to ensure the production and dissemination of a given category of work, especially given the wide range of subject matter that copyright protects.

...

Deontological Justifications for Copyright

The economic arguments for copyright assume that the regime exists to serve a public purpose. But it may be that the regime exists, not to advance the common weal, but to give force to certain ethical obligations owed to creators.

...

The Argument from Desert

It is a claim frequently made that the creator of a work 'deserves' control over its use. There are two ways in which such a desert claim may be established. First, a creator might deserve control over the use of the work as a reward for her efforts in producing it. Second, a creator might deserve control over the use of the work as a reward for the contribution that it makes to her culture ... Desert is an uncertain concept that has only recently become the subject of rigorous philosophical analysis. But, even assuming that the concept of desert can be clearly expounded, it proves a difficult basis for the justification of copyright. This is for three reasons.

First, there is no direct correlation between a creator's effort or contribution and the works which copyright might be expected to protect. If it is effort that is deserving of reward, then the question arises what the minimum threshold of effort might be for a work to be deserving of protection and whether works that required little effort should be protected. Copyright would be in danger of protecting only the perspiring, and not the inspired, creator. If it is contribution that is deserving of reward, then the question becomes what level of contribution is deserving.

...

Second, even if the creator of a work can establish her desert there may be good reasons for not recognizing her claim to control the use of the work. She may already have been rewarded in other ways...She may have been amply rewarded in the payment she receives and copyright protection might be more than she deserves.

...

Third, there is no reason why, even if the creator of the work deserves something as a reward for effort or contribution, it ought necessarily to be the control over the use of the work that copyright affords. We reward those who work hard to establish world peace and thereby contribute to our public life, with gratitude, praise and, perhaps, a Nobel prize. It is hard to see that the creator of an artistic work expends more effort, or contributes more, than such people.

...

The Argument from Personhood

This argument is that a work is an embodiment of the personality of the creator. Control over the work is essential to secure the creator's control over her own personality...There are two principal difficulties with this approach.

First, it is questionable just how many works constitute, or are intended to constitute, an embodiment of the creator's personality.

...

Second, even assuming personality to mean something as discernible as self-presentation, it is unclear precisely how much control over her self-presentation a creator ought to be afforded...such control might be appropriate in contexts in which there is a threat that unauthorized use will change the meaning of the work in a way that does the creator harm. But that she ought to have control over her self-presentation to the extent of being able to prohibit the reproduction or publication of her work in a way which is perfectly faithful to its meaning though, perhaps, at a time or by someone not of her choosing, is far more questionable.

...

The Argument from Personal Autonomy

This attractive argument flows from the intuition that valuing personal autonomy must involve granting an individual at least some control over those things with which she is most closely associated: to allow her to carve out an area of individual dominion. If a creator can show a close association with a particular work, then respect for her personal autonomy may require that she be given at least some degree of control over its use.

...

First, none of the usual arguments from personal autonomy can establish a nexus between the creator and her work such that recognition of her right to control the work is essential to recognition of her personal autonomy.

...

Second, against the claim that control over a creator's work is essential to the protection of her personal autonomy, must be set the claim that the grant of such control is a limitation of the autonomy of those who would seek to use the work without her permission. It is therefore necessary to demonstrate that the impact on the creator's personal autonomy of refusing her control over the work would outweigh the impact on the world-be user's autonomy of granting the creator such control.

In your view, which is the most persuasive justification when it comes to copyright—is it economic or deontological (i.e. natural rights) and why? How important is it, do you think, for rationales to underpin a copyright system, i.e. what should be their role? Finally, which, if any, of the above justifications is likely to be favoured in the UK? Numerous commentators associate common law copyright systems, such as the UK, with economic or utilitarian justifications. Others, however, are less convinced that UK copyright law has a clear rationale. By way of contrast, commentators frequently cite *droit d'auteur* (i.e. civil law authors' rights) systems, such as France, as having clear natural-rights foundations that are reflected in robust protection for authors. As you progress through this chapter, it will be important to bear in mind the various copyright justifications and to reflect on whether any one of them adequately explain the principles of UK copyright law.

FURTHER READING

T. Aplin, *Copyright Law in the Digital Society* (Oxford: Hart, 2005), ch. 2.

S. Breyer, 'The uneasy case for copyright: a study of copyright in books, photocopies and computer programs' (1970) 84 Harv. L. R. 281,

P. Geller, 'Must copyright be for ever caught between marketplace and authorship norms?' in B. Sherman and A. Strowel (eds), *Of Authors and Origins* (Oxford: Clarendon, 1994), pp. 159–201.

W. M. Landes and R. A. Posner, 'An economic analysis of copyright law' (1989) 18 J. Legal Studies 325.

B. W. Tyerman, 'The economic rationale for copyright protection for published books: a reply to Professor Breyer' (1971) 18 UCLA L. R. 1100.

A. C. Yen, 'Restoring the natural law: copyright as labor and possession' (1990) 51 Ohio State L. J. 517.

2.4 SOURCES OF LAW

2.4.1 INTERNATIONAL

A collection of international conventions and treaties exists to regulate copyright law. As such, it is vital to understand the extent of the obligations imposed by these instruments. Those we consider the most important are as follows.

2.4.1.1 Berne Convention on the Protection of Literary and Artistic Works 1886 (Berne Convention)

The Berne Convention occupies an extremely important place in international copyright law since it was the first multilateral treaty on copyright law. Signed in 1886, membership of the Berne Union has grown from ten to 183 countries.[1] As such, the Berne Convention has had a dominant influence on the development of copyright standards at an international, regional, and national level and this has been reinforced by the TRIPS Agreement 1994, which incorporates most of the Berne Convention obligations.

Since its inception, the Berne Convention has been revised on several occasions—in 1908 at the Berlin Revision Conference, in 1928 at the Rome Revision Conference, in 1948 at the Brussels Revision Conference, and in 1967 and 1971 at the Stockholm and Paris Revision Conferences, respectively.[2] In terms of membership, the UK, France, and Germany were three of the original signatories to the Convention. Other major countries did not join until much later—the US on 1 March 1989, Russia on 13 March 1995, and China on 15 October 1992.

The ambit of the Berne Convention is succinctly summarized by Article 1, which states:

> The countries to which this Convention applies constitute a Union for the protection of the rights of authors in their literary and artistic works.

According to Article 3 of the Berne Convention, protection applies to the following categories of persons:

- authors who are nationals of a Union country for their unpublished or published works;
- authors who are not nationals of a Union country, but have their habitual residence in a Union country for their unpublished or published works;
- authors who are *not* nationals of a Union country, but whose works are first published in a Union country or simultaneously published in a Union country and non-Union country.[3]

In relation to cinematographic works, Article 4 states that protection shall apply, even if Article 3 is not fulfilled to:

- authors of cinematographic works the maker of which has his headquarters or habitual residence in a Union country;
- authors of architectural works erected in a country of the Union or of other works incorporated in a building or other structure located in a Union country.

Two fundamental principles underpin the Berne Convention—that of national treatment and minimum rights. They are both contained in Article 5(1) of the Berne Convention, which states:

> Authors shall enjoy, in respect of works for which they are protected under this Convention, in countries of the Union other than the country of origin, the rights which their respective laws do now or may hereafter grant to their nationals, as well as the rights specially granted by this Convention.

---

[1] As at 1 August 2016—see <www.wipo.int/treaties/en/ip/berne/>.
[2] There are also the 1896 and 1914 protocols to the Berne Convention.
[3] Simultaneous publication is publication in a Union country within 30 days of first publication in a non-Union country.

The principle of national treatment may be explained as follows: Union country A is obliged to confer the same rights on an author from Union country B as it confers on nationals of Union country A. In other words, a country of the Berne Union cannot discriminate, when it comes to copyright protection, between its own nationals and authors from other countries of the Union. This means that UK authors can expect to go to France and receive the same copyright protection that is offered to French authors and vice versa.

There are four exceptions to the principle of national treatment. These relate to: the *droit de suite*, which is a right to receive a percentage of the sale price on original works of art and original manuscripts that are subsequently sold;[4] duration of protection;[5] works of applied art and industrial designs and models;[6] and the exception in Article 6 that was crafted to deal with the US before it became a member of the Berne Union.

The principle of minimum rights requires Union country A to offer the rights specially granted by the Berne Convention to authors of all Union countries, except Union country A. In other words, the minimum standards of protection that are contained in the Berne Convention apply only to authors from *other* Berne countries and no Berne member is obliged to accord this protection to their own authors. That said, most Berne countries do offer the minimum rights to their own authors as well. For a Berne member to do otherwise would be to privilege foreign authors and create a sense of unfairness, as well as unpopularity.

The minimum rights that must be offered have steadily expanded since the Convention was signed in 1886. They include a collection of economic rights (which may be subject to certain permitted reservations, exceptions, or limitations), moral rights, and duration of protection. Of course, if Berne countries so wish they may offer protection in excess of these minimum standards. As and when the Berne Convention minimum rights are relevant to explaining UK copyright law, they will be discussed later in this chapter.

FURTHER READING

L. Bently and B. Sherman, 'Great Britain and the signing of the Berne Convention in 1886' (2001) 48 Journal of the Copyright Society of the USA 311.

P. Goldstein and P. B. Hugenholtz, *International Copyright* (3rd edn, Oxford: Oxford University Press, 2012).

S. von Lewinski, *International Copyright Law and Policy* (Oxford: Oxford University Press, 2008).

S. Ricketson and J. Ginsburg, *International Copyright and Neighbouring Rights: The Berne Convention and Beyond* (2nd edn, Oxford: Oxford University Press, 2005).

2.4.1.2 International Convention for the Protection of Performers, Producers of Phonograms and Broadcasting Organizations 1961 (Rome Convention)

Technological developments post-World War I led to a new trio of interests that sought copyright protection. These were producers of phonograms (i.e. sound recordings), performers, and broadcasters. Sound recordings lacked any kind of international protection and were vulnerable to use without remuneration, particularly by broadcasters. Broadcasters had no

---

[4] Art. 14*ter*(2).   [5] Art. 7(8).   [6] Art. 2(7).

rights in relation to the broadcasts that they made and for performers their live performances could be fixed and disseminated in a manner not previously possible. Thus, it was at the Brussels Revision Conference 1948 that performers, sound recording producers, and broadcasters sought protection under the Berne Convention. This was unsuccessful, however, because these persons were not seen as 'authors of literary and artistic works' within the meaning of the Convention. Instead, a resolution was passed that the governments of the Union should study the way in which protection could be granted to these interests, without prejudice to the rights of authors. Negotiations subsequently occurred during the 1950s between three organizations: the International Federation of Musicians (representing performers), the International Federation of the Phonographic Industry (representing phonogram producers), and the European Broadcasting Union (representing broadcasting organizations in Europe). The International Federation of Actors and the International Federation of Variety Artists were also involved. Three international governmental organizations promoted and sustained the progress of the negotiations: the ILO, UNESCO, and WIPO (known then as the United International Bureaux for the Protection of Intellectual Property (BIRPI)). The conference for the preparation of the Draft Convention was held at The Hague in 1960 and this was followed in 1961 by the Diplomatic Conference on the Protection of Performers, Producers of Phonograms and Broadcasting Organizations, in which a total of 41 states participated. The signatories to this Convention have now grown to 86,[7] of which the UK is one.

The protection under the Rome Convention in no way affects the protection of copyright in literary and artistic works.[8] The beneficiaries of protection are, unsurprisingly, performers, phonogram producers, and broadcasting organizations. The two basic principles of the Rome Convention are national treatment and the obligation of Contracting States to afford minimum rights.

The conditions for national treatment differ depending on whether it is being claimed for performers, phonogram producers, or broadcasting organizations. For performers, national treatment shall be granted if either: (1) the performance takes place in another Contracting State; (2) the performance is incorporated in a phonogram which is protected by Article 5 of the Rome Convention; or (3) the performance is carried by a broadcast which is protected by Article 6 of the Convention.[9] In the case of producers of phonograms, national treatment shall be granted by Contracting States if: (1) the producer of the phonogram is a national of another Contracting State; (2) the first fixation of the sound was made in another Contracting State; or (3) the phonogram was first published in another Contracting State.[10] Finally, each Contracting State shall grant national treatment to broadcasting organizations if either of the following conditions is met: the headquarters of the broadcasting organization is situated in another Contracting State or the broadcast was transmitted from a transmitter situated in another Contracting State.[11]

According to Article 7, performers are to be granted the possibility of preventing the broadcasting and communication to the public, without their consent, of their performance; the fixation without their consent of their unfixed performance; and the reproduction without their consent of a fixation of their performance if the original fixation itself was made without their consent or the reproduction is made for purposes different from those for which the performers gave their consent. It is important to note that once a performer

---

[7] See <www.wipo.int/treaties/en/ip/rome>. [8] Art. 1. [9] Art. 4. [10] Art. 5.
[11] Art. 6.

has consented to the incorporation of his or her performance in a visual or audiovisual fixation, these rights do not apply.

Both producers of phonograms and broadcasting organizations have stronger rights, insofar as they are exclusive rights, as opposed to merely 'the possibility of preventing' certain acts. This latter formulation was included for performers' rights in order to allow Contracting States flexibility as to how they protected performers. This enabled, for example, the UK to continue to protect performers through the use of criminal sanctions only.

Producers of phonograms are granted the right to authorize or prohibit the direct or indirect reproduction of their phonograms.[12] Where a phonogram is published for commercial purposes, or a reproduction of such phonogram is used directly for broadcasting or any communication to the public, then a single equitable remuneration is to be paid by the user to the performers, or the producers, or to both.[13]

Broadcasting organizations are granted the right to authorize or prohibit: (1) the rebroadcasting of their broadcasts; (2) the fixation of their broadcasts; and (3) the reproduction of fixations, made without their consent, of their broadcasts or of fixations of their broadcasts made in accordance with the stipulated exceptions in Article 15, if the reproduction is made for purposes different from those stated in Article 15. They are also granted the exclusive right to authorize or prohibit the communication to the public of their television broadcasts if such communication is made in places accessible to the public against payment of an entrance fee.[14]

The above rights must last for at least 20 years from the end of the year in which the fixation was made (in the case of phonograms or performances incorporated therein); or when the performance took place (for performances not incorporated in phonograms); or, in the case of broadcasts, when the broadcast took place. Notably, there are no obligations concerning moral rights.

FURTHER READING

G. Davies, 'The 50th anniversary of the Rome Convention for the protection of performers, producers of phonograms and broadcasting organizations: reflections on the background and importance of the Convention' (2012) 2 QMJIP 206.

2.4.1.3 Agreement on Trade Related Aspects of Intellectual Property Rights 1994 (TRIPS Agreement)

As explained in Chapter 1,[15] the TRIPS Agreement forms part of the WTO Agreement and thus binds all WTO members, currently standing at 153. The UK has been a WTO member since 1 January 1995.

The TRIPS Agreement incorporates, inter alia, the key provisions of the Berne Convention. It does this via Article 9, which stipulates that members shall comply with Articles 1 to 21 of the Berne Convention (as revised in 1971). Importantly, however, there is no obligation to comply with Article 6*bis* of the Berne Convention, which deals with moral rights.

The TRIPS Agreement also contains a number of provisions that seek to clarify and also extend the minimum standards of copyright protection. For example, Article 9(2) of TRIPS emphasizes that 'Copyright protection shall extend to expressions and not to ideas, procedures, methods of operation or mathematical concepts as such' and Article 10(1) clarifies

---

[12] Art. 10.   [13] Art. 12.   [14] Art. 13.   [15] See 1.3.1.2.

that computer programs shall be protected as literary works under the Berne Convention. An example of extending protection is Article 11, which provides that for at least computer programs and cinematographic works, Member States shall provide authors and their successors in title with the right of commercial rental to the public.

The TRIPS Agreement also provides for protection of performers, producers of phonograms (i.e. sound recordings), and broadcasters in Article 14. This protection mirrors that stated in the Rome Convention, except that the term of protection for performers and phonogram producers is increased to 50 years from the end of the calendar year in which the fixation was made or the performance took place.[16]

As discussed in Chapter 1,[17] an important feature of the TRIPS Agreement is that it makes disputes between WTO members about compliance with TRIPS obligations subject to the dispute settlement procedures of the WTO. This has created both formal and informal pressure to implement TRIPS obligations. Given that TRIPS incorporates Berne Convention obligations (except for Article 6*bis*), it has provided an effective mechanism for (indirectly) enforcing the Berne Convention.

2.4.1.4 WIPO Copyright Treaty 1996 (WCT)

Developments in technology during the 1980s and 1990s created various problems and uncertainties for copyright law. For example, it was unclear whether computer programs and electronic databases fell within the scope of the Berne Convention and whether the Convention minimum rights covered transmission of works via electronic networks, such as the internet. There was also the more general problem of how to ensure effective enforcement of copyright in an increasingly global, networked society.

In 1991 and succeeding years, WIPO summoned Committees of Experts to consider these problems and to draft a possible protocol to the Berne Convention. Revision of the Berne Convention itself was not feasible, in light of the fact that amendments to the substantive provisions of Berne require unanimity of votes[18] and it was felt that such unanimity would be difficult to achieve given the diversity of opinions and the complexity of problems to be solved. Therefore, a more practical option was to establish a protocol to the Berne Convention.

The Diplomatic Conference on Certain Copyright and Neighbouring Rights Questions was held in Geneva between 2 and 20 December 1996. It was one of the largest diplomatic conferences on copyright law, with over 120 Berne countries being represented, together with a special delegation of the EC, and representatives of seven intergovernmental organizations, 76 non-governmental organizations, and the International Bureau of WIPO. Two treaties sprang from this conference, one of which was the WIPO Copyright Treaty 1996 (WCT). The relationship of this treaty to the Berne Convention is that it is a special agreement within the meaning of Article 20 of Berne, i.e. an agreement entered into by Berne Union countries.

The WCT contains clarifying provisions such as Article 4, which states that computer programs are protected as literary works within the meaning of Article 2 of the Berne Convention; and Article 5, which says the same for databases. Article 2 emphasizes that copyright protection extends to expressions and not to ideas, procedures, methods of operation, or mathematical concepts as such.

---

[16] Art. 14(5).   [17] See 1.3.1.2.   [18] See Berne Convention, Art. 27(3).

In terms of exclusive rights, Article 1(4) of the WCT states that Contracting Parties shall comply with Articles 1 to 21 (Article 6*bis* inclusive) of Berne (Paris Act, 1971). The effect is to institute or confirm the regime of the Berne Convention in all countries which are Contracting Parties to the Treaty, whether they are members of the Berne Convention or not. The WCT also introduces two new economic rights not provided for in the Berne Convention—the right of distribution[19] and the right of rental[20]—and extends the right of communication to the public to include on-demand transmissions.[21]

By virtue of incorporating the Berne Convention obligations, the minimum term of protection is 50 years *post mortem auctoris* (*pma*). However, it is important to note that Article 9 of the WCT stipulates that Contracting Parties shall not apply Article 7(4) of the Berne Convention. This provision allows countries of the Union to determine the term of protection for photographic works and works of applied art (insofar as they are protected as artistic works), provided it is a minimum of 25 years from the making of the work. The effect of Article 9 of the WCT is that 50 years *pma* will now be applicable to photographic works and works of applied art.

In an attempt to combat widespread digital piracy of copyright works, Article 11 of the WCT imposes obligations to provide adequate legal protection and effective legal remedies against the circumvention of effective technological measures. To facilitate the exploitation of copyright works in a digital environment, Article 12 creates obligations in respect of rights management information that is applied to copyright works. The role and scope of these provisions is discussed further in Chapter 4.[22]

2.4.1.5 WIPO Performances and Phonograms Treaty 1996 (WPPT)

Developments in digital technology also created pressures on the protection of related rights, in particular those applicable to performers, phonograms (i.e. sound recordings), and broadcasters. In order to amend the Rome Convention, which governs these related rights, it would have been necessary to bring together the three organizations responsible for the Convention and to balance the interests of the three groups. It was thought to be more practical to focus on a separate treaty and one that dealt with the rights of performers and phonogram producers (the rights of broadcasters to be dealt with later). Thus, the second treaty to emerge from the 1996 Diplomatic Conference was the WIPO Performances and Phonograms Treaty 1996 (WPPT).

There is no provision in the WPPT imposing an obligation on Contracting States to comply with the Rome Convention, but nothing in the WPPT is taken to derogate from the existing obligations that Contracting Parties have to each other under the Rome Convention.[23]

The protection given to performers improves significantly on that available under the Rome Convention. This is because performers are given exclusive rights in relation to their performances[24] and also moral rights in respect of live aural performances or performances fixed in phonograms.[25] Producers of phonograms are given exclusive rights of authorizing the reproduction,[26] distribution,[27] and commercial rental[28] of their phonograms, as well as the making available of their phonograms via on-demand transmissions, such as the internet.[29] There is also a right to equitable remuneration for the use of phonograms published for commercial purposes for broadcasting or for any communication to the public, which can be claimed by the performer or producer or both.[30]

---

[19] Art. 6.   [20] Art. 7.   [21] Art. 8.   [22] See 4.3.9.   [23] Art. 1.
[24] See Arts 6–10.   [25] Art. 5.   [26] Art. 11.   [27] Art. 12.   [28] Art. 13.
[29] Art. 14.   [30] Art. 15.

The term of protection for both performers and phonogram producers is 50 years, measured, in the case of the former, from the end of the year in which the performance was fixed in a phonogram and, in terms of the latter, 50 years from the end of the year in which the phonogram was published or, failing publication within 50 years of fixation, 50 years from the end of the year in which the fixation was made.[31]

As with the WCT, there are obligations in the WPPT concerning adequate legal protection and effective legal remedies in respect of circumvention of technological measures and the removal or altering of rights management information.[32]

FURTHER READING

M. Ficsor, *The Law of Copyright and the Internet: The 1996 WIPO Treaties, Their Interpretation and Implementation* (Oxford: Oxford University Press, 2002).

J. Reinbothe and S. von Lewinski, *The WIPO Treaties 1996* (London: Butterworths, 2002).

2.4.1.6 WIPO Beijing Treaty on Audiovisual Performances (Beijing Treaty)

We have seen that the Rome Convention and WPPT provide for minimum standards of protection for performers at the international level. However, if you look back at our discussion of the Rome Convention and WPPT you will notice that the protection is largely for audio performers or sound performances and that audiovisual performers (e.g. film actors) are largely unprotected by international standards. After an unsuccessful attempt at adopting an international treaty on the protection of audiovisual performances at a WIPO Diplomatic Conference in 2000, and subsequent extensive consultation by the WIPO Standing Committee on Copyright and Related Rights, the Beijing Treaty on Audiovisual Performances was adopted at the WIPO Diplomatic Conference held in Beijing from 20 to 26 June 2012.[33] The Treaty will enter into force once it has been ratified by 30 eligible parties.[34]

The Treaty accords protection to performers who are nationals of, or are habitually resident in, other Contracting Parties[35] and imposes the requirement of national treatment on each Contracting Party.[36] Performers are defined in Article 2(a) as 'actors, singers, musicians, dancers, and other persons who act, sing, deliver, declaim, play in, interpret, or otherwise perform literary or artistic works or expressions of folklore'. Audiovisual fixations are defined in Article 2(b) as 'the embodiment of moving images, whether or not accompanied by sounds or by the representations thereof, from which they can be perceived, reproduced or communicated through a device'.

The Beijing Treaty requires Contracting Parties to offer certain minimum rights to performers. According to Article 5, performers, in relation to their live performances or performances fixed in audiovisual fixations, have the rights of attribution and integrity. Also, performers can enjoy the exclusive rights of reproduction, distribution, commercial rental, and making available to the public by wire or wireless means, broadcasting,

---

[31] Art. 17.   [32] Arts 18–19.

[33] For details see <www.wipo.int/copyright/en/activities/audio_visual.html>.

[34] See Art. 26. Eligible parties must first sign and then ratify the treaty. Note that neither the EU nor the UK has yet signed the treaty.

[35] See Art. 3. Compare the Rome Convention and TRIPS on this point.   [36] See Art. 4.

and communication to the public of their performances fixed in audiovisual fixations (see Articles 7 to 11). The term of protection of these rights must last at least 50 years from the end of the year in which the performance was fixed. There are also obligations on Contracting Parties to provide the same kinds of limitations or exceptions in respect of performers' rights as they provide in connection with the protection of copyright in literary and artistic works (Article 13) and to provide adequate and effective legal remedies in relation to circumvention of technological protection measures and the removal or alteration of rights management information (Articles 15 and 16).

The provision particularly to note, however, is Article 12 dealing with transfer of rights because it deals with the issue that led to the faltering of the efforts to adopt a treaty in Geneva in 2000. Article 12(1) states:

> A Contracting party may provide in its national law that once a performer has consented to fixation of his or her performance in an audiovisual fixation, the exclusive rights of authorization provided for in Articles 7 to 11 of this Treaty shall be owned or exercised by or transferred to the producer of such audiovisual fixation subject to any contract to the contrary between the performer and the producer of the audiovisual fixation as determined by the national law.

What is the nature of this provision—is it mandatory or permissive? Whose interests does it seek to protect and which countries or copyright systems would you expect to want to invoke such a provision?

2.4.1.7 WIPO Treaty on Visually Impaired Persons (Marrakesh Treaty)

The Marrakesh Treaty to Facilitate Access to Published Works for Persons Who are Blind, Visually Impaired, or Otherwise Print Disabled was adopted at a WIPO Diplomatic Conference on 27 June 2013. The Treaty mandates Contracting Parties to provide for limitations or exceptions to the rights of reproduction, distribution, and making available to the public in relation to accessible format copies for the visually impaired (Article 4(1)(a)). Contracting Parties may also provide such limitations or exceptions in relation to the right of public performance (Article 4(1)(b)). Article 3 defines the beneficiaries of such limitations or exceptions as persons who are blind, visually impaired, or with a perceptual or reading disability, or otherwise unable 'through physical disability, to hold or manipulate a book or to focus or move the eyes to the extent that would be normally acceptable for reading'. According to Article 2(b) an 'accessible format copy' is a 'copy of a work in an alternative manner or from which gives a beneficiary person access to the work, including to permit the person to have access as feasibly and comfortably as a person without visual impairment or other print disability'. Contracting Parties may fulfil their obligations by creating limitations or exceptions that permit authorized entities (i.e. non-profit, government-approved providers of education, instructional training, adaptive reading, or information access to beneficiary persons) or the beneficiary persons themselves, or someone acting on their behalf to make accessible format copies (Article 4(2)). Importantly, the Treaty also mandates the cross-border exchange of accessible format copies by authorized entities (Articles 5 and 6).

The Marrakesh Treaty is unique insofar as its focus is on mandatory (as opposed to optional) copyright exceptions for the visually impaired. However, Article 1 of the Treaty stresses that rights and obligations under other treaties are not affected and, according to Article 11, that the three-step test in the Berne Convention, TRIPS Agreement, and the WCT applies to Contracting Parties when adopting measures necessary to ensure the application of the Marrakesh Treaty. The Treaty is also without prejudice to other limitations and exceptions for persons with disabilities provided by national law.

While the Marrakesh Treaty might be lauded for its objectives of enabling persons with visual impairments or other print disabilities to participate in cultural life and, in doing so, benefiting many in developing and least developed countries, Professors Ricketson and Ginsburg have queried whether such a copyright-limiting treaty is consistent with the Berne Convention. Nevertheless, they see the Marrakesh Treaty as a 'small but important step in healing some of the rancor that has beset relations between developed and developing countries for over four decades' while at the same time maintaining the respect for authorship at the heart of the Berne Convention.[37]

FURTHER READING

S. Ricketson and J. Ginsburg, 'The Berne Convention: historical and institutional aspects' in D. J. Gervais (ed.), *International Intellectual Property* (Cheltenham: Edward Elgar, 2015), ch. 1, pp. 3–36.

A. Brown and C. Waelde, 'Human rights, persons with disabilities and copyright' in C. Geiger (ed.), *Research Handbook on Human Rights and Intellectual Property* (Cheltenham: Edward Elgar, 2015), ch. 31, pp. 577–602.

2.4.2 REGIONAL

Since 1991, the EU (and previously the European Community) has issued numerous harmonizing directives in the field of copyright law (and rights related to copyright) with the object of promoting the smooth functioning of the internal market. As such, there has been a major intervention by the EU in the field of copyright and this has had a significant impact on the shape of UK copyright law.

The directives may be broadly classed into three types. The first type deals with specific subject matter, such as the Software Directive[38] and Database Directive.[39] The second type are directives dealing with specific rights or specific issues, namely the Rental Right Directive,[40] the Cable and Satellite Directive,[41] the Term Directive,[42] the Droit de Suite Directive,[43] the

---

[37] S. Ricketson and J. Ginsburg, 'The Berne Convention: historical and institutional aspects' in D. J. Gervais (ed.), *International Intellectual Property* (Cheltenham: Edward Elgar, 2015), ch. 1, p. 36.

[38] Directive 91/250/EEC on the legal protection of computer programs [1991] OJ L122/42, subsequently codified as Directive 2009/24/EC of 23 April 2009 on the legal protection of computer programs [2009] OJ L111/16.

[39] Directive 96/9/EC of the European Parliament and of the Council of 11 March 1996 on the legal protection of databases [1996] OJ L77/20.

[40] Directive 92/100/EEC of 19 November 1992 on rental and lending rights and on certain rights related to copyright in the field of intellectual property [1992] OJ L346/61, codified in Directive 2006/115/EC of the European Parliament and of the Council of 12 December 2006 on rental right and lending right and on certain rights related to copyright in the field of intellectual property [2006] OJ L367/28.

[41] Directive 93/83/EEC of 27 September 1993 on the coordination of certain rules concerning copyright and rights related to copyright applicable to satellite broadcasting and cable retransmission [1993] OJ L248/15.

[42] Directive 93/98/EEC, which was subsequently codified by Directive 2006/116/EC of 12 December 2006 on the term of protection of copyright and certain related rights [2006] OJ L372/12 and amended by Directive 2011/77/EU amending Directive 2006/1116/EC on the term of protection of copyright and certain related rights [2011] OJ L265/1.

[43] Directive 2001/84/EC of the European Parliament and of the Council of 27 September 2001 on the resale right for the benefit of the author of an original work of art [2001] OJ L272/32.

Orphan Works Directive,[44] and the Collective Rights Management Directive.[45] The final type is that focusing on broader harmonization across several copyright areas. Only one directive falls into this category, namely the Information Society Directive.[46]

 There is no need here to list the details of all directives concerning copyright law since, as and when the directives relate to UK copyright law, they will be discussed later in the chapter. The main point to note is that the UK has had to implement a substantial amount of EU law in the copyright field over the past two decades and this has not always been done in the most faithful or elegant fashion. It also seems increasingly likely that the EU will move towards codification of copyright law, in which case we may expect further changes to the fabric of UK law.[47]

FURTHER READING

T. Cook and E. Derclaye, 'An EU Copyright Code: what and how, if ever?' [2011] IPQ 259.

E. Derclaye (ed.), *Research Handbook on the Future of EU Copyright Law* (Cheltenham: Edward Elgar, 2009).

M. van Eechoud, P. B. Hugenholtz, S. van Gompel, L. Guibault, and N. Helberger, *Harmonizing European Copyright Law: The Challenges of Better Lawmaking* (Alphen aan den Rijn: Kluwer, 2009).

B. Lindner and T. Shapiro, *Copyright in the Information Society: A Guide to National Implementation of the European Directive* (Cheltenham: Edward Elgar, 2011).

T. Synodinou, *Codification of European Copyright Law: Challenges and Perspectives* (Alphen aan den Rijn: Kluwer, 2012).

M. Walter and S. von Lewinski, *European Copyright Law: A Commentary* (Oxford: Oxford University Press, 2010).

2.4.3 NATIONAL

The history of copyright protection in the UK has been discussed already at 2.2. The statute that presently governs UK copyright law is the CDPA, as amended.

2.5 SUBSISTENCE OF COPYRIGHT

As we have seen, copyright began life as a registered right. However, since the beginning of the 20th century it has been an unregistered right, meaning that protection arises automatically without having to satisfy any formalities, such as registration, deposit, or notice. The absence of formalities is mandated by the Berne Convention, specifically Article 5(2)

---

[44] Directive 2012/28/EU on certain permitted uses of orphan works [2012] OJ L299/5.

[45] Directive 2014/26/EU on collective management of copyright and related rights and multi-territorial licensing of rights in musical works for online use in the internal market [2014] OJ L84/72.

[46] Directive 2001/29/EC on the harmonization of certain aspects of copyright and related rights in the information society [2001] OJ L167/10.

[47] Leading scholars have already attempted to draft a European Copyright Code: see the efforts of the Wittem Group at <www.copyrightcode.eu/index.php?websiteid=1>. They believe that 'the design of a European Copyright Code might serve as an important reference tool for future legislatures at the European and national levels'.

which states that 'The enjoyment and the exercise of these rights shall not be subject to any formality.' This principle was introduced at the Berlin 1908 Revision Conference and the current wording of Article 5(2) was refined at the Stockholm and Paris Revision Conferences. Despite this clear prohibition on formalities, there have been some less than faithful attempts to abide by Article 5(2) (e.g. in the US) and also suggestions by scholars for their reintroduction, albeit in a more limited form.

The absence of formalities makes it much easier and less expensive to acquire and maintain copyright protection than other forms of IPRs, such as trade marks and patents. But when it comes to enforcing copyright through infringement proceedings, owners may have to establish that they are entitled to copyright protection because the defendant puts this matter in issue. This is when it will become necessary to show that the requirements for subsistence of copyright have been satisfied.

In the UK, for copyright to subsist, it is necessary to show appropriate subject matter and qualification and, in the case of literary, dramatic, musical, and artistic works, originality and fixation. We turn now to consider these requirements.

FURTHER READING

J. C. Ginsburg, 'The US experience with mandatory copyright formalities: a love/hate relationship' (2010) 33 Columbia Journal of Law & the Arts 311.

S. van Gompel, *Formalities in Copyright Law: An Analysis of Their History, Rationales and Possible Future* (Alphen aan den Rijn: Kluwer, 2011).

2.5.1 SUBJECT MATTER

2.5.1.1 'Open' and 'closed' lists of subject matter

According to the Berne Convention, the principles of national treatment and minimum rights apply 'in respect of works for which [authors] are protected under this Convention'.[48] These are 'literary and artistic works' and Article 2(1) of the Berne Convention states that 'the expression "literary and artistic works" shall include every production in the literary, scientific and artistic domain, whatever may be the mode or form of its expression' and goes on to provide an extensive but non-exhaustive list of examples. Some of the more notable works listed are: books, lectures, dramatic works, musical compositions, cinematographic works, paintings, sculptures, photographic works, and works of applied art. It is clear that the works enumerated in Article 2(1) are to be protected by members of the Berne Union, but there are no definitions of these works and also no stipulations about how this is to be achieved. This leaves open the possibility of different approaches to subject matter in the national laws of Union members. One of the major differences is the 'open list' versus 'closed list' approach, exemplified by France and the UK.

An 'open list' approach is one that broadly identifies the subject matter of protection and usually provides an illustrative list of such subject matter. For example, in France, article L112-1 of the Intellectual Property Code 1992 refers to, 'the rights of authors in all works of the mind, whatever their kind, form of expression, merit or purpose'. Article L112-2 then goes on to provide an illustrative list of 'works of the mind' that largely corresponds to Article 2(1) of Berne, but has some additional illustrations, namely that of software and its

---

[48] Berne Convention, Art. 5(1).

preparatory design material and 'creations of the seasonal industries of dress and articles of fashion'. Notably, there are no statutory definitions of what can or cannot constitute protectable subject matter and implicit within the French notion of 'work of the mind' is that it is original in the sense of displaying the imprint of the author's personality.

By contrast, the UK is a prime example of a 'closed list' system. This is where copyright protection is given to stipulated categories of subject matter. Thus, the CDPA grants protection to eight—and *only* eight—types of works. These are literary, dramatic, musical, and artistic works; films; sound recordings; broadcasts; and typographical arrangements of published editions.[49] As such, a person must bring his or her creation within one or more of these categories in order to obtain copyright—failure to do so will preclude protection. The scope of the eight categories is elaborated upon, in varying degrees, via statutory definitions. Some definitions are exhaustive in nature, such as that for 'artistic work',[50] whereas others are inclusive, such as that for 'dramatic work'.[51] In the case of literary, dramatic, artistic, and musical works once the subject matter hurdle is surmounted it is still necessary to establish that the works are original (a requirement examined in the next section).

It is important to note, however, that in light of recent CJEU rulings the UK may not be able to retain its closed list approach to subject matter. In *Bezpečnostní softwarová asociace v Ministerstvo kultury*,[52] the Court concluded that the graphic user interface of a computer program was not part of the expression of that program within the meaning of the Software Directive.[53] However, the Court went on to find that, in reliance on *Infopaq International A/S v Danske Dagblades Forening*[54] (discussed at 2.5.2.3.2), copyright could subsist in a graphic user interface provided it was original in the sense of the author's own intellectual creation.[55] In other words, the Court implicitly suggested that where there was an intellectual creation it was unnecessary further to categorize it as a particular type of work. Similarly, in *Football Association Premier League v QC Leisure; Murphy v Media Protection Services*,[56] the CJEU considered whether football matches could be copyright protected works under the Information Society Directive.[57] The Court accepted that, in principle, this was possible if sporting events were original 'in the sense that it is its author's own intellectual creation' but they rejected the claim that sporting events could be intellectual creations since the rules of football left 'no room for creative freedom'.[58]

Bezpečnostní and *FAPL* are unlikely to trouble those Member States, such as France, that take an 'open' list approach to authors' rights. But will the rulings force the UK to move away from its closed list, 'pigeonhole' approach and link the notion of work entirely to originality? In *Nova v Mazooma*,[59] Jacob LJ observed (prior to these CJEU rulings) that identifying the type of work was 'untouched by any EU harmonization'. Can we continue to say that this is the case?

In the next section we consider some of the more contentious categories of subject matter in the CDPA. In reading this section, it is worth reflecting upon the following

---

[49] CDPA, s. 1(1).   [50] CDPA, s. 4.   [51] CDPA, s. 3.

[52] Case C-393/09 [2011] ECDR 3, [2011] FSR 18.

[53] Directive 91/250/EEC on the legal protection of computer programs [1991] OJ L122/42, subsequently codified as Directive 2009/24/EC of 23 April 2009 on the legal protection of computer programs [2009] OJ L111/16.

[54] Case C-5/08 [2010] FSR 20, [33]–[37].   [55] *Bezpečnostní*, [45]–[46].

[56] Joined Cases C-403 and 429/08 [2012] FSR 1.

[57] Directive 2001/29/EC on the harmonization of certain aspects of copyright and related rights in the information society [2001] OJ L167/10.

[58] [97], [98].   [59] [2007] EWCA Civ 219, [2007] RPC 25.

questions: (1) what are the advantages and disadvantages of the open list and closed list approaches to subject matter; (2) do these approaches lead to fundamentally different results; (3) how might the requirements of subject matter and originality interrelate; and (4) how might the UK give effect to the CJEU rulings discussed above?

FURTHER READING

T. Aplin, 'Subject matter' in E. Derclaye (ed.), *Research Handbook on the Future of EU Copyright Law* (Cheltenham: Edward Elgar, 2008), pp. 94–135, available at <http://papers.ssrn.com/sol3/papers.cfm?abstract_id=2437006>.

A. Christie, 'A proposal for simplifying United Kingdom copyright law' [2001] EIPR 26.

J. Griffiths, '*Infopaq, BSA* and the "Europeanisation" of United Kingdom copyright law' (2011) 16 MALR 59.

J. Pila, 'An intentional view of the copyright work' (2008) 71 Modern Law Review 535.

J. Pila, 'Copyright and its categories of original works' (2010) 30 Oxford Journal of Legal Studies 229.

E. Rosati, 'Closed subject-matter systems are no longer compatible with EU copyright' (2014) 12 GRUR Int 1112, available at <http://papers.ssrn.com/sol3/papers.cfm?abstract_id=2468104>.

B. Sherman, 'What is a copyright work?' (2011) 12 Theoretical Inquiries in Law 99.

2.5.1.2 Literary work

Section 3 of the CDPA defines 'literary work' to mean:

> any work, other than a dramatic or musical work, which is written, spoken or sung, and accordingly includes—
>
> (a) a table or compilation other than a database,
>
> (b) a computer program,
>
> (c) preparatory design material for a computer program, and
>
> (d) a database.

Several things are apparent from this definition, the first being that literary works are mutually exclusive of dramatic and musical works. This means that in the case of a song, the copyright works will be split into two—the literary work (for the lyrics) and the musical work (for the music). This is not the case in other Member States, such as Germany, where the musical composition includes both music and lyrics. This different characterization of musical creations into separate works (literary and musical) impacts upon authorship and also the term of protection. Directive 2006/116/EC (as recently amended) has sought to deal with this discrepancy in Member States' characterization of musical creations by instituting a special rule concerning term of protection (which is discussed in the next chapter at 3.5.1).[60]

---

[60] Directive 2011/77/EU amending Directive 2006/116/EC on the term of protection of copyright and certain related rights [2011] OJ L265/1, Art. 1, inserting para. (7) to Art. 1 of Directive 2006/116/EC.

The second point to emerge from the above definition of literary works is that they include technological works, namely software and databases. The history of these inclusions and some of the challenges that they pose are dealt with later in this section.[61]

Finally, it should be noted that literary works are works that are 'written, spoken or sung'. 'Writing' is defined in section 179 to mean, 'any form of notation or code, whether by hand or otherwise and regardless of the method by which, or medium in or on which, it is recorded' and 'written' shall be construed accordingly. Thus, the fact that a work is stored in digital or electronic form will not preclude it from being a literary work. Nor will the fact that it is recorded in notation (e.g. shorthand) or code (e.g. source or object code used in computer programs). The definition of 'written' also highlights that aesthetic or qualitative criteria are irrelevant when it comes to identifying a literary work. This was a principle established in the early case law.

University of London Press v University Tutorial Press [1916] 2 Ch 601

The issue was whether mathematics examination papers were 'original literary works' within the meaning of section 1(1) of the Copyright Act 1911. On the question of whether they were 'literary works', Peterson J held as follows:

Peterson J, at p. 608:

It may be difficult to define 'literary work' as used in this Act, but it seems to be plain that it is not confined to 'literary work' in the sense in which that phrase is applied, for instance, to Meredith's novels and the writings of Robert Louis Stevenson. In speaking of such writings as literary works, one thinks of the quality, the style, and the literary finish which they exhibit. Under the Act of 1842, which protected 'books', many things which had no pretensions to literary style acquired copyright; for example, a list of registered bills of sale, a list of foxhounds and hunting days, and trade catalogues; and I see no ground for coming to the conclusion that the present Act was intended to curtail the rights of authors. In my view the words 'literary work' cover work which is expressed in print or writing, irrespective of the question whether the quality or style is high. The word 'literary' seems to be used in a sense somewhat similar to the use of the word 'literature' in political or electioneering literature and refers to written or printed matter. Papers set by examiners are, in my opinion, 'literary work' within the meaning of the present Act.

Does it make sense, as Peterson J does, to avoid aesthetic or qualitative judgments when it comes to identifying a literary work? Is this approach in keeping with the justifications for copyright?

2.5.1.2.1 *Words, titles, and headlines*

When we think of literary works what may spring to mind are appreciable amounts of text, in the form of, say, a letter, a set of instructions, a poem, or a book. But what about very short forms of text, such as names, single words, titles, or short phrases? Do these, and should these, qualify as 'literary works'? The Court of Appeal in the following case

---

[61] See 2.5.1.2.2 and 2.5.1.2.3.

considered whether a single word, which was the name of a company, could be protected as a literary work.

Exxon v Exxon Insurance [1982] Ch 119

'Exxon' was an invented word developed as a result of considerable research and expenditure and used as the corporate name of several of the claimant companies. The defendant used Exxon in its corporate name and, as a result, the claimants sought injunctions against them, alleging both copyright infringement and passing off. At first instance, Graham J held that the claimants were entitled to an injunction to restrain passing off by the continued use of Exxon but refused the injunction to restrain an infringement of copyright, on the basis that Exxon was not an original literary work within the meaning of section 2 of the Copyright Act 1956. This decision was upheld on appeal. In the Court of Appeal, Stephenson LJ referred to the observations of Davey LJ in *Hollinrake v Truswell*,[62] a case that raised the issue of whether copyright could subsist in a cardboard pattern sleeve featuring scales, figures, and descriptive words on it. Davey LJ in *Hollinrake v Truswell* stated that, 'a literary work is intended to afford either information and instruction, or pleasure, in the form of literary enjoyment'[63] and found that the sleeve chart did not satisfy this test. Stephenson LJ, after referring to the test in *Hollinrake v Truswell*, made the following comments:

Stephenson LJ, at p. 143:

The words do, however, appeal to me as stating the ordinary meaning of the words 'literary work'. I would have thought, unaided or unhampered by authority, that unless there is something in the context of the Act which forbids it, a literary work would be something which was intended to afford either information and instruction, or pleasure in the form of literary enjoyment, whatever those last six words may add to the word 'pleasure'. Mr Price has not convinced me that this word 'Exxon' was intended to do, or does do, either of those things; nor has he convinced me that it is not of the essence of a literary work that it should do one of those things. Nor has he convinced me that there is anything in the Act, or in what Peterson J said about the words in the earlier Act, or in any authority, or in principle, which compels me to give a different construction from Davey LJ's to the words 'literary work'. As I have already said, I agree with the way in which Graham J put the matter; I am not sure whether this can be said to be a 'work' at all, I am clearly of the opinion that it cannot be said to be a 'literary work'. I therefore agree with Graham J and I would dismiss this appeal.

Oliver LJ was in agreement:

Oliver LJ, at pp. 144–5:

Stephenson LJ has already referred to the judgment of Davey LJ in *Hollinrake v Truswell* [1894] 3 Ch 420, 428, where he said: 'Now, a literary work is intended to afford either information and instruction, or pleasure, in the form of literary enjoyment.' Admittedly, that was

---

[62] [1894] 3 Ch 420.   [63] At 427–8.

said in relation to the preamble of the Act of 1842, which referred to affording 'encourage-ment to the production of literary works of lasting benefit to the world'. But it does seem to me, as it seems to Stephenson LJ, that what Davey LJ said was a fair summary of what the expression means in ordinary language. We have been referred to a number of cases in which copyright has been successfully claimed in, for instance, examination papers, football cou-pons and tables of ciphers; but all these—and I do not exclude the case of the telegraphic code in *DP Anderson & Co Ltd v Lieber Code Co* [1917] 2 KB 469—seem to me to fall fairly within Davey LJ's commonsense formulation. But that for which protection is sought in the instant case does not appear to me to have any of the qualities which commonsense would demand. It conveys no information; it provides no instruction; it gives no pleasure that I can conceive; it is simply an artificial combination of four letters of the alphabet which serves a purpose only when it is used in juxtaposition with other English words, to identify one or other of the companies in the plaintiffs' group. Whether, as might perhaps be the case if one followed up the suggestion made in the judgment of Graham J, the insertion of the extra 'x' was to avoid the risk of involving the Bishop of Exeter in proceedings for infringe-ment every time he wrote to 'The Times' newspaper, I do not pause to inquire. I am clearly of the opinion that Graham J arrived at the correct conclusion when he held that this was not an 'original literary work' in which copyright subsists, and I agree that the appeal should be dismissed.

Do you agree with the test for 'literary work' adopted by the Court of Appeal in *Exxon*? If so, do you think the court correctly applied it to the facts of the case? For the sake of argu-ment, assume that the facts involved an ordinary English word, rather than an invented one—would the application of the *Exxon* test lead to a different result? What about if the subject of protection was a short phrase or title of a song, as in *Francis, Day and Hunter v 20th Century Fox*?

Francis, Day and Hunter v 20th Century Fox [1940] AC 112 (PC)

In this case, the Privy Council considered whether a song title, 'The Man Who Broke the Bank at Monte Carlo', had been infringed.

Lord Wright (delivering the judgment of the Privy Council):

... [I]n general a title is not by itself a proper subject-matter of copyright. As a rule a title does not involve literary composition, and is not sufficiently substantial to justify a claim to protection. That statement does not mean that in particular cases a title may not be on so extensive a scale, and of so important a character, as to be a proper subject of protection against being copied. As Jessel M.R. said in *Dicks v. Yates* [(1881) 18 Ch D 76, 89] ... there might be copyright in a title 'as, for instance, in a whole page of title or something of that kind requiring invention.' But this could not be said of the facts in the present case. There may have been a certain amount, though not a high degree, of originality in thinking of the theme of the song, and even in choosing the title, though it is of the most obvious. To 'break the bank' is a hackneyed expression, and Monte Carlo is, or was, the most obvious place at which that achievement or accident might take place. The theme of the film is different from that of the song, and their Lordships see no ground in copyright law to justify the appellants' claim to prevent the use by the respondents of these few obvious words, which are too unsubstantial to constitute an infringement, especially when used in so different a connection.'

Does the above extract from *Francis, Day* suggest that a title will not usually be protected by copyright because it is not a literary work or because it lacks originality? As well, does the Privy Council consider that a title forms part of a literary work (the lyrics) and the question is whether copying only the title infringes the entire literary work?

Whether words, short phrases, or titles can be protected by copyright is not an idle, academic question but one that can have significant legal and practical consequences. This is highlighted by the litigation in *Newspaper Licensing Agency Ltd v Meltwater*.[64]

Newspaper Licensing Agency v Meltwater Holding BV, Meltwater News UK Ltd, Public Relations Consultants Association Ltd [2010] EWHC 3099 (Ch), [2011] RPC 7, [2011] EWCA Civ 890

The first claimant, Newspaper Licensing Agency (NLA), manages the copyright of its members, largely publishers of newspapers, and licenses the copying of newspaper content. The remaining claimants are publishers of national newspapers and members of NLA. The first defendant is the Dutch holding company for a group of companies carrying on business as commercial media-monitoring organizations, the second defendant is the first defendant's UK subsidiary, and the third defendant is the Public Relations Consultations Association (PRCA), an organization that represents the interests of public relations consultants operating in the UK. PRCA members subscribe to the services of Meltwater News.

Those services involve Meltwater using computer software to monitor news websites in order to identify references to particular search terms relevant to their subscribers. It then makes this information available to its subscribers by setting out a hyperlink to the relevant article; the headline from the article; the opening words of the article after the headline; and an extract from the article in which the relevant search term is identified, with some words immediately preceding and following it.

NLA put forward two licensing schemes under the CDPA that were contested by the defendants. One was the Web Database Licence which was a licence for media-monitoring organizations, such as Meltwater; the other was the Web End User Licence, which was a licence for the users of media-monitoring organizations (such as PRCA). The Web Database Licence required the clients of the media-monitoring organization to hold a Web End User Licence. Meltwater and the PRCA sought to challenge these licensing schemes before the Copyright Tribunal pursuant to section 119 of the CDPA. Both argued that the licences were unnecessary for them lawfully to offer and use the Meltwater service. In response, NLA brought a claim against both parties seeking declarations that a licence *was* necessary in order for the defendants to carry out their activities. Meltwater subsequently agreed to take a Web Database Licence, regardless of whether it was obliged to do so, so that it could continue to operate its service while also

---

[64] [2010] EWHC 3099 (Ch), [2011] RPC 7, [2011] EWCA Civ 890, [2013] UKSC 18, [2013] 2 All ER 852.

maintaining its reference to the Copyright Tribunal. As a result, the part of the action that came before Proudman J at first instance was that relating to PRCA. Various legal issues were raised, including whether headlines were original literary works, whether the extracts from the articles were a substantial part of the literary work that was the article, and whether relevant exceptions applied. In the following extract, Proudman J analyses whether headlines are original literary works.

Proudman J:

[Proudman J briefly referred to UK authorities and then cited with approval the Australian decision *Fairfax Media Publications Pty Ltd v Reed International Books Australia Pty Ltd* [2010] FCA 984 which dealt with copyright in newspaper headlines.]

62. *Fairfax* is the only authority directly to address the status in copyright law of a headline in a newspaper. Bennett J. said at [40]–[50],

'In my view, the headline of each article functions as the title of the article…It may be a clever title. That is not sufficient. Headlines are, like titles, simply too insubstantial and too short to qualify for copyright protection as literary works. The function of the headline is as a title to the article as well as a brief statement of its subject, in a compressed form comparable in length to a book title or the like. It is, generally, too trivial to be a literary work, much as a logo was held to be too trivial to be an artistic work…It may be that evidence directed to a particular headline, or a title of so extensive and of such a significant character, could be sufficient to warrant a finding of copyright protection…but that is not the case here…'

…To continue the citation from Bennett J.'s judgment,

'The need to identify a work by its name is a reason for the exclusion of titles from copyright protection in the public interest. A proper citation of a newspaper article requires not only reference to the name of the newspaper but also reproduction of the headline…If titles were subject to copyright protection, conventional bibliographic references to an article would infringe. Such considerations may well be a reason for the fact that headlines and "short phrases" are excluded from copyright in the United States…

In my view, to afford published headlines, as a class, copyright protection as literary works would tip the balance too far against the interest of the public in the freedom to refer or be referred to articles by their headlines.'

63. In some of the cases analysed, copyright protection was apparently denied to titles on the ground of lack of originality. For example, 'Splendid Misery' for a book title in *Dick v Yates* (that expression obviously being one in universal use at the time although as far as I know it has now completely fallen out of use) or 'the Lawyer's Diary' in *Rose v Information Services Limited* [1978] FSR 254. In other cases, it seems that there was sufficient originality in a heading but the status of literary work was still denied, such as 'Opportunity Knocks', 'Dr Martens', 'Exxon' and, notably, 'the Man Who Broke the Bank at Monte Carlo'. Cases in which headings were, to the contrary, given the status of literary work are distinguishable. In *Shetland v Wills* the case proceeded on the basis of a concession and in *Lamb v Evans* the whole purpose of the trade directory under consideration was to arrange and compile the entries under headings.

…

66. The issues I have to decide about the headlines in this case are (a) can they have the necessary quality of originality to qualify as a literary work? In any case, (b) are they part of the articles to which they relate?

[Proudman J then discussed the CJEU ruling in *Infopaq* which is discussed at 2.5.2.3.2 before going on to conclude as follows:]

70. The evidence in the present case (incidentally much fuller than that before Bennett J. in *Fairfax*—see her observations at [28]) is that headlines involve considerable skill in devising and they are specifically designed to entice by informing the reader of the content of the article in an entertaining manner.

71. In my opinion headlines are capable of being literary works, whether independently or as part of the articles to which they relate…

72. …I find that some of the headlines are independent literary works; those that are not form part of the articles to which they relate.

On appeal, the defendant PRCA argued, inter alia, that Proudman J's conclusion that headlines could be original literary works was wrong. The Court of Appeal, without examining the relevant authorities in any great detail, rejected this argument and held that a 'headline is plainly literary as it consists of words' and that Proudman J's conclusion was 'plainly correct'.[65] This issue was not appealed to the Supreme Court. Do you think it appropriate for the court to take into account the sorts of policy considerations raised by Bennett J in *Fairfax* and cited with approval by Proudman J? Might there be other policy considerations at stake? What impact, for example, would a finding of copyright in headlines or titles have on hyperlinking on the internet?[66] Finally, if a work qualifies as a 'literary work' simply because it comprises words, is the subject matter threshold for this category of works almost non-existent and the sole issue really one of originality?

FURTHER READING

J. Cullabine, 'Copyright in short phrases and single words' [1992] EIPR 205.

J. Davis and A. Durant, 'To protect or not to protect? The eligibility of commercially used short verbal texts for copyright and trade mark protection' [2011] IPQ 345.

J. Klink, 'Titles in Europe: trade names, copyright works or title marks' [2004] EIPR 291.

2.5.1.2.2 Computer programs

Yet another controversial example of what can constitute a literary work arose with the emergence of computer programs. At the international level, *sui generis* protection for software was initially proposed by WIPO in 1977. However, software producers were keen to rely on copyright because it offered an established and 'ready-made' solution, for which the benefit of national treatment and minimum rights under the Berne Convention could be claimed. Those who objected to computer programs being literary works within the meaning of Article 2(1) of the Berne Convention argued, inter alia, that while source code (which is close to natural language) was superficially analogous to literary works, machine code (which is in binary notation) was not, and the final addressee of the instructions was a

---

[65] See Chancellor Morritt, [19] and [22], delivering the only reasoned judgment and with whom Jackson LJ and Elias LJ agreed.

[66] On the lawfulness of linking, see *Svensson and Ors v Retreiver Sverige AB* Case C-466/12 [2015] EMLR 5.

computer (which then carried out a function) and not an individual. They argued further that computer programs lacked intellectual creativity (i.e. originality).

Nevertheless, in the early to mid-1980s national laws of various countries (including the US, France, Germany, Australia, and the UK[67]) readily began to accept copyright protection of computer programs as literary works.[68] Eventually, Article 4 of the WIPO Copyright Treaty 1996 and Article 10(1) of the TRIPS Agreement 1996 clarified that computer programs are protected as literary works within Article 2 of the Berne Convention. At a regional level, Article 1(1) of the EU Software Directive[69] makes clear that Member States must protect computer programs as literary works within the meaning of the Berne Convention. Article 1(2) states that protection extends 'to the expression in any form of a computer program', but not to the ideas and principles underlying any element of a computer program. Aside from stipulating that a computer program includes preparatory design material,[70] there was no attempt to provide a harmonized, exhaustive definition of what constitutes a computer program.

UK courts have explored what comprises a 'computer program'. In *Navitaire v Easyjet Airline Co.*,[71] which concerned software for a 'ticketless' airline-booking system, Pumfrey J held that individual command names used in the system could not be literary works. Referring to *Exxon*, he held it was 'clear that single words in isolation are not to be considered as literary works'.[72] A series of commands were also excluded from protection because they amounted, in effect, to a computer language and recital 14 of the Software Directive stated that 'to the extent that … programming languages comprise ideas and principles those … are not protected under this Directive'. Pumfrey J admitted, however, that this point was not entirely clear and would require a reference to the CJEU at some point.[73]

This reference came from Arnold J in *SAS Institute Inc. v World Programming Ltd*[74] and the CJEU delivered its ruling in May 2012.

SAS Institute Inc. v World Programming Ltd Case C-406/10 [2012] 3 CMLR 4 (Grand Chamber)

The claimant had developed a sophisticated software system, the SAS system, over many years. The system enabled its users to carry out various data processing and analytical tasks, in particular statistical analysis. A core component of the SAS system, Base SAS, allowed users to write and run application programs in SAS Language. Additional components (the SAS components) enabled Base SAS to be extended in various ways. In

---

[67] See *Sega Enterprises Ltd v Richards* [1983] FSR 73.

[68] Although note that Arnold J in the recent *SAS Institute* decision (see fn 74) observed at [198] that 'it is nevertheless inescapable for the reasons so eloquently explained by Pumfrey J in *Navitaire*, in particular at [112] and [125], that computer programs are different from other kinds of literary works and present peculiar problems for copyright law'.

[69] Directive 91/250/EEC on the legal protection of computer programs [1991] OJ L122/42, subsequently codified as Directive 2009/24/EC of 23 April 2009 on the legal protection of computer programs [2009] OJ L111/16 (Software Directive).

[70] As stated in recital 7, this means 'preparatory design work leading to the development of a computer program provided that the nature of the preparatory work is such that a computer program can result from it at the later stage'.

[71] [2006] RPC 3.   [72] [80].   [73] [88].

[74] See *SAS Institute Inc. v World Programming Ltd* [2011] RPC 1 (Ch D). After the CJEU ruling, there were two further decisions: *SAS Institute Inc. v World Programming Ltd* [2013] EWHC 69 (Ch), [2013] RPC 17 and *SAS Institute Inc. v World Programming Ltd* [2013] EWCA Civ 1482, [2014] RPC 8.

order for customers to continue running application programs written in SAS Language and to develop new ones, they had to continue to license use of the SAS system, otherwise they faced the burdensome task of rewriting all of their application programs. The defendant, WPL, developed software that executed application programs written in SAS Language and, in so doing, sought to closely emulate the functionality of the SAS components. WPL did not have access to the source code of the SAS system and did not copy the source code (including its structural design). The claimants alleged, inter alia, that the defendants had indirectly copied (through using the SAS manuals) the computer programs that comprised the SAS components. In order to resolve this claim, Arnold J referred several questions to the CJEU. The Court ruled as follows:

[29] By these questions, the national court asks, in essence, whether art.1(2) of Directive 91/250 must be interpreted as meaning that the functionality of a computer program and the programming language and the format of data files used in a computer program in order to exploit certain of its functions constitute a form of expression of that program and may, as such, be protected by copyright in computer programs for the purposes of that directive.

[30] In accordance with art.1(1) of Directive 91/250, computer programs are protected by copyright as literary works within the meaning of the Berne Convention.

[31] Article 1(2) of Directive 91/250 extends that protection to the expression in any form of a computer program. That provision states, however, that the ideas and principles which underlie any element of a computer program, including those which underlie its interfaces, are not protected by copyright under that directive.

[32] The 14th recital in the preamble to Directive 91/250 confirms, in this respect, that, in accordance with the principle that only the expression of a computer program is protected by copyright, to the extent that logic, algorithms and programming languages comprise ideas and principles, those ideas and principles are not protected under that directive. The 15th recital in the preamble to Directive 91/250 states that, in accordance with the legislation and jurisprudence of the Member States and the international copyright conventions, the expression of those ideas and principles is to be protected by copyright.

[33] With respect to international law, both art.2 of the WIPO Copyright Treaty and art.9(2) of the TRIPs Agreement provide that copyright protection extends to expressions and not to ideas, procedures, methods of operation or mathematical concepts as such.

[34] Article 10(1) of the TRIPs Agreement provides that computer programs, whether in source or object code, are to be protected as literary works under the Berne Convention.

[35] In a judgment delivered after the reference for a preliminary ruling had been lodged in the present case, the Court interpreted art.1(2) of Directive 91/250 as meaning that the object of the protection conferred by that directive is the expression in any form of a computer program, such as the source code and the object code, which permits reproduction in different computer languages (*Bezpečnostní softwarová asociace - Svaz softwarové ochrany v Ministerstvo kultury* (C-393/09) [2011] FSR 18 at [35]).

[36] In accordance with the second phrase of the seventh recital in the preamble to Directive 91/250, the term 'computer program' also includes preparatory design work leading to the development of a computer program, provided that the nature of the preparatory work is such that a computer program can result from it at a later stage.

[37] Thus, the object of protection under Directive 91/250 includes the forms of expression of a computer program and the preparatory design work capable of leading, respectively,

to the reproduction or the subsequent creation of such a program (*Bezpečnostní softwarová asociace* [2011] FSR 18 at [37]).

[38] From this the Court concluded that the source code and the object code of a computer program are forms of expression thereof which, consequently, are entitled to be protected by copyright as computer programs, by virtue of art.1(2) of Directive 91/250. On the other hand, as regards the graphic user interface, the Court held that such an interface does not enable the reproduction of the computer program, but merely constitutes one element of that program by means of which users make use of the features of that program (*Bezpečnostní softwarová asociace* [2011] FSR 18 at [34] and [41]).

[39] On the basis of those considerations, it must be stated that, with regard to the elements of a computer program which are the subject of Questions 1–5, neither the functionality of a computer program nor the programming language and the format of data files used in a computer program in order to exploit certain of its functions constitute a form of expression of that program for the purposes of art.1(2) of Directive 91/250.

[40] As the A.G. states in point AG57 of his Opinion, to accept that the functionality of a computer program can be protected by copyright would amount to making it possible to monopolise ideas, to the detriment of technological progress and industrial development.

[41] Moreover, point 3.7 of the explanatory memorandum to the Proposal for Directive 91/250 [COM(88) 816] states that the main advantage of protecting computer programs by copyright is that such protection covers only the individual expression of the work and thus leaves other authors the desired latitude to create similar or even identical programs provided that they refrain from copying.

[42] With respect to the programming language and the format of data files used in a computer program to interpret and execute application programs written by users and to read and write data in a specific format of data files, these are elements of that program by means of which users exploit certain functions of that program.

[43] In that context, it should be made clear that, if a third party were to procure the part of the source code or the object code relating to the programming language or to the format of data files used in a computer program, and if that party were to create, with the aid of that code, similar elements in its own computer program, that conduct would be liable to constitute partial reproduction within the meaning of art.4(a) of Directive 91/250.

[44] As is, however, apparent from the order for reference, WPL did not have access to the source code of SAS Institute's program and did not carry out any decompilation of the object code of that program. By means of observing, studying and testing the behaviour of SAS Institute's program, WPL reproduced the functionality of that program by using the same programming language and the same format of data files.

[45] The Court also points out that the finding made in [39] of the present judgment cannot affect the possibility that the SAS language and the format of SAS Institute's data files might be protected, as works, by copyright under Directive 2001/29 if they are their author's own intellectual creation (see *Bezpečnostní softwarová asociace* [2011] FSR 18 at [44]–[46]).

[46] Consequently, the answer to Questions 1–5 is that art.1(2) of Directive 91/250 must be interpreted as meaning that neither the functionality of a computer program nor the programming language and the format of data files used in a computer program in order to exploit certain of its functions constitute a form of expression of that program and, as such, are not protected by copyright in computer programs for the purposes of that directive.

The CJEU ruled that protection of a computer program pursuant to the Software Directive extends to its expression and this includes the source and object code in which it is written. It excludes, however, the program's functionality, programming language, graphic user interface, and the format of the data files that it uses. Do you agree with this conclusion? Of note is the fact that the CJEU reiterated the possibility that some of these elements (the graphic user interface, programming language, and format of data files) could be protected as copyright expression pursuant to the Information Society Directive if they were the result of the author's own intellectual creation. When the case returned to the English High Court after the CJEU ruling, Arnold J rejected the claimant's argument that the SAS Language and file formats were protectable as copyright works because they were the author's own intellectual creation. He found that the CJEU had not ruled on whether the SAS programming language or data file formats were protected works under the Information Society Directive, but merely observed the possibility that they might be so protected.[75] Further, it was not an issue that arose in this case because it had not been pleaded or proved by the claimants.[76] On appeal, the Court of Appeal held that the CJEU ruling had indicated that the functionality of a computer program was neither protected under the Software Directive nor the Information Society Directive.[77]

Once again, in the UK context, the question arises whether it is still necessary for courts first to find a relevant category of subject matter—for example, a literary work—before considering whether there is an *original* work. Or is *originality* the crucial criterion for determining protectable subject matter?

FURTHER READING

D. Gervais and E. Derclaye, 'The scope of computer program protection after *SAS*: are we closer to answers? [2012] EIPR 565.

2.5.1.2.3 Databases

In the early 1990s the European Commission became extremely keen to nurture and protect the European database industry. However, it saw the differences between Member States in their protection of databases, as well as the lack of appropriate protection, as obstacles to achieving this goal. The result was a directive harmonizing the legal protection of databases[78] (Database Directive), which was adopted on 11 March 1996. The directive adopted a two-fold approach to protecting databases: first, it sought to harmonize copyright protection and, second, it introduced a new *sui generis* right for databases. The *sui generis* right is discussed further at 4.4.

Harmonization of copyright protection of databases covers most areas, including the definition of subject matter, originality, authorship, exclusive rights, and exceptions. Relevant here is the definition of database in Article 1(2) of the Database Directive. A database is defined as:

> a collection of independent works, data or other materials arranged in a systematic or methodical way and individually accessible by electronic or other means.

---

[75] *SAS Institute Inc. v World Programming Ltd* [2013] EWHC 69 (Ch), [2013] RPC 17, [21].

[76] [22], [24]. This issue was not appealed to the Court of Appeal.

[77] *SAS Institute Inc. v World Programming Ltd* [2013] EWCA Civ 1482, [2014] RPC 8, [51]–[52].

[78] Directive 96/9/EC of the European Parliament and of the Council of 11 March 1996 on the legal protection of databases [1996] OJ L77/20.

A wide range of materials may comprise a database, as confirmed by recital 17 of the Database Directive, which states that databases include 'literary, artistic, musical or other collections of works or collections of other material such as texts, sounds, images, numbers, facts, and data'. However, it seems that a database does not extend to collections of tangible objects, such as a group of artworks in a gallery. This is because the purpose of the directive was to protect databases as informational works.[79]

The collection must comprise independent works, data, or other materials, but what is meant by independent? Recital 17 provides some guidance. It states that a 'recording or an audiovisual, cinematographic, literary or musical work as such does not fall within the scope of this Directive'. The CJEU has held that 'independent' materials refer to those materials 'which are separable from one another without their informative, literary, artistic, musical or other value being affected'.[80] The CJEU has also ruled that 'a decline in the informative value of material linked to its being extracted from the collection of which it forms a part' does not mean that it is not independent provided it 'retains autonomous informative value' and this is to be assessed 'not for a typical user of the collection concerned, but for each third party interested by the extracted material'.[81] Works, data, or other material will be arranged in a systematic or methodical way where they are presented in an organized manner as opposed to being physically stored as such.[82] This includes presentation in an alphabetical, chronological, or subject order. Also, it is clear from the words 'individually accessible by electronic or other means' that both electronic and non-electronic (or hard copy) databases are included. As for the requirement that materials are 'individually accessible' this is best understood as where the collection of materials is searchable and the materials can be perceived distinctly.[83]

Article 1(3) of the Database Directive provides that protection shall not apply to 'computer programs used in the making or operation of databases accessible by electronic means'. It thus appears that computer programs cannot be protected as databases, although distinguishing between the two may not always be straightforward.[84]

Section 3A of the CDPA implements verbatim the definition of database in Article 1(2) of the directive. Section 3(1) of the CDPA, however, characterizes 'databases' as 'literary works' and this classification suggests that in the UK a narrower range of works may comprise a 'database'. However, the better view is that the amendments implementing the Database Directive should be construed as far as possible to comply with that directive, so that the broad definition of 'database' contained in section 3A be given its full effect. Article 1(3) was not explicitly incorporated into the CDPA; however, it seems that computer programs will not amount to a 'database' because section 3(1) of the CDPA draws a clear distinction between computer programs and databases and the legislation should be construed in conformity with the directive. A remnant of poor implementation of the Database Directive is that section 3(1) of the CDPA distinguishes between 'databases' and 'tables or compilations other than databases'. Given how widely 'database' is defined, it is hard to think of many examples of tables or compilations that are *not* databases—a randomized shopping list perhaps?

---

[79] See recital 9 and also E. Derclaye, 'What is a database? A critical analysis of the definition of a database in the European Database Directive and suggestions for an international definition' (2002) 5 Journal of World Intellectual Property 981, 998–1003.

[80] *Fixtures Marketing Ltd v Organismos prognostikon agonon podosfairou AE (OPAP)* Case C-444/02 [2004] ECR I-10549, [29].

[81] *Freistaat Bayern v Verlag Esterbauer GmbH* Case C-490/14 [2016] ECDR 6, [24] and [27].

[82] See recital 21.   [83] T. Aplin, *Copyright Law in the Digital Society* (Oxford: Hart, 2005), p. 51.

[84] Especially once recital 20 is taken into account.

> **FURTHER READING**
>
> E. Derclaye, 'What is a database? A critical analysis of the definition of a database in the European Database Directive and suggestions for an international definition' (2002) 5 Journal of World Intellectual Property 281.

2.5.1.3 Musical work

Section 3(1) of the CDPA defines 'musical work' as:

> a work consisting of music, exclusive of any words or action intended to be sung, spoken or performed with the music.

The above definition again highlights the mutual exclusivity between musical, literary, and dramatic works. Its usefulness is limited, however, because 'a work consisting of music' is left undefined. What, then, can we say constitutes music? Can John Cage's '4 minutes 33 seconds', a work in three parts in which the performer is required to remain absolutely silent at his instrument for exactly this length of time, qualify as music?[85] What about Steve Reich's 'Clapping Music for Two Performers'[86] in which two performers clap together rhythmically? Or music which comes from the 'industrial' genre?[87] Some guidance on the meaning of 'music' has fortunately been provided by the Court of Appeal in *Hyperion Records v Sawkins*.

Hyperion Records v Sawkins [2005] RPC 32, [2005] 1 WLR 3281

This was a case involving the music of 17th- and 18th-century baroque composer Michel-Ricard de Lalande. The claimant, Dr Lionel Sawkins, is a musicologist of high repute and the leading authority on the music of Lalande. In relation to some of Lalande's pieces (namely his grand motets), he produced modern performing editions—i.e. scores from which today's performers can play Lalande's music. In producing the modern performing editions, Dr Sawkins aimed to reproduce Lalande's music as faithfully as possible. He therefore consulted and drew upon manuscript and printed sources from the 17th and 18th centuries and transcribed music from the original scores into modern notation. In addition, to make the music playable Dr Sawkins made numerous corrections and additions to the notation, figured the bass line, and recreated missing parts. Producing these editions required considerable expertise, as well as skill and effort—approximately 300 hours on each of the performing editions of the four pieces. The defendants recorded a performance of Lalande's music from the modern performing editions prepared by Dr Sawkins. The claimant alleged that he owned copyright in the editions as original musical works and that the defendants' actions had infringed his copyright. Dr Sawkins argued that he had expended considerable effort in producing the editions and they contained musical information in the form of conventional modern notation and directions to the performers. The defendant denied that the performing editions were original or musical. The originality point is dealt with later in this

---

[85] For a performance of this by David Tudor see <http://uk.youtube.com/watch?v=HypmW4Yd7SY>.
[86] For a performance of this work see <http://uk.youtube.com/watch?v=BhhIZscEE_g>.
[87] See e.g. the music of the band 'Throbbing Gristle'.

chapter. What is relevant here is the approach to whether the work was a 'musical work'. On this point, the defendants argued that the performing edition did not amount to a new and substantive musical work in itself—it simply reproduced Lalande's music. The court rejected this argument.

Mummery LJ:

42. On the approach advocated by the defendant most of the exertions of the claimant, such as researching the source materials, selecting the best versions to edit, transcribing them into modern notation, making them playable, or more easily playable, correcting errors, inserting missing material from other sources, the inclusion of the figured bass and determining such matters as layout of the scores on the page and inserting 'advisory' or courtesy indications, such as tempo and ornamentation, are irrelevant to the issue whether he created an original musical work. They were not part of the music. Thus the material shown on the marked up copies of the scores adduced in evidence by the claimant, in order to illustrate the nature and extent of the editorial interventions by him to the text bar by bar, might be academically sound and valuable, but was insufficient to attract musical copyright…

43. …I do not accept the narrow approach advocated by the defendant as to the type and nature of the work required to attract musical copyright.

…

53. In the absence of a special statutory definition of music, ordinary usage assists: as indicated in the dictionaries, the essence of music is combining sounds for listening to. Music is not the same as mere noise. The sound of music is intended to produce effects of some kind on the listener's emotions and intellect. The sounds may be produced by an organised performance on instruments played from a musical score, though that is not essential for the existence of the music or of copyright in it. Music must be distinguished from the fact and form of its fixation as a record of a musical composition. The score is the traditional and convenient form of fixation of the music and conforms to the requirement that a copyright work must be recorded in some material form. But the fixation in the written score or on a record is not in itself the music in which copyright subsists. There is no reason why, for example, a recording of a person's spontaneous singing, whistling or humming or of improvisations of sounds by a group of people with or without musical instruments should not be regarded as 'music' for copyright purposes.

…

55. In principle, there is no reason for regarding the actual notes of music as the *only* matter covered by musical copyright, any more than, in the case of a dramatic work, only the words to be spoken by the actors are covered by dramatic copyright. Added stage directions may affect the performance of the play on the stage or on the screen and have an impact on the performance seen by the audience. Stage directions are as much part of a dramatic work as plot, character and dialogue.

…

56. It is wrong in principle to single out the notes as uniquely significant for copyright purposes and to proceed to deny copyright to the other elements that make some contribution to the sound of the music when performed, such as performing indications, tempo and performance practice indicators, if they are the product of a person's effort, skill and time, bearing in mind, of course, the 'relatively modest' level…of the threshold for a work to qualify for protection. The work of Dr Sawkins has sufficient aural and musical significance to attract copyright protection.

Is Mummery LJ's approach to determining what constitutes a 'musical work', for copyright purposes, a sensible one? Would it embrace a wide variety of musical creations and, if not, is this problematic?

FURTHER READING

A. Barron, 'Introduction: harmony or dissonance? Copyright concepts and musical practice' (2006) 15 Social and Legal Studies 25.

A. Rahmatian, 'Music and creativity as perceived by copyright law' [2005] IPQ 267.

2.5.1.4 Dramatic work

Section 3(1) of the CDPA defines 'dramatic work' as including a 'work of dance or mime'. This is an inclusive definition, but one that sheds little light on the scope of this particular category of subject matter. The main questions that have arisen about the scope of 'dramatic works' are whether they include television formats and also films. We turn first to consider the protection of television formats.

Green v Broadcasting Corporation of New Zealand [1989] RPC 700

The appellant (Green) was a well-known personality who was the author and presenter of a highly successful television show in England entitled *Opportunity Knocks*. The show was essentially a talent contest and featured several characteristic catch phrases, the use of sponsors to introduce competitors, and the use of a 'clapometer' to measure audience reaction to the performances of competitions. The respondent (Broadcasting Corporation of New Zealand) broadcast a similar television show under the same title in New Zealand. As a result, the appellant commenced proceedings, claiming damages for passing off and infringement of copyright. In respect of the copyright claim, the appellants argued that copyright subsisted in the scripts and dramatic format of the show. The action was dismissed by the New Zealand High Court and the appeal to the Court of Appeal was unsuccessful. The appellant then appealed on the copyright issue to the Privy Council.

Lord Bridge of Harwich (delivering the opinion of the Privy Council), **at p. 702:**

[His Lordship began by agreeing with the Court of Appeal that what little evidence of scripts that existed pointed to no more than a general idea or concept for a talent contest and as such could not attract copyright. He then considered the alternative argument that copyright subsisted in the 'dramatic format' of the show.]

It is stretching the original use of the word 'format' a long way to use it metaphorically to describe the features of a television series such as a talent, quiz or game show which is presented in a particular way, with repeated but unconnected use of set phrases and with the aid of particular accessories. Alternative terms suggested in the course of argument were 'structure' or 'package'. This difficulty in finding an appropriate term to describe the nature of the 'work' in which the copyright subsists reflects the difficulty of the concept that a number of allegedly distinctive features of a television series can be isolated from the changing material presented in each separate performance (the acts of the performers in the talent show, the questions and answers in the quiz show etc.) and identified as an 'original dramatic work'. No case was cited to their Lordships in which copyright of the kind claimed had been established.

The protection which copyright gives creates a monopoly and 'there must be certainty in the subject matter of such monopoly in order to avoid injustice to the rest of the world': *Tate v Fulbrook* [1908] 1 KB 821, per Farwell J at page 832. The subject matter of the copyright claimed for the 'dramatic format' of 'Opportunity Knocks' is conspicuously lacking in certainty. Moreover, it seems to their Lordships that a dramatic work must have sufficient unity to be capable of performance and that the features claimed as constituting the 'format' of a television show, being unrelated to each other except as accessories to be used in the presentation of some other dramatic or musical performance, lack that essential characteristic.

For these reasons their Lordships will humbly advise Her Majesty that the appeal should be dismissed. The appellant must pay the respondent's costs of the appeal to the Board.

In the last decade or so we have seen a plethora of highly successful television shows, such as *Big Brother, The Weakest Link, Who Wants to be a Millionaire?, I'm a Celebrity Get Me Out of Here!, Strictly Come Dancing,* and *The X Factor.* Do you think that *Green* precludes protection for these types of shows and, if so, does this seem unduly harsh on their creators? In Australia, the Federal Court in *Nine Films & TV Pty Ltd v Ninox TV Ltd*[88] recognized that a particularized format for a reality television programme broadcast in New Zealand, entitled *Dream Home* and which concerned a house-renovation competition between two couples, was protected as a dramatic work. However, the judge found that the defendants had not infringed the claimant's dramatic work by broadcasting a reality television programme about renovation of four apartments, entitled *The Block.* This was because the latter programme had been independently created and differed in key respects. Tamberlin J concluded: 'Having regard to technique, context, character of contestants, mood, music, image, style and basic theme content, the two productions and formats are a long way apart and are quite different in their essential features.'[89] Thus, even if television formats are protected as dramatic works in the UK, infringement may be difficult to establish and require difficult assessments of whether there has been substantial copying of idea versus expression. These general principles are explored in more detail at 4.2.

The issue of whether a film can qualify as a dramatic work was raised in the *Norowzian* litigation.

Norowzian v Arks Ltd (No. 2) [2000] FSR 363

Mr Norowzian had created and produced a film, entitled *Joy,* which depicted a man, casually dressed, dancing to music in a quirky manner against a plain backdrop. The film was shot with a camera in a fixed position and the editing process heavily used the 'jump cutting' technique. This is a process whereby the editor excises pieces of film, joining together the remaining pieces. When shown, the film depicted a series of movements by the actor that appeared to be performed successively, but which in real life could not be so. The defendants produced an advertisement for Guinness, called 'Anticipation'.[90]

---

[88] [2005] FCA 1404. See also *Ukulele Orchestra of GB v Erwin* [2015] ETMR 40, [100]–[104].   [89] [91].
[90] The advertisement may be viewed at <http://uk.youtube.com/watch?v=3MuEtGPXLPI>.

This also used the 'jump cutting' technique and showed a man dancing around to music in a quirky manner, waiting for his pint of Guinness to settle.

Initially, Mr Norowzian sought to rely on his film copyright. Section 5B of the CDPA provides that 'film' means 'a recording on any medium from which a moving image may by any means be produced'. Mr Norowzian's film clearly fell within this definition and was protected by copyright as a 'film' work. It was on this basis that he initially sued the defendants in *Norowzian v Arks Ltd (No. 1)* [1998] FSR 394. However, this claim was unsuccessful because Mr A. G. Steinfeld QC held that the scope of protection for films is limited to copying the actual images, i.e. the recording from which the moving image constituting the film has been produced, and the defendants had made their own film that had allegedly similar images. In relation to dramatic works, however, the scope of protection is not limited in this way and this is why the claimant sought to argue that his film also qualified for copyright protection as a 'dramatic work'. Before Rattee J this argument was rejected. He held that a film could record a dramatic work, but could not itself be a dramatic work. This was not a record of a dramatic work since, as a result of the 'jump cutting' technique, what was depicted in the claimant's film could not actually be performed. In *obiter*, he stated that even if *Joy* was a dramatic work it was not infringed by 'Anticipation' because of the differences between the two films.

The claimant appealed. The Court of Appeal disagreed with Rattee J that a film per se could not be a dramatic work, but agreed that a substantial part of the claimant's dramatic work was not reproduced in the defendant's film.

Nourse LJ (Brooke LJ in agreement; Buxton LJ delivering a concurring judgment)**, at pp. 366–7:**

Rattee J was of the opinion that a film per se cannot be a dramatic work within the meaning of the 1988 Act, though it can be a recording of such a work for the purpose of section 3(2); see page 77. His view was based partly on the different categorisations adopted by paragraphs (a) and (b) of section 1(1) and partly on the express exclusion of films from the definition of dramatic work in the Copyright Act 1956; see section 48(1) of that Act. Although we were not referred to transcripts of the arguments in the court below, my strong impression is that the judge's view was influenced by the submissions of counsel then representing the claimant, who do not appear to have argued that *Joy* was itself a dramatic work. At page 77 the judge records the submission of the claimant's leading counsel as being that 'Joy is clearly a work of dance and mime which has been recorded on film.'

...

In my judgment a film can be a dramatic work for the purposes of the 1988 Act. The definition of that expression being at large, it must be given its natural and ordinary meaning. We were referred to several dictionary and textbook definitions. My own, substantially a distilled synthesis of those which have gone before, would be this: a dramatic work is a work of action, with or without words or music, which is capable of being performed before an audience. A film will often, though not always, be a work of action and it is capable of being performed before an audience. It can therefore fall within the expression 'dramatic work' in section 1(1)(a) and I disagree with the judge's reasons for excluding it.

As to those reasons, no mutual exclusivity between paragraphs (a) and (b) is expressed, and the absence of the requirement of originality in paragraph (b) is sufficient ground for none to be implied. Moreover, it is unsafe to base any construction of the material provisions of the 1988 Act on those of the 1956 Act. Indeed, it might be said that Parliament's omission to repeat the exclusion of films from the definition of dramatic work points rather towards their inclusion. But whether that be right or wrong, the material provisions of the 1988 Act must be construed as they stand. Where a film is both a recording of a dramatic work and a dramatic work in itself they do not exclude an overlap. In other cases there will be no overlap. Sometimes a film will simply be a recording of something which is not a dramatic work. At other times it will not be a recording of a dramatic work but a dramatic work in itself.

Once it is established that a film can be a dramatic work for the purposes of the 1988 Act it is clear that *Joy*, being a work of action capable of being performed before an audience, is such a work. Clearly, it is an original work. Two further points must be mentioned in relation to the primary question. First, in support of his argument on the 1988 Act, Mr Arnold relied on certain European materials, in particular the Berne Copyright Convention (as revised and amended up to 1979). In my view it is unnecessary to have to resort to those materials as an aid to the construction of the 1988 Act. Secondly, Mr Arnold submitted, in the alternative, that *Joy* was a recording of a dramatic work. In agreeing with Rattee J that that submission must be rejected, I need do no more than read the following passage from his judgment at page 78:

> *Joy*, unlike some films, is not a recording of a dramatic work, because, as a result of the drastic editing process adopted by Mr Norowzian, it is not a recording of anything that was, or could be, performed or danced by anyone…It may well be, in the case of *Joy*, that the original unedited film of the actor's performance, what I believe are called 'the rushes', was a recording of a dramatic work, but Mr Norowzian's claim is not in respect of copyright in them or their subject matter. His claim is in respect of the finished film.
>
> *Joy*, just like many cartoon films, is, without being a recording of one, a dramatic work in itself.

Does the Court of Appeal's decision in *Norowzian* distort the meaning of 'dramatic work'? Or does the case reflect a sensible interpretation to achieve a legitimate result, i.e. proper protection for films/cinematographic works? What sorts of complications could arise by being able to treat films as both 'film works' and 'dramatic works'? In considering this question, it is worth asking whether there will be different authors, owners, and terms of protection depending on the classification of the subject matter.

FURTHER READING

R. Arnold, '*Joy*: a reply' [2001] IPQ 10.

S. Bechtold, 'The fashion of TV show formats' (2013) 2 Mich. St. L. Rev. 451.

L. Golding, 'Opportunity knocks for dramatic copyright in television formats' in M. Richardson and S. Ricketson (eds) *Research Handbook on Intellectual Property in Media and Entertainnment*, ch. 14.

P. Kamina, 'British film copyright and the incorrect implementation of the EC Copyright Directives' (1998) 9 Ent. L. R. 109.

U. Klement, 'Protecting television show formats under copyright law: new developments in common law and civil law countries' [2007] EIPR 52.

M. Kretschmer, S. Singh, and J. Wardle, 'The Exploitation of Television Formats, ESRC Digital Resource, Bournemouth University' (Bournemouth University, 2009) <http://tvformats.bournemouth.ac.uk>.

I. Stamatoudi, ' "Joy" for the claimant: can a film also be protected as a dramatic work?' [2000] IPQ 117.

2.5.1.5 Artistic work

An artistic work, according to section 4 of the CDPA means:

> (a) a graphic work, photograph, sculpture or collage, irrespective of artistic quality,
>
> (b) a work of architecture being a building or model for a building, or
>
> (c) a work of artistic craftsmanship.

A number of these subcategories—building, graphic work, photograph, and sculpture—are further defined in section 4. Importantly, 'graphic work' is defined to include:

> (a) any painting, drawing, diagram, map, chart or plan, and
>
> (b) any engraving, etching, lithograph, woodcut or similar work.

It is apparent from the definition of artistic work that it covers a range of artistic creations, from the purely aesthetic to those of a more functional kind. The fact that section 4(1)(a) specifically states that certain subcategories of artistic work are protected 'irrespective of artistic quality' highlights that courts should not engage in a subjective evaluation of the artistic merits of a work. This also facilitates the protection of works of a more functional or industrial nature. As such, this has, and still does, create tension between copyright protection of industrial or functional items and the protection available under designs law, a point which is explored in greater detail in Chapter 14.[91]

In interpreting the scope of the 'artistic works' category, courts have, on occasions, been fairly conservative. An example of this conservatism is the following case, where the court considered whether facial make-up could be protected as a painting.

Merchandising Corporation of America Inc. v Harpbond [1983] FSR 32

The case concerned the facial make-up of performer Adam Ant (from 'Adam and the Ants'). He adopted a new style (his Prince Charming look) in the early 1980s, in which he wore make-up that comprised two red stripes, with a light blue stripe in the middle, running diagonally from nose to jaw on one cheek, as well as a heart over the left eyebrow and a beauty spot near the left nostril. The claimants made photographs and sketches of him in his Prince Charming look. The defendants reproduced these images in a variety of ways—by reproducing one of the photographs, altering existing photographs to erase the old make-up and superimposing the new, and painting a portrait of Adam Ant in his new style based on one of the claimants' photographs. The claimants sought interim relief for, inter alia, copyright infringement. Walton J granted such relief in respect of reproduction of one of the photographs, but not for the altered photograph or portrait. The claimants appealed, arguing that copyright existed in the facial make-up of Adam Ant. The Court of Appeal dismissed the appeal.

---

[91] See 14.4 and 14.5.

Lawton LJ (with whom Oliver LJ and Brightman LJ agreed)**, at p. 46:**

Mr Wilson's bold submission at the beginning of his presentation of his clients' case was that the marks on Mr Goddard's face by way of facial make-up were painting. That caused me very considerable surprise, because, although there are various statutory provisions in the Act defining various words used in it, there is no statutory definition of a painting. 'Painting' is a word in the ordinary usage of the English language and it is a question of fact in any particular case whether that which is under discussion is or is not a painting. It seemed to me, right at the beginning of Mr Wilson's submissions (and I want to be restrained in my language), that it was fantastic to suggest that make-up on anyone's face could possibly be a painting.

Mr Swift, in his succinct and concise reply, pointed out what had occurred to me and I had mentioned to Mr Wilson in the course of argument, that a painting must be on a surface of some kind. The surface upon which the startling make-up was put was Mr Goddard's face and, if there were a painting, it must be the marks plus Mr Goddard's face. If the marks are taken off the face there cannot be a painting. A painting is not an idea: it is an object; and paint without a surface is not a painting. Make-up, as such, however idiosyncratic it may be as an idea, cannot possibly be a painting for the purposes of the Copyright Act 1956.

Do you think that the Court of Appeal's interpretation of 'painting', albeit in the Copyright Act 1956, is a sound one? Would it exclude other forms of body art, such as tattoos?

The following is another case in which the court was asked to test the boundaries of the 'artistic work' category.

Creation Records Ltd v News Group Newspapers Ltd [1997] EMLR 444

Noel Gallagher arranged an ensemble of objects for the purposes of a 'photo shoot', the results of which were to be used for the front sleeve of the Oasis album, 'Be Here Now'. The defendant newspaper engaged a freelance photographer to take an unauthorized photograph of the scene, which it subsequently published and offered for sale. In an action for an interlocutory injunction restraining further publication of the photograph, Lloyd J considered whether copyright subsisted in the 'photo shoot' scene as a dramatic or artistic work.

Lloyd J, at pp. 447–50:

Mr Gallagher exhibits to his affidavit a photograph which, he says, he envisaged as being used for the front sleeve of the album. This has the swimming pool in the foreground with the Rolls Royce seemingly emerging from the water towards the camera. The hotel is beyond and to the right. In the far distance is a wooded area with a partly clouded sky above. The five members of the group are posed round the pool, one on a scooter, one climbing out of the pool and others with or near other objects seemingly unrelated to each other. The various objects were ordered two days before from a warehouse in London; none of them was made for the purpose.

...

It is said, first, that the scene itself (the arrangement or composition of the members of the group, the various objects and the site) is a copyright work. I do not see how that can be so. Mr Merriman argued faintly that it was a dramatic work. Since the scene is inherently static, having no movement, story or action, I cannot accept this. Primarily, he argued that it was an artistic work, as a sculpture or collage within section 4(1)(a) of the Copyright, Designs and Patents Act 1988 or a work of artistic craftsmanship within section 4(1)(c) of that Act.

I do not regard this as seriously arguable. I do not see how the process of assembling these disparate objects together with the members of the group can be regarded as having anything in common with sculpture or with artistic craftsmanship. No element in the composition has been carved, modelled or made in any of the other ways in which sculpture is made (see *Breville (Europe) plc v Thorn EMI Domestic Appliances Ltd* [1995] FSR 77 at 94). Nor does it seem to me to be the subject or result of the exercise of any craftsmanship (see *George Hensher Ltd v Restawile Upholstery (Lancs) Ltd* [1976] AC 64, especially Lord Simon at 91).

I should also mention in this context the case of *Shelley Films Ltd v Rex Features Ltd* [1994] EMLR 134. In this case Mr Martin Mann QC, sitting as a deputy judge of this division, held it to be seriously arguable that a film set prepared for the film to be called 'Mary Shelley's Frankenstein' was a work of artistic craftsmanship so that an unauthorised photograph taken of an actor on the set was a breach of copyright in the set as well, for different reasons, as of other elements in the photograph. That seems to me quite different on the facts. I can readily accept that a film set does involve craftsmanship. It is not merely an assembly of 'objets trouvés'. I will need to come back to another aspect of that case later.

As for collage, a subject of copyright new to English law in the 1988 Act, the traditional understanding of that word is that it involves the use of glue or some other adhesive in the process of making a work of visual art, being derived from the French. Two Oxford Dictionary definitions were put before me. *The Oxford English Dictionary* (2nd edn, 1989) has this:

> An abstract form of art in which photographs, pieces of paper, newspaper cuttings, string etc are placed in juxtaposition and glued to the pictorial surface; such a work of art.

It then goes on to quote examples which include some loose uses of the word, for example, in relation to poems and music. *The Concise Oxford Dictionary* (9th edn) has a shorter version of these two definitions, but also as its third:

> A collection of unrelated things.

Mr Merriman submits that it is at least seriously arguable that the composition which Mr Gallagher put together as the subject of the photography is within the definition of collage in this sense, even though it did not involve the use of any adhesive. More generally, he submitted that this composition is the result of the exercise of artistic creativity and originality and that at a time when the creativity of visual artists is finding outlets in a great variety of novel forms the 1988 Act should not be construed so as to deny such novel works of art the possibility of copyright protection as artistic works within section 4. He asked forensically how it might be found that copyright subsisted in Carl Andre's bricks, in stone circles created by Richard Long, in Rachel Whiteread's house, in the living sculptures of Gilbert and George and in examples of installation art generally. I do not find it necessary or appropriate to answer that question. I would distinguish Mr Gallagher's composition from all of those examples as being put together solely to be the subject matter of a number of photographs and disassembled as soon as those were taken. This composition was intrinsically ephemeral, or indeed less than ephemeral, in the original sense of that word of living only for one day. This existed for a few hours on the ground. Its continued existence was to be in the form of a photographic image. Accordingly, it seems to me materially different from all the particular examples put to me in this context by Mr Merriman.

Even if it were otherwise, I would not accept that it is seriously arguable that this composition is a collage. In my view a collage does indeed involve as an essential element the sticking of two or more things together. It does not suffice to point to the collocation, whether or not with artistic intent, of such random, unrelated and unfixed elements as is seen in the photographs in question.

Accordingly, I am not prepared to regard the plaintiffs' case based on copyright in the subject matter of the shoot as sufficiently arguable to be the basis of an interlocutory injunction.

Although the claimants failed on the copyright claim, they were successful in obtaining an injunction on the basis of breach of confidence (the scene was treated as confidential as regards photography).[92] Nevertheless, does their failure to establish copyright in the scene highlight an unduly narrow interpretation of artistic works? What impact would it have on the protection of works of modern art, such as those mentioned in the above extract? Finally, does this case reflect the limitations of a 'closed list' approach to subject matter? Bearing in mind the CJEU rulings in *Bezpečnostní* and *FAPL* discussed at 2.5.1.1, would UK courts have to adopt a different approach if facts similar to *Creation Records* were to arise again? Would it, and should it, simply be enough that Mr Gallagher exercised intellectual creativity in putting together the ensemble of objects for the photo shoot?

The apparent restrictiveness of the *Harpbond* and *Creation Records* decisions may be contrasted with those involving protection of functional items. For example, in *Wham-O Manufacturing Co. v Lincoln Industries*[93] the New Zealand Court of Appeal protected a wooden prototype of a Frisbee as a 'sculpture' and the moulds for manufacturing Frisbees as 'engravings'. While in *Hi Tech Autoparts Ltd v Towergate Two Ltd (No. 2)*[94] Christopher Floyd QC held that metal plates for the manufacture of rubber car mats were protected as engravings and in *Breville Europe plc v Thorn EMI Domestic Appliances Ltd*[95] Falconer J held that plaster casts of a sandwich maker were 'sculptures' within the meaning of section 3 of the Copyright Act 1956. However, by way of contrast, Laddie J in *Metix (UK) Ltd v GH Maughan (Plastics) Ltd*[96] favoured a test that a 'sculpture is a three-dimensional work made by an artist's hand' and rejected a claim that moulds used for making cartridges were artistic works. Similarly, in *Davis (J & S) (Holdings) Ltd v Wright Health Group Ltd*[97] Whitford J refused to protect a model of a dental impression tray as a sculpture, largely because of its ephemeral nature.

Does it make sense for courts to interpret the 'artistic works' category generously when it comes to industrial or functional items, but less so in relation to other types of creations, such as facial make-up, arrangements of objects, or modern art?

In the recent *Star Wars* litigation, the meaning and scope of 'sculpture' was examined by the High Court, Court of Appeal, and eventually the Supreme Court. We turn to consider these decisions.

---

[92] See 9.4.3.   [93] [1985] RPC 127.   [94] [2002] FSR 16.   [95] [1995] FSR 77.
[96] [1997] FSR 718, 721–2.   [97] [1988] RPC 403.

Lucasfilm Ltd v Ainsworth [2011] UKSC 39, [2012] 1 AC 208

The case concerned the first *Star Wars* film, i.e. the film released in 1977, now known as *Episode IV: The New Hope* and the costumes of the 'Imperial Stormtrooper' characters, in particular the white helmets and armour worn by them. Paintings and drawings of the stormtroopers in their helmets and armour had been created, along with a clay model of a stormtrooper helmet. The first defendant, Mr Ainsworth, using vacuum-moulding techniques, had produced the final plastic version of the helmets and armour. Some 30 years after the film was released, Mr Ainsworth found his moulds and decided to supply stormtrooper outfits to zealous *Star Wars* fans, who like dressing up as Imperial Stormtroopers. The claimants objected to this activity and obtained a default judgment for trade mark and copyright infringement against Mr Ainsworth in the US for damages amounting to $20 million (Mr Ainsworth's sales in the US had amounted to only $14,500). The claimants sought to enforce the US judgment in England (where Mr Ainsworth resides); and, in the event that they were unsuccessful, also sought to bring an action in England for infringement of US copyright; and a claim for copyright infringement under UK law. It is this latter claim that we are focusing on here.

In determining whether the defendants had infringed UK copyright, one of the key issues was whether the helmets and armour were 'sculptures' within section 4(2) of the CDPA (which defines 'sculpture' to include 'a cast or model made for purposes of sculpture'). Whether or not the helmets and armour were sculptures was relevant to whether Mr Ainsworth would be able to invoke the defences in sections 51 and 52 of the CDPA. (For an explanation of these defences, refer to 14.4). If the stormtrooper costumes were *not* 'sculptures' then Mr Ainsworth would *not* be liable for making three-dimensional reproductions of the underlying artistic works, i.e. the paintings and drawings (as design documents) in accordance with section 51. Further, in reliance on section 52 (a provision dealing with artistic works that have been industrially exploited) Mr Ainsworth would not be liable for copyright infringement because the claimants' term of protection in their artistic works would have been limited to 25 years and thus would have expired.

At first instance,[98] Mann J reviewed a series of authorities and from these gleaned the following guidance factors for determining a sculpture for copyright purposes:

Mann J:

118. From those authorities, and those approaches, a number of guidance factors can be extracted…

(i) Some regard has to be had to the normal use of the word.

(ii) Nevertheless, the concept can be applicable to things going beyond what one would normally expect to be art in the sense of the sort of things that one would expect to find in art galleries.

(iii) It is inappropriate to stray too far from what would normally be regarded as sculpture.

(iv) No judgment is to be made about artistic worth.

---

[98] [2008] EWHC 1878 (Ch), [2009] FSR 2.

(v)   Not every three dimensional representation of a concept can be regarded as a sculpture. Otherwise every three dimensional construction or fabrication would be a sculpture, and that cannot be right.

(vi)   It is of the essence of a sculpture that it should have, as part of its purpose, a visual appeal in the sense that it might be enjoyed for that purpose alone, whether or not it might have another purpose as well. The purpose is that of the creator. This reflects the reference to 'artist's hand' in the judgment of Laddie J. in *Metix*, with which I respectfully agree. An artist (in the realm of the visual arts) creates something because it has visual appeal which he wishes to be enjoyed as such. He may fail, but that does not matter (no judgments are to be made about artistic merit). It is the underlying purpose that is important. I think that this encapsulates the ideas set out in the reference works referred to in *Wham-O* and set out above (and in particular the *Encyclopaedia Britannica*).

(vii)   The fact that the object has some other use does not necessarily disqualify it from being a sculpture, but it still has to have the intrinsic quality of being intended to be enjoyed as a visual thing. Thus the model soldier in Britain might be played with, but it still, apparently, had strong purely visual appeal which might be enjoyed as such. Similarly, the Critters in Wildash had other functions, but they still had strong purely visual appeal. It explains why the Frisbee itself should be excluded from the category, along with the moulds in *Metix* and *Davis*. It would also exclude the wooden model in *Wham-O* and the plaster casts in *Breville*, and I would respectfully disagree with the conclusions reached by the judges in those cases that those things were sculptures. Those decisions, in my view, would not accord with the ordinary view of what a sculpture is, and if one asks why then I think that the answer is that the products fail this requirement and the preceding one—there is no intention that the object itself should have visual appeal for its own sake, and every intention that it be purely functional.

(viii)   I support this analysis with an example. A pile of bricks, temporarily on display at the Tate Modern for two weeks, is plainly capable of being a sculpture. The identical pile of bricks dumped at the end of my driveway for two weeks preparatory to a building project is equally plainly not. One asks why there is that difference, and the answer lies, in my view, in having regard to its purpose. One is created by the hand of an artist, for artistic purposes, and the other is created by a builder, for building purposes. I appreciate that this example might be criticised for building in assumptions relating to what it seeks to demonstrate, and then extracting, or justifying, a test from that, but in the heavily subjective realms of definition in the artistic field one has to start somewhere.

(ix)   The process of fabrication is relevant but not determinative. I do not see why a purely functional item, not intended to be at all decorative, should be treated as a sculpture simply because it is (for example) carved out of wood or stone.

119. Those factors are guidelines, not rigid requirements. The question: 'What is a sculpture?' has some of the elements about it of the unanswerable question: 'What is Art?'. However, they do, in my view, represent what one can extract from the cases, definitions and statutes in order to assist in answering the question whether any particular article is a sculpture or not. They are an attempt to extract elements from what plainly are sculptures, to distinguish what makes something plainly *not* a sculpture, and to arrive at some factors which result from that exercise. I would no more attempt a definition than any of the judges in the other authorities.

On the facts, Mann J concluded that the stormtrooper helmet and armour were not sculptures because they lacked artistic purpose and this would overstretch 'the ordinary perception of what is a sculpture'. Rather, their primary function was utilitarian, i.e. to be worn as items of costume and to identify and portray characters in a film.[99]

The Court of Appeal,[100] like Mann J, were critical of certain decisions, such as *Wham-O* and *Breville Europe* (see [65]–[66]). They also agreed with Mann J on the sculpture and sections 51 and 52 issues, in particular with the judge's multifactorial approach:

Jacob LJ (delivering the judgment of the court):

75. The issue in this case and the judge's approach to it does not turn on the purpose for which it is actually used but on the purposive nature of the object: what the judge described as its 'intrinsic quality of being intended to be enjoyed as a visual thing'. As we read his judgment, the purpose of the object is simply one of the relevant guides to whether it qualifies as a sculpture. A precise definition of that term is not possible which is why the judge has outlined a number of considerations which should act as signposts to the right answer. One can demonstrate this by an example. Most people would not regard a real soldier's helmet as a sculpture. Although made of pressed metal from a mould, its essential functionality as such is to take it outside any reasonable use of that term. A medieval suit of armour, however highly decorated, is no different. Although now of largely historical interest, it was made for a practical purpose which, again, characterises it as an object of utility rather than an artistic work. This view of these objects would not change if they were used as props for a play or film. Their use in that context would not alter their nature or their description.

76. But if the soldier's helmet appears on a bronze statue of a soldier as part of an artistic representation of the man and his kit no one would, we think, dispute that it formed part of a sculpture. It has no practical utility. It cannot be used as a helmet and, to that extent, it is not one.

77. The result of this analysis is that it is not possible or wise to attempt to devise a comprehensive or exclusive definition of 'sculpture' sufficient to determine the issue in any given case. Although this may be close to adopting the elephant test of knowing one when you see one, it is almost inevitable in this field. We therefore consider that the judge was right to adopt the multi-factorial approach which he did.

The Supreme Court also expressed doubts about the conclusions reached in *Wham-O* and *Breville* (at [30]–[32]) and then went on to consider the claimants' contention that Mann J and the Court of Appeal were wrong to conclude that the helmet's purpose was utilitarian.

Lord Walker and Lord Collins (with whom Lord Phillips and Baroness Hale agreed):

42. In this court the claimants have challenged the reasoning of the judge and the Court of Appeal. Mr Sumption QC said that it was eccentric of the judge to describe the helmet's purpose as utilitarian, and that the Court of Appeal could find it to have a functional purpose only by treating it as having the same functional purpose as a real helmet 'within the confines of a film'.

[99] [121]–[122].   [100] [2009] EWCA Civ 1328, [2010] FSR 10.

43. This is quite a puzzling point. The Star Wars films are set in an imaginary, science-fiction world of the future. War films set in the past (*Paths of Glory*, for instance, depicting the French army in the First World War, or *Atonement* depicting the British Expeditionary Force at Dunkirk) are at least based on historical realities. The actors and extras in the trenches or on the beaches may be wearing real steel helmets, or (because real steel helmets of the correct style are unobtainable in sufficient numbers) they may be wearing plastic helmets painted khaki. In either case the helmets are there as (in the judge's words) 'a mixture of costume and prop' in order to contribute to the artistic effect of the film as a film. They are part of a production process, as Laddie J said in the *Metix* case [1997] FSR 718, 721, citing Whitford J in *J & S Davis (Holdings) Ltd v Wright Health Group Ltd* [1988] RPC 403, 410–412. In this case the production process was the making of a full-length feature film.

44. It would not accord with the normal use of language to apply the term 'sculpture' to a 20th century military helmet used in the making of a film, whether it was the real thing or a replica made in different material, however great its contribution to the artistic effect of the finished film. The argument for applying the term to an Imperial Stormtrooper helmet is stronger, because of the imagination that went into the concept of the sinister cloned soldiers dressed in uniform white armour. But it was the Star Wars film that was the work of art that Mr Lucas and his companies created. The helmet was utilitarian in the sense that it was an element in the process of production of the film.

45. Those were the concurrent findings of both the judge [2009] FSR 193 and the Court of Appeal [2010] Ch 75, in paras 121 and 80 of their respective judgments. The type of judgmental conclusion that often has to be reached in intellectual property cases—on issues such as obviousness, inventiveness, and copying—are matters on which appellate courts should be slow to interfere with the judgment of the trial judge.

46. …He did not err in law or reach an obviously untenable conclusion, and the Court of Appeal was right to uphold his decision on this point.

Although the Supreme Court upheld the judgments of Mann J and the Court of Appeal 'very largely for the reasons that they [gave]', it did state that it was unenthusiastic about the Court of Appeal's 'elephant test' ('knowing a sculpture when you see it') and stressed the need for a judge to evaluate the evidence, weigh the various factors, and provide reasons for reaching their conclusion.[101] As well, the Supreme Court disagreed with the Court of Appeal's view that the legislative history of the relationship between copyright and designs did not lend any assistance. Rather, it believed the legislative history indicated that protection of three-dimensional objects should be gradual and that the court should not 'encourage the boundaries of full copyright protection to creep outwards'.[102]

Do you agree with the multifactorial test for 'sculpture' that was approved by the Supreme Court? What are its advantages and disadvantages? It is also interesting to note that the court found factors (i) to (v) relatively straightforward and uncontroversial. However, factors (vi) and (vii) (the purpose of the work being its visual appeal and the object, where it has some other use, having the intrinsic quality of being enjoyed as a visual thing) were controversial, particularly in their application. Do you agree that these factors were applied correctly to the facts of the case?

Another vexed aspect of the 'artistic works' category is the scope of the subcategory 'works of artistic craftsmanship'. The difficulty stems mainly from determining whether or

[101] [47].   [102] [48].

not the work is one of *artistic* craftsmanship. In the following decision, the House of Lords formulated a variety of approaches to this assessment.

George Hensher Ltd v Restawile Upholstery (Lancs) Ltd [1976] AC 64

The appellants produced a prototype of a suite of furniture (comprising two chairs and a settee), known as the 'Bronx' suite. It subsequently offered the suite (and variations of it) for sale to the general public. The respondents manufactured a suite of furniture (known as the 'Amazon' suite), which the appellants alleged infringed copyright in their suite and prototypes of the suites as artistic works. Graham J held that the prototype of the 'Bronx' suite was a work of artistic craftsmanship within the meaning of section 3(1)(c) of the Copyright Act 1956. An appeal by the respondents to the Court of Appeal was allowed. The appellants then appealed to the House of Lords. The respondents admitted that the prototype was a work of craftsmanship but not that it was of 'artistic craftsmanship'. Each of the law lords delivered a speech.

Lord Reid, at pp. 78–9:

But here two questions must be determined. What precisely is the meaning of 'artistic' in this context and who is to judge of its application to the article in question? There is a trend of authority with which I agree that a court ought not to be called on to make an aesthetic judgment. Judges have to be experts in the use of the English language but they are not experts in art or aesthetics. In such a matter my opinion is of no more value than that of anyone else. But I can and must say what in my view is the meaning of the word 'artistic'.

...

It is I think of importance that the maker or designer of a thing should have intended that it should have an artistic appeal but I would not regard that as either necessary or conclusive. If any substantial section of the public genuinely admires and values a thing for its appearance and gets pleasure or satisfaction, whether emotional or intellectual, from looking at it, I would accept that it is artistic although many others may think it meaningless or common or vulgar.

I think that it may be misleading to equate artistic craftsmanship with a work of art. 'Work of art' is generally associated more with the fine arts than with craftsmanship and may be setting too high a standard. During last century there was a movement to bring art to the people. I doubt whether the craftsmen who set out with that intention would have regarded all their products as works of art, but they were certainly works of artistic craftsmanship whether or not they were useful as well as having an artistic appeal.

...

In the present case I find no evidence at all that anyone regarded the appellants' furniture as artistic. The appellants' object was to produce something which would sell. It was, as one witness said, 'a winner' and they succeeded in their object. No doubt many customers bought the furniture because they thought it looked nice as well as being comfortable. But looking nice appears to me to fall considerably short of having artistic appeal. I can find no evidence that anyone felt or thought that the furniture was artistic in the sense which I have tried to explain. I am therefore of opinion that this appeal should be dismissed.

Lord Morris, at pp. 81–2:

So I would say that the object under consideration must be judged as a thing in itself. Does it have the character or virtue of being artistic? In deciding as to this some persons may take something from their ideas as to what constitutes beauty or as to what satisfies their notions of taste or as to what yields pleasure or as to what makes an aesthetic appeal. If, however, there is a resort to these or other words which may themselves have their own satellites of meanings there must follow a return to the word 'artistic' which is apt without exposition to contain and convey its own meaning.

As to the second question, I consider that as in all situations where a decision is required upon a question of fact the court must pay heed to the evidence that is adduced. Though it is a matter of individual opinion whether a work is or is not artistic there are many people who have special capabilities and qualifications for forming an opinion and whose testimony will command respect. In practice a court will not have difficulty in weighing their evidence and in deciding whether it clearly points to some conclusion. In cases where the court is able to see the work which is in question that will not warrant a decision on the basis of a spot opinion formed by the court itself but it will be a valuable aid to an appreciation of the evidence.

In the present case the evidence fell short of establishing that the knock-up qualified to be characterised as a work of artistic craftsmanship.

I would dismiss the appeal.

Viscount Dilhorne, at p. 87:

I am conscious, as was the Court of Appeal, of the need to avoid judicial assessment of artistic merits or quality, but I do not think that any such assessment is involved in deciding whether a work is an artistic work.

This question of fact in relation to copyright is decided not by a jury but by a judge sitting alone. Evidence may be called with regard to it. Expert witnesses may testify. At the end of the day, it will be for the judge to decide whether it is established that the work is one of artistic craftsmanship. If that is not established, the claim to copyright on that ground will fail. I do not think that it suffices to show that some section of the public considers the work to be artistic, though that fact will be one for the judge to take into account, for the decision has to be made by the judge and cannot be delegated.

In this case there was no evidence before Graham J that the prototype as a whole or that part of it which has been called a plinth was a work of an artistic character.

…

I would therefore dismiss this appeal.

Lord Simon, at pp. 94–6:

Not only is artistic merit irrelevant as a matter of statutory construction, evaluation of artistic merit is not a task for which judges have any training or general aptitude. Words are the tools and subject matter of lawyers; but even in matters of literary copyright the court will not concern itself with literary merit: *Walter v Lane* [1900] AC 539. Since the tribunal will not attempt a personal aesthetic judgment (Stewart J in *Hay and Hay Construction Co Ltd v Sloan* (1957) 16 Fox Pat C 185, 190), it follows, again, that whether the subject matter is or is not a work of artistic craftsmanship is a matter of evidence; and the most cogent evidence is likely to be from those who are either themselves acknowledged artist-craftsmen or concerned with the training of artist-craftsmen—in other words, expert evidence.

…

Against this construction of the statutory phrase, the result of the instant appeal cannot be in doubt: there was no, or certainly no adequate, evidence that the prototype of the Bronx chair was a work of artistic craftsmanship.

…

I would therefore dismiss the appeal.

Lord Kilbrandon, at p. 97:

The conscious intention of the craftsman will be the primary test of whether his product is artistic or not; the fact that many of us like looking at a piece of honest work, especially in the traditional trades, is not enough to make it a work of art.

Whether a given object is a work of artistic craftsmanship can be posed as a question of fact, but only after the meaning of the word 'artistic' has been determined; what that meaning is, is a question of law, since it involves a decision of what Parliament meant by the word Parliament used. I do not believe that it is possible, as matter of law or of exegesis, to arrive at a comprehensive definitive interpretation of such a familiar English word, so as to be armed with a test which will enable one, by the application of it, at a glance, to exclude all that does not properly fall within the scope of the simple word itself. It is, indeed, seldom that a simple word can, by translation into some easier or more difficult phrase, be rendered the more capable of furnishing such a test. But it is quite plain, in my opinion, that you cannot get on without exercising, in any case in which this kind of dispute arises, the judicial function of holding whether the facts bring the object within the meaning of the statutory definition. You will get no assistance, until you have exercised that judicial function, by asking the opinion of an expert; if he says 'I regard that object as artistic', the next question which must be asked in order to make his last answer intelligible is 'What do you mean by artistic?' That question is incompetent, because the answer would be irrelevant. Since the word is a word of common speech, it requires, and permits of, no interpretation by experts. It is for the judge to determine whether the object falls within the scope of the common meaning of the word.

…

In the result I have failed, perhaps inevitably, to find a substitute formula which will replace the word 'artistic,' and be one which will serve to qualify as artistic or non-artistic any given piece of craftsmanship. I do not think it is necessary to do so. I would put it in this way, that in my opinion the common meaning of the word 'artistic' does not permit that word to be used as a description of the craftsmanship involved in the production of the prototype 'Bronx' chair, having regard to all the evidence of the circumstances surrounding its manufacture, and I have endeavoured to show the reason why that should be so.

Is it possible to discern a *ratio decidendi* from the above speeches of the House of Lords? Or do the law lords each propound different tests for determining whether something qualifies as a 'work of artistic craftsmanship'? If so, which in your view is the preferable test?

In *Merlet v Mothercare*,[103] one of the issues raised was whether a prototype of a rain-cape for children (the 'Raincosy') was a work of artistic craftsmanship. At first instance, Walton J took the following view of *Hensher*:

At any rate in the first instance, it is not for the court to make a value judgment: the question is primarily the intention of the artist-craftsman. If his intention was to create a work of art

---

[103] [1986] RPC 115.

and he has not manifestly failed in that intent, that is all that is required. It is not for the court to say that he has merely done the equivalent of flinging a paint pot in the face of the public. But, of course, he may have manifestly failed in his object, and his own *ipse dixit* cannot therefore be the sole, although it is the initial and predominant, test.

There is one further reflection. Although there must always come a first time when an artist-craftsman seeks to create a work of art, and the court may well look with just suspicion upon the first claim of this nature, it will be much easier to recognise the claim if the craftsman is already a recognised artist.

Finally, I say nothing as to the evidence which should be properly admitted as to whether the artist has succeeded in his aim of creating a work of art. There was a diversity of views in the House as to what evidence (apart of course from the intentions of the presumed artist-craftsman) was properly admissible, and especially on this last point. I do not think it would be right, since it is not required for the purposes of this case, to express any opinion thereon.[104]

Walton J concluded that the Raincosy was not a work of artistic craftsmanship because, in designing the cape, the claimant had in mind purely utilitarian considerations, namely complete protection from inclement weather.

Does Walton J's interpretation of the ratio in *Hensher v Restawhile* reflect your understanding of the case? In any event, do you agree with the approach that he adopts, judging whether something is a work of artistic craftsmanship according to the intention of the artist-craftsman?

In *Lucasfilm Ltd v Ainsworth*,[105] Mann J had to consider whether the stormtrooper helmets and armour were works of artistic craftsmanship (both for the purpose of deciding whether section 51 of the CDPA applied but also if copyright subsisted in these items). After reviewing *Hensher*, Mann J concluded that it was 'with respect, not easy to obtain much general guidance from this case' but that it did indicate that 'the intention of the creator has some real evidence' and 'the composite phrase is important and has to be borne in mind'.[106] In rejecting the argument that the helmet worn by the stormtrooper characters was a work of artistic craftsmanship, Mann J found that it was not the creators' purpose that the helmet should in any way have aesthetic appeal. This finding was not pursued on appeal.

The Australian High Court in *Burge v Swarbuck*[107] has also considered the scope of works of artistic craftsmanship and held that the primary concern is 'the extent to which the particular work's artistic expression, in its form, is unconstrained by functional considerations'.[108]

Which, if any, of the approaches discussed above is preferable in your view?

Another issue that has arisen in the context of works of artistic craftsmanship is the extent to which the elements of artistry and craftsmanship can derive from different persons, as opposed to from the same person. In the New Zealand decision *Bonz Group (Pty) Ltd v Cooke*,[109] Tipping J stated that the author must be both a craftsman and an artist. The former is 'a person who makes something in a skilful way and takes justified pride in his workmanship' whereas an artist 'is a person with creative ability who produces something which has aesthetic appeal'.[110] Tipping J went on to comment that '[i]f two or more people combine to design and make the ultimate product I cannot see why that ultimate product should not be

104 At 126–7.   105 [2008] ECDR 17.   106 [130].   107 [2007] FSR 27, [63]–[65].
108 [83].   109 [1994] NZLR 216.   110 At 223.

regarded as a work of artistic craftsmanship'.[111] This approach was adopted by Evans-Lombe J in *Vermaat and Powell v Boncrest*.[112]

FURTHER READING

A. Barron, 'Copyright law and the claims of art' [2002] IPQ 368.

J. Pila, 'Works of artistic craftsmanship in the High Court of Australia: the exception as paradigm copyright work' (2008) 36 Fed. L. Rev. 365.

J. Pila, 'The "Star Wars" copyright claim: an ambivalent view of the Empire' (2012) 128 LQR 15.

2.5.2 ORIGINALITY

2.5.2.1 Introduction

A requirement of 'originality' is not expressly mandated by international copyright law. However, the *travaux préparatoires* for the Brussels Revision Conference of the Berne Convention indicate that the requirement of 'intellectual creation' is implicit in the concept of 'literary and artistic work'.[113] This view is arguably reinforced by the fact that Article 2(5) of the Berne Convention expressly refers to 'collections of literary or artistic works' being 'intellectual creations' by virtue of the 'selection and arrangement of their contents'. Professors Ricketson and Ginsburg argue that, 'while such a stipulation is necessary in the case of these kinds of borderline works, it hardly needs to be stated in relation to the "mainline" works covered by article 2(1)'.[114] There is, however, very little guidance on what constitutes 'intellectual creation' and, as a result, Berne Union members may, and do, differ in their approach to originality. Different jurisdictions have in fact adopted varying tests, including 'labour, skill and judgment',[115] 'skill and judgment',[116] 'minimal level of creativity',[117] 'imprint of the author's personality', 'intellectual contribution',[118] 'personal intellectual creation',[119] and 'author's own intellectual creation'.[120] The variation in tests may be indicative of the particular copyright philosophy operating in that jurisdiction or they may simply reflect the difficulties associated with defining this particular concept.

---

[111] At 223.   [112] [2001] FSR 5.

[113] S. Ricketson and J. Ginsburg, *International Copyright and Neighbouring Rights: The Berne Convention and Beyond* (2nd edn, Oxford: Oxford University Press, 2005), para. 8.03.

[114] Ricketson and Ginsburg, *International Copyright*, para. 8.03.

[115] See House of Lords decision in *Ladbroke (Football) Ltd v William Hill (Football) Ltd* [1964] 1 WLR 273.

[116] See Canadian Supreme Court decision in *CCH Canadian Ltd v Law Society of Upper Canada* [2004] 236 DLR (4th) 395, [2004] 1 SCR 339.

[117] See US Supreme Court decision in *Feist Publications v Rural Telephone*, 111 S Ct 1282 (1991).

[118] See French Supreme Court ruling in *Pachot Decision* (1986) 129 RIDA 130.

[119] See German Federal Supreme Court decision in *Unauthorised Reproduction of Telephone Directories on CD-Rom* [2002] ECDR 3 (6 May 1999) (BGH).

[120] See Directive 91/250/EEC on the legal protection of computer programs [1991] OJ L122/42, subsequently codified as Directive 2009/24/EC of 23 April 2009 on the legal protection of computer programs [2009] OJ L111/16, Art. 1(3); Directive 93/98/EEC, which was subsequently codified by Directive 2006/116/EC of 12 December 2006 on the term of protection of copyright and certain related rights, Art. 6 and Directive 96/9/EC of the European Parliament and of the Council of 11 March 1996 on the legal protection of databases [1996] OJ L77/20, Art. 3.

What, do you think, is the *purpose* of the originality requirement in copyright law? Is it supposed to operate as a filtering mechanism for determining which intangible creations are deserving of protection? If so, what sorts of consideration would you expect to inform the content of an originality test? For example, would or should you expect underlying justifications—such as the utilitarian and deontological justifications discussed by Spence earlier in this chapter at 2.3—to shape the originality requirement? Further, are there other roles for originality? Does it, for example, have a role to play in determining the scope of protection, i.e. infringement, where only parts of a work are copied and, what role does, or should, originality play alongside subject matter, i.e. the concept of a literary, dramatic, musical, or artistic work? Finally, should we expect originality to mean different things depending on the type of work involved or to reflect a universal, consistent standard?

In the UK, section 1(1)(a) of the CDPA makes clear that literary, dramatic, musical, and artistic works must be 'original' in order for copyright to subsist. For all other types of work, i.e. films, sound recordings, broadcasts, and typographical arrangements of published editions, there is *no* requirement of originality. Instead, the CDPA provides that copyright does not subsist in a sound recording, film, or published edition to the extent that it is itself copied from a previous work of the same kind.[121] For broadcasts, copyright does not subsist in a broadcast to the extent that it infringes copyright in another broadcast.[122] Thus, literary, dramatic, musical, and artistic works will need to satisfy a higher threshold for protection than entrepreneurial works (i.e. films, sound recordings, broadcasts, and published editions).

Aside from databases (a subcategory of literary works) where section 3A of the CDPA defines originality as the 'author's own intellectual creation', the Act is otherwise silent on the content of the originality requirement. This has meant that, for the most part, the meaning of 'originality' has been developed by the courts. We begin by examining the way in which UK courts have traditionally defined originality before turning to examine the influence of EU copyright law, in particular the harmonization of the originality concept via both directives and CJEU jurisprudence. These European developments have undoubtedly impacted on the traditional UK test and made originality an especially complex area of copyright law.

2.5.2.2 Traditional UK approach

One of the seminal cases that has shaped the standard of originality in the UK is *Walter v Lane*.

Walter v Lane [1900] AC 539

The Earl of Rosebery (who made no claim in the action) gave public speeches on five occasions. Reporters from *The Times* newspaper took down the speeches verbatim in shorthand and later transcribed them, adding punctuation, revisions, and corrections. The respondent published a book, which included Lord Rosebery's speeches taken substantially from the reports in *The Times*. The newspaper brought an action against the respondents for infringement of copyright under the Literary Copyright Act 1842. The issue that arose was whether or not the reporters of a speech could be considered 'authors'. If so, *The Times* would be entitled to copyright since the reporters were their

---

[121] CDPA, ss. 5A(2), 5B(4), and 8(2).   [122] CDPA, s. 6(6).

employees and had assigned their rights to them. The Court of Appeal held that the reporters were not 'authors'. This was reversed in the House of Lords.

Lord Davey, at pp. 551–2:

In my opinion the reporter is the author of his own report. He it was who brought into existence in the form of a writing the piece of letterpress which the respondent has copied. I think also that he and he alone composed his report. The materials for his composition were his notes, which were his own property, aided to some extent by his memory and trained judgement. Owing to the perfection which the art of shorthand writing has attained in recent years, memory and judgement bear a less important part in the composition of a report of a speech than was formerly the case. But the question whether the composer has copyright in his report does not seem to me to vary inversely with or to depend on his skill in stenography. Nor, as it appears to me, does the fact that the subject-matter of the report had been made public property, or that no originality or literary skill was demanded for the composition of the report, have anything to do with the matter. Again, it is said that the lucidity of diction and perfection of expression which characterise the eminent person named render an exact reproduction of his words a comparatively easy and almost mechanical task. But is it argued that the reporter of the hesitating or half-completed utterances of an inferior speaker might have copyright, though the reporter of Lord Rosebery may not? Or does the question of copyright in the report depend on the clearness of thought and speech of the orator? In my opinion the question must be decided on general considerations, and not on any grounds which are personal either to the orator or to the reporter. Copyright has nothing to do with the originality or literary merits of the author or composer. It may exist in the information given by a street directory: *Kelly v Morris*; or by a list of deeds of arrangement: *Cate v Devon and Exeter Constitutional Newspaper Co*; or in a list of advertisements: *Lamb v Evans*. I think those cases right, and the principle on which they proceed directly applicable to the present case. It was of course open to any other reporter to compose his own report of Lord Rosebery's speech, and to any other newspaper or book to publish that report; but it is a sound principle that a man shall not avail himself of another's skill, labour, and expense by copying the written product thereof.

Lord James, at pp. 553–5:

Whilst the Act supplies no definition of the word 'author', and whilst it may be difficult for any judicial authority to give a positive definition of that word, certain considerations controlling the meaning of it seem to be established. A mere copyist of written matter is not an 'author' within the Act, but a translator from one language to another would be so. A person to whom words are dictated for the purpose of being written down is not an 'author'. He is the mere agent or clerk of the person dictating, and requires to possess no art beyond that of knowing how to write. The person dictating takes a share in seeing that the person writing follows the dictation, and makes it his care to give time for the writing to be made. But an 'author' may come into existence without producing any original matter of his own. Many instances of the claim to authorship without the production of original matter have been given at the bar. The compilation of a street directory, the reports of proceedings in courts of law, and the tables of the times of running of certain railway trains have been held to bring the producers within the word 'author'; and yet in one sense no original matter can be found in such publications. Still there was a something apart from originality on the one hand and mere mechanical transcribing on the other which entitled those who gave these works to the world to be regarded as their authors.

Now, what is it that a reporter does? Is he a mere scribe? Does he produce original matter or does he produce the something I have mentioned which entitles him to be regarded as an 'author' within the Act? I think that from a general point of view a reporter's art represents more than mere transcribing or writing from dictation. To follow so as to take down the words of an ordinary speaker, and certainly of a rapid speaker, is an art requiring considerable training, and does not come within the knowledge of ordinary persons. Even amongst professional reporters many different degrees of skill exist. Some reporters can take down the words of a speaker however rapidly he speaks; others less practised or proficient cannot, as the term is, keep up with the rapid speaker. Apart from the dealing with the rapidity of speech, there are some reporters whose ears and thoughts and hands never fail them, and who therefore produce reports of complete accuracy. On the other hand, reporters less skilled may be so deficient in this quality of accuracy as to produce reports which certainly tend to perturb the speakers whom they have endeavoured to report. Thus there seems to be a degree of skill in one class of reporters over the other...

After taking such matters as these into consideration, I have, after some doubt, come to the conclusion that a reporter of a speech under the conditions existing in this case is the meritorious producer of the something necessary to constitute him an 'author' within the meaning of the Copyright Act of 1842, and that therefore the judgement of the Court of Appeal should be reversed.

Lord Brampton, at p. 556:

The material facts which have led me to the opinion I am about to express are admitted, and may be very briefly stated. On the several occasions when the speeches were delivered, reporters for *The Times* and other newspapers attended by invitation to enable them to compose and write, for publication in their respective journals, descriptive articles of the occurrences, containing full and accurate reports of the speeches as they were delivered from the lips of the speaker. The reporters who represented *The Times*, with whom alone I have now to deal, were undoubtedly gentlemen of education, great ability, and long and varied experience in the duties of their vocation. They wrote the descriptive parts of their reports from personal observation, the speeches they took down in shorthand, word for word, transcribed them verbatim in longhand, carefully corrected and revised and punctuated them, so that when they appeared in the columns of *The Times* they might, as perfectly as printed words could do, convey to the readers all that was to be seen or heard upon those occasions. From these reports all that appeared in *The Times* was first published to the world. It is obvious that the preparation of them involved considerable intellectual skill and brain labour beyond the mere mechanical operation of writing.

[**Lord Halsbury** delivered a speech, in which he reversed the Court of Appeal's decision. **Lord Robertson** delivered a dissenting speech.]

Given that the Literary Copyright Act 1842 did not have an express requirement of 'originality' and that their lordships were considering the meaning of 'author', how is it that this House of Lords decision remains relevant to 'originality' under existing copyright law? An answer is that originality and authorship are in fact heavily interrelated concepts. Professor Ginsburg has gone so far as to describe authorship as synonymous with originality.[123]

---

[123] J. C. Ginsburg, 'The concept of authorship in comparative copyright law' (2003) 52 DePaul L. Rev. 1063, 1078–82.

As we shall see at 3.2.1, identifying an author usually involves identifying the creator, who will invariably be the person who has contributed the skill, labour, creativity, or personality (depending on your test of originality). Thus, it is perhaps unsurprising that later decisions have treated *Walter v Lane* as authoritative on the meaning of 'originality'.[124] What principles do you think emerge from *Walter v Lane* in relation to originality? Will courts be required to assess the merits of the contribution made by a putative author? And what types of contribution are required—simply originating the work, or are there additional requirements of (intellectual) skill and (brain) labour? The House of Lords had occasion to consider originality in a later decision, this time in the context of compilations.

Ladbroke (Football) Ltd v William Hill (Football) Ltd [1964] 1 WLR 273

The respondents (William Hill) claimed copyright in their football betting coupons and alleged that the appellants (Ladbroke) had produced infringing coupons. The judge at first instance found against the respondents, but the Court of Appeal reversed this decision, finding that the respondents' coupons were entitled to copyright, and granted an injunction to restrain the appellants. On appeal to the House of Lords, the appellants argued, inter alia, that the coupons were not original literary works under section 2(1) of the Copyright Act 1956. They submitted that while a considerable amount of skill, judgment, and labour went into deciding what bets to include in the coupons, the expression of these bets in the coupon lacked skill, judgment, and labour since it only involved them writing down the bets.

Lord Reid, at pp. 277–8:

A wrong result can easily be reached if one begins by dissecting the plaintiffs' work and asking, could section A be the subject of copyright if it stood by itself, could section B be protected if it stood by itself, and so on. To my mind, it does not follow that, because the fragments taken separately would not be copyright, therefore the whole cannot be. Indeed, it has often been recognised that if sufficient skill and judgement have been exercised in devising the arrangements of the whole work, that can be an important or even decisive element in deciding whether the work as a whole is protected by copyright.

...

The appellants' main argument was based on quite a different ground. They deny that the respondents' coupon is an original compilation. There is no dispute about the meaning of the term 'original'. 'The word "original" does not in this connection mean that the work must be the expression of original or inventive thought. Copyright Acts are not concerned with the originality of ideas, but with the expression of thought, and, in the case of "literary work", with the expression of thought in print or writing. The originality which is required relates to the expression of the thought. But the Act does not require that the expression must be in an original or novel form, but that the work must not be copied from another work— that it should originate from the author.' *Per* Peterson J in *University of London Press Ltd v University Tutorial Press Ltd*. And it is not disputed that, as regards compilation, originality

---

[124] e.g. see *Express Newspapers plc v News (UK) Ltd* [1990] 1 WLR 1320, 1325–6; *Sands & McDougall Proprietary Ltd v Robinson* (1917) 23 CLR 49.

is a matter of degree depending on the amount of skill, judgement or labour that has been involved in making the compilation.

In the present case, if it is permissible to take into account all the skill, judgement and labour expended in producing the respondents' coupon, there can be no doubt that it is 'original'. But the appellants say that the coupon must be regarded as having been produced in two stages: first, the respondents had to decide what kind of business they would do—what kinds of bets they would offer to their clients—and then they had to write these out on paper. The appellants say that it is only the skill, judgement and labour involved in the latter stage that can be considered and that that part of their operation involved so little skill, judgement or labour that it cannot qualify as 'original'. In fact, the respondents did not proceed in that way. Their business was to devise a coupon which would appeal to the betting public, and its form and arrangement were not something dictated by previous decisions about the nature of the bets to be offered. The appellants likened the coupon to a trader's catalogue of his wares, and argued that in considering whether a catalogue is entitled to copyright you must disregard the trader's skill and work in deciding what wares he will stock for sale and only consider the skill and labour involved in the actual preparation of the catalogue. I do not think that that is a true analogy. And even in the case of a catalogue there may be a question whether the work, in deciding what to sell, and the work, in deciding how to sell it, are not so inter-connected as to be inseparable. Copyright in a catalogue in no way prevents honest competition—any other trader can decide to stock and sell any or all of the catalogued articles, and he can thereafter make a new catalogue of his own wares. What he must not do is simply to copy the other trader's catalogue.

Lord Pearce, at pp. 292–3:

…In each case it is a question of degree whether the labour or skill or ingenuity or expense involved in the compilation is sufficient to warrant a claim to originality in a compilation. Applying those principles to the present case I feel little doubt that the plaintiff's coupon is entitled to copyright. The plaintiffs have been pioneers in this field and had invented various bets and nomenclatures some of which have been adopted by their rivals…. The coupon must contain an assorted selection of bets that will attract a customer and induce him to fill up the coupon in preference to rival coupons. To this end, the plaintiffs have devoted much work and money and ingenuity. Out of the vast number of bets that can be offered, they select and devise those which, while being profitable to them, will fill the coupon with the greatest allure.

The appellants seek to say that this work is preliminary and has been directed to decisions as to what types of bets the plaintiffs shall pursue in the business; that such decisions are merely ideas and as such not the subject of copyright; and that the work of actually writing down those ideas in the coupon is too easy and negligible to justify any claim to originality.

An argument on those lines was unsuccessful in the cases of the *British Broadcasting Co v Wireless League Gazette Publishing Co* and *Football League Ltd v Littlewoods Pools Ltd.* There may be cases where such a dichotomy might be justified between some preliminary work and the actual transcription of a compilation, if the work was done with no ultimate intention of a compilation. But on the facts of the present case such an argument cannot succeed. The whole of the plaintiff's efforts from the beginning were devoted to arranging a coupon that would attract punters and be the basis of the plaintiffs' business. Types of bets were not considered *in vacuo* but only in relation to the part which they would play in the coupon.

In my opinion, the majority of the Court of Appeal rightly held that the plaintiffs had established copyright in the coupon.

[**Lord Devlin**, **Lord Hodson**, and **Lord Evershed** delivered concurring speeches.]

Having considered both *Walter v Lane* and *Ladbroke*, how would you describe the originality test in UK copyright law? Is it the same as the novelty or inventive step requirements found in patent law and, if not, in what ways does it differ (see Chapter 12 for a discussion of the patent requirements)? What type of contribution must the person claiming copyright make? Would you describe this as a requirement that the work must originate from the author and be the result of skill, labour, and judgment? Finally, when it comes to the originality of compilations must the relevant skill, judgment, and labour be directed to the selection and/or arrangement of materials (in this case bets) or can the efforts in generating the material in the first place be taken into account?

Walter v Lane and *Ladbroke v William Hill* concerned literary works. Can we say that the originality principles articulated in these cases apply equally to all other types of work, i.e. artistic, musical, and dramatic? Whether there is a universal test of originality, applicable to every type of work, was doubted by the Privy Council in *Interlego v Tyco*.

Interlego v Tyco [1989] AC 217

The appellants (Interlego) were the manufacturers of Lego and Duplo toy bricks for children. They previously had patent and registered design protection for the design of their bricks, which had expired. Design drawings from pre-1973 existed for both types of bricks. These pre-1973 drawings were later redrawn (the post-1972 drawings). The main features of the pre-1973 drawings were reproduced, the only changes being to the written information on the drawings, which had technical importance for manufacturing purposes. The respondents (Tyco), a US toy manufacturing company, decided to make and sell in Hong Kong toy bricks that were compatible with those of the appellants. They achieved this by studying the appellants' bricks and copying the principal features of the design. The appellants brought an action in the High Court of Hong Kong, alleging infringement of copyright in the design drawings. An injunction was granted at first instance. An appeal was partly allowed by the Court of Appeal, which held that copyright did not subsist in the pre-1973 drawings because the designs were capable of registration under the Registered Designs Act 1949, but that the post-1972 drawings were original artistic works that had been infringed. The appellants appealed on the issue of copyright in the pre-1973 drawings, while the respondents cross-appealed in relation to the post-1972 drawings.

Lord Oliver, delivering the opinion of the Privy Council, held that the Court of Appeal were correct in denying copyright protection to the pre-1973 design drawings. He then turned to the cross-appeal.

Lord Oliver (delivering the opinion of the Privy Council), **at pp. 256–63:**

[Perhaps indicating the policy concerns of the Privy Council, Lord Oliver began by summarizing the key legal issue as follows.]

Thus the primary question on Tyco's appeal can be expressed in this way: can Lego, having enjoyed a monopoly for the full permitted period of patent and design protection in reliance upon drawings in which no copyright any longer subsists, continue their monopoly for yet a further, more extensive period by redrawing the same designs with a number of minor alterations and claiming a fresh copyright in the redrawn designs?

...

The significant thing about all these changes is that they involve no substantial alteration to the drawing as such. The outline of the object depicted is, in each case, virtually identical save for the minute differences occasioned by the abandonment of the flow-rib, the depicting of radii on the edges of the knobs and the abandonment of the radius on the outer diameter of the tubes. The significant changes, however important technically, are not indicated by any substantial alteration of the drawing as an artistic work. That remains basically the same and was admittedly copied from the 1968 drawing in the same way as if it had been actually traced ... What is important about a drawing is what is visually significant and the redrawing of an existing drawing with a few minimal visual alterations does not make it an original *artistic* work, however much labour and skill may have gone into the process of reproduction or however important the technical significance of the verbal information that may be included in the same document by way of information or instruction.

...

Not altogether surprisingly there is no statutory definition of the word 'originality' but there is a classical statement of what is comprised in the concept of originality in the context of copyright in the judgement of Peterson J in *University of London Press Ltd v University Tutorial Press Ltd* [1916] 2 Ch 601, 608–9:

> The word 'original' does not in this connection mean that the work must be the expression of original or inventive thought. Copyright Acts are not concerned with the originality of ideas, but with the expression of thought, and, in the case of 'literary work,' with the expression of thought in print or writing. The originality which is required relates to the expression of the thought. But the Act does not require that the expression must be in an original or novel form, but that the work must not be copied from another work—that it should originate from the author.

That statement is, of course, not complete in itself because there may clearly be original work which makes use of material obtained by the author from pre-existing sources. Perhaps the most useful exegesis is to be found in three passages from the opinion of the Board delivered by Lord Atkinson in the Privy Council case of *Macmillan & Co Ltd v Cooper* (1924) 40 TLR 186, a case concerned with university textbooks consisting of abridgements of or excerpts from existing works with appropriate notes for students. Lord Atkinson observed, at p. 188:

> it is the product of the labour, skill, and capital of one man which must not be appropriated by another, not the elements, the raw material, if one may use the expression, upon which the labour and skill and capital of the first have been expended. To secure copyright for this product it is necessary that labour, skill and capital should be expended sufficiently to impart to the product some quality or character which the raw material did not possess, and which differentiates the product from the raw material.

...

Originality in the context of literary copyright has been said in several well known cases to depend upon the degree of skill, labour and judgement involved in preparing a compilation. *Macmillan & Co Ltd v Cooper*, 40 TLR 186 was such a case. So was *GA Cramp & Son Ltd v Frank Smythson Ltd* [1944] AC 329. Similarly in the speeches of Lord Reid and Lord Hodson in *Ladbroke (Football) Ltd v William Hill (Football) Ltd* [1964] 1 WLR 273, 277 (Lord Reid) and at pp. 285 and 287 (Lord Hodson) it is stressed that the amount of skill, judgement or labour is likely to be decisive in the case of compilations. To apply that, however, as a universal test of originality in all copyright cases is not only unwarranted by the context in which the observations were made but palpably erroneous. Take the simplest case of artistic copyright, a painting or a photograph. It takes great skill, judgement and labour to produce a good copy by painting or to produce an enlarged photograph from a positive print, but no one would reasonably contend that the copy painting or enlargement was an 'original' artistic work in which the copier is entitled to claim copyright. Skill, labour or judgement merely in the process of copying cannot confer originality. In this connection some reliance was placed on a passage from the judgement of Whitford J in *LB (Plastics) Ltd v Swish Products Ltd* [1979] RPC 551, 568–9, where he expressed the opinion that a drawing of a three-dimensional prototype, not itself produced from the drawing and not being a work of artistic craftsmanship, would qualify as an original work. That may well be right, for there is no more reason for denying originality to the depiction of a three-dimensional prototype than there is for denying originality to the depiction in two-dimensional form of any other physical object. It by no means follows, however, that that which is an exact and literal reproduction in two-dimensional form of an existing two-dimensional work becomes an original work simply because the process of copying it involves the application of skill and labour. There must in addition be some element of material alteration or embellishment which suffices to make the totality of the work an original work. Of course, even a relatively small alteration or addition quantitatively may, if material, suffice to convert that which is substantially copied from an earlier work into an original work. Whether it does so or not is a question of degree having regard to the quality rather than the quantity of the addition. But copying, per se, however much skill or labour may be devoted to the process, cannot make an original work. A well executed tracing is the result of much labour and skill but remains what it is, a tracing. Moreover it must be borne in mind that the Copyright Act 1956 confers protection on an original work for a generous period. The prolongation of the period of statutory protection by periodic reproduction of the original work with minor alterations is an operation which requires to be scrutinised with some caution to ensure that that for which protection is claimed really is an original artistic work.

What is the ratio of *Interlego*? Is it that an (exact) copy of an existing artistic work will never satisfy the test of originality? Or is the ratio more limited than this? As well, the Privy Council recognized that significant skill and labour could go into redrawing or reproducing existing works but this would not necessarily be enough—why not? *Walter v Lane*, where a report (i.e. copy) of a speech was protected, does not appear to have been cited to the Privy Council. Can *Interlego* be reconciled with *Walter v Lane*?

The originality requirement as it relates to artistic works has been the subject of further judicial comment, as well as academic debate. In the US decision of *Bridgeman Art Library Ltd v Corel*,[125] District Judge Kaplan commented *obiter* that, if the governing law was UK copyright law, photographic reproductions of paintings could not qualify as original artistic works because of the *Interlego* decision. This gave rise to a debate in the UK about the originality requirement for artistic works, particularly for photographs. In the UK decision of *Antiquesportfolio.com plc v Rodney Fitch & Co. Ltd*,[126] an issue arose as to whether a photograph of a static three-dimensional object (such as a vase) could qualify as an original artistic work. Neuberger J (as he then was) distinguished the *Bridgeman* decision on the basis that it involved a photograph of a two-dimensional work. He stated:

36. In the case of photographs of a three-dimensional object, with which I am concerned in the present case, it can be said that the positioning of the object (unless it is a sphere), the angle at which it is taken, the lighting and the focus, and matters such as that, could all be matters of aesthetic or even commercial judgement, albeit in most cases at a very basic level.

[125] 36 F Supp 2d 191 (SDNY 1999).   [126] [2001] FSR 23.

80. Both textbooks maintain that view despite what was said obiter in the *Interlego case* [1989] AC 217, 255–6, per Lord Oliver:

Take the simplest case of artistic copyright, a painting or a photograph. It takes great skill, judgement and labour to produce a good copy by painting or to produce an enlarged photograph from a positive print, but no one would reasonably contend that the copy painting or enlargement was an 'original' artistic work in which the copier is entitled to claim copyright. Skill, labour or judgement merely in the process of copying cannot confer originality.

81. The authors of *The Modern Law of Copyright* comment on this passage at para. 4.39. Although the comment is long it is worth setting it out:

However, whilst the remarks made in *Interlego* may be valid if confined to the subject matter then before the Privy Council, they are stated too widely. The Privy Council was there considering fairly simple technical drawings. This is a rather special subject matter. While the drawing of such a work is more laborious than it looks, it is a fact that any competent draftsman (perhaps, any conscientious amateur) who sets out to reproduce it exactly will almost certainly succeed in the end, because of the mathematical precision of the lines and measurements. This should be contrasted with, e.g. a painting by Vermeer, where it will be obvious that very few persons, if any, are capable of making an exact replica. Now, assume a number of persons do set out to copy such a painting, each according to his own personal skill. Most will only succeed in making something which all too obviously differs from the original—some of them embarrassingly so. They will get a copyright seeing that in each instance the end result does differ from the original yet it took a measure of skill and labour to produce. If, however, one of these renders the original with all the skill and precision of a Salvador Dali, is he to be denied a copyright where a mere dauber is not? The difference between the two cases (technical drawing and old master painting) is that in the latter there is room for individual interpretation even where faithful replication is sought to be attempted while in the former there is not. Further, a photographer who carefully took a photograph of an original painting might get a copyright and, if this is so, it is rather hard to see why a copy of the same degree of fidelity, if rendered by an artist of the calibre forementioned, would not be copyright. These considerations suggest that the proposition under discussion is suspect. It is therefore submitted that, for example, a picture restorer may get a copyright for the result of his efforts. Be that as it may, it is submitted that the *Interlego* proposition is anyway distinguishable where the replicator succeeds in preserving for posterity an original to which access is difficult.

82. The authors of *Copinger on Copyright*, para. 3-142, likewise take the view that the passage should be read as confined.

83. I agree with the textbooks. I do not think the comment as a generality is consistent with *Walter v Lane* [1900] AC 539. I think the true position is that one has to consider the extent to which the 'copyist' is a mere copyist—merely performing an easy mechanical function. The more that is so the less is his contribution likely to be taken as 'original'. Professor Jane C. Ginsburg ('The concept of authorship in comparative copyright law', 10 January 2003, Columbia Law School, Public Law Research Paper No. 03-51, http://ssrn.com/abstract=368481) puts it this way, at p. 21:

reproductions requiring great talent and technical skill may qualify as protectable works of authorship, even if they are *copies* of pre-existing works. This would be the case for photographic and other high quality replicas of works of art.

In the end the question is one of degree—how much skill, labour and judgement in the making of the copy is that of the creator of that copy? Both individual creative input and sweat of brow may be involved and will be factors in the overall evaluation.

...

85. Therefore, as it seems to me, one is bound to have to consider whether what the claimant did involved enough to confer originality—did it go beyond mere servile copying? Patten J held that it did. He applied this test, at para. 58:

The question to ask in any case where the material produced is based on an existing score is whether the new work is sufficiently original in terms of the skill and labour used to produce it.

86. That seems to me to be exactly right. Of course the test involves a question of degree—mere photocopying or merely changing the key would not be enough. But a high degree of skill and labour was involved. This must be considered as a whole—it would not be right to look at each contribution and say 'that is not enough' and conclude that the same goes for the whole. The claimant started by choosing which original manuscript(s) to use (actually he used mainly two out of four, using one to correct ambiguities in the other), he checked every note and supplied 27 'corrections' (i.e. his personal evaluation as to what note Lalande really intended), supplied many suggestions for the figured bass, and put the whole into modern notation. This was not mere servile copying. It had the practical value (unchallenged) of making the work playable. He recreated Lalande's work using a considerable amount of personal judgement. His recreative work was such as to create something really new using his own original (not merely copied) work.

87. I therefore think Patten J was right and agree that this appeal should be dismissed.

[**Mance LJ** agreed with both Mummery LJ and Jacob LJ.]

Do you agree that the contribution of Dr Sawkins was enough to satisfy the test as set out in *Walter v Lane*? Further, does Jacob LJ satisfactorily reconcile the tension between *Walter v Lane* and *Interlego v Tyco*? Does his interpretation of *Interlego v Tyco* mean that there is now a common approach to originality for literary, musical, artistic, and dramatic works?

Situations where an allegedly original literary, dramatic, musical, or artistic work is in fact a copy of pre-existing material have arisen in other jurisdictions, as the Israeli 'Dead Sea Scrolls' case highlights.[127] In this case an unpublished Dead Sea Scroll from several thousand years ago was discovered and subsequently an expert physically reconstructed the fragments of that scroll. Even so, about one-third of the scroll was missing, so another expert, Professor Qimron, spent 11 years deciphering the existing text and using his expertise to fill in the gaps, so to speak. One of the issues in the case was whether Professor Qimron was the author of an original literary work (that work being the final 'deciphered' text). The Israeli Supreme Court held that he was the author and owner of an original literary work. How do you think UK courts would and should treat this type of creativity and would your view change depending on whether the pre-existing material that was being reconstructed or copied was in the public domain or not?

---

[127] For a discussion, see M. Birnhack, 'The Dead Sea Scrolls case: who is an author? [2001] EIPR 128.

> **FURTHER READING**
>
> M. Birnhack, 'The Dead Sea Scrolls case: who is an author?' [2001] EIPR 128.
>
> D. Nimmer, 'Copyright in the Dead Sea Scrolls: authorship and originality' (2001) 38 Houston L. Rev. 1.
>
> A. Rahmatian, 'Music and creativity as perceived by copyright law' [2005] IPQ 267.
>
> A. Rahmatian, 'The concepts of "musical work" and "originality" in UK copyright law—*Sawkins v Hyperion* as a test case' (2009) 40 IIC 560.

2.5.2.3 Influence of EU copyright law

2.5.2.3.1 *Legislative harmonization*

EU copyright directives have sought to harmonize originality for specific types of subject matter, namely computer programs, photographs, and databases. These works will be protected where they are original in the sense that they are the 'author's own intellectual creation'.[128] This new EU standard of originality applies to computer programs after 1 January 1993,[129] photographs after 1 July 1995,[130] and databases after 11 March 1996.[131]

Why has harmonization of originality been limited to these three types of works? The short answer is that the greatest disparities between Member States' approaches to originality manifested themselves in relation to computer programs, photographs, and databases.

In the case of computer programs, this was the first time the originality threshold was harmonized and it was thought necessary because of the stark differences between the UK, French, and German tests in particular. The UK used its traditional, 'labour, skill, and judgment' test, while France applied a test of 'intellectual contribution'.[132] Meanwhile, Germany applied a very strict standard, as evidenced in *Inkasso-Program*,[133] where the German Federal Supreme Court applied a test of 'significant level of creativity', i.e. creativity which exceeds that which could have been achieved by the average programmer.

The requirement of 'author's own intellectual creation' was not expressly incorporated into six Member States' laws (the UK being one) on the basis that it was an implied condition of their laws. The European Commission, however, took issue with the UK because of its arguably lower standard of originality and because the standard was subsequently incorporated for databases in the CDPA. In Germany, Article 69(a) was introduced into the German Copyright Law 1965 in order to implement the originality criterion and reject the 'level of creativity' approach previously taken by the German courts.

Harmonization of the originality standard for photographs was thought necessary because the various Member States' tests (especially the UK test versus the German test) were thought to produce different outcomes (with the UK being the most generous in its approach). In order to accommodate the position of some Member States (such as Germany),

---

[128] See Software Directive, Art. 1(3); Term Directive, Art. 6; and Database Directive, Art. 3.

[129] Software Directive, Art. 9(2).   [130] Term Directive, Art. 10(1).

[131] Database Directive, Art. 14(2) and (4). But note that databases which existed before 27 March 1996 retain copyright if they satisfied the previous UK test of originality, even if they would now fail the EU test of author's own intellectual creation: see the Copyright and Rights in Databases Regulations 1997 (SI 1997/3032), reg. 29.

[132] *Pachot Decision* (1986) 129 RIDA 130. This was instead of its usual imprint of the author's personality test.

[133] (1986) 17 IIC 681.

where photographs (where original) were protected by copyright and (where non-original) by related rights, Article 6 of the Term Directive permits protection for 'other photographs', i.e. those that do not result from the author's own intellectual creation. Therefore, under EU law two types of photographs may be protected: 'original' photographs and 'other' (non-original) photographs. Given that the UK did not incorporate explicitly a test of 'author's own intellectual creation' into the CDPA for photographs, can we say that UK law adequately distinguishes between original photographs and photographs which fail to meet this standard?

Finally, in the case of databases, variations in protection existed, although these were less pronounced than in the case of computer programs. France applied its originality test of 'imprint of the author's personality', while in Germany the test was 'personal intellectual creation'. In both jurisdictions, courts were reasonably generous in their application of these tests to tables and compilations. However, they were less willing than English courts to protect very mundane compilations. Thus, in Germany, telephone directories were held not to satisfy the test of 'personal intellectual creation'[134] and, in France, a table of wine information (listing wines by region, year, and quality) was held not to reflect the author's 'imprint of personality'.[135] In the UK, however, mundane compilations were regularly protected as literary works, including trade directories,[136] indexes of information,[137] betting coupons,[138] and football fixture lists.[139] UK courts appeared to take a generous approach to compilations and there were cases where compilations featuring marginal skill or judgment in their selection or arrangement of materials, but which involved considerable labour or expense, were protected.[140] Further, as we have seen from *Ladbroke v William Hill* discussed in the previous section, courts were prepared to consider the labour, skill, and judgment applied in collecting or generating data for a compilation, as well as that used in selecting or arranging data.[141] Finally, the scope of protection given to compilations was extensive, in that copying data, as opposed to the selection or arrangement of the contents of the compilation, was often treated as infringing.[142]

After being criticized by the European Commission for not implementing a test of 'author's own intellectual creation' in its legislation, the UK decided to incorporate this test into section 3A of the CDPA for databases. However, as was noted previously, implementation was clumsy because section 3 of the CDPA distinguishes between 'databases' and 'tables or compilations other than databases'. In other words, if a collection constitutes a 'database' according to the definition in section 3A, it will be classified as such and, as a result, will need to satisfy the test of author's own intellectual creation. But what about 'tables or compilations other than databases'? Will the traditional UK test of 'labour, skill, and judgment' (and its generous interpretation to compilations) apply? This point is addressed later when we briefly examine the ruling in *Football Dataco Ltd v Yahoo! UK Ltd*.[143] It is submitted,

---

[134] *Unauthorised Reproduction of Telephone Directories on CD-Rom* [2002] ECDR 3.
[135] *Compagnie des Courtiers Jures Piqueurs de Vins de Paris v Société DDB Needham* [2000] ECC 128.
[136] *Morris v Ashbee* (1868–9) LR 7 Eq 34; *Kelly v Morris* (1865–6) LR 1 Eq 697.
[137] *Blacklock v Pearson* [1915] 2 Ch 376.
[138] *Ladbroke (Football) Ltd v William Hill (Football) Ltd* [1964] 1 WLR 273.
[139] *Football League v Littlewoods* [1959] Ch 637.
[140] *Football League v Littlewoods* [1959] Ch 637.
[141] *Ladbroke (Football) Ltd v William Hill (Football) Ltd* [1964] 1 WLR 273.
[142] e.g. see *Waterlow Directories Ltd v Reed Information Services Ltd* [1992] FSR 409; *Waterlow Publishers Ltd v Rose* [1995] FSR 207; and *Elanco Products Ltd v Mandops Ltd* [1979] FSR 409.
[143] Case C-604/10 [2013] FSR 1.

however, that given the breadth of the definition of 'database' (discussed at 2.5.1.2.3) there are very few collections that will fall outside it. As such, there will be a minimal number of works that are tables or compilations *other* than databases and subject to the traditional UK originality test.

2.5.2.3.2 Judicial interpretation and harmonization

There have been several CJEU rulings addressing the originality standard under EU law. However, it is fair to say that the decision in *Infopaq* has had the most dramatic and far-reaching effect of them all. We turn, therefore, to consider this case.

Infopaq International A/S v Danske Dagblades Forening Case C-5/08 [2009] ECDR 16 (CJEU Fourth Chamber)

Infopaq is a media-monitoring organization that provides summaries of selected articles from Danish newspapers to its subscribers. Danske Dagblades Forening (DDF) is the professional body representing Danish newspapers in copyright matters. They complained that the Infopaq service involved several infringing reproductions of their members' copyright-protected newspaper articles. The data capture process used by Infopaq to provide its summaries consisted of manually registering the relevant publications in a database; scanning in the physical publications and creating a TIFF image file; translating the TIFF file into a text format; searching the text file to find certain search words; and finally producing a cover sheet which lists the page of the newspaper on which the search term was found in the newspaper and an 11-word extract comprising the search term plus the five words which come before and after the search word in the article.

The Dutch court referred several questions to the Court of Justice that centred on whether Infopaq's activities amounted to reproductions of part of the articles (i.e. literary works) within Article 2 of the Information Society Directive (Directive 2001/29) and whether some of these acts could be exempt as transient reproductions pursuant to Article 5(1) of the same directive. In order to answer the question concerning the scope of the reproduction right in Article 2, the Court of Justice considered that it had to investigate the basis for protection of a work, as the following extract shows.

Court of Justice (Fourth Chamber):

30 By its first question, the national court asks, essentially, whether the concept of 'reproduction in part' within the meaning of Directive 2001/29 is to be interpreted as meaning that it encompasses the storing and subsequent printing out on paper of a text extract consisting of 11 words.

31 It is clear that Directive 2001/29 does not define the concept of either 'reproduction' or 'reproduction in part'.

32 In those circumstances, those concepts must be defined having regard to the wording and context of art.2 of Directive 2001/29, where the reference to them is to be found and in the light of both the overall objectives of that Directive and international law (see, to that effect, *SGAE*, [34] and [35] and case-law cited).

33 Article 2(a) of Directive 2001/29 provides that authors have the exclusive right to authorise or prohibit reproduction, in whole or in part, of their works. It follows that protection of the author's right to authorise or prohibit reproduction is intended to cover 'work'.

34 It is, moreover, apparent from the general scheme of the Berne Convention, in particular arts 2(5) and (8), that the protection of certain subject-matters as artistic or literary works presupposes that they are intellectual creations.

35 Similarly, under arts 1(3) of Directive 91/250, 3(1) of Directive 96/9 and 6 of Directive 2006/116, works such as computer programs, databases or photographs are protected by copyright only if they are original in the sense that they are their author's own intellectual creation.

36 In establishing a harmonised legal framework for copyright, Directive 2001/29 is based on the same principle, as evidenced by recitals 4, 9–11 and 20 in the preamble thereto.

37 In those circumstances, copyright within the meaning of art.2(a) of Directive 2001/29 is liable to apply only in relation to a subject-matter which is original in the sense that it is its author's own intellectual creation.

…

39 In the light of the considerations referred to in [37] of this judgment, the various parts of a work thus enjoy protection under art.2(a) of Directive 2001/29, provided that they contain elements which are the expression of the intellectual creation of the author of the work.

The Court of Justice took the rather radical step of making the exception as regards harmonization of originality the rule. More specifically, it inferred that because the Berne Convention protects literary and artistic works that are 'intellectual creations' and the EU protects computer programs, photographs, and databases by copyright where they are the author's own intellectual creation, copyright applies to *all* works of authors covered by the Information Society Directive *only* where they are original in the sense of being the author's own intellectual creation. In other words, it stipulated a generalized test of originality for *all* authorial works and thus in effect harmonized originality in the EU via the back door.

The Court went on to consider the scope of protection of a work and in so doing elaborated on what sorts of contribution might satisfy the originality standard of 'author's own intellectual creation'.

44 As regards newspaper articles, their author's own intellectual creation, referred to in [37] of this judgment, is evidenced clearly from the form, the manner in which the subject is presented and the linguistic expression. In the main proceedings, moreover, it is common ground that newspaper articles, as such, are literary works covered by Directive 2001/29.

45 Regarding the elements of such works covered by the protection, it should be observed that they consist of words which, considered in isolation, are not as such an intellectual creation of the author who employs them. It is only through the choice, sequence and combination of those words that the author may express his creativity in an original manner and achieve a result which is an intellectual creation.

46 Words as such do not, therefore, constitute elements covered by the protection.

It might have been thought that because *Infopaq* was a decision of the Fourth Chamber and the facts of the case involved infringement of newspaper articles, the ruling on originality could be viewed as an anomaly, or as not binding on matters of subsistence or, at the very least, limited to literary works. However, subsequent CJEU rulings have confirmed the wider application of *Infopaq*. Thus, in *Bezpečnostní softwarová asociace v Ministerstvo kultury*[144] the CJEU relied on *Infopaq* to support the conclusion that a graphic user interface might be protected under the Information Society Directive (but not as a computer program under the Software Directive) where it was original in the sense of the author's own intellectual creation.[145] And in *Football Association Premier League v QC Leisure; Murphy v Media Protection Services*[146] the CJEU relied on *Infopaq* in stating that, in principle, a football match could be protected under the Information Society Directive if it was original 'in the sense that it is its author's own intellectual creation'. However, they went on to hold that sporting events were not in fact intellectual creations because the rules of football left 'no room for creative freedom'.[147]

Should we welcome this judicial harmonization of the originality standard? On the one hand, we could say that it at least ensures the same test of originality is applied to all works. As well, we could say that a general test of originality makes up for the fact that there is no harmonized approach to subject matter, i.e. what can constitute a 'work' under copyright law. Then again, perhaps this indirectly harmonizes the approach to subject matter so that the sole criterion is whether it is the author's own intellectual creation, and a Member State, such as the UK, would have to abandon its closed list approach to subject matter. As well, is it legitimate for the Court of Justice to generalize the test of originality in this way given that EU legislation has only intervened to harmonize originality for three specific types of subject matter? Considerable uncertainty also arises, not least in whether national courts will have to entirely abandon their 'home grown' approaches to originality.

In subsequent rulings of the CJEU, some light has been shed on the content of the 'author's own intellectual creation' standard. In *SAS Institute*, which concerned computer programs (and was discussed at 2.5.1.2.2), two of the questions related to whether the reproduction of certain elements of a user manual for a computer program (which was protected as a literary work) in another computer program was an infringement within Article 2(a) of the Information Society Directive (Directive 2001/29). The Court of Justice (Grand Chamber) ruled as follows:

66 In the present case, the keywords, syntax, commands and combinations of commands, options, defaults and iterations consist of words, figures or mathematical concepts which, considered in isolation, are not, as such, an intellectual creation of the author of the computer program.

67 It is only through the choice, sequence and combination of those words, figures or mathematical concepts that the author may express his creativity in an original manner and achieve a result, namely the user manual for the computer program, which is an intellectual creation (see, to that effect, *Infopaq International* [2009] ECR I-6569 at [45]).

68 It is for the national court to ascertain whether the reproduction of those elements constitutes the reproduction of the expression of the intellectual creation of the author of the user manual for the computer program at issue in the main proceedings.

Once again we see originality being considered in the context of infringement (a point that we return to at 4.2.1.2). However, this discussion also allows us to glean what the CJEU might consider as relevant to intellectual creation—is this the exercise of creative choice(s)?

---

[144] Case C-393/09 [2011] ECDR 3, [2011] FSR 18.   [145] [45]–[46].
[146] Joined Cases C-403 and 429/08 [2012] FSR 1.   [147] [97], [98].

In a later ruling, *Painer v Standard Verlags GmbH*,[148] the Court of Justice (Third Chamber) had to consider whether a portrait photograph could be protected by copyright.

Painer v Standard Verlags GmbH Case C-145/10 [2012] ECDR 6

Ms Painer was a freelance photographer who had taken portrait photographs of a young girl, then aged ten. The photographs were sold but without granting any rights over them or consenting to publish them. The girl was subsequently abducted and then escaped from her captor some eight years later. The defendants, who were newspaper and magazine publishers, published Ms Painer's photographs of the young girl without proper attribution of her as the author. In an action brought by Ms Painer to stop the defendants from reproducing and publishing her photographs without her consent, the Austrian court referred several questions to the CJEU including whether Article 6 of the Term Directive, which protects photographs that are the result of the author's own intellectual creation, applied here.

Court of Justice (Third Chamber):

86 Therefore, the referring court's question must be understood as asking, in essence, whether art.6 of Directive 93/98 must be interpreted as meaning that a portrait photograph can, under that provision, be protected by copyright and, if so, whether, because of the allegedly too minor degree of creative freedom such photographs can offer, that protection, particularly as regards the regime governing reproduction of works provided for in art.2(a) of Directive 2001/29, is inferior to that enjoyed by other works, particularly photographic works.

87 As regards, first, the question whether realistic photographs, particularly portrait photographs, enjoy copyright protection under art.6 of Directive 93/98, it is important to point out that the Court has already decided, in *Infopaq International A/S v Danske Dagblades Forening* (C-5/08) [2009] E.C.R. I-6569; [2009] E.C.D.R. 16 at [35], that copyright is liable to apply only in relation to a subject-matter, such as a photograph, which is original in the sense that it is its author's own intellectual creation.

88 As stated in recital 17 in the preamble to Directive 93/98, an intellectual creation is an author's own if it reflects the author's personality.

89 That is the case if the author was able to express his creative abilities in the production of the work by making free and creative choices (see, *a contrario*, *Football Association Premier League Ltd v QC Leisure* (C-403/08 & C-429/08) [2012] FSR 1 at [98]).

90 As regards a portrait photograph, the photographer can make free and creative choices in several ways and at various points in its production.

91 In the preparation phase, the photographer can choose the background, the subject's pose and the lighting. When taking a portrait photograph, he can choose the framing, the angle of view and the atmosphere created. Finally, when selecting the snapshot, the photographer may choose from a variety of developing techniques the one he wishes to adopt or, where appropriate, use computer software.

92 By making those various choices, the author of a portrait photograph can stamp the work created with his 'personal touch'.

---

[148] Case C-145/10 [2012] ECDR 6.

93 Consequently, as regards a portrait photograph, the freedom available to the author to exercise his creative abilities will not necessarily be minor or even non-existent.

94 In view of the foregoing, a portrait photograph can, under art.6 of Directive 93/98, be protected by copyright if—which it is for the national court to determine in each case—such photograph is an intellectual creation of the author reflecting his personality and expressing his free and creative choices in the production of that photograph.

The CJEU uses the language of 'free and creative choices' and the author stamping the work with her 'personal touch' to elaborate upon the EU originality standard of author's own intellectual creation. Referring back to our discussion of originality of artistic works at 2.5.1.5, do you think that the traditional UK test is consistent with the approach adopted in *Painer*? Would we expect the photographs at issue in *Bridgeman* (photographs of paintings) and *Antiquesportfolio* (photographs of 3D artworks) to satisfy the 'author's own intellectual creation' test?

In *Temple Island Collections Ltd v New English Teas Ltd*,[149] one of the issues was whether a photograph of a red Routemaster bus travelling across Westminster Bridge, with the Houses of Parliament and Big Ben in the background, was protected by copyright. HHJ Birss QC noted that it was common ground that, based on *Infopaq* and *Painer*, copyright may subsist in a photograph if it is the author's own intellectual creation.[150] He went on to indicate that while the language of intellectual creation differed 'from the way in which an English court would traditionally express itself in a copyright case' there was little difference in approach.[151] Do you agree? He went on to add: 'What is decisive are the arrangements (motif, visual angle, illumination, etc.) selected by the photographer himself or herself.'[152] Further, that the 'composition of the image can be the product of the skill and labour (or intellectual creation) of a photographer and it seems to me that skill and labour/intellectual creation directed to that end can give rise to copyright'.[153] HHJ Birss QC concluded that the claimant's work was plainly original. The expression of skill and labour or the author's intellectual creation had been demonstrated, 'both in terms of his choices relating to the basic photograph itself: the precise motif, angle of shot, light and shade, illumination, and exposure and also in terms of his work after the photograph was taken to manipulate the image to satisfy his own visual aesthetic sense'.[154] The fact that the photograph featured iconic images of London did not detract from this conclusion.

It is interesting to note that in *Temple Islands* the traditional UK test of 'skill and labour' was treated as interchangeable with or equivalent to 'intellectual creation'. Would you agree? In *Newspaper Licensing Agency v Meltwater and the PRCA*,[155] Chancellor Morritt went further and observed that *Infopaq* referred to intellectual creation in the sense of origin and, as such, did not qualify the long-standing test established by *University of London Press Ltd v University of London Tutorial Press Ltd*[156] and *Ladbroke v William Hill* (discussed earlier). By way of contrast, the Court of Appeal in *SAS Institute* observed that, '[i]f the Information Society Directive has changed the traditional domestic test … it has raised rather than lowered the hurdle to obtaining copyright protection'.[157] As such, the EU originality test is having a mixed reception in UK courts. Does this represent a judicial resistance to the EU originality standard or reflect the difficulties of translating EU 'autonomous' concepts into Member States' domestic law?

[149] [2012] EWPCC 1, [2012] FSR 9.   [150] [18].   [151] [20].   [152] [20].   [153] [27].
[154] [51].   [155] [2011] EWCA Civ 890, [19]–[20].   [156] [1916] 2 Ch 601.
[157] *SAS Institute Inc. v World Programming Ltd* [2013] EWCA Civ 1482, [2014] RPC 8, [37].

A final example of where the European harmonization of originality has caused friction and uncertainty, at least in its application in the UK to databases, is illustrated by *Football Dataco v Yahoo! Ltd*.

Football Dataco v Yahoo! UK Ltd Case C-604/10 [2013] FSR 1 (CJEU Third Chamber)

The case involved, inter alia, whether the football league fixture lists for England and Scotland were the subject of copyright. At first instance, Floyd J found that the process of producing the fixture list entailed very significant skill and labour and not merely 'sweat of the brow', particularly in order to reconcile the various competing parameters, such as the number of fixtures to be played, allowing for international matches, facilitating requests from clubs, and ensuring that no club had more than three consecutive home or away matches. Floyd J also found that Article 3 of the Database Directive, which refers to the selection or arrangement of contents of the database being the author's own intellectual creation, did not exclude selection decisions that were made in the process of creating the contents. Finally, he rejected the argument that databases could still be protected if they satisfied the traditional UK test of originality. On appeal, the Court of Appeal believed that the points raised were not *acte claire* and so referred several questions to the CJEU. Question 1, in essence, concerned the content of the 'author's own intellectual creation' originality standard for databases and question 2 asked whether the directive precluded national copyright protection of databases other than that provided for by the Database Directive. The CJEU ruled as follows on question 1:

> 38 As regards the setting up of a database, that criterion of originality is satisfied when, through the selection or arrangement of the data which it contains, its author expresses his creative ability in an original manner by making free and creative choices (see, by analogy, *Infopaq International* [2010] FSR 20 at [45]; *Bezpečnostní softwarová asociace* [2011] FSR 18 at [50]; and *Painer* [2012] ECDR 6 at [89]) and thus stamps his 'personal touch' (*Painer* [2012] ECDR 6 at [92]).
>
> 39 By contrast, that criterion is not satisfied when the setting up of the database is dictated by technical considerations, rules or constraints which leave no room for creative freedom (see, by analogy, *Bezpečnostní softwarová asociace* [2011] FSR 18 at [48] and [49], and *Football Association* [2012] FSR 1 at [98]).
>
> 40 As is apparent from both art.3(1) and recital 16 of Directive 96/9, no other criteria than that of originality is to be applied to determine the eligibility of a database for the copyright protection provided for by that directive.
>
> 41 Therefore, on the one hand, provided that the selection or arrangement of the data—namely, in a case such as the one in the main proceedings, data corresponding to the date, the time and the identity of teams relating to the different fixtures of the league concerned (see [26] of the present judgment)—is an original expression of the creativity of the author of the database, it is irrelevant for the purpose of assessing the eligibility of the database for the copyright protection provided for by Directive 96/9 whether or not that selection or arrangement includes 'adding important significance' to that data, as mentioned in s.(b) of the referring court's first question.

42 On the other hand, the fact that the setting up of the database required, irrespective of the creation of the data which it contains, significant labour and skill of its author, as mentioned in s.(c) of that same question, cannot as such justify the protection of it by copyright under Directive 96/9, if that labour and that skill do not express any originality in the selection or arrangement of that data.

43 In the present case, it is for the referring court to assess, in the light of the factors set out above, whether the football fixture lists in question in the main proceedings are databases which satisfy the conditions of eligibility for the copyright protection set out in art.3(1) of Directive 96/9.

44 In that respect, the procedures for creating those lists, as described by the referring court, if they are not supplemented by elements reflecting originality in the selection or arrangement of the data contained in those lists, do not suffice for the database in question to be protected by the copyright provided for in art.3(1) of Directive 96/9.

Having digested the above extract, do you think it is fair to say that the EU test of originality for databases is more stringent than the traditional UK test of 'labour, skill, and judgment' (also referred to as 'skill and labour' by some courts) and, if so, in what ways?

On the second question, the Court noted that Article 3 of the Database Directive sought to harmonize the criteria for determining copyright protection of a database. As such, it made no sense for national laws, other than honouring the transitional arrangements contained in Article 14(2) of the directive, to grant copyright to databases under conditions different to those stipulated in Article 3(1).[158] While this ruling clarifies that compilations that fall within the definition of database in section 3A must satisfy the test of author's own intellectual creation, it leaves untouched the oddity that tables or compilations *other* than databases (i.e. those which fall outside the definition of 'database') are subject to the traditional UK test of originality. As has been mentioned already, this is likely to concern only a marginal number of compilations.

FURTHER READING

R. Casas Vallés, 'The requirement of originality' in E. Derclaye (ed.), *Research Handbook on the Future of EU Copyright Law* (Cheltenham: Edward Elgar, 2009), pp. 102–32.

E. Derclaye, '*Infopaq International A/S v Danske Dagblades Forening* (C-5/08): wonderful or worrisome? The impact of the ECJ ruling in *Infopaq* on UK copyright law' [2010] EIPR 247.

J. Griffiths, 'Dematerialization, pragmatism, and the European copyright resolution' (2013) 33 Oxford Journal of Legal Studies 767.

G. W. G. Karnell, 'European originality: a copyright chimera' in J. Kabel et al. (eds), *Intellectual Property and Information Law* (The Hague: Kluwer, 1998), pp. 201–9.

A. Rahmatian, 'Originality in UK copyright law: the old 'skill and labour' doctrine under pressure' (2013) 44 IIC 4.

E. Rosati, *Originality in EU Copyright: Full Harmonisation through Case Law* (Cheltenham: Edward Elgar, 2013).

---

[158] *Football Dataco*, [48]–[50].

E. Rosati, 'Towards an EU-wide copyright? (Judicial) pride and (legislative) prejudice' [2013] IPQ 47.

S. Vousden, '*Infopaq* and the Europeanisation of copyright law' [2010] WIPO J 197.

N. Walravens, 'The concept of originality and contemporary art' in D. McClean and K. Schubert (eds), *Dear Images: Art, Copyright and Culture* (Manchester: Ridinghouse, 2002), pp. 171–95.

2.5.3 FIXATION

Although Article 5(2) of the Berne Convention prohibits formalities, Article 2(2) states that it shall be for Union members 'to prescribe that works in general or any specified categories of works shall not be protected unless they have been fixed in some material form'. The UK adopts a 'fixation' requirement expressly in relation to literary, dramatic, and musical works, since section 3(2) of the CDPA stipulates that copyright will not subsist in these works 'unless and until it is recorded, in writing or otherwise'. The definition of 'writing' in section 178 is such that this would include digital or electronic recordings. It is important to note that, according to section 3(3) of the CDPA, someone other than the author can record the work and that it is immaterial whether the work is recorded by or with the permission of the author. Where the work is recorded by someone other than the author, section 3(3) envisages that distinct copyrights may arise—one in the content and one in the recording as such.

In relation to artistic works, there is no express requirement of fixation. However, is it possible to argue that fixation is implicit in the notion of an artistic work? In considering this question, it is worthwhile reconsidering the extracts from *Merchandising Corporation of America v Harpbond* and also *Creation Records* that were referred to at 2.5.1.5.

For films, sound recordings, and typographical arrangements of published editions, fixation is inherent in their definitions. Thus, a 'film' is 'a recording on any medium from which a moving image may by any means be produced'[159] and a 'sound recording' is 'a recording of sounds, from which the sounds may be reproduced'.[160] With typographical arrangements of published editions, the notion of 'published edition' seems to assume fixation.

The only category that clearly does not have a fixation requirement is that of 'broadcast'. This is because 'broadcast' is defined as 'an electronic transmission of visual images, sounds or other information' and so by its very nature is ephemeral. However, as a matter of practice it is often the case that broadcasts, whilst they are being transmitted, are recorded.

Why is it, particularly in relation to literary, musical, and dramatic works, that UK copyright law requires fixation? What kinds of work does such a requirement exclude and is this defensible? Does it make sense to retain fixation as a requirement of protection, as opposed to, say, as an evidential requirement (which is the position in France)? Finally, is it still possible for the UK to retain its fixation requirement in light of EU case law that suggests that all

---

[159] CDPA, s. 5B(1).   [160] CDPA, s. 5A(1)(a).

that is required for subject matter to be classified as copyright works is that they are original in the sense of being an author's own intellectual creation?

FURTHER READING

D. J. Brennan and A. F. Christie, 'Spoken words and copyright subsistence in Anglo-American law' [2000] IPQ 309.

Y. Gendreau, 'The criterion of fixation in copyright law' (1994) 159 RIDA 110.

A. Latreille, 'From idea to fixation: a view of protected works' in E. Derclaye (ed.), *Research Handbook on the Future of EU Copyright Law* (Cheltenham: Edward Elgar, 2009), pp. 133–47.

2.5.4 QUALIFICATION

Qualification is a prerequisite to copyright protection[161] and may arise via the author, the place of publication, or, in the case of a broadcast, the place from where the broadcast was made.

A work will qualify for copyright protection if, at the material time, the author was a qualifying person.[162] A qualifying person is either:

(1) a British citizen;

(2) an individual domiciled or resident in the UK or another country to which the relevant provisions of Chapter IX of the CDPA extend;

(3) a body incorporated under the law of a part of the UK or of another country to which the relevant provisions of Chapter IX extend or are applied.

The material time for literary, dramatic, musical, or artistic works is, in the case of unpublished works, when the work was made and in the case of published works, when the work was first published.[163] In the case of sound recordings, films, and broadcasts it is when the work was made. For typographical arrangements of published editions, it is when the edition was first published.[164]

Literary, dramatic, musical, and artistic works; films; sound recordings; and typographical arrangements may also qualify for protection if first published in the UK or in another country to which the relevant provisions of Chapter IX extend or are applied.

Finally, a broadcast qualifies for protection if it is made from a place in the UK or a country to which the relevant provisions of Chapter IX extend or are applied.

Countries to which Chapter IX extends include England, Wales, Scotland, and Northern Ireland and may include any of the Channel Islands, the Isle of Man, and any colony.[165] Countries to which Chapter IX does not extend but may be applied by Order in Council are Convention countries[166] and Member States of the EU.

---

[161] See CDPA, ss. 1(3) and 153(1). Except this does not apply to Crown or parliamentary copyright.

[162] CDPA, s. 154.   [163] CDPA, s. 154(4).   [164] CDPA, s. 154(5).   [165] CDPA, s. 157.

[166] s. 159(4) defines 'Convention country' to mean 'a country which is a party to a Convention relating to copyright to which the United Kingdom is also a party'. This would include, e.g., the Berne Convention, Rome Convention, and TRIPS Agreement.

2.5.5 PUBLIC POLICY EXCLUSION

Even if the above requirements for subsistence of copyright have been satisfied, courts retain, as part of their inherent jurisdiction, the ability to deny protection on public policy grounds. Courts may refuse to recognize the existence of copyright in a work or they may recognize copyright but deny a remedy to the owner. The public policy grounds that have warranted such intervention in the past include immorality[167] and fraudulent and deceptive works.[168] Also, in *Attorney-General v Guardian Newspapers Ltd (No. 2)*[169] Lord Jauncey commented *obiter* that because the book *Spycatcher* was published in breach of a confidential obligation owed to the Crown, his action 'reeked of turpitude' and it was 'inconceivable that a United Kingdom court would afford to him or his publishers any protection in relation to any copyright which either of them may possess in the book'.[170]

> **FURTHER READING**
>
> A. Sims, 'The denial of copyright protection on public policy grounds' [2008] EIPR 189.

---

[167] *Glyn v Weston Feature Film Co.* [1916] 1 Ch 261.
[168] *Slingsby v Bradford Patent Truck and Trolley Co.* [1905] WN 122, [1906] WN 51.
[169] [1990] 1 AC 109.
[170] *Attorney-General v Guardian Newspapers Ltd (No. 2)* [1990] 1 AC 109, 294.

3

COPYRIGHT II:
AUTHORSHIP, OWNERSHIP, EXPLOITATION, TERM, MORAL RIGHTS, AND ECONOMIC RIGHTS

3.1 INTRODUCTION

In this chapter we consider which persons are designated as the authors and owners of copyright works and the significance of this designation. As we will see, the concept of originality that we explored at length in the previous chapter has relevance to questions of authorship. We also examine how owners of copyright can exploit their works by either assignment or licence and the circumstances in which courts can imply terms in the absence of parties having agreed as to how a copyright work can be exploited. The term of copyright protection and the extensions that have recently been adopted are also discussed. Finally, we examine the exclusive rights, both moral and economic in nature, that authors and owners respectively have in their copyright works.

3.2 AUTHORSHIP

3.2.1 IDENTIFYING THE AUTHOR

Being able to identify the author is important for several reasons. First, as discussed in the previous chapter at 2.5.4, a work will qualify for copyright protection if, at the material time, the author was a qualifying person. Second, for literary, dramatic, musical, and artistic works, the term of protection is calculated *post mortem auctoris*, i.e. 70 years after the death of the author. Finally, as a general rule, the author of the work will be its first owner according to section 11(1) of the Copyright, Designs and Patents Act 1988 (CDPA) and thus able to exercise the economic rights that inhere in that work. As well, moral rights will vest in the author of a literary, dramatic, musical, or artistic work and one of the authors of a film (the principal director).

At the international level, there is no definition of 'author', despite the fact that authors are central to the Berne Convention (directed, as it is, at the protection of *authors* of literary and artistic works). We can, however, infer that authors of literary and artistic works (within the meaning of Article 2(1) of Berne) must be natural persons, as opposed to legal persons.[1] This is because, as already mentioned at 2.5.2.1, literary and artistic works must be intellectual creations and it would be counterintuitive to think that legal persons could exercise the requisite mental effort. Further, the *post mortem auctoris* calculation of term (i.e. fixed term after death) makes sense in the context of natural persons, who clearly will die whereas this cannot be guaranteed for legal persons. It is also the case that requiring, as minimum rights, the right of attribution and integrity (i.e. moral rights) makes most sense in the context of natural persons as authors. Finally, the fact that Article 4(a) of Berne refers to *makers* of cinematographic works suggests legal persons are encompassed for this type of work, and *a contrario* that the general rule is that authors must be natural persons.

Turning to UK copyright law, who, then, is the author of the work? Section 9(1) of the CDPA stipulates that it is the person who *creates* the work. Thus, there is a clear link between the notions of authorship and originality, a point that was aptly illustrated by *Walter v Lane* discussed at 2.5.2.2. The person who contributes the relevant originality (whether that be 'skill and labour' or 'intellectual creation' will be the person who creates the work and thus its author).

In the case of sound recordings, broadcasts, typographical arrangements of published editions, and films, further guidance as to authorship is provided by section 9(2) of the CDPA. It is the producer for sound recordings, the person making the broadcast in the case of broadcasts, the publisher in the case of typographical arrangements, and, finally, the principal director *and* producer in the case of films. Note that the inclusion of the principal director as one of the co-authors of a film was the result of EU copyright harmonization.[2] Prior to this, only the producer was the author of a film under UK law. 'Producer' is further defined in section 178 of the CDPA as 'the person by whom the arrangements necessary for the making of the sound recording or film are undertaken'. For these types of work, do you think that it is possible for legal entities to be authors and if so, why? Does this conflict with the Berne Convention at all?

For literary, dramatic, musical, or artistic works, identifying the author will involve asking who has contributed the relevant originality. The difficulty, of course, as we explored in the previous chapter, is which test of originality will be used—the traditional UK test of 'labour, skill, and judgment' or the EU test of 'author's own intellectual creation'? Even if it is clear that it should be the EU test, UK courts may struggle effectively to apply the EU test because of a lack of clarity or understanding about how the two tests differ. In the case of sound recordings and films, the enquiry is whether or not someone is the 'producer' and this involves identifying the person who has undertaken the necessary arrangements for making the sound recording or film. The following case reviews the various authorities and the sorts of considerations that point to whether someone is a producer or not.

---

[1] See S. Ricketson and J. Ginsburg, *International Copyright and Neighbouring Rights: The Berne Convention and Beyond* (2nd edn, Oxford: Oxford University Press, 2005), pp. 369–72, paras 7.12–7.14.

[2] See Directive 92/100/EEC of 19 November 1992 on Rental and Lending Rights codified by Directive 2006/115/EC, Art. 2 and Directive 93/98/ EEC of 29 October 1993, Harmonising the Term of Protection of Copyright and Certain Related Rights codified by Directive 2006/116/EC, Art. 2.

Bamgboye v Reed [2004] EMLR 5

The case concerned disputed ownership of copyright in the musical work and sound recording of a song called 'Bouncing Flow'. The first claimant (Mr Bamgboye) had worked as a trainee tape operator and sound engineer at a particular recording studio. The track 'Bouncing Flow' was conceived and recorded at sessions at the recording studio, during which sessions the first claimant alleged that he had contributed drum and bass-line parts and cymbal effects. After the track was recorded, the first defendant (Mr Reed) used equipment at the first claimant's home to further work on and master the recording. Deputy Judge Hazel Williamson QC held that Mr Bamgboye was a joint author of the musical work. However, in relation to the sound recording she found that the first defendant was the producer.

Deputy Judge Hazel Williamson QC:

47. Identifying the relevant person is said to be a matter of fact, and I have been referred helpfully to various authorities that deal with that. These show, in particular, that 'undertaking these arrangements' effectively means to be responsible for producing the sound recording in the financial sense or generally.

48. Mr Harbottle, in his closing submissions, drew my attention to certain authorities giving examples of the way in which the court had approached the question of who had undertaken the arrangements for the making of sound recordings and films, because the same principles obviously apply. He referred me to *Adventure Film Productions v Tully* [1993] EMLR 376 in which on an application for interim relief, the claimant who provided the funds for a film that was actually shot by others on its behalf, the funds coming from Channel 4, was held to be sufficiently likely to be the owner of a film copyright that a serious issue should go forward to trial. In *Mad Hat Music v Pulse 8 Records* [1993] EMLR 172, there was a claim that the second defendant owned copyright in a sound recording because, as the first claimant's manager, it had made her available for the recording sessions, although others, namely the defendants, had made other arrangements which included paying for the studio time. It was held again that this raised a serious question to be tried.

49. The case I probably found must useful was *Century Communications Ltd v Mayfair Entertainment Ltd* [1993]. This was a case in which a film had been produced by E on the Chinese mainland, but to do this it had had to bring in assistance from another company known as C, and it was held that even though C was responsible for obtaining the permissions and shooting the film, arrangements for making it had in fact been made by E, since E had initiated its making and organised the activity necessary for its making and paid for it. The particular passage that deals with this is briefly at p. 342 of the authority, where the learned judge said: 'Looking at the documents and appreciating that Era Communications could not make a film in mainland China without the help of CCP, it is plain to me that the arrangements necessary for the making of the film were undertaken by Era Communications. There never would have been a film had Era Communications not initiated its making and organised the activity necessary for its making and paid for it. To achieve that purpose they had to invoke the help of CCP and that Era Communications did. CCP made no arrangements, they simply helped Era Communications to make the film. Accordingly, I find that copyrights subsist in the film in that Era Communications was its author and, as is agreed, Era Communications is a body which qualifies for copyright protection. By documents that are not challenged, C is the present owner of the copyright and Era has distribution rights.' So the copyright in the film was given to E in that situation.

50. Finally, I should refer to the case of *Beggars Banquet Records v Carlton Television* [1993] EMLR at 349. A similar question arose as to who had undertaken the arrangements necessary for the making of a film, and it was in that case decided they do include finance, but the question arising is who, in fact, is directly responsible for the payment of the production costs rather than who is the person who might be the ultimate source of the funds. There is a passage in the judgment of Warner J which emphasises that in any case it is a question of fact who, in fact, made the arrangements.

...

86. The cases are often concerned with financial arrangements. No payments were involved here, so the real question, is who instigated the relevant recording and organised the activity necessary for its making? Mr Bamgboye has agreed that he would have regarded Bouncing Flow as finished, and it was Mr Reed who decided that further editing, recording and mastering was necessary. I find that it was Mr Reed who arranged, as it were, to get Mr Bamgboye to make available the house and the equipment. If this had not happened, it could have been done elsewhere. If that had happened it would have had to have been done by payment, but nonetheless the moving force, the person who got this recording made at the end of the day, seems to me to have been Mr Reed in substance, rather than it being a joint operation by Mr Reed and Mr Bamgboye.

87. As I have said, I found the *Century Communications v Mayfair Entertainment* case helpful in this regard. Without Mr Reed there would not have been the recording because he instigated everything, and the arrangements that he got Mr Bamgboye to make were subsidiary. It is right to say that Mr Bamgboye was assisting in the recording and, indeed, possibly even contributing to parts of the recording, but I find that that was a part of the artistic, or creative element of creating a musical piece, rather than part of undertaking the necessary arrangements for the sound recording as such. In so far as Mr Bamgboye did have any input that might be described as that, it was done at Mr Reed's behest to this extent that it was even anything that he did on his own behalf, perhaps by asking his father to let them have the computer in the relevant room, it was really not significant enough, and would have effectively been done as part of having been asked by Mr Reed to get the premises, and so forth, into position to make the final recording which Mr Reed was organising.

What are the key factors for determining who is the producer of a sound recording or film? How influential is the provision of finance to this assessment?

When it comes to identifying the author of a copyright work, it is important to remember that the CDPA sets out certain presumptions.[3] Thus, in the case of literary, dramatic, musical, or artistic works, where a name purporting to be that of the author appears on copies of the work, the person named shall be presumed, until the contrary is proved, to be the author of the work.[4] The same presumption applies in the case of works of joint authorship.[5] Likewise, with respect to sound recordings, if copies of the recording as issued to the public bear a label or other mark stating that a named person is the owner of copyright in the recording, this shall be presumed to be correct until the contrary is proved.[6] In the case of films, where copies of the film as issued to the public state that a named person is the director or producer of the film this shall be presumed to be correct until the contrary is proved.[7] The

---

[3] Note that the Berne Convention, Art. 15 permits such evidential presumptions.
[4] CDPA, s. 104(2)(a).   [5] CDPA, s. 104(3).   [6] CDPA, s. 105(1)(a).   [7] CDPA, s. 105(2)(a).

provisions on presumptions in sections 104 and 105 of the CDPA repay closer inspection. The general point to remember, however, is that these provisions create evidential presumptions that can be very valuable when it comes to litigation, a point that is highlighted by *Brighton v Jones*,[8] which is discussed at 3.2.2.2.

3.2.2 JOINT AUTHORSHIP

UK copyright law recognizes that works may be jointly authored. In section 10(1) of the CDPA it defines 'works of joint authorship' as:

> a work produced by the collaboration of two or more authors in which the contribution of each is not distinct from that of the other author or authors.

Notably, films are deemed to be works of joint authorship between the producer and principal director, unless these two persons are the same.[9]

3.2.2.1 Significance of joint authorship

A finding of joint authorship is significant to both duration and ownership of copyright. The term of protection, generally speaking, will be calculated according to 70 years after the death of the last remaining author.[10] Further, as a general rule, joint authorship will lead to joint ownership[11] and, as a result, this will constrain the behaviour of all co-owners in the manner described below.

Robin Ray v Classic FM [1988] FSR 622

The facts are described at 3.4.2.

> **Lightman J, at pp. 637–8:**
>
> It is common ground that joint authors hold copyright in the subject of the joint authorship as tenants in common entitled in equal shares. The defendant contends that, if it was a joint author of the copyright in the above five documents and the catalogue, as tenant in common it was entitled to exploit the copyright in the way it has because: (1) such exploitation did no damage to the copyright; and, (2) the only right of the plaintiff as co-owner is to an account of the profits earned.
>
> It is unnecessary to consider whether the use made of the copyright material did any damage, for it is quite clear that, even if the defendant was joint author of the five documents and the catalogue, joint ownership could not without the consent of the plaintiff justify the making of copies for the purpose of exploitation of the copyright abroad. The 1988 Act itself provides in section 16(2) that it is an infringement of copyright to do any of the restricted

---

[8] [2004] EMLR 26.   [9] CDPA, s. 10(1A).
[10] CDPA, s. 12(8). There are exceptions to this rule, including for Crown copyright and parliamentary copyright works: see ss. 163 and 166 respectively.
[11] CDPA, s. 11(1).

acts (which include making copies) without the consent of the 'copyright owner', and section 173(2) expressly provides that in case of joint owners this means the consent of all the owners. This result is in accord with the decision in *Cescinsky v George Routledge & Sons Ltd* [1916] 2 KB 325 and the view expressed by Laddie J in *Cala* (at 836). I reject the defendant's submission that the defendant as a joint owner is free to do a restricted act so long as he accounts to the plaintiff as its joint owner for a share of the profits, or that the right of the plaintiff is limited to claiming an account: the plaintiff is entitled to sue for infringement, claiming damages and an injunction.

What is the reason, do you think, for requiring all joint owners to consent to *any* exploitation of the work? Would it make more sense to allow each co-owner to exploit the work in certain circumstances (and, if so, which), but to account to each other for any profits that they make from such use?

For those that raise the issue of joint authorship and joint ownership many years after the work was created, there is the risk that the courts will refuse the claim based on the equitable doctrines of laches and estoppel, provided the defendant can establish detrimental reliance. In *Fisher v Brooker*,[12] the claimant waited some 38 years before claiming joint authorship and ownership of the musical work, 'A Whiter Shade of Pale', based on his contribution of the distinctive organ sections. Nevertheless, on the facts, the House of Lords held that the claimant was not prevented from successfully bringing his action since the respondents had not suffered detrimental reliance (indeed they had benefited from the delay in terms of receiving all the royalties). The claimant was thus declared joint author and joint owner of copyright in the work with a share of 40 per cent and able to claim future royalties on this basis.[13] Others, however, have not always been as successful.[14]

3.2.2.2 Requirement of 'contribution'

Joint authorship has been raised in numerous cases. Of the requirements contained in section 10(1) of the CDPA that of 'contribution' has received the most judicial attention. The principles for determining whether there is a relevant contribution are neatly summarized in the following case.

Brighton v Jones [2004] EMLR 26

The case involved a dispute about copyright in the play, *Stones In His Pockets*. The defendant had written the script of the play in 1996 and had been listed as the sole author on publicity material, whilst the first claimant had directed the first production of the play. The defendant rewrote elements of the script in 1999 and exploited it in various ways, achieving major commercial success. The first claimant alleged, inter alia, that she was a joint author, and therefore joint owner, of the play as a result of contributions made during rehearsals of the 1996 version, including suggested changes to plot and dialogue.

---

[12] [2009] UKHL 41, [2009] FSR 25.

[13] The claim that the claimant was estopped from asserting joint ownership was also rejected in *Beckingham v Hodgens* [2003] EWCA Civ 143, [2004] ECDR 6.

[14] *Godfrey v Lees* [1995] EMLR 307.

Park J:

[He began by rehearsing the principles of joint authorship:]

34. ... The Act itself does not expand upon the concept of joint authorship, but there have been a number of cases which have examined it. In my opinion three propositions can be extracted from the cases which may be relevant to this case.

(i) If someone claims to be a joint author, although the contribution which he needs to have made to the creation of the work does not have to be equal in magnitude to the contribution of the other joint author or authors, it still needs to be significant. In the *Robin Ray* case ... Lightman J said that he had to be someone 'who (as an author) provides a significant creative input'. In *Godfrey v Lees* [1995] EMLR 307 at 325 Blackburne J said: 'What the claimant to joint authorship of a work must establish is that he has made a significant and original contribution to the creation of the work ... It is not necessary that his contribution to the work is equal in terms of either quantity, quality or originality to that of his collaborators.' In *Hadley v Kemp* [1999] EMLR 589 at 643 I noted that, where a person is a joint author, the effect was that he had an equal share in the copyright, and I added: 'It would be surprising if a slight contribution was enough to make a person a joint author and thereby make him an equal owner with another or others who had contributed far more than he had.' I should, however, add that in the recent case of *Bamgboye v Reed* [2002] EWHC 2922 (QB); [2004] EMLR 5, the claimant was held to have been a joint author by reason of his contributions, but with a one-third share, not a half share: see [77] of the judgment of Hazel Williamson QC.

(ii) The contribution which a person claiming to be a joint author makes must be a contribution towards the creation of the work. A contribution, even a significant one, of a different kind will not cause him or her to be a joint author. *Fylde Microsystems Ltd v Key Radio Systems Ltd* [1998] FSR 449 concerned the ownership of the copyright in software which, on the face of it, had been written by Fylde Microsystems (acting by its employees). Key Radio Systems argued unsuccessfully that it was a joint author because of contributions which its employees had made. They had put much skill, time and effort into testing the software and ensuring that it would achieve the performance which was intended. Laddie J accepted that their contributions were extensive and technically sophisticated, and that they had required considerable time and effort; but he held that they were not contributions to the 'authoring' of the software. The skill was like a proof reader's skill, not authorship skill. Key Radio Systems had not contributed 'the right kind of skill and labour'. *Hadley v Kemp* (*supra*) is another example of the same point, this time in the context of a pop group. One member of the group devised the songs (the musical works), and the group as a whole performed them with much skill and flair. I held that the other members of the group were not joint authors. I said (at 643): '... contributions by the plaintiffs, however significant and skilful, to the performance of the musical works are not the right kind of contributions to give them shares in the copyrights. The contributions need to be to the creation of the musical works, not to the performance or interpretation of them.' The case can interestingly be compared with *Stuart v Barrett* [1994] EMLR 449, in which the songs of another group emerged from a process of 'collective jamming', and all the members were found to be joint authors.

(iii) However, a person can become a joint author even if he has not himself put pen to paper, but someone else has done that, effectively writing what the first person had created. *Cala Homes (South) Ltd v Alfred McAlpine Homes East Ltd* [1995] FSR 818 was about the copyright in drawings for aspects of house designs. The physical drawings had been prepared by staff of a business called Crawley Hodgson. However, the Crawley Hodgson staff had been very closely instructed, verbally and sometimes by means of sketches, by the design director of Cala Homes. Laddie J held that, on the facts, Cala Homes was a joint author. In the *Robin Ray* case … Lightman J ascribed a fairly narrow ambit to this concept: 'But in my judgment what is required is something which approximates to penmanship. What is essential is a direct responsibility for what actually appears on the paper … As it appears to me the architects in that case [Cala Homes] were in large part acting as "scribes" for the director. In practice such a situation is likely to be exceptional.'

…

[Park J went on to apply these principles to the facts:]

55. It must be remembered that, by virtue of s. 104(2), the burden of proof rests on Miss Brighton. The person described on the script of the play as the author was Miss Jones alone. She was also billed as the sole author in publicity material and in programmes. It never occurred to Miss Brighton to say that she ought to be regarded as a joint author until she commenced this case. None of that is conclusive against her, but it does at the least raise a substantial evidential hurdle for her to overcome.

56. I agree that, on all versions of what happened in the rehearsals, changes were made to Miss Jones' original script, and that the changes resulted from the experience of the rehearsals and the discussions in the rehearsals. I agree that Miss Brighton was involved in the rehearsals throughout, and I would accept (though the point was not specifically covered) that she probably knew about all the changes before they were made and had played a part in what had led to each of them. However, there are still several reasons why, in my opinion, she was not a joint author.

(i) In terms of the dialogue of the final play, I believe that 100 per cent of the words spoken (or as near to 100 per cent as makes no difference) were actually composed by Miss Jones. Miss Brighton no doubt identified passages and places where some rewriting was desirable, but it was Miss Jones who (if she agreed that there should be some rewriting at those points) actually chose the words which the actors were to use. There is a sentence in Miss Brighton's witness statement which reads: 'In respect of each Act, I was heavily responsible for the actual form of expression of the dialogue on paper.' That appears to be saying that Miss Brighton was responsible not just for determining where some rewriting was to take place, but also for determining what the precise new words were to be. All of the other evidence is contrary to that, and I do not accept it.

(ii) The point made in (i) above concerns the actual words used, and it is not in itself decisive. Copyright can subsist in a story or a plot, so that if what happened in rehearsals was that Miss Brighton determined what the plot of the play was to be (or Miss Brighton and Miss Jones determined in collaboration what it was to be), and then Miss Jones actually wrote the words to give effect to the plot, I can see that Miss Brighton might have been a joint author. But in my opinion that was not how it was. I believe that the script which Miss Jones provided in advance of the rehearsals, plus the fairly small part which she had not written before the rehearsals began but did write before the rehearsals got round to that part, contained a complete plot for the play. It was a dramatic work, and at that stage the copyright in it was solely owned by Miss Jones. (That conclusion is not changed by the use which Miss Jones made of Miss Brighton's draft opening script, as I will explain later.) I am sure that there were some changes to the plot before the final form of the 1996 script was reached, and I accept that Miss Brighton made her own input into what those changes were; but I do not believe that the changes were nearly significant enough to mean that a different dramatic work, of which Miss Brighton and Miss Jones were joint authors, had been created.

(iii) Just focusing on the changes, Miss Brighton had played a part in what led up to them, but in my view, on the general thrust of the evidence and bearing in mind the burden of proof, she has not established that the contributions which she made were contributions to the creation of the dramatic work rather than contributions to the interpretation and theatrical presentation of the dramatic work. In the expression used in the Fylde Microsystems case (see [34(ii)] above), they were not 'the right sort of contributions'.

(iv) It cannot be said that, whenever Miss Brighton wanted a change to be made to the script, Miss Jones simply and unquestioningly made it. I accept that she expected to have suggestions for changes made to her, that she was fully prepared to consider them, that she probably expected that she would agree to many of them, and that she did agree to many of them. But it is clear from the evidence which I summarised earlier that she would not make changes to the script if she did not agree to them. The decision whether to make a change or not was hers, and that was not just a theoretical position: it was also the reality of what actually happened.

(v) It is in any case unrealistic to distinguish, so far as the present issue is concerned, between what Miss Brighton did in the rehearsals and what the two actors did. The actors do not claim to have become joint authors simply by doing well one of the things which led to them being engaged: working on the rehearsals of a newly commissioned play which had not yet been performed, and by doing so assisting in making the script better than it had been before the rehearsals. It seems to me that Miss Brighton is in essentially the same position. Miss Jones presented her with a play upon which, during the rehearsals, she was expected to exercise her director's skills, together with Mr Murphy and Mr Hill exercising their actors' skills, in order to get it ready to be performed before live audiences. The actors did not become joint authors by reason of what they did, and I do not think that Miss Brighton became a joint author by reason of what she did either.

...

59. For the foregoing reasons my decision on Miss Brighton's joint authorship claim is that it fails.

What are the relevant principles for assessing whether a person has made a contribution sufficient to qualify for joint authorship? Do you agree with them? Can a clear distinction be drawn between contributions to the creation of a work and contributions to its performance? Also, why is it necessary for a person to have direct responsibility for expression in order to make an appropriate contribution?

3.2.2.3 Requirement of collaboration

A work of joint authorship also requires collaboration between two or more persons. In the following case, the Court of Appeal explored whether this means an intention to be joint authors.

Beckingham v Hodgens [2003] EWCA Civ 143, [2003] EMLR 18

The claimant in this case was a professional fiddle player who had been hired as a session musician for the recording of the song 'Young at Heart' by the Bluebells. He claimed that he had composed the violin part that featured in the introduction to the song and recurred several times throughout the song. At first instance, the claimant was held to have contributed the violin part and, as such, was a joint author and joint owner of the musical work. On appeal, it was argued, inter alia, that joint authorship in section 11(3) of the Copyright Act 1956 (which is in very similar terms to section 10(1) of the CDPA) required an intention to create a joint work, which was absent in this case.

Jonathan Parker LJ (with whom Laws LJ and Ward LJ agreed):

49. I reject the submission that s. 11(3) requires, as one of the elements of joint authorship, the existence of a common intention as to joint authorship. I do so for essentially the reasons which the judge gave.

50. In the first place, I agree with the judge that there is nothing in the express wording of s. 11(3) which warrants the imposition of such a requirement. The only requirements for a 'work of joint authorship' expressed in s. 11(3) are that the authors should have collaborated and that their contributions should not be 'separate'.

51. As *Levy v Rutley* makes clear, these requirements will not be met unless there has been 'joint labouring in furtherance of a common design' (see ibid. p. 529, per Keating J). But the 'common design' in that context is not an intention that there should be joint authorship.
    What Keating J was describing, as I read his judgment, was the process of jointly creating the work in question: as the judge in the instant case put it in para. 48 of the judgment, a 'common design to produce the work'. So much is clear, in my judgment, from the passage in Keating J's judgment which follows his reference to 'common design', where he says:

> I fail to discover any evidence that there was any co-operation of the two in the design of this piece [a play], or in its execution, or in any improvements either in the plot or the general structure … If the plaintiff and the author had agreed together to rearrange the plot, and so to produce a more attractive piece out of the original materials, possibly that might have made them joint authors of the whole. So, if two persons undertake jointly to write a play, agreeing in the general outline and design, and sharing the labour of working it out, each would be contributing to the whole production, and they might be said to be joint authors of it. But, to constitute joint authorship, there must be a common design. Nothing of the sort appears here. The plaintiff made mere additions to a complete piece, which did not in themselves amount to a dramatic piece, but were intended only to make the play more attractive to the audience.

52. As to the Canadian case of *Darryl Neudorf*, on which Mr Engelman naturally relies strongly, I agree with the judge that there is no basis in the English cases for importing the requirement of an intention as to joint authorship. In *Darryl Neudorf*, Cohen J followed the United States case of *Childress v Taylor* 945 F 2d 500. At p. 962 of the report of *Darryl Neudorf*, Cohen J said this:

> the creation of the intent to co-author requirement in *Childress v Taylor* happened despite the statutory definition of joint authorship…, not because of it. The court looked beyond the language of the section and moved on to review policy considerations in the application of the section. In particular, the court could not accept that Congress intended to extend joint

authorship to, for example, editors and researchers. It was for this reason that the court created the intent to co-author requirement.

53. In my judgment, the judge in the instant case was clearly right to confine his consideration to the language of s. 11(3) and not to look beyond the section into the uncertain realms of policy. So doing, he plainly reached the correct conclusion.

54. I would accordingly refuse permission to appeal on the s. 11(3) issue, confirming my earlier refusal of permission on the papers.

Thus, we see from the above case that collaboration means acting pursuant to a 'common design', as opposed to an intention to be joint authors, which is the case in the US and which is often judged according to whether each participant intended that all would be identified as co-authors. What are the benefits and disadvantages of omitting an intention requirement?

3.2.2.4 Requirement of 'not distinct'

According to section 10(1) of the CDPA, contributions must be 'not distinct' from those of the other author(s). This requirement has received little attention in the case law, but, at first instance in *Beckingham v Hodgens*,[15] Deputy Judge Christopher Floyd QC commented upon the requirement of 'not separate' in the Copyright Act 1956 as follows:

46. Finally there is the negative requirement: non-separateness. A work will not be a work of joint authorship if the contribution of the co-authors is separate. The example often given is of a literary work where separate authors contribute specific chapters, but there are other examples where the distinction made in the section may not be so easy to apply. I do not believe that a contribution to the arrangement of a song of the kind I am concerned with in this case is 'separate' in the sense in which that word is used in the section. The added part is heavily dependent on what is there already. Stripped of the voices and other instruments, the violin part would sound odd, and lose meaning. The final musical expression—what the audience will hear—is a joint one.

Does it make sense to adopt a test that asks whether or not the contribution is dependent on the other parts, in order to judge whether it is 'not distinct'? If not, what could be an alternative, workable test? What is the purpose of retaining the 'not distinct' requirement? Here, it is interesting to note that in the US a joint work requires the contribution to be 'merged into inseparable or interdependent parts of a unitary whole'.[16] Would it make sense to follow this approach instead?

FURTHER READING

W. R. Cornish, 'Authors in law' (1995) 58 Modern Law Review 1.

J. Ginsburg, 'The concept of authorship in comparative copyright law' (2003) 52 DePaul L. Rev. 1063.

S. Ricketson and J. Ginsburg, *International Copyright and Neighbouring Rights: The Berne Convention and Beyond* (2nd edn, Oxford: Oxford University Press, 2005), ch. 7.

---

[15] [2003] ECDR 6.   [16] US Copyright Act 1976, s. 101.

3.3 OWNERSHIP

3.3.1 EMPLOYEES

As a general rule the first owner of copyright in a work is its author.[17] However, this is not the case for works of Crown or parliamentary copyright. For works made by Her Majesty or by an officer or servant of the Crown in the course of his duties, the first owner of copyright in the work will be Her Majesty.[18] Where a work is made by or under the direction or control of either the House of Commons or House of Lords, or both Houses, then that House or both Houses will be the first owner or joint owners of copyright in the work. Another important exception to this general rule exists in relation to literary, dramatic, musical, and artistic works and films. Where the work is made by an employee in the course of his or her employment, in the absence of an agreement to the contrary, ownership will vest in the employer.[19] What is the rationale, do you think, behind such an exception to first ownership? Here, it is interesting to note the contrasting approach of civil law systems, such as France, where there is no presumed transfer of ownership of economic rights to the employer. Instead, article L111-1 of the Intellectual Property Code provides that 'the existence or conclusion of a contract for hire or of service by the author ... shall in no way derogate from the enjoyment of the right'. Instead, employers in France have to negotiate with employees to agree a transfer of such rights. Would this difference in the default rule of employee ownership produce different results in practice, do you think? French law, however, has had to soften its author-centric approach in order to implement Article 2(3) of the Software Directive, which provides that for computer programs created by an employee 'in the execution of his duties or following the instructions given by his employer, the employer exclusively shall be entitled to exercise all economic rights in the program so created, unless otherwise provided by contract'.[20]

Returning to the UK position, under section 11(2), an author must be an employee in order for that section to apply. Section 178 of the CDPA defines this as employment under a contract of service or of apprenticeship. The indicia of a contract of service, as opposed to a contract for services, were explored in the following case.

Beloff v Pressdram [1973] FSR 33

Ms Beloff had written a memorandum, excerpts of which were used by the defendant in its *Private Eye* publication. A key issue was whether or not Ms Beloff was an employee of *The Observer* newspaper. If so, she had created the memorandum in the course of employment and her employer owned copyright in the literary work, such that she did not have standing to bring the action against the defendant. Ungoed Thomas J held that Ms Beloff was an employee.

---

[17] CDPA, s. 11(1).   [18] CDPA, s. 163(1).   [19] CDPA, s. 11(2).
[20] Art. L113-9 of the French Intellectual Property Code 1992 provides: 'Unless otherwise provided by statutory provision or stipulation, the economic rights in the software and its documentation created by one or more employees in the execution of their duties or following the instructions given by their employer shall be the property of the employer and he exclusively shall be entitled to exercise them.' See also Art. 69b of German Copyright Law 1965.

Ungoed-Thomas J, at pp. 42, 45–6:

It thus appears, and rightly in my respectful view, that, the greater the skill required for an employee's work, the less significant is control in determining whether the employee is under a contract of service. Control is just one of many factors whose influence varies according to circumstances. In such highly skilled work as that of the plaintiff it seems of no substantial significance.

...

The plaintiff writes for the Observer a weekly article headed 'Politics-Nora Beloff': it is usually on one theme. She also writes profiles, and on the major speeches of politicians, and she even writes leaders. The Editor described her as 'a very active member of the general editorial staff' and said that she shared in the editorial responsibility of the newspaper. She is a regular attendant at weekly and ad hoc editorial meetings presided over by the Editor and whose wide scope is indicated by the functions of those who attend—deputy and assistant editors, chief reporters, the Business Editor, the Leader Writer, the News Editor, and others as advisable from time to time. The plaintiff said its purpose was to plan the paper for the next issue, to look ahead and to have a general discussion and exchange ideas. She said that her article for the following issue was very often discussed. The Editor said that she tells him what she is going to write and that discussion only arises if it overlaps with something else. The Editor has certainly some strong-minded persons attending these meetings and, as might be expected from his experience and wisdom, he said that 'my government is as a rule consensual'. The plaintiff said that she was free to decline to write on a suggested topic. Of course, she could not be forced to do so, nor can I imagine Mr Astor attempting to force her. The editorial meetings are for discussion, without power of decision; that rests solely with the Editor, and not the less so, although as a rule consensually exercised by him.

I come to other recognised indications of contract of service, in addition to her substantial regular salary for her full-time job and her holidays. Apart from an electric typewriter, which the plaintiff has at home, the plaintiff does not provide any equipment of her own which she uses for her work. All the Observer's resources are available to her to carry out her job. She has an office in the Observer building, and a secretary who is provided by the Observer. She does not use her own capital for the job, nor is her remuneration affected by the financial success or otherwise of the Observer. In addition to PAYE deductions, deduction for the pension scheme to which she belongs is also made by the Observer from her salary. All these indications are in favour of her contract being a contract of service.

It is not enough that the author is an employee—he or she must also have created the work in the course of employment in order for ownership to vest in the employer. The sorts of factors relevant to determining this question are explored in the case below.

Noah v Shuba [1991] FSR 14

Dr Noah had been employed as a consultant epidemiologist at the Public Health Laboratory Service (PHLS). He had written 'A Guide to Hygienic Skin Piercing' at home in the evenings and weekends, but had used the PHLS library and secretarial assistance. The guide had been first published by the PHLS. The defendant had written and published an article, which reproduced substantial extracts from Dr Noah's guide. The claimant brought proceedings alleging, inter alia, copyright infringement under the

Copyright Act 1956. The defendant argued that the owner of copyright in the guide was not Dr Noah but his employer.

Mummery J (as he then was), at pp. 25–6:

The primary submission made on behalf of Dr Noah is that the copyright in the Guide did not vest in the PHLS as his employer because he had not made it 'in the course of his employment' with PHLS. His evidence, which I accept, is that he wrote the Guide at home in the evenings and at weekends and not at the instigation of or on the direction of PHLS.

On behalf of Mr Shuba many points have been taken on the evidence as indicating that Dr Noah wrote the Guide in the course of his employment. It has been pointed out that under the terms of his conditions of service, which do not expressly deal with the matter of copyright, he was expected to report on research work by means of contributions to appropriate scientific journals and before recognised learned societies. Regulation 11 of the Staff Regulations provided that before doing so he should inform the Director of the Service and follow the normal practice of consulting colleagues who have been associated with him in collaborative investigations. It was, however, also provided in regulation 11 that the writing of scientific books or monographs, if undertaken, was 'not expected to be done in working hours'. It is also clear from regulation 3(b) and (c) that the writing of books and articles was in general to be regarded as something done 'in addition to official duties', though staff were entitled to undertake such work at the laboratory or elsewhere and to receive fees, provided that the work would not interfere with their official duties.

Mr Price, on behalf of Mr Shuba, pointed out that the PHLS functions included the provision to persons perceived as needing it information relevant to the control of infectious diseases; that the Guide fell within those functions and had been printed and published by PHLS at public expense; that Dr Noah's duties included the making of investigations and provision of information on subjects which were covered by the Guide; that the Guide had been designed to enable health authorities and other bodies to set and observe high and uniform standards in the implementation of the 1928 Act; that it could not be said that Dr Noah had undertaken the writing of the book in any private capacity and that the preparation of the Guide was part of the official duties which fell within the terms of his conditions of service. It was pointed out that the Guide could not be properly described as a 'private' venture by Dr Noah, since it was clear from the cover and the title page that it was a PHLS guide. The previous 1979 Tattooing Guide had been signed by Dr Noah in his official capacity as a consultant at the Communicable Diseases Surveillance Centre. The evidence showed that Dr Noah had used PHLS notepaper in order to send out letters to those from whom he solicited comments and views before settling on the final version of the Guide. The typescript of the Guide had been produced by his secretary at the Centre using PHLS time and equipment. In brief, it was submitted that the Guide was a PHLS venture involving the collaboration of staff at PHLS premises, including Dr Noah's colleague, Mr Peter Hoffman, who wrote one of the appendices in the Guide. Mr Price submitted that, if the court accepted Dr Noah's contention, this would result in the surprising consequence that Dr Noah, as owner of the copyright, would be in a position to invoke that copyright in order to prevent PHLS from reprinting and disseminating the Guide without his permission. This was surprising, it was argued, in view of the public functions of PHLS and the public interest in the whole question of hygiene and infectious diseases. I have not been persuaded by these points that Mr Shuba has discharged the burden of proving that Dr Noah made the Guide in the course of his employment. In my judgment, Dr Noah's position is very similar to that of the accountant in *Stevenson Jordan and Harrison Limited v McDonald and Evans* [1952] 1 TLR 101 in relation to copyright in lectures delivered by the accountant author who was employed under a contract of service. It was held that the provisions of the Copyright Act 1911 equivalent to section 4(4) did not apply. At page 111 Denning LJ pointed out that it had to be remembered that a man employed under a contract of service may sometimes perform services outside the contract. He gave the instance of a doctor on the staff of a hospital or the master on the staff of a school employed under a contract of service giving lectures or lessons orally to students. He expressed the view that if, for his own convenience, he put the lectures into writing then his written work was not done under the contract of service. It might be a useful accessory to his contracted work, but it was not part of it and the copyright vested in him and not in his employers. Morris LJ also pointed out at page 113 that, even though the employer in that case paid the expenses of the lecturer incurred in the delivery of a lecture and was prepared to type the lectures as written by any lecturer and even though it would not have been improper for that lecturer to have prepared his lecture in the company's time and used material obtained from its library, it had not been shown that the accountant could have been ordered to write or deliver the lectures or that it was part of his duty to write or deliver them. In those circumstances the lectures were not written in the course of his employment.

Assessing whether a work has been created in the course of employment is very much a question of fact, to be determined in light of the factors discussed by Mummery J. Do you think it makes sense for the overriding factor to be whether or not the employee could have been ordered to create the particular work?

It is important to remember that if there is an agreement to the contrary, ownership of copyright works created in the course of employment may remain with the employee. In *Noah v Shuba*, Mummery J commented *obiter* that there was an agreement to the contrary.

Mummery J (as he then was), at pp. 26–7:

Although that conclusion is sufficient to dispose of the issue on ownership of copyright, I should add that, even if I had found that the Guide had been written by Dr Noah in the course of his employment, I would have found on the evidence before me that there was an implied term of his contract of service excluding the operation of the statutory rule in section 4(4) vesting the copyright in the work so made in the employer PHLS. Evidence was given by Dr Noah and also by Dr Christine Miller, who was a consultant epidemiologist at PHLS from 1967 to 1987 and the author of numerous publications on vaccination, that it had for long been the practice at PHLS for employees there to retain the copyright in work written by them, usually in the form of articles, in the course of their employment there. If, for example, the articles were published in learned journals, it was the author of the article and not the PHLS who, at the insistence of most learned journals, assigned the copyright to the publishers of the journal in question. At no relevant time has the copyright in those articles been claimed by PHLS. It has acquiesced in a practice under which that copyright was retained and then assigned by the employee authors. The position of the PHLS in relation to this case is consistent with that practice. It has accepted that the copyright in the Guide is vested in Dr Noah. In my judgment, this longstanding practice is sufficient material from which I can and do imply that it was a term of Dr Noah's appointment as consultant that he should be entitled to retain the copyright in works written by him in the course of his employment.

Mummery J implied an agreement (or more specifically a term in his employment contract) to the contrary because of the conduct of the PHLS. For employees wishing to retain copyright in the works it would be preferable to rely on an express, rather than implied, agreement to the contrary. Yet, is it a realistic possibility that employees will be able to negotiate such an agreement? If the UK followed a civil law approach and did not presumptively transfer ownership to employers, would this lead to more employees retaining ownership of the works they create?

3.3.2 EU HARMONIZATION

There has been little EU harmonization of copyright authorship and ownership principles. The most significant harmonization measure, particularly from the point of view of the UK, relates to authors of cinematographic works. Article 2(2) of the Rental and Lending Rights Directive and Article 2 of the Term Directive provide that the 'principal director of a cinematographic or audiovisual work shall be considered as its author or one of its authors' and adds that Member States are 'free to designate other co-authors'. Consequently, UK law had to be amended to include the principal director as an author of a film, alongside the producer. The EU provisions on authorship of cinematographic works were the subject of a ruling in *Luksan v van der Let*.[21] In this case the CJEU considered whether a provision of Austrian law that vested all economic rights in the producer was consistent with EU law. After reviewing the relevant EU directives, international conventions, and the EU Charter on Fundamental Rights and Freedoms, the Court concluded that the rights to exploit a cinematographic work had to vest by operation of law 'directly and originally, in the principal director'.[22] As a result, Member States were precluded from including in their national legislation provisions that allocated 'exploitation rights by operation of law exclusively to the producer of the work in question'.[23] Some commentators have suggested that *Luksan* is yet another example of judicial activism on the part of the CJEU because the Court strays into laying down rules of ownership and does not deal simply with authorship.[24]

3.3.3 ORPHAN WORKS

Orphan works are those works where the copyright owner cannot be identified or located by a person who wishes to make use of the work in a manner that would require permission. These differ from 'out-of-print' works, which are works that are not currently being commercially exploited or are commercially unavailable.[25] The obstacles to identifying and locating copyright owners include inadequate information on the work itself,[26] along with changes of ownership or changes in the circumstances of the owner, ranging from change

---

[21] Case C-277/10, Judgment of the Court (Third Chamber), 9 February 2012.   [22] [72].
[23] [72].
[24] J. Griffiths, 'Constitutionalising or harmonising? The Court of Justice, the right to property and European copyright law' (2013) 38 E. L. Rev. 65.
[25] United States Copyright Office, 'Report on Orphan Works: A Report of the Register of Copyrights' (January 2006), pp. 21, 34; and i2010, Digital Libraries High Level Expert Group—Copyright Subgroup, 'Final Report on Digital Preservation, Orphan Works and Out-of-Print Works' (4 June 2008), s. 6.1.
[26] i.e. no details about the author or copyright owner, or no copyright notice, which is a particular problem for works of visual art, such as photographs, and audiovisual works.

of address to death or dissolution. Arguably, the absence of formalities for copyright protection exacerbates the orphan works problem as a user must generally assume that a work he wishes to use is subject to copyright.[27]

It is feared that if adequate solutions are not found for the problem of orphan works this will hamper institutional users, such as libraries, archives, or museums, as well as commercial users, from digitizing and making available online large collections of works. The extent of the orphan works 'problem' in the UK was suggested, in a research study published by JISC,[28] to be some 5 to 10 per cent of the holdings of most public sector institutions, and between 11 and 20 per cent of the holdings of archives. Given that it estimated that these institutions might hold as many as 13 million orphan works, it could take 6.5 million working days (estimating half a day per work) to locate the rightholders.

Various solutions have been discussed: a limitation on remedies, provided a diligent search has been undertaken; statutory exceptions; licences granted by a statutory copyright board or other authority; extended collective licences (which involves collecting societies representing the unlocatable rightholders of a class of works); and certain collective agreements with rightholders.[29] Although reinstating the registration and notice requirements has been mooted as a possible solution, this is unfeasible because of the prohibition on formalities contained in Article 5(2) of the Berne Convention. Indeed, even where formalities are structured as *incentives*, as opposed to prerequisites, for copyright protection these would seem to fall foul of Article 5(2).[30]

At a European level, the EU has adopted the Orphan Works Directive 2012/28/EU applicable only to uses made of orphan works by publicly accessible libraries, educational establishments and museums, and archives and public service broadcasting organizations. An 'orphan work' according to Article 2 is a work or phonogram where the rightholders are unable to be identified or located after a diligent search has been conducted in accordance with Article 3. Once a work or phonogram is considered an orphan work in one Member State it shall be considered such in all other Member States (see Article 4). Member States are obliged by Article 6(1) to establish an exception or limitation to the reproduction and communication to the public rights so that the organizations specified above are able to make the orphan work available to the public or reproduce it for the purposes of digitization, making available, indexing, cataloguing, preservation, or restoration. Fair compensation shall be payable to rightholders where they have put an end to the orphan work status of their work (see Articles 5 and 6(5)). It is up to Member States to 'determine the circumstances under which the payment of such compensation may be organized' and also the level of the compensation (Article 6(5)). For users other than those specified in the Directive (e.g. commercial entities or private libraries), no preference has been expressed for any one particular solution and Member States have been left to decide on the best path for solving

---

[27] See O. Huang, 'U.S. Copyright Office Orphan Works Inquiry: finding homes for the orphans' (2006) 21 Berkeley Tech. L. J. 265, 268–9; and 268–76 for a discussion of the various causes of the orphan works problem. See also United States Copyright Office, 'Report on Orphan Works: A Report of the Register of Copyrights' (January 2006), p. 43.

[28] JISC, 'In from the Cold: An Assessment of the Scope of Orphan Works and its impact on the delivery of services to the public' (August 2009).

[29] See United States Copyright Office, 'Report on Orphan Works: A Report of the Register of Copyrights' (January 2006).

[30] See S. Perlmutter, 'Freeing copyright from formalities' (1994–5) 13 Cardozo Arts & Ent. L. J. 565, 575. But contrast P. Samuelson, 'Preliminary thoughts on Copyright Report' (2007) Utah L. Rev. 551, 563 who argues that 'copyright formalities may have a useful role in reshaping copyright norms and practices in the more complex world that has evolved in recent years'.

this problem. Dr Rosati has been critical of the Orphan Works Directive because it allows for considerable flexibility in how Member States implement it and thus creates the potential for significant divergences. Moreover, it does not address private or commercial entities and solutions for these users are left to Member States, thus also creating the likelihood of divergences.[31]

In the UK, the Orphan Works Directive has been implemented by the Copyright and Rights in Performances (Certain Permitted Uses of Orphan Works) Regulations 2014.[32] These Regulations create an exception for certain uses of orphan works by publicly accessible libraries, educational establishments or museums, archives, film or audio heritage institutions, and public service broadcasting organizations.[33] In order to qualify as an orphan work, the relevant body must ensure that a good faith diligent search is undertaken.[34] In relation to 'fair compensation' to rightholders who put an end to the orphan work status of their works, it is up to the relevant body using the orphan work to calculate what is 'fair' and, in the event that the relevant body and rightholder disagree on what is 'fair compensation', either may apply to the Copyright Tribunal to determine the amount.[35] In addition, the UK introduced the Enterprise and Regulatory Reform Act 2013,[36] section 77 of which grants powers to the Secretary of State to make regulations to allow for an orphan works licensing scheme[37] and to make regulations for the authorization of voluntary extended collective licensing schemes.[38] These regulations have now been introduced.[39] The Copyright and Rights in Performances (Licensing of Orphan Works) Regulations 2014[40] permits users to apply to the Comptroller-General of Patents, Designs and Trade Marks for an orphan licence once they have carried out a diligent search to identify the rightholders and these have either not been identified or located. A diligent search must at least include a search of the relevant register maintained by the Comptroller, the relevant databases maintained by OHIM, and certain other relevant sources specified in Schedule ZA1 to the CDPA (as inserted by SI 2014/2861). An orphan licence is valid for seven years, with a possibility of renewal for a further term not exceeding seven years and permits non-exclusive use of an orphan work in the UK. Licensees must pay a reasonable licence fee to the Comptroller, which will hold these fees and distribute them to rightholders when identified. The Comptroller must also maintain a register of orphan works. By contrast, the Copyright and Rights in Performances (Extended Collective Licensing) Regulations 2014 grants the Secretary of State the power to authorize a relevant licensing body (such as a collecting society) to operate an extended collective licensing scheme, i.e. a licensing scheme for classes of rightholders.

---

[31] E. Rosati, 'The Orphan Works Directive, or throwing a stone and hiding the hand' (2013) 8 JIPLP 303, 309–310.

[32] SI 2014/2861; these came into force on 29 October 2014.   [33] See SI 2016/2861, regs 1 and 2.

[34] See SI 2016/2861, reg. 4.   [35] See SI 2016/2861, reg. 7(4).

[36] See <www.legislation.gov.uk/ukpga/2013/24/contents/enacted>.

[37] Orphan works only being characterized as such where a diligent search has already been undertaken by potential licensee(s). It is thought that the proposed Digital Copyright Exchange might facilitate diligent searches being undertaken: see UK IPO, 'Copyright works: Streamlining copyright licensing for the digital age: An independent report by Richard Hooper CBE and Dr Ros Lynch' (July 2012), available at <www.copyrighthub.co.uk/Documents/dce-report-phase2.aspx>.

[38] For more details see the Explanatory Memorandum, [510]–[512].

[39] The Copyright and Rights in Performances (Licensing of Orphan Works) Regulations 2014 (SI 2014/2863; in force 29 October 2014) and the Copyright and Rights in Performances (Extended Collective Licensing) Regulations 2014 (SI 2014/2588; in force 1 October 2014).

[40] SI 2014/2863.

FURTHER READING

J. de Beer and M. Bouchard, 'Canada's "orphan works" regime: unlocatable copyright owners and the Copyright Board' (2010) 10 OUCLJ 215.

R. Burrell and E. Hudson, 'Property concepts in European copyright law: the case of abandonment' in H. Howe and J. Griffiths (eds), *Concepts of Property in Intellectual Property Law* (Cambridge: Cambridge University Press, 2013), ch. 9.

S. van Gompel, 'The orphan works chimera and how to defeat it: a view from across the Atlantic' (2012) 27 Berkeley Technology L. J. 1347.

D. R. Hansen et al., 'Solving the orphan works problem for the United States' (2013) 37 Columbia Journal of Law and the Arts 1.

E. F. Schulze, 'Orphan works and the other orphan material under national, regional and international law: analysis, proposals and solutions' [2012] EIPR 313.

3.4 EXPLOITATION

3.4.1 EXPRESS ASSIGNMENTS AND LICENCES

Copyright is a property right,[41] which can be exploited in two main ways: assignment and licence. An assignment is a transfer of ownership. It may be partial, in the sense of transferring only some of the owner's exclusive rights or in transferring ownership for only a limited period, as opposed to the whole term of copyright.[42] To be effective, an assignment must be in writing signed by or on behalf of the assignor.[43] Why do you think such a requirement exists?

Unlike assignment, a licence does not involve a transfer of ownership. Rather, it is a grant of permission to carry out certain acts that fall within the exclusive rights of the owner. A variety of types of licence may be granted. An important distinction is between exclusive, sole, and non-exclusive licences. An exclusive licence is one that grants to the licensee the right to carry out the right(s) stipulated in the licence that would otherwise be exercisable by the copyright owner, to the exclusion of all other persons, including the person granting the licence (usually the copyright owner). By way of contrast, a sole licence differs from an exclusive licence in that the copyright owner remains free to exercise the licensed rights. Finally, a non-exclusive licence is where a licensee has the right to carry out the licensed rights, but this is not to the exclusion of third parties or the copyright owner.

Section 92 of the CDPA defines an exclusive licence as 'a licence in writing signed by or on behalf of the copyright owner'. In other words, as with assignments, exclusive licences must satisfy formal requirements. Why do you think this is the case? It is also important to note that section 101 of the CDPA grants exclusive licensees the same rights and remedies (except as against the copyright owner) in respect of matters occurring after the grant of the licence as if the licence had been an assignment. Given the nature of an exclusive licence, why would it be preferable to obtain an assignment?

Another broad distinction that can be made in respect of licences is between contractual and gratuitous licences. The former are contractual promises to license certain rights, while

---

[41] CDPA, s. 1(1).   [42] CDPA, s. 90(2).   [43] CDPA, s. 90(3).

the latter are non-contractual in nature. When it comes to revocation, what do you think are the main differences between contractual and gratuitous licences?[44]

3.4.2 IMPLIED ASSIGNMENTS AND LICENCES

Where a copyright work has been commissioned, i.e. it has been created pursuant to a contract *for* services, as opposed to in the course of a contract *of* service, first ownership will vest in the author according to the general rule in section 11(1) of the CDPA. Yet, the commissioning party will undoubtedly want to be able to exploit or use the copyright work that it has commissioned. In this situation, what would you advise the commissioning party to do?

It sometimes happens, however, that the parties to a contract *for* services fail to mention or stipulate anything about ownership of copyright or permission to carry out certain acts in relation to the copyright work. In such situations, courts may intervene to imply terms of assignment or terms of licence in favour of the commissioning party. The principles governing the implication of such terms were set out in *Robin Ray v Classic FM*.

Robin Ray v Classic FM [1988] FSR 622

The claimant had entered into a consultancy agreement with the defendant, under which he was to provide advice on their classical musical repertoire and catalogue its recorded music library. Nothing was mentioned about intellectual property rights in any work created by the claimant when acting as a consultant for the defendant. The claimant supplied various documents and a catalogue to the defendant and these formed a crucial part of their programming database. The defendant radio station became highly successful and, as a result, proposed to grant licences to foreign radio stations to use the database. The claimant objected to this use, but the defendant nevertheless went ahead with granting these licences. The claimant then commenced proceedings for infringement of copyright in the documents and catalogue he had produced. The defendant argued, inter alia, that because it had commissioned the claimant to produce these works, it had been granted an implied assignment of copyright or an implied licence.

Lightman J, at pp. 640–5:

[Lightman J began by stating the principles governing the implication of such terms:]
The general principles governing the respective rights of the contractor and client in the copyright in a work commissioned by the client appear to me to be as follows:

(1) the contractor is entitled to retain the copyright in default of some express or implied term to the contrary effect;

(2) the contract itself may expressly provide as to who shall be entitled to the copyright in work produced pursuant to the contract. Thus under a standard form Royal Institute

---

[44] For the circumstances in which a gratuitous, implied licence may be revoked see *Brighton v Jones*. For a discussion of how dedications of a copyright work to the public domain create a licence (as opposed to extinguishing the copyright) see P. Johnson, '"Dedicating" copyright to the public domain' (2008) 71 MLR 587.

of British Architects ('RIBA') contract between an architect and his client, there is an express provision that the copyright shall remain vested in the architect;

(3) the mere fact that the contractor has been commissioned is insufficient to entitle the client to the copyright. Where Parliament intended the act of commissioning alone to vest copyright in the client, e.g. in case of unregistered design rights and registered designs, the legislation expressly so provides (see section 215 of the 1988 Act and section 2(1A) of the Registered Designs Act 1949 as amended by the 1988 Act). In all other cases the client has to establish the entitlement under some express or implied term of the contract;

(4) the law governing the implication of terms in a contract has been firmly established (if not earlier) by the decision of the House of Lords in *Liverpool City Council v Irwin* [1977] AC 239 ('Liverpool'). In the words of Lord Bingham MR in *Philips Electronique v British Sky Broadcasting Ltd* [1995] EMLR 472 ('Philips') at 481, the essence of much learning on implied terms is distilled in the speech of Lord Simon of Glaisdale on behalf of the majority of the Judicial Committee of the Privy Council in *BP Refinery (Westernport) Pty Ltd v The President, Councillors and Ratepayers of the Shire of Hastings* (1978) 52 ALJR 20 at 26:

Their Lordships do not think it necessary to review exhaustively the authorities on the implication of a term in a contract which the parties have not thought fit to express. In their view, for a term to be implied, the following conditions (which may overlap) must be satisfied: (1) it must be reasonable and equitable; (2) it must be necessary to give business efficacy to the contract, so that no term will be implied if the contract is effective without it; (3) it must be so obvious that 'it goes without saying'; (4) it must be capable of clear expression; (5) it must not contradict any express term of the contract.

[Lord Bingham added an explanation and warning:]

The courts' usual role in contractual interpretation is, by resolving ambiguities or reconciling apparent inconsistencies, to attribute the true meaning to the language in which the parties themselves have expressed their contract. The implication of contract terms involves a different and altogether more ambitious undertaking: the interpolation of terms to deal with matters for which, *ex hypothesi*, the parties themselves have made no provision. It is because the implication of terms is so potentially intrusive that the law imposes strict constraints on the exercise of this extraordinary power…

The question of whether a term should be implied, and if so what, almost inevitably arises after a crisis has been reached in the performance of the contract. So the court comes to the task of implication with the benefit of hindsight, and it is tempting for the court then to fashion a term which will reflect the merits of the situation as they then appear. Tempting, but wrong.

(5) where (as in the present case) it is necessary to imply the grant of some right to fill a lacuna in the contract and the question arises how this lacuna is to be filled, guidance is again to be found in *Liverpool*. The principle is clearly stated that in deciding which of various alternatives should constitute the contents of the term to be implied, the choice must be that which does not exceed what is necessary in the circumstances (see Lord Wilberforce at 245F–G). In short a minimalist approach is called for. An implication may only be made if this is necessary, and then only of what is necessary and no more;

(6) accordingly if it is necessary to imply some grant of rights in respect of a copyright work, and the need could be satisfied by the grant of a licence or an assignment of the copyright, the implication will be of the grant of a licence only;

(7) circumstances may exist when the necessity for an assignment of copyright may be established. As Mr Howe has submitted, these circumstances are, however, only likely to arise if the client needs in addition to the right to use the copyright works the right to exclude the contractor from using the work and the ability to enforce the copyright against third parties. Examples of when this situation may arise include: (a) where the purpose in commissioning the work is for the client to multiply and sell copies on the market for which the work was created free from the sale of copies in competition with the client by the contractor or third parties; (b) where the contractor creates a work which is derivative from a pre-existing work of the client, e.g. when a draughtsman is engaged to turn designs of an article in sketch form by the client into formal manu-facturing drawings, and the draughtsman could not use the drawings himself without infringing the underlying rights of the client; (c) where the contractor is engaged as part of a team with employees of the client to produce a composite or joint work and he is unable, or cannot have been intended to be able, to exploit for his own benefit the joint work or indeed any distinct contribution of his own created in the course of his engagement: see *Nichols Advanced Vehicle Systems Inc v Rees* [1979] RPC 127 at 139 and consider *Sofia Bogrich v Shape Machines*, unreported, November 4, 1994, Pat Ct and in particular page 15 of the transcript of the judgment of Aldous J. In each case it is necessary to consider the price paid, the impact on the contractor of assignment of copyright and whether it can sensibly have been intended that the contractor should retain any copyright as a separate item of property;

(8) if necessity requires only the grant of a licence, the ambit of the licence must be the minimum which is required to secure to the client the entitlement which the parties to contract must have intended to confer upon him. The amount of the purchase price which the client under the contract has obliged himself to pay may be relevant to the ambit of the licence. Thus in *Stovin-Bradford v Volpoint Properties Ltd* [1971] 1 Ch 1007, where the client agreed to pay only a nominal fee to his architect for the preparation of plans, he was held to have a licence to use the plans for no purpose beyond the antici-pated application for planning permission. By contrast in *Blair v Osborne and Tompkins* [1971] 2 QB 78, where the client was charged the full RIBA scale fee, his licence was held to extend to using the plans for the building itself. Guidance as to the approach to be adopted is provided in a passage in the judgment of Jacobs J in *Beck v Montana Constructions Pty* [1964–5] NSWR 229 at 235 cited with approval by Widgery LJ in *Blair v Osborne and Tompkins*, supra at 87:

it seems to me that the principle involved is this; that the engagement for reward of a person to produce material of a nature which is capable of being the subject of copyright implies a permission, or consent, or licence in the person giving the engagement to use the material in the manner and for the purpose in which and for which it was contemplated between the parties that it would be used at the time of the engagement.

(9) the licence accordingly is to be limited to what is in the joint contemplation of the parties at the date of the contract, and does not extend to enable the client to take advantage of a new unexpected profitable opportunity (consider *Meikle v Maufe* [1941] 3 All ER 144).

[Lightman J then applied these principles to the facts of the case:]

It is common ground that upon the true construction of the consultancy agreement some form of right in respect of the intellectual property rights in the five documents and the catalogues must have been intended in favour of the defendant, for without it the contract for the provision of his services by the plaintiff would be without purpose or value: the defendant could make no use and obtain no benefit from their product. The question raised is the content of the implication. The plaintiff says that the implication should be of a licence limited to use of the database and the making of copies for the purpose of the defendant's existing business. The defendant says that the implication should be of a grant of the copyright in the five documents and the catalogue or at least of a licence broad enough to permit the making of copies for the purposes of exploitation of the copyright abroad.

It seems quite clear to me upon the true construction of the consultancy agreement in its matrix of facts that the limits of what was contemplated at the date of the consultancy agreement were that the plaintiff's work would be used for the purpose of enabling the defendant to carry on its business as set out in recital A, namely to broadcast in the United Kingdom. The only necessary implication to give purpose and effect to the consultancy agreement is accordingly the grant of a licence to the defendant to use the copyright material for the indefinite future for this purpose and for this purpose only.

...

The defendant can accordingly make copies of the database if this was reasonably required for carrying on the business of a broadcaster in the United Kingdom, but cannot do so for the purpose of exploiting the database abroad. The making of the copies in question in this case accordingly constituted an infringement of the plaintiff's copyright.

The principles governing the implication of terms of assignment or terms of licence set out in *Robin Ray* were approved and followed by the Court of Appeal in *Griggs Group Ltd v Evans & Raben Footwear*.[45] On the facts, however, the court found an implied term of assignment. In this case the claimants had commissioned an advertising agency to produce a combined logo for their 'Doc Martens' footwear. The advertising agency in turn commissioned the first defendant (a freelance artist) to produce the logo and paid him at their standard rate. Subsequently, the first defendant assigned copyright in the combined logo to the second defendant, who was an Australian footwear company. The claimants asserted that they were equitable owners of copyright in the logo and sought a declaration to that effect and an order that copyright be formally assigned to them. The claimants were successful at first instance and the defendant's appeal was dismissed. Jacob LJ (with whom Chadwick and Lloyd LJJ agreed) held:

If an officious bystander had asked at the time of contract whether Mr Evans was going to retain rights in the combined logo which could be used against the client by Mr Evans (or anyone to whom he sold the rights) anywhere in the world, other than in respect of point of sale material in the UK, the answer would surely have been 'of course not'. Mr Evans had no conceivable further interest in the work being created ...[46]

Do you agree with courts' implying terms of assignment or licence? If so, how can this practice be reconciled with the requirements in sections 90(3) and 92(1) of the CDPA that assignments and exclusive licences must be in writing signed by or on behalf of the assignor/copyright owner?

---

[45] [2005] FSR 31.   [46] [19].

3.5 TERM

3.5.1 CALCULATION OF TERM

The rules for calculating term of protection are generally straightforward. For literary, dramatic, musical, and artistic works, copyright expires 70 years from the end of the calendar year in which the author dies.[47] Currently, copyright in sound recordings expires 50 years after the end of the calendar year in which the recording is made or, if during that period the recording is published or made available to the public by being played in public or communicated to the public, 50 years from the end of the calendar year in which first publication takes place or the work is so made available.[48] This 50-year term, however, has been extended to 70 years pursuant to the EU Term Extension Directive and the UK introduced this change in 2013.[49] For broadcasts, copyright lasts for 50 years from the end of the calendar year when the broadcast is made[50] and, for typographical arrangements, 25 years from the end of the calendar year in which the edition was first published.[51] Finally, literary, dramatic, musical, and artistic works subject to Crown copyright are protected for 125 years from the end of the calendar year in which they were made or for 50 years from the end of the calendar year in which the work was published commercially where that publication occurs within 75 years of the work being made. Literary, dramatic, musical, and artistic works that are subject to parliamentary copyright are protected for 50 years from the end of the calendar year in which the work was made.[52]

Calculating the term of protection for films differs in that it does not coincide with a fixed term after the death of the author(s). Instead, section 13B of the CDPA provides that copyright expires 70 years after the end of the calendar year in which the death of the last of the following persons occurs: the principal director, the author of the screenplay, the author of the dialogue, or the composer of music specially created for and used in the film. Only one of these persons—i.e. the principal director—is the author of a film. The explanation for this apparent oddity is the Term Directive,[53] which sought to harmonize the terms of protection for all copyright works.

Prior to the Term Directive, the CDPA stipulated that the author of a film was its producer and that protection would last for 50 years from the time the film was made. However, in other Member States, such as Germany, films were protected as cinematographic works and copyright expired 70 years after the death of the relevant authors: these included persons who made a creative contribution to the film which was inseparably incorporated into the film work, such as the principal director, cameraman, or cutter.[54] Thus, in harmonizing the length of protection for films, the Term Directive needed to come up with a common approach to calculating term, but at the same time respect the different approaches to authorship of films. The result was partial harmonization of film authorship, whereby Article 2(1) of the Term Directive states that the principal director of a cinematographic work shall be considered as one of its authors. UK copyright law was

---

[47] CDPA, s. 12(2).   [48] CDPA, s. 13A(2).

[49] See Directive 2011/77/EU, Art. 2(1) and The Copyright and Duration of Rights in Performances Regulations 2013 No. 1782.

[50] CDPA, s. 14.   [51] CDPA, s. 15.   [52] CDPA, s. 165(3).

[53] The terms of protection for copyright and related rights were harmonized by Directive 93/98/EEC, which was subsequently codified by Directive 2006/116/EC of 12 December 2006 on the term of protection of copyright and certain related rights (Term Directive), Art. 2(2).

[54] Art. 65 of the German Law on Copyright and Neighbouring Rights of 9 September 1965.

amended accordingly. However, commentators have queried whether the UK properly implemented the provisions relating to cinematographic works, given the limited scope of protection for film works. Further, although films may now be classified as dramatic works and thus obtain a greater scope of protection,[55] it seems that Article 2(1) of the Term Directive, as implemented in section 13B of the CDPA, does not apply to films that are protected as dramatic works.

The Term Extension Directive,[56] as explained at 3.5.3, has sought to deal with the divergences in the way Member States characterize musical creations (i.e. treating the lyrics and music as one collaborative work or as two separate works), by instituting a special rule concerning term of protection. This rule provides that the term of protection for a musical composition with words will expire 70 years after the death of the author of the lyrics or the composer of the musical composition (whichever is the last person to die), whether or not they are designated as co-authors, provided that 'both contributions were specifically created for the respective musical composition with words'.[57] Commentators have queried whether such a rule was needed in the first place and its clarity of application. Moreover, harmonizing the term of protection in this way indirectly harmonizes approaches to subject matter and also approaches to authorship.[58] The Copyright and Duration of Rights in Performances Regulations 2013[59] implemented this rule by inserting a new section 10A of the CDPA. Section 10A deems works produced by the collaboration of the author of a musical work and the author of a literary work, where the two works are created in order to be used together, as a work of co-authorship. As such, the term of protection is measured according to the last of the co-authors to die.

> **FURTHER READING**
>
> M. van Eechoud, P. B. Hugenholtz, S. van Gompel, L. Guibault, and N. Helberger, *Harmonizing European Copyright Law: The Challenges of Better Lawmaking* (Alphen aan den Rijn: Kluwer, 2009), ch. 6.
>
> P. Kamina, 'Authorship of films and implementation of the Term Directive: the dramatic tale of two copyrights' [1994] EIPR 319.
>
> P. Kamina, 'British film copyright and the incorrect implementation of the EC Copyright Directives' (1998) 9 Ent. L. R. 109.

3.5.2 IMPACT OF TERM DIRECTIVE 2006/116/EC ON EXPIRED COPYRIGHT WORKS

When it came to harmonization of the term of protection in Directive 93/98/EEC, which was subsequently codified by Directive 2006/116/EC, it was thought that upwards

---

[55] See 2.5.1.4.

[56] Directive 2011/77/EU amending Directive 2006/116/EC on the term of protection of copyright and certain related rights [2011] OJ L265/1, Art. 1, inserting para. (7) to Art. 1 of Directive 2006/116/EC.

[57] Directive 2011/77/EU, Art. 1.

[58] M. van Eechoud, P. B. Hugenholtz, S. van Gompel, L. Guibault, and N. Helberger, *Harmonizing European Copyright Law: The Challenges of Better Lawmaking* (Alphen aan den Rijn: Kluwer, 2009), ch. 6.

[59] SI 2013/1782.

harmonization to 70 years *post mortem auctoris* for authorial works would be least disruptive. Thus, countries like the UK, which hitherto offered 50 years *post mortem auctoris* for literary, dramatic, musical, and artistic works, were required to extend the term to the life of the author plus 70 years.[60] This EU-wide increase in the duration of protection generated little controversy, unlike the most recent EU Term Extension Directive,[61] discussed at 3.5.3, and the later US proposal to increase the term by 20 years, which provoked a constitutional challenge in *Eldred v Ashcroft*.[62]

An important provision of the Term Directive is Article 10(2) which states that the extended term of 70 years applies to all works and subject matter still protected *in at least one* Member State. Thus, even if copyright in, say, a literary work has expired in the UK if, at the relevant time, it is still protected in Germany (which has always had a rule of life plus 70 years), copyright will revive in that work in *all* Member States. The CJEU ruling that held that Member States could not discriminate between its national authors and authors from other EU Member States invariably meant that such works would be protected in Germany and as such copyright would revive in the remaining Member States.[63] Thus, the Term Directive not only extends the term of protection for works in which copyright still exists, it also revives copyright in works that have fallen into the public domain in some Member States. To deal with the possible hardship and unfairness that third parties might suffer as a result of these rules, Article 10(3) of the Term Directive permits Member States to 'adopt the necessary provisions to protect in particular acquired rights of third parties'. The CJEU has ruled in *Butterfly Music*[64] that Member States are obliged to protect rights of third parties, although there is a discretion as to how they do so, provided the exercise of this discretion does not effectively undermine the rules introduced by the Term Directive.

The UK implemented the Term Directive via the Duration of Copyright and Rights in Performances Regulations 1995.[65] Of particular note are regulations 23 and 24, which protect the interests of third parties when it comes to works in which copyright has been revived.

Regulation 23(1) states that no act done before commencement of the Regulations (i.e. 1 January 1996) shall be treated as infringing revived copyright in a work. Regulation 23(2) states that it is also not infringement of revived copyright in a work to do anything 'in pursuance of arrangements made before 1st January 1995 at a time when copyright did not subsist in the work' or 'to issue to the public after commencement copies of the work made before 1st July 1995 at a time when copyright did not subsist in the work'. 'Arrangements' are defined in regulation 23(5) to mean 'arrangements for the exploitation of the work in question'.

---

[60] Term Directive, Art. 1(1).

[61] Directive 2011/77/EU amending Directive 2006/116/EC on the term of protection of copyright and certain related rights [2011] OJ L265/1.

[62] 123 S Ct 769 (2003), discussed in C. Seville, 'Copyright's bargain—defining our terms' [2003] IPQ 312.

[63] See *Phil Collins Decision* Joined Cases C-92 and 326/92 [1993] 3 CMLR 773, [1994] FSR 166 (ECJ) and the discussion of the implications of this ruling in G. Dworkin and J. A. L. Sterling, 'Phil Collins and the Term Directive' [1994] EIPR 187. The principle of non-discrimination between Member States' authors applies even where the author was dead at the time the EEC Treaty came into force—see *Land Hessen v Ricordi* Case C-360/00 [2004] 2 CMLR 20.

[64] Case C-60/98 [2000] 1 CMLR 587.   [65] SI 1995/3297.

Regulation 24 differs insofar as it creates a form of compulsory licence. It states that in relation to works in which copyright has revived, 'any acts restricted by the copyright shall be treated as licensed by the copyright owner, subject only to the payment of such reasonable royalty or other remuneration as may be agreed or determined in default of agreement by the Copyright Tribunal'. Importantly, a person seeking to rely on this provision must give reasonable notice of his intention to the copyright owner.[66] The scope of regulations 23 and 24 was analysed in the following case.

Sweeney v Macmillan Publishers Ltd [2002] RPC 35

James Joyce had died in 1941 and, as such, copyright in *Ulysses* had expired in the UK as from 1 January 1992. In 1992, the second defendant (Mr Rose), a Joyce scholar, contacted the first defendant (Macmillan Publishers) with a view to him producing a Reader's Edition of *Ulysses*. He started work on the project during 1992 and completed most of the work by the end of 1993. He entered into an agreement with the second defendant to publish the text in early 1996 and publication occurred in 1997. As a result of the Duration of Copyright and Rights in Performances Regulations 1995, copyright in *Ulysses* was revived, with effect from 1 January 1996, until the end of 2011. The claimants (Sweeney), who were the trustees of James Joyce's estate, commenced proceedings against the defendants, alleging infringement of copyright. The defendants sought to rely on regulations 23 and 24.

Lloyd J:

[Discussing the scope and application of regulation 23:]

57. I do not propose to attempt a definition of 'arrangements'. I can accept Mr Burkill's proposition that they are not necessarily limited to arrangements by way of contract. Nevertheless they must be of some degree of solidity or certainty, such that it can be said that acts done later are done in pursuance of the arrangements. Regulations 23(2)(a) and (3)(b) are not so wide as to extend to anything done after commencement in consequence of anything at all which has been done, or any steps of any kind taken, with a view to exploiting the work in question, before January 1, 1995. Apart from anything else a very wide reading of 'arrangements' would produce a very odd contrast with the fairly narrow and specific provisions of regulation 23(2)(b). That deals only with the distribution of stock in hand on July 1, 1995...

58. I accept Mr Rose's evidence that he did not start on his Reader's Edition project until after January 1, 1992. All that he did in respect of the project before January 1, 1995 was done while the 1922 edition was in the public domain. But what did that amount to? He started work on the project, and no doubt achieved a great deal of what he intended by the end of 1994. He got into discussion with Penguin, to whom he was already talking about Finnegans Wake. He told me that he was confident that Penguin would publish the Reader's Edition, but he was wrong. In 1993 he approached Macmillan, and may at that stage have showed them some sample text. They were encouraging but without any commitment. Mr Rose was again confident that they would publish the Reader's Edition, once Penguin withdrew, and this confidence was enhanced when Mr Riley moved from Penguin to Macmillan in September 1993. It does not seem to me that these limited contacts with

[66] Reg. 24(2).

publishers can fairly be described as amounting to 'arrangements for the exploitation of the work'. That aside, what he relies on is his having done a great deal, even the vast bulk, of the work needed to prepare his new edition. That, by itself, does not seem to me to be arrangements in pursuance of which it could be said that the eventual publication was done. If it were sufficient it is difficult to see how a distinction could be made between this case and one in which only a small amount of the work had been done before January 1, 1995, but the work was thereafter carried on, eventually brought to completion, and finally published. The publication could be said to have been done in that case too in pursuance of the work started before January 1, 1995. Such an interpretation of the regulation would, in my judgment, be far too wide, even in its own terms, and the more so with the guidance of the European Court of Justice given in the passages from *Butterfly Music* which I have quoted above. It would interfere to an excessive extent with the rights conferred by the revived copyright.

[Lloyd J then discussed the scope and application of regulation 24:]

62. In order to qualify for the compulsory licence afforded by regulation 24, all that has to be done is for the person intending to avail himself of the right conferred by the regulation to give reasonable notice of his intention to the copyright owner, stating when he intends to begin to do the acts. The first question is whether Macmillan, when they told the estate, via Mr Monro, of their intention in March 1997, stated when they intended to begin the acts. The letter of 1996 does not contain that information. But it seems to me that, in the context of the exchanges that took place in March 1997, it would be wrong to regard Macmillan as not having given notice of that simply because the intended publication date of June 1997 was not stated in that letter. Normally it would be sensible for a notice which is intended to take effect under regulation 24 itself to state the intended date. But here Mr Monro already knew the intended date from the publicity which had been drawn to his attention, and this was confirmed by Mr Riley in their telephone conversation. I am not prepared to hold that no sufficient notice was given because the intended publication date was not included in the 1996 letter, as received in March 1997.

63. A puzzle about regulation 24 is the requirement for 'reasonable' notice, which must refer to the period of notice. Since the copyright owner cannot do anything to stop the intended acts once notice is given, so long as they are within the regulation, it seems to be arguable that only quite short notice needs to be given. The requirement of notice means that the acts must be open and not clandestine, and that a person who hoped to get away with publication in breach of copyright in secret cannot justify his acts retrospectively by reference to the regulation. But on any basis notice in March for publication in June would be reasonable, and I need not say anything about what is required to make the period of notice reasonable. Mr Baldwin submitted that the notice had to include full particulars of what was to be done, including, he said, a copy of the intended publication. I cannot get that out of the text of the regulation, and it seems to me that it would not be compatible with a notice given at all well in advance, since the text may well not be finalised until near the time of publication. In my judgment Macmillan's notice was not invalid on this account.

64. The other question is whether it is open to the person seeking to take advantage of the regulation to give notice on a contingent basis, as a fall-back to, for example, an argument under regulation 23 as here … It seems to me that it would be reading a great deal too much into regulation 24(2) to say that the notice can only ever be given unequivocally, and that no such notice can be given in the alternative to an argument that it is not necessary.

…

66. Accordingly, as to whether a valid notice was given under regulation 24, I find for the defendants. If and in so far as their acts would otherwise infringe revived copyright, they would be entitled to do them but would have to pay a sum to be agreed or determined under the regulations.

Do you think regulations 23 and 24, as interpreted in *Sweeney*, strike a fair balance between the interests of the owner of revived copyright and those of third parties? If not, what would be your suggested alternatives?

FURTHER READING

H. Cohen Jehoram, 'The E.C. copyright directives, economics and authors' rights' (1994) 25 IIC 821.

G. Dworkin and J. A. L. Sterling, 'Phil Collins and the Term Directive' [1994] EIPR 187.

B. Lindner, 'Revival of rights v protection of acquired rights' [2000] EIPR 133.

B. Sherman and L. Bently, 'Balance and harmony in the duration of copyright: the European Directive and its consequences' in P. Parrinder and W. Chernaik (eds), *Textual Monopolies: Literary Copyright and the Public Domain* (London: Office for Humanities Communication, 1997).

3.5.3 EU TERM EXTENSION DIRECTIVE

While the basic rules for calculating term are reasonably straightforward, the policy considerations underlying the length of copyright protection and whether it should be extended further are highly contested. Generally speaking, the term of copyright has continually expanded for authorial works, moving from two 14-year fixed terms in the Statute of Anne, to life of the author plus seven years in the 1842 Literary Copyright Act, to life of the author plus 50 years in the Copyright Act 1911, to the current life plus 70 years formulation in the CDPA (as amended).

In respect of related rights, such as the rights given to sound recordings, broadcasts, and performers, Article 3 of the Term Directive harmonized the length of protection to a fixed term of 50 years. This harmonization was relatively uncontroversial. However, when the EU proposed to increase the term of protection for sound recordings and performers' rights to a fixed term of 95 years, much disagreement ensued, with academics, government policy makers, record companies, and other interested parties vociferously joining the debate.

The question of term extension for sound recordings and performers was first aired in the UK when the Gowers Review of Intellectual Property[67] actually recommended against such an increase in term. However, the proposal quickly shifted to the European Commission who firmly supported an increased term of protection to 95 years and issued a Proposed Directive[68] to that effect.

In the Explanatory Memorandum to the Proposed Term Extension Directive, the Commission set out it main reasons for the change, which are examined below.

---

[67] See <www.gov.uk/government/uploads/system/uploads/attachment_data/file/228849/0118404830.pdf> at paras 4.20–4.47.

[68] Proposal for a European Parliament and Council directive amending Directive 2006/116/EC of the European Parliament and of the Council on the term of protection of copyright and certain related rights, Brussels, COM (2008) 464/3.

Explanatory Memorandum to Proposal for a European Parliament and Council Directive amending Directive 2006/116/EC of the European Parliament and of the Council on the term of protection of copyright and certain related rights, Brussels, COM (2008) 464/3, pp. 8–9

[This option] would increase the pool of A&R resources available to phonogram record producers and could thus have an additional positive impact on cultural diversity. The [Impact Assessment] also demonstrates that the benefits of a term extension are not necessarily skewed in favour of famous featured performers. While featured performers certainly earn the bulk of the copyright royalties that are negotiated with record companies, all performers, be it featured artists or session musicians, are entitled to so-called 'secondary' income sources, such as single equitable remuneration when the sound recording incorporating their performances is broadcast or performed in public. A term extension would ensure that these income sources do not cease during the performer's lifetime. Even incremental increases in income are used by performers to buy more time to devote to their artistic careers, and to spend less time on part time employment. Moreover, for the thousands of anonymous session musicians who were at the peak of their careers in the late fifties and sixties, 'single equitable remuneration' for the broadcasting of their recordings is often the only source of income left from their artistic career.

...

On the other hand, the impact on users would be minimal. This is true in relation to statutory remuneration claims and for the sale of CDs:

- First, the 'single equitable remuneration' due for broadcasting and performances of music in public venues would remain the same as these payments are calculated as a percentage of the broadcasters or other operators revenue (a parameter independent of how many phonograms are in or out of copyright).

- Empirical studies also show that the price of sound recordings that are out of copyright are not lower than that of sound recordings in copyright. A study by Price Waterhouse Coopers concluded that there was no systematic difference between prices of in-copyright and out-of copyright recordings. It is the most comprehensive study to date and covers 129 albums recorded between 1950 and 1958. On this basis, it finds no clear evidence that records in which the related rights have expired are systematically sold at lower prices than records which are still protected.

...

Overall the extended term should have a positive impact on consumer choice and cultural diversity. In the long run, this is because a term extension will benefit cultural diversity by ensuring the availability of resources to fund and develop new talent. In the short to medium term, a term extension provides record companies with an incentive to digitize and market their back catalogue of old recordings. It is already clear that internet distribution offers unique opportunities to market an unprecedented quantity of sound recordings.

The impact on so-called public domain producers would be minimal. While those companies could [argue] that they have to wait longer to produce phonograms in which the performers and phonogram producers' rights have expired, the works performed in a phonogram would not lose protection once the term of protection for the phonogram expires. This is because the work performed on a phonogram remains protected for the life of the author (songwriter and composer) who wrote the work.

The Commission's proposal attracted vehement and wide-ranging criticism, particularly from the academic community. One of the major criticisms was that the real problem for performers was not the length of protection, but rather their poor bargaining position such that they bargain away their rights in return for a one-off payment. Thus, scholars argued, a better means of improving the position of performers would be to restrict the lawfulness of these contracts.[69] Scholars also pointed out that the majority of performers earn an inadequate sum and a prolongation of protection would merely extend the receipt of this fairly minimal income, rather than substantially increase it.[70] Further, doubts were expressed about whether the losses in revenue to the record industry were due to peer-to-peer activities and indeed whether an increase in term of protection would be an adequate countermeasure to alleged widespread piracy.[71] Finally, commentators were sceptical that an increase in term would not negatively impact on users, in terms of access and the price paid for recordings that would otherwise be out of copyright.[72]

The Proposed Directive was subsequently amended so that the term extension was limited to an additional 20 years, i.e. to an overall term of 70 years. Moreover, various 'safeguards' were introduced into the directive in order to address some of the concerns that performers would not benefit from the increased protection. Thus, where a phonogram producer fails adequately to exploit the sound recording in the additional term period, the performer has a right to terminate the contract of transfer or assignment. This unwaivable right may only be exercised where the performer has given notice to the producer of his intention to terminate the contract and the phonogram producer has not adequately exploited the sound recording within a year of that notice. Further, there is an obligation on phonogram producers to put aside, at least once per year during the additional term period of 20 years, 20 per cent of revenue from the distribution, reproduction, and making available of sound recordings. This is for the benefit of performers whose performances were assigned for a lump sum and who will be entitled to an unwaivable right of annual supplementary remuneration to be administered by collecting societies. Finally, for those performers who have transferred their exclusive rights to a phonogram producer on a royalty basis, the performer is entitled to a 'clean slate' for the additional 20-year term, meaning that producers will not be able to deduct advance payments or other contractually defined deductions during this period.

The Term Extension Directive was subsequently adopted on 27 September 2011 and was implemented in the UK via the Copyright and Duration of Rights in Performances Regulations 2013.[73] The arguments on both sides of the debate as to whether to increase term of protection for sound recordings and performers repay much closer attention. However, based on what has been discussed, and bearing in mind the justifications for copyright addressed at 2.3, do you agree with the adoption of the Term Extension Directive?

---

[69] R. Hilty et al., 'Comment by the Max-Planck Institute on the Commission's proposal for a directive to amend Directive 2006/116 concerning the term of protection for copyright and related rights' [2009] EIPR 59, 61.

[70] Hilty et al., 'Comment by the Max-Planck Institute', 62–3; M. Kretschmer et al., 'Creativity stifled? A joint academic statement on the proposed copyright term extension for sound recordings' [2008] EIPR 341, 342.

[71] Hilty et al., 'Comment by the Max-Planck Institute', 64–5.

[72] Hilty et al., 'Comment by the Max-Planck Institute', 69; Kretschmer et al., 'Creativity stifled?', 343–4.

[73] SI 2013/1782.

FURTHER READING

C. Angelopolous, 'The myth of European term harmonisation—27 public domains for 27 Member States' (2012) 43 IIC 567.

N. Helberger et al., 'Never forever: why extending the term of protection for sound recordings is a bad idea' [2008] EIPR 174.

R. Hilty et al., 'Comment by the Max-Planck Institute on the Commission's proposal for a directive to amend Directive 2006/116 concerning the term of protection for copyright and related rights' [2009] EIPR 59.

M. Kretschmer et al., 'Creativity stifled? A joint academic statement on the proposed copyright term extension for sound recordings' [2008] EIPR 341.

A. Rahmatian, 'The Gowers review on copyright term extension' [2007] EIPR 353.

S. Ricketson, 'The copyright term' (1992) 23 IIC 753.

3.6 MORAL RIGHTS

In this section, we discuss a very particular set of rights—called moral rights—that inhere in authors of copyright works regardless of whether they retain ownership of the economic rights.

Moral rights were developed in the civil law countries, primarily Germany and France, during the 18th and 19th centuries. They are rights of a non-pecuniary nature and the main ones include: the right to divulge the work, the right to be attributed as author of the work (or the right of paternity), the right of integrity in the work, and the right to withdraw the work from circulation. Article 6*bis* of the Berne Convention, however, obliges Union members to implement only the rights of attribution and integrity. This provision was inserted into Berne at the Rome Revision Conference in 1928 and represented a compromise between civil law countries, represented by France, and common law countries such as the UK and Australia. The latter countries had resisted the introduction of moral rights into the Berne Convention on the basis that it was a concept 'alien' to common law systems and that, in any event, such interests were adequately protected by the laws of contract, defamation, and passing off.

Moral rights are said to be about protecting the personality interests of the author, as embodied in the copyright work. In the following extract, Professor Ginsburg suggests that this justification is at odds with common law systems and investigates whether or not alternative justifications may be found.

J. Ginsburg, 'Moral rights in the common law system'
(1990) 1 Ent. L. R. 121 at 122

Why Protect Moral Rights?

The denomination 'moral rights' may appear rhetorically charged. Does the 'moral' label suggest that these rights are somehow better or more sacrosanct than other rights associated with copyright? Does it cast the opponent of these rights as some kind of unethical bully? Although some moral rights advocates may subscribe to those sentiments, the derivation of the term is not so invested with 'moral' meaning. The term is a translation from the French 'droit moral', where it does not address 'morality', but rather, non-pecuniary interests. For example, the broader term 'dommage moral' denotes non-economic damages, such as psychological suffering, incurred by the victim of a tort. The justification of 'droit moral', as understood on the Continent, comes from the notion that the work incorporates the personality of the author because the authorial persona permeates and pervades the work. Therefore, when something happens to the work—such as a deformation or a mutilation—that constitutes an attack on the person or the personality of the author herself.

Such a deeply personalist justification may seem alien to copyright systems derived from the English copyright law. But that does not mean that moral rights are some kind of bizarre irruption into our intellectual property regimes. Rather, it means that an effort should be made to understand moral rights on our copyright terms. What are those terms? The 1710 English Statute of Anne enunciates a public benefit policy of copyright law. Protection is afforded because we believe it will induce authors to create works. The Statute of Anne states that its purpose is 'for the encouragement of learned men to write useful books'. Copyright creates a climate conducive to the production of works of authorship. Copyright benefits authors, and by so doing, enhances our scientific and cultural heritage.

How do moral rights fit into this socially-oriented scheme? It is often said that 'Anglo' copyright concerns only economic rights. This has generally been true, but it does not follow that our copyright laws are therefore incapable of protecting non-pecuniary personality rights. To say that a law has not yet done something does not imply that the law is inherently hostile to that goal. One strong argument for moral rights—an argument that strongly resonates with our copyright heritage—is that protection of creators' interests in attribution and integrity will improve the climate in which they create works of authorship. A writer who feels secure that she will receive name credit for her work, or an artist who can rely on the continued existence of his sculpture, may find this background knowledge more conducive to creative activity. Indeed, for some creators, the non-pecuniary rewards such as recognition and hoped-for immortality through preservation of the work, may be more important than immediate material gain. Adoption of moral rights sends a message that a society cares about creation, and about authorship. I cannot prove that the existence of moral rights would in fact make a difference to any given author, any more than I can prove that their absence forestalls creation. Nor indeed, by the same token, can I, or moral rights' detractors, prove that the existence of moral rights would in fact hurt the production of works. Adequate evidence is lacking on these issues. As a result, then, the question of moral rights should be viewed partly as a question of tone and primarily as a question of social policy.

Another argument for moral rights, which also echoes our collective copyright tradition, concerns the public benefit flowing from the enactment of moral rights. In addition to presenting the prospect of more productive creators, a moral rights regime furthers several public concerns. The right of attribution enhances the public interest because it affords, or it should afford, the fullest possible public information about who created a work, about the source of the work. The public has at least as much of an interest in knowing who the author is, as in knowing who the producer of a brand of detergent is. Moreover, the reverse side of the attribution right helps avoid public deception, as it prevents misattribution of the author's name to works the author did not create, or perhaps to works for which the author is only partially responsible, and for which she is receiving undue attribution. The integrity right promotes the public interest perhaps most strongly in the context of conservation of works of the visual arts, but it also plays an important public role to the extent that it avoids misrepresentation of deformed or altered works as those of an aggrieved artist or author.

Of course, as already indicated, these arguments do not represent the only possible vision of the relationship between moral rights and the public interest. One might contend that moral rights impede the efficient exploitation of works of authorship, and that this will discourage investment in creation. Essentially, this view articulates an investment model of copyright. In the United States we say: 'money talks'. In this 'investment' view, it also means that money writes, composes, paints and sculpts. Whatever the power of the dollar, it does not wreak these acts on its own. Indeed, the US Constitution acknowledges that the progress of learning is achieved by awarding copyright, not to publishers or investors, but to authors. But behind most works, even those in which there is third-party investment, there is a person or persons that have to do the creating. Moral rights are about society's commitment to the person. Not because she is superior, but because that commitment benefits all of us in ways not readily captured by a pure investment model of copyright.

Do you agree with Professor Ginsburg that the personality-based justification for moral rights is alien to UK copyright law? Are there any other problems with a personality-based justification that you can identify? For example, as Loughlan has argued, would it give too much primacy to the author and potentially disrupt the transformative practices of users of the work?[74] In any case, could the UK approach change as a result of the EU harmonization of originality that we examined at 2.5.2.3.1, specifically because the EU test involves taking into account creative choices and the 'stamp' of the author? Or, are Professor Ginsburg's alternative justifications a sound basis for protecting moral rights in the UK? According to her justifications, what sort of moral-rights regime would you expect to see, particularly when there is a conflict between the economic interests of the owner and the moral rights of the author?

Although Article 6bis of Berne was inserted in 1928, the UK did not implement this obligation until the Copyright, Designs and Patents Act 1988. Prior to the adoption of the Copyright Act 1956, the Gregory Committee report took the view that the obligations in Article 6bis were satisfied indirectly by the common law torts of defamation and passing off, and the law of contract. However, the Whitford Committee in 1977 expressed scepticism about whether such indirect provisions in English law were adequate and recommended the express introduction of moral rights.[75] They were expressly introduced in 1988.

The moral-rights provisions are contained in sections 77 to 85 and include the right to be identified as the author or director (s. 77 attribution right); the right to object to derogatory treatment of the work (s. 80 integrity right); the right to object to false attribution of the work (s. 84 false attribution right); and the right to privacy in certain photographs and films (s. 85 privacy right).

Although the false attribution right and privacy right are grouped under the heading 'Chapter IV Moral Rights', one needs to ask whether they are moral rights in the strict sense. This is especially so since neither right is concerned with the link between an author and his or her work, and the focus is on personal interests more generally. In the case of false attribution, it is the right to ensure that a person is not misattributed as the author of a work not created by him or her. In the case of the privacy right, it is the right to control the exploitation of photographs or films that have been commissioned for private and domestic purposes.

---

[74] P. Loughlan, 'Moral rights (a view from the town square)' (2000) 5 MALR 1.
[75] G. Dworkin, 'Moral rights in English law: the shape of rights to come' [1986] EIPR 329.

3.6.1 FALSE ATTRIBUTION

The false attribution right was first inserted in the Copyright Act 1956.[76] It is now contained in section 84 of the CDPA, which states that a person has a right to object to having a literary, dramatic, musical, or artistic work or film falsely attributed to him or her. The right is only infringed, however, where there is some kind of dealing with a work or copies of the work in or on which there is a false attribution.[77] Unlike the other moral rights, which endure for as long as copyright subsists in the work, this right lasts for 20 years after a person's death.

Below we consider one of the few decisions concerning section 84 of the CDPA.

Clark v Associated Newspapers Ltd [1998] 1 WLR 1558

The claimant (Clark) was a well-known Conservative MP, who had published diaries documenting his public and private life. The defendant (Associated Newspapers Ltd), who published the *Evening Standard* newspaper in London, ran a series of articles parodying the claimant's diaries. They were headed with the titles 'Alan Clark's Secret Election Diary' or 'Alan Clark's Secret Political Diaries' and were accompanied by a small masthead photograph of the claimant. Underneath the title was an introductory paragraph containing the name of the real author (Mr Peter Bradshaw) in capital letters and a statement that the author was imagining how the claimant would record the day's events. The claimant brought an action under section 84 of the CDPA and also for passing off.

Lightman J, at pp. 1564, 1568, 1571:

Legal principles

The plaintiff invokes two rights to protection from false attribution of authorship, one statutory and one common law. The plaintiff can succeed in this action if he establishes that either right has been infringed. The statutory right is that conferred by section 84(1)(a) of the Copyright, Designs and Patents Act 1988 'not to have a literary ... work falsely attributed to him as author'. (Section 84 of the Act of 1988 re-enacts the provision to like effect in section 43 of the Copyright Act 1956.) An 'attribution' in relation to such a work means 'a statement (express or implied) as to who is the author', and the right is infringed 'by a person who—(a) issues to the public copies of a work of any of those descriptions in or on which there is a false attribution': see section 84(2). An example of the commission of this tort is to be found in *Moore v News of the World Ltd* [1972] 1 QB 441. The newspaper in that case published an article under the headline: 'The Girl Who Lost The Saint. When Love Turns Sour by Dorothy Squires talking to Weston Taylor.' The words attributed to the plaintiff (Dorothy Squires) were not her words: they were the words of Weston Taylor. The issue was whether the article pretended to be written by Dorothy Squires. The trial judge directed the jury to make up their minds what the impression was to the reader. The jury found that the article did pretend to be written by Dorothy Squires. The Court of Appeal approved the direction by the trial judge and affirmed the decision that the tort had been committed.

---

[76] Although there was a predecessor in the Fine Arts Copyright Act 1862.

[77] CDPA, s. 84(2)–(6).

Two distinctive features of the statutory tort are: (a) that it is unnecessary that the plaintiff be a professional author and accordingly that he has any goodwill or reputation as an author to protect or which may be damaged by false attribution; and (b) consequently the tort is actionable per se without proof of damage. In short section 84 of the Act of 1988 confers a personal or civic right on everyone not to have authorship of any literary work falsely attributed to him. The plaintiff is accordingly entitled to relief under section 84 if he merely establishes the false attribution alleged.

...

Section 84 of the Act of 1988

The law of passing off embraces the concept that one and the same representation may mean something different to different members of the public and in order to succeed it is sufficient for the plaintiff to establish that one of those meanings misleads a substantial number of people. Mr Prescott has argued that the position is different under section 84 of the Act of 1988, and that upon the true construction of section 84 for the purposes of that section a representation can only have one single correct meaning and, if the tort is to be established, that meaning must be the false attribution of authorship.

Some support may be found in the direction to the jury of Cantley J approved by the Court of Appeal in *Moore v News of the World Ltd* [1972] 1 QB 441, 444d, 451g, 453. No other judicial or textbook guidance was cited to me.

In my judgment, Mr Prescott's submission is correct and to succeed in a claim under section 84 of the Act of 1988 a plaintiff must establish that the work in question contains what is a false attribution of authorship, and not merely what is or may be understood by some or more people to be a false attribution. The proper approach (as under the law of defamation) is to determine what is the single meaning which the literary work conveys to the notional reasonable reader: compare *Charleston v News Group Newspapers Ltd* [1995] 2 AC 65, 71. I must accordingly read the articles and decide whether they contain what would be understood by a reasonable reader to be a false attribution of authorship to the plaintiff.

...

Section 84

In my judgment (as I have already held) the headings of the articles contain a clear and unequivocal false statement attributing their authorship to the plaintiff, and the vice of this statement is not cured by the various counter-messages relied on by the defendant. I would be minded to accept that (as in certain cases of false trade description) the effect of such a false statement can be neutralised by an express contradiction, but (as in the case of a false trade description) it has to be as bold, precise and compelling as the false statement (consider the citation from the judgment of Lord Widgery CJ in *Norman v Bennett* [1974] 1 WLR 1229, 1232), and in this case the contradiction lacks the required prominence and is less likely to get home to the readers, as is confirmed (if confirmation is necessary) by the evidence in this case.

The plaintiff is accordingly entitled to relief in respect of the commission of the statutory tort.

The statement regarding the actual author was held to be insufficient to neutralize the false attribution of authorship to Mr Alan Clark. But if the counter-statement had been as 'bold, precise and compelling as the false statement' how effective would the parody have been? Should parodies be given greater leeway when it comes to false attribution?

In the subsequent case of *Harrison v Harrison*,[78] Fysh J in the Patents County Court held that false attribution arose where a second edition of a book, written by a person different to the author of the first edition, was published without any reference to an author. Testimonials praising the first edition had been included on the back cover of the second edition and, as such, the judge concluded that the single meaning to be assumed by a reasonable reader was that the updated second edition had been written by the same author as the first edition, which in fact was not the case.

3.6.2 ATTRIBUTION

We turn now to examine the first of the two proper moral rights in the CDPA. The right of attribution (also known as the paternity right) applies to authors of literary, dramatic, musical, or artistic works and directors of films and is the right to be identified as such. However, the right is only infringed where the work is dealt with in certain ways, without the proper attribution.[79]

An important precondition to exercising the right of attribution is that the right is asserted.[80] Failure to do so can destroy a claim to infringement of an attribution right, as was illustrated in *Christoffer v Poseidon Film Distributors Ltd*.[81] Assertion can occur by including, in an instrument of assignment of copyright in the work, a statement that the author or director asserts his right of attribution in relation to that work, or by an instrument in writing signed by the author or director.[82] In the case of public exhibition of artistic works, the right may also be asserted by ensuring that the author is identified on the original or copy of the artistic work, or on a frame, mount, or other thing to which it is attached.[83] Alternatively, by including in a licence by which the making of copies of the work is authorized a statement signed by or on behalf of the person granting the licence that the author asserts his right to be identified in the event of a public exhibition of a copy of the work.[84] What is the purpose, do you think, behind an assertion requirement? Is it problematic, particularly in light of the 'no formalities' rule specified in Article 5(2) of the Berne Convention?

What if an author uses a pseudonym or indeed wishes to remain anonymous? Does this fall within the scope of his or her right of attribution? Section 77(8) makes clear that if an author or director 'specifies a pseudonym, initials or some other particular form of identification be used, that form shall be used'. In the absence of a specified form of identification, it is acceptable to use any reasonable form of identification. It does not appear to be the case, however, that an author can insist on anonymity. How does this aspect of the right of attribution relate to the justification(s) for moral rights?

Commentators, such as Professor Ginsburg, have been critical of the UK's implementation of the attribution right. In the following extract, the main criticisms are discussed.

J. Ginsburg, 'Moral rights in the common law system' (1990) 1 Ent. L. R. 121 at 128–9

The CDPA announces a general right of attribution benefiting authors of literary, dramatic, musical or artistic works. But the right must be 'asserted', and binds only those who receive actual or constructive notice of the assertion. This precondition derives from a peculiar, not

---

[78] [2010] EWPCC 3, [2010] ECDR 12 (PCC).   [79] CDPA, s. 77(2)–(7).   [80] CDPA, s. 78.
[81] [2000] ECDR 487.   [82] CDPA, s. 78(2).
[83] CDPA, s. 78(3)(a).   [84] CDPA, s. 78(3).

to say perverse, reading of article 6 *bis* of the Berne Convention. The Berne Convention declares that the 'author shall have the right to claim authorship of the work'. From a provision entitling authors to recognition of their status as creators, the drafters of the CDPA fashioned an *obligation* to assert authorship before the right to be recognised can take effect. Not only does the UK text torture the Berne text, but the assertion requirement may well violate the Berne Convention's rule that 'the enjoyment and exercise' of authors' rights, including moral rights, 'shall not be subject to any formality'.

Multiple exceptions qualify the attribution right, notably the exclusions of creators of computer programs and employees creating works pursuant to their employment. Similarly, unlicensed uses of the work that are non-infringing uses (for example, fair dealing for purposes of news reporting) are not subject to the attribution right. In addition, the right is subject to waiver both formal and informal. As a result, an author who fails to 'assert' the right in her contract in effect may have no attribution right, and even if she does assert the right, a court may find overall conditions pointing to a waiver of the right.

Moreover, one may inquire how the assertion requirement affects third parties. The text of the CDPA appears to leave significant gaps in coverage. The text holds two classes of persons bound by an author's assertion of attribution rights: assignees and persons 'claiming through' them, when the assignment contained an assertion; and 'anyone to whom notice is brought of an instrument in writing [containing the assertion] signed by the author or director'. The structure of the statute prompts several questions. With respect to the second class of persons, what kind of written instrument is contemplated, and how is notice brought to third parties? It appears that identification of the author on the book, on the screen credits, etc., does not satisfy the statute, because even if this form of identification gives general notice of who the author is, it is not an 'instrument in writing signed' by the author. An author might, at least in theory, execute a document proclaiming herself to be the author, but how would this document be brought to the notice of third parties? A registry of claims of authorship, like a land-title registry, might afford notice, but would clash with the Berne Convention's proscription of formalities. Presentation of the document to third parties following their failure to credit the author should oblige them in the future, but will the notice receive retroactive effect to entitle the author to damages for prior non-attribution? A contract, such as a licence agreement, would meet the signed written instrument requirement, but, again, third parties would at least initially remain unaffected.

Finally, the distinction between an assignment and other written instruments points up further anomalies. Persons 'claiming through' an assignee of copyright are bound by the assertion in the assignment, even without actual notice. (Note, however, that third-party infringers appear to escape liability for violation of attribution rights; as infringers, they certainly do not 'claim through' the assignee.) But the sub-licensee of a licensee would not be obliged to credit the author, unless the sub-licensee had known of the author's assertion of the attribution right in the original licence agreement. Thus, for example, suppose an author executes a book-publishing agreement which includes an assertion of authorship, and entitles the publisher-licensee to license film rights in the book; the publisher licenses the film rights, but the sub-licence neither mentions the original assertion, nor obligates the film production company to attribute the work to the author. It appears that the author would have no attribution right against the film company: although the film company 'claims through' the publisher, the publisher was a licensee, not an assignee. Had the publisher been an assignee, the author would have had an attribution claim against the film company. This analysis indicates that the protection of authors' moral interests could come at the expense of their economic interests: for purposes of enforcing the attribution right, authors might be better off assigning all rights under the copyright, than retaining some rights and merely granting licences.

In light of the above discussion, would it be advisable for the UK to remove the requirement of assertion? What objections do you envisage to such a reform and are these outweighed by the disadvantages of the requirement?

A notable example of where there has been a successful claim for infringement of the attribution right is *Hyperion v Sawkins* (discussed at 2.5.1.3). The sleeve on the CDs acknowledged and thanked the claimant for his preparation of performance materials for the recording; however, the trial judge and Court of Appeal held that this was inadequate to identify the claimant as the author of the modern performing editions of Lalande's music.[85]

FURTHER READING

C. Fisk, 'Credit where it's due: the law and norms of attribution' (2006) 95 Geo. L. J. 49.

3.6.3 INTEGRITY

The second moral right in the CDPA, the right of integrity, has the potential to cause the greatest conflict between the interests of the author and those of the copyright owner. For example, the owner of a copyright in an artistic work (e.g. a painting) created by A may want to publish a reduced-size version of the work in a catalogue. The copyright owner is entitled to exercise the right of reproduction, but at the same time the author, A, objects that the reduction in size is a derogatory treatment of his painting because the subtleties of the brushstrokes and colours are lost. Clearly, there is a clash of interests and the question is how will these be balanced and whose interests will prevail? A closer examination of the right of integrity will indicate where the preference lies.

Section 80 of the CDPA grants authors of literary, dramatic, musical, and artistic works and directors of films the right, in certain circumstances, not to have their work subjected to derogatory treatment. Those circumstances are set out in section 80(3)–(6) and include such things as exhibiting in public a derogatory treatment of an artistic work or commercially publishing, performing in public, or communicating to the public a derogatory treatment of a literary, dramatic, or musical work.

3.6.3.1 Treatment

Both 'treatment' and 'derogatory' are defined. 'Treatment' means 'any addition to, deletion from or alteration to or adaptation of the work' but does not include a translation of a literary or dramatic work or an arrangement or transcription of a musical work involving no more than a change of key or register.[86] Is this definition a broad one? Would it encompass uses of a work that do not change the physical structure of the work, but alter its meaning or perception, such as a portrait of the Royal Family hung amongst an exhibition of pornography or a modern piece of classical music used as part of a television advertisement selling washing powder? Arguably, the definition of 'treatment' does not embrace such instances of recontextualization. As a result, the UK provision on 'treatment' is probably contrary to Article 6*bis*(1) of the Berne Convention, which refers to 'other derogatory action in relation to' the work. However, in *Harrison v Harrison*, Judge Fysh suggested, in *obiter*, that 'treatment'

---

[85] [2005] EWCA Civ 565, [2005] RPC 32, [69].   [86] CDPA, s. 80(2).

of a work is 'a broad, general concept ... [that] implies a spectrum of possible acts carried out on the work, from the addition of say, a single word to a poem to the destruction of the entire work' and that the limit to the generality of 'treatment' was 'surely to be found ... in the possible prejudice to the honour or reputation of the author'.[87] This dicta, while encouraging, still does not seem directed towards recontextualization of works where no physical change has been made.

3.6.3.2 Derogatory

Treatment of a work is 'derogatory', 'if it amounts to distortion or mutilation of the work or is otherwise prejudicial to the honour or reputation of the author or director'.[88] There are very few cases on the UK integrity right and even fewer that discuss the meaning of 'derogatory'. One of the leading cases is examined below.

Confetti Records v Warner Music UK Ltd [2003] ECDR 31

The third claimant (Mr Alcee) had composed a piece of garage music called 'Burnin', which he sold to the first claimant (Confetti Records). The defendant (Warner Music) had been in negotiations with the first claimant to use the 'Burnin' track on a compilation album, but these fell through late in the day, by which time the defendant had recorded and mixed their album and made a quantity of copies. The original version of 'Burnin' comprised an insistent instrumental beat accompanied by the vocal repetition of the word 'burning'. The version produced by the defendant featured the Heartless Crew, a garage trio of DJ Fonti and MCs Mighty Mo and Bushkin. The Heartless Crew used the original version of 'Burnin' as a backing track, over which they rapped lyrics. The third claimant alleged that this was a derogatory treatment of his work because the rap lyrics were suggestive of violence and drug usage.

Lewison J:

149. Mr Howe submitted that there could be no derogatory treatment unless the treatment was prejudicial to the honour or reputation of the author. Mr Shipley, on the other hand, said that treatment was derogatory if it was a distortion or mutilation of the work, even if it did not prejudice the honour or reputation of the author. Both Laddie Prescott and Vitoria on The Modern Law of Copyrights and Designs (3rd ed.) paragraph 13.18, and Copinger and Skone James on Copyright (14th ed.) paragraph 11–42, disagree with this view. So do I. Section 80 is clearly intended to give effect to Art. 6 bis of the Berne Convention. That article gives the author the right to object: 'to any distortion, mutilation or other modification of, or other derogatory action in relation to, the said work, which would be prejudicial to his honour or reputation'.

150. It is clear that in Art. 6 bis the author can only object to distortion, mutilation or modification of his work if it is prejudicial to his honour or reputation. I do not believe that the framers of the 1988 Act meant to alter the scope of the author's moral rights in this respect. Moreover, in the compressed drafting style of the United Kingdom legislature, the word

---

[87] [2010] EWPCC 3, [2010] ECDR 12 (PCC), [60].   [88] CDPA, s. 80(2)(b).

'otherwise' itself suggests that the distortion or mutilation is only actionable if it is prejudicial to the author's honour or reputation. HH Judge Overend adopted this construction in *Pasterfield v Denham* [1999] FSR 168, and in my judgment he was correct to do so. I hold that the mere fact that a work has been distorted or mutilated gives rise to no claim, unless the distortion or mutilation prejudices the author's honour or reputation.

151. The nub of the original complaint, principally advanced by Mr Pascal, is that the words of the rap (or at least that part contributed by Elephant Man) contained references to violence and drugs. This led to the faintly surreal experience of three gentlemen in horsehair wigs examining the meaning of such phrases as 'mish mish man' and 'shizzle (or sizzle) my nizzle'.

152. The 'author' in the present case is the third claimant, Mr Alcee. The assignment of his copyright to the first and/or second claimants does not affect his authorship. The first and second claimants are not entitled to complain of prejudice to their honour or reputation. Thus the evidence that I heard about the kinds of songs produced by Confetti, and in particular about the meaning of the lyrics of 'Champion Puffa', is, to my mind, irrelevant.

153. When played at normal speed the words of the rap overlying 'Burnin' are very hard to decipher, and indeed the parties disagreed on what the words were. Even when played at half speed there were disagreements about the lyrics. The very fact that the words are hard to decipher itself militates against the conclusion that the treatment was 'derogatory' in the statutory sense.

154. Mr Pascal did not himself claim to know what street meanings were to be attributed to the disputed phrases, but said that he had been told what they were by an unnamed informant conversant with the use of drugs. Mr Howe submitted, correctly in my opinion, that the meaning of words in a foreign language could only be explained by experts. He also submitted, again correctly in my opinion, that the words of the rap, although in a form of English, were for practical purposes a foreign language. Thus he submitted that Mr Pascal's evidence, not being the evidence of an expert, was inadmissible. I think that he is right, although the occasions on which an expert drug dealer might be called to give evidence in the Chancery Division are likely to be rare.

155. But even if I pay regard to Mr Pascal's evidence on this topic, I do not find that the meaning of the disputed words has been proved. Mr Pascal's evidence was hearsay, and the source of his information was not identified. Mr Hunter, one of the MCs with The Heartless Crew, (professionally known as MC Bushkin) had not heard of the meanings that Mr Pascal attributed to the disputed phrases. Nor had Mr Thomas. A search on the Internet discovered the Urban Dictionary which gave some definitions of 'shizzle my nizzle' (and variants) none of which referred to drugs. Some definitions carried sexual connotations. The most popular definitions were definitions of the phrase 'fo' shizzle my nizzle' and indicated that it meant 'for sure'. There were no entries for 'sizzle my nizzle' or for 'mish mish man', and Mr Hunter said that Elephant Man (the MC who uttered the disputed phrases) often made up words for their rhyming effect.

156. To be fair, Mr Shipley did not press this complaint in his closing submissions. Instead he sought to advance a new case. First he said that the treatment was derogatory because all coherence of the original work has been lost as a result of the superimposition of the rap. Secondly he said, whatever a 'mish mish man' was, the words of the rap 'string dem up one by one' was an invitation to lynching. It is by no means clear that the words on the rap are in fact 'string dem up'. Moreover, I am not at all sure that the meaning Mr Shipley attributes to the phrase 'string dem up' is the only possible meaning. A proponent of capital punishment

who says that murderers should be 'strung up' would usually be taken to advocate the return of a hangman, rather than lynching.

157. However, it seems to me that the fundamental weakness in this part of the case is that I have no evidence about Mr Alcee's honour or reputation. I have no evidence of any prejudice to either of them. Mr Alcee himself made no complaint about the treatment of 'Burnin' in his witness statement. Mr Shipley invites me to infer prejudice. Where the author himself makes no complaint, I do not consider that I should infer prejudice on his behalf.

158. I do not infer any prejudice from the fact that The Heartless Crew rode the rhythm right through the track. If I am to draw any inference, the inference I would draw, having listened to the original mix of 'Burnin', is that it was designed to be the background track to a rap. Indeed the proposed mix for the single of 'Burnin' by the Ant'ill Mob (called the vocal mix) was itself a rap which rode the rhythm throughout the track.

159. There was a suggestion that Mr Alcee is the only permanent member of the Ant'ill Mob. He did not say this in his own witness statement, and Mr Pascal said in his witness statement that the Ant'ill Mob 'do not have identifiable members in the traditional sense of a group'. He also said that when they perform Confetti hire session musicians to form the group.

160. If, however, Mr Alcee is a member (or perhaps the only member) of the Ant'ill Mob, then the way in which they are presented may impinge on his own honour and reputation. It is clear to me, despite Mr Pascal's protestations to the contrary, that the Ant'ill Mob were costumed to look like 1930s gangsters. As it was put in a newspaper article in February 2002, the release of 'Burnin' was twinned 'with a video showing the Mob in true 1930s gangster style'. My own viewing of the video confirmed this impression. I do not therefore infer any prejudice from the invitation to 'string up' 'mish mish men', even if it bears the meaning that Mr Shipley attributes to it.

From reading the above extract, would you say that to establish derogatory treatment it is enough that an author objects to what has been done to his or her work? If not, what must be established and what is the relevance of both honour and reputation? Would you describe the approach for determining whether treatment is derogatory as an objective or subjective one? In France, which represents the par excellence of moral-rights protection, it is enough that the author objects to what has been done to his or her work. For example, the estate of John Huston was successful in restraining the owners of copyright in the black-and-white film *Asphalt Jungle*, which he co-directed, from showing a colour version of it in France.[89] In your view, is the French approach preferable to that adopted in the UK?

FURTHER READING

E. Adeney, 'The moral right of integrity: the past and future of "honour"' [2005] IPQ 111.

T. Cheng-Davies, 'Honour in UK copyright law is not "A Trim Reckoning" – its impact on the integrity right and the destruction of works of art' (2016) 36 OJLS 272.

S. Teilmann, 'Framing the law: the right of integrity in Britain' [2005] EIPR 19.

---

[89] See *Huston v Turner Entertainment Co.* [1992] ECC 334.

3.6.4 EXCEPTIONS

There are a raft of exceptions in relation to both the attribution and integrity rights, the more important of which will be mentioned here.

The rights do not apply to computer programs or any computer-generated works[90] and, in the case of the attribution right, also designs of typefaces. The rights also do not apply in relation to any work made for the purpose of reporting current events.[91] In addition, where an act would not infringe copyright because it is fair dealing for the purpose of reporting current events by means of a sound recording, film, or broadcast, the attribution right will not be infringed.[92]

The publishing industry was successful in obtaining exceptions in their favour. Thus, neither the attribution nor the integrity right applies:

> in relation to the publication in (a) a newspaper, magazine or similar periodical, or (b) an ency-clopaedia, dictionary, yearbook or other collective work of reference, of a literary, dramatic, musical or artistic work made for the purposes of such publication or made available with the consent of the author for the purposes of such publication.[93]

Perhaps the most important exclusions are those relating to employee-created works. The right of attribution does not apply to anything done by or with the authority of the owner of copyright in a work, where ownership originally vested in the author's or director's employer under section 11(2).[94] As such, employee authors have their right of attribution severely limited. When it comes to the right of integrity, this does not apply to anything done in relation to an employee-created work unless the author or director is identified at the time of the relevant act or has previously been identified in or on published copies of the work and there is no sufficient disclaimer.[95] Given that employers will usually own copyright in works created by their employees in the course of employment, does it seem fair also to deprive employees of their moral rights in relation to such works?

3.6.5 WAIVER

If an author consents to a particular act being done, it will not amount to an infringement of moral rights.[96] In addition, an author may *waive* his or her moral rights by an instrument in writing.[97] The waiver may potentially be broad-ranging, in that it can relate to works of a specified description or to works generally and to existing or future works. If it is made in favour of the owner or prospective owner of copyright in the work to which it relates, it shall be presumed to extend to his licensees and successors in title, unless a contrary intention is expressed.[98]

Does the ability to waive moral rights, particularly in the way possible under the CDPA, seriously undermine the effectiveness of those rights? If so, would it be desirable to prevent waiver or at least limit the circumstances in which it can be used?

---

[90] CDPA, ss. 79(2) and 81(2).   [91] CDPA, ss. 79(5) and 81(3).   [92] CDPA, s. 79(4)(a).
[93] CDPA, ss. 79(6) and 81(4).   [94] CDPA, s. 79(3).   [95] CDPA, s. 82(1)–(2).
[96] CDPA, s. 87(1).   [97] CDPA, s. 87(2).   [98] CDPA, s. 87(3).

3.6.6 ALTERNATIVE APPROACH?

As mentioned earlier, France represents the par excellence of moral-rights regimes. In the following extract, Dr Irini Stamatoudi highlights the main features of the French approach.

I. Stamatoudi, 'Moral rights of authors in England: the missing emphasis on the role of creators' [1997] IPQ 478 at 498–500

The French paradigm

France was the first country in Europe to recognise the '*droit moral*'. This legal concept was first formed in a piecemeal way through case law at the end of the 19th century, while in the mid-20th century moral rights were given statutory recognition. Today moral rights in France are enshrined in the 1994 CPI. There are five moral rights, namely the right of divulgation (*droit de divulgation*), the right of integrity (*droit au respect*), the right of paternity (*droit de paternité*), the right of revocation (*droit de repentir*) and the right of access to the work (*droit d'accès a l'oeuvre*).

The right of divulgation or publication of the work is in fact the author's right to decide whether or not to publish a work and in what form. The paternity and integrity rights have the same content as their counterparts in the Berne Convention, although the requirement in relation to the integrity right of harm to the author's honour or reputation, has been dropped. More specifically, the integrity right, apart from harm to the author's honour or reputation, also covers situations where the material integrity of a work has not been affected and no direct harm to the author's honour or reputation has ensued, but where, for example, the image of the author has suffered due to the circumstances in which the work was exhibited to the public. The right of revocation is supposed to be a corollary to the right to publication. According to this right the author of a work can withdraw it from sale because he has changed his views. That right is, of course, not unrestricted. Essentially the author has to compensate the publisher for all the expenses he has incurred in marketing the work. However, if the owner of the work at issue is affected as well, relief under the right might not be given by the court. And lastly, there is the right of access to the work. The author has the right to see his work in order to be able to make reproductions, observe details or just enjoy it. This right is to be exercised under certain rather restrictive conditions (e.g. without being a constant nuisance to the owner of the work, and with the obligation to visit the owner's residence and not expect the owner to bring the work over to him).

Contrary to common law countries, France has adopted the dualistic approach to moral rights. It distinguishes moral rights from the economic rights of authors and considers them to be separate rights. They are also said to be perpetual, imprescriptible, non-assignable and discretionary. These characteristics are indicative of the degree of protection accorded to authors under French copyright law. However, these characteristics are not without restrictions. Apart from express exceptions, such as in the case of computer programs and films where certain alterations are held not to infringe the right of integrity, there are implied exceptions as well. In fact, the scope of these rights is to be interpreted purposively, which in practice includes the rights being balanced against other legal rights which other parties may hold, as well as the practical circumstances of the specific case being taken into account. First, in relation to their existence in perpetuity, one may wonder how moral rights can be exercisable when neither the author, nor members of his family are left alive. It must be mentioned here that the courts are reluctant to accept claims from people who are not family members. As Dietz points out, '[I]n spite of the recognised principle [of perpetuity] the reduced number of persons able to sue for infringement of moral rights makes the perpetuity of its protection considerably less important'.

Secondly by 'discretion' one does not mean that the author has the unrestricted right to exercise his moral rights whenever he thinks appropriate. This right is given to him, only if he exercises his moral rights in a way that is consistent with their purpose. If that is not the case the court will prevent him from exercising them abusively or to another end; for example, to get a better deal by concluding another more lucrative publishing contract after he frees himself from the one at issue.

Lastly, assertion and waiver are not provided for under French law. Moral rights constitute *ius cogens* and they cannot be contracted out of, by the parties.

Having considered the UK regime of moral rights and briefly also the French regime, would you say that the UK takes moral rights protection seriously? What does the UK approach to moral rights tell you about its copyright system as a whole? Finally, it is worth noting that moral rights is one of the areas left untouched by EU legislative harmonization. If the UK and France represent opposite ends of the spectrum of moral rights protection, what is the likelihood that harmonization will be possible? Moreover, how pressing a need is there, do you think, to harmonize moral rights within the EU?

FURTHER READING

E. Adeney, *The Moral Rights of Authors and Performers* (Oxford: Oxford University Press, 2006).

G. Davies and K. Garnett QC, *Moral Rights* (London: Sweet & Maxwell, 2010).

I. Harding and E. Sweetland, 'Moral rights in the modern world: is it time for a change?' (2012) 7 JIPLP 565.

G. Lea, 'Moral rights and the internet: some thoughts from a common law perspective' in F. Pollaud-Dulian (ed.), *Perspectives on Intellectual Property: The Internet and Author's Rights* (London: Sweet & Maxwell, 1999), p. 94.

P. Loughlan, 'Moral rights (a view from the town square)' (2000) 5 Media and Arts L. Rev. 1.

S. Newman, 'The development of copyright and moral rights in the European legal systems' [2011] EIPR 677.

G. Pessach, 'The author's moral right of integrity in cyberspace—a preliminary normative framework' (2003) 34 IIC 250.

L. de Souza, 'Moral rights and the internet: squaring the circle' [2002] IPQ 265.

3.7 ECONOMIC RIGHTS

According to section 16 of the CDPA, the copyright owner has the exclusive right to:

- copy the work;
- issue copies of the work to the public;
- rent or lend the work to the public;

- perform, show, or play the work in public;
- communicate the work to the public;
- make an adaptation of the work or do any of the above in relation to an adaptation.

These economic rights comprise the copyright owner's monopoly and allow the owner to exploit the work in a variety of ways. From the time of the Statute of Anne (1710), which prohibited only copying, it is clear that the bundle of rights granted to an owner has grown steadily. It is also interesting to note that the CDPA enumerates the exclusive rights, meaning that it specifically states the acts that belong to the copyright owner. Thus, if a new mode of exploitation arises it is a matter of seeing whether it can be encompassed within the existing rights; if not, the practice is to amend the legislation accordingly. The most recent example of this was the insertion of the right of communication to the public, particularly to include internet transmissions.[99] This approach may be contrasted with that taken in France, where two broad rights are granted—that of reproduction and performance—and courts have interpreted these rights to include new forms of exploitation as and when they have emerged, thus avoiding the need for regular legislative amendment.

The following sections discuss the scope of the exclusive rights in the CDPA in more detail.

3.7.1 REPRODUCTION

The right to copy the work is the oldest of the exclusive acts, being first recognized in the Statute of Anne 1710. Section 17 of the CDPA elaborates upon the scope of this right and emphasizes several important features. For literary, dramatic, musical, and artistic works, the right means 'reproducing the work in any material form' and this includes 'storing the work in any medium by electronic means'.[100] As such, simply digitizing a work (e.g. by scanning a document or converting an analogue musical recording to digital) will amount to a copy.

In addition, for any description of work, copying includes transient or incidental copies. Thus, running a computer program or browsing an internet webpage will involve copying since transient copies are made in the Random Access Memory (RAM) of one's computer. The fact that transient copying is a prohibited act has been a controversial issue. For example, at the WIPO Diplomatic Conference in December 1996, there was considerable disagreement about the scope of the reproduction right contained in Article 9(1) of the Berne Convention and whether the WIPO Copyright Treaty (WCT) should stipulate that transient copies were included within its scope. Those against including any technical copy of a work argued that this would create a right of *access* and would be too far-reaching. A stalemate occurred on this issue and the most that was achieved was an agreed statement that:

> The reproduction right, as set out in Article 9 of the Berne Convention, and the exceptions permitted thereunder, fully apply in the digital environment, in particular to the use of works in digital form. It is understood that the storage of a protected work in digital form in an electronic medium constitutes a reproduction within the meaning of Article 9 of the Berne Convention.[101]

---

[99] See CDPA, s. 20 and 3.7.6.   [100] CDPA, s. 17(2).

[101] There was an equivalent Agreed Statement for performers and phonogram producers in the WIPO Performances and Phonograms Treaty 1996, discussed at 2.4.1.5.

This statement achieved little apart from stating the obvious, namely that a reproduction could occur where it was in digital or electronic format. It did not answer the question of whether temporary or transient copies of a work would also constitute a 'reproduction' in legal terms.

At the EU level, Article 2 of the Information Society Directive obligates Member States to provide:

> the exclusive right to authorise or prohibit direct or indirect, temporary or permanent reproduction by any means and in any form, in whole or in part.[102]

This provision, read together with recital 2 of the Information Society Directive, clearly shows that the reproduction right is to be broadly construed as a matter of EU law and this view has been confirmed by CJEU rulings.[103]

The fact that reproduction extends to transient copying has been criticized by some commentators for taking a factual or technical approach to defining the scope of this right, as opposed to a normative approach.[104] Indeed, Professor Litman has argued that '[t]he centrality of copying to use of digital technology is precisely why reproduction is no longer an appropriate way to measure infringement'.[105] As well, there is concern that an over-expansive interpretation of reproduction in this manner will lead to undue overlap with the right of communication to the public.[106] It may be, however, that any harshness of this broad definition of 'reproduction' is mitigated somewhat by the mandatory exception for temporary copying contained in Article 5(1) and implemented in section 28A of the CDPA, discussed at 4.3.3.

In relation to artistic works, section 17(3) of the CDPA stipulates that copying includes changes of dimension, from two-dimensional to three-dimensional form and vice versa. Thus, an owner of copyright in a drawing of, say, a cartoon character will be able to prevent an unauthorized third party from making a cuddly toy of that character. Further, an owner of copyright in sculpture will be able to prevent unauthorized photographs of it being made. The fact that copying of artistic works includes changes of dimension is particularly useful to those creating industrial or functional designs and can create a tension between copyright and designs law.[107]

An issue that has arisen is whether reproduction in a different dimension or material form is prohibited for works other than artistic works. For example, does following a set of instructions (such as a recipe or knitting pattern) and producing a resultant article according to those instructions amount to an infringement of the literary work represented by the instructions? This issue was discussed in *obiter* in the following case.

---

[102] Note that the UK did not have to amend the CDPA in order to implement Art. 2 of the Information Society Directive as regards temporary copying since s. 17(6) already defined 'copying' to include 'the making of copies which are transient or are incidental to some other use of the work'.

[103] *Infopaq International A/S v Danske Dagblades Forening* Case C-5/08 [2010] FSR 20, [40]–[43]. See also *Football Association Premier League v QC Leisure; Murphy v Media Protection Services* Joined Cases C-403 and 429/08 [2012] FSR 1, [157]–[159] where the CJEU ruled that fragments of works stored transiently in the memory of a satellite decoder and on a television screen could constitute reproductions 'provided those fragments contain elements which are the expression of the author's own intellectual creation', [159].

[104] e.g. see P. B. Hugenholtz, 'Caching and copyright: the right of temporary copying' [2000] EIPR 482, 485.

[105] J. Litman, *Digital Copyright* (New York: Prometheus, 2001), p. 178.

[106] M. F. Makeen, *Copyright in a Global Information Society: The Scope of Copyright Protection under International, US, UK and French Law* (London: Kluwer, 2000), pp. 308–14.

[107] See 14.4.

Autospin (Oil Seals) Ltd v Beehive Spinning [1995] RPC 683

The claimant (Autospin) had designed and developed a new type of oil seal. There were three dimensions of critical importance to manufacturing this seal and the claimant had produced charts containing instructions that allowed these dimensions to be calculated. The defendants (Beehive Spinning), who were all ex-employees of the claimant, began manufacturing oil seals, which the claimants alleged, inter alia, infringed copyright in the compilation of measurements in their charts. Laddie J considered whether or not a three-dimensional article could reproduce a literary work, in this case the compilation.

Laddie J, at pp. 697–8, 700:

Argument in favour of a three dimensional article being a reproduction of a literary work:

...

It is well established that the copyright in a two dimensional drawing (an 'artistic work' under the relevant legislation) may be infringed by reproducing it in a three dimensional article. This was the law well before the legislation expressly provided that it was so (See *King Features Syndicate Inc v O and M Kleeman Ltd* [1941] AC 417). By parity of reasoning, since copyright in a literary work may be infringed by reproducing it in any material form, why should it not be an infringement to take a compilation of dimensions and reproduce it in the form of a three dimensional article which embodies those dimensions? After all, the alleged infringer has made use of the author's skill and effort in discovering and bringing together the relevant dimensions.

The argument can also be put another way. As I have mentioned, copyright in a drawing can be infringed by reproducing it in a three dimensional form. It is possible to define any shape in words and letters. Therefore a design in a drawing can be defined equally accurately in non-graphic notation. In fact many three dimensional articles are now designed on computers. A literary work consisting of computer code therefore represents the three dimensional article. Surely if it is an infringement of copyright in a two dimensional drawing to make a three dimensional article from it, it must follow that it should also be an infringement to produce the article from the equivalent literary work which contains the same design information and is just as much a product of the author's design skill ... Against this, my attention was drawn to statements in two cases. In the Privy Council in *Interlego AG v Tyco Industries Inc* [1988] RPC 343, Lord Oliver said:

> 'It has always to be borne in mind that infringement of copyright by three dimensional copying is restricted to artistic copyright (section 48(1)). To produce an article by following written instructions may be a breach of confidence or an infringement of patent, but it does not infringe the author's copyright in his instructions.' [page 373]

...

The second case was *Brigid Foley Ltd v Ellott* [1982] RPC 433 in which the plaintiff was seeking to enforce the copyright in a knitting guide. Megarry V-C stated:

> 'I did not call upon Mr Pumphrey to argue this point, since it seems to me quite plain that there is no reproduction of the words and numerals in the knitting guides in the knitted garments produced by following the instructions. The essence, I think, of a reproduction (and I do not attempt to be exhaustive) is that the reproduction should be some copy of or

representation of the original. I do not see how anyone looking at the knitted garment could then say "Well, that is a copy of, or a reproduction of, the words and numerals to be found in the knitting guide". By a process of counting up the number of stitches, and so on, in the knitted garment one might be able to work back and produce the knitting instructions; but that is a very different matter from saying that the garment is a reproduction of those instructions.' [page 434]

… In my view the court should ask the question 'is it accurate to say that the alleged infringer's article is, from a common sense point of view, a reproduction of this particular type of literary work?' In answering that question in this case, it is potentially misleading to look over one's shoulder to see what the response would have been if the compilation had been an artistic work or even a different form of literary work. Thus it may well be sensible to say that making a three dimensional article from a data file in a computer (a literary work) which precisely defines the shape of the article is to reproduce it. However, in my view, even if the plaintiff's charts in this case had included the three critical dimensions of some of the parts used for making a seal, it would not be right to say that making a seal to those dimensions is to reproduce the charts. Those dimensions say virtually nothing about the shape of the seal, they merely indicate some critical dimensions used in the manufacturing process which results in the creation of the seal.

Indeed, in my view, on the facts, this case is even weaker that [sic] that. The charts do not contain even the three critical dimensions. They contain instructions for the calculation of those dimensions…

The charts say nothing more about how a seal is to be constructed. In my view, just as it cannot be a reproduction of literary copyright in a recipe for a cake to make a cake to the recipe, so it is not a reproduction to follow such mathematical instructions.

For these reasons I hold that the claim to infringement of copyright in the charts also fails.

Do you agree with the approach taken by Laddie J? In what sorts of situations do you imagine there could be a three-dimensional reproduction of a literary work?

FURTHER READING

S. Dusollier, 'Technology as an imperative for regulating copyright: from the public exploitation to the private use of the work' [2005] EIPR 201.

P. B. Hugenholtz, 'Adapting copyright to the information superhighway' in Hugenholtz (ed.), *The Future of Copyright in a Digital Environment* (The Hague: Kluwer, 1996), pp. 81–102.

P. B. Hugenholtz, 'Caching and copyright: the right of temporary copying' [2000] EIPR 482.

M. F. Makeen, *Copyright in a Global Information Society: The Scope of Copyright Protection under International, US, UK and French Law* (London: Kluwer, 2000), pp. 308–14.

P. Recht, 'Should the Berne Convention include a definition of the right of reproduction?' [1965] Copyright 82.

3.7.2 ADAPTATION

It is important to note that, unlike under US copyright law, the right of adaptation in the CDPA does not amount to a right to control the creation of all adaptations or derivative works. Rather, it is restricted to certain types of works—literary, dramatic, and musical works—and is defined narrowly.[108] For example, it includes a translation of a literary or dramatic work or converting a dramatic work into non-dramatic form (and vice versa).[109] In relation to musical works, adaptation means an arrangement or transcription of the work.[110] For a subset of literary works, specifically computer programs, 'adaptation' means 'an arrangement or altered version of the program or a translation of it'[111] and according to section 21(4) of the CDPA, a 'translation' of the program includes where a version of the program in one language or code is converted into another language or code. Important to note is that the right of adaptation is left unharmonized by the EU Information Society Directive (2001/29);[112] and, further, it may not be straightforward to identify the dividing line between reproduction (which is harmonized by Article 2 of the Information Society Directive) and adaptation. In *Art & Allposters International BV v Stichting Pictoright*, Advocate General Villalón opined that the concept of 'adaptation' was 'an artistic expression which *recreates* the subject-matter of that work in its own language and its own conceptual and expressive universe, which differ from those in which it was originally conceived',[113] and that the canvas transfer was not an adaptation because it did not affect the image reproduced.[114] The CJEU chose not to interpret the concept of 'adaptation', but instead ruled that the transfer of an image (i.e. an artistic work) from a poster to a canvas was 'actually sufficient to constitute a new reproduction of that work, within the meaning of art. 2(a) of Directive 2001/29'.[115]

An adaptation of a literary, dramatic, or musical work may itself separately qualify for protection under the CDPA assuming the originality requirement has been satisfied. This usually will be the case according to the 'labour, skill, and judgment' test and the fact that the adaptation is carried out without permission and is thus infringing will not preclude it from being protected by copyright.[116] Whether adaptations of literary, dramatic, or musical works will satisfy the EU test of 'author's own intellectual creation' will depend on whether creative choices have been exercised. Even for straightforward translations from, for example, English to French, there are likely to be creative decisions made about which terminology to employ. In the case of musical arrangements or adaptations, whether there is sufficient intellectual creation could depend on their simplicity. For example, if a person was adapting a musical work to a different key, the functional constraints on what is required to achieve this may preclude any exercise of creative choice. The same may be said for simple arrangements from one instrument to another.

3.7.3 DISTRIBUTION

The right to issue copies of a work to the public was first introduced by section 18 of the CDPA. Prior to this legislation, there existed only a right to publish the work for the first time.[117] In other words, there was a shift from a right of divulgation to a right of distribution of the work. Section 18 has been amended twice, in order to implement Article 4 of

---

[108] CDPA, s. 21.   [109] CDPA, s. 21(3)(a).   [110] CDPA, s. 21(3)(b).

[111] CDPA, s. 21(ab).

[112] *Art & Allposters International BV v Stichting Pictoright* Case C-419/13 [2016] FSR 6, [26].

[113] [AG57].   [114] [AG59] and [AG60].   [115] [43].

[116] See e.g. *Redwood Music v Chappell* [1982] RPC 109 and *ZYX v King* [1995] FSR 566 (both involving musical arrangements).

[117] See *Infabrics Ltd v Jaytex Ltd* [1981] 1 All ER 1057, 1067.

the Software Directive and Article 9 of the Rental Rights Directive (it did not have to be amended in order to implement Article 4 of the Information Society Directive).[118] These amendments have resulted in a complex provision that gives rise to several uncertainties. One of the major uncertainties is identifying the point at which there has been a distribution or issuing *to the public*.

Professors Phillips and Bently have examined this issue at length, largely focusing on the ambiguities present within section 18 and have suggested two alternative interpretations of when issuing to the public occurs. The first is at the point of *disposition* (when the work is first put into circulation) and the second is at the point of *destination* (i.e. when the work is sold to the consumer, i.e. the general public).[119] Resolving which is the correct interpretation is crucial to distinguishing acts of primary and secondary infringement[120] under UK copyright law (and to the tenability of that distinction), and to identifying when the distribution right has been exhausted.

The 'disposition' interpretation is supported by three main arguments. The first is that the language of section 18(2), which defines issuing copies to the public as 'the act of putting into circulation', 'implies an act of alienation early in the chain of distribution'.[121] Second, this interpretation would permit the UK to maintain its distinction between primary and secondary infringement. In particular, it would ensure that retailers are not held strictly liable for selling infringing copies of copyright works but are only held liable where they import or deal in infringing copies with the requisite knowledge.[122] The converse would happen under the 'destination' interpretation and this would undermine 'the traditional dichotomy in English law between primary and secondary infringement'.[123] Finally, the Court of Justice has held that the distribution right is exhausted when the goods are placed on the market in the EU by or with the consent of the copyright owner,[124] and 'placed on the market' has not been interpreted to require sale to members of the general public.[125]

However, there are also three main arguments supporting a 'destination' interpretation. First, the language of Article 4[126] refers to 'any form of distribution *to the public* by sale or otherwise',[127] which language suggests distribution to a more general audience and not a

---

[118] The CDPA introduced a right of distribution in s. 18, which was later amended by SI 1992/3233, reg. 4 to implement Art. 4, Directive 2009/24/EC of 23 April 2009 on the legal protection of computer programs [2009] OJ L111/16 (replacing Directive 91/250/EEC [1991] OJ L122/42); and by SI 1996/2967 to implement Art. 9, Directive 2006/115/EC of 12 December 2006 on rental right and lending right and on certain rights related to copyright in the field of intellectual property [2006] OJ L376/28 (replacing Directive 92/100/EEC [1992] OJ L346/61).

[119] See J. Phillips. and L. Bently, 'Copyright issues: the mysteries of section 18' [1999] EIPR 133–41.

[120] Primary infringement is governed by the CDPA, s. 16. This provision creates a strict liability tort for carrying out one of the exclusive rights without the owner's permission. Ss. 22–7 are the secondary infringement provisions and they create liability, inter alia, for importing or dealing in infringing copies of a work with actual or constructive knowledge. See 4.2.1 and 4.2.2 for further discussion.

[121] Phillips and Bently, 'Copyright issues', 134.

[122] Phillips and Bently, 'Copyright issues', 135–6.

[123] Phillips and Bently, 'Copyright issues', 136.

[124] *Deutsche Grammophon v Metro* Case 78/70 [1971] ECR 487; *Musikvertrieb v GEMA* Case 55/80 [1981] ECR 147.

[125] *Peak Holding AB v Axolin-Elinor AB* Case C-16/03 [2005] 2 WLR 650. See also Phillips and Bently, 'Copyright issues', 140; and Directive 2001/29/EC, Art. 4(2) and recital 28, according to which the distribution right is exhausted where there is a 'first sale or other transfer of ownership in the Community of that object' by the rightholder or with his consent.

[126] See also Art. 9 of Directive 2006/115/EC on rental and lending.   [127] Emphasis supplied.

limited audience of wholesalers or distributors. Second, this interpretation would provide a high level of protection to copyright owners,[128] which is what the directive mandates,[129] because those further down the chain of distribution (such as retailers) would be held liable for unauthorized sales of copyright works. Under a 'disposition' approach, on the other hand, the distribution right would heavily overlap with the reproduction right and be of relatively minor significance.[130] Finally, in two first instance decisions, English courts have implicitly accepted the 'destination' approach.[131]

Clarification of the scope of Article 4 of the Information Society Directive is undoubtedly required. While the language and purpose of the directive suggest that distribution to the public occurs when a copy of the work is sold to the general public,[132] this interpretation does not sit comfortably with the jurisprudence of the Court of Justice concerning exhaustion of the distribution right.[133] The uncertainties of section 18 of the CDPA are symptomatic of those reflected in Article 4 of the directive, but these are compounded by the reluctance of the UK to revisit its long-standing distinction between primary and secondary infringement and also the tendency to use language that does not closely follow the provision to be implemented.

While the CJEU may not yet have ruled on the issue of when the act of distribution to the public occurs, it has elucidated the distribution right in other respects. It is important to note here that the distribution right for computer programs, as harmonized in EU law by Article 4 of the Software Directive, differs in scope from the distribution right harmonized in Article 4 of the Information Society Directive and applicable to all types of authorial works. Article 4(c) of the Software Directive states a rightholder of copyright in a computer program is given the exclusive right to carry out 'any form of distribution to the public, including the rental, of the original computer program or copies thereof'. Thus, rental is included within the scope of the distribution right for computer programs (but is a separately listed right for other authorial works). Also, the CJEU (Grand Chamber) ruled in *UsedSoft GmbH v Oracle International Corp.*[134] that the right of distribution of a copy of a computer program can be exhausted through authorized downloading of that copy from the internet where the rightholder has also conferred, in return for a payment of a fee, a right to use that copy for an unlimited period. This ruling has caused some consternation because it suggests that exhaustion is not limited to copies of a work embodied in tangible articles and can extend to online, intangible copies.[135]

[128] Contrast the 'disposition theory' which would, as Phillips and Bently, 'Copyright issues', 135 explain, result in s. 18 being of 'relatively minor significance because the "reproduction right" conferred by section 17 operates, in most circumstances, to enable the copyright owner to control whether copies are disseminated, and, if so, when and how'.

[129] Recitals 4 and 9.   [130] Phillips and Bently, 'Copyright issues', 135.

[131] *KK Sony Computer v Pacific Game Technology* [2006] EWHC 2509 (Ch) and *Independiente Ltd v Music Trading On-Line (HK) Ltd* [2007] FSR 21.

[132] Or at least, distribution cannot mean first sale or disposition because otherwise there is no point in the language 'to the public'.

[133] As well, some commentators support the 'disposition' interpretation: see C. Stothers, *Parallel Trade in Europe* (Oxford: Hart, 2007), p. 387, arguing that this is a more natural reading of s. 18 and 'one that is in line with the concept of "putting on the market" for the purposes of Community exhaustion'. See also K. M. Garnett, K. Davies, and G. Harbottle (eds), *Copinger and Skone James on Copyright* (16th edn, London: Sweet & Maxwell, 2010), p. 428.

[134] Case C-128/11 [2012] ECDR 19, [72].

[135] F. Maclean, 'European Union (CJEU) has delivered its long awaited decision in *UsedSoft v Oracle International Corp*' [2013] CTLR 1. On the impact more generally, see C. Stothers, 'When is copyright exhausted by a software licence?: *UsedSoft v Oracle*' [2012] EIPR 787.

Article 4 of the Information Society Directive obliges Member States to 'provide for authors, in respect of the original of their works or of copies thereof, the exclusive right to authorize or prohibit any form of distribution to the public by sale or otherwise'. This right, according to Article 4(2), is not exhausted except where there is a first sale or other transfer of ownership within the EU with the rightholder's consent.

In contrast to computer programs and the ruling in *UsedSoft*, online dissemination of works or copies thereof will not exhaust the right of distribution. This view is supported by recitals 28 and 29 of the Information Society Directive, which state that distribution is the right to control 'distribution of the work incorporated in a tangible article' and that 'the question of exhaustion does not arise in the case of services and on-line services in particular'. The CJEU in *Art & Allposters International BV v Stichting Pictoright* reiterated this position, ruling that 'exhaustion of the distribution right applies to the tangible object into which a protected work or its copy is incorporated if it has been placed onto the market with the copyright holder's consent'.[136]

Art & Allposters International is significant for also clarifying when the distribution right is exhausted in relation to tangible objects that are subsequently altered. In this case, artistic works embodied in posters had been transferred to canvas and sold in that form. The defendant argued that the distribution right of the copyright owner had been exhausted by sale of the poster embodying the artistic work and thus there was no infringement. However, the CJEU rejected this argument, ruling that 'the consent of the copyright holder does not cover the distribution of an object incorporating his work if that object has been altered after its initial marketing in such a way it constitutes a new reproduction of that work'.[137]

In *Peek & Cloppenburg v Cassina*,[138] the CJEU refused to adopt an overly extensive interpretation of the distribution right in Article 4 of the Information Society Directive to include the display of artistic works in a shop window, but held that distribution was limited to 'acts which entail a transfer of the ownership of that object'.[139] However, in *Dimensione Direct Sales Srl and Labianca v Knoll International SpA*[140] the CJEU ruled that 'an infringement of the distribution right can be observed where consumers located in the territory of the Member State in which that work is protected are invited, by targeted advertising, to acquire ownership of the original or a copy of that work'.[141]

> **FURTHER READING**
>
> S. Karapapa, 'Reconstructing copyright exhaustion in the online world' [2014] IPQ 307.

3.7.4 RENTAL AND LENDING

Prior to the CDPA there was no rental or lending right and an attempt to fill this gap by arguing that a record-lending library was authorizing the infringement of its users failed in *CBS Inc. v Ames Records and Tapes*.[142] The CDPA included a limited right to control the rental of copies of sound recordings, films, and computer programs. However, it was the implementation of the Rental and Lending Rights Directive which led to section 18A(1). This section provides for the exclusive right of rental or lending of copies of the work to the public in

---

[136] Case C-419/13 [2016] FSR 6, [40].   [137] [46].   [138] Case C-456/06 [2009] ECDR 9.
[139] [36].   [140] Case C-516/13 [2015] ECDR 12.   [141] [33].   [142] [1982] Ch 91.

respect of literary, dramatic, musical, and artistic works (other than a work of architecture or work of applied art), films, and sound recordings.

Rental is defined in section 18A(2)(a) as 'making a copy of the work available for use, on terms that it will or may be returned, for direct or indirect economic or commercial advantage'. Lending is defined in section 18A(2)(b) to mean making a copy of the work available for use, on terms that it will or may be returned, otherwise than for direct or indirect economic or commercial advantage, through an establishment which is accessible to the public. Section 18A(3) excludes from the scope of rental and lending:

- making available for the purpose of public performance, playing or showing in public, or communication to the public;
- making available for the purpose of exhibition in public; and
- making available for on-the-spot reference use.

Further, lending 'does not include making available between establishments which are accessible to the public' (e.g. inter-library loans) and such lending will not be for direct or indirect commercial advantage where the payment only covers the necessary operating costs of the establishment.[143] Recently, questions have been referred to the CJEU about the scope of the lending right in the digital environment, in particular whether it extends to libraries making e-books available to their users (i.e. digital or e-lending). Advocate General Szpunar issued his Opinion on 16 June 2016. In it, he opines that acts of borrowing a book from a library, whether a hard copy or e-copy, are the same and, as such, '[t]he interpretation of Directive 2006/115 must therefore take that reality into account and align the legal framework for the lending of electronic books with that for the lending of traditional books'.[144] This includes Member States benefiting from the ability to derogate from the lending right in respect of public lending (provided authors receive remuneration for such lending) as permitted by Article 6(1) of the directive. The ruling of the CJEU is awaited.

The rental or lending right extends to the original, as well as copies, of the work. Unlike the distribution right, the right is not exhausted by distribution of copies of the work. As the CJEU ruled in *Metronome Musik GmbH v Music Point Hokamp GmbH*:

> the release into circulation of a sound recording cannot render lawful other forms of exploitation of the protected work, such as rental, which are of a different nature from sale or any other lawful form of distribution … The rental right remains one of the prerogatives of the author and producer notwithstanding sale of the physical recording.[145]

The right of rental or lending is also not exhausted by prior acts of rental or lending in an EU Member State. As the CJEU held in *Foreningen AF Danske Videogramdistributorer v Laserdisken*:[146]

> the exclusive right to hire out various copies of the work contained in a video film can, by its very nature, be exploited by repeated and potentially unlimited transactions, each of which involves the right to remuneration. The specific right to authorise or prohibit rental would be rendered meaningless if it were held to be exhausted as soon as the object was first offered for rental.

---

143 CDPA, s. 18A(4) and (5).
144 Vereniging Openbare Bibliotheken v Stichting Leenrecht Case C-174/15, ECLI:EU:C:2016:459, [32].
145 Case C-200/96 [1999] FSR 576, [1998] ECR I-1953, [18].
146 Case C-61/97 [1999] EMLR 681, [18].

3.7.5 PERFORMANCE IN PUBLIC

Section 19 of the CDPA grants the exclusive right to perform a literary, dramatic, or musical work in public, and the right to play or show a sound recording, film, or broadcast in public. The main difficulty with this right is identifying when the performance is *in public*. Although courts have interpreted the scope of the right on several occasions, they have not produced a consistent set of factors for determining when performances are 'in public' as opposed to private. Two cases in particular highlight the different approaches adopted by the courts.

Harms Ltd and Chappell v Martans Club Ltd [1927] 1 Ch 526

The case involved the performance of a musical work, 'That Certain Feeling' at an exclusive London club, the Embassy Club. Approximately 1,800 people were members of the club, but on the night in question 150 members and 50 of their guests had been present. The claimants (who were the owner and musical publisher of the work) brought an action for infringement under the Copyright Act 1911. The defendants admitted the performance but argued that it was not 'in public'. At first instance Eve J held that the claimants' right had been infringed. The defendants appealed, on the basis that he had incorrectly interpreted the words 'in public'. The appeal was dismissed.

Lord Hanworth MR, at pp. 532–3:

In considering here whether or not there has been within s. 2, sub-s. 1, an infringement of the author's sole right, one must see whether or not, upon the facts as a whole, the true view is that there has been a representation of this composition in public. In dealing with the tests which have been applied in the cases, it appears to me that one must apply one's mind to see whether there has been any injury to the author. Did what took place interfere with his proprietary rights? As to that, profit is a very important element. Next, you must consider whether there has been admission of any portion of the public, with or without payment, and when you are considering what you mean by any portion of the public you will find in *Duck v Bates* that according to Brett MR it means the public who would go either with or without payment—the class of persons who would be likely to go to a performance if there was a performance at a public theatre for profit. Then one has also to consider whether or not the performance is a domestic one so as to exclude the notion of 'public'—domestic in the sense that it was private and domestic, a matter of family and household concern only. Then again you must consider where the performance took place, bearing in mind that the place need not be one which is kept habitually for the exhibition of dramatic entertainments. I do not say that I have catalogued all the suggestions made as tests of the facts to be considered, but it appears to me that I have tabled enough to support the conclusion that Eve J was right in his judgment.

[**Sargant** and **Lawrence LJJ** delivered concurring judgments.]

What are the factors identified by Lord Hanworth MR? Does it make sense to take all of these into account or should there be an overriding or definitive factor and, if so, which one?

Jennings v Stephens [1936] Ch 469

A play was performed without consent by a dramatic society at a meeting of the Duston Women's Institute. No guests were present at the performance, only 62 of the 109 members of the Duston Women's Institute.

Lord Wright MR, at pp. 479–81:

The presence or absence of visitors is thus not the decisive factor, nor does it matter whether the performance is paid or gratuitous, nor is it conclusive that admission is free or for payment, nor is the number of the audience decisive…The antithesis adopted by the cases between performances in public and performances domestic or quasi-domestic cannot be said necessarily to depend on these factors either separately or in combination. The true criterion seems to be the character of the audience. If the performance of 'The Rest Cure' in the Duston Village Institute had been before an audience of exactly the same women as constituted it in fact, drawn from the village, but they had been brought together by a general invitation or advertisement, all other conditions being the same, it cannot be doubted that it would have been a performance in public. In the actual facts, the audience was limited to members of the institute in the village, but all the adult women in the village could be members, and were invited to be members. Election if desired was, in the absence of special disability, a matter of course. If payment was to be considered, the annual 2s. subscription included such performances, and thus corresponded to a small payment for the performance. There was no other qualification for membership except residence in the village, but mere residence in the same village in different homes cannot be regarded as constituting a domestic or quasi-domestic audience. There was nothing like the fact of the hospital as the common home which gave a quasi-domestic complexion to the performance in *Duck v Bates*. Thus it would certainly be a great extension of *Duck v Bates* to apply the decision there to this case; and, as already stated, that case was, in the opinion of Brett MR a border-line and extreme case. The words of Bowen LJ quoted above with reference to a club of persons united for purposes of good fellowship seem to indicate that a dramatic performance given to its members would generally fall within the prohibition of the statute. Furthermore, the institute is a society of a quasi-public character…The Court cannot be influenced by feelings of sympathy for the Women's Institute movement, and must decide the case as if it related to an ordinary village social club open to all village women who chose to take the necessary steps to join, which gave to its members a dramatic entertainment by means of performers from outside, whether amateur or professional. Probably no one would question that the performance was in public if the audience, other circumstances being the same, had been, not sixty-two, but 600, as I suppose in one of the larger villages it might have been. If that were not a performance in public, and might be repeated indefinitely all over the country, the performing right would not be of much value. The quality of domesticity or quasi-domesticity seems to me to be absent. I think such performances are in public within the meaning of the statute. The case seems to me to be within the principle laid down in *Harms'* case rather than within the principle applied in *Duck v Bates*. With great respect to the learned judge, I have come to the conclusion that the performance in question of 'The Rest Cure' was a performance in public.

Greene LJ, at p. 485:

It is, I think, important, in approaching the question whether a particular performance is 'in public', to bear in mind that by s. 2, sub-s. 1, of the Copyright Act, 1911, infringement is defined by reference to the things the sole right to do which is by the Act conferred on the owner of the copyright. The owner of the copyright is by s. 1, sub-s. 2, given the sole right to perform the work in public, and any person who does this without the consent of the owner infringes his copyright. The question may therefore be usefully approached by inquiring whether or not the act complained of as an infringement would, if done by the owner of the copyright himself, have been an exercise by him of the statutory right conferred upon him. In other words, the expression 'in public' must be considered in relation to the owner of the copyright. If the audience considered in relation to the owner of the copyright may properly be described as the owner's 'public' or part of his 'public', then in performing the work before that audience he would in my opinion be exercising the statutory right conferred upon him; and any one who without his consent performed the work before that audience would be infringing his copyright.

[**Romer LJ** delivered a concurring judgment.]

Do Lord Wright MR and Greene LJ adopt the same overriding test for determining whether a performance is 'in public'? If not, how do their approaches differ and which approach is preferable? In your view, is it desirable to identify when performances are in public according to a combination of factors or a single factor? Dr Makeen, in an article that extensively reviews UK case law interpreting the phrase 'in public', argues that courts have employed several criteria. These are the 'nature of the place; nature of the gathering; the "for profit" requirement; and the potential financial injury to the copyright owner', but that 'the importance of the nature of the place and that of the "for profit" requirement faded away. As a result, it was only the potential financial injury and the nature of the gathering that were consistently considered to be decisive.'[147] Dr Makeen argues that it is preferable to adopt a sole criterion for measuring when a performance is 'in public' and that this ought to be the 'nature of the gathering'.

3.7.6 COMMUNICATION TO THE PUBLIC

The right of communication to the public contained in section 20 of the CDPA has been significantly influenced by international and EU law and so we turn briefly to examine these frameworks in order to place the domestic right in context.

The right of communication to the public is recognized as a minimum standard of protection in several provisions of the Berne Convention. According to Article 11*bis*(1)(i), authors of literary and artistic works have the exclusive right of authorizing the 'the broadcasting of their works or the communication thereof to the public by any other means of wireless diffusion of signs, sounds or images'. Whereas, Article 11*bis*(1)(ii) grants authors of literary and artistic works the exclusive right to authorize 'any communication to the public by wire or by rebroadcasting of the broadcast of the work', other provisions grant the exclusive right of authorizing the communication to the public of performances of dramatic, dramatico-musical, and musical works (Article 11(1)(ii)) and recitations of literary works (Article 11*ter*(1))(ii)). Further, there is the exclusive right of communication to the public by wire of cinematographic adaptations or reproductions of works (Article 14(1)(ii)) and Article 14*bis*(1) confirms that cinematographic works also attract these rights of communication to the public.

---

[147] M. F. Makeen, 'Rationalising performance "in public" under UK copyright law' [2016] IPQ 117, 133.

As is apparent from the language of these Berne provisions, the rights of communication to the public are not comprehensive in scope, nor do they seem to embrace digital transmissions. Thus, Article 8 of the WCT aims to supplement and expand the existing communication to the public rights in the Berne Convention, in particular to accommodate changes to exploitation methods arising from new technologies, such as the internet. Article 8 of the WCT states:

> Without prejudice to the provisions of Articles 11(1)(ii), 11*bis* (1)(i) and (ii), 11*ter* (1)(ii), 14(1)(ii) and 14*bis* (1) of the Berne Convention, authors of literary and artistic works shall enjoy the exclusive right of authorising any communication to the public of their works, by wire or wireless means, including the making available to the public of their works in such a way that members of the public may access these works from a place and at a time individually chosen by them.

Of particular note is that Article 8 of the WCT introduces a new right of making available to the public as a subset of the right of communication to the public. In relation to performers and phonogram producers, the obligation to introduce a right of making available to the public by wire or wireless means is contained in Articles 10 and 14 of the WIPO Performances and Phonograms Treaty (WPPT).

The adoption of Article 8 of the WCT came after much debate about the appropriate means to protect authors from unauthorized transmission of their works over digital networks. In the lead-up to the adoption of the final text of the WCT, various solutions had been proposed, such as treating digital dissemination as an act of distribution, an act of public display or rental, an act of communication to the public, or establishing a new specific digital transmission right. In the end, an 'umbrella' solution was adopted, namely to create an obligation to grant an exclusive right to authorize on-demand transmission, but described in a neutral way so that the legal characterization of the right granted would be left to national law.[148]

In terms of what constitutes making available *to the public*, this is left to national law. Commentators have suggested that the concept of 'public' excludes the close family circle and closest social acquaintances, such that material stored on domestic intranets would not constitute making available to the public.[149] If this is correct, then situations where material is placed on the internet without being accessible to anyone but family and friends should also be excluded. The notion of 'public' would not necessarily exclude material made available via school or company intranets. Further, 'making available to the public' would clearly embrace placing a protected work on an internet server, without restriction, along with an individual accessing that work.

The WCT is silent on where the act of making available occurs and how this is to be determined. This is an important issue because internet transmissions by their very nature may be made to persons across the globe. As we shall see, this question is also unclear in the context of EU and UK copyright law.

The Information Society Directive seeks to implement the international obligations contained in the WCT and WPPT and also to harmonize certain substantive aspects of copyright law to prevent distortion of the internal market. Article 3 of the Information Society Directive mandates that all rightholders (i.e. of both authorial and entrepreneurial works) have an exclusive right to make available to the public copyright works by way of interactive

---

[148] M. Ficsor, *The Law of Copyright and the Internet: The 1996 WIPO Treaties, their Interpretation and Implementation* (Oxford: Oxford University Press, 2002), paras C8.06–C8.07.

[149] J. Reinbothe and S. von Lewinski, *The WIPO Treaties 1996* (London: Butterworths, 2002), p. 111.

on-demand transmission, which are characterized by the fact that members of the public may access them from a place and at a time individually chosen by them. Authors of traditional works, however, will acquire this right as part of the broader right of communication to the public, which right, according to recital 23, is to be:

> understood in a broad sense covering all communication to the public not present at the place where the communication originates ... [and] should cover any such transmission or retransmission of a work to the public by wire or wireless means, including broadcasting.

Article 3 of the Information Society Directive, like the WCT and WPPT whose obligations it seeks to implement, does not address *where* the act of making available takes place.

Prior to implementing the Information Society Directive, the old section 20 of the CDPA referred to the exclusive acts of broadcasting the work or including it in a cable programme service. Broadcasting was limited to transmissions by wireless means and inclusion in a cable programme service covered transmissions *other* than by wireless telegraphy.[150] With the intention of implementing Article 3 of the Information Society Directive, section 20 was amended by the 2003 Regulations[151] to replace these two rights with the right to authorize or prohibit any communication of the work to the public.[152] Section 20(2) of the CDPA provides:

> References in this Part to communication to the public are to communication to the public by electronic transmission, and in relation to a work include—
>
> (a) the broadcasting of the work;
>
> (b) the making available to the public of the work by electronic transmission in such a way that members of the public may access it from a place and at a time individually chosen by them.

The right of communication to the public applies to all categories of works,[153] with the exception of typographical arrangements, and includes—but is not restricted to—broadcasting and making available to the public. As Kitchin J in *TV Catchup* observed:[154]

> Consistently with art.3 of the Information Society Directive, subs.(2) defines communication to the public as communication to the public by electronic transmission. The

---

[150] For a discussion of the previous legislation and amendments inserted by the Copyright and Related Rights Regulations 2003 (SI 2003/2498), see *ITV Broadcasting Ltd v TV Catchup Ltd (No. 2)* [2011] EWHC 1874 (Pat), [2011] FSR 40, [37]–[45].

[151] The Copyright and Related Rights Regulations 2003 (SI 2003/2498).

[152] This has been held to be an effective transposition of Art. 3—see *FAPL v QC Leisure* [2012] EWCA Civ 1708, [2013] FSR 20.

[153] Including broadcasts and films. Even though protection of broadcasts in this way went further than the obligation contained in Art. 3(2) of the Information Society Directive this has been held *not* to have required primary legislation but to fall within the powers given to the Secretary of State under s. 2(2) of the European Communities Act 2002: see *ITV v TV Catchup (No. 2)* [2011] EWHC 1874 (Pat), [2011] FSR 40, [49]–[79]. The 2003 Regulations also went further in providing the right of communication to the public (and not the more limited right of making available to the public) to films under the CDPA. They went further because films under the CDPA offer in effect protection for first fixations of films (i.e. related rights) and the cinematic content is protected as a dramatic work, following *Norowzian v Arks (No. 2)* [2000] FSR 363, [2000] EMLR 67 (CA). This extension of the right of communication to the public of first fixations of films has been held permissible by Arnold J in *Dramatico Entertainment Ltd v British Sky Broadcasting Ltd* [2012] EWHC 268 (Ch), [2012] RPC 27.

[154] *ITV Broadcasting Ltd v TV Catchup Ltd* [2010] EWHC 3063 (Ch), [2011] FSR 16, [16].

definition then identifies two specific ways in which such communication may take place, namely: (a) broadcasting the work and (b) making the work available by electronic transmission on demand. But I do not read the definition in subs.(2) as being limited to these forms of communication. To the contrary, it says in terms that it includes them. In my judgment it also covers all other acts which constitute communication to the public of the work by electronic transmission.

So, while section 20 clearly includes both broadcasting and making available to the public, it is not limited to these two acts and can encompass other communications to the public. The definition of broadcast in section 6 of the CDPA was amended to refer to wire or wireless transmission of visual images, sounds, or other information, excluding internet transmissions, except of a limited kind akin to traditional broadcasting. 'Making available to the public', rather than 'broadcasting', is thus relevant to on-demand, internet transmissions.[155]

The scope of the right of communication to the public in Article 3 of the Information Society Directive has been the subject of several decisions from the CJEU and English courts.[156] A key issue has been the line dividing public performance (which is not harmonized by the Information Society Directive and was discussed in the previous section) and communication to the public. A question to this effect was referred by the English High Court to the CJEU in the joined cases of *Football Association Premier League Ltd v QC Leisure* and *Murphy v Media Protection Services Ltd.*[157] In the following extract, which is from the referring court's application of the ruling, we see how communication to the public has been defined.

Football Association Premier League v QC Leisure (No. 3) [2012] EWHC 108 (Ch), [2012] FSR 12

A dispute arose from the supply of (genuine) Greek satellite decoder cards to pubs and bars in the UK. The Football Association Premier League grants exclusive territorial licences to broadcasters in different Member States. In the UK, the exclusive licensee is Sky and in Greece it is Nova, and the subscription fees charged by these broadcasters varies by thousands of pounds. In this case, Greek satellite decoder cards, which cost considerably less, were used by the operators of UK premises to receive live broadcasts of English Premier League football matches from satellite channels outside the UK (i.e. from Greece). A series of complex legal issues were raised in this litigation. However, for our purposes it is enough to focus on one particular issue, namely whether the publicans were communicating the relevant copyright works to the public by either *re-broadcasting* from the receiving satellite dish to the bar area; or by *displaying* the works on the pub's TV screens and playing the works on the TV speakers. In the following extract, the referring court analyses and applies the CJEU ruling on this issue.

---

[155] This has been confirmed in *Polydor Ltd v Brown* [2005] EWHC 3191 (Ch).

[156] For a useful summary of several of these decisions see *Dramatico Entertainment Ltd v British Sky Broadcasting Ltd* [2012] EWHC 268 (Ch), [2012] RPC 27, [44]–[64].

[157] Joined Cases C-403 and 429/08 [2012] FSR 1 (Grand Chamber).

Kitchin LJ:

7. …I referred a question to the Court of Justice asking, in essence, whether the phrase 'communication to the public' in art.3(1) of the Copyright Directive must be interpreted as covering transmission of the broadcast works, via a television screen and speakers, to the customers present in a public house.

8. In answering that question, the Court of Justice observed that Article 3(1) does not define the concept of 'communication to the public' and accordingly its meaning and scope has to be determined in the light of the objectives pursued by the Copyright Directive and the context in which the provision is set. In that regard, the Court noted first, that the principal objective of the Copyright Directive is to establish a high level of protection for authors and that 'communication to the public' must therefore be interpreted broadly; second, given the requirements of unity of the European Union legal order and its coherence, concepts used in the various directives in the area of intellectual property should generally be interpreted as having the same meaning; and third, Article 3(1) must, so far as possible, be interpreted in a manner consistent with international law, in particular taking account of the Berne Convention and the WIPO Copyright Treaty.

9. The Court then explained the concept of communication in these terms:

191. As regards, first, the concept of communication, it is apparent from Article 8(3) of the Related Rights Directive and Articles 2(g) and 15 of the Performance and Phonograms Treaty that such a concept includes 'making the sounds or representations of sounds fixed in a phonogram audible to the public' and that it encompasses broadcasting or 'any communication to the public'.

192. More specifically, as Article 11*bis* (1)(iii) of the Berne Convention expressly indicates, that concept encompasses communication by loudspeaker or any other instrument transmitting, by signs, sounds or images, covering—in accordance with the explanatory memorandum accompanying the proposal for a copyright directive (COM(97) 628 final)—a means of communication such as display of the works on a screen.

193. That being so, and since the European Union legislature has not expressed a different intention as regards the interpretation of that concept in the Copyright Directive, in particular in Article 3 thereof (see paragraph [188] of the present judgment), the concept of communication must be construed broadly, as referring to any transmission of the protected works, irrespective of the technical means or process used.

10. Applying these principles to the present case, the Court held that the proprietor of a public house does effect a communication when he intentionally transmits broadcast works, via a television screen and speakers, to the customers present in that establishment:

195. In Case C-403/08, the proprietor of a public house intentionally gives the customers present in that establishment access to a broadcast containing protected works via a television screen and speakers. Without his intervention the customers cannot enjoy the works broadcast, even though they are physically within the broadcast's catchment area. Thus, the circumstances of such an act prove comparable to those in *SGAE*.

196. Accordingly, it must be held that the proprietor of a public house effects a communication when he intentionally transmits broadcast works, via a television screen and speakers, to the customers present in that establishment.

11. The Court then identified a second requirement, namely that it is also necessary for the work broadcast to be transmitted to a new public, that is to say, to a public which was not taken into account by the author of the protected work when he authorised its use by the communication to the original public (at [197]).

12. In the present case, the Court continued, when the authors authorise a broadcast of their works, they consider, in principle, only the owners of television sets who, either personally or within their own private or family circles, receive the signal and follow the broadcasts. Where a broadcast work is transmitted, in a place accessible to the public, for an additional public which is permitted by the owner of the television set to hear or see the work, an intentional intervention has occurred which must be regarded as an act by which the work in question is communicated to a new public (at [198]).

13. It followed that the publicans were transmitting the broadcast works to a new public:

199. That is so when the works broadcast are transmitted by the proprietor of a public house to the customers present in that establishment, because those customers constitute an additional public which was not considered by the authors when they authorised the broadcasting of their works.

14. The Court then identified a third requirement founded on recital 23 in the preamble to the Copyright Directive, namely that the work must be transmitted to a public not present at the place where the communication originates. This requirement, the Court considered, is intended to exclude direct public representation and performance from the scope of the concept of communication to the public (at [200] to [202]).

15. That third requirement is also satisfied here, as the Court explained:

203. Such an element of direct physical contact is specifically absent in the case of transmission, in a place such as a public house, of a broadcast work via a television screen and speakers to the public which is present at the place of that transmission, but which is not present at the place where the communication originates within the meaning of recital 23 in the preamble to the Copyright Directive, that is to say, at the place of the representation or performance which is broadcast (see, to this effect *SGAE* paragraph [40]).

16. Finally, the Court observed that 'it is not irrelevant that a "communication" within the meaning of Article 3(1) of the Copyright Directive is of a profit-making nature'. This consideration is also material in this case, as the Court elaborated:

205. In a situation such as that in the main proceedings, it is indisputable that the proprietor transmits the broadcast works in his public house in order to benefit therefrom and that that transmission is liable to attract customers to whom the works transmitted are of interest. Consequently, the transmission in question has an effect upon the number of people going to that establishment and, ultimately, on its financial results.
   206. It follows that the communication to the public in question is of a profit-making nature.

17. The Court therefore answered the referred question in these terms:

207. In light of all the foregoing, the answer to the question referred is that 'communication to the public' within the meaning of Article 3(1) of the Copyright Directive must be interpreted as covering transmission of the broadcast works, via a television screen and speakers, to the customers present in a public house.

The CJEU in *FAPL v QC Leisure; Murphy v Media Protection Services* adopted a broad interpretation of Article 3. Where did it draw the line between public performance and communication to the public? On this issue, the Court was influenced by Article 11*bis*(1)(iii) of the Berne Convention, which refers to authors of literary and artistic works having the exclusive right of 'public communication by loudspeaker or any other analogous instrument transmitting, by signs, sounds or images, the broadcast of the work'. However, as Dr Makeen has persuasively argued, Article 11*bis*(1)(iii) (unlike sub-paragraphs (i) and (ii)) deals with acts of reception *in* public (i.e. public performance) and not communication *to* the public. He explains that this sub-paragraph was erroneously included in Article 11*bis* in order to ensure that all of the provisions dealing with broadcasters came under the one article.[158] Therefore, significant doubts can be raised about the CJEU's conclusion that the publicans' showing of Premier League football broadcasts was a communication *to* the public, as opposed to a communication *in* public (i.e. public performance) of the relevant copyright works.[159] In the later case of *Circul Globus Bucuresti v Uniunea Compozitorilor si Muzicologilor din Romania*,[160] the CJEU followed the *FAPL* and *Murphy* rulings in finding that Article 3 of the Information Society Directive was *not* intended to cover live presentation or performance of a work, so that live circus and cabaret performances of musical works were not covered. Nevertheless, the effect of the *FAPL* and *Murphy* rulings is that playing a radio broadcast or showing a television broadcast that includes copyright works may amount to communication to the public within the meaning of Article 3. In terms of UK law, it is actually section 19 of the CDPA that expressly covers 'the playing or showing of the work in public' in the case of sound recordings, films, and broadcasts. However, Kitchin LJ held that section 20 of the CDPA was an effective transposition of Article 3(1) of the Information Society Directive and that the publicans' activities fell within section 20 of the CDPA (even if they could also fall within section 19):

> 57. That brings me to s.20 CDPA and the question whether or not it is an effective transposition of art.3(1) of the Directive into national law. In my judgment it is. In words which reflect the explanatory note to the 2003 Regulations, it defines communication to the public as communication to the public by 'electronic transmission'. Further, when considered in light of the reasoning and answer provided by the Court of Justice, I believe this expression is entirely apt to encompass the activities of the publicans. They are 'transmitting' FAPL's relevant copyright works, including its artistic works, to a 'new public'. Are they doing so by electronic means? In my view they are. They are using televisions and speakers which are electronic instruments. If and insofar as there may be any doubt about this, I see no difficulty in a conforming interpretation of s.20 and in meeting the obligation upon this court to interpret s.20, so far as possible, in light of the wording and purpose of the Copyright Directive and in order to achieve the result pursued by it.

The fact that the publicans' activities fell within both sections 19 and 20 of the CDPA impacted upon which of the relevant exceptions could be invoked by the defendants. However, Kitchin LJ held that section 72 of the CDPA applied to both infringements under sections 19 and 20. This view was upheld on appeal.[161]

There have been several CJEU rulings on the right of communication to the public, some of which have caused more confusion than clarification.[162] However, in a recent decision, the CJEU has helpfully synthesized its previous rulings.

---

[158] M. F. Makeen, *Copyright in a Global Information Society: The Scope of Copyright Protection under International, US, UK and French Law* (London: Kluwer, 2000), pp. 75–7.

[159] T. Aplin, ' "Reproduction" and "communication to the public" rights in EU copyright law: *FAPL v QC Leisure*' (2011) 22 KLJ 209, 215–18.

[160] Case C-283/10, Judgment of the Court (Third Chamber), 24 November 2011.

[161] *FAPL v QC Leisure* [2012] EWCA Civ 1708.

[162] e.g. see *Società Consortile Fonografici (SCF) v Del Corso* Case C-135/10 [2012] ECDR 16; *ITV Broadcasting Ltd v TV Catchup Ltd* Case C-607/11 [2013] FSR 36; *Svensson v Retriever Sverige AB* Case C-466/12 [2015] EMLR 5.

Reha Training v GEMA Case C-117/15, Judgment of the Court (Grand Chamber), 31 May 2016

GEMA, a German collecting society, claimed that Reha Training was carrying out acts of communication to the public, for which royalties were owed. These acts were the screening of television programmes on television sets installed in waiting rooms and training rooms at the rehabilitation centre operated by Reha Training. An issue that arose was whether the same interpretation of 'communication to the public' should be given to Article 3 of the Information Society Directive and Article 8(2) of the Rental and Lending Rights Directive. The latter refers to communication to the public in the context of sound recordings and the obligation to pay equitable remuneration to the relevant performers and sound recording producers. Further, whether the acts of Reha Training did constitute a communication to the public.

Court of Justice (Grand Chamber):

31 …[T]here is no evidence that the EU legislature wished to confer on the concept of 'communication to the public' a different meaning in the respective contexts of Directives 2001/29 and 2006/115.

32 As the Advocate General noted, in point 34 of his Opinion, the different nature of the rights protected under those directives cannot hide the fact that, according to the wording of those directives, those rights have the same trigger, namely the communication to the public of protected works.

33 It follows from the foregoing that, in a case such as that in the main proceedings, concerning the broadcast of television programmes which allegedly affects not only copyright but also, inter alia, the rights of performers or phonogram producers, both Article 3(1) of Directive 2001/29 and Article 8(2) of Directive 2006/115 must be applied, whilst giving the concept of 'communication to the public' in both those provisions the same meaning.

34 Therefore, that concept must be assessed in accordance with the same criteria in order to avoid, inter alia, contradictory and incompatible interpretations depending on the applicable provision.

35 In that connection, the Court has already held that, in order to determine whether there has been a communication to the public, account has to be taken of several complementary criteria, which are not autonomous and are interdependent. Since those criteria may, in different situations, be present to widely varying degrees, they must be applied both individually and in their interaction with one another (see, to that effect, judgment of 15 March 2012 in *Phonographic Performance (Ireland)*, C-162/10, EU:C:2012:141, paragraph 30 and the case-law cited).

36 Furthermore, it must be recalled that the concept of 'communication to the public' must be interpreted broadly, as recital 23 of Directive 2001/29 indeed expressly states (see, to that effect, judgment of 7 March 2013 in *ITV Broadcasting and Others*, C-607/11, EU:C:2013:147, paragraph 20 and the case-law cited).

37 The Court has also previously held that the concept of 'communication to the public' includes two cumulative criteria, namely, an 'act of communication' of a work and the communication of that work to a 'public' (judgment of 19 November 2015 in *SBS Belgium*, C-325/14, EU:C:2015:764, paragraph 15 and the case-law cited).

38 That said, it must be stated, first, as regards the concept of the 'act of communication', that that refers to any transmission of the protected works, irrespective of the technical means or process used (see, to that effect, judgment of 19 November 2015 in *SBS Belgium*, C-325/14, EU:C:2015:764, paragraph 16 and the case-law cited).

39 Moreover, every transmission or retransmission of a work which uses a specific technical means must, as a rule, be individually authorised by the author of the work in question (judgment of 19 November 2015 in *SBS Belgium*, C-325/14, EU:C:2015:764, paragraph 17 and the case-law cited).

40 Secondly, in order to fall within the concept of 'communication to the public', within the meaning of Article 3(1) of Directive 2001/29, it is necessary, as stated in paragraph 37 of the present judgment, that protected works must actually be communicated to a 'public'.

41 In that connection, it follows from the case-law of the Court, in the first place, that the term 'public' refers to an indeterminate number of potential recipients and implies, moreover, a fairly large number of persons (see, to that effect, judgment of 7 December 2006 in *SGAE*, C-306/05, EU:C:2006:764, paragraphs 37 and 38 and the case-law cited).

42 As regards, to begin with, the 'indeterminate' nature of the public, the Court has observed that it means making a work perceptible in any appropriate manner to 'persons in general', that is, not restricted to specific individuals belonging to a private group (see, to that effect, judgment of 15 March 2012 in *SCF*, C-135/10, EU:C:2012:140, paragraph 85).

43 Next, as regards, the criterion of 'a fairly large number of people', this is intended to indicate that the concept of 'public' encompasses a 'certain *de minimis* threshold', which excludes from the concept groups of persons which are too small, or insignificant (see, to that effect, judgment of 15 March 2012 in *SCF*, C-135/10, EU:C:2012:140, paragraph 86).

44 In order to determine the size of that audience, account must be taken of the cumulative effects of making works available to potential audiences (see, to that effect, judgment of 7 December 2006 in *SGAE*, C-306/05, EU:C:2006:764, paragraph 39). It is relevant, inter alia, to know how many persons have access to the same work at the same time and how many of them have access to it in succession (see, to that effect, judgment of 15 March 2012 in *Phonographic Performance (Ireland)*, C-162/10, EU:C:2012:141, paragraph 35).

45 In the second place, the Court has held that, in order to fall within the concept of 'communication to the public' the work broadcast must be transmitted to a 'new public', that is to say, to a public which was not taken into account by the authors of the protected works when they authorised their use by the communication to the original public (see, to that effect, judgments of 7 December 2006 in *SGAE*, C-306/05, EU:C:2006:764, paragraphs 40 and 42, and 4 October 2011 in *Football Association Premier League and Others*, C-403/08 and C-429/08, EU:C:2011:631, paragraph 197).

46 In that context, the Court emphasised the indispensable role of the user. It has held that, in order for there to be a communication to the public, that user must, in full knowledge of the consequences of its actions, give access to the television broadcast containing the protected work to an additional public and that it appears thereby that, in the absence of that intervention those 'new' viewers are unable to enjoy the broadcast works, although physically within the broadcast's catchment area (see, to that effect, judgments of 7 December 2006 in *SGAE*, C-306/05, EU:C:2006:764, paragraph 42 and 4 October 2011 in *Football Association Premier League and Others*, C-403/08 and C-429/08, EU:C:2011:631, paragraph 195).

47 Thus, the Court has already held that the operators of a café-restaurant, a hotel or a spa establishment are such users and make a communication to the public if they intentionally

broadcast protected works to their clientele, by intentionally distributing a signal by means of television or radio sets that they have installed in their establishment (see, to that effect, judgments of 7 December 2006 in *SGAE*, C-306/05, EU:C:2006:764, paragraphs 42 and 47; 4 October 2011 in *Football Association Premier League and Others*, C-403/08 and C-429/08, EU:C:2011:631, paragraph 196; and 27 February 2014 in *OSA*, C-351/12, EU:C:2014:110, paragraph 26).

48 It is therefore understood that the public which is the subject of the communication in these establishments is not merely 'caught' by chance, but is targeted by their operators (see, to that effect, judgment of 15 March 2012 in *SCF*, C-135/10, EU:C:2012:140, paragraph 91).

49 It must also be stated that although it is true that the profit-making nature of the broadcast of a protective work does not determine conclusively whether a transmission is to be categorised as a 'communication to the public' (see, to that effect, judgment of 7 March 2013 in *ITV Broadcasting and Others*, C-607/11, EU:C:2013:147, paragraph 43), it is not however irrelevant (see, to that effect, judgment of 4 October 2011 in *Football Association Premier League and Others*, C-403/08 and C-429/08, EU:C:2011:631, paragraph 204 and the case-law cited), in particular, for the purpose of determining any remuneration due in respect of that transmission.

...

51 Thus, the Court held that the broadcast of protected works has a profit-making nature where the user is likely to obtain an economic benefit related to the attractiveness of, and, therefore, the greater number of people attending the establishment in which it makes those broadcasts (see, to that effect, judgment of 4 October 2011 in *Football Association Premier League and Others*, C-403/08 and C-429/08, EU:C:2011:631, paragraphs 205 and 206).

The Court went on to apply these principles to the facts of the case and concluded that there was a communication to the public. Reha Training was said to communicate works because it intentionally broadcast TV programmes to patients via the installed TV sets. The patients attending the centre were persons in general and so constituted a public, as well as a 'new public' because of the 'targeted intervention' of Reha Training. Further, there was an economic advantage to the broadcasting of these programmes insofar as Reha Training supplied 'additional services' which affected the 'establishment's standing and attractiveness, thereby giving it a competitive advantage'.[163] *Reha Training* is similar to the *FAPL* and *Murphy* rulings, in terms of some of the legal principles it articulates and because it treats acts of reception in public as acts of communication to the public rather than as public performance.

Despite the ruling in *Reha Training*, uncertainties in the interpretation of the right of communication to the public persist. Although the CJEU in *Reha Training* referred to communication as involving transmission by any means, the Court in *Svensson v Retreiver Sverige AB*[164] suggested that providing access to a work (in this case by the provision of hyperlinks), as opposed to transmitting it, was an act of 'making available' and therefore an act of communication.[165] A question arises whether this interpretation applies only to the notion of 'making available' or extends to 'communication' more broadly. It is worth noting here that the CJEU in the *FAPL* ruling, in the context of deciding whether there was a communication, referred to the fact that 'the proprietor of a public house intentionally gives the customers present in that establishment access to a broadcast containing protected works

---

[163] [63].   [164] Case C-466/12 [2015] EMLR 5.   [165] [18]–[20].

via a television screen and speakers'.[166] The English High Court in *Twentieth Century Fox Films v Newzbin*[167] has followed this broader interpretation in finding that the act of 'making available to the public' (which, as noted earlier, is a subset of the right of communication to the public in section 20 of the CDPA) does not require that a person is responsible for actually transmitting the work but can embrace situations where a person provides the technological capacity which enables the transmission of the copyright work.[168]

Another difficulty to note is that in *ITV Broadcasting v TV Catchup Ltd*,[169] the CJEU held that it was not necessary always to apply the requirement of 'new public', even though it had been applied in several previous rulings. The justification for departing from this requirement was that the 'transmission of works included in a terrestrial broadcast and the making available of those works over the internet' were made 'under specific technical conditions, using a different means of transmission … intended for a public'.[170] Does this explanation for departing from the 'new public' criterion seem persuasive? Of course, the requirement of a 'new public' may itself cause concern because it refers to 'a public that was not taken into account by the copyright holders when they authorized the initial communication to the public'.[171] How can this be objectively assessed? And what are the consequences of adopting such a test? Here, it may be worth noting that a 'new public' approach was rejected at an international level when members of the Berne Union were deciding on how to deal with cable retransmissions in Article 11*bis*(1)(ii) of the Berne Convention. Instead, the criterion of 'organisation other than the original one' was adopted as a means of identifying which types of cable retransmissions were prohibited.[172]

While the CJEU has clarified that the 'profit-making nature' of an activity can influence whether it is a communication to the public, the application of this factor has not always been consistent. In *Società Consortile Fonografici (SCF) v Del Corso*,[173] the Court ruled that the playing of sound recordings via the radio in a private dental practice was not a communication to the public because the listeners involved were a limited and determinate group of patients and the playing of the radio did not encourage people to make appointments and so did not contribute to the income of the dentist. In your view, how does this situation differ from that in *Reha Training*? Why did the playing of radio broadcasts not increase the attractiveness of the dental practice in *SCF* but the showing of TV programmes in *Reha Training* increase the attractiveness of the rehabilitation clinic?

Finally, there has been controversy surrounding whether hyperlinking amounts to communication to the public. In *Svensson*, as noted earlier, the CJEU ruled that provision of hyperlinks did amount to an act of communication, but that it was not 'to the public' because the communication was not directed to a 'new public'. This was because the 'public targeted by

---

[166] [195].   [167] [2010] EWHC 608 (Ch), [2010] FSR 21.

[168] Interestingly, a similar conclusion was reached in relation to who is responsible for making copies of a work in the Australian decision *National Rugby League Investments Pty Ltd v Singtel Optus Pty Ltd* [2012] FCAFC 59. In this case the defendants provided the technical means for subscribers to record free to air broadcasts so that they could be watched later on their mobile device or computer, but it was the subscriber who initiated requests for particular broadcasts to be recorded. The Full Federal Court of Australia held that either Optus was the maker of copies of copyright works or Optus and the subscriber were jointly and severally liable for making the copies because they had acted in concert.

[169] Case C-607/11 [2013] FSR 36.   [170] [39].   [171] *Svensson*, [24] and *Reha Training*, [45].

[172] See M. F. Makeen, 'The Controversy of Simultaneous Cable Retransmission to Hotel Rooms under International and European Copyright Laws' (2010) 57 Journal of the Copyright Society of the USA 59. M. F. Makeen, *Copyright in a Global Information Society: The Scope of Copyright Protection under International, US, UK and French Law* (London: Kluwer, 2000), pp. 241–2.

[173] Case C-135/10 [2012] ECDR 16.

the initial communication consisted of all potential visitors to the site concerned, since, given that access to the works on that site was not subject to any restrictive measures, all Internet users could therefore have free access to them'.[174] Critics of the ruling suggest that this use of the 'new public' criterion risks leading to a type of 'exhaustion' of the communication to the public right.[175] A reference to the CJEU in *GS Media BV v Sanoma Media Netherlands BV*[176] raises further issues about whether hyperlinks can amount to a communication to the public. In this case, photographs commissioned by *Playboy* magazine were stored (without authorization) on various websites. The defendant, GS Media, included hyperlinks to these photographs, which were subsequently removed from the websites. Questions have been referred to the CJEU about whether hyperlinks to copyright material on third party websites can amount to communication to the public within Article 3 of the Information Society Directive and whether it makes a difference if the work has not previously been communicated, with the rightholder's consent, to the public. Advocate General Wathelet issued his Opinion on 7 April 2016 and, contrary to *Svensson*, takes the view that the hyperlinks that direct users to copyright works freely accessible on another website are not acts of communication since they are not indispensable to accessing those works.[177] Further, that the criterion of 'new public' is applicable only where the initial communication to the public was authorized by the copyright holder, which was not the case here.[178] However, if the 'new public' criterion were to be applied then, following *Svensson*, this would not be satisfied where photographs were freely accessible to the general internet public.[179] This, of course, begs the question of when copyright works are 'freely accessible'. Would this be the case where restrictions exist in accessing third party websites? *Svensson* suggests that the answer is 'yes'.[180] Also pending is a reference about whether products that have add-ons installed in them which contain hyperlinks to websites that store copyright works can be a communication to the public.[181] And a reference concerning whether a system (i.e. BitTorrent) that allows indexation and categorization of copyright works stored on users' computers to enable their tracing and upload and download amounts to a communication to the public.[182] Based on the principles articulated by the CJEU thus far and summarized in *Reha Training*, what do you the think the answers might be?

Like the WIPO treaties and directive, the CDPA is silent on where the act of communication to the public takes place, with the exception of satellite broadcasts. For broadcasts, section 6(4) of the CDPA designates that a wireless broadcast is made from the place:

> where, under the control and responsibility of the person making the broadcast, the programme-carrying signals are introduced into an uninterrupted chain of communication (including, in the case of a satellite transmission, the chain leading to the satellite and down towards earth).

---

[174] [26].

[175] See ALAI, 'Opinion Proposed to the Executive Committee and adopted at its meeting, 17 September 2014 on the criterion of "New Public", developed by the Court of Justice of the European Union (CJEU)' (2014). For a contrary view to ALAI see European Copyright Society, 'Opinion on the Reference to the CJEU in Case C-466/12 *Svensson*, 15 February 2013' available at <https://europeancopyrightsociety.org/opinion-on-the-reference-to-the-cjeu-in-case-c-46612-svensson/>.

[176] Case C-160/15, EU:C:2016:221.   [177] [59]–[60].   [178] [67].   [179] [69]–[71].

[180] *Svensson*, [31]. See C-160/15 *GS Media* EU:C:2016:644.

[181] See *Stichting Brein v Filmspeler* Case C-527/15, reference lodged on 5 October 2015 by the Rechtbank Midden-Nederland.

[182] *Stichting Brein v Ziggo BV* Case C-610/15, reference lodged on 18 November 2015 by the Hoge Raad der Nederlanden.

However, no guidance is provided in respect of communication to the public *other* than satellite broadcasting and, in particular, in relation to making available to the public. One school of thought is to apply the 'emission theory', i.e. the applicable law in the context of the making-available right would be the law of the country from which the interactive transmission originates. This begs the question, of course, from where does the interactive transmission originate—is it the place of upload or the place where the server is located? Another school of thought is the 'communication theory', where the applicable law would be the laws of the countries where the work is accessed or accessible or the law of the country of emission (whether place of upload or place of the server) and the laws of the countries of reception. Of these two theories, which do you think is preferable for identifying where communication to the public, in respect of internet transmissions, occurs? While this issue of *where* the act of communication to the public occurs has been raised in passing in an English decision,[183] it has not yet been referred to the CJEU.[184]

FURTHER READING

T. Aplin, *Copyright Law in the Digital Society* (Oxford: Hart: 2005), pp. 131–7.

E. Bonadio and M. Santo, ' "Communication to the public" in *FAPL v QC Leisure* and *Murphy v Media Protection Services* (C-403/08 and C-429/08)' [2012] EIPR 277.

J. Ginsburg, 'The (new?) right of making available to the public' in D. Vaver and L. Bently (eds), *Intellectual Property in the New Millennium* (Cambridge: Cambridge University Press, 2004), pp. 234–47.

M. Makeen, *Copyright in a Global Information Society: The Scope of Copyright Protection under International, US, UK and French Law* (London: Kluwer, 2000).

A. Ross and C. Livingstone, 'Communication to the public: Part 1 and Part 2' (2012) 23 Ent. L. R. 160; (2012) 23 Ent. L. R. 209.

A. Tsoutsanis, 'Why copyright and linking can tango' (2014) 9 JIPLP 495.

---

[183] In *Dramatico Entertainment Ltd v British Sky Broadcasting Ltd* [2012] EWHC 268 (Ch), [2012] RPC 27, [68] this legal issue was raised in passing but not did not have to be resolved because the UK users of the Pirate Bay were involved in both uploading and downloading and so it was immaterial whether the act of communication occurred at the place of upload or download. See *EMI Records Ltd v British Sky Broadcasting Ltd* [2013] EWHC 379 (Ch), [2013] FSR 31, [48]–[51] where Arnold J suggests that the act of communication to the public occurs within the UK when acts are targeted at the UK.

[184] Although note that the CJEU has ruled on where the act of reutilization occurs for *sui generis* databases. Reutilization is defined in Art. 7(2)(b) of the Database Directive as 'any form of making available to the public all or a substantial part of the contents of a database'. The CJEU ruled that the mere fact that a website containing data is accessible in a particular national territory is not enough to establish that the database contents are made available to the public. Rather, there must be evidence from which to conclude that there was an intention to target persons in that territory for the purposes of determining where the act of making available to the public occurs: see *Football Dataco v Sportradar* Case C-173/11 [2013] FSR 4, [33]–[47].

4

COPYRIGHT III:

INFRINGEMENT, EXCEPTIONS, AND DATABASE RIGHT

4.1 INTRODUCTION

In the previous chapter we explored the exclusive rights granted to authors and owners, namely moral rights and economic rights respectively. In this chapter we turn to examine the circumstances in which an owner's economic rights may be infringed. This chapter also considers some of the major exceptions that may be relied upon to excuse copyright infringement and how technological protection measures interrelate with copyright exceptions. Finally, the chapter concludes by briefly examining an important related right, the *sui generis* right for databases.

4.2 INFRINGEMENT

Chapter 3 discussed the economic rights that belong to the copyright owner. This section explores the infringement of those rights. At the outset, it is important to distinguish between primary and secondary infringement. Primary infringement occurs where, without the licence of the copyright owner, a person does, or authorizes another to do, one of the exclusive acts restricted by the copyright.[1] Importantly, there is no requirement of knowledge on the part of the infringer and so innocently doing one of the acts will not constitute a defence.[2] Secondary infringement, by way of contrast, occurs where a person facilitates primary infringing activities or deals in infringing copies of a work.[3] A key difference is the requirement of knowledge since a person has to know or have reason to believe that he or she was facilitating an infringement or dealing with an infringing copy of a work.

---

[1] CDPA, s. 16.

[2] It may, however, be relevant to an award of damages—see CDPA, s. 97(1) and see Chapter 15.

[3] CDPA, ss. 22–6.

4.2.1 PRIMARY INFRINGEMENT

To establish a primary infringement it is necessary to ask whether a person has carried out one of the exclusive acts or authorized the doing of one of them. The scope of these acts has been discussed at 3.7. The main additional point to note here is that, because copyright is a territorially limited right, the infringing act must occur within the UK. However, when it comes to authorizing the doing of an exclusive act, it is possible for the act of authorization to occur outside the UK, provided the exclusive act itself occurs within the UK.[4] The next question to ask is whether or not the alleged infringing activity falls within the scope of an express or implied licence. If so, it will not amount to an infringement and if not, it may amount to an infringement depending on whether the remaining elements are established.

What are those remaining elements? First, there must be a causal connection or copying of the copyright work. The causal connection may be direct (e.g. copying onto one's computer a music CD) or indirect (e.g. copying drawings by copying an article that has been manufactured according to those drawings). Second, the act must be done in relation to the whole or *substantial* part of the work.

4.2.1.1 Causal connection

It is important to remember that independently creating the same or similar work will not amount to an infringement. Rather, it is essential to show that the allegedly infringing work was copied or derived from the relevant copyright work. This is described as the requirement of 'copying' or 'causal connection'.[5] Often this issue is not disputed, the defendant conceding that he or she copied from the claimant's work, but arguing that it was not a substantial part or that a relevant exception applies. But sometimes a defendant will argue that the circumstances in which they created their work had absolutely nothing to do with the claimant's copyright work, as occurred in the following case.

Designer Guild v Russell Williams [1998] FSR 803 (Ch D)

The claimant (Designer Guild) owned copyright in a painting from which it had produced its Ixia fabric design, a design which consisted of a vertically striped pattern scattered with flowers. The claimant complained that the defendant (Russell Williams) had infringed copyright in its painting, by virtue of copying the Ixia design in its own Marguerite fabric design, i.e. this was a case of indirect copying. The defendant vigorously denied this allegation, claiming that it was not aware of the Ixia design at the time of creating its own Marguerite design. There was, however, evidence that the Ixia design had been displayed at a trade show that the defendant had attended.

Deputy Judge Lawrence Collins QC, at pp. 810–11, 813, 818, 820:

(6) There must be a causal connection between the copyright work and any infringing work; infringement may be negatived by acceptable evidence of independent design, and

---

[4] *ABKCO Music and Records Inc. v Music Collection International Ltd* [1995] RPC 657.
[5] See *Francis, Day & Hunter Ltd v Bron* [1963] Ch 587.

copying may not be an infringement if it fails to create a sufficient resemblance to amount to a reproduction: *Billhöfer Maschinenfabrik GmbH v TH Dixon & Co Ltd* [1990] FSR 105, 107, *per* Hoffmann J.

(7) There is no infringement if a person arrives by independent work at a substantially similar result to that sought to be protected; but the beginning of the necessary proof of copying normally lies in the establishment of similarity combined with proof of access to the plaintiff's productions: *LB (Plastics) Ltd v Swish Products Ltd* [1979] RPC 619, *per* Lord Wilberforce. If there is proof of access and a sufficient similarity, there will be a shift to the defendant of the evidential burden, i.e. *prima facie* evidence of copying which the party charged may refute by evidence that, notwithstanding the similarity, there was no copying but independent creation: *ibid.* at 625, *per* Lord Hailsham of St Marylebone, citing *King Features Syndicate Inc v O&M Kleeman Ltd* [1941] AC 417, 436, *per* Lord Wright. [Applying these principles to the facts, the judge held that copying had occurred:] The similarities are these:

1. Each fabric consists of vertical stripes, with spaces between the stripes equal to the width of the stripe, and in each fabric flowers and leaves are scattered over and between the stripes, so as to give the same general effect.

2. Each is painted in a similar neo-Impressionistic style. Each uses a brush-stroke technique, i.e. the use of one brush to create a stripe, showing the brush marks against the texture.

3. In each fabric the stripes are formed by vertical brush strokes, and have rough edges which merge into the background.

4. In each fabric the petals are formed with dryish brushstrokes and are executed in a similar way (somewhat in the form of a comma).

5. In each fabric parts of the colour of the stripes shows through some of the petals.

6. In each case the centres of the flower heads are represented by a strong blob, rather than by a realistic representation.

7. In each fabric the leaves are painted in two distinct shades of green, with similar brush strokes, and are scattered over the design.

The overall impression is very similar, but there are differences. The *Ixia* design is smaller and more delicate and the detail is different. In *Marguerite* the effect of the stripes showing through the petals is not as marked as it is in *Ixia*. The leaves in *Marguerite* are distinctly less impressionistic than those in *Ixia*. The impression of similarity is more marked on a comparison of the pink colourways.

…[I]t is extremely improbable that the similarities between *Ixia* and *Marguerite* could be the result of coincidence. There are simply too many, and too many obvious, similarities, any one of which could of itself be coincidental, but the combination of which could not.

…In my judgment the effect of the (1) many and obvious similarities; (2) the opportunity to copy; (3) the complementary nature of the acetate and the striped artwork: and (4) the false provenance given to the acetate, is that Designers Guild has convincingly discharged the burden of proving that Russell Williams copied *Ixia*.

What of situations where a creator has been unconsciously or subconsciously influenced by the claimant's work? Will this amount to causal connection? According to *Francis, Day & Hunter v Bron*,[6] this is possible. The case involved alleged infringement of copyright

---

[6] [1963] Ch 587. For the approach in the US see *Bright Tunes Music Corp. v Harrisongs Music, Ltd*, 420 F Supp 177 (SDNY, 1976).

in a musical work, 'In a Little Spanish Town', first published in 1926 and extensively exploited in the US and elsewhere since that time. The claimants alleged that the defendant's work, 'Why', published in 1959, was an infringement because it reproduced the first eight bars of the chorus of the claimants' work. The defendants denied that they had copied the claimants' work, the composer giving evidence that he had not consciously copied the claimants' song and had not heard it (accepting that if he had heard it, it must have been when he was young). The judge (Wilberforce J) found a considerable degree of similarity between the two songs, but accepted the evidence of the composer of 'Why' that there had been no conscious copying. He also found insufficient evidence to prove unconscious copying. On appeal, the Court of Appeal held that proof of similarity between the allegedly infringing work and the original, coupled with proof of access to the original, creates a prima facie case but not an irrebuttable presumption of copying. As to the issue of subconscious or unconscious copying, Willmer LJ stated that, 'if subconscious copying is to be found, there must be proof (or at least a strong inference) of de facto familiarity with the work alleged to be copied. In the present case, on the findings of Wilberforce J, this element is conspicuously lacking'.[7] Upjohn LJ did not stipulate the same requirement of de facto familiarity with the allegedly copied work, but stressed that strong evidence would be required in order to draw an inference of unconscious copying and that 'the possibility that the defendant had heard it, or even played it in his early youth, is quite insufficient'.[8]

4.2.1.2 Substantial part

It is prima facie infringement where a defendant, without permission of the owner, does one of the exclusive acts in relation to the whole of a copyright work. However, where the dealing is in relation to only part of the work it becomes necessary to establish that this amounts to a substantial part. What constitutes a 'substantial' part is difficult to predict and the courts have developed fairly general guidelines to assist in this assessment. Several of those guidelines are set out in the House of Lords' decision in *Designer Guild*.

Designer Guild v Russell Williams [2000] 1 WLR 2416, [2001] FSR 11 (HL)

The facts of this case were discussed at 4.2.1.1. At first instance, the judge found that a substantial part of the design had been copied; the Court of Appeal, however, overturned this decision. The claimants appealed to the House of Lords.

Lord Bingham, at p. 2418:

While not accepting the judge's finding of copying, the defendant recognised the virtual impossibility of dislodging it in the Court of Appeal and did not challenge it. The defendant's challenge was accordingly directed to the judge's finding that a substantial part of the *Ixia* design had been copied. The Court of Appeal upheld this challenge. But in doing so, as it seems to me, it fell into error. First, by analysing individual features of the two designs and highlighting certain dissimilarities the court failed to give effect to the judge's conclusion, not challenged before it, that the similarities between the two designs were so marked as to

---

[7] *Francis, Day & Hunter v Bron*, p. 613.   [8] pp. 620–1.

warrant a finding that the one had been copied from the other. While the finding of copying did not in theory conclude the issue of substantiality, on the facts here it was almost bound to do so. Secondly, the Court of Appeal approached the issue of substantiality more in the manner of a first instance court making original findings of fact than as an appellate court reviewing findings already made and in very important respects not challenged. It was not for the Court of Appeal to embark on the issue of substantiality afresh, unless the judge had misdirected himself, which in my opinion he had not.

There was, I conclude, no ground for interfering with the judge's conclusion.

Lord Hoffmann, at pp. 2422–3:

[Lord Hoffmann began by emphasizing that the question of substantiality is one of mixed law and fact and that, as such, the Court of Appeal should not have reversed the trial judge's decision unless he had made an error of principle, which he had not. He therefore allowed the appeal.]

It is often said, as Morritt LJ said in this case, that copyright subsists not in ideas but in the form in which the ideas are expressed. The distinction between expression and ideas finds a place in the Agreement on Trade-Related Aspects of Intellectual Property Rights (TRIPS) (OJ 1994 L 336, p. 213), to which the United Kingdom is a party (see article 9.2: 'Copyright protection shall extend to expressions and not to ideas . . .'). Nevertheless, it needs to be handled with care. What does it mean? As Lord Hailsham of St Marylebone said in *LB (Plastics) Ltd v Swish Products Ltd* [1979] RPC 551, 629, 'it all depends on what you mean by "ideas"'.

Plainly there can be no copyright in an idea which is merely in the head, which has not been expressed in copyrightable form, as a literary, dramatic, musical or artistic work. But the distinction between ideas and expression cannot mean anything so trivial as that. On the other hand, every element in the expression of an artistic work (unless it got there by accident or compulsion) is the expression of an idea on the part of the author. It represents her choice to paint stripes rather than polka dots, flowers rather than tadpoles, use one colour and brush technique rather than another, and so on. The expression of these ideas is protected, both as a cumulative whole and also to the extent to which they form a 'substantial part' of the work. Although the term 'substantial part' might suggest a quantitative test, or at least the ability to identify some discrete part which, on quantitative or qualitative grounds, can be regarded as substantial, it is clear upon the authorities that neither is the correct test. *Ladbroke (Football) Ltd v William Hill (Football) Ltd* [1964] 1 WLR 273 establishes that substantiality depends upon quality rather than quantity (Lord Reid, at p. 276, Lord Evershed, at p. 283, Lord Hodson, at p. 288, Lord Pearce, at p. 293). And there are numerous authorities which show that the 'part' which is regarded as substantial can be a feature or combination of features of the work, abstracted from it rather than forming a discrete part. That is what the judge found to have been copied in this case. Or to take another example, the original elements in the plot of a play or novel may be a substantial part, so that copyright may be infringed by a work which does not reproduce a single sentence of the original. If one asks what is being protected in such a case, it is difficult to give any answer except that it is an idea expressed in the copyright work.

My Lords, if one examines the cases in which the distinction between ideas and the expression of ideas has been given effect, I think it will be found that they support two quite distinct propositions. The first is that a copyright work may express certain ideas which are not protected because they have no connection with the literary, dramatic, musical or artistic nature of the work. It is on this ground that, for example, a literary work which describes a system or invention does not entitle the author to claim protection for his system or invention as such. The same is true of an inventive concept expressed in an artistic work. However striking or original it may be, others are (in the absence of patent protection) free to express it in works of their own: see *Kleeneze Ltd v DRG (UK) Ltd* [1984] FSR 399. The other proposition is that certain ideas expressed by a copyright work may not be protected because, although they are ideas of a literary, dramatic or artistic nature, they are not original, or so commonplace as not to form a substantial part of the work. *Kenrick & Co v Lawrence & Co* (1890) 25 QBD 99 is a well known example. It is on this ground that the mere notion of combining stripes and flowers would not have amounted to a substantial part of the plaintiff's work. At that level of abstraction, the idea, though expressed in the design, would not have represented sufficient of the author's skill and labour as to attract copyright protection.

Generally speaking, in cases of artistic copyright, the more abstract and simple the copied idea, the less likely it is to constitute a substantial part. Originality, in the sense of the contribution of the author's skill and labour, tends to lie in the detail with which the basic idea is presented. Copyright law protects foxes better than hedgehogs. In this case, however, the elements which the judge found to have been copied went well beyond the banal and I think that the judge was amply justified in deciding that they formed a substantial part of the originality of the work.

Lord Millett, at p. 2426:

Once the judge has found that the defendant's design incorporates features taken from the copyright work, the question is whether what has been taken constitutes all or a substantial part of the copyright work. This is a matter of impression, for whether the part taken is substantial must be determined by its quality rather than its quantity. It depends upon its importance to the copyright work. It does not depend upon its importance to the defendant's work, as I have already pointed out. The pirated part is considered on its own (see *Ladbroke (Football) Ltd v William Hill (Football) Ltd* [1964] 1 WLR 273, 293, *per* Lord Pearce) and its importance to the copyright work assessed. There is no need to look at the infringing work for this purpose.

The Court of Appeal were concerned only with this second stage. They were not entitled to reverse the judge's finding that the defendant's design reproduced features of the copyright work, nor his identification of the features in question. The only issue was whether those features represented a substantial part of the copyright work. A visual comparison of the two designs was not only unnecessary but likely to mislead.

My noble and learned friend, Lord Scott of Foscote, has drawn attention to the differences between the copying of a discrete part of the copyright work and the altered copying of the whole, or the copying with or without modifications of some but not all the features of the copyright work. The distinction is not material in the present case. Whether or not it is alleged that a discrete part of the copyright work has been taken, the issues of copying and substantiality are treated as separate questions. Where, however, it is alleged that some but not all the features of the copyright work have been taken, the answer to the first question will almost inevitably answer both, for if the similarities are sufficiently numerous or extensive to justify an inference of copying they are likely to be sufficiently substantial to satisfy this requirement also.

For these reasons, as well as those given by my noble and learned friends, Lord Hoffmann and Lord Bingham of Cornhill, I would allow the appeal.

Lord Scott of Foscote, at pp. 2430–2:

Substantiality

Section 16(3) of the Act of 1988 says that copying a copyright work is a copyright infringement if the copying is of 'the work as a whole or any substantial part of it'. Section 16(3) may come into play in two quite different types of case. One type of case is, obviously, where an identifiable part of the whole, but not the whole, has been copied. For example, only a section of a picture may have been copied, or only a sentence or two, or even only a phrase, from a poem or a book, or only a bar or two of a piece of music, may have been copied: see the examples given at pp. 88–89, para. 2–102 of *Laddie, Prescott and Vitoria, The Modern Law of Copyright and Designs*, 2nd edn (1995), vol. 1 (which, for convenience, I will refer to as '*Laddie*'). In cases of that sort, the question whether the copying of the part constitutes an infringement depends on the qualitative importance of the part that has been copied, assessed in relation to the copyright work as a whole. In *Ladbroke (Football) Ltd v William Hill (Football) Ltd* [1964] 1 WLR 273 Lord Reid said, at p. 276, that: 'the question whether he has copied a substantial part depends much more on the quality than on the quantity of what he has taken'.

The present case is not a case of that type. The judge did not identify any particular part of *Ixia* and hold that that part had been copied. His finding of copying related to *Ixia* as a whole.

The other type of case in which a question of substantiality may become relevant is where the copying has not been an exact copying of the copyright work but a copying with modifications. This type of copying is referred to in *Laddie* as 'altered copying'. A paradigm of this type of case would be a translation of a literary work into some other language, or the dramatisation of a novel. The translation, or the play or film, might not have a single word in common with the original. But, assuming copyright existed in the original, the 'copy' might well, and in the case of a word-by-word translation certainly would, constitute an infringement of copyright.

The present case is an 'altered copying' case. Helen Burke put together a number of artistic ideas derived from various sources in order to produce her *Ixia* design, an original artistic design as it is accepted to be. Miss Ibbotson and Mrs Williams, as the judge found, copied the *Ixia* design in order to produce their *Marguerite* design. But they did so with modifications. The *Marguerite* design is not an exact copy of *Ixia*. Nor is any specific part of the *Marguerite* design an exact copy of any corresponding part of the *Ixia* design. It is an altered copy.

The question, then, where an altered copy has been produced, is what the test should be in order to determine whether the production constitutes a copyright infringement. If the alterations are sufficiently extensive it may be that the copying does not constitute an infringement at all. The test proposed in *Laddie*, at pp. 92–93, para. 2–108, to determine whether an altered copy constitutes an infringement is: 'Has the infringer incorporated a substantial part of the independent skill, labour etc contributed by the original author in creating the copyright work ...'

My Lords, I think this is a useful test, based as it is on an underlying principle of copyright law, namely, that a copier is not at liberty to appropriate the benefit of another's skill and labour.

My noble and learned friend, Lord Millett, has made the point that once copying has been established, the question of substantiality depends on the relationship between what has been copied on the one hand and the original work on the other, similarity no longer being relevant. My Lords, I respectfully agree that that would be so in the first type of case. But in an altered copying case, particularly where the finding of copying is dependant, in the absence of direct evidence, upon the inferences to be drawn from the extent and nature of the similarities between the two works, the similarities will usually be determinative not only of the issue of copying but also of the issue of substantiality. And even where there is direct evidence of copying, as, for example, where it is admitted that the copier has produced his 'copy' with the original at his elbow, the differences between the original and the 'copy' may be so extensive as to bar a finding of infringement. It is not a breach of copyright to borrow an idea, whether of an artistic, literary or musical nature, and to translate that idea into a new work. In 'altered copying' cases, the difficulty is the drawing of the line between what is a permissible borrowing of an idea and what is an impermissible piracy of the artistic, literary or musical creation of another. In drawing this line, the extent and nature of the similarities between the altered copy and the original work must, it seems to me, play a critical and often determinative role. In particular, this must be so where there is no direct evidence of copying and the finding of copying is dependant on the inferences to be drawn from the similarities.

[**Lord Hope** agreed with Lord Bingham.]

According to *Designer Guild*, when will it be appropriate for an appellate court to overturn a first instance decision regarding substantiality? Where the similarities between the copyright work and allegedly infringing work are so extensive as to support a finding of copying or causal connection, to what extent will this justify a finding that a substantial part of the work has been copied? In this situation is Lord Scott of Foscote's characterization of copying as either 'discrete' or 'altered' a helpful tool? How does his approach differ from that of Lord Millett's?

Lords Hoffmann, Millett, and Scott of Foscote all held that substantiality is a qualitative assessment, a principle that was reiterated by the House of Lords in *Newspaper Licensing Agency v Marks & Spencer Ltd*.[9] In this case the defendant had obtained press cuttings from an agency licensed by the claimant. However, the defendant made further copies of some of the press cuttings for circulation within its organization. The claimant (who represented national and provincial newspapers) alleged infringement of copyright in the typographical arrangement of published editions of certain newspapers. At first instance, the judge held that copyright in the typographical arrangement related to both the newspaper as a whole and the individual articles. Further, that even if typographical arrangement copyright was restricted to the whole newspaper, copying individual articles amounted to a 'substantial part'. The Court of Appeal allowed the appeal, holding that typographical arrangement copyright subsisted in the newspaper as a whole and none of the individual cuttings constituted a substantial part of the newspaper from which they were derived. The claimant's appeal was unsuccessful. In the House of Lords, Lord Hoffmann (who delivered the leading speech) observed that the qualitative aspect of 'substantial part' had to be answered 'by reference to the reason why the work is given copyright protection'.[10] In the case of literary works, this was literary originality and in the case of artistic works, this was artistic originality (irrespective, in both cases, of literary and artistic merit). For typographical arrangements, the question of substantiality was to be decided according to the same principles. However, the court had to take into account the fact that reproduction of typographical arrangements was limited to facsimile copies (by virtue of section 17(5) of the Copyright Designs and Patents Act 1988 (CDPA)).[11] Lord Hoffmann held that:

[9] [2003] 1 AC 551.   [10] [19].   [11] [20].

23. In the case of a modern newspaper, I think that the skill and labour devoted to typographical arrangement is principally expressed in the overall design. It is not the choice of a particular typeface, the precise number or width of the columns, the breadth of margins and the relationship of headlines and strap lines to the other text, the number of articles on a page and the distribution of photographs and advertisements but the combination of all of these into pages which give the newspaper as a whole its distinctive appearance. In some cases that appearance will depend upon the relationship between the pages; for example, having headlines rather than small advertisements on the front page. Usually, however, it will depend upon the appearance of any given page. But I find it difficult to think of the skill and labour which has gone into the typographical arrangement of a newspaper being expressed in anything less than a full page. The particular fonts, columns, margins and so forth are only, so to speak, the typographical vocabulary in which the arrangement is expressed.

...

25. ... The test is quantitative in the sense that, as there can be infringement only by making a facsimile copy, the question will always be whether one has made a facsimile copy of enough of the published edition to amount to a substantial part. But the question of what counts as enough seems to me to be qualitative, depending not upon the proportion which the part taken bears to the whole but on whether the copy can be said to have appropriated the presentation and layout of the edition.

Although Lord Hoffmann describes substantiality as a qualitative and quantitative test, is the assessment really only a qualitative one? Do you agree that the best mechanism for determining whether a substantial part has been copied, from a qualitative point of view, is whether the originality reflected in that type of work has been appropriated? How does this approach operate for those categories of works (i.e. films, sound recordings, broadcasts, and typographical arrangements) where there is no originality requirement in order for copyright to subsist? Can we really assess whether the part copied for these categories reflects originality and according to what standard would this be assessed?

As in other areas of copyright, CJEU jurisprudence threatens to disrupt established UK law and, as we will see, the *Infopaq* ruling leads to a possible rethinking of infringement principles.

Infopaq International A/S v Danske Dagblades Forening Case C-5/08 [2009] ECDR 16 (CJEU Fourth Chamber)

The facts were discussed in Chapter 2. Refer back and re-read the facts and extract at 2.5.2.3.2.

39 In the light of the considerations referred to in [37] of this judgment, the various parts of a work thus enjoy protection under art.2(a) of Directive 2001/29, provided that they contain elements which are the expression of the intellectual creation of the author of the work.

40 With respect to the scope of such protection of a work, it follows from recitals 9–11 in the preamble to Directive 2001/29 that its main objective is to introduce a high level of protection, in particular for authors to enable them to receive an appropriate reward for the use of their works, including at the time of reproduction of those works, in order to be able to pursue their creative and artistic work.

41 Similarly, recital 21 in the preamble to Directive 2001/29 requires that the acts covered by the right of reproduction be construed broadly.

42 That requirement of a broad definition of those acts is, moreover, also to be found in the wording of art.2 of that Directive, which uses expressions such as 'direct or indirect', 'temporary or permanent', 'by any means' and 'in any form'.

43 Consequently, the protection conferred by art.2 of Directive 2001/29 must be given a broad interpretation.

44 As regards newspaper articles, their author's own intellectual creation, referred to in [37] of this judgment, is evidenced clearly from the form, the manner in which the subject is presented and the linguistic expression. In the main proceedings, moreover, it is common ground that newspaper articles, as such, are literary works covered by Directive 2001/29.

45 Regarding the elements of such works covered by the protection, it should be observed that they consist of words which, considered in isolation, are not as such an intellectual creation of the author who employs them. It is only through the choice, sequence and combination of those words that the author may express his creativity in an original manner and achieve a result which is an intellectual creation.

46 Words as such do not, therefore, constitute elements covered by the protection.

47 That being so, given the requirement of a broad interpretation of the scope of the protection conferred by art.2 of Directive 2001/29, the possibility may not be ruled out that certain isolated sentences, or even certain parts of sentences in the text in question, may be suitable for conveying to the reader the originality of a publication such as a newspaper article, by communicating to that reader an element which is, in itself, the expression of the intellectual creation of the author of that article. Such sentences or parts of sentences are, therefore, liable to come within the scope of the protection provided for in art.2(a) of that Directive.

48 In the light of those considerations, the reproduction of an extract of a protected work which, like those at issue in the main proceedings, comprises 11 consecutive words thereof, is such as to constitute reproduction in part within the meaning of art.2 of Directive 2001/29, if that extract contains an element of the work which, as such, expresses the author's own intellectual creation; it is for the national court to make this determination.

49 It must be remembered also that the data capture process used by Infopaq allows for the reproduction of multiple extracts of protected works. That process reproduces an extract of 11 words each time a search word appears in the relevant work and, moreover, often operates using a number of search words because some clients ask Infopaq to draw up summaries based on a number of criteria.

50 In so doing, that process increases the likelihood that Infopaq will make reproductions in part within the meaning of art.2(a) of Directive 2001/29 because the cumulative effect of those extracts may lead to the reconstitution of lengthy fragments which are liable to reflect the originality of the work in question, with the result that they contain a number of elements which are such as to express the intellectual creation of the author of that work.

51 In the light of the foregoing, the answer to the first question is that an act occurring during a data capture process, which consists of storing an extract of a protected work comprising 11 words and printing out that extract, is such as to come within the concept of reproduction in part within the meaning of art.2 of Directive 2001/29, if the elements thus reproduced are the expression of the intellectual creation of their author; it is for the national court to make this determination.

In *Infopaq*, the CJEU held that reproduction should be broadly construed and that reproduction of a work 'in part' could extend to copying sentences or parts of sentences of a literary work, provided such extracts reflected the author's 'intellectual creation'. In so holding, did the Court inextricably tie the notion of infringement to originality? Is this consistent with the UK approach to substantial part? Assuming it is consistent, is it at all problematic that originality will be determinative in deciding whether a substantial part of a work has been reproduced? Finally, if the originality standard is that of intellectual creation, as opposed to skill and labour, would we expect to see different outcomes when it comes to infringement?

Subsequent CJEU rulings and English decisions have reiterated the importance of originality—in the EU sense—to determining infringement. For example, in *NLA v Meltwater*[12] Proudman J observed that: 'originality rather than substantiality is the test to be applied to the part extracted'.[13] She also commented that, based on *Infopaq*, the question of whether text extracts constituted a substantial part of a literary work depended on whether some or all of the text extracts expressed the author's intellectual creation.[14] On appeal, the Court of Appeal endorsed Proudman J's approach.[15] In *SAS Institute Inc. v World Programming Ltd*,[16] Arnold J observed that: 'when considering whether a substantial part has been reproduced, it is necessary to focus upon what has been reproduced and to consider whether it expresses the author's own intellectual creation. To that extent, some dissection is not merely permissible, but required. On the other hand, the Court of Justice also held in *Infopaq* at [49] that it is necessary to consider the cumulative effect of what has been reproduced.'[17] Further, in *England and Wales Cricket Board Ltd v Tixdaq Ltd and Fanatix Ltd* ('*Fanatix*')[18] Arnold J considered how reproduction in part would be assessed for broadcasts and first fixations of films. He held that parts of these works enjoy protection 'provided that they contain elements which reflect the rationale for protecting broadcasts and first fixations, that is to say, the investment made by the broadcaster or producer'.[19] He stressed that this did not mean that reproduction of *any* part would be an infringement, and that the test was quantitative and qualitative. In the context of this case, which involved clips from sports broadcasts (discussed later at 4.3.2.2), Arnold J observed that 'the footage is not undifferentiated either in terms of its interest to viewers or in terms of its commercial value or in terms of the equipment and skills that is required to produce it'.[20] He went on to find that an eight-second clip from a broadcast or film of two to three hours in length did constitute a substantial part.[21]

The CJEU has reiterated the importance of originality to assessing when there has been a reproduction 'in part'. In the joined cases *FAPL v QC Leisure* and *Murphy v Media Protection Services*,[22] the CJEU ruled that the reproduction right would apply to transient fragments of works stored within the memory of a satellite decoder or on a television screen provided that 'those fragments contain elements which are the expression of the authors' own intellectual creation'.[23] Further, in *Painer*[24] the CJEU expressed

[12] [2010] EWHC 3099 (Ch), [2011] RPC 7.   [13] [69].   [14] [78].
[15] [2011] EWCA Civ 890.   [16] [2011] RPC 1.
[17] *SAS Institute Inc. v World Programming Ltd*, [243].
[18] [2016] EWHC 575 (Ch), [2016] Bus. L. R. 641.   [19] [66].   [20] [66].   [21] [99].
[22] Joined Cases C-403 and 429/08 [2012] FSR 1 (Grand Chamber).
[23] *FAPL* and *Murphy*, [188]. See also *ITV Broadcasting v TV Catchup Ltd (No. 2)* [2011] EWHC 1874 (Pat), [109] where Lloyd J adopted the provisional view that there was a reproduction of a substantial part of films in internet server buffers and on users' computer screens.
[24] Case C-145/10 [2012] ECDR 6.

the view that the extent of protection should not 'depend on possible differences in the degree of creative freedom in the production of various categories of works'.[25] As such, the protection conferred by the reproduction right had to be the same for portrait photographs as for any other photographic works.[26] A possible interpretation of this ruling is that when assessing reproduction 'in part' according to the intellectual creation of the part taken, the degree of creative freedom (or constraint) for that type of work is not relevant. However, this view is problematic because the creative freedom or functional constraints available must surely affect whether the author has made creative choices and the degree of intellectual creation reflected in the work. As well, it seems strange that it might be easier to prove a reproduction 'in part' for a work that, while original, features less creativity because of functional constraints than a work which displays significant creativity due to there being a lot of creative choices available. Therefore, arguably the preferable interpretation of this ruling is that the Court meant that once any work has overcome the originality threshold of 'author's own intellectual creation' then the right of reproduction in Article 2(a) of the Information Society Directive applies to it. Further, it is silent about how to assess reproduction in part, not least because the entirety of the photograph was copied in *Painer* and so the issue did not arise.

FURTHER READING

I. Alexander, 'The concept of reproduction and the "temporary and transient" exception' [2009] CLJ 520.

E. Derclaye, '*Infopaq International A/S v Danske Dagblades Forening* (C-5/08): wonderful or worrisome? The impact of the ECJ ruling in *Infopaq* on UK copyright law' [2010] EIPR 247.

J. Pila, 'An Australian copyright revolution and its relevance for UK jurisprudence: *IceTv* in the light of *Infopaq v Danske*' (2010) 9 Oxford University Commonwealth L. J. 77.

Another issue that emerges from *Infopaq* and subsequent CJEU rulings is whether determining a reproduction 'in part' according to the 'intellectual creation' of the part taken applies only to when the literal expression is copied or extends to non-literal expression as well. In *Designer Guild*, Lord Scott of Foscote describes this as a distinction as between discrete or altered copying. In your view, are *Infopaq*, *Painer*, and *SAS Institute*[27] examples of copying of discrete (literal) expression or altered (non-literal) expression? Further, does the approach adopted by the House of Lords in *Designer Guild* apply to both literal and non-literal expression? Finally, is it possible for factors, aside from originality, such as the idea/expression distinction, to be used in determining whether a substantial part has been copied? In this regard, consider again Lord Hoffmann's and Lord Scott's speeches in *Designer Guild* (extracted at 4.2.1.2).

The idea/expression distinction and its relationship to whether the part taken is 'substantial' has been further explored by the Court of Appeal in the '*Da Vinci Code*' case.

---

[25] [97].   [26] [98].   [27] Refer back to the extract at 2.5.1.2.2.

Baigent v Random House [2007] FSR 24

The case involved a dispute between two of the authors of *The Holy Blood and the Holy Grail* (HBHG), a work of historical conjecture, and the UK publisher of Dan Brown's *Da Vinci Code* (DVC), a work of fiction. The claimants alleged that a substantial part of HBHG had been reproduced in DVC. In particular, they alleged copying of 15 elements of what was described as the 'central theme' of HBHG and very minor examples of language similarity. The defendant argued that they had copied only ideas and, as such, no infringement had occurred. At first instance, Peter Smith J dismissed the claimants' action. The claimants appealed.

Mummery LJ (Rix LJ in agreement):

153. I appreciate that the Central Theme and its elements particularised in the VSS [Voluntary Supplemental Schedule] are important to the claimants. They are by-products of their years of research, discussion and speculation. Viewed objectively, however, in the context of the necessary and sufficient conditions for infringement, they are not 'a substantial part' of HBHG. They are not substantial *in the copyright sense*, any more than a fact or theory that took a lifetime to establish, or a discovery that cost a fortune to make.

154. The position is that the individual elements of the Central Theme Points distilled from HBHG in the VSS are not of a sufficiently developed character to constitute a substantial part of HBHG. In the words of the judge they are 'too generalised' to be a substantial part of HBHG. They are an assortment of items of historical fact and information, virtual history, events, incidents, theories, arguments and propositions. They do not contain detailed similarities of language or 'architectural' similarities in the detailed treatment or development of the collection or arrangement of incidents, situations, characters and narrative, such as is normally found in cases of infringement of literary or dramatic copyright. The 11 aspects of the Central Theme in DVC are differently expressed, collected, selected, arranged and narrated.

155. Of course, it takes time, effort and skill to conduct historical research, to collect materials for a book, to decide what facts are established by the evidence and to formulate arguments, theories, hypotheses, propositions and conclusions. It does not, however, follow, as suggested in the claimants' submissions, that the use of items of information, fact and so on derived from the assembled material is, in itself, 'a substantial part' of HBHG simply because it has taken time skill and effort to carry out the necessary research.

156. The literary copyright exists in HBHG by reason of the skill and labour expended by the claimants in the original composition and production of it and the original manner or form of expression of the results of their research. Original expression includes not only the language in which the work is composed but also the original selection, arrangement and compilation of the raw research material. It does not, however, extend to clothing information, facts, ideas, theories and themes with exclusive property rights, so as to enable the claimants to monopolise historical research or knowledge and prevent the legitimate use of historical and biographical material, theories propounded, general arguments deployed, or general hypotheses suggested (whether they are sound or not) or general themes written about.

157. The reported cases in which infringement claims have succeeded in relation to historical works or semi-historical works do not assist the claimants' case. They are decisions by experienced Chancery judges at first instance correctly applying well established general

principles to the particular facts of the case. For example, in *Ravenscroft v Herbert* [1980] RPC 193 Brightman J found that there was copying of a substantial part of a work of non-fiction (The Spear of Destiny) in the form of a novel. To an appreciable extent they were competing works. The defendant's novel was alleged to contain as many as 50 instances of deliberate language copying, as well as copying of the same historical characters, historical incidents and interpretation of the significance of historical events.

158. *Harman Pictures NV v Osborne* [1967] 1 WLR 723 is another well known example of a case in which the author of a historical work (The Reason Why) obtained an interlocutory injunction in a copyright claim against the writer of a film script, which had much in common with the original copyright work in its selection of incidents and quotations supplemented by some alterations and additions attributed to other sources. Goff J found 'many similarities of detail' in John Osborne's film script (p. 735) and he was impressed by 'the marked similarity of the choice of incidents...and by the juxtaposition of ideas' for which there was a lack of explanation on the defendant's side.

159. In my judgment, the judge rightly held that the claimants have not established that a substantial part of HBHG has been copied, either as to the original composition and expression of the work or as to the particular collection, selection and arrangement of material and its treatment in HBHG.

[**Lloyd LJ** also dismissed the appeal.]

How would you characterize the idea/expression distinction? How was it characterized by Lord Hoffmann in *Designer Guild* as compared with the Court of Appeal in *Baigent v Random House*? Which sorts of contribution might fall within the domain of unprotectable ideas? Finally, do you think there is still room for UK courts to take account of the idea/expression distinction in determining infringement post-*Infopaq*?

In relation to computer programs, the idea/expression distinction has been expressly articulated in legislation (in Article 1(2) and recital 14 of the Software Directive) and elucidated by a handful of CJEU and English decisions.[28] In *Navitaire v Easjyet*, Pumfrey J made the following remarks on the difficulties of identifying idea versus expression in the case of computer programs.

124. ...I would with respect accept what is said by Jacob J in *Ibcos* [at p. 291]:

'The true position is that where an "idea" is sufficiently general, then even if an original work embodies it, the mere taking of that idea will not infringe. But if the "idea" is detailed, then there may be infringement. It is a question of degree. The same applies whether the work is functional or not, and whether visual or literary. In the latter field the taking of a plot (i.e. the "idea") of a novel or play can certainly infringe—if that plot is a substantial part of the copyright work. As Judge Learned Hand said (speaking of the distinction between "idea" and "expression"): Nobody has ever been able to fix that boundary and nobody ever can.'

---

[28] *Bezpečnostní softwarová asociace v Ministerstvo kultury* Case C-393/09 [2011] ECDR 3, [2011] FSR 18; *SAS Institute Inc. v World Programming Ltd* [2011] RPC 1 (Ch D); *SAS Institute Inc. v World Programming Ltd* Case C-406/10 [2012] 3 CMLR 4 (Grand Chamber); *Navitaire v Easyjet Airline Co.* [2006] RPC 31; *Nova Productions Ltd v Mazooma Games Ltd* [2007] RPC 25.

125. This does not answer the question with which I am confronted, which is peculiar, I believe, to computer programs. The reason it is a new problem is that two completely different computer programs can produce an identical result: not a result identical at some level of abstraction but identical at any level of abstraction. This is so even if the author of one has no access at all to the other but only to its results. The analogy with a plot is for this reason a poor one. It is a poor one for other reasons as well. To say these programs possess a plot is precisely like saying that the book of instructions for a booking clerk acting manually has a plot: but a book of instructions has no theme, no events, and does not have a narrative flow. Nor does a computer program, particularly one whose behaviour depends upon the history of its inputs in any given transaction. It does not have a plot, merely a series of pre-defined operations intended to achieve the desired result in response to the requests of the customer.

Do you agree that computer programs pose unique difficulties when it comes to distinguishing between idea and expression? Is it preferable, as Pumfrey J went on to do, to ask instead whether relevant skill and labour (or intellectual creation) has been copied by the defendant? The Court of Appeal in *Nova Productions Ltd v Mazooma Games Ltd*[29] applied *Navitaire*, reiterating that the idea/expression principle applies to computer programs protected as literary works and emphasizing that the behaviour or appearance generated by a program falls within the realm of 'idea'. However, as the CJEU indicated in *Bezpečnostní softwarová asociace v Ministerstvo kultury*,[30] this does not prevent elements of software, such as the graphic user interface, possibly obtaining protection as a separate work if originality, in the sense of an author's own intellectual creation, can be established.[31] The other major ruling on the scope of protection for computer programs was in *SAS Institute Inc. v World Programming Ltd*.[32] If you turn back to Chapter 2 and re-read the extract at 2.5.1.2.2, what was the CJEU's view about the functionality of software and its programming languages and data file formats? Why were these *not* classed as protectable expression?

FURTHER READING

S. Ang, 'The idea–expression dichotomy and merger doctrine in the copyright laws of the US and UK' (1994) 2 IJL & IT 111.

E. Barker and I. Harding, 'Copyright, the idea/expression dichotomy and harmonization: digging deeper into *SAS*' (2012) 7 JIPLP 673.

R. H. Jones, 'The myth of the idea/expression dichotomy in copyright law' (1990) 10 Pace L. R. 551.

P. Masiyakurima, 'The futility of the idea/expression dichotomy in UK copyright law' (2007) 38 IIC 548.

4.2.1.3 Authorization

Where a person authorizes, without permission of the copyright owner, another to carry out one of the exclusive acts, this will amount to primary infringement. But in what

---

[29] [2007] RPC 25.　　[30] Case C-393/09 [2011] ECDR 3, [2011] FSR 18.　　[31] [45]–[46].
[32] Case C-406/10 [2012] 3 CMLR 4.

circumstances will 'authorization' occur? This issue was explored at length in the following House of Lords' decision.

CBS Songs v Amstrad [1988] AC 1013

The defendant (Amstrad) manufactured and sold a dual-tape cassette deck machine, which enabled high-speed recording from pre-recorded cassette tapes to blank cassette tapes. The claimants (CBS Songs) sued on behalf of themselves and other owners of copyright in the music trade alleging, inter alia, that the defendant by making, advertising, and selling its machine had authorized members of the public to infringe their copyright under the Copyright Act 1956. The defendants applied to strike out the writ and statement of claim as disclosing no cause of action. This was refused by Whitford J, but allowed by the Court of Appeal. There was an appeal to the House of Lords.

Lord Templeman (with whom the other law lords agreed)**, at pp. 1052–5:**

Section 1(1) of the Act of 1956 confers on the copyright owners in a record the 'exclusive right...to authorise other persons' to copy the record. BPI submit that by selling a model which incorporates a double-speed twin-tape recorder Amstrad 'authorise' the purchaser of the model to copy a record in which copyright subsists and therefore Amstrad infringe the exclusive right of the copyright owner. My Lords, twin-tape recorders, fast or slow, and single-tape recorders, in addition to their recording and playing functions, are capable of copying on to blank tape, directly or indirectly, records which are broadcast, records on discs and records on tape. Blank tapes are capable of being employed for recording or copying. Copying may be lawful or unlawful. Every tape recorder confers on the operator who acquires a blank tape the facility of copying; the double-speed twin-tape recorder provides a modern and efficient facility for continuous playing and continuous recording and for copying. No manufacturer and no machine confers on the purchaser authority to copy unlawfully. The purchaser or other operator of the recorder determines whether he shall copy and what he shall copy. By selling the recorder Amstrad may facilitate copying in breach of copyright but do not authorise it.

   BPI's next submission is that Amstrad by their advertisement authorise the purchaser of an Amstrad model to copy records in which copyright subsists. Amstrad's advertisement drew attention to the advantages of their models and to the fact that the recorder incorporated in the model could be employed in the copying of modern records. But the advertisement did not authorise the unlawful copying of records; on the contrary, the footnote warned that some copying required permission and made it clear that Amstrad had no authority to grant that permission. If Amstrad had considered the interests of copyright owners, Amstrad could have declined to incorporate double-tape double-speed recorders in Amstrad's models or could have advertised the illegality of home copying. If Amstrad had deprived themselves of the advantages of offering improved recording facilities, other manufacturers would have reaped the benefit. The effect of double-tape double-speed recorders on the incidence of home copying is altogether speculative. If Amstrad had advertised the illegality of home copying the effect would have been minimal. Amstrad's advertisement was deplorable because Amstrad thereby flouted the rights of copyright owners. Amstrad's advertisement was cynical because Amstrad advertised the increased efficiency of a facility capable of being employed to break the law. But the operator of an Amstrad tape recording facility, like all other operators, can alone decide whether to record or play and what material is to be recorded. The Amstrad advertisement is open to severe criticism but no purchaser of an Amstrad model could reasonably deduce from the facilities incorporated in the model or from Amstrad's advertisement that Amstrad possessed or purported to possess the authority to grant any required permission for a record to be copied.

...

In the present case, Amstrad did not sanction, approve or countenance an infringing use of their model and I respectfully agree with Atkin LJ and with Lawton LJ in the present case [1986] FSR 159, 207 that in the context of the Copyright Act 1956 an authorisation means a grant or purported grant, which may be express or implied, of the right to do the act complained of. Amstrad conferred on the purchaser the power to copy but did not grant or purport to grant the right to copy.

In *Moorhouse v University of New South Wales* [1976] RPC 151 in the High Court of Australia where the facilities of a library included a photocopying machine, Gibbs J said, at p. 159:

a person who has under his control the means by which an infringement of copyright may be committed—such as a photocopying machine—and who makes it available to other persons, knowing, or having reason to suspect, that it is likely to be used for the purpose of committing an infringement, and omitting to take reasonable steps to limit its use to legitimate purposes, would authorise any infringement that resulted from its use.

Whatever may be said about this proposition, Amstrad have no control over the use of their models once they are sold...

In *CBS Inc v Ames Records & Tapes Ltd* [1982] Ch 91, Whitford J held that a record library which lent out records and simultaneously offered blank tapes for sale at a discount did not authorise the infringement of copyright in the records. He said, at p. 106:

Any ordinary person would, I think, assume that an authorisation can only come from somebody having or purporting to have authority and that an act is not authorised by somebody who merely enables or possibly assists or even encourages another to do that act, but does not purport to have any authority which he can grant to justify the doing of the act.

This precisely describes Amstrad.

In *RCA Corporation v John Fairfax & Sons Ltd* [1982] RPC 91 in the High Court of Australia, Kearney J, at p. 100, approved a passage in Laddie, Prescott & Vitoria, *The Modern Law of Copyright* (1980), para. 12.9, p. 403, in these terms:

a person may be said to authorise another to commit an infringement if the one has some form of control over the other at the time of infringement or, if he has no such control, is responsible for placing in the other's hands materials which by their nature are almost inevitably to be used for the purpose of infringement.

This proposition seems to me to be stated much too widely. As Whitford J pointed out in the *Ames* case, at p. 107:

you can home tape from bought records, borrowed records, borrowed from friends or public libraries, from the playing of records over the radio, and indeed, at no expense, from records which can be obtained for trial periods on introductory offers from many record clubs who advertise in the papers, who are prepared to let you have up to three or four records for a limited period of trial, free of any charge whatsoever.

> These borrowed records together with all recording machines and blank tapes could be said to be 'materials which by their nature are almost inevitably to be used for the purpose of an infringement'. But lenders and sellers do not authorise infringing use.
>
> For these reasons, which are to be found also in the judgments of the Court of Appeal, at pp. 207, 210 and 217, I am satisfied that Amstrad did not authorise infringement.

CBS v Amstrad was decided at a time when the threat of music piracy came from dual-tape cassette deck machines. But today, piracy is more likely to arise from peer-to-peer file-sharing activities of varying degrees of sophistication. How would the principles stated in *CBS v Amstrad* apply to modern-day piracy? Could it be argued that operators of peer-to-peer file-sharing facilities authorize the infringing uploading and downloading activities of their users? This was one of the issues considered in the following case.

Dramatico Entertainment Ltd v British Sky Broadcasting Ltd [2012] EWHC 268 (Ch), [2012] RPC 27

The claimants were record companies who sought an injunction, pursuant to section 97A of the CDPA, against the defendants, a group of internet service providers, requiring them to block or impede access to the (now infamous) peer-to-peer file-sharing website, the Pirate Bay. In order to obtain the injunction it was necessary for the claimants to show that their copyrights were being infringed by the users and/or operators of the Pirate Bay. Arnold J considered that users of the Pirate Bay were communicating copyright works to the public (as was discussed at 3.7.6). On the issue of whether the operators of the Pirate Bay were liable for copyright infringement, Arnold J considered whether they were authorizing the infringing activities of the website's users.

Authorisation

73. The law with regard to authorisation was considered by Kitchin J. in *20C Fox v Newzbin* at [85]–[95]. At [89] he cited a passage from the speech of Lord Templeman in *CBS Songs Ltd v Amstrad Consumer Electronics Plc* [1988] 1 AC 1013, [1988] R.P.C. 567, HL at 1053–1055 in which Lord Templeman approved the definition of 'to authorise' given by Atkin L.J. in *Monckton v Pathe Freres Pathephone Ltd* [1914] 1 KB 395, CA at 499, namely 'to grant or purport to grant to a third person the right to do the act complained of'. Kitchin J. continued at [90]:

> 'In my judgment it is clear from this passage that "authorise" means the grant or purported grant of the right to do the act complained of. It does not extend to mere enablement, assistance or even encouragement. The grant or purported grant to do the relevant act may be express or implied from all the relevant circumstances. In a case which involves an allegation of authorisation by supply, these circumstances may include the nature of the relationship between the alleged authoriser and the primary infringer, whether the equipment or other material supplied constitutes the means used to infringe, whether it is inevitable it will be used to infringe, the degree of control which the supplier retains and whether he has taken

any steps to prevent infringement. These are matters to be taken into account and may or may not be determinative depending upon all the other circumstances.'

[He went on at [98]–[102] to conclude on the fact of that case that Newzbin Ltd had indeed authorized infringements of the claimants' copyrights by its premium members.]

74. I shall consider each of the factors identified by Kitchin J. in turn.

The nature of the relationship.

75. TPB provides a sophisticated and user-friendly environment in which its users are able to search for and locate content. John Hodge, BPI's Head of Internet Investigations, describes in his witness statement how the website is organised and the functions that are available to users. As he explains:

(i) TPB indexes and arranges torrent files so that users can choose between various different search facilities to assist them in browsing for content to download or in locating specific content or categories of content.

(ii) When uploading a torrent file, users are required to provide detailed information about it. This information provides TPB with the ability to index it and make it available for searching. It also assists users in deciding whether or not to download it.

(iii) TPB does not merely receive the upload of the torrent file, it processes it. For example, TPB deletes any tracker server that may have been nominated by the uploader in the torrent file and replaces it with tracker servers of TPB's choosing.

(iv) Users are provided with assistance and advice as to how to download from the site and as to the trustworthiness of particular torrents. Status badges are awarded to uploaders to provide an indication of number and popularity of their uploads.

(v) Users are also provided with assistance and advice as to how to circumvent blocking measures taken as a result of court orders.

(vi) Users are offered links to 'cyberlocker' storage facilities for downloaded material.

(vii) Registered users are able to set preferences which allow them to choose what material can be downloaded and how information is displayed on the website.

(viii) TPB provides a forum for users to share information about content and even to ask other users to upload particular content which might not currently be available.

(ix) Users are offered a choice of 35 different languages to facilitate and encourage the widest possible participation in the use of its services by those engaged in P2P file-sharing.

76. These features are plainly designed to afford to users of TPB the easiest and most comprehensive service possible. TPB is in no sense a passive repository of torrent files. It goes to great lengths to facilitate and promote the download of torrent files by its users.

The means used to infringe.

77. The torrent files which are so conveniently indexed, arranged and presented by TPB constitute precisely the means necessary for users to infringe. It is the torrent files which provide the means by which users are able to download the "pieces" of the content files and/or to make them available to others.

Inevitability of infringement.

78. Infringement is not merely an inevitable consequence of the provision of torrent files by TPB. It is the operators of TPB's objective and intention. That is clear from the following:

(i)   Its name—The Pirate Bay—and associated pirate ship logo are clearly a reference to the popular terminology applied to online copyright infringement: online piracy.

(ii) According to a statement published on its site, it was founded by a 'Swedish anti copyright organisation'.

(iii) The matters described in para.13 above.

(iv) In the first instance judgment in the Swedish criminal proceedings, Lundström was recorded as stating that 'the purpose of the site was pirate copying'.

(v)   It is also evident from the numerous proceedings in other European jurisdictions that the operators of TPB are well aware that it is engaged in copyright infringement. Injunctions and other orders against the operators of TPB have been ignored. Orders against TPB's hosting service providers have been circumvented by moving TPB to new providers.

Degree of control.

79. TPB would be able to prevent infringement of copyright, should its operators so wish. As the website makes clear, torrents can be removed. They will be removed if 'the name isn't in accordance with the content' or if they are 'child porn, fakes, malware, spam and miscategorised torrents'. As a matter of policy, however, the rights of copyright owners are excluded from the criteria by which the operators of TPB choose to exercise this power.

Steps to prevent infringement.

80. Despite their ability to do so and despite the judicial findings that have been made against them, the operators of TPB take no steps to prevent infringement. On the contrary, as already explained, they actively encourage it and treat any attempts to prevent it (judicial or otherwise) with contempt. Indeed, according to a statement on the website, the reason for its recent adoption of Magnet links as the default option is that 'it's not as easy to block as torrent files'. This confirms the operators' determination to do whatever they can to provide users with unrestricted access to torrent files and thereby enable the users to continue to infringe. As noted above, BPI has asked TPB to cease infringing its members' and PPL's members' copyrights, but this request has been ignored.

Conclusion.

81. In my judgment, the operators of TPB do authorise its users' infringing acts of copying and communication to the public. They go far beyond merely enabling or assisting. On any view, they 'sanction, approve and countenance' the infringements of copyright committed by its users. But in my view they also purport to grant users the right to do the acts complained of. It is no defence that they openly defy the rights of the copyright owners. I would add that I consider the present case to be indistinguishable from *20C Fox v Newzbin* in this respect. If anything, it is a stronger case.

Given the facts of this case, Arnold J's conclusion that the operators of the Pirate Bay were authorizing infringement by its users seems unsurprising. But are there other examples of internet operators or facilities where authorization may seem less clear? In the Australian decision *Roadshow Films Pty Ltd v iiNet*,[33] the High Court of Australia had to consider whether the defendant internet service provider (ISP) authorized the infringing activities of its customers (who had been using BitTorrent to download copyright protected films). The court unanimously held that there was no authorization on the part of the ISP. The following factors—that the defendant provided the internet connections which enabled its customers to use BitTorrent unlawfully; that the defendant could suspend or terminate customers' subscriptions; that notices were received and were not acted upon (albeit for good cause)—did not suffice to establish authorization on the part of the defendant ISP.

FURTHER READING

A. Strowel (ed.), *Peer-to-Peer File Sharing and Secondary Liability in Copyright Law* (Cheltenham: Edward Elgar, 2009).

4.2.2 SECONDARY INFRINGEMENT

Secondary infringement occurs where, broadly speaking, a person facilitates primary infringing activities or deals in infringing copies of a work. More specifically, a person who permits a place of public entertainment to be used for an infringing performance will be liable unless there were reasonable grounds for believing that the performance would not infringe copyright.[34] Further, a person who supplies apparatus by which an infringing public performance occurs will be liable where they knew or had reason to believe the apparatus was likely to be used to infringe copyright.[35] Importing into the UK, other than for private and domestic use, an article, which a person knows or has reason to believe is an infringing copy of a work, will amount to infringement.[36] Similarly, possessing, selling, hiring, commercially dealing with, or prejudicially distributing an article, which a person knows or has reason to believe is an infringing copy of a work, will constitute infringement. Finally, a person will be liable if they make, import, possess in the course of business, sell, or let for hire, an article specifically designed or adapted for making copies of that work, knowing or having reason to believe that it is to be used to make infringing copies.[37]

A key feature of the secondary infringement provisions is actual knowledge or having reason to believe. 'Reason to believe' has been interpreted as meaning knowledge of facts from which a reasonable person would arrive at the relevant belief (and not merely suspect the relevant conclusion) and allowing for a period of time to evaluate the relevant facts.[38]

---

[33] [2012] HCA 16. [34] CDPA, s. 25. [35] CDPA, s. 26.
[36] CDPA, s. 22. [37] CDPA, s. 24.
[38] *LA Gear Inc. v Hi-Tec Sports Plc* [1992] FSR 121. In *Pensher Security Door Co. Ltd v Sunderland City Council* [2000] RPC 249, the Court of Appeal held that the relevant belief may be established by the surrounding circumstances.

4.3 EXCEPTIONS AND LIMITATIONS

4.3.1 INTRODUCTION

The CDPA has a range of exceptions and limitations to copyright infringement. Exceptions are provisions that allow a person to carry out an exclusive act in relation to a copyright work, without having to remunerate the owner, whereas limitations are provisions that allow a person to do an exclusive act, in return for paying remuneration of some kind. Exceptions and limitations are important mechanisms for facilitating a balance of interests between copyright owners and users. Where to strike that balance, however, is frequently a matter of contention and is arguably influenced by the underlying rationale(s) for copyright protection.

UK copyright exceptions are influenced by both international and EU copyright law. We therefore briefly turn to examine these legislative influences.

The Berne Convention contains only one mandatory exception, in Article 10(1), for quotations from works that have already been lawfully made available to the public, where 'their making is compatible with fair practice, and their extent does not exceed that justified by the purpose'. Otherwise, all other exceptions in Berne are permissive. They include, for example, use for teaching purposes (Article 10(2)) and use of works in reporting current events (Article 10*bis*(2)). They also include the now infamous Article 9(2), which permits Union members to stipulate exceptions to the reproduction right in: (1) certain special cases; (2) provided the reproduction does not conflict with a normal exploitation of the work; and (3) does not unreasonably prejudice the legitimate interests of the author. This is known as the 'three-step' test for introducing exceptions to the reproduction right. It has, however, been extended via Article 13 of the TRIPS Agreement to all exclusive rights covered by TRIPS, and by Article 10 of the WIPO Copyright Treaty 1996 (WCT) and Article 16 of the WIPO Performances and Phonograms Treaty 1996 (WPPT) to the minimum rights established by those treaties. As such, the 'three-step' test has taken on a much wider significance and spawned a great deal of scholarly discussion about the nature of its conditions. It has also found its way into EU law via Article 5(5) of the Information Society Directive, although the effect of this provision is also contentious. Is it a matter for the legislature when implementing exceptions from Article 5 to do so in accordance with the three-step test or must national courts interpret exceptions in light of the three-step test or instead apply Article 5(5) as a separate and additional threshold?[39]

An important development at the international level has been the WIPO treaties. We have seen that the WCT and WPPT introduced exclusive rights to cater for new forms of exploitation in an internet and digital environment. However, it was important also that the interests of users were catered for. To that end, Article 10 of the WCT states that Contracting Parties may provide for exceptions or limitations in their national legislation in respect of the rights granted under the treaty. This is provided there is compliance with the three-step test. The agreed statement to the WCT highlights that the intention of Article 10 is to allow Contracting Parties 'to carry forward and appropriately extend into the digital environment limitations and exceptions in their national laws which have been considered acceptable under the Berne Convention'. A similar approach is taken in the WPPT in Article 16 and its corresponding agreed statement.

---

[39] For discussion see R. Arnold and E. Rosati, 'Are national courts addressees of the Info-Soc three-step test?' (2015) 10 JIPLP 741.

In terms of EU law, exceptions and limitations have been harmonized in the case of computer programs (by the Software Directive), databases (by the Database Directive), and for all other types of work (by the Information Society Directive). Undoubtedly, the greatest harmonization impact has occurred via the Information Society Directive. Article 5(1), which is explored at 4.3.3, sets out a mandatory exception for certain acts of temporary reproduction, which acts as an important counterbalance to the very broad right of reproduction in Article 2 and is particularly relevant to the internet. Articles 5(2)–(3) contain an optional, but exhaustive, list of exceptions and limitations, some of which are particularly applicable to the internet or online context. In terms of the harmonization goal, this is somewhat thwarted by the optional nature of the list and the fact that there are 20 exceptions in total. This approach, however, does have the advantage of allowing different legal traditions in the Member States comfortably to coexist and the exhaustive nature of the list means that some headway is being made towards harmonization.

An issue that the Information Society Directive virtually ignores is the extent to which exceptions may be overridden by contract.[40] This is surprising, particularly given that it deals with the situations in which exceptions may be constrained or overridden by technological protection measures.[41] As well, there are other fields, namely computer programs and databases, where there has been a real and more explicit attempt to determine which exceptions are fundamental enough not to be overridden by contract.[42] Certainly this is a matter that requires further consideration and has arisen in the context of recent UK reforms to exceptions, where certain exceptions have been stipulated as unable to be contractually overridden.[43]

As well as having to navigate the constraints imposed by international and EU copyright law, UK copyright exceptions face the significant challenge of coping with major technological developments that have occurred since the 1990s. The calls in the WIPO treaties to make exceptions relevant to the digital environment have, until recently, gone unheeded. Following the Gowers Review of Intellectual Property in December 2006, the UK Intellectual Property Office published a consultation paper[44] in which reforms were proposed in order to provide clarity regarding the scope of certain exceptions and limitations in a digital context and also balance and flexibility in the copyright system. These, however, fell by the wayside and the impetus for reform was not revived until the Hargreaves Review in 2011.[45] In the wake of that review, the government broadly accepted the Hargreaves recommendations

---

[40] Note that R. Burrell and A. Coleman, *Copyright Exceptions: The Digital Impact* (Cambridge: Cambridge University Press, 2005), pp. 67–70, are somewhat less concerned by this issue than other commentators. This is because it is not clear how often owners will seek to use contracting-out terms, and doubts remain about whether contractual terms seeking to exclude the operation of copyright exceptions would be deemed to be validly incorporated, are enforceable, and how they may be interpreted. Also, there is a growing list of exceptions (for software and databases) that cannot be contracted-out of.

[41] See discussion at 4.3.9.1.

[42] For a discussion see T. Aplin, *Copyright Law in the Digital Society: The Challenges of Multimedia* (Oxford: Hart, 2005), pp. 163–4, 166–9, 172–3, 176.

[43] i.e. contractual terms seeking to prevent or restrict the doing of the permitted acts will be unenforceable—see ss. 29(4B), 29A(5), 30(4), 30A(2), 32(3), 41(5), 42(7), and 42A(6). For discussion see A. Aronsson-Storrier, 'Copyright exceptions and contract in the UK: the impact of recent amendments' (2016) 6 QMJIP 111.

[44] 'Taking forward the Gowers Review of Intellectual Property: proposed changes to copyright exceptions', available at <http://webarchive.nationalarchives.gov.uk/20140603093549/http://www.ipo.gov.uk/c-notice-2008-exceptions.htm>.

[45] See 'Digital Opportunity: A Review of Intellectual Property and Growth' (May 2011), available at <http://webarchive.nationalarchives.gov.uk/20140603093549/http://www.ipo.gov.uk/ipreview.htm>.

(a number of which resonated with the earlier Gowers review) and set about consulting on various changes to the law, including reforms to copyright.[46] In December 2012, the government published the final part of its response to its copyright consultation in the report 'Modernising Copyright: a modern, robust and flexible framework'[47] and, in 2014, introduced new exceptions (fair dealing for quotation and also for parody,[48] a text and data-mining exception[49], an exception for libraries and archives to make works available through dedicated terminals,[50] and an exception for orphan works[51]). Amendments to existing exceptions were also introduced (concerning fair dealing for research and private study,[52] and exceptions for educational institutions, libraries and archives,[53] and disabled persons[54]).

Although Chapter III of the CDPA features a raft of exceptions and limitations (from sections 28A to 76), the following discussion will examine only some of the more important and controversial ones and also briefly consider the newly introduced and amended exceptions.

FURTHER READING

R. Burrell and A. Coleman, *Copyright Exceptions: The Digital Impact* (Cambridge: Cambridge University Press, 2005).

E. Rosati, 'Copyright in the EU: in search of (in)flexibilities' (2014) 9 JIPLP 585.

M. Senftleben, *Copyright, Limitations and the Three Step Test* (The Hague: Kluwer, 2004).

4.3.2 FAIR DEALING

The CDPA contains fair-dealing exceptions in respect of certain specific uses—these are research or private study,[55] reporting current events,[56] criticism or review,[57] quotation,[58] and parody, caricature, or pastiche.[59] It is important to remember that these specific uses or purposes are exhaustive, meaning that a defendant must bring their actions within one or more of them in order for the exception to apply. This may be contrasted with the 'fair use' exception in section 107 of the US Copyright Act 1976, which features an illustrative open list of purposes to which the defence may apply.[60] Given the importance in UK copyright

---

[46] See <http://webarchive.nationalarchives.gov.uk/20140603093549/http://www.ipo.gov.uk/types/hargreaves.htm>.

[47] 'Modernising Copyright Paper', available at <http://webarchive.nationalarchives.gov.uk/20140603093549/http://www.ipo.gov.uk/response-2011-copyright-final.pdf>.

[48] See the Copyright and Rights in Performances (Quotation and Parody) Regulations 2014 (SI 2014/2356), introducing s. 30(1ZA) on quotation and s. 30A on caricature, parody, and pastiche.

[49] See the Copyright and Rights in Performances (Research, Education, Libraries and Archives) Regulations 2014 (SI 2014/1372), reg. 3 introducing s. 29A CDPA.

[50] The Copyright and Rights in Performances (Research, Education, Libraries and Archives) Regulations 2014, reg. 5 inserting a new s. 40B CDPA.

[51] Discussed already at 3.3.3.

[52] The Copyright and Rights in Performances (Research, Education, Libraries and Archives) Regulations 2014, amending s. 29 CDPA.

[53] The Copyright and Rights in Performances (Research, Education, Libraries and Archives) Regulations 2014, amending ss. 32, 35, 36 CDPA relating to educational establishments, and amending ss. 41–3 CDPA relating to libraries and archives.

[54] The Copyright and Rights in Performances (Disability) Regulations 2014, amending ss. 31A–F CDPA.

[55] CDPA, s. 29.   [56] CDPA, s. 30(2).   [57] CDPA, s. 30(1).   [58] CDPA, s. 30(1ZA).

[59] CDPA, s. 30A.

[60] Note that the Hargreaves Review was specifically tasked with investigating whether the UK should adopt a fair-use approach and recommended against its introduction: see paras 5.12–5.19. Not only were the

law of fitting within the fair-dealing purposes, we turn to examine the scope of research or private study, reporting current events, criticism or review, parody, and quotation in more detail before moving on to examine the factors that relate to whether a dealing is 'fair'. When considering the scope of these exceptions, it is worth asking to what extent the collection of UK fair-dealing exceptions approximates the US fair-use exception.

4.3.2.1 Research or private study

Fair dealing for the purpose of research or private study previously was limited to literary, dramatic, musical, and artistic works and also typographical arrangements of published editions. However, it has now been extended to all works (including films, sound recordings, and broadcasts) as a result of recent amendment.[61] What will be the benefits and risks of such a change, do you think?[62]

What is the meaning of 'research' and 'private study'? Section 29(1) of the CDPA, as a result of implementing Article 5(2) of the Information Society Directive, stipulates that research must be for a non-commercial purpose and section 178 states that 'private study' does not include any study that is directly or indirectly for a commercial purpose. This gives rise to some uncertainties. Is it the case that research must be wholly for a non-commercial purpose, i.e. not directly or indirectly for a commercial purpose? Also, what is meant by a 'commercial' purpose?[63] Is it a purpose that involves direct or indirect profit-making? If so, does that mean educational purposes, such as research within universities, are excluded? Further, what is the difference between the activities of 'research' and 'private study'? The latter suggests an activity carried out by individuals for their own benefit or gratification, possibly as part of pursuing a formal qualification. By way of contrast, 'research' could connote work done by an individual for the benefit of an organization or that which has some kind of public dimension, such as publication. Even so, the distinction between the two types of activity is fairly unclear and this matters because, in the case of research for non-commercial purposes, there is a further requirement that it is accompanied by a sufficient acknowledgement, unless this would be impossible for reasons of practicality.[64] Sufficient acknowledgement is defined in section 178 as an acknowledgement identifying the work in question by its title or other description and identifying the author.

Can a person copying on behalf of researchers or students rely on this exception? According to section 29(3), it is possible for librarians, or a person acting on behalf of a librarian, to rely on this fair-dealing exception provided they do not supply more than one copy of the same article to the same person. Further, a person cannot rely on this exception if they know or have reason to believe that copies of substantially the same material will be provided to more than one person at substantially the same time and for substantially the

---

benefits of introducing such an exception thought to be overstated, it was noted that there were real legal obstacles to its implementation, given the constraints of EU law.

[61] The Copyright and Rights in Performances (Research, Education, Libraries and Archives) Regulations 2014, reg. 3.

[62] The Modernising Copyright Paper at p. 34 observes that the changes will directly benefit the person conducting research or private study but there are also spill-over benefits from fundamental research, so improvements to research exceptions should have broader positive consequences.

[63] An example of where research was held to be for a commercial purpose is *HMSO v Green Amps* [2007] EWHC 2755 (Ch).

[64] CDPA, s. 29(1) and (1B).

same purpose. Thus, this exception would not permit a lecturer to supply copies of an article that is prescribed reading to all the students in his or her class.

4.3.2.2 Reporting current events

Fair dealing for the purpose of reporting current events applies to all copyright works *except* for photographs. Why is it, do you think, that photographs have been excluded from the scope of this exception? With regard to the interpretation of 'reporting current events' in *British Broadcasting Corp. v British Satellite Broadcasting Ltd*,[65] a case involving the scope of fair dealing with respect to broadcasters' rights, Scott J held that it extends to the inclusion of material in sports news programmes. As a result, the use of very short excerpts from the BBC broadcasts of 1990 World Cup football matches in the defendant's sports news programmes was held to fall within the scope of this exception.

In the following case, the Court of Appeal considered whether publication of an article can itself constitute a 'current event'.

Newspaper Licensing Agency Ltd v Marks & Spencer plc [2003] 3 WLR 1256

The facts of this case were discussed at 4.2.1.2. One of the arguments raised by the defendant was that the further copies it had made of press cuttings had been for the purpose of reporting current events to those within its organization. This argument was rejected at first instance and, on appeal, by a majority of the Court of Appeal.

Peter Gibson LJ:

40. It is common ground that in the light of the decision of this court in *Pro Sieben Media AG v Carlton UK Television Ltd* [1999] FSR 610: (1) 'for the purpose of reporting current events' in section 30(2) should be construed as a composite phrase; (2) for that phrase there could be substituted 'in the context of' or 'as part of an exercise in' [reporting current events] without any significant alteration of meaning, the intentions and motives of the user of another's copyright work being of little importance save for considering whether the dealing was fair; (3) the words 'reporting current events' are of wide and indefinite scope and require a liberal interpretation.

41. It is also not in dispute that the defence of fair dealing is directed, as the judge put it [1999] RPC 536, 545, to achieving a proper balance between protection of the rights of a creative author or the wider public interest, of which free speech is a very important ingredient. The judge said, at p. 546, that the publication of a report or article in the press may itself constitute a current event and a publication may constitute fair dealing for the purpose of reporting current events though it contains no analysis or comment or any matter other than use of the copyright material, but that did not mean that whatever was reported in the press was a current event. He added that the term 'current events' was narrower than the term 'news', and that reporting of current events does not extend to publishing matters of current interest, whether generally or to particular persons like M & S, but which were not current events.

42. We were shown a number of cuttings. Many were of articles in the press which referred to M & S, whether reporting a news item (e.g. the announced intention to expand

---

[65] [1992] Ch 141.

the workforce) or commenting on or displaying an M & S product. Others were of articles about matters (e.g. the launch of the Euro) which could affect M & S in its business activities or about M & S's competitors. There can be no doubt but that the copying of the articles for the benefit of M & S executives was for a genuine business purpose and put before those recipients matters which they had a good commercial reason to see.

43. The fact that an article appears in the press can be said to be an event. As the cutting is copied promptly the event might be said to be current. The circulating of a copy to an M & S executive can be said to be reporting the current event of the appearance of that article. But is that what was intended by the phrase 'for the purpose of reporting current events?' I think not for two reasons. First, the language of the subsection to my mind naturally connotes the public reporting of a recent newsworthy event. It is not natural to read it as meaning that the defence applies where the dealing lies in reporting the mere fact that an article has appeared in the press, however interesting that fact may be to M & S, for example that a fashion editor of a journal has featured an M & S garment, when that event has no other significance. Although the scope of the defence has been widened in successive Acts since it first appeared in section 2(1)(i) of the Copyright Act 1911 as 'Any fair dealing with any work for the purposes of … newspaper summary' and willing though I am to give the phrase a liberal interpretation, I cannot see that the language, read naturally, permits a meaning as wide as Mr Silverleaf would urge on us. Second, to interpret section 30(2) as providing a defence to copyright infringement in a case like the present would seem to me to have nothing to do with the public interest and everything to do with serving the private commercial interests of M & S. I can see no public interest reason why the legislature should want to provide a defence to an infringement of copyright for the copying within a commercial organisation for commercial reasons of material subject to copyright, whereas a public interest can be discerned in the public reporting of newsworthy current events. I would therefore hold, in agreement with the judge, that if what M & S did was an infringement of copyright, it would not come within the defence of section 30(2).

[**Mance LJ** delivering a judgment in which he agreed with **Peter Gibson LJ**, while **Chadwick LJ** delivered a dissenting judgment.]

Apparent from the above extract is that 'current events' is not synonymous with 'news' How would you describe the difference between the two concepts? Also, it seems possible for the publication of an article itself to constitute a current event, even if that was not held to be so on the facts of *NLA v Marks & Spencer*. A case in which it was successfully argued that the fact of media coverage can itself qualify as a 'current event' is *Hyde Park Residence v Yelland*.[66] The defendants had published in *The Sun* newspaper stills from a security video, which showed Princess Diana and Dodi Al Fayed arriving and departing from a Paris villa. The claimant company, which was responsible for security at the Paris villa, brought an action alleging infringement of copyright and sought summary judgment. The defendants argued, inter alia, that publication of the stills was for the purpose of reporting current events because it refuted allegations recently made by Mohammed Al Fayed that the couple had been visiting the Paris villa in order to make wedding plans. Aldous LJ (with whom Mance and Stuart-Smith LJJ agreed), accepted that use of the security video stills was for the purpose of reporting current events, in the sense that it related to the recent media coverage

---

[66] [2001] Ch 143.

of Mr Al Fayed's claims about his son and Princess Diana. Although the purpose was satisfied, he went on to hold that the use was not a 'fair' dealing.

In the recent decision of *England and Wales Cricket Board Ltd v Tixdaq Ltd and Fanatix Ltd*[67] Arnold J had occasion to interpret the scope of fair dealing for the purpose of reporting current events in light of EU law, CJEU jurisprudence, and a different technological matrix.

England and Wales Cricket Board Ltd v Tixdaq Ltd and Fanatix Ltd
[2016] EWHC 575 (Ch)

The claimants owned copyright in television broadcasts and films incorporated within these broadcasts (e.g. action replays) of cricket matches played by the England men's and women's cricket teams. The defendant operated a website www.fanatix.com and mobile applications, which enabled users to upload eight-second clips of broadcasts of cricket matches. The clips can be posted moments after they have been broadcast, thus allowing users to create and view highlights on a near-live basis. Users in later versions were required to add at least 70 characters of commentary and could not upload more than two eight-second clips per hour and users were restricted in the amount of footage they could view from a single sports event in a 24-hour period (60 to 90 seconds and an overall limit of 360 seconds per day). The defendants argued that their activities were not infringing the claimant's copyright because they constituted fair dealing for the purposes of reporting current events. (No defence of fair dealing for the purposes of quotation was advanced and fair dealing for the purposes of criticism or review was not pursued.)

Arnold J:

69. Two points should be noted. The first is that it follows that article 5(3)(c) must be construed in accordance with article 10*bis*(2) of the Berne Convention and article 15(1)(b) of Rome; but otherwise it should be given an autonomous European interpretation.

70. The second is that, if section 30(2) is compared to article 5(3)(c), it can be seen that the expression 'for the purpose of reporting currents' in section 30(2) is very close to the expression 'in connection with the reporting of current events' in article 5(3)(c), but that article 5(3)(c) permits use 'to the extent justified by the informatory purpose' whereas section 30(2) permits use which is 'fair dealing'. It follows, in my judgment, that an important consideration in the assessment of fair dealing is whether the extent of the use is justified by the informatory purpose.

...

74. I was referred to a number of domestic authorities on the interpretation and application of section 30(2) and its predecessors in the Copyright Acts of 1911 and 1956, most of which I shall mention below. In my judgment, however, these authorities must be treated with a degree of caution, since they were mostly decided prior to the implementation of the Information Society Directive and all of them were decided well before the recent jurisprudence of the Court of Justice concerning the interpretation of that Directive. Moreover, as discussed below, there is no consideration in any of them of the three-step test.

---

[67] [2016] EWHC 575 (Ch), [2016] Bus LR 641.

...

76. Although recital (34) of the Information Society Directive refers to 'news reporting', there is no warrant for interpreting 'reporting current events' as being restricted to 'news reporting'. As noted above, article 5(3)(c) of the Information Society Directive gives effect to both article 10*bis*(2) of the Berne Convention and article 15(1)(b) of the Rome Convention, both of which refer to 'reporting current events', and the same language is employed in article 5(3)(c).

...

80. Consistently with the general approach outlined above, it is clear that 'current events' are not confined to events which are very recent, particularly where the ramifications of an event continue to be a matter of public debate or concern: see in particular the *Pro Sieben* case [1999] 1 WLR 605, 619, *Hyde Park Residence Ltd v Yelland* [2001] Ch 143, paras 28–32, per Aldous LJ, and the *Ashdown* case [2002] Ch 149, paras 62–64.

81. On the other hand, there has been very little consideration in any of the case law of what amounts to 'reporting' a current event. This is no doubt because most of the decided cases have involved what might be termed traditional media outlets, that is to say, newspapers and linear television channels ...

...

112. In considering these submissions, the starting point is that the verb 'reporting' is capable of bearing a broad or narrow meaning depending on context. It follows that it is necessary to construe it purposively. The purpose of section 30(2) of the 1988 Act, article 5(3)(c) of the Information Society Directive, article 10*bis*(2) of the Berne Convention and article 15(1)(b) of the Rome Convention is to provide an exception to, or limit upon, copyright protection in the public interest, namely freedom of expression. As discussed above, this favours a broad interpretation. Furthermore, the exception is not an unqualified one: even if a use is for the purpose of reporting current events, it will not be protected unless it satisfies the additional criteria considered above. Again, this favours a broad interpretation. In addition, the exception must be given a 'living' interpretation, at least in the sense that it must be interpreted in manner that takes into account recent developments in technology and the media.

113. In these circumstances I consider that these provisions should now be interpreted more broadly than they may have been in the past. Thus I consider that it is clear that they are not restricted to the kind of situation which was under consideration when what is now article 10*bis* of the Berne Convention was first introduced, such as a radio or newsreel report of a public ceremonial occasion which incorporated part of a musical work performed by a military band: see Ricketson and Ginsburg, *International Copyright and Neighbouring Rights: The Berne Convention and Beyond*, 2nd ed (2007), para 13.54.

114. Accordingly, I consider that counsel for the claimants was right to accept that section 30(2) and article 5(3)(c) are not restricted to traditional media and that 'citizen journalism' can qualify as reporting current events. If a member of the public captures images and/or sound of a newsworthy event using their mobile phone and uploads it to a social media site like Twitter, then that may well qualify as reporting current events even if it is accompanied by relatively little in the way of commentary. Thus such a person may well have defence under section 30(2) and article 5(3)(c) if the images and/or sound happen to include a substantial part of a copyright work.

[Arnold J then turned to apply these principles to the facts and concluded as follows.]

129. In my judgment the use made of the copyright works in versions 8.2 and 8.3 of the App was not for the purpose of reporting current events. The clips were not used in order to

inform the audience about a current event, but presented for consumption because of their intrinsic interest and value. Furthermore, although the fact that a news service is a commercial one funded by advertising revenue does not prevent its use from being for the purpose of reporting current events, I consider that the defendants' objective was purely commercial rather than genuinely informatory.

[Arnold J also concluded that the use was not 'fair' because it was commercially damaging to the claimants and the extent of the use was not justified by the informatory purpose and, as such, the exception did not apply to exempt the defendant's activities.]

Do you agree with Arnold J's decision to interpret 'reporting current events' purposively to cover new types of online activities? Do you also agree with his conclusion that the uploading of clips by users to Fanatix was not for the purpose of reporting current events?

The final point to note in relation to this exception is that, in order to rely on it, there must be sufficient acknowledgement (as discussed earlier). However, section 30(3) states that where the current events are reported by means of a sound recording, film, or broadcast, no acknowledgement is required where this would be impossible for reasons of practicality or otherwise.

FURTHER READING

C. Kelly, 'Current events and fair dealing with photographs: time for a revised approach' [2012] IPQ 242.

4.3.2.3 Criticism or review

Fair dealing for the purpose of criticism or review applies to all types of works. Importantly, the criticism or review must be directed to the work that is allegedly infringed or else another work or a performance of a work[68]—it cannot be criticism or review generally. The scope of this purpose and how it is to be assessed is explained in the following case.

Pro Sieben Media AG v Carlton UK Television Ltd [1999] 1 WLR 605

Pro Sieben had broadcast a programme (the TAFF programme), which included an exclusive interview with Mandy Allwood, a woman who was pregnant with octuplets. The second defendant had produced a current affairs programme, *The Big Story: Selling Babies*, which featured a 30-second extract from the TAFF programme and this was broadcast by the first defendant. The second defendant had also copied the whole of the TAFF programme in order to select the appropriate extract to be used. The claimant alleged copyright infringement and the defendants argued that their use of the extract was fair dealing for the purpose of criticism or review, or for reporting current events. Laddie J at first instance rejected both of these defences. There was an appeal to the Court of Appeal.

---

[68] CDPA, s. 30(1).

Robert Walker LJ (Henry and Nourse LJJ in agreement), **at pp. 613–15:**

This court has by contrast heard quite lengthy submissions as to whether the words 'for the purpose of' in section 30(1) and section 30(2) import a subjective or an objective test. The judge did not discuss this point at length, but rejected the submission made on behalf of Pro Sieben that even if the critic had the necessary purpose, the defence is not made out unless the purpose was understood by the audience.

...

The fact that there is no authority on the point after nearly 90 years suggests that the issue may not be of much practical importance; indeed, that it may not be a significant point of construction at all. In *Sweet v Parsley* [1970] AC 132 the House of Lords emphasised the importance of construing a composite phrase rather than a single word. It seems to me that in the composite phrases 'for the purposes of criticism or review' and 'for the purpose of reporting current events' the mental element on the part of the user is of little more importance than in such everyday composite expressions as 'for the purpose of argument' or 'for the purpose of comparison'. The words 'in the context of' or 'as part of an exercise in' could be substituted for 'for the purpose of' without any significant alteration of meaning.

That is not to say that the intentions and motives of the user of another's copyright material are not highly relevant for the purposes of the defences available under section 30(1) and section 30(2). But they are most highly relevant on the issue of fair dealing, so far as it can be treated as a discrete issue from the statutory purpose (arguably the better course is to take the first 24 words of section 30(1), and the first 16 words of section 30(2), as a single composite whole and to resist any attempt at further dissection). It is not necessary for the court to put itself in the shoes of the infringer of the copyright in order to decide whether the offending piece was published 'for the purposes of criticism or review'. This court should not in my view give any encouragement to the notion that all that is required is for the user to have the sincere belief, however misguided, that he or she is criticising a work or reporting current affairs. To do so would provide an undesirable incentive for journalists, for whom facts should be sacred, to give implausible evidence as to their intentions.

...

'Criticism or review' and 'reporting current events' are expressions of wide and indefinite scope. Any attempt to plot their precise boundaries is doomed to failure. They are expressions which should be interpreted liberally, but I derive little assistance from comparisons with other expressions such as 'current affairs' or 'news' ...

Criticism of a work need not be limited to criticism of style. It may also extend to the ideas to be found in a work and its social or moral implications. So in *Time Warner Entertainments Co v Channel Four Television Corporation Plc* [1994] EMLR 1 this court, in allowing an interlocutory appeal and discharging an injunction, accepted that a television programme criticising the withdrawal of the film 'A Clockwork Orange' from distribution in the United Kingdom amounted to criticism of the film itself, since the content of the film and the decision to withdraw it were inseparable: see Henry LJ, at p. 15, and Neill LJ, at p. 13. The defendants relied on that case. Pro Sieben on the other hand pointed out that section 30(1) requires use for the purpose of criticism or review 'of that or another work' and that the judge was not persuaded that criticism of the TAFF report, as opposed to the decision to pay for an interview, was in Ms Byrne's mind when the Carlton programme was made or broadcast.

[Robert Walker LJ concluded that the judge had erred in principle in his approach to this defence, mainly because he had focused too much on the expressed purpose, intention, and motive of those involved in producing the programme and too little on the likely impact on the audience. He went on to consider whether the use of the clip had been for the purpose of fair dealing for criticism or review:]

The Carlton programme as a whole was, in my judgment, made for the purpose of criticism of works of chequebook journalism in general, and in particular the (then very recent) treatment by the media of the story of Ms Allwood's multiple pregnancy. Mr Clifford, the 'News of the World' and Pro Sieben were on the side of the 'haves'; other newspapers were 'have nots' and the programme vividly depicted how payments to peripheral figures (such as Ms Allwood's former husband and one of Mr Hudson's former girlfriends) could produce material for 'spoilers'. The criticism of the TAFF report was relatively mild because the report itself was, to use one of Ms Byrne's milder expressions, bland … Nevertheless the criticism was not, in my view, limited to what the judge called the 'throw away' comment: 'After ten days of muckraking, a sanitised version of the truth, tightly controlled by Max Clifford.' … Mr Clifford's involvement with the TAFF report was therefore featured prominently, rather than being limited to the single 'sanitised version' remark which came at the end of the 30-second extract showing the teddy bears. The element of criticism was also strengthened by the final part of the Carlton programme, immediately after the extract, in which Mr Clifford made the very candid remarks which I have already quoted ('We lie all the time. You know, that's, that's what it's about … lying, corruption, deceit').

When it comes to assessing whether a work, or part of a work, has been used for the purposes of criticism or review, the courts will adopt an objective test. When will the subjective intentions of the parties be relevant, if at all? The Court of Appeal accepted that criticism of a work includes criticism of a genre of works, in this case works of chequebook journalism. This liberal interpretation of 'criticism or review' has also been applied in *Fraser-Woodward Ltd v BBC*[69] where Mann J accepted that photographs of the Beckham family were being used for the purpose of criticism or review of works of tabloid journalism. Do you agree with such a generous approach to the scope of the purpose?

To rely on this exception, there must be sufficient acknowledgement. In *Pro Sieben*, the defendant's programme included the title 'TAFF' and also the Pro Sieben logo (a stylized number seven). While it was accepted that 'TAFF' shown on the screen identified the title of the work, the question was whether or not the television transmission of the Pro Sieben logo was sufficient to identify the author of the work. The Court of Appeal held that it was because 'the logo was the means by which the author of a television programme was accustomed to identify itself'.[70]

Another prerequisite to relying on this exception is that the work has been made available to the public. This requirement was introduced in order to implement Article 5(3)(d) of the Information Society Directive. Section 30(1A) of the CDPA states that a work will have been made available to the public by a variety of means (e.g. making the work available by means of an electronic retrieval system or communicating it to the public), but importantly that act must have been authorized. No account is to be taken of any unauthorized act of making the work available to the public. Which users of copyright do you think this requirement will affect most? Does it reflect an appropriate balance between the interests of the author or owner in divulging the work and the public interest in permitting criticism or review?

---

[69] [2005] FSR 36.   [70] [1999] 1 WLR 605, 618.

4.3.2.4 Quotation

Article 5(3)(d) of the Information Society Directive allows Member States to provide for exceptions or limitations for 'quotations for purposes such as criticism or review'. This is provided the work has 'already been lawfully made available to the public' and that 'the source, including the author's name, is indicated', unless this turns out to be impossible, and that the 'use is in accordance with fair practice, and to the extent required by the specific purpose'. In turn, Article 5(3)(d) is based on Article 10(1) of the Berne Convention.

New section 30(1ZA) was introduced as a 'minor amendment' to remove unnecessary restrictions to freedom of expression and better align UK copyright law with international and EU copyright standards.[71] This provision states:

> Copyright in a work is not infringed by the use of a quotation from the work (whether for criticism or review or otherwise) provided that—
>
> (a) the work has been made available to the public,
>
> (b) the use of the quotation is fair dealing with the work,
>
> (c) the extent of the quotation is no more than is required by the specific purpose for which it is used, and
>
> (d) the quotation is accompanied by a sufficient acknowledgement (unless this would be impossible for reasons of practicality or otherwise).

Some of the features of this exception are now familiar from other fair-dealing exceptions, such as the requirement that the work is made available to the public, that the dealing is fair, and the requirement of sufficient acknowledgement. However, an issue that arises is whether quotation can be for any purpose. It is submitted that quotation is not restricted to 'criticism or review' and can be for any purpose. This is because the language of Article 10(1) of the Berne Convention is not restricted to a particular purpose and this is confirmed by the preparatory documents. Further, the language in Article 5(3)(d) of the Information Society Directive refers to purposes *such as* criticism or review and section 30(1ZA) of the CDPA refers to criticism or review *or otherwise*, thus indicating that quotation is not restricted to these purposes. It is also argued that quotation is not necessarily restricted to use of small parts, rather this is a matter to assess as part of the 'fairness' enquiry.

A difference to other fair-dealing exceptions is the separate requirement of proportionality (i.e. the extent of the quotation does not exceed what is required by the specific purpose). It is submitted that this does not require strict necessity in the sense of being essential for achieving the stated purpose.[72] Rather, it arguably requires that there is a plausible, causal link between the extent of the quotation and the purpose for which it is being used. It is perhaps also a factor that is inextricably tied to the notion of a fair dealing.

[71] Modernising Copyright Paper, p. 26.
[72] This strict interpretation was adopted by Aldous LJ in *Hyde Park Residence v Yelland*, [37]: 'it is appropriate to take into account ... the extent and purpose of the use, and whether that extent was necessary for the purpose ...' Note that Aldous LJ went on to find at [40] 'the extent of the use was excessive' because, it was not necessary, in order to convey the time of arrival and departure, to show photographs—a simple description in the article of having seen the photographs would have sufficed. (See in agreement Mance LJ at [78].)

Although the UK government envisaged the quotation as a minor amendment, the quotation exception has the potential significantly to liberalize the notion of fair dealing under UK copyright law. As such, its relevance may extend to everything from academic citation to use of hyperlinks to music sampling and film quotation.

4.3.2.5 Parody

Until recently, the UK did not have a separate parody exception or indeed specific principles in the case of parodies.[73] Instead, one had to rely on fair dealing for the purposes of criticism or review for protecting parodies; however, this was seen as an inadequate mechanism.[74] The UK now features a specific exception[75] for parody, caricature, and pastiche in section 30A of the CDPA.[76] Section 30A(1) states: 'Fair dealing with a work for the purposes of caricature, parody or pastiche does not infringe copyright in the work.' In introducing this legislative amendment, the UK government suggested that various benefits would ensue, such as the encouragement of creative activity, the removal of administrative costs, the promotion of legal clarity, and the development of freedom of expression.[77] Do you agree that these are the likely benefits of such an exception?

The English courts have not yet had an opportunity to interpret the scope of section 30A; however, Article 5(3)(k) of the Information Society Directive on which this provision is based was the subject of a CJEU ruling in *Deckmyn*.

Deckmyn v Vandersteen Case C-201/13 [2014] ECDR 21 (Grand Chamber)

Mr Deckmyn, a member of a right-wing political party, edited and distributed a calendar that featured a drawing on its cover page that resembled a drawing created by Mr Vandersteen and which had featured on the cover of the *Suske en Wiske* comic book. This drawing represented one of the main characters of the comic book throwing coins to people who were collecting them. The drawing on the calendar replaced this main character with the Mayor of the City of Ghent and the people collecting the coins were people wearing veils and people of colour. Mr Vandersteen and others brought an action for copyright infringement and, in his defence, Mr Deckmyn argued that the drawing was a political cartoon that fell within the parody exception. The Brussels Court of Appeal referred questions to the CJEU about the interpretation of 'parody' and the conditions that have to be met. The CJEU held that 'parody' is an autonomous concept of EU law that must be interpreted uniformly throughout the EU.[78] The Court went on to consider the conditions that a parody has to meet.

---

[73] See *Williamson Music Ltd v Pearson Partnership* [1987] FSR 97.

[74] See R. Deazley, 'Copyright and parody: taking backward the Gowers Review?' (2010) 73 MLR 785.

[75] Australia also features a specific exception, for parody and satire, in ss. 41A and 103AA of the Australian Copyright Act 1968 (Cth). This was introduced by the Australian Copyright Amendment Act 2006 (Cth).

[76] Inserted by the Copyright and Rights in Performances (Quotation and Parody) Regulations 2014 (SI 2014/2356), reg. 5.

[77] See Modernising Copyright Paper, Annex C.   [78] [14]–[17].

19 It should be noted that, since Directive 2001/29 gives no definition at all of the concept of parody, the meaning and scope of that term must, as the Court has consistently held, be determined by considering its usual meaning in everyday language, while also taking into account the context in which it occurs and the purposes of the rules of which it is part (see, to that effect, judgment in *Diakité v Commissaire General aux Refugies et aux Apatrides* (C-285/12) [2014] 1 W.L.R. 2477 at [27] and the case law cited).

20 With regard to the usual meaning of the term 'parody' in everyday language, it is not disputed, as the Advocate General stated in point 48 of his Opinion, that the essential characteristics of parody are, first, to evoke an existing work while being noticeably different from it, and, secondly, to constitute an expression of humour or mockery.

21 It is not apparent either from the usual meaning of the term 'parody' in everyday language, or indeed, as rightly noted by the Belgian Government and the European Commission, from the wording of art.5(3)(k) of Directive 2001/29, that the concept is subject to the conditions set out by the referring court in its second question, namely: that the parody should display an original character of its own, other than that of displaying noticeable differences with respect to the original parodied work; could reasonably be attributed to a person other than the author of the original work itself; should relate to the original work itself or mention the source of the parodied work.

...

27 It follows that the application, in a particular case, of the exception for parody, within the meaning of art.5(3)(k) of Directive 2001/29, must strike a fair balance between, on the one hand, the interests and rights of persons referred to in arts 2 and 3 of that directive, and, on the other, the freedom of expression of the user of a protected work who is relying on the exception for parody, within the meaning of art.5(3)(k).

28 In order to determine whether, in a particular case, the application of the exception for parody within the meaning of art.5(3)(k) of Directive 2001/29 preserves that fair balance, all the circumstances of the case must be taken into account.

29 Accordingly, with regard to the dispute before the national court, it should be noted that, according to *Vandersteen and Others*, since, in the drawing at issue, the characters who, in the original work, were picking up the coins were replaced by people wearing veils and people of colour, that drawing conveys a discriminatory message which has the effect of associating the protected work with such a message.

30 If that is indeed the case, which it is for the national court to assess, attention should be drawn to the principle of non-discrimination based on race, colour and ethnic origin, as was specifically defined in Council Directive 2000/43/EC of 29 June 2000 implementing the principle of equal treatment between persons irrespective of racial or ethnic origin [2000] OJ L180/22, and confirmed, inter alia, by art.21(1) of the Charter of Fundamental Rights of the European Union.

31 In those circumstances, holders of rights provided for in arts 2 and 3 of Directive 2001/29, such as *Vandersteen and Others*, have, in principle, a legitimate interest in ensuring that the work protected by copyright is not associated with such a message.

32 Accordingly, it is for the national court to determine, in the light of all the circumstances of the case in the main proceedings, whether the application of the exception for parody, within the meaning of art.5(3)(k) of Directive 2001/29, on the assumption that the drawing at issue fulfils the essential requirements set out in [20] above, preserves the fair balance referred to in [27] above.

According to the CJEU, which are the essential characteristics of a parody? And which criteria are *not* required in order to rely on the parody exception? In interpreting the scope of the parody exception, the Court emphasized the need to achieve a 'fair balance' between rightholders' interests and users' freedom of expression.[79] Did the Court strike a 'fair balance' in suggesting that a discriminatory parody would not be justified? What will constitute a 'discriminatory' message and to what extent does this raise issues better dealt with by the moral right of integrity (which is not harmonized at EU level) or indeed other laws (such as those regulating hate speech)?[80]

FURTHER READING

R. Deazley, 'Copyright and parody: taking backward the Gowers Review?' (2010) 73 MLR 785.

S. McCausland, 'Protecting "a fine tradition of satire": the new fair dealing exception for parody or satire in the Australian Copyright Act' [2007] EIPR 287.

J. McCutcheon, 'The new defence of parody or satire under Australian copyright law' [2008] IPQ 163.

E. Rosati, 'Just a laughing matter? Why the decision in *Deckmyn* is broader than parody' (2015) 52 CML Rev. 511.

C. Rutz, 'Parody: a missed opportunity?' [2004] IPQ 284.

M. Spence, 'Intellectual property and the problem of parody' (1998) 114 LQR 594.

4.3.2.6 Fair-dealing factors

It is not enough that the activity satisfies the requisite purpose, sufficient acknowledgement is required and, in the case of criticism or review and quotation, the work must have been made available to the public. The dealing must also be *fair*. There is no statutory guidance, however, as to what constitutes fair dealing. This may be contrasted with the approach in the US, where section 107 of the US Copyright Act 1976 sets out factors to be included in the assessment of whether the use is a fair one. These are:

(1) the purpose and character of the use,

(2) including whether such use is of a commercial nature or is for nonprofit educational purposes;

(3) the nature of the copyrighted work;

(4) the amount and substantiality of the portion used in relation to the copyrighted work as a whole; and

(5) the effect of the use upon the potential market for or value of the copyrighted work.

The fact that a work is unpublished shall not itself bar a finding of fair use if such finding is made upon consideration of all the above factors.

---

[79] [27].

[80] See C. Geiger et al., 'Limitations and exceptions as key elements of the legal framework for copyright in the European Union: opinion of the European Copyright Society on the CJEU ruling in Case C-201/13 *Deckmyn*' (2015) 46 IIC 93, 99.

In the UK it has been left to the courts to develop guidance for determining whether or not there is fair dealing. In *Hubbard v Vosper*,[81] Lord Denning MR held that the following factors ought to be taken into account:

> It is impossible to define what is 'fair dealing'. It must be a question of degree. You must consider first the number and extent of the quotations and extracts. Are they altogether too many and too long to be fair? Then you must consider the use made of them. If they are used as a basis for comment, criticism or review, that may be fair dealing. If they are used to convey the same information as the author, for a rival purpose, that may be unfair. Next, you must consider the proportions. To take long extracts and attach short comments may be unfair. But, short extracts and long comments may be fair. Other considerations may come to mind also. But, after all is said and done, it must be a matter of impression. As with fair comment in the law of libel, so with fair dealing in the law of copyright. The tribunal of fact must decide. In the present case, there is material on which the tribunal of fact could find this to be fair dealing.[82]

How would you describe the factors discussed by Lord Denning MR?

Additional guidance on assessing fair dealing is set out in the following extract from Aldous LJ's judgment in *Hyde Park Residence v Yelland*,[83] the facts of which were discussed at 4.3.2.2.

> **Aldous LJ:**
>
> 38. … Thus the court must judge the fairness by the objective standard of whether a fair minded and honest person would have dealt with the copyright work, in the manner that 'The Sun' did, for the purpose of reporting the relevant current events, in this case the published untruthful statements of Mr Al Fayed.
>
> …
>
> 40. I reject Mr Spearman's submission. I have come to the conclusion that the defence of fair dealing cannot succeed. I do not believe that a fair minded and honest person would pay for the dishonestly taken driveway stills and publish them in a newspaper knowing that they had not been published or circulated when their only relevance was the fact that the Princess and Mr Dodi Fayed only stayed the 28 minutes at the Villa Windsor—a fact that was known and did not establish that the Princess and Mr Dodi Fayed were not to be married. To describe what 'The Sun' did as fair dealing is to give honour to dishonour. Further the extent of the use was excessive. The only part of the driveway stills relevant to the alleged purpose was the information as to the timing of arrival and departure. That information could have been given in the articles by Mr Thompson stating that he had seen the photographs which proved the Princess and Mr Dodi Fayed only stayed at the Villa Windsor for 28 minutes. If he needed confirmation he could have relied upon the statement by Mr Cole. Despite that, 'The Sun' used the driveway stills so that they covered over one-third of page 4. The information as to the time of arrival and departure did not establish that Princess Diana and Mr Dodi Fayed were not going to be married or that the other statements made by Mr Al Fayed, that are said to be untrue, were false.
>
> 41. The suggestion that the use of the driveway stills was a fair dealing for the purposes of reporting the events of 30 August 1997 is, to draw upon the words of Henry LJ in *Time*

---

[81] [1972] 2 QB 84.   [82] At 94.   [83] [2001] Ch 257.

Warner Entertainment Co Ltd v Channel Four Television Corpn plc [1994] EMLR 1, 14, an attempt to dress up the infringement of Hyde Park's copyright in the guise of reporting an event. In my view the judge came to the wrong conclusion and the allegation of fair dealing by the defendants could not provide them a defence to the action.

How do the factors identified by Aldous LJ compare with those set out by Lord Denning MR? Which factors overlap and which are additional? In your view, should it be relevant to consider matters from the perspective of the 'fair minded and honest person' and to give weight to whether the work has been dishonestly obtained? Does this not put the media in a difficult position when it comes to bringing matters of public interest to light? Also, do you agree that the use of the driveway stills was excessive—was the alternative method of corroborating the story a realistic one?

 Further guidance on the factors relevant to 'fair' dealing is to be found in the following Court of Appeal decision.

Ashdown v Telegraph Group Ltd [2002] Ch 149

This case concerned a meeting between the then Labour Prime Minister Tony Blair and the then leader of the Liberal Democrats, Mr Paddy Ashdown, five months after the Labour Party came to power in 1997. The meeting was to discuss a possible coalition government between the two political parties. Mr Ashdown wrote a minute of the meeting, which he kept confidential. Two copies were made—one was kept with Mr Ashdown's diaries and the other was shown to his closest advisors and then destroyed. A couple of years later, when it was imminent that Mr Ashdown would stand down as the Liberal Democrat leader, he made it known that he was contemplating publishing his diaries. Some of his material, including the minute of the meeting, was shown confidentially to potential publishers. It transpired that a copy of the minute was leaked to the political editor of the *Sunday Telegraph* and substantial extracts from the minute were copied verbatim in several articles published in that newspaper. The claimant sued for breach of confidence and copyright infringement and brought a motion for summary judgment on the latter claim. This motion was successful at first instance before Sir Andrew Morritt V-C. The defendant newspaper appealed. The court accepted the findings of Sir Andrew Morritt V-C that the defendant's use was not for the purposes of criticism or review, because it criticized the Prime Minister's and the claimant's actions, as opposed to the minute. In terms of fair dealing for the purpose of reporting current events, it also upheld the judge's finding that this was arguable, on the basis that 'reporting current events' should be interpreted liberally and the meeting between the claimant and Prime Minister was still a matter of current interest to the public. The court then went on to consider whether the dealing was arguably a fair one.

Lord Phillips MR (delivering the judgment of the court):

 70. Authority is very sparse in relation to the defence of fair dealing in the context of reporting current events: see the comment of Scott J in *British Broadcasting Corpn v British Satellite Broadcasting Ltd* [1992] Ch 141, 148. Sir Andrew Morritt V-C commented with approval, however, on the summary of the authors of *Laddie, Prescott and Vitoria, The Modern Law of*

Copyright and Designs, 3rd edn (2000), para. 20.16 on the test of fair dealing in the general context of section 30. We also have found this an accurate and helpful summary and set it out for the purpose of discussion.

> It is impossible to lay down any hard-and-fast definition of what is fair dealing, for it is a matter of fact, degree and impression. However, by far the most important factor is whether the alleged fair dealing is in fact commercially competing with the proprietor's exploitation of the copyright work, a substitute for the probable purchase of authorised copies, and the like. If it is, the fair dealing defence will almost certainly fail. If it is not and there is a moderate taking and there are no special adverse factors, the defence is likely to succeed, especially if the defendant's additional purpose is to right a wrong, to ventilate an honest grievance, to engage in political controversy, and so on. The second most important factor is whether the work has already been published or otherwise exposed to the public. If it has not, and especially if the material has been obtained by a breach of confidence or other mean or underhand dealing, the courts will be reluctant to say this is fair. However this is by no means conclusive, for sometimes it is necessary for the purposes of legitimate public controversy to make use of 'leaked' information. The third most important factor is the amount and importance of the work that has been taken. For, although it is permissible to take a substantial part of the work (if not, there could be no question of infringement in the first place), in some circumstances the taking of an excessive amount, or the taking of even a small amount if on a regular basis, would negative fair dealing.

71. These principles are based on a summary of the authorities before the Human Rights Act 1998 came into force. They are still important when balancing the public interest in freedom of expression against the interests of owners of copyright. It is, however, now essential not to apply inflexibly tests based on precedent, but to bear in mind that considerations of public interest are paramount. With that consideration in mind, we turn to consider each of the important factors identified in *Laddie, Prescott and Vitoria* in turn.

Commercial competition

72. In a passage of its defence quoted by Sir Andrew Morritt V-C [2001] Ch 685, 698, at para. 25, Telegraph Group contended that its publication 'in no or no appreciable way competed ... with any publication or publications which the claimant might issue in the future'. The Vice-Chancellor rejected this assertion, and we consider that he was right to do so. There was evidence, as he pointed out, that the publication in the 'Sunday Telegraph' destroyed a part of the value of the memoirs which it had been Mr Ashdown's intention to sell, and which he did in fact sell. Equally, we are in no doubt that the extensive quotations of Mr Ashdown's own words added a flavour to the description of the events covered which made the article more attractive to read and will have been of significant commercial value in enabling the 'Sunday Telegraph' to maintain, if not to enhance, the loyalty of its readership.

Prior publication

73. In the same passage of their defence the Telegraph Group asserted that Mr Ashdown had already revealed some details of the matters covered in the articles in his radio interview about 'Resigning Issues'. Sir Andrew Morritt V-C roundly rejected this contention, at p. 699, para. 28:

> The claimant had taken great care to limit the number of people who read it and to impose on them obligations of secrecy. Moreover the 'Sunday Telegraph' knew not only that the minute

had not been published, indeed Mr Murphy described it as secret, but that, as the claimant revealed on the 'Resigning Issues' interview, he was thinking of doing so in the not so distant future. It is not the case that during the interview for 'Resigning Issues' the claimant had already disclosed the important matters covered in the articles.

74. While we endorse these conclusions, it does not seem to us that they are wholly in point. Mr Spearman, for Mr Ashdown, argued that much of the information in the minute had already been made public and that this fact made it even harder to justify the 'Sunday Telegraph' publication. We consider that there is force in this point and will return to it in due course. What is at issue in a claim for breach of copyright is publication of the form of the literary work, not the information that it contains. It is beyond any doubt that the copyright work had never been published or otherwise exposed to the public before the publication in the 'Sunday Telegraph'.

75. At the same time, the fact that the minute was undoubtedly obtained in breach of confidence is a material consideration when considering the defence of fair dealing. Sir Andrew Morritt V-C rightly attached importance to the fact that the minute was secret and had been obtained by Telegraph Group without Mr Ashdown's knowledge or approval.

The amount and importance of the work taken

76. Here again we consider that Sir Andrew Morritt V-C correctly found that this aspect of the test of fair dealing weighed against the defence of fair dealing. A substantial portion of the minute was copied and it is reasonable to conclude, for the reasons given by Sir Andrew Morritt V-C, at p. 699, para. 29, that the most important passages in the minute were selected for publication.

77. All these considerations point in one direction and satisfy us that Sir Andrew Morritt V-C was correct to conclude that if the established authorities fell to be applied without any additional regard to the effect of Article 10 there was no realistic prospect that a defence of fair dealing would be made out.

Having read the above extracts from *Hubbard v Vosper*, *Hyde Park Residence v Yelland*, and *Ashdown*, what factors would you identify as the ones that courts are most likely to take into account when assessing whether there is a 'fair' dealing? Do you think that there are additional factors that courts should consider? Jonathan Griffiths has argued that, in order to give proper effect to Article 10 of the ECHR, right to freedom of expression, courts should also weigh up the subject matter of the defendant's article and the nature of the claimant's work.

J. Griffiths, 'Copyright law after *Ashdown*: time to deal fairly with the public'
[2002] IPQ 240 at 257–9

Principles relating to factors not considered by the Court of Appeal in *Ashdown*

In addition, however, it is also possible to identify two further principles that could usefully be applied. These relate to significant issues that were largely overlooked by the Court of Appeal in *Ashdown*.

The subject-matter of the defendant's article

The article within which the claimant's minute was reproduced concerned matters of considerable political significance to the United Kingdom. In finding that the meeting recorded in the minute was of continuing interest at the time of the *Sunday Telegraph's* publication, the Court of Appeal itself noted that:

> In a democratic society, information about a meeting between the Prime Minister and an opposition party leader during the then current Parliament to discuss possible close co-operation between those parties is very likely to be of legitimate and continuing public interest. It might impinge upon the way in which the public voted at the next general election.

Information about matters of public importance is strongly protected under Article 10. Indeed, the single guiding principle of the jurisprudence of the European Court of Human Rights on that Article appears to be that interference with 'public speech' requires a very high degree of justification. The Court is extremely suspicious of sanctions on publications concerning matters of legitimate public concern. This suspicion is also a feature of other areas of domestic law concerning the disclosure of information. In *Ashdown*, however, the Court of Appeal conceded only that the significance of the subject-matter of the newspaper's disclosure justified 'making limited quotation' from the minute. This grudging approach does not do justice to the crucial significance of this factor in the Strasbourg jurisprudence.

Thus, as a further principle, it can be suggested that in assessing 'fairness' under section 30, courts should apply a strong presumption in favour of a defendant where publication raises issues of legitimate public concern. Of course, the scope of 'public speech' is not clearly defined. However, guidance can be derived from case law, both domestic and at Strasbourg. The information contained in Paddy Ashdown's minute would clearly fall within any definition of such protected 'public speech'. However, disclosure should not only be favoured in high political matters, but also in other matters of legitimate public interest.

The nature of the claimant's work

The second significant aspect of the case to which the Court of Appeal failed to pay sufficient, or indeed any, attention was the nature of the claimant's work. The structure of Article 10 required the Court of Appeal to consider, first, whether the *Sunday Telegraph's* disclosure fell within the scope of Article 10(1). It was then required to decide whether it was 'necessary in a democratic society' for this right to be outweighed by the need to protect the claimant's copyright interest. In taking this decision, the Court of Appeal ought to have weighed up the relative significance of the newspaper's right to freedom of expression and of the claimant's right under copyright law. Such an exercise is, however, only possible where an appropriate value, or weight, is attributed to the copyright interest in question. Not all copyright interests have equal value. For example, entrepreneurial or related rights are not as well protected by copyright law as 'original' works. Within the category of works requiring originality, there is also an established hierarchy. Greater protection is granted to works invested with a higher degree of labour and skill and relatively simple works receive a 'thinner' form of protection. The more convincingly copyright protection can be justified in relation to a particular work, the stronger the powers granted to the copyright owner.

However, in the past, in considering the fair dealing defence, courts have been reluctant to identify different qualities of copyright protection. Copyright interests have tended to be regarded as property rights with a settled, and universally applicable value. Courts have frequently questioned the value of the *defendant's* claim, but have tended not explicitly to evaluate the significance of the competing claim of the claimant. The Court of Appeal in *Ashdown* adopted this traditional approach. Even before October 2, 2000, this omission was rather peculiar. However, under the Human Rights Act, it is quite improper. In *Ashdown* itself, it could be strongly argued that the nature of the claimant's property interest ought to have favoured a finding of 'fair dealing'. The minute did not represent the culminating expression of extensive 'labour and skill'. It was simply a factual record of a meeting attended by the claimant. Furthermore, the claimant was present at this meeting in his capacity as the leader of a national political party. He would, undoubtedly, have regarded himself as being engaged in public service at the time of the meeting. As such, his claim to be entitled to use copyright law to protect the fruits of this opportunity to secure personal financial advantage does not seem a strong one. As a further principle, then it can be suggested that, in assessing fairness under section 30, courts should pay regard to the nature of the claimant's work. The more strongly that copyright protection is justified in the case of a work, the less likely are dealings with that work to be 'fair'.

The Court of Appeal in *Ashdown* did not give effect to the right to freedom of expression in the way suggested by Jonathan Griffiths. Instead, the court used the public interest defence as the vehicle for reconciling copyright with the right to freedom of expression. This defence is considered at 4.3.6.

A final issue to mention in the context of fair-dealing factors is their relationship to the three-step test in Article 5(5) of the Information Society Directive. In the *Fanatix* decision, Arnold J accepted that national courts had to apply Article 5(5) when deciding individual cases and took the view that this required 'consideration of essentially the same factors as fair dealing'.[84] Arnold J accepted that 'reporting current events' was a 'certain special case' (thus satisfying limb 1 of the three-step test) and considered the commercial harm to the claimant's copyright (i.e. whether the defendant's use conflicted with the normal exploitation of the copyright works) and the proportionality of the interference with the claimant's interests (corresponding to the third limb of the three-step test).[85] Interestingly, in *Newspaper Licensing Agency v Meltwater*[86] the CJEU considered the three-step test in Article 5(5) in addition to Article 5(1) for temporary reproduction. However, it is fair to say that the reasoning employed by the Court in assessing Article 5(5) was synonymous with the reasoning they had used for interpreting whether the requirements of Article 5(1) were met.[87] Thus, at least in substance, the CJEU approach seems to accord with that taken by Arnold J in *Fanatix*.

FURTHER READING

D. K. Mendis, 'Back to the drawing board: pods, blogs and fair dealing—making sense of copyright exceptions in an online world' [2010] EIPR 582.

A. Sims, 'Appellations of piracy: fair dealing's prehistory' [2011] IPQ 3.

---

[84] [89].   [85] [90]–[91].   [86] Case C-360/13 [2014] AC 1438.   [87] [54]–[62].

4.3.3 TEMPORARY REPRODUCTION

At 3.7.1 we discussed the broad scope of the reproduction right. Article 5(1) of the Information Society Directive creates an exception for temporary copies that may restrict the concept of reproduction so that it does not go too far. Article 5(1) states:

> Temporary acts of reproduction referred to in Article 2, which are transient or incidental, which are an integral and essential part of a technological process whose sole purpose is to enable:
>
> (a) a transmission in a network between third parties by an intermediary, or
>
> (b) a lawful use
>
> of a work or other subject matter to be made, and which have no independent economic significance, shall be exempted from the right provided for in Article 2.

The transmission of material over the internet, from an originating server to a user, is made possible by packets of data being routed via a series of ISPs. Each of these ISPs will make fleeting copies of the material during the process. Article 5(1) permits temporary, technical acts of reproduction that occur as part of a network transmission and thus excludes this type of copying from infringement.

Article 5(1) would also appear to exempt acts of local and proxy caching. Local caching refers to the situation where the web-browser software of an internet user stores recently accessed webpages. This allows a user to call up these webpages faster than if the computer had to fetch them from their source server on the internet. Proxy caching occurs at the network level on proxy servers. Proxy servers act as intermediaries between local client servers and remote content servers. They store copies of the most frequently requested pages, so that these copies can be delivered to users, rather than having to search out the data from the original source. That, generally, caching should be exempt under Article 5(1) is emphasized by recital 33 of the Information Society Directive, which states:

> To the extent that they meet these conditions, this exception should include acts which enable browsing as well as acts of caching to take place, including those which enable transmission systems to function efficiently, provided that the intermediary does not modify the information and does not interfere with the lawful use of technology, widely recognised and used by industry, to obtain data on the use of information.

Section 28A of the CDPA implemented Article 5(1), using virtually identical language. Note, however, that computer programs and copyright databases are excluded from this exception. Article 5(1) has proved a controversial provision and, as such, has been the subject of several rulings from the CJEU in *Infopaq I & II*[88] and *FAPL* and *Murphy*[89] and was also at the centre of the appeal to the UK Supreme Court in *Public Relations Consultants Association Ltd v Newspaper Licensing Agency Ltd*.[90]

---

[88] *Infopaq International A/S v Danske Dagblades Forening* Case C-5/08 [2010] FSR 20 (*Infopaq I*) and *Infopaq International A/S v Danske Dagblades Forening* C-302/10 (*Infopaq II*).

[89] *Football Association Premier League v QC Leisure* and *Murphy v Media Protection Services* Joined Cases C-403 and 429/08 [2012] FSR 1.

[90] [2013] UKSC 18, [2013] RPC 19.

In *Infopaq I*, the CJEU ruled that the conditions within Article 5(1) are cumulative and that the provision must be interpreted strictly because it derogates from the right of reproduction in Article 2 (and also in light of Article 5(5)). Further, the Court held that:

> an act can be held to be 'transient' … only if its duration is limited to what is necessary for the proper completion of the technological process in question, it being understood that that process must be automated so that it deletes the act automatically without human intervention, once its function of enabling the completion of such a process has come to an end.[91]

As a result of this interpretation, the reproduction made by Infopaq in printing out files containing text extracts could not be classified as 'transient'. In *Infopaq II*, the CJEU went on to consider whether the other acts of reproduction carried out by Infopaq could fall within Article 5(1). These acts were the creation of an image file from the scanned documents, the creation of a data file from the image file, and the digital storage of the 11-word extracts. The Court ruled that the acts were an integral and essential part of a technological process; and that their sole purpose was to enable lawful use of a protected work, namely the more efficient drafting of summaries of newspaper articles. Finally, the Court found that the acts did not have independent economic significance. On this issue the CJEU ruled:

> 50. However, those acts must not have independent economic significance, in that the economic advantage derived from their implementation must not be either distinct or separable from the economic advantage derived from the lawful use of the work concerned and it must not generate an additional economic advantage going beyond that derived from that use of the protected work (see, to that effect, *Football Association Premier League and Others*, paragraph 175).
>
> 51. The efficiency gains resulting from the implementation of the acts of temporary reproduction, such as those in issue in the main proceedings, have no such independent economic significance, inasmuch as the economic advantages derived from their application only materialise during the use of the reproduced subject matter, so that they are neither distinct nor separable from the advantages derived from its use.
>
> 52. On the other hand, an advantage derived from an act of temporary reproduction is distinct and separable if the author of that act is likely to make a profit due to the economic exploitation of the temporary reproductions themselves.

The question of what amounts to 'independent economic significance' was also raised in *FAPL v QC Leisure*. The acts in issue were the transient reproductions of copyright works made in the satellite decoder and on the television screen. The CJEU ruled that although Article 5(1) had to be interpreted strictly because it derogated from Article 2, the interpretation of the conditions had to enable the effectiveness of the exception. The Court observed:

> [Article 5(1)] must allow and ensure the development and operation of new technologies and safeguard a fair balance between the rights and interests of right holders on the one hand, and of users of protected works who wish to avail themselves of those new technologies on the other.[92]

---

[91] *Infopaq I*, [64].   [92] [164].

The Court held that the first three conditions were satisfied. On the question of independent economic significance, the Court observed that making access to the works possible had an economic value but that if Article 5(1) was 'not to be rendered redundant, that significance must also be independent in the sense that it goes beyond the economic advantage derived from mere reception of a broadcast containing protected works'.[93] The Court concluded that the transient copies made within the satellite decoder memory and on the TV screen were 'an inseparable and non-autonomous part of the process of reception of the broadcasts transmitted … performed without influence or even awareness on the part of the persons thereby having access to the protected works'[94] and as such were 'not capable of generating an additional economic advantage'.[95]

In *NLA v Meltwater*, Proudman J at first instance rejected a defence based on section 28A of the CDPA. She held:

> 109. …A person making a copy of a webpage on his computer screen will not have a defence under s. 28A CDPA simply because he has been browsing. He must first show that it was lawful for him to have made the copy. The copy is not part of the technological process; it is generated by his own volition. The whole point of the receipt and copying of Meltwater News is to enable the End User to receive and read it. Making the copy is not an essential and integral part of a technological process but the end which the process is designed to achieve. Storage of the copy and the duration of that storage are matters within the End User's control. It begs the question for decision whether making the copy is to enable a lawful use of the work. Moreover, making the copy does have an independent economic significance as the copy is the very product for which the End Users are paying Meltwater

The Court of Appeal upheld Proudman J's decision.[96] However, on appeal, the Supreme Court reached the opposite conclusion.[97] Lord Sumption (with whom the rest of the court agreed), reviewed the leading CJEU rulings on Article 5(1) in *Infopaq I*, *Infopaq II*, and *FAPL v QC Leisure* and summarized their effect:

> 26. The effect of this body of authority can be summarized as follows:
>
> (1) Subject to the limitations which I shall summarise in the following sub-paragraphs, the exception in article 5.1 applies to copies made as an integral and necessary part of a 'technological process', in particular the digital processing of data. For this purpose, the making of copies is a 'necessary' part of the process if it enables it to function 'correctly and efficiently': *Infopaq II*, at paras 30, 37.
>
> (2) These copies must be temporary. This requirement is explained and defined by the words which follow, namely that the making of the copies must be 'transient or incidental and an integral and essential part of a technological process'. It means (i) that the storage and deletion of the copyright material must be the automatic consequence of the user's decision to initiate or terminate the relevant technological process, as opposed to being dependent on some further discretionary human intervention, and (ii) that the duration of the copy should be limited to what is necessary for the completion of the relevant technological process: see *Infopaq I*, at paras 62 and 64.

---

[93] [175].   [94] [176].   [95] [177].   [96] [2011] EWCA Civ 890, [2012] RPC 1.
[97] *Public Relations Consultants Association Ltd v Newspaper Licensing Agency Ltd* [2013] UKSC 18, [2013] RPC 19.

(3) The exception is not limited to copies made in order to enable the transmission of material through intermediaries in a network. It also applies to copies made for the sole purpose of enabling other uses, provided that these uses are lawful. These other uses include internet browsing: *Infopaq I*, at para 63 and *Infopaq II*, at para 49.

(4) For the purpose of article 5.1, a use of the material is lawful, whether or not the copyright owner has authorized it, if it is consistent with EU legislation governing the reproduction right, including article 5.1 itself: *Premier League*, at paras 168–173, *Infopaq II*, at para 42. The use of the material is not unlawful by reason only of the fact that it lacks the authorization of the copyright owner.

(5) The making of the temporary copy must have no 'independent economic significance'. This does not mean that it must have no commercial value. It may well have. What it means is that it must have no *independent* commercial value, i.e. no value additional to that which is derived from the mere act of digitally transmitting or viewing the material: *Premier League*, at para 175, *Infopaq II*, at para 50.

(6) If these conditions are satisfied no additional restrictions can be derived from article 5.5.

Lord Sumption observed that the rulings in *Infopaq II* and *FAPL v QC Leisure* had been given after Proudman J and the Court of Appeal had delivered their decisions in *Meltwater* and concluded that neither could have arrived at the conclusions they did if they had had the benefit of the CJEU rulings:

> 37. In particular, the far broader meaning given by the Court of Justice in these cases to the concept of 'lawful use' makes it impossible to confine the scope of the exception to the internal plumbing of the internet. Once it is accepted that article 5.1 extends in principle to temporary copies made for the purpose of browsing by an unlicensed end-user, much of the argument which the courts below accepted unravels.

Despite the Supreme Court's conclusion on the merits of the Article 5(1) issue, it nevertheless decided to refer questions to the CJEU because of the importance of the issue.[98] Those questions essentially asked whether the on-screen and cached copies made when an internet user is browsing are temporary, transient, and incidental in nature and constitute an integral and essential part of a technological process.

The CJEU in *PRCA v Meltwater* reiterated that Article 5(1) had to be interpreted strictly because it is a derogation from Article 2 of the Information Society Directive, but that the exemption 'must allow and ensure the development and operation of new technologies' and ensure a fair balance between rightholders and users.[99] The Court held that the on-screen copies were temporary because they were deleted when a user moved away from a webpage, and in terms of the cached copies they were 'normally automatically replaced by other content after a certain time'.[100] The Court also ruled that the copies were incidental in nature because they did not 'exist independently of, nor [had] a purpose independent of, the technological process at issue'.[101] Finally, the Court ruled that the on-screen and cached copies were an integral and essential part of the technological process used for viewing a website.[102] It did not matter that the process was activated and terminated by a user.[103] In terms of the

---

[98] [38].   [99] *Newspaper Licensing Agency Ltd v Meltwater* Case C-360/13 [2014] AC 1438, [24].
[100] [26].   [101] [50].   [102] [38].   [103] [29]–[31].

cached copies, it was an essential part of the process used for viewing websites because, without it, 'the Internet would be unable to cope with the current volumes of data transmitted online'.[104]

4.3.4 INCIDENTAL INCLUSION

Section 31(1) of the CDPA states that the incidental inclusion of a copyright work in an artistic work, sound recording, film, or broadcast will not constitute an infringement. Further, copyright is not infringed by issuing to the public copies, or playing, showing, or communicating to the public, anything the making of which was not an infringement because it was an incidental inclusion.[105]

There is little guidance regarding what is meant by 'incidental', except for section 31(3) of the CDPA, which states that it does not encompass *deliberate* inclusion of either a musical work, words spoken or sung with music, or so much of a sound recording or broadcast as includes a musical work or such words. Further light was shed on the meaning of 'incidental' in the following decision.

Football Association Premier League Ltd v Panini UK Ltd [2004] FSR 1

The defendant (Panini) distributed for sale within the UK collectible stickers of famous football players, together with an album into which the stickers could be placed. The stickers and album in dispute were 'Panini's Football 2003 Sticker Collection'. Each sticker in the collection depicted a photographic image of a player typically in their club 'strip', but occasionally in their international 'strip', and in total 396 football players were included. On the footballer's strip the individual club badge and the Premier League emblem were depicted. The defendant's album collection was marketed as unofficial. The 'official' collection was marketed by a company, Topps Europe Ltd, which had been licensed by the first claimant (Football Association Premier League Ltd) to use and reproduce official team crests and logos in the production of stickers and albums. The first claimant, together with Topps and 14 of the 20 clubs that are members of the Premier League, brought proceedings against Panini for infringement of copyright in the club badges and emblems (as artistic works). Panini argued that its reproduction of the claimant's copyright works in its stickers and albums was an incidental inclusion within section 31 of the CDPA. This defence was rejected at first instance and also on appeal.

Chadwick LJ (Brooke LJ in agreement):

24. ...It is plain that the decision to leave the word 'incidental' undefined was intentional. As the minister responsible for the progress of the Bill (Lord Beaverbrook) put it (Hansard, December 8, 1987, p. 123 lhc): 'What is incidental will depend on all the circumstances of each case and it would be impossible to provide a satisfactory definition for all circumstances.' It is plain, also, that 'incidental' was not intended to mean 'unintentional'. That is clear, not only from the debate in the House of Lords but also from the explanation which

---

[104] [35].   [105] CDPA, s. 31(2).

was given to the House of Commons (Hansard, May 19, 1988, p. 218) in respect of the provision which has become s. 31(3) of the 1988 Act. But it is unnecessary to have resort to proceedings in Parliament in order to reach that conclusion. It is obvious, when subss. (1) and (3) of s. 31 of the Act are read together, that 'incidental', in the context of subs. (1), is not confined to unintentional, or non-deliberate, inclusion. If it were, subs. (3)—which deals with the particular case of incidental, or background, music in (say) a film or broadcast—would be unnecessary. There is, in my view, nothing else in the material which we were shown which throws light upon what Parliament meant by the word 'incidental'; and, for my part, I doubt whether there was any proper basis upon which that material could have been put before the judge. Be that as it may, we may, perhaps, take some comfort from the evident intention of the promoter of the Bill that 'What is incidental will depend on all the circumstances of each case...'; and his recognition that 'it would be impossible to provide a satisfactory definition for all circumstances'. The relevant question, as the judge pointed out, is whether, in the circumstances of this case, the inclusion on the stickers and in the album of the FAPL emblem and the individual club badges is or is not incidental.

...

26. ...That, as it seems to me, turns on the question: why—having regard to the circumstances in which work 'B' was created—has work 'A' been included in work 'B'? And, in addressing that question, I can see no reason why, if the circumstances so require, consideration should not be given as well to the commercial reason why work 'A' has been included in work 'B' as to any aesthetic reason. In particular, in a case (such as the present) where work 'B' is created, primarily if not exclusively, to serve a commercial purpose, it seems to me wholly artificial to test the 'incidentality' of the inclusion of work 'A' by reference (or primarily by reference) to artistic considerations—if, by that is meant aesthetic considerations. It is, I think, pertinent to keep in mind that, for the purposes of the 1988 Act, 'artistic works' are not confined to works of artistic quality—s. 4(1)(a) of the Act.

27. If, as I would hold, the relevant question, for the purposes of testing 'incidentality' in the context of s. 31(1) of the 1988 Act, is why has work 'A' been included in work 'B', the answer, in the present case, is indeed (as the judge thought) self-evident. The objective, when creating the image of the player as it appears on the sticker or in the album, was to produce something which would be attractive to a collector. That conclusion does not depend on any inquiry into the subjective intent of the individual employee who created the image—or (as I have said) of the photographer who took the photograph from which that image was derived. It depends on an objective assessment of the circumstances in which the image was created.

It is not, I think, a matter about which there can be any doubt. Nor can there be any doubt that it was of importance, in order to achieve that objective, that the player should appear in the appropriate club strip; and that the club strip be authentic. An image of a player in strip which an informed collector would recognise as not authentic would not achieve that objective. But if the strip were to be authentic it must include the club badge and (where appropriate) the FAPL emblem. That, as it seems to me, is what the judge had in mind when he described the inclusion of the badge as 'an integral part of the artistic work comprised of the photograph of the professional footballer in his present-day kit'. The authenticity of the image of the player as it appears on the sticker or in the album (work 'B') depends on the inclusion in work 'B' of the individual badge and the FAPL emblem (work 'A') in which copyright subsists. It is impossible to say that the inclusion of the individual badge and the FAPL emblem is 'incidental'. The inclusion of the individual badge and the FAPL emblem is essential to the object for which the image of the player as it appears on the sticker or in the album was created.

Is the approach to determining whether inclusion of a copyright work is 'incidental' an objective or subjective one? Is it safe to conclude that where the inclusion has a commercial purpose of some kind it can never be incidental? In what circumstances can you envisage the requirement of 'incidental' being satisfied, particularly where the inclusion is intentional or deliberate?

FURTHER READING

K. Garnett, 'Incidental inclusion under section 31' [2003] EIPR 579.

4.3.5 RECENT REFORMS

Some of the recent reforms have already been discussed in the context of the fair-dealing exceptions. In this section we outline some of the other key changes that the government made to copyright exceptions in 2014. Many of these were attempts to make existing copyright exceptions more workable and relevant in a digital context.

The UK introduced a limited private copying exception in section 28B of the CDPA, in reliance on Article 5(2)(b) of the Information Society Directive.[106] However, in *BASCA v Secretary of State for Business, Innovation and Skills*[107] this exception was subsequently held to be unlawful. Section 28B (if lawful) would have applied to all types of copyright work and all types of private storage (including cloud services). It would have applied to persons who are lawful owners or purchasers of a copy of a work and would not have permitted them to share copies with friends or other persons. However, it would have allowed, for example, a purchaser of an e-book to make a back-up copy on their computer but not to send a copy to their friend. Likewise, it would have allowed a purchaser of an MP3 file to transfer it from their computer to their iPod but not to make it available via a peer-to-peer service or to their friends via Skype.

In introducing section 28B, the Secretary of State for Business, Innovation and Skills took the view that it would cause minimal harm to rightholders, particularly because the value of any private copying was likely to be priced in at the point of sale,[108] and, as such, fair compensation was not required. This approach was said to be justified by recital 35 of the Information Society Directive which states that '[i]n certain situations where the prejudice to the rightholder would be minimal, no obligation for payment may arise'. However, it was exactly on this issue that the new exception ran aground. In an application for judicial review, Green J in *BASCA v Secretary of State for Business, Innovation and Skills*[109] held that there had been insufficient evidence that 'pricing-in was so extensive as to render harm [to rightholders] minimal or non-existent'[110] and therefore 'the decision to introduce s. 28B in the absence of a compensation mechanism [was] unlawful'.[111]

Changes to the educational exceptions in sections 32, 35, and 36 of the CDPA have been introduced. Section 32 is now framed as a fair-dealing exception for the sole purpose of illustration for instruction. This exception applies provided the dealing is for a non-commercial

---

[106] The Copyright and Rights in Performances (Personal Copies for Private Use) Regulations 2014 (SI 2014/2361).

[107] [2015] EWHC 1723 (Admin), [2015] RPC 26.

[108] On this see UK IPO, *Private Copying* (2013), which examines the music, film, publishing, and software sectors.

[109] [2015] EWHC 1723 (Admin), [2015] RPC 26.   [110] [272].   [111] [274].

purpose and is by a person giving or receiving instruction (or preparing for giving or receiving instruction) and where there is sufficient acknowledgement (unless impossible for reasons of practicality). 'Giving or receiving instruction' includes but is not limited to 'setting examination questions, communicating the questions to pupils and answering the questions' (section 32(2)). Sections 35 and 36 were seen as broadly fit for purpose, but they were updated with a view to ensuring modern teaching tools, such as interactive whiteboards and distance learning platforms, can be used. Section 35 permits educational establishments to record and use broadcasts for non-commercial educational purposes where there is a sufficient acknowledgement (unless impossible for reasons of practicality) and to the extent that licences for these activities do not exist. The use has been extended to communication of recordings of broadcasts to the pupil and staff of educational establishments, including outside the premises of the establishment provided it is via a secure network accessible only to those persons. Section 36 has been extended to apply to all copyright works (previously it was limited to published literary, dramatic, or musical works) and permits extracts of works to be copied provided they are made for non-commercial instructional purposes and there is sufficient acknowledgement (unless impossible due to reasons of practicality). Further, extracts may be communicated by an educational establishment to its pupils and staff, including outside the premises of the establishment, provided it is over a secure electronic network accessible only to those persons. Similar to section 35, the acts permitted under section 36 are permitted to the extent that licences are not available authorizing the acts in question.

Recent amendments have also broadened the existing exception for archiving and preservation so that cultural institutions are better positioned to preserve creative content. Section 42 permits librarians, archivists, and curators at prescribed libraries, archives, and museums to make a copy of any type of work in their permanent collection for preservation or replacement purposes, where it is not reasonably practicable to purchase a copy of the item to fulfil this purpose. Previously, section 42 was limited to literary, dramatic, and musical works and did not apply to museums. Moreover, this exception may not be overridden by contract. A new exception for libraries, archives, museums, and educational establishments has been introduced by section 40B of the CDPA, in reliance on Article 5(3)(n) of the Information Society Directive. Section 40B stipulates that copyright is not infringed if these institutions communicate the work to the public by means of a dedicated terminal on their premises. This is provided the work has been 'lawfully acquired by the institution, is communicated ... to individuals ... for the purposes of research or private study, and is communicated ... in compliance with any purchase or licensing terms to which the work is subject'.[112] The CJEU in *Technische Universität Darmstadt v Ulmer*[113] interpreted Article 5(3)(n) of the Information Society Directive and ruled that 'purchase or licensing terms' meant 'a licensing agreement in respect of the work in question that sets out the conditions in which that establishment may use that work',[114] that Member States may permit the institutions covered by this exception to digitize the works in their collection, if this is necessary for the purpose of making those works available to users via dedicated terminals.[115] Finally, the Court ruled that the exception did not extend to permitting users of dedicated terminals to print out those works on paper or store them on a USB stick.[116]

---

[112] CDPA, s. 40B(3).   [113] Case C-117/13 [2014] ECDR 23.   [114] [35].
[115] [49].   [116] [57].

The disability exceptions included within section 31A–F of the CDPA have been simplified and broadened. These exceptions previously targeted visual and aural impairments, but now include all types of disability that prevent someone from accessing a copyright work.[117] Sections 31B and 31BA permit authorized bodies to make and supply accessible copies (including intermediate copies in order to make the accessible copies) for the personal use of disabled persons, provided the same kind of copies are not commercially available on reasonable terms. Further, these exceptions now extend to all types of work, whereas previously they were limited to literary, dramatic, musical, and artistic works. As such, the changes seem to be consistent with the Marrakesh Treaty (discussed at 2.4.1.7). Contractual terms will be unenforceable if they seek to override these exceptions.[118]

Finally, the government has introduced a controversial new exception for text and data-mining activities in section 29A of the CDPA. Text and data mining refers to the use of analytic technology to copy and analyse large quantities of data in order to determine patterns, trends, and other useful information which is potentially very valuable for scientific research. The technology achieves on a larger and faster scale what could be undertaken by individual researchers scouring published journal articles. Publishers opposed this exception, because they were concerned about the security of access to their copyright works and also argued that licensing provided a solution. The exception applies to persons who have lawful access to the work and permits copies made for 'computational analysis of anything recorded in the work for the sole purpose of research for a non-commercial purpose' and provided there is sufficient acknowledgement (unless this is impossible for reasons of practicality) (section 29A(1)). Contractual terms that purport to override this exception will be unenforceable (section 29A(5)). There is debate about whether to introduce such an exception at the EU level and whether it should extend to research for commercial *and* non-commercial purposes.[119]

FURTHER READING

B. Batchelor et al., 'Copyright levies: moving towards harmonization? The European Court rules on the concept of fair compensation for rightholders' [2011] ECLR 277.

S. Karapapa, *Private Copying* (Oxford/New York: Routledge, 2012).

4.3.6 PUBLIC INTEREST DEFENCE

The public interest defence was originally developed in the context of the law of confidence,[120] but later appeared in copyright cases, such as *Beloff v Pressdram*[121] where Ungoed-Thomas J accepted that public interest could override copyright, although this was not the case on the facts. In Chapter 2 at 2.5.5 the public policy exclusion to copyright protection was briefly discussed. In reading this next section, try to identify how that exclusion differs from the public interest defence.

Section 171(3) of the CDPA arguably preserves the public interest defence since it states, 'Nothing in this Part affects any rule of law preventing or restricting the enforcement of

---

[117] CDPA, s. 31F(2). [118] CDPA, s. 31F(8).

[119] European Commission, *Standardisation in the area of innovation and technological development, notably in the field of Text and Data Mining: Report from the Expert Group* (2014) available at <http://ec.europa.eu/research/innovation-union/pdf/TDM-report_from_the_expert_group-042014.pdf>, 5.2. See now proposed directive on copyright in the Digital Single Market, Brussels 14.9.2016, Art. 3.

[120] See 9.5.2. [121] [1973] FSR 33, 57.

copyright, on grounds of public interest or otherwise.' However, in *Hyde Park Residence v Yelland* the Court of Appeal held that this did not reflect a *defence* of public interest, but rather the court's inherent jurisdiction to refuse to enforce copyright in work.

Hyde Park Residence v Yelland [2001] Ch 143

The facts were discussed at 4.3.2.2.

Aldous LJ (Stuart-Smith LJ in agreement):

Public interest

...

43. Mr Bloch's submission that no public interest defence exists starts with an analysis of the 1988 Act. As he correctly pointed out, copyright is an intellectual property right provided for by the 1988 Act. That Act contains detailed provisions in the 51 sections in Chapter III of Part I of the types of acts that are permitted to be carried out by persons without the copyright owner's consent. They range from fair dealing to use for education, by libraries and for public administration. They are, as he submitted, provisions directed towards achieving a proper balance between the protection of copyright and the wider public interest. They would therefore appear to set out in detail the extent to which the public interest overrides copyright. I agree. The 1988 Act does not give a court general power to enable an infringer to use another's property, namely his copyright in the public interest. Thus a defence of public interest outside those set out in Chapter III of Part I of the 1988 Act, if such exists, must arise by some other route.

44. The courts have an inherent jurisdiction to refuse to allow their process to be used in certain circumstances. It has long been the law that the courts will not give effect to contracts which are, for example, illegal, immoral or prejudicial to family life because they offend against the policy of the law. In my view that inherent jurisdiction can be exercised in the case of an action in which copyright is sought to be enforced, as is made clear by section 171(3) of the 1988 Act: 'Nothing in this Part affects any rule of law preventing or restricting the enforcement of copyright, on grounds of public interest or otherwise.'

...

54. There are other cases where the courts have refused to grant interlocutory injunctions to restrain a breach of confidence upon the basis of public interest. The principle is, as stated by Lord Denning MR in *Woodward v Hutchins* [1977] 1 WLR 760, 764: 'In these cases of confidential information it is a question of balancing the public interest in maintaining the confidence against the public interest in knowing the truth.'

55. That principle has particular relevance to an action for breach of confidence. Such an action is brought to enforce an obligation of confidence in respect of information of a confidential nature imparted in circumstances where the courts import an obligation of confidence: see *Coco v A N Clark (Engineers) Ltd* [1969] RPC 41. The court can therefore weigh the public interest in knowing the truth against the public interest in maintaining the confidence in the light of the facts of each case. That cannot be the test to be applied where copyright infringement has taken place for three reasons. First, copyright is a property right which is given by the 1988 Act. Chapter III of Part I of the Act provides for exceptions in the public interest. It would therefore be wrong for a court which had rejected a defence of, for

example, fair dealing, because there was not a sufficient acknowledgement, to uphold a defence because publication was in the public interest. That would result in a disregard of an important requirement set out in the Act. Second, copyright is concerned with protection of the form of works in which copyright can subsist and not with protection of information. That can be illustrated with the facts of the present case. Nobody has suggested nor could it be suggested that the information recorded on the driveway stills could be the subject of copyright or that use of that information would be an infringement of the copyright which subsists in the film. It follows that the weighing operation is not apt when the information can be published even though the action for infringement of copyright succeeds. Third, the 1988 Act gives effect to the United Kingdom's obligations pursuant to the Conventions of the International Union for the Protection of Literary and Artistic Works (Berne, 9 September 1886) and the International Convention further revising the Berne Convention (Paris, 24 July 1971–31 January 1972) (Cmnd 5002) and certain EC Council Directives. Those Conventions came into being to provide for uniform and effective protection of copyright amongst the signatories. Article 10 of the Berne Convention allows quotations from copyright works provided that the quotation is compatible with fair practice. Section 30 of the 1988 Act is thought to be within the terms of that article. However there is no general power for courts of the signatories to such Conventions to refuse to enforce copyright if it is thought to be in the public interest of that state that it should not be enforced. Thus a general defence of public interest would appear to be contrary to this country's international obligations.

...

64. I have pointed out earlier in this judgment that the basis of the defence of public interest in a breach of confidence action cannot be the same as the basis of such defence to an action for infringement of copyright. In an action for breach of confidence the foundation of the action can fall away if that is required in the public interest, but that can never happen in a copyright action. The jurisdiction to refuse to enforce copyright, which I believe has been recognised, comes from the court's inherent jurisdiction. It is limited to cases where enforcement of the copyright would offend against the policy of the law. The *Lion Laboratories* case [1985] QB 526 was such a case. Lion Laboratories sought to obtain an interlocutory injunction to restrain publication of documents which showed that they had suppressed information leading to or which might lead to the wrongful conviction of motorists. The action was based upon documents which in the circumstances reeked of turpitude. As Lord Mansfield CJ said in *Holman v Johnson* (1775) 1 Cowp 341, 343: 'No court will lend its aid to a man who founds his cause of action upon an immoral or an illegal act.'

65. To rely upon copyright to suppress documents which could exonerate motorists convicted of drink driving or which might lead to their acquittal is, in my view, to found a cause of action upon an immoral act.

66. The circumstances where it is against the policy of the law to use the court's procedure to enforce copyright are, I suspect, not capable of definition. However it must be remembered that copyright is assignable and therefore the circumstances must derive from the work in question, not ownership of the copyright. In my view a court would be entitled to refuse to enforce copyright if the work is: (i) immoral, scandalous or contrary to family life; (ii) injurious to public life, public health and safety or the administration of justice; (iii) incites or encourages others to act in a way referred to in (ii).

Mance LJ:

83. Whilst account must be taken of the different nature of the right involved in copyright, I prefer to state no more in this case than that the circumstances in which the public interest

may override copyright are probably not capable of precise categorisation or definition. I would not as at present advised agree with Aldous LJ's suggestion that 'the circumstances must derive from the work in question, not ownership of the copyright'. No doubt this would normally be so. But the possibility of assignment does not appear to me to lead to a conclusion that it must always be so. Of course, if copyright has been assigned, e.g. to a purchaser having no notice of circumstances which might have affected its enforceability in the hands of the assignor, that would be a very relevant circumstance when considering whether the public interest overrode copyright. But, aside from situations of assignment, it seems to me possible to conceive of situations where a copyright document itself appeared entirely innocuous, but its publication—as a matter of fair dealing or, in circumstances outside the scope of section 30, in the public interest—was justified by its significance in the context of other facts. It might conceivably represent the relevant, though by itself apparently meaningless, piece needed to complete a whole jigsaw.

Do you find Aldous LJ's reasons for rejecting a public interest defence persuasive? Certainly, they have been heavily criticized by some commentators, such as Robert Burrell.[122] What difference, if any, is there between a defence of public interest and, as the court in *Yelland* found, its inherent jurisdiction to refuse to enforce copyright? With respect to the circumstances in which a court can refuse to enforce copyright, do you agree with the approach of Aldous LJ or that of Mance LJ?

Subsequent to *Yelland* the Human Rights Act 1998 came into effect and the issue of how courts should give effect to Article 10 of the ECHR, the right to freedom of expression, arose. At first instance in *Ashdown v Telegraph Group Ltd*[123] Sir Andrew Morritt V-C concluded:

Article 10 cannot be relied on to create defences to the alleged infringement over and above those for which the 1988 Act provides. The balance between the rights of the owner of the copyright and those of the public has been struck by the legislative organ of the democratic state itself in the legislation it has enacted. There is no room for any further defences outside the code which establishes the particular species of intellectual property in question.

The Court of Appeal, however, took a different approach to this issue.

Ashdown v Telegraph Group Ltd [2002] Ch 149

The facts were described at 4.3.2.6.

Lord Phillips MR (delivering the judgment of the court):

39. We have already observed that, in most circumstances, the principle of freedom of expression will be sufficiently protected if there is a right to publish information and ideas set out in another's literary work, without copying the very words which that person has employed to convey the information or express the ideas. In such circumstances it will normally be necessary in a democratic society that the author of the work should have his property in his own creation protected. Strasbourg jurisprudence demonstrates, however,

---

[122] See R. Burrell, 'Defending the public interest' [2000] EIPR 394.   [123] [2001] Ch 658, 696.

that circumstances can arise in which freedom of expression will only be fully effective if an individual is permitted to reproduce the very words spoken by another.

...

43. *Fressoz and Roire* was not a copyright case, but it illustrates a general principle. Freedom of expression protects the right both to publish information and to receive it. There will be occasions when it is in the public interest not merely that information should be published, but that the public should be told the very words used by a person, notwithstanding that the author enjoys copyright in them. On occasions, indeed, it is the form and not the content of a document which is of interest.

44. Where the subject matter of the information is a current event, section 30(2) of the 1988 Act may permit publication of the words used. But it is possible to conceive of information of the greatest public interest relating not to a current event, but to a document produced in the past. We are not aware of any provision of the 1988 Act which would permit publication in such circumstances, unless the mere fact of publication, and any controversy created by the disclosure, is sufficient to make them 'current events'. This will often be a 'bootstraps' argument of little merit, but on other occasions (such as disclosure by the Public Record Office under the 30-year rule) it may have a more solid basis.

45. For these reasons, we have reached the conclusion that rare circumstances can arise where the right of freedom of expression will come into conflict with the protection afforded by the 1988 Act, notwithstanding the express exceptions to be found in the Act. In these circumstances, we consider that the court is bound, in so far as it is able, to apply the Act in a manner that accommodates the right of freedom of expression. This will make it necessary for the court to look closely at the facts of individual cases (as indeed it must whenever a 'fair dealing' defence is raised). We do not foresee this leading to a flood of litigation.

46. The first way in which it may be possible to do this is by declining the discretionary relief of an injunction. Usually, so it seems to us, such a step will be likely to be sufficient. If a newspaper considers it necessary to copy the exact words created by another, we can see no reason in principle why the newspaper should not indemnify the author for any loss caused to him, or alternatively account to him for any profit made as a result of copying his work. Freedom of expression should not normally carry with it the right to make free use of another's work.

Public interest

47. In the rare case where it is in the public interest that the words in respect of which another has copyright should be published without any sanction, we have been concerned to consider why this should not be permitted under the 'public interest' exception, the possibility of which is recognised by section 171(3). Sir Andrew Morritt V-C considered that he was precluded from so holding by the decision of this court in *Hyde Park Residence Ltd v Yelland* [2001] Ch 143. [Referring to *Yelland*:]

52. Stuart-Smith LJ agreed that the appeal should be allowed for the reasons given by Aldous LJ. It does not seem to us that those reasons depended on the precise scope of the public interest exception identified by Aldous LJ...[Referring to *Lion Laboratories v Evans* [1985] QB 526:]

58. In the light of these judgments, we do not consider that Aldous LJ was justified in circumscribing the public interest defence to breach of copyright as tightly as he did. We prefer the conclusion of Mance LJ that the circumstances in which public interest may override

copyright are not capable of precise categorisation or definition. Now that the Human Rights Act 1998 is in force, there is the clearest public interest in giving effect to the right of freedom of expression in those rare cases where this right trumps the rights conferred by the 1988 Act. In such circumstances, we consider that section 171(3) of the Act permits the defence of public interest to be raised.

59. We do not consider that this conclusion will lead to a flood of cases where freedom of expression is invoked as a defence to a claim for breach of copyright. It will be very rare for the public interest to justify the copying of the form of a work to which copyright attaches. We would add that the implications of the Human Rights Act 1998 must always be considered where the discretionary relief of an injunction is sought, and this is true in the field of copyright quite apart from the ambit of the public interest defence under section 171(3).

There are two important strands to the Court of Appeal's reasoning. The first is that rare circumstances may arise in which it is necessary to use the precise form of the copyright work, but the existing exceptions in the CDPA cannot be relied upon. In these circumstances, the court will have to apply the CDPA in a manner that accommodates the right to freedom of expression. This may occur by refusing discretionary relief (such as an injunction). Alternatively, and this constitutes the second strand of the court's reasoning, it may be appropriate to rely upon the public interest defence. Here, the court held that Aldous LJ's definition of public interest was not the *ratio decidendi* of *Yelland* and preferred to adopt the approach of Mance LJ, whereby instances of public interest are not capable of precise categorization or definition. The court also reverted to the language of public interest *defence*. It held that the defence of public interest may be invoked in those rare circumstances where the right to freedom of expression outweighs the property rights of a copyright owner.

On the facts, the Court of Appeal held that substantial parts of the minute had been reproduced 'most likely to add flavour to the article and thus to appeal to the readership of the newspaper'[124] and in furtherance of the commercial interests of the defendant. As such, the Article 10 interests of the defendant did not outweigh the copyright interests of the claimant.

Jonathan Griffiths has remarked that the Court of Appeal in *Ashdown* crafted 'an extremely elegant solution to the challenge presented by the Human Rights Act'.[125] But, as previously mentioned, in his view it does not go far enough and the court, when it comes to applying the fair-dealing exceptions, should take into account additional factors. Further, Robert Burrell argues that although *Ashdown* 'represents a welcome relaxation of the approach taken in *Yelland*' the judgment 'is not an unqualified boost for users' because the defence will apply only in 'rare' circumstances.[126]

FURTHER READING

J. Griffiths, 'Pre-empting conflict—a re-examination of the public interest defence in UK copyright law' (2014) 34 Legal Studies 76.

P. Johnson, 'The public interest: is it still a defence to copyright infringement?' (2005) 16 Ent. L. R. 1.

---

[124] [2002] Ch 149, [82].
[125] J. Griffiths, 'Copyright law after *Ashdown*: time to deal fairly with the public' [2002] IPQ 240, 247.
[126] R. Burrell, 'Reining in copyright law: is fair use the answer?' [2001] IPQ 361, 381.

4.3.7 COMPUTER PROGRAMS

Articles 5 and 6 of the Software Directive obligate Member States to include exceptions to infringement to permit reverse engineering, decompilation, error correction, and back-up copies.

4.3.7.1 Reverse engineering

The Software Directive draws a distinction between reverse engineering that involves studying the operation of a computer program and reverse engineering that involves decompilation. Article 5(3) deals with the former situation whereas Article 6 deals with the latter.

Studying a computer program involves running it and this in turn involves reproduction of the program in the RAM of the computer. As such, unless the person running a computer program (or copy thereof) has the copyright owner's permission to do so, this temporary reproduction will constitute a prima facie infringement of copyright. It may also amount to an infringing adaptation (because the source code will be converted to object code in order to operate). Yet, the purpose in running the computer program is simply to observe what it does and how it functions, in other words to understand the ideas and principles underlying the program, and it is clear from Article 1(2) that such matter is not protected by copyright. Thus, an exception was crafted to deal with the apparent conflict between a prima facie infringement (through copying) and the need to ensure underlying ideas and principles are not protected. Article 5(3) was the solution. This provision states:

> The person having a right to use a copy of a computer program shall be entitled, without the authorisation of the rightholder, to observe, study or test the functioning of the program in order to determine the ideas and principles which underlie any element of the program if he does so while performing any of the acts of loading, displaying, running, transmitting or storing the program which he is entitled to do.

The UK did not insert an express provision into the CDPA corresponding to Article 5(3) of the Software Directive and was criticized by the Commission for failing to do so. As a result of the Copyright and Related Rights Regulations 2003,[127] however, a new section 50BA was inserted into the CDPA, which mirrors Article 5(3) and Article 8.

Only the person having a 'right to use a copy of a computer program' can rely on this exception. There has been uncertainty about what this phrase means, given that Article 5(1) refers to a 'lawful acquirer' and Article 5(2) refers to 'a person having a right to use the computer program'. However, it is now understood that all three expressions mean the same concept of 'lawful user': that is, a person who *lawfully* acquires the program (e.g. via purchase, gift, public lending, or rental contracts).[128] Thus, where an illicit or pirated copy of the program is used the exception cannot be relied upon.

Article 8 of the Software Directive (previously Article 9(1) of Directive 91/250) emphasizes that any contractual provision contrary to Article 5(3) will be null and void. Thus, it seems that the owner of copyright in the program cannot override the user's right to reverse engineer. However, the terms of Article 5(3), which state that reverse engineering has to

---

[127] SI 2003/2498.
[128] T. Aplin, *Copyright Law in the Digital Society: The Challenges of Multimedia* (Oxford: Hart, 2005), p. 164.

occur 'while performing any of the acts of loading, displaying, running or transmitting or storing the program *which he is entitled to do*' (emphasis supplied), read in combination with recital 19, which provides that the acts of reverse engineering 'do not infringe copyright in the program', suggest that the copyright owner could license the use of the program in such a way that restricted the user's ability to carry out acts of reverse engineering. This was indeed one of the key questions referred to the CJEU in *SAS Institute Inc. v World Programming Ltd*.[129] In this case the defendants had purchased the Learning Edition of the SAS system and the terms of the licence prohibited users from using this version to produce anything (as opposed simply to learning and understanding how to use the SAS Language, scripts, and system). The ruling of the CJEU (Grand Chamber) on the scope of Article 5(3) was not, however, particularly clear, as the following extract shows.

SAS Institute Inc. v World Programming Ltd Case C-406/10 (Grand Chamber)

50 The Court observes that, from the wording of that provision, it is clear, first, that a licensee is entitled to observe, study or test the functioning of a computer program in order to determine the ideas and principles which underlie any element of the program.

51 In this respect, art. 5(3) of Directive 91/250 seeks to ensure that the ideas and principles which underlie any element of a computer program are not protected by the owner of the copyright by means of a licensing agreement.

52 That provision is therefore consistent with the basic principle laid down in art. 1(2) of Directive 91/250, pursuant to which protection in accordance with that directive applies to the expression in any form of a computer program and ideas and principles which underlie any element of a computer program are not protected by copyright under that directive.

53 Article 9(1) of Directive 91/250 adds, moreover, that any contractual provisions contrary to the exceptions provided for in art. 5(2) and (3) of that directive are null and void.

54 Secondly, under art. 5(3) of Directive 91/250, a licensee is entitled to determine the ideas and principles which underlie any element of the computer program if he does so while performing any of the acts of loading, displaying, running, transmitting or storing that program which he is entitled to do.

55 It follows that the determination of those ideas and principles may be carried out within the framework of the acts permitted by the licence.

56 In addition, the 18th recital in the preamble to Directive 91/250 states that a person having a right to use a computer program should not be prevented from performing acts necessary to observe, study or test the functioning of the program, provided that these acts do not infringe the copyright in that program.

57 As the A.G. states in point AG95 of his Opinion, the acts in question are those referred to in art. 4(a) and (b) of Directive 91/250, which sets out the exclusive rights of the rightholder to do or to authorise, and those referred to in art.5(1) thereof, relating to the acts necessary for the use of the computer program by the lawful acquirer in accordance with its intended purpose, including for error correction.

58 In that latter regard, the 17th recital in the preamble to Directive 91/250 states that the acts of loading and running necessary for that use may not be prohibited by contract.

---

[129] Case C-406/10 [2012] 3 CMLR 4.

59 Consequently, the owner of the copyright in a computer program may not prevent, by relying on the licensing agreement, the person who has obtained that licence from determining the ideas and principles which underlie all the elements of that program in the case where that person carries out acts which that licence permits him to perform and the acts of loading and running necessary for the use of the computer program, and on condition that that person does not infringe the exclusive rights of the owner in that program.

60 As regards that latter condition, art. 6(2)(c) of Directive 91/250 relating to decompilation states that decompilation does not permit the information obtained through its application to be used for the development, production or marketing of a computer program substantially similar in its expression, or for any other act which infringes copyright.

61 It must therefore be held that the copyright in a computer program cannot be infringed where, as in the present case, the lawful acquirer of the licence did not have access to the source code of the computer program to which that licence relates, but merely studied, observed and tested that program in order to reproduce its functionality in a second program.

62 In those circumstances, the answer to Questions 6 and 7 is that art. 5(3) of Directive 91/250 must be interpreted as meaning that a person who has obtained a copy of a computer program under a licence is entitled, without the authorisation of the owner of the copyright, to observe, study or test the functioning of that program so as to determine the ideas and principles which underlie any element of the program, in the case where that person carries out acts covered by that licence and acts of loading and running necessary for the use of the computer program, and on condition that that person does not infringe the exclusive rights of the owner of the copyright in that program.

Having read the Court's ruling on the scope of Article 5(3), do you think that the acts of World Programming Ltd in using the SAS system to produce competing, but non-infringing, software would be exempt? Were their acts within the scope of the licence? If not, and if this is fatal to reliance on Article 5(3), will it simply be a matter of stipulating as a term of the licence that certain reverse-engineering activities are not permitted? If so, will this make a mockery of Article 8 of the Software Directive?

FURTHER READING

D. Gervais and E. Derclaye, 'The scope of computer program protection after *SAS*: are we closer to answers?' [2012] EIPR 565.

A. van Rooijen, *The Software Interface Between Copyright and Competition Law: A Legal Analysis of Interoperability in Computer Programs* (Alphen aan den Rijn: Wolters Kluwer, 2010).

4.3.7.2 Decompilation

Decompilation allows a software engineer or programmer to access the original source code, or a version as near as possible to the source code, so that he can appreciate the ideas and principles underlying a computer program, how the program functions, and its interfaces. This may allow a competitor to imitate the program, design a competing program that improves upon the existing program, or create a program or hardware device that complements the program. However, decompilation necessarily involves either a reproduction or adaptation of the underlying source code (or code written in another higher level language) and, in the absence of an applicable exception or express licence, will constitute an infringement of copyright.

Article 6(1) creates a fairly detailed and complex exception for decompilation. It provides that a rightsholder's permission is not required for reproduction or translation of a computer program where these acts are '*indispensable* to obtain the information necessary to achieve the *interoperability* of an *independently created computer program* with other programs'.[130] Indispensability means, for example, that the information needed to achieve interoperability cannot already be obtained by reverse engineering in reliance on Article 5(3). The purpose of decompilation must be to achieve interoperability and it is clear that the independently created program may be one that competes with the program that is decompiled.

Certain circumstances have to exist before a person can rely on Article 6 of the Software Directive. First, pursuant to Article 6(1)(a), the person performing the acts of reproduction or translation must be the licensee, or another person having a right to use a copy of a program, or a person authorized by the licensee or a person having a right to use the program. Second, Article 6(1)(b) requires that the information necessary to achieve interoperability has not previously been readily available to the persons just mentioned. It is unclear, however, what will constitute 'readily available'. Finally, Article 6(1)(c) states that the acts of reproduction and translation must be 'confined to the parts of the original program which are necessary to achieve interoperability'. The difficulty with this requirement is that it is not always possible to ascertain at the beginning of the decompilation process which parts of the work are essential to achieving interoperability.

Once information necessary to achieve interoperability has been obtained, Article 6(2) imposes further obligations on what may be done with this information. First, the information obtained cannot be used for purposes other than to achieve interoperability of the independently created computer program. Second, the information cannot be passed on to others, except for the purposes of interoperability. Finally, the information cannot be used to create a substantially similar computer program, 'or for any other act which infringes copyright'.

Article 8 of the Software Directive makes clear that any contractual provision contrary to Article 6 will be null and void. Even so, it seems that Article 8 does not prohibit Article 6 from being overridden by other forms of legal protection, such as the law of confidence.

Article 6 is implemented in the UK via section 50B of the CDPA. This provision departs from the language of Article 6 in two respects. First, 'decompiling' is not described as 'reproduction of the code and translation, of its form' but rather in terms of converting a copy of a computer program expressed in a low level language into a version in a higher level language; or, incidentally while doing so, copying the program. Arguably, the UK language has a more restricted meaning. Second, section 50B refrains from using the term 'interoperability' and instead refers to obtaining the information necessary *to create an independent program* which can be operated with the program decompiled or another program. It seems, therefore, that under the UK provision a person will not be able to decompile another program in order to obtain information that could lead to the interoperability of a program that already exists.

---

[130] Emphasis supplied.

4.3.7.3 Back-up copies and error correction

Article 5(2) of the Software Directive creates an exception for back-up copies. This was implemented in the UK by section 50A(1) of the CDPA. Section 50A(1) creates an exception for a lawful user of a copy of a computer program, 'to make any back up copy of it which it is necessary for him to have for the purposes of his lawful use'. The right to make a back-up copy cannot be excluded by contract.[131] However, what amounts to a 'back-up copy' is not defined in the Software Directive or CDPA, but seems to include a copy made by a user as a reserve in case of loss or damage to the original. While it may be desirable to make a back-up copy, it is questionable whether it is generally necessary to do so. The requirement of 'necessity' probably limits the lawful user to making only one back-up copy.

Article 5(1) of the Software Directive provides that a lawful acquirer of a computer program may carry out the acts of reproduction, translation, adaptation, and any other alteration of a computer program, 'where they are necessary for use of the computer program by the lawful acquirer in accordance with its intended purpose, including for error correction'. Unlike the other exceptions, Article 5(1) states that the exception applies in the absence of specific contractual provisions, thus it appears permissible to override via contract. This provision is implemented in the UK in section 50C of the CDPA.

4.3.8 COPYRIGHT DATABASES

When it comes to exceptions to infringement of copyright-protected databases, Article 6 of the Database Directive contains one mandatory and four optional exceptions. The mandatory exception is contained in Article 6(1) and states that the performance by a lawful user of any exclusive act 'which is necessary for the purpose of access to the contents of the databases and normal use of the contents by the lawful user' shall not require authorization. Any contractual provision that seeks to override this exception will be null and void according to Article 15 of the Database Directive. Importantly, the exception applies only to the *lawful user* of a database, the meaning of which is not entirely certain. However, it has been argued that the preferable interpretation of 'lawful user' is that it refers to any person who lawfully acquires the database (e.g. via sale, gift, public lending, and rental contracts).[132] Article 6(1) has been implemented in the CDPA as section 50D. This provision is similar in terms to Article 6(1), except that instead of referring to 'lawful user' it refers to 'a person who has a right to use the database or any part of the database (whether under a licence to do any of the acts restricted by the copyright in the database or otherwise)'. This wording is possibly inconsistent with the concept of 'lawful user' in the Database Directive insofar as it may include persons who rely upon an implied licence.

---

[131] CDPA, ss. 50A(3) and 296A.

[132] T. Aplin, *Copyright Law in the Digital Society: The Challenges of Multimedia* (Oxford: Hart, 2005), p. 177.

Member States, according to Article 6(2), may also provide for exceptions in the following cases:

(a) in the case of reproduction for private purposes of a non-electronic database;

(b) where there is use for the sole purpose of illustration for teaching or scientific research, as long as the source is indicated and to the extent justified by the non-commercial purpose to be achieved;

(c) where there is use for the purposes of public security or for the purposes of an administrative or judicial proceeding;

(d) where other exceptions to copyright which are traditionally authorised under national law are involved, without prejudice to points (a), (b) and (c).

The scope of the above exceptions is discussed in the following extract.

T. Aplin, *Copyright Law in the Digital Society: The Challenges of Multimedia* (Oxford: Hart, 2005), pp. 179–80

The first optional exception is limited, in that it exempts only the act of reproduction carried out in relation to non-electronic databases. It reflects a private use type exception for hard-copy databases. This exception was not implemented into the CDPA probably because a private use exception does not exist in UK copyright law, as compared with certain civil law Member States.

The scope of the second optional exception is difficult to ascertain. It is unclear, for example, what will amount to '*illustration* for teaching or scientific research'. Does 'illustration' confine the use to providing examples of what is being taught or researched? If so, this would not allow a teacher or researcher to use the database simply in preparing their teaching or as an aid to their research. Further, does 'illustration for teaching' mean that use for the purpose of learning, in other words, private study, is excluded? Finally, illustration for teaching or scientific research must be the sole purpose and must not exceed the non-commercial purpose. Thus, it appears that the use must be non-commercial, which may be a difficult requirement to satisfy in the light of realities of education and research institutions. This exception was not specifically implemented in UK law. However, the exception of fair dealing for the purpose of (non-commercial) research and private study, along with the exceptions relating to copying by educational establishments in sections 32–36 of the CDPA will embrace the sorts of activities contemplated by Article 6(2)(b) of the Database Directive.

The third optional exception, namely, Article 6(2)(c) concerning the purposes of public security and administrative and judicial proceedings, would appear to be catered for by sections 45–50 of the CDPA. These provisions create exceptions relating to public administration.

The fourth optional exception, namely, exceptions to copyright traditionally authorised under national law, was the subject of consideration in *Mars v Teknowledge* (discussed above in relation to computer programs). In *Mars*, Jacob J considered that such exceptions had to be adopted by Member States and did not encompass judge-made exceptions, such as the common law 'right to repair' or 'spare parts' exception that originated in *British Leyland v Armstrong*, and was subsequently narrowed by the Privy Council in *Canon Kabushiki Kaisha v Green Cartridge*. In relation to Article 6(2)(d) of the Database Directive, Jacob J commented—

that provision is an option for Member States to adopt by way of limitation of database rights. It can hardly be for the judges of a particular Member State of their own to act as though they are exercising the option on behalf of that State. If Parliament had wanted to adopt an option

> in relation to the use of database rights for updating equipment, that is a matter for it, not the judges. I cannot regard section 173(2) [sic] as adopting such an option. Moreover it is far from certainly the case that the use of copyright in databases (which, before the Directive, were generally protected in the UK as literary works in the form of compilations) was 'traditionally authorised' in this country.
>
> Jacob J's comments about Article 6(2)(d), strictly speaking, are obiter dicta since the case concerned the applicability of the 'spare parts' defence to the *database right* and Article 6(2)(d) relates only to copyright databases.

Would you agree with the comments made in the above extract about the scope of exceptions in Article 6(2)(a)–(b) of the Database Directive? If so, how would you seek to broaden the scope of these exceptions?

4.3.9 THE RELATIONSHIP OF EXCEPTIONS TO TECHNOLOGICAL PROTECTION MEASURES

4.3.9.1 Introduction

As a means of helping to enforce copyright, online rightholders have resorted to using digital 'locks', otherwise known as technological protection measures (TPMs). Various types of TPM can be used, ranging from passwords, to encryption, to copy-protection software. What they have in common is the aim of controlling unauthorized copying and/or distribution of copyright works in digital form. TPMs, however, can and have been circumvented. Therefore, copyright owners looked to bolster the practical obstacle of digital 'locks' with a legal obstacle, namely the prohibition of circumvention and circumvention means. This was achieved via Article 11 of the WCT and Article 18 of the WPPT.

Article 11 of the WCT provides:

> Contracting Parties shall provide adequate legal protection and effective legal remedies against the circumvention of effective technological measures that are used by authors in connection with the exercise of their rights under this Treaty or the Berne Convention and that restrict acts, in respect of their works, which are not authorized by the authors concerned or permitted by law.

Article 18 of the WPPT is in virtually identical terms, except that it refers to performers and their performances and phonogram producers and their phonograms. The language of Article 11 of the WCT and Article 18 of the WPPT is broad, thus permitting signatories a wide discretion as to how to implement their obligations. In particular, the WIPO treaties' provisions are ambiguous about how any anti-circumvention provisions will relate to copyright exceptions. Will it be possible to circumvent TPMs in order to carry out exceptions or not? Certainly, there have been divergent approaches to implementing these provisions, including the interface between TPMs and exceptions. We turn now to examine the EU position.

4.3.9.2 EU position

Article 6 of the Information Society Directive implements the above obligations in the WCT and WPPT. Article 6(1)–(2) obliges Member States to provide adequate legal protection against circumvention of any effective technological measure and 'trafficking' in circumvention devices or services.

A 'technological measure' is defined by Article 6(3) to mean:

> Any technology, device or component that, in the normal course of its operation, is designed to prevent or restrict acts, in respect of works or other subject-matter, which are not authorised by the rightholder of any copyright or any right related to copyright as provided for by law or the *sui generis* right provided for in Chapter III of Directive 96/9/EC.

Article 6(3) goes on to state that technological measures shall be deemed 'effective':

> where the use of a protected work or other subject-matter is controlled by the rightholders through application of an access control or protection process, such as encryption, scrambling or other transformation of the work or other subject-matter or a copy control mechanism, which achieves the protection objective.

Thus, a 'technological measure' appears to include access control and copy-protection technology. This is implicit in Article 6(3) which refers to 'any technology ... designed to prevent or restrict acts'. Further, in defining 'effective', Article 6(3) explicitly refers to an access control process and copy control mechanism.

In *Nintendo Co. Ltd v PC Box Srl*,[133] the CJEU had occasion to consider the meaning of 'effective technological measure' in Article 6(3) of the Information Society Directive. In this case, Nintendo had installed a recognition system in its videogame consoles and applied an encrypted code onto the housing of the videogames. These measures were designed to interact in order to prevent unlawful copies of Nintendo videogames from being played on the consoles. PC Box sold equipment that allowed the Nintendo protection system to be circumvented and claimed that it enabled lawful independent software to be played on Nintendo consoles. Following a reference from the Milan District Court, the CJEU ruled that the concept of 'effective technological measures' is defined broadly and includes measures such as those utilized in this case, i.e. partly within the housing of the videogames and partly in the games consoles. However, the Court went on to stress that Article 6(3) only grants legal protection to technological measures which aim to restrict or eliminate acts not authorized by the rightholder and, as such, '[t]hose measures must be suitable for achieving that objective and must not go beyond what is necessary for this purpose'.[134] It was for the referring court to make this assessment, taking into account whether other measures could have caused less interference with the legitimate activities of third parties (such as playing independent software on the consoles) and the relative costs of these different measures and their comparative effectiveness.[135]

Article 6(1) obligates Member States to 'provide adequate legal protection against the circumvention of any effective technological measures' in situations where the person carries out the circumvention with actual or constructive knowledge that she is pursuing that objective. It is clear that circumvention of both access control and copy control measures is prohibited.

---

[133] Case C-355/12 [2014] ECDR 6.   [134] [31].   [135] [32]–[36].

Article 6(2) obligates Member States to prohibit the 'trafficking' in circumvention devices or services. Specifically, it states:

> Member States shall provide adequate legal protection against the manufacture, import, distribution, sale, rental, advertisement for sale or rental, or possession for commercial purposes of devices, products or components or the provision of services which:
>
> (a) are promoted, advertised or marketed for the purpose of circumvention of, or
>
> (b) have only a limited commercially significant purpose or use other than to circumvent, or
>
> (c) are primarily designed, produced, adapted or performed for the purpose of enabling or facilitating the circumvention of,
>
> any effective technological measures.

Unlike the prohibition against circumvention per se, the above prohibition against 'trafficking' in circumvention devices or services does not contain a knowledge requirement. Article 6(2) also targets those devices or services that have circumvention as their primary or commercial purpose (as opposed to sole intended purpose).

Importantly, Article 6(1)–(2) applies to copyright works *other than computer programs* and databases protected by the *sui generis* right. This creates a disparity in the regulation of TPMs as applied to computer programs and those applied to other works. This is because Article 7(1)(c) of the Software Directive does not prohibit circumvention per se and prohibits commercially dealing in circumvention devices or services whose *sole intended purpose* is to facilitate circumvention and where there is actual or constructive knowledge. Although this inconsistency has been criticized by commentators, the European Commission has no intention of amending Article 7 of the Software Directive until more experience has been gained from application of Article 6 of the Information Society Directive.[136] However, this disparity may not matter as much after the above ruling in *Nintendo*, where the CJEU acknowledged that Article 6 of the Information Society Directive was applicable to videogames, even though they incorporated computer programs, because videogames were complex products that included other works, such as graphic and sound elements.[137]

A major concern, and one that almost brought the adoption of the Information Society Directive to a halt, is the extent to which TPMs may override copyright exceptions. More specifically, should it be the case that circumvention of TPMs is unlawful, even where it is done for the purpose of carrying out an act that is excused by one of the exceptions? The solution to this clash of interests was to insert Article 6(4), which provides:

> 4. Notwithstanding the legal protection provided for in *paragraph 1, in the absence of voluntary measures taken by rightholders, including agreements* between rightholders and other parties concerned, Member States *shall take appropriate measures* to ensure that rightholders make available to the beneficiary of an exception or limitation provided for in national law in accordance with *Article 5(2)(a), (2)(c), (2)(d), (2)(e), (3)(a), (3)(b) or (3)(e) the means of benefiting from that exception or limitation*, to the extent necessary to benefit from that exception or limitation and *where that beneficiary has legal access to* the protected work or subject-matter concerned.

---

[136] *Commission Staff Working Paper on the review of the EC legal framework in the field of copyright and related rights*, Brussels, 19 July 2004, SEC (2004) 995, para. 2.2.1.4.

[137] [23].

A Member State *may* also take such measures in respect of a beneficiary of an exception or limitation provided for in accordance with *Article 5(2)(b)*, unless reproduction for private use has already been made possible by rightholders to the extent necessary to benefit from the exception or limitation concerned and in accordance with the provisions of Article 5(2)(b) and (5), without preventing rightholders from adopting adequate measures regarding the number of reproductions in accordance with these provisions.

The technological measures applied voluntarily by rightholders, including those applied in implementation of voluntary agreements, and technological measures applied in implementation of the measures taken by Member States, shall enjoy the legal protection provided for in paragraph 1.

The provisions of the first and second subparagraphs shall not apply to works or other subject-matter made available to the public on agreed contractual terms in such a way that members of the public may access them from a place and at a time individually chosen by them.

When this Article is applied in the context of Directives 92/100/EEC and 96/9/EC, this paragraph shall apply *mutatis mutandis*. [Emphasis supplied]

Article 6(4) does not create exceptions that an alleged infringer can rely upon to exclude liability for circumvention of technological measures. Instead, it introduces 'a unique legislative mechanism which foresees an ultimate responsibility on the rightsholders to accommodate certain exceptions to copyright or related rights'.[138]

Sub-paragraph (1) of Article 6(4) imposes a mandatory obligation on Member States. However, this only applies in relation to persons seeking to circumvent technological measures and *not* in relation to persons 'trafficking' in circumvention devices or services. Further, the obligation arises only in the *absence of voluntary measures* taken by rightsholders. Article 6(4) and recital 51 of the Information Society Directive indicate that voluntary measures include 'agreements' between rightsholders and other parties concerned. Apart from agreements, however, it is unclear what else might constitute a 'voluntary measure'. Recital 51 also indicates that Member States do not have an obligation to adopt appropriate measures *unless* a rightsholder has failed to take voluntary measures within a 'reasonable period' of time. What constitutes a 'reasonable period' is also unclear.

The obligation on Member States imposed by sub-paragraph 1 of Article 6(4) only relates to *specific* exceptions listed in Article 5(2)–(3) (assuming they exist in the law of the respective Member State) and not to all exceptions. These exceptions are: reproductions on paper and any similar medium (Article 5(2)(a)); specific acts of reproduction by libraries, educational establishments, museums, or archives (Article 5(2)(b)); ephemeral recording by broadcasting organizations (Article 5(2)(c)); reproduction of broadcasts made by certain social institutions (Article 5(2)(e)); use for illustration for teaching or scientific research (Article 5(3)(a)); use for the benefit of people with disability (Article 5(3)(b)); and use for the purposes of public security or for administrative, parliamentary, or judicial proceedings (Article 5(3)(e)). The basis upon which these seven exceptions have been singled out as important matters of public policy has not been made clear, nor why the remaining exceptions listed under Article 5(2)–(3) have been omitted. This is particularly a concern since Member States are not under any obligation to ensure that beneficiaries of the remaining

---

[138] N. Braun, 'The interface between the protection of technological measures and the exercise of exceptions to copyright and related rights: comparing the situation in the United States and the European Community' [2003] EIPR 496, 499.

exceptions or limitations can benefit from them. Indeed, it is arguable that a natural reading of Article 6(4) is that Member States would not be permitted to assist beneficiaries in respect of the exceptions omitted from sub-paragraphs (1) and (2).

Article 6(4), sub-paragraph (1) obligates Member States to *take appropriate measures* to ensure that rightsholders make available, to the beneficiary of the listed specific exception or limitation, the *means* of benefiting from it. The Information Society Directive is not particularly illuminating on what will constitute 'appropriate measures' and 'means', although recital 51 indicates that 'means' could include modifying an implemented technological measure.

Finally, sub-paragraph (1) of Article 6(4) emphasizes that the beneficiary of a specific exception or limitation must have *legal access* to the protected work or subject matter. This requirement indicates that the obligation on a Member State to take appropriate measures exists only in relation to *copy control* measures and not access control measures. This undoubtedly reduces the value of Article 6(4) to those where lack of access stands in the way of relying upon copyright exceptions.

The scheme described above is narrowed considerably by sub-paragraph (4) of Article 6(4). This is because it stipulates that the obligation under sub-paragraph (1) and the discretion under sub-paragraph (2) shall not apply 'to works or other subject-matter made available to the public on *agreed contractual terms* in such a way that members of the public may access them from a place and at a time individually chosen by them' (emphasis supplied). Recital 53 indicates that the exclusion relates to where interactive on-demand services are governed by contractual arrangements. Thus, the assistance created by Article 6(4), sub-paragraphs (1) and (2) can be potentially overridden by the use of click-wrap and browse-through licences.

Article 6(4) represents one model of balancing the interests of owners who wish to utilize TPMs and users who wish to rely on copyright exceptions. Having considered its scope, would you agree that it is a desirable model? Alternative models are available. These include: (1) leaving the use of TPMs completely unregulated; (2) permitting the sale of circumvention devices or services, but punishing those persons who use such devices to infringe copyright; (3) prohibiting the manufacture and sale of circumvention devices, but allowing individual users to circumvent TPMs; or (4) regulating TPMs but creating a list of exceptions to circumvention or trafficking in circumvention devices (as in the US). What would be the advantages or disadvantages of these alternative models? Here, it is important to consider whether they would comply with the WCT and WPPT and also whether the correct balance between owner and user interests would be struck. As well, we might note that because Article 6(4) has been implemented in various ways in different Member States, it has created rather a loose harmonization of the way in which copyright owners' and users' interests are balanced when TPMs are applied to copyright works and *sui generis* databases.

4.3.9.3 UK position

In the UK, the Copyright and Related Rights Regulations 2003[139] inserted new sections 296ZA to 296ZF in the CDPA to implement Article 6 of the Information Society Directive.

Here it is interesting to note the way in which the UK has implemented Article 6(4), which governs the relationship between exceptions and TPMs. This has occurred via section 296ZE

---

[139] SI 2003/2498.

of and Schedule 5A to the CDPA. According to section 296ZE, where the application of any effective technological measure to a copyright work prevents a person from carrying out a permitted act then that person, or a person representative of a class of persons prevented from carrying out a permitted act, may issue a notice of complaint to the Secretary of State. A 'permitted act' is an act which may be done in relation to copyright works by virtue of a provision in the CDPA listed in Part 1 of Schedule 5A. Upon receiving a notice of complaint, the Secretary of State may give relevant directions to the copyright owner, for the purpose of establishing whether any voluntary measure or agreement subsists in relation to the copyright work under complaint. Where it is established that there is no subsisting voluntary measure or agreement, the Secretary of State may give relevant directions ensuring that the copyright owner or exclusive licensee makes available to the complainant the means of carrying out the permitted act to the extent necessary to so benefit from it. The Secretary of State may also give directions as to the form and manner in which the notice of complaint, or evidence of any voluntary measure, may be delivered to him, and generally as to the procedure to be followed in relation to a complaint made under section 296ZE. Directions given by the Secretary of State under this provision must be in writing and may be varied or revoked by a subsequent direction under this provision.

FURTHER READING

N. Braun, 'The interface between the protection of technological measures and the exercise of exceptions to copyright and related rights: comparing the situation in the United States and the European Community' [2003] EIPR 496.

S. Dusollier, 'Exceptions and technological measures in the European Copyright Directive of 2001: an empty promise' (2003) 34 IIC 62.

S. Dusollier, 'The protection of technological measures: much ado about nothing or silent remodeling of copyright?' in R. C. Dreyfuss and J. C. Ginsburg (eds), *Intellectual Property at the Edge: The Contested Contours of IP* (Cambridge: Cambridge University Press, 2014), ch. 12, 253–67.

M. Favale, 'Approximation and DRM: can digital locks respect copyright exceptions?' (2011) 19 IJL & IT 306.

4.4 DATABASE RIGHT

4.4.1 INTRODUCTION

As well as harmonizing copyright protection of databases, the Database Directive introduced a new *sui generis* right for databases. This 'database right' was implemented in the UK via the Copyright and Rights in Databases Regulations 1997.[140] As the recitals to the directive indicate,[141] databases were seen as vital components of an information market within the Community, but vulnerable to piracy. Protection additional to that offered by copyright was thought necessary in order to prevent the unauthorized extraction and reuse of database contents and hence to safeguard the considerable investment required to produce databases. It was seen as particularly important to encourage this type of investment because of

---

[140] SI 1997/3032.   [141] See especially recitals 6–12, 38–40.

the 'very great imbalance in the level of investment in the database sector both as between the Member States and between the Community and the world's largest database-producing third countries'.[142] A *sui generis* right was adopted as the form of protection, rather than unfair competition law, because of the difficulties of harmonizing the law of unfair competition (not least because some countries, such as the UK and Ireland, do not have this type of protection). Thus, it is now the case that a database may be protected both by copyright *and* the *sui generis* right and this protection is irrespective of the eligibility of individual contents for protection by copyright or related rights.[143] Copyright protects the selection or arrangement of the contents in a database, while the *sui generis* right protects the contents of the database as a whole.

4.4.2 REQUIREMENTS FOR PROTECTION

The definition of 'database' is the same for the *sui generis* right as it is for copyright.[144] As such, the scope of that definition, previously discussed at 2.5.1.2.3, also applies here.

Chapter III of the Database Directive sets out the *sui generis* right. According to Article 7(1), the maker of a database only acquires the right where there has been 'qualitatively and/or quantitatively a substantial investment in either the obtaining, verification or presentation of the contents'. Where that threshold is met, the *maker* of the database will have the right to prevent extraction and/or reutilization of the whole or a substantial part of the database contents.

The exact nature of the threshold requirement of substantial investment and so on has been the source of uncertainty and so it was that several references on the same issue were made to the CJEU.[145] For our purposes, it suffices to focus on the reference from the Court of Appeal, which is dealt with below.

British Horseracing Board Ltd v William Hill Organization Ltd
Case C-203/02 [2004] ECR I-10415

The British Horseracing Board (BHB) is the governing authority for the British racing industry, formed in 1993. Its functions include compiling data related to horseracing, establishing the dates and programme contents for race fixtures, and creating the fixture list for each year's racing. William Hill is one of the leading providers of off-course betting services in the UK and elsewhere and mainly provides fixed-odds bets on sporting and other events from its licensed betting offices. It also provides online betting services.

Racing information in the BHB database was distributed in two main ways. First, via a company called Racing Pages Ltd, which operated a declarations feed. The declarations feed contained a list of races, declared runners and jockeys, distance and name of races, race times, and number of runners in each race together with other information

---

[142] Recital 11.   [143] Database Directive, Art. 7(4).   [144] Database Directive, Art. 1(2).
[145] *Fixtures Marketing Ltd v Svenska Spel AB* Case C-338/02 [2004] ECR I-10497; *Fixtures Marketing Ltd v Organismos prognostikon agnon podosfairou AE (OPAP)* Case C-444/02 [2004] ECR I-10549; *Fixtures Marketing Ltd v Oy Veikkaus Ab* Case C-46/02 [2004] ECR I-10365; *British Horseracing Board Ltd v William Hill Organization Ltd* Case C-203/02 [2004] ECR I-10415.

and this data was forwarded to subscribers usually the day before the race. The second form of distribution was via Satellite Information Services, a subscriber of Racing Pages, who supplied this data to its own subscribers in the form of a raw-data feed. William Hill subscribed to both the declarations feed and the raw-data feed, for the purpose of its betting operations from its licensed betting offices.

The dispute arose from William Hill's use of data from the raw-data feed in relation to its online betting services. BHB claimed that William Hill's activities amounted to unauthorized extraction or reutilization of a substantial part of the contents of its database, contrary to Article 7(1), or else repeated and systematic extraction or reutilization of insubstantial parts of the contents contrary to Article 7(5). BHB succeeded in the High Court before Laddie J.[146] The Court of Appeal referred a series of questions to the ECJ for interpretation.[147]

28. By its second and third questions the referring court seeks clarification of the concept of investment in the obtaining and verification of the contents of a database within the meaning of Art. 7(1) of the directive.

29. Article 7(1) of the directive reserves the protection of the *sui generis* right to databases which meet a specific criterion, namely to those which show that there has been qualitatively and/or quantitatively a substantial investment in the obtaining, verification or presentation of their contents.

30. Under the 9th, 10th and 12th recitals of the preamble to the directive, its purpose, as William Hill points out, is to promote and protect investment in data 'storage' and 'processing' systems which contribute to the development of an information market against a background of exponential growth in the amount of information generated and processed annually in all sectors of activity. It follows that the expression 'investment in … the obtaining, verification or presentation of the contents' of a database must be understood, generally, to refer to investment in the creation of that database as such.

31. Against that background, the expression 'investment in … the obtaining … of the contents' of a database must, as William Hill and the Belgian, German and Portuguese Governments point out, be understood to refer to the resources used to seek out existing independent materials and collect them in the database, and not to the resources used for the creation as such of independent materials. The purpose of the protection by the *sui generis* right provided for by the directive is to promote the establishment of storage and processing systems for existing information and not the creation of materials capable of being collected subsequently in a database.

32. That interpretation is backed up by the 39th recital of the preamble to the directive, according to which the aim of the *sui generis* right is to safeguard the results of the financial and professional investment made in 'obtaining and collection of the contents' of a database. As the Advocate General notes in points AG41 to AG46 of her Opinion, despite slight variations in wording, all the language versions of the 39th recital support an interpretation which excludes the creation of the materials contained in a database from the definition of obtaining.

33. The 19th recital of the preamble to the directive, according to which the compilation of several recordings of musical performances on a CD does not represent a substantial enough

---

[146] *British Horseracing Board Ltd v William Hill Organization Ltd* [2001] CMLR 12.
[147] *British Horseracing Board Ltd v William Hill Organization Ltd* [2002] ECDR 4.

investment to be eligible under the *sui generis* right, provides an additional argument in support of that interpretation. Indeed, it appears from that recital that the resources used for the creation as such of works or materials included in the database, in this case on a CD, cannot be deemed equivalent to investment in the obtaining of the contents of that database and cannot, therefore, be taken into account in assessing whether the investment in the creation of the database was substantial.

34. The expression 'investment in … the … verification … of the contents' of a database must be understood to refer to the resources used, with a view to ensuring the reliability of the information contained in that database, to monitor the accuracy of the materials collected when the database was created and during its operation. The resources used for verification during the stage of creation of data or other materials which are subsequently collected in a database, on the other hand, are resources used in creating a database and cannot therefore be taken into account in order to assess whether there was substantial investment in the terms of Art. 7(1) of the directive.

35. In that light, the fact that the creation of a database is linked to the exercise of a principal activity in which the person creating the database is also the creator of the materials contained in the database does not, as such, preclude that person from claiming the protection of the *sui generis* right, provided that he establishes that the obtaining of those materials, their verification or their presentation, in the sense described in [31] to [34] of this judgment, required substantial investment in quantitative or qualitative terms, which was independent of the resources used to create those materials.

36. Thus, although the search for data and the verification of their accuracy at the time a database is created do not require the maker of that database to use particular resources because the data are those he created and are available to him, the fact remains that the collection of those data, their systematic or methodical arrangement in the database, the organisation of their individual accessibility and the verification of their accuracy throughout the operation of the database may require substantial investment in quantitative and/or qualitative terms within the meaning of Art. 7(1) of the directive.

37. In the case in the main proceedings, the referring court seeks to know whether the investments described in [14] of this judgment can be considered to amount to investment in obtaining the contents of the BHB database. The plaintiffs in the main proceedings stress, in that connection, the substantial nature of the above investment.

38. However, investment in the selection, for the purpose of organising horse racing, of the horses admitted to run in the race concerned relates to the creation of the data which make up the lists for those races which appear in the BHB database. It does not constitute investment in obtaining the contents of the database. It cannot, therefore, be taken into account in assessing whether the investment in the creation of the database was substantial.

39. Admittedly, the process of entering a horse on a list for a race requires a number of prior checks as to the identity of the person making the entry, the characteristics of the horse and the classification of the horse, its owner and the jockey.

40. However, such prior checks are made at the stage of creating the list for the race in question. They thus constitute investment in the creation of data and not in the verification of the contents of the database.

41. It follows that the resources used to draw up a list of horses in a race and to carry out checks in that connection do not represent investment in the obtaining and verification of the contents of the database in which that list appears.

Do you agree with the distinction made by the Court between investment in creating data (which is irrelevant) and investment in obtaining or verifying existing data (which is relevant)? Will this be a straightforward distinction to apply in practice? According to Jacob LJ in *Football Dataco v Sportradar*,[148] a database of 'live' information about football matches in English and Scottish leagues, which cost approximately £600,000 per season to operate, was protected. He rejected the defendants' submission that this substantial investment was of the wrong kind because it was directed to creation of data. In particular, Jacob LJ was dismissive of the argument that the act of recording a fact is an act of creation. Jacob LJ observed:

> the factual data provided by the FBA [football analyst] to the SIP [sports information processor] and then recorded by the SIP (sometimes after some conversation to verify its accuracy) in [the claimant's] database is pre-existing data. Only a metaphysicist would say a goal is not scored until the FBA tells the SIP that it has been scored…I am entirely confident that a scientist who takes a measurement would be astonished to be told that she was creating data. She would say she is creating a record of pre-existing fact, recording data, not creating it.[149]

After reviewing the directive, relevant case law, and scholarly writing Jacob LJ added:

> I do not think this Directive is concerned with deep abstract aspects of informational theory or that the Court would consider it to be so concerned. The Directive is concerned with creating a commercial right so as to encourage the creation of valuable databases. There is no realistic chance of the Court striking down the many large database protected industries of Europe on the grounds that they consist of objective information recorded for the first time by their creators.[150]

In terms of investment in the presentation of contents, this issue was not addressed in *British Horseracing*, but it was dealt with in the other three references to the CJEU. The Court held in *Fixtures Marketing v Svenska, Fixtures Marketing v OPAP*, and *Fixtures Marketing v Veikkaus*, that investment in presentation of the database contents refers to 'the resources used for the purpose of giving the database its function of processing information, that is to say those used for the systematic or methodical arrangement of the materials contained in that database and the organization of their individual accessibility'.[151] The Court held that in relation to the database in issue, i.e. football fixtures, there was no relevant investment because the presentation of the list was too closely linked to the creation of the data.[152]

An issue that none of the above rulings addressed is, what constitutes *substantial* investment? The Advocate General in her Opinion in *Fixtures Marketing v Svenska* took the view that substantial investment should be construed in relative terms 'first in relation to costs and their redemption and second in relation to the scale, nature and contents of the database and the sector to which it belongs'.[153] However, the Advocate General went on to explain that 'the criterion "substantial" cannot be construed only in relative terms.

---

[148] [2013] EWCA Civ 27, [2013] 2 CMLR 36. Lewison and Lloyd LJJ were in agreement.
[149] [39].   [150] [60].   [151] *Svenska*, [27]; *OPAP*, [43]; *Veikkaus*, [37].
[152] *Svenska*, [35]; *OPAP*, [51]; *Veikkaus*, [46].
[153] *Fixtures Marketing Ltd v Svenska Spel AB* C-338/02, Opinion of the Advocate General delivered on 8 June 2004, [38].

The directive requires an absolute lower threshold for investments worthy of protection as a sort of *de minimis* rule. That is implied by the 19th recital, according to which the investment must be "substantial enough".[154] Further, that this threshold should be set at a low level, consistent with the purpose of the directive to create incentives for investment in databases. In its ruling in *Svenska*, the CJEU observed that 'the quantitative assessment refers to quantifiable resources and the qualitative assessment to efforts which cannot be quantified, such as intellectual effort and energy, according to the 7th, 39th and 40th recitals'.[155] Unfortunately, however, the Court did not express any views on whether substantial investment is to be measured in absolute or relative terms or whether the threshold of investment is low or high. In your view, what would be the preferable approach bearing in mind the objectives of the directive?

4.4.3 OWNERSHIP

When it comes to ownership of the *sui generis* right, this lies with the maker of a database who, according to recital 41 of the Database Directive, is 'the person who takes the initiative and the risk of investing'. The directive is silent on the position of employees. However, regulation 14(2) of the UK Database Regulations provides that the employer shall be regarded as the maker of the database where it is made by an employee in the course of employment.

Importantly, Article 11 of the Database Directive imposes territorial qualifications on makers (or rightsholders) of databases. A maker or rightsholder must be a national of a Member State or else have their habitual residence in the EU. Where the maker or rightsholder is a company formed in accordance with the law of a Member State, their registered office, central administration, or principal place of business must be within the EU. What is the purpose of this territorial requirement and whom does it benefit? Further, what is the position of those database makers that fail to meet the requirement? Article 11(3), read in conjunction with recital 56, is helpful on this latter point. The *sui generis* right can be extended by the European Council to databases made in countries that are not Member States where those countries provide 'comparable protection' to databases made by EU nationals or those habitually resident in the EU. In other words, the *sui generis* right, unlike copyright, is not subject to the principle of national treatment but instead is based on the principle of material reciprocity. Where a country such as the US protects its databases only by copyright law, what is the impact do you think of the territorial requirement plus material reciprocity rule?

4.4.4 SCOPE OF PROTECTION

What are the rights given to the database maker? According to Article 7(1), it is the right to prevent unauthorized extraction or reutilization of the whole or substantial part of the database contents. Article 7(2)(a) of the Database Directive defines 'extraction' to mean:

> the permanent or temporary transfer of all or a substantial part of the contents of a database to another medium by any means or in any form.

---

[154] *Svenska*, [39].   [155] [28].

'Reutilization' is defined in the same provision to mean:

> Any form of making available to the public all or a substantial part of the contents of a database by the distribution of copies, by renting, by on-line or other forms of transmission. The first sale of a copy of a database within the Community by the rightholder or with this consent shall exhaust the right to control resale of that copy within the Community.

Questions regarding the scope of the above rights were referred to the CJEU in *British Horseracing*, so we turn once again to the ruling in that case.

British Horseracing Board Ltd v William Hill Organization Ltd Case C-203/02 [2004] ECR I-10415

For the facts, see 4.4.2.

Note that the Court of Appeal referred questions to the CJEU as to whether extraction includes indirect transfer of the database contents and whether reutilization includes making available to the public the contents of the database indirectly from the database. These questions arose because the defendant had obtained the racing fixtures data indirectly via newspapers published the day before the race and via the raw-data feed from one of BHB's licensed distributors.

The Court of Appeal also referred questions about the meaning of 'substantial part, evaluated qualitatively and/or qualitatively, of the contents' of the database.

Judgment of the Court (Grand Chamber):

45. The terms extraction and re-utilisation must be interpreted in the light of the objective pursued by the *sui generis* right. It is intended to protect the maker of the database against 'acts by the user which go beyond [the] legitimate rights and thereby harm the investment' of the maker, as indicated in the 42nd recital of the preamble to the directive.

46. According to the 48th recital of the preamble to the directive, the *sui generis* right has an economic justification, which is to afford protection to the maker of the database and guarantee a return on his investment in the creation and maintenance of the database.

...

49. In Art. 7(2)(a) of the directive, extraction is defined as 'the permanent or temporary transfer of all or a substantial part of the contents of a database to another medium by any means or in any form', while in Art. 7(2)(b), re-utilisation is defined as 'any form of making available to the public all or a substantial part of the contents of a database by the distribution of copies, by renting, by on-line or other forms of transmission'.

50. The reference to 'a substantial part' in the definition of the concepts of extraction and re-utilisation gives rise to confusion given that, according to Art. 7(5) of the directive, extraction or re-utilisation may also concern an insubstantial part of a database. As the Advocate General observes, in point AG90 of her Opinion, the reference, in Art. 7(2) of the Directive, to the substantial nature of the extracted or re-utilised part does not concern the definition of those concepts as such but must be understood to refer to one of the conditions for the application of the *sui generis* right laid down by Art. 7(1) of the directive.

51. The use of expressions such as 'by any means or in any form' and 'any form of making available to the public' indicates that the Community legislature intended to give the concepts of extraction and re-utilisation a wide definition. In the light of the objective pursued by the directive, those terms must therefore be interpreted as referring to any act of appropriating and making available to the public, without the consent of the maker of the database, the results of his investment, thus depriving him of revenue which should have enabled him to redeem the cost of the investment.

52. Against that background, and contrary to the argument put forward by William Hill and the Belgian and Portuguese Governments, the concepts of extraction and re-utilisation cannot be exhaustively defined as instances of extraction and re-utilisation directly from the original database at the risk of leaving the maker of the database without protection from unauthorised copying from a copy of the database. That interpretation is confirmed by Art. 7(2)(b) of the directive, according to which the first sale of a copy of a database within the Community by the rightholder or with his consent is to exhaust the right to control 'resale', but not the right to control extraction and re-utilisation of the contents, of that copy within the Community.

53. Since acts of unauthorised extraction and/or re-utilisation by a third party from a source other than the database concerned are liable, just as much as such acts carried out directly from that database are, to prejudice the investment of the maker of the database, it must be held that the concepts of extraction and re-utilisation do not imply direct access to the database concerned.

...

68. By its fourth, fifth and sixth questions, the referring court raises the question of the meaning of the terms 'substantial part' and 'insubstantial part' of the contents of a database as used in Art. 7 of the directive. By its first question it also seeks to know whether materials derived from a database do not constitute a part, substantial or otherwise, of that database, where their systematic or methodical arrangement and the conditions of their individual accessibility have been altered by the person carrying out the extraction and/or re-utilisation.

69. In that connection, it must be borne in mind that protection by the *sui generis* right covers databases whose creation required a substantial investment. Against that background, Art. 7(1) of the directive prohibits extraction and/or re-utilisation not only of the whole of a database protected by the *sui generis* right but also of a substantial part, evaluated qualitatively or quantitatively, of its contents. According to the 42nd recital of the preamble to the directive, that provision is intended to prevent a situation in which a user 'through his acts, causes significant detriment, evaluated qualitatively or quantitatively, to the investment'. It appears from that recital that the assessment, in qualitative terms, of whether the part at issue is substantial, must, like the assessment in quantitative terms, refer to the investment in the creation of the database and the prejudice caused to that investment by the act of extracting or re-utilising that part.

70. The expression 'substantial part, evaluated quantitatively', of the contents of a database within the meaning of Art. 7(1) of the directive refers to the volume of data extracted from the database and/or re-utilised, and must be assessed in relation to the volume of the contents of the whole of that database. If a user extracts and/or re-utilises a quantitatively significant part of the contents of a database whose creation required the deployment of substantial resources, the investment in the extracted or re-utilised part is, proportionately, equally substantial.

71. The expression 'substantial part, evaluated qualitatively', of the contents of a database refers to the scale of the investment in the obtaining, verification or presentation of the contents of the subject of the act of extraction and/or re-utilisation, regardless of whether that subject represents a quantitatively substantial part of the general contents of the protected database. A quantitatively negligible part of the contents of a database may in fact represent, in terms of obtaining, verification or presentation, significant human, technical or financial investment.

72. It must be added that, as the existence of the *sui generis* right does not, according to the 46th recital of the preamble to the directive, give rise to the creation of a new right in the works, data or materials themselves, the intrinsic value of the materials affected by the act of extraction and/or re-utilisation does not constitute a relevant criterion for the assessment of whether the part at issue is substantial.

73. It must be held that any part which does not fulfil the definition of a substantial part, evaluated both quantitatively and qualitatively, falls within the definition of an insubstantial part of the contents of a database.

The CJEU indicated that the activities carried on by William Hill did amount to extraction and reutilization, but that they did not relate to a substantial part of the contents of the database. This was because extracting and reusing the names of the horses in the race, the details of the race, and the name of the racecourse, represented a very small proportion of the whole of the BHB database. Further, the resources used to establish this data represented an investment in the *creation* of data and thus had to be ignored. As such, the data extracted and reused could not represent a qualitatively substantial part of the BHB database (even though the data was incredibly useful to William Hill).

Is the Court's ruling that 'extraction' and 'reutilization' is not limited to direct access to the database a sensible one? In particular, is this interpretation consistent with the language and objective of the Database Directive? What about the Court's approach to determining 'substantial part', particularly in qualitative terms? Does it make sense to link the notion of substantial part with the notion of substantial investment, as opposed to looking at the intrinsic value of the materials that have been extracted or reutilized? Is this reminiscent of an approach that we have dealt with so far?

A more recent ruling has further elaborated upon the scope of the 'extraction' right. In *Directmedia Publishing GmbH v Albert-Ludwigs-Universität Freiburg*,[156] a list of verse titles, known as the 'The 1,100 most important poems in German literature between 1730 and 1900', had been drawn up as part of the 'Vocabulary of the Classics' project directed by Professor Knoop of the University of Freiburg. DirectMedia marketed a CD-Rom, '1000 poems everyone should have' in which 856 of the poems included were also featured in the claimant's list. In selecting the poems for inclusion on its CD-Rom, DirectMedia had consulted the claimant's list of titles, but used additional selection criteria in deciding whether to include a poem. The Bundesgerichtshof (German Federal Supreme Court) referred a question to the ECJ on the meaning of 'extraction', in particular whether it covered transfer of data following individual assessments resulting from consultation of the database or was limited to physical copying of data. The Court held that a broad construction of 'extraction' was supported by the objectives of introducing a *sui generis* right. Further, that it was

---

[156] Case C-304/07 [2009] 1 CMLR 7.

immaterial whether the transfer of contents is based on a technical process of copying or simply a manual process, since the latter type of copying could be equally as harmful to the interests of the database maker. Where a person transferred data to another database only after a critical assessment of whether to include it did not prevent this from being 'extraction', but rather went to determining the eligibility of that other database for protection. Finally, the ECJ addressed the arguments that a broad construction of 'extraction' would limit the ability freely to access information and could lead to abusive monopolies on the part of database makers. It held that the *sui generis* right does not prevent third parties from consulting a database for information purposes only and that the rules of competition law would regulate any abusive monopolies. Thus, the CJEU ruled that 'extraction' did include transfer of material from a protected database to another database following an on-screen consultation of the first database and an individual assessment of the material contained in that first database.

The CJEU in *Football Dataco v Sportradar*[157] has also pronounced upon the scope of the reutilization right, specifically where an act of making database contents available to the public occurs. The Court ruled that the mere fact that a website containing data is accessible in a particular national territory is not enough to establish that the database contents are made available to the public. Rather, there must be evidence from which to conclude that there was an intention to target persons in that territory for the purposes of determining where the act of making available to the public occurs.[158]

The ruling in *Innoweb v Wegener* also signals a broad interpretation of the reutilization right. The claimants (Wegener) operated a website (the Autotrack website) featuring car advertisements, which users could search. Approximately 40,000 of the 200,000 advertisements featured were solely available on Autotrack. The defendant (Innoweb) offered via its website (GasPedaal) a meta search engine, which sent user queries to search engines on third party sites. This enabled users to search several websites with car advertisements (including Autotrack) at the same time. On a daily basis, GasPedaal carried out approximately 100,000 searches on the Autotrack website, but only displayed a small part of the contents of the collection. The CJEU was asked to rule on whether the defendants had reutilized a substantial part of the claimants' database by virtue of making it possible to search the whole or a substantial part of the contents of a database in real time. The Court emphasized that 'reutilization' should be given a broad construction[159] and held that it included 'any act of making available to the public, without the consent of the database maker, the results of his investment, thus depriving him of revenue which should have enabled him to redeem the cost of the investment'.[160] The Court went on to note that the defendant's website enabled the end user to search the entire contents of the claimant's database and that this created a risk that the claimant would lose income, in particular advertising revenue, which would affect its ability to redeem the cost of the investment in setting up and maintaining the database.[161] Moreover, the CJEU saw the defendant as having created what came close to a 'parasitical competing product ... albeit without copying the information stored in the database concerned'.[162] As such, the CJEU concluded that Innoweb were reutilizing a substantial part of the database contents.

Do you think the CJEU's construction of 'reutilization' was correct in *Innoweb*? In particular, was the Court right to assume that income was lost by the defendant's activities?

---

[157] *Football Dataco Ltd v Sportradar GmbH* Case C-173/11 [2013] FSR 4.   [158] [33]–[47].
[159] C-202/12 [2014] Bus. L. R. 308, [34].   [160] [37].   [161] [40]–[41].   [162] [48].

Further, what is the impact of the ruling for other types of meta search engines and thus for internet users?[163] Also, is the reference to a 'parasitical competing product' adopting an unfair competition approach to the database right and, if so, is this problematic?

Where the extraction or reutilization of database contents relates to an insubstantial part, logic would suggest that no infringement of the *sui generis* right occurs. This view is supported by Article 8(1), which provides that a maker of a database may not prevent a lawful user of the database from extracting or reutilizing insubstantial parts of its contents. However, Article 7(5) prohibits the repeated and systematic extraction and/or reutilization of insubstantial parts of the database contents where this conflicts with a normal exploitation of that database or unreasonably prejudices the legitimate interests of the maker of the database. In *British Horseracing*, the CJEU ruled that an insubstantial part is whatever does not constitute a substantial part. Further, that to infringe Article 7(5) there is the need for the cumulative effect of the acts of extraction and reutilization in relation to insubstantial parts of the database contents to reconstitute the database, either as a whole or in a substantial part. This seems to require looking at the insubstantial extractions or reutilizations in their totality, even if individually they are not still retained or are no longer being used.[164]

The CJEU in *British Horseracing* indicated that William Hill's acts of extraction and reutilization were repeated and systematic because they were carried out each time a race was held. However, these acts were not intended to circumvent Article 7(1) because their cumulative effect was not to reconstitute and make available to the public a substantial part of the contents of the BHB database. This was because the insubstantial parts that were taken and reused reflected investment in creation of data, as opposed to obtaining, verifying, or presenting its contents.

4.4.5 TERM

An important point of difference between the *sui generis* right for databases and copyright is the term of protection available. In the case of the *sui generis* right, Article 10 stipulates that the right lasts for 15 years. This is calculated from 1 January of the year following the date of completion of the database. Alternatively, where the database is not yet completed, it is calculated from 1 January of the year following the date when the database was first made available to the public. On the face of it, therefore, the *sui generis* right is much shorter than copyright protection, which will last for 70 years after the death of the author(s). However, the difference is not quite so great when Article 10(3) of the Database Directive is considered. This section provides:

> Any substantial change, evaluated qualitatively or quantitatively, to the contents of a database, including any substantial change resulting from the accumulation of successive additions, deletions or alterations, which would result in the database being considered to be a substantial new investment, evaluated qualitatively or quantitatively, shall qualify the database resulting from that investment for its own term of protection.

---

[163] For criticism see S. Vousden, 'Innoweb, search engines and engineering legitimacy in EU law' [2014] IPQ 280 and P. Virtanen, '*Innoweb v Wegener*: CJEU, sui generis database right and making available to the public—the war against the machines' (2014) 5 European Journal of Law and Technology 1.

[164] *BHB v William Hill*, [86]–[89].

Article 10(3) thus provides for a further 15-year term of protection if a substantial new investment is made to the database. This provision is meant to deal with the problem raised by dynamic databases, which require a steady stream of maintenance to ensure their currency, which in turn demands continuing investment. The provision may also benefit owners of reasonably static, but long-term, databases where what is required is continual verification of material.

There is, however, ambiguity over how Article 10(3) will operate: is the database 'resulting from that investment' referring to the entirety of the new (modified) database or only the new part of the database that is created with the later investment? The scope of Article 10(3) was raised in the *British Horseracing* case. The defendant argued that in updating and verifying the BHB database, new databases came into existence, each of which was protected for its own new term. As such, the defendant argued that it had not infringed the *sui generis* right because it had made insubstantial extractions or reutilizations from a series of related databases as opposed to from the one database. The Court of Appeal referred a question on Article 10(3) to the CJEU. However, in light of its rulings on Article 7(1) and (5) (that no infringement had occurred), the CJEU did not consider it necessary to reply to the question. This is a great shame since this is an important issue and, depending on how Article 10(3) is interpreted, leaves open the way for potentially perpetual protection of databases.

4.4.6 EXCEPTIONS

When it comes to balancing the interests of database makers and users, Article 9 permits Member States to introduce exceptions for lawful users of databases, to enable them to extract or reutilize a substantial part of the database contents in the following situations:

> a. in the case of extraction for private purposes of the contents of a non-electronic database;
>
> b. in the case of extraction for the purposes of illustration for teaching or scientific research, as long as the source is indicated and to the extent justified by the non-commercial purpose to be achieved;
>
> c. in the case of extraction and/or re-utilisation for the purposes of public security or an administrative or judicial procedure.

Criticisms similar to those raised in respect of the exceptions available against infringement of copyright in databases are applicable here. When it comes to private purposes, the exception is limited to the extraction right and to hard copy databases. In respect of the exception for teaching or scientific research, this is also limited to extraction and is further narrowed by the requirement of non-commercial purpose. As such, the exceptions in Article 9 may be said to provide a weak counterbalance against the wide protection that is available to database makers under Article 7.[165]

---

[165] C. D. Freedman, 'Should Canada enact a new sui generis database right?' (2002) 13 Fordham Intellectual Property Media & Entertainment L. J. 35, 97; J. Lipton, 'Databases as intellectual property: new legal approaches' [2003] EIPR 139, 141–2.

4.4.7 EVALUATION OF THE *SUI GENERIS* RIGHT

The European Commission, in its first (and so far only) evaluation of the directive,[166] has considered the impact of the *sui generis* right on the European database industry's rate of growth. The Commission concludes that EU database production has recently fallen back to pre-directive levels and that, at present, the economic impact of the *sui generis* right on database production is 'unproven'.[167] Further, it appears that the *sui generis* right has not significantly improved the competitiveness of the European database industry vis-à-vis the US.[168] Faced with an absence of empirical evidence about the success of the *sui generis* provisions, the Commission has suggested four possible options for the future, as set out in the following extract.

First evaluation of Directive 96/9/EC on the legal protection of databases
(12 December 2005)

6.1. Option 1: Repeal the whole Directive

Withdrawing the Directive in its entirety would allow Member States to revert to the situation that applied in national law prior to the adoption of the Directive. This would allow *droit d'auteur* Member States to keep their threshold of 'originality', to protect 'original' databases under copyright law and to choose other means e.g. unfair competition or the law of misappropriation, to protect 'non-original' compilations. Common law Member States, for their part, would be allowed to revert to the 'sweat of the brow' standard as a relevant copyright test.

But withdrawing the Directive in its entirety would give rise to a pre-directive scenario where Member States could protect 'original' databases under diverging levels of 'originality'. In particular, the UK and Ireland would be allowed to revert to the 'sweat of the brow' copyright test and Sweden, Denmark and Finland (and Norway and Iceland) would be allowed to revert to their 'catalogue rule'.

In this scenario, one could expect that the terms of use for collections of data or compilations would be dealt with only by contract law and right-holders would increasingly protect their databases (especially online databases) by means of access control systems. However, this option would have the disadvantage of doing away with the harmonised level of copyright protection for 'original' databases which has not caused major problems so far.

6.2. Option 2: Withdraw the 'sui generis' right

Another possibility would therefore be to withdraw the 'sui generis' right in isolation and thus maintain the harmonised level of copyright protection for 'original' databases.

Arguably, this partial withdrawal would still allow *droit d'auteur* Member States to keep their threshold of 'originality', to protect 'original' databases under copyright law and to choose other means e.g. unfair competition or the law of misappropriation to protect 'non-original' compilations. It would also allow common law Member States to revert to the 'sweat of the brow' standard as a relevant test to protect 'non-original' compilations.

---

[166] Commission of the European Communities, DG Internal Market and Services Working Paper, *First evaluation of Directive 96/9/EC on the legal protection of databases*, Brussels, 12 December 2005 (Evaluation Paper).

[167] Evaluation Paper, paras 1.4 and 4.2.   [168] Evaluation Paper, para. 4.4.

The arguments for partial withdrawal would largely be based on a strict application of the 'better regulation' principles. These principles would probably suggest that the 'sui generis' right be withdrawn as it has revealed itself to be an instrument that is ineffective at encouraging growth in the European database industry and, due to its largely untested legal concepts, given rise to significant litigation in national and European courts. Empirical data underlying this evaluation show that its economic impact is unproven. In addition, no empirical data that proves that its introduction has stimulated significant growth in the production of EU databases could be submitted so far.

Furthermore, withdrawal of the 'sui generis' right appears to be in line with an emerging trend in common law jurisdictions as the high standard of 'originality' introduced by the Directive would put them on a par with the US, thereby protecting fewer rather than more databases. It may thus well be that even the common law jurisdictions within the Community (UK and Ireland) would maintain the higher threshold for protection, thereby only protecting 'original' databases. The ruling in the *Feist* case and the economic evidence that points at the US as being a leader in database production could lead to significant reluctance in reintroducing 'sweat of the brow'.

Finally, withdrawing the 'sui generis' right would still leave companies with factual compilations that may not be fully protected under the standard of 'originality' as prescribed in copyright law, free to protect their works by other means such as contract law or use of technological protection measures or other forms of access control when the work is delivered on-line. It would also not exclude producers of compilations to claim protection by stating that their arrangements met the threshold of 'originality'. However, this paper acknowledges that European publishers and database producers would clearly prefer to retain the 'sui generis' protection.

6.3. Option 3: Amend the 'sui generis' provisions

Another option would be to amend and clarify the scope of protection awarded under the 'sui generis' provisions. Attempts could be made to reformulate the scope of the 'sui generis' right in order to also cover instances where the 'creation' of data takes place concurrently with the collection and screening of it. Amendments could also clarify the issue of what forms of 'official' and thereby single source lists would be protected under the 'sui generis' provisions.

Amendments could also be proposed to clarify the scope of protection and clarify whether the scope would only cover 'primary' producers of databases (i.e. those producers whose main business is to collect and assemble information they do not 'create' themselves) or would also include producers for whom production of a databases is a 'secondary' activity (in other words, a spin-off from their main activity). Amendments could, in addition, clarify the issue of what actually constitutes a substantial investment in either the obtaining, verification or presentation of the contents of a database. On the other hand, reformulating the scope of the 'sui generis' right entails a serious risk that yet another layer of untested legal notions would be introduced that will not withstand scrutiny before the ECJ.

6.4. Option 4: Maintaining the status quo

On the other hand, even if a piece of legislation has no proven positive effects on the growth of a particular industry, withdrawal is not always the best option. Removing the 'sui generis' right and thereby allowing Member States to revert to prior forms of legal protection for all forms of 'non-original' databases that do not meet the threshold of 'originality', might be more costly than keeping it in place. Arguably, the limitations imposed by the judgments of the ECJ mean that the right is now only available to 'primary' producers of databases and not those for whom databases are a 'secondary' activity.

The EU Commission has not actively pursued options 1 to 3, but by default have adopted option 4. In your view, which of the four options is preferable? If another jurisdiction were looking to introduce the *sui generis* database right, would you recommend adopting the EU model as it stands or with changes or not at all?

The role of the Database Directive in relation to online databases which are not protected either by copyright or the *sui generis* right arose in *Ryanair Ltd v PR Aviation BV*.[169] PR Aviation operated a website for checking and comparing prices of low-cost flights and for booking these flights. Ryanair operated their website, which featured terms of use prohibiting the use of automated systems to extract data from the website for commercial purposes. The domestic courts in the Netherlands dismissed Ryanair's claims of copyright and database infringement and the Supreme Court referred a question to the CJEU, which essentially asked whether the Database Directive applied to online databases not protected by copyright or the *sui generis* right. In particular, whether the prohibition in Article 15 on contractually overriding the exceptions to copyright databases in Article 6 and the rights of lawful users of *sui generis* databases in Article 8 applied to such databases. The Court ruled that it was clear from the 'purpose and structure' of the Database Directive 'that it does not prevent the adoption of contractual clauses concerning the conditions of use' of a database not protected either by copyright or the *sui generis* right.[170] Commentators have expressed concern that 'non-protected sole-source databases benefit from the full scope of contractual protection' and that this has the potential to allow monopolization of data in an online context and defeat the aims of the safeguards built into the Database Directive.[171]

FURTHER READING

T. Aplin, 'The EU database right: recent developments' [2005] IPQ 52.

M. Borghi and S. Karapapa, 'Contractual restrictions on lawful use of information: sole-source databases protected by the back door?' [2015] EIPR 505.

M. Davison and P. B. Hugenholtz, 'Football fixtures, horseraces and spin offs: the ECJ domesticates the database right' [2005] EIPR 113.

E. Derclaye, 'The Court of Justice interprets the database sui generis right for the first time' [2005] European L. R. 420.

E. Derclaye, *The Legal Protection of Databases: A Comparative Analysis* (Cheltenham: Edward Elgar, 2008).

A. Kur et al., 'First evaluation of Directive 96/9/EC on the legal protection of databases: comment by the Max Planck Institute for Intellectual Property, Competition and Tax Law, Munich' (2006) 37 IIC 551.

---

[169] Case C-30/14 [2015] ECDR 13.   [170] [39].
[171] M. Borghi and S. Karapapa, 'Contractual restrictions on lawful use of information: sole-source databases protected by the back door?' [2015] EIPR 505, 513.

5

PASSING OFF

5.1 INTRODUCTION

Trade marks may be either registered or unregistered. The following chapters will consider the law of registered trade marks. The subject of this chapter is the protection which the law affords to unregistered trade marks through the tort of passing off. According to Lord Oliver in the leading case on passing off, 'Jif Lemon':[1] 'The law of passing off can be summarised in one short general proposition—no man may pass off his goods as those of another.'

5.1.1 THE DEFINITION OF PASSING OFF

5.1.1.1 The classic trinity

In 'Jif Lemon', Lord Oliver set out the three basic elements which are necessary to bring an action in passing off. These have come to be known as the 'classic trinity'.

> **Lord Oliver, at p. 499:**
>
> First, [the claimant] must establish a goodwill or reputation attached to the goods or services which he supplies in the mind of the purchasing public by association with the identifying 'get-up' (whether it consists simply of a brand name or a trade description, or the individual features of labelling or packaging) under which his particular goods or services as offered to the public, such that the get-up is recognised by the public as distinctive specifically of the plaintiff's goods or services. Secondly, he must demonstrate a misrepresentation by the defendant to the public (whether or not intentional) leading or likely to lead the public to believe that goods or services offered by him are the goods or services of the plaintiff.
>
> ...
>
> Thirdly, he must demonstrate that he suffers or, in a quia timet action that he is likely to suffer, damage by reason of the erroneous belief engendered by the defendant's misrepresentation that the source of the defendant's goods or services is the same as the source of those offered by the plaintiff.

---

[1] *Reckitt & Coleman Products Ltd v Borden Inc. (No. 3)* [1990] 1 WLR 491, 499.

The 'classic trinity' identified in 'Jif Lemon' as necessary for a passing off action are:

(1) goodwill;

(2) a misrepresentation;

(3) damage or in a *quia timet* action, the likelihood of damage.

5.1.1.2 The 'Advocaat' definition

Earlier in the 'Advocaat' case,[2] Lord Diplock had set out the general background to the tort of passing off. He identified five elements which he held must be present in order to bring a passing off action:

Lord Diplock, at pp. 740–2:

The action for what has become known as 'passing off' arose in the nineteenth century out of the use in connection with his own goods by one trader of the trade name or trade mark of a rival trader so as to induce in potential purchasers the belief that his goods were those of the rival trader. Although the cases up to the end of the century had been confined to the deceptive use of trade names, marks, letters or other indicia, the principle had been stated by Lord Langdale MR as early as 1842 as being: 'A man is not to sell his own goods under the pretence that they are the goods of another man'; *Perry v Truefitt*, 6 Beav 66. At the close of the century in *Reddaway v Banham* [1896] AC 199, it was said by Lord Herschell that what was protected by an action for passing off was not the proprietary right of the trader in the mark, name or get-up improperly used. Thus the door was opened to passing off actions in which the misrepresentation took some other form than the deceptive use of trade names, marks, letters or other indicia; but as none of their Lordships committed themselves to identifying the legal nature of the right that was protected by a passing off action it remained an action sui generis which lay for damage sustained or threatened in consequence of a misrepresentation of a particular kind.

Reddaway v Banham, like all previous passing off cases, was one in which Banham had passed off his goods as those of Reddaway, and the damage resulting from the misrepresentation took the form of the diversion of potential customers from Reddaway to Banham. Although it was a landmark case in deciding that the use by a trader of a term which accurately described the composition of his own goods might nevertheless amount to the tort of passing off if that term were understood in the market in which the goods were sold to denote the goods of a rival trader, *Reddaway v Banham* did not extend the nature of the particular kind of misrepresentation which gives rise to a right of action in passing off beyond what I have called the classic form of misrepresenting one's own goods as the goods of someone else nor did it provide any rational basis for an extension.

This was left to be provided by Lord Parker in *Spalding v Gamage* (1915) 32 RPC 273. In a speech which received the approval of the other members of this House, he identified the right the invasion of which is the subject of passing off actions as being the 'property in the business or goodwill likely to be injured by the misrepresentation'.

...

The goodwill of a manufacturer's business may well be injured by some-one else who sells goods which are correctly described as being made by that manufacturer but being of an inferior class or quality are misrepresented as goods of his manufacture of a superior

---

[2] *Erven Warnink BV v J. Townend & Sons (Hull) Ltd* [1979] AC 731.

class or quality. This type of misrepresentation was held in *Spalding v Gamage* to be actionable and the extension to the nature of the misrepresentation which gives rise to a right of action in passing off which this involved was regarded by Lord Parker as a natural corollary of recognising that what the law protects by a passing off action is a trader's property in his business or goodwill.

The significance of this decision in the law of passing off lies in its recognition that misrepresenting one's own goods as the goods of someone else was not a separate genus of actionable wrong but a particular species of wrong included in a wider genus of which a premonitory hint had been given by Lord Herschell in *Reddaway v Banham* when, in speaking of the deceptive use of a descriptive term, he said: 'I am unable to see why a man should be allowed in this way more than any other to deceive purchasers into the belief that they are getting what they are not, and thus to filch the business of a rival.'

...

Spalding v Gamage led the way to recognition by judges of other species of the same genus, as where although the plaintiff and the defendant were not competing traders in the same line of business, a false suggestion by the defendant that their businesses were connected with one another would damage the reputation and thus the goodwill of the plaintiff's business.

...

My Lords, *Spalding v Gamage* and the later cases make it possible to identify five characteristics which must be present in order to create a valid cause of action for passing off: (1) a misrepresentation (2) made by a trader in the course of trade, (3) to prospective customers of his or ultimate consumers of goods or services supplied by him, (4) which is calculated to injure the business or goodwill of another trader (in the sense that this is a reasonably foreseeable consequence) and (5) which causes actual damage to a business or goodwill of the trader by whom the action is brought or (in a *quia timet* action) will probably do so.

Also in 'Advocaat', Lord Fraser identified five criteria which should be present for a successful passing off action. Lord Fraser's criteria are generally complementary to those of Lord Diplock, but his do emphasize the importance of goodwill subsisting in England, an issue that will be considered later in this chapter.

Lord Fraser, at p. 755:

It is essential for the plaintiff in a passing off action to show at least the following facts: (1) that his business consists of, or includes, selling in England a class of goods to which the particular trade name applies; (2) that the class of goods is clearly defined, and that in the minds of the public, or a section of the public, in England, the trade name distinguishes that class from other similar goods; (3) that because of the reputation of the goods, there is goodwill attached to the name; (4) that he, the plaintiff, as a member of the class of those who sell the goods, is the owner of goodwill in England which is of substantial value; (5) that he has suffered, or is really likely to suffer, substantial damage to his property in the goodwill by reason of the defendants selling goods which are falsely described by the trade name to which the goodwill is attached. Provided these conditions are satisfied, as they are in the present case, I consider that the plaintiff is entitled to protect himself by a passing off action.

The definitions set out by Lord Oliver in 'Jif Lemon' and Lord Diplock in 'Advocaat' are not incompatible. In many cases of passing off, the courts have preferred to adhere to Lord

Oliver's 'classic trinity'. What Lord Diplock suggests in 'Advocaat' is that the types of mis-representation which might give rise to a passing off action are constantly evolving. In some instances, the particular circumstances of a misrepresentation may make the application of Lord Diplock's five elements more appropriate. As Lord Diplock points out, the classic mis-representation that 'A man is not to sell his own goods under the pretence that they are the goods of another man'[3] has now expanded to encompass the situation where the defendant may sell inferior goods as if they were superior,[4] he may suggest a business connection with the claimant where none exists,[5] and, as was the case in 'Advocaat' itself, he may claim that his goods are the goods of a limited class of traders, to which the defendant does not belong. This latter misrepresentation characterizes what has come to be known as the extended form of passing off—and it is in such cases that Lord Diplock's formulation (together with that of Lord Fraser) might be most usefully applied.[6]

5.1.2 THE RELATIONSHIP BETWEEN PASSING OFF AND UNFAIR COMPETITION

In 'Advocaat', Lord Diplock expressed his anxiety that an action for passing off might, but should not, be used to hamper legitimate competition. Thus, he took the view that it should not be available in every instance where one trader makes untrue assertions about another's goods.

> **Lord Diplock, at p. 742:**
>
> In seeking to formulate general propositions of English law, however, one must be par-ticularly careful to beware of the logical fallacy of the undistributed middle. It does not follow that because all passing off actions can be shown to present these characteristics, all factual situations which present these characteristics give rise to a cause of action for passing off. True it is that their presence indicates what a moral code would censure as dishonest trading, based as it is upon deception of customers and consumers of a trader's wares but in an economic system which has relied on competition to keep down prices and to improve products there may be practical reasons why it should have been the policy of the common law not to run the risk of hampering competition by providing civil remedies to every one competing in the market who has suffered damage to his business or goodwill in consequence of inaccurate statements of whatever kind that may be made by rival traders about their own wares. The market in which the action for passing off originated was no place for the mealy mouthed; advertisements are not on affidavit; exaggerated claims by a trader about the quality of his wares, assertions that they are better than those of his rivals, even though he knows this to be untrue, have been permitted by the common law as venial 'puffing' which gives no cause of action to a competitor even though he can show he has suffered actual damage in his business as a result.

Despite Lord Diplock's strictures, in the later case of *Arsenal FC v Reed*,[7] Aldous LJ opined that the tort of passing off is 'perhaps best referred to as unfair competition'. Four years later,

---

[3] *Perry v Truefitt* (1842) 6 Beav 66, per Lord Langdale MR.
[4] *Spalding & Bros v A. W. Gamage* (1915) 84 LJ Ch 449.
[5] *Harrods Ltd v R. Harrod Ltd* (1924) 41 RPC 74.   [6] See 5.2.1.8.   [7] [2003] 1 All ER 137.

in *L'Oréal v Bellure* (2009), Jacob LJ asserted the opposite when he said, 'So I think the tort of passing off cannot and should not be extended into some general law of unfair competition.'[8]

A proper retort to these statements might be to ask what precisely is meant by a law of unfair competition. Does it mean generally regulating the way traders and consumers interact in the marketplace? If so, then the UK has numerous statutes and regulations which set out to do just that, in addition to passing off and other torts which might be invoked in instances of dishonest trading, such as defamation and trade libel. Thus, the Competition Act 1998 harmonizes domestic law with Articles 101 and 102 of the TFEU, inter alia, regulating anti-competitive agreements and the abuse of a dominant position.[9] Legislation aimed more directly at providing a remedy for unfair competition in the UK includes the Enterprise Act 2002, as well as the Business Protection from Misleading Marketing Regulations 2008 (BPRs)[10] and the Consumer Protection from Unfair Trading Regulations 2008 (CPRs), both based on EU Directives.[11] The BPRs are designed to protect traders against unfair trading practices, for example in the area of comparative advertising. The CPRs protect the interests of consumers. Regulation 3 of the CPRs contains a general prohibition against unfair commercial practices. A commercial practice is deemed unfair if it is not professionally diligent and if it materially distorts, or is likely to materially distort, the economic behaviour of the average consumer. Regulations 5 to 7 prohibit misleading and aggressive practices. These are practices which cause or are likely to cause the average consumer to take a different decision. They include practices which might also fall within the remit of passing off. For example, the CPRs regulate misleading information which creates confusion with a competitor's products, trade marks, or any other distinguishing indicia. They also regulate false information about the main characteristics of a product, including for example its composition or its geographical or commercial origin, a misrepresentation which as we shall see falls squarely within the extended form of passing off.

Nonetheless, the reason the UK is often accused of not having a law of unfair competition is because, unlike many other European countries, it does not have a general law against 'misappropriation'. As we saw in Chapter 1, at the heart of misappropriation is the unjust enrichment of one trader who misappropriates the value created by another. For example, in the case of *L'Oréal v Bellure*,[12] which concerned both registered trade mark infringement and passing off, the defendant sold cheap perfumes which it claimed in advertisements were smell-alikes of the claimant's far more expensive and well-known brands. In this case, the claimant neither suffered damage from lost sales, nor was the public deceived into believing the defendant's perfumes were associated with the claimants. The defendant was, however, able to appropriate some of the cachet residing in the claimant's luxury products for its own. Despite this, the claimant failed in its claim for passing off. According to Jacob LJ, 'those who support some wider tort of unfair competition, use the word misappropriation of goodwill to designate it'. He went on:

> I wish to state that I think it very unhelpful. We are all against misappropriation, just as we are all in favour of mother and apple pie. To use the word in the context of a debate about

---

[8] *L'Oréal v Bellure* [2007] EWCA Civ 968, [160]–[161].   [9] See 1.3.2.3.

[10] SI 2008/1276; implements the Comparative and Misleading Marketing Directive (MCAD) and replaces requirements set out under the Control of Misleading Advertising Regulations 1998 (CMARs).

[11] SI 2008/1277; implements the Directive 2005/29/EC on Unfair Commercial Practices.

[12] *L'Oréal SA v Bellure NV* [2007] EWCA Civ 968. The trade mark aspects of this case will be considered in detail in the following three chapters.

> the limits of the tort of passing off and its interface with legitimate trade is at best muddling and at worse tendentious.[13]

Instead, according to Jacob LJ, at the heart of the tort of passing off is a misrepresentation or a deception and neither was present in this case. The claimant's claim for passing off failed (although, as we shall see in the next chapter, its claim for infringement of its registered trade marks succeeded).

It is perhaps worth asking why the UK has not traditionally been sympathetic to laws preventing such misappropriation, given the normative appeal of arguments against unjust enrichment. Does one answer lie in the consistent support which UK courts have given to relatively unfettered markets; support which was clearly expressed in the speech of Lord Diplock in 'Advocaat'? At the end of this chapter we shall return to the question of whether passing off should extend its remit to encompass misappropriation and whether in fact, despite Jacob LJ's statement to the contrary, it has already done so.

FURTHER READING

R. Arnold, 'English unfair competition law' (2013) 44 IIC 63.

H. Carty, *An Analysis of Economic Torts* (Oxford: Oxford University Press, 2010).

P. Johnson and J. Gibson, 'The "new" tort of passing off' (2015) 131 LQR 476.

C. Wadlow, *The Law of Passing-Off: Unfair Competition by Misrepresentation* (London: Sweet & Maxwell, 2011).

5.2 THE ELEMENTS OF PASSING OFF

5.2.1 GOODWILL

5.2.1.1 The definition of goodwill

Traditionally, goodwill has been the property protected by a passing off action. As was put by Sir John Mummery in *Starbucks (HK) Ltd v British Sky Broadcasting Group Plc*:[14]

> 102. First, there is the strong flavour of property in the foundations of the tort of passing off, though not, of course, being the same in all respects as property in land or in things. Although the common law does not recognise any property in the word, mark or sign itself as such, it does recognise that a goodwill, to which the name or mark has become attached in a market, may be entitled to protection from damage inflicted by express or implied misrepresentation.

For a definition of goodwill, courts commonly revert to Lord Macnaghten's famous description in *The Commissioners of Inland Revenue v Muller & Co.'s Margarine*.[15]

---

13 [160].   14 [2013] EWCA Civ 1465.   15 [1901] AC 217.

Lord Macnaghten, at pp. 223–4:

It is the benefit and advantage of the good name, reputation and connection of a business. It is the attractive force which brings in custom…However widely extended or diffused its influence may be, goodwill is worth nothing unless it has the power of attraction sufficient to bring customers home to the source from which it emanates.

In a passing off action, the misrepresentation may result from the improper use of a trader's trade name or other indicia which distinguishes this goodwill. But while passing off will protect a trader's goodwill, it will not necessarily protect a trader's reputation. The two are not synonymous. This was made clear in the *Harrods* case.

Harrods Ltd v Harrodian School Ltd [1996] RPC 697

The claimant owned the Harrods department store. The defendants ran a preparatory school under the name 'The Harrodian School'. The school was on the site of what had previously been 'The Harrodian Club', a sports club run by the claimant but which had closed in 1990. The claimant brought an action for passing off. In the course of the action, it was established that the claimant did not run a school nor did it intend to do so. Furthermore, the word 'Harrodian' had not been used for 40 or 50 years in the claimant's dealings with customers, although it had been applied to the claimant's employees and some staff associations during that period. In his judgment, Millett LJ acknowledged that the claimant enjoyed 'a long-established reputation and goodwill in the business of a department store, carried on under the name "Harrods"'. He also acknowledged that it offered a 'vast' range of services.

Lord Justice Millett, at p. 702:

The plaintiffs have always been very proud of the name 'Harrods'. They claim that it has come to represent an unsurpassed level of quality in the range of goods and services which they provide. But while their range is of astonishing breadth, it would be a mistake to be dazzled into thinking that the range of the plaintiffs' commercial activities is virtually unlimited, or that they have acquired a reputation for excellence in every field of activity. They are retail suppliers of goods and services of every kind; but that is all. They sell theatre tickets; they do not run a theatre: they supply medical equipment; they do not run a hospital: they act as insurance agents; they do not underwrite policies of insurance: they supply school uniforms; they do not run a school.

[The question then arose whether, given the wide reputation which resided in the name 'Harrods', any use by the defendant of the 'Harrods' name would inevitably trespass on the claimant's goodwill. Lord Justice Millett concluded it would not. He noted that it is goodwill, alone, that is protected by a passing off action:]

At p. 711:

It is this fundamental principle of the law of passing off which leads me to reject the main way in which the plaintiffs have put their case before us. 'Harrodian', they submit, is synonymous with 'Harrods'; the name 'Harrods' is universally recognised as denoting the plaintiffs' business—it has, as counsel put it (borrowing and adapting an expression used by Falconer J in *Lego System A/S v Lego M Lemelstrich Ltd* ('the *Lego* case') [1983] FSR 155 at page 187) an unlimited 'field of recognition'; the defendants were, therefore, unarguably guilty of misrepresenting their business as that of the plaintiffs; given the huge number of persons who are customers or potential customers of the plaintiffs it is a simple matter to infer that an appreciable number of them will be deceived into thinking that 'The Harrodian School' is owned by or otherwise connected in some way with Harrods; and damage may likewise easily be inferred. But in referring to the possibility of a plaintiff having only 'a limited field of recognition', Falconer J was referring to the limited field of commercial activity with which the plaintiff's reputation was associated by the public; he was not referring to the extent to which the plaintiff's reputation in that limited field was familiar to the public. The name 'Harrods' may be universally recognised, but the business with which it is associated in the minds of the public is not all embracing. To be known to everyone is not to be known for everything.

The claimant failed in its action for passing off. Harrods is obviously a widely known name. Do you think Millett LJ was correct to assert that customers or potential customers of the store would assume it was not connected with the school? Or is the Harrods store sufficiently famous so if any other business traded under that name, consumers would inevitably assume a connection with the store? This was the conclusion reached by Kerr LJ in a dissenting judgment and it raises the issue of whether goodwill can reside in the value of the name alone, not just the underlying business.[16]

5.2.1.2 The location of goodwill

To bring a passing off action, goodwill must be situated in the UK. It is worth remembering that having a reputation in the UK is not the same as having goodwill. This principle is clearly demonstrated by the Court of Appeal decision in the 'Budweiser' case.[17] In this case, the American brewers of Budweiser beer brought a passing off action against the defendants who supplied beer under the name 'Budweiser' in the UK. Although it was accepted that the American 'Budweiser' beer was well known in the UK, the claimant supplied its beer only to US army bases. In the Court of Appeal, Oliver LJ held that the claimants did not have the goodwill necessary for a passing off action. He noted that it is not possible to assume 'the existence of the goodwill apart from the market, and that, as it seems to me, is to confuse goodwill, which cannot exist in a vacuum, with mere reputation which may, no doubt, and frequently does, exist without any supporting local business, but which does not by itself constitute a property which the law protects'.[18]

In 'Budweiser', Oliver LJ held that the claimant must have a 'market' in the UK for its goods to have the requisite goodwill. The question then arises as to what constitutes the relevant market. In the early case of *Alain Bernardin et Cie v Pavilion Propertie*[19] the claimants, who carried on a restaurant business in Paris under the title 'The Crazy Horse Saloon', had for many years advertised their establishment by publicity material distributed to tourist

---

[16] See 5.2.2.4. [17] *Anheuser-Busch Inc. v Budějovický Budvar NP* [1984] FSR 413.
[18] At p. 470. See also *The Athletes' Foot Marketing Associates Inc. v Cobra Sports Ltd* [1980] RPC 343.
[19] [1967] RPC 581.

organizations and hotels in the UK. They failed to restrain the defendants from carrying on a restaurant in London under the same name because the court held that a trader could not acquire goodwill without some sort of use in the UK. By merely advertising, a foreign trader might acquire a reputation in the UK but not the requisite domestic goodwill. The 'Crazy Horse' decision suggested that for goodwill to subsist in services, the claimant must not only have customers in the UK but also a place of business. However, in the subsequent 'Hit Factory' decision, Browne-Wilkinson V-C refused to follow the reasoning in 'Crazy Horse', arguing that it neither accorded with earlier authorities nor reflected modern trading realities.

Pete Waterman Ltd v CBS United Kingdom Ltd [1993] EMLR 27

The claimants (PWL) were a successful pop record-producing organization who were known to the public as 'The Hit Factory'. The claimants did not trade under the name 'Hit Factory', but had released three compilation albums of their hits entitled 'The Hit Factory', 'The Hit Factory 2', and 'The Hit Factory 3'. The defendant was a record company which owned a recording studio in London. The defendant had entered into a joint venture agreement with the owner of a studio in New York for the refurbishment and running of the London studio. The New York studio had traded since about 1970 as 'The Hit Factory'. Under the agreement, the owner of the New York studio had granted the defendant a licence to use the name 'The Hit Factory'. The defendant proposed to rename its studio in London 'The Hit Factory'. The New York studio had an international reputation and clientele, including many from the UK. Bookings had been made direct from the UK. In addition, $3.5 million of business had been done by the New York studio with US record companies relating to English artists, including bookings placed at the behest of UK companies through their US affiliates. However, all services rendered by the New York studio had been rendered in New York. The New York studio had no agent or place of business in the UK. The claimants brought an action for passing off. As part of its defence, the defendant argued that it had established its own goodwill in the UK on the basis of UK customers for its studio in New York. PWL responded, relying on 'Crazy Horse', that the Hit Factory, New York, had no goodwill in the UK since it had no place of business, nor an agent, nor did it carry on business in the UK, and all its services had been provided outside the UK. One issue for the court was whether, assuming that PWL had demonstrated that the name the Hit Factory was distinctive of their goodwill, the defendant's claim to concurrent goodwill in the UK was defeated by the Crazy Horse principle. The Vice-Chancellor called that question 'the Crazy Horse issue'.

Browne-Wilkinson V-C, at p. 50:

The issue is whether the English court will protect the trade connection with the United Kingdom customers of non-UK traders. In the passage I quoted of Lord Diplock in the *General Electric* case [*GE Trade Mark* [1972] FSR 225] he demonstrated how the principle of honest concurrent use was developed in 19th century England to meet the problem where two traders using similar marks in separate areas of the United Kingdom were brought into the same market within the United Kingdom by improvements in internal communications. The changes in the second half of the 20th century are far more fundamental than those in 19th century England. They have produced worldwide marks, worldwide goodwill and brought separate markets into competition one with the other. Radio and television with their attendant advertising cross national frontiers. Electronic communication via satellite produces virtually instant communication between all markets. In terms of travel time, New York by air is as close as Aberdeen by rail. This has led to the development of the international reputation in certain names, particularly in the service fields, for example Sheraton Hotels, Budget Rent A Car.

In my view, the law will fail if it does not try to meet the challenge thrown up by trading patterns which cross national and jurisdictional boundaries due to a change in technical achievement.

The problem is particularly acute with service industries. A first division recording studio is catering to a market which treats crossing the Atlantic as an everyday incident. Similar problems arise in relation to professional and other services. For example, an internationally famous hospital in Paris or Boston, Massachusetts draws its patients from worldwide. Is it unable to protect its goodwill otherwise than in its home country?

As a matter of legal principle, I can see no reason why the courts of this country should not protect the trading relationship between a foreign trader and his United Kingdom customers by restraining anyone in this country from passing himself off as the foreign trader. The essence of a claim in passing off is that the defendant is interfering with the goodwill of the plaintiff. The essence of the goodwill is the ability to attract customers and potential customers to do business with the owner of the goodwill. Therefore any interference with the trader's customers is an interference with his goodwill. The rules under which for certain purposes a specific local situation is attributed to such goodwill appear to me to be irrelevant. Even if under such rules the situs of the goodwill is not in England, any representation made to customers in England is an interference with that goodwill wherever it may be situate. Only if English law refuses to recognise the existence of rights locally situate abroad should the English courts refuse to protect such rights. But English law in general is not so chauvinistic; it does recognise and protect rights which are locally situate abroad. The rights of a beneficiary under a New York trust in assets in England will be protected by an English court even though the situs of his right is in New York. Therefore, when a foreign trader has customers here, one would expect the English courts to protect his goodwill with those customers.

The Vice-Chancellor then rehearsed the authorities which preceded the 'Crazy Horse' decision. He concluded that in the earlier case law, 'there is no reference to the local situation of the goodwill being important. The critical questions have been (a) the use of the name in this country and (b) the presence of customers here.' The Vice Chancellor then detailed the cases which had followed the 'Crazy Horse' decision. Among the conclusions he reached were the following:

At pp. 57–8:

...

A. The presence of customers in this country is sufficient to constitute the carrying on of business here whether or not there is otherwise a place of business here and whether or not the services are provided here. Once it is found that there are customers, it is open to find that there is a business here to which the local goodwill is attached;

B. To the extent that the *Crazy Horse* case is authority to the contrary, I prefer not to follow it.

> It follows that since at all material times The Hit Factory Inc. has had a substantial number of customers here, it would have been entitled to protect its name here against third parties and is therefore entitled to continue to use its name here concurrently with PWL even if, contrary to my view, PWL has itself acquired a goodwill in the name.

The approach taken by Browne-Wilkinson V-C in the 'Hit Factory' case to services provided abroad was later confirmed by the Court of Appeal in *Hotel Cipriani v Cipriani (Grosvenor Street)*.

Hotel Cipriani v Cipriani (Grosvenor Street) [2010] EWCA Civ 110

The Hotel Cipriani is a 'famous and luxurious' hotel in Venice. There is also a well-known bar in Venice named Harry's Bar. Both of these enterprises were founded by Giuseppe Cipriani in the early 20th century. However, by the time of these proceedings, ownership had divided. The hotel is now owned by the claimant company, which has no connection to the family. The bar is run by a company controlled by the founder's grandsons. The latter company has a number of restaurants in New York operating under the 'Cipriani' name and modelled on Harry's Bar. In 2004, the defendants opened a similar bar in London under the name 'Cipriani London' (or 'Cipriani' for short). The claimants, who have a registered community trade mark (EUTM), 'Cipriani', sued for both trade mark infringement and passing off. They succeeded in both actions in the High Court and the defendants appealed. One basis for the appeal was the defendants' contention that contrary to the findings of Arnold J in the High Court, the claimants did not have the requisite goodwill in the UK to bring an action for passing off. Another was that, alternatively, both they and the claimants had sufficient concurrent goodwill in their respective enterprises, so that when the defendants started trading, they could not be found liable for passing off. After rehearsing the earlier authorities and endorsing Browne-Wilkinson V-C's judgment in the 'Hit Factory'/'Peter Waterman case', Lloyd LJ identified the key question in this case as 'what is necessary for the reputation of a business abroad and its mark to qualify as goodwill in this country'.[20] He then identified two subsidiary questions: is what the claimant can show sufficient and, if it is, why is what the defendant can show not sufficient? He then set out his answer:

> 117. In Budweiser in relation to sales of beer, the court regarded it as necessary that, in addition to an international reputation, there should have been significant sales of the product in this country. How does the matter stand when one is considering not goods but services?
>
> [Lloyd LJ then considered the suggestion made by Wadlow in *The Law of Passing-off* (3rd edn, 2004) at para. 3-80 that the test for whether services supplied abroad have generated domestic goodwill might be whether English residents are prepared to travel abroad to use them. He continued:]
>
> 118. That is an interesting proposition which might provide a suitable line of distinction between businesses abroad with a genuinely international reputation and clientele, on the

---

[20] [116].

one hand, and those which have English customers abroad, and therefore may be known of in this country, but whose reputation here does not in practice bring in significant custom from the public in England. However, it does not seem to me that it is necessary or appropriate to adopt a general principle such as that in order to decide this appeal. Like the judge, I would hold that the first claimant did have goodwill here on the basis that, in April 2004 (the relevant moment for passing-off) it had a substantial reputation in England and a substantial body of customers from England, in part as a result of significant marketing efforts directed at the relevant public here, and a significant volume of business was placed directly from this country, either by individual clients by telephone or the like, or via travel agents or tour operators. On that basis it seems to me clear that the international reputation of Hotel Cipriani, and the use of the mark Cipriani, was something that brought in business from England—it was an attractive force that brought in English custom—and accordingly the business had goodwill in England at the relevant time.

119. Turning then to the defendants and the Cipriani group, on the judge's findings the defendants showed that Harry's Bar had a significant number of English customers, and that it had a substantial reputation in England, but not that it had a sufficient association with the mark Cipriani. That, therefore, could not justify a finding of goodwill in England in relation to the Cipriani mark.

120. As for the New York Cipriani restaurants, despite some slight reputation in England, they failed to prove any significant English custom at the relevant time. The evidence relied on by the defendants in this respect, to which I have referred at para. [47] above, was very limited and indirect, and I am not surprised that the judge found it of little assistance or persuasive weight. That too, therefore, is inadequate to show that the name Cipriani brought in any worthwhile English custom to the Cipriani restaurants in New York.

121. It seems to me that it must be necessary to show more than this in order to establish goodwill in England for a mark used by a business based abroad for services which it supplies abroad. Therefore, whatever test might be applied to determine whether a business supplying services abroad which has a reputation in England also has goodwill in England, the defendants do not satisfy it.

[Lloyd LJ went on to confirm the High Court's decision that while the claimants had goodwill in the UK, the defendants did not and that the passing off action should succeed. He then noted *obiter* how the test for domestic goodwill might have to be revisited in the future.]

124. It is fair to say that, especially in the circumstances of the present day, with many establishments worldwide featuring on their own or shared websites, through which their services and facilities can be booked directly (or their goods can be ordered directly) from anywhere in the world, the test of direct bookings may be increasingly outmoded. It would be salutary for the test to be reviewed in an appropriate case. However, it does not seem to me that this case offers a suitable opportunity. I therefore decide the case on the basis indicated above, without wishing to prejudice an argument in a later case that the true test may be wider, other than to the extent of my decision that, whatever the exact test may be, the defendants do not pass it.

In 'Hotel Cipriani', the Court of Appeal recognized that customers or their agents are now quite likely to make direct bookings with overseas service providers, such as hotels, and this practice might provide sufficient domestic goodwill. Lloyd LJ noted, however, that the test might change again in recognition of the increasing number of bookings for overseas services, which are made via websites.

5.2.1.3 The relationship between a reputation, goodwill, and location

In considering goodwill thus far, it is clear that there are three fundamental and related questions which may arise in an action for passing off, especially one which involves overseas commerce. These are: how to differentiate between reputation and goodwill; whether it is necessary to have actual goodwill in the UK to bring an action for passing off; and, third, how is one to assess the extent of that goodwill. The Supreme Court recently addressed all three of these questions in *Starbucks (HK) Ltd v British Sky Broadcasting Group Plc*. It did so fully conscious that the advent of the internet has fundamentally changed how we now do business.

Starbucks (HK) Ltd v British Sky Broadcasting Group Plc [2015] UKSC 31

The claimants, PCCM, supply a closed circuit internet television (IPTV) subscription service in Hong Kong, which has operated under the name 'NOW TV' since 2006. It has approximately 1.2 million subscribers and provides 200 channels, many with names including the word 'NOW'. The vast majority of its programmes are in Mandarin or Cantonese. The service cannot be received nor have any set top boxes been supplied in the UK. There are no subscribers to NOW TV with UK billing addresses. And PCCM has never held an OFCOM licence for UK broadcasting. Nonetheless, many Chinese-speaking residents of the UK would be aware of NOW TV, either through its Hong Kong service or because, since 2007, NOW TV Chinese content has been available on PCCM's website, its YouTube 'channel', and as video on demand on flights to the UK. PCCM has also been considering expanding its service into the UK, launching a NOW TV app which by October 2012 had been downloaded by 2,200 people. In July 2012, the defendants, collectively known as Sky, launched an IPTV service named 'NOW TV', available across all internet platforms. The claimants sued for passing off. PCCM argued that they had both a reputation in this country with those who might subscribe to its service in Hong Kong and it also had customers in this country because of the significant number of people who were exposed to its programmes on its website and on some international flights. The lower courts disagreed and PCCM appealed. On appeal, PCCM made the additional argument that even if it were held that they did not have customers in this country, the Supreme Court should acknowledge that in an age of e-commerce it was both impractical and unrealistic to treat goodwill as limited only to jurisdictions where a trader had customers and should instead allow a passing off action where the trader has a reputation but no goodwill. This was particularly the case, PCCM argued, in relation to electronically communicated services and should apply even if, as in this instance, users did not actually pay for such services. In his judgment, Lord Neuberger reiterated that to find passing off the three elements identified by Lord Oliver in 'Jif Lemon' must be present. He then identified the focus of the appeal in this case as being on the first element: 'namely the requirement that PCCM must establish what Lord Oliver referred to as "a goodwill or reputation attached to the goods or services which he supplies in the mind of the purchasing public by association" with the relevant "get-up", viz. the mark NOW TV with PCCM's IPTV service.'[21] Lord Neuberger noted

---

[21] [17].

that the lower courts had found that it had been insufficient for PCCM to show that it had a reputation among 'a significant number of people' in the UK, if it had no goodwill. He then affirmed, citing *Budweiser* as authority, the need for a claimant to demonstrate that its goodwill is situated in the UK, in the form of custom for its goods and services, in order to succeed in passing off. Accepting that PCCM had made a strong argument, Lord Neuberger nonetheless found for the defendants:

Lord Neuberger:

47 ...I have reached the conclusion that this appeal should be dismissed on the same ground on which it was decided in the courts below. In other words, I consider that we should reaffirm that the law is that a claimant in a passing off claim must establish that it has actual goodwill in this jurisdiction, and that such goodwill involves the presence of clients or customers in the jurisdiction for the products or services in question. And, where the claimant's business is abroad, people who are in the jurisdiction, but who are not customers of the claimant in the jurisdiction, will not do, even if they are customers of the claimant when they go abroad.

Lord Neuberger also declined to accept the claimant's suggestion that the court jettison the idea that claimants, with an online presence, must necessarily establish goodwill as opposed to a mere reputation in the relevant jurisdictions. He acknowledged that the court certainly had the power to adapt the common law to changed 'practical or commercial realities', if it chose.[22] But he held that he would not depart from the 'hardline approach' adopted in UK cases. He took this view not least because he believed that changing the law in this way could undermine legal certainty. However, he believed that two related aspects of the case required further elucidation. These were: what constitutes sufficient business to give rise to goodwill; and whether that goodwill has to be in England.

52. As to what amounts to a sufficient business to amount to goodwill, it seems clear that mere reputation is not enough, as the cases cited at [21]–[26] and [32]–[36] above establish. The claimant must show that it has a significant goodwill, in the form of customers, in the jurisdiction, but it is not necessary that the claimant actually has an establishment or office in this country. In order to establish goodwill, the claimant must have customers within the jurisdiction, as opposed to people in the jurisdiction who happen to be customers elsewhere. Thus, where the claimant's business is carried on abroad, it is not enough for a claimant to show that there are people in this jurisdiction who happen to be its customers when they are abroad. However, it could be enough if the claimant could show that there were people in this jurisdiction who, by booking with, or purchasing from, an entity in this country, obtained the right to receive the claimant's service abroad. And, in such a case, the entity need not be a part or branch of the claimant: it can be someone acting for or on behalf of the claimant. That is why, as explained in *Athlete's Foot*, the decision in *Panhard et Levassor* and the observations in *Pete Waterman* are compatible with the decision in *Alain Bernardin*.

53. As to Lord Diplock's statement in *Star Industrial* that, for the purpose of determining whether a claimant in a passing off action can establish the first of Lord Oliver's three elements, an English court has to consider whether the claimant can establish goodwill in

[22] [49]–[50].

England, I consider that it was correct. In other words, when considering whether to give protection to a claimant seeking relief for passing off, the court must be satisfied that the claimant's business has goodwill within its jurisdiction.

54. It would be wrong to suggest that there is a rule of law that, whatever the point at issue, goodwill has to be divided between jurisdictions, not least because (unsurprisingly) we have not had an exhaustive analysis of all the circumstances in which goodwill may have to be considered by the court. However, it seems to me that, when it comes to a domestic, common law issue such as passing off, an English court has to consider the factual position in the UK. That is well illustrated by the fact that, even if PCCM's argument was accepted and it was enough for a claimant merely to establish a reputation, that reputation would still have to be within the jurisdiction.

55. The notion that goodwill in the context of passing off is territorial in nature is also supported by refusal of judges to accept that a court of one jurisdiction has power to make orders in relation to the goodwill in another jurisdiction.

[Lord Neuberger then listed the various authorities for this stance. He continued:]

56. My view on the two issues discussed at [49]–[53] above is supported by a brief extract from Lord Fraser's speech in *Erven Warnink* at p.755, where he said that 'the meaning of the name in … countries other than England is immaterial because what the court is concerned to do is to protect the plaintiffs' property in the goodwill attaching to the name in England and it has nothing to do with the reputation or meaning of the name elsewhere'.

Lord Neuberger also thought it relevant that the CJEU in relation to registered trade mark law had adopted a similar approach, for example holding that genuine use of a registered trade mark necessitated the commercial exploitation of the mark in order to establish an actual market share. He then went on to say that maintaining that there is a difference between goodwill and reputation could lead to 'difficult decisions'. But he believed that there would be 'more unfairness' if he were to find for PCCM rather than for the defendant. Finally, Lord Neuberger identified an overriding public interest concern which he believed justified the current approach which stipulated the need for goodwill rather than a mere reputation to establish passing off.

61. It is also necessary to bear in mind the balancing exercise underlying the law of passing off, which Somers J described in *Dominion Rent A Car* at p.116 as 'a compromise between two conflicting objectives, on the one hand the public interest in free competition, on the other the protection of a trader against unfair competition by others'. More broadly, there is always a temptation to conclude that, whenever a defendant has copied the claimant's mark or get-up, and therefore will have benefitted from the claimant's inventiveness, expenditure or hard work, the claimant ought to have a cause of action against the defendant. Apart from the rather narrower point that passing off must involve detriment to the claimant, it is not enough for a claimant to establish copying to succeed. All developments, whether in the commercial, artistic, professional or scientific fields, are made on the back of other people's ideas: copying may often be an essential step to progress. Hence, there has to be some balance achieved between the public interest in not unduly hindering competition and encouraging development, on the one hand, and on the other, the public interest in encouraging, by rewarding through a monopoly, originality, effort and expenditure—the argument which is reflected in Turner LJ's observation at p.312 in *Maxwell v Hogg* to the effect that a plaintiff

who has merely advertised, but not marketed, his product, has given no consideration to the public in return for his claimed monopoly. In the instant case, the assessment of the appropriate balance between competition and protection, which arises in relation to any intellectual property right, must be made by the court, given that passing off is a common law concept.

62. If it was enough for a claimant merely to establish reputation within the jurisdiction to maintain a passing off action, it appears to me that it would tip the balance too much in favour of protection. It would mean that, without having any business or any consumers for its product or service in this jurisdiction, a claimant could prevent another person using a mark, such as an ordinary English word, 'now', for a potentially indefinite period in relation to a similar product or service. In my view, a claimant who has simply obtained a reputation for its mark in this jurisdiction in respect of his products or services outside this jurisdiction has not done enough to justify granting him an effective monopoly in respect of that mark within the jurisdiction.

63. I am unpersuaded that PCCM's case is strengthened by the fact that we are now in the age of easy worldwide travel and global electronic communication. While I accept that there is force in the point that the internet can be said to render the notion of a single international goodwill more attractive, it does not answer the points made at [51]–[59] above. Further, given that it may now be so easy to penetrate into the minds of people almost anywhere in the world so as to be able to lay claim to some reputation within virtually every jurisdiction, it seems to me that the imbalance between protection and competition which PCCM's case already involves (as described at [60]–[62] above) would be exacerbated. The same point can be made in relation to increased travel: it renders it much more likely that consumers of a claimant's product or service abroad will happen to be within this jurisdiction and thus to recognise a mark as the claimant's. If PCCM's case were correct, it would mean that a claimant could shut off the use of a mark in this jurisdiction even though it had no customers or business here, and had not spent any time or money in developing a market here—and did not even intend to do so.

Lord Neuberger's reasoning in *Starbucks* has been questioned. According to David Brophy,[23] its definition of 'customers' is too narrow:

However, the *Starbucks* decision is disappointing in its conservative approach to 'customers'. It is respectfully suggested that the decision does not satisfactorily explain why a UK intermediary is required for a UK resident to be a 'customer' of a foreign business. If someone in the UK is prepared to seek out and provide custom to a foreign business it appears artificial to hold that the business has no goodwill.

The most cited definition of goodwill is the 'attractive force which brings in custom'. Goodwill is the 'attractive force' in this definition, not the 'custom' itself or the (implied) destination towards which the force draws that custom. Attractive forces are not limited by borders, and imposing artificial requirements such as the need to book locally seems to add nothing positive to the cause of action, while potentially denying the remedy of passing-off to companies which do enjoy significant UK goodwill and custom.

Others have suggested that the requirement for a claimant to have more than a reputation in the UK constitutes an ultimately futile attempt to close the floodgates of global commerce

---

[23] 'Case comment: The Supreme Court decision in *Starbucks (HK) v British Sky Broadcasting*: is that crazy horse still running?' [2015] EIPR 661, 665.

which the internet has opened. Or do you agree with Lord Neuberger that accepting mere reputation rather than actual goodwill would allow a trader to monopolize an ordinary English word such as 'now' against its use by third parties? And that this monopoly might arise, particularly in the context of the internet, without the necessity of the trader committing the time and resources to developing an actual market, and hence goodwill, in any particular jurisdiction.

5.2.1.4 Local goodwill

Within the UK, goodwill may be local rather than national. For example, in *Associated Newspapers, Daily Mail and General Trust v Express Newspapers*,[24] it was held sufficient that the publishers of the *Daily Mail* had goodwill in London and the south-east of England in order to stop publication of the defendant's local newspaper, the *London Evening Mail*. However, the local nature of the claimant's goodwill may affect the reach of any subsequent injunction circumscribing the defendant's trading activities.[25]

5.2.1.5 The timing of goodwill

Goodwill may arise before a trader has begun trading. In *My Kinda Bones v Dr Pepper*, the claimant, trading as the Chicago Rib Shack, was able to persuade the court that its business had generated sufficient goodwill for a passing off action through a pre-launch advertising campaign.[26] Goodwill may also be abandoned[27] or conversely it may survive even after the cessation of a business. According to Arnold J in *Maslyukov v Diageo Distilling Ltd*,[28] 'the test is whether the relevant business has been abandoned so as to destroy the goodwill. Mere cessation of business is not enough.'[29] Hazel Carty has suggested that the test as to whether goodwill survives the cessation of a business is a multifactorial one and includes looking at the length of non-use, the size of the reputation before cessation of trading, whether the goods or services continue to have public recognition, and whether the purported owner of the goodwill has taken action to nurture its reputation.[30] An example of a case where goodwill was held to have survived cessation of trading is *Ad-Lib Club v Granville*.[31] Here, the claimant ran a successful nightclub which had been forced to close five years previously because of complaints about noise. However, the claimant was seeking alternative premises, and succeeded in a passing off action. One question raised by such cases is what damage might be suffered by a claimant who is not actively pursuing his business. The attitude of the court has been that the value of goodwill may derive not simply from its present use, but also any advantage that it may give to a claimant's future business plans. This point is illustrated by the decision in *Jules Rimet (JRCL) v The Football Association (FA)*.[32] The case concerned 'World Cup Willie', a cartoon lion dressed in a Union flag shirt, which the Football Association had created for the 1966 World Cup. Although it was very popular at the time, the FA did not continue to exploit the mascot. In 2005, JRCL sought to

---

[24] [2003] EWHC 1322 (Ch).
[25] *Clock v Clock House Hotel* (1936) 53 RPC 269 (CA); *Associated Newspapers v Express Newspapers.*
[26] *My Kinda Bones v Dr Pepper* [1984] FSR 289.
[27] *Star Industrial Co Ltd v Yap Kwee Kor* [1976] FSR 256.   [28] [2010] EWHC 443 (Ch).
[29] [80].
[30] H. Carty, 'The dissipation of goodwill in the tort of passing off: an analysis' [2015] IPQ 177.
[31] [1967] RPC 581.   [32] [2007] EWHC 2376 (Ch).

register the mascot's name and image as trade marks. In turn, the FA successfully opposed the application on the basis that it owned the goodwill in the name 'World Cup Willie'. Mr Roger Wyand QC, after considering the claimant's evidence which included references to the mascot in the press 'from time to time' and the 'odd' approach from traders seeking a licence, concluded that there was sufficient residual goodwill in the mascot for an action in passing off. There have been a number of cases where goodwill has been held to survive over lengthy periods without use but this is perhaps a record.[33] What distinguishes this case, it might be argued, is that JRCL made the decision to adopt the word and design marks in 2005 precisely because they still embodied valuable goodwill. On that basis, once it was held that the FA owned the goodwill in 1966, it would seem difficult to argue convincingly that it had now dissipated.

FURTHER READING

H. Carty, 'The dissipation of goodwill in the tort of passing off: an analysis' [2015] IPQ 177.

J. Davis, 'The continuing importance of local goodwill in passing off' [2015] CLJ 419.

D. Fields, 'Case comment: Supreme Court confirms that mere reputation in the UK is insufficient to establish passing off' (2015) 26 Ent. L. R. 217.

K. H. F. Kwok, 'Protection of a reputable foreign trader's legitimate interests under the law of passing-off' (2016) 132 LQR 186.

R. Swindells, 'Case comment: *Jules Rimet Cup Ltd v The Football Association Ltd*' (2008) 19 Ent. L. R. 41.

5.2.1.6 The definition of a trader

In order to bring a passing off action, the claimant must be a 'trader', for it is only a trader who will have ownership of the requisite goodwill.[34] In this context, 'trader' has been given a very wide definition by the courts. Claimants in passing off actions have included a famous diarist (Alan Clark),[35] ballroom dancers,[36] and a racing car driver, Eddie Irvine, whose goodwill resided in his business of endorsing products.[37] Trade associations, such as the Society of Accountants and Auditors, have been held to have the necessary goodwill to bring a passing off action,[38] as have non-profit and charitable organizations such as the Law Society,[39] the British Legion,[40] and a state- run community college.[41] Political organizations may also have goodwill. The Court of Appeal held that the Countryside Alliance, a non-profit political organization, which had never put up a candidate for election, could succeed in a passing off action against a former member of the far-right British National Party, who ran for Parliament describing himself on the ballot paper as 'Countryside Alliance'. The Countryside Alliance had significant trading activities designed to generate revenue for campaigning and lobbying. The claimants gave evidence that the reputation of the Alliance

---

[33] *Sutherland v V2 Music Ltd* [2002] EWHC 14 (Ch).
[34] See e.g. Lord Diplock in 'Advocaat'.
[35] *Clark v Associated Newspapers Ltd* [1998] 1 WLR 1558.
[36] *Henderson v Radio Corpn Pty Ltd* [1969] RPC 218.
[37] *Irvine v Talksport Ltd* [2002] 1 WLR 2355.
[38] *Society of Accountants and Auditors v Goodway & London Association of Accountants Ltd* [1907] Ch 489.
[39] *Law Society of England and Wales v Society of Lawyers* [1996] RSR 739.
[40] *British Legion v British Legion Club (Street) Ltd* (1931) 48 RPC 555.
[41] *Cranford Community College v Cranford College Ltd* [2014] EWHC 2999 (IPEC).

would be damaged by association with somebody with perceived racist views.[42] During the course of the action, the question arose as to whether the Alliance, being a non-commercial organization, could be said to have the requisite goodwill. According to Brooke LJ:[43]

> 61. … This line of authority shows that a claimant in a passing off action may be a charitable organisation or a professional institution which does not carry on commercial activity in the ordinary sense of the word, but which has unquestionably in the eyes of the law a valuable property in the sense of its goodwill which it is entitled to protect by bringing a passing off action if the three classic ingredients of a passing off action are present.

5.2.1.7 The ownership of goodwill

Goodwill is property. As such it can be sold or assigned. It cannot, however, be separated from the business to which it attaches. This was made clear by Lord Diplock in *Star Industrial Company Ltd v Yap Kwee Kor.*[44]

> **Lord Diplock, at p. 269:**
>
> Goodwill, as the subject of proprietary rights, is incapable of subsisting by itself. It has no independent existence apart from the business to which it is attached. It is local in character and divisible; if the business is carried on in several countries a separate goodwill attaches to it in each. So when the business is abandoned in one country in which it has acquired a goodwill, the goodwill in that country perishes with it although the business may continue to be carried on in other countries.

There may be more than one owner of goodwill. In a partnership or a joint venture, goodwill may be shared. In *Fine & Country Ltd v Okotoks Ltd,*[45] it was suggested the goodwill might also be shared between a licensor and licensee. It might also be shared by the owners of a business which has been divided, for instance between the founder's heirs (*Sir Robert McAlpine Ltd v Alfred McAlpine Plc*).[46] Alternatively, a number of traders may have goodwill in the same mark, such as the title 'mail' which is commonly attached to newspapers (*Associated Newspapers v Express Newspapers* [2003] FSR 51). Goodwill may also be shared between traders in goods which have distinctive characteristics in common, such as champagne, advocaat, and Swiss chocolate. In these circumstances, passing off may arise when the defendant misrepresents its own goods as sharing these characteristics. Such actions have come to be known as the extended form of passing off.

5.2.1.8 Shared goodwill/the extended form of passing off

It has been argued, by at least one observer,[47] that the novelty which characterizes the extended form of passing off is that it is not concerned with an 'origin misrepresentation'

---

[42] *Burge v Haycock* [2001] EWCA Civ 900, [2002] RPC 28.

[43] Brooke LJ distinguished this case from *Kean v McGivan* [1982] FSR 119, where the claimant also ran a political party, which was held to be not sufficiently known to have the necessary goodwill.

[44] [1976] FSR 256.   [45] [2012] EWHC 2230 (Ch).

[46] [2004] EWHC 630 (Ch), [2004] RPC 36.

[47] H. Carty, 'Dilution and passing off: cause for concern' (1996) 112 LQR 632–66.

but rather 'product misrepresentation'. In other words, the defendant does not misrepresent its goods as originating from a particular source, but rather it misrepresents the fact that its goods share the same characteristics as a certain category of goods. The extended form of passing off has commonly been associated with names of alcoholic drinks, since the first 'modern' case which involved the defendant selling a Spanish sparkling wine as 'Spanish champagne'.[48] Later cases involved sherry[49] and whisky.[50] In more recent times, it has expanded to include other products, such as chocolate.[51] It is 'Advocaat' which provides the authoritative definition of the extended form of passing off. In this case, Lord Diplock set out the circumstances in which a limited class of traders might share the goodwill in a particular product.

Erven Warnink BV v J. Townend & Sons (Hull) Ltd [1979] AC 731

The first claimants and other Dutch traders had for many years manufactured in the Netherlands a liquor called 'advocaat,' which was exported to Britain and distributed by the second claimants. The essential ingredients were the spirit brandewijn, egg yolks, and sugar as required by statutory regulations in the Netherlands, though the British regulations were not so specific. The liquor acquired a substantial reputation in Britain as a distinct and recognizable beverage. From 1974, a drink described as 'Keeling's Old English Advocaat' composed of dried egg powder mixed with Cyprus sherry was made and marketed in England by the defendants. Though it could not be shown that it was mistaken for Dutch advocaat, it captured a substantial part of the claimants' English market. In the passing off action in the High Court, Goulding J gave judgment for the claimants. The Court of Appeal reversed his decision and the case reached the House of Lords. Having set out the facts of the case and the general background to passing off, Lord Diplock first turned to the 'Champagne' case.

Lord Diplock, at p. 743:

The Champagne case came before Danckwerts J in two stages: the first (reported at [1960] RPC 16) on a preliminary point of law, the second (reported at [1961] RPC 116) on the trial of the action. The assumptions of fact on which the legal argument at the first stage was based were stated by the judge to be:

(1) The plaintiffs carry on business in a geographical area in France known as Champagne; (2) the plaintiffs' wine is produced in Champagne and from grapes grown in Champagne; (3) the plaintiffs' wine has been known in the trade for a long time as 'Champagne' with a high reputation; (4) members of the public or in the trade ordering or seeing wine advertised as 'Champagne' would expect to get wine produced in Champagne from grapes grown there; and (5) the defendants are producing a wine not produced in that geographical area and are selling it under the name of 'Spanish Champagne'.

---

[48] *Bollinger v Costa Brava Wine Co. Ltd* [1960] Ch 262.
[49] *Vine Products v Mackenzie* [1969] RPC 1.
[50] *John Walker & Sons Ltd v Douglas McGibbon & Co.* [1975] RPC 506.
[51] *Chocosuisse Union des Fabricants Suisse de Chocolat v Cadbury Ltd* [1998] RPC 117 (HC); [1999] RPC 286 (CA) ('the Swiss Chalet case').

These findings disclose a factual situation (assuming that damage was thereby caused to the plaintiffs' business) which contains each of the five characteristics which I have suggested must be present in order to create a valid cause of action for passing off. The features that distinguished it from all previous cases were (a) that the element in the goodwill of each of the individual plaintiffs that was represented by his ability to use without deception (in addition to his individual house mark) the word 'Champagne' to distinguish his wines from sparkling wines not made by the champenois process from grapes produced in the Champagne district of France, was not exclusive to himself but was shared with every other shipper of sparkling wine to England whose wines could satisfy the same condition and (b) that the class of traders entitled to a proprietary right in 'the attractive force that brings in custom' represented by the ability without deception to call one's wines 'Champagne' was capable of continuing expansion, since it might be joined by any future shipper of wine who was able to satisfy that condition. My Lords, in the Champagne case the class of traders between whom the goodwill attaching to the ability to use the word 'Champagne' as descriptive of their wines was shared was a large one, 150 at least and probably considerably more, whereas in the previous English cases of shared goodwill the number of traders between whom the goodwill protected by a passing off action was shared had been two ...

...

At p. 744:

It seems to me, however, as it seemed to Danckwerts J, that the principle must be the same whether the class of which each member is severally entitled to the goodwill which attaches to a particular term as descriptive of his goods, is large or small. The larger it is the broader must be the range and quality of products to which the descriptive term used by the members of the class has been applied, and the more difficult it must be to show that the term has acquired a public reputation and goodwill as denoting a product endowed with recognisable qualities which distinguish it from others of inferior reputation that compete with it in the same market. The larger the class the more difficult it must also be for an individual member of it to show that the goodwill of his own business has sustained more than minimal damage as a result of deceptive use by another trader of the widely shared descriptive term. As respects subsequent additions to the class, mere entry into the market would not give any right of action for passing off; the new entrant must have himself used the descriptive term long enough on the market in connection with his own goods and have traded successfully enough to have built up a goodwill for his business.

For these reasons the familiar argument that to extend the ambit of an actionable wrong beyond that to which effect has demonstrably been given in the previous cases would open the floodgates or, more ominously, a Pandora's box of litigation leaves me unmoved when it is sought to be applied to the actionable wrong of passing off.

I would hold the Champagne case to have been rightly decided and in doing so would adopt the words of Danckwerts J where he said (at [1960] RPC 31):

There seems to be no reason why such licence (*sc.* to do a deliberate act which causes damage to the property of another person) should be given to a person competing in trade, who seeks to attach to his product a name or description with which it has no natural association, so as to make use of the reputation and goodwill which has been gained by a product genuinely indicated by the name or description. In my view, it ought not to matter that the persons truly entitled to describe their goods by the name and description are a class producing goods in a certain locality, and not merely one individual. The description is part of their goodwill and a right of property. I do not believe that the law of passing off, which arose to prevent unfair trading, is so limited in scope.

...

At p. 747:

Of course it is necessary to be able to identify with reasonable precision the members of the class of traders of whose products a particular word or name has become so distinctive as to make their right to use it truthfully as descriptive of their product a valuable part of the goodwill of each of them; but it is the reputation that that type of product itself has gained in the market by reason of its recognisable and distinctive qualities that has generated the relevant goodwill. So if one can define with reasonable precision the type of product that has acquired the reputation, one can identify the members of the class entitled to share in the goodwill as being all those traders who have supplied and still supply to the English market a product which possesses those recognisable and distinctive qualities.

In 'Advocaat', Lord Diplock made it clear that the extended form of passing off is not confined to goods produced in a particular geographical area. In the later 'Chocosuisse' case,[52] the class of goods at issue was Swiss chocolate. A question raised in the High Court was whether descriptive words, such as these, could embody goodwill in the same manner as designations such as 'champagne' or 'Advocaat'. It was held that the words 'Swiss chocolate' were clearly descriptive. However, evidence from members of the public and the relevant trade sector showed that the words indicated a smoother chocolate, of high quality, and of Swiss origin. As a result, the words 'Swiss chocolate' had acquired in England a distinct reputation and manufacturers of Swiss chocolate shared the goodwill which attached to those words.

The question of which type of goods might be the subject of an action brought under the extended form of passing off was revisited in *Diageo v Intercontinental Brands*.

Diageo North America Inc. v Intercontinental Brands (ICB) Ltd
[2010] EWCA Civ 920

The defendants manufactured a mixed drink, containing vodka, which was sold under the name 'VODKAT'. The claimant, one of the world's leading producers of alcoholic drinks, including vodka, sued for passing off. At the time of the trial, vodka was the highest selling alcoholic beverage in the UK, while 'Vodkat' had been on the market for over four years and had sold at least 13 million bottles. Diageo claimed that by marketing its drink under the name 'VODKAT', the defendant was misrepresenting to the public that it was vodka. In its defence, ICB argued not only that the extended form of passing off was meant only to apply to products which had 'cachet' but also that the product 'vodka' did not denote a sufficiently precisely defined class of goods to be the subject of a passing off action. In the High Court, Arnold J found

---

[52] *Chocosuisse Union des Fabricants Suisses de Chocolat v Cadbury Ltd* [1998] ETMR 205.

that there had been passing off. The defendants appealed on the issue of goodwill and the claimants cross-appealed on the issue of the form of the injunction given. In the Court of Appeal, Patten LJ considered whether vodka was sufficiently clearly defined to be the subject of a passing off action. He suggested that like whisky, vodka fell into the category, defined by Wadlow in *The Law of Passing Off*, as 'generic terms with well-defined meanings, which may consequently be protected despite the fact that they are not distinctive in the traditional sense of denoting a specific producer'. Patten LJ continued:

26. Vodka and whisky fall into this category. Although they do not denote and are not derived from any particular geographical location, they have, as a matter of language, come to be used to describe particular types of spirit distilled in a particular way. To that extent they are no different in descriptive terms from the other examples of well-known commodities relied on by Mr Wyand such as beer or butter.

Patten LJ went on to say that if products of this kind 'are to qualify for protection under the extended form of passing-off it can only be because they have acquired a reputation and goodwill in their own name by dint of the qualities or characteristics which they possess'. He then cited with approval the judgment of the Court of Appeal in the 'Chocosuisse' case, before returning to the present action.

28. The switch in focus from the name and reputation of the seller to that of the product ought not in principle to impose a less stringent test in terms of what is required to establish the necessary goodwill in the product and an actionable misrepresentation on the part of the defendant in relation to his own goods. In ordinary cases of passing-off the claimant has to show that the use of a particular mark or get-up has become distinctive of his goods and will be treated in the public mind as an indication that when used in relation to goods of that kind, the goods in question will be seen to be his goods or goods connected with him. This requirement that the name or mark should be distinctive is critical to any finding of goodwill subsisting in the use of the mark. The mark has to distinguish the goods sold under it from those of other traders. It may also be determinative of the allegation of misrepresentation. A trader who uses a name which is primarily descriptive of the product is likely to have more difficulty in proving misrepresentation against a defendant who uses the same name to describe a similar product of his own.

29. But there is no legal requirement that the distinctiveness of the claimant's mark should also be a badge of quality. Whether it generates goodwill in relation to the goods or services sold will inevitably be determined by the impact which they have on consumers. Doubtless the better the quality or the more fashionable they are, the more likely it is that the necessary reputation and goodwill will be acquired. But this factor is evidential in character and largely co-incidental. The law of passing-off is there to protect the unlawful appropriation of goodwill through misrepresentation. It is not there to guarantee to the general consumer the quality of what he buys. For that he must look elsewhere.

[After reviewing the authorities on the extended form of passing off, Patten LJ took up the defendant's argument that for goods to have sufficient goodwill in the extended form of passing off they must have 'cachet'.]

51. It seems clear to me from this and the other statements of principle in *ADVOCAAT* that there is no support in the authorities for Mr Wyand's submission that in cases of extended

passing-off some cachet must be found in the sense of the product being a superior or luxury brand. Of course if, by a cachet, one means no more than distinctiveness then there is no difficulty. But I endorse the view of the judge that the argument that the product must be a premium or luxury one is in fact contrary to the principle which underlies all these cases. So-called premium brands are likely (perhaps more likely) in many cases to acquire the distinctiveness required. But goodwill may attach to a product simply because consumers come to like and value it for its inherent qualities rather than its status. In fairness to Mr Wyand, I think that he ultimately recognised that this may be the wrong emphasis. What he is essentially contending for is a high degree of distinctiveness which he says is not apparent in generally available products such as vodka.

52. Whether or not any particular product has acquired the kind of public reputation described by Lord Diplock is a question of fact for the trial judge. One of the dangers about highlighting the references in cases on champagne, sherry and advocaat to the product having superior or special qualities is that it risks elevating the facts of those cases into a principle. The criteria to be satisfied are those set out by Lord Diplock and Lord Fraser in *ADVOCAAT* and the judge in this case directed himself in accordance with them. Mr Wyand's example of white paint is unlikely to qualify on these principles. As a term it is imprecise and purely descriptive and could apply to any type of paint which might arguably be described as the colour white. It is difficult therefore to see how, as a product, it could ever acquire the necessary distinctiveness of kind or how any paint manufacturer could establish goodwill in the product itself divorced from the goodwill attaching to the manufacturer's own name and reputation. This is not therefore a serious example, in my view, of the range of goods which might qualify for protection under the *ADVOCAAT* principles. Butter, on the other hand, might be different. But I have to say that I find these hypothetical examples largely unhelpful. Vodka has, on the judge's findings in this case, become known and recognised for its distinctive qualities as a particular kind of alcoholic drink. Why then, one asks, should it not be entitled to the same protection as champagne given that it satisfies the criteria which the House of Lords has laid down in *ADVOCAAT*?

53. The judge in this case has found that the conditions described in Lord Fraser's speech in *ADVOCAAT* have all been satisfied and there is no challenge to any of those findings; in particular that relating to distinctiveness. Its qualities as a clear, tasteless, distilled, high strength spirit have given vodka a following which has created significant goodwill in the name. That is sufficient in my view to entitle Diageo to protection for their product against VODKAT which, on the judge's findings, passes itself off as the same product. Mr Wyand's difficulty in formulating a precise definition of the level of distinctiveness necessary to create the cachet he contends for is because the concept of distinctiveness which is effective to produce the necessary goodwill provides a sufficient and comprehensive yardstick for deciding which products qualify for protection. Nothing more is needed or, in my view, justified. The argument that one should graft on to this some additional cachet requirement amounts to an attempt to by-pass or undermine the judge's findings on reputation and goodwill which are not the subject of this appeal.

Patten LJ upheld the High Court decision and dismissed the defendant's appeal. In his judgment in the High Court, Arnold J had said of consumers of vodka, 'They may not know precisely what it is, what it is made from or where it is made, but they use the term "vodka" to get what they want and to distinguish it from other similar products.' Laddie J had made a similar point about the lack of agreement between consumers of Swiss chocolate as to what distinguished that product, apart from the fact that it is made in Switzerland. And so did the Court of Appeal in an action concerning 'Greek Yoghurt'.[53] We might ask, on that basis, what product could not, in principle, be the subject of a passing off action? Patten LJ, for example, suggested white paint could not, but butter might. But would bread? After all, it is surely the case that every consumer will have his or her view of what constitutes bread and what does not, but these views will vary widely.

In 'Chocosuisse', the question was also raised as to when a trader might join the ranks of those who bring an extended form of passing off action. In his judgment, Laddie J observed that it is open to any trader to participate provided the term at issue, here Swiss chocolate, properly describes and designates its own goods (thus appearing to differ from Lord Diplock in 'Advocaat' who opined that prospective claimants would need to build up individual goodwill in relation to the products at issue). Conversely, those who already trade in these goods cannot use the term on goods which do not share their defining characteristics without misrepresentation. Or as Laddie J noted: 'it is not open to any existing user of the protected name to use it on products for which it is not an accurate description or designation. Messrs Taittinger are no more entitled to use the word Champagne on a non-alcoholic cola drink than anyone else.'[54] Nonetheless, it has been argued that the extended form of passing off, which protects designations which are not only distinctive but also descriptive, might be anti-competitive. This point was considered by Kitchin LJ in the 'Greek yoghurt' case, where a maker of yoghurt manufactured in Greece alleged passing off against a manufacturer selling as Greek, a yoghurt made in the US. Kitchin LJ noted:

> 148. Whether the current state of the law has drawn the line between what is capable of protection and what is not in the correct place may well be the subject of debate. I share some of the concerns expressed by Rix L.J. in the *Diageo* case that this form of passing off risks stifling healthy competition in relatively low cost generic goods. But in my judgment the location of the line has been drawn by *Chocosuisse*, by which we are bound; and for as long as that remains the law, it means that the judge was entitled to reach the conclusions that he did.

Recently, in *NOCN v Open College Network*,[55] the High Court did draw the line. The court held that despite a number of years of use exclusively by members of one organization, the term 'Open College Network', to describe services rendered to adult education colleges, lacked the distinctiveness necessary for an action in the extended form of passing off. However, might this judgment simply suggest that services can be even harder to define in any concrete way than goods?

5.2.2 DISTINGUISHING CRITERIA

According to Lord Jauncey in 'Jif Lemon': 'Get-up is the badge of the plaintiff's goodwill, that which associates the goods with the plaintiff in the mind of the public' (p. 511). It is a matter of fact in each case whether the mark, get-up, or trade name under which a product is sold is distinctive of the claimant's goodwill.

---

[53] *Fage UK Ltd v Chobani UK Ltd* [2014] EWCA Civ 5.   [54] *Chocosuisse*, p. 214.
[55] *NOCN (formerly National Open College Network) v Open College Network Credit4Learning* [2015] EWHC 2667 (IPEC).

5.2.2.1 The definition of distinguishing criteria

Passing off protects goodwill attached to the goods or services which the claimant supplies by association with an 'identifying indicia' or get-up. A passing off action most commonly protects the claimant against deceptive use by the defendant of this identifying or distinctive indicia which attaches to the claimant's goodwill. It is not necessary for the consumer to know the ultimate owner of the goodwill, as long as the public believes that all goods or services sold under a distinctive insignia derive from a single source which is the claimant.[56] A useful way of determining whether any particular indicia is distinctive is to ask: may only the claimant use it in relation to its goods or services without deception or misrepresentation? If that is the case, then the indicia is distinctive. It follows that when an indicia is distinctive, the claimant will have an effective monopoly on its use. As was put by Lord Jauncey in 'Jif Lemon': 'The common law will protect goodwill against misrepresentation by recognizing a monopoly in a particular get-up.' The fact that the law of passing off effectively recognizes a monopoly in the use of distinguishing insignia by the claimant has raised particular difficulties in relation to descriptive insignia and get-up which is common to the trade.

5.2.2.2 The limits to distinctiveness (1): descriptive insignia and get-up common to the trade

If any insignia, be it a word, a colour, or even a shape, is in practice descriptive of the goods or services to which it applies then it would appear to be a hard thing to prevent any other supplier from using such insignia to accurately describe its own goods and services. The same might be true of get-up which is commonly used by a number of suppliers of particular goods or services. Nonetheless, it also possible that, because of the way in which a claimant uses such insignia on the market, the insignia may come to be associated exclusively with its goods or services in the mind of the public. If it does, it will have acquired a 'secondary meaning'. In other words, it will be not just descriptive of the claimant's goods or services, but also distinctive of its goodwill. Descriptive insignia or get-up common to the trade which has acquired a secondary meaning, will be protected against use by other traders in passing off. It is possible, therefore, once such insignia has acquired a secondary meaning that a single trader may monopolize its use. Such a result raises public interest concerns. It seems reasonable to ask whether competition between traders will be unduly inhibited if only one trader may use a word, colour, or shape which may accurately describe the goods or services supplied by other traders or which other traders have been accustomed to use.

The question of when such insignia may acquire a secondary meaning was central to the 'Jif Lemon' case. So, too, was the issue of whether it was in the public interest to allow descriptive insignia and get-up common to the trade, which had acquired a secondary meaning, to be protected by a passing off action. In their speeches Lords Oliver and Jauncey looked at the first question. Lord Bridge considered the public interest issue.

Reckitt & Colman Products Ltd v Borden Inc. (No. 3) [1990] 1 WLR 491

The claimants sold lemon juice in yellow plastic containers that were similar in size and shape to a lemon. The containers had the word 'Jif' embossed on them and also had a yellow cap and a green label. The product had been sold for over 30 years and had

---

[56] *Edge (William) & Sons Ltd v William Niccolls & Sons Ltd* [1911] AC 693 (HL).

become known as 'Jif lemon'. In 1985, the defendants began selling lemon juice also in lemon-shaped containers with a green cap. Both the products were sold in supermarkets. The claimants began an action in passing off. They obtained an interim injunction in the High Court. The defendants' appeal was dismissed by the Court of Appeal and the defendants unsuccessfully appealed to the House of Lords.

The first issue raised in the case was whether the claimants had proved that the get-up under which their lemon juice had been sold since 1956 had become associated in the minds of the public specifically and exclusively with the claimant's (or 'Jif') lemon juice. The defendants' first argument was that the claimants were not seeking to protect the goodwill associated with the get-up of their product, but rather the product itself. Lord Oliver addressed this issue.

Lord Oliver, at p. 503:

There is not and cannot be any proprietary right in an idea nor can a trader claim a monopoly in the manufacture or sale of a non-patented article or, in the absence of a registered design, in the configurations of shape in which an article is manufactured. What the respondents are seeking to do, it is said, is to separate the article sold from the label under which it is sold, treat the article itself as its own trade mark and, by protecting a claim to monopoly in the mark, to establishing in the manufacture and sale of the article itself a monopoly which the law does not permit.

[Second, the defendants argued that the claimants' get-up could not be protected because it was common to the trade. Thirdly, they maintained that the get-up was descriptive, albeit in shape form, of the product. Lords Oliver and Jauncey dismissed all three arguments. Lord Oliver continued:]

At p. 504:

It is, no doubt, true that the plastic lemon-shaped container serves, as indeed does a bottle of any design, a functional purpose in the sale of lemon juice. Apart from being a container *simpliciter*, it is a convenient size; it is capable of convenient use by squeezing; and it is so designed as conveniently to suggest the nature of its contents without the necessity for further labelling or other identification. But those purposes are capable of being and indeed are served by a variety of distinctive containers of configurations other than those of a lemon-sized lemon. Neither the appellants nor the respondents are in the business of selling plastic lemons. Both are makers and vendors of lemon juice and the only question is whether the respondents, having acquired a public reputation for Jif juice by selling it for many years in containers of a particular shape and design which, on the evidence, has become associated with their produce, can legitimately complain of the sale by the appellants of similar produce in containers of similar, though not identical, size, shape, and colouring.

So I, for my part, would reject the suggestion that the plastic lemon container is an object in itself rather than part of the get-up under which the respondents' produce is sold.

[Lord Oliver then addressed the question of whether when two traders use the same descriptive insignia or get up for their products such that confusion results, this necessarily give rise to an action in passing off. He held that it did not. In such circumstances there would be no actionable misrepresentation, since both traders would be using the insignia correctly to describe their goods. The defendants claimed that such was the case here, and that the claimants were 'asking the court to protect no more than use by them of a descriptive term, embodied in a plastic lemon instead of expressed verbally, which is common to the trade'.

At p. 506:

Every case depends upon its own peculiar facts. For instance, even a purely descriptive term consisting of perfectly ordinary English words may, by a course of dealing over many years, become so associated with a particular trader that it acquires a secondary meaning such that it may properly be said to be descriptive of that trader's goods and of his goods alone, as in *Reddaway v Banham* [1896] AC 199. In the instant case, what is said is that there was nothing particularly original in marketing lemon juice in plastic containers made to resemble lemons. The respondents were not the first to think of it even though they have managed over the past 30 years to establish a virtual monopoly in the United Kingdom. It is, in fact, a selling device widely employed outside the United Kingdom. It is a natural, convenient and familiar technique—familiar at least to those acquainted with retail marketing methods in Europe and the United States. If and so far as this particular selling device has become associated in the mind of the purchasing public with the respondents' Jif lemon juice, that is simply because the respondents have been the only people in the market selling lemon juice in this particular format. Because there has been in fact a monopoly of this sale of this particular article, the public is led to make an erroneous assumption that a similar article brought to the market for the first time must emanate from the same source. This has been referred to in the argument as 'the monopoly assumption'. The likelihood of confusion was admitted by the appellants themselves in the course of their evidence, but it is argued that the erroneous public belief which causes the product to be confused arises simply from the existing monopoly and not from any deception by the appellants in making use of what they claim to be a normal, ordinary and generally available selling technique.

The difficulty about this argument is that it starts by assuming the only basis upon which it can succeed, that is to say, that the selling device which the appellants wish to adopt is ordinary and generally available or, as it is expressed in some of the cases, 'common to the trade': see e.g. *Payton & Co Ltd v Snelling, Lampard & Co Ltd* (1900) 17 RPC 48. In one sense, the monopoly assumption is the basis of every passing off action. The deceit practised on the public when one trader adopts a get-up associated with another succeeds only because the latter has previously been the only trader using that particular get-up. But the so called 'monopoly assumption' demonstrates nothing in itself. As a defence to a passing off claim it can succeed only if that which is claimed by the plaintiff as distinctive of his goods and his goods alone consists of something either so ordinary or in such common use that it would be unreasonable that he should claim it as applicable solely to his goods, as for instance where it consists simply of a description of the goods sold. Here the mere fact that he has previously been the only trader dealing in goods of that type and so described may lead members of the public to believe that all such goods must emanate from him simply because they know of no other. To succeed in such a case he must demonstrate more than simply the sole use of the descriptive term. He must demonstrate that it has become so closely associated with his goods as to acquire the secondary meaning not simply of goods of that description but specifically of goods of which and he alone is the source.

...

At p. 507:

In the instant case the submission that the device of selling lemon juice in a natural size lemon-shaped squeeze pack is something that is 'common to the trade' and therefore incapable of protection at the suit of a particular trader begs the essential question. If 'common to the trade' means 'in general use in the trade' then, so far as at least as the United

Kingdom is concerned, the evidence at the trial clearly established that the lemon-sized squeeze pack was not in general use. If, on the other hand, it means, as the appellants submit, 'available for use by the trade' then it is so available only if it has not become so closely associated with the respondents' goods as to render its use by the appellants deceptive; and that is the very question in issue. The trial judge here has found as a fact that the natural size squeeze pack in the form of a lemon has become so associated with Jif lemon juice that the introduction of the appellants' juice in any of the proposed get-ups will be bound to result in many housewives purchasing that juice in the belief that they are obtaining Jif juice. I cannot interpret that as anything other than a finding that the plastic lemon-shaped container has acquired, as it were, a secondary significance. It indicates not merely lemon juice but specifically Jif lemon juice.

In his speech, Lord Jauncey looked at earlier cases regarding goodwill in the shapes of products. He continued:

Lord Jauncey, at p. 519:

In my view these two cases are merely examples of the general principle that no man may sell his goods under the pretence that they are the goods of another. This principle applies as well to the goods themselves as to their get-up. A markets a ratchet screwdriver with a distinctively shaped handle. The screwdriver has acquired a reputation for reliability and utility and is generally recognised by the public as being the product of A because of its handle A would be entitled to protection against B if the latter sought to market a ratchet screwdriver with a similarly shaped handle without taking sufficient steps to see that the public were not misled into thinking that his product was that of A. It is important to remember that such protection does not confer on A a monopoly in the sale of ratchet screwdrivers not even in the sale of such screwdrivers with similarly distinctive handles if other appropriate means can be found of distinguishing the two products. Once again it will be a question of fact whether the distinguishing features are sufficient to avoid deception.

In the end of the day this is a very simple case notwithstanding the able and attractive arguments addressed to your Lordships and the plethora of authority referred to. It is not in dispute that the respondents have acquired over many years a reputation in the market for their lemon juice got up in plastic lemons. There is abundant evidence that customers would be deceived if any of the three Marks of the appellants' lemons were put on the market in their present form. No reason in law has been made out why this evidence should not have been accepted. The respondents have accordingly established the facts necessary to succeed. The decisions in the courts below and in this House do not have the effect of conferring on the respondents a monopoly right to sell lemon juice in plastic lemons. They merely decide that on the facts as found, the appellants in seeking to enter the plastic lemon market have not taken adequate steps to differentiate their get-up from that of the respondents so that consumers will not be deceived.

For the foregoing reasons and for the reasons given by my noble and learned friend, Lord Oliver of Aylmerton, I would dismiss the appeal.

In 'Jif Lemon', both Lord Oliver and Lord Jauncey raised the question of whether the claimants' victory would endow them with a monopoly of selling lemon juice in plastic lemons. They both took the view it would not. Anyone could sell their products in the same way, if they sufficiently differentiated their own product from that of the claimants. As we shall see, in the next section on misrepresentation, this is something the defendants singularly failed to do. Nonetheless, both Lords Oliver and Jauncey concluded that it is in principle possible for a trader to have an effective monopoly on certain descriptive insignia or the shape of goods, in this case the shape of a plastic lemon, if it can be shown that they have acquired a secondary meaning. We may think that it would be unlikely that another trader would choose to sell its product in a lemon-shaped container given the outcome of the 'Jif Lemon' case, even if it had differentiating features. Certainly, the outcome troubled Lord Bridge who saw it as anti-competitive.

> ### Lord Bridge, at p. 494:
>
> When plastic containers made in the shape, colour and size of natural lemons first appeared on the market in the United Kingdom as squeeze packs containing preserved lemon juice the respondents were astute enough to realise their potential and to buy up the businesses of the two companies who first marketed preserved lemon juice in this way. They thereby acquired a de facto monopoly which, by the periodical threat or institution of passing off actions over the years, they have succeeded in preserving ever since. This is the first such action to come to trial.
>
> The idea of selling preserved lemon juice in a plastic container designed to look as nearly as possible like the real thing is such a simple, obvious and inherently attractive way of marketing the product that it seems to me utterly repugnant to the law's philosophy with respect to commercial monopolies to permit any trader to acquire a de jure monopoly in the container as such. But, as Mr Jacob for the respondents, quite rightly pointed out, the order made by the trial judge in this case does not confer any such de jure monopoly because the injunction restrains the appellants from marketing their product 'in any container so nearly resembling the plaintiffs' Jif lemon-shaped container as to be likely to deceive *without making it clear to the ultimate purchaser that it is not of the goods of the plaintiff*' [emphasis added]. How then are the appellants, if they wish to sell their product in plastic containers of the shape, colour and size of natural lemons, to ensure that the buyer is not deceived? The answer, one would suppose, is by attaching a suitably distinctive label to the container. Yet here is the paradox: the trial judge found that a buyer reading the labels proposed to be attached to the appellants' Mark I, II or III containers would know at once that they did not contain Jif lemon juice and would not be deceived; but he also enjoined the appellants from selling their product in those containers because he found, to put it shortly, that housewives buying plastic lemons in super markets do not read the labels but assume that whatever they buy must be Jif. The result seems to be to give the respondents a de facto monopoly of the container as such which is just as effective as de jure monopoly. A trader selling plastic lemon juice would never be permitted to register a lemon as his trade mark,[57] but the respondents have achieved the result indirectly that a container designed to look like a real lemon is to be treated, per se, as distinctive of their goods.

In his speech, Lord Bridge shows his concern that the claimants were able to obtain a 'de facto' monopoly over a container (in this case a plastic lemon) through their successful passing off action. He took the view that allowing the claimants a monopoly of such an obvious and attractive way of marketing lemon juice undermined competition and, as a result, was detrimental to the public interest. Presumably, one response to such a

---

[57] At the time, a shape could not be registered as a trade mark. The 1994 Trade Mark Act allowed the registration of shapes.

concern would be that it is equally in the public interest that consumers should not be deceived, as would be the case were others to use the claimants' distinctive insignia. Another might be that 'Jif Lemon' is a rarity. In most cases, goodwill will be distinguished not by get-up or a descriptive sign alone, but through the addition of another distinguishing mark such as a trade name.[58] It is also true that placing a combination of a trade name and a descriptive mark on goods or services may present its own dangers, as we shall see below.

5.2.2.3 The limits to distinctiveness (2): generic marks

A trader may introduce a new product onto the market. In doing so, the trader will give the product a name. The name chosen may be an entirely made-up word. Or it might alternatively be descriptive in some way of the product. If the latter, the question arises as to whether the name will have a 'built in' secondary meaning because the trader is the only one providing the product. Or, if the name is descriptive (or indeed if it is entirely made up), will the name lose any secondary meaning it may have had and come to be seen as synonymous with the product precisely because it is the only such product on the market? Should the latter occur, then the name has become generic and use of a generic mark will not be protected by a passing off action. Each of these possible outcomes was rehearsed in the 'McCain Oven Chips' case.

McCain International v Country Fair Foods [1981] RPC 69 (CA)

In 1979, the claimants introduced a new product into the UK market: chips which could be cooked in the oven. They sold the product under the name 'McCain Oven Chips'. A year later, the defendants introduced their own version of the product which they sold under the names, 'Country Fair Oven Chips' and 'Birds Eye Oven Chips'. The claimants obtained an injunction in the High Court to restrain the defendants from marketing their product under the name 'oven chips' with or without their own brand names. The defendants appealed. The defendants argued that the name 'Oven Chip' was descriptive of the product, that it had not subsequently acquired distinctiveness, and that where a descriptive name had been applied to a product by the sole supplier of that product that name could not easily acquire distinctiveness. The claimants argued that 'oven chips' was not descriptive but was a fancy name because it was an ungrammatical combination of two words which had not previously been associated together and, further, that by virtue of the claimants' extensive sales and advertising it had acquired a secondary meaning.

Templeman LJ, at p. 73:

The authorities, many of which, unavoidably, were not considered by the learned judge, disclose that there is a very real distinction in passing off litigation between a fancy name and a descriptive name. A fancy name which is not descriptive of a product can only indicate that the product bearing that name is, or is licensed by, or is derived from one and the same supplier. Thus in *Spalding & Bros v Gamage Ltd* (1915) 32 RPC 273, the plaintiffs described

---

[58] *Moroccanoil Israel Ltd v Aldi Stores Ltd* [2014] EWHC 1686 (IPEC), [30]–[31].

their football as 'Orb football'. Mr Harman submitted that might be a descriptive phrase, but in my judgment it was a fancy name in that nobody would have dreamed of connecting a football with an orb in normal speech, and as it was a fancy name the defendants could not use the same fancy name without thereby representing that their goods were the goods of the plaintiff. In my judgment a fancy name is an indication of a single source and that is why it is impossible, generally speaking, for a defendant to appropriate the same fancy name without committing the tort of passing off.

A descriptive name, on the other hand, does not indicate the source of the goods, but the nature of the goods. In the present case, the name 'oven chips' is a descriptive name which is not so far-fetched or fanciful as to indicate that all oven chips emanate from the same source. Indeed the plaintiffs themselves appear to have recognised that the expression 'oven chips' is not in itself a fancy name which indicates as single source or origin. That is why they have consistently referred in their literature and in their packaging to 'McCain oven chips'. In my judgment they found it necessary or prudent to do so in order to distinguish their brand of oven chips from any other brand. The expression 'oven chips' in my judgment identifies the product and the name 'McCain', identifies the manufacturer who is responsible for that particular brand of that product.

[Templeman LJ then distinguished the present case from *Reddaway v Banham* (1896)[59] in which it was held that the claimant's product, 'Camel-hair Belting', had acquired a secondary meaning in connection with belting, in that it did not convey to persons dealing in belting the idea that it was made of camel's hair, but rather that it was belting manufactured by the claimant. He continued:]

At p. 73:

In the present case, not only is the period [of trading] only 18 months, but it seems to me that it is quite impossible for the plaintiffs to establish that a secondary meaning has been attached to anything other than that which is claimed on their own packet and what is claimed on their own packet is 'McCain oven chips'. I have no doubt that in the trade, both as regards consumers and retailers, the name 'McCain oven chips' means those oven chips made by the plaintiffs, but the words 'oven chips' *simpliciter* never have been used in isolation by the plaintiffs. There has been neither the opportunity nor the time for people to form the impression that the only makers of oven chips are and will remain McCain. It must be remembered that in the field of frozen foods the consumer is accustomed to different brands of the same or similar products and is accustomed to competing brands coming on to the market at different times.

...

At p. 75:

In my judgment, the distinction is between a name which is descriptive of the product and a name which is distinctive of the manufacturer. In the present case the words 'oven chips' are distinctive of the product, and the words 'McCain oven chips' refer to the brand of the product which is put on sale by the plaintiffs.

...

---

[59] [1896] AC 199.

At pp. 80–1:

It does not seem to me in the light of the admitted facts and of the evidence, and in the light of the authorities to which I have referred, that the plaintiffs have established a triable issue which justifies the granting of an injunction pending trial. Shortly, the words 'oven chips' are in my judgment descriptive of the product and the defendants will not, by using those words in conjunction with their own brand name represent, and no reasonable person would infer, that the goods sold by the defendants are to have some association with the plaintiffs' goods. There is no danger of actual confusion and the plaintiffs, by their advertisements and by their evidence, have not succeeded in establishing that the words 'oven chips' mean, and must mean, potato chips supplied by the plaintiffs and nobody else.

[Templeman LJ also disagreed with the High Court judgment which found the fact that McCain was the only manufacturer using the phrase 'oven chips' significant.]

In my judgment that is falling into the trap of saying that because the product was novel and the name was novel, therefore the plaintiffs are entitled to a monopoly in the name. As I think I have shown from the authorities, that is not the law. On the contrary if the plaintiffs introduce a novel product with novel words, but they take the risk of choosing descriptive words, then they run the risk that the defendants cannot be prevented from using those same descriptive words so long as they make it clear that their brands of the product are not the same as the brand of the plaintiffs.

The learned judge continued:

there has been a substantial volume of sales of oven chips and I am satisfied on the evidence that 'Oven Chips' has become distinctive of the plaintiffs' product and no one else's.

With respect it seems to me impossible to reach that conclusion when there has not been a substantial sale of oven chips, but a substantial sale of McCain oven chips and there is not, and there could not be, any evidence of what the reaction of consumers would be if what had been sold over the counter were oven chips without the name McCain.

The claimants failed in the 'McCain' case. How important to this failure is the fact that they only sold their 'oven chips' in conjunction with their brand name, 'McCain'? Bearing in mind the earlier comments about 'Jif Lemon', do you think that the outcome would have been different if the claimants had sold their new product from its inception only under the name 'Oven Chips'?

5.2.2.4 The protection given to distinctive insignia as such

It has been noted that the property protected by an action in passing off is goodwill. There is a strong argument that more recently the courts have come to accept that a passing off action will protect not simply damage to a claimant's goodwill caused by a defendant's misrepresentation, but also damage to the claimant's distinctive insignia. According to Kerr LJ in his dissenting judgment in the *Harrods* case, 'a trader's distinctive name can in some cases in itself form part of its goodwill and constitute a property interest'. From this perspective, damage can be said to occur because the defendant, by employing the claimant's insignia to misrepresent the origin or characteristics of its own goods, will 'dilute' the distinctiveness of the claimant's insignia and hence its value. For example, in the 'Elderflower champagne' case, the defendant described its cheap, non-alcoholic drink as 'champagne'.[60] The Court of Appeal accepted that not only would some consumers buy the defendant's product instead of champagne, but that by using the word champagne to describe its inferior product, the defendant was also 'diluting' the value of the word more generally. At the heart of this development is the question of where the damage lies. Is it damage to goodwill or damage to the insignia as such which passing off protects or both? For this reason, the issue of 'dilution' will be considered more fully in the section of this chapter which is devoted to the third element of passing off: damage.

FURTHER READING

J. Agnew, 'Misleading use of geographical marks: extending passing-off for Greek yoghurt' [2013] EIPR 692.

H. Carty, 'Passing off: frameworks for liability debated' [2012] IPQ 106.

D. Stone and B. Heard, 'VODKAT is not vodka: "extended" passing off extended' [2010] JIJIP 842.

C. Wadlow, 'The House of Lords ruling in Jif Lemon' (1990) 2(2) IPB Rev. 19.

5.2.3   MISREPRESENTATION

The second element in a passing off action is a misrepresentation. The misrepresentation must be actionable or material.

5.2.3.1 The definition

An actionable misrepresentation will be one which deceives the consumer and, as a result, the claimant suffers or is likely to suffer damage. For instance, the defendant may misrepresent to the consumer that his product originates from the claimant. As a result of that misrepresentation, the consumer may purchase the defendant's product. To be an actionable misrepresentation, a substantial number of customers must be confused. Lord Jauncey considered the nature of a misrepresentation in the 'Jif Lemon' case.

Lord Jauncey, at p. 510:

The basic underlying principle of such an action was stated in 1842 by Lord Langdale MR in *Perry v Truefitt* (1842) 6 Beav 66, 73 to be: 'A man is not to sell his own goods under the pretence that they are the goods of another man...' Accordingly, a misrepresentation achieving such a result is actionable because it constitutes an invasion of proprietary rights vested in the plaintiff. However, it is a prerequisite of any successful passing off action that the plaintiff's goods have acquired a reputation in the market and are known by some distinguishing feature. It is also a prerequisite that the misrepresentation has deceived or is likely to deceive and that the plaintiff is likely to suffer damage by such deception. Mere confusion which does not lead to a sale is not sufficient. Thus, if a customer asks for a tin of black shoe polish without specifying any brand and is offered the product of A which he mistakenly believes to be that of B, he may be confused as to what he has got but he has not been deceived into getting it. Misrepresentation has played no part in his purchase.

---

[60] *Taittinger SA v Allbev Ltd* [1993] FSR 641 (the 'Elderflower champagne' case).

5.2.3.2 A misrepresentation and mere confusion

As was suggested by Lord Jauncey, there is a difference between an actionable misrepresentation in a passing off action and 'mere' confusion. The latter may affect a consumer's actions in relation to the product or service, but does not result in damage to the claimant's goodwill. In *Phones 4u v Phone 4u*, Jacob LJ examined the distinction between a misrepresentation which is vital to an action for passing off and mere confusion.

Phones 4u Ltd v Phone4u.co.uk Internet Ltd [2007] RPC 5

The claimants had, since 1995, owned and operated a nationwide chain of shops under the name, 'Phones 4u', which sold mobile phones and arranged customer contracts. It also had a domain name, 'phones4u.co.uk'. In 1999, the defendant registered the domain name 'phone4u.co.uk'. It sold mobile phones from this site, although, in 2000, it offered to sell its domain name to the claimant for a considerable sum. The claimant sued for passing off. The Court of Appeal found that, by the time the defendant commenced trading, the claimant had substantial goodwill in the name 'Phones 4u'. A considerable number of people sought to contact the claimant via the defendant's website. Once on the site, the defendant offered to sell them phones, but also stated it was unconnected with the claimant's business. Among the questions for the Court of Appeal was whether the defendant's actions amounted to an actionable misrepresentation or 'mere confusion'. In his judgment, Jacob LJ examined the difference between the two.

Jacob LJ:

16. The next point of passing off law to consider is misrepresentation. Sometimes a distinction is drawn between 'mere confusion' which is not enough, and 'deception', which is. I described the difference as 'elusive' in *Reed Executive v Reed Business Information* [2004] RPC 767 at 797. I said this, [111]:

> Once the position strays into misleading a substantial number of people (going from 'I wonder if there is a connection' to 'I assume there is a connection') there will be passing off, whether the use is as a business name or a trade mark on goods.

17. This of course is a question of degree—there will be some mere wonderers and some assumers—there will normally (see below) be passing off if there is a substantial number of the latter even if there is also a substantial number of the former.

18. The current (2005) edition of *Kerly* contains a discussion of the distinction at paragraphs 15-043–15-045. It is suggested that:

> The real distinction between mere confusion and deception lies in their causative effects. Mere confusion has no causative effect (other than to confuse lawyers and their clients) whereas, if in answer to the question: 'what moves the public to buy?', the insignia complained of is identified, then it is a case of deception.

19. Although correct as far as it goes, I do not endorse that as a complete statement of the position. Clearly if the public are induced to buy by mistaking the insignia of B for that which they know to be that of A, there is deception. But there are other cases too—for

instance those in the *Buttercup* case. A more complete test would be whether what is said to be deception rather than mere confusion is really likely to be damaging to the claimant's goodwill or divert trade from him. I emphasise the word 'really'.

20. *HFC Bank v Midland Bank* [2000] FSR 176, relied upon by Miss Lane, is a case about 'mere confusion'. The claimant Bank was known, but not very well known, as HFC. It sought to restrain the Midland with its very many branches from changing its name to HSBC. That was said to be passing off. It relied upon some 1,200 instances of alleged deception. Lloyd J analysed the ten best (pp. 189–104). None really amounted to deception. And in any event, given the scale of the parties' respective operations, the totality of what was relied upon was trivial. The case was one on its facts. It decided no question of principle.

21. In this discussion of 'deception/confusion' it should be remembered that there are cases where what at first sight may look like deception and indeed will involve deception, is nonetheless justified in law. I have in mind cases of honest concurrent use and very descriptive marks. Sometimes such cases are described as 'mere confusion' but they are not really—they are cases of tolerated deception or a tolerated level of deception.

22. An example of the former is the old case of *Dent v Turpin* (1861) 2 J&H 139. Father Dent had two clock shops, one in the City, the other in the West End. He bequeathed one to each son—which resulted in two clock businesses each called Dent. Neither could stop the other; each could stop a third party (a villain rather appropriately named Turpin) from using 'Dent' for such a business. A member of the public who only knew of one of the two businesses would assume that the other was part of it—he would be deceived. Yet passing off would not lie for one son against the other because of the positive right of the other business. However it would lie against the third-party usurper.

23. An example of the latter is *Office Cleaning Services v Westminster Window and General Cleaners* (1946) 63 RPC 39. The differences between 'Office Cleaning Services Ltd' and 'Office Cleaning Association', even though the former was well-known, were held to be enough to avoid passing off. Lord Simmonds said:

> Where a trader adopts words in common use for his trade name, some risk of confusion is inevitable. But that risk must be run unless the first user is allowed unfairly to monopolise the words. The Court will accept comparatively small differences as sufficient to avert confusion. A greater degree of discrimination may fairly be expected from the public where a trade name consists wholly or in part of words descriptive of the articles to be sold or the services to be rendered (p. 43).

In short, therefore, where the 'badge' of the plaintiff is descriptive, cases of 'mere confusion' caused by the use of a very similar description will not count. A certain amount of deception is to be tolerated for policy reasons—one calls it 'mere confusion'.

In his judgment, Jacob LJ defined the difference between an actionable misrepresentation and confusion as: 'whether what is said to be deception rather than mere confusion is really likely to be damaging to the claimant's goodwill or divert trade from him'. In this particular case, Jacob LJ concluded that customers or potential customers of the claimant were being deceived into contacting the defendant's website and, once there, the defendant sought to take advantage of this initial deception. This was more than 'mere deception' and since the other elements of a passing off action, goodwill and damage, were also present the claimant's case was made out. An opposite conclusion was reached in the earlier case of *BP Amoco*

Plc v John Kelly Ltd.[61] In this case, the claimants operated service stations all decorated in a particular shade of green. It claimed one purpose of this was so that approaching motorists could identify the stations even if they were too far away to be able to read the BP logo. The defendant operated service stations in Ireland and Northern Ireland, under the name 'TOP'. In 1996, it adopted green as the main colour of its service stations. BP sued, inter alia, for passing off. BP was unsuccessful in its action, because as Carswell CJ held, a normally observant motorist would realize once he reached the defendant's service station that it was not run by the claimant.[62] According to Carswell CJ: 'it is a necessary ingredient of the tort that the customer is deceived into making a purchase by reason of the confusion engendered by the defendant's get-up …'

5.2.3.3 Initial interest confusion

not remain confused at point of sale

In *BP v John Kelly*, the court held that there would be no passing off because, even if a passing motorist were initially confused, he would not remain confused at the point of sale. In *Och-Ziff Management Europe Ltd v Och Capital LLP*,[63] Arnold J looked at what has come to be termed 'initial interest' confusion and took a different view. The claimant was part of a leading asset management group. The defendant was an independent investment house. The claimant alleged both infringement of its registered trade marks, 'Och-Ziff' and 'Och', and also passing off. In response, the defendant argued that since the two businesses were not in competition, a customer who initially confused them would be disabused of any such confusion by the time of his entering into a contract with the defendant and the claimant would suffer no damage. Arnold J held for the claimant on the basis that 'initial interest confusion' was sufficient for a finding of passing off. According to Arnold J, initial interest confusion can be identified as 'a doctrine which has been developing in US trade marks cases since the 1970s, which allows for a finding of liability where a plaintiff can demonstrate that a consumer was confused by a defendant's conduct at the time of interest in a product or service, even if that initial confusion is corrected by the time of purchase'.[64] Arnold J then examined its application to both registered trade mark infringement and passing off. On the issue of passing off, he took the view that there can be passing off through advertising goods for sale even if none are actually sold. The only question would be whether there was a misrepresentation and subsequent damage resulting from such advertising. In this case, according to Arnold J, there had been a misrepresentation or, as he termed it, initial interest confusion. He then turned to the question of damage. He held that there would be damage to the claimant's goodwill by association and damage to the 'exclusivity' of the claimant's mark through dilution. (Both of these heads of damage will be examined later in the chapter.) In the more recent case of *Moroccanoil v Aldi*,[65] Hacon J returned to the issue of initial interest confusion in passing off and took a markedly more cautious approach than Arnold J. According to Hacon J:

> 28. By contrast, as I have just indicated, it seems to me that where 'initial interest confusion' as defined by Arnold J is dispelled before that confusion is acted upon, generally by making a purchase, in circumstances such that the claimant suffers no damage, this is not sufficient to give rise to passing off.

---

[61] [2002] FSR 5.   [62] p. 48.   [63] [2010] EWHC 2599 (Ch).   [64] [80].
[65] *Moroccanoil Israel Ltd v Aldi Stores Ltd* [2014] EWHC 1686 (IPEC).

Since the decision in *Och Ziff*, the Court of Appeal has held that initial interest confusion has no place in registered trade mark law, not least because it might stifle legitimate competition when consumers shop online.[66] It will be interesting to see whether in future a higher court might take the same view about its deployment in passing off.

5.2.3.4 The circumstances in which an actionable misrepresentation may arise

The question of whether or not a misrepresentation is actionable may depend upon the nature of the goods or services at issue, the typical customers for such goods or services, and the circumstances in which the misrepresentation is made, or a combination of each or all of these factors.[67]

In 'Jif Lemon', Lord Oliver considered the circumstances in which customers were likely to be deceived by the sale of the defendant's product. He began by accepting that 'a careful shopper who read the labels attached respectively to the appellants and the respondents products would have no difficulty whatever in distinguishing them'.

> **Lord Oliver, at p. 508:**
>
> The essence of the action for passing off is a deceit practised upon the public and it can be no answer, in a case where it is demonstrable that the public has been or will be deceived, that they would not have been if they had been more careful, more literate or more perspicacious. Customers have to be taken as they are found.
>
> [He then noted previous cases where the court had asked whether the marks at issue would deceive 'incautious' customers:]
>
> **At p. 509:**
>
> It is also the question to be asked in this case. It has, however, to be asked in every case against the background of the type of market in which the goods are sold, the manner in which they are sold, and the habits and characteristics of purchasers in that market. The law of passing off does not rest solely upon the deceit of those whom it is difficult to deceive.
>
> In the instant case, side-by-side visual comparison does not in fact take place. Moreover the trial judge was satisfied of the fact that a substantial part of the purchasing public requires specifically Jif lemon juice, associates it with the lemon-shape, lemon-size container which is the dominant characteristic of the get-up and pays little or no attention to the label. It is no answer to say that the diversion of trade which he was satisfied would take place would be of relatively short duration, since the public would ultimately become educated to the fact that there were two brands of lemon juice marketed in such containers and would then be likely to pay more attention to the labels to be sure that they got the brand which they required. His finding was that the diversion would be likely to run into millions of units. It inevitably follows from these findings that the appellants have not in fact sufficiently and effectively distinguished their goods from those of the respondents and it is not for the respondents or for the court to suggest what more they should do, although some suggestions were made

---

[66] *Interflora Inc. and another v Marks & Spencer plc (No. 5)* [2014] EWCA Civ 1403.
[67] *Cadbury-Schweppes Pty Ltd v The Pub Squash Co.* [1981] 1 WLR 193.

by Slade LJ in the course of his judgment in the Court of Appeal. In the light of the trial judge's finding, I see no escape from the proposition that the respondents were entitled to an injunction which they obtained in the form in which it was granted.

The facts of the 'Jif Lemon' case led Lord Oliver to assume that shoppers would be confused between the two products. According to Lord Oliver, it is irrelevant that the public will not be deceived if they are more careful, literate, or perspicacious. Instead, in passing off actions, customers must be taken as they are found. Generally, as it did in 'Jif Lemon', the court will assess the likelihood of the public's being deceived by reference to the type of goods or services concerned. So the public is likely to be more careful and less likely to be deceived when dealing with a bank[68] than when reading an evening paper on the Tube during rush hour.[69] Or, indeed, when buying lemon juice in a supermarket.

5.2.3.5 Definition of a substantial number in passing off

In determining whether there has been an actionable misrepresentation, it is necessary to ask whether a sufficient number of customers have been misled. The general rule is that it is necessary for a *substantial* number of customers to be misled but not necessarily a majority. As Lightman J stated in the 'Alan Clark diaries' case, 'it is no defence that many people are not deceived'.[70] Indeed, it would be fair to say that the definition of 'substantial' in relation to passing off is a relative one. For example, in the 'Chocosuisse' case, Laddie J in the High Court concluded that a 'substantial' number of potential customers need not even comprise a majority.

Chocosuisse Union des Fabricants Suisses de Chocolat v Cadbury Ltd
[1998] RPC 117

The claimants were manufacturers and retailers of chocolate made in Switzerland. The defendant, Cadbury, manufactured its chocolate in the UK and in 1994 launched a new chocolate bar called 'Swiss Chalet'. The claimants alleged that the defendant had passed off 'Swiss Chalet' as Swiss chocolate. In the High Court, Laddie J found that there had been passing off. The defendant unsuccessfully appealed. One question that arose for the court was whether a substantial section of the public would have been confused by the defendant's misrepresentation.

Laddie J, at p. 413:

I think it is clear that for many people, including some of those for whom the words Swiss chocolate mean a product of quality from Switzerland, the prominent use of the famous Cadbury name and get-up will be enough to prevent them thinking that Swiss Chalet is a Swiss chocolate. Furthermore there are very many for whom the origin or connections of

---

[68] *HFC Bank plc v HSBC Bank plc* [2000] FSR 176.
[69] *Clark v Associated Newspapers Ltd* [1998] 1 WLR 1558.
[70] *Clark v Associated Newspapers Ltd*, p. 1566.

Swiss Chalet will be irrelevant. In addition to this, I think that in some cases it is likely that the questions asked in both the plaintiffs' and defendant's surveys may have resulted in the interviewees entering into an area of speculation which would not normally have crossed their minds. Many people, and particularly those who are more observant, would not be confused. For them the words 'Swiss Chalet' will signify nothing but a pretty sounding name for a bar of chocolate. They will convey no other message. However I have come to the conclusion that there are some who will be struck by the largest and most prominent word on the defendant's packaging namely 'Swiss' and think that it is a reference to an attribute of the product itself. I think it is likely that some will think that it is an indication that the product is Swiss chocolate. Some, like Mr Crocker, may not see the reference to Cadbury. Others might not believe that all Cadbury chocolate is made in England. In fact it is not all made here. Cadbury like many other manufacturers has set up factories or formed alliances abroad. Further, for some the get-up of the packaging with its typical Swiss scene will tend to reinforce the message of the word 'Swiss'. Finally some may be left in confusion as to whether Swiss Chalet is Swiss chocolate or not.

I have found this the most difficult issue in the case. However, I have come to the conclusion that a substantial number of members of the public who regard Swiss chocolate as the name for a group of products of repute will be confused into thinking that Swiss Chalet is a member of that group by reason of the use of the name Swiss Chalet. It is likely that the number who think that will be smaller than the number for whom there will be no confusion but, in my view, it is still likely to be a substantial number. It follows that on this issue the plaintiffs succeed.

Laddie J's conclusion that there was sufficient customer confusion for the claimants to succeed in their passing off action was subsequently upheld by the Court of Appeal. And this approach was adopted by the Court of Appeal in the more recent 'Greek yoghurt' case.

Fage UK Ltd v Chobani UK Ltd [2014] EWCA Civ 5

The claimants had, since the 1980s, marketed yoghurt in the UK which was imported from Greece. It was sold under the name FAGE but described as 'Greek yoghurt'. By 2012 it had 95 per cent of the market for all yoghurt sold in the UK as Greek yoghurt. The defendants, Chobani, introduced a yoghurt into the UK in 2012 which was described as 'Greek yoghurt' but was made in the US. The claimants argued that Greek yoghurt had acquired goodwill in the UK, in which they shared, and that using the phrase 'Greek yoghurt' for yoghurt not made in Greece was a misrepresentation. This was the case even though the defendant's method used to produce its yoghurt, which gave it a 'thick and creamy' texture, was the same as that applied in Greece to the same effect. It was also the case that in the UK (unlike in the US) only yoghurt made in Greece was described as 'Greek yoghurt'. At trial, the judge looked at a variety of evidence, including market surveys and newspaper articles, to reach his conclusion that for a substantial proportion of actual or potential buyers, Greek yoghurt meant a thick and creamy yoghurt which was specifically made in Greece. The claimant succeeded in its claim and the defendant appealed. In particular, the defendant argued that the term 'Greek yoghurt' is descriptive of a broad range of products, sharing the same method of manufacture, which were not necessarily made in Greece. And that even if a significant proportion of the yoghurt-buying public believed Greek yoghurt came from Greece, this was not important to them when buying yoghurt and hence Greek yoghurt did not have the necessary goodwill which might be protected by passing off.

Lord Justice Kitchin:

37. This is one of those cases in which it is alleged that a geographical name has become so distinctive of particular goods made in that geographical area that its use in relation to other goods amounts to a misrepresentation which is calculated to lead to the deception of members of the public and to cause damage to those traders who enjoy a goodwill in their businesses of supplying goods which are in fact made in that area. It therefore involves an allegation of so called extended passing off. It gives rise to fundamental questions as to the meaning of distinctiveness in this context, and the degree of distinctiveness which must be established to sustain such a claim.

Lord Justice Kitchin examined the authority for the extended form of passing off, including 'Advocaat' and finally the 'Swiss Chocolate' case. He took a number of lessons from the authorities, in particular on the question of how many customers need to be misled. He noted that not all potential customers must find descriptive terms have acquired a secondary meaning but, as per Chadwick LJ in 'Swiss Chocolate', a 'significant' section of the public must. He then turned to what constituted a significant number and in particular how it might be assessed in cases of the extended form of passing off.

66. Fifthly, it is no more necessary in a case of extended passing off than in a case of conventional passing off for a claimant to establish that all members of the public understand how the goods are made. Thus in the *Spanish Champagne* case the degree of understanding of the meaning of the term 'champagne' varied from consumer to consumer, with the less knowledgeable consumers being most likely to be confused. This mattered not because, as Cross J. so precisely identified in the *British sherry* case, those less knowledgeable consumers might well think a bottle labelled 'Spanish champagne' was the genuine article. Similarly, in the *Advocaat* case, the reputation attaching to the name was simply that of a drink having recognisable qualities of appearance, taste, strength and satisfaction and for that reason the defendants' product, labelled as it was 'Old English Advocaat', would lead them into believing they were in fact buying genuine advocaat.

[After a further discussion about damage, Lord Justice Kitchin turned to the question of whether the claimant had established its case.]

70. So I must now consider whether the judge was entitled to reach the conclusion he did in light of the principles which I have summarised. I have set out in some detail the approach the judge took to the evidence, the findings he made, his analysis of the law and his reasoning in arriving at his ultimate conclusion. In dealing with the critical issue on this aspect of the appeal, that is to say distinctiveness, he found (at [112]–[116]) that a substantial proportion, and probably a clear majority, of the buyers of Greek yoghurt believed that it came from Greece and further, that the description conveyed to them that the yoghurt to which it was applied was in some way special. Adopting Laddie J.'s illustrations at first instance in the *Chocosuisse* case, 'Greek yoghurt' is not one of those descriptions such as 'French ball bearings' or 'Italian pencils' which do not have associated with them any goodwill which acts as an attractive force which brings in custom. To the contrary and notwithstanding that few know how or why Greek yoghurt has its distinctive thick and creamy texture, a substantial

proportion of the relevant public not only believe that Greek yoghurt comes from Greece but also believe it to be special. I am satisfied the judge was entitled to make these findings on the evidence. Indeed they had powerful support from the trade witnesses, the unwritten labelling convention, the advice given to Chobani and the premium price which Greek yoghurt commands in the marketplace. Furthermore, the evidence given by Chobani through Mr Bevers betrayed not only a recognition of the reputation enjoyed by Greek yoghurt but also a determination to take commercial advantage of it.

71. The judge returned to this issue later in his judgment (at [133]–[135]) in dealing with goodwill. There he reiterated that a substantial proportion of those who buy Greek yoghurt think that it is made in Greece and that the proportion of those Greek yoghurt buyers to whom it matters is also substantial. It followed, he thought, that FAGE had demonstrated that a substantial goodwill attached to the phrase.

The defendant's appeal failed on this basis as did its further argument that the protection of the designation 'Greek yoghurt' should more properly be achieved through an action based on European legislation relating to geographical indications.

In the case of both Greek yoghurt and Swiss chocolate, the courts found that even though only a minority of purchasers of the products would share a common view of their particular characteristics or think they were significant in making a purchasing decision, as long as it was a substantial number of purchasers that was sufficient. The question then arises as to how a substantial number is to be identified and assessed by the court.

5.2.3.6 Measuring customer confusion in passing off

It is sometimes the case that when passing off is alleged to have been continuing for some time, the court may take the absence of evidence of confusion as telling.[71] In *Moroccanoil v Aldi* [2015] FSR 4, the claimant sold a hair oil under the name 'Moroccanoil'. It sued the defendant, a supermarket chain, for passing off when it introduced a hair oil named 'Miracle Oil' with some similarity of packaging. In finding for the defendant, Hacon J held that the lack of evidence of actual confusion was a relevant factor. He noted:

45. There was no direct evidence of there having been a misrepresentation—nothing to show that any identified individuals had assumed that Aldi's miracle oil had a trade connection with Moroccanoil because of Miracle Oil's name and/or get-up. I think in the present case that if a significant proportion of the public believed that Aldi's product was Moroccanoil, there is a fair chance that at least one or two people with complaints about something, possibly quality or the divergence in price, would have written to one or other of the parties expressing that complaint.

Conversely, as was pointed out by Jacob LJ in *Phones4u*: 'It should also be remembered here that it is seldom the case that all instances of deception come to light—the more perfect the deception the less likely that will be so.'[72]

If, to establish passing off, the claimant must nonetheless convince the court that a substantial number of the relevant public have been or are likely to be misled, the question arises of how that 'substantial number' is to be measured. In the 'Chocosuisse' case, both

---

[71] *Arsenal Football Club plc v Reed* [2001] RPC 46, [24].   [72] [45].

parties initiated surveys in order to demonstrate either that customers were or were not likely to be misled. Although this may appear to be an obvious course to take in a passing off action, it is by no means the norm. Such evidence is bound to be contentious and the court, as it did in 'Chocosuisse', may take a view that the questions addressed to potential customers are leading ones. Furthermore, the speed with which many passing off actions reach the court may make the collection of such data impractical. In fact, the courts have generally taken the view that the question of whether enough people will be misled is one for the judge to answer. As was put by Jacob J in *Neutrogena v Golden Ltd* and approved by the Court of Appeal:[73]

> The proper approach of the court to the question was not in dispute. The judge must consider the evidence adduced and use his own common sense and his own opinion as to the likelihood of deception. It is an overall 'jury' assessment involving a combination of all these factors, see 'GE' Trade Mark [1973] RPC 297 at 321. Ultimately the question is one for the court, not for the witnesses. It follows that if the judge's own opinion is that the case is marginal, one where he cannot be sure whether there is a likelihood of sufficient deception, the case will fail in the absence of enough evidence of the likelihood of deception.

It is perhaps not surprising that, for all these reasons, the introduction of survey evidence into passing off actions has tended to be the exception rather than the rule and that the subject has received little attention from the courts. However, the recent controversy over the value of survey evidence in registered trade mark disputes, which arose in *Interflora v Marks & Spencer*, has meant that similar questions are now being raised in relation to passing off.[74]

The question in *Interflora* of when it is legitimate to produce survey evidence arose from an anterior question: whether, as was put by Lewison LJ, assessing confusion in registered trade mark cases is 'a matter of counting heads'.[75] Lewison LJ thought it was not. But he also held 'that the average consumer (in trade mark infringement) is conceptually different from the "substantial proportion of the public" test applied in passing off …'[76] as in the latter case the actual number of people who are or might be misled is relevant. Nonetheless, where the two actions do overlap is on the question of the circumstances under which there is 'real value' to be had from introducing customer surveys, as an aid to assessing confusion. In *Zee Entertainment Enterprises Ltd v Zeebox Ltd*, the Court of Appeal addressed this question in relation to passing off.

Zee Entertainment Enterprises Ltd v Zeebox Ltd [2014] EWCA Civ 82

The claimant was an Indian cable television channel which provided programmes in Hindi and other Indian languages. The defendant produced an app, 'Zeebox', providing information about television programmes. The claimant sought to introduce a survey of 'British Asian people' which, among other things, was intended to assess whether there was a likelihood of a misrepresentation in that they would make a connection between

---

[73] *Neutrogena Corp. and Anr v Golden Ltd and Anr* [1996] RPC 473 at 482.
[74] *Interflora Inc. v Marks & Spencer* [2012] EWCA Civ 1501 (*Interflora I*); *Interflora Inc. v Marks & Spencer* [2013] EWCA Civ 319 (*Interflora II*). For a discussion of the trade mark issues, see 7.2.2.4.
[75] *Interflora I*, [36].   [76] *Interflora I*, [34].

the claimant's service and the defendant's app. In the High Court, Birss J refused the claimant's request and the claimant appealed. In the Court of Appeal, the claimant argued that such a survey was justified because the misrepresentation would be occurring among 'a people and a culture with whom the judge may be unfamiliar'.[77] In his judgment, Floyd LJ confirmed that whether the defendants were making a 'misrepresentation calculated to deceive is ultimately a question for the trial judge'.[78] He then looked to see whether there was what he termed 'a cost benefit' in admitting the claimant's survey in this instance. He first considered the claimant's argument for admitting survey evidence.

Floyd LJ:

31. I should add that Mr. Malynicz [for the claimant] made detailed oral submissions to us as to the potential value of survey evidence in passing off cases. First, a survey could, for example, provide reassurance for a judge that his or her view was not idiosyncratic. Secondly, it could ensure that the judge is aware of the views of the relevant public, in the present case, watchers of the appellant's channel and users of apps, tablets and smartphones. Thirdly, this was particularly so where linguistic or cultural factors to come into play.

32. As was pointed out in the course of argument, however, many of these factors would be present in all passing off cases. In my judgment, one factor which might be of importance is where there is some special factor about the goods or services, or their consumers, which makes evidence of the kind likely to be of real value.

Ground 2: the relevant public

33. The appellants' survey was targeted at members of the British Asian community. The appellants say that given the nature of the services offered by the claimant, which are also targeted at that community, the judge will be assisted by evidence of the reactions of the interviewees. They say that the trial judge is likely to have little familiarity with the appellant's channel or the reactions of the ethnically distinct market to which it is directed.

...

36. Although Mr. Malynicz accepts that the passing off in the present case is not taking place in a distant country, he submits that it is taking place amongst a people and culture with whom the trial judge may be unfamiliar. He submits that in saying that the passing off case was concerned with matters which were not esoteric, the judge lost sight of this aspect of the case.

37. I do not think there is anything in these points. First, whilst of course the trial judge may not be a watcher of Zee TV, or indeed of any television channel at all, I have real difficulty in accepting that, when equipped with knowledge of the extent and popularly of the appellant's channel, he will not be able to assess the susceptibility of watchers of that channel to confusion or deception when confronted with the signs complained of. Judges in passing off cases are familiar with taking into account any relevant characteristics of the purchasing public and making allowances for it.

38. Secondly, the attempted analogy with *White Horse v Gregson* seems to me to be misplaced. In that case the impact of the defendant's advertising in a foreign language was relevant, as were the ways in which whisky was sold in a foreign country.

---

[77] *Zee Entertainment Enterprises v Zeebox* (CA), [84].　　[78] [25].

39. This case, in contrast, is about a very short English trade mark and logo delivered to the public in the way that television services are the delivered to the public in this country. There is nothing in that which is likely to be unfamiliar or not readily understandable to the trial judge.

40. Thirdly, if the justification of the survey is the need to target speakers of Hindi because the appellant's channels are in Hindi, then the survey has failed to do that. As Mr. Roberts has demonstrated, significant numbers of interviewees speak nothing but English.

[Floyd LJ then looked at the reliability of the survey and concluded that it was conducted under 'artificial circumstances', in that participants were not introduced to the defendant's app in the way they would come across it in real life. He also took the view that the high cost of the survey, agreed to be £150,000, must be a significant factor in allowing its admissibility. He concluded that it should not be admitted.]

58. By far the most significant factor is that the survey is flawed in the way I have described. Any marginal value it might have is outweighed by the significant and, in my view, disproportionate cost. The appellants have other avenues open of them to prove their case. Against that, one must of course bear in mind that one is preventing the appellants from adducing some potentially relevant evidence. I consider that in this case the balance comes down heavily in favour of refusing permission for the survey evidence.

59. For my part I would not grant permission for this survey. If follows that I would dismiss the appeal.

Lewison LJ who had given the leading judgments in *Interflora v M&S* agreed. He made clear that those judgments should be read to mean that survey evidence, in both passing off and registered trade mark disputes, should only be admitted 'in special cases' such as when the judge is dealing with 'specialized' or 'esoteric' goods or services. Otherwise, he thought that 'surveys have very limited value'.[79] In 'Zee TV', the court was being asked to take a view on whether a very particular social group would be misled about a product aimed specifically at that group. Nonetheless, the Court of Appeal agreed that the judge could make up his or her own mind, without depending upon survey evidence. This raises the question of just how 'specialized' or 'esoteric' goods or services must be before a survey is deemed cost-effective in a passing off action.

5.2.3.7 The deception does not have to be deliberate

[handwritten margin note: Shun didn't need to know the Csproducts]

In order to show passing off, there is no need to prove that the defendant intended to make a misrepresentation. However, the court may choose to see the reason why the defendant chose to adopt a particular insignia as relevant, as was explained in *Specsavers v Asda*.[80]

[handwritten margin note: court may want to know why you adopted certain words.]

Specsavers v Asda Stores [2012] EWCA Civ 24

The claimant owned a chain of opticians and the defendant supermarket also had opticians in some of its stores. The claimant had a number of registered trade marks, including the word 'Specsavers' and a device of two intersecting shaded ellipses. The defendant launched an advertising campaign which featured, inter alia, the slogan 'Be a real spec saver at Asda' and two non-intersecting ellipses. The claimant sued for trade mark

---

[79] [64].   [80] The trade mark aspects of this case will be examined in Chapter 8.

infringement. Kitchin LJ, in the course of his judgment, described the circumstances in which a defendant's decision to 'live dangerously' by alluding to the claimant's insignia might affect the likelihood that the court would find passing off.

> 114. Finally, I come to the 'living dangerously' point. Mr Mellor submitted that if a trader takes a decision to live dangerously he recognises a risk of a successful legal action and so also recognises a likelihood that his activity will deceive some people. This submission was founded upon an observation of Robert Walker J. in United Biscuits (UK) Ltd v Asda Stores Ltd [1997] R.P.C. 513, a case in which Asda designed its own chocolate-coated sandwich biscuit called 'Puffin' which was intended as a 'brand-beater' to be matched against the well-known 'Penguin' biscuit. In that case, as in this, Asda made changes to its initial designs so as to lessen the risk of confusion, but only such changes as were needed in order to avoid what it judged to be an unacceptable risk of being attacked for copying while maintaining Puffin's position as an obvious competitor and parody. Robert Walker J. said at p.531:
>
>> 'I cannot escape the conclusion that, while aiming to avoid what the law would characterise as deception, they were taking a conscious decision to live dangerously. That is not in my judgment something that the court is bound to disregard.'
>
> 115. In my judgment it is important to distinguish between a defendant who takes a conscious decision to live dangerously and one who intends to cause deception and deliberately seeks to take the benefit of another trader's goodwill. It has long been established that if it is shown that a defendant has deliberately sought to take the benefit of a claimant's goodwill for himself the court will not 'be astute to say that he cannot succeed in doing that which he is straining every nerve to do': see Slazenger & Sons v Feltham & Co (1889) 6 R.P.C. 130 at p.538 per Lindley L.J. A trader who has taken the decision to live dangerously is in a different position, however. He has appreciated the risk of confusion and has endeavoured to adopt a sign which is a safe distance away. All must depend upon the facts of the particular case…

The issue of whether the defendant was living dangerously when they marketed Miracle Oil was raised in *Moroccanoil v Aldi*. Hacon J took the view that 'Aldi intended to make the public think of Moroccanoil when they saw Miracle Oil in its packaging and I think Aldi succeeded. But purchases of Miracle Oil have not been and are not likely to be made with any relevant false assumption in the mind of the purchasers. There is not even likely to be any initial interest confusion. There is no likelihood of an actionable misrepresentation.'[81]

5.2.3.8 The common field of activity

A recurring question, which has now been definitively answered, has been whether there must be direct competition between the claimant and the defendant, in other words must they share 'a common field of activity', for a passing off action to succeed. There have been a number of authoritative decisions which have made clear that it is not necessary for there to be a common field.[82] Among them is that of the Court of Appeal in *Harrods*. Millett LJ first considered the authorities.

---

[81] [61].

[82] It should be noted that the need to show a common field has had greater longevity in cases involving character merchandising (see e.g. *McCulloch v May* (1948) 65 RPC 58). However, in *Irvine v Talksport Ltd* [2002] FSR 60, Laddie J held that in these cases too there was no need to show a 'common field' between the parties. Both cases will be examined in Chapter 10.

Millett LJ, at p. 714:

There is no requirement that the defendant should be carrying on a business which competes with that of the plaintiff or which would compete with any natural extension of the plaintiff's business. The expression 'common field of activity' was coined by Wynn-Parry J in *McCulloch v May* (1948) 65 RPC 58, when he dismissed the plaintiff's claim for want of this factor. This was contrary to numerous previous authorities (see, for example, *Eastman Photographic Materials Co Ltd v John Griffiths Cycle Corporation Ltd* (1898) 15 RPC 105 (cameras and bicycles); *Walter v Ashton* [1902] 2 Ch 282 (The Times newspaper and bicycles)) and is now discredited. In the Advocaat case Lord Diplock expressly recognised that an action for passing off would lie although 'the plaintiff and the defendant were not competing traders in the same line of business'. In the Lego case Falconer J acted on evidence that the public had been deceived into thinking that the plaintiffs, who were manufacturers of plastic toy construction kits, had diversified into the manufacture of plastic irrigation equipment for the domestic garden. What the plaintiff in an action for passing off must prove is not the existence of a common field of activity but likely confusion among the common customers of the parties.

[Millett LJ then went on to suggest that while a common field of activity is not necessary, it is nonetheless suggestive of passing off. He continued:]

At p. 714:

The absence of a common field of activity, therefore, is not fatal; but it is not irrelevant either. In deciding whether there is a likelihood of confusion, it is an important and highly relevant consideration:

> whether there is any kind of association, or could be in the minds of the public any kind of association, between the field of activities of the plaintiff and the field of activities of the defendant (*Annabel's (Berkeley Square) Ltd v G Schock (trading as Annabel's Escort Agency)* [1972] RPC 838, at page 844 per Russell LJ).

In the Lego case Falconer J likewise held that the proximity of the defendant's field of activity to that of the plaintiff was a factor to be taken into account when deciding whether the defendant's conduct would cause the necessary confusion.

Where the plaintiff's business name is a household name the degree of overlap between the fields of activity of the parties' respective businesses may often be a less important consideration in assessing whether there is likely to be confusion, but in my opinion it is always a relevant factor to be taken into account.

Where there is no or only a tenuous degree of overlap between the parties' respective fields of activity the burden of proving the likelihood of confusion and resulting damage is a heavy one.

It is clear from Millett LJ's comments and also from earlier authorities, in particular the 'Lego' case, that what is needed to establish passing off is evidence of confusion and a likelihood of damage whether or not there is a common field of activity between the parties. However, both confusion (and damage) will be easier to prove if there is a common field of activity or where, as in the 'Lego' case, the claimant is a household name. Millett LJ went on in *Harrods* to assess whether, in the absence of any common field, there was a likelihood of either confusion or damage to the claimant. He concluded there was not.

Millett LJ, at p. 717:

(3) The absence of any common field of activity.

This is of particular significance in the present case. The judge correctly directed himself as to the law; he cannot be faulted in the way in which he applied it. It is not merely that the plaintiffs have never run a school and have no established reputation for doing so; or even that the nature of the parties' respective businesses are as dissimilar as can well be imagined. It is rather that the commercial reputation for excellence as a retailer which the plaintiffs enjoy would be regarded by the public as having no bearing upon their ability to run a school. Customers of the plaintiffs would be surprised to learn that Harrods had ventured into the commercial theatre; they would, I think, be incredulous if they were told that Harrods had opened a preparatory school.

The last two features must be taken together, for they reinforce each other. Nothing in the judge's decision compels the conclusion that the defendants would have been permitted to call their school 'Harrods' or 'Harrods School'; or that an enterprising trader would be permitted to set up a retail shop under the name 'The Harrodian'. The question is whether there is a real risk that members of the public will be deceived into thinking that a school called 'The Harrodian School' (not written in the distinctive Harrods' script or livery) is owned or managed by Harrods or under Harrods' supervision or control. Whether there is a real likelihood of such confusion is a question of fact. It is primarily a question of impression. The judge decided that there was not. I would have reached the same conclusion myself. More to the point, I am satisfied that the judge made no discernible error of law and that his conclusion was one to which he was entitled to come.

In *Harrods*, the Court of Appeal held that the absence of a common field between the department store and the school meant that the public would not be misled into believing that there was any connection between the parties. By contrast, where there is a common field of activity between the parties, the courts will be more likely to find both an actionable misrepresentation and the likelihood of damage. To understand how, in an area of law which regulates unfair competition, there may be no direct competition between the parties, we need to examine the various types of misrepresentation which might lead to a finding of passing off.

FURTHER READING

A. Blythe, 'Misrepresentation, confusion and the average consumer: to what extent are the tests for passing off and likelihood of confusion within trade mark law identical?' [2015] EIPR 484.

J. Davis, 'Revisiting the average consumer: an uncertain presence in European trade mark law' [2015] IPQ 15.

P. Ellis and G. Parsons, 'A "blink blink eye rub" does not amount to passing off' (2014) 9 JIPLP 799.

B. Trimmer, 'Another supermarket lookalike fight—why Aldi has won first round' [2014] WIPR 45.

5.2.4 TYPES OF ACTIONABLE MISREPRESENTATIONS

The very early cases of passing off generally involved a misrepresentation by the defendant that its goods were those of the claimant. Over time, the tort has expanded to encompass many other types of misrepresentation. Indeed, at its simplest, it may be argued that any misrepresentation might give rise to an action in passing off, provided that it is material and that the other constituents of the tort are also present. Below we shall look at the most common types of actionable misrepresentations. They are:

(1) the defendant's goods or services are those of the claimant or originate from him or, if they are the claimant's goods, that they are, for example, of a different quality;

(2) there is a business connection between the claimant and the defendant;

(3) the defendant's goods are of the same origin or nature as the claimant's goods;

(4) the defendant claims that the goods or services of the claimant are his own;

(5) there is a licensing agreement between the claimant and the defendant;[83]

(6) the claimant has endorsed the defendant's goods.[84]

5.2.4.1 The defendant's goods or services are those of the claimant or are of a different quality

'Jif Lemon' is of course a classic example of a misrepresentation that the defendant's goods originated with the claimant. The early case of *Spalding v Gamage* established that a misrepresentation by the defendant as to the quality of the claimant's goods could also amount to passing off. The claimants manufactured rubber footballs which were sewn and sold as the 'Improved Sewn Orb'. The defendants obtained a stock of moulded footballs, which the claimants had manufactured and rejected, which the defendants advertised under the same name. This was held to be an actionable misrepresentation. Other cases have concerned the claimant's second-hand goods which were sold by the defendant as if they were new[85] and goods which were manufactured to the claimant's specification but sold without its authorization.[86]

5.2.4.2 There is a business connection between the claimant and the defendant

It has also been long established that passing off may occur if the defendant wrongly claims that there is a business connection between himself and the claimant. However, not all such misrepresentations will be actionable. This was made clear by Millett LJ in the *Harrods* case.

> **Millett LJ, at p. 712:**
>
> The relevant connection
>
> In its classic form the misrepresentation which gave rise to an action for passing off was an implied representation by the defendant that his goods were the goods of the plaintiff, but

---

[83] This will be considered again in Chapter 10.   [84] This will be considered in Chapter 10.
[85] *Gillette Safety Razor v Diamond Edge* (1926) 43 RPC 310.
[86] *Primark Stores Ltd v Lollypop Clothing Ltd* [2001] FSR 637.

by the beginning of the present century the tort had been extended beyond this. As Lord Diplock explained in the 'Advocaat' case [1979] AC 731 at pages 741–2, it came to include the case:

> where although the plaintiff and the defendant were not competing traders in the same line of business, a false suggestion by the defendant that their businesses were connected with one another would damage the reputation and thus the goodwill of the plaintiff's business.

In a written summary of the plaintiffs' points in reply which was prepared by their junior counsel and presented to us at the conclusion of the argument, and to the excellence of which I would like to pay tribute, it was submitted:

> In this case the belief engendered [in the minds of the public] is probably that Harrods sponsor or back the school. Obviously not every connection will found an action for passing off … but where the representation is to the effect that the plaintiff is *behind* the defendant in some way, that is a classic case.

This is too widely stated. In my judgment the relevant connection must be one by which the plaintiffs would be taken by the public to have made themselves responsible for the quality of the defendant's goods or services. In *British Legion v British Legion Club (Street) Ltd* (1931) 48 RPC 555 Farwell J considered that the public would take the defendant club to be 'connected in some way' with the plaintiff. But he explained this by saying that some persons would think that it was 'either a branch of the plaintiff or a club in some way amalgamated with or under the supervision of the plaintiff *and for which the plaintiff had in some way made itself responsible*' [my emphasis].

At p. 713:

This, in my opinion, is the gist of the matter.

…

It is not in my opinion sufficient to demonstrate that there must be a connection of some kind between the defendant and the plaintiff, if it is not a connection which would lead the public to suppose that the plaintiff has made himself responsible for the quality of the defendant's goods or services. A belief that the plaintiff has sponsored or given financial support to the defendant will not ordinarily give the public that impression. Many sporting and artistic events are sponsored by commercial organisations which require their name to be associated with the event, but members of the public are well aware that the sponsors have no control over and are not responsible for the organisation of the event. Local teams are often sponsored in similar fashion by local firms, but their supporters are well aware that the sponsors have no control over and are not responsible for the selection or performance of the players.

Schools and colleges are not normally sponsored or promoted in the same way, but they are often financially supported by commercial and professional organisations. Scholarships and professorial chairs are increasingly established by professional firms which stipulate that their name is publicly associated with the endowment. But it is generally recognised that those who provide financial support to such institutions do not expect to have any control over or to be held responsible for the institution or the quality of the teaching. Many ancient schools still bear the names of the guilds which founded them, not as part of their trading activities, but as charitable institutions for the benefit of children of their members. The connection is now largely if not entirely historical; but it was probably never one which was capable of adversely affecting the goodwill and business reputation of the founder.

Millett LJ took the view that, at the very least, the public must believe that the claimant was responsible for the quality of the defendant's goods or services. In *Harrods*, the court found there was no misrepresentation because the two businesses were too remote from each other for the public to assume that the claimant would have control of or be responsible for the quality of the defendant's goods or services. Where the claimant and the defendant are in the same line of business, such as financial services for example, the court may find there is a real risk that such a connection will be made, and as a result the claimant may lose control of its reputation.[87] Do you think that Millett LJ's approach is realistic given that today a wide variety of goods might be sold under a single 'mark' or identifying insignia? The mark 'Virgin' springs to mind.

5.2.4.3 The defendant's goods are of the same origin or nature as the claimant's goods

This misrepresentation is characteristic of what has become known as the extended form of passing off. In the extended form, the defendant will make the misrepresentation that its goods share the same origin or nature as those of the claimant's goods, not that they originate from the claimant, as in the classic form of passing off. The 'Advocaat' case provided the authoritative definition of the extended form of passing off.

Lord Diplock, at p. 739:

[T]he question of law for your Lordships is whether this House should give the seal of its approval to the extended concept of the cause of action for passing off that was applied in the champagne, sherry and Scotch whisky cases. This question is essentially one of legal policy.

[Lord Diplock then examined the facts of the case and the High Court decision that there had been passing off (in effect, by finding that the five factors were present which Lord Diplock identifies in this same case as necessary for a successful action in passing off). He continued:]

At p. 739:

True it is that it could not be shown that any purchaser of 'Keeling's Old English Advocaat' supposed or would be likely to suppose it to be goods supplied by Warnink or to be Dutch advocaat of any make. So Warnink had no cause of action for passing off in its classic form. Nevertheless, the learned judge was satisfied: (1) that the name 'advocaat' was understood by the public in England to denote a distinct and recognisable species of beverage; (2) that Warnink's product is genuinely indicated by that name and has gained reputation and goodwill under it; (3) that Keeling's product has no natural association with the word 'advocaat'; it is an egg and wine drink properly described as an 'egg flip,' whereas advocaat is an egg and spirit drink; these are different beverages and known as different to the public; (4) that members of the public believe and have been deliberately induced by Keeling to believe that in buying their 'Old English Advocaat' they are in fact buying advocaat; (5) that Keeling's deception of the public has caused and, unless prevented, will continue to cause, damage to Warnink in the trade and the goodwill of their business both directly in the loss of sale and indirectly in the debasement of the reputation attaching to the name 'advocaat' if it is

[87] *Dawnay Day & Co. Ltd v Cantor Fitzgerald International* [2000] RPC 669 (CA).

permitted to be used of alcoholic egg drinks generally and not confined to those that are spirit based.

These findings, he considered, brought the case within the principle of law laid down in the champagne case by Danckwerts J and applied in the sherry and Scotch whisky cases. He granted Warnink an injunction restraining Keeling from selling or distributing under the name or description 'advocaat' any product which does not basically consist of eggs and spirit without any admixture of wine.

[The Court of Appeal, in reversing the High Court decision, had distinguished the present case from the 'Champagne' case. They had found that while champagne was a product that could only be made by a particular class of producers, advocaat was merely the description of a particular type of drink. Lord Diplock believed this was not a useful distinction.]

At p. 747:

It cannot make any difference in principle whether the recognisable and distinctive qualities by which the reputation of the type of product has been gained are the result of its having been made in, or from ingredients produced in, a particular locality or are the result of its having been made from particular ingredients regardless of their provenance; though a geographical limitation may make it easier (a) to define the type of product; (b) to establish that it has qualities which are recognisable and distinguish it from every other type of product that competes with it in the market and which have gained for it in that market a reputation and goodwill; and (c) to establish that the plaintiff's own business will suffer more than minimal damage to its goodwill by the defendant's misrepresenting his product as being of that type.

In this case, Lord Diplock took the view that although most of the 'advocaat' on the English market came from the Netherlands, this was not its distinctive feature. Rather, any drink made in conformity to the official Dutch recipe wherever it was made, had the same recognizable and distinctive features which have gained 'advocaat' recognition and goodwill on the English market. It followed that Keeling were seeking to take advantage of this goodwill by misrepresenting that their own product was of that type. Furthermore, in 'Advocaat' it was accepted that because members of the public believed that in buying Keeling's 'Old English Advocaat' they were in fact buying advocaat made to the Dutch recipe, this misrepresentation would cause damage to the makers of the latter both directly through loss of sales and indirectly through the 'debasement' of the reputation attaching to the name 'advocaat'. In the later 'Elderflower Champagne' case, the defendant marketed a product, 'Elderflower Champagne' in a champagne-style bottle. It was, in fact, a non-alcoholic drink which sold at £2.35 a bottle. The Court of Appeal accepted that there had been a misrepresentation that the defendant's drink was champagne or in some way associated with it. They also concluded that it was a reasonably foreseeable consequence of the misrepresentation that there would be injury to the claimant's goodwill, both in loss of sales and the debasement of champagne's reputation. However, the court went on to suggest that the misrepresentation would also dilute the exclusivity of the name 'champagne' itself. The question of whether the 'Elderflower Champagne' case and later passing off decisions have extended the tort of passing off to encompass not merely damage to goodwill but also damage to the exclusivity of the distinguishing indicia as such will be discussed at 5.2.5 on damage. We shall also ask whether this is a legitimate extension of the tort of passing off.

5.2.4.4 The defendant claims that the goods or services of the claimant are its own

Following *Bristol Conservatories Ltd v Conservatories Custom Built Ltd*,[88] it is now generally accepted that inverse or reverse passing off falls within the wider tort of passing off. A key problem to be overcome in this situation is that characteristically the public would not be in a position to know of the claimant, and hence would not be misled into thinking there was an association between the claimant and the defendant. In *Bristol Conservatories*, the defendants' salesman showed prospective customers photographs of conservatories, as if they were samples of their own work. In fact, they were photographs of the claimant's conservatories. An action for passing off failed in the High Court, because the judge held that the public would not associate the conservatory in the photographs with the claimant; that there would be no confusion; and that the claimant had no goodwill which was affected by the showing of the photographs. The decision was overturned in the Court of Appeal. Gibson LJ held that the defendants, by their misrepresentation, were seeking to induce customers to purchase their conservatories in order to get a conservatory from the commercial source which had designed and constructed the conservatories shown in the photographs. However, if a customer ordered a conservatory they would not get one from this source, but rather one made by the defendants. This was passing off. As to goodwill, by showing the photographs to prospective customers goodwill was created for the supplier (that is, the claimant) and at the same time misappropriated by the defendants. In reaching his decision, Gibson LJ stated that, 'I do not intend to decide whether there is a form of the tort to be known as reverse passing-off. It is sufficient, I think, to hold that the facts alleged can properly be regarded as within the tort of passing off.'[89]

However, at least one commentator has noted that, like the extended form of passing off, most commonly reverse (or inverse) passing off will be concerned with a 'quality' misrepresentation rather than a misrepresentation as to origin and argues that this has led to an expansion in the ambit of passing off.[90]

5.2.4.5 Instruments of fraud

It is possible that a defendant may make available the means of making an actionable misrepresentation to others. For example, D may register the domain name of a well-known retailer such as Marks & Spencer. While not using the domain name itself, D may offer to sell the domain name on the open market. These were the facts in the case of *BT v One in a Million Ltd*,[91] where the defendants registered a number of domain names of well-known companies including marksandspencer.co.uk. In the Court of Appeal, the defendants were found to have created an instrument of fraud.[92] In other words, unless the purchaser of the domain name was Marks & Spencer (which may well have been the defendant's hope and intention when registering the name), the use of the domain name by any other purchaser would almost certainly amount to an actionable misrepresentation in relation to Marks & Spencer's goodwill. The defendants would, therefore, have

---

[88] [1989] RPC 455.   [89] p. 464.

[90] H. Carty, 'Inverse passing off: a suitable addition to passing off?' [1993] EIPR 370.

[91] [1999] 1 WLR 903.

[92] The defendant was also found liable for passing off, because those who checked to see who had registered the domain name would believe that One in a Million was associated in some way with Marks & Spencer.

furnished the purchaser with an 'instrument of fraud'. By making an instrument of fraud available for others, the defendant was found liable in passing off. The decision in *BT v One in a Million Ltd* has been criticized as an unacceptable extension of passing off, since the questions arise where the misrepresentation lies in this situation and what would be the resulting damage. One commentator has argued that the basis of the judgment seems to be that the claimants have ownership in their names as such and are, in principle, entitled to stop any other party from using the same names whether or not that use might be entirely legal.[93] Despite this and like criticisms, the doctrine of instruments of fraud has continued to be applied and not just in cases involving domain names.[94] Recently, in *Hearst Holdings v Avela*,[95] the doctrine was applied to a defendant who 'granted' licences to third parties to use the name and image of the cartoon character Betty Boop. The third parties placed the name and image on merchandise which they were obliged to mark 'officially licensed', even though the goodwill in Betty Boop's name and image was owned by the claimant. As a result, the third parties' customers were deceived. The same third parties also supplied Betty Boop merchandise to retailers. The court held this merchandise to be instruments of fraud, since because the merchandise were marked 'official' retailers might deceive consumers, albeit unwittingly. The claimant was successful in an action for passing off.

FURTHER READING

H. Carty, 'Inverse passing off: a suitable addition to passing off?' [1993] EIPR 370.

J. Davis, 'Passing off and joint liability: the rise and fall of "instruments of deception"' [2011] EIPR 204.

D. Fields, 'Registering trade marks as domain names with view to selling for profit constitutes passing off' [2014] CTLR 209.

J. Griffiths, 'Misattribution and misrepresentation: the claim for reverse passing off as "patenting right"' [2006] IPQ 34.

5.2.5 DAMAGE

5.2.5.1 Introduction

Damage is the third element identified by Lord Oliver in 'Jif Lemon' as necessary to establish an action in passing off. According to Lord Oliver, the claimant:

> must demonstrate that he suffers or, in a *quia timet* action, that he is likely to suffer damage by reason of the erroneous belief engendered by the defendant's misrepresentation that the source of the defendant's goods or services is the same as the source of those offered by the plaintiff.[96]

---

[93] A. Sim, 'Rethinking *One in a Million*' [2004] EIPR 442–6.

[94] See *Global Projects Management v Citigroup* [2005] FSR 39; *Vertical Leisure Ltd v Poleplus Ltd* [2014] EWHC 2077 (IPEC).

[95] *Hearst Holdings Inc. & Fleischer Studios Inc. v AVELA Inc., Poeticgem Ltd, The Partnership (Trading) Ltd, U Wear Ltd & J. Fox Ltd* [2014] EWHC 439 (Ch). See also the case of *L'Oréal SA v Bellure NV* [2006] EWHC 2355 (Ch).

[96] p. 499.

It is, in fact, possible to state two general principles about the role of damage in a passing off action.

(1) The damage must be as a consequence of the defendant's misrepresentation.

(2) There is no need for actual damage, as long as the claimant can show that there is a likelihood of damage.

A third principle would seem to be implicit in these dicta—that the damage must be to the claimant's goodwill. However, a number of recent cases have suggested that passing off may also protect against damage to the distinctiveness of a claimant's insignia as such through dilution, rather than to the claimant's goodwill. It has also been argued that courts have found passing off where the claimant has not suffered damage but there has been unjust enrichment of the defendant. Finally, it would be fair to say that the courts will frequently assume that there is damage, or a likelihood of damage, once the claimant has convinced the court that there is goodwill and a misrepresentation.[97] Thus, in 'Hotel Cipriani' in the High Court, Arnold J noted: 'Counsel for the defendants did not seriously dispute that, if the claimants established goodwill and misrepresentation, damage followed.'[98]

It is possible to identify five key heads of damage in passing off:

(1) direct loss of sales;

(2) loss of reputation or control over reputation;

(3) dilution;

(4) loss of a licensing opportunity;[99]

(5) damages for false endorsement.[100]

5.2.5.2   Direct loss of sales

'Jif Lemon' is an example of a situation where the claimant would have lost sales to the defendant if the latter had continued to misrepresent its goods as those of the claimant. Similar damage would have occurred in 'Advocaat'. In 'Vodkat', in the High Court, Arnold J accepted the claimant would suffer direct loss of sales of its vodka at pubs, off-licences, and convenience stores, as some customers would opt for the cheaper Vodkat. Direct loss of sales may also occur when a defendant sells the claimant's goods but misrepresents their quality, as in *Spalding v Gamage*.

5.2.5.3 Loss of reputation or control over reputation

In the leading case of *Annabel's v Schock*, the Court of Appeal held that the claimants would suffer potential loss of earnings, because of the damage to their goodwill resulting from the association which the public would make between the claimants' and the defendant's business.

---

[97] *Stringfellow v McCain Foods (GB)* [1984] FSR 175, [1984] RPC 501; *Harrods*, per Millett LJ, at p. 714.
[98] *Hotel Cipriani Srl v Cipriani (Grosvenor Street) Ltd* [2008] EWHC 3032 (Ch), [234].
[99] This will be discussed in relation to character merchandising in Chapter 10.
[100] This will be discussed in relation to personality merchandising in Chapter 10.

Annabel's (Berkley Square) Ltd v G. Schock (t/a Annabel's Escort Agency)
[1972] FSR 261

The claimants were proprietors of a well-known London club, named Annabel's. They sought an interim injunction to restrain the defendant from carrying on the business of an escort agency under the name Annabel's Escort Agency. An injunction was granted in the High Court and the defendant appealed. A key question for the Court of Appeal was what was the nature of the misrepresentation and the consequent damage.

Russell LJ, at p. 269:

Here I have no doubt at all as at present advised that there is a sufficient association between what the public would consider the field of activity in which Annabel's Club is conducted and the field of activity in which Mr Schock indulges in the course of his escort business.

Both are concerned with what might be described as 'night life' or 'hight [sic] entertainment'. Put another way, it can be said that Annabel's Club provides facilities to men for dining and dancing with female partners—though not in the sense that they are made available on the premises, as is the case, I understand, in some or perhaps many night clubs, where they are known as 'hostesses'. Turning it round slightly, Mr Schock's business is concerned with supplying for men facilities of female partners for the purpose, among other things, of dining and dancing with them.

I should have thought there was a relevant association between the fields of activities sufficient to make it impossible to say that the general public could not be confused into thinking that Mr Schock's business under the name of 'Annabel's' was something to do with or was associated with the plaintiffs' business also under the name of 'Annabel's'.

Now it is said, as I have previously remarked, that it may be that in terms of pounds and pence between now and the trial, when the whole matter will be finally decided, it is improbable having regard to their flourishing condition, that the plaintiffs through their club will actually lose money by the activities of Mr Schock trading under the business name of 'Annabel's Escort Agency'. Indeed, I think it is fair to remark that Mr Schock said: 'It may very well be that I have had one or two members of Annabel's who have applied to me for an escort to take them there, and no doubt have taken them there.' I dare say that has swollen the takings of the plaintiffs' club, though perhaps if it had not been that escort it would have been one of Jeannie's or another girl; one does not know. This may be so; but the crucial point seems to me in this case to be this: First of all, I absolutely and entirely agree with the learned judge that on the evidence there is a probability of confusion, and that some members of the public though not all will think that there is some association between the plaintiffs' club and Annabel's Escort Agency.

Having reached that stage we are then faced with this situation which has got nothing to do with immediate possible loss of takings by Annabel's Club, or even immediate falling off in membership, both of which seem unlikely. But the fact is, as Mr Schock very properly, rightly and honestly faced and agreed with, that escort agencies have, as yet, as a general activity, to say the least but an indifferent public image. I am prepared, of course, to accept from Mr Schock that everything to do with his particular agency has always been run with the strictest regard to public and private morals, and so on. But as he says, as yet one cannot but be tarred (I am not using his words) to some extent with the brush which the general public are inclined to think is appropriate to these escort agencies, though, according to Mr Schock they are satisfying a present and increasing want, and it may be that they will come to be thought to be a good thing or a better thing than they are thought to be now.

> This seems to me to be the important matter. This seems to me to entitle Annabel's Club or the proprietors to now say what in my judgment is correct at this stage, namely: 'If it is going to be thought by a sufficient number of people that we are somehow associated with the running of an escort agency, some of the tar will come off on us, and we have no tar on us at all.' This is the real ground upon which it seems to me an interlocutory injunction is justified, because it is that kind of attack, albeit unintended, on the general good will of a plaintiff that requires the protection of an interlocutory injunction, because there is never going to be any means at the end of the road to see how much harm has been done by this kind of possible reputation being acquired in the mind of the public in regard to a perfectly respectable organisation and activity such as is the plaintiffs' and as is run by the plaintiffs.
>
> For those reasons it appears to me that the learned judge was right in coming to his conclusion that this was a case in which an interlocutory injunction should be ordered, of course with an undertaking as to damages should the matter turn out differently on the evidence given at the trial. For those reasons I would dismiss the appeal.

An interesting aspect of this judgment is that Russell LJ accepted that it might not be possible to assess the actual damage to the claimant's goodwill which might result from the defendant's misrepresentation. As a result, he held that it was appropriate to order an interim injunction. 'Anticipated' damage, through both damage to the claimant's reputation because of an association with the defendant and also through loss of control over its reputation in the future, was also the issue in *McAlpine v McAlpine*.

Sir Robert McAlpine Ltd v Alfred McAlpine Plc [2004] EWHC 630 (Ch)

The claimant and the defendant were both construction companies which were established when the original company founded by Sir Robert McAlpine divided along geographical lines. When the defendant decided to trade simply under the name 'McAlpine', the claimant sued for passing off, claiming that the defendant would misrepresent either that he was associated with the claimant or had the sole goodwill in the 'McAlpine' name. The question arose of what would be the damage that the claimant might suffer. The claimant alleged such damage might result, inter alia, (1) if Robert does not get on a tender list because Alfred had attracted bad publicity; or (2) Alfred does something which attracts bad publicity which generally rubs off on Robert, such as something involving a railway accident. In that latter case, there might also be general damage to the goodwill of the McAlpine name. Mann J held that this might amount to damage which would be covered by a claim in passing off.

Mann J:

> 43. I shall take heads (a) and (b) together. As a matter of principle they ought to amount to damage if the risk is sufficiently great. I have already set out some extracts from authority which deal with the question of damage. That authority indicates, and it indeed is accepted by Alfred, that the relevant damage, for the purposes of passing off, is not limited to loss of sales to an opponent, or cases where the defendant's goods or services are inferior to those of the claimant. As Mr Thorley put it, injurious association or dilution of exclusivity can, in an appropriate case, amount to damage...

44. I therefore have to weigh and assess the risks of damage relied on by Robert in the light of the evidence. First, there is the question of the level of risk of a tarnishing of the McAlpine name. This is impossible to quantify, but it is a possibility. With one exception, no witness suggested that Alfred enjoyed anything other than a good current reputation in terms of its work, payment record, creditworthiness, health and safety matters and all other things that would establish a good business reputation...There were no positive indications that its good reputation was about to change. However, that is not entirely the point. There is a risk. A number of things might plausibly happen. Alfred's business reputation in one or more of the areas might change; or its reputation might be affected by some engineering misfortune which gains some publicity. Since Alfred is involved in railway maintenance, fears were expressed by one witness that accidents in that area might affect its reputation, though it was pointed out that Alfred's railway maintenance activities related to such fixtures as embankments, and not to such things as the track and signalling, where reputations might be said to be more vulnerable. Other work was put forward as possibly causing public opprobrium, such as participating in an environmentally sensitive road building project.

[Having pointed out that the defendant's actions risked damaging the claimant's reputation in the future, Mann J then looked at various ways in which the claimant might be negatively associated with the defendant. He continued:]

47. I bear in mind that the customers of Robert and Alfred operate in a relatively sophisticated and well-informed market. Many will be sufficiently well-informed to be able to distinguish between the two, and not to let an adverse impression attaching to one affect its judgments in relation to the other. However, I am satisfied that there is still scope for the sort of adverse effects referred to above, and that that scope presents a sufficiently high risk to the reputation of Robert as to amount to damage for the purposes of passing off. After the rebranding there is greater scope for adverse publicity and reputation to be attached to 'McAlpine' (after all, putting the name forward prominently is part of the purpose of the rebranding exercise) without a distinguishing 'Alfred', and for that to rub off on Robert because of the shared goodwill and shared name. I accept that some of the risks tend to be more speculative than others—for example, the risk of being excluded from PFI work at the pre-qualification stage—but I have to look at the matter in the round and realistically, and doing so leads me to the conclusion that the risks are real enough to amount to the sort of damage that the law of passing off is intended to prevent, as Warrington LJ stated.

In the 'Ukulele' case,[101] Hacon J held that the claimant, which performed under the name 'The Ukulele Orchestra of Great Britain' (UOGB) should succeed in passing off against the defendant because the latter's use of the name 'The United Kingdom Ukulele Orchestra' had 'caused damage to UOGB's goodwill, particularly by way of loss of control over UOGB's reputation as performers.'[102] However, it is possible to argue that in the 'McAlpine' case, Mann J went further. He held that damage caused by the defendant's misrepresentation would be not only to the claimant's reputation (or goodwill) but also to the value of the claimant's 'name'. Sometimes known as 'dilution', there has been considerable controversy as to what extent passing off covers this head of damage.

---

[101] *The Ukulele Orchestra of Great Britain v Erwin Clausen & Yellow Promotion GmbH & Co. Kg (t/a the United Kingdom Ukulele Orchestra)* [2015] EWHC 1772 (IPEC).
[102] [92].

5.2.5.4 Does passing off recognize damage by dilution?

The case which is generally credited with recognizing damage which dilutes the value of the claimant's identifying insignia (most usually its name) rather than directly damaging its goodwill is the 'Elderflower Champagne' case.

Taittinger v Allbev Ltd (Discovery) [1993] FSR 641

The claimants produced champagne and French wines. Previous actions taken by them had ensured that the name 'champagne' was used only for sparkling wine produced in the Champagne district of France. The defendants produced a cheap drink under the name 'Elderflower Champagne'. The drink was non-alcoholic, but was carbonated and was sold in champagne-style bottles with labels and wired corks similar to those used on champagne bottles. The claimants sued for passing off. They were unsuccessful in the High Court. The court accepted that there had been a misrepresentation, but did not believe that there was a likelihood of serious damage, because only a small number of people were likely to be confused. The claimants appealed. In the Court of Appeal, Peter Gibson LJ in his leading judgment concluded that it was 'at least as likely that a not insignificant number of members of the public would think that it [the defendant's product] had some association with champagne, if it was not actually champagne'. In addition, he held that there was ample evidence that as a reasonably foreseeable consequence of that misrepresentation injury to the champagne houses' goodwill would result. Furthermore, even though the activities of the defendant were on a 'small scale' he believed that the claimants would suffer damage through loss of sales. He then identified an additional head of damage which might result from the defendant's misrepresentation, but which had been rejected by Sir Mervyn Davies in the High Court.

Peter Gibson LJ, at p. 669:

But in my judgment the real injury to the champagne houses' goodwill comes under a different head and although the judge refers to Mr Sparrow [the plaintiff's counsel] putting the point in argument, he does not deal with it specifically or give a reason for its undoubted rejection by him. Mr Sparrow had argued that if the defendants continued to market their product, there would take place a blurring or erosion of the uniqueness that now attends the word 'champagne', so that the exclusive reputation of the champagne houses would be debased. He put this even more forcefully before us. He submitted that if the defendants are allowed to continue to call their product Elderflower Champagne, the effect would be to demolish the distinctiveness of the word champagne, and that would inevitably damage the goodwill of the champagne houses.

In the Advocaat case at first instance ([1980] RPC 31 at 52) Goulding J held that one type of damage was 'a more gradual damage to the plaintiffs' business through depreciation of the reputation that their goods enjoy'. He continued:

Damage of [this] type can rarely be susceptible of positive proof. In my judgment, it is likely to occur if the word 'Advocaat' is permitted to be used of alcoholic egg drinks generally or of the defendants' product in particular.

In the House of Lords in that case Lord Diplock referred to that type of damage to goodwill as relevant damage, which he described as caused 'indirectly in the debasement of the reputation attaching to the name "advocaat" ' ([1979] AC 731 at 740).

In *Vine Products Ltd v MacKenzie & Co Ltd* [1969] RPC 1 at 23 Cross J, commenting with approval on the decision of Danckwerts J in *Bollinger v Costa Brava Wine Co Ltd (No 2)* said:

[Danckwerts J] thought, as I read in his judgment, that if people were allowed to call sparkling wine not produced in Champagne 'Champagne', even though preceded by an adjective denoting the country of origin, the distinction between genuine Champagne and 'champagne type' wines produced elsewhere would become blurred; that the word 'Champagne' would come gradually to mean no more than 'sparkling wine'; and that the part of the plaintiffs' goodwill which consisted in the name would be diluted and gradually destroyed.

[Peter Gibson LJ then identified later cases in both Australia and New Zealand which had approved Danckwerts J's approach in the 'champagne' case to the blurring of its distinctive name. He continued:]

At p. 670:

It seems to me inevitable that if the defendants, with their not insignificant trade as a supplier of drinks to Sainsbury and other retail outlets, are permitted to use the name Elderflower Champagne, the goodwill in the distinctive name champagne will be eroded with serious adverse consequences for the champagne houses.

In my judgment therefore the fifth characteristic identified in the Advocaat case is established. I can see no exceptional feature to this case which would justify on grounds of public policy withholding from the champagne houses the ordinary remedy of an injunction to restrain passing off. I would therefore grant an injunction to restrain the defendant from selling, offering for sale, distributing and describing, whether in advertisements or on labels or in any other way, any beverages, not being wine produced in Champagne, under or by reference to the word champagne. That injunction, I would, emphasise, does not prevent the sale of the defendants' product, provided it is not called champagne.

[Both Mann LJ and Lord Bingham MR concurred that the claimants would suffer sufficient damage, both to their goodwill and to the exclusivity of their name.]

Mann LJ, at pp. 673–4:

Their case was and is, that the word 'Champagne' has an exclusiveness which is impaired if it is used in relation to a product (particularly a potable product) which is neither Champagne nor associated or connected with the businesses which produce Champagne. The impairment is a gradual debasement, dilution or erosion of what is distinctive.

...

The consequences of debasement, dilution or erosion are not demonstrable in figures of lost sales but that they will be incrementally damaging to goodwill is in my opinion inescapable. On this basis I would grant injunctive relief as claimed.

Bingham LJ, at p. 678:

Any product which is not Champagne but is allowed to describe itself as such must inevitably, in my view, erode the singularity and exclusiveness of the description Champagne and so cause the first plaintiffs damage of an insidious but serious kind.

As we have seen, Peter Gibson LJ had cited a number of cases, including previous drinks cases, to support his finding that damage to the exclusivity of the claimant's name fell within the parameters of a passing off action. However, this view was not shared by Millett LJ in *Harrods*. He took the view that, following the 'Elderflower Champagne' case, the law of passing off was in danger of operating in areas which he for one found inappropriate.

Millett LJ, at p. 715:

Damage

In the classic case of passing off, where the defendant represents his goods or business as the goods or business of the plaintiff, there is an obvious risk of damage to the plaintiff's business by substitution. Customers and potential customers will be lost to the plaintiff if they transfer their custom to the defendant in the belief that they are dealing with the plaintiff. But this is not the only kind of damage which may be caused to the plaintiff's goodwill by the deception of the public. Where the parties are not in competition with each other, the plaintiff's reputation and goodwill may be damaged without any corresponding gain to the defendant. In the Lego case, for example, a customer who was dissatisfied with the defendant's plastic irrigation equipment might be dissuaded from buying one of the plaintiff's plastic toy construction kits for his children if he believed that it was made by the defendant. The danger in such a case is that the plaintiff loses control over his own reputation.

In *Taittinger SA v Allbev Ltd* [1993] FSR 641 the court appears to have recognised a different head of damage. If the defendants were allowed to market their product under the name Elderflower Champagne

there would take place a blurring or erosion of the uniqueness that now attends the word 'champagne', so that the exclusive reputation of the champagne houses would be debased.
(per Peter Gibson LJ at page 669)

It is self-evident that the application of the plaintiff's brand name to inferior goods is likely to injure the plaintiff's reputation and damage his goodwill if people take the inferior goods to be those of the plaintiff. That is a classic head of damage in cases of passing off. But Peter Gibson LJ may have had more in mind than this. He referred without disapproval to the submission of counsel for the plaintiffs that if the defendants were allowed to continue to call their product Elderflower Champagne 'the effect would be to demolish the distinctiveness of the word champagne, and that would inevitably damage the goodwill of the champagne houses'.

This is a reference to the debasement of the distinctiveness of the name champagne which would occur if it gradually came to be used by the public as a generic term to describe any kind of sparkling wine. Erosion of the distinctiveness of a brand name has been recognised as a form of damage to the goodwill of the business with which the name is connected in a number of cases, particularly in Australia and New Zealand; but unless care is taken this could mark an unacceptable extension to the tort of passing off. To date the law has not sought to protect the value of the brand name as such, but the value of the goodwill which it generates; and it insists on proof of confusion to justify its intervention. But the erosion of the distinctiveness of a brand name which occurs by reason of its degeneration into common use as a generic term is not necessarily dependent on confusion at all. The danger that if the defendant's product was called champagne then all sparkling wines would eventually come to be called champagne would still exist even if no one was deceived into thinking that such wine really was champagne. I have an intellectual difficulty in accepting the concept

> that the law insists upon the presence of both confusion and damage and yet recognises as sufficient a head of damage which does not depend on confusion. Counsel for the plaintiffs relied strongly on the possibility of damage of this nature, but it is in my opinion not necessary to consider it further in the present case. There is no danger of 'Harrods' becoming a generic term for a retail emporium in the luxury class, and if such a danger existed the use of a different name in connection with an institution of a different kind would not advance the process.

Millett LJ observed that he was uncomfortable with a head of damage in passing off which did not rely on a misrepresentation, but rather on a simple association made by the public between the name of the claimant's product and that of the defendant's, which might damage the exclusivity of the former. In his dissenting judgment in the same case, Sir Michael Kerr showed no such reservations. He noted, for example, that Harman J in the High Court appears to have given 'no or insufficient weight to the fact that a trader's distinctive name can in some cases in itself form part of its goodwill and constitute a property interest, and that this is the position here'. He then considered the issue of damage.

Sir Michael Kerr, at p. 724:

The standard remedy in passing-off actions is an injunction; an account to assess damages is rare. In the great majority of cases the relevant damage will not be measurable in pounds and pence, but consist in the probability of damage to the plaintiff's reputation and goodwill which is ultimately liable to lead indirectly to a reduction in trade. Loss of distinctiveness causes damage to a reputation for excellence, and loss of trade will ultimately follow. The authorities show two relevant propositions in this regard. First, a debasement or dilution of the plaintiff's reputation, as the result of the action of the defendant, is a relevant head of damage. Secondly, if the act which constitutes the passing-off has the effect of raising in people's minds the mistaken belief of a connection between the defendant and the plaintiff, but which is in fact non-existent, then the court will have regard to the fact that the plaintiff has, to that extent, lost control of his reputation, and that he has therefore suffered damage to his goodwill by a potentially injurious association with the defendant against which the court will protect him by injunction.

A number of passages bear out these propositions. Inevitably, the factual contexts were different, but the aspects of principle are not open to question.

[Sir Michael Kerr then quoted approvingly the comments of Peter Gibson LJ, Bingham LJ, and Mann LJ in the 'Elderflower Champagne' case in which each recognized loss of distinctiveness in the name champagne as a head of damage. He continued:]

At p. 725:

In fairness to the defendants, it cannot of course be said in the present case that a similar consequence [to those] would necessarily follow, and indeed it is greatly to be hoped that this would not be the case. But that is not the test. The crucial point, as stated in the second of the foregoing propositions, is the plaintiff's inevitable loss of control of his reputation and the consequent risk of damage to it.

Later decisions show that Lord Justice Millett's suspicion of this apparent extension to passing off has not been generally shared by the judiciary. Indeed, it is Sir Michael Kerr's judgment which proved to be more prescient in terms of the future direction of passing off. Since *Harrods*, judges have, with growing frequency, accepted 'dilution' as a legitimate head of damage.[103]

A number of commentators have viewed the use of passing off to protect against the erosion (or dilution) of the distinctive nature of a claimant's sign as a worrying extension of the tort, not least because it appears to favour the trader with a powerful brand. Thus, Hazel Carty in her article 'Dilution and passing off: cause for concern'[104] suggests that introducing dilution into passing off without adequately defining its remit would be 'dangerous'.

This is because, according to Carty, protecting the advertising function of a mark through passing off will not serve consumers' interests, since consumer loyalty will become tied to the brand and not to the qualities of the goods to which it attaches. Indeed, she goes further to suggest that allowing 'dilution' into passing off may actually be a way of protecting a trader against misappropriation or unjust enrichment. Thus, she quotes Sir Thomas Bingham in *Taittinger* which was ostensibly about lost sales and dilution, to the effect that it would be unfair to allow others to 'cash in on the reputation they have done nothing to establish'. She concludes that raising the question of whether competition is fair or unfair in a passing off action undermines the rationale of the tort, which is primarily to promote efficient competition for the benefit of consumers.

mimicking?

5.2.5.5 Passing off and misappropriation

The idea that passing off recognizes misappropriation as a head of damage or indeed should do so, as was suggested by Bingham LJ's comment in *Taittinger*, is a controversial one. Misappropriation can occur without a misrepresentation and will not necessarily damage the trader's goodwill. For example, it could be argued that in the *Taittinger* case what was at issue was not loss of sales, which in any event would have been nugatory, and not even (or not only) the 'dilution' of the exclusivity of the name 'champagne' but rather the fact that, by mimicking the packaging and the name, the defendants were appropriating that exclusivity for themselves. Similarly, it is possible to argue in cases of reverse passing off, that there is unlikely to be any damage to the claimant but there will be advantage taken by the third party who presents the claimant's goods as its own.[105] This has led some to argue that judges have in practice often recognized misappropriation as a basis for a finding of passing off despite the claims, for example, of Jacob LJ *in L'Oréal v Bellure*,[106] that passing off is not a law of unfair competition.[107] However, others such as Carty are unsympathetic to suggestions that passing off should extend to encompass misappropriation or even dilution. She would prefer passing off not to inhibit competition, since she takes the view that unfettered competition generally benefits consumers through providing more choice and lower prices. Conversely, she believes that remedies against dilution and misappropriation would primarily benefit traders at the expense of consumers' interests. In the following article, Carty argues for a return to the 'classic trinity' in passing off.

---

[103] See e.g. *Och-Ziff Management Europe v Och Capital LLP* [2010] EWHC 2599 (Ch), [158].
[104] (1996) 112 LQR 632–66.
[105] *Bristol Conservatories Ltd v Conservatories Custom Build* [1989] RPC 455.
[106] [2007] EWCA Civ 968, [160].
[107] J. Davis, 'Why the United Kingdom should have a law against misappropriation' [2010] CLJ 561.

H. Carty, 'Passing off: frameworks for liability debated' [2012] IPQ 106 at 107–110

Strict classic trinity

The standard framework for the tort of passing off is provided by the trinity of goodwill; misrepresentation; damage. Though Lord Diplock provided a more detailed framework in *Erven Warnink BV v Townend (Advocaat)* the trinity provides a clearer emphasis on the need to link the ingredients of the tort and was the test favoured by the House of Lords in *Reckitt & Colman Products Ltd v Borden Inc (Jif Lemon)* [1990] 1 W.L.R. 491 HL, and the Court of Appeal in *Consorzio del Prosciutto di Parma v Marks and Spencer Plc (Parma Ham)*, in *Harrods Ltd v Harrodian School* and in *Diageo NA Inc v Intercontinental Brands (ICB) Ltd (Vodkat)*.

The fact that the tort is based on a trinity underlines the important fact that all three ingredients are to be understood and applied as interlinked concepts; each ingredient helps to fashion and (importantly) limit the other ingredients. So the tort involves the defendant making a (mis)representation that draws on the claimant's goodwill and damages it. As will be seen this also means that when applying the classic trinity it is dangerous to substitute analogous concepts such as reputation for goodwill and confusion for misrepresentation. Though reputation lurks behind the concept of goodwill and confusion is often present as a result of a misrepresentation, such substitution of concepts may weaken the linkage of the trinity ingredients.

The classic trinity reveals that the only valuable intangible that the tort protects is 'goodwill', the property interest identified at the heart of the tort by the House of Lords in *Spalding v Gamage*. Goodwill involves an existing customer connection in this jurisdiction that is valuable because it attracts and retains a customer base: hence Lord Eldon's assertion that it was 'the value of that probability that the old customers will resort to the old place'. So customer connection is based on the market familiarity with or the perceived quality of 'the old place'. This means that for the strict classic trinity goodwill has to be seen as a vehicle for information, not merely a vehicle for persuasion (a point reinforced by the need for materiality, discussed below). Thus care must be taken when applying the classic definition of goodwill, taken from Lord Macnaghten's speech in a tax case, *Inland Revenue Commissioners v Muller & Co's Margarine Ltd*. That definition of goodwill as 'the benefit and advantage of the good name, reputation and connection of a business … the attractive force that brings in custom' has to be read as a whole to appreciate that goodwill is about customer connection, not simply reputation per se or its equivalents. Case law reveals that customer connection is not simply market recognition/reputation; an attractive name; or brand 'aura'.

And of course within the framework of the trinity, goodwill is only protected against misrepresentations (regardless of fault). To be relevant the misrepresentation must involve the defendant referencing the claimant's goodwill in his (the defendant's) own trade—hence the name 'passing off'—and in so doing misinforming consumers. This linkage between the misrepresentation and goodwill and misrepresentation and consumer information requires that to be actionable a misrepresentation must be material in two senses. First, it must be material to customers in making their market choices: they base their decision on the referencing of the claimant's goodwill. Secondly, that effect on consumer choice must be in a way that is harmful to the claimant's existing customer connection. As Jacob J. noted in *Hodgkinson & Corby Ltd v Wards Mobility Services Ltd* [1995] F.S.R. 169 Ch D, 'there is no tort of making use of another's goodwill as such'.

Of course the most obvious way that a misrepresentation could be so material in both senses is where it causes customer confusion as to source. But the tort does not focus on confusion: a lack of confusion does not rule out the presence of a material misrepresentation and not all confusing misrepresentations are material misrepresentations. Nor is it limited to source misrepresentations: material misrepresentations—those that reference the claimant's goodwill and shape customer choice—may relate to quality, a connection or a distinctive product rather than source per se. The strict classic trinity simply requires that the defendant's misrepresentation lead (or be likely to lead) to a material reliance by the customer *and* that reliance be likely to harm the claimant's customer connection. By so doing it helps to protect the market information passing between trader and consumer, but it does not as such serve to protect the persuasive effect (subliminal or otherwise) of reputation or aura. And the trinity framework means that only damage to the valuable intangible being protected is relevant. There must be harm to customer connection, though a likelihood of harm suffices. And such damage must be real rather than speculative. In *Stringfellow v McCain Foods (GB) Ltd* the claimant's famous night club was referenced in advertising by the defendant frozen chips manufacturer. However, despite the possible consumer misassociation between the parties the Court of Appeal found there to be no likely harm: the claimant's argument that he might begin merchandising the club name in the future and might be prejudiced was rejected as 'pure speculation'. Thus recently the Singapore Court of Appeal in *Novelty Pte Ltd v Amanresorts Ltd* stressed that the requirement of harm should not be 'rendered otiose' and applied a test of 'real tangible risk of substantial damage'.

A real risk of damage may arise from possible harm to the claimant's goodwill by tarnishing the reputation behind it or through lost sales. However, free riding or 'unfair advantage' is not damage. For this reason the strict classic trinity demands that 'dilution' be rejected as a spurious head of damage. The theory behind it—that unauthorised referencing will erode the exclusivity of a mark—is controversial (even under its own terms dilution is not claimed to affect the information passing between trader and consumer) and unsubstantiated (as a head of damage it is revealingly often alluded to as 'insidious' or 'subtle' harm to the claimant's goodwill). It has no place within the classic trinity as such. In reality 'dilution' (or the equivalent allegations of *speculative* lost licensing or control opportunities) is the label offered to the courts when in fact 'misappropriation' is the heart of the claimant's complaint. So though Laddie J. cited erosion as the harm in *Irvine v Talksport*, he also referred to the defendant 'squatting' and taking the 'lustre' of the famous claimant in order to enhance 'the attractiveness of the product to the target audience'.

Thus the classic trinity—as strictly applied in *Mars v Burgess Group; Bulmer v Bollinger; Harrods v Harrodian School*—only protects the claimant's existing customer connection against real harm inflicted by the defendant's misrepresentation which draws on the claimant's goodwill. And what is clear (despite Davis's assertion otherwise) is that the two modern variants of the tort—extended passing off and inverse passing off—are capable of falling within this strict classic trinity frame.

[Carty sees the 'strict classic trinity' as superior to passing off which recognizes misappropriation. She concludes at 121:]

The classic trinity—linking misrepresentation, goodwill and damage by the cement of materiality—protects successful claimants where it is in the public interest so to do. (Indeed failing to protect goodwill against harmful misrepresentations 'would have serious negative consequences in the commercial marketplace'.) It protects information not persuasion per se, does not encourage litigation over competition and requires more than moral opprobrium to set the ground rules for the rat race of competition. The strict classic trinity is a clever mechanism that combines the claimant's interests, the consumers' interests and the public interest. Thus this cautious framework avoids taking the common law into areas best suited to legislation: namely competition rules, consumer laws and intellectual property rights. And it means that not all appropriations, imitations, referencing of the market leader, attention-grabbing on the back of the claimant's success or riding on the brand leader's coat-tails will give rise to liability. Correctly applied, this tort does not seek to protect the psychological 'pull' or commercial magnetism of a name—though that is what the big brands seek. Nor does it seek to protect the psychological 'glow' of consumer lifestyle choices— what Davis terms their 'investment' in the aura or exclusivity offered by the 'real thing'. The tort is seen as having a limited constructive part to play in the process of regulating competitive practices.

Given the enormous value of many trade marks and their significant role in the global economy, it is perhaps unsurprising that the tort of passing off has evolved to give such marks additional protection. In her article, Carty suggests that the primary purpose of passing off is not to protect the interests of traders in this way but rather to protect the interests of consumers who both benefit from unrestricted competition and who may be confused. Yet is it not a fact that unlike statutes aimed at protecting consumers, a passing off action brought by one trader against another will inevitably have as its goal the protection of the interests of the claimant? Of course, it is also true that the court must balance the claimant's interests against the legitimate interests of the defendant. However, it would seem to follow that in passing off cases, consumers' interests will play an important but not a central role in this balancing exercise.

> **FURTHER READING**
>
> H. Carty, 'Heads of damage in passing off' [1996] EIPR 487.
>
> J. Davis 'Why the United Kingdom should have a law against misappropriation' [2010] CLJ 561.
>
> F. Russell, 'The Elderflower Champagne case: is this a further expansion of the tort of passing off?' [1993] EIPR 379.
>
> C. Wadlow, 'Passing off at the crossroads again, a review article for Hazel Carty, An Analysis of the Economic Torts' [2011] EIPR 447.

5.3 DEFENCES

The three most common defences in passing off are:

(1) delay or acquiescence;

(2) bona fide use of the defendant's own name;

(3) concurrent use.

5.3.1 DELAY OR ACQUIESCENCE

If a claimant delays in bringing an action for passing off, it does not forfeit its right to do so as long as the alleged passing off is continuing. However, such delay may bring other unwelcome consequences. The claimant may be unlikely to succeed in obtaining an interim injunction. Or the defendant may have built up its own goodwill in the product or services which is independent of the claimant. Thus, in *DaimlerChrysler AG v Alavi*,[108] the claimant was the owner of the Mercedes-Benz motor car company. The claimant's car was often referred to by the term, 'Merc'. The defendant owned a clothes shop called 'Merc' and also sold clothes under the name 'Merc', and had been doing so since 1967. DaimlerChrysler had registered trade marks for both 'Mercedes' and 'Merc' for, inter alia, clothing. It sued Alavi for both passing off and trade mark infringement. The claim for passing off failed. The court held that there had been no deception by the defendant, because by 1975 the defendant had established its own goodwill trading under the name 'Merc'. In the more recent case of *Blinkx UK Ltd v Blinkbox Entertainment Ltd*,[109] the defendant and the claimant had rival internet businesses. The claimant started its business in 2004 and the defendant three years later. However, the claimant waited a further two years before bringing an action for passing off. In light of this delay, Floyd J refused to grant the claimant an interim injunction. He noted that 'the defendant's business has grown from very small beginnings to a very substantial one during the period of the delay'.[110] And he concluded:

> Had the claimant acted promptly while the defendant's business was still in its trial phase, the balance of convenience might have favoured an injunction. But two years later it seems to me that the position has reversed. If one asks whether I should permit a short further period of coexistence or stop all use of the name by the defendant except within the narrow confines proposed, I come down very heavily in favour of the former. Whichever way one looks at the matter, I consider that the claimant's delay here is fatal to the grant of interim relief, and I dismiss the application.[111]

In some circumstances, the court may take the claimant's delay in bringing an action as evidence of acquiescence to the defendant's conduct, particularly if the defendant has altered its position in reliance on the claimant's action or on its failure to act, or on a representation by the claimant that 'would make it inequitable for the claimant to enforce his rights'.[112] Acquiescence was found by the Court of Appeal in *Habib Bank v Habib Bank AG Zurich*.[113] However, the court did not find acquiescence in the 'Merc' case. According to Pumfrey J:

> It is an essential component in a defence of acquiescence that the failure of the plaintiff to act should have induced the defendant to believe that the wrong was being assented to. But in this case there was no such reliance by Mr Alavi … in any event, DaimlerChrysler (or their predecessors) were not aware of his trading activities until 1997. These facts cannot support a plea of acquiescence. But the period of trading is long. Had I found that Mr Alavi had infringed one or more of the Mercedes marks, but that there was no passing off, and that there had been no damage, perhaps the question of delay should have to be considered in the context of relief. But the question does not arise. This defence fails.[114]

5.3.2 BONA FIDE USE OF THE DEFENDANT'S OWN NAME

Use by a defendant of his own name may provide a defence in passing off, but it is a narrow one. For example, the defence has never been held to apply to names of new companies 'as

---

[108] [2001] RPC 42.   [109] [2010] EWHC 1624 (Ch).
[110] See also *Fine and Country Ltd v Okotoks Ltd (formerly SpicerHaart Ltd)* [2012] EWHC 2230 (Ch).
[111] [28].   [112] C. Wadlow, *The Law of Passing Off*, p. 790.   [113] [1981] 1 WLR 1265.
[114] p. 850.

otherwise a route to piracy would be obvious'.[115] The limited nature of this defence was confirmed by the Court of Appeal in *Reed Executive v Reed Business Information*.

Reed Executive Plc v Reed Business Information Ltd [2004] RPC 40

The claimants had operated employment agencies since 1960 and recently through a website, 'reed.co.uk'. They had a registered trade mark 'Reed' for employment agency services since 1996. The defendants published, inter alia, business and science journals and magazines and had used the word Reed in relation to their business since 1983. In 1999, the defendants started their own website, totaljobs.com, which, inter alia, advertised jobs which had traditionally been advertised in the journals. Initially, the names 'Reed Elsevier' and 'Reed Business Information' logos appeared on the website. Furthermore, the word Reed was used as a metatag for the website and as a reference word for a variety of web advertising, although none of the advertisements actually used the word Reed. In addition, the Yahoo search engine linked the search terms 'recruitment' and 'job' to the totaljobs.com website and Yahoo gave the defendants free use of their own name. The name Reed was chosen by Yahoo rather than Reed Elsevier. There was some minor evidence of confusion, in the form of enquiries being made to the claimants about jobs advertised by the defendants on their website. By the date of the trial, the only use of Reed on the defendants' website was to be found in the use of the name Reed Business Information Ltd in the copyright notices on the site and the Reed Business Information logo, which was on the home page. The claimants sued for both trade mark infringement and passing off. In relation to the latter, the defendants argued both that there was no actionable misrepresentation and in addition that they had a defence of bona fide use of their own name. Although the Court of Appeal found that there had been neither trade mark infringement nor passing off, Jacob LJ did go on to examine the scope of the own name defence in passing off.

Jacob LJ:

The own name defence to passing off

109. It is long and well settled that it is no defence to passing off that the defendant has or had no intention to deceive. It is also settled that there is only a very limited own name defence. It was put this way by Romer J in *Joseph Rodgers & Sons Ltd v WN Rodgers & Co* (1924) 41 RPC 277, a passage approved by the majority of the House of Lords in *Parker-Knoll Ltd v Knoll International Ltd* [1962] RPC 265:

> To the proposition of law [that no man is entitled to carry on his business in such a way as to represent that it is the business of another, or is in any way connected with the business of another], there is an exception, that a man is entitled to carry on his business in his own name so long as he does not do anything more than that to cause confusion with the business of another, and so long as he does it honestly. To the proposition of law that [no man is entitled so to describe his goods as to represent that the goods are the goods of another,] there is no exception.

[115] *Asprey & Garrard Ltd v WRA (Guns) Ltd and Asprey* [2002] ETMR 47, per Peter Gibson LJ.

110. Thus the English law of passing off abounds with cases where people have been prevented from using their own name. This particularly happens when a scion of some well-known family business has sought to cash in on his name at the expense of that business, as for instance Dunhill (*Alfred Dunhill Ltd v Sunoptic SA* [1979] FSR 337), Gucci (*Guccio Gucci SpA v Paulo Gucci* [1991] FSR 89) and Asprey (*Asprey & Garrard Ltd v WRA (Guns) Ltd* [2002] FSR 31).

111. I have already observed that the difference between mere confusion and deception is elusive. I suppose the sort of background non-damaging confusion in this case might be the sort of thing Romer J had in mind. Once the position strays into misleading a substantial number of people (going from 'I wonder if there is a connection' to 'I assume there is a connection') there will be passing off, whether the use is as a business name or a trade mark on goods.

112. The judge [in the High Court] rightly observed that the passing-off defence is narrow. Actually no case comes to mind in which it has succeeded. Because the test is honesty, I do not see how any man who is in fact causing deception and knows that to be so can possibly have a defence to passing off.

113. Thus in this case if RBI had been causing significant deception, the fact that it was using its own name would have afforded no defence to the passing-off claim, even though it had no intention to deceive. That is the admitted position as regards Version 1 [of their web site]. But in relation to later versions there is at best no more than some minimal degree of confusion—significant deception is not shown and so, narrow though it is, I think RBI come within Romer J's exception.

The own name defence in registered trade mark actions has proved more effective.[116] Do you think that the courts are interpreting this defence too narrowly? After all, the idea that there may be a defence in passing off which has never been known to succeed is an interesting one.

5.3.3 CONCURRENT USE

This defence arises when two or more traders have acquired the right to use the same name or indicia. Although such concurrent use may initially have caused confusion, it is also the case that if the trader with the earlier right does not take action, then the public may come, over time, to distinguish between them. Cases where the courts have found concurrent use, where both parties have a right to use the name, include the 'Hit Factory', 'Merc', and 'Reed' cases.[117] In *Woolley v Ultimate Products*,[118] the claimant sold watches under the name 'Henley' and the defendant sold clothing under the name 'Henleys'. Arden LJ in the Court of Appeal accepted that both the defendant and the claimant had acquired goodwill distinguished by their respective names through concurrent use. However, the defendant's goodwill attached to its clothing products, not to the watches which it had begun selling under the name 'Henleys'. The defendant did not have a defence to passing off.

---

[116] Jacob LJ also went on to examine the 'own name defence' in trade mark law and this will be examined in Chapter 8.

[117] See also *Habib Bank v Habib Bank AG Zurich* [1981] 2 All ER 277.

[118] [2012] EWCA Civ 1038.

FURTHER READING

K. Stephens, Z. Fuller, and H. Atherton, 'Passing off: honest concurrent use' [2013] CIPAJ 212.

C. Wadlow, 'The own-name defence in passing-off: six pennyworth of thoughts from the other side' (2011) 1 QMJIP 130.

D. Wells and P. Sherrell, 'Trade marks—infringement—passing off' [2001] EIPR N93.

5.4 CONCLUSION

It was suggested at the beginning of this chapter, that the UK does not have a general law of unfair competition. In its absence, the tort of passing off has provided the most important recourse for traders who believe they have been subjected to unfair trade practices by their rivals. Consumer protection has generally been left to other areas of the law. The recognition by the courts in passing off cases of damage to a trader's goodwill through dilution underscores the emphasis of the tort on protecting traders' interests. In this respect, in recent years the protection given to a mark or other identifying insignia by passing off has moved closer to that given by trade mark registration. But the substantial differences between these two actions remain important. Passing off has often offered protection to the distinctive get-up by which products and services are identified which would not necessarily be registrable as a trade mark. Furthermore, as trade mark registration has become increasingly international, passing off is also offering traders' insignia domestic protection when its international protection comes under threat. The differences and overlaps between registered trade marks and passing off will be considered in the following chapters.

6

TRADE MARKS I:

JUSTIFICATIONS, REGISTRATION, AND ABSOLUTE GROUNDS FOR REFUSAL OF REGISTRATION

6.1 INTRODUCTION

For some companies, trade marks may be their most valuable commercial assets. The trade mark, 'Coca-Cola' is almost universally recognizable; and in this age of global commerce, the product to which it attaches is almost universally available too. Indeed, the value of the Coca-Cola brand far exceeds the worth either of the company's tangible assets or of the trade secret which is the Coca-Cola recipe. An attractive trade mark may sustain the value of a medicine, even when its patent protection has expired and there are cheaper generic alternatives on the market. The difficulty of enforcing copyright in an age of digital technology and the internet has increased the importance to rightsholders of merchandising as a means of profiting from their works, whether they be movies, books, or music. Trade marks play a crucial role in merchandising, both of products and of characters.[1]

In recent years, and certainly in large measure as a consequence of the growing value of trade marks, there has been considerable legal activity concerning their protection in the EU. The EU agreed the Trade Marks Directive (TMD) in 1988.[2] In the UK, the directive was incorporated into national law with the passage of the Trade Marks Act 1994 (TMA). At substantially the same time, the EU introduced its Community Trade Mark (CTM).[3] After the implementation of the directive across the EU and the introduction of the CTM, there developed a substantial jurisprudence relating to trade marks, emanating from both

---

[1] Character and personality merchandising is addressed in Chapter 10.

[2] First Council Directive of 21 December 1988 to approximate the laws of the Member States relating to trade marks (2008/95 EC; formerly, 89/104/EEC). It was updated in 2008.

[3] Council Regulation (EC) No. 40/94 of 20 December 1993. Under the 2016 Regulation it is now called the European Union Trade Mark (EUTM).

domestic courts and the CJEU. Much of this jurisprudence was concerned with establishing how the terms of the directive (and the CTM Regulation[4]) should be interpreted and applied. In 2015, the EU incorporated key lessons learned from this jurisprudence into a new directive and regulations, which are designed not only to build on the original legislation but also to iron out some of the unforeseen difficulties which have arisen in its interpretation. The new directive[5] (henceforth the TMD 2016) was adopted in January 2016 and Member States have been given three years to implement the changes. The regulations[6] which affect the CTM, renamed the European Union Trade Mark (EUTM), came into effect in March 2016.[7]

The 1988 Trade Mark Directive was not intended to harmonize trade mark law across the EU but rather to 'approximate' trade mark law. In fact, it had more or less a harmonizing effect. Behind the directive was an acknowledgement that differing trade mark regimes across the EU could place barriers in the way of trade between Member States or, as it was put in the recitals to the directive:

> Whereas the trade mark laws at present applicable in the Member States contain disparities which may impede the free movement of goods and freedom to provide services and may distort competition within the common market; whereas it is therefore necessary, in view of the establishment and functioning of the internal market, to approximate the laws of Member States…

The recitals to the TMD 2016 again emphasize the importance of a 'single market for intellectual property rights' in order, as it states: 'to meet increased demands from stake holders for faster, higher quality, more streamlined trade mark registration systems'. But the new directive is also based on a recognition that is it necessary 'to modernize the trade mark system in the Union as a whole and adapt it to the internet era'. And that, in addition, 'in spite of the previous partial harmonization of national laws, there remain areas where further harmonization could have a positive impact on competitiveness and growth'.

A number of key issues which have preoccupied the courts in interpreting European trade mark law are sought to be addressed through the introduction of the TMD 2016. These issues will be examined in this and subsequent chapters. But first this chapter will explore the main justifications which have been proffered for the legal protection afforded to trade marks through registration. The chapter will then consider the practicalities of the trade mark registration process and the substantive law relating to the subject matter of registration. The following chapters will be concerned with the scope of the protection which is afforded by trade mark registration. Chapter 7 will look at the relative grounds for refusal to register a trade mark and infringement. Chapter 8 will consider the limitations to trade mark protection, including the defences to infringement and the various ways that it is possible to lose a mark. It will also examine the exhaustion of registered trade mark rights.

---

[4] Council Regulation (EC) No. 207/2009; formerly, Council Regulation (EC) No. 40/94.

[5] Directive (EU) 2015/2436 of the European Parliament and of the Council to approximate the laws of the Member States relating to trade marks (Recast).

[6] Regulation (EU) No. 2015/2424 of the European Parliament and of the Council of 16 December 2015.

[7] Exceptionally, the elimination of the requirement for graphic representation of a sign in an application for registration will not come into force for a further 21 months.

6.2 THE JUSTIFICATIONS FOR THE PROTECTION OF REGISTERED TRADE MARKS

6.2.1 TRADE MARKS AS A BADGE OF ORIGIN

The CJEU has recognized in a number of cases that the primary function of a registered trade mark is that of an indicator of origin and hence as a guarantee of quality for the consumer. This view of the origin function of registered trade marks, which was recently confirmed in recital 16 of the TMD 2016, had been set out by the CJEU in the early case of *Arsenal v Reed*.

Arsenal Football Club v Reed [2003] CMLR 481

47. Trade mark rights constitute an essential element in the system of undistorted competition which the Treaty is intended to establish and maintain. In such a system, undertakings must be able to attract and retain customers by the quality of their goods or services, which is made possible only by distinctive signs allowing them to be identified (see, inter alia, Case C-10/89 *HAG GF* [1990] ECR I-3711, paragraph 13, and Case C-517/99 *Merz & Krell* [2001] ECR I-6959, paragraph 21).

48. In that context, the essential function of a trade mark is to guarantee the identity of origin of the marked goods or services to the consumer or end user by enabling him, without any possibility of confusion, to distinguish the goods or services from others which have another origin. For the trade mark to be able to fulfil its essential role in the system of undistorted competition which the Treaty seeks to establish and maintain, it must offer a guarantee that all the goods or services bearing it have been manufactured or supplied under the control of a single undertaking which is responsible for their quality (see, inter alia, Case 102/77 *Hoffman[n]-La Roche* [1978] ECR 1139, paragraph 7, and *Koninklijke Philips Electronics v Remington Consumers Products Ltd* (Case C-299/99) [2003] Ch 159, para 30.

49. The Community legislature confirmed that essential function of trade marks by providing, in Article 2 of the Directive, that signs which are capable of being represented graphically may constitute a trade mark only if they are capable of distinguishing the goods or services of one undertaking from those of other undertakings (see, inter alia, *Merz & Krell*, paragraph 23).

50. For that guarantee of origin, which constitutes the essential function of a trade mark, to be ensured, the proprietor must be protected against competitors wishing to take unfair advantage of the status and reputation of the trade mark by selling products illegally bearing it (see, inter alia, *Hoffmann-La Roche*, paragraph 7, and Case C-349/95 *Loendersloot* [1997] ECR I-6227, paragraph 22).

As this extract makes clear, the CJEU sees the system of trade mark registration as designed to protect the interests of the proprietors of the marks as well as consumers. In their influential essay, written from a 'law and economics' perspective, William Landes and Richard Posner identify what they believe to be the key economic benefits offered by the legal protection of trade marks, among which the trade mark's function as an indicator of origin is, in their view, paramount.

W. Landes and R. Posner, 'Trademark law: an economic perspective' (1987)
30 Journal of Law and Economics 265 at 268–70

1. Benefits of Trademarks

Suppose you like decaffeinated coffee made by General Foods. If General Food's brand has no name, then to order it in a restaurant or grocery store you would have to ask for 'the decaffeinated coffee made by General Foods'. This takes longer to say, requires you to remember more, and requires the waiter or clerk to read and remember more than if you can just ask for 'Sanka'. The problem would be even more serious if General Foods made more than one brand of decaffeinated coffee, as in fact it does. The benefit of the brand name is analogous to that of designating individuals by last as well as first names, so that instead of having to say 'the Geoffrey who teaches constitutional law at the University of Chicago Law School—not the one who teaches corporations'. You can say 'Geoffrey Stone—not Geoffrey Miller'.

To perform its economizing function a trademark or brand name (these are rough synonyms) must not be duplicated. To allow another maker of decaffeinated coffee to sell its coffee under the name 'Sanka' would destroy the benefit of the name in identifying a brand of decaffeinated coffee made by General Foods (whether there might be offsetting benefits is considered later). It would be like allowing a second rancher to graze his cattle on a pasture the optimal use of which required that only one herd be allowed to graze. The failure to enforce trademarks would impose two distinct costs—one in the market for trademarked goods and the other in the distinct (and unconventional) market in language.

a) *The Market for Trademarked Goods*. The benefit of trademarks in reducing consumer search costs requires that the producer of a trademarked good maintain a consistent quality over time and across consumers. Hence trademark protection encourages expenditures on quality. To see this, suppose a consumer has a favorable experience with brand X and wants to buy it again. Or suppose he wants to buy brand X because it has been recommended by a reliable source or because he has a favourable experience with brand Y, another brand produced by the same producer. Rather than investigating the attributes of all goods to determine which one is brand X or is equivalent to X, the consumer may find it less costly to search by identifying the relevant trademark and purchasing the corresponding brand. For this strategy to be efficient, however, not only must it be cheaper to search for the right trademark than for the desired attributes of the good, but also past experience must be a good predictor of the likely outcome of current consumption choices—that is, the brand must exhibit consistent quality. In short, a trademark conveys information that allows the consumer to say to himself, 'I need not investigate the attributes of the brand I am about to purchase because the trade mark is a shorthand way of telling me that the attributes are the same as that of the brand I enjoyed earlier.'

Less obviously, a firm's incentive to invest resources in developing and maintaining (as through advertising) a strong mark depends on its ability to maintain consistent product quality. In other words, trademarks have a self-enforcing feature. They are valuable because they denote consistent quality, and a firm has an incentive to develop a trademark only if it is able to maintain consistent quality. To see this, consider what happens when a brand's quality is inconsistent. Because consumers will learn that the trademark does not enable them to relate their past to future consumption experiences, the branded product will be like a good without a trademark. The trademark will not lower the search costs, so consumers will be unwilling to pay more for the branded than for the unbranded good. As a result, the firm will not earn a sufficient return on its trademark promotional expenditures to justify making them. A similar argument shows that a firm with a valuable trademark would be reluctant to lower the quality of its brand because it would suffer a capital loss of its investment in the trademark.

Landes and Posner argue that the legal protection of trade marks lowers consumer search costs and also affords an incentive for proprietors both to ensure that the goods which attach to their mark are of a desirable and consistent quality and to maintain that quality over time. Furthermore, without such legal protection, others might free-ride on the original trade mark and it would lose its value as an indicator of origin and a guarantee of quality for the public. Nor do Landes and Posner believe that the legal protection of trade marks has any notable costs. They continue at 274–5:

> We may seem to be ignoring the possibility that, by fostering product differentiation, trademarks may create deadweight costs, whether of monopoly or of (excessive) competition. We have assumed that a trademark induces its owner to invest in maintaining uniform product quality, but another interpretation is that it induces the owner to spend money on creating, through advertising and promotion, a spurious image of high quality that enables monopoly rents to be obtained by deflecting consumers from lower-price substitutes of equal or even higher quality. In the case of products that are produced according to an identical formula, such as aspirin or household liquid bleach, the ability of name-brand goods (Bayer aspirin, Clorox bleach) to command higher prices than generic (nonbranded) goods has seemed to some economists and more lawyers an example of the power of brand advertising to bamboozle the public and thereby promote monopoly. And brand advertising presupposes trademarks—they are what enable a producer readily to identify his brand to the consumer. Besides the possibility of creating monopoly rents, trademarks may transform rents into costs, as one firm's expenditure on promoting its marks cancels out that of another firm. Although no monopoly profits are created, consumers may pay higher prices, and resources may be wasted in a sterile competition.
>
> The short answer to these arguments is that they have gained no foothold at all in trade mark law, as distinct from anti-trust law. The implicit economic model of trademarks that is used in that law is our model, in which trademarks lower search costs and foster quality control rather than create social waste and consumer deception. A longer answer, which we shall merely sketch, is that the hostile view of brand advertising has been largely and we think correctly rejected by economists. The fact that two goods have the same chemical formula does not make them of equal quality to even the most coolly rational consumer. That consumer will be interested not in the formula but in the manufactured product and may therefore be willing to pay a premium for greater assurance that the good will actually be manufactured to the specifications of the formula. Trademarks enable the consumer to economize on a real cost because he spends less time searching to get the quality he wants. If this analysis is correct, the rejection by trademark law of a monopoly theory of trademarks is actually a mark in favor of the economic rationality of that law.

The arguments made by Landes and Posner might be especially convincing if applied to fanciful trade names (such as 'Google' for example) because it is possible to argue that there is potentially an unlimited supply of such marks. But what of trade marks which are proper names, perhaps geographical indications, or are descriptive of the goods to which they are applied? Of course, the supply of such names is not unlimited. Other traders apart from the proprietor may wish to use them. We will see later in the chapter that whether and how much protection should be given to descriptive signs has been a matter of much debate.

6.2.2 THE TRADE MARK AS AN ADVERTISING TOOL

Landes and Posner also argue that there are benefits to be gained from protecting trade marks which have moved beyond their role as a badge of origin to embody other meanings.

For example, they identify the added value of a trade mark which through advertising attracts consumers, even if the product to which it attaches is no different from competing products. As early as 1927, Frank I. Schechter argued in his seminal essay that the advertising functions of a mark should also be protected along with its function as a badge of origin. In his essay, Schechter equates the trade mark's role as a badge of origin to the manner in which goodwill is protected by a distinctive insignia in passing off.

F. I. Schechter, 'The rational basis for trade mark protection' (1926–7)
40 Harv. L. R. 813 at 818–19

The true functions of the trademark are, then, to identify a product as satisfactory and thereby to stimulate further purchases by the consuming public. The fact that through his trademark the manufacturer or importer may 'reach over the shoulder of the retailer' and across the latter's counter straight to the consumer cannot be over-emphasized, for therein lies the key to any effective scheme of trademark protection. To describe a trademark merely as a symbol of goodwill will, without recognizing in it an agency for the actual creation and perpetuation of goodwill, ignores the most potent aspect of the nature of a trademark and that phase most in need of protection. To say that a trademark 'is merely the visible manifestation of the more important business goodwill, which is the "property" to be protected against invasion', or that 'the goodwill is the substance, the trademark merely the shadow', does not accurately state the function of a trade mark today and obscures the problem of adequate protection. The signboard of a inn in stagecoach-days, when the golden lion or the green cockatoo actually symbolized to the hungry and weary traveller a definite smiling host, a tasty meal from a particular cook, a favourite brew and a comfortable bed, was merely 'the visible manifestation' of the goodwill or probability of custom of the house; but today the trademark is not merely the symbol of goodwill but often the most effective agent for the creation of goodwill, imprinting upon the public mind an anonymous and impersonal guaranty of satisfaction, creating a desire for further satisfactions. The mark actually *sells* the goods. And, self-evidently, the more distinctive the mark, the more effective is its selling power.

Schechter then questions whether the protection afforded to trade marks, as in passing off, should apply only when the consumer may be confused as to the origin of the defendant's goods. Schechter suggests such a view is outmoded. He argues that protection should also be offered where there is likely to be no confusion as to origin, such as, for example, when a third party uses the trade mark on quite different goods from those for which it is registered. He then sets out what he views as the key principles relating to trade mark protection:

(1) that the value of the modern trademark lies in its selling power; (2) that this selling power depends for its psychological hold upon the public, not merely upon the merit of the goods upon which it is used, but equally upon its own uniqueness and singularity; (3) that such uniqueness or singularity is vitiated or impaired by its use upon either related or non-related goods; and (4) that the degree of protection depends in turn upon the extent to which, through the efforts or ingenuity of its owner, it is actually unique and different from other marks.[8]

---

[8] At 831.

Schechter concludes that the 'preservation of the uniqueness of a trademark should constitute the only rational basis for its protection'. Or, in other words, the mark's uniqueness (or distinctiveness) should be protected from 'dilution'. In his opinion, in *Arsenal v Reed*, which concerned football merchandising, Advocate General Colomer appeared to go further and suggest that, at times, it may be the trade mark itself which the consumer seeks to own, with the underlying product simply acting as a vehicle for the mark.

Arsenal Football Club plc v Reed Case C-206/01 [2002] ECR I-10273

AG Colomer:

A46. It seems to me to be simplistic reductionism to limit the function of the trade mark to an indication of trade origin … Experience teaches that, in most cases, the user is unaware of who produces the goods he consumes. The trademark acquires a life of its own, making a statement, as I have suggested, about quality, reputation and even, in certain cases, a way of seeing life.

A47. The messages it sends out are, moreover, autonomous. A distinctive sign can indicate at the same time trade origin, the reputation of its proprietor and the quality of the goods it represents, but there is nothing to prevent the consumer, unaware of who manufactures the goods or provides the services which bear the trade mark, from acquiring them because he perceives the mark as an emblem of prestige or a guarantee of quality. When I regard the current functioning of the market and the behaviour of the average consumer, I see no reason whatever not to protect those other functions of the trade mark and to safeguard only the function of indicating the trade origin of the goods and services.

Subsequent decisions by the CJEU have endorsed Advocate General Colomer's view that the value of trade marks may extend beyond their function as a badge of origin. In *L'Oréal v Bellure*,[9] for example, the Court held that a trade mark might also embody communication, advertising, and investment functions.[10] The recognition that a registered trade mark might fulfil some or all of these wider functions has important implications for how far they might be protected from third party use. It is one that has preoccupied the CJEU and is also a concern of the TMD 2016. It will be examined in the following chapter which looks at infringement. However, at this point it is worth asking whether in general there is a price to be paid for protecting these additional functions of a trade mark. You may, for example, agree that the value of some trade marks is greater than and not necessarily dependent upon the products to which they attach. Thus, in the case of football merchandise, a football fan may well purchase goods carrying his club's logo because they demonstrate his allegiance to the club, rather than because the trade mark acts as a badge of origin. Indeed, there is a strong argument made by cultural critics and others that a great deal of modern commerce, not just that involving football merchandise, depends upon the production and consumption of attractive brands rather than of the underlying product.[11] For such critics, there are costs involved in extending legal protection to cover not just a trade mark's origin function

---

[9] *L'Oréal SA and others v Bellure NV and others* Case C-487/07 [2009] ECR I-5185.

[10] See also *Interflora Inc. v Marks & Spencer plc* Case C-323/09 [2012] ETMR 1 and *L'Oréal SA v eBay International AG* Case C-324/09 [2010] ETMR 52.

[11] This was the argument made, e.g., by Naomi Klein in her best-selling book, *No Logo* (London: Flamingo, 2000).

but also the wider brand values which it might embody. These possible costs were identified by Jessica Litman. Litman raises the question of whether the 'atmospherics' (advertising functions) which are now embodied in trade symbols should be afforded legal protection, together with their origin function.

J. Litman, 'Breakfast with Batman: the public interest in the advertising age'
(1999) 108 Yale L. J. 1717 at 1728–30

To say that many consumers seem to attach real value to atmospherics, however, doesn't itself demonstrate that those atmospherics should be afforded legal protection. As Ralph Brown reminded us often, the essence of any intellectual property regime is to divide the valuable stuff subject to private appropriation from the valuable stuff that, precisely because of its importance, is reserved for public use. In the law of trade symbols, for instance, it has long been the rule that functional product features may not be protected, because they have too much value, not too little. Value, without more, does not tell us whether a particular item for which protection is sought belongs in the proprietary pile or in public use.

To agree to treat a class of stuff as intellectual property, we normally require a showing that, if protection is not extended, bad things will happen that will outweigh the resulting good things. But it would be difficult to argue that the persuasive values embodied in trade symbols are likely to suffer from underprotection. Indeed, the Mattels, Disneys, and Warner Brothers of the world seem to protect their atmospherics just fine without legal assistance. Not only can their target audiences tell the difference between, say, a Barbie doll and some other thirteen-inch fashion doll, but, regardless of features, they seem well-trained in the art of insisting on the Mattel product. Nor is the phenomenon limited to the junior set. The popularity of Ralph Lauren's Polo brand shirts or Gucci handbags is an obvious example.

To the extent that consumers want to purchase the higher-priced spread, they ought to be able to be sure that they are paying the higher price for the genuine branded article. If the concept of branding is itself legitimate, then we want to ensure consumers' protection against confusion or deception. Conventional trademark law does that. But, to stick with Lauren's Polo for a minute, what about consumers who want to pick up a polo shirt with some design on the chest at a good price? What if instead, they want to buy this month's issue of polo magazine (which follows the sport, not the fashion)? It seems obvious why Lauren might want to hinder the first and collect a licence fee from the second, so it would hardly be perplexing if his company threatened to sue. There seems, nonetheless, to be no good reason why we should help him.

If competition is still the American way of doing business, then before we give out exclusive control of some coin of competition, we need, or should need, a justification. Protecting consumers from deception is the justification most familiar to trademark law, but it does not support assigning broad rights to prevent competitive or diluting use when no confusion seems likely. Supplying incentives to invest in the item that's getting the protection is another classic justification for intellectual property, and it is equally unavailing here. An argument that we would have an undersupply of good commercials if advertisers were not given plenary control over the elements of their ads cannot be made with a straight face. Finally, there is the perennially popular justification of desert. Producers have invested in their trade symbols, the argument goes; they have earned them, so they're entitled to them.

But so have we. The argument that trade symbols acquire intrinsic value—apart from their usefulness in designating the source—derives from consumers' investing those symbols with value for which they are willing to pay real money. We may want our child to breakfast with Batman. It may well increase the total utils [sic] in our society if every time a guy drinks a Budweiser or smokes a Camel, he believes he's a stud. We may all be better off if, each time a woman colours her hair with a L'Oreal product, she murmurs to herself *and I'm worth it'*. If that's so, however, Warner Brothers, Anheuser-Busch, R.J. Reynolds, and L'Oreal can hardly take all the credit. They built up all that mystique with their customer's money and active collaboration. If the customers want to move on, to get in bed with other products that have similar atmospherics, why shouldn't they? It's not very sporting to try to lock up the atmospherics.

Litman concludes that no useful social purpose is to be gained by protecting the advertising function of brands, even though she recognizes that a trade mark which embodies attractive 'atmospherics' can be extremely valuable. Do you agree with Litman that the public have a role in creating the various meanings carried by a famous trade mark? And that, as a consequence, such meaning should be left in the public sphere? Or do you think that trade mark proprietors have a right to argue that since they put considerable investment into nurturing these further meanings, they should be able to protect that investment through trade mark registration? We shall see that the present law of trade marks does protect certain marks from the dilution of their distinctive character, even if there is no customer confusion. But we shall also see that the extent to which the law should go on to protect other advertising functions of trade marks remains a contentious issue.

FURTHER READING

R. S. Brown, Jr, 'Advertising and the public interest: the protection of trade symbols' (1948) 57 Yale L. J. 1165, 1206.

A. Griffiths, 'A law-and-economics perspective on trade marks' in L. Bently, J. Davis, and J. C. Ginsburg (eds), *Trade Marks and Brands: An Interdisciplinary Perspective* (Cambridge: Cambridge University Press, 2008), p. 241.

J. Linford, 'A linguistic justification for "generic" trademarks' (2015) 17 Yale J. Law & Tech. 110.

L. McDonagh, 'From brand performance to consumer performativity: assessing European trade mark law after the rise of anthropological marketing' (2015) 42 J. Law & Soc. 611.

6.3 THE SUBJECT MATTER OF REGISTRATION

In this part of the chapter, we will look first at the practical routes to protecting a trade mark through registration. We will then turn to the substantive law of trade marks and, in particular, how the subject matter of a registered trade mark is defined in Articles 2 and 3 of the TMD.[12]

---

[12] TMA, s. 1(1); TMD 2016, Arts 3 and 4.

6.3.1 REGISTERING A TRADE MARK

6.3.1.1 Domestic registrations

In the UK, applications to register a trade mark are made to the Trade Mark Registry at the UK Intellectual Property Office (UK IPO). Applications are made to register the mark in respect of specific goods or services. There is an International Classification of Goods and Services which was drawn up under the Nice Agreement and is administered by the World Intellectual Property Organization (WIPO). Applications may be made for the mark to be registered in respect of goods or services which will fall into one or a number of classes. For example, when the Jif lemon shape was registered as a trade mark following the passage of the TMA, it was registered in respect of 'Class 29: Lemon Juice' and 'Class 32: Fruit juices and non-alcoholic fruit extracts: all being lemon flavoured'. In the CJEU decision, *Chartered Institute of Patent Agents v Registrar of Trade Marks*,[13] the UK Chartered Institute of Patent Agents sought to register the mark 'IP TRANSLATOR' for Class 41: education and training. The institute made the application solely in order to obtain a ruling on the breadth of the protection which will be given when an applicant seeks to register a mark for an entire class of goods (or services), as was the case here. In its judgment, the CJEU stated that the purpose of the classification system is that a single form of wording should mean the same to everyone who reads it. It followed that it may be possible to use the class heading where all the goods within that class fall within the natural meaning of the words in the heading. But for other classes this may not be the case. An example of the latter might be using the heading, Class 34: tobacco; smokers' articles; matches, when the applicant intends to use his mark only on snuff boxes. It is submitted that in this example the use of the heading, alone, would not be appropriate. The TMD 2016 reflects the decision in the *Chartered Institute* case. Article 39(2) of the new directive states that the designation of goods and services should be identified with clarity and precision and, at Article 39(5), that class headings of the Nice classification should be interpreted to include only goods and services clearly covered by the literal meaning of the term.[14]

An application is examined by the Registry to see if there are any grounds for refusing registration. Until 2008, these grounds included whether the sign to be registered conflicted with any earlier registered mark.[15] Now, the Registry will only concern itself with the question of whether the sign avoids any of the absolute grounds for refusal of registration.[16] If the Registry finds the mark acceptable, it will be published in the Trade Marks Journal. This allows third parties to view the application and gives them a period of three months to oppose the registration if they believe there are grounds for doing so. For example, a third party may have an earlier identical, but unregistered, mark which is protected by the law of passing off.[17] Oppositions are dealt with first by the Registrar and, if there is an appeal, by the Appointed Person. If the dispute is not settled at the Registry level, it may proceed through the courts. Trade marks are registered for ten years, but the registration may be renewed an indefinite number of times so long as the mark remains distinctive.

---

[13] Case C-307 [2012] ETMR 42.   [14] See TM Reg 2016, Art. 28.
[15] Trade Marks (Relative Grounds) Order 2007 (SI 2007/1976) and the Trade Marks (Amendment) Rules 2007 (SI 2007/2076).
[16] See 6.3.3.   [17] See Chapter 5.

6.3.1.2 European and international applications

It is also possible to obtain a EUTM (previously a Community Trade Mark (CTM)). This is a single mark which is valid for the entire European Union. Applications may be made through the UK IPO or directly to the European Union Intellectual Property Office (EU IPO) (previously the OHIM) in Alicante. The EU IPO looks to see whether the mark fulfils the formal requirements for registration. It also searches to ensure that the mark applied for does not conflict with an earlier registered mark or EUTM registration. The EU IPO then publishes the mark. The results of the search are purely advisory, and it is left to the owner of the earlier mark or right to oppose the application. Oppositions are dealt with first by the EU IPO, then by the Board of Appeal. An appeal may then go to the General Court all the way to the CJEU. Infringement actions are, however, heard in the national courts of Member States. The EUTM is valid across the EU. Therefore, if it is unregistrable because of, for example, a conflict in one Member State, then the application will fail entirely. Finally, it is possible to register an already-registered trade mark in any of the other 97 countries which are members of the Madrid Protocol, through a single application. Applications to register a UK registered trade mark in other countries which are members of the Madrid Protocol (an International Registration) are made to the UK IPO, which will forward the application to WIPO. The application will then be examined in each of the countries for which the application is made. Unlike the EUTM, if the application fails in one country, it may nonetheless go on to be successfully registered in others.

6.3.1.3 Trade marks as property

Once it is registered, a trade mark is a form of personal property (section 22 of the TMA). Like other sorts of personal or moveable property, a registered trade mark can be assigned (section 24 of the TMA).[18] It may also be licensed[19] (Article 8 of the TMD; sections 28–31 of the TMA).

FURTHER READING

A. Kur, 'Fundamental concerns in the harmonisation of (European) trademark law' in G. B. Dinwoodie and M. D. Janis (eds), *Trade Mark Law and Theory* (Cheltenham: Edward Elgar, 2008), p. 177.

A. A. Machnicka, 'Territorial aspects of Community trade marks: the Single Market's splendid sovereignty' [2014] IIC 915.

6.3.2 THE SUBJECT MATTER OF TRADE MARK REGISTRATION

This section of the chapter will look to see how the directive (and the regulation) have been interpreted by both European and domestic courts in order to delineate the universe of signs which may be the subject matter of a trade mark registration. As we shall see, a key issue for the courts has been how wide that universe of protected signs should be. On the one hand, there is a widely shared concern that allowing a broad range of signs to be registered will

---

[18] TMD 2016, Art. 22.   [19] TMD 2016, Art. 25.

hamper competition by allowing a single proprietor to monopolize a sign which other traders, as well as the proprietor, may legitimately wish to use. These may include, for example, descriptive marks and colours. On the other hand, there are those who argue that offering to protect a broad category of signs will encourage traders to invest in their trade marks and maintain the quality of the products or services to which they attach. It will also ensure that the public can rely on trade marks to guarantee the source and quality of their purchases. As we shall see, the CJEU has been engaged, since the implementation of the 1998 directive, in seeking to balance these two imperatives.

6.3.2.1 Registrable signs: an introduction

Article 2 of the TMD identifies the subject matter of a trade mark registration:[20]

> A trade mark may consist of any sign capable of being represented graphically, particularly words, including personal names, designs, letters, numerals, the shape of goods or of their packaging, provided that such signs are capable of distinguishing the goods or services of one undertaking from those of other undertakings.

Article 3 of the TMD 2016 makes some significant amendments to this definition. It reads:

> A trade mark may consist of any signs, in particular words, including personal names, or designs, letters, numerals, colours, shapes of goods or the packaging of goods, or sounds, provided that such signs are capable of:
>
> (a) distinguishing the goods or services of one undertaking from those of other undertakings; and
>
> (b) being represented on the register in a manner which enables the competent authorities and the public to determine the clear and precise subject matter of the protection afforded to its proprietor.

Even if a trade mark meets the criteria set out in Article 2,[21] there may still be bars to its registration. Article 3 of the directive[22] sets out the absolute grounds for the refusal of registration of a trade mark.[23] It states, inter alia, that the following signs shall not be registered or, if registered, shall be declared invalid:

> a. signs which cannot constitute a trade mark;[24]
>
> b. trade marks which are devoid of distinctive character;[25]
>
> c. trade marks which consist exclusively of signs or indications which may serve to designate the kind, quality, quantity, intended purpose, value, geographical origin, or the time of production of the goods or rendering of the service, or other characteristics of the goods or service;[26]

---

[20] TMA, s. 1; TMD 2016, Art. 3.   [21] TMD 2016, Art. 3.   [22] TMD 2016, Art. 4.
[23] TMA, s. 3.
[24] This means signs which do not fall within the Art. 2 definition of a trade mark. The comparable section of the TMA is s. 3(1)(a); TMD 2016, Art. 4(1)(a).
[25] TMA, s. 3(1)(b); TMD 2016, Art. 4(1)(b).   [26] TMA, s. 3(1)(c); TMD 2016, Art. 4(1)(c).

> d. trade marks which consist exclusively of signs or indications which have become customary in the current language or in the bona fide and established practices of the trade.[27]

There is, however, a proviso. According to Article 3(3) of the directive, signs which fall under the categories in Article 3(1)(b)–(d):

> shall not be refused registration or be declared invalid…if, before the date of application for registration and following the use which has been made of it, it has acquired a distinctive character.[28]

There is also a further category of signs identified in Article 3 which will not be registered under any circumstances. The most important are the following:

(e) signs which consist exclusively of:
- the shape which results from the nature of the goods themselves, or
- the shape of goods which is necessary to obtain a technical result, or
- the shape which gives substantial value to the goods;

(f) trade marks which are contrary to public policy or to accepted principles of morality;

(g) trade marks which are of such a nature as to deceive the public, for instance as to the nature, quality or geographical origin of the goods or service;

In addition, under Article 3(2)(d), a trade mark application will be rejected if it was made in bad faith.[29] The TMD 2016 adds a further important ground for refusal of registration and that is if the application is for a trade mark which clashes with a sign protected as a designation of origin or geographical indication.[30]

6.3.2.2 Signs which may be registered (Article 2)

Article 2 tells us what signs may be registered. They must be capable of graphic representation, they must be distinctive, and they must be capable of acting as a badge of origin. Under the TMD 2016 signs will no longer need to be represented graphically. Instead they must be capable of being represented in a way which allows the authorities and the public to determine the clear and precise subject matter of the registration. Both directives appear to leave open the possibility that any sign might be registered so long as it is distinctive and can be adequately represented. Indeed, in listing possible signs, the TMD 2016 adds to the list colours and sounds. However, the decision by the CJEU in *Dyson Ltd v Registrar of Trade Marks* shows that not all signs may constitute a trade mark.

---

[27] TMA, s. 3(1)(d); TMD 2016, Art. 4(1)(d).   [28] TMA, s. 3(1); TMD 2016, Art. 4(4)(b)–(d).
[29] TMA, s. 3(6); TMD 2016, Art. 4(2). Trade marks will also not be registered if they fail the relative grounds for refusal of registration; that is, they conflict with an earlier registered mark or an earlier right. These grounds are set out in Art. 4 of the TMD and are discussed in the following chapter.
[30] TMD 2016, Art. 4(1)(i).

Dyson Ltd v Registrar of Trade Marks Case C-321/03 [2007] ECR I-687

Since 1993, Dyson has made and sold 'bagless' vacuum cleaners. It sought to register the following trade marks: 'a transparent bin or collection chamber forming part of the external surface of a vacuum cleaner as shown in the representation'. Illustrations of two bagless vacuum cleaners were attached to the applications. Both the Registrar and the High Court took the view that, on the face of it, the bagless illustrations were entirely descriptive of the product. The High Court went on to ask the CJEU how distinctiveness should be assessed in light of Article 3 of the TMD. But the CJEU chose to answer a different question: did the subject matter of Dyson's application meet the requirements of Article 2—i.e. was it a sign which could in principle be registered? The CJEU held that it was not.

35. In this present case it is common ground that the subject matter in the main proceedings is not a particular type of transparent collecting bin forming part of the external surface of the vacuum cleaner, but rather, in a general and abstract manner, all the conceivable shapes of such a collecting bin. ...

38. Given the exclusivity inherent in a trade mark right the holder of a trade mark relating to such a non-specific subject matter would obtain an unfair competitive advantage, contrary to the purpose pursued by Art. 2 of the Directive, since it would be entitled to prevent its competitors from marketing vacuum cleaners having any kind of transparent collecting bin on their external surface regardless of its shape.

39. It follows that the subject matter of the application at issue in the main proceedings is, in fact, a mere property of the product concerned and does not therefore constitute a 'sign' within the meaning of Art. 2 of the Directive.

In *Dyson*, the CJEU held that the transparent collecting bin was not a sign at all but rather a concept which other traders might wish to use. We may question whether, in this case, the CJEU's primary concern was actually with protecting competition between traders rather than limiting the universe of what constituted a sign, since the application itself did have an illustration of what was intended to be registered. Another related question that this open-ended definition of registrable signs raises is whether marks which cannot be perceived visually might be registered. Under the original directive, no sign could be registered, no matter how distinctive, unless it was capable of graphic representation. However, this requirement begged the question of how intangible signs, such as sounds and smells, might be properly represented graphically. This question was addressed by the CJEU in *Sieckmann v Deutsches Patent- und Markenamt*, which concerned an application to register an odour.

Sieckmann v Deutsches Patent- und Markenamt Case C-273/00 [2002] ECR I-11737

The applicant sought to register a mark which it described on its application as a 'balsamically fruity odour with a slight hint of cinnamon' for goods within Classes 35, 41, and 42, including advertising and business management. When making its application, apart from offering the verbal description of the smell, the applicant had also deposited with the German Patent and Trade Mark Office its chemical breakdown and the location of local laboratories where a sample of the smell could be obtained. It also submitted an odour sample in a container. The CJEU addressed itself to the question of whether an intangible sign might be registered. In making its judgment, the CJEU clearly set out why the necessity for graphic representation is so important to a system of trade mark registration, the aim of which is to enhance competition between traders.

Findings of the Court

...

43. The purpose of Art. 2 of the Directive is to define the types of signs of which a trade mark may consist. That provision states that a trademark may consist of 'particularly words, including personal names, designs, letters, numerals, the shape of goods or of their packaging ...' Admittedly, it mentions only signs which are capable of being perceived visually, are two-dimensional or three-dimensional and can thus be represented by means of letters or written characters or by a picture.

44. However, as is clear from the language of both Art. 2 of the Directive and the seventh recital in the preamble thereto, which refers to a 'list [of] examples' of signs which may constitute a trade mark, that list is not exhaustive. Consequently, that provision, although it does not mention signs which are not in themselves capable of being perceived visually, such as odours, does not, however, expressly exclude them.

45. In those circumstances, Art. 2 of the Directive must be interpreted as meaning that a trade mark may consist of a sign which is not in itself capable of being perceived visually, provided that it can be represented graphically.

46. That graphic representation must enable the sign to be represented visually, particularly by means of images, lines or characters, so that it can be precisely identified.

47. Such an interpretation is required to allow for the sound operation of the trade mark registration system.

48. First, the function of the graphic representability requirement is, in particular, to define the mark itself in order to determine the precise subject of the protection afforded by the registered mark to its proprietor.

49. Next, the entry of the mark in a public register has the aim of making it accessible to the competent authorities and the public, particularly to economic operators.

50. On the one hand, the competent authorities must know with clarity and precision the nature of the signs of which a mark consists in order to be able to fulfil their obligations in relation to the prior examination of registration applications and to the publication and maintenance of an appropriate and precise register of trade marks.

51. On the other hand, economic operators must, with clarity and precision, be able to find out about registrations or applications for registration made by their current or potential competitors and thus to receive relevant information about the rights of third parties.

52. If the users of that register are to be able to determine the precise nature of a mark on the basis of its registration, its graphic representation in the register must be self-contained, easily accessible and intelligible.

53. Furthermore, in order to fulfil its role as a registered trade mark a sign must always be perceived unambiguously and in the same way so that the mark is guaranteed as an indication of origin. In the light of the duration of a mark's registration and the fact that, as the Directive provides, it can be renewed for varying periods, the representation must be durable.

54. Finally, the object of the representation is specifically to avoid any element of subjectivity in the process of identifying and perceiving the sign. Consequently, the means of graphic representation must be unequivocal and objective.

55. In the light of the foregoing observations, the answer to the first question must be that Art. 2 of the Directive must be interpreted as meaning that a trade mark may consist of a sign which is not in itself capable of being perceived visually, provided that it can be represented graphically, particularly by means of images, lines or characters, and that the representation is clear, precise, self-contained, easily accessible, intelligible, durable and objective.

The CJEU then turned to the question of whether the applicant had adequately represented the odour which it wished to register. It held that neither a chemical formula nor a description of an odour is sufficiently clear and precise. In addition, neither these nor an odour sample, nor a combination of all three, is sufficiently clear and precise to constitute an adequate graphic representation. The formula devised by the CJEU in *Sieckmann* that adequate graphic representation must be 'self-contained, easily accessible, intelligible, durable and objective' was subsequently applied to other intangible signs and also to colours. The questions as to whether a single colour might constitute a sign and how it might be represented in order to meet the Sieckmann criteria was considered by the CJEU in *Libertel Groep BV v Benelux-Merkenbureau*.

Libertel Groep BV v Benelux-Merkenbureau Case C-104/01 [2003] ECR I-3793

Libertel was a Dutch mobile phone company. It sought to register a trade mark for the colour orange for certain telecommunications goods and services. In the space for reproducing the trade mark, the application form contained an orange rectangle and, in the space for describing the trade mark, the word 'orange' without reference to any colour code. The application was initially refused on the grounds that the proposed mark was devoid of distinctive character and would not be registered without proof that it had acquired distinctiveness through use. Libertel appealed, and the Dutch court subsequently addressed a number of questions to the CJEU concerning distinctiveness. The CJEU began by answering the question of whether a single colour could fulfil the requirements of Article 2.

27. In that regard it must be pointed out that a colour per se cannot be presumed to constitute a sign. Normally a colour is a simple property of things. Yet it may constitute a sign. That depends on the context in which the colour is used. None the less, a colour per se is capable, in relation to a product or service, of constituting a sign.

[The CJEU then went on to consider whether a single colour was capable of graphic representation, in that it fulfilled the requirements set out in *Sieckmann*. It noted as follows:]

32. ...[A] sample of a colour may deteriorate with time. There may be certain media on which it is possible to reproduce a colour in permanent form. However with other media, including paper, the exact shade of the colour cannot be protected from the effects of the passage of time. In these cases, the filing of a sample of a colour does not possess the durability required by Art. 2 of the Directive (see Sieckmann, para. 53).

33. It follows that filing a sample of a colour does not per se constitute a graphic representation within the meaning of Art. 2 of the Directive.

34. On the other hand, a verbal description of a colour, in so far as it is composed of words which themselves are made up of letters, does constitute a graphic representation of the colour (see Sieckmann, para. 70).

35. A description in words of the colour will not necessarily satisfy the conditions set out in paras. 28 and 29 of this judgment in every instance. That is a question which must be evaluated in the light of the circumstances of each individual case.

36. A sample of a colour, combined with a description in words of that colour, may therefore constitute a graphic representation within the meaning of Art. 2 of the Directive, provided that the description is clear, precise, self-contained, easily accessible, intelligible, durable and objective.

37. For the same reasons as those set out at para. 34 of this judgment, the designation of a colour using an internationally recognised identification code may be considered to constitute a graphic representation. Such codes are deemed to be precise and stable.

38. Where a sample of a colour, together with a description in words, does not satisfy the conditions laid down in Art. 2 of the Directive in order for it to constitute a graphic representation because, *inter alia*, it lacks precision or durability, that deficiency may, depending on the facts, be remedied by adding a colour designation from an internationally recognised identification code.

[Finally, the CJEU looked at the third element for defining a trade mark as identified in Article 2 of the TMD, and considered whether a single colour was capable of acting as a badge of origin:]

39. As to the question whether a colour per se is capable of distinguishing the goods or services of one undertaking from those of other undertakings, within the meaning of Art. 2 of the Directive, it is necessary to determine whether or not colours per se are capable of conveying specific information, in particular as to the origin of a product or service.

40. In that connection, it must be borne in mind that, whilst colours are capable of conveying certain associations of ideas, and of arousing feelings, they possess little inherent capacity for communicating specific information, especially since they are commonly and widely used, because of their appeal, in order to advertise and market goods or services, without any specific message.

41. However, that factual finding would not justify the conclusion that colours per se cannot, as a matter of principle, be considered to be capable of distinguishing the goods or services of one undertaking from those of other undertakings. The possibility that a colour per se may in some circumstances serve as a badge of origin of the goods or services of an undertaking cannot be ruled out. It must therefore be accepted that colours per se may be capable of distinguishing the goods or services of one undertaking from those of other undertakings, within the meaning of Art. 2 of the Directive.

42. It follows from the foregoing that, where the conditions described above apply, a colour per se is capable of constituting a trade mark within the meaning of Art. 2 of the Directive.

The decisions in *Sieckmann* and subsequent cases suggest that while intangible signs may in principle be registered, there are hurdles to be crossed in order to ensure that they are properly represented graphically. In the case of odours, tastes, and onomatopoeic sounds,[31]

[31] See *Shield Mark BV v Joost Kist* Case C-283/01 [2004] ECR I-14313 for onomatopoeic sounds; see *Eli Lilly's & Co.'s CTM Application* [2004] ETMR 4 for tastes.

it appears that these hurdles are practically insurmountable, whereas in the case of colours the issue might be resolved by using a recognized colour code. The TMD 2016 recognizes that for certain categories of signs graphic representation may not in fact be possible. Instead it states that to be registered a sign must be capable of representation in a manner which is 'clear, precise, self contained, easily accessible, intelligible, durable and objective'.[32] In other words, its representation must meet the *Sieckmann* criteria. And, it also states that this might be achieved by using any 'generally available technology'. It is notable that those categories of signs which are produced by nature and consequently are in limited supply have been seen to meet the criterion of graphic representation only with difficulty, if at all, perhaps reflecting a reluctance on the part of the CJEU to see such signs monopolized by a single trader. And we might ask once the necessity for graphic representation has been dropped whether this will continue to be the case. The judgment of the Court of Appeal in *Nestlé v Cadbury* recognized the public interest in protecting public access to certain signs, in this case the colour purple. Interestingly, it also demonstrated that whether something constitutes a sign for the purposes of registration and whether it can be adequately represented might be interdependent.

Société des Produits Nestlé SA v Cadbury UK Ltd [2013] EWCA Civ 1174

Cadbury applied to register in the UK a sign consisting of a purple rectangular block. In the application the mark was described as:

> The colour purple (Pantone 2685C) as shown on the form of application, applied to the whole visible surface, or being the predominant colour applied to the whole visible surface, of the packaging of the goods.

The application was for, inter alia, 'Milk chocolate in bar and tablet form; milk chocolate for eating; drinking chocolate; preparations for making drinking chocolate.'

Cadbury filed evidence of distinctiveness acquired through use of the mark. The application was accepted by the UK IPO despite an opposition from Nestlé and Nestlé appealed. Nestlé lost in the High Court but succeeded in the Court of Appeal. The basis of Nestlé's appeal was that the application did not meet the requirement of a sign nor did its graphic representation satisfy the *Sieckmann* criteria. Nestlé argued that the application was not simply for a colour mark but for a colour plus a verbal description of how the colour would be used on the packaging, with the result that the mark might be used in a number of different visual forms and, if so, then it was not a sign per se as it would not meet the requirement of specificity. Furthermore, the use of the word 'predominant' introduced a 'vagueness and subjectivity' which meant that the description did not meet the *Sieckmann* criteria. Cadbury replied that this was an application for a single colour and there was no authority that it was necessary to show the different ways a registered colour might be used. Cadbury added that the word 'predominant' had been used in other successful colour applications and, in any event, it had been agreed that purple was distinctive of Cadbury and so capable of distinguishing. Nor would registration give Cadbury a competitive advantage as purple was not a characteristic of chocolate and competitors did not need to use the same colour on their goods. In the

---

[32] Recital 13.

Court of Appeal, Sir John Mummery began by referring to the judgment of Birss J in the High Court.

Sir John Mummery:

13. The judge recognised that unconventional or 'exotic' marks, such as colours, sounds and smells, give rise to conceptual problems, which are not encountered with more conventional trade names and logos. As the registration of a trade mark creates a form of intellectual property conferring a potentially perpetual monopoly in the mark and excluding everybody else from use in various ways, the point of principle has some public importance.

Mummery LJ then examined the key decisions of the CJEU which had dealt with the registrability of 'exotic' trade marks. He identified these as *Libertel, Sieckmann, Dyson*, and also *Heidelberger Bauchemie GmbH v Bundespatentgericht*.[33] The latter case concerned an application to register a combination of the colours blue and yellow 'in every conceivable form' as a trade mark. The CJEU had held that such a sign could be registered so long as the application included a systematic arrangement showing how the colours would be used in a predetermined and uniform way. Mummery LJ then looked at Article 2 of the TMD. He began with the conditions it imposed and then turned to their purpose.

15.... (2) The purpose of the requirements is to prevent abuse of trade mark law in order to obtain an unfair competitive advantage.

Identification

(3) Identification requirements for entry of a trade mark on the public register of trade marks include clarity, intelligibility, specificity, precision, accessibility, uniformity, self-containment and objectivity.

Multitude of forms

(4) The identification requirements are not satisfied, if the mark could take on a multitude of different appearances, which would create problems for registration of the mark and give an unfair competitive advantage over competitors.

Colour without a message

(5) Colours are normally a simple property of things, or a means of decorating things. They are not normally capable of being a sign. A sign conveys a message. The sign is capable of being registered as a trade mark, if the message is about the source of goods or services.

Colour as a sign conveying a message

(6) Depending on the facts and circumstances of the case, colours, or combinations of colours, designated in the abstract and without contours and used in relation to a product or service are capable of being 'a sign.'

---

[33] Case C-49/02 [2004] ECR I-6129.

Graphic representation of colour

(7) As for the second condition of graphical representation, in a mark consisting of two or more colours designated in the abstract and without contours, qualities of precision and uniformity are required. The colours must be arranged by associating them in a predetermined and uniform way.

Colour without form/in a multitude of forms

(8) Those requirements are not met by the mere juxtaposition of colours without shape or contours, or by reference to colours in every conceivable form, so that the consumer would not be able to recall or repeat with certainty the experience of a purchase. The scope of protection afforded by such a mark would be unknown both to the competent authorities responsible for maintaining the register and to economic competitors. Registration would confer unfair competitive advantages on the proprietor of the mark.

[Mummery LJ then discussed the arguments of both parties, and continued:]

50. The crucial point stems from the misinterpretation of the verbal description of the graphic representation of the mark for which application is made. The description refers not only to the colour purple as applied to the whole visible surface of the packaging of the goods, but also to an alternative i.e. 'or being the predominant colour applied to the whole visible surface…' The use of the word 'predominant' opens the door to a multitude of different visual forms as a result of its implied reference to other colours and other visual material not displayed or described in the application and over which the colour purple may predominate. It is an application for the registration of a shade of colour 'plus' other material, not of just of an unchanging application of a single colour, as in *Libertel*.

51. In my judgment, that description, properly interpreted, does not constitute 'a sign' that is 'graphically represented' within art 2. If the colour purple is less than total, as would be the case if the colour is only 'predominant', the application would cover other matter in combination with the colour, but not graphically represented or verbally described in the specific, certain, self-contained and precise manner required. The result would not be an application to register 'a sign', in the accepted sense of a single sign conveying a message, but to register multiple signs with different permutations, presentations and appearances, which are neither graphically represented nor described with any certainty or precision, or at all.

52. The appearance and number of such other signs would be unknown both to the Registrar, who is responsible for the proper functioning of the registration system and is faced with the decision whether or not to register it on a public register, and to competitors, who would not be able to tell from inspecting the register the full scope and extent of the registration. To allow a registration so lacking in specificity, clarity and precision of visual appearance would offend against the principle of certainty. It would also offend against the principle of fairness by giving a competitive advantage to Cadbury and by putting Nestlé and its other competitors at a disadvantage.

Mummery LJ concluded that Nestlé's appeal should be allowed.[34]

---

[34] Following this decision, Cadbury sought unsuccessfully to withdraw what they argued was an already registered mark using the word 'predominant' in its description: *Cadbury UK Ltd v The Comptroller General of Patents, Designs and Trade Marks* [2016] EWHC 79 (Ch).

In *Nestlé v Cadbury*, the Court of Appeal took a cautious approach to expanding the universe of registrable signs. In the recent case of *Apple v Deutsches Patent- und Markenamt*,[35] the CJEU adopted a more generous approach. The Court allowed Apple to register a three-dimensional trade mark of the distinctive design and layout of a retail store, for services 'aimed at inducing the consumer to purchase its products'. The Court held that the design of the store did constitute a sign and it was adequately represented even though the application lacked a description of the layout or any indication of the specific measurements as to the size and proportions of the store. Some might argue that registering a store design, especially without any designated measurements, presents similar problems to registering a vacuum cleaner bin. In the case of *Apple*, is it possible to suggest that the Court was influenced by the distinctiveness of the Apple mark which would be attached to these stores? Turning to Article 3 and the absolute grounds for refusal of registration, we will again see that the key question for the CJEU and domestic courts has been how wide to draw the boundaries of registrable signs.

FURTHER READING

P. Bricknell, '*Société des Produits Nestlé SA v Cadbury UK Ltd*: single colour marks predominantly applied to the whole visible surface of the goods' [2014] EIPR 200.

R. Burrell and M. Handler, 'Making sense of trade mark law' [2003] IPQ 388.

J. C. Ginsburg, '"See me, feel me, touch me, hea[r] me (and maybe smell and taste me too)— I am a trademark": a US perspective' in L. Bently, J. Davis, and J. C. Ginsburg (eds), *Trade Marks and Brands: An Interdisciplinary Critique* (Cambridge: Cambridge University Press, 2008), pp. 92–105.

E. Smith, '*Dyson* and the public interest: an analysis of the Dyson trade mark case' [2007] EIPR 469.

J. Tizon Mirza, 'CJEU expands trade mark law to include the design of a store layout: *Apple Inc v Deutsches Patent- und Markenamt* (German Patent and Trade Mark Office)' [2014] EIPR 813.

6.3.3 THE ABSOLUTE GROUNDS FOR REFUSAL OF REGISTRATION (ARTICLE 3)

Article 3(1)(a)–(d) of the TMD[36] covers signs which do not fulfil the requirements of Article 2(1) and so cannot be registered and signs which may be registered only with evidence of distinctiveness acquired through use.

6.3.3.1 Article 3(1)(a)

Article 3 begins by providing that a sign may not be registered if it cannot constitute a trade mark. This provision seems to raise the question of whether there is a category of signs which are inherently incapable of acting as a badge of origin. It was a question put to the CJEU by the Court of Appeal in the *Philips* case.

---

[35] Case C-421/13 [2015] RPC 14.   [36] TMA, s. 3(1)(a)–(d); TMD 2016, Art. 4(1)(a)–(d).

Koninklijke Philips Electronics NV v Remington Consumer Products Ltd
Case C-299/99 [2002] ECR I-5475

In 1966, Philips developed a new type of three-headed rotary electric shaver. In 1985, Philips filed an application to register a trade mark consisting of a graphic representation of the shape and configuration of the head of such a shaver, comprising three circular heads with rotating blades in the shape of an equilateral triangle. In 1995, Remington, a competing company, began to manufacture and sell in the UK the DT 55, which was a shaver with three rotating heads forming an equilateral triangle, shaped similarly to that used by Philips. Philips sued Remington for infringement of its trade mark. Remington counterclaimed for revocation of the trade mark registered by Philips on the grounds, inter alia, that it lacked distinctiveness. In the High Court, Jacob J held that the mark was incapable of distinguishing under Article 2, in that it could only ever convey the message, 'Here is a three-headed shaver.' The Court of Appeal also took the view that the sign was incapable of distinguishing because it had no features which were of trade mark significance. Rather, the Court of Appeal held that a trade mark such as the Philips mark which consisted of the shape of the goods could only be registered if it had some addition to its shape, some capricious element, which made it capable of distinguishing. But it also decided to ask the CJEU, inter alia, whether there existed a category of marks which were excluded from registration under Article 3(1)(a) of the directive whether or not they had acquired distinctiveness through use and also whether there was a category of descriptive signs (in this case a shape of goods sign) which would be registered only if they incorporated a 'capricious' element. The CJEU gave the following answer:

38. ...Article 3(1)(a) of the Directive, like the rule laid down by Article 3(1)(b), (c) and (d), precludes the registration of signs or indications which do not meet one of the two conditions imposed by Article 2 of the Directive, that is to say, the condition requiring such signs to be capable of distinguishing the goods or services of one undertaking from those of other undertakings.

39. It follows that there is no class of marks having a distinctive character by their nature or by the use made of them which is not capable of distinguishing goods or services within the meaning of Article 2 of the Directive.

40. In the light of those considerations, the answer to the first question must be that there is no category of marks which is not excluded from registration by Article 3(1)(b), (c) and (d) and Article 3(3) of the Directive which is none the less excluded from registration by Article 3(1)(a) thereof on the ground that such marks are incapable of distinguishing the goods of the proprietor of the mark from those of other undertakings.

[In relation to the second question concerning the 'capricious addition', the CJEU held:]

48. ...Article 2 of the Directive makes no distinction between different categories of trade marks. The criteria for assessing the distinctive character of three-dimensional trade marks, such as that at issue in the main proceedings, are thus no different from those to be applied to other categories of trade mark.

49. In particular, the Directive in no way requires that the shape of the article in respect of which the sign is registered must include some capricious addition. Under Article 2 of

the Directive, the shape in question must simply be capable of distinguishing the product of the proprietor of the trade mark from those of other undertakings and thus fulfil its essential purpose of guaranteeing the origin of the product.

50. In the light of those considerations, the answer to the second question must be that, in order to be capable of distinguishing an article for the purposes of Article 2 of the Directive, the shape of the article in respect of which the sign is registered does not require any capricious addition, such as an embellishment which has no functional purpose.

The implication of the CJEU's judgment in *Philips* is that the directive dictates that any sign may in principle either be initially distinctive (a good example here would be an invented sign such as 'Esso', or a sign which bears no relation to the goods and services to which it is applied, such as 'Apple' for computers) or else may acquire distinctiveness through use (the categories of signs set out in Article 3(1)(b)–(d)). This conclusion is confirmed by later CJEU decisions. In *OHIM v BORCO*, the applicant sought to register a single Greek letter for alcoholic beverages as a EUTM. The OHIM (now the EU IPO) refused the application on the grounds that a single letter cannot in principle be distinctive. On appeal, the CJEU held that, in determining whether a sign is distinctive, it is always necessary to look at the particular facts of each application. These may include the specific goods and services on which the mark will be used, the view of the average consumer, and any other evidence produced by the applicant.[37]

In other words, following *Philips*, there would appear to be no category of signs which by their *nature* are incapable of acting as a trade mark. It follows that when the relevant authority is judging whether a sign might be registered, it should turn first to look at whether it fails to fulfil the requirements of Article 3(1)(b)–(d) in that it has failed to acquire distinctiveness through use. If that is the case, then there is no need to measure the sign against the Article 3(1)(a) requirements. Indeed, we may ask whether the decision in *Philips* has effectively made these requirements irrelevant. Do you think that the result is an unacceptable widening of the signs which may be registered?

6.3.3.2 Signs which have acquired distinctiveness through use: an introduction

We shall now look at the second category of signs: those which may be registered only with evidence of acquired distinctiveness. As we have seen, this provision covers signs which are devoid of distinctive character, descriptive signs, and signs which are customary in the trade (including generic marks). There has been considerable case law concerned with identifying signs which fall into each of these categories (or into more than one—for example, the Philips three-headed razor mark which was held to be both descriptive and devoid of distinctive character). In the leading CJEU case of *Linde*,[38] the Court noted that each of these grounds for refusal listed in Article 3(1) 'is independent of the others and calls for separate

---

[37] *OHIM v Borco* Case C-265/09 P [2011] ETMR; see also *Agencja Wydawnicza Technopol sp. z o.o. v OHIM* Case C-51/10 P [2011] ETMR 34, where the CJEU made a similar point about signs consisting of numerals, which are presented neither in a stylized nor an artistic way.

[38] *Linde AG, Winward Industries Inc., Rado Uhren AG v Deutsches Patent- und Markenamt* Joined Cases C-53–55/01 [2003] ECR I-3161.

examination'.[39] In addition, the Court also noted that, 'the various grounds for refusing registration set out in Article 3 of the directive must be interpreted in the light of the public interest underlying each of them'.[40] Article 3 raises two important questions. First, what is the scope of each of the absolute grounds for refusal of registration? Second, in the case of those signs which are initially refused registration, how should acquired distinctiveness be judged? The first major case concerning both these questions is generally agreed to be *Windsurfing*, which was concerned with a descriptive sign, in this case a geographical indication. It therefore makes sense first of all to consider how the CJEU has interpreted the scope of Article 3(1) in relation to descriptive signs.

6.3.3.3 Descriptive signs

Windsurfing Chiemsee Produktions- und Vertriebs GmbH v Boots- und Segelzubehör Walter Huber Joined Cases C-108 and 109/97 [1999] ECR I-2779

Windsurfing concerned a geographical sign, the word 'Chiemsee' which is a large Bavarian lake and tourist attraction. Windsurfing Chiemsee, based near the shores of the Chiemsee, sold sporting goods which were manufactured elsewhere. The goods bore the designation 'Chiemsee'. Windsurfing Chiemsee had registered the word 'Chiemsee' in Germany as a picture trade mark in the form of various graphic designs, but there was no German trade mark for the word 'Chiemsee' as such because the German registration authorities had hitherto regarded the word 'Chiemsee' as an indication which might serve to designate geographical origin and which was consequently incapable of registration as a trade mark. The defendants had been selling sports clothing since 1995 in a town also near the shores of the Chiemsee. Their clothing also bore the designation 'Chiemsee', but depicted in a different graphic form from that of the trade marks which identified Windsurfing Chiemsee's products. In the main proceedings, Windsurfing Chiemsee challenged the use by the defendants of the name 'Chiemsee', claiming that, notwithstanding the differences in graphic representation of the marks on the products in question, there was a likelihood of confusion with its designation 'Chiemsee' with which, it claimed, the public was familiar and which had in any case been in use since 1990. In reply, the defendants contended that, since the word 'Chiemsee' was an indication which designated geographical origin and must consequently remain available for other traders to use, it was not capable of protection. It was this latter contention which concerned the CJEU.

Questions on Article 3(1)(c) of the Directive

19. By those questions, which may conveniently be considered together, the national court is essentially asking in what circumstances Article 3(1)(c) of the Directive precludes registration of a trade mark which consists exclusively of a geographical name. In particular, it is asking: if the application of Article 3(1)(c) depends on whether there is a real, current or serious need to leave the sign or indication free; and what connection there must be between

---

[39] [67].   [40] [73].

the geographical location and the goods in respect of which registration of the geographical name for that location as a trade mark is applied for.

...

24. It should first of all be observed that Article 3(1)(c) of the Directive provides that registration is to be refused in respect of descriptive marks, that is to say marks composed exclusively of signs or indications which may serve to designate the characteristics of the categories of goods or services in respect of which registration is applied for.

25. However, Article 3(1)(c) of the Directive pursues an aim which is in the public interest, namely that descriptive signs or indications relating to the categories of goods or services in respect of which registration is applied for may be freely used by all, including as collective marks or as part of complex or graphic marks. Article 3(1)(c) therefore prevents such signs and indications from being reserved to one undertaking alone because they have been registered as trade marks.

26. As regards, more particularly, signs or indications which may serve to designate the geographical origin of the categories of goods in relation to which registration of the mark is applied for, especially geographical names, it is in the public interest that they remain available, not least because they may be an indication of the quality and other characteristics of the categories of goods concerned, and may also, in various ways, influence consumer tastes by, for instance, associating the goods with a place that may give rise to a favourable response.

...

29. Article 3(1)(c) of the Directive is not confined to prohibiting the registration of geographical names as trade marks solely where they designate specified geographical locations which are already famous, or are known for the category of goods concerned, and which are therefore associated with those goods in the mind of the relevant class of persons, that is to say in the trade and amongst average consumers of that category of goods in the territory in respect of which registration is applied for.

30. Indeed, it is clear from the actual wording of Article 3(1)(c), which refers to '... indications which may serve ... to designate ... geographical origin', that geographical names which are liable to be used by undertakings must remain available to such undertakings as indications of the geographical origin of the category of goods concerned.

31. Thus, under Article 3(1)(c) of the Directive, the competent authority must assess whether a geographical name in respect of which application for registration as a trade mark is made designates a place which is currently associated in the mind of the relevant class of persons with the category of goods concerned, or whether it is reasonable to assume that such an association may be established in the future.

32. In the latter case, when assessing whether the geographical name is capable, in the mind of the relevant class of persons, of designating the origin of the category of goods in question, regard must be had more particularly to the degree of familiarity amongst such persons with that name, with the characteristics of the place designated by the name, and with the category of goods concerned.

33. In that connection, Article 3(1)(c) of the Directive does not in principle preclude the registration of geographical names which are unknown to the relevant class of persons—or at least unknown as the designation of a geographical location—or of names in respect of which, because of the type of place they designate (say, a mountain or lake), such persons are unlikely to believe that the category of goods concerned originates there.

34. However, it cannot be ruled out that the name of a lake may serve to designate geographical origin within the meaning of Article 3(1)(c), even for goods such as those in the main proceedings, provided that the name could be understood by the relevant class of persons to include the shores of the lake or the surrounding area.

35. It follows from the foregoing that the application of Article 3(1)(c) of the Directive does not depend on there being a real, current or serious need to leave a sign or indication free ('Freihaltebedürfnis') under German case law, as outlined in the third indent of paragraph 16 of this judgment.

36. Finally, it is important to note that, whilst an indication of the geographical origin of goods to which Article 3(1)(c) of the Directive applies usually indicates the place where the goods were or could be manufactured, the connection between a category of goods and a geographical location might depend on other ties, such as the fact that the goods were conceived and designed in the geographical location concerned.

37. In view of the foregoing, the answer to the questions on Article 3(1)(c) of the Directive must be that Article 3(1)(c) is to be interpreted as meaning that:

- it does not prohibit the registration of geographical names as trade marks solely where the names designate places which are, in the mind of the relevant class of persons, currently associated with the category of goods in question; it also applies to geographical names which are liable to be used in future by the undertakings concerned as an indication of the geographical origin of that category of goods;

- where there is currently no association in the mind of the relevant class of persons between the geographical name and the category of goods in question, the competent authority must assess whether it is reasonable to assume that such a name is, in the mind of the relevant class of persons, capable of designating the geographical origin of that category of goods;

- in making that assessment, particular consideration should be given to the degree of familiarity amongst the relevant class of persons with the geographical name in question, with the characteristics of the place designated by that name, and with the category of goods concerned; it is not necessary for the goods to be manufactured in the geographical location in order for them to be associated with it.

Of course, geographical names are not the only signs which may fall within the category of descriptive signs and it was assumed, following *Windsurfing*, that the identification of the public interest behind Article 3(1)(c) which had been made by the CJEU applied more generally to other types of descriptive signs. However, this assumption was called into question by the CJEU's controversial judgment in *Proctor & Gamble v OHIM*,[41] which appeared to lower the high barrier to registering descriptive marks which it had itself set in *Windsurfing*. In this case, the applicant sought to register the mark 'Baby-Dry' as a EUTM for nappies, without evidence of distinctiveness acquired through use. The EU IPO refused the application on the grounds that the mark was descriptive, consisting exclusively of an indication which might serve in trade to designate the intended purpose of the goods. The applicant's appeal eventually reached the CJEU. Perhaps surprisingly, in light of the *Windsurfing* decision, the CJEU held that 'Baby-Dry' could be registered. In particular, the Court concluded that only 'purely' descriptive signs should not be registered. It defined such signs as those which,

[41] Case C-383/99 P [2001] ECR I-6251.

because they are no different from the usual way of designating goods or services, cannot by definition be distinctive. It followed that in the case of word marks: 'Any perceptible difference between the combination of words submitted for registration and the terms used in the common parlance of the relevant class of consumers to designate the goods or services or their essential characteristics is apt to confer distinctive character on the word combination enabling it to be registered as a trade mark.' In this case, the CJEU took the view that while the words 'Baby-Dry' were unquestionably allusive and might, in combination, be used as part of expressions in everyday speech to designate the function of babies' nappies, 'their syntactically unusual juxtaposition is not a familiar expression in the English language, either for designating babies' nappies or for describing their essential characteristics.' The combination was not descriptive.

In explaining its reasoning in 'Baby-Dry', a factor which weighed with the Court was that under the regulation (Article 12) and the directive, it is a defence to trade mark infringement if a registered trade mark is used by a third party purely descriptively and not as a badge of origin, thus tempering the potentially strong monopoly that registration affords to the proprietors of descriptive marks. But might it not be equally possible to argue that the courts should always be slow to give such protection to words which other traders might legitimately wish to use? When a case with similar facts to the 'Baby-Dry' decision subsequently came before the CJEU, the Court took a stance much more in keeping with its earlier decision in *Windsurfing*: that case was *Wrigley*.

Office for Harmonisation in the Internal Market v Wm Wrigley Jr Co.
Case C-191/01 P [2003] ECR I-12447

The EU IPO rejected an application from Wrigley to register as a EUTM the word 'Doublemint' for various classes of goods including chewing gum, because it was held to be descriptive (Article 7(1)(c) of the EUTM Regulation).[42] The applicant appealed. The First Board of Appeal of the EU IPO dismissed the appeal on the grounds that the word 'Doublemint', a combination of two English words without additional fanciful or imaginative elements, was descriptive of certain characteristics of the goods in question, namely their mint-based composition and their mint flavour. This decision was overturned by the Court of First Instance (CFI) (now the General Court). The CFI appeared to have followed the 'Baby-Dry' decision, and held that since the term was not the ordinary English way of describing the goods (i.e. it had other meanings and was not exclusively descriptive), the mark should be registered. The CJEU, however, disagreed.

> 32. In order for OHIM to refuse to register a trade mark under Art. 7(1)(c) of Reg. 40/94, it is not necessary that the signs and indications composing the mark that are referred to in that article actually be in use at the time of the application for registration in a way that is descriptive of goods or services such as those in relation to which the application is filed, or of characteristics of those goods or services. It is sufficient, as the wording of that provision itself indicates, that such signs and indications could be used for such purposes. A sign must therefore be refused registration under that provision if at least one of its possible meanings designates a characteristic of the goods or services concerned.

---

[42] Equivalent to TMD, Art. 3(1)(a).

33. In the present case, the reason given by the Court of First Instance, at para. 20 of the contested judgment, for holding that the word at issue could not be refused registration under Art. 7(1)(c) was that signs or indications whose meaning goes beyond the merely descriptive are capable of being registered as Community trade marks and, at para. 31 of the contested judgment, that that term cannot be characterised as exclusively descriptive. It thus took the view that Art. 7(1)(c) of Reg. 40/94 had to be interpreted as precluding the registration of trade marks which are exclusively descriptive of the goods or services in respect of which registration is sought, or of their characteristics.

34. In so doing, the Court of First Instance applied a test based on whether the mark is exclusively descriptive, which is not the test laid down by Art. 7(1)(c) of Reg. 40/94.

35. It thereby failed to ascertain whether the word at issue was capable of being used by other economic operators to designate a characteristic of their goods and services.

36. It follows that it erred as to the scope of Art. 7(1)(c) of Reg. 40/94.

The widely held view that *Wrigley* followed the CJEU's approach to descriptive signs set out in *Windsurfing*, rather than the more expansive approach to their registration set out in the 'Baby-Dry' case, is confirmed in later judgments. In *Campina Melkunie BV v Benelux-Merkenbureau*,[43] which concerned the application 'Biomild' for a mild-flavoured yoghurt, the CJEU held that a neologism would be unregistrable if it were descriptive. In *Koninklijke KPN Nederland NV v Benelux-Merkenbureau*,[44] concerning an application to register 'Postkantoor', the Dutch word for post office, for a range of goods including stamps, paper, and advice, the CJEU held that a mark which is composed of elements, each of which is descriptive, may itself be considered descriptive unless it creates an impression far removed from its descriptive elements. The CJEU also noted that even if synonyms exist for a descriptive word, such a word might not be registered if it is the normal way of referring to the relevant goods or services.

In *Technopol v OHIM*, the CJEU summarized the principles relating to the registration and non-registration of descriptive marks.

Agencja Wydawnicza Technopol sp. z o.o. v Office for Harmonisation in the Internal Market (Trade Marks and Designs) (OHIM) Case C-51/10 P [2011] ETMR 34

The mark at issue was '1000', which the applicant sought to register as a EUTM for, inter alia, brochures and periodicals containing crossword puzzles. The OHIM denied the mark registration on the basis of Article 7(1)(c) of the EUTM Regulation, because, if used on its own, it would lack distinctiveness and be descriptive of the contents of the goods concerned (e.g. because it might describe the number of puzzles in the periodical). Technopol appealed unsuccessfully to the General Court. Among its arguments was that used alone, the sign '1000' was not descriptive, because consumers would make no direct link with the goods at issue. It also argued that since there were 10,000 possible combinations of four-digit numbers, there was no need to keep this particular sign free for others to use. Finally, the applicant appealed to the CJEU. The Court made clear

[43] Case C-45/06 [2004] ECR I-1699.   [44] Case C-363/99 [2004] ECR I-1619.

that just because a mark is made up simply of numerals, without graphic modification or stylization, this certainly does not mean it is in principle incapable of registration. However, it went on to confirm the decision of the General Court that this particular mark was descriptive. It began by looking at Technopol's argument that only signs which are the usual way of describing the characteristics of the goods at issue should be refused registration.

37 The general interest underlying art.7(1)(c) of Regulation 40/94 is that of ensuring that descriptive signs relating to one or more characteristics of the goods or services in respect of which registration as a mark is sought may be freely used by all traders offering such goods or services (see, to that effect, *Wrigley* [2004] E.T.M.R. 9 at [31] and the case law cited).

38 With a view to ensuring that that objective of free use is fully met, the Court has stated that, in order for OHIM to refuse to register a sign on the basis of art.7(1)(c) of Regulation 40/94, it is not necessary that the sign in question actually be in use at the time of the application for registration in a way that is descriptive. It is sufficient that the sign could be used for such purposes (*Wrigley* [2004] E.T.M.R. 9 at [32]; *Campina Melkunie* [2004] E.T.M.R. 58 at [38]; and the order of February 5, 2010 in *Mergel v Office for Harmonisation in the Internal Market (Trade Marks and Designs) (OHIM)* (C-80/09 P), not yet reported, para. 37).

39 By the same token, the Court has stated that the application of that ground for refusal does not depend on there being a real, current or serious need to leave a sign or indication free and that it is therefore of no relevance to know the number of competitors who have an interest, or who might have an interest, in using the sign in question (*Windsurfing Chiemsee Produktions- und Vertriebs GmbH (WSC) v Boots- und Segelzubehör Walter Huber* (C-108/97 & C-109/97) [1999] E.C.R. I-2779; [1999] E.T.M.R. 585 at [35], and *Koninklijke KPN Nederland NV v Benelux-Merkenbureau* (C-363/99) [2004] E.C.R. I-1619; [2004] E.T.M.R. 57 at [58]). It is, furthermore, irrelevant whether there are other, more usual, signs than that at issue for designating the same characteristics of the goods or services referred to in the application for registration (*Koninklijke KPN Nederland* [2004] E.T.M.R. 57 at [57]).

40 It follows from the foregoing that the application of art.7(1)(c) of Regulation 40/94 does not require the sign at issue to be the usual means of designation.

...

[The CJEU then went on to examine Technopol's argument that the General Court wrongly applied these principles by defining a sign which is 'characteristic of goods and services' and hence too broadly descriptive.]

50 The fact that the legislature chose to use the word 'characteristic' highlights the fact that the signs referred to in art.7(1)(c) of Regulation 40/94 are merely those which serve to designate a property, easily recognisable by the relevant class of persons, of the goods or the services in respect of which registration is sought. As the Court has pointed out, a sign can be refused registration on the basis of art.7(1)(c) of Regulation 40/94 only if it is reasonable to believe that it will actually be recognised by the relevant class of persons as a description of one of those characteristics (see, by analogy, as regards the identical provision laid down in art.3 of Directive 89/104, *Windsurfing Chiemsee* [1999] E.T.M.R. 585 at [31], and *Koninklijke KPN Nederland* [2004] E.T.M.R. 57 at [56]).

51 Those specific points are of particular relevance as regards signs which are composed exclusively of numerals.

> 52 Given that such signs are generally equated with numbers, one of the things that they can do, in trade, is to designate a quantity. Nevertheless, in order for a sign which is composed exclusively of numerals to be refused registration on the basis of art.7(1)(c) of Regulation 40/94 on the ground that it designates a quantity, it must be reasonable to believe that, in the mind of the relevant class of persons, the quantity indicated by those numerals characterises the goods or services in respect of which registration is sought.
>
> 53 As is apparent from [26] et seq. of the judgment under appeal, the General Court based its decision on the fact that the sign '1000' can indicate the number of pages in the goods covered by the application for registration and on the fact that ranking lists and collections of data and puzzles—in respect of which there is a preference for the content to be indicated by one or more words coupled with round numbers—are frequently published in those goods.

The CJEU concluded that the General Court had been right to find that '1000' was descriptive.

A recent succinct and practical summary of how descriptiveness will be assessed was given by Advocate General Mengozzi in *BGW Beratungs-Gesellschaft Wirtschaft mbH v Bodo Scholz*:[45]

> 23 …Thus, it has been held that the distinctiveness of a sign can only be assessed, first, in relation to the goods or services concerned and, second, in relation to the perception of the section of the public targeted, which is composed of the consumers of those goods or services. It has also been held that the signs and indications to which the abovementioned provisions refer are those which may serve in normal usage, from the point of view of the public targeted, to designate, either directly or by reference to one of their essential characteristics, the goods or services in respect of which registration is sought, and that, for a sign to be caught by the prohibition set out in those provisions, there must be a sufficiently direct and specific relationship between the sign and the goods and services concerned to enable the relevant public immediately to perceive, without further thought, a description of the category of goods and services concerned or one of their characteristics. Although those criteria have often been applied strictly by the EU judicature, a sign can be refused registration on the ground of its descriptiveness only if it is reasonable to believe that it will actually be recognised by the relevant class of persons as the description of one of the 'characteristics' of the goods or the services in respect of which registration is sought, namely 'a property, easily recognisable by the relevant class of persons'.

Technopol provided confirmation that it is to *Windsurfing* rather than to 'Baby-Dry' that we must look to measure the height of the bar to the registration of descriptive marks. In other words, the CJEU appears to have taken the view that it is important to protect the public interest in keeping descriptive signs free for others to use even though, as some believe, this may militate against market efficiency. Do you think this is the correct approach?

6.3.3.4 Signs which are devoid of distinctive character

These signs will be registered only if there is evidence of distinctiveness acquired through use. In *Henkel KgaA v OHIM*,[46] the CJEU ruled that the particular public interest consideration underlying this absolute ground for refusal is that there is no public benefit in

---

[45] Case C-20/14, EU:C:2015:714.   [46] Case C-144/06 P [2005] ECR I-1725.

conferring legal protection on a trade mark which does not fulfil its essential function as a badge of origin. Signs which are descriptive will, of course, lack distinctiveness. *Philips* provides one example. Another is *Linde v Deutsches Patent Markenamt*,[47] where the applicant sought to register the shape of a fork-lift truck for fork-lift trucks. The CJEU held that the proposed 'shape of goods' mark would be both descriptive and lack distinctiveness. However, other signs may lack distinctiveness, but will not be descriptive, such as for example a common name or a colour. The criteria for deciding whether a sign is devoid of distinctive character have been examined in a number of CJEU decisions. We have already seen in *Libertel*, which concerned an application to register the colour orange, that the CJEU held that in principle single-colour marks might be registrable provided they have adequate graphic representation. Later in the *Libertel* judgment, the CJEU also addressed the question of whether and under what circumstances a colour mark may be sufficiently distinctive to satisfy Article 3(1)(b).

> 65. The perception of the relevant public is not necessarily the same in the case of a sign consisting of a colour per se as it is in the case of a word or figurative mark consisting of a sign that bears no relation to the appearance of the goods it denotes. While the public is accustomed to perceiving words or figurative marks instantly as signs identifying the commercial origin of the goods, the same is not necessarily true where the sign forms part of the look of the goods in respect of which registration of the sign is sought. Consumers are not in the habit of making assumptions about the origin of goods based on their colour or the colour of their packaging, in the absence of any graphic or word element, because as a rule a colour per se is not, in current commercial practice, used as a means of identification. A colour per se is not normally inherently capable of distinguishing the goods of a particular undertaking.
>
> 66. In the case of a colour per se, distinctiveness without any prior use is inconceivable save in exceptional circumstances, and particularly where the number of goods or services for which the mark is claimed is very restricted and the relevant market very specific.

In *Libertel*, the CJEU was also asked to identify the circumstances in which it was likely such distinctiveness would be present. It noted that:

> 71. ... [T]he reply to Question 2(b) must be that the fact that registration as a trade mark of a colour per se is sought for a large number of goods or services, or for a specific product or service or for a specific group of goods or services, is relevant, together with all the other circumstances of the particular case, to assessing both the distinctive character of the colour in respect of which registration is sought, and whether its registration would run counter to the general interest in not unduly limiting the availability of colours for the other operators who offer for sale goods or services of the same type as those in respect of which registration is sought.

In *Libertel*,[48] the CJEU makes the point that whether a mark is initially devoid of distinctive character may depend upon the nature of the goods and services to which it attaches: a parallel approach to that summarized by Advocate General Mengozzi in *BGW* in relation

---

[47] *Linde AG, Winward Industries Inc., Rado Uhren AG v Deutsches Patent und Markenamt* Joined Cases C-53–55/01 [2003] ECR I-3161.
[48] See also *Linde*.

to descriptive marks. For example, we might agree that the colour orange would be more readily viewed by the public as a badge of origin, if it were used in relation to telecommunications rather than foodstuffs.[49] Similarly, in the earlier case of *Proctor & Gamble*,[50] the CJEU held that:

> 37. ... Only a trade mark which departs significantly from the norm or customs of the sector and thereby fulfils its essential function of indicating origin, is not devoid of any distinctive character for the purposes of that provision (see, in relation to the identical provision in Art. 3(1)(b) of First Directive 89/104, *Henkel*, para. 49).[51]

Thus, in *Proctor & Gamble*, which concerned an application to register the shape of washing-up tablets, the CJEU took the view that because they are everyday items, consumers would not pay particular attention to their shape and, as a result, they would not be viewed as a badge of origin. More recently, and perhaps surprisingly, the General Court took a similar approach to 'shape of goods marks' when dealing with expensive, luxury items, in this case handbags. In *Louis Vuitton v OHIM*,[52] it held that the shape of the applicant's locking device for bags would be seen by the public as a representation of a particularly interesting or attractive detail of the product in question rather than as an indication of its commercial origin.

6.3.3.5 Trade marks which consist exclusively of signs or indications which have become customary in the current language or in the bona fide and established practices of the trade (Article 3(1)(d) of the TMD; Article 4(1)(d) of the TMD 2016)

The key case for interpreting this exclusion is the case of *Merz & Krell GmbH & Co.* In particular, in *Merz & Krell*, the CJEU discussed the difference between these signs and descriptive signs.

Merz & Krell GmbH & Co. Case C-517/99 [2000] ECR I-6959

Merz & Krell sought to register the mark 'Bravo' for writing instruments at the German Patent and Trade Mark Office. Registration was refused on the basis that 'Bravo' was seen by the relevant consumers as a word of praise, and therefore devoid of distinctive character. Merz & Krell then appealed to the Bundespatentgericht. It took the view that 'Bravo' could not be registered under paragraph 8(2)(3) of the Markengesetz (the German Trade Marks Act) because the word is traditionally used in advertising for a variety of goods, and therefore had become customary in the current language or in the bona fide and established practices of the trade, even if that use was for a variety of goods

---

[49] In fact, following the CJEU decision, Libertel succeeded with its trade mark application.
[50] *Procter & Gamble v OHIM* Joined Cases C-468–472/01 P [2004] ECR I-5141.
[51] This judgment was followed in *Mag Instrument Inc. v Office for Harmonisation in the Internal Market* Case C-136/02 P [2004] ECR I-9165.
[52] *Louis Vuitton Malletier v OHIM, FriiS Group International APD Intervening* Case C-97/12 P [2014] ETMR 42.

and not necessarily writing instruments. It went on to address the following question to the CJEU: should Article 3(1)(d) be interpreted restrictively to mean that only signs which are descriptive would be denied registration? Or alternatively, does Article 3(1)(d) also cover signs which have become customary in current language in the sector in question, for instance as a persuasive advertising tool, but which are not directly descriptive? The CJEU answered in the positive.

> 35. It must first of all be observed that, although there is a clear overlap between the scope of Articles 3(1)(c) and 3(1)(d) of the Directive, marks covered by Article 3(1)(d) are excluded from registration not on the basis that they are descriptive, but on the basis of current usage in trade sectors covering trade in the goods or services for which the marks are sought to be registered.
>
> 36. It follows that, in order for Article 3(1)(d) of the Directive to be effective, the scope of the provision in respect of which the Court's interpretation is sought should not be limited solely to trade marks which describe the properties or characteristics of the goods or services covered by them.
>
> ...
>
> 39. It also follows that, where the signs or indications concerned have become customary in the current language or in the bona fide and established practices of the trade to designate the goods or services covered by the mark, it is of little consequence that they are used as advertising slogans, indications of quality or incitements to purchase those goods or services.
>
> 40. However, registration of a trade mark which consists of signs or indications that are also used as advertising slogans, indications of quality or incitements to purchase the goods or services covered by that mark is not excluded as such by virtue of such use. It is for the national court to determine in each case whether the signs or indications have become customary in the current language or in the bona fide and established practices of the trade to designate the goods or services covered by that mark.

Looking back over the series of cases which have allowed the CJEU to interpret the reach of the absolute grounds for refusal of registration as it applies to descriptive, non-distinctive marks and marks that are common in the trade, it is clear that beginning with *Windsurfing*, the CJEU has generally sought to protect such marks from the monopoly afforded by registration on the basis that, in the interests of competition, they should be left available for other traders to use. A related question then arises. If there is a public interest in leaving certain signs free for others to use unless they have acquired distinctiveness, should it be more difficult for a would-be proprietor to persuade the Court that such distinctiveness has indeed been achieved? In a number of cases, including *Windsurfing*, the CJEU has made it clear that there should be no higher hurdle to proving that a mark has acquired distinctiveness through use even if it falls into one of the categories of marks which should initially be left free for others to use.[53] The question of how acquired distinctiveness is to be assessed is considered in the following section. But, if this is the case, do you think the CJEU has actually struck the correct balance between trade mark protection and the initial public interest in leaving certain signs free?

---

[53] e.g. see *Linde*, [46].

FURTHER READING

A. Griffiths, 'Modernising trade mark law and promoting economic efficiency: an evaluation of the Baby-Dry judgment and its aftermath' [2003] IPQ 37.

M. Handler, 'The distinctive problem of European trade mark law' [2005] EIPR 306.

N. Lee, 'Public domain at the interface of trade mark and unfair competition law: the case of referential use of trade marks' in N. Lee, G. Westkamp, A. Kur, and A. Ohly (eds), *Intellectual Property, Unfair Competition and Publicity: Convergences and Development* (Cheltenham: Edward Elgar, 2014), pp. 309–39.

J. Phillips, 'Trade mark law and the need to keep free' (2005) 36 IIC 389.

6.3.3.6 The proviso at Article 3(3) (Article 4(4) of the TMD 2016)

In *British Sugar*,[54] Jacob J held that mere use of a mark does not necessarily equal distinctiveness. *Windsurfing* tells us that in the case of a geographical mark which is very well known, it may be that only long-standing and intensive use will endow the mark with the necessary distinctiveness to be registered. Although *Windsurfing* was specifically concerned with geographical names, in its judgment the CJEU also set out the general criteria for assessing distinctiveness under Article 3(3).[55]

Windsurfing Chiemsee Produktions und Vertriebs GmbH v Boots und Segelzubehör Walter Huber Joined Cases C-108 and 109/97 [1999] ECR I-2779

49. In determining whether a mark has acquired distinctive character following the use made of it, the competent authority must make an overall assessment of the evidence that the mark has come to identify the product concerned as originating from a particular undertaking, and thus to distinguish that product from goods of other undertakings.

...

51. In assessing the distinctive character of a mark in respect of which registration has been applied for, the following may also be taken into account: the market share held by the mark; how intensive, geographically widespread and long-standing use of the mark has been; the amount invested by the undertaking in promoting the mark; the proportion of the relevant class of persons who, because of the mark, identify goods as originating from a particular undertaking; and statements from chambers of commerce and industry or other trade and professional associations.

52. If, on the basis of those factors, the competent authority finds that the relevant class of persons, or at least a significant proportion thereof, identify goods as originating from a particular undertaking because of the trade mark, it must hold that the requirement for registering the mark laid down in Article 3(3) of the Directive is satisfied. However, the circumstances in which that requirement may be regarded as satisfied cannot be shown to exist solely by reference to general, abstract data such as predetermined percentages.

53. As regards the method to be used to assess the distinctive character of a mark in respect of which registration is applied for, Community law does not preclude the competent

---

[54] *British Sugar plc v James Robertson & Sons* [1996] RPC 281.   [55] TMD 2016, Art. 4(4).

authority, where it has particular difficulty in that connection, from having recourse, under the conditions laid down by its own national law, to an opinion poll as guidance for its judgment (see, to that effect, Case C-210/96 *Gut Springenheide and Tusky* [1998] ECR I-4657, paragraph 37).

Crucial to the test for distinctiveness set out in *Windsurfing* is that a 'significant portion of the relevant class of persons' have come to see the mark as a badge of origin. Later cases have elaborated on the question as to how the registering authorities might define the relevant consumer. Emerging from the case law is what has come to be known as the 'average-consumer test'.

6.3.3.7 Assessing distinctiveness: the average-consumer test

The issue of how to judge acquired distinctiveness was a key issue in *Philips*.

Koninklijke Philips Electronics NV v Remington Consumer Products Ltd
Case C-299/99 [2002] ECR I-5475

Specific to the case, as we have seen, was that until Remington marketed their own three-headed shaver, Philips was the only company to supply such a product. The CJEU was asked 'whether, when a trader has been the only supplier of particular goods to the market, extensive use of a sign which consists of the shape of those goods is sufficient to give the sign a distinctive character for the purposes of Article 3(3) of the directive in circumstances where, as a result of that use, a substantial proportion of the relevant class of persons associates the shape with that trader, and no other undertaking, or believes that goods of that shape come from that trader in the absence of a statement to the contrary'.

In answering this question, the CJEU first cited the *Windsurfing* test for distinctiveness, but added the following important caveat. It noted that acquired distinctiveness:

> 63. ... must be assessed in the light of the presumed expectations of an average consumer of the category of goods or services in question, who is reasonably well-informed and reasonably observant and circumspect (see, to that effect, the judgment in *Gut Springenheide and Tusky*, Case C-210/96 [1998] ECR I-4657, paragraph 31). [It then concluded:]

> 65. ... [W]here a trader has been the only supplier of particular goods to the market, extensive use of a sign which consists of the shape of those goods may be sufficient to give the sign a distinctive character for the purposes of Article 3(3) of the Directive in circumstances where, as a result of that use, a substantial proportion of the relevant class of persons associates that shape with that trader and no other undertaking or believes that goods of that shape come from that trader. However, it is for the national court to verify that the circumstances in which the requirement under that provision is satisfied are shown to exist on the basis of specific and reliable data, that the presumed expectations of an average consumer of the category of goods or services in question, who is reasonably well-informed and reasonably observant and circumspect, are taken into account and that the identification, by the relevant class of persons, of the product as originating from a given undertaking is as a result of the use of the mark as a trade mark.

The CJEU identifies the average consumer as being reasonably well informed, reasonably observant, and circumspect.[56] In a number of recent cases concerned with the use of trade marks on the internet, the CJEU has identified a different average consumer. The relevant consumer in internet cases, according to the CJEU, is the 'average internet user'.[57] It is worth speculating whether the average consumer who frequents stores on the 'high street' and the average internet user who buys from virtual stores would really be distinct individuals at a time when the internet has become, for many, a normal avenue for purchases of all kinds. And, indeed, the CJEU has not given any general insight as to how the two types of consumer might differ.

How are the views of the average consumer, whether on or off the internet, to be assessed? Of particular importance for the average-consumer test is the nature of the goods or services which attach to the mark or marks at issue. In other words, the courts will assume that the attention the average consumer will pay to the mark at issue will vary according to the nature of the goods or services.[58] This was made clear in the recent case of *Nestlé v Cadbury*,[59] on a question from the English High Court to the CJEU. The question was whether in judging whether a sign which has only been used in conjunction with a registered mark has acquired distinctiveness, must that judgment be made on the basis of that sign alone and not together with the mark with which it has been used. In this case, the issue was whether the four-finger shape of the 'KitKat' chocolate bar had acquired sufficient distinctiveness to be registered as a trade mark given that it had never been used without the registered mark 'KitKat' embossed on each finger. When the case[60] returned to the High Court, Arnold J understood the CJEU judgment to mean that when assessing whether an applicant has proved that a sign has acquired distinctiveness, it is necessary to ask whether the average consumer would explicitly rely upon the sign as denoting the origin of the goods if it were used on its own rather than simply view the sign as distinct from other signs.[61] In this case, Arnold J agreed with the Registry that consumers would not rely on the four-finger shape of the 'KitKat' as denoting the origin of the chocolate bar not least because the shape is hidden by packaging when the bar is bought. Nor would consumers use the shape of the chocolate bar, once purchased, to check that it is the product they intended to buy. We might speculate whether, if the sign had not been a piece of chocolate hidden by a foil wrapper, the decision might have been different. And, indeed, some years ago Nestlé had successfully registered the slogan 'Have a Break', which was also invariably used with the name 'KitKat', but this time on the outside of the packaging. In this case, the CJEU held that it was possible for the slogan to acquire distinctiveness even though it had not been used independently from a registered mark.[62] And the registering authority accepted that 'Have a Break' had acquired sufficient distinctiveness to be registered.

In *Picasso v OHIM*,[63] the CJEU looked at the question of whether, if a mark is highly distinctive in one field, it will be harder to persuade the public that it is distinctive for goods

---

[56] The average-consumer test originated in EU cases concerned with misleading advertising. As both *Windsurfing* and *Philips* make clear, the first appearance of the average consumer was in *Gut Springenheide and Tusky* Case C-210/96 [1998] ECR I-4657.

[57] See e.g. *Interflora v Marks & Spencer* Case C-323/09 [2011].

[58] *Proctor & Gamble.*

[59] *Société des Produits Nestlé SA v Cadbury UK Ltd* Case C-215/14 [2015] Bus. L. R. 1034.

[60] *Société de Produits Nestlé SA v Cadbury UK Ltd* [2016] EWHC 50 (Ch).   [61] [60].

[62] For the relevant CJEU decision, see: *Société de Produits Nestlé SA v Mars* Case C-353/03 [2005] ECR I-6135.

[63] *Claude Ruiz-Picasso v Office for Harmonisation in the Internal Market (Trade Marks and Designs), DaimlerChrysler AG* Case C-361/04 P [2006] ECR I-643.

and services in another, quite unrelated, field. This case concerned the proprietors of the 'Picasso' trade mark for cars who sought to prevent the registration of the mark 'Picaro' also for cars on the grounds that it was confusingly similar, under Article 8(1)(b) and Article 9(1)(b) of the TMD. The question arose as to whether 'Picasso' was a particularly distinctive sign. There was no argument that it was well known to the public as the name of a famous painter. However, it was held by the Court of First Instance and confirmed by the CJEU that simply because 'Picasso' was well known in one context did not mean that it possessed a highly distinctive character when applied to motor vehicles.

In *Oberbank*, the CJEU summarized the approach to be taken in assessing the distinctiveness of signs in the eyes of the average consumer for the purposes of registration.

Oberbank AG v Deutscher Sparkassen- und Giroverband eV Banco Santander SA and another v Same Joined Cases C-217 and 218/13, EU:C:2014:2012, [2014] WLR (D) 274

An association of German banks, DSGV, had a registered trade mark for the colour red for retail banking services on the basis of distinctiveness acquired through use. Three other banks which also used red as their corporate colour sought to have the mark declared invalid arguing that it had not acquired distinctiveness. One of the questions addressed to the CJEU by the German court was whether Article 3(1) and (3) of the TMD should be interpreted as meaning that in order to show a non-distinctive sign, such as a colour, has acquired distinctiveness, customer surveys must show a degree of recognition of at least 70 per cent. The CJEU addressed a more general question: how should it be determined whether, following the use which has been made of it, a mark has acquired a distinctive character within the meaning of Article 3(3) and, in particular, should that assessment depend, in significant part, on the results of a consumer survey. In making its judgment, the CJEU set out the general criteria to be employed in assessing distinctiveness.

40 As regards the question how to determine whether a mark has acquired a distinctive character through use, it is settled case law that the competent authority for registering trade marks must carry out an examination by reference to the actual situation (the *Libertel case* [2004] Ch 83, para 77, and *Nichols plc v Registrar of Trade Marks* (Case C-404/02) [2005] 1 WLR 1418; [2004] ECR I-8499, para 27) and make an overall assessment of the evidence that the mark has come to identify the goods or services concerned as originating from a particular undertaking: see the *Windsurfing Chiemsee case* [2000] Ch 523, para 49, and the *Nestlé case* [2005] ECR I-6135, para 31. Moreover, that evidence must relate to use of the mark as a trade mark, that is to say for the purposes of such identification by the relevant class of persons: see the *Philips case* [2003] Ch 159, para 64, and the *Nestlé* case[64] at paras 26 and 29.

The CJEU then repeated the evidence that may be taken into consideration and which was set out in *Windsurfing* at [51]. This included, as we have seen, the use of opinion polls. The CJEU continued:

---

[64] *Société des Produits Nestlé SA v Mars UK Ltd* Case C-353/03 [2005] ECR I-6135.

45 In that regard, it must be observed that, in an overall assessment of the evidence that the mark has acquired a distinctive character through use, it may indeed appear, inter alia, that the perception of the relevant public is not necessarily the same for each of the categories of marks and that, accordingly, it could prove more difficult to establish the distinctive character, including distinctiveness acquired through use, of trade marks in certain categories than that of those in other categories: see *Henkel KGaA* (Case C-218/01) [2004] ECR I-1725, para 52 and the case law cited, and the *Nichols case* [2005] 1 WLR 1418, para 28.

46 However, article 2 and article 3(1)(b) and (3) of Directive 2008/95 make no distinction between different categories of trade marks. The criteria for assessing the distinctive character of contourless colour marks, such as the mark at issue in the main proceedings, including whether that mark has acquired a distinctive character following the use which has been made of it, are thus no different from those to be applied to other categories of trade mark: see, by analogy, the *Philips case*, at para 48, and the *Nichols case*, at paras 24 and 25.

47 The difficulties in establishing distinctive character which may be associated with certain categories of marks because of their nature—difficulties which it is legitimate to take into account—do not therefore justify laying down stricter criteria supplementing or derogating from application of the criterion of distinctiveness as interpreted in the case law on other categories of marks: see the *Nichols case*, at para 26, and, by analogy, the *OHIM case* [2010] ECR I-8265, para 34.

48 It follows from the foregoing that it is not possible to state in general terms, for example by referring to predetermined percentages relating to the degree of recognition attained by the mark within the relevant section of the public, when a mark has acquired a distinctive character through use and that, even with regard to contourless colour marks, such as the mark at issue in the main proceedings, and even if a consumer survey may be one of the factors to be taken into account when assessing whether such a mark has acquired a distinctive character through use, the results of a consumer survey cannot be the only decisive criterion to support the conclusion that a distinctive character has been acquired through use.

49 In the light of those considerations, the answer to the first question is that article 3(1) and (3) of Directive 2008/95 must be interpreted as precluding an interpretation of national law according to which, in the context of proceedings raising the question whether a contourless colour mark has acquired a distinctive character through use, it is necessary in every case that a consumer survey indicate a degree of recognition of at least 70%.

In *Oberbank* and earlier cases such as *Windsurfing* and *Philips*, the CJEU has made it clear that a variety of empirical evidence may be employed to determine whether a sign has acquired distinctiveness. However, in *Marks and Spencer Plc v Interflora Inc.*,[65] the Court of Appeal held that the empirical approach to assessing the distinctiveness of signs, including the use of survey evidence, might not be appropriate when judging the separate question of the extent of consumer confusion in cases of infringement. The reason for making a qualitative and not a quantitative judgment in the latter circumstance is discussed in the next chapter.

6.3.3.8 Trade mark protection and the public domain

Thus far, in discussing the TMD and its interpretation, we have suggested that a crucial concern for the CJEU has been the need to balance the public interest in offering legal protection

---

[65] [2012] EWCA Civ 1501.

to signs, which are acting as trade marks, against the public interest in keeping certain signs free for others to use. Before the passage of the TMA, the UK courts had taken the view that certain signs, including geographical signs, although they might be acting as a badge of origin, should never be registered because they should be free for all to use. In a famous example, *Yorkshire Copper Works Ltd v Registrar of Trade Marks*,[66] a company which manufactured most of its products in Yorkshire applied to register as a trade mark, 'Yorkshire', for copper fittings. No one else manufactured these goods in Yorkshire and the applicants produced evidence that the mark had become '100 per cent distinctive' through use. The Registrar refused registration on the grounds that certain geographical words, including this one, could never be distinctive in law of a trader's goods, even though they were distinctive in fact. The House of Lords concurred that certain signs are too important to other traders for them to be reserved to a single proprietor. However, we have seen that the directive does not allow for such an approach, since following *Windsurfing*, any descriptive signs (including geographical signs) may be registered provided they have acquired distinctiveness through use. In her article, Jennifer Davis considered why, in interpreting the directive, the CJEU had not recognized a public domain or a 'trade mark commons', containing certain trade marks, which should be refused registration in the public interest.

J. Davis, 'The need to leave free for others to use and the trade mark common' in J. Phillips and I. Simon (eds), *Trade Mark Use* (Oxford: Oxford University Press, 2005), pp. 39–45

3.22 The question remains as to what extent the ECJ has been willing to recognise and hence to balance the different and conflicting interests which may be affected by a trade mark registration, something which we have argued was fundamental to the delineation of the English trade mark common. Clearly, the ECJ's freedom of action in this regard has been constrained by the market led approach to trade mark registration embodied in Art. 3(3) of the Directive, which determines that any sign which is acting as a trade mark, that is as a badge of origin in the market, can be registered. Furthermore, there has been some argument, put most forcefully by Advocate General Jacobs in his BABY-DRY opinion and followed by the ECJ in its ruling, that allowing proprietors to appropriate even minimally distinctive signs did not unduly impede access to the public domain, since it is a defence to trade mark infringement if a third party uses the mark descriptively. Not surprisingly it was an English judge, Jacob J, who presented what was perhaps the most cogent criticism of this view. He pointed out that such an approach inevitably favoured 'powerful traders', who will 'naturally assert their rights even in marginal cases'. Indeed, in such cases, he believed that:

defendants, SMEs particularly, are likely to back off when they receive a letter before action. It is cheaper and more certain to do that than stand and fight, even if in principle they have a defence.

3.23 It is submitted that, since BABY-DRY, the ECJ has backed away from the robust view of registration embodied in the judgment. Without the option of creating a protected trade mark common to protect the interest of 'the public in general and weaker and less organised companies', the ECJ has instead emphasised that the relevant authorities should be more

---

[66] [1954] 1 WLR 554.

rigorous in their examination of an applicant's sign before allowing a mark to be removed from the public domain in the first place. In other words, it is the 'competent authorities' who should be the gatekeepers as to which marks are removed from the public domain, rather than transferring such responsibility, *ex post facto*, to the courts. In *Libertel* the ECJ noted that:

the large number of and detailed nature of the obstacles to registration set out in Articles 2 and 3 of the Directive, and the wide range of remedies available in the event of refusal, indicate that the examination carried out at the time of the application for registration must not be a minimal one. It must be a stringent and full examination, in order to prevent trade marks from being improperly registered.

3.24 In fact, by advocating this approach, the ECJ was once again reaching a destination which had been sign-posted 90 years earlier by Lord Parker in *W & G du Gros*.[67] He stated:

In my opinion, in order to determine whether a mark is distinctive it must be considered quite apart from the effects of registration. The question, therefore, is whether the mark itself, if used as a Trade Mark, is likely to become actually distinctive of the goods of the persons so using it. The applicant for registration in effect says, 'I intend to use this mark as a Trade Mark, i.e., for the purpose of distinguishing my goods from the goods of other persons', and the Registrar or the court has to determine, before the mark be admitted to registration, whether it is of such a kind that the applicant, quite apart from the effects of registration, is likely or unlikely to attain the object he has in view. The applicant's chance of success, in this respect, must, I think, largely depend upon whether other traders are likely, in the ordinary course of their business and without any improper motive, to desire to use the same mark, or some mark nearly resembling it, upon or in connection with, their own goods.

D. Conclusion: The Balance Between Leaving Marks Free for Others to Use and Recognising Distinctiveness Acquired through Use

3.25 In its White Paper preceding the implementation of the Directive, the British Government noted:

At present it is possible for it to be established beyond doubt that a particular trade mark is distinctive in fact and yet for it to held in law to be not capable of distinguishing. Examples are geographical names and laudatory epithets. This position has been described as unattractive, but the Registry and the courts have considered themselves bound by a long history of case law, much of it dating from a period in which trading conditions were very different from today. The government intends to take the opportunity offered by a new law to clarify the position so that any trade mark which is demonstrated to be distinctive in fact will in future be regarded as distinctive in law and therefore be registrable.

3.26 As we have seen, the effect of Art. 3(3) of the Directive has been precisely to ensure that any mark which has acquired distinctiveness through use may indeed be capable of registration. As a corollary, it is also no longer possible for certain marks to be reserved for

[67] *W. & G. Du Cros Ltd's Application* (1913) 30 RPC 661.

the 'English language common', so they may be left free for others to use despite acquired distinctiveness.

3.27 It can be argued that such an approach to trade mark registration has the virtue of both simplicity and consistency. In a long line of trade mark cases, many of which preceded the Directive, the ECJ has held that:

> the essential function of a trade mark is to guarantee the identity of origin of the marked goods or services to the consumer or end user by enabling him, without any possibility of confusion, to distinguish the goods or services from others which have another origin.

3.28 It follows that if a descriptive mark or a non-distinctive mark reaches the requisite level of distinctiveness through use, it will fulfil the essential function of a trade mark and should be capable of registration. Such was the simple logic followed by the ECJ in *Windsurfing* and *Philips*, for example. Indeed, it may be further argued that to allow otherwise would be precisely to allow for the possibility of such confusion. Finally, in its reference to contemporary 'trading conditions', the White Paper was surely recognising the contemporary importance of branding. It would certainly be a hard thing to deny a trader the economic rewards for the investment he has made in ensuring that his mark, which might initially have been descriptive or lacking in distinctiveness, has indeed acquired distinctiveness through use.

FURTHER READING

A. Blythe, 'In search of Mr Average: attempting to identify the average consumer and his role within trade mark law' [2015] EIPR 209.

J. Davis, 'Revisiting the average consumer: an uncertain presence in European trade mark law' [2015] IPQ 15.

A. Folliard-Monguiral, 'Distinctive character acquired through use: the law and the case law' in J. Phillips and I. Simon (eds), *Trade Mark Use* (Oxford: Oxford University Press, 2005), pp. 49–70.

E. Rosati, 'CJEU says that mere recognition/association is not sufficient to prove acquired distinctiveness' (2016) 11 JIPLP 77.

6.3.4 SIGNS WHICH MAY NEVER BE REGISTERED

6.3.4.1 Shape marks

The TMD allows, as we have seen, for the registration of shape marks: both fanciful shapes and also shape of goods marks which have acquired distinctiveness. However, the directive contains a prohibition against the registration of functional shapes. Article 3(1)(e) of the TMD[68] prohibits registration of signs which consist exclusively of:

- the shape which results from the nature of the goods themselves;
- the shape of goods which is necessary to obtain a technical result;
- the shape of goods which give substantial value to the goods.

---

[68] TMA, s. 3(2); TMD 2016, Art. 4(1)(e).

The TMD 2016 has added the words 'or another characteristic' to these three exclusions. Thus, under the new directive, a sign will also not be registered if it consists of another characteristic, for example a sound or a smell, which results from the nature of the goods, is necessary to obtain a technical result, or gives substantial value to the goods.

6.3.4.2 Interpreting the shapes exclusion

Until the decision in *Lego v OHIM*, the leading case for interpreting Article 3(1)(e) was *Philips*. We have looked at the facts. Apart from arguing that the three-headed shaver lacked distinctiveness under section 3(1)(b) and was descriptive, Remington also argued that the Philips trade mark, viewed as a three-dimensional mark, was invalidly registered because it fell within Article 3(1)(e). When the case reached the Court of Appeal, the court addressed a number of questions to the CJEU, of which the most pertinent in relation to Article 3(1)(e) was whether Article 3(1)(e) of the TMD should be interpreted to mean that a sign consisting exclusively of the shape of a product is unregistrable if it is established that the essential functional features of the shape are attributable only to the technical result. It also asked whether the ground for refusal or invalidity of the registration imposed by that provision could be overcome by establishing that there are other shapes which can obtain the same technical result. The CJEU answered that even if other shapes were available which could obtain the same technical result, if the essential features of a sign are necessary to obtain that technical result it cannot be registered. The full implications of prohibiting the registration of functional shapes were set out in the *Lego* case.

Lego Juris A/S v Office for Harmonisation in the Internal Market (OHIM), Mega Brands, Inc. Case C-48/09 [2010] ETMR 63

This was an appeal against a decision of the General Court. In particular, it concerned the correct interpretation of Article 7(1)(e)(ii) of the EUTM Regulation,[69] which denies registration to signs which consist exclusively of shapes which are necessary to obtain a technical result. Lego had a EUTM for 'Games and Playthings' in Class 28 in the shape of its highly distinctive, red, three-dimensional toy-brick. Almost immediately after the registration was obtained in 1999, the predecessor-in-title to Mega Brands applied for a declaration that the mark was invalid in relation to construction toys on the basis that, inter alia, it was a shape necessary to obtain a technical result. Following the judgment in *Philips*, the Cancellation Division declared the mark invalid for that reason. Lego appealed. The General Court confirmed the finding of invalidity and Lego then appealed to the CJEU. The first subject of its appeal was that the General Board had incorrectly interpreted both the 'subject matter and the scope of art 7(1)(e)(ii)'. In particular, Lego argued that a shape should only be denied registration if it would create a monopoly on either technical solutions or on functional characteristics. It followed, according to Lego, that the term 'technical solution' should be distinguished from 'technical result', because the latter can be achieved by many different shapes. Thus, where there are several shapes which can also achieve the same result, registration of one would not prevent competitors from reaching the same technical solution. In its turn,

---

[69] TMA, s. 3(2)(b); TMD, Art. 3(1)(e)(ii).

the OHIM (now the EU IPO) argued that the inclusion of the words 'necessary' and 'exclusively' in Article 7(1)(e)(ii) does not mean that only shapes which are necessary as such for the function sought should not be registered. Instead, the article covers all essentially functional shapes which are attributable to achieving the desired result. In finding against Lego, the CJEU first of all accepted that the shape of the Lego brick was distinctive. It then turned to the question of whether it should be denied registration as a functional shape. It first identified the general principle behind the prohibition.

45 First, the inclusion in art.7(1) of Regulation 40/94 of the prohibition on registration as a trade mark of any sign consisting of the shape of goods which is necessary to obtain a technical result ensures that undertakings may not use trade mark law in order to perpetuate, indefinitely, exclusive rights relating to technical solutions.

46 When the shape of a product merely incorporates the technical solution developed by the manufacturer of that product and patented by it, protection of that shape as a trade mark once the patent has expired would considerably and permanently reduce the opportunity for other undertakings to use that technical solution. In the system of intellectual property rights developed in the European Union, technical solutions are capable of protection only for a limited period, so that subsequently they may be freely used by all economic operators ...

...

48 Secondly, by restricting the ground for refusal set out in art.7(1)(e)(ii) of Regulation 40/94 to signs which consist 'exclusively' of the shape of goods which is 'necessary' to obtain a technical result, the legislature duly took into account that any shape of goods is, to a certain extent, functional and that it would therefore be inappropriate to refuse to register a shape of goods as a trade mark solely on the ground that it has functional characteristics. By the terms 'exclusively' and 'necessary', that provision ensures that solely shapes of goods which only incorporate a technical solution, and whose registration as a trade mark would therefore actually impede the use of that technical solution by other undertakings, are not to be registered.

[The CJEU then looked to see whether the General Court had applied Article 7(1)(e)(ii) correctly.]

51 As regards the fact that the ground for refusal covers any sign consisting 'exclusively' of the shape of goods which is necessary to obtain a technical result, the General Court stated, at [38] of the judgment under appeal, that that condition is fulfilled when all the essential characteristics of a shape perform a technical function, the presence of non-essential characteristics with no technical function being irrelevant in that context.

52 That interpretation is consistent with [79] of *Philips* [2002] E.T.M.R. 81. Moreover, it reflects the idea underlying that judgment, as set out by Advocate General Ruíz-Jarabo Colomer at point 28 of his Opinion in that case and also at point 72 of his Opinion in *Koninklijke KPN Nederland NV v Benelux-Merkenbureau* (C-363/99) [2004] E.C.R. I-1619; [2004] E.T.M.R. 57, that is to say, that the presence of one or more minor arbitrary elements in a three-dimensional sign, all of whose essential characteristics are dictated by the technical solution to which that sign gives effect, does not alter the conclusion that the sign consists exclusively of the shape of goods which is necessary to obtain a technical result. In addition, since that interpretation implies that the ground for refusal under art.7(1)(e)(ii) of Regulation 40/94 is applicable only where all the essential characteristics of the sign are functional, it ensures that such a sign cannot be refused registration as a trade mark under that provision

if the shape of the goods at issue incorporates a major non-functional element, such as a decorative or imaginative element which plays an important role in the shape.

53 As regards the condition that registration of a shape of goods as a trade mark may be refused under art.7(1)(e)(ii) of Regulation 40/94 only if the shape is 'necessary' to obtain the technical result intended, the General Court rightly found, at [39] of the judgment under appeal, that that condition does not mean that the shape at issue must be the only one capable of obtaining that result.

54 It is true, as the appellant points out, that, in some cases, the same technical result may be achieved by various solutions. Thus, there may be alternative shapes, with other dimensions or another design, capable of achieving the same technical result.

55 However, contrary to the appellant's submission, that fact does not in itself mean that registering the shape at issue as a trade mark would have no effect on the availability, to other economic operators, of the technical solution which it incorporates.

56 In that connection, it should be observed, as OHIM points out, that under art.9(1) of Regulation 40/94 registration as a trade mark of a purely functional product shape is likely to allow the proprietor of that trade mark to prevent other undertakings not only from using the same shape, but also from using similar shapes. A significant number of alternative shapes might therefore become unusable for the proprietor's competitors.

57 That would be particularly so if various purely functional shapes of goods were registered at the same time, which might completely prevent other undertakings from manufacturing and marketing certain goods having a particular technical function.

…

59 To the extent that the appellant also submits, and OHIM does not dispute, that in order to use the same technical solution, its competitors do not need to place on the market toy bricks whose shape and dimensions are in all respects identical to those of the Lego brick, it is sufficient to observe that that fact cannot prevent application of the rules laid down by the European Union's legislature, interpreted above, under which a sign consisting of the shape of a product that, without the inclusion of significant non-functional elements, merely performs a technical function cannot be registered as a trade mark. Such a registration would unduly impair the opportunity for competitors to place on the market goods whose shapes incorporate the same technical solution.

60 That applies a fortiori in a case of this kind, where it has been found by the competent authority that the solution incorporated in the shape of goods examined is the technically preferable solution for the category of goods concerned. If the three-dimensional sign consisting of such a shape were registered as a trade mark, it would be difficult for the competitors of the proprietor of that mark to place on the market shapes of goods constituting a real alternative, that is to say, shapes which are not similar and which are nevertheless attractive to the consumer from a functional perspective.

Another argument put forward by Lego was that the 'essential characteristics' of a shape should be understood as meaning its 'dominant and distinctive elements' and that these should be identified from the perspective of the average consumer. Only once these have been identified by the average consumer, should experts be asked whether they are necessary to obtain a technical result. Both Megabrands and the OHIM disagreed, the latter maintaining that both the identification of essential elements and determining whether they are essential for the function of the shape are part of the same exercise. The CJEU agreed. Identification should be made not by the average consumer but by the relevant authority carrying out the assessment on a case-by-case basis, considering either the overall impression produced by the sign or each of its components. Such an assessment could take into account surveys, expert opinions, or other relevant data if necessary. It concluded that on this criteria the General Court was correct to find that all the elements of the Lego brick shape, except for its colour, were functional. In rejecting Lego's appeal, the CJEU confirmed that the general purpose of the prohibition against the registration of functional shapes is to stimulate healthy competition. Such competition would be inhibited if a trader could continue to monopolize a functional shape once its patent or design protection had expired. This is especially true because the length of protection for both patents and designs is limited, whereas for trade marks it is open-ended.

Lego looked at signs which were necessary to obtain a technical result. In *Hauck v Stokke*, the CJEU considered the first and third exclusions under Article 3(1)(e): shapes which consist exclusively of the nature of the goods themselves and shapes which give substantial value to the goods.

Hauck GmbH & Co. KG v Stokke A/S and other Case C-205/13 [2014] ETMR 60

Hauck applied for the annulment of Stokke's 1998 Benelux trade mark registration for a three-dimensional shape of a children's chair. The chair was called the 'Tripp Trapp'. Its design, which was acknowledged to have a high level of originality, had won a number of prizes. Hauck, which also marketed children's chairs, claimed that the trade mark was invalid on the grounds that the shape of the chair was determined by the nature of the product, in that it was a safe, reliable, children's chair and that its attractive appearance gave it substantial value. Hauck succeeded in the Dutch Court of Appeal and Stokke appealed. The Dutch court addressed a number of questions to the CJEU. One concerned the first exclusion under Article 3(1)(e) of the TMD: whether a shape resulted from the nature of the goods. The Dutch court asked whether the exclusion should be interpreted to mean that the ground for refusal refers only to a sign which consists exclusively of a shape which is indispensable to the function of the product in question. Or whether it also applies to a sign which consists exclusively of a shape which has one or more characteristics which are essential to the function of the product, which consumers may look for in the products of competitors. In answer, the CJEU began by considering the rationale behind the second exclusion under Article 3(1)(e) which, following *Philips* and *Lego*, was to prevent trade mark protection granting a monopoly on technical solutions or functional aspects of a product. It held that this same rationale applied to all three exclusions under Article 3(1)(e). It then considered the breadth of the first exclusion.

22 In that regard, it must be emphasised that the ground for refusal of registration set out in the first indent of article 3(1)(e) of the Trade Marks Directive cannot be applicable where the trade mark application relates to a shape of goods in which another element, such as a decorative or imaginative element, which is not inherent to the generic function of the goods, plays an important or essential role: see the *Lego Juris* case, paras 52 and 72.

23 Thus, an interpretation of the first indent of that provision whereby that indent is to apply only to signs which consist exclusively of shapes which are indispensable to the function of the goods in question, leaving the producer of those goods no leeway to make a

personal essential contribution, would not allow the objective of the ground for refusal set out therein to be fully realised.

24 Indeed, an interpretation to that effect would result in limiting the products to which that ground for refusal could apply to (i) 'natural' products (which have no substitute) and (ii) 'regulated' products (the shape of which is prescribed by legal standards), even though signs consisting of the shapes formed by such products could not be registered in any event because of their lack of distinctive character.

25 Instead, when applying the ground for refusal set out in the first indent of article 3(1)(e) of the Trade Marks Directive, account should be taken of the fact that the concept of a 'shape which results from the nature of the goods themselves' means that shapes with essential characteristics which are inherent to the generic function or functions of such goods must, in principle, also be denied registration.

26 As the Advocate General indicated in point 58 of his opinion, reserving such characteristics to a single economic operator would make it difficult for competing undertakings to give their goods a shape which would be suited to the use for which those goods are intended. Moreover, it is clear that those are essential characteristics which consumers will be looking for in the products of competitors, given that they are intended to perform an identical or similar function.

27 Consequently, the answer to the first question is that the first indent of article 3(1)(e) of the Trade Marks Directive must be interpreted as meaning that the ground for refusal of registration set out in that provision may apply to a sign which consists exclusively of the shape of a product with one or more essential characteristics which are inherent to the generic function or functions of that product and which consumers may be looking for in the products of competitors.

The second question addressed to the CJEU concerned shapes which give substantial value to the goods. The Dutch court asked whether this exclusion should be interpreted to cover not just the aesthetic aspects of a sign but also functional elements. According to the CJEU:

29 It can be seen from the order for reference that the doubts expressed by the referring court regarding the interpretation of that provision stem from the fact that, according to that court, although the shape of the 'Tripp Trapp' chair gives it significant aesthetic value, at the same time it has other characteristics (safety, comfort and reliability) which give it essential functional value.

30 In that regard, the fact that the shape of a product is regarded as giving substantial value to that product does not mean that other characteristics may not also give the product significant value.

31 Thus, the aim of preventing the exclusive and permanent right which a trade mark confers from serving to extend indefinitely the life of other rights which the EU legislature has sought to make subject to limited periods requires—as the Advocate General observed in point 85 of his opinion—that the possibility of applying the third indent of article 3(1)(e) of the Trade Marks Directive not be automatically ruled out when, in addition to its aesthetic function, the product concerned also performs other essential functions.

32 Indeed, the concept of a 'shape which gives substantial value to the goods' cannot be limited purely to the shape of products having only artistic or ornamental value, as there

is otherwise a risk that products which have essential functional characteristics as well as a significant aesthetic element will not be covered. In that case, the right conferred by the trade mark on its proprietor would grant that proprietor a monopoly on the essential characteristics of such products, which would not allow the objective of that ground for refusal to be fully realised.

On the related question whether the views of the average consumer are decisive in deciding if a shape gives substantial value, the CJEU followed its ruling in *Lego* and held that they were not.[70] It was a question for the relevant authority which could also take into account a variety of further evidence such as the nature of the goods concerned, the shape's artistic value, and its dissimilarity to other shapes in common use in the relevant market. The Court then turned to a third question which was whether the three exclusions under Article 3(1)(e) can be applied in combination in order to prevent a sign from being registered. According to the CJEU:

39 ...[T]he three grounds for refusal of registration set out in that provision operate independently of one another: the fact that they are set out as successive points, coupled with the use of the word 'exclusively', shows that each of those grounds must be applied independently of the others.

40 Thus, if any one of the criteria listed in article 3(1)(e) of the Trade Marks Directive is satisfied, a sign consisting exclusively of the shape of the product or of a graphic representation of that shape cannot be registered as a trade mark: the *Koninklijke Philips case* [2003] Ch 159, para 76, and *Benetton Group SpA v G-Star International BV* (Case C-371/06) [2007] ECR I-7709, para 26, third indent.

41 In that regard, the fact that the sign in question could be denied registration on the basis of a number of grounds for refusal is irrelevant so long as any one of those grounds fully applies to that sign.

42 In addition, it must be pointed out that—as the Advocate General indicated in point 99 of his opinion—the public interest objective underlying the application of the three grounds for refusal of registration set out in article 3(1)(e) of the Trade Marks Directive precludes refusal of registration where none of those three grounds is fully applicable.

43 In those circumstances, the answer to the third question is that article 3(1)(e) of the Trade Marks Directive must be interpreted as meaning that the grounds for refusal of registration set out in the first and third indents of that provision may not be applied in combination.

Recently, in *Société des Produits Nestlé SA v Cadbury UK Ltd* which, as we have seen, concerned an attempt by Nestlé to register the shape of the iconic four-fingered 'KitKat' chocolate bar, the CJEU was asked whether when a shape consists of three essential features, one of which results from the nature of the goods themselves and two of which are necessary to obtain a technical result, it is precluded from registration under Article 3(1)(e)(i) of the TMD. The Court held that at least one of the grounds for refusal of registration set out in that provision must be fully applicable to the shape at issue for registration to be refused. Also in *Nestlé*, the CJEU held that Article 3(1)(e) should not be interpreted to preclude the registration of shapes which are necessary to obtain a technical result with regard to the manner in which they are manufactured rather than the manner in which they function. More recently,

[70] [35].

the CJEU has been asked whether the exclusion under Article 3(1)(e)(iii) can include two-dimensional characteristics, in this case a colour, rather than only three-dimensional shapes. At issue are the famous red soles which characterize Louboutin shoes. The question for the Court is whether the red soles are a figurative mark, rather than either a shape or a colour or a hybrid of both.[71]

What may be surprising about the *Lego* and *Hauck* cases is precisely the fact that, although functional, both shapes at issue had a very high degree of distinctiveness. The outcome of these cases underlines the fact that under the directive (and the EUTM Regulation), there are times when freedom of competition will be deemed to outweigh the need to protect a trader's substantial and long-term investment in making its sign distinctive. It may also be argued that the addition by the TMD 2016 of 'another characteristic' to the exclusion previously confined to the shape of goods may have a similar balancing effect. We have seen that the removal of the requirement for graphic representation may make it easier to register unconventional signs such as smells and sounds. Might not this new exclusion ensure that any attempt to register these and other unconventional attributes of a product will continue to face substantial checks?

6.3.4.3 Other grounds for the refusal of registration

Article 3 of the TMD[72] identifies a number of further signs that will not be registered, of which the most significant are the following:

(1) Article 3(1)(f) (section 3(3)(a) of the TMA): trade marks which are contrary to public policy or to accepted principles of morality;

(2) Article 3(1)(g) (section 3(3)(b) of the TMA): trade marks which are of such a nature as to deceive the public, for instance as to the nature, quality, or geographical origin of the goods or service;

(3) Article 3(2)(d) (section 3(6) of the TMA): trade marks for which the application is made in bad faith.

6.3.4.4 Marks contrary to public policy or morality

These may, of course, vary widely over time, as social mores change. The general standard against which such signs will be judged was set out by the Appointed Person in *French Connection*.

French Connection Ltd's Trade Mark Application [2007] ETMR 8

The proprietor had a trade mark for the word 'FCUK' for a variety of goods, including watches and jewellery. A Mr Woodman applied for a declaration of invalidity on the basis that the mark was contrary to accepted principles of morality. According to the Appointed Person:

60 ... (1) The applicability of section 3(3)(a) depends on the intrinsic qualities of the mark itself and not on circumstances relating to the conduct of the applicant.

---

[71] *Louboutin SAS v Van Haren Schoenen BV* [2016] (C-163/16) OJ C211/39.   [72] TMD 2016, Art. 4.

...

(3) Section 3(3)(a) should be interpreted and applied consistently with Article 10 ECHR. It follows that registration should be refused only where this is justified by a pressing social need and is proportionate to the legitimate aim pursued. Furthermore, any real doubt as to the applicability of the objection should be resolved by upholding the right to freedom of expression and thus by permitting the registration.

(4) Section 3(3)(a) must be objectively applied. The personal views of the tribunal are irrelevant.

(5) While section 3(3)(a) may apply to a mark whose use would not be illegal, the legality or otherwise of use of the mark is a relevant consideration.

(6) For section 3(3)(a) to apply, there must be a generally accepted moral principle which use of the mark would plainly contravene.

(7) Mere offence to a section of the public, in the sense that that section of the public would consider the mark distasteful, is not enough for section 3(3)(a) to apply.

(8) Section 3(3)(a) does apply if the use of the mark would justifiably cause outrage, or would be the subject of justifiable censure, amongst an identifiable section of the public as being likely significantly to undermine current religious, family or social values.

(9) In the case of a word mark, it is necessary to consider the applicability of section 3(3)(a) on the basis of any usage that the public makes of the word or words of which the mark is comprised. Thus the slang meaning of a word may lead to an objection even if its normal meaning does not.

(10) A mark which does not proclaim an opinion, or contain an incitement or convey an insult is less likely to be objectionable than one that does.

The Appointed Officer ruled against a declaration of invalidity. Among the grounds for so doing was his finding that FCUK was not a swear word as such, although it could be used in that way, nor was there any evidence that its extensive use had caused significant public offence. Further clarification of Article 3(3)(f)[73] was given at the EU level in *Dennis Nazir v George V Entertainment (SA) (BUDDHA-BAR)*, 16 February 2011. The Cancellation Division of the EU IPO noted that:

(14) A judicious application of Article 7(1)(f) CTMR necessarily entails balancing the right of traders to freely employ words and images in the signs they wish to register as trade marks against the right of the public not to be confronted with disturbing, abusive, insulting and even threatening trade marks. In deciding whether a trade mark should be barred from registration on grounds of public policy or morality, the Office must apply the standards of a reasonable person with normal levels of sensitivity and tolerance. The Office should not refuse to register a trade mark which is only likely to offend a small minority of exceptionally puritanical citizens. It is necessary to consider the context in which the mark is likely to be encountered, assuming normal use of the mark in connection with the goods covered by the registration ('SCREW YOU', *loc. cit.*,[74] paragraph 21).

---

[73] Art. 7(1)(f) Reg.
[74] *Kenneth (t/a Screw You)'s Community Trade Mark Application* Case R495/2005 G [2007] ETMR7.

If FCUK was deemed to be acceptable as a trade mark in the UK, applications have been refused for 'Tiny Penis'[75] and 'Jesus'[76] for clothes. In the European context, the General Court upheld the decision not to allow registration of the coat of arms of the former USSR, that is the hammer and sickle, as a EUTM for clothing on the grounds that it was a symbol of oppression and would cause outrage to a significant number of people, particularly but not exclusively in Hungary where the Soviet emblem was legally identified as a 'symbol of despotism' and its use contrary to public policy.[77] We might argue the refusal to register marks on the basis of what is in effect a subjective judgment of the authorities potentially inhibits free speech. However, it is of course also the case that because a sign is not allowed registration as a trade mark does not mean it cannot be used freely in other contexts, a point made by the Appointed Person in the 'FCUK' decision.

6.3.4.5 Deceptive marks

Trade marks may be found to be deceptive if they mislead the public as to the quality of the goods to which they attach. The standard necessary for deception, according to the CJEU in *Consorzio per la tutela del formaggio Gorgonzola*,[78] is that there is 'the existence of actual deceit or a sufficiently serious risk that the consumer will be deceived'. The CJEU looked at the question of deceptive marks in *Emanuel v Continental Shelf*.

Elizabeth Florence Emanuel v Continental Shelf 128 Ltd Case C-259/04 [2006] ECR I-3089

The fashion designer, Elizabeth Emanuel, who designed Princess Diana's wedding dress, registered the mark 'Elizabeth Emanuel' in 1997. She then sold her business to a third party and assigned the trade mark to them. She was also employed by them, but subsequently left. The third party then assigned the business on to Continental Shelf who sought to register a further trade mark, 'Elizabeth Emanuel'. Elizabeth Emanuel opposed the registration on the basis that it would be deceptive of the origin of the goods. Among the questions referred to the CJEU by the Appointed Person was the following: should a trade mark be refused registration because it is deceptive where the goodwill associated with that mark has been assigned together with the business making the goods to which the mark relates and that trade mark, which corresponds to the name of the designer and first manufacturer of those goods, was previously registered in a different graphic form. The CJEU found that such a registration would not be deceptive.

> 45. A trade mark such as 'ELIZABETH EMANUEL' may have that function of distinguishing the goods manufactured by an undertaking, particularly where that trade mark has been assigned to that undertaking and the undertaking manufactures the same type of goods as those which initially bore the trade mark in question.

---

[75] *Ghazilian's Trade Mark Application* [2002] ETMR 56.

[76] *Basic Trade Mark SA's Trade Mark Application* [2006] ETMR 24.

[77] *Couture Tech Ltd v OHIM* Case T-232/10 [2012] ETR 5. See also *Pooja Sweets & Savouries Ltd v Pooja Sweets Ltd* (O-195-15), Appointed Person, 9 February 2015.

[78] *Consorzio per la tutela del formaggio Gorgonzola v Käserei Champignon Hofmeister GmbH & Co. KG* Case C-87/97 [1999] ECR I-1301.

46. ... [I]n the case of a trade mark corresponding to the name of a person, the public interest ground which justifies the prohibition laid down by Art. 3(1)(g) of Directive 89/104 to register a trade mark which is liable to deceive the public, namely consumer protection, must raise the question of the risk of confusion which such a trade mark may engender in the mind of the average consumer, especially where the person to whose name the mark corresponds originally personified the goods bearing that mark.

47. Nevertheless, the circumstances for refusing registration referred to in Art. 3(1)(g) of Directive 89/104 presuppose the existence of actual deceit or a sufficiently serious risk that the consumer will be deceived (Case C-87/97) *Consorzio per la tutela del formaggio Gorgonzola* [1999] ECR I-1301 at paragraph 41).

48. In the present case, even if the average consumer might be influenced in his act of purchasing a garment bearing the trade mark 'ELIZABETH EMANUEL' by imagining that the appellant in the main proceedings was involved in the design of that garment, the characteristics and the qualities of that garment remain guaranteed by the undertaking which owns the trade mark.

49. Consequently, the name Elizabeth Emanuel cannot be regarded in itself as being of such a nature as to deceive the public as to the nature, quality or geographical origin of the product it designates.

It is submitted that the CJEU was correct in this approach. It would be difficult to see how a business could be assigned together with its trade mark if subsequent use of the trade mark, by the party that had acquired it, was found to be deceptive. However, others might argue that the average consumer when purchasing a gown with the label 'Elizabeth Emanuel' would assume that the gown, like Princess Diana's wedding dress, was designed by Elizabeth Emanuel herself.

6.3.4.6 Trade marks registered in bad faith

The most common circumstances in which a trade mark may be registered in bad faith are those instances where the applicant does not intend to use the trade mark or where there are better third party rights to the mark.[79] Where the applicant does not intend to use his mark against all the goods and services for which it is registered, the courts have not generally made a finding of bad faith.[80] In *Harrison's Trade Mark Application*[81] in the Court of Appeal, Aldous LJ defined bad faith as where the applicant's actions fall below the standard of acceptable commercial behaviour observed by reasonable and experienced persons in the particular commercial area being examined. The bar against registrations in bad faith was further considered by the CJEU in the *Lindt* case.

Chocoladefabriken Lindt & Sprüngli AG v Franz Hauswirth GmbH
Case C-529/07 [2009] ETMR 56

Chocolate bunnies have been marketed in Austria and Germany since 1930. Since the 1950s, Lindt has produced and marketed a chocolate bunny in Austria. In 2000,

---

[79] See e.g. *Ferrero SpA's Trade Marks* [2004] RPC 29.
[80] *Knoll AG's Trade Mark* [2003] EWHC 899.   [81] [2005] FSR 10.

Lindt became the proprietor of a three-dimensional mark representing a gold-coloured chocolate bunny, with a red ribbon and a bell, for chocolate and chocolate products carrying the words 'Lindt GOLDHASE'. Hauswirth has marketed chocolate bunnies in Austria since 1962 of a similar shape and colour. After the registration of the mark, Lindt began proceedings against Hauswirth for trade mark infringement. In turn, Hauswirth argued that Lindt was acting in bad faith when it registered its mark. Hauswirth offered two reasons for this claim. First, it argued that when Lindt applied to register the mark Lindt knew that Hauswirth was already using a same or similar sign in a Member State and that its motive was to stop Hauswirth from continuing to do so. Alternatively, Hauswirth argued that Lindt acted in bad faith when it applied to register its mark, because it was aware that Hauswirth had acquired a prior right to use a same or similar mark in Austria. The CJEU identified some of the factors which might determine whether an applicant was acting in bad faith under Article 5(1)(b) of the EUTM Regulation.[82]

46 Equally, the fact a third party has long used a sign for an identical or similar product capable of being confused with the mark applied for and that that sign enjoys some degree of legal protection is one of the factors relevant to the determination of whether the applicant was acting in bad faith.

47 In such a case, the applicant's sole aim in taking advantage of the rights conferred by the Community trade mark might be to compete unfairly with a competitor who is using a sign which, because of characteristics of its own, has by that time obtained some degree of legal protection.

48 That said, it cannot however be excluded that even in such circumstances, and in particular when several producers were using, on the market, identical or similar signs for identical or similar products capable of being confused with the sign for which registration is sought, the applicant's registration of the sign may be in pursuit of a legitimate objective.

49 That may in particular be the case, as stated by the Advocate General in point 67 of her Opinion, where the applicant knows, when filing the application for registration, that a third party, who is a newcomer in the market, is trying to take advantage of that sign by copying its presentation, and the applicant seeks to register the sign with a view to preventing use of that presentation.

50 Moreover, as the Advocate General states in point 66 of her Opinion, the nature of the mark applied for may also be relevant to determining whether the applicant is acting in bad faith. In a case where the sign for which registration is sought consists of the entire shape and presentation of a product, the fact that the applicant is acting in bad faith might more readily be established where the competitors' freedom to choose the shape of a product and its presentation is restricted by technical or commercial factors, so that the trade mark proprietor is able to prevent his competitors not merely from using an identical or similar sign, but also from marketing comparable products.

51 Furthermore, in order to determine whether the applicant is acting in bad faith, consideration may be given to the extent of the reputation enjoyed by a sign at the time when the application for its registration as a Community trade mark is filed.

---

[82] TMA, s. 3(6); TMD, Art. 3(2)(d).

> 52 The extent of that reputation might justify the applicant's interest in ensuring a wider legal protection for his sign.
>
> 53 Having regard to all of the foregoing, the answer to the questions referred is that, in order to determine whether the applicant is acting in bad faith within the meaning of art.51(1)(b) of Regulation No.40/94, the national court must take into consideration all the relevant factors specific to the particular case which pertained at the time of filing the application for registration of the sign as a Community trade mark, in particular:
>
> – the fact that the applicant knows or must know that a third party is using, in at least one Member State, an identical or similar sign for an identical or similar product capable of being confused with the sign for which registration is sought;
>
> – the applicant's intention to prevent that third party from continuing to use such a sign; and
>
> – the degree of legal protection enjoyed by the third party's sign and by the sign for which registration is sought.

In fact, Lindt did not lose its EUTM registration subsequent to this case and, in 2011, an Austrian court ruled that Hauswirth could no longer sell its gold, bunny-shaped chocolate. Ironically, when Lindt sought to register more recently the same three-dimensional sign as a EUTM but without the words 'Lindt GOLDHASE' on the packaging, its application was refused by the EU IPO because the sign was deemed to lack distinctiveness, given the large number of gold-wrapped chocolate bunnies also on the market in the EU.[83]

The bar against the registration of marks in bad faith would appear to be directed at protecting the public interest in ensuring that there is fair competition between traders. By contrast, the bar against the registration of deceptive marks is obviously relevant to a different but no less important concern, that of ensuring that the essential function of the mark is maintained and that it continues to act as a badge of origin for the benefit of consumers.

6.3.4.7 The absolute grounds for refusal of registration: a summary

As we have seen, some of the categories of signs identified in Article 3(1) may be registered with evidence of acquired distinctiveness. Others may not be registered under any circumstances. Annette Kur, in her discussion of trade mark protection given to product shapes, sets out the public interest behind these latter exclusions.

A. Kur, 'Too common, too splendid, or "just right"?: trade mark protection for product shapes', Max Planck Institute for Innovation and Competition Research Paper No. 14-17 (2014), pp. 1–2

1. Introduction

The option to protect shapes as marks designating the goods they incorporate is not easily reconciled with the basic structure of intellectual property (IP) law. As a general maxim

---

[83] *Chocoladefabriken Lindt v OHIM* Case C-98/11 P, 24 May 2012.

governing the interface of intellectual property and freedom of competition it is postulated that to prohibit competition by imitation of goods embodying creative or inventive achievements is necessary to incentivize competition, but that the market exclusivity thus granted shall only last for a limited period of time, upon the lapse of which copying shall be permitted. Trade marks, on the other hand, are not captured by that scheme, and can therefore be protected without fixed limits in time: As marks are not destined to protect commercial achievements as such, but only serve to indicate their commercial origin so as to channel the flow of revenues procured on the market back to their proper commercial source, they are not considered as interfering with competition on the production level: as a matter of principle (and absent protection under other IP rights), competitors are free to offer exactly the same product, if only they use a different mark for indicating origin.

This scheme is disrupted when trade marks and the goods they designate are so closely intertwined that one cannot be protected without also ensuring market exclusivity of the other, meaning that the product necessarily shares the 'eternal' protection granted to the mark. Trade mark protection for the shape of goods therefore inevitably results in an irregular feature being added to the systemic pattern of legal protection for IP rights.

On the other hand, this is no cogent reason to deny protection as a matter of principle. After all, protection will only be obtained if shapes, in addition to being perceived as goods of a particular kind, description and utility, are recognized by consumers as a badge of origin and are thus able to fulfill genuine trade mark functions. If protection was denied and the shape were free for everyone to copy this might result in the public being misled as to the commercial origin of the imitations. Furthermore, although protection is not finite in time, the mark will only maintain its protection if and as long as it is genuinely used as a mark in commerce. Finally and most importantly, the principle that products should not enjoy market exclusivity for an unlimited time is not an end in itself, but reflects the public interest in maintaining meaningful and efficient competition in the production of goods. As long as that interest is sufficiently safeguarded by other means than a strict enforcement of the rule that protection must end after a certain time period, there is no predominant harm in trade mark protection per se.

Kur suggests that there is a balance to be struck between the public interest in rewarding the investment proprietors may make in nurturing the distinctiveness of their marks and in protecting consumers against confusion and the public interest in limiting the protection given to shape of goods marks. As we have seen, the CJEU has consistently sought, in interpreting the absolute grounds for refusal of registration, to find an acceptable balance between the two. We have also seen that at times this balance has shifted. We might take the view that the CJEU has achieved a fair compromise between these competing claims. But we should also be aware that it is possible for that balance to shift again. This is particularly the case as the new directive introduces new parameters for protection.

FURTHER READING

L. Brancusi, 'Designs determined by the product's technical function: arguments for an autonomous test' [2016] EIPR 23.

N. M. Dawson, 'Bad faith in European trade mark law' [2011] IPQ 229.

C. Howell, 'Trade marks, registered designs and the monopolisation of functional shapes: a consideration of *Lego* and *Dyson*' [2011] EIPR 60.

J. Hunter and J. Thomas, 'Lego and the system of intellectual property, 1955–2015' [2016] IPQ 1.

A. Santani, 'Trade marks that are contrary to public policy or morality: the search for the right thinking man' [2012] IPQ 39.

I. Simon Fhima, 'Trade marks and free speech' (2013) 44 IIC 293.

TRADE MARKS II:

THE RELATIVE GROUNDS FOR REFUSAL OF REGISTRATION, INFRINGEMENT, AND REMEDIES

7.1 THE RELATIVE GROUNDS FOR REFUSAL OF REGISTRATION

7.1.1 INTRODUCTION

The previous chapter was concerned with those signs which might be registered as trade marks and those signs which, in the public interest, should be left free for others to use or registered only with acquired distinctiveness. The first section of this chapter will examine the relative grounds for refusal of registration. The second section will look at the rights conferred by registration, most notably, the right to act against infringers. In considering the scope of protection afforded to trade marks, the CJEU has had to consider the extent to which the functions of a trade mark might extend beyond that of acting as a badge of origin. In the previous chapter, we saw that the Court has identified these additional functions as including: communication, investment, and advertising functions. In this chapter we shall see that a key question for the courts has been the extent to which these functions should not only be recognized but also protected, particularly against unauthorized third party use.

7.1.2 ARTICLE 4

Article 4 of the Trade Marks Directive (TMD)[1] (Article 5 of the TMD 2016) identifies the circumstances in which the proprietor of a registered trade mark (or the owner of an earlier right) may prevent the registration of a later sign. Article 4 thus defines the penumbra of protection which is endowed on a trade mark by registration. The grounds for finding a conflict at the time

---

[1] Its equivalent in English law is the Trade Marks Act 1994 (TMA), s. 5; TMD 2016, Art. 5.

of registration are the same as the grounds for a finding of infringement. The provisions of the directive dealing with infringement will be examined later in this chapter. Nonetheless, when discussing the relative grounds for refusal of registration, we shall have considerable recourse to judgments which have turned upon whether an earlier registered mark has been infringed. In the same way, we shall see later that interpretations of the infringement provisions of the directive frequently derive from judgments relating to conflict at the time of registration.

7.1.3 ARTICLE 4(1): CONFUSION AS TO ORIGIN

Article 4(1)[2] reads as follows:

> a trade mark shall not be registered or, if registered, shall be liable to be declared invalid:
>
> a. if it is identical with an earlier trade mark, and the goods or services for which the trade mark is applied for or is registered are identical with the goods or services for which the earlier trade mark is protected.
>
> b. if because of its identity with, or similarity to the earlier trade mark and the identity or similarity of the goods or services covered by the trade marks, there exists a likelihood of confusion on the part of the public, which includes the likelihood of association with the earlier trade mark.

Article 4(2)[3] defines earlier trade marks as including EU trade marks, trade marks already registered in the Member State or in a Member State via the Madrid Protocol, and well-known marks as defined under Article 6*bis* of the Paris Convention.

Article 4(4)[4] (Article 5(4)) adds other grounds for conflict, both at the registration stage and in relation to infringement which were optional for Member States to recognize. The most important are the following:

> a. the trade mark is identical with, or similar to, an earlier national trade mark within the meaning of paragraph 2 and is to be, or has been, registered for goods or services which are not similar to those for which the earlier trade mark is registered, where the earlier trade mark has a reputation in the Member State concerned and where the use of the later trade mark without due cause would take unfair advantage of, or be detrimental to the distinctive character or the repute of the earlier trade mark
>
> b. rights to a non-registered trade mark or to another sign used in the course of trade were acquired prior to the date of application for registration of the subsequent trade mark, or the date of the priority claimed for the application for registration of the subsequent trade mark and the non-registered trade mark or other sign confers on its proprietor the right to prohibit the use of the subsequent trade mark
>
> c. the use of the trade mark may be prohibited by virtue of an earlier right other than the rights referred to in paragraphs 2 and 4(b) and in particular:
>
> (i) a right to a name;
>
> (ii) a right of personal portrayal;
>
> (iii) a copyright;
>
> (iv) an industrial property right.

---

[2] The equivalent provisions in the TMA are s. 5(1) and s. 5(2)(a)–(b); TMD 2016, Art. 5(1).
[3] TMA, s. 6(1); TMD 2016, Art. 5(2).   [4] TMA, s. 5(4); TMD 2016, Art. 5(4).

The UK has chosen to incorporate these provisions into the TMA. Thus section 5(4) of the TMA refuses registration to a mark whose use is liable to be prevented either by virtue of any rule of law (in particular, the law of passing off) protecting an unregistered trade mark or other sign used in the course of trade (section 5(4)(a)) or by virtue of an earlier right (section 5(4)(b)). The latter would include a copyright or a patent, but not a right of personality which does not exist in the UK.[5] Under the TMD 2016, the protection offered by Article 4(4)(a) is no longer optional for Member States.[6]

7.1.3.1 Article 4(1)(a) (section 5(1)(a) of the TMA; Article 5(1)(a) of the TMD 2016): identical marks on identical goods

In this case, the later sign will be refused registration, without the necessity of proving that the public would be confused if both marks are on the Register. The CJEU considered when marks should be considered identical for the purposes of conflict in the case *LTJ Diffusion v SA Sadas*.[7]

LTJ Diffusion v SA Sadas Case C -291/000 [2003] ECR I-2799

50. The criterion of identity of the sign and the trade mark must be interpreted strictly. The very definition of identity implies that the two elements compared should be the same in all respects...

51. There is therefore identity between the sign and the trade mark where the former reproduces, without any modification or addition, all the elements constituting the latter.

52. However, the perception of identity between the sign and the trade mark must be assessed globally with respect to an average consumer who is deemed to be reasonably well informed, reasonably observant and circumspect. The sign produces an overall impression on such a consumer. That consumer only rarely has the chance to make a direct comparison between signs and trade marks and must place his trust in the imperfect picture of them that he has kept in his mind. Moreover, his level of attention is likely to vary according to the category of goods or services in question (see, to that effect, Case C- 342/97 *Lloyd Schuhfabrik Meyer* [1999] ECR I-3819, para. 26).

53. Since the perception of identity between the sign and the trade mark is not the result of a direct comparison of all the characteristics of the elements compared, insignificant differences between the sign and the trade mark may go unnoticed by an average consumer.

54. In those circumstances, the answer to the question referred must be that Art. 5(1)(a) of the directive must be interpreted as meaning that a sign is identical with the trade mark where it reproduces, without any modification or addition, all the elements constituting the trade mark or where, viewed as a whole, it contains differences so insignificant that they may go unnoticed by an average consumer.

There is rather less case law which relates specifically to whether the goods or services are identical for the purposes of Article 4(1)(a). Instead, the question of whether goods or

---

[5] See Chapter 10 on character merchandising and publicity rights.   [6] TMD 2016, Art. 5(3)(a).
[7] This case arose out of an infringement action and therefore addressed the meaning of Art. 5(1)(a).

services are similar or identical has been addressed more frequently in cases concerned with Article 4(1)(b) of the directive, which covers, inter alia, similar marks on similar goods or services. It is to the interpretation of this provision that we now turn.

7.1.3.2 Article 4(1)(b) (section 5(2)(a)–(b) of the TMA; Article 5(1)(b) of the TMD 2016): identical or similar signs on identical or similar goods or services and the proviso

There are three elements which must be proved for conflict to arise under Article 4(1)(b). First, the earlier registered mark and the later sign must be identical or similar. Second, the goods must be identical or similar. If both these conditions obtain, then conflict between the earlier registered mark and the sign will still only arise if, third, the proviso applies and there exists a likelihood of confusion on the part of the public, which includes the likelihood of association with the earlier trade mark. In a succession of cases following the implementation of the directive, beginning with the judgment in *Sabel v Puma*,[8] the CJEU has made clear that all these conditions are interdependent. It has developed what has become known as 'the global approach' for assessing conflict under Article 4(1)(b).

Sabel BV v Puma AG and Rudolf Dassler Sport Case C-251/95 [1998] ECR I-6191

The applicant sought to register a mark consisting of a 'leaping cat' device together with the word 'Sabel' in Germany for a variety of goods in classes 19 and 25, including clothing and leather goods. The application was opposed by the proprietors of two German registered trade marks, each of which featured a 'leaping cat' device that was also registered for clothing and leather goods. Since the marks were clearly not identical, the application therefore fell to be decided under Article 4(1)(b). The German court asked the CJEU first whether it was sufficient for a finding of conflict that there is a likelihood of confusion between a sign composed of text and a picture and a sign consisting merely of a picture, which is registered for identical and similar goods and is not especially well known to the public, where the two signs coincide as to their semantic content (in this case, a bounding feline) and second whether, in relation to this connection, does the likelihood of confusion include the likelihood that a mark may be associated with an earlier mark? The CJEU first set out the differing views of the Member States. It summarized the broad view of trade mark protection taken by the Benelux countries and then set out its own interpretation of the proviso.

> 18. In that connection, it is to be remembered that Article 4(1)(b) of the Directive is designed to apply only if, by reason of the identity or similarity both of the marks and of the goods or services which they designate, 'there exists a likelihood of confusion on the part of the public, which includes the likelihood of association with the earlier trade mark'. It follows from that wording that the concept of likelihood of association is not an alternative to that of likelihood of confusion, but serves to define its scope. The terms of the provision itself exclude its application where there is no likelihood of confusion on the part of the public.
>
> ...

---

[8] *Sabel BV v Puma AG and Rudolf Dassler Sport* Case C-251/95 [1998] ECR I-6191.

22. As pointed out in paragraph 18 of this judgment, Article 4(1)(b) of the Directive does not apply where there is no likelihood of confusion on the part of the public. In that respect, it is clear from the tenth recital in the preamble to the Directive that the appreciation of the likelihood of confusion 'depends on numerous elements and, in particular, on the recognition of the trade mark on the market, of the association which can be made with the used or registered sign, of the degree of similarity between the trade mark and the sign and between the goods or services identified'. The likelihood of confusion must therefore be appreciated globally, taking into account all factors relevant to the circumstances of the case.

23. That global appreciation of the visual, aural or conceptual similarity of the marks in question, must be based on the overall impression given by the marks, bearing in mind, in particular, their distinctive and dominant components. The wording of Article 4(1)(b) of the Directive—'...there exists a likelihood of confusion on the part of the public...'—shows that the perception of marks in the mind of the average consumer of the type of goods or services in question plays a decisive role in the global appreciation of the likelihood of confusion. The average consumer normally perceives a mark as a whole and does not proceed to analyse its various details.

24. In that perspective, the more distinctive the earlier mark, the greater will be the likelihood of confusion. It is therefore not impossible that the conceptual similarity resulting from the fact that two marks use images with analogous semantic content may give rise to a likelihood of confusion where the earlier mark has a particularly distinctive character, either *per se* or because of the reputation it enjoys with the public.

25. However, in circumstances such as those in point in the main proceedings, where the earlier mark is not especially well known to the public and consists of an image with little imaginative content, the mere fact that the two marks are conceptually similar is not sufficient to give rise to a likelihood of confusion.

26. The answer to the national court's question must therefore be that the criterion of 'likelihood of confusion which includes the likelihood of association with the earlier mark' contained in Article 4(1)(b) of the Directive is to be interpreted as meaning that the mere association which the public might make between two trade marks as a result of their analogous semantic content is not in itself a sufficient ground for concluding that there is a likelihood of confusion within the meaning of that provision.

The CJEU then turned its attention to the circumstances in which marks might be found to be confusingly similar and held that the marks should be viewed through the perspective of the average consumer who will take account of the overall impression created by them. In *Sabel*, the CJEU also made clear that non-origin confusion is a matter for Articles 4(3) and 5(2)[9] of the directive, which are intended to address the issue of dilution when the earlier mark has a 'reputation'. Nonetheless, in *Sabel*, the CJEU did hold that where the earlier mark is particularly distinctive or has a reputation, there would be a greater likelihood that origin confusion will arise. Such a view was confirmed in *Marca Mode CV v Adidas AG*,[10] where the CJEU stated that where it is the case that the earlier mark may be particularly distinctive, such a mark may receive broader protection under Article 4(1)(b) than a mark which is not as distinctive. However, in *Marca Mode*, the CJEU also went on to find that a likelihood of confusion cannot

[9] TMA, ss. 5(3) and 10(3); TMD 2016, Art. 5(3)(b). See 7.1.4.2 for a discussion of the dilution provisions of the directive.
[10] Case C-425/98 [2000] ECR I-4861.

be assumed simply because an earlier mark has a reputation which might give rise to the possibility of it being associated with a later mark. Another factor a court may take into account when assessing the likelihood of confusion is whether, when the mark and the sign are identical, they have been able to 'peacefully coexist' on the market for a sufficient period of time before the application for registration of the latter.[11]

7.1.3.3 Confusingly similar goods and services

In *Sabel*, the CJEU held that it is necessary to take a 'global approach' to finding confusion under Article 4(1)(b). In other words, whether there is confusion under this provision will depend upon the interaction between the distinctiveness of the mark and the similarity of the goods. The global approach was further elaborated by the CJEU in *Canon v MGM* in which the Court addressed the issue of when goods are confusingly similar.[12]

Canon Kabushiki Kaisha v Metro-Goldwyn-Mayer Inc. Case C-39/97
[1998] ECR I-5507

MGM applied to register in Germany the mark 'Cannon' to be used, inter alia, on video film cassettes, production, and distribution of films. The application was opposed by Canon which had a registered trade mark 'Canon' in respect, inter alia, of cameras and projectors. The question before the CJEU was whether, on a proper construction of Article 4(1)(b) of the directive, the distinctive character of the earlier trade mark, and in particular its reputation, must be taken into account when determining whether the similarity between the goods or services covered by the two trade marks is sufficient to give rise to the likelihood of confusion. The CJEU first summarized the global test for conflict which had been set out in *Sabel*. It then went on to consider the issue of the similarity of goods.

> 22. It is, however, important to stress that, for the purposes of applying Article 4(1)(b), even where a mark is identical to another with a highly distinctive character, it is still necessary to adduce evidence of similarity between the goods or services covered.
>
> ...
>
> 23. In assessing the similarity of the goods or services concerned, as the French and United Kingdom Governments and the Commission have pointed out, all the relevant factors relating to those goods or services themselves should be taken into account. Those factors include, *inter alia*, their nature, their end users and their method of use and whether they are in competition with each other or are complementary.
>
> 24. In the light of the foregoing, the answer to be given to the first part of the question must be that, on a proper construction of Article 4(1)(b) of the Directive, the distinctive character of the earlier trade mark, and in particular its reputation, must be taken into account when determining whether the similarity between the goods or services covered by the two trade marks is sufficient to give rise to the likelihood of confusion.

---

[11] *Vimeo LLC v OHIM* Case T-96/14 [2016] ETMR 10.
[12] The question of how to assess the similarity between goods had earlier been considered in the UK in *British Sugar plc v James Robertson & Sons Ltd* [1997] ETMR 118.

7.1.3.4 Summarizing the global approach

In the recent case of *Specsavers v Asda Stores*, Lord Justice Kitchin offered a summary of the global approach to assessing the likelihood of confusion. It suggests the myriad of ways that courts have elaborated upon the global approach since its introduction in *Sabel* and *Canon*.

Specsavers International Healthcare Ltd v Asda Stores Ltd [2012] EWCA Civ 24

Lord Kitchin:

52. On the basis of these and other cases the Trade Marks Registry has developed the following useful and accurate summary of key principles sufficient for the determination of many of the disputes coming before it:

(a) the likelihood of confusion must be appreciated globally, taking account of all relevant factors;

(b) the matter must be judged through the eyes of the average consumer of the goods or services in question, who is deemed to be reasonably well informed and reasonably circumspect and observant, but who rarely has the chance to make direct comparisons between marks and must instead rely upon the imperfect picture of them he has kept in his mind, and whose attention varies according to the category of goods or services in question;

(c) the average consumer normally perceives a mark as a whole and does not proceed to analyse its various details;

(d) the visual, aural and conceptual similarities of the marks must normally be assessed by reference to the overall impressions created by the marks bearing in mind their distinctive and dominant components, but it is only when all other components of a complex mark are negligible that it is permissible to make the comparison solely on the basis of the dominant elements;

(e) nevertheless, the overall impression conveyed to the public by a composite trade mark may, in certain circumstances, be dominated by one or more of its components;

(f) and beyond the usual case, where the overall impression created by a mark depends heavily on the dominant features of the mark, it is quite possible that in a particular case an element corresponding to an earlier trade mark may retain an independent distinctive role in a composite mark, without necessarily constituting a dominant element of that mark;

(g) a lesser degree of similarity between the goods or services may be offset by a greater degree of similarity between the marks, and vice versa;

(h) there is a greater likelihood of confusion where the earlier mark has a highly distinctive character, either per se or because of the use that has been made of it;

(i) mere association, in the strict sense that the later mark brings the earlier mark to mind, is not sufficient;

(j) the reputation of a mark does not give grounds for presuming a likelihood of confusion simply because of a likelihood of association in the strict sense; and

(k) if the association between the marks causes the public to wrongly believe that the respective goods [or services] come from the same or economically-linked undertakings, there is a likelihood of confusion.

It is perhaps worth emphasizing that this summary contains an important limitation to the global approach. Point (j) reflects the decision in *Calvin Klein Trademarks Trust v OHIM*,[13] where the CJEU pointed out that if there is no 'objective' similarity between a mark and a sign, the application of the global approach will not lead to a finding that they are confusingly similar even though the earlier mark has a strong reputation. And, as we shall see below, there are further factors which may be taken into account when assessing the likelihood of confusion in an infringement action, where the allegedly infringing sign is actually being used on the market, rather than when a comparison is being made between a sign and an earlier registered mark for the purposes of registration.

FURTHER READING

I. Fhima and C. Denvir, 'An empirical analysis of the likelihood of confusion factors in European trade mark law' (2015) 47 IIC 310.

A. Griffiths, 'The trade mark monopoly: an analysis of the core zone of absolute protection under Article 5(1)(a)' [2007] IPQ 312.

7.1.4 ARTICLE 4(4)(A): DILUTION, TARNISHMENT, AND TAKING UNFAIR ADVANTAGE

According to Article 4(4)(a),[14] conflict arises between a registered mark and a later sign where the mark and the sign are identical or similar and the goods are similar or dissimilar and the earlier mark has a reputation, plus the proviso applies. We have noted that it was up to Member States to decide whether they wished to adopt Article 4(4)(a) of the TMD although this will not be the case under the TMD 2016. The UK chose to do so. While this provision originally applied only to situations in which the goods concerned were dissimilar, in *Davidoff v Gofkid*,[15] the CJEU ruled that it also applied where the goods were identical or similar. The UK amended the TMA to reflect this decision in 2004. The intent of Article 4(4)(a) is to protect trade marks with a reputation against dilution, tarnishment and the taking of unfair advantage. In *Adidas-Salomon v Fitnessworld*, Advocate General Jacobs offered an excellent summary of the sorts of harm against which Article 4(4)(a) (and Article 5(2) under infringement) is intended to protect.

Adidas-Salomon AG and Adidas Benelux BV v Fitnessworld Trading Ltd
Case C-408/01 [2003] ECR I-12537

36. Article 5(2) protects the proprietor of a mark with a reputation against use of an identical or similar sign where use of that sign without due cause takes unfair advantage of, or is detrimental to, the distinctive character or the repute of the trade mark. There are thus in principle four types of use which may be caught: use which takes unfair advantage of the mark's distinctive character, use which takes unfair advantage of its repute, use which is detrimental to the mark's distinctive character and use which is detrimental to its repute.

---

[13] *Calvin Klein Trademarks Trust v OHIM, Zafra Marroquinros SL* Case C-254/09 P [2011] ETMR 5.
[14] TMA 1994, s. 5(3); TMD 2016, Art. 5(3)(a).
[15] *Davidoff & Cie SA v Gofkid Ltd* Case C-292/00 [2003] ECR I-389.

37. The concept of detriment to the distinctive character of a trade mark reflects what is generally referred to as dilution. That notion was first articulated by Schechter, who advocated protection against injury to a trade mark owner going beyond the injury caused by use of an identical or similar mark in relation to identical or similar goods or services causing confusion as to origin. Schechter described the type of injury with which he was concerned as the 'gradual whittling away or dispersion of the identity and hold upon the public mind' of certain marks. The courts in the United States, where owners of certain marks have been protected against dilution for some time, have added richly to the lexicon of dilution, describing it in terms of lessening, watering down, debilitating, weakening, undermining, blurring, eroding and insidious gnawing away at a trade mark. The essence of dilution in this classic sense is that the blurring of the distinctiveness of the mark means that it is no longer capable of arousing immediate association with the goods for which it is registered and used. Thus, to quote Schechter again:

> for instance, if you allow Rolls Royce restaurants and Rolls Royce cafeterias, and Rolls Royce pants, and Rolls Royce candy, in 10 years you will not have the Rolls Royce mark any more.

38. In contrast, the concept of detriment to the repute of a trade mark, often referred to as degradation or tarnishment of the mark, describes the situation where—as it was put in the well-known *Claeryn/Klarein* decision of the Benelux Court of Justice—the goods for which the infringing sign is used appeal to the public's senses in such a way that the trade mark's power of attraction is affected. That case concerned the identically pronounced marks 'Claeryn' for a Dutch gin and 'Klarein' for a liquid detergent. Since it was found that the similarity between the two marks might cause consumers to think of detergent when drinking 'Claeryn' gin, the 'Klarein' mark was held to infringe the 'Claeryn' mark.

39. The concepts of taking unfair advantage of the distinctive character or repute of the mark in contrast must be intended to encompass instances where there is clear exploitation and free-riding on the coattails of a famous mark or an attempt to trade upon its reputation. Thus by way of example Rolls Royce would be entitled to prevent a manufacturer of whisky from exploiting the reputation of the Rolls Royce mark in order to promote his brand. It is not obvious that there is any real difference between taking advantage of a mark's distinctive character and taking advantage of its repute; since however nothing turns on any such difference in the present case, I shall refer to both as free-riding.

In *Adidas*, the Advocate General identified three types of third party use which may be covered by the proviso to Article 4(4)(a). These are: use which takes unfair advantage of the mark's distinctive character and use which takes unfair advantage of its repute ('free-riding'); use which is detrimental to the mark's distinctive character (blurring); and, finally, use which is detrimental to its repute (tarnishment). It is particularly interesting to note that the Advocate General, in describing these types of injury, refers to the article written by Schechter over half a century ago, which we looked at in the previous chapter.[16] This would appear to suggest that dilution is not a new phenomenon, even if in certain jurisdictions, the UK for example, protection against dilution is. Does it suggest, on the contrary, that what is new is a willingness by a number of European governments, including the UK, to afford broader protection to registered marks, in particular those with a reputation, than has been true in the past?

---

[16] See 6.2.2.

7.1.4.1 The nature of a reputation

The provisions of Article 4(4)(a) are intended to protect marks with a strong advertising function: that is, marks with a 'reputation'. In *General Motors v Yplon*,[17] the CJEU was asked in essence to explain the meaning of 'reputation' for the purpose of Article 5(2) of the directive. In this case, General Motors (GMC) had registered the mark 'Chevy' in the Benelux countries, inter alia, for cars. Yplon had registered the mark 'Chevy' for detergents and cleaning fluids. GMC applied for an order to prevent Yplon using the 'Chevy' mark on the basis that it would damage the value of its own. One question posed to the CJEU was how to assess whether a mark has a reputation. According to the CJEU, first, the public amongst whom the mark must have a reputation will either be the public at large or a more specialized public, depending on the type of product or service concerned. Second, there is no rule that a given percentage of the population must know of the mark. Third, the mark must be known to a significant part of the relevant public. In determining whether it is so known, the national court may take into consideration the relevant facts of the case, including the market share of the mark, and the intensity, geographical extent, and duration of its use and the size of the investment in promoting it. Finally, the CJEU held that it is not necessary for the mark to be known in the whole of the territory concerned (e.g. in this case, the whole of the Benelux) as long as it is known by the public in a substantial part of that territory. Perhaps surprisingly, in *Iron & Smith v Unilever*,[18] the CJEU held that it is sufficient for a EUTM to have a reputation in only one Member State to prevent the use of an identical or similar sign in another. This inevitably raises the question of whether such expansive protection given to a mark with a reputation might overly inhibit market entry within the EU.

7.1.4.2 The meaning of the proviso: dilution and tarnishment

It is interesting to note that thus far there have been no major cases either at the European or domestic level which have looked solely or mainly at tarnishment. In *L'Oréal v Bellure*,[19] the CJEU described the effects of tarnishment:

> ...[T]the trade mark's power of attraction is reduced. The likelihood of such detriment may arise in particular from the fact that the goods or services offered by the third party possess a characteristic or quality which is liable to have a negative impact on the image of the mark.

By contrast, the issue of what constitutes dilution has been extensively canvassed, and judgments of the CJEU have made clear that the general principles which apply to a finding of dilution, similarly apply to a finding of tarnishment.[20] It is thus to dilution that we now turn.

Fundamental to anti-dilution protection is that it protects trade marks with a reputation not against confusion as to origin but rather against the damage which might result if the public 'associates' a later mark or sign with the earlier registered mark. The concept of dilution was introduced into US federal trade mark law by the Federal Trademark Dilution Act 1995,

---

[17] *General Motors Corp. v Yplon SA* Case C-375/97 [1999] ECR I-5421.
[18] *Iron & Smith kft v Unilever NV* Case C-125/14 [2015] ETMR 45.
[19] *L'Oréal SA v Bellure NV* [2006] EWHC 2355 (Ch), [40].
[20] e.g. *Interflora v Marks & Spencer* Case C-323/09 [2012] ETMR 1.

which has now been amended by the Trademark Dilution Revision Act 2006. In 1971, the Benelux Trade Marks Act also appeared to recognize the concept of dilution. Following the passage of the directive, there was general agreement that Article 4(4)(a) was intended to protect trade marks with a reputation from dilution. This understanding was confirmed in a number of judgments, including *Sabel v Puma*, which made clear that to find conflict under Articles 4(3) and (4)(3)(a), and 5(2) of the directive, there is no need for proof of a likelihood of confusion, even where there is no similarity between the goods in question.[21] In *Adidas-Salomon*,[22] the CJEU elaborated further on the difference between origin confusion and association. It ruled:

> 2. The protection conferred by Art. 5(2) of Directive 89/104 is not conditional on a finding of a degree of similarity between the mark with a reputation and the sign such that there exists a likelihood of confusion between them on the part of the relevant section of the public. It is sufficient for the degree of similarity between the mark with a reputation and the sign to have the effect that the relevant section of the public establishes a link between the sign and the mark.

The leading case on the anti-dilution provisions of the directive is *Intel Corp. Inc. v CPM*. A key question for the CJEU in *Intel* was how to identify the necessary 'link' made by consumers, first identified in *Adidas*, which would lead to the dilution of the exclusiveness of the claimant's trade mark.

Intel Corp. Inc. v CPM United Kingdom Ltd Case C-252/07 [2009] ETMR 13

Intel held a number of UK and Community trade marks for the words INTEL and INTELINSIDE for, inter alia, computers and related products. CPM registered the mark INTELMARK for marketing and telemarketing. Intel sought a declaration of invalidity for the CPM mark. It argued that CPM's use of the INTELMARK was without due cause and would take unfair advantage of and be detrimental to the distinctive character or the repute of its own marks. The Hearing Officer rejected Intel's application for a declaration of invalidity because he was not persuaded by Intel that use by CPM of its mark on its own products would damage the distinctiveness or repute of the Intel mark. Intel appealed and the case eventually reached the Court of Appeal. In the Court of Appeal,[23] Jacob LJ accepted that 'Intel' was an invented word in that it had no other meaning beyond its identification with the products of Intel Corp., that it was unique in that it had not been used by any other trader in relation to other goods or services and that it had a 'huge reputation' in the UK for computers and related products. Jacob LJ also accepted that the marks were similar and that the goods were dissimilar. Further, he assumed that the use of the INTELMARK did not suggest that there was a trade connection with Intel Corp. Jacob LJ then sought a ruling from the CJEU whether, under these circumstances, the INTELMARK should be revoked. The CJEU summarized the questions put by the Court of Appeal.

---

[21] [20].
[22] *Adidas-Salomon AG and Adidas Benelux BV v Fitnessworld Trading Ltd* Case C-408/01 [2003] ECR I-12537.
[23] *Intel Corp. Ltd v CPM United Kingdom Ltd* [2007] EWCA Civ 431.

23. Accordingly, the Court of Appeal (England and Wales) (Civil Division) decided to stay the proceedings and to refer the following questions to the Court for a preliminary ruling:

(1) For the purposes of Article 4(4)(a) of the [Directive], where:

    (a) the earlier mark has a huge reputation for certain specific types of goods or services,

    (b) those goods or services are dissimilar or dissimilar to a substantial degree to the goods or services of the later mark,

    (c) the earlier mark is unique in respect of any goods or services,

    (d) the earlier mark would be brought to mind by the average consumer when he or she encounters the later mark used for the services of the later mark, are those facts sufficient in themselves to establish (i) 'a link' within the meaning of paragraphs 29 and 30 of [*Adidas-Salomon and Adidas Benelux*], and/or (ii) unfair advantage and/or detriment within the meaning of that Article?

(2) If no, what factors is the national court to take into account in deciding whether such is sufficient? Specifically, in the global appreciation to determine whether there is a 'link', what significance is to be attached to the goods or services in the specification of the later mark?

(3) In the context of Article 4(4)(a) [of the Directive], what is required in order to satisfy the condition of detriment to distinctive character? Specifically, (i) does the earlier mark have to be unique, (ii) is a first conflicting use sufficient to establish detriment to distinctive character and (iii) does the element of detriment to distinctive character of the earlier mark require an effect on the economic behaviour of the consumer?

The CJEU then made some preliminary observations. It noted that Article 4(4)(a) provides for three types of injury to marks with a reputation, as we have seen, and held that any one of these was sufficient for the provision to apply. Such injury will only occur where, because of the similarity between the marks, the public establishes a link between them. Such a link does not involve confusion—but the existence of such a link is not enough to establish that injury has occurred. The CJEU also considered the nature of the public whose perceptions are relevant to assessing whether the provision applies. Not surprisingly, it concluded that this public consisted of average consumers of the goods and services in question, who are reasonably well informed, reasonably observant, and circumspect.[24] And it is the perceptions of the average consumer which determines whether a mark has a reputation, whether it is distinctive, and whether injury has occurred to the distinctive character and repute of the mark. Finally, the CJEU held that to obtain protection under Article 4(4)(a), the proprietor of the earlier mark must adduce proof that use of the later mark would take 'unfair advantage of, or be detrimental to, the distinctive character' of his mark. It did, however, accept that it might be difficult to demonstrate actual damage, and indeed that it would be wrong to expect the proprietor of the earlier mark to have to wait to bring an action until actual damage had occurred. The CJEU thus held it sufficient for the proprietor to prove 'that there was a serious risk that such an injury will occur in the future'.[25] Should the proprietor of the earlier mark show actual or potential damage, then it falls to the proprietor of the later mark to establish that there was due cause for his use of the mark. The CJEU then went on to answer the questions posed by the Court of Appeal. It held first that in assessing whether

---

[24] For a full discussion in relation to registration and distinctiveness, see 6.3.3.6.   [25] [38].

there is a relevant link, in the sense described in *Adidas-Salomon*, it is necessary to take a global approach, taking into account a number of factors:

42. Those factors include:
   - the degree of similarity between the conflicting marks;
   - the nature of the goods or services for which the conflicting marks were registered, including the degree of closeness or dissimilarity between those goods or services, and the relevant section of the public;
   - the strength of the earlier mark's reputation;
   - the degree of the earlier mark's distinctive character, whether inherent or acquired through use;
   - the existence of the likelihood of confusion on the part of the public.

43. In that respect, the following points must be made.

44. As regards the degree of similarity between the conflicting marks, the more similar they are, the more likely it is that the later mark will bring the earlier mark with a reputation to the mind of the relevant public. That is particularly the case where those marks are identical.

45. However, the fact that the conflicting marks are identical, and even more so if they are merely similar, is not sufficient for it to be concluded that there is a link between those marks.

46. It is possible that the conflicting marks are registered for goods or services in respect of which the relevant sections of the public do not overlap.

47. The reputation of a trade mark must be assessed in relation to the relevant section of the public as regards the goods or services for which that mark was registered. That may be either the public at large or a more specialised public (see *General Motors*, [24]).

48. It is therefore conceivable that the relevant section of the public as regards the goods or services for which the earlier mark was registered is completely distinct from the relevant section of the public as regards the goods or services for which the later mark was registered and that the earlier mark, although it has a reputation, is not known to the public targeted by the later mark. In such a case, the public targeted by each of the two marks may never be confronted with the other mark, so that it will not establish any link between those marks.

49. Furthermore, even if the relevant section of the public as regards the goods or services for which the conflicting marks are registered is the same or overlaps to some extent, those goods or services may be so dissimilar that the later mark is unlikely to bring the earlier mark to the mind of the relevant public.

50. Accordingly, the nature of the goods or services for which the conflicting marks are registered must be taken into consideration for the purposes of assessing whether there is a link between those marks.

51. It must also be pointed out that certain marks may have acquired such a reputation that it goes beyond the relevant public as regards the goods or services for which those marks were registered.

52. In such a case, it is possible that the relevant section of the public as regards the goods or services for which the later mark is registered will make a connection between the conflicting marks, even though that public is wholly distinct from the relevant section of the public as regards goods or services for which the earlier mark was registered.

53. For the purposes of assessing where there is a link between the conflicting marks, it may therefore be necessary to take into account the strength of the earlier mark's reputation in order to determine whether that reputation extends beyond the public targeted by that mark.

54. Likewise, the stronger the distinctive character of the earlier mark, whether inherent or acquired through the use which has been made of it, the more likely it is that, confronted with a later identical or similar mark, the relevant public will call that earlier mark to mind.

55. Accordingly, for the purposes of assessing whether there is a link between the conflicting marks, the degree of the earlier mark's distinctive character must be taken into consideration.

56. In that regard, in so far as the ability of a trade mark to identify the goods or services for which it is registered and used as coming from the proprietor of that mark and, therefore, its distinctive character are all the stronger if that mark is unique—that is to say, as regards a word mark such as INTEL, if the word of which it consists has not been used by anyone for any goods or services other than by the proprietor of the mark for the goods and services it markets—it must be ascertained whether the earlier mark is unique or essentially unique.

57. Finally, a link between the conflicting marks is necessarily established when there is a likelihood of confusion, that is to say, when the relevant public believes or might believe that the goods or services marketed under the earlier mark and those marketed under the later mark come from the same undertaking or from economically-linked undertakings (see to that effect, inter alia, *Lloyd Schuhfabrik Meyer & Co GmbH v Klijsen Handel BV* (C-342/97) [1999] ECR I-3819 and *O₂ Holdings Ltd v Hutchinson 3G UK Ltd* (C-533/06) [2008] ETMR 55 ECJ at [59].

58. However, as is apparent from [27]–[31] of the judgment in *Adidas-Salomon and Adidas Benelux*, implementation of the protection introduced by Article 4(4)(a) of the Directive does not require the existence of a likelihood of confusion.

In defining the nature of the 'link' necessary for the dilution provisions of the proviso to apply, the CJEU suggested the courts take a global approach which acknowledges the importance of a mark's distinctiveness or reputation. But it also warned that the presence of a 'reputation' for certain goods, that the goods involved are dissimilar, and the earlier mark is 'unique' do not necessarily mean that there is such a 'link'. The CJEU then went on to look at the relevant criteria for assessing whether use of the later mark would be detrimental to the distinctive character of the earlier mark. It held that this also called for a global assessment based on the criteria set out in paragraph 42.[26] It continued:

71. …[T]he existence of a link between the conflicting marks does not dispense the proprietor of the earlier trade mark from having to prove actual and present injury to its mark, for the purposes of Article 4(4)(a) of the Directive, or a serious likelihood that such an injury will occur in the future.

72. Lastly, as regards, more particularly, detriment to the distinctive character of the earlier mark, the answer to the second part of the third question must be that, first, it is not necessary for the earlier mark to be unique in order to establish such injury or a serious likelihood that it will occur in the future.

---

[26] It is submitted that the factors identified in *Intel* which are relevant to finding the link necessary for dilution would also be the same for finding tarnishment.

73. A trade mark with a reputation necessarily has distinctive character, at the very least acquired through use. Therefore, even if an earlier mark with a reputation is not unique, the use of a later identical or similar mark may be such as to weaken the distinctive character of that earlier mark.

74. However, the more 'unique' the earlier mark appears, the greater the likelihood that the use of a later identical or similar mark will be detrimental to its distinctive character.

75. Secondly, a first use of an identical or similar mark may suffice, in some circumstances, to cause actual and present detriment to the distinctive character of the earlier mark or to give rise to a serious likelihood that such detriment will occur in the future.

76. Thirdly, as was stated on [29] of this judgment, detriment to the distinctive character of the earlier mark is caused when that mark's ability to identify the goods or services for which it is registered and used as coming from the proprietor of that mark is weakened, since use of the later mark leads to dispersion of the identity and hold upon the public mind of the earlier mark.

77. It follows that proof that the use of the later mark is or would be detrimental to the distinctive character of the earlier mark requires evidence of a change in the economic behaviour of the average consumer of the goods or services for which the earlier mark was registered consequent on the use of the later mark, or a serious likelihood that such a change will occur in the future.

78. It is immaterial, however, for the purposes of assessing whether the use of the later mark is or would be detrimental to the distinctive character of the earlier mark, whether or not the proprietor of the later mark draws real commercial benefit from the distinctive character of the earlier mark.

Do you think that the CJEU, in *Intel*, found the correct balance between the interests of the proprietors of distinctive marks and those of other traders? It is certainly the case that the CJEU held that even if the earlier mark is unique, has a huge reputation, and the later mark calls to mind the earlier mark, this will not necessarily establish the necessary 'link'. It also held that for detriment to the distinctive character of the mark with a reputation, there must be evidence of a change in the economic behaviour of the average consumer which has or is likely to cause injury to the earlier mark. On the other hand, the CJEU found that use of the later mark by a third party may cause damage to the earlier mark even if the latter is not unique. Indeed, even first use of the mark by a third party may be sufficient to damage the distinctive character of the earlier mark. We might also wonder quite how one is to prove that the distinctiveness of a mark has been 'injured' or indeed is likely to be so in the future. Is there an obvious economic measurement to calculate this injury or would we need to canvass the views of the putative, average consumer?

7.1.4.3 The meaning of 'unfair advantage'

The third sort of harm covered by Article 4, together with dilution and tarnishment, is the taking of unfair advantage. The meaning of 'taking unfair advantage' in relation to a mark with a reputation was examined in *L'Oréal v Bellure*, first in the UK courts and then on appeal to the CJEU.[27]

---

[27] The case was concerned with infringement under Art. 5(2) of the TMD, but the judgment applies equally to Art. 4(4)(a).

L'Oréal SA v Bellure NV [2007] EWCA Civ 968

The claimant manufactured expensive perfumes and cosmetics, sold under registered trade marks, including 'Trésor', 'Miracle', 'Anaïs Anaïs', and 'Noa'. These products were sold through exclusive outlets and had expensive packaging, which also had trade mark protection. The defendants manufactured and distributed perfumes under their 'Creation Lamis' range which were sold in down-market outlets. These products were intended to have a 'smell-alike' relationship to the claimant's perfumes. Furthermore, the defendants' packaging was designed to call to mind the claimant's packaging. After complaints from the claimant, the defendants altered their packaging so it would be less likely to call to mind the claimant's packaging. Nonetheless, the claimant contended that the defendants had infringed its trade marks by using signs which were similar to its registered marks. The defendants also produced a product comparison list which was designed to show which of the defendants' perfumes smelt like those of the claimant and which they argued was a legitimate use of comparative advertising.[28] In the High Court, Lewison J held that two of the defendants' bottles were sufficiently similar to the claimant's marks so as to give rise to an association between them in the eyes of the relevant consumers and that, while there was no likelihood of confusion, the defendants' products took unfair advantage of the character or reputation of the claimant's registered marks. The defendants appealed, arguing in particular that their use of the claimant's marks was descriptive. Jacob LJ agreed with Lewison J that there was 'no causative link between the application of the sign and the tarnishing or blurring complained of'. This left the question of whether Lewison J was right to find that the defendants had taken unfair advantage of the claimant's mark. Jacob LJ's own view was that taking advantage need not necessarily be unfair. As a result, he chose to address the question to the CJEU of when taking an advantage is unfair.[29]

> 5. Where a trader uses a sign which is similar to a registered trade mark which has a reputation, and that sign is not confusingly similar to the trade mark, in such a way that:
>
> (a) the essential function of the registered trade mark of providing a guarantee of origin is not impaired or put at risk;
>
> (b) there is no tarnishing or blurring of the registered trade mark or its reputation or any risk of either of these;
>
> (c) the trade mark owner's sales are not impaired; and
>
> (d) the trade mark owner is not deprived of any of the reward for promotion, maintenance or enhancement of his trade mark;
>
> (e) but the trader gets a commercial advantage from the use of his sign by reason of its similarity to the registered mark
>
> does that use amount to the taking of 'an unfair advantage' of the reputation of the registered mark within the meaning of Art. 5(2) of the Trade Mark Directive? ...

Is it not possible to suggest that Jacob LJ's own answer is implicit in how he drafted the question? Indeed, he went on to say explicitly that 'the answer ought to be no.'[30] However, when the CJEU considered Jacob LJ's question, they took a contrary view.

---

[28] See 8.2 for a discussion of comparative advertising.

[29] Jacob LJ also asked the CJEU to address the issue of comparative advertising. This is looked at in Chapter 8 at 8.2.

[30] [93].

L'Oréal v Bellure Case C-487/07 [2009] ECR I-5185

The CJEU first set out what it understood as the meaning of unfair advantage of the distinctive character or repute of the mark with a reputation.

41 As regards the concept of 'taking unfair advantage of the distinctive character or the repute of the trade mark', also referred to as 'parasitism' or 'free-riding', that concept relates not to the detriment caused to the mark but to the advantage taken by the third party as a result of the use of the identical or similar sign. It covers, in particular, cases where, by reason of a transfer of the image of the mark or of the characteristics which it projects to the goods identified by the identical or similar sign, there is clear exploitation on the coat-tails of the mark with a reputation.

[In its judgment, the CJEU also identified the circumstances in which the taking of unfair advantage might be proved.]

44 In order to determine whether the use of a sign takes unfair advantage of the distinctive character or the repute of the mark, it is necessary to undertake a global assessment, taking into account all factors relevant to the circumstances of the case, which include the strength of the mark's reputation and the degree of distinctive character of the mark, the degree of similarity between the marks at issue and the nature and degree of proximity of the goods or services concerned. As regards the strength of the reputation and the degree of distinctive character of the mark, the Court has already held that, the stronger that mark's distinctive character and reputation are, the easier it will be to accept that detriment has been caused to it. It is also clear from the case-law that, the more immediately and strongly the mark is brought to mind by the sign, the greater the likelihood that the current or future use of the sign is taking, or will take, unfair advantage of the distinctive character or the repute of the mark or is, or will be, detrimental to them (see, to that effect, *Intel Corporation* (C-252/07) [2009] E.T.M.R. 13 at [67] to [69]).

The CJEU noted that the British courts had found there was a link between the claimant's marks and those of the defendants. It went on to conclude that this link 'confers a commercial advantage on the defendants'. It further concluded that the similarity between the marks, 'was created intentionally in order to create an association in the mind of the public between fine fragrances and their imitations, with the aim of facilitating the marketing of those imitations'.[31] It held that in disposing of the case, the British court would therefore have to ask whether the defendant's imitation of the claimant's marks was intended to take advantage, for promotional purposes, of the distinctive character and the repute of the claimant's marks.[32] It continued:

49 In that regard, where a third party attempts, through the use of a sign similar to a mark with a reputation, to ride on the coat-tails of that mark in order to benefit from its power of attraction, its reputation and its prestige, and to exploit, without paying any financial compensation and without being required to make efforts of his own in that regard, the marketing effort expended by the proprietor of that mark in order to create and maintain the image of that mark, the advantage resulting from such use must be considered to be an advantage that has been unfairly taken of the distinctive character or the repute of that mark.

[31] [47].   [32] [48].

50 In the light of the above, the answer to the fifth question is that art.5(2) of Directive 89/104 must be interpreted as meaning that the taking of unfair advantage of the distinctive character or the repute of a mark, within the meaning of that provision, does not require that there be a likelihood of confusion or a likelihood of detriment to the distinctive character or the repute of the mark or, more generally, to its proprietor. The advantage arising from the use by a third party of a sign similar to a mark with a reputation is an advantage taken unfairly by that third party of the distinctive character or the repute of the mark where that party seeks by that use to ride on the coat-tails of the mark with a reputation in order to benefit from the power of attraction, the reputation and the prestige of that mark and to exploit, without paying any financial compensation, the marketing effort expended by the proprietor of the mark in order to create and maintain the mark's image.

L'Oréal then returned to the Court of Appeal for a final judgment.[33] By this point, the only outstanding issue was the lawfulness of the comparison lists. Following the CJEU judgment, Jacob LJ took the view that he had no choice but to find against the defendants in relation to the lists on the basis that they both breached the rules on comparative advertising[34] and they took unfair advantage of the claimant's marks. However, for Jacob LJ, the overall outcome was to be regretted. In particular, he saw the broad definition which the CJEU had given to the taking of unfair advantage as inimical both to free speech and to healthy competition.

Jacob LJ:

14. The ECJ's decision in this case means that poor consumers are the losers. Only the poor would dream of buying the defendants' products. The real thing is beyond their wildest dreams. Yet they are denied their right to receive information which would give them a little bit of pleasure; the ability to buy a product for a euro or so which they know smells like a famous perfume.

15. Moreover there is no harm to the trade mark owner—other than possibly a 'harm' which, to be fair, L'Oréal has never asserted. That 'harm' would be letting the truth out— that it is possible to produce cheap perfumes which smell somewhat like a famous original. I can understand that a purveyor of a product sold at a very high price as an exclusive luxury item would not like the public to know that it can be imitated, albeit not to the same quality, cheaply—there is a bit of a message that the price of the real thing may be excessive and that the 'luxury image' may be a bit of a delusion. But an uncomfortable (from the point of view of the trade mark owner) truth is still the truth: it surely needs a strong reason to suppress it.

[Jacob LJ then turned to the issue of competition and continued:]

16 ... If a trader cannot (when it is truly the case) say: 'my goods are the same as Brand X (a famous registered mark) but half the price', I think there is a real danger that important areas of trade will not be open to proper competition ...

[He then offered examples such as referring to a generic drug under the mark of its branded equivalent or listing replacement cartridges under the mark of those printers or cartridges with which they are compatible. He concluded:]

17 ... I regret that the ECJ in this case has not addressed the competition aspects of what it calls 'riding on the coattails'. The trouble with deprecatory metaphorical expressions such as this ('free-riding' is another), containing as they do clear disapproval of the defendants' trade as such, is that they do not provide clear rules by which a trader can know clearly what he can and cannot do.

---

[33] *L'Oréal SA v Bellure NV* [2010] EWCA Civ 535.   [34] See Chapter 8.

The *L'Oréal* decision was welcomed by those who took the view that the provisions of Article 4(4) of the TMD were not intended to benefit consumers first and foremost, but rather the trade mark proprietors who have succeeded in nurturing a valuable brand. It could also be argued that in this age of brand awareness, consumers who pay a premium for branded products would feel unhappy if the brand value was not protected. However, there were others who argued that the purpose of the TMD is to ensure that there is competition in the marketplace and this is better provided for if the protection given to registered trade marks is limited. For those who take the latter view, the decision in *Intra-Press SAS v OHIM*[35] undoubtedly raises further concerns. The CJEU held that the amount of similarity between a mark and a sign sufficient to ground an assumption that the public might make a 'link' between them for the purposes of finding dilution or unfair advantage, is less than is necessary to identify a likelihood of confusion. Even a 'low degree of similarity' might be sufficient to find such a link provided other factors, for example the reputation of or the recognition enjoyed by the mark, are sufficient to compensate.[36] In their comment on the *L'Oréal* decision, Gangjee and Burrell argue that the law might now be overly protective of trade marks at the expense of desirable competition.

D. Gangjee and R. Burrell, 'Because you're worth it: *L'Oréal* and the prohibition on free riding' (2010) 73 MLR 282

Introduction

In *L'Oreal v Bellure* the European Court of Justice decided that free riding, or taking advantage of the reputation enjoyed by an earlier mark, is actionable per se. In reaching this conclusion, the ECJ significantly expanded the scope of trade mark protection with little justification for doing so. Referencing activity and building on the efforts of others are fundamental to creative and competitive processes. This comment argues that *L'Oreal*'s broad prohibition on free riding is theoretically unsound, runs counter to the thrust of the European trade mark law and could negatively impact on the competitiveness of the European marketplace.

[The authors then go on to look at background to the dispute and describe the CJEU judgment. They continue at 788:]

L'Oreal's Blemishes

Is a prohibition on free riding desirable?

We acknowledge the marketplace reality that brands attract custom and are valuable to trade mark proprietors. However, it does not necessarily follow that the law should intervene to protect this value. In effect, the ECJ has recognised property rights in reputation per se. Unlike previous decisions where a renowned mark's reputation was in danger of being damaged, the Court (a) formally acknowledged that trademarks possess a 'communication, investment or advertising' function, signalling not only objective information about product

---

[35] *Intra-Presse SAS v OHIM* Case C-581/13 P [2015] ETMR 6.   [36] [74].

quality, but also attributes such as style and luxury; (b) this constitutes the mark's image and (c) the prohibition against taking 'unfair advantage of ... repute' prevents exploitation through the 'transfer of image'. In protecting reputation absent any harm, the Court recognised the investment in creating an attractive brand image. Since granting property rights to one group inevitably takes away freedoms from others, we ask whether protection is justified. A precondition to this inquiry is to clarify the meaning of free riding. One frustrating aspect of the ECJ's judgment is that it provides no explanation of its understanding of free riding, even though this language brings with it elements of both economic theory and moral disapprobation.

In economic terms we normally understand free rider problems as flowing from the generation of some positive externality, that is, a benefit that is conferred on another person by an economic actor outside of any transaction between the parties. Positive externalities are of concern because they may lead to underinvestment in the activity that generates the benefit in question. This is because the market signal will fail to reflect the full value of the activity. The allocation of property rights is widely accepted as providing one way in which the state can intervene to try to ensure that externalities (whether positive or negative) are internalised. However, it is imperative not to leap from the identification of some positive externality to the conclusion that legal intervention to correct for this externality is justified. On the contrary, positive externalities are ubiquitous. The person who maintains an attractive front garden has no claim against neighbours who see their property values increase; the person who buys and uses a handkerchief when suffering from a cold receives no compensation from acquaintances and passers-by who avoid becoming ill as a result. These examples could be multiplied more or less indefinitely and the point we want to stress is that legal intervention is the exception, not the rule. Particularly notable is the fact that we make no general attempt to intervene in cases where a person introduces a new product to the market. For example, the person who (re)introduced absinthe to the UK market received no compensation from subsequent importers even though they benefitted from the marketing efforts of the first mover. Absent copyright, design or patent protection, the same applies to any copyist. Bellure was entitled to copy L'Oreal's fragrances and if Bellure could trade off L'Oreal's efforts to this extent why should it be prevented from communicating the fact of its copying to the market?

Furthermore, even in situations where we determine that some form of legal intervention is required, there is a strong case that such intervention should go no further than is required to provide the incentive to invest. One of the reasons why patent and copyright law have become so controversial is because these regimes now provide a level of protection that would seem to go well beyond that which is required to preserve incentives. Given the advantages that accrue to the owner of an established brand it is difficult to see that there is any danger of 'undersupply' that trademark law needs to guard against. Certainly David Barnes, the leading scholar to take externalities in trade mark law seriously, comes to this conclusion and, more specifically, Barnes is dismissive of the idea that a free rider argument could ever justify providing a right to prohibit the type of referential use made by Bellure in its comparative lists.

The ECJ gave no indication that it had thought through the economic implications of its decision. Its departure from the default assumption that imitation is permissible remains unexplained, as do the implications of its decision for consumer welfare. It also showed no hesitation about its institutional competence in the field of economic policy making. Thus, judged in economic terms, L'Oreal is deeply problematic.

The authors, after concluding that the decision in *L'Oreal* could not be justified on economic grounds, ask whether there are more normative justifications for the decision. They argue that since consumers play a key role in creating a brand, it is not clear why all of its value should accrue to the proprietor. They then go on to look at 'unjust enrichment'.[37]

> Turning to arguments derived from preventing 'unjust enrichment', the unjustness of another's gain is usually the trickiest element to explain. It 'is neither possible nor necessarily desirable for a competitor to rely completely on his own unaided efforts. We neither live in [a] romantic world of perfectly self-sufficient individualists…nor would want to.' Since we inhabit a world where we are enriched by those around us, the unjustness often rests on an assumption that the defendant is appropriating the claimant's (intangible) property without consent, but this is entirely circular. If property is the label given to that which the law protects, why should we concede property in reputation in the first place? Here powerful rhetorical devices that can suggest moral blameworthiness, such as free riding and the Biblical language of 'reaping without sowing' are to be treated with considerable care. In the course of this litigation, Jacob LJ commented that
>
> > 'free riding' is 'subtly and dangerously emotive: it carries the unwritten message that, it ought to be stopped. That is far from being necessarily so. The needs of proper competition and lawful free trade will involve an element [of it]. The problem for trade mark law is where to draw the line between permissible and impermissible "free riding". Using the epithet does not solve the problem.'

One problem the author's identify with the *L'Oréal v Bellure* decision is that the Court did not shed light on what evidence must be adduced to show that there has been unjust enrichment. Indeed, we could go further and question how, even if such evidence is produced, the precise economic gain to the defendant will be calculated. Indeed, perhaps the key difference between dilution and taking unfair advantage concerns the question of damage. In *Intel*, the CJEU made clear that dilution depends upon there being damage or the likelihood of damage to the claimant's mark. However, in the case of unfair advantage, following the *L'Oréal v Bellure* decision, it would appear that the claimant's mark need suffer no damage at all. In *Helena Rubenstein v OHIM*,[38] the CJEU held that in the case of both dilution and unjust enrichment:[39]

> the proprietor of the earlier mark is not required to demonstrate actual and present harm to its mark but must, however, adduce prima facie evidence of a future risk, which is not hypothetical, of unfair advantage or detriment, and such a conclusion may be established, in particular, on the basis of logical deductions made from an analysis of the probabilities and by taking account of the normal practice in the relevant commercial sector as well as all the other circumstances of the case.

While the Court offers some guidance on how to assess the likelihood of damage from dilution or to identify the taking of unfair advantage, it arguably brings us no closer to answering the question of how any monetary remedy should subsequently be calculated.

---

[37] At 291.　　[38] *Helena Rubinstein SNC v OHIM* Case C-100/11 P [2012] ETMR 40.　　[39] [95].

7.1.4.4 Without due cause

The phrase, 'without due cause', of course, implies that there may be times when a third party can legitimately make use of a mark with a reputation. The meaning of due cause was addressed by the CJEU in the *Red Bull* case. In its judgment, the CJEU drew a distinction between objective reasons for finding due cause and what it termed 'subjective' reasons. The latter might consist of particular circumstances in which it would be justifiable for a third party to use a sign which is the same or similar to a registered mark; use which would otherwise fall foul of Article 4(4)(3). It identified such circumstances in the *Red Bull* case.

Leidseplein Beheer BV and another v Red Bull GmbH and another
Case C-65/12 [2014] Bus. L. R. 280

In 1983, Red Bull registered the word and figurative trade mark, 'Red Bull Krating-Daeng' for, inter alia, non-alcoholic drinks in the Benelux. The defendant, Mr de Vries, is the proprietor of the Benelux word and figurative mark, 'The Bulldog', registered in 1983, the word mark, 'The Bulldog' registered in 1999, and the word and figurative mark 'The Bulldog Energy Drink' registered in 2000 all for non-alcoholic drinks. It was common ground that before Red Bull filed for its mark in 1983, Mr de Vries had been using the sign 'The Bulldog' on a hotel, restaurant, and cafe. It was also accepted that 'Red Bull Krating-Daeng' has a reputation in the Benelux. Red Bull began an action in 2005 alleging that use of the sign 'The Bulldog' adversely affected its mark and asked that Mr de Vries cease production of his energy drinks in packaging carrying the word 'Bull' or any other sign confusingly similar to its trade mark. Red Bull failed at first instance but on appeal succeeded; the court holding that because of the reputation of Red Bull's mark the public would make a 'link' between that and the defendant's marks and that by so doing the defendant would be 'riding on the coat tails' of the claimant's mark. Mr de Vries appealed on the basis that the court had not taken account of the fact that he had due cause to use the sign 'The Bulldog' as it was a continuation of commercial use dating from before the claimant had registered its mark. The Dutch Supreme Court referred the following question to the CJEU: must Article 5(2) of the directive be interpreted as meaning that the use by a third party of a sign that is similar to a trade mark with a reputation in relation to goods identical to those for which that mark is registered be considered to be with 'due cause', within the meaning of that provision, if it is demonstrated that that sign was being used before that mark was filed? The CJEU noted that the purpose and scope of protection of a registered trade mark under Article 5(2) differs from that under Article 5(1)(a), which is intended to ensure that a trade mark can fulfil its functions most notably as a badge of origin and under Article 5(1)(b) where it is necessary for there be to a likelihood of confusion. It also noted that in *Levi Strauss v Casucci*,[40] it had held that the protection afforded by the directive to registered trade marks must be balanced against the interests of other market operators. It continued:

42 It follows that the protection of rights which the proprietor of a trade mark derives from that Directive is not unconditional, since in order to maintain the balance between those

---

[40] *Levi Strauss & Co. v Casucci SpA* Case C-145/05 [2006] ECR I-3703.

interests that protection is limited, in particular, to those cases in which that proprietor shows himself to be sufficiently vigilant by opposing the use, by other operators, of signs likely to infringe his mark: see the *Levi Strauss case*, para 30.

43 In a system for the protection of marks such as that adopted, on the basis of Directive 89/104 by the Benelux Convention, however, the interests of a third party in using, in the course of trade, a sign similar to a mark with a reputation must be considered, in the context of article 5(2) of that Directive, in the light of the possibility for the user of that sign to claim 'due cause'.

44 Where the proprietor of the mark with a reputation has demonstrated the existence of one of the forms of injury referred to in article 5(2) of Directive 89/104 and, in particular, has shown that unfair advantage has been taken of the distinctive character or the repute of that mark, the onus is on the third party using a sign similar to the mark with a reputation to establish that he has due cause for using such a sign: see, by analogy, *Intel Corpn Inc v CPM United Kingdom Ltd* (Case C-252/07) [2009] Bus LR 1079; [2008] ECR I-8823, para 39.

45 It follows that the concept of 'due cause' may not only include objectively overriding reasons but may also relate to the subjective interests of a third party using a sign which is identical or similar to the mark with a reputation.

46 Thus, the concept of 'due cause' is intended, not to resolve a conflict between a mark with a reputation and a similar sign which was being used before that trade mark was filed or to restrict the rights which the proprietor of that mark is recognised as having, but to strike a balance between the interests in question by taking account, in the specific context of article 5(2) of Directive 89/104 and in the light of the enhanced protection enjoyed by that mark, of the interests of the third party using that sign. In so doing, the claim by a third party that there is due cause for using a sign which is similar to a mark with a reputation cannot lead to the recognition, for the benefit of that third party, of the rights connected with a registered mark, but rather obliges the proprietor of the mark with a reputation to tolerate the use of the similar sign.

47 The court thus held in *Interflora Inc v Marks & Spencer plc* [2012] Bus LR 1440, para 91 (a case concerning the use of keywords for Internet referencing) that where the advertisement displayed on the Internet on the basis of a keyword corresponding to a trade mark with a reputation puts forward—without offering a mere imitation of the goods or services of the proprietor of that trade mark, without being detrimental to the repute or the distinctive character of that mark and without, moreover, adversely affecting the functions of the trade mark concerned—an alternative to the goods or services of the proprietor of the trade mark with a reputation, it must be concluded that such a use falls, as a rule, within the ambit of fair competition in the sector for the goods or services concerned and is thus not without 'due cause'.

48 Consequently, the concept of 'due cause' cannot be interpreted as being restricted to objectively overriding reasons.

[The CJEU then turned to the facts of the present case to ask under what conditions the prior use of a sign which is similar to a trade mark with a reputation may be covered by the concept of 'due cause'.]

54 In the first place, such an assessment requires a determination as to how that sign has been accepted by, and what its reputation is with, the relevant public. In the present case, it is not disputed that the sign 'The Bulldog' has been used for a range of hotel, restaurant and café services since 1983 or before. The date from which Mr de Vries has offered energy drinks for sale is, however, not specified in the order for reference.

55 In the second place, it is necessary to examine the intention of the person using that sign.

56 In this regard, in order to determine whether the use of the sign similar to the mark with a reputation was in good faith, it is necessary to take account of the degree of proximity between the goods and services for which that sign has been used and the product for which that mark was registered, as well as to have regard for when that sign was first used for a product identical to that for which that mark was registered, and when that mark acquired its reputation.

57 First, where a sign has been used prior to the registration of a mark with a reputation in relation to services and goods which may be linked to the product for which that mark has been registered, the use of that sign in relation to that latter product may appear to be a natural extension of the range of services and goods for which that sign already enjoys a certain reputation with the relevant public.

58 In the present case, it is not disputed that Mr de Vries uses the sign 'The Bulldog' in relation to hotel, restaurant and café goods and services which include the sale of drinks. Consequently, in the light of the recognition enjoyed by that sign among the relevant public, and in the light of the nature of the goods and services for which it has been used, the sale of energy drinks contained in packaging which displays that sign may therefore be perceived, not as an attempt to take advantage of the repute of the mark 'Red Bull', but rather as a genuine extension of the range of goods and services offered by Mr de Vries. That impression would be strengthened even further if the sign 'The Bulldog' was used for energy drinks before the mark 'Red Bull Krating-Daeng' acquired its reputation.

59 Secondly, the greater the repute of the sign used, prior to the registration of a similar mark with a reputation, for a certain range of goods and services, the more its use will be necessary for the marketing of a product identical to that for which the mark was registered, a fortiori as that product is close, by its nature, to the range of goods and services for which that sign was previously used.

60 Consequently, it follows from all of the foregoing considerations that the answer to the question referred is that article 5(2) of Directive 89/104 must be interpreted as meaning that the proprietor of a trade mark with a reputation may be obliged, pursuant to the concept of 'due cause' within the meaning of that provision, to tolerate the use by a third party of a sign similar to that mark in relation to a product which is identical to that for which that mark was registered, if it is demonstrated that that sign was being used before that mark was filed and that the use of that sign in relation to the identical product is in good faith. In order to determine whether that is so, the national court must take account, in particular, of: how that sign has been accepted by, and what its reputation is with, the relevant public; the degree of proximity between the goods and services for which that sign was originally used and the product for which the mark with a reputation was registered; and the economic and commercial significance of the use for that product of the sign which is similar to that mark.

In other words, the CJEU concluded that Mr de Vries had a very strong argument that his use of the mark 'Bulldog' was covered by the concept of 'due cause'.

By identifying those occasions when the concept of 'due cause' applies, the CJEU has taken a step towards delimiting the extent of the monopoly afforded by trade mark registration, particularly in the case of potentially powerful brands. It has ruled that 'due cause' might arise from subjective reasons which would apply specifically to the defendant and from objective reasons deriving from a rule of law. But it has also made clear that a finding of due cause does not give the defendant a new right to use its mark, simply an exemption from infringement in the particular circumstances of the case. Do you think that this approach successfully protects the interests of third parties, who may or may not be competitors of the trade mark owner?

FURTHER READING

V. di Cataldo, 'The trade mark with a reputation in EU law—some remarks on the negative condition "without due cause"' (2011) 42 IIC 883.

A. Chronopoulos, 'Legal and economic arguments for the protection of advertising value through trade mark law' (2014) 4 QMJIP 256.

C. Greenhalgh and E. Webster, 'Have trademarks become deceptive?' [2015] WIPO J 109.

S. Malynicz, 'Applying the law on trade mark dilution' [2015] ERA Forum 49.

I. Simon Fhima, 'Exploring the roots of European dilution' (2015) 16 IPQ 25.

A. Smith, 'Every BULLDOG has its day: an analysis of "due cause": *Leidseplein Beheer BV and de Vries v Red Bull GmBH*' [2014] EIPR 536.

7.2 INFRINGEMENT

The registration of a trade mark confers upon its proprietor the right to prevent third parties from infringing his mark. The acts which constitute infringement are set out in Article 5 of the TMD.[41] The key provisions mirror those which give rise to conflict under Article 4 of the TMD. According to Article 5(1), infringement will arise when a third party uses in the course of trade:

(a) any sign which is identical with the trade mark in relation to goods or services which are identical with those for which the trade mark is registered;

(b) any sign where, because of its identity with, or similarity to, the trade mark and the identity or similarity of the goods or services covered by the trade mark and the sign, there exists a likelihood of confusion on the part of the public, which includes the likelihood of association between the sign and the trade mark.

There is also an anti-dilution provision under Article 5(2), which again was optional and which the UK incorporated into the 1994 TMA.[42] Thus, under Article 5(2):

Any Member State may also provide that the proprietor shall be entitled to prevent all third parties not having his consent from using in the course of trade any sign which is identical with, or similar to, the trade mark in relation to goods or services which are not similar to those for which the trade mark is registered, where the latter has a reputation in the Member State and where use of that sign without due cause takes unfair advantage of, or is detrimental to, the distinctive character or the repute of the trade mark.

---

[41] TMA, s. 10(1)–(2); TMD 2016, Art. 10.

[42] TMA, s. 10(3). Following *Davidoff v Gofkid*, infringement under Art. 5(2) also encompasses an identical or similar mark used on similar goods. Under the TMD 2016, it will no longer be optional.

The global approach to finding conflict under Article 4(1)(b) is also to be applied to finding infringement under Article 5(1)(b). As a result, it follows that if the earlier registered mark has a reputation or is particularly distinctive, then the court will be more likely to find that it has been infringed by the use of the later mark. There are also a number of limitations to the rights conferred by registration, which are more commonly thought of as defences to infringement. These include use by a third party of a trade mark descriptively or to indicate the intended purpose of goods or services. These limitations will be looked at in the following chapter.

7.2.1 INFRINGING ACTS

The acts which constitute use of a trade mark and which may be prohibited are set out in Article 5(3) of the TMD.[43] They include: affixing the sign to goods or packaging; offering goods or putting them on the market or stocking them for these purposes under the sign; offering or supplying services under the sign; importing or exporting goods under the sign; and using the sign on business papers and in advertising.[44] In *Google v Louis Vuitton*,[45] the CJEU noted that this list is not exhaustive. It includes the use of a registered trade mark as a link to a third party's website, even if the trade mark is not mentioned on the website itself. As the CJEU noted, the list was drawn up 'before the full emergence of electronic commerce' and advertising, which can 'typically give rise to uses which differ from those listed in art. 5(3)'. Two additions to prohibited acts which are incorporated into the TMD 2016 are using the sign in comparative advertising in a manner contrary to the Comparative Advertising Directive[46] and using the sign as a company name.[47]

Infringing use must also be use 'in the course of trade'. In *Arsenal v Reed*, the CJEU confirmed that use in the course of trade means use which 'takes place in the context of commercial activity with a view to economic advantage and not as a private matter'.[48] The question of when unauthorized use of a registered trade mark is in the course of trade was re-examined by the CJEU in *Google v Louis Vuitton*. This case is just one example of how the realities of conducting commerce on the internet have raised new questions regarding the interpretation of the directive.

Google France, Google Inc. v Louis Vuitton Malletier and others
Joined Cases C-236, 237, and 238/08 [2010] ECR I-2417

Google operates an internet search engine. Louis Vuitton manufactures and sells luxury leather goods and has a number of EUTMs and national registrations for 'Louis Vuitton' and 'LV'. The dispute arose over Google's 'AdWords' service, a major source of revenue for the company. When an individual searches for words using Google,

---

[43] TMA, s. 10(4); TMD 2016, Art. 10(3).

[44] For an example of what constitutes an infringing act, see *Frisdranken Industrie Winters BV v Red Bull GmbH* Case C-119/10 [2012] CEC 957: placing soft drinks in cans carrying an infringing mark affixed by a third party was not an infringing act.

[45] Joined Cases C-236–238/08 [2010] ECR I-2417, [67].

[46] Directive 2006/114/EC. See Chapter 8 for a discussion of comparative advertising.

[47] TMD 2016, Art. 10(3)(d) and (f).

[48] *Arsenal Football Club plc v Reed* Case C-206/01 [2002] ECR I-10273.

the result displays sites which are the 'natural' results of the search. Google also offers the paid referencing service, 'AdWords', which enables a trader to reserve so-called 'keywords'. When an internet user searches for these words, both the natural results and an advertising link with a short commercial message are displayed, the latter together with the words 'sponsored links'. The link directs the user to the advertiser's website. Each time a user clicks on to one of these sites, the advertiser pays a fee to Google. In the case of Louis Vuitton, traders were able to select keywords corresponding to its trade marks. Some advertisers were also using expressions such as 'imitation' and 'copy' together with the Louis Vuitton marks. Louis Vuitton (and the other claimants) sued both Google and the advertisers for trade mark infringement. The French courts found for the claimants but addressed a number of questions to the CJEU. One set of questions pertained to whether the advertisers and Google were infringing by using the trade marks as keywords. This raised the anterior question of whether either the advertisers or Google were using the registered marks 'in the course of trade'. The CJEU held that the advertisers were using the marks in the course of trade but Google was not.

51 With regard, first, to the advertiser purchasing the referencing service and choosing as a keyword a sign identical with another's trade mark, it must be held that that advertiser is using that sign within the meaning of that case law.

52 From the advertiser's point of view, the selection of a keyword identical with a trade mark has the object and effect of displaying an advertising link to the site on which he offers his goods or services for sale. Since the sign selected as a keyword is the means used to trigger that ad display, it cannot be disputed that the advertiser indeed uses it in the context of commercial activity and not as a private matter.

53 With regard, next, to the referencing service provider, it is common ground that it is carrying out a commercial activity with a view to economic advantage when it stores as keywords, for certain of its clients, signs which are identical with trade marks and arranges for the display of ads on the basis of those keywords.

54 It is also common ground that that service is not supplied only to the proprietors of those trade marks or to operators entitled to market their goods or services, but, at least in the proceedings in question, is provided without the consent of the proprietors and is supplied to their competitors or to imitators.

55 Although it is clear from those factors that the referencing service provider operates 'in the course of trade' when it permits advertisers to select, as keywords, signs identical with trade marks, stores those signs and displays its clients' ads on the basis thereof, it does not follow, however, from those factors that that service provider itself 'uses' those signs within the terms of art.5 of Directive 89/104 and art.9 of Regulation 40/94.

56 In that regard, suffice it to note that the use, by a third party, of a sign identical with, or similar to, the proprietor's trade mark implies, at the very least, that that third party uses the sign in its own commercial communication. A referencing service provider allows its clients to use signs which are identical with, or similar to, trade marks, without itself using those signs.

We may find the CJEU approach here surprising. As the Court acknowledges, Google is making money through offering its AdWords service. However, because it is the service itself rather than the use of the marks as such which is the source of profit, the Court found Google was not using the marks in the course of trade. It followed that Google could not have infringed the claimant's marks. The CJEU reached an opposite conclusion in *Logistics v Bacardi*.

Logistics BV and another v Bacardi & Co. Ltd and another Case C-379/14, EU:C:2015:497

The claimants sold alcoholic drinks. Several consignments of their goods were imported into the Netherlands from outside the EEA without their consent. These goods were placed in a warehouse by customs and excise. The goods could not be released and the question arose as to whether storing the goods in the warehouse constituted 'use in the course of trade' of the marks placed on the goods for the purposes of an infringement action under Article 5(3). According to the CJEU, it did despite the goods being held in a warehouse.

40 It is true that, in importing and storing goods bearing a sign identical to another's trade mark for goods identical to those in respect of which that mark is registered, that economic operator does not use that sign in the course of dealings with consumers. However, at the risk of depriving Directive 89/104 of any useful effect, the terms 'using' and 'in the course of trade' used in paragraph 1 of that article cannot be interpreted as meaning that they refer only to immediate relationships between a trader and a consumer.

41 First, concerning the notion of 'using', the court has previously held that there is use of a sign identical to the trade mark, within the meaning of article 5 of Directive 89/104, where the economic operator concerned uses the sign in its own commercial communications: *Google France SARL v Louis Vuitton Malletier SA* (Joined Cases C-236/08 to C-238/08) [2011] Bus LR 1; [2010] ECR I-2417, para 56.

42 That is the case, for example, where an economic operator imports or sends to a warehousekeeper goods bearing a trade mark of which it is not a proprietor with a view to releasing them for marketing. If it were otherwise, the acts of import and of stocking for the purpose of placement on the market, mentioned in article 5(3) of Directive 89/104 and normally carried out without direct contact with potential consumers, could not be qualified as 'using' within the meaning of that article and could not be prohibited, even though the EU legislature has expressly identified them as being prohibited.

43 Concerning the expression 'in the course of trade', it is settled case law that the use of a sign identical to a trade mark constitutes use in the course of trade where it occurs in the context of commercial activity with a view to economic advantage and not as a private matter: *Arsenal Football Club plc v Reed* (Case C-206/01) [2002] ECR I-10273, para 40; *Céline SARL v Céline SA* (Case C-17/06) [2007] ECR I-7041, para 17 and the *Google France case*, para 50.

44 That is evidently the case where, as in the case in the main proceedings, an economic operator active in the parallel trade of trade marked goods, imports and stores such goods.

It is important to note here that it is not the warehouse owner, in this case customs and excise, which is being held to account but the importers of the claimant's goods. Such a result would seem to follow the reasoning in *Google*. But do you think the result would have been the same if the warehouse were owned by a private company aware of the origin of the goods? We return below to whether the same might be said for the advertisers who bought AdWords from Google.[49]

7.2.2 INFRINGING USE

We have seen that trade mark registration affords the proprietor a monopoly over the use of his mark in certain circumstances. For example, it allows the trade mark proprietor to prevent third parties from using his mark in those circumstances set out in Article 5(1) and (2). There are also limitations to this monopoly. The defences to trade mark infringement circumscribe the monopoly endowed by registration. The question of how broad the monopoly afforded by registration should be is also implicit in another key question relating to a finding of infringement, which is whether a third party needs to use the registered mark as a trade mark, that is as a badge of origin, to infringe the mark.

7.2.2.1 Trade mark use: the judgment in *Arsenal v Reed*

The CJEU examined the question of whether it is necessary for there to be trade mark use of the later sign or mark for a finding of infringement in *Arsenal v Reed*.

Arsenal Football Club plc v Reed Case C-206/01 [2002] ECR I-10273

Matthew Reed sold merchandise outside the Arsenal football ground. These goods carried a number of Arsenal's trade marks, which had been registered for the same goods. Reed had placed a notice on his stall, stating that his goods were not 'official' Arsenal merchandise. Arsenal alleged passing off and trade mark infringement by Reed. In his defence to the latter, Reed claimed, inter alia, that to be infringing, his use of Arsenal's trade marks had to be trade mark use. He argued that he did not use the Arsenal marks as a badge of origin, but rather as badges of allegiance. Laddie J agreed. In his High Court judgment, he held that the Arsenal marks on Mr Reed's merchandise were viewed as badges of 'support, loyalty or affiliation' by the relevant public. However, he also noted that although in his view the directive suggested that a mark had to be used in a trade mark sense to infringe, crucially previous UK decisions, including by the Court of Appeal in *Philips*, had held the opposite. Laddie J therefore chose to ask the CJEU whether infringing use must be trade mark use. The CJEU held first of all that the use of the Arsenal sign was use in the course of trade and that it prima facie fell under Article 5(1)(a) of the directive, as use of an identical sign on identical goods. The CJEU then identified the essential function of the mark which was to act as a badge of origin.

> 51. It follows that the exclusive right under Art. 5(1)(a) of the Directive was conferred in order to enable the trade mark proprietor to protect his specific interests as proprietor, that is, to ensure that the trade mark can fulfil its functions. The exercise of that right must therefore be reserved to cases in which a third party's use of the sign affects or is liable to affect the functions of the trade mark, in particular its essential function of guaranteeing to consumers the origin of the goods.

---

[49] See 7.2.3.1.

52. The exclusive nature of the right conferred by a registered trade mark on its proprietor under Art. 5(1)(a) of the Directive can be justified only within the limits of the application of that article.

53. It should be noted that Art. 5(5) of the Directive provides that Art. 5(1) to (4) does not affect provisions in a Member State relating to protection against the use of a sign for purposes other than that of distinguishing goods or services.

54. The proprietor may not prohibit the use of a sign identical to the trade mark for goods identical to those for which the mark is registered if that use cannot affect his own interests as proprietor of the mark, having regard to its functions. Thus certain uses for purely descriptive purposes are excluded from the scope of Art. 5(1) of the Directive because they do not affect any of the interests which that provision aims to protect, and do not therefore fall within the concept of use within the meaning of that provision (see, with respect to a use for purely descriptive purposes relating to the characteristics of the product offered, Case C-2/00 *Hölterhoff* [2002] ECR I-4187, paragraph 16).

55. In this respect, it is clear that the situation in question in the main proceedings is fundamentally different from that in *Hölterhoff*.[50] In the present case, the use of the sign takes place in the context of sales to consumers and is obviously not intended for purely descriptive purposes.

56. Having regard to the presentation of the word 'Arsenal' on the goods at issue in the main proceedings and the other secondary markings on them … the use of that sign is such as to create the impression that there is a material link in the course of trade between the goods concerned and the trade mark proprietor.

57. That conclusion is not affected by the presence on Mr Reed's stall of the notice stating that the goods at issue in the main proceedings are not official Arsenal FC products … Even on the assumption that such a notice may be relied on by a third party as a defence to an action for trade mark infringement, there is a clear possibility in the present case that some consumers, in particular if they come across the goods after they have been sold by Mr Reed and taken away from the stall where the notice appears, may interpret the sign as designating Arsenal FC as the undertaking of origin of the goods.

58. Moreover, in the present case, there is also no guarantee, as required by the Court's case law …, that all the goods designated by the trade mark have been manufactured or supplied under the control of a single undertaking which is responsible for their quality.

59. The goods at issue are in fact supplied outside the control of Arsenal FC as trade mark proprietor, it being common ground that they do not come from Arsenal FC or from its approved resellers.

60. In those circumstances, the use of a sign which is identical to the trade mark at issue in the main proceedings is liable to jeopardise the guarantee of origin which constitutes the essential function of the mark, as is apparent from the Court's case … It is consequently a use which the trade mark proprietor may prevent in accordance with Art. 5(1) of the Directive.

61. Once it has been found that, in the present case, the use of the sign in question by the third party is liable to affect the guarantee of origin of the goods and that the trade mark proprietor must be able to prevent this, it is immaterial that in the context of that use the sign is perceived as a badge of support for or loyalty or affiliation to the proprietor of the mark.

---

[50] *Hölterhoff* is discussed at 8.1.2 under the exceptions to trade mark infringement.

7.2.2.2 Trade mark use after *Arsenal v Reed*

When the case returned to the High Court, Laddie J disagreed with the CJEU's conclusion that there would be confusion among those who acquired the goods after sale and who might not be aware that they were unofficial (what had become known as the 'Christmas Present Issue') and also that the use of the sign by Reed was liable to affect the origin function of the marks. Laddie J, by contrast, concluded that because the defendant's use of the mark was not intended by him nor understood by the public to be a designation of origin, there could be no infringement as such use did not prejudice the essential function of the mark. He held that Reed had not infringed the Arsenal mark. The case then proceeded to the Court of Appeal, where it is generally agreed that the court endorsed the CJEU's decision. In his judgment, Aldous LJ[51] summarized the CJEU judgment in the following terms:

> 37. It is important to note that the ECJ is not concerned with whether the use complained about is trade mark use. The consideration is whether the third party's use affects or is likely to affect the functions of the trade mark. An instance of where that will occur is given, namely where a competitor wishes to take unfair advantage of the reputation of the trade mark by selling products illegally bearing the mark. That would happen whether or not the third party's use was trade mark use or whether there was confusion.

He added that at no stage had the CJEU suggested that use of the mark which was not understood by the public as use as a badge of origin could not infringe. Instead, what was required was consideration of whether the function of the trade mark was liable to be harmed by such use. In the case, Aldous LJ held that Reed was using the Arsenal marks in a trade mark sense, in that some of his customers would inevitably understand them as denoting the origin of the goods. Reed had infringed the Arsenal mark. The Court of Appeal's approach was confirmed in later CJEU decisions, most notably *Adam Opel AG v Autec AG*.[52] In this case, the claimant, Opel, manufactured cars and had a registered trade mark in Germany, inter alia, for cars and toys. The defendant manufactured model cars. It sold a model of the claimant's Opel Astra, carrying its mark. One question for the Court was whether such use could be infringing, since Autec was not using the Opel mark as a badge of origin. The CJEU, referring back to its decision in *Arsenal v Reed*, confirmed that infringing use of a trade mark is use which affects the functions of a trade mark, in particular its function as a badge of origin. If, in this case, the average consumer understood the use of the mark to be to indicate that this was a scale model of an Opel car, then the origin function of the mark would not be affected and there would be no infringement. The TMD 2016 underlines the reasoning in this line of cases by stating in its preamble that:

> (18) It is appropriate to provide that an infringement of a trade mark can only be established if there is a finding that the infringing mark or sign is used in the course of trade for the purposes of distinguishing goods and services. Use of a sign for purposes other than for distinguishing goods and services should be subject to the provisions of national law.

---

[51] *Arsenal Football Club Plc v Reed (No. 2)* [2003] RPC 39.
[52] *Adam Opel AG v Autec AG* Case C-48/05 [2007] ECR I-1017.

7.2.2.3 The functions of a trade mark and infringement

A key element of both the *Arsenal* and *Opel* decisions is that, in defining infringing use, the CJEU consistently referred not only to the essential function of a trade mark as a badge of origin, but also to its functions in the plural. In *L'Oréal v Bellure*, the Court of Justice set out the implications for a finding of infringement under Article 5(1)(a), that is the use of identical marks on identical goods, once it has been acknowledged that a trade mark's function may extend beyond its role as a badge of origin.

58 The Court has already held that the exclusive right under art.5(1)(a) of Directive 89/104 was conferred in order to enable the trade mark proprietor to protect his specific interests as proprietor, that is, to ensure that the trade mark can fulfil its functions and that, therefore, the exercise of that right must be reserved to cases in which a third party's use of the sign affects or is liable to affect the functions of the trade mark (*Arsenal Football Club* (C-206/01) [2002] E.C.R I-10273 at [51]; *Anheuser-Busch* (C-245/02) [2004] E.C.R. I-10989 at [59]; and *Adam Opel* (C-48/05) [2007] E.C.R. I-1017 at [21]). These functions include not only the essential function of the trade mark, which is to guarantee to consumers the origin of the goods or services, but also its other functions, in particular that of guaranteeing the quality of the goods or services in question and those of communication, investment or advertising.

59 The protection conferred by art.5(1)(a) of Directive 89/104 is thus broader than that provided by art.5(1)(b), the application of which requires that there be a likelihood of confusion and accordingly the possibility that the essential function of the mark may be affected (see, to that effect, *Davidoff* [2003] E.C.R. I-389 at [28], and *O2 Holdings and O2 (UK)* [2008] E.C.R. I-4231 at [57]). By virtue of the 10th recital in the preamble to Directive 89/104, the protection afforded by the registered trade mark is absolute in the case of identity between the mark and the sign and also between the goods or services, whereas, in case of similarity between the mark and the sign and between the goods or services, the likelihood of confusion constitutes the specific condition for such protection.

60 It is apparent from the case-law cited in paragraph 58 of this judgment that the proprietor of the mark cannot oppose the use of a sign identical with the mark on the basis of art.5(1)(a) of Directive 89/104 if that use is not liable to cause detriment to any of the functions of that mark (see also *Arsenal Football Club* [2002] E.C.R. I-10273 at [54], and *Adam Opel* [2007] E.C.R. I-1017 at [22]).

61 Thus, the Court has already held that certain uses for purely descriptive purposes are excluded from the scope of application of art.5(1) of Directive 89/104, because they do not affect any of the interests which that provision is intended to protect and accordingly do not constitute 'use' within the meaning of that provision (see, to that effect, *Hölterhoff* (C-2/00) [2002] E.C.R. I-4187 at [16]).

62 It must, however, be made clear that the situation described in the main proceedings is fundamentally different from that which gave rise to the judgment in *Hölterhoff*, in that the word marks belonging to L'Oréal and Others are used in the comparison lists distributed by Malaika and Starion not for purely descriptive purposes, but for the purpose of advertising.

63 It is for the referring court to determine whether, in a situation such as that which arises in the main proceedings, the use which is made of the marks belonging to L'Oréal and Others is liable to affect one of the functions of those marks, such as, in particular, their functions of communication, investment or advertising.

In *L'Oréal v Bellure*, the Court of Justice made clear that while a finding of infringement under Article 5(1)(b) is contingent on a finding of confusion, a finding of infringement under Article 5(1)(a) rests on one of the functions of the mark having been affected. The CJEU's approach to interpreting Article 5(1)(a) has attracted criticism. The general assumption had been that, under this provision, if the mark and sign and the goods and services are identical then it is presumed the mark has been infringed. Such an assumption arises from the fact that given the overlap, the origin function of the mark would inevitably be affected. Now the CJEU seemed to be suggesting that there was no such presumption, and it was necessary to look further to see if any of the mark's functions had been damaged including but not restricted to its origin function. The TMD 2016 seeks to undo what many have seen as an unnecessary complication in 'double-identity' infringement cases, that is cases involving identical signs and identical goods and services. The TMD 2016 states:

> The protection afforded by the registered trade mark, the function of which is in particular to guarantee the trade mark as an indication of origin should be absolute in the event of there being identity between the mark and the sign and the goods or services.

7.2.2.4 Assessing confusion

In infringement actions when assessing a likelihood of confusion, the court will apply the global approach. However, there are a number of key differences between assessing confusion at the point of registration and in an infringement action, where the mark and the sign have both been used on the market. First of all, in an infringement action, the use of the allegedly infringing sign is not to be considered stripped of its context. Rather, all the circumstances of its actual use which are likely to operate in the average consumer's mind, including the impression it is likely to make on him or her, should be considered. In addition, if both sign and mark have been used and there has been actual confusion between them, this may be powerful evidence that their similarity is such that there exists a likelihood of confusion. The reverse may also be the case, although the lack of evidence of confusion is not decisive.[53] Second, the court may take a different approach to measuring consumer confusion in infringement cases than it will in cases concerning conflict between a mark and a sign at the point of registration. We have seen that when looking at the latter, the court will take into account a variety of empirical evidence, including surveys. However, in a series of cases relating to the dispute between Interflora and Marks & Spencer (the facts of which are set out at 7.2.3.2), the English courts have suggested a different approach to assessing consumer confusion in cases of trade mark infringement. In particular, they have taken a contrasting view of the utility of survey evidence in making such an assessment. Thus, in *Interflora v Marks & Spencer*, the claimant sought to introduce evidence of surveys it had conducted, in order to show that there had been sufficient customer confusion for a finding of trade mark infringement. It was accepted by the claimant that these surveys were not statistically reliable. In the High Court it was held that some of this survey evidence might be admitted. Marks & Spencer appealed. In upholding the appeal, Lewison LJ set out the circumstances in which a court would be likely to accept survey evidence in trade mark cases. An important question for the court was whether actual evidence of customer confusion would be probative of the fact that the average consumer of the goods and services at

---

[53] *Roger Maier, Assos of Switzerland SA v ASOS Plc, ASOS.com Ltd* [2015] EWCA Civ 220, [79]–[80].

issue had been confused or whether the question would be one for the judge.[54] In his judgment, Lewison LJ framed what has come to be known as 'the real value test' for admitting survey evidence.

Marks & Spencer Plc v Interflora Inc. and Interflora British Unit
[2012] EWCA Civ 1501

Lewison LJ:

76. ... But the remaining objections still hold good: viz. that the selected witnesses are not (or at least cannot be shown to be) a fair sample of the class of reasonably well-informed and reasonably observant internet users, with the consequence that there is no ground for any extrapolation on a statistical basis, or on the basis of any mathematical or logical probability, of the views of the selected witnesses as representing the effect of the M & S advertisement on the hypothetical reasonably well-informed and reasonably observant internet user. If evidence of this kind cannot form the basis for extrapolation on the basis of any mathematical or logical probability leading to a conclusion about the effect of M & S's advertisement on the hypothetical reasonably well-informed and reasonably observant internet user, then in the absence of special circumstances it cannot be useful. And if it cannot be useful, it should not be allowed to distract the focus of the trial even if it is technically admissible.

...

135. The upshot of this review is that courts have allowed the calling of evidence of the kind that Interflora wishes to call and have considered it, either in conjunction with or in the absence of a statistically valid and reliable survey. But it is generally of little or no value. Sometimes it does no more than confirm the conclusion that the judge would have reached without the evidence. In passing off cases it sometimes has greater effect, but as I have said more than once, passing off raises a different legal question. Unless the court can be confident that the evidence of their evidence may be probative. But unless the court can extrapolate from their evidence, it is not probative.

...

137. That is not to say that there can never be evidence called in a case of trade mark infringement. The court may need to be informed of shopping habits; of the market in which certain goods or services are supplied; the means by which goods or services are marketed and so on. In addition I must make it clear, however, that different considerations may come into play where:

i) evidence is called consisting of the spontaneous reactions of members of the relevant public to the allegedly infringing sign or advertisement;

ii) evidence from consumers is called in order to amplify the results of a reliable survey;

iii) the goods or services in question are not goods or services supplied to ordinary consumers and are unlikely to be within the judge's experience;

iv) the issue is whether a registered mark has acquired distinctiveness; or

v) where the cause of action is in passing off, which requires a different legal question to be answered.

[54] Because this case concerned trade mark infringement on the internet, the average consumer was identified as the reasonably well-informed and reasonably observant internet user. However, the average internet user was held to be no different from the average consumer (see e.g. [38]).

138. Outside these kinds of cases there may be others where a judge might think that it would be useful to hear from consumers. I would not wish to rule out the possibility. So I would not accept the proposition that evidence from respondents to a questionnaire can never be called in the absence of a statistically valid and reliable survey. But (apart from those I have mentioned) the cases in which that kind of evidence might be of real use are difficult to imagine. I would not therefore hold that such evidence is inadmissible as a matter of law.

...

144. The current practice, which Arnold J. understandably followed, is to allow the evidence in unless the judge can be satisfied that it will be valueless. In my judgment that is the wrong way round. I consider that, even if the evidence is technically admissible, the judge should not let it in unless (a) satisfied that it would be valuable and (b) that the likely utility of the evidence justifies the costs involved.

...

146. In the present case I do not consider that Interflora has demonstrated that the evidence it wishes to call would be of real value. To put it bluntly, Interflora starts with an unreliable dataset from which it proposes to select the witnesses most favourable to itself. I would hold, therefore that Mr Hobbs' macro objection is well founded. I would therefore allow the appeal on that basis.[55]

When *Interflora v M&S* returned to the High Court,[56] Arnold J followed Lewison LJ's judgment and allowed evidence of the extent to which internet users in 2008 would be able to differentiate between the natural results of an internet search and a paid advertisement but not surveys assessing consumer confusion. Do you agree with Lewison LJ that because the average consumer is a hypothetical construct, the question of whether he or she would be confused is one that should normally be left to the judgment of the court? As Lewison LJ suggests, such an approach has the advantage of avoiding costly and often lengthy disputes which might arise over the admissibility of survey evidence, of which *Interflora v Marks & Spencer* presents a clear example. However, the advantage of such an approach might be less clear when the goods at issue are not everyday items but more esoteric and less likely to be familiar to the judge, such as specialist bicycling gear.[57] In *Shoe Branding Europe v Adidas AG, OHIM*,[58] the CJEU has confirmed: 'that Community law does not preclude a national court, if it encounters particular difficulties in assessing the misleading nature of the indication in question, from making use, within the parameters established by national law, of market surveys or expert reports in order to deliver a more enlightened judgment.'[59] Is it possible that when recognizing national parameters, the CJEU had the UK courts in mind?

Third, in a recent case, *Comic Enterprises v Twentieth Century Fox Film Corp.*,[60] the UK courts accepted the principle of 'wrong way round confusion' in an infringement action. In this case the claimant, which ran four comedy clubs across the UK, had a registered trade mark which included the words 'the glee CLUB'. It sued Fox for trade mark infringement for its use of the word 'Glee', the title of its very popular television series, on related sound recordings, concert tours, and merchandise. In the High Court, it was held that in assessing

[55] See also *Interflora Inc. v Marks & Spencer plc* [2013] EWHC 273 (Ch) and *Interflora Inc., Interflora British Unit v Marks & Spencer plc* [2013] EWCA Civ 319.
[56] *Interflora Inc. v Marks & Spencer* [2013] EWHC 1291 (Ch), [2013] ETMR 35.
[57] *Maier v ASOS Plc* [2015] EWCA Civ 220.
[58] *Shoe Branding Europe BVBA v Adidas AG, OHIM* Case C-296/15 P, 17 February 2016.
[59] [29].   [60] *Comic Enterprises Ltd v Twentieth Century Fox Film Corp.* [2016] EWCA Civ 41.

the likelihood of confusion it was a relevant factor for finding confusion that the defendant's sign was very widely known, in this case more so than the claimant's mark. The claimant succeeded in the High Court and the defendant appealed, inter alia, arguing that 'wrong way round confusion' was inadmissible. According to Kitchin LJ:

Against this background I can see no basis for saying that, as a matter of law, evidence of 'wrong way round confusion' is inadmissible. It will be recalled that Mr Purvis defines a 'right way round' confusion case as being one in which a consumer familiar with the mark is confused upon seeing the accused sign; and a 'wrong way round' confusion case as being one in which a consumer familiar with the accused sign is confused upon seeing the mark. It seems to me that whether a particular instance of confusion is 'right way round' or 'wrong way round' may be a consequence of nothing more meaningful than the order in which the consumer happened to come across the mark and the sign. Further, in both cases the consumer thinks that the goods or services in issue come from the same undertaking or economically linked undertakings, and they may be equally damaging to the distinctiveness and functions of the mark. Moreover, as I think Mr Purvis was disposed to accept, evidence of 'wrong way round' confusion may be probative of a risk of 'right way round' confusion in any event.[61]

> **FURTHER READING**
>
> J. Davis, 'Revisiting the average consumer: an uncertain presence in European trade marks law' [2015] IPQ 15.
>
> N. M. Dawson, 'Non trade mark use' [2012] IPQ 204.
>
> A. Horton, 'The implications of *L'Oréal v Bellure*: the essential functions of a trade mark and when is an advantage unfair?' [2011] EIPR 550.
>
> A. Kur, 'Trade marks function, don't they? CJEU jurisprudence and unfair competition practices' (2014) 45 IIC 434.
>
> C. Rowden et al., 'When trade mark use is not infringement' [2015] MIP 36.

7.2.3 TRADE MARK INFRINGEMENT AND THE INTERNET

Earlier in this chapter we noted that the rise of e-commerce has resulted in the CJEU looking again at a number of aspects of the TMD. This is no more so than in the area of infringing use, and in particular the use of registered trade marks as keywords and on auction sites. In revisiting infringement in these new contexts, the CJEU has added to our understanding of how the TMD, and its provisions on infringement, should be more generally interpreted.

7.2.3.1 Trade mark infringement and the internet: Article 5(1)(a)

The TMD 2016 aims to adapt EU trade mark law 'to the internet era'. Certainly, the growth of online commerce has raised particular problems for trade mark protection. One of the most urgent has been the use of trade marks as keywords on internet search engines. We have

---

[61] [160].

already seen that Google was not liable for infringement when supplying advertisers with AdWords, as it was not using the trade marks 'in the course of trade'. The advertisers were, however, found to be using the marks in the course of trade and the CJEU also confirmed that their use was in relation to the goods and services at issue. The CJEU was then asked to consider whether their use was infringing under Article 5(1)(a).

> 83 The question whether that function of the trade mark is adversely affected when internet users are shown, on the basis of a keyword identical with a mark, a third party's ad, such as that of a competitor of the proprietor of that mark, depends in particular on the manner in which that ad is presented.
>
> 84 The function of indicating the origin of the mark is adversely affected if the ad does not enable normally informed and reasonably attentive internet users, or enables them only with difficulty, to ascertain whether the goods or services referred to by the ad originate from the proprietor of the trade mark or an undertaking economically connected to it or, on the contrary, originate from a third party (see, to that effect, *Céline* [2007] E.T.M.R. 80 at [27] and the case law cited).
>
> 85 In such a situation, which is, moreover, characterised by the fact that the ad in question appears immediately after entry of the trade mark as a search term by the internet user concerned and is displayed at a point when the trade mark is, in its capacity as a search term, also displayed on the screen, the internet user may err as to the origin of the goods or services in question. In those circumstances, the use by the third party of the sign identical with the mark as a keyword triggering the display of that ad is liable to create the impression that there is a material link in the course of trade between the goods or services in question and the proprietor of the trade mark (see, by way of analogy, *Arsenal Football Club* [2003] E.T.M.R. 19 at [56], and *Anheuser-Busch Inc v Budějovický Budvar, Národní Podnik* (C-245/02) [2004] E.C.R. I-10989; [2005] E.T.M.R. 27 at [60]).
>
> …
>
> 88 It is for the national court to assess, on a case-by-case basis, whether the facts of the dispute before it indicate adverse effects, or a risk thereof, on the function of indicating origin as described at [84] of the present judgment.
>
> 89 In the case where a third party's ad suggests that there is an economic link between that third party and the proprietor of the trade mark, the conclusion must be that there is an adverse effect on the function of indicating origin.
>
> 90 In the case where the ad, while not suggesting the existence of an economic link, is vague to such an extent on the origin of the goods or services at issue that normally informed and reasonably attentive internet users are unable to determine, on the basis of the advertising link and the commercial message attached thereto, whether the advertiser is a third party vis-à-vis the proprietor of the trade mark or, on the contrary, economically linked to that proprietor, the conclusion must also be that there is an adverse effect on that function of the trade mark.

7.2.3.2 Trade mark infringement and the internet: Article 5(2)

Following *Google*, the CJEU was again asked to address the implications of the use of trade marks as key words on the internet in *Interflora v Marks & Spencer*. In this case, the claimant alleged infringement of its trade marks under both Article 5(1) and (2) of the TMD.

Interflora v Marks & Spencer Case C-323/09 [2012] ETMR 1

Interflora operates a worldwide, flower delivery service. The address of its main website is www.interflora.com. The site redirects customers to country-specific websites such as www.interflora.co.uk. Orders for flowers are made on the website, and the orders are filled by the florist closest to the delivery site. Interflora has a EUTM and a UK registered trade mark, 'Interflora'. Marks & Spencer (M&S), which is a well-known UK retailer, has its own website from which customers can order flowers: www.marksandspencer.com. M&S selected 'Interflora' and variants as a keyword from Google's AdWords service. As a result, if Interflora was entered into the Google search engine an M&S advertisement for its flower delivery service appeared as a sponsored link. Interflora sued M&S for trade mark infringement. It was accepted by both parties that Interflora had a reputation for the purposes of Article 5(2). Arnold J in the High Court addressed a number of questions to the CJEU. Among these were the following. First, if a trader selects a trade mark as a keyword but the sponsored link does not include the sign or a similar sign, as the M&S site did not, does that constitute use within Article 5(1)(a)? The CJEU held that it did. Second, is such use 'in relation to the goods or services identical to those for which the trade mark is registered even if the sign does not appear on the competitor's website'? Once again, the CJEU held that it did.[62] Third, does such use constitute infringement under Article 5(1)(a) and Article 5(2)? Finally, should Article 5(2) be interpreted as meaning that the proprietor of a trade mark with a reputation is entitled to prevent a competitor from basing its advertising on a keyword corresponding to that trade mark which the competitor has, without the proprietor's consent, selected in an internet referencing service? Turning first to the questions regarding Article 5(1)(a), the Court of Justice chose to expand upon the circumstances in which a trade mark's origin, advertising, and investment functions might be put in jeopardy. Thus, in relation to the adverse effect on the origin function of a keywords advertisement, the Court cited its decision in *Google* to the effect that the origin function will be adversely affected if the advertisement does not enable reasonably well-informed and reasonably observant internet users, or enables them only with difficulty, to ascertain whether the goods or services referred to by the advertisement originate from the proprietor of the trade mark or an undertaking economically connected to it or, on the contrary, originate from a third party. The Court then turned to the advertising and investment functions. Again, it cited the decision in *Google*, this time to the effect that use of a trade mark as a keyword does not necessarily affect its advertising function.

57 However, the mere fact that the use, by a third party, of a sign identical with a trade mark in relation to goods or services identical with those for which that mark is registered obliges the proprietor of that mark to intensify its advertising in order to maintain or enhance its profile with consumers is not a sufficient basis, in every case, for concluding that the trade mark's advertising function is adversely affected. In that regard, although the trade mark is an essential element in the system of undistorted competition which European law seeks to establish (see, in particular, *Copad SA v Christian Dior Couture SA* (C-59/08) [2009] E.C.R. I-3421; [2009] E.T.M.R. 40 at [22]), its purpose is not, however, to protect its proprietor against practices inherent in competition.

[62] See *Google v Louis Vuitton* at 7.2.1.

58 Internet advertising on the basis of keywords corresponding to trade marks constitutes such a practice in that its aim, as a general rule, is merely to offer internet users alternatives to the goods or services of the proprietors of those trade marks (see, to that effect, *Google France* [2010] E.T.M.R. 30 at [69]).

59 The selection of a sign identical with another person's trade mark, in a referencing service with the characteristics of 'AdWords', does not, moreover, have the effect of denying the proprietor of that trade mark the opportunity of using its mark effectively to inform and win over consumers (see, in that regard, *Google France* [2010] E.T.M.R. 30 at [96] and [97]).

[The CJEU then turned to the relationship between the investment function and key words advertising.]

60 In addition to its function of indicating origin and, as the case may be, its advertising function, a trade mark may also be used by its proprietor to acquire or preserve a reputation capable of attracting consumers and retaining their loyalty.

61 Although that function of a trade mark—called the 'investment function'—may overlap with the advertising function, it is nonetheless distinct from the latter. Indeed, when the trade mark is used to acquire or preserve a reputation, not only advertising is employed, but also various commercial techniques.

62 When the use by a third party, such as a competitor of the trade mark proprietor, of a sign identical with the trade mark in relation to goods or services identical with those for which the mark is registered substantially interferes with the proprietor's use of its trade mark to acquire or preserve a reputation capable of attracting consumers and retaining their loyalty, the third party's use must be regarded as adversely affecting the trade mark's investment function. The proprietor is, as a consequence, entitled to prevent such use under art.5(1)(a) of Directive 89/104 or, in the case of a Community trade mark, under art.9(1)(a) of Regulation 40/94.

...

64 However, it cannot be accepted that the proprietor of a trade mark may—in conditions of fair competition that respect the trade mark's function as an indication of origin—prevent a competitor from using a sign identical with that trade mark in relation to goods or services identical with those for which the mark is registered, if the only consequence of that use is to oblige the proprietor of that trade mark to adapt its efforts to acquire or preserve a reputation capable of attracting consumers and retaining their loyalty. Likewise, the fact that that use may prompt some consumers to switch from goods or services bearing that trade mark cannot be successfully relied on by the proprietor of the mark.

[The CJEU then turned to the questions relating to Article 5(2) of the TMD and looked first at dilution.]

78 In support of its contention that detriment is caused to its trade mark's distinctive character, Interflora maintains that the use by M&S and other undertakings of the word 'interflora' within a referencing service such as that at issue in the main proceedings gradually persuades internet users that the word is not a trade mark designating the flower-delivery service provided by florists in the Interflora network but is a generic word for any flower-delivery service.

79 It is true that the use, by a third party in the course of trade, of a sign identical with or similar to a trade mark with a reputation reduces the latter's distinctiveness and is thus detrimental to the distinctive character of that trade mark for the purposes of art.5(2) of Directive

89/104 or, in the case of a Community trade mark, of art.9(1)(c) of Regulation 40/94, when it contributes to turning the trade mark into a generic term.

80 However, contrary to Interflora's contention, the selection of a sign which is identical with or similar to a trade mark with a reputation as a keyword within an internet referencing service does not necessarily contribute to such a development.

81 Thus, when the use, as a keyword, of a sign corresponding to a trade mark with a reputation triggers the display of an advertisement which enables the reasonably well informed and reasonably observant internet user to tell that the goods or services offered originate not from the proprietor of the trade mark but, on the contrary, from a competitor of that proprietor, the conclusion will have to be that the trade mark's distinctiveness has not been reduced by that use, the latter having merely served to draw the internet user's attention to the existence of an alternative product or service to that of the proprietor of the trade mark.

[The CJEU then turned to the issue of the taking of unfair advantage.]

85 It is also apparent that the fact that a trade mark enjoys a reputation makes it likely that a large number of internet users will use the name of that mark as a keyword when carrying out an internet search to find information or offers relating to the goods or services covered by that trade mark.

86 In those circumstances, as the Advocate General observes at para.96 of his Opinion, it cannot be denied that, where a competitor of the proprietor of a trade mark with a reputation selects that trade mark as a keyword in an internet referencing service, the purpose of that use is to take advantage of the distinctive character and repute of the trade mark. In fact, that selection is liable to create a situation in which the probably large number of consumers using that keyword to carry out an internet search for goods or services covered by the trade mark with a reputation will see that competitor's advertisement displayed on their screens.

87 Nor can it be denied that, when internet users, having studied the competitor's advertisement, purchase the product or service offered by the competitor instead of that of the proprietor of the trade mark to which their search originally related, that competitor derives a real advantage from the distinctive character and repute of the trade mark.

88 Furthermore, it is not disputed that, in the context of a referencing service, an advertiser which selects signs identical with or similar to the trade marks of other persons does not, as a general rule, pay the proprietors of the trade marks any compensation in respect of that use.

89 It is clear from those particular aspects of the selection as internet keywords of signs corresponding to trade marks with a reputation which belong to other persons that such a selection can, in the absence of any 'due cause' as referred to in art.5(2) of Directive 89/104 and art.9(1)(c) of Regulation 40/94, be construed as a use whereby the advertiser rides on the coat-tails of a trade mark with a reputation in order to benefit from its power of attraction, its reputation and its prestige, and to exploit, without paying any financial compensation and without being required to make efforts of its own in that regard, the marketing effort expended by the proprietor of that mark in order to create and maintain the image of that mark. If that is the case, the advantage thus obtained by the third party must be considered to be unfair (*L'Oréal* [2009] E.T.M.R. 55 at [49]).

90 As the Court has already stated, that is particularly likely to be the conclusion in cases in which internet advertisers offer for sale, by means of the selection of keywords corresponding to trade marks with a reputation, goods which are imitations of the goods of the proprietor of those marks (*Google France* [2010] E.T.M.R. 30 at [102] and [103]).

> 91 By contrast, where the advertisement displayed on the internet on the basis of a keyword corresponding to a trade mark with a reputation puts forward—without offering a mere imitation of the goods or services of the proprietor of that trade mark, without causing dilution or tarnishment and without, moreover, adversely affecting the functions of the trade mark concerned—an alternative to the goods or services of the proprietor of the trade mark with a reputation, it must be concluded that such use falls, as a rule, within the ambit of fair competition in the sector for the goods or services concerned and is thus not without 'due cause' for the purposes of art.5(2) of Directive 89/104 and art.9(1)(c) of Regulation 40/94.

In its decision in *Interflora v Marks & Spencer*, the CJEU explicitly sought to draw a balance between those activities of an advertiser which might undermine the earlier mark's origin, advertising, and investment functions or might dilute its distinctiveness or ride on its coat-tails, and those activities which would represent legitimate competition, if carried on by a third party. Do you think the CJEU got the balance right?[63]

7.2.3.3 Trade mark infringement, keywords, and auction sites

Trade mark infringement and trade mark use were also considered in *L'Oréal v eBay*.[64] In this case, the online auction site was sued by L'Oréal for infringing a number of its EUTMs. An important issue in this case concerned the repacking and reselling of L'Oréal's products, and this will be examined when we consider exhaustion of rights in the next chapter. However, questions relating to eBay's use of Google's AdWords service were also raised. One question was whether eBay made 'use' of L'Oréal's marks, within the meaning of Article 5(1)(a) of the TMD, when the marks appeared as sponsored links directing internet users to the auction site, as a result of eBay registering them as keywords with Google. The CJEU held that they did not when they were used as a general link to eBay's auction site, although eBay might be liable for their use under Article 5(2), which of course involves the use of marks with a reputation on dissimilar goods.[65] However, where eBay used keywords to promote customer–sellers offers, then it was using the sign against goods or services for the purposes of Article 5(1)(a) and as a result it might be liable for infringement.[66] Thus, the Court of Justice concluded that:

> the proprietor of a trade mark is entitled to prevent an online marketplace operator from advertising —on the basis of a keyword which is identical to his trade mark and which has been selected in an internet referencing service by that operator—goods bearing that trade mark which are offered for sale on the marketplace, where that advertising does not enable reasonably well-informed and reasonably observant internet users, or enables them only with difficulty, to ascertain whether the goods concerned originate from the proprietor of the trade mark or from an undertaking economically linked to that proprietor or, on the contrary, originate from a third party.[67]

---

[63] In the High Court, Arnold J found the defendant liable under Art. 5(1)(a); on appeal, the Court of Appeal ordered a retrial because of what were held to be procedural irregularities: *Interflora v Marks & Spencer* [2013] EWHC 1291 (Ch); *Interflora v Marks & Spencer* [2014] EWCA Civ 1403.

[64] *L'Oréal v eBay International AG* Case C-324/09 [2011] ETMR 52.   [65] [90].   [66] [91].

[67] [97].

However, the CJEU took a different view regarding whether eBay made 'use' of a trade mark, when that mark was being displayed by one of the sellers on the site. Here the CJEU concluded:

> 102 If a sign identical with, or similar to, the proprietor's trade mark is to be 'used', within the meaning of Article 5 of Directive 89/104 and Article 9 of Regulation No 40/94, by a third party, that implies, at the very least, that that third party uses the sign in its own commercial communication. In so far as that third party provides a service consisting in enabling its customers to display on its website, in the course of their commercial activities such as their offers for sale, signs corresponding to trade marks, it does not itself use those signs within the meaning of that EU legislation (see, to that effect, *Google France and Google*, paragraphs 56 and 57).

It is an interesting question whether, had the CJEU found otherwise, eBay's entire business model might have been undermined, as indeed might have been the result if Google's AdWords service had been held to constitute infringing use. A related problem arose in the more recent case of *Cartier v BSB*.[68] *Cartier* concerned the sale of counterfeit goods on the internet under the claimant's marks. In the High Court, Arnold J issued an order for ISPs to apply technological measures to prevent access to websites dedicated to selling these counterfeit goods. And a website-blocking order was subsequently made against a number of ISPs.[69] On appeal, the Court of Appeal upheld Arnold J's judgment.[70] Kitchin LJ took the view that the UK courts had the jurisdiction to make blocking orders against intermediaries even though they, themselves, were innocent of any infringement. The Court of Appeal also held that the costs of such orders must be borne by the intermediaries. And, in making such orders, the courts must be sure that they are proportionate, striking a fair balance between the interests of the intermediaries and those of the rightsholder. Previously, so-called 'blocking injunctions' had been applied only in cases of copyright infringement. All these cases underline the novelty and importance of the questions which the growth of e-commerce raise for the protection of intellectual property generally and for trade marks in particular.[71]

FURTHER READING

A. Blythe, 'Trade marks as adwords: an aid to competition or a potential infringement? An evaluation of the law in the light of recent decisions' [2015] EIPR 225.

D. Leviens 'L'Oreal v. eBay—welcomed in France, resented in England' (2012) 43 IIC 68.

E. Moro, 'Protection of reputed trademarks and keywords: looking for Ariadne's thread among flowers, perfumes and bags' [2013] UCL J. L. & J. 64.

F. Rizzuto, 'The liability of online service providers for infringement of intellectual property rights' [2012] CTLR 4.

---

[68] *Cartier International AG v British Sky Broadcasting Ltd* [2014] EWHC 3354 (Ch).

[69] *Cartier International Ltd v British Sky Broadcasting Ltd* [2014] EWHC 3354 (Ch).

[70] *Cartier International Ltd v British Sky Broadcasting Ltd* [2016] EWCA (Civ) 658. This case is examined in detail in Chapter 15.

[71] In both *Google v Louis Vuitton* and *L'Oréal v eBay*, the CJEU also suggested there were certain circumstances in which the defendants would be liable under Art. 14(1) of the e-Commerce Directive; in particular, if Google failed to act expeditiously to prevent access to infringing data or, in the case of eBay, to remove infringing data from its site.

7.3 REMEDIES

In trade mark cases, infringement proceedings cannot begin until the date upon which the trade mark is first registered, although damages for infringement will be recoverable from the mark's priority date. In all legal proceedings relating to a registered trade mark, the registration of a person as proprietor of a trade mark shall be prima facie evidence of the validity of the original registration (section 72 of the TMA). Specific remedies for trade mark infringement include an order for the erasure of an infringing sign (section 15) or for the delivery up of goods, materials, or articles which bear it (section 16). There are also criminal sanctions for trade mark infringement. The prerequisite to finding an offence has been committed is that the defendant must have acted with a view to gain for himself or another or with intent to cause loss to another and without the consent of another (section 92 of the TMA). This is an offence of strict liability, in that there is no need to show that at the time the defendant knew that there was a registered trade mark (*Torbay Council v Satnam Singh*[72]). It is a defence for the accused to show that he believed or that he had reasonable grounds to believe that the use of the sign in the manner in which it was used or was to be used was not an infringement of the registered trade mark (section 92(5)). On the other hand, it is not a defence to an action that the quality of the infringing goods was so poor that the public would not be confused into believing they were legitimate merchandise.[73]

7.4 CONCLUSION

Arguably, two of the most important developments we have considered in this chapter on the relative grounds for refusal of registration and infringement have resulted in the expansion of the monopoly accorded to trade mark proprietors. First, there is the finding by the CJEU that the investment, advertising, and commercial functions of a trade mark will be protected as well as its role as a badge of origin in cases of 'double identity' under Article 5(1)(a): a protection which applies to all registered trade marks, not just those with a reputation. The second development has been what many observers believe is the CJEU's overly broad interpretation of cases where a third party is deemed to have taken unfair advantage of a trade mark with a reputation. For example, we have seen serious doubt expressed that taking advantage should always be deemed unfair. And there have also been arguments that the *L'Oréal v Bellure* decision will inhibit legitimate competition and limit consumer choice. We have also seen, that at least in the case of the functions of a mark and 'double identity' infringement, the TMD 2016 has sought to both clarify the law and to limit its impact on third parties. On a more general level, one response to those expressing concerns that trade mark law has become unbalanced in favour of proprietors might be that there are number of important exceptions to trade mark infringement which will limit the monopoly afforded by registration. These limitations are the subject of the following chapter.

---

[72] [2000] FSR 158.   [73] *R v Boulter (Gary)* [2008] EWCA Crim 2375.

8

TRADE MARKS III:

DEFENCES, THE LOSS OF A TRADE MARK, AND EXHAUSTION OF RIGHTS

8.1 EXCLUSIONS FROM PROTECTION

This chapter considers the limits to the protection afforded by trade mark registration. We will first consider the defences to infringement which are set out in Article 6 of the TMD and section 11 of the TMA.[1] We will then go on to consider the various ways in which it is possible to lose registered trade mark protection, the two most important of which are revocation (Article 12 of the TMD; section 46 of the TMA[2]) and a finding of invalidity (Article 3 of the TMD; section 47 of the TMA[3]). Finally, we will look at how trade mark rights might be exhausted.

8.1.1 DEFENCES TO TRADE MARK INFRINGEMENT

There are three main defences to trade mark infringement (or, as they are termed in the TMA, 'limits on the effect' of a registered trade mark). These are set out in Article 6 of the TMD.[4] Provided the use is in accordance with honest practices in industrial or commercial matters, the defences are:

(1) use by a person of his own name and address (Article 6(1)(a) of the TMD; section 11(2)(a) of the TMA);

---

[1] TMD 2016, Art. 14.   [2] TMD 2016, Art. 19.   [3] TMD 2016, Art. 4.

[4] TMA, s. 11; TMD 2016, Art. 14. Another defence is the use in the course of trade in a particular locality of an earlier right which applies only in that locality (s. 11(3); Art. 6(2)). This earlier sign will be protected by virtue of any rule of law (in particular the law of passing off). An example might be a pub sign which is the subject of another's registered trade mark.

(2) use of indications concerning the kind, quality, quantity, intended purpose, value, geographical origin, the time of production of the goods or of rendering of services, or other characteristics of goods or services (Article 6(1)(b) of the TMD; section 11(2) (b) of the TMA);

(3) use of a trade mark where it is necessary to indicate the intended purpose of a product or service (in particular accessories or spare parts) (Article 6(1)(c) of the TMD; section 11(2)(c) of the TMA).

It is also possible to include in the defences to infringement the use of a registered trade mark in comparative advertising and this will be considered at 8.2.

8.1.2 USE OF OWN NAME AND THE DEFINITION OF HONEST PRACTICES

This defence applies to company names and personal names. Although it was suggested by the Court of Appeal in *Hotel Cipriani*, that the own name defence may also apply to the trading names of companies, the TMD 2016 is taking the law in an opposite direction. The TMD 2016 confines the defence to the use of personal names of individuals only and will not be available to companies. According to Article 6 of the present TMD, a third party may only rely on any of the defences set out above, including the use of the own name, if use of the registered mark is in accordance with honest practices in industrial or commercial matters. The CJEU considered the own name defence, together with what constitutes honest practices, in *Céline Sarl v Céline SA*.[5] The Court held that, in assessing whether use is honest, account should be taken first of the extent to which the mark is understood by the relevant public, or a significant section of it, as indicating a link between the third party's goods or services and those of the trade mark proprietor and, second, the extent to which the third party ought to be aware that a link is being made. A third factor to be taken into account is whether the trade mark concerned enjoys a reputation in the Member State in which it is registered from which the third party might profit.[6] Recently, in *Maier v Asos*, the Court of Appeal considered the own name defence and also gave detailed consideration as to what is meant by the phrase: 'honest practices in industrial or commercial matters'.

Roger Maier, Assos of Switzerland SA v ASOS Plc, ASOS.com Ltd
[2015] EWCA Civ 220

The claimants registered the mark ASSOS for, inter alia, 'clothing, footwear and headgear' as a EUTM in 2006. It has since the 1970s sold specialist cycling clothing. It does so primarily through specialist cycling goods stores across the EU and does not have an online store or encourage sales of its clothing over the internet. Its goods are highly designed and expensive and have been used by national cycling teams and Olympic gold medallists. The defendant has run a very successful global online fashion shop since 1999. It has only ever operated on the internet and it adopted the name 'ASOS' in 2002 (an acronym for 'as seen on screen'). By 2004, it was selling its own brand clothing

---

[5] Case C-17/06 [2007] ECR I-7041.
[6] See also *Hotel Cipriani v Cipriani (Grosvenor Street)* [2010] EWCA Civ 110, discussed at 5.2.1.2.

under the name ASOS. It has a high media profile, including a YouTube channel. Its business is now valued at over £2 billion. ASOS has never sold ASSOS goods or specialist cycling gear. In 2005, ASOS sought to register its name as a EUTM. This was successfully opposed by ASSOS although ASOS does have a UK registered trade mark for a wide range of goods. In 2011, ASSOS brought infringement proceedings against ASOS under Article 9(1)(b) and (c) of the Regulation and also claimed ASOS's UK trademark was invalid. ASOS counterclaimed, among other things, that the ASSOS mark had not been used for the goods for which it was registered and should be revoked.[7] ASOS also asserted that is was entitled to rely upon the 'own name defence' under Article 12(a) of the Regulation. The case reached the Court of Appeal. The court held that the ASSOS registration was too broad but it also held that ASOS had infringed the claimant's mark under Article 9(1)(b) and (c) of the Regulation. It then turned to the defendant's own name defence. It held that the defendant did have such a defence. In making this finding, Kitchin LJ first rehearsed the law relating to honest practices in commercial matters.

Kitchin LJ:

147. It is accepted that the defence is available to legal persons (that is to say, corporations) as well as natural persons. It also applies to the use of a name as a trade mark. That is what Asos has done. The crucial question, therefore, is whether the use that Asos has made of the sign ASOS has been in accordance with honest practices in industrial or commercial matters. This condition qualifies all of the defences in art.12 of the Regulation and has been interpreted by the Court of Justice on numerous occasions as importing a duty to act fairly in relation to the legitimate interests of a trade mark proprietor. It also involves the balancing or reconciliation of potentially conflicting fundamental interests. The Court put it this way in BMW v Deenik (C-63/97) ECR I-905 [EU:C:2003:145] at [61]–[62] (in connection with what is now art.6 of the Directive):

'61. Lastly, the condition requiring use of the trade mark to be made in accordance with honest practices in industrial or commercial matters must be regarded as constituting in substance the expression of a duty to act fairly in relation to the legitimate interests of the trade mark owner, similar to that imposed on the reseller where he uses another's trade mark to advertise the resale of products covered by that mark.

62. Just like Article 7, Article 6 seeks to reconcile the fundamental interests of trade-mark protection with those of free movement of goods and freedom to provide services in the common market in such a way that trade mark rights are able to fulfil their essential role in the system of undistorted competition which the Treaty seeks to establish and maintain (see, in particular, HAG II, para.13).'

148. In considering whether a defendant is acting fairly in relation to the legitimate interests of the trade mark proprietor it will be relevant to consider, among other things, whether there exists a likelihood of confusion; whether the trade mark has a reputation; whether use of the sign complained of takes advantage of or is detrimental to the distinctive character or repute of the trade mark; and whether the possibility of conflict was something of which the defendant was or ought to have been aware. The national court must carry out an overall assessment of all the circumstances and determine whether the defendant is competing unfairly. This emerges from the guidance given by the Court of Justice in Anheuser-Busch Inc

---

[7] Revocation for non-use is looked at below at 8.3.2.

v Budějovický Budvar Narodni Podnik (C-245/02) ECR I-10989 [EU:C:2004:717] and reiterated in *Céline SARL v Céline* (C-17/06) ECR I-7041 [EU:C:2007:497] at [34]–[35]:

'34. In that regard, it must be noted that, in assessing whether the condition of honest practice is satisfied, account must be taken first of the extent to which the use of the third party's name is understood by the relevant public, or at least a significant section of that public, as indicating a link between the third party's goods or services and the trade mark proprietor or a person authorised to use the trade mark, and secondly of the extent to which the third party ought to have been aware of that. Another factor to be taken into account when making the assessment is whether the trade mark concerned enjoys a certain reputation in the Member State in which it is registered and its protection is sought, from which the third party might profit in marketing his goods or services (*Anheuser-Busch* at [83]).'

...

149. The possibility of a limited degree of confusion does not preclude the application of the defence, however. It all depends upon the reason for that confusion and all the other circumstances of the case. So for example in *Gerolsteiner Brunnen GmbH & Co v Putsch GmbH* (C-100/02) ECR I-691 [EU:C:2004:11] the Court of Justice said at [25]–[26]:

'25. The mere fact that there exists a likelihood of aural confusion between a word mark registered in one Member State and an indication of geographical origin from another Member State is therefore insufficient to conclude that the use of that indication in the course of trade is not in accordance with honest practices. In a Community of 15 Member States, with great linguistic diversity, the chance that there exists some phonetic similarity between a trade mark registered in one Member State and an indication of geographical origin from another Member State is already substantial and will be even greater after the impending enlargement.

26. It follows that, in a case such as that in the main proceedings, it is for the national court to carry out an overall assessment of all the relevant circumstances. Since the case concerns bottled drinks, the circumstances to be taken into account by that court would include in particular the shape and labelling of the bottle in order to assess, more particularly, whether the producer of the drink bearing the indication of geographical origin might be regarded as unfairly competing with the proprietor of the trade mark.'

150. The relevance of this latter point to the own name defence was recognised by Jacob LJ (with whom Rix and Auld LJJ agreed) in *Reed Executive Plc v Reed Business Information Ltd* [2004] EWCA Civ 159; [2004] E.T.M.R. 56; [2004] R.P.C. 40 at [129]:

'129. I conclude from *Gerri/Kelly* [*Gerolsteiner*] that a man may use his own name even if there is some actual confusion with a registered trade mark. The amount of confusion which can be tolerated is a question of degree—only if objectively what he does, in all the circumstances, amounts to unfair competition, will there also be infringement. In practice there would have to be significant actual deception—mere possibilities of confusion, especially where ameliorated by other surrounding circumstances (mere aural confusion but clearly different bottles) can be within honest practices. No doubt in some cases where a man has set out to cause confusion by using his name he will be outside the defence (*cf.* the English passing-off cases cited above)—in others he may be within it if he has taken reasonable precautions to reduce confusion. All will turn on the overall circumstances of the case.'

Having looked closely at what constitutes honest practices, the Court of Appeal then turned to the defendant's claim to have a defence to infringement based on the use of its own name in accordance with honest practices in industrial and commercial matters. It held (with Sales LJ dissenting) that the claim was justified. It founded its decision on a number of factors: that the names were adopted independently and Asos had no intention of damaging the claimant's business; that even though Asos failed to conduct a trade mark search before adopting the trading name Asos, had it done so it would not have believed its business would impact on the defendant's; that both companies have expanded their businesses and acquired substantial reputations and goodwill; that there had been no confusion in the marketplace and none was likely and that Asos had not taken advantage of the claimant's reputation; and, finally, that Asos has taken steps to ensure it does not sell cycling-inspired fashion wear. Sales LJ dissented. He believed that the own name defence failed. In particular, he took the view that the defendant's failure to undertake a trade mark search before adopting the mark ASOS did not constitute honest practice.[8] Had they made such a search he believed they would not, or at least should not, have chosen ASOS as a mark as it would have both 'trampled' on Assos' existing rights and interests and would have also risked consumer confusion.

In this case two powerful companies were challenging each other. It is unlikely that an individual would feel able to challenge an infringement allegation in the same way. We might also ask whether by removing the own name defence from companies, it is small or medium-sized enterprises, which may have adopted their names entirely honestly, that will be disproportionately disadvantaged if a more powerful company trading under the same name alleges infringement.

8.1.3 THE DEFENCE OF DESCRIPTIVE USE (ARTICLE 6(1)(B); SECTION 11(2)(B))

The availability of this defence helps to define the scope of the monopoly accorded by trade mark registration. As we have seen, the CJEU has made clear in a number of cases, most notably *Libertel*,[9] that the relevant authorities should not take an *a posteriori* view of registration. Instead, they should ensure that trade marks, whose use can be successfully challenged because, for example, they are descriptive, will not be registered. However, there have also been parallel developments which might be said to have whittled down the availability of the descriptive use defence. Thus, in *Arsenal v Reed*[10] and later cases, the CJEU has held that any use which affects the functions of a registered mark, even if it is not trade mark use, is infringing. As a result, it appears possible that even descriptive use of a registered mark by a third party might be infringing. Under the new directive, however, this will no longer be the case. Only if a sign is used as a badge of origin will it be infringing. In the CJEU decision in *Arsenal v Reed*, the case of *Hölterhoff v Freiesleben* was cited as a clear example of non-infringing, descriptive use. It continues to be authoritative.[11]

Michael Hölterhoff v Ulrich Freiesleben Case C-2/00 [2002] ECR I-4187

Freiesleben was the proprietor of two trade marks, 'Spirit Sun' and 'Context Cut' for precious stones of a particular cut. Hölterhoff also dealt in precious stones. He sold two

---

[8] [245].   [9] *Libertel Groep BV v Benelux-Merkenbureau* Case C-104/01 [2003] ECR I-3793.
[10] *Arsenal Football Club plc v Reed* Case C-206/01 [2002] ECR I-10273.
[11] See e.g. *Supreme Petfoods Ltd v Henry Bell & Co. (Grantham) Ltd* [2015] EWHC 256 (Ch), [2015] ETMR 20.

garnets which were identified in a delivery note and invoice as 'rhodolites'. However, in the course of oral negotiations with the purchaser, Hölterhoff referred to the trade marks 'Spirit Sun' and 'Context Cut' and the order was for two stones in the Spirit Sun cut. Freiesleben sued for trade mark infringement. The German court held that Hölterhoff had used the names 'Spirit Sun' and 'Context Cut' purely descriptively to identify the way the stones had been cut, and not to suggest that they had originated from him. The CJEU agreed.

16. In that regard, it is sufficient to state that, in a situation such as that described by the national court, the use of the trade mark does not infringe any of the interests which Article 5(1) is intended to protect. Those interests are not affected by a situation in which:

— the third party refers to the trade mark in the course of commercial negotiations with a potential customer, who is a professional jeweller,

— the reference is made for purely descriptive purposes, namely in order to reveal the characteristics of the product offered for sale to the potential customer, who is familiar with the characteristics of the products covered by the trade mark concerned,

— the reference to the trade mark cannot be interpreted by the potential customer as indicating the origin of the product.

In *Arsenal*, the CJEU distinguished *Hölterhoff* (where the trade marks had been used to describe a method of cutting precious stones, rather than to identify their producer) from the use of the Arsenal marks by Reed. It noted that under the directive:

54. The proprietor may not prohibit the use of a sign identical to the trade mark for goods identical to those for which the mark is registered if that use cannot affect his own interests as proprietor of the mark, having regard to its functions. Thus certain uses for purely descriptive purposes are excluded from the scope of Art. 5(1) of the Directive because they do not affect any of the interests which that provision aims to protect, and do not therefore fall within the concept of use within the meaning of that provision (see, with respect to a use for purely descriptive purposes relating to the characteristics of the product offered, Case C-2/00 *Hölterhoff* [2002] ECR I-4187, paragraph 16).

55. In this respect, it is clear that the situation in question in the main proceedings is fundamentally different from that in *Hölterhoff*. In the present case, the use of the sign takes place in the context of sales to consumers and is obviously not intended for purely descriptive purposes.

The decision in *Arsenal* made clear that 'purely' descriptive use will not be infringing. What the courts will not countenance is a defence where the sign is used partly in a trade mark sense and partly descriptively. Thus, in *Adidas v Fitnessworld* C-408/01 [2004] Ch 120, the CJEU held that the public must see a mark 'purely' as an embellishment for it not to infringe the earlier mark. Given the importance of geographical names and the need to leave free, which we discussed in Chapter 6, we may not be surprised that particular concerns have been expressed when the trade mark at issue indicates the geographical origin of goods. According to the CJEU, in such cases, the registered mark may be used by a third party to indicate the origin of the goods, but not their trade origin (an example is *Gerolsteiner v Putsch* C-100/02 [2004] RPC 39).

8.1.4 USE OF A TRADE MARK WHERE IT IS NECESSARY TO INDICATE THE INTENDED PURPOSE OF A PRODUCT OR SERVICE (IN PARTICULAR ACCESSORIES OR SPARE PARTS) (ARTICLE 6(1)(C); SECTION 11(2)(C))

This defence allows traders to refer to a registered trade mark in order to indicate the nature of the goods or services which they offer to the public. It is frequently referred to as the 'spare parts defence', although its use is not limited to trade marks used by third parties in supplying spare parts. Its purpose is to ensure that competition to supply spare parts and other goods which might be identified by reference to a registered trade mark is not inhibited by the threat of an infringement action. The scope of the defence was considered by the CJEU in *BMW v Deenik*.[12] The defendant had a business selling and repairing BMW cars, but he was not an authorized dealer. He advertised that he sold second-hand BMWs and repaired them. BMW sued Deenik for trade mark infringement, and he raised the defence of intended purpose. Eventually, the CJEU was called upon to give guidance as to when the defence might succeed. The Court held that use must be 'necessary' to indicate the intended purpose of the goods or services. It then set out the following guidelines:

> Articles 5 to 7 of the directive do not entitle the proprietor of a trade mark to prohibit a third party from using the mark for the purpose of informing the public that he carries out the repair and maintenance of goods covered by that trade mark and put on the market under that mark by the proprietor or with his consent, or that he has specialised or is a specialist in the sale or the repair and maintenance of such goods, unless the mark is used in a way that may create the impression that there is a commercial connection between the other undertaking and the trade mark proprietor, and in particular that the reseller's business is affiliated to the trade mark proprietor's distribution network or that there is a special relationship between the two undertakings.[13]

Later, in *Gillette*, the CJEU was asked to rule, inter alia, upon what constitutes 'necessity' under Article 6(1)(c) and what constitutes acceptable use of the registered trade mark.

Gillette Co. v LA-Laboratories Ltd Oy Case C-228/03 [2005] ECR I-2337

The claimants marketed razors in Finland, including replaceable blades, under the registered marks 'Gillette' and 'Sensor'. LA also manufactured razors and replaceable blades similar to the claimant's products under a different mark, 'Parason Flexor'. But LA fixed a sticker to their packaging bearing the words 'all Parason Flexor and Gillette Sensor handles are compatible with this blade'. Gillette sued for trade mark infringement. LA claimed a defence under Article 6(1)(c) of the TMD. It was Gillette's argument that the use of its mark would lead the public to assume there was a link between the two companies and that, furthermore, the defendant could state that the blade was compatible with other razors without using the Gillette mark. The questions for the CJEU, inter alia, were whether a trader may only refer to the third party mark if it is strictly

---

[12] *Bayerische Motorenwerke AG (BMW) and BMW Nederland BV v Deenik* Case C-63/97 [1999] ECR I-905.
[13] [64].

necessary, even if such a prohibition puts the consumer at a disadvantage and, second, what constitutes fair use. In particular, the CJEU was asked whether fair use necessarily means that the product to which the third party attaches the mark is thus presented as being of the same quality as, or having equivalent properties to, those of the proprietor's product bearing the trade mark.

39. Use of the trade mark by a third party who is not its owner is necessary in order to indicate the intended purpose of a product marketed by that third party where such use in practice constitutes the only means of providing the public with comprehensible and complete information on that intended purpose in order to preserve the undistorted system of competition in the market for that product ... It is for the national court to determine whether, in the case in the main proceedings, such use is necessary, taking account of the nature of the public for which the product marketed by the third party in question is intended.

...

[The CJEU then turned its attention to the questions of what constitutes honest practices and, second, whether use of a trade mark by a third party implies its products are equivalent to those of the original proprietor:]

42. In that regard, use of the trade mark will not comply with honest practices in industrial or commercial matters where, first, it is done in such a manner that it may give the impression that there is a commercial connection between the re-seller and the trade mark proprietor (*BMW*, para. 51).

43. Nor may such use affect the value of the trade mark by taking unfair advantage of its distinctive character or repute (*BMW*, para. 52).

44. In addition, as the UK Government and the Commission have rightly pointed out in their observations, use of the trade mark will not be in accordance with Art. 6(1)(c) of Directive 89/104 if it discredits or denigrates that mark.

45. Finally, where the third party presents its product as an imitation or replica of the product bearing the trade mark of which it is not the owner, such use of that mark does not comply with honest practices within the meaning of Art. 6(1)(c).

46. It is for the national court to determine whether, in the case in the main proceedings, the use made of the trade marks owned by Gillette Company has been made in accordance with honest practices, taking account, in particular, of the conditions referred to in paras. 42 to 45 of this judgment. In that regard, account should be taken of the overall presentation of the product marketed by the third party, particularly the circumstances in which the mark of which the third party is not the owner is displayed in that presentation, the circumstances in which a distinction is made between that mark and the mark or sign of the third party, and the effort made by that third party to ensure that consumers distinguish its products from those of which it is not the trade mark owner.

47. Concerning the second part of that question, as the UK Government has rightly pointed out in its observations, the fact that a third party uses a trade mark of which it is not the owner in order to indicate the intended purpose of its product, does not necessarily mean that it is presenting that product as being of the same quality as, or having equivalent properties to, those of the product bearing the trade mark. Whether there has been such a presentation depends on the facts of the case, and it is for the referring court to determine whether it has taken place by reference to the circumstances.

> 48. Moreover, whether the product marketed by the third party has been represented as being of the same quality as, or having equivalent properties to, the product whose trade mark is being used, is a factor which the referring court must take into consideration when it verifies that such use is made in accordance with honest practices in industrial or commercial matters.

In *Portakabin v Primakabin*,[14] the CJEU looked at the defence provided by Article 6(1)(c) when the trade mark at issue is used as a keyword on the internet. In this case, the 'Portakabin' trade mark was used by a company selling second-hand Portakabin products. In its judgment, which will be considered in more detail when this chapter turns to 'exhaustion of rights', the CJEU looked at the meaning of honest practices. It held that an advertiser cannot, in general, rely on the exception for 'intended use' in order to avoid liability for infringement.

> 70 In that regard, it must be held, first, that one of the characteristics of the situation referred to in [68] above lies precisely in the fact that the ad is likely to cause at least a significant section of the target public to establish a link between the goods or services to which it refers and the goods or services of the trade mark proprietor or persons authorised to use that trade mark. Secondly, in the event that the national court finds that the ad does not enable average internet users, or enables them only with difficulty, to ascertain whether the goods or services referred to by the ad originate from the trade mark proprietor or from a third party, it is unlikely that the advertiser can genuinely claim not to have been aware of the ambiguity thus caused by its ad. It is the advertiser itself, in the context of its professional strategy and with full knowledge of the economic sector in which it operates, which chose a keyword corresponding to another person's trade mark and which, alone or with the assistance of the referencing service provider, designed the ad and therefore decided how it should be presented.
>
> 71 Taking account of those factors, it must be concluded that, in the situation described in [54] and [68] above, the advertiser cannot, in principle, claim to have acted in accordance with honest practices in industrial or commercial matters. It is, however, for the national court to carry out an overall assessment of all the relevant circumstances in order to determine whether there may be evidence to justify a contrary finding (see, to that effect, *Gerolsteiner & Brunnen GmbH & Co. v Putsch GmbH* (C-100/02) [2004] E.C.R. I-691; [2004] E.T.M.R. 40 at [26], and *Anheuser-Busch* [2005] E.T.M.R. 27 at [84] and the case law cited).

The preamble to the 2016 Directive states that: 'Use of a trade mark by third parties to draw the consumer's attention to the resale of genuine goods that were originally sold by or with the consent of the proprietor of the trade mark'[15] is fair as long as it is in accordance with honest practices. However, one implication of the *Portakabin* decision is that it may well prove difficult, if not impossible, for a third party to make use of keyword advertising on the internet where it is selling second-hand goods or spare parts which relate to that keyword (assuming it is a registered trade mark). It is worth asking whether the CJEU would have been similarly concerned if the reference had not been made in the course of e-commerce. And whether, as a result, registered trade marks, at least in relation to the Article 6(1)(c) defence, will receive greater protection in the virtual world than the real world.

---

[14] Case C-558/08 [2011] CEC 552, [2010] ETMR 52. For a fuller discussion regarding exhaustion of rights see 8.4.

[15] Recital 27.

FURTHER READING

H. Hartwig, 'Spare parts under European design and trade mark law' (2016) 11 JIPLP 121.

R. Knaak, 'Geographical indications and their relationship with trade marks in EU law' (2015) 46 IIC 843.

D. Meale, 'Your name in lights? Just so long as it's honest: the "own name" defence in trade mark and passing off law' (2013) 8 JIPLP 603.

A. Peukert, 'The coexistence of trade mark laws and rights on the Internet, and the impact of geolocation technologies' (2016) 47 IIC 60.

A. Roughton, 'The own-name defence in relation to registered trade mark law' in I. Simon Fhima (ed.), *Trade Mark Law and Sharing Names: Exploring Use of the Same Mark by Multiple Undertakings* (Cheltenham: Edward Elgar, 2009), p. 141.

8.2 COMPARATIVE ADVERTISING

In advertising their goods and services, commercial enterprises may wish to make comparisons with the goods and services of others. As a short cut, the advertiser may choose to refer to these latter goods and services by using the registered trade mark under which they are sold. Initially, following the passage of the TMA 1994, comparative advertising was regulated under the relevant provision of the Act. More recently, the courts have held that the use by third parties of a registered trade mark in comparative advertising is regulated by the EU Directive on Comparative Advertising (CAD).[16] This is confirmed in the 2016 Directive, which states in its preamble that:

In order to ensure legal certainty and full consistency with specific Union legislation, it is appropriate to provide that the proprietor of a trade mark should be entitled to prohibit a third party from using a sign in comparative advertising where such comparative advertising is contrary to Directive 2006/114/EC of the European Parliament and of the Council.[17]

8.2.1 COMPARATIVE ADVERTISING AND THE TMA

Comparative advertising involving third party use of a registered trade mark is explicitly allowed under section 10(6) of the TMA 1994 which reads:

Nothing in the preceding provisions of this section[18] shall be construed as preventing the use of a registered trade mark by any person for the purpose of identifying goods or services as those of the proprietor or a licensee.

But any such use otherwise than in accordance with honest practices in industrial or commercial matters shall be treated as infringing the registered trade mark if the use without due cause takes unfair advantage of or is detrimental to, the distinctive character or repute of the trade mark mark.

---

[16] Directive on Comparative Advertising (EC) 97/55, amending the Directive (EEC) 84/450 on Misleading Advertising. Now Directive 2006/114/EC, OJ L376/21.

[17] Recital 20.

[18] Which, as we have seen, deals with infringement.

Section 10(6) was not taken from the TMD or the CTM Regulation, but was a purely domestic addition to the TMA. It is possible to think of this section as an exception to infringement rather than as a defence. Following the passage of the TMA, there were a number of cases which interpreted the meaning and scope of this exception, usually in a way which was favourable to comparative advertising.[19] However, the decisions in *O2 Holdings v Hutchinson*[20] both in the domestic courts and at the CJEU made clear that the use of trade marks in comparative advertising is regulated by CAD.

8.2.2 COMPARATIVE ADVERTISING AND CAD

The case of *O2 v Hutchison 3G* examined the relationship between the Comparative Advertising Directive and the Trade Mark Directive.

O2 Holdings Ltd v Hutchison 3G UK Ltd Case C-533/06 [2008] ECR I-4231, [2007] 2 CMLR 15

The claimant, O2, a mobile phone service provider, had various registered trade marks including one for 'O2' and another for bubbles used in relation to, inter alia, telecommunications apparatus and telecommunications services. The defendant, H3G, was also a mobile phone service provider. H3G started an advertising campaign in which it compared its services to other providers, including O2. In the case of O2, it used as a reference both the trade mark 'O2' and bubbles which were similar but not identical to the bubbles registered by O2 as a trade mark. O2 did not contest the accuracy of the comparison, but alleged infringement of its registered trade mark, through use of a similar mark on identical goods (Article 5(1)(b)). In the High Court, Mr J Pumfrey found for the defendant, holding that the use of the bubbles fell within Article 5(1)(b); that the advertisement complied with Article 3a(1) of the Unfair Commercial Practices Directive 84/450/EEC as amended by CAD; and that such compliance provided a defence of descriptive use provided for by Article 6(1)(b) of the TMD. O2 appealed. In the Court of Appeal, Jacob LJ took the view that there were a number of issues raised by the case which should be considered by the CJEU. They were:

> 28 ...
>
> 1. Where a trader, in an advertisement for his own goods or services, uses a registered trade mark owned by a competitor for the purpose of comparing the characteristics (and in particular the price) of goods or services marketed by him with the characteristics (and in particular the price) of the goods or services marketed by the competitor under that mark in such a way that it does not cause confusion or otherwise jeopardise the essential function of the trade mark as an indication of origin, does his use fall within either (a) or (b) of Article 5[(1)] of Directive 89/104?
>
> 2. Where a trader uses, in a comparative advertisement, the registered trade mark of a competitor, in order to comply with Article 3a[(1)] of Directive 84/450 ... must that use be 'indispensable' and if so what are the criteria by which indispensability is to be judged?

---

[19] Most notably, *British Airways plc v Ryanair Ltd* [2001] ETMR 24.

[20] *O2 Holdings (formerly O2 Ltd) and O2 (UK) Ltd v Hutchison 3G Ltd* [2006] EWCA Civ 1656.

3. In particular, if there is a requirement of indispensability, does the requirement preclude any use of a sign which is not identical to the registered trade mark but is closely similar to it?

Article 3a(1) of CAD essentially said that comparative advertising is permitted when it is not misleading; does not create confusion between the advertiser's trade mark and those of a competitor; does not take unfair advantage of the reputation of a trade mark, trade name, or other distinguishing marks; and it does not present the goods or services as imitations or replicas of goods or services bearing a protected trade mark or trade name.

The CJEU began its judgment by considering the relationship between CAD and the TMD. It held that use by an advertiser of a sign identical or similar to a competitor's mark constituted use within the meaning of Article 5(1) and (2) of the TMD. It would therefore be possible for a comparative advertiser under certain circumstances to infringe the competitor's sign. On the other hand, it is an aim of the CAD to promote comparative advertising and in doing so it may allow the competitor's mark or a similar mark to be used in order to do so. It went on:

43. The test for determining whether an advertisement is comparative in nature is thus whether it identifies, explicitly or by implication, a competitor of the advertiser or goods or services which the competitor offers (*Toshiba Europe*, paragraph 29, and *De Landtsheer Emmanuel*, paragraph 17).

44. Therefore, when the use, in an advertisement, of a sign similar to the mark of a competitor of the advertiser is perceived by the average consumer as a reference to that competitor or to the goods and services which he offers—as in the case in the main proceedings—there is comparative advertising within the meaning of Article 2(2a) of Directive 84/450.

45. Consequently, in order to reconcile the protection of registered marks and the use of comparative advertising, Article 5(1) and (2) of Directive 89/104 and Article 3a(1) of Directive 84/450 must be interpreted to the effect that the proprietor of a registered trade mark is not entitled to prevent the use, by a third party, of a sign identical with, or similar to, his mark, in a comparative advertisement which satisfies all the conditions, laid down in Article 3a(1) of Directive 84/450, under which comparative advertising is permitted.

In effect, a comparative advertisement would not satisfy Article 3a(1) of CAD if such use presents a risk of origin confusion because of the way the comparative advertiser deploys the competitor's mark. Rather, such use will fall within Article 5(1)(b) of the TMD. It will be infringing use. The CJEU then turned to the first question asked by the Court of Appeal which is whether the proprietor of a registered trade mark is entitled to prevent the use by a third party in comparative advertising of a sign similar to his own for identical or similar goods where there is no likelihood of confusion. It answered:

61. It is also clear that H3G used that sign without the consent of O2 and O2 (UK), the proprietors of the bubbles trade marks.

62. Furthermore, that sign was used for services identical with those for which those marks are registered.

63. By contrast, in accordance with the referring court's own findings, the use by H3G, in the advertisement in question, of bubble images similar to the bubbles trade marks did not give rise to a likelihood of confusion on the part of consumers. The advertisement, as a whole, was not misleading and, in particular, did not suggest that there was any form of commercial link between O2 and O2 (UK) on the one hand, and H3G, on the other.

...

69. Consequently, the answer to the first question must be that Article 5(1)(b) of Directive 89/104 is to be interpreted as meaning that the proprietor of a registered trade mark is not entitled to prevent the use, by a third party, in a comparative advertisement, of a sign similar to that mark in relation to goods or services identical with, or similar to, those for which that mark is registered where such use does not give rise to a likelihood of confusion on the part of the public, and that is so irrespective of whether or not the comparative advertisement satisfies all the conditions laid down in Article 3a of Directive 84/450 under which comparative advertising is permitted.

With its decision in *O2*, the CJEU made clear that if a comparative advertisement causes customer confusion, it is infringing. *L'Oréal v Bellure* was also a case of comparative advertising (see the facts at 7.1.4.3). However, in this case, as we have seen, there was no allegation by the claimant that consumers would be confused by the use of its signs in the defendant's advertisements, under Article 5(1)(b) of the TMD. Rather, the defendant was alleged to have taken unfair advantage of the claimant's trade marks, under Article 5(2) of the TMD. The CJEU was asked about the relationship between Article 5(2) of the TMD and CAD. In particular, it was asked what would be the situation where a defendant was marketing imitations or replicas of a claimant's products through comparative advertising, as was the case with Bellure. It first set out the preconditions for comparative advertising. It continued:

72 It follows that the use of a competitor's trade mark in comparative advertising is permitted by Community law where the comparison objectively highlights differences and the object or effect of such highlighting is not to give rise to situations of unfair competition, such as those described inter alia in art.3a(1)(d), (e), (g) and (h) of Directive 84/450 (see, to that effect, *Pippig Augenoptik* [2003] E.C.R. I-3095 at [49]).

73 As regards, in the first place, art.3a(1)(h) of Directive 84/450, which provides that comparative advertising must not present goods or services as imitations or replicas of goods or services bearing a protected trade mark or trade name, it is clear from the wording of that provision and that of recital 19 in the preamble to Directive 97/55 that that condition applies not only to counterfeit goods but also to any imitation or replica.

74 In addition, it follows from a systematic interpretation of art.3a(1)(h) of Directive 84/450 that that provision does not require either that the comparative advertising be misleading in nature or that there be a likelihood of confusion. The requirement that there be no misleading effect and the requirement that there be no likelihood of confusion are distinct conditions as regards the question whether comparative advertising is permitted, set out under art.3a(1) (a) and (d).

...

78 Given that it was found in paragraph 76 of this judgment that the comparison lists used by the defendants in the main proceedings present the perfumes which they market as being an imitation or a replica of goods bearing a protected trade mark within the meaning

of art.3a(1)(h) of Directive 84/450, the third question must be understood as meaning that it seeks to ascertain whether, in such circumstances, the use of those lists results in the taking of an unfair advantage of the reputation of that protected mark for the purposes of art.3a(1)(g).

79 In that regard, it must be held that since, under Directive 84/450, comparative advertising which presents the advertiser's products as an imitation of a product bearing a trade mark is inconsistent with fair competition and thus unlawful, any advantage gained by the advertiser through such advertising will have been achieved as the result of unfair competition and must, accordingly, be regarded as taking unfair advantage of the reputation of that mark.

The CJEU has now elucidated the correct approach to the use of registered trade marks in comparative advertising. And, as we have noted, the TMD 2016 makes clear that use of a trade mark which is contrary to CAD will be infringing, although the courts are still left to take a view on the facts as to when such use is contrary to CAD. However, for those concerned with the proper limits of trade mark protection, a more general question is raised: is it more important for competitors to have the opportunity to give consumers relevant information about two competing products than it is to protect the 'reputation' of the trade mark with which comparisons are to be made? In *L'Oréal*, the CJEU expressed the view that the law should be interpreted in a way most favourable to comparative advertising, so long as the advertisements are not infringing. Brand holders may well disagree, holding that any use of their marks in comparative advertising is in effect taking advantage of their attractiveness. On the other hand, there have been some, most notably Jacob LJ, in his judgment in *L'Oréal*, who are concerned that the CJEU's approach places a limit on free speech, preventing traders from making 'honest statements about their products'.[21] More generally, it has been suggested that perhaps using registered trade marks in a referential manner (that is, not as a badge of origin) even if done in a commercial context should have general and explicit protection: the use by Bellure of the L'Oréal marks is a case in point. Nari Lee argues for such an approach in the excerpt below.

N. Lee, 'Public domain at the interface of trade mark and unfair competition law: the case of referential use of trade marks' in N. Lee, G. Westkamp, A. Kur, and A. Ohly (eds), *Intellectual Property, Unfair Competition and Publicity: Convergences and Development* (Cheltenham: Edward Elgar, 2014), pp. 334–338

3.3 Referential Use of Trade Marks in Commercial Communication

More controversial developments in trade mark laws for the last decades have been in the area of referential uses in commercial communication. Referential uses of another's trade mark typically include comparative advertising, descriptive and qualitative references for spare parts or interoperable products, satire or parody in a commercial context. As explored in the above, using a trade mark in the course of trade is precisely the conduct that the trade mark law aims to regulate and national laws often have limited exceptions allowing referential use in commercial communications.

Article 17 of the TRIPs agreement allows members to provide 'limited exceptions' for the rights 'such as *fair use of descriptive terms*, provided that such exceptions take account of

---

[21] *L'Oréal SA v Bellure* [2010] EWCA Civ 535, [8].

the legitimate interests of the owner of the trademark and third parties.' However, it does not provide sufficient clarity for limitation nor the substantive ceiling for the restriction that may be imposed. Although it mentions the 'fair use of descriptive terms' which is typically found in national laws as an example of such exceptions, referential uses may go beyond this limited notion of fair use. More elaboration is found in the MPI TRIPs Amendment Proposal.[22] The proposal suggests the amendment of article 17 and it includes uses in the course of trades:

(i) *for descriptive purposes*, like indications concerning the kind, quality, quantity, intended purpose, value, geographical origin, the time of production of goods or of rendering of the service, or other characteristics of goods or services;

(ii) *in order to provide information* in connection with the sales or goods or services that are legitimately commercialised on the market concerned;

(iii) *for other marketing purposes providing relevant information, in particular comparative advertising;*

(iv) *in a satirical or parodist manner*, or in other modes of use covered by rules applying to freedom of speech and/or freedom of art in the Member concerned;

(v) of a natural persons own name ....

Descriptive, informational, comparative and satirical or parodist uses are all examples of referential uses of trade marks in commercial communications. As argued above a trade mark is a device that allows communication of meaning, and due to their symbolic nature, trade marks are a highly effective communication tool to provide information. For example, to inform the consumers of the nature of the products, such as smell-alike perfume, it would be easier to describe the smell by comparison that product X smells like the famous Y, rather than to describe the product by listing the elements and chemical qualities. Consumers are not likely to be confused as they will see the reference to the well known mark, not as an indication of source or an indication that the producer of the famous Y endorsed the smell-alike perfume, but would see the smell alike product 'for what it is and no more.'

National laws include limitations to trade mark rights or at least against claims of trade mark infringement for these types of communication. For example, the US has a statute acknowledging a fair use defence. Accordingly, a fair use of a trade mark as a name, a descriptive use of goods or service or geographic origin would benefit from this defence. At the same time the notion of use of a trade mark limits liability, when the trade mark was not used 'on or in connection with goods or services.' Similarly in Europe, the Trademark Directive provides exceptions, aimed at honest business practices, as to the use as a name or address, use as indications concerning the kind, quality, quantity, intended purpose, value, geographical origin, the time of production of goods or of rendering of the service, or other characteristics of goods or services, necessary indication of the intended purpose of a product or service, in particular as accessories or spare parts. In Korea and Japan similar exceptions are found. Thus uses of an own name, common name or indication, descriptive indication, customary indication, or as an indispensable functional shape are exempted. In Korea and Japan, courts tend to rely on the principle of use as a trade mark to excuse the referential use that is necessary to communicate the information for selling the goods and so this is allowed by case law. For example, the Tokyo District Court in Japan found no trade mark use when ink cartridges for a Brother printer were marketed, bearing the label 'for Brother printers,' as the word 'for' makes it clear that the use is for referential purposes. Likewise, the Supreme Court of Korea found that using a trade mark relating to a computer program for a manual for that computer program or using a trade mark to indicate a technical or a quality standard did not constitute trade mark use, as these uses were made for referential purposes.

---

[22] See <www.ip.mpg.de/shared/data/pdf/proposed_amendments_to_trips_20110504.pdf>.

The above observation shows that while the concrete articulation of the exceptions in the statutes has the benefit of certainty, a catalogue of exceptions might hinder the application of exceptions to new uses. Thus even when there are concrete exceptions found in statutes, when new practices emerge such as comparative advertising and keyword advertising, the courts often either need to invent a new function of a trade mark right to restrict the use, or to search for an elastic notion through interpretation of the law. Use of a trade mark which is tied to the core function of a trade mark has been one such notion. Use as a trade mark may not only be used to limit the scope of a right; when a court finds a new function such as 'investment function,' when the use affects that aspect of a trade mark, the court could find infringement. Courts in Japan and Korea have sometimes used to extend the protection against a reference use [sic]. In other words, a judicially created doctrine, 'use as a trade mark' may depend on the facts of each use, and thus may not provide a predictable outcome. For most of the prevailing communication in internet and social media, to make allowing referencing possible, a general exception of such as 'fair use' based on statutes, other than use in trade or commercial use or trade mark use theory, may provide both predictability and flexibility.

The TMD 2016 has acknowledged some of the concerns expressed by critics, such as Lee, who believe trade mark protection might inhibit free speech. The preamble to the TMD 2016 states that:

Use of a trade mark by third parties for the purpose of artistic expression should be considered as being fair as long as it is at the same time in accordance with honest practices in industrial and commercial matters. Furthermore this Directive should be applied in a way that ensures full respect for fundamental rights and freedoms, and in particular the freedom of expression.[23]

Do you think it right that registered trade marks should face limitations similar to those which are applied to works under copyright law? Or does the fact that trade mark disputes are generally concerned with commercial speech mean that the rights of proprietors, who may have invested heavily in their marks, should be given higher priority? It will be interesting to see the extent to which, having acknowledged concerns regarding free expression, the TMD 2016 will be interpreted to ensure they are addressed.

FURTHER READING

C. J. Craig, 'Perfume by any other name may smell as sweet … but who can say?: a comment on *L'Oreal v. Bellure*' [2010] IP Journal 32.

V. Glockner, 'The regulatory framework for comparative advertising in Europe: time for a new round of harmonization' (2012) 12 IIC 3.

V. McEvedy, 'Keywords and resales and other fair and referential uses' (2012) IPQ 149.

L. P. Ramsey and J. Schovsbo, 'Mechanisms for limiting trade mark rights to further competition and free speech' (2013) 13 IIC 671.

M. Senftleben et al., 'The recommendation on measures to safeguard freedom of expression and undistorted competition: guiding principles for the further development of EU trade mark law' [2015] EIPR 337.

---

[23] Recital 27.

8.3 THE LOSS OF A REGISTERED TRADE MARK

The two key routes to losing a trade mark registration are either through revocation or a finding of invalidity. According to the TMA, any person may seek a declaration of invalidity (section 47(3)) or make an application for revocation (section 46(4)).[24] In practice, a declaration of invalidity is most likely to be sought and an application for revocation made by a defendant in infringement proceedings.

8.3.1 INVALIDITY

For the most part, the grounds for a finding of invalidity are the same as the absolute and relative grounds for refusal of registration. They are set out in Articles 3 and 4 of the TMD.[25] A trade mark may be declared invalid because it is in breach of the absolute grounds for refusal of registration, for example because it is not sufficiently distinctive.[26] However, a trade mark which is found to have lacked the requisite distinctiveness when it was registered, may not be declared invalid if subsequent to registration it has acquired distinctiveness through use.[27] In *Sofa Workshop v Sofaworks*,[28] the claimant had a EUTM for 'Sofa Workshop' for furniture. It alleged that the defendant had infringed its mark. In response, the defendant argued that the claimant's mark should be declared invalid as it was descriptive and had not acquired distinctiveness through use. The High Court found that although the mark had acquired distinctiveness in the UK, it had not done so in other English-speaking areas of the EU and as a result should be declared invalid. A trade mark may also be declared invalid because it is in breach of the relative grounds for refusal of registration, in that there is an earlier registered mark (or EUTM) with which it conflicts. In addition, under Article 4(4)(b) and (c) of the TMD,[29] a trade mark may be declared invalid if it conflicts with an earlier right, such as copyright, or with a non-registered trade mark which, in the case of the UK, is protected under the law of passing off.[30] Finally, a trade mark may be declared invalid if it was registered in bad faith. If a mark is found to be invalidly registered, the effect is as if the mark had never been registered. As a result, infringement proceedings may cover the period during which it was on the Register. However, any past or closed proceedings relating to the expunged trade mark are not reopened.

In cases of conflict with an earlier registered mark or other right, a trade mark may escape a finding of invalidity if the proprietor of the earlier mark or rights consents or if he has acquiesced in the use of the later registered mark for a period of five years, being aware of such use. The exception is if the later mark is registered in bad faith. Finally, a declaration of invalidity may be refused if there has been honest concurrent use of the two marks. In *Budějovický Budvar NP v Anheuser-Busch Inc.*,[31] the CJEU identified the circumstances in

---

[24] Trade marks may also be voluntarily surrendered in respect of some or all of the goods and services for which it is registered (s. 45).

[25] TMA, s. 47; TMD 2016, Arts 4 and 5.

[26] For a recent case see *The Ukulele Orchestra of Great Britain v Erwin Clausen* [2015] EWHC 1772 (IPEC).

[27] *Hasbro Inc. v 123 Nahrmittel GmbH and Marketing and Promotional Services* [2011] EWHC 199 (Ch).

[28] *The Sofa Workshop Ltd v Sofaworks Ltd* [2015] EWHC 1773 (IPEC).

[29] TMA, s. 47(2)(a) and (b); TMD 2016, Art. 5(4)(a) and (b).

[30] The equivalent provision under the CTM Regulation is Art. 8(4). For an example, see *Tresplain Investments Ltd v OHIM* [2012] ETMR 22.

[31] [2012] ETMR 2.

which there would be a finding of honest concurrent use, where both the marks and goods at issue are identical:

> 3. Article 4(1)(a) of Directive 89/104 must be interpreted as meaning that the proprietor of an earlier trade mark cannot obtain the cancellation of an identical later trade mark designating identical goods where there has been a long period of honest concurrent use of those two trade marks where, in circumstances such as those in the main proceedings, that use neither has nor is liable to have an adverse effect on the essential function of the trade mark which is to guarantee to consumers the origin of the goods or services.

8.3.2 REVOCATION

Article 12 of the TMD sets out the grounds for revocation.[32] If a trade mark is revoked, the mark ceases to have protection from that date or earlier if the Registrar believes that the conditions for revocation were present at an earlier date. There are three main reasons for revocation. A trade mark may be revoked because, as a consequence of the way it has been used, it has become either generic or misleading (Article 12(2)(a)–(b)). Or it may be revoked for non-use (Article 12(1)).[33] In *Backaldrin Österreich The Kornspitz Co. GmbH v Pfahnl Backmittel GmbH (PBG)*[34] the CJEU looked at the first two grounds for revocation. At issue were the circumstance under which a trade mark is liable to be revoked because as a consequence of the acts or inactivity of the proprietor it has become the common name in the trade for the product or service against which it is registered. In *Backaldrin*, the proprietor sold a pastry mix to bakers under the registered mark 'KORNSPITZ'. The mix produced a distinctively-shaped oblong roll. PBG applied to have the mark declared invalid on the basis that it had become the common name for rolls with that particular shape. The CJEU was asked a number of questions by the Austrian court including how to assess whether a mark is a common name in the trade, what is regarded as 'inactivity' for the purposes of losing the mark and whether, even if there are other names for the same product, the mark can be declared invalid and revoked. As to the first question, the CJEU held that a trade mark may be declared invalid and revoked if, as a result of the acts or inactivity of the proprietor, it has become the common name for the product. And this assessment may be made from the point of view solely of end users of the product even if the sellers of the products, in this case the bakers, are aware that the name is a trade mark. Second, the CJEU was asked what constituted inactivity. It answered:

> 33 The court has already held that the concept of 'inactivity' may cover a failure on the part of the proprietor of a trade mark to have recourse to the exclusive rights referred to in article 5 of that Directive in due time, for the purposes of applying to the competent authority to prevent third parties from using a sign in respect of which there is a likelihood of confusion with that mark, since the purpose of such applications is to preserve the distinctive character of the mark in question: see the *Levi Strauss & Co case* [2006] ECR I-3703, para 34.
>
> 34 However, unless the pursuit of the balance described in para 32 of this judgment is be abandoned, that concept cannot in any way be restricted to that kind of omission, but includes all those by which the proprietor of a trade mark shows that he is not sufficiently vigilant as

---

[32] TMA, s. 46; TMD 2016, Art. 19.
[33] TMA, s. 46(1)(c)–(d). For a discussion of deceptive marks see 6.3.4.5.
[34] Case C-409/12 [2014] Bus. L. R. 320.

regards the preservation of the distinctive character of his trade mark. Consequently, in a case such as that described by the referring court, in which the sellers of the product made using the material supplied by the proprietor of the trade mark do not generally inform their customers that the sign used to designate the product in question has been registered as a trade mark and thus contribute to the transformation of that trade mark into the common name, that proprietor's failure to take any initiative which may encourage those sellers to make more use of that mark may be classified as inactivity within the meaning of article 12(2)(a) of Directive 2008/95/EC.

35 It is for the referring court to examine whether, in the present case, Backaldrin took any initiative to encourage the bakers and foodstuffs distributors selling the bread rolls made using the baking mix it had supplied to make more use of the trade mark 'KORNSPITZ' in their commercial contact with customers.

36 It follows from all of the foregoing considerations that the answer to the second question referred is that article 12(2)(a) of Directive 2008/95/EC must be interpreted as meaning that it may be classified as 'inactivity' within the meaning of that provision if the proprietor of a trade mark does not encourage sellers to make more use of that mark in marketing a product in respect of which the mark is registered.

Finally, the CJEU held that a trade mark which has become the common name in the trade can still be held to be revoked even if there are alternative names for the same product.

We will now turn to the third circumstance which may give rise to revocation: non-use of the registered mark (Articles 10 and 12 of the TMD).[35] Article 10 states:

1. If, within a period of five years following the date of the completion of the registration procedure, the proprietor has not put the trade mark to genuine use in the Member State in connection with the goods or services in respect of which it is registered, or if such use has been suspended during an uninterrupted period of five years, the trade mark shall be subject to the sanctions provided for in this Directive unless there are proper reasons for non-use.

Article 12(1) states that if the above conditions apply, the registered trade mark shall be liable to revocation. The onus is on the trade mark proprietor to prove that there has been genuine use of its trade mark.[36]

In her essay, Belinda Isaac sets out the justification for this provision.

B. Isaac, 'Use for the purpose of resisting an application for revocation for non-use' in J. Phillips and I. Simon (eds), *Trade Mark Use* (Oxford: Oxford University Press, 2005), p. 223

It is a fundamental principle of trade mark law, and indeed it is expressly stated in European law, that registered trade marks must actually be used if the proprietor is to continue to benefit from the exclusive rights granted by virtue of registration. In Europe, if a registered

[35] TMA, s. 46(1); TMD 2016, Arts 16 and 19. The wording of the TMD and s. 46(1) in relation to revocation for non-use differs slightly. It was held by the Court of Appeal that the relevant provisions should be given the same meaning (*Laboratoires Goemar SA v La Mer Technology Inc.* [2005] EWCA Civ 978).
[36] *Galileo International Tech LLC v European Union* [2011] EWHC 35 (Ch).

trade mark is not used, it will become liable to revocation unless legitimate reasons for non-use exist.

...

One of the reasons for the necessity to use a registered trade mark given by the Directive is:

to reduce the total number of trade marks registered and protected in the Community and, consequently, the number of conflicts which arise between them...

A consequence of the sheer number of trade marks being registered within the Community and the number of conflicts (oppositions) encountered is that there is a strong public interest in the removal from the register of marks that are not being used. Indeed, some would argue that there are only a finite number of useful or valuable marks and that revocation therefore helps to ensure that unused marks are recycled. If such unused marks were not removed the register would become clogged and the number of conflicts would soon make the system unworkable. Revocation therefore restricts the protection conferred by registration to the proprietor's legitimate and actual trade requirements, avoiding the inconvenience, cost and interference with trade that would result from allowing trade marks to be registered by traders who have no intention of using them, but only wish to prevent other traders from using them.

The key questions posed by Article 10 are first what constitutes genuine use and second what are to be considered proper reasons for non-use.[37] The first question was addressed in the CJEU decision *Ansul v Ajax*.[38] It was also considered by the UK Court of Appeal in *Laboratoires Goemar v La Mer Technology*.[39] When the *Goemar* case, which concerned the revocation of trade mark for non-use, had been heard by the High Court, Jacob J referred a number of questions to the CJEU regarding the definition of genuine use. These were answered by the CJEU in a Reasoned Order, in which it stated generally that the definition of what constituted genuine use had been given in the *Ansul* case. *Goemar* then returned to the High Court and subsequently it reached the Court Appeal. In the Court of Appeal, Mummery LJ set out the proper understanding of what constitutes 'genuine use' of a trade mark following *Ansul* and the CJEU's order on *Goemar*.

Laboratoires Goemar SA v La Mer Technology Inc. [2005] EWCA Civ 978, [2006] FSR 5

Goemar was a French company which made seaweed-based products. Goemar's goods were sold under the registered mark, 'Laboratoire de la Mer'. The mark had been registered in 1989. La Mer Technology (a US company) sought to have the mark revoked for non-use. Initially, the Registrar refused to revoke the mark. But in the High Court, Blackburne J revoked the mark for non-use as of 1998. Goemar appealed to the Court of Appeal. The use relied upon by Goemar was described by Mummery LJ in the Court of Appeal judgment.

---

[37] It is possible to avoid revocation for non-use of a mark if the proprietor uses a mark which incorporates the distinctive features of the registered mark (TMD, Art. 10(2); TMA, s. 46(2)). See *Elle Trade Marks, Re* [1997] FSR 529 and *Cabañas Habana (Device) Trade Mark, Re* [2000] RPC 26.

[38] *Ansul BV v Ajax Brandbeveiliging BV* Case C-40/01 [2003] ECR I-2439.

[39] *Laboratoires Goemar SA v La Mer Technology Inc.* [2005] EWCA Civ 978.

Mummery LJ:

9. It [Goemar] appointed a small enterprise with which it had no connection, Health Scope Direct Ltd (formerly Meadow Breeze Ltd) of the Old Brewery, Banff on the Moray Firth in Scotland as its agent in the United Kingdom. The agent traded as 'Health Scope Direct' until it ceased business and was struck off the register of companies on 21 October 1997.

10. Limited sales of the relevant products bearing the mark were made by Goemar pursuant to five separate repeat orders placed by Health Scope Direct. The orders amounted to £8,000 in all. The sales took place over the six-month period between 14 November 1996 and 16 May 1997. There were five deliveries of goods. The products imported were within the Class 3 registration…

11. There was no evidence of any sales of the goods to members of the public or consumers and end-users. The agent has been making preparations to sell the products by appointing members of the public as sub-agencies via private parties, based on the 'Tupperware' model, but there was no evidence that this method of sale to the public ever got off the ground.

[In his judgment, **Mummery LJ** considered the CJEU authority on genuine use. He noted, in particular, the issues concerning what criteria or factors should be taken into account in deciding whether a mark has been put to genuine use, what types of use can be considered, and specifically whether importation by a single importer could count as genuine use.]

Ansul

18. Let us begin with *Ansul*, to which the Court of Justice looked in answering the questions posed in the *La Mer* reference. The Court of Justice said (para. 35 of *Ansul*) that 'Genuine use means actual use of the mark.' This is not altogether surprising, as trade marks are made for and matter in markets, in which goods and services are bought and sold and in which their different origins need to be identified and distinguished.

19. The Court of Justice expounded the concept of genuine use:

36. 'Genuine use' must therefore be understood to denote use that is not merely token, serving solely to preserve the rights conferred by the mark. Such use must be consistent with the essential function of a trade mark, which is to guarantee the identity of the origin of the goods or services to the consumer or end-user by enabling him, without any possibility of confusion, to distinguish the product or service from others which have another origin.

37. It follows that 'genuine use' of the mark entails use of the mark on the market for the goods or services protected by the mark and not just internal use by the undertaking concerned. The protection the mark confers and the consequences of registering in terms of enforceability *vis-a-vis* third parties cannot continue to operate if the mark loses its commercial *raison d'etre*, which is to create and preserve an outlet for the goods or services that bear the sign of which it is composed, as distinct from the goods or services of other undertakings. Use of the mark must therefore relate to goods or services already marketed or about to be marketed and for which preparations by the undertaking to secure customers are under way, particularly in the form of advertising campaigns. Such use may be either by the trade mark proprietor or, as envisaged in Article 10(3) of the Directive, by a third party with authority to use the mark.

38. Finally when assessing whether there has been genuine use of the trade mark, regard must be had to all the facts and circumstances relevant to establishing whether the commercial exploitation of the mark is real, in particular whether such use is viewed as warranted in

the economic sector concerned to maintain or create a share in the market for the goods or services protected by the mark.

39. Assessing the circumstances of the case may thus include giving consideration, *inter alia*, to the nature of the goods or service at issue, the characteristics of the market concerned and the scale and frequency of use of the mark. Use of the mark need not therefore always be quantitatively significant for it to be deemed genuine, as that depends on the characteristics of the goods or service concerned on the corresponding market.

Reasoned order in *La Mer*

20. The questions in *La Mer*, which were, of course, framed without the benefit of the subsequent judgment in *Ansul*, sought rulings about the extent of use, the amount of use and types of use that can be considered when deciding whether a mark has been put to genuine use in a Member State. The Court of Justice considered the questions together on the basis of paras. 35 to 39 of *Ansul* (see paras. 18 and 19 of *La Mer*) and continued:

20. It follows from those considerations that the preservation by a trade mark proprietor of his rights is predicated on the mark being put to genuine use in the course of trade, on the market for the goods or services for which it was registered in the Member State concerned.

21. Moreover, it is clear from para. [39] of *Ansul* that use of the mark may in some cases be sufficient to establish genuine use within the meaning of the Directive even if that use is not quantitatively significant. Even minimal use can therefore be sufficient to qualify as genuine, on condition that it is deemed to be justified, in the economic sector concerned, for the purpose of preserving or creating market share for the goods or services protected by the mark.

22. The question whether use is sufficient to preserve or create market share for those products or services depends on several factors and on a case by case assessment which is for the national court to carry out. The characteristics of those products or services, the frequency or regularity of the use of the mark, whether the mark is used for the purpose of marketing all the identical products or services of the proprietor or merely some of them, or evidence which the proprietor is able to provide, are among the factors which may be taken into account.

23. Similarly, as emerges from paras. [35]–[39] of *Ansul* set out above, the characteristics of the market concerned, which directly affect the marketing strategy of the proprietor of the mark, may also be taken into account in assessing genuine use of the mark.

24. In addition, use of the mark by a single client which imports the products for which the mark is registered can be sufficient to demonstrate that such use is genuine, if it appears that the import operation has a genuine commercial justification for the proprietor of the mark.

Mummery LJ then went on to consider Blackburne J's reasoning in the High Court. Unlike Blackburne J, he came down on the side of the claimant. He took the view that Blackburne J had wrongly interpreted the *Ansul* decision, in that he had applied a qualitative and quantitative test based on the number of end users of the product, for assessing whether there had been sufficient market use to comprise genuine use.

Mummery LJ:

33. Trade marks are not only used on the market in which goods bearing the mark are sold to consumers and end-users. A market exists in which goods bearing the mark are sold by

foreign manufacturers to importers in the United Kingdom. The goods bearing the LA MER mark were sold by Goemar and bought by Health Scope Direct on that market in arm's length transactions. The modest amount of the quantities involved and the more restricted nature of the import market did not prevent the use of the mark on the goods from being genuine use on the market. The Court of Justice made it clear that, provided the use was neither token nor internal, imports by a single importer could suffice for determining whether there was genuine use of the mark on the market.

According to Lord Justice Mummery in *Goemar*, the decision as to whether use of a mark has been genuine should be based on objective factors, most notably whether the goods bearing the mark have been placed on the market, even if there have been no final consumers for the goods. Furthermore, use of the mark can be modest. Other circumstances which might give rise to non-use and hence to the revocation of the registered mark are: that the mark as it is used does not incorporate the distinctive features of the registered mark, as was argued in *Bud and Budweiser Budbrau Trade Marks*,[40] or that the mark is not used on the goods for which it is registered.[41] This was the case in *Thomas Pink Ltd v Victoria's Secret UK*.[42] The claimant had a EUTM registration for the word 'Pink' for a wide range of goods including clothing and footwear. The defendant began selling lingerie under the sign 'Pink'. The claimant succeeded in showing infringement. The defendant counterclaimed for revocation of the registration of 'Pink' both for clothing and footwear arguing that the registration was too broad. The court agreed that the registration of 'Pink 'for footwear should be revoked on the basis that while the claimant sold wellington boots, this did not justify a registration for footwear in general.

There are also defences to an accusation of non-use. It is possible to argue that the proprietor has used a registered mark when he uses a mark which incorporates its distinctive elements (Article 10(1)(a) of the TMD).[43] This was one of the issues raised in *Specsavers v Asda*.

Specsavers International Healthcare Ltd, Specsavers BV, Specsavers Optical Group Ltd and Specsavers Optical Superstores Ltd v Asda Stores Ltd and The Registrar of Trade Marks (Intervening) [2014] EWCA Civ 1294

The claimant operated a chain of opticians. The issue of non-use concerned two of the claimant's EUTMs. These were a registered mark which consisted simply of two overlapping ellipses (the 'wordless logo mark') and a registration for the same ellipses but containing the word SPECSAVERS ('the shaded logo mark'). When the defendant began advertising its own optical service with a logo of two overlapping ellipses carrying the words 'ASDA OPTICIANS', the claimant sued for infringement of both these trade marks. In turn, ASDA claimed that the 'wordless logo mark' should be revoked for non-use as it had never been used alone. Specsavers answered that use of the shaded logo mark also constituted use of the wordless logo mark. The Court of Appeal asked the CJEU if, where a trader has two separate EUTMs for a graphic mark and a word mark and uses the two together, such use constitutes use of the graphic mark and how

---

[40] [2002] RPC 747.   [41] TMD, Art. 13.   [42] [2014] FSR 40.
[43] TMA, s. 46(2) TMA; TMD 2016, Art. 19(2).

such use is to be assessed. In the Court of Appeal judgment which followed the CJEU decision,[44] Kitchin LJ summarized the CJEU's response:

13. In its judgment and answer to the first three questions, the Court of Justice pointed out first, that the superimposition of the word 'Specsavers' over the Wordless logo mark changes the form of the mark because parts of the mark are hidden by the word. However, the Court continued, it follows from the wording of art.15 that the use of a mark in a form which differs from the form in which it is registered is nevertheless considered as use of the registered mark to the extent that its distinctive character is not altered.

14. Turning to the assessment of the distinctive character of a registered trade mark, the Court reiterated (at [22]) that, in accordance with well established principles, the mark must serve to identify the product in relation to which it is used as a product originating from a particular undertaking, and so distinguish that product from those of other undertakings. It then explained that the distinctive character of a mark might be the result of its use as part of or in conjunction with another mark:

'23. That distinctive character of a registered trade mark may be the result both of the use, as part of a registered trade mark, of a component thereof and of the use of a separate mark in conjunction with a registered trade mark. In both cases, it is sufficient that, in consequence of such use, the relevant class of persons actually perceive the product or service at issue as originating from a given undertaking (see, by analogy, Case C-353/03 *Société des Produits Nestlé SA v Mars UK Ltd* [2005] E.C.R. I-6135, paragraph 30).'

15. The Court then reasoned as follows in relation to the particular circumstances of this case:

'24. It follows that the use of the wordless logo mark with the superimposed word sign "Specsavers", even if, ultimately, it amounts to a use as a part of a registered trade mark or in conjunction with it, may be considered to be a genuine use of the wordless logo mark as such to the extent that that mark as it was registered, namely without a part of it being hidden by the superimposed word sign "Specsavers", always refers in that form to the goods of the Specsavers group covered by the registration, which is to be determined by the referring court.'

16. If the Wordless logo mark does refer to the goods of Specsavers, it matters not that the word Specsavers and the combination of the Wordless logo and the word Specsavers (that is to say, the Shaded logo) are themselves registered, as emerges clearly from [25]–[27]:

'25. That conclusion is not affected by the fact that the word sign "Specsavers" and the combination of the wordless logo with the superimposed word sign "Specsavers" are also registered as Community trade marks.
26. The Court has already held that the condition of genuine use of a trade mark, within the meaning of Article 15(1) of Regulation 207/2009, may be satisfied where the trade mark is used only through another composite mark, or where it is used only in conjunction with another mark, and the combination of those two marks is, furthermore, itself registered as a trade mark (see, to that effect, Case C-12/12 *Colloseum Holding AG v Levi Strauss & Co* [2012] ECR I-0000, paragraphs 35 and 36).

[44] *Specsavers International Healthcare Ltd, Specsavers BV, Specsavers Optical Group Ltd, Specsavers Optical Superstores Ltd v Asda Stores Ltd* Case C-252/12 [2013] ETMR 46.

27. Moreover, the Court has also held, in relation to Article 10(2)(a) of First Council Directive 89/104/EEC of 21 December 1988 to approximate the laws of the Member States relating to trade marks (OJ 1989 L 40, p.1), which provision corresponds, in essence, to the second subparagraph of Article 15(1)(a) of Regulation 207/2009 , that the proprietor of a registered trade mark is not precluded from relying, in order to establish use of the trade mark for the purposes of that provision, on the fact that it is used in a form which differs from the form in which it was registered, without the differences between the two altering the distinctive character of that trade mark, even though that different form is itself registered as a trade mark (Case C-553/11 *Rintisch v Eder* (C-553/11) [2012] ECR I-0000, paragraph 30).'

17. The Court therefore answered the first three referred questions in these terms:

'31. In view of all the foregoing considerations, the answer to the first three questions is that Article 15(1) and Article 51(1)(a) of Regulation 207/2009 must be interpreted as meaning that the condition of "genuine use", within the meaning of those provisions, may be fulfilled where a Community figurative mark is used only in conjunction with a Community word mark which is superimposed over it, and the combination of those two marks is, furthermore, itself registered as a Community trade mark, to the extent that the differences between the form in which that trade mark is used and that in which it was registered do not change the distinctive character of that trade mark as registered.'

Applying the CJEU judgment to the facts of the case, Kitchin LJ held that the wordless logo mark had been put to genuine use and should not be revoked. He looked amongst other things at the length of time the shaded logo had been used and he accepted that the average consumer would find the wordless logo to be distinctive, since when the shaded logo was seen from a distance the word SPECSAVERS would not stand out. He concluded:

34. Drawing the threads together, I have come to the conclusion that, in the rather unusual circumstances of this case and notwithstanding my initial impression to the contrary, Specsavers have established that much of the use they have made of the Shaded logo mark including, in particular, its use on signage, does also constitute use of the Wordless logo mark, for the evidence in this case shows that it has been such that the Wordless logo mark has served and does serve to identify the goods and services of Specsavers, and that the average consumer has perceived and does perceive the Wordless logo mark as indicative of the origin of the goods and services supplied by Specsavers. In short, much of that use has been such that the differences between the Shaded logo mark and the Wordless logo mark have not changed the distinctive character of the Wordless logo mark; and the Wordless logo mark has itself been seen as a trade mark and not simply as background. It follows that Specsavers have established that they have made genuine use of the Wordless logo mark.

A second defence against revocation for non-use is if there are 'proper reasons' for non-use of the mark (Article 12(1) of the TMD). The General Court considered what constitutes 'proper reasons' in *Naazneen Investments Ltd v OHIM, Energy Brands Inc.*,[45] which concerned Naazneen's 2002 registration of the EUTM 'SMART WATER' for, inter alia, beverages. Energy Brands sought to have the mark revoked for non-use for a period of five years. Among its

[45] Case T-250/13 [2015] ETMR 21.

arguments, Naazneen asserted that there were proper reasons for non-use. Its beverages were produced by a third party. It had had to interrupt the marketing of them under the mark since the goods were defective. In effect, it argued that it had had the choice either to stop using the mark at issue or to put consumers' health in danger. The General Court defined proper reasons only as obstacles having a sufficiently direct relationship with a trade mark as to make its use impossible or unreasonable and which arise independently of the will of the proprietor of that mark. These reasons must be assessed on a case-by-case basis, including asking whether a change in the strategy of the undertaking to circumvent the obstacle under consideration would make the use of that mark unreasonable. In this case, since it was for Naazneen to supervise and control the manufacture of the goods in question, even though they were being manufactured by a third party, the interruption to the marketing of those goods could not be regarded as independent of the will of Naazneen. According to the General Court:

> 68 Naazneen is wrong to claim that it had no choice other than to stop using the mark at issue or to put consumers' health in danger. This is because further products could have been manufactured and placed on the market within a reasonable period. The additional economic investments necessary for the manufacture of further products form part of the risks that an undertaking must face.

It is clearly important to recognize that registration accords the proprietor a monopoly over the use of the mark in the course of trade and hence prevents its use by competitors in the market. What the decision in *Naazneen* appears to recognize, as do the penalties for non-use more generally, is that with such a monopoly also comes a responsibility to take all reasonable measures to ensure that the mark is exploited.

FURTHER READING

S. Burke and J. Smith, 'Court of Appeal finds genuine use of the Specsavers logo' (2015) 10 JIPLP 79.

J. Davis and A. Durant, 'HAVE A BREAK and the changing demands of trade mark registration' (2015) 5 QMJIP 132.

C. Howell, 'Trade marks: what constitutes "genuine use"? *Laboratoires Goemar SA v La Mer Technology*' [2006] EIPR 118.

8.4 TRADE MARKS AND THE EXHAUSTION OF RIGHTS

Article 7 of the TMD[46] deals with the exhaustion of those rights which are endowed on a trade mark by registration. It reads:

> (1) The trade mark shall not entitle the proprietor to prohibit its use in relation to goods which have been put on the market in the Community under that trade mark by the proprietor or with his consent.

---

[46] TMA, s. 12; TMD 2016, Art. 15.

> (2) Paragraph 1 shall not apply where there exist legitimate reasons for the proprietor to oppose further commercialisation of the goods, especially where the condition of the goods is changed or impaired after they have been put on the market.

This provision, like the defences to trade mark infringement and the grounds for invalidity and revocation, is concerned with setting the limits to the monopoly afforded by registration. Article 7 primarily deals with the parallel importation of goods from one Member State to another by a party other than the trade mark proprietor. It has been suggested that Article 7 exhaustion marks a recognition that, under conditions of resale, the trade mark will continue to play its role as an indication of origin and quality. Its use will not deceive the public and might well serve the public interest by encouraging competition and hence lower prices. On the other hand, if the mark is used by the third party in such a way that its value is diminished, Article 7(2) affords the proprietor the power to prevent such an outcome.

8.4.1 INTERPRETING ARTICLE 7

The interpretation of both parts of Article 7 has caused considerable controversy. In interpreting Article 7(1), the key issue has been whether a trade mark proprietor is entitled to prohibit use of his mark in relation to goods which were put on the market *outside* the EEA (European Economic Area) with his consent but are then imported into the EEA by a third party. In relation to Article 7(2), the debate has focused on what constitutes legitimate reasons for a proprietor to oppose the resale of his goods which have been put on the market with his consent within the EEA. More recently, the courts have considered under what conditions is it 'necessary' for the parallel importer to use the registered mark.

8.4.1.1 International exhaustion of rights

The TMD introduced regional exhaustion, applying the principle to trade both within Member States and between them. However, given the global nature of trade (and more particularly of branding), it is not surprising that shortly after the directive was incorporated into the national law of Member States, the issue of international exhaustion (i.e. in relation to goods placed on the market outside the EEA) was raised. The general approach to this question, which remains authoritative today, was set out by the CJEU in *Silhouette*.

Silhouette International Schmied GmbH & Co. KG v Hartlauer Handelsgesellschaft mbH Case C-355/96 [1998] ECR I-4799

Silhouette is an Austrian company producing expensive spectacle frames which it sells worldwide under the name 'Silhouette', a registered trade mark in Austria and many other countries. In Austria, Silhouette supplied its frames directly to opticians. Elsewhere, it distributed them through subsidiary companies or distributors. Hartlauer sold spectacles among other cut-priced goods through its Austrian subsidiaries. As noted by the CJEU, Hartlauer 'was not supplied by Silhouette because that company considers that distribution of its products by Hartlauer would be harmful to its image as a manufacturer of top-quality fashion spectacles'. In 1995, Hartlauer purchased 21,000 Silhouette spectacle frames. These spectacles had originally been supplied by Silhouette to a Bulgarian company which had been instructed only to sell the frames in Bulgaria or the former USSR. It is not clear from whom Hartlauer had purchased the frames. In Austria, Silhouette sought an injunction to prevent Hartlauer from selling the frames under its trade mark as they had not been put on the market in the EEA by Silhouette or with its consent. In other words, it argued that it had not exhausted its trade mark rights in the EEA. In the course of the proceedings, the Austrian courts referred to the CJEU the question of whether Article 7(1) should be understood to mean that the trade mark entitles a proprietor to prohibit a third party from using the mark for goods which have been put on the market in a state which is not part of the EEA. The CJEU held that it did not.

19. No argument has been presented to the Court that the Directive could be interpreted as providing for the exhaustion of the rights conferred by a trade mark in respect of goods put on the market by the proprietor or with his consent irrespective of where they were put on the market.

...

24. The first recital in the preamble to the Directive notes that the trade mark laws applicable in the Member States contain disparities which may impede the free movement of goods and freedom to provide services and may distort competition within the common market, so that it is necessary, in view of the establishment and functioning of the internal market, to approximate the laws of Member States. The ninth recital emphasises that it is fundamental, in order to facilitate the free movement of goods and services, to ensure that registered trade marks enjoy the same protection under the legal systems of all the Member States, but that this should not prevent Member States from granting at their option more extensive protection to those trade marks which have a reputation.

25. In the light of those recitals, Articles 5 to 7 of the Directive must be construed as embodying a complete harmonisation of the rules relating to the rights conferred by a trade mark. That interpretation, it may be added, is borne out by the fact that Article 5 expressly leaves it open to the Member States to maintain or introduce certain rules specifically defined by the Community legislature. Thus, in accordance with Article 5(2), to which the ninth recital refers, the Member States have the option to grant more extensive protection to trade marks with a reputation.

26. Accordingly, the Directive cannot be interpreted as leaving it open to the Member States to provide in their domestic law for exhaustion of the rights conferred by a trade mark in respect of products put on the market in non-member countries.

27. This, moreover, is the only interpretation which is fully capable of ensuring that the purpose of the Directive is achieved, namely to safeguard the functioning of the internal market. A situation in which some Member States could provide for international exhaustion while others provided for Community exhaustion only would inevitably give rise to barriers to the free movement of goods and the freedom to provide services.

...

30. Finally, the Community authorities could always extend the exhaustion provided for by Article 7 to products put on the market in non-member countries by entering into international agreements in that sphere, as was done in the context of the EEA Agreement.

31. In the light of the foregoing, the answer to be given to the first question must be that national rules providing for exhaustion of trade mark rights in respect of products put on the market outside the EEA under that mark by the proprietor or with his consent are contrary to Article 7(1) of the Directive, as amended by the EEA Agreement.

The decision in *Silhouette* that the directive neither allowed for international exhaustion nor enabled states within the EEA to adopt their own approach was criticized by a number of commentators. It was suggested that by not endorsing international exhaustion, the CJEU was allowing trade mark rights to be used as a barrier to international trade, with the result that prices of goods put on the market in the EEA might be kept artificially high if they were protected from competition from goods with the same trade mark but put on the market at a lower price outside the EEA. It was also suggested by some commentators that difficulties would arise around the question of when a trade mark owner would be deemed to have consented to the distribution of his goods in the EEA and when he would be deemed to have withheld consent. The meaning of consent was subsequently examined by the CJEU in *Sebago*.[47] In this case, the CJEU held that for there to be consent, such consent must relate to each individual item of the product imported and sold in the EEA by the parallel importer. However, perhaps the key case dealing with consent is *Zino Davidoff v A & G Imports*.

Zino Davidoff SA v A & G Imports Ltd; Levi Strauss & Co. Ltd v Tesco Stores Ltd, Tesco Plc and Costco Wholesale UK Ltd Joined Cases C-414–416/99 [2001] ECR I-8691

Zino Davidoff was the proprietor of two trade marks, 'Cool Water' and 'Davidoff Cool Water' registered in the UK for toiletries and other cosmetic products. Davidoff sold its products in the EEA and outside. In 1996, it contracted with a trader in Singapore to sell its products to distributors in a defined territory outside the EEA and to impose on these distributors a contractual term not to resell outside the defined territory. A & G acquired these products (identified by batch code numbers placed on them by Davidoff) and then imported and sold them in the UK. Davidoff alleged that its trade mark had been infringed by this importation and sale. A & G argued that given the circumstances in which the goods had been placed on the market in Singapore, Davidoff should be deemed to have given consent to the importation and sale of the goods in the UK. Davidoff denied it had given consent. Levi Strauss sold jeans under the marks 'Levis' and '501'. It distributed its goods in the UK through a selective distribution system, which did not include the defendants. Tesco and Costco obtained Levi jeans which had been manufactured and sold outside the EEA. The contracts by which they had acquired the jeans did not contain any terms which would prevent their sale in the UK. Indeed, the jeans had originally been sold to authorized dealers outside the UK and acquired by a third party. Levis alleged trade mark infringement. Among the questions addressed to the CJEU by the High Court was whether and in what circumstances it was possible to imply consent by a trade mark proprietor for the importation and sale of his goods in the EEA. In its judgment, the CJEU first looked at whether consent could be implied, noting that different Member States had differing definitions of consent.

> 43. It therefore falls to the Court to supply a uniform interpretation of the concept of 'consent' to the placing of goods on the market within the EEA as referred to in Article 7(1) of the Directive.
>
> …

---

[47] *Sebago Inc. and Ancienne Maison Dubois et Fils SA v GB-Unic SA* Case C-173/98 [1999] ECR I-4103.

45. In view of its serious effect in extinguishing the exclusive rights of the proprietors of the trade marks in issue in the main proceedings (rights which enable them to control the initial marketing in the EEA), consent must be so expressed that an intention to renounce those rights is unequivocally demonstrated.

46. Such intention will normally be gathered from an express statement of consent. Nevertheless, it is conceivable that consent may, in some cases, be inferred from facts and circumstances prior to, simultaneous with or subsequent to the placing of the goods on the market outside the EEA which, in the view of the national court, unequivocally demonstrate that the proprietor has renounced his rights.

47. The answer to the first question referred in each of Cases C414/99 to C-416/99 must therefore be that, on a proper construction of Article 7(1) of the Directive, the consent of a trade mark proprietor to the marketing within the EEA of products bearing that mark which have previously been placed on the market outside the EEA by that proprietor or with his consent may be implied, where it is to be inferred from facts and circumstances prior to, simultaneous with or subsequent to the placing of the goods on the market outside the EEA which, in the view of the national court, unequivocally demonstrate that the proprietor has renounced his right to oppose placing of the goods on the market within the EEA.

[Having concluded that consent could be implied, the CJEU then went on to consider whether consent may be inferred from the mere silence of a trade mark proprietor:]

53. It follows from the answer to the first question referred in the three cases C-414/99 to C-416/99 that consent must be expressed positively and that the factors taken into consideration in finding implied consent must unequivocally demonstrate that the trade mark proprietor has renounced any intention to enforce his exclusive rights.

54. It follows that it is for the trader alleging consent to prove it and not for the trade mark proprietor to demonstrate its absence.

55. Consequently, implied consent to the marketing within the EEA of goods put on the market outside that area cannot be inferred from the mere silence of the trade mark proprietor.

56. Likewise, implied consent cannot be inferred from the fact that a trade mark proprietor has not communicated his opposition to marketing within the EEA or from the fact that the goods do not carry any warning that it is prohibited to place them on the market within the EEA.

57. Finally, such consent cannot be inferred from the fact that the trade mark proprietor transferred ownership of the goods bearing the mark without imposing contractual reservations or from the fact that, according to the law governing the contract, the property right transferred includes, in the absence of such reservations, an unlimited right of resale or, at the very least, a right to market the goods subsequently within the EEA.

58. A rule of national law which proceeded upon the mere silence of the trade mark proprietor would not recognise implied consent but rather deemed consent. This would not meet the need for consent positively expressed required by Community law.

59. In so far as it falls to the Community legislature to determine the rights of a trade mark proprietor within the Member States of the Community it would be unacceptable on the basis of the law governing the contract for marketing outside the EEA to apply rules of law that have the effect of limiting the protection afforded to the proprietor of a trade mark by Articles 5(1) and 7(1) of the Directive.

60. The answer to be given to the second question and to Question 3(a)(i), (vi) and (vii) in Cases C-415/99 and C-416/99, and to the second question in Case C-414/99, must therefore be that implied consent cannot be inferred:

— from the fact that the proprietor of the trade mark has not communicated to all subsequent purchasers of the goods placed on the market outside the EEA his opposition to marketing within the EEA;

— from the fact that the goods carry no warning of a prohibition of their being placed on the market within the EEA;

— from the fact that the trade mark proprietor has transferred the ownership of the products bearing the trade mark without imposing any contractual reservations and that, according to the law governing the contract, the property right transferred includes, in the absence of such reservations, an unlimited right of resale or, at the very least, a right to market the goods subsequently within the EEA.

It is submitted that the judgment in *Zino Davidoff* came down firmly on the side of the trade mark proprietor on the question of consent. Although consent might be implied, according to the CJEU, strict conditions need to be met in order to infer implied consent. Do you think that the CJEU was correct to favour the proprietor in this regard, or does this approach give too much power to proprietors to control the cost of their products, which may be sold more cheaply abroad, at the expense of the consumer? In a later case concerning the issue of consent, *Van Doren + Q GmbH v Lifestyle Sports + Sportswear*,[48] the CJEU appeared to shift the balance somewhat towards that of the importer. It held that where a third party succeeds in establishing that there is a real risk of partitioning of national markets if he himself bears that burden of proof, particularly where the trade mark proprietor markets his products in the EEA using an exclusive distribution system, it is for the proprietor of the trade mark to establish that the products were initially placed on the market outside the EEA by him or with his consent. If such evidence is adduced, it is for the third party to prove the consent of the trade mark proprietor to subsequent marketing of the products in the EEA.[49]

Questions have also been raised as to when goods are deemed to have been 'put on the market'. In *Peak Holding AB v Axolin-Elinor AB*,[50] the claimant had imported its own goods, carrying its trade mark, into the EEA where they had been offered for sale to the public but had remained unsold. This was held by the CJEU not to constitute putting the goods on the market for the purpose of exhaustion. According to the CJEU, importing the goods or offering them for sale in the EEA cannot be equated to putting them on the market there.[51] The problem of ascertaining when exactly goods are put on the market has, not surprisingly, been exacerbated by the rise of e-commerce. It was raised in the case of *L'Oréal v eBay*.[52] One question for the Court was whether goods which were advertised on the auction site, which had not been put on the market in the EEA by the proprietor

---

[48] *Van Doren + Q GmbH v Lifestyle Sports + Sportswear Handelsgesellschaft GmbH* Case C-244/00 [2003] ECR I-3051.

[49] In *Makro Zelfbedieningsgroothandel CV v Diesel SPA* [2009], the CJEU held that the same principles for finding in the context of international exhaustion applied to exhaustion within the EEA.

[50] Case C-16/03 [2005] ECR I-11313.   [51] [43].   [52] [2011]; see also Chapter 7.

or with his consent, would be considered to be infringing under Article 5. According to the CJEU:

> 1. Where goods located in a third State, which bear a trade mark registered in a Member State of the European Union or a Community trade mark and have not previously been put on the market in the European Economic Area or, in the case of a Community trade mark, in the European Union, (i) are sold by an economic operator on an online marketplace without the consent of the trade mark proprietor to a consumer located in the territory covered by the trade mark or (ii) are offered for sale or advertised on such a marketplace targeted at consumers located in that territory, the trade mark proprietor may prevent that sale, offer for sale or advertising by virtue of the rules set out in Article 5 of First Council Directive 89/104/EEC of 21 December 1988 to approximate the laws of the Member States relating to trade marks, as amended by the Agreement on the European Economic Area of 2 May 1992, or in Article 9 of Council Regulation (EC) No 40/94 of 20 December 1993 on the Community trade mark. It is the task of the national courts to assess on a case-by-case basis whether relevant factors exist, on the basis of which it may be concluded that an offer for sale or an advertisement displayed on an online marketplace accessible from the territory covered by the trade mark is targeted at consumers in that territory.

The CJEU held that sample products and 'testers' which L'Oréal had provided free to its distributors and which were marked 'not for sale' had not been put on the market for the purposes of Article 7 of the TMD (Article 13 of the Trade Mark Regulation). On a related point, we have seen, in *Logistics v Bacardi*, that in the case of the marks on parallel imports held in a warehouse, this was deemed to be use of the marks 'in the course of trade'.[53] We may wonder whether the decision in *Logistics* is compatible with the decision in *L'Oréal*.

8.4.1.2 Free movement of trade marked goods within the EU

Article 36 of the TFEU (previously Article 30 of the Treaty of Rome) protects the specific subject matter of industrial property rights. In the case of trade marks, the CJEU has identified this to be the guarantee to the proprietor of a trade mark that he has the exclusive right to use the trade mark for the purpose of putting the product into circulation for the first time, and therefore to protect him against competitors wishing to take advantage of the status and the reputation of the mark by selling products illegally bearing the mark.[54] But Article 36 also states that 'prohibitions or restrictions on imports between Member States which are justified on grounds of protection of industrial and commercial property are permissible, provided they do not constitute a means of arbitrary discrimination or a disguised restriction on trade between Member States'.[55] Typically, early cases which dealt with the parallel importation of trade marked goods within the EU concerned the situation where a proprietor may have marketed the same goods under different registered marks in different Member States. In *Centrafarm BV v American Home Products*,[56] the CJEU held that a proprietor could not rely on its trade mark registrations to prevent parallel import of goods from one Member State to another if its intention was to artificially partition the market. In *Bristol-Myers Squibb v Paranova*, the CJEU held that Article 7 should be

---

[53] *Logistics BV and another v Bacardi & Co. Ltd and another* Case C-379/14, EU:C:2015:497. See 7.2.1.
[54] *Centrafarm BV and Adriaan De Peijper v Sterling Drug Inc.* Case 15/74 [1974] ECR 1147.
[55] *Bristol-Myers Squibb v Paranova A/S* Case C-427/93 [1996] ECR I-3457, [3].
[56] *Centrafarm BV v American Home Products Corp.* Case 3/78 [1978] ECR 1823.

understood in light of Article 36 and was an objective test: that is, the intentions of the proprietor were irrelevant.

8.4.1.3 Reasons to oppose further dealings (1): changing the physical condition of the goods

The specific question raised by Article 7 is under what circumstances a proprietor may object to the further marketing of his goods because of the way they are being marketed by the parallel importer. This was the issue raised in *Bristol-Myers Squibb v Paranova*, which concerned changes to the physical condition of the goods.

Bristol-Myers Squibb v Paranova A/S Case C-427/93 [1996] ECR I-3457

Paranova sold pharmaceuticals in Denmark which Bristol-Myers Squibb (BMS) had first placed on the market in other EU states. Paranova repackaged the drugs in a design which was distinctive of its own goods but also retained the design of the original packaging. Paranova left the original trade mark on the packaging, but stated that the goods had been 'imported and repackaged by Paranova'. In some cases, Paranova also changed the size of the packaging. In others it relabelled the drugs, so that they carried both the BMS marks and its own trade mark. BMS brought an action in the Danish courts claiming that Paranova had infringed its trade marks. The Danish court asked the CJEU a number of questions. The first was whether Article 7(1) precludes a proprietor from objecting to goods put on the market and with his consent where the importer has repackaged the product and reaffixed the trade mark without the proprietor's consent.

34. The Court's case law on Article 36 of the Treaty shows that the owner's exclusive right to affix a trade mark to a product must in certain circumstances be regarded as exhausted in order to allow an importer to market under that trade mark products which were put on the market in another Member State by the owner or with his consent (see Case 102/77 *Hoffmann-la Roche v Centrafarm* [1978] ECR 1139; Case 3/78 *Centrafarm v American Home Products Corporation* [1978] ECR 1823; and the judgment given today in *Eurim-Pharm Arzeneimittel GmbH v Beiersdorf AG* (Joined Cases C-71-73/94) [1996] ECR I-3603 and *MPA Pharma GmbH v Rhone-Poulenc Pharma GmbH* (Case C-232/94) [1996] ECR I-3671).

35. To accept the argument that the principle of exhaustion under Article 7(1) cannot apply if the importer has repackaged the product and reaffixed the trade mark would therefore imply a major alteration to the principles flowing from Articles 30 and 36 of the Treaty.

36. There is nothing to suggest that Article 7 of the Directive is intended to restrict the scope of that case law. Nor would such an effect be permissible, since a Directive cannot justify obstacles to inter-Community trade save within the bounds set by the Treaty rules. The Court's case law shows that the prohibition on quantitative restrictions and measures having equivalent effect applies not only to national measures but also to those emanating from Community institutions (see, most recently, Case C-51/93 *Meyhui v Schott Zwiesel Glaswerke* [1994] ECR I-3879, paragraph 11).

37. The answer to the first question in Cases C-427/93 and C-429/93 must therefore be that, save in the circumstances defined in Article 7(2), Article 7(1) of the Directive precludes the owner of a trade mark from relying on his rights as owner to prevent an importer from

marketing a product which was put on the market in another Member State by the owner or with his consent, even if that importer repackaged the product and reaffixed the trade mark to it without the owner's authorisation.

[The second question addressed to the CJEU was when might a proprietor fall back on Article 7(2) to prevent the re-marketing of its goods. The CJEU first pointed out that earlier cases had found that a trade mark owner could not rely upon its trade mark rights to artificially partition the market. The CJEU went on to identify those situations when artificial partitioning might occur:]

Artificial partitioning of the markets between Member States

52. Reliance on trade mark rights by their owner in order to oppose marketing under that trade mark of products repackaged by a third party would contribute to the partitioning of markets between Member States in particular where the owner has placed an identical pharmaceutical product on the market in several Member States in various forms of packaging, and the product may not, in the condition in which it has been marketed by the trade mark owner in one Member State, be imported and put on the market in another Member State by a parallel importer.

53. The trade mark owner cannot therefore oppose the repackaging of the product in new external packaging when the size of packet used by the owner in the Member State where the importer purchased the product cannot be marketed in the Member State of importation by reason, in particular, of a rule authorising packaging only of a certain size or a national practice to the same effect, sickness insurance rules making the reimbursement of medical expenses depend on the size of the packaging, or well-established medical prescription practices based, inter alia, on standard sizes recommended by professional groups and sickness insurance institutions.

54. Where, in accordance with the rules and practices in force in the Member State of importation, the trade mark owner uses many different sizes of packaging in that State, the finding that one of those sizes is also marketed in the Member State of exportation is not enough to justify the conclusion that repackaging is unnecessary. Partitioning of the markets would exist if the importer were able to sell the product in only part of his market.

55. The owner may, on the other hand, oppose the repackaging of the product in new external packaging where the importer is able to achieve packaging which may be marketed in the Member State of importation by, for example, affixing to the original external or inner packaging new labels in the language of the Member State of importation, or by adding new user instructions or information in the language of the Member State of importation, or by replacing an additional article not capable of gaining approval in the Member State of importation with a similar article that has obtained such approval.

56. The power of the owner of trade mark rights protected in a Member State to oppose the marketing of repackaged products under the trade mark should be limited only in so far as the repackaging undertaken by the importer is necessary in order to market the product in the Member State of importation.

57. Finally, contrary to the argument of the plaintiffs in the main actions, the Court's use of the words 'artificial partitioning of the markets' does not imply that the importer must demonstrate that, by putting an identical product on the market in varying forms of packaging in different Member States, the trade mark owner deliberately sought to partition the markets

between Member States. By stating that the partitioning in question must be artificial, the Court's intention was to stress that the owner of a trade mark may always rely on his rights as owner to oppose the marketing of repackaged products when such action is justified by the need to safeguard the essential function of the trade mark, in which case the resultant partitioning could not be regarded as artificial.

[Key to the CJEU judgment is that repackaging undertaken by a parallel importer must be 'necessary' in order for the latter to enter the market. In the judgment, the CJEU also set out the conditions which must be met by a parallel importer so as not to fall foul of Article 7(2). They include, inter alia, that:]

79. ...

(c) the new packaging clearly states who repackaged the product and the name of the manufacturer in print such that a person with normal eyesight, exercising a normal degree of attentiveness, would be in a position to understand; similarly, the origin of an extra article from a source other than the trade mark owner must be indicated in such a way as to dispel any impression that the trade mark owner is responsible for it; however, it is not necessary to indicate that the repackaging was carried out without the authorisation of the trade mark owner;

(d) the presentation of the repackaged product is not such as to be liable to damage the reputation of the trade mark and of its owner; thus, the packaging must not be defective, of poor quality, or untidy; and

(e) the importer gives notice to the trade mark owner before the repackaged product is put on sale, and, on demand, supplies him with a specimen of the repackaged product.

We should not be surprised that following the *Bristol-Myers Squibb v Paranova* decision, the question was raised of when repackaging or relabelling was 'necessary' and therefore acceptable under Article 7. The leading case on the scope of necessity is *Boehringer Ingelheim KG v Swingward Ltd*

Boehringer Ingelheim KG and Boehringer Ingelheim Pharma KG v Swingward Ltd Case C-143/00 [2002] ECR I-3759

The pharmaceutical products involved in this action had been marketed by the claimants in the EU, and the defendants had imported them into the UK. The defendants had altered the packaging of the products in various ways. For example, they attached labels to the original packets which identified themselves and the licence number of the product but left the original trade mark visible. Alternatively, the defendant had repackaged the products but reproduced the original trade mark. Finally, in other cases, the product had been repackaged without the original trade mark visible on the outside, although the original trade mark was visible inside the box but 'over-stickered' with a label giving the product's generic name and identifying the manufacturer and the parallel importer. All the packages also included an information leaflet bearing the claimants' trade marks but translated into English. The claimants argued that such changes were not 'necessary' to market the products in the UK. A key question addressed to the CJEU was whether repackaging is by definition detrimental to the specific subject matter of a trade mark even if it does not affect the essential function of the mark to act as a badge of origin. In its judgment, the CJEU looked at the scope of the test of 'necessity', which had been identified in *Bristol-Myers Squibb v Paranova*.

Findings of the Court

45. According to the Court's case law, where a trade mark proprietor relies on its trade mark rights to prevent a parallel importer from repackaging where that is necessary for the pharmaceutical products concerned to be marketed in the importing State, that contributes to artificial partitioning of the markets between Member States, contrary to Community law.

46. The Court has found in that respect that it is necessary to take account of the circumstances prevailing at the time of marketing in the importing Member State which make repackaging objectively necessary in order that the pharmaceutical product can be placed on the market in that State by the parallel importer. The trade mark proprietor's opposition to the repackaging is not justified if it hinders effective access of the imported product to the market of that State (see, to that effect, *Upjohn*, para. 43).

47. Such an impediment exists, for example, where pharmaceutical products purchased by the parallel importer cannot be placed on the market in the Member State of importation in their original packaging by reason of national rules or practices relating to packaging, or where sickness insurance rules make reimbursement of medical expenses depend on a certain packaging or where well-established medical prescription practices are based, inter alia, on standard sizes recommended by professional groups and sickness insurance institutions. In that regard, it is sufficient for there to be an impediment in respect of one type of packaging used by the trade mark proprietor in the Member State of importation (see *Bristol-Myers Squibb and Others*, paras. 53 and 54).

48. In contrast, the trade mark proprietor may oppose the repackaging if it is based solely on the parallel importer's attempt to secure a commercial advantage (see, to that effect, *Upjohn*, para. 44).

49. In that context, it has also been held that the trade mark proprietor may oppose replacement packaging where the parallel importer is able to reuse the original packaging for the purpose of marketing in the Member State of importation by affixing labels to that packaging (see *Bristol-Myers Squibb and Others*, para. 55).

50. Thus, while the trade mark proprietor may oppose the parallel importer's use of replacement packaging, that is conditional on the relabelled pharmaceutical product being able to have effective access to the market concerned.

51. Resistance to relabelled pharmaceutical products does not always constitute an impediment to effective market access such as to make replacement packaging necessary, within the meaning of the Court's case law.

52. However, there may exist on a market, or on a substantial part of it, such strong resistance from a significant proportion of consumers to relabelled pharmaceutical products that there must be held to be a hindrance to effective market access. In those circumstances, repackaging of the pharmaceutical products would not be explicable solely by the attempt to secure a commercial advantage. The purpose would be to achieve effective market access.

53. It is for the national court to determine whether that is the case.

54. The answer to the third question must therefore be that replacement packaging of pharmaceutical products is objectively necessary within the meaning of the Court's case law if, without such repackaging, effective access to the market concerned, or to a substantial part of that market, must be considered to be hindered as the result of strong resistance from a significant proportion of consumers to relabelled pharmaceutical products.

In *Boehringer*, the CJEU found that a trade mark proprietor could rely on its trade mark rights to prevent repackaging unless to do so would artificially partition the market. However, repackaging is necessary if simply relabelling goods would lead consumers to resist their purchase. When *Boehringer* returned to the Court of Appeal,[57] Jacob LJ interpreted the CJEU decision to mean that repackaging or rebranding is not necessary if it affects the condition of the goods or if it damages the reputation of the mark. However, because the Court of Appeal felt the situation was still unclear despite the earlier findings of the CJEU, it addressed a further question to the CJEU. It asked whether the test of necessity was relevant only to repackaging or whether it extended to the way the repackaged product was presented. It is submitted that in its judgment,[58] which was relevant solely to pharmaceutical products, the CJEU took a stance favourable to the trade mark proprietors. It held, inter alia, that a trade mark owner may legitimately oppose the re-marketing of its product where an external label has been applied unless to do so would contribute to the artificial partitioning of the market or unless the new label does not affect the original condition of the product or damage the reputation of the original trade mark, and notice is given. However, the right of a proprietor to oppose the re-marketing of a product, which has been repackaged or relabelled, because it damages the reputation of the mark is not confined to instances where the repackaging is of poor quality, defective, or untidy. It might arise when, for example, the parallel importer prints its own mark in capital letters or fails to affix the original trade mark to the new exterior packaging ('de-branding'). It is up to the national courts to decide in light of the particular circumstances whether the mark's reputation has been damaged. And, it is for the parallel importer to prove not only the existence of the conditions which made such repackaging necessary but also that the repackaging will not affect the original condition of the product or the reputation of the mark.

In *Boehringer*, the CJEU suggested that consumers might be wary of purchasing goods (especially, pharmaceuticals) which may appear to have been interfered with and, as a result, in order to achieve effective market access it might be necessary for the parallel importer to repackage and rebrand the goods. This assumption was recently confirmed by the Court of Appeal in *Speciality European Pharma Ltd v Doncaster Pharmaceuticals Group Ltd & Madus GmbH*[59] which held that the test of necessity was met even if the parallel importer would have some market access. The case concerned the parallel import of pharmaceutical products. The defendant argued that without repackaging or rebranding, it was unable to overcome artificial barriers to market access which, in this case, arose from a resistance from many, but not all, doctors and pharmacists to prescribe medicines which did not carry the original registered trade mark of the claimant. The Court of Appeal held that the defendant was unable to access a substantial part of the market without rebranding the products with the claimant's mark and hence the test of necessity was met.

8.4.1.4 Reasons to oppose further dealings (2): changing the 'mental' condition of the goods

The *Boehringer* case raised the issue of when the parallel imports could be resisted by a trade mark proprietor if the way they were re-marketed damaged the reputation of the mark. In *Bristol-Myers Squibb v Paranova*, the CJEU suggested that an Article 7(2) objection might

---

[57] *Boehringer Ingelheim KG, Ingelheim Pharma GmbH & Co. KG v Swingward Ltd* [2004] ETMR 65 (CA).
[58] *Boehringer Ingelheim KG v Swingward Ltd* Case C-348/04 [2007] ECR I-3391.
[59] [2015] EWCA Civ 54.

be raised where the poor presentation of the goods after repackaging damaged the mark's reputation. This was the specific issue in the *Dior* case, where the CJEU was asked whether legitimate reasons for opposing further dealing in parallel imports extended to use of the trade mark which would impair or change the 'mental' condition of the goods rather than their physical condition.

Parfums Christian Dior SA v Evora BV Case C-337/95 [1997] ECR I-6013

Dior France, which sold a number of high-profile perfumes, sought to protect the high prices paid for its goods and their luxurious image by distributing them only through exclusive outlets. Evora operated a chain of chemist shops in the Netherlands. It sold Dior perfumes which it had obtained through parallel imports. It advertised the perfumes in leaflets which reproduced Dior's marks and which also advertised other perfumes which were not of a similar quality. The CJEU was asked whether a reseller may use the marks attached to the goods for advertising purposes.

34. On the one hand, Article 5 of the Directive, which determines the rights conferred by a trade mark, provides, in paragraph (1), that the proprietor is to be entitled to prevent all third parties from using his trade mark in the course of trade and, in paragraph (3)(d), that he may prohibit all third parties from using the trade mark in advertising.

35. On the other hand, Article 7(1) of the Directive, which concerns the exhaustion of the rights conferred by a trade mark, provides that a trade mark is not to entitle its proprietor to prohibit its use in relation to goods which have been put on the market in the Community under that trade mark by its proprietor or with his consent.

36. If the right to prohibit the use of his trade mark in relation to goods, conferred on the proprietor of a trade mark under Article 5 of the Directive, is exhausted once the goods have been put on the market by himself or with his consent, the same applies as regards the right to use the trade mark for the purpose of bringing to the public's attention the further commercialisation of those goods.

[The CJEU ruled that:]

…[O]n a proper interpretation of Articles 5 and 7 of the Directive, when trade-marked goods have been put on the Community market by the proprietor of the trade mark or with his consent, a reseller, besides being free to resell those goods, is also free to make use of the trade mark in order to bring to the public's attention the further commercialisation of those goods.

[Having held that a parallel importer can make use of the original trade mark to market the goods, the ECJ then considered the question of whether the proprietor could object to the way the mark was used by the reseller because it might endanger the advertising function or reputation of the mark. It held the following:]

43. The damage done to the reputation of a trade mark may, in principle, be a legitimate reason, within the meaning of Article 7(2) of the Directive, allowing the proprietor to oppose further commercialisation of goods which have been put on the market in the Community by him or with his consent. According to the case law of the Court concerning the repackaging of trade-marked goods, the owner of a trade mark has a legitimate interest, related to the specific subject-matter of the trade mark right, in being able to oppose the commercialisation

of those goods if the presentation of the repackaged goods is liable to damage the reputation of the trade mark (*Bristol-Myers Squibb*, cited above, paragraph 75).

44. It follows that, where a reseller makes use of a trade mark in order to bring the public's attention to further commercialisation of trade-marked goods, a balance must be struck between the legitimate interest of the trade mark owner in being protected against resellers using his trade mark for advertising in a manner which could damage the reputation of the trade mark and the reseller's legitimate interest in being able to resell the goods in question by using advertising methods which are customary in his sector of trade.

45. As regards the instant case, which concerns prestigious, luxury goods, the reseller must not act unfairly in relation to the legitimate interests of the trade mark owner. He must therefore endeavour to prevent his advertising from affecting the value of the trade mark by detracting from the allure and prestigious image of the goods in question and from their aura of luxury.

46. However, the fact that a reseller, who habitually markets articles of the same kind but not necessarily of the same quality, uses for trade-marked goods the modes of advertising which are customary in his trade sector, even if they are not the same as those used by the trade mark owner himself or by his approved retailers, does not constitute a legitimate reason, within the meaning of Article 7(2) of the Directive, allowing the owner to oppose that advertising, unless it is established that, given the specific circumstances of the case, the use of the trade mark in the reseller's advertising seriously damages the reputation of the trade mark.

47. For example, such damage could occur if, in an advertising leaflet distributed by him, the reseller did not take care to avoid putting the trade mark in a context which might seriously detract from the image which the trade mark owner has succeeded in creating around his trade mark.

48. In view of the foregoing, the answer to be given to the third, fourth and fifth questions must be that the proprietor of a trade mark may not rely on Article 7(2) of the Directive to oppose the use of the trade mark, by a reseller who habitually markets articles of the same kind, but not necessarily of the same quality, as the trade-marked goods, in ways customary in the reseller's sector of trade, for the purpose of bringing to the public's attention the further commercialisation of those goods, unless it is established that, given the specific circumstances of the case, the use of the trade mark for this purpose seriously damages the reputation of the trade mark.

Following *Dior*, in two cases, *Zino Davidoff v A & G Imports*[60] and *Glaxo Group Ltd v Dowelhurst Ltd*,[61] the High Court took a narrow view as to what constituted unacceptable commercialization by a parallel importer. In the former case, it was held that damage to the registered trade mark must be 'substantial'. In the latter, it was held that damage must be to the specific subject matter of the trade mark (i.e. to its ability to act as a badge of origin).

8.4.2 ARTICLE 7 AND THE INTERNET

Two CJEU cases looked at Article 7(2) specifically in relation to the sale of goods on the internet. They are *Portakabin* and *L'Oréal v eBay*. The former raised the issue of the resale of goods

---

[60] *Zino Davidoff SA v A & G Imports Ltd* [2000] Ch 127.   [61] [2004] ETMR 39.

using the original producer's trade mark as a keyword. The second concerned the question of repackaging and the possible damage to a mark's reputation that this might entail.

Portakabin Ltd and Portakabin BV v Primakabin BV Case C-558/08 [2010] ETMR 52

Portakabin Ltd manufactures and supplies mobile buildings. It has a trade mark in Benelux, PORTAKABIN, registered inter alia for metal and non-metal buildings, goods, and building materials. Primakabin sells and leases new and second-hand mobile buildings. It also sells and leases second-hand units, including some manufactured by Portakabin. Primakabin used the AdWords referencing service, and chose as its key words, 'portakabin', 'portacabin', 'portokabin', and 'portocabin'. The heading of Primakabin's advertisement was 'used portakabins'. Portakabin sued for trade mark infringement. The Hoge Raad addressed a number of questions to the CJEU. Among these was whether the use of the keywords by Primakabin is infringing use, and if so, whether Article 7 is relevant; that is, would Article 7(1)(c) provide a defence for Primakabin to trade mark infringement or, alternatively, could the claimant argue that there were legitimate reasons for opposing resale under Article 7(2). According to the CJEU:

75 At the outset, as is apparent from the order for reference, Primakabin's advertising, carried out with the assistance of keywords identical with, or similar to, Portakabin's trade mark, concerns to a large degree the resale of used mobile buildings originally manufactured by Portakabin. It is also common ground that those goods have been placed on the market in the EEA by Portakabin, under the trade mark PORTAKABIN.

76 Next, it cannot be disputed that the resale by a third party of second-hand goods, which had originally been placed on the market under the trade mark by the proprietor of that mark or by a person authorised by him, constitutes a 'further commercialisation of the goods' within the meaning of art.7 of Directive 89/104, and that use of that mark for the purposes of that resale can therefore be prohibited by that proprietor only where there are 'legitimate reasons', within the meaning of art.7(2), such as to justify his opposition to that commercialisation (see, by analogy, *BMW* [1999] E.T.M.R. 339 at [50]).

77 Lastly, it is settled case law that, when trade-marked goods have been placed on the market in the EEA by the proprietor of the trade mark or with his consent, a reseller, besides being free to resell those goods, is also free to make use of the trade mark in order to bring to the public's attention the further commercialisation of those goods (*Parfums Christian Dior SA v Evora BV* (C-337/95) [1997] E.C.R. I-6013; [1998] E.T.M.R. 26 at [38], and *BMW* [1999] E.T.M.R. 339 at [48]).

78 It follows from the foregoing that a trade mark proprietor is not entitled to prohibit an advertiser from advertising, on the basis of a keyword identical with, or similar to, that trade mark, which the advertiser has chosen for an internet referencing service without the consent of the proprietor, the resale of second-hand goods originally placed on the market in the EEA under that trade mark by the proprietor or with his consent, unless there are legitimate reasons, within the meaning of art.7(2) of Directive 89/104, which would justify that proprietor's opposition to such advertising.

79 Such a legitimate reason exists, inter alia, when the advertiser's use of a sign identical with, or similar to, a trade mark seriously damages the reputation of that mark (*Parfums Christian Dior* [1998] E.T.M.R. 26 at [46], and *BMW* [1999] E.T.M.R. 339 at [49]).

80 The fact that the reseller, through its advertising based on a sign identical with, or similar to, the trade mark, gives the impression that there is a commercial connection between the reseller and the trade mark proprietor, and in particular that the reseller's business is affiliated to the proprietor's distribution network or that there is a special relationship between the two undertakings, also constitutes a legitimate reason within the meaning of art.7(2) of Directive 89/104. Advertising which is liable to give such an impression is not essential to the further commercialisation of goods placed on the market under the trade mark by its proprietor or with his consent or, therefore, to the purpose of the exhaustion rule laid down in art.7 of Directive 89/104 (see, to that effect, *BMW* [1999] E.T.M.R. 339 at [51] and [52], and *Boehringer Ingelheim KG v Swingward Ltd* (C-348/04) [2007] E.C.R. I-3391; [2007] E.T.M.R. 71 at [46]).

81 It follows that the circumstances, referred to in [54] above, in which a trade mark proprietor is, pursuant to art.5(1) of Directive 89/104, entitled to prohibit use by an advertiser of a sign identical with, or similar to, that trade mark as a keyword—that is to say, circumstances in which use of that sign by the advertiser does not enable normally informed and reasonably attentive internet users, or enables them only with difficulty, to ascertain whether the goods or services referred to by the ad originate from the proprietor of that mark or from an undertaking economically linked to it or, on the contrary, originate from a third party—correspond to a situation in which art.7(2) of that directive applies and in which, accordingly, the advertiser cannot rely on the exhaustion rule laid down in art.7(1) of Directive 89/104.

82 As has been pointed out in [34]–[36] and [52] and [53] above, it is for the national court to assess whether or not Primakabin's ads, as they were displayed in the event of a search performed by internet users on the basis of the terms 'portakabin', 'portacabin', 'portokabin' and 'portocabin', would enable a normally informed and reasonably attentive internet user to ascertain whether Primakabin is a third-party vis-à-vis Portakabin, or, on the contrary, is economically linked to it.

The CJEU then provided some guidance for national courts where the particular goods being resold are second-hand. It suggested that Article 7(2) will not apply simply because the reseller is advertising the goods as 'second-hand' or 'used' as the average consumer, used to seeing second-hand goods advertised, will not necessarily make the required link. However, a trade mark proprietor might oppose resale where the goods are 'rebranded' by the seller, as was the case here, as such rebranding or relabelling would affect the trade mark's function as a badge of origin. The CJEU then looked to see whether Primakabin's use of the claimant's trade marks gave it an unfair advantage. It concluded:

89 However, as the Court has already held, the mere fact that a reseller derives an advantage from using another person's trade mark in so far as advertisements for the sale of goods covered by the mark, which are in other respects honest and fair, lend an aura of quality to his own business does not constitute a legitimate reason within the meaning of art.7(2) of Directive 89/104 (*BMW* [1999] E.T.M.R. 339 at [53]).

90 It must be held, in that regard, that a reseller who markets second-hand goods under another person's trade mark, and who is specialised in the sale of those goods, will have difficulty communicating such information to his potential customers without using that mark (see, by analogy, *BMW* [1999] E.T.M.R. 339 at [54]).

> 91 In those circumstances, in which a reseller specialises in the resale of goods under another person's trade mark, the reseller cannot be prohibited from using that mark in order to advertise its resale activities which include—apart from the sale of second-hand goods under that mark—the sale of other second-hand goods, unless the resale of those other goods risks, in the light of their volume, their presentation or their poor quality, seriously damaging the image which the proprietor has succeeded in creating for its mark.

In *L'Oréal v eBay*, the perfume manufacturer alleged that some of its products being resold on the auction site had been removed from their packaging. The question arose whether this would be sufficient to oppose their resale, either because the labelling contained important information about, inter alia, the content of the products or because the removal of the labels would harm their trade marks' image. In return, eBay argued that it was not the packaging which gave perfumes their luxury aura but more frequently the shape of the bottle. The CJEU held that either might constitute a reason to oppose resale:

> 3. Article 5 of Directive 89/104 and Article 9 of Regulation No 40/94 must be interpreted as meaning that the proprietor of a trade mark may, by virtue of the exclusive right conferred by the mark, oppose the resale of goods such as those at issue in the main proceedings, on the ground that the person reselling the goods has removed their packaging, where the consequence of that removal is that essential information, such as information relating to the identity of the manufacturer or the person responsible for marketing the cosmetic product, is missing. Where the removal of the packaging has not resulted in the absence of that information, the trade mark proprietor may nevertheless oppose the resale of an unboxed perfume or cosmetic product bearing his trade mark, if he establishes that the removal of the packaging has damaged the image of the product and, hence, the reputation of the trade mark.

In *Portakabin*, the CJEU sought to balance the interests of the proprietor in protecting its marks and the reputation they embody against the obvious fact that for there to be a second-hand market in its goods, it will be necessary for the second-hand dealer to make use of those marks. In *L'Oréal v eBay*, the CJEU needed to conduct a similar balancing of interests, in this case between the trade mark proprietor and the competing interests of the reseller of its goods on an auction site. Do you think it got the balance right in both cases? This issue of the relationship and competition law, more generally, was brought in to sharp focus in the case of *Oracle v M-Tech Data*, which reached the UK Supreme Court in 2012.

8.4.3 EXHAUSTION OF RIGHTS AND COMPETITION LAW

Oracle America Inc. (Formerly Sun Microsystems Inc.) v M-Tech Data Ltd
[2012] UKSC 27

The claimant, at the time of the events at issue, was known as Sun Microsystems. Sun manufactures computer systems, workstations, and related goods. It is the proprietor of five relevant CTMs and two UK trade marks, which are registered, inter alia, for computer hardware. The defendant, located in Manchester, supplied both new and used hardware and in 1999 it supplied to KSS Associates (in a trap purchase) 64 new Sun disk drives, originally supplied by Sun to purchasers in China, Chile, and the US but not the UK. The drives had been bought by M-Tech through a broker in the US and M-Tech imported them into the UK. It was agreed by all the parties that Sun had not consented to their importation into the UK. Thus, on the face of it, M-Tech had infringed Sun's marks as its rights had not been exhausted under Article 7(1). M-Tech's defence was that Sun's trade marks were not enforceable because, inter alia, the object and effect of enforcement would be to partition the EEA market in Sun hardware contrary to the Treaty provisions relating to the free movement of goods (Articles 34–36 of the TFEU) and that the effect of the enforcement of Sun's trade marks would constitute an abuse of rights as that concept is understood in EU law in relation to Article 101 of the TFEU (the 'Euro-defence'). In particular, M-Tech alleged that Sun had indulged in anti-competitive practices first by withholding information which would enable a dealer in its products, both new and second-hand, from knowing whether they had been first marketed in the EU or brought into the EU with Sun's consent and, second, by being extremely proactive in enforcing its trade mark rights, if they had not been exhausted. As a result of these practices, M-Tech alleged that Sun had effective control of the second-hand market in its products. In the High Court, the defendant was found to have infringed Sun's trade marks. On appeal, the Court of Appeal suggested that M-Tech might have a valid defence under competition law. However, Lord Sumption in the Supreme Court disagreed. A particular problem for M-Tech was that, on the facts of the case, it was not dealing with second-hand goods but with goods which Sun had first marketed outside the EEA. According to Lord Sumption this fatally undermined its defence.

25. The first and main reason follows directly from the scheme of those articles. On the agreed facts, these goods were never marketed in the EEA until they were imported and marketed there by M-Tech without Sun's consent. It is therefore not in dispute that the only right derived from its trade marks which Sun is seeking to enforce by these proceedings is its right to control the first marketing of the goods in the EEA. This is an exercise of rights which does not engage the principle of the free movement of goods between Member States embodied in arts 34–36 of the Treaty. It affects only the entry of the goods onto the EEA market, not the movement of the goods within it. It is specifically authorised by arts 5 and 7(1) of the Trade Mark Directive, which are part of an exhaustive code that itself fully reflects the requirements of arts 34–36 of the Treaty. M-Tech's argument to the contrary, and the decision of the Court of Appeal accepting it, are both substantially based on decisions of the Court of Justice under art.7(2) concerning the use of trade mark rights to obstruct the trading between Member States of goods already legitimately in circulation within the EEA. That is a different, and for present purposes irrelevant situation.

26. Secondly, what produces the impediment to the free movement of goods is not the enforcement of Sun's right to control the first marketing of its products in the EEA. On M-Tech's account of the facts, the adverse effect on the free movement of goods arises from the partitioning of the market through Sun's controlled distribution network. That is made possible by the disappearance of the independent secondary market for

its hardware, which removes any alternative source of supply. The disappearance of the independent secondary market is in turn the result of Sun's refusal to disclose where any particular goods were first marketed and, if it was in the EEA, whether it happened with its consent. This is said to achieve the 'chilling effect' on both the legitimate and the illegitimate parallel trade, which has served to eliminate independent resellers in both categories. This is the only economically intelligible way in which M-Tech's case may be understood. It is also the mechanism which is clearly being put forward in the evidence of the two witnesses, Mr Marion and Mr Buta, who deal with this matter on their behalf. The difficulty about M-Tech's argument is that the act of a trade mark proprietor in seeking to control the first marketing of his products in the EEA is in principle an ordinary exercise of the essential right conferred on him by arts 5 and 7(1) of the directive. He may or may not also engage in activities such as withholding information about provenance, which are designed to eliminate the independent parallel trade. But Sun cannot be prevented from doing something which is in itself entirely lawful and consistent with the principle of the free movement of goods, simply because it proposes to do something else as well which is unlawful and inconsistent with that principle. It does not advance the argument to say, as M-Tech does, that Sun's policy of withholding information about provenance is effective only because it is combined with a policy of 'vigorously' enforcing its trade mark rights. The only conceivable relevance of the fact that Sun seeks to control the first marketing of its trade-marked products in the EEA is that if they did not do this, then it would be impossible to eliminate independent resellers by withholding information about provenance, because they could supply themselves with stock from outside the EEA regardless of provenance and market it in the EEA regardless of Sun's objection. But that is the very thing that EU law unquestionably says that they cannot do. It cannot therefore follow that because Sun enforces its trade mark rights 'vigorously' it should have no trade mark right to enforce in those circumstances. Nor, in my view, does it advance the argument to refer to the enforcement of Sun's trade mark rights as part of a 'scheme' to eliminate the independent resellers from the secondary market. This is simply a pejorative way of making the same unsustainable point.

[Lord Sumption also rejected the third plank of M-Tech's defence which was that Sun was using Article 7(2) to partition the market. According to Lord Sumption, considering the cases relating to Article 7(2):]

27. ... They are authority for the proposition that a trade mark proprietor cannot claim a right under the directive to oppose the 'further commercialisation' of the goods if the exercise of that right would *itself* unjustifiably impede the free movement of goods between Member States. However, none of the cases go so far as to hold non-existent or unenforceable rights whose exercise would in itself have no impact on trade between Member States, merely because they are accompanied by other acts which do. The law responds to this situation by restraining the acts which do. It does not pull down the whole temple.

Furthermore, Lord Sumption did not accept the defendant's argument that withholding information about their products' provenance partitioned the market, since any such argument must apply throughout the EEA and in relation to any party, even industrial counterfeiters, and this would be an 'extreme' outcome. Finally, Lord Sumption rejected the argument that the fact that Sun makes its network of authorized dealers agree to obtain their supplies only from Sun or authorized Sun dealers, which Sun accepted might be contrary to Article 101, undermined its right to rely on Article 7(2) of the TMD. He noted:

> 32. There are two insuperable difficulties about this part of M-Tech's case. The first is that there is no relevant connection between the policy of withholding information about provenance and the prevention, restriction and distortion of competition by means of the distribution agreements. The whole premise of the argument is that the policy of withholding information has no anti-competitive effect on the choices of Sun's authorised distributors. The second difficulty is that there is no relevant connection between the policy of withholding information about provenance and the enforcement of Sun's right to control the first marketing of its trade-marked products in the EEA, for the same reasons as there is no such connection in the context of arts 34–36. More generally, neither the trade marks nor the rights conferred on their proprietor by the directive can be characterised as the subject, the means or the result of an agreement or concerted practice contravening art.101.

8.4.4 CONCLUSION

Like many of the key issues raised by the TMD, the interpretation of Article 7 concerns the scope of the monopoly which should be afforded through trade mark registration. In the case of parallel imports, the courts have again been bound to weigh the interests of the proprietor against those of his competitors and consumers at large. It can be argued that where changing the physical condition of the goods is an issue, the CJEU, and indeed the domestic courts, have sought to circumscribe the ability of the proprietor to use his registration to interfere with parallel importation. In relation to re-marketing which affects the mental condition of the goods, the CJEU has been more willing to protect the proprietor's interest. This approach would seem to accord with the more general view taken by commentators that while the origin function of a mark is essentially for the benefit of consumers, the dilution provisions of the directive are primarily concerned with protecting the proprietor's investment in nurturing the advertising functions of his mark. Perhaps the most interesting question to emerge from the CJEU's judgments on exhaustion of rights, and particularly its interpretation of Article 7(2), is why it was ready in 1997 in the *Dior* case to recognize the need for very broad protection for marks against dilution in relation to re-marketing, but waited another decade before defining the scope of dilution more generally, and in a far more limited way. Could it be because, in relation to parallel imports, such goods can always be re-marketed in such a way that does not dilute the trade mark's reputation and hence the interest of the consumer in having access to cheaper goods need not inevitably be disturbed?

FURTHER READING

I. Avgoustis, 'Parallel imports and exhaustion of trade mark rights: should steps be taken towards an international exhaustion regime?' [2012] EIPR 108.

J. Davis, 'The "exhaustion approach" to trade mark protection: a parallel universe or a better way?' (2014) 9 JIPLP 742.

T. Hays, 'The free movement (or not) of trademark protected goods in Europe' in G. B. Dinwoodie and M. D. Janis (eds), *Trademark Law and Theory: A Handbook of Contemporary Research* (Cheltenham: Edward Elgar, 2008), pp. 204–28.

O. Owoeye, 'Access to medicines and parallel trade in patented pharmaceuticals' [2015] EIPR 359.

M. Senftleben, 'Function theory and international exhaustion: why it is wise to confine the double identity rule in EU trade mark law to cases affecting the origin function' [2014] EIPR 518.

9

BREACH OF CONFIDENCE

9.1 INTRODUCTION

The protection of confidentiality dates back to at least the 17th century and not, as is popularly thought, from the mid-18th-century decision in *Prince Albert v Strange*.[1] From the 17th century onwards, courts used a variety of legal doctrines, including employment law, patents, express and implied contract, copyright in unpublished works, criminal law, and equity to protect confidential information.[2] The 'modern' action for breach of confidence (i.e. the one that we recognize today), however, emerged in the 20th century following the Court of Appeal decision in *Saltman Engineering v Campbell Engineering*[3] and quickly developed to embrace a range of information, including commercial, personal, government, and artistic secrets.

The protean nature of the action for breach of confidence is one of its strengths, allowing it to be moulded to new forms of protection.[4] For example, in the wake of the Human Rights Act 1998, UK courts have developed the action to protect against misuse of private information. This 'extended' action, referred to as the tort of misuse of private information, is discussed in some detail in Chapter 10. In this chapter, however, we focus primarily on the action for breach of confidence as it relates to commercial secrets.

It is perhaps in the field of commercial secrets—or trade secrets as they are more commonly known—that the economic importance of confidentiality is emphasized. In particular, various studies and scholars have observed that secrecy is often relied upon by commercial enterprises as a means of protecting their innovations.[5] This can be prior to

---

[1] *Prince Albert v Strange* (1849) 1 MacN & G 25, 41 ER 1171. See T. Aplin, L. Bently, P. Johnson, and S. Malynicz, *Gurry on Breach of Confidence* (Oxford: Oxford University Press, 2012), ch. 2.

[2] See *Gurry*, ch. 2.   [3] (1948) 65 RPC 203.

[4] See also M. Richardson, M. Bryan, M. Vranken, and K. Barnett, *Breach of Confidence: Social Origins and Modern Developments* (Cheltenham: Edward Elgar, 2012).

[5] UK Innovation Survey 2007, Statistical Analysis at <http://webarchive.nationalarchives.gov.uk/20121212135622/http://www.bis.gov.uk/policies/science/science-innovation-analysis/cis>; R. Levin, A. Klevorick, R. Nelson, and S. Winter, 'Appropriating the returns from industrial R&D', Brookings Paper on Economic Activity (1987), 783–820; R. L. Amara and N. Traoré, 'Managing the protection of innovations in knowledge-intensive business services' (2008) 37 Research Policy 1530.

patent protection (to avoid anticipation of the invention), in addition to it, or as an alternative to, patent protection.[6] However, there is frequently an assumption that patents will be preferred to trade secret protection where the former is available.[7] Why do you think this is? During the course of this chapter it will be worth considering the relative advantages and disadvantages of patent protection versus confidentiality protection.

The justifications for protecting commercial or trade secrets vary and do not map neatly onto the justifications usually invoked for intellectual property rights, which were explored in Chapter 1.[8] Particularly prominent are economic justifications, i.e. to incentivize innovation and to prevent an undesirable expenditure of resources in order to preserve secrecy. On the first argument—to incentivize innovation—it may be queried whether this really is necessary given the patent system, other intellectual property rights (IPRs), and market forces more generally (e.g. operating a competitive business). On the second argument, the costs of keeping information secret are not entirely avoided by protecting confidentiality because, in order to enforce protection, the information must remain confidential, and for those 'trading' in commercial secrets there are usually obligations on the licensee to keep it confidential.

9.2 JURISDICTIONAL BASIS AND ELEMENTS OF THE ACTION

There has been extensive scholarly debate about the jurisdictional basis of the action for breach of confidence, more specifically, whether it is grounded in contract, property, equity, or is *sui generis* in nature.[9] This jurisdictional issue recently reared its head once again, this time in the context of determining whether confidential information is a type of IPR. In *Phillips v Mulcaire*,[10] the Supreme Court had to consider whether, for the purposes of section 72 of the Senior Courts Act 1981, which removes the privilege against self-incrimination for 'rights pertaining to any intellectual property or passing off', confidential technical or commercial information could be regarded as intellectual property. The actions had been brought by Steve Coogan (a comedian) and Nicola Phillips (a former assistant to publicist Max Clifford) for breach of confidence/misuse of private information against News Group Newspapers Ltd, the publishers of the now defunct *News of the World* with regard to the interception and misuse of voicemail messages on their mobile telephones. Actions were also brought against Mr Mulcaire and the claimants sought information from Mr Mulcaire as to the identity of persons who had required him to intercept the phone messages; and to whom he had supplied the information obtained. In his defence, Mr Mulcaire relied on the privilege against self-incrimination; however, at first instance, Mann J and Vos J (for Phillips and Coogan respectively) held that section 72 of the Senior Courts Act 1981 applied to deprive Mr Mulcaire of the privilege against self-incrimination. This was because the information involved fell within section 72(5) which defines 'intellectual property' to mean 'any patent, trade mark, copyright, design right, registered design, *technical or commercial information* or other intellectual property' (emphasis supplied). An appeal was dismissed,

---

[6] A. Arundel, 'The relative effectiveness of patents and secrecy for appropriation' (2001) 30 Research Policy 611, 613; K. Jorda, 'Patent and trade secret complementariness: an unsuspected synergy' (2008) 48 Washburn L. J. 1.

[7] *Kewanee Oil Co. v Bicron Corp.*, 416 US 470, 94 S Ct 1879 (1974).   [8] *Gurry*, ch. 3.

[9] For an authoritative discussion see *Gurry*, ch. 4.   [10] [2012] UKSC 28, [2013] 1 AC 1.

the Court of Appeal holding that 'technical or commercial information' means confidential information which is technical or commercial in character.[11] In response to the argument that confidential information was not *property* and thus could not fall within the phrase 'commercial information or other intellectual property', the court concluded: 'while the prevailing current view is that confidential information is not strictly property, it is not inappropriate to include it as an aspect of intellectual property'.[12] The Supreme Court held, dismissing the appeal, that 'there is no particular potency about the expression "intellectual property" because there is a general consensus as to its core content ... but no general consensus as to its limits'. Further, it was irrelevant that confidential information 'ought not, strictly speaking, to be regarded as property' since it was clear from the statutory language of section 72 that technical or commercial information was to fall within 'intellectual property' for the purposes of this provision.[13] Technical or commercial information, however, was held not to include personal or private information –an opposite conclusion to that reached below in the Court of Appeal.[14]

The Supreme Court decision in *Phillips v Mulcaire* thus supports the position that confidential information is not property and further that it is not necessarily (or not always) intellectual *property*. Does this mean, therefore, that the jurisdictional basis of the action for breach of confidence is contractual or equitable (given that it is not proprietary)? While courts may use the language of contract or equity when discussing duties of confidence, it is submitted that in fact the action is *sui generis* in nature, and that courts invoke these different jurisdictions in a pragmatic way in order to enforce confidences. In other words, courts seek to enforce confidences and protect confidential information because it is important to do so and will utilize which jurisdictional basis best achieves that aim. The history of protection for confidential information supports this position, as do certain appellate decisions, such as the Supreme Court of Canada decision *Lac Minerals Ltd v International Corona Resources Ltd*,[15] where Sopinka J observed:

> The foundation of action for breach of confidence does not rest solely on one of the traditional jurisdictional bases for action of contract, equity or property. The action is sui generis relying on all three to enforce the policy of the law that confidences be respected.[16]

Despite the *sui generis* jurisdictional basis for breach of confidence, it is possible to point to core elements of the action that courts will assess. These were helpfully articulated by Megarry J in the following seminal case.

Coco v A. N. Clark (Engineers) Ltd [1969] FSR 415

The claimant had designed a new 'Coco' moped, which featured special engine parts, and had entered into negotiations with the defendants with a view to them ultimately

---

[11] [2012] EWCA Civ 48, [2012] FSR 29, [31].   [12] [39].
[13] [2012] EWCA Civ 48, [2012] FSR 29, [20].   [14] [27]–[33].   [15] [1989] 2 SCR 574.
[16] [171]. Followed by the Supreme Court of Canada in *Cadbury Schweppes Inc. v FBI Foods Ltd* [1999] 1 SCR 142. See also the New Zealand Court of Appeal in *Hunt v A* [2008] 1 NZLR 368, [64]: 'the jurisdiction is based on a broad principle of good faith ... [it] does not depend upon the existence of a contract between the parties or there being "property" in the subject-matter of the confidence. Nor does it depend upon the existence of a fiduciary relationship. Breach of confidence is not a tort. The doctrine is a sui generis cause of action.'

manufacturing it. He showed the defendants a prototype and also supplied them with information, drawings, and other aids towards the production of the moped. After several months of discussions, the defendants broke off negotiations and subsequently began manufacturing and selling their own 'Scamp' moped, which was highly successful. The defendants admitted that the piston and carburettor were of the same types as the 'Coco' moped. The claimant then sought an injunction against the manufacture and sale of any machines in which the defendants had made use, directly or indirectly, of any confidential information which was the property of the claimant. This was refused by Megarry J.

Megarry J, at p. 419:

The equitable jurisdiction in cases of breach of confidence is ancient; confidence is the cousin of trust. The Statute of Uses, 1535, is framed in terms of 'use, confidence or trust'; and a couplet, attributed to Sir Thomas More, Lord Chancellor avers that;

> Three things are to be helpt in Conscience; Fraud, Accident and things of Confidence.

(See 1 Rolle's Abridgement 374). In the middle of the last century, the great case of *Prince Albert v Strange* (1849) 1 MacN & G 25 reasserted the doctrine. In the case before me, it is common ground that there is no question of any breach of contract, for no contract ever came into existence. Accordingly, what I have to consider is the pure equitable doctrine of confidence, unaffected by contract. Furthermore, I am here in the realms of commerce, and there is no question of any marital relationship such as arose in *Duchess of Argyll v Duke of Argyll* [1967] Ch 302. Thus limited, what are the essentials of the doctrine?

Of the various authorities cited to me, I have found *Saltman Engineering Co Ltd v Campbell Engineering Co Ltd* (1948) 65 RPC 203; *Terrapin Ltd v Builders' Supply Co (Hayes) Ltd* [1960] RPC 128 and *Seager v Copydex Ltd* [1967] 1 WLR 923; [1967] RPC 349; of the most assistance. All are decisions of the Court of Appeal. I think it is quite plain from the *Saltman* case that the obligation of confidence may exist where, as in this case, there is no contractual relationship between the parties. In cases of contract, the primary question is no doubt that of construing the contract and any terms implied in it. Where there is no contract, however, the question must be one of what it is that suffices to bring the obligation into being; and there is the further question of what amounts to a breach of that obligation.

In my judgment, three elements are normally required if, apart from contract, a case of breach of confidence is to succeed. First, the information itself, in the words of Lord Greene MR in the *Saltman* case on page 215, must 'have the necessary quality of confidence about it'. Secondly, that information must have been imparted in circumstances importing an obligation of confidence. Thirdly, there must be an unauthorised use of that information to the detriment of the party communicating it.

Megarry J outlines a three-limb test—known as the *Coco v Clark* test—for establishing a breach of confidence. He refused, however, to grant the injunction since the claimant had not made out the first and third limbs. While Megarry J's statements seem to link this test to equity and thus suggest breach of confidence is an equitable action, as was argued earlier, it is possible to see the jurisdictional basis of breach of confidence as *sui generis* or multifaceted. Even so, the elements outlined in *Coco v Clark* are used with regularity, regardless of whether courts locate their analysis within contract or equity.

The *Coco v Clark* test was approved by the House of Lords and has been applied in numerous decisions.[17] A fourth limb, or at least a gloss to the third limb, of the test should be added, however. This is that an unauthorized use of confidential information may be justified where the disclosure is in the public interest.

The remainder of this chapter examines the elements for establishing a breach of confidence in more detail, starting first with the requirement that there must be confidential information.

FURTHER READING

T. Aplin, L. Bently, P. Johnson, and S. Malynicz, *Gurry on Breach of Confidence* (Oxford: Oxford University Press, 2012), chs 1–4.

L. Bently, 'Patents and trade secrets' in N. Wilkof and S. Basheer (eds), *Overlapping Intellectual Property Rights* (Oxford: Oxford University Press, 2012), ch. 3.

L. Bently, 'Trade secrets: "intellectual property" but not "property"?' in H. Howe (ed.) (and J. Griffiths, consultant ed.), *Concepts of Property in Intellectual Property Law* (Cambridge: Cambridge University Press, 2013), ch. 13.

R. G. Hammond, 'The origins of the equitable duty of confidence' (1979) 8 Anglo-American L. R. 71.

W. M. Landes and R. A. Posner, *The Economic Structure of Intellectual Property Law* (Cambridge, MA: Harvard University Press, 2003), ch. 3.

M. Richardson, M. Bryan, M. Vranken, and K. Barnett, *Breach of Confidence: Social Origins and Modern Developments* (Cheltenham: Edward Elgar, 2012).

S. Ricketson, 'Confidential information: a new proprietary interest? Part I' (1977) 11 Melbourne University L. R. 223.

9.3 CONFIDENTIAL INFORMATION

9.3.1 TYPE OF INFORMATION THAT IS PROTECTABLE

The flexibility of the action for breach of confidence is demonstrated by the width of the information that it encompasses. This includes literary and artistic material, such as ideas for a television series,[18] photographic images of articles assembled for the purpose of a record album cover,[19] and the costumes and design of a film set.[20] It also embraces government information, such as Cabinet discussions and advice,[21] and details of the security services.[22] Business or trade secrets may be protected, such as the design of a carpet grip,[23] the design of prefabricated portable buildings,[24] a moulding system for decorative gas fires,[25] and design

---

[17] e.g. *Attorney-General v Observer Ltd* [1990] 1 AC 109, 268 (Lord Griffiths) and *Douglas v Hello! Ltd* [2008] 1 AC 1, [13] (Lord Nicholls) and [111]–[115] (Lord Hoffmann).

[18] *Fraser v Thames TV* [1984] 1 QB 44.

[19] *Creation Records Ltd v News Group Newspapers Ltd* [1997] EMLR 444.

[20] *Shelley Films v Rex* [1994] EMLR 134.   [21] *Attorney-General v Cape* [1976] QB 752.

[22] *Attorney-General v Observer Ltd* [1990] 1 AC 109.

[23] *Seager v Copydex (No. 1)* [1967] 2 All ER 415.

[24] *Terrapin Ltd v Builders' Supply Co. (Hayes) Ltd* [1967] RPC 375.

[25] *Lancashire Fires v SA Lyons* [1966] FSR 629.

elements of a Formula One racing car.[26] Finally, personal information may qualify as confidential, including marital secrets,[27] private telephone conversations,[28] details of a homosexual affair,[29] photographic images of a wedding reception,[30] details of narcotics addiction therapy,[31] and details of a sadomasochistic sex party.[32]

9.3.2 INFORMATION MUST BE IDENTIFIABLE, ORIGINAL, NOT TRIVIAL NOR IMMORAL

Although diversity of confidential information may be protected, important threshold requirements, as outlined in the following case, must be satisfied.

Fraser v Thames TV [1984] 1 QB 44

The claimants had developed a well-formed idea for a television series concerning the formation of a female rock group and their subsequent experiences and adventures. It was to be partly fictional and partly based upon the experiences of the second claimants, who had formed a group called 'Rock Bottom' in 1973. The idea for the series was orally communicated in confidence by one of the claimants to the second defendant (the scriptwriter), who in turn communicated the idea to the third defendant (the producer). The first defendant television company were also made aware of the idea for the series and decided to make the series, *Rock Follies*, except using different actresses. The claimants claimed, inter alia, damages for breach of confidence. The defendants argued that while confidence can, in principle, protect a literary or dramatic idea, it can only do so when it is fully developed in the form of a synopsis or embodied in a material form.

> **Hirst J, at pp. 65–6:**
>
> In my judgment there is no reason in principle why an oral idea should not qualify for protection under the law of confidence, provided it meets the other criteria I discuss below. Neither the originality nor the quality of an idea is in any way affected by the form in which it is expressed. No doubt both the communication and the content of an oral idea may be more difficult to prove than in the case of a written idea, but difficulties of proof should not affect the principle any more than in any other branches of the law where similar problems arise (e.g. contract and defamation).
>
> ...
>
> I accept that to be capable of protection the idea must be sufficiently developed, so that it would be seen to be a concept which has at least some attractiveness for a television programme and which is capable of being realised as an actuality: see *per* Harris J in *Talbot v General Television Corporation Pty Ltd* [1981] RPC 1, 9, lines 20–22. But I do not think this requirement necessitates in every case a full synopsis. In some cases the nature of the idea

---

[26] *Force India Formula One Team Ltd v 1 Malaysia Facing Team Sdn Bhd* [2012] EWHC 616 (Ch), [2012] RPC 29, [2013] EWCA Civ 780, [2013] RPC 36.
[27] *Argyll (Duchess) v Argyll (Duke)* [1967] 1 Ch 302.
[28] *Francome v Mirror Group Newspapers Ltd* [1984] 2 All ER 408.
[29] *Barrymore v News Group Newspapers Ltd* [1997] FSR 600.
[30] *Douglas v Hello! (No. 3)* [2006] QB 125.
[31] *Campbell v Mirror Group Newspapers Ltd* [2004] 2 AC 457.
[32] *Mosley v News Group Newspapers Ltd* [2008] EMLR 20.

may require extensive development of this kind in order to meet the criteria. But in others the criteria may be met by a short unelaborated statement of an idea. In *Talbot's* case itself I do not think the detailed submission, quoted at p. 5, added very much of substance to the idea which is set out in one sentence starting at line 10 on p. 5.

Unquestionably, of course, the idea must have some significant element of originality not already in the realm of public knowledge. The originality may consist in a significant twist or slant to a well known concept (*Talbot's* case). This is, I think, by analogy, consistent with the statements in *Saltman Engineering Co Ltd v Campbell Engineering Co Ltd* 65 RPC 203 and *Coco v AN Clark (Engineers) Ltd* [1969] RPC 41, that novelty in the industrial field can be derived from the application of human ingenuity to well known concepts.

…

This of course does not mean that every stray mention of an idea by one person to another is protected. To succeed in his claim the plaintiff must establish not only that the occasion of communication was confidential, but also that the content of the idea was clearly identifiable, original, of potential commercial attractiveness and capable of being realised in actuality.

[Hirst J accepted that these requirements were satisfied on the facts and that the script-writer, producer, and Thames were fixed with an obligation of confidence.]

How does the type of information that can be protected by confidence differ from the subject matter that can be protected by copyright? Further, what are the requirements for protection set out in *Fraser v Thames TV*? An example of where these requirements were not satisfied is *De Maudsley v Palumbo*.[33] In this case, the claimant had revealed to the defendant, during a dinner party at the defendant's flat, his idea for a new nightclub. Subsequently, a nightclub—the Ministry of Sound—was opened by the defendants, in which the claimant had no involvement. The claimant argued, inter alia, breach of confidence. Knox J held that the information disclosed by the claimant was not capable of protection. The information included the idea that the club would legally operate all night long; that top disc jockeys from the UK and worldwide would appear at the club; that there would be separate areas for dancing, resting, and socializing; and that the club would be big, decorated in a 'high-tech industrial' warehouse style. Knox J described the information as either too general or vague, or lacking in originality, to constitute confidential information.

Information of a grossly immoral nature will not be the subject of a confidential obligation.[34] It seems, however, that what can be regarded as grossly immoral is judged according to a fairly high standard and courts are unlikely to characterize sexual activities as such because '[t]here is no common view that sexual conduct of any kind between consenting adults is grossly immoral'.[35]

9.3.3 INFORMATION MUST BE SECRET

A crucial threshold requirement for protection is that the information is secret or confidential, i.e. not in the public domain. This general principle was set out by Lord Greene MR in *Saltman Engineering v Campbell Engineering*:[36]

The information, to be confidential, must, I apprehend, apart from contract, have the necessary quality of confidence about it, namely, it must not be something which is public property

---

[33] [1996] FSR 447.   [34] *Stephens v Avery* [1988] Ch 449.   [35] *Stephens v Avery*, 449, 453.
[36] (1948) 65 RPC 203, 215.

and public knowledge. On the other hand, it is perfectly possible to have a confidential document, be it a formula, a plan, a sketch, or something of that kind, which is the result of work done by the maker on materials which may be available for use of anybody; but what makes it confidential is the fact that the maker of the document has used his brain and this produced a result which can only be produced by somebody who goes through the same process.

As Lord Greene MR emphasizes, information must not be in the public domain, but confidentiality can arise where materials in the public domain are developed or processed as a result of human skill or creativity.[37] An example of where information was held to have entered the public domain is *Mustad & Son v Dosen*.

O. Mustad & Son v Dosen and Allcock [1963] 3 All ER 416

The appellants, Mustad, had purchased a company called Thoring and Co. and with it the benefit of Thoring's trade secrets, which included confidential information relating to a machine for the manufacture of fish hooks. The first respondent, Dosen, had originally been employed by Thoring and had come under an express contractual obligation of confidence. The appellants commenced proceedings and sought an injunction against Dosen from communicating confidential information relating to the machine to Dosen's new employer, the second respondents, Allcock & Co. Ltd.

The appellant had filed a patent application in respect of the information alleged to be confidential in Germany in 1925 and the patent specification was published in 1926. The respondents contended that, as such, the information was no longer secret. The appellant argued that Dosen possessed more information than appeared in the patent specification. A final injunction was granted by Rowlatt J, which was set aside by the Court of Appeal. The appeal to the House of Lords was dismissed.

Lord Buckmaster (the other law lords in agreement)**, at p. 418:**

Of course, the important point about the patent is not whether it was valid or invalid, but what it was that it disclosed, because after the disclosure had been made by the appellants to the world, it was impossible for them to get an injunction restraining the respondents from disclosing what was common knowledge. The secret, as a secret, had ceased to exist. But the appellants say—and I think say with considerable force—that it might well have been that in the course of the experience which Dosen had gained in their service he had obtained knowledge of ancillary secrets connected with the patented invention which were not in fact included in the invention but which would be of very great service to any person who proceeded to make the machine to which the invention related.

[The onus of showing this knowledge ancillary to the patent specification lay with the appellants, who failed to adduce this evidence.]

Cases show that the secrecy requirement, unlike in patent law, is not an absolute one. Thus, in *Prince Albert v Strange*,[38] an injunction was granted even though the confidential

---

[37] See also *Coco v Clark* [1969] FSR 415, 420 (Megarry J).   [38] (1849) 1 MacN & G 25, 41 ER 1171.

information, in the form of etchings of Queen Victoria and Prince Albert, had been circulated amongst friends of the claimant. Further, in *Exchange Telegraph Co. Ltd v Central News Ltd*[39] Stirling J rejected the argument that race information was no longer protected because it had become public to those present at the racecourse. As he explained: 'the information was not made known to the whole world; it was no doubt known to a large number of persons, but a great many more were ignorant of it'.[40] In the following case, an obligation of confidence was maintained even though the allegedly confidential information could have been obtained from public sources.

Schering Chemicals Ltd v Falkman Ltd [1982] QB 1

The claimant made and marketed a drug, Primodos, as a pregnancy test. Subsequently, it was suspected that the drug was responsible for causing abnormalities in unborn children and, unsurprisingly, this attracted large media coverage. The claimant engaged the services of the first defendant to provide training sessions for their executives to assist them in handling the adverse publicity. For the purpose of training the claimant's executives, a great deal of information was disclosed to the first defendant, which they agreed to keep confidential. The instructors also accepted that the information was confidential. One of the instructors, the second defendant, came up with the idea of making a documentary on Primodos, which the claimant rejected. Nevertheless, the second defendant went ahead with making the documentary. The claimant issued proceedings against the defendants and obtained an interim injunction to prevent the broadcasting of the film. A majority of the Court of Appeal dismissed the appeal against the award of an injunction, rejecting the argument that the information was not confidential because it could be derived from public domain sources.

Shaw LJ, at pp. 27–8:

The second proposition put forward on behalf of Mr Elstein and Thames was to this effect. When Mr Elstein undertook as an associate of Falkman to participate in the course for Schering, he had no intimate knowledge of the controversy and contentions which surrounded Primodos. By that time there had been numerous articles in scientific papers and journals and the first Sunday Times article had given publicity to the matter in the popular press. Mr Elstein's mind had, however, not been prompted to look in that direction. What he learned at the course came new to him. It is now said that all the information upon which the programme of the projected documentary is based could have been derived from sources available to the public before the Schering course with Executive Television Training. It is asserted also that Mr Elstein, with the assistance of a colleague at Thames, has assiduously explored and collated all those sources. The relevant facts and opinions are all to be found in what has been described as 'the public domain' or 'the public sector'. No principle of confidentiality can apply, so it is contended, to matters which have become notorious. Whatever may have been the fiduciary duty on the part of Mr Elstein not to disclose anything of a confidential nature that he had learned on the course it had been entirely dissipated when the Primodos affair emerged into public view. What obligation of reticence can apply to what has long been an open secret? So the argument ran.

[39] [1897] 2 Ch 48.   [40] *Exchange Telegraph Co. Ltd v Central News Ltd* [1897] 2 Ch 48, 53.

It is an argument which at best is cynical; some might regard it as specious. Even in the commercial field, ethics and good faith are not to be regarded as merely opportunist or expedient. In any case, though facts may be widely known, they are not ever-present in the minds of the public. To extend the knowledge or to revive the recollection of matters which may be detrimental or prejudicial to the interests of some person or organisation is not to be condoned because the facts are already known to some and linger in the memories of others.

Templeman LJ, at pp. 37–8:

In my judgment, when Mr Elstein agreed for reward to take part in the training course and received and absorbed information from Schering, he became under a duty not to use that information and impliedly promised Schering that he would not use that information for the very purpose which Schering sought to avoid, namely, bad publicity in the future, including publicity which Schering reasonably regarded as bad publicity. Schering reasonably regard the film 'The Primodos Affair' as bad publicity based on information which they supplied to Mr Elstein to enable him to advise Schering. Mr Elstein could have made a film based on Primodos if he had not taken part in the training programme, but 'The Primodos Affair' film only came into existence because Mr Elstein received from Schering information for one purpose and used that information for another purpose, for his own gain and to the detriment, as they reasonably believe, of Schering.

The information supplied by Schering to Mr Elstein had already been published, but it included information which was damaging to Schering when it was first published and which could not be republished without the risk of causing further damage to Schering. Any republication and recycling by Mr Elstein of any of the information supplied to him by Schering could be unwelcome to Schering, could be inimical to the best interests of Schering and could reasonably be regarded by Schering as further bad publicity. Mr Elstein must have realised that if he revived and recycled and republished information which he received from Schering, that action on his part was liable to be damaging. Mr Elstein must have realised that Schering would not supply Mr Elstein with any information at all if they thought for one moment that there was any possibility that he might make use of that information for his own purposes and in a manner which Schering might find unwelcome or harmful. That Mr Elstein realised and accepted this is shown by his letter dated July 4, 1979. As between Schering and Mr Elstein, if Mr Elstein had obtained information from sources other than Schering, then it would of course not have been confidential in his hands but, by agreeing to advise Schering and by accepting information from them to enable him to advise Schering, Mr Elstein placed himself under a duty, in my judgment, not to make use of that information without the consent of Schering in a manner which Schering reasonably considered to be harmful to their cause. As between Schering and Mr Elstein, the information which Mr Elstein received from Schering was confidential and cannot be published by Mr Elstein in the film 'The Primodos Affair'. Thames made the film 'The Primodos Affair' with full knowledge of all the circumstances and with knowledge of the claim by Schering that the film would constitute a breach of confidentiality and could not be broadcast without the prior consent of Schering.

[**Lord Denning MR** delivered a dissenting judgment, holding that an injunction should be refused because the information was not confidential and it was in the public interest to disclose the information.]

The majority in *Schering* found that even though the information previously had been the subject of extensive media coverage, this did not preclude the information from being confidential and subject to an obligation of confidence. Does this mean that information will fall into the public domain only when it is generally accessible on a large scale? Or is the test of confidentiality tied to whether or not further prejudice or harm can be suffered by further circulation? Are either of these approaches a desirable way to determine confidentiality? Another view of the case is that, even though much of the information was already in the public domain, the defendants had contractually promised not to disclose the information and this had been defined in the agreement as 'information, some of which is public and some of which is private'. It could be argued that, even though much of the information used by the defendants *was* in the public domain, they had been privy to some information that was still secret and, as such, were in breach of their obligation. Alternatively, it could be argued that the defendants' obligation was not dependent on the information being secret and was simply a promise not to use the information that had been disclosed to them. Such an approach, however, would mean that contractual obligations of confidence could be created in respect of information that was not confidential. Is this acceptable?

It appears that there is no 'bright line' test for determining when information enters the public domain. Nevertheless, courts have sought to provide guidance on this issue, as illustrated by the House of Lords decision in *Attorney-General v Observer Ltd*.

Attorney-General v Observer Ltd [1990] 1 AC 109

The case concerned the publication of the memoirs of former senior MI5 agent, Peter Wright. The book, entitled *Spycatcher*, was published in Australia, the US, Canada, the Republic of Ireland, and elsewhere. Although the book had not been published in the UK, it could be readily imported into the country. Litigation in England was commenced in relation to the activities of certain newspapers. *The Guardian* and *Observer* newspapers had published articles about the litigation in Australia to restrain the publication of the work and the *Sunday Times* had published the first extract of an intended serialization of *Spycatcher*. At first instance and in the Court of Appeal, it was held that the Attorney-General was not entitled to an injunction against the newspapers. A majority of the House of Lords dismissed the appeal.

Lord Keith, at pp. 259–60:

In relation to Mr Wright, there can be no doubt whatever that had he sought to bring about the first publication of his book in this country, the Crown would have been entitled to an injunction restraining him. The work of a member of MI5 and the information which he acquires in the course of that work must necessarily be secret and confidential and be kept secret and confidential by him. There is no room for discrimination between secrets of greater or lesser importance, nor any room for close examination of the precise manner in which revelation of any particular matter may prejudice the national interest. Any attempt to do so would lead to further damage. All this has been accepted from beginning to end by each of the judges in this country who has had occasion to consider the case and also by counsel for the respondents ... The question whether Mr Wright or those acting for him would be at liberty to publish *Spycatcher* in England under existing circumstances does not arise for immediate consideration. These circumstances include the world-wide dissemination of the contents of the book which has been brought about by Mr Wright's wrongdoing. In my opinion general publication in this country would not bring about any significant damage to the public interest beyond what has already been done. All such secrets as the book may contain have been revealed to any intelligence services whose interests are opposed to those of the United Kingdom. Any damage to the confidence reposed in the British Security and Intelligence Services by those of friendly countries brought about by Mr Wright's actions would not be materially increased by publication here ... I have not been persuaded that the effect of publication in England would be to bring about greater damage in the respects founded upon than has already been caused by the widespread publication elsewhere in the world. In the result, the case for an injunction now against publication by or on behalf of Mr Wright would in my opinion rest upon the principle that he should not be permitted to take advantage of his own wrongdoing.

...For the reasons which I have indicated in dealing with the position of Mr Wright, I am of the opinion that the reports and comments proposed by *The Guardian* and the *Observer* would not be harmful to the public interest, nor would the continued serialisation by *The Sunday Times*. I would therefore refuse an injunction against any of the newspapers. I would stress that I do not base this upon any balancing of public interest nor upon any considerations of freedom of the press, nor upon any possible defences of prior publication or just cause or excuse, but simply upon the view that all possible damage to the interest of the Crown has already been done by the publication of *Spycatcher* abroad and the ready availability of copies in this country.

It is possible, I think, to envisage cases where, even in the light of widespread publication abroad of certain information, a person whom that information concerned might be entitled to restrain publication by a third party in this country. For example, if in the *Argyll* case the Duke had secured the revelation of the marital secrets in an American newspaper, the Duchess could reasonably claim that publication of the same material in England would bring it to the attention of people who would otherwise be unlikely to learn of it and who were more closely interested in her activities than American readers. The publication in England would be more harmful to her than publication in America. Similar considerations would apply to, say, a publication in America by the medical adviser to an English pop group about diseases for which he had treated them. But it cannot reasonably be held in the present case that publication in England now of the contents of *Spycatcher* would do any more harm to the public interest than has already been done.

Lord Brightman, at p. 265:

A member of the Security Service is under a lifelong duty of confidence towards the Crown. The purpose of that duty is to preserve intact the secrets of the service which it would be against the public interest to disclose. If the member departs abroad and publishes his memoirs there, he breaches his lifelong duty of confidence. Thereafter such duty is incapable of existing *quoad* the matter disclosed. The reason why the duty of confidence is extinguished is that the matter is no longer secret and there is therefore no secrecy in relation to such matter remaining to be preserved by the duty of confidence. It is meaningless to talk of a continuing duty of confidence in relation to matter disclosed world-wide. It is meaningful only to discuss the remedies available to deprive the delinquent confidant or his successors in title of benefits flowing from the breach, or in an appropriate case to compensate the confider.

Lord Goff, at p. 281:

To this broad general principle [of when an obligation of confidence arise], there are three limiting principles to which I wish to refer. The first limiting principle (which is rather an expression of the scope of the duty) is highly relevant to this appeal. It is that the principle of confidentiality only applies to information to the extent that it is confidential. In particular, once it has entered what is usually called the public domain (which means no more than that the information in question is so generally accessible that, in all the circumstances, it cannot be regarded as confidential) then, as a general rule, the principle of confidentiality can have no application to it. I shall revert to this limiting principle at a later stage.

The second limiting principle is that the duty of confidence applies neither to useless information, nor to trivia. There is no need for me to develop this point.

Attorney-General v Observer Ltd illustrates that confidentiality will be destroyed by information entering the public domain. But in what circumstances, broadly speaking, will this be the case? Will the assessment differ depending on the type of information involved, i.e. whether it is personal or not and, if so, should this matter?

9.4 OBLIGATION OF CONFIDENCE

9.4.1 GENERAL PRINCIPLES

The second element required to establish a breach of confidence is that the defendant comes under an obligation of confidence. When will such an obligation arise? The test that emerges from the case law is a 'notice of confidentiality' test. The following observations of Lord Goff in *Attorney-General v Observer Ltd* set out this test:[41]

I start with the broad general principle (which I do not intend to be definitive) that a duty of confidence arises when *confidential information comes to the knowledge of a person* (the confidant) in circumstances where he has *notice or is held to have agreed, that the information is confidential*, with the effect that it would be just in all the circumstances that he should be precluded from disclosing the information to others. [Emphasis supplied]

Lord Goff's dicta has been followed or cited with approval on several occasions.[42]

The notice of confidentiality test is also consistent with *Coco v Clark*, another decision that has been cited and followed on numerous occasions.[43]

---

[41] [1990] 1 AC 109, 281B.

[42] See *Shelley Films Ltd v Rex Features Ltd* [1994] EMLR 134; *Hellewell v The Chief Constable of Derbyshire* [1995] 1 WLR 804, 809; *Douglas v Hello! Ltd* [2001] QB 967, 999 (Sedley LJ), 1012 (Keene LJ); *Campbell v Mirror Group Newspapers Ltd* [2004] 2 AC 457, [14] (Lord Nicholls) and [48] (Lord Hoffmann); *Tchenguiz v Imerman* [2010] EWCA Civ 908, [2011] 1 All ER 555; [64] (Lord Neuberger giving the judgment of the court); *BBC v HarperCollins Publishers, Ben Collins and Collins Autosport Ltd* [2010] EWHC 2424 (Ch), [47] (Morgan J); *Force India Formula One Team Ltd v 1 Malaysia Facing Team Sdn Bhd* [2012] EWHC 616 (Ch), [2012] RPC 29, [224] and *ABC v Lenah Game Meats Pty Ltd* [2001] HCA 63, (2001) 208 CLR 199, [36] (Gleeson CJ).

[43] e.g. see *Aveley v Boman* [1975] FSR 139, 145–6; *Stephens v Avery* [1988] Ch 449, 456 (Browne-Wilkinson V-C); *DeMaudsley v Palumbo* [1996] FSR 447, 457; *Dunford & Elliott Ltd v Johnson & Firth Brown Ltd* [1977] 1 Lloyd's LR 505, 509 (Lord Denning MR); *G. D. Searle & Co. Ltd v CellTech Ltd* [1982] FSR 92, 100 (Cumming Bruce LJ); *Union Carbide Corp. v Naturin* [1987] FSR 538, 544–5 (Slade and Ralph Gibson LJJ); *Malone v Metropolitan Police Commissioner* [1979] Ch 344 (Megarry V-C), 376; *Douglas v Hello!* [2003] EMLR 31 (Ch), [184] (Lindsey J) and [2006] QB 125 (CA), [83].

Coco v A. N. Clark (Engineers) Ltd [1969] FSR 415, [1969] RPC 41

The facts were described at 9.2.

> #### Megarry J, at pp. 420–1:
>
> It may be that that hard-worked creature, the reasonable man, may be pressed into service once more; for I do not see why he should not labour in equity as well as at law. It seems to me that if the circumstances are such that any reasonable man standing in the shoes of the recipient of the information would have realised that upon reasonable grounds the information was being given to him in confidence, then this should suffice to impose upon him the equitable obligation of confidence. In particular, where information of commercial or industrial value is given on a business-like basis and with some avowed common object in mind, such as a joint venture or the manufacture of articles by one party for the other, I would regard the recipient as carrying a heavy burden if he seeks to repel a contention that he was bound by an obligation of confidence: see the *Saltman* case at page 216.

In essence, Megarry V-C's comments amount to asking whether a reasonable person acquiring or receiving information would know that the information was being disclosed in confidence.[44] What is crucial here is knowledge or notice that the information is *confidential*. The relevant factors for establishing such knowledge or notice include: the nature of the information (whether it is common knowledge, commercially valuable, banal, trivial, or intimately personal);[45] the steps taken to preserve or emphasize the secrecy of the information (e.g. whether it is marked 'confidential' or 'private'; or if special care is taken that there is a restricted disclosure to others);[46] the manner in which the information was disclosed or obtained (whether it is informal, social, commercial, or professional);[47] the understanding of the parties involved (i.e. did they in fact regard the information as confidential or themselves as being under an obligation of confidence);[48] and where the information is disclosed for a specific, limited purpose and it is understood, from the legal and cultural context of the disclosure, that the information will not be used for another purpose.[49]

---

[44] This approach was adopted in *Ocular Sciences v Aspect Vision Care* [1997] RPC 289, 369 (Laddie J); *De Maudsley v Palumbo* [1996] FSR 447, 457 (Knox J); and *Carflow Products v Linwood Securities* [1996] FSR 424, 428.

[45] e.g. see *Ocular Sciences v Aspect Vision Care* [1997] RPC 289, 369 (Laddie J): 'Where a piece of technology is regarded by those in the trade as common currency, then the reasonable man standing in the shoes of the recipient is unlikely to think that it is being transmitted to him in circumstances importing an obligation of confidence. If technology was treated by the parties as if it was common knowledge, it is likely to be reasonable for them to assume that it is being treated in the same way when it is passed on between them.'

[46] e.g. see *New Zealand Needle Manufacturers Ltd v Taylor* [1975] 2 NZLR 33, 36 (McMullin J) and where no such measures were taken *Yates Circuit Foil Co. v Electrofoils Ltd* [1976] FSR 345, 377, 379 (Whitford J), [2007] FCA 2054, [89]–[91].

[47] *Coco v Clark* [1969] RPC 41, 48 (Megarry J). *De Maudsley v Palumbo* [1996] FSR 447, 458 (Knox J): 'the occasion was a social and not a business one. Nothing was said, even on Mr de Maudsley's evidence, to take the occasion out of the social, and put it into a business sphere.'

[48] See *Fraser v Thames TV Ltd* [1984] QB 44, 65 (Hirst J) and *De Maudsley v Palumbo* [1996] FSR 447, 457 (Knox J).

[49] See e.g. *Saltman Engineering Co. Ltd v Campbell Engineering Co. Ltd* (1948) 65 RPC 203, 213 and 216 (Lord Greene MR).

The 'notice of confidentiality' test requires knowledge or notice on an *objective* rather than subjective basis. However, it may be queried whether the actual understanding or knowledge of the parties (i.e. their subjective views) should be relevant to this objective assessment. In *Carflow Products (UK) Ltd v Linwood Securities*,[50] Jacob J (as he then was) took the following view:

> There are two possible approaches in law: what did the parties themselves think they were doing by way of imposing or accepting obligations and what would a reasonable man think they were doing? The difference between the two approaches is that the former takes into account the subjective unspoken views of the parties. One would not do so in relation to the making of a contract, but in relation to the equitable obligation of confidence it seems right to do so—equity looks at the conscience of the individual. So I prefer the subjective view. As it happens, overall I do not think in this case it matters whether one approaches the problem from the subjective or objective points of view.[51]

On the facts of *Carflow Products* it did not matter whether a subjective or objective test was applied since, on either approach, there was no obligation. However, the dichotomy drawn by Jacob J in *Carflow Products* is unnecessary because it is submitted that an objective test can be informed by subjective views and understandings. This was the approach adopted by Knox J in *De Maudsley v Palumbo*,[52] when he had to consider whether disclosure of an idea for a nightclub venture at a dinner party gave rise to an obligation of confidence. Knox J held:

> The test in my view is objective—the question is were the circumstances such as to import a duty of confidence and, if so, the obligation is not to be avoided simply by not addressing the problem. On the other hand I accept that a factor, and it may be an important factor, is whether the parties did in fact regard themselves as under an obligation to preserve confidence, just as is a proven trade or industry usage in that regard but I do not accept that the test is exclusively subjective as to the parties' intentions.[53]

As well, the balance of authority favours an objective test. Arnold J in *Force India Formula One Team Ltd v 1 Malaysia Facing Team Sdn Bhd*, after referring to a series of authorities, held: 'An equitable obligation of confidence will arise as a result of the acquisition or receipt of confidential information if, but only if, the acquirer or recipient either knows or has notice (objectively assessed by reference to a reasonable person standing in his shoes) that the information is confidential'.[54]

9.4.2 THIRD PARTY RECIPIENTS

What is the position if A communicates a commercial secret to B, who in turn and without authorization from A communicates it to C, a third party? Will A be able to restrain C from using or disclosing the secret to others? The position of third party recipients of confidential information was discussed *obiter dicta* in *Attorney-General v Observer Ltd*.

---

[50] [1996] FSR 424.   [51] At 428.   [52] [1996] FSR 447.   [53] At 457.
[54] [2012] EWHC 616 (Ch), [2012] RPC 29, [224]. See also *Primary Group (UK) Ltd v The Royal Bank of Scotland plc* [2014] EWHC 1082 (Ch), [223] and *Vestergaard Frandsen A/S v Bestnet Europe Ltd* [2013] UKSC 31, [23].

Attorney-General v Observer Ltd [1990] 1 AC 109

The facts were discussed at 9.3.3.

Lord Keith, at p. 260:

The newspapers which are the respondents in this appeal were not responsible for the world-wide dissemination of the contents of *Spycatcher* which has taken place. It is a general rule of law that a third party who comes into possession of confidential information which he knows to be such, may come under a duty not to pass it on to anyone else. Thus in *Duchess of Argyll v Duke of Argyll* [1967] Ch 302 the newspaper to which the Duke had communicated the information about the Duchess was restrained by injunction from publishing it.

Lord Griffiths, at p. 268:

The duty of confidence is, as a general rule, also imposed on a third party who is in possession of information which he knows is subject to an obligation of confidence: see *Prince Albert v Strange* (1849) 1 Mac & G 25 and *Duchess of Argyll v Duke of Argyll* [1967] Ch 302. If this was not the law the right would be of little practical value: there would be no point in imposing a duty of confidence in respect of the secrets of the marital bed if newspapers were free to publish those secrets when betrayed to them by the unfaithful partner in the marriage. When trade secrets are betrayed by a confidant to a third party it is usually the third party who is to exploit the information and it is the activity of the third party that must be stopped in order to protect the owner of the trade secret.

Their lordships point to a rule, recognized in various other cases as well, that a third party may come under an obligation of confidence where he or she knows that it has been disclosed to them in breach of confidence. This knowledge must exist at the time of receipt of the information and may be actual or constructive.[55] However, it is possible also to restrain a third party who initially receives confidential information innocently but later learns that it was disclosed to him without authorization. As Megarry V-C explained in *Malone v Commissioner of Police of the Metropolis (No. 2)*:[56]

If A makes a confidential communication to B, then A may not only restrain B from divulging or using the confidence, but also may restrain C from divulging or using it if C has acquired it from B, even if he acquired it without notice of any impropriety ... In such cases it seems plain that, however innocent the acquisition of the knowledge, what will be restrained is the use or disclosure of it after notice of the impropriety.[57]

---

[55] See also *Aveley/Cybervox Ltd v Boman* [1975] FSR 139, 147 (Plowman V-C); *Butler v Board of Trade* [1971] Ch 680, 690 (Goff J); *Fraser v Evans* [1969] 1 QB 349, 361 (Lord Denning MR); *Malone v Commissioner of Police of the Metropolis (No. 2)* [1979] 2 All ER 620, 634 (Megarry V-C); *Prince Albert v Strange* (1849) 2 De Gex & Sm 652, 64 ER 293 (on appeal, (1849) 1 Mac & G 25, 41 ER 1171); *Printers and Finishers Ltd v Holloway* [1965] RPC 239; *Rex v Muirhead* (1927) 44 RPC 38; *Stevenson Jordan & Harrison Ltd v MacDonald & Evans* (1951) 68 RPC 190 (revd on other grounds, (1952) 69 RPC 10).

[56] [1979] 2 All ER 620.

[57] At 634. See also *Fraser v Evans* [1969] 1 QB 349, 361 (Lord Denning MR); *Johns v Australian Securities Commission* (1993) 178 CLR 408, 459–60 (Gaudron J); and *Vestergaard Frandsen A/S v Bestnet Europe Ltd* [2013] UKSC 31, [25] and [39].

What is the policy, do you think, of restraining third parties in these circumstances? Is it to preserve and reinforce the confidential obligation between A and B or is there another reason?

9.4.3 PERSONS WHO ACCIDENTALLY OR SURREPTITIOUSLY ACQUIRE CONFIDENTIAL INFORMATION

What of the situations where A does not intentionally communicate confidential information to B, but B accidentally comes across it (by, say, finding an envelope containing secret formulae on a train) or intentionally acquires it using surreptitious means, such as stealing a confidential product[58] or document;[59] secretly photographing, filming, or otherwise recording the activities of a business;[60] or 'tapping' a telephone.[61] In *Attorney-General v Observer Ltd*, Lord Goff uttered his seminal dicta which subsequently shaped courts' responses to these types of situations.

Attorney-General v Observer Ltd [1990] 1 AC 109

Lord Goff, at p. 281:

I start with the broad general principle (which I do not intend in any way to be definitive) that a duty of confidence arises when confidential information comes to the knowledge of a person (the confidant) in circumstances where he has notice, or is held to have agreed, that the information is confidential, with the effect that it would be just in all the circumstances that he should be precluded from disclosing the information to others....

I realise that, in the vast majority of cases, in particular those concerned with trade secrets, the duty of confidence will arise from a transaction or relationship between the parties—often a contract, in which event the duty may arise by reason of either an express or an implied term of that contract. It is in such cases as these that the expressions 'confider' and 'confidant' are perhaps most aptly employed. But it is well settled that a duty of confidence may arise in equity independently of such cases; and I have expressed the circumstances in which the duty arises in broad terms, not merely to embrace those cases where a third party receives information from a person who is under a duty of confidence in respect of it, knowing that it has been disclosed by that person to him in breach of his duty of confidence, but also to include certain situations, beloved of law teachers—where an obviously confidential document is wafted by an electric fan out of a window into a crowded street, or where an obviously confidential document, such as a private diary, is dropped in a public place, and is then picked up by a passer-by. I also have in mind the situations where secrets of importance to national security come into the possession of members of the public—a point to which I shall refer in a moment.

---

[58] *Franklin v Giddins* [1978] Qd R 72 (competing farmer stole budwood of a special nectarine variety).

[59] *J. N. Dairies Ltd v Johal Dairies Ltd and Singh* [2009] EWHC 1331 (Ch) (former employee stole invoices).

[60] *EI duPont deNemours & Co. v Christopher* 341 F 2d 1012 (1970) (aerial photographs of the construction of a new factory); *Australian Broadcasting Corp. v Lenah Game Meats Pty Ltd* (2001) 208 CLR 199 (filming of a possum meat processing facility); *Tillery Valley Foods v Channel Four Television* [2004] EWHC 1075 (Ch) (filming of a factory producing frozen meals for hospitals).

[61] As in *Malone v Metropolitan Police Commissioner* [1979] Ch 344 and *Francome v Mirror Group Newspapers Ltd* [1984] 2 All ER 408.

Lord Goff clearly envisages that accidental acquisition of confidential information can give rise to a duty of confidence on the part of the recipient. On what basis is this obligation imposed? Is it the 'notice of confidentiality' test that was discussed at 9.4.1 and can this be applied to other situations, such as where information is obtained in an underhand manner?

In reliance on Lord Goff's dicta, Laws J in *Hellewell v Chief Constable of Derbyshire* made the following observations about surreptitious acquisition of confidential information:[62]

> If someone with a telephoto lens were to take from a distance and with no authority a picture of another engaged in some private act, his subsequent disclosure of the photograph would, in my judgment, as surely amount to a breach of confidence as if he had found or stolen a letter or diary in which the act was recounted and proceeded to publish it. In such a case, the law would protect what might reasonably be called a right of privacy, although the name accorded to the cause of action would be breach of confidence. It is, of course, elementary that, in all such cases, a defence based on the public interest would be available.

The above dicta suggests that certain privacy intrusions may be actionable as a breach of confidence, a topic that is explored further in the next chapter. But what about commercial or artistic secrets? Would surreptitious or intrusive means of acquiring such secrets also be actionable? Several cases suggest yes, and seem to apply a notice of confidentiality test in their analysis.

In *Shelley Films v Rex Features Ltd*,[63] Deputy Judge Martin Mann QC held, in an application for an interim injunction, that it was seriously arguable that the defendant's knowledge of the circumstances in which the photograph was taken was sufficient to place it under an obligation of confidence. In this case, a photograph from a scene of the (then forthcoming) film *Mary Shelley's Frankenstein* was credited to the defendant and published in *The People* newspaper. In granting the injunction the judge referred to the *obiter dicta* of Lord Goff extracted above and took into account the following circumstances: the film studio was fenced, with security guards at the main gate; there were signs clearly stating that the property was private and entry was by permission only; there were notices that photography within the studios was not permitted; and the set itself was patrolled by security guards and featured signs at the entrance prohibiting entrance to other than authorized persons.

A similar conclusion to that in *Shelley Films* was reached in *Creation Records*.

Creation Records Ltd v News Group Newspapers Ltd [1997] EMLR 444

The case concerned a photographic shoot for the cover of a forthcoming record album. The shoot was directed at a scene outside a country hotel. A freelance photographer took photographs of the same scene and these were published in *The Sun* newspaper. In considering whether to grant an interim injunction, Lloyd J accepted that while the freelance photographer was permitted to view the scene, he was not authorized to photograph it.

---

[62] [1995] 1 WLR 804, 807.   [63] [1994] EMLR 134.

Lloyd J, at p. 455:

Here, while admittedly Mr Seeburg was lawfully at the hotel and with others was able to gain access to the restricted area and his presence there was tolerated and even the taking of photographs was tolerated before the shoot as such began, the plaintiff's evidence, if accepted, shows that thereafter a tighter regime of security was imposed as regards preventing photography, the tight ring of security men and minders of which the *Sun's* first article spoke. It would of course have been clearer if each of the strangers to the shoot who were allowed to stay in the restricted area had been told that they may not take photographs thereafter. But what the plaintiff's witnesses depose to amounts to much the same as that, although in a more general and less explicit form. I accept also that they were of course allowed to observe the scene and could therefore have gone away and told the world the ingredients of the picture, or even made a sketch of it from memory. But being lawfully there does not mean that they were free to take photographs and it seems to me that to be able to record it as a photographic image is different in kind, not merely in degree, from being able to relate it verbally or even by way of a sketch. That is above all because it was in photographic form that it was intended to be preserved for the group. It is the photographic record of the scene, the result of the shoot in fact, that was to be confidential.

I accept it as well arguable that the nature of the operation together with the imposition of security measures as described by the plaintiffs' witnesses made it an occasion of confidentiality at any rate as regards photography. In that context I also accept it as sufficiently arguable that in order to get his picture Mr Seeburg must have conducted himself a good deal less openly than he suggests and indeed surreptitiously, as the plaintiffs suggest. If so, it is an easy inference that he did so because he knew that photography was not permitted and that he was being allowed to remain in the restricted area only on the basis that photographs would not be taken of the actual shoot.

On that footing it seems to me that the plaintiffs do have a sufficiently arguable case for saying that the taking of the photograph and its publication is in breach of confidence and that future publication can be restrained by injunction at any rate until the image is fully released into the public domain, presumably on publication of the album, if it does come out with this cover.

Thinking about *Shelley Films* and *Creation Records*, is it possible to conclude that it is the underhand or surreptitious means of acquiring confidential information which provides the justification for imposing an obligation of confidence? Or is it that the method of acquisition points to knowledge or notice of the information's confidential nature? In *J. N. Dairies Ltd v Johal Dairies Ltd and Singh*[64] the second defendant, an ex-employee of the claimant, entered the claimant's premises in the early hours of the morning two days after his employment was terminated, stole invoices detailing important customer information, and gave these to his new employer (the first defendant). The first defendant immediately started to approach the claimant's customers, with a view to persuading them to transfer their custom. HHJ David Cooke held that the invoices were commercial secrets and that the ex-employee owed an obligation of confidence. In reaching this conclusion he observed:

It is clear that when he [the second defendant] took it *he knew that it was the claimant's commercially valuable information*, and that he had no right to obtain it or to pass it on to anyone else without the claimant's authority. That is sufficient to impose upon him a duty of confidentiality.[65]

---

[64] [2009] EWHC 1331 (Ch).   [65] [113] (emphasis supplied).

In other words, the judge appeared to be applying a notice of confidentiality test and theft of the confidential information was key to establishing the requisite knowledge. The first defendant was also held to owe an obligation of confidence, but as a third party because it 'knew full well of the confidential nature of the material and the circumstances in which it had been obtained'.[66]

A decision which perhaps takes Lord Goff's dicta in *Attorney-General v Observer* too far is *Tchenguiz v Imerman*.[67] In the context of a marital dispute and fearing that Mr Imerman would conceal his assets, Mrs Imerman's brother accessed and copied confidential information relating to Mr Imerman. This information had been stored on a server located in an office shared between Mr Imerman and the brother. The confidential documents were passed to Mrs Imerman's lawyers so that they could be used in the ancillary relief proceedings and it was argued that this was justified on the basis of the so-called Hildebrand rules. The Court of Appeal, in finding that there was an actionable privacy intrusion, referred to Lord Goff's dicta and concluded:

> If confidence applies to a defendant who adventitiously, but without authorization, obtains information in respect of which he must have appreciated that the claimant had an expectation of privacy, it must, *a fortiori*, extend to a defendant who intentionally, and without authorization, takes steps to obtain such information. It would seem to us to follow that intentionally obtaining such information, secretly and knowing that the claimant reasonably expects it to be private, is itself a breach of confidence.[68]

To reach this conclusion, the Court of Appeal took the view that 'traditional' breach of confidence (which includes all types of information, including commercial secrets) and misuse of private information actions (which are discussed in the next chapter) should be 'developed and applied consistently and coherently'.[69] *Attorney-General v Observer* was relied upon as authority for the proposition that a *breach* of confidence arises where an obviously confidential document comes into a person's hands adventitiously and it was a logical extension to find that intentionally obtaining a confidential document was also a breach of confidence.

While we may sympathize with the conclusion that Mr Imerman's privacy had been invaded, there are some key problems with the reasoning of the Court of Appeal. The first is that the court misinterprets Lord Goff's dicta. Lord Goff's statements emphasize that a *duty* of confidence may arise in situations where confidential information is accidentally acquired where the recipient has notice of confidentiality. It does *not* say that a *breach* of that duty occurs by virtue of acquiring that information in the first place. Rather, breach of the duty would occur through subsequent (mis)use or disclosure. This view is supported by later cases, such as *Hellewell*.

A second problem with the application of the *Imerman* principle is that, in the case of commercial secrets, reverse engineering per se would prima facie amount to a breach of confidence. This is because reverse engineering clearly involves an intentional attempt to acquire any commercial secrets that are embodied in a product. What impact would this have on reverse engineering practices and competition more generally? Should the *Imerman* decision be confined to its facts or to cases of private information only?

---

[66] [113].   [67] [2010] EWCA Civ 908, [2011] 1 All ER 555.   [68] [68].   [69] [67].

FURTHER READING

T. Aplin, 'Reverse engineering commercial secrets' (2013) 66 Current Legal Problems 1.

T. Aplin, L. Bently, P. Johnson, and S. Malynicz, *Gurry on Breach of Confidence* (Oxford: Oxford University Press, 2012), ch. 7.

M. Richardson, 'Breach of confidence, surreptitiously or accidentally obtained information and privacy: theory versus law' (1994) 19 Melbourne University L. R. 673.

9.4.4 STANDING TO SUE

When it comes to the issue of who is entitled to sue for breach of confidence, the general principle, as laid down by the Court of Appeal in *Fraser v Evans*, is that the claimant must be owed a duty of confidence: 'the party complaining must be the person who is *entitled* to the confidence and to have it respected. He must be a person to whom the duty of good faith is owed'.[70]

Determining whether a person is owed a duty of confidence may be a complicated matter, as illustrated by *Fraser v Evans*. The claimant, Fraser, had prepared a report for the Greek government, pursuant to a written contract with his firm, which contained an express obligation not to disclose to any person any information obtained during the course of the contract. The Greek government did not, however, give a corresponding undertaking. The report was translated by the firm's office into Greek and copies were sent to the Greek government. One of the copies was obtained surreptitiously by a third party and eventually made its way into the hands of a *Sunday Times* journalist, who had the document translated into English and later interviewed Mr Fraser. Fearing that the *Sunday Times* would publish an article damaging to his reputation, the claimant obtained an *ex parte* injunction before Shaw J and a continuation of this injunction (*inter partes*) from Crichton J, who held that there were mutual obligations of confidence owed between the claimant and the Greek government and that the defendants were in no better a position than the person who had surreptitiously acquired a copy of the report.

On appeal, however, Lord Denning MR (with whom Davies and Widgery LJJ agreed) held that the Greek government was under neither an express nor implied obligation of confidence to the claimant and, further, that the Greek government was entitled to the information, having commissioned and paid for it. It thus followed that they alone had standing to sue for unauthorized use of the confidential information.[71] The key divergence between the first instance and appellate decisions was whether the Greek government owed any duty of confidence to the claimant. Crichton J held that the Greek government owed such a duty because 'the document being confidential it necessarily contained items which, if made public, might tend to injure the reputation of the claimant who had written the document in complete confidence to his client'.[72] In other words, the Greek government appeared to be under a duty to the claimant to keep (at the very least) the *identity* of the author of the report confidential. The Court of Appeal's divergence from Crichton J on this point is inadequately addressed, with Lord Denning MR simply remarking that there was no express or implied contractual obligation imposed on the Greek government.[73] Are there other

---

[70] *Fraser v Evans* [1969] 1 QB 349, 361 (Lord Denning MR) (emphasis added).
[71] At 361.   [72] At 351.   [73] At 361.

possible explanations for why a duty of confidence was not owed by the *Sunday Times* to Fraser in this case?

The *Fraser v Evans* decision highlights a more general point which is that multiple persons may have an interest in the same confidential information and, as such, more than one person may be owed an obligation (or obligations) of confidence and have standing to sue. This is the case whether we are talking about trade secrets, government secrets, or personal confidential information.

A fairly recent and controversial case in which a key issue was which parties had standing to sue for breach of confidence was *Douglas v Hello!*. In this case *OK!* magazine had, by virtue of contract, acquired exclusive rights to the coverage of the Douglases' wedding. At first instance Lindsay J found that *Hello!* magazine owed an obligation of confidence to the Douglases *and also* to *OK!*.[74] He explained:

> They knew that *OK!* had an exclusive contract; as persons long engaged in the relevant trade, they knew what sort of provisions any such contract would include and that it would include provisions intended to preclude intrusion and unauthorized photography. Particularly would that be so where, as they knew, a very considerable sum would have had to have been paid for the exclusive rights which had been obtained. As to their knowledge of steps taken to protect the secrecy of the event, their own written text in their Issue 639 spoke of 'elaborate security procedures'. The surrounding facts were such that a duty of confidence should be inferred from them … The unauthorized pictures themselves plainly indicated they were taken surreptitiously. Yet these defendants firmly kept their eyes shut lest they might see what they undeniably knew would have become apparent to them. Breach of confidence apart, had the *Hello!* defendants opened their eyes they would have seen that the taking of the photographs which they bought had involved at least a trespass.

According to Lindsay J, the benefit of the obligation of confidence could be shared between the claimants and, in support of this view, he cited *Gilbert v The Star Newspaper Co. Ltd*[75] and *Mustad v Dosen*.[76]

It was on this point that the Court of Appeal overturned Lindsay J. The court held that Lindsay J had incorrectly 'treated the information about the wedding as if it were property when he referred to its benefit being 'shared between and … enforceable by co-owners or by a successor in title'.[77] Further, *Gilbert* and *Mustad v Dosen* were said to be distinguishable because the *OK!* contract only purported to transfer or share with *OK!* the right to use *approved* photographs and not *any* photographs of the wedding and any rights not expressly granted to *OK!* were retained by the Douglases.[78] The Court of Appeal explained:

> The grant to *OK!* of the right to use the approved photographs was no more than a licence, albeit an exclusive licence, to exploit commercially those photographs for a nine-month period. This licence did not carry with it any right to claim, through assignment or otherwise, the benefit of any other confidential information vested in the Douglases.[79]

On appeal to the House of Lords, Lord Hoffmann (who delivered the leading speech of the majority) held that Lindsay J had been correct in holding that the obligation of confidence was also owed to *OK!* magazine on the basis that 'everyone knew that the obligation

---

[74] *Douglas v Hello! Ltd* [2003] EMLR 31, [198].   [75] (1894) 11 TLR 3.
[76] [1963] 3 All ER 416.   [77] [128].   [78] [132].   [79] [134].

of confidence was imposed for the benefit of *OK!* as well as the Douglases'.[80] Further, the obligation was owed in respect of *any* photographs and not just the authorized photographs:

> The point of which one should never lose sight is that *OK!* had paid £1 million for the benefit of the obligation of confidence imposed upon all those present at the wedding in respect of *any* photographs of the wedding. That was quite clear. Unless there is some conceptual or policy reason why they should not have the benefit of that obligation, I cannot see why they were not entitled to enforce it. And in my opinion there are no such reasons. Provided that one keeps one's eye firmly on the money and why it was paid, the case is, as Lindsay held, quite straightforward.[81]

Lord Brown also shared Lord Hoffmann's view that the obligation of confidence owed to *OK!* included all photographs and not just the approved photographs.[82]

This aspect of the House of Lords decision is perplexing for at least two reasons. First, it did not address the reasoning of the Court of Appeal. Second, the basis for the duty being owed to *OK!* is unclear. It appears that it is simply that *Hello!* had knowledge that the wedding was being kept secret for the benefit of *OK!*. If so, this approach is a considerable extension of Lord Goff's dicta in *Attorney-General v Observer Ltd* and opens up a broad spectrum of situations in which persons for whose benefit confidentiality is sought will be owed an obligation of confidence. As Richard Arnold QC comments: 'the effect of it will be to give many exclusive, and indeed non-exclusive, licensees of confidential information a right of action. Whether this is a good thing or not remains to be seen'.[83]

FURTHER READING

T. Aplin, L. Bently, P. Johnson, and S. Malynicz, *Gurry on Breach of Confidence* (Oxford: Oxford University Press, 2012), ch. 8.

R. Arnold, 'Confidence in exclusives: *Douglas v Hello!* in the House of Lords' [2007] EIPR 339.

9.4.5 DURATION OF THE OBLIGATION: SPRINGBOARD DOCTRINE

The 'springboard' doctrine deals with situations where a person uses confidential information to get an illegitimate head start, yet the information subsequently enters the public domain. The doctrine was first articulated in the case below.

Terrapin Ltd v Builders' Supply Co. (Hayes) Ltd [1967] RPC 375

The defendant made prefabricated portable buildings to the claimant's design as part of a joint venture. For this purpose, the claimant communicated information concerning manufacturing details, technical information, and know-how to the defendant. After the joint venture came to an end, the defendant offered prefabricated buildings

---

[80] *Douglas v Hello! Ltd* [2008] 1 AC 1, [114].   [81] [117].   [82] [327].
[83] R. Arnold, 'Confidence in exclusives: *Douglas v Hello!* in the House of Lords' [2007] 29 EIPR 339, 343.

incorporating many of the features of the claimant's design for sale. The defendant argued that sale of the claimant's buildings, together with publication of brochures, had disclosed all the relevant design features to the public and, since the information was no longer secret, their obligation of confidence had been discharged.

Roxburgh J, at p. 391:

[Referring to Lord Greene MR's judgment in *Saltman Engineering*:]

As I understand it, the essence of this branch of the law, whatever the origin of it may be, is that a person who has obtained information in confidence is not allowed to use it as a spring-board for activities detrimental to the person who made the confidential communication, and spring-board it remains even when all the features have been published or can be ascertained by actual inspection by any member of the public. The brochures are certainly not equivalent to the publication of the plans, specifications, other technical information and know-how. The dismantling of a unit might enable a person to proceed without plans or specifications, or other technical information, but not, I think, without some of the know-how, and certainly not without taking the trouble to dismantle. I think it is broadly true to say that a member of the public to whom the confidential information had not been imparted would still have to prepare plans and specifications. He would probably have to construct a prototype, and he would certainly have to conduct tests. Therefore, the possessor of the confidential information still has a long start over any member of the public. The design may be as important as the features. It is, in my view, inherent in the principle upon which the *Saltman* case rests that the possessor of such information must be placed under a special disability in the field of competition in order to ensure that he does not get an unfair start; or, in other words, to preclude the tactics which the first defendants and the third defendants and the managing director of both of those companies employed in this case.

The above passage from *Terrapin* has been the subject of considerable debate and discussion. In particular, subsequent cases have struggled to reconcile the statement by Roxburgh J that 'spring-board it remains even when all the features have been published' with the House of Lords decision in *Mustad v Dosen*. Refer back to the discussion of *Mustad v Dosen* at 9.3.3—what is the apparent conflict between this decision and *Terrapin*?

Courts have sought to resolve the tension between *Terrapin* and *Mustad v Dosen* in various ways. One such example is illustrated by *Cranleigh Precision Engineering Ltd v Bryant*.

Cranleigh Precision Engineering Ltd v Bryant [1965] 1 WLR 1293

The claimant company manufactured above-ground swimming pools to a design invented by the defendant, Bryant, its managing director. Bryant learned from the company's patent agent of a British patent owned by a third party which covered features of the Cranleigh design. Instead of informing the claimant, Bryant took steps to set up a rival business and he purchased the patent for this purpose. The claimant sued, inter alia, for an injunction against the defendant making use of confidential information obtained while a managing director of Cranleigh. To this, Bryant pleaded that the relevant information, the existence of the patent, was in the public domain and that, in accordance with *Mustad v Dosen*, it could not be protected as confidential.

Roskill J, at pp. 1318–19:

[Referring to *Terrapin*:]

The judgment of Roxburgh J was strongly criticised by counsel for the defendants in the Court of Appeal. Although Sellers LJ dissented from the majority judgments of Lord Evershed MR and of Romer LJ dismissing the appeal, the ground of dissent was not that the judge had misstated the law. Whilst it is true that nowhere in the judgments of the Court of Appeal is there any approval of the passage which Mr Sieghart criticised, there is equally no indication of disapproval. It is difficult to believe that had anyone thought that the judge's statement of the law was wrong in principle, some criticism would not have been advanced since it would have afforded an easy way of securing the reversal of the judge's order. Furthermore, the language of the judge appears to me to echo certain language used earlier by Luxmoore J in *Reid & Sigrist v Moss & Mechanism Ltd* a case to which I have already referred.

The question whether this passage in the judgment of Roxburgh J was correct also arose in a very recent case before Pennycuick J, *Peter Pan Manufacturing Corporation v Corsets Silhouette Ltd*, but that judge found it unnecessary to determine the point. The passage was also cited by Havers J in *Ackroyds (London) Ltd v Islington Plastics Ltd* a case to which I have already referred—not only without disapproval but as stating the law which he proceeded to apply. It may be that, strictly speaking, Mr Sieghart is right in saying that in those circumstances it would be open to me to hold that the passage in Roxburgh J's judgment misstated the law. I apprehend that it would be my duty to so do if I were convinced that it conflicted with the decision in the *Mustad* case, but in my judgment there is no such conflict because the two matters are separate and distinct. I would respectfully borrow and adopt the passage as correctly stating the law which I have to apply, and I respectfully agree with the judge in stating that the principle, as he stated it, is a logical consequence of the decision of the Court of Appeal in *Saltman's* case. *Mustad* was, as I have said, a case where the employer made the publication in question. In the present case, Bryant, as possessor of what I have held to be the plaintiffs' confidential information, is seeking to free himself from his obligations of confidence, not because of what the plaintiffs have published, for they have published nothing, but because of what Bischoff published—a publication of which Bryant only became aware because of his contractual and confidential relationship with the plaintiffs.

I have dealt with this question at length for the matter was argued at length before me. Applying the law as I conceive it to be, I have no doubt that Bryant acted in grave dereliction of his duty to the plaintiffs in concealing from the plaintiffs' board the information which he received from the plaintiffs' patent agents, and in taking no steps whatsoever to protect the plaintiffs against the possible consequences of the existence and publication of the Bischoff patent. I also have no doubt that Bryant acted in breach of confidence in making use, as he did as soon as he left the plaintiffs, of the information regarding the Bischoff patent which he had acquired in confidence and about its various effects on the plaintiffs' position, for his own advantage and for that of the defendant company. Any other conclusion would involve putting a premium on dishonesty by managing directors.

What ratio emerges from the above passage? Is it that Bryant acted in breach of fiduciary duty? Or is it that Bryant acted in breach of confidence by disclosing not the existence of the patent or the information contained within it (which were in the public domain), but the relevance of the patent to the claimant's business? Do you find the basis upon which Roskill J distinguished *Mustad* from the facts at hand persuasive? If information was confidential but subsequently entered the public domain, should the issue of whether an obligation of confidence arises depend upon *who* disclosed the information to the public? The Court of

Appeal in *Speed Seal Products Ltd v Paddington*[84] favoured this type of approach. However, Lord Goff in *Attorney-General v Observer Ltd* was much more sceptical. Lord Goff's dicta shed helpful light on the 'springboard' doctrine and its relationship to information entering the public domain.

Attorney-General v Observer Ltd [1990] 1 AC 109

The facts were described at 9.3.3.

Lord Goff, at pp. 285-7:

As I have already indicated, it is well established that a duty of confidence can only apply in respect of information which is confidential: see *Saltman Engineering Co Ltd. v Campbell Engineering Co Ltd* 65 RPC 203, 215, *per* Lord Greene MR. From this it should logically follow that, if confidential information which is the subject of a duty of confidence ceases to be confidential, then the duty of confidence should cease to bind the confidant. This was held to be so in *O Mustad & Son v Dosen* (Note) [1964] 1 WLR 109. That was however a case in which the confidential information was disclosed by the confider himself; and stress was placed on this point in a later case where the disclosure was not by the confider but by a third party and in which *O Mustad & Son v Dosen* was distinguished: see *Cranleigh Precision Engineering Ltd v Bryant* [1965] 1 WLR 1293. It was later held, on the basis of the *Cranleigh Precision Engineering* case, that, if the confidant is not released when the publication is by a third party, then he cannot be released when it is he himself who has published the information: see *Speed Seal Products Ltd v Paddington* [1985] 1 WLR 1327. I have to say however that, having studied the judgment of Roskill J in the *Cranleigh Precision Engineering* case [1965] 1 WLR 1293, it seems to me that the true basis of the decision was that, in reliance on the well known judgment of Roxburgh J in the 'springboard' case, *Terrapin Ltd v Builders' Supply Co (Hayes) Ltd* [1967] RPC 375, the defendant was in breach of confidence in taking advantage of his own confidential relationship with the plaintiff company to discover what a third party had published and in making use, as soon as he left the employment of the plaintiff company, of information regarding the third party's patent which he had acquired in confidence: see [1965] 1 WLR 1293, 1319. The reasoning of Roskill J in this case has itself been the subject of criticism (see e.g. Gurry, *Breach of Confidence*, at pp. 246–7); but in any event it should be regarded as no more than an extension of the springboard doctrine, and I do not consider that it can support any general principle that, if it is a third party who puts the confidential information into the public domain, as opposed to the confider, the confidant will not be released from his duty of confidence. It follows that, so far as concerns publication by the confidant himself, the reasoning in the *Speed Seal* case [1985] 1 WLR 1327 (founded as it is upon the *Cranleigh Precision Engineering* case [1965] 1 WLR 1293) cannot, to my mind, be supported. I recognise that a case where the confider himself publishes the information might be distinguished from other cases on the basis that the confider, by publishing the information, may have implicitly released the confidant from his obligation. But that was not how it was put in *O Mustad & Son v Dosen* (Note) [1964] 1 WLR 109, 111, in which Lord Buckmaster stated that, once the disclosure had been made by the confider to the world, 'The secret, as a secret, had ceased to exist.' For my part, I cannot see how the secret can continue to exist when the publication has been made not by the confider but by a third party.

[84] [1986] FSR 309, 313 (Fox LJ).

> … On this approach, it is difficult to see how a confidant who publishes the relevant confidential information to the whole world can be under any further obligation not to disclose the information, simply because it was he who wrongfully destroyed its confidentiality. The information has, after all, already been so fully disclosed that it is in the public domain: how, therefore, can he thereafter be sensibly restrained from disclosing it? Is he not even to be permitted to mention in public what is now common knowledge? For his wrongful act, he may be held liable in damages, or may be required to make restitution; but, to adapt the words of Lord Buckmaster, the confidential information, as confidential information, has ceased to exist, and with it should go, as a matter of principle, the obligation of confidence.

From the above passage it is apparent that Lord Goff found the reasoning in *Speed Seal Products* unpersuasive and that *Cranleigh Precision Engineering v Bryant* does not support a continuing duty of confidence even where the information has been made public, whether by a third party or the defendant.

The first instance decision in *Vestergaard Frandsen A/S v Bestnet Europe Ltd*[85] reviewed the authorities discussed above, as well as others, and sought to set out key statements of principle concerning the 'springboard' doctrine. One of these was that publication of confidential information brings the obligation of confidence to an end, regardless of *who* has published the information—the confider, a stranger, or the confidant himself. To the extent that the springboard doctrine was understood to mean that an injunction could be obtained for misuse of confidential information, even once the information was no longer confidential, this doctrine 'should now be regarded as having been laid to rest'.[86] According to Arnold J, the authorities gave rise to two possible understandings of what is meant by the 'springboard' doctrine. The first is that information may have a limited degree of confidentiality even though it can be ascertained by reverse engineering or through compilation of public domain sources. In this situation, an injunction may be granted but only for a limited period, i.e. for as long as it would take someone to reverse engineer or compile the information. Or, as the Court of Appeal in *Roger Bullivant v Ellis*[87] put it, the injunction should not 'normally extend beyond the period for which the unfair advantage may reasonably be expected to continue'.[88] The second interpretation of the 'springboard' doctrine is that an injunction may be granted to stop the defendant from benefiting from a *past* misuse of confidential information even if the information is no longer confidential. Arnold J accepted that the usual remedy in this situation would be a financial one, but that there was some support for allowing the grant of an injunction,[89] although considerable caution would be required 'both as to whether to grant such an injunction at all and, if so, as to its form and duration'.[90]

Arnold J's reconciliation of the 'springboard' cases is a welcome synthesis and clarification of this difficult area of the law. However, another interpretation of the *Terrapin* decision is that although *some* of the commercial secrets had become (or would become) public, there was a considerable amount of other information—in the form of technical specifications and know-how—that was not apparent from either sales of the buildings, reverse engineering, or publication of the brochures. In other words, there was still commercial information that would remain confidential. *Cranleigh Precision v Bryant* can also be seen in the

---

[85] [2009] EWHC 1456 (Ch), [2010] FSR 2.   [86] [76].   [87] [1987] FSR 172.
[88] *Roger Bullivant v Ellis*, 183, per Nourse LJ (May LJ in agreement).
[89] *Terrapin*, *Roger Bullivant Ltd v Ellis* [1987] FSR 172; *Universal Thermosensors Ltd v Hibben* [1992] 1 WLR 840.
[90] *Vestergaard*, [93].

same way, namely, that because of Bryant's position as managing director of the claimant company and his intimate knowledge of the claimant's business, he knew the relevance and impact of the patent specification on the claimant's business and this is not something that would have been disclosed by distribution of the pools or the publication of the patent specification. If these two cases are viewed in this way, the 'springboard' is the fact that use of the confidential information *enabled* much faster or more effective use of information that had entered the public domain.

9.5 UNAUTHORIZED USE

9.5.1 REQUIREMENT OF DETRIMENT

The third element of a breach of confidence requires an unauthorized use of the information to the detriment of the person communicating it. However, doubts have been expressed about whether detriment is in fact necessary, including by Megarry J in *Coco v Clark*:

> Thirdly, there must be an unauthorised use of the information to the detriment of the person communicating it. Some of the statements of principle in the cases omit any mention of detriment; others include it. At first sight, it seems that detriment ought to be present if equity is to be induced to intervene; but I can conceive of cases where a plaintiff might have substantial motives for seeking the aid of equity and yet suffer nothing which could fairly be called detriment to him, as when the confidential information shows him in a favourable light but gravely injures some relation or friend of his whom he wishes to protect. The point does not arise for decision in this case, for detriment to the plaintiff plainly exists. I need therefore say no more than that although for the purposes of this case I have stated the proposition in the stricter form, I wish to keep open the possibility of the true proposition being that in the wider form.[91]

Determining whether the information has been used in an unauthorized manner will depend on the scope of the confidential obligation that is owed. For example, if Company A, a travel operator, communicates to Company B details of its confidential software system because they want B to develop for them a new type of online booking system, then it seems highly likely that B will owe A an obligation of confidence not to disclose details of A's software system to competitors or other third parties. Further, it is unlikely that B will be authorized to use A's software in order to devise an improved travel booking system for competitor D or indeed a hotel booking system for third party E. However, it may be that the circumstances permit some disclosure to, or use by, third parties, when Company B is, say, using expert independent consultants to assist them in devising the improved online booking system.

How will the scope of any confidential obligation be ascertained? In the case of contractual obligations of confidence, courts are most likely to interpret the language of the relevant provisions. In the absence of contractual terms, or where courts are supplementing contractual duties with additional (equitable) duties, then the notice of confidentiality test will also have a role to play here. In other words, the factors that were relevant to determining whether an obligation exists in the first place will also influence the nature and scope of

---

[91] *Coco v Clark*, 421.

that obligation. Especially relevant, but not necessarily determinative, will be A's purpose in giving the confidential information to B.[92]

9.5.2 PUBLIC INTEREST DEFENCE

It is a well-recognized principle that unauthorized use or disclosure of confidential information may be excused on the grounds of public interest. But what constitutes 'public interest'? Is it where information will be of interest to the public or must the information relate to an act or issue of a sufficiently serious nature? The Court of Appeal, in the following decision, sought to tease out the type of public interest that would justify unauthorized use of confidential information.

Lion Laboratories v Evans [1985] QB 526

The claimant was a company which manufactured and sold the Lion Intoximeter 3000, an instrument for measuring blood-alcohol levels. The device was one of two devices approved by the Home Office for police use in carrying out breathalyser tests in drivers of motor vehicles. The first and second defendants, who were former employees of the claimant, leaked confidential documents to a journalist at the *Daily Express* (the fourth defendant), in breach of the duty of confidence owed to their former employer. An *ex parte* injunction was granted against the *Daily Express* and its editor (the third defendant) restraining them from publishing the contents of the confidential documents. Nevertheless, the *Daily Express* published an article in which it alleged that the Intoximeter was liable to serious error and could lead to wrongful conviction. The interim injunction was confirmed at an *inter partes* hearing. The defendants appealed. There was no dispute that the documents were confidential and that publication of the documents would be in breach of confidence. However, the defendants contended that publication was justified on the grounds of public interest. The Court of Appeal discharged the injunction.

Stephenson LJ (O'Connor LJ in agreement), **at pp. 536–7:**

… The problem before the judge and before this court is how best to resolve, before trial, a conflict of two competing public interests. The first public interest is the preservation of the right of organisations, as of individuals, to keep secret confidential information. The courts will restrain breaches of confidence, and breaches of copyright, unless there is just cause or excuse for breaking confidence or infringing copyright. The just cause or excuse with which this case is concerned is the public interest in admittedly confidential information. There is confidential information which the public may have a right to receive and others, in particular the press, now extended to the media, may have a right and even a duty to publish, even if the information has been unlawfully obtained in flagrant breach of confidence and irrespective of the motive of the informer. The duty of confidence, the public interest in maintaining it, is a restriction on the freedom of the press which is recognised by our law, as well as by article 10(2) of the Convention for the Protection of Human Rights and

---

[92] *R v Department of Health, ex p Source Informatics* [1999] EWCA Civ 3011. Cf *Smith Kline & French Laboratories (Australia) Ltd v Secretary to the Department of Community Services and Health* [1990] FSR 617.

Fundamental Freedoms (1953) (Cmd 8969); the duty to publish, the countervailing inter-est of the public in being kept informed of matters which are of real public concern, is an inroad on the privacy of confidential matters. So much is settled by decisions of this court, and in particular by the illuminating judgments of Lord Denning MR in *Initial Services Ltd v Putterill* [1968] 1 QB 396; *Fraser v Evans* [1969] 1 QB 349; *Hubbard v Vosper* [1972] 2 QB 84; *Woodward v Hutchins* [1977] 1 WLR 760; and *per* Lord Denning MR (dissenting) in *Schering Chemicals Ltd v Falkman Ltd* [1982] QB 1. I add to those the speeches of Lord Wilberforce, Lord Salmon and Lord Fraser of Tullybelton in *British Steel Corporation v Granada Television Ltd* [1981] AC 1096.

There are four further considerations. First, 'there is a wide difference between what is inter-esting to the public and what it is in the public interest to make known' said Lord Wilberforce in *British Steel Corporation v Granada Television Ltd*, at p. 1168. The public are interested in many private matters which are no real concern of theirs and which the public have no pressing need to know. Secondly, the media have a private interest of their own in publishing what appeals to the public and may increase their circulation or the numbers of their viewers or listeners; and I quote from Sir John Donaldson MR in *Francome v Mirror Group Newspapers Ltd* [1984] 1 WLR 892, 898B, 'they are peculiarly vulnerable to the error of confusing the public interest with their own interest'. Thirdly, there are cases in which the public interest is best served by an informer giving the confidential information, not to the press but to the police or some other responsible body, as was suggested by Lord Denning MR in *Initial Services Ltd v Putterill* [1968] 1 QB 396, 405–6 and by Sir John Donaldson MR in *Francome v Mirror Group Newspapers Ltd* [1984] 1 WLR 892, 898. Fourthly, it was said by Wood V-C in 1856, in *Gartside v Outram* (1856) 26 LJ Ch 113, 114, 'there is no confidence as to the disclosure of iniquity'; and though Mr Hoolahan concedes on the plaintiffs' behalf that, as Salmon LJ said in *Initial Services Ltd v Putterill* [1968] 1 QB 396, 410, 'what was iniquity in 1856 may be too narrow or … too wide for 1967', and in 1984 extends to serious misdeeds or grave misconduct, he submits that misconduct of that kind is necessary to destroy the duty of confidence or excuse the breach of it, and nothing of that sort is alleged against the plaintiffs in the evidence now before the court.

Mr Alexander, on behalf of the third and fourth defendants, and Mr Bloch on behalf of the first and second defendants, have not been able to find any case where a defendant has been able to rely on public interest in defence of a claim for breach of confidence and the plaintiff has not also been guilty of such misconduct, and there are passages in the speeches of Lord Wilberforce and Lord Fraser of Tullybelton in *British Steel Corporation v Granada Television Ltd* [1981] AC 1096, 1165, 1195 in which they appear to be satisfied with describing the 'public interest rule' as the 'iniquity rule'. But I nowhere find any authority for the proposition, except perhaps in the judgment of Ungoed-Thomas J in *Beloff v Pressdram Ltd* [1973] 1 All ER 241, 260, that some modern form of iniquity on the part of the plaintiffs is the only thing which can be disclosed in the public interest; and I agree with the judge in rejecting the 'no iniquity, no public interest' rule; and in respectfully adopting what Lord Denning MR said in *Fraser v Evans* [1969] 1 QB 349, 362, that some things are required to be disclosed in the public interest, in which case no confidence can be prayed in aid to keep them secret, and '[iniquity] is merely an instance of just cause or excuse for breaking confidence'.

Griffiths LJ put this case in argument. Suppose the plaintiffs had informed the police that their Intoximeter was not working accurately nor safe to use, and the police had replied that they were nevertheless going to continue using it as breath test evidence. Could there then be no defence of public interest if the defendants sought to publish that confidential informa-tion, simply because the plaintiffs themselves had done nothing wrong but the police had? There would be the same public interest in publication, whichever was guilty of misconduct; and I cannot think the right to break confidence would be lost, though the public interest remained the same. Bearing this last consideration in mind, in my opinion we cannot say that the defendants must be restrained because what they want to publish does not show misconduct by the plaintiffs.

...

The issue raised by the defendants is a serious question concerning a matter which affects the life, and even the liberty, of an unascertainable number of Her Majesty's subjects, and though there is no proof that any of them has been wrongly convicted on the evidence of the plaintiffs' Intoximeter, and we certainly cannot decide that any has, we must not restrain the defendants from putting before the public this further information as to how the Lion Intoximeter 3000 has worked, and how the plaintiffs regard and discharge their responsibility for it, although the information is confidential and was unlawfully taken in breach of confidence.

[**Griffiths LJ** delivered a concurring judgment.]

As the Court of Appeal emphasized, the public interest defence does not equate to that which is of interest to the public. Neither does it have to relate necessarily to wrongful or iniquitous conduct on the part of the claimant. But the matter or issue that is sought to justify the unauthorized disclosure must be of sufficient importance or gravity. Thus, we see that the public interest defence has succeeded where publication concerned disclosure of criminal or other unlawful activities[93] or protected the public from medically dangerous practices[94] or from a potentially dangerous mental patient likely to be discharged into the community.[95] However, the defence has, on occasion, succeeded in relation to matters of apparently lesser importance, such as where the disclosure sought to correct a misleading public image that famous pop stars were wholesome.[96]

In *Lion Laboratories*, Stephenson LJ noted that upholding a duty of confidence is a restriction on the freedom of the press, as recognized by Article 10(2) of the ECHR. Since the enactment of the Human Rights Act 1998 (HRA) the role of Article 10 of the ECHR has come into sharper focus. This is because section 6 of the HRA makes it unlawful for a public authority (including a court) to act in a manner incompatible with a Convention right and this includes Article 10 of the ECHR, which sets out a right to freedom of expression. A significant amount of case law has been concerned with weighing a claimant's Article 8 right to privacy against a defendant's Article 10 right to freedom of expression and this is explored in the next chapter. What is of interest here is whether, in the case of commercial secrets in particular, there is a countervailing right to weigh against Article 10.

Where a claimant is seeking to restrain a defendant from misusing or unlawfully disclosing his commercial secrets, the defendant may argue that this restricts his Article 10 right to freedom of expression. For example, where Company A seeks to restrain B, a former employee, from disclosing commercial secrets that illustrate A's fraudulent and unethical practices to C, a newspaper, and to restrain C from publishing them, B and C may argue that their rights to freedom of expression will be encroached upon if an injunction is granted. If Article 10 is the only Convention right to be engaged then it is arguable that B and C's rights to freedom of expression will take precedence and the court would have to assess, pursuant to Article 10(2), whether upholding the duties of confidence owed to A is a justified

---

[93] *Malone v Metropolitan Police Commissioner* [1979] Ch 344; *Initial Services v Putterill* [1968] 1 QB 396.
[94] *Hubbard v Vosper* [1972] 2 QB 84.   [95] *W v Edgell* [1990] 1 Ch 359.
[96] *Woodward v Hutchins* [1977] 1 WLR 760.

interference with B and C's Article 10 rights. There is little support for treating commercial secrets as within the Article 8 right to privacy (mainly because this requires acceptance of a notion of corporate privacy). However, it may be possible to treat commercial secrets as 'property' within Article 1 Protocol 1 of the ECHR. If this characterization is accepted by the courts then a balancing exercise would ensue. Thus, to continue with our example, the court would have to weigh A's right to property under Article 1 Protocol 1 against B and C's right to freedom of expression under Article 10. Is this type of balancing exercise the same as weighing a public interest in confidentiality against a public interest in disclosure of the information that was discussed in *Lion Laboratories*? Can we say that the public interest defence is synonymous with Article 10 of the ECHR or a distinct defence? Courts have been frustratingly opaque on the relationship between the public interest defence and Article 10 of the ECHR. Paul Stanley has argued that the two are distinct:

> the right to freedom of expression constitutes a defence to an action for breach of confidence that is, in principle, distinct from the public interest defence, albeit closely related, historically and as a matter of practice. The former tends to apply to specific and narrow disclosures, the latter to general and public disclosures. There may be cases where they overlap; but in principle they are distinct.[97]

FURTHER READING

T. Aplin, 'Commercial confidences after the Human Rights Act' [2007] EIPR 411.

T. Aplin, 'A right of privacy for corporations?' in P. Torremans (ed.), *IP & Human Rights* (The Hague: Kluwer, 2008), pp. 475–505.

9.6 EMPLOYEE AND EX-EMPLOYEE OBLIGATIONS

Employees are the lifeblood of any organization and are usually entrusted with, or are privy to, important and valuable details of their employer's business, including commercial secrets. Disclosure of such information to competitors or other misuse by an employee, or ex-employee, can be highly damaging to organizations and, yet, for ex-employees in particular, there is a need to be able freely to use their acquired expertise. The sorts of duties that apply to employees, both during and after employment, is therefore an important and highly complex area of the law. In the next section we review the main confidentiality obligations that apply to employees and ex-employees when it comes to commercial secrets.

9.6.1 OBLIGATIONS DURING EMPLOYMENT

When it comes to regulating the sorts of duties owed by employees to their employer, the preferable way of doing this is via express terms in their contract of employment. This is because express terms allow the obligation to be tailored to the terms of the particular relationship; and to be articulated transparently and with clarity. The sorts of express duties that employers will wish to impose on their employees include a duty not to use or disclose

---

[97] Review of P. Stanley, *The Law of Confidentiality: A Restatement* (Oxford: Hart, 2008), p. 88.

confidential information of the organization to third parties; and a duty not to compete with the organization for whom they work.

Implied obligations undoubtedly still have a role to play, including alongside express contractual obligations. There is extensive case law that supports an implied duty of fidelity or loyalty being imposed on employees. An early case in which the duty of fidelity was held to preclude activities by employees to build up a rival business is *Hivac Ltd v Park Royal*.

Hivac Ltd v Park Royal Scientific Instruments Ltd [1946] 1 Ch 169

The claimant company was the sole manufacturer of small thermionic valves for use in hearing aids. Five of its skilled manual employees worked on Sundays for the defendant company, which had been established to make hearing aids with valves that competed with the claimant's. The claimant could not dismiss the five employees without following a complex statutory procedure. Thus, it instead sought interlocutory relief enjoining the defendant from procuring breach by the workers of their employment contracts.

Lord Greene MR (Bucknill LJ in agreement)**, at pp. 174–5:**

It has been said on many occasions that an employee owes a duty of fidelity to his employer. As a general proposition that is indisputable. The practical difficulty in any given case is to find exactly how far that rather vague duty of fidelity extends. Prima facie it seems to me on considering the authorities and the arguments that it must be a question on the facts of each particular case. I can very well understand that the obligation of fidelity, which is an implied term of the contract, may extend very much further in the case of one class of employee than it does in others. For instance, when you are dealing, as we are dealing here, with mere manual workers whose job is to work five and a half days for their employer at a specific type of work and stop their work when the hour strikes, the obligation of fidelity may be one the operation of which will have a comparatively limited scope. The law would, I think, be jealous of attempting to impose on a manual worker restrictions, the real effect of which would be to prevent him utilising his spare time. He is paid for five and a half days in the week. The rest of the week is his own, and to impose upon a man, in relation to the rest of the week, some kind of obligation which really would unreasonably tie his hands and prevent him adding to his weekly money during that time would, I think, be very undesirable. On the other hand, if one has employees of a different character, one may very well find that the obligation is of a different nature. A manual worker might say: 'You pay me for five and a half days work. I do five and a half days work for you. What greater obligation have I taken upon myself? If you want in some way to limit my activities during the other day and a half of the week, you must pay me for it.' In many cases that may be a very good answer. In other cases it may not be a good answer because the very nature of the work may be such as to make it quite clear that the duties of the employee to his employer cannot properly be performed if in his spare time the employee engages in certain classes of activity. One example was discussed in argument, that of a solicitor's clerk who on Sundays it was assumed went and worked for another firm in the same town. He might find himself embarrassed because the very client for whom he had done work while working for the other firm on the Sunday might be a client against whom clients of his main employer were conducting litigation, or something of that kind. Obviously in a case of that kind, by working for another firm he is in effect, or may be, disabling himself from performing his duties to his real employer and placing himself in an embarrassing position. I can well understand it being said: 'That is a breach of the duty of fidelity to your employer because as a result of what you have done you have disabled yourself from giving to your employer that undivided attention to his business which it is your duty to give.' I merely put that forward, not for the purpose of laying down the law or expressing any concluded opinion, but merely as illustrating the danger of laying down any general proposition and the necessity of considering each case on its facts.

[**Morton LJ** delivered a short concurring judgment.]

Lord Greene MR went on to conclude that the deliberate and secret action by the employees was a prima facie breach of their duty of fidelity.

The relationship between an implied duty of fidelity and an express contractual obligation of confidence was explored in the following case.

Thomas Marshall (Exporters) Ltd v Guinle [1979] Ch 227

The defendant was managing director of the claimant company. His appointment was for ten years and his service agreement provided that during his employment he was not to engage in other business without the company's consent; that during and after his employment he was not 'to disclose' confidential information relating to the company; and that after ceasing to be managing director he was neither 'to use or disclose' confidential information about the suppliers and customers of the group nor, for a period of five years, employ any person who had worked for the company during the last two years of his appointment.

Unbeknown to the claimant, the defendant began to trade on his own account and on behalf of his two companies in competition with the claimant. He bought from the claimant's suppliers and sold to the claimant's customers. He also employed several former employees of the claimant. He purported to resign part way through his contract. The claimant brought proceedings against the defendant and his companies and sought interim injunctions against them.

Megarry V-C, at pp. 244–6:

[Sir Robert Megarry V-C considered, inter alia, whether there was a breach of the defendant's implied duty of fidelity and also his contractual duty not to disclose confidential information relating to the company.]

First, then, there is the servant's implied duty of fidelity and good faith. For this, Mr Morritt cited two decisions of the Court of Appeal, *Wessex Dairies Ltd v Smith* [1935] 2 KB 80 and *Hivac Ltd v Park Royal Scientific Instruments Ltd* [1946] Ch 169. In the Wessex case, a milk roundsman employed by a company solicited the company's customers to transfer their custom to him when he ceased to be employed by the company. The Court of Appeal held that, apart from any express term of his employment, to do this was a breach of the servant's implied obligation to serve his master with good faith and fidelity, and to look after his master's interests and not his own, and he was held liable in damages. I need not set out the rather more complex facts of the *Hivac* case, which related to skilled workers secretly working in their spare time for a trade rival of their employers. I need only say that in it the Court of Appeal reaffirmed the servant's implied duty of fidelity, and applied it to acts done by the servant outside his hours of work for his employer, in addition to acts done within those hours. An interlocutory injunction was granted to restrain the rival firm from employing the workers in question.

… It is impossible to deny that the defendant has been guilty of gross and repeated breaches of his implied obligation to be faithful to the company. While still in office as managing director of the company he travelled abroad, ostensibly on the company's business, and without the company's knowledge placed orders for the benefit of himself and his companies with the company's suppliers. He also, while still managing director and without the company's knowledge, sold goods for the benefit of himself and his companies to customers of the company. In the *Boston* case, 39 Ch D 339, the receipt by the managing director of what may have been a single secret commission was said in the Court of Appeal to be dishonest and a fraud. I can apply no milder description to the defendant's prolonged duplicity. His contention is that he is entitled to go on doing this, and that the company is not entitled to any injunction restraining him from doing it. The injunctions claimed do not seek to restrain him from carrying on a similar business: all that is claimed is that he should not solicit orders from the company's customers or suppliers, or otherwise deal with them, and that he should not disclose or use any confidential information or trade secrets of the company. Subject to what I shall say later, particularly about confidential information, I think it clear that injunctions to this effect ought to be granted.

…

Third, there is clause F.7 of the service agreement. The obligation of the defendant not to 'disclose any confidential information relating to the affairs customers or trade secrets of the group' of which he became possessed while in the company's service is clear enough; and it plainly continues after the service agreement terminates. However, Mr Hutchison contended, as I have mentioned, that this provision did not justify the injunctions claimed. He contended that the only obligation was against disclosure.

…

I return, then, to Mr Hutchison's distinction between 'disclose' and 'use or disclose'. Mr Morritt contended that the obligation in clause F.7 not to 'disclose' any confidential information should be read as including an obligation not to use that information: the words 'or use' ought, he said, to be implied into it. I can see no basis upon which such an implication could be made, especially in view of the contrast with the 'use or disclose' of the first proviso to clause J.2. I think 'disclose' means what it says, and does not extend to 'use'. Of course, I can conceive of methods of use which would amount to making a disclosure. If an employee were to use his secret knowledge in such a way as to make it plain to others what the secret process or information was, that might well amount to a disclosure. The mode and circumstances of use may be so ostentatious that they plainly constitute a disclosure. But apart from such cases, I do not think that a prohibition on disclosure prevents use. It therefore seems to me that clause F.7 provides no basis for granting an injunction to restrain the defendant from using confidential information or trade secrets, as distinct from disclosing them.

…

With that, I turn to the injunctions sought by the company. First, there is the soliciting order, to restrain the defendant from soliciting orders from, or otherwise dealing with, any of the company's customers for goods of the nature of those sold by the company, and from soliciting orders for the supply of such goods from, or otherwise dealing with, any of the company's suppliers. From what I have said it can be seen that in my judgment the implied duty of fidelity and good faith plainly warrants the grant of an injunction in such terms.

…

> Second, there is the breach of confidence order. This, in its wide form, restraining the disclosure or use of confidential information or trade secrets, seems to me to be fully supported by the implied duty of fidelity and good faith … [Also] clause F.7 fully supports the breach of confidence order so far as disclosing is concerned, but not as to using.

As the above case highlights, express contractual duties of confidence must be interpreted according to their terms. However, this does not inhibit courts from implying a duty of fidelity (the scope of which may include an obligation of confidence) that extends wider than those contractual terms. Do you think it is appropriate for courts to place more onerous confidentiality obligations on employees than those that were explicitly agreed in the employment contract?

9.6.2 GARDEN LEAVE CLAUSES

A so-called 'garden leave' clause refers to an express clause in a contract of employment whereby the employer requires an employee to remain away from work whilst his contract of employment (and remuneration) continues. Why would an employer pay their employee *not* to come to work? This type of clause is often invoked once an employee has given notice that they are leaving their employment and moving elsewhere. Garden leave clauses emerged as a way of addressing two types of problem. The first problem is where employees seek to leave their employment before their contractual notice period has expired. In this case, courts will not usually order specific performance requiring the employee to work out their notice period. The second problem relates to where an employee is content to work out their notice period, but there is a significant risk of that person taking valuable confidential information away with them. Simply keeping the employee away from their job, however, for the notice period would amount to a repudiation of the employment contract by the employer.

In a series of cases beginning in the late 1980s, the courts developed principles concerning garden leave.[98] Where employers attempt to enforce garden leave, they do not seek enforcement of the garden leave clause per se but instead ask the court to restrain the employee from working for another employer before the termination of his employment. It is advisable for employers to include an express garden leave clause and as well to include ancillary provisions to strengthen their position, such as terms that during the garden leave period an employee should not compete with their employer, solicit customers, or approach fellow employees; and to return all company property. Because doubts have been expressed that the implied duty of fidelity or loyalty continues to apply to the same extent or at all during the garden leave period, it is also wise for the employment contract expressly to provide that the duty of fidelity continues during this time.[99]

In order for courts to enforce garden leave clauses, the employer will need to show that they have legitimate interests that require protection, such as confidential information,[100] client connections,[101] or the stability of their workforce.[102] As well, courts are mindful of

---

[98] e.g. see the Court of Appeal decisions in *Evening Standard Co. v Henderson* [1987] ICR 588; *Provident Financial Group v Hayward* [1989] ICR 160; *William Hill Organisation Ltd v Tucker* [1999] ICR 291; *Symbian v Christensen* [2000] EWCA Civ 517, [2001] IRLR 77; and *Tullet Prebon Plc v BGC Brokers LP & Ors* [2011] EWCA Civ 131, [2011] IRLR 420.

[99] See *Symbian v Christensen* [2000] EWCA Civ 517, [2001] IRLR 77 (CA).

[100] *Provident Financial Group v Hayward* [1989] ICR 160; *Symbian v Christensen* [2000] (Ch), [2001] IRLR 77.

[101] *GFI Group v Eaglestone* [1994] IRLR 119.

[102] *Crystal Palace v Stephen Bruce* [2002] SLR 81.

the tendency of employers to use garden leave clauses instead of (or perhaps in addition to) post-termination restrictive covenants. Post-termination restrictive covenants are terms that seek to restrict what an employee can do once his contract of employment has come to an end, for example prohibiting an ex-employee from working for a particular competitor or any competitors for a fixed period of time. In *William Hill Organisation Ltd v Tucker*, Millett LJ commented *obiter*:[103]

> there appears to be a trend towards increasing reliance on garden leave provisions in pref-
> erence to conventional restrictive covenants, no doubt because hitherto the courts have
> treated the former with greater flexibility than the latter, as explained by Neill LJ in *Credit
> Suisse Management Ltd v Armstrong* [1996] ICR 882, 892. But the reported cases dealing
> with the court's approach to the grant of injunctions in this field show that if injunctive relief
> is sought then it has to be justified on similar grounds to those necessary to the validity of
> an employee's covenant in restraint of trade. It seems to me that the court should be careful
> not to grant interlocutory relief to enforce a garden leave clause to any greater extent than
> would be covered by justifiable covenant in restraint of trade previously entered into by an
> employee.[104]

9.6.3 OBLIGATIONS POST-EMPLOYMENT

When it comes to regulating the duties owed by ex-employees to their former employer, the use of express clauses is even more advisable than in the case of employees. This is because the implied duty of fidelity discussed at 9.6.1 comes to an end when the contract of employment terminates and, further, the duty of confidentiality is argu-ably more limited in post-employment circumstances insofar as it applies only to *trade secrets* and not confidential information more generally. These express terms—known as post-termination restrictive covenants—can take different forms. They may seek to restrict an ex-employee's ability to use or disclose confidential information; or to prevent an ex-employee from competing with their former employer for a period of time; or to prohibit the solicitation or enticement of their ex-employer's customers or workers. Of these restrictions which, ideally, do you think an employer would seek to use and why?

Post-termination restrictive covenants undoubtedly restrict the type of activities and employment that an ex-employee can enter into and, as such, they amount to a prima facie restraint of trade. It is only where this restraint is reasonable that it will be upheld by the courts. The reasonableness of the restraint will be judged having regard to the interests of the parties and the public interest more generally and courts will take into account factors such as the width of the covenant and the types of legitimate interests that the employer is seeking to protect.

In the absence of any post-termination restrictive covenants, employers will seek to rely on an implied duty of confidentiality. As the following decision shows, however, this

---

[103] [1999] ICR 291, 301–2.

[104] See also *Tullet Prebon Plc v BGC Brokers LP & Ors* [2010] EWHC 484 (QB), [219] per Jack J: 'Courts will approach enforcement of garden leave by injunction in a similar way in part to that in which it approaches the enforcement of a post-termination restraint, often called a restrictive covenant'. On appeal see [2011] EWCA Civ 131, [2011] IRLR 420.

obligation on ex-employees is more restricted in scope than the implied duties imposed on employees. Why would this be?

Faccenda Chicken Ltd v Fowler [1987] Ch 117

The claimant company (Faccenda) carried on the business of rearing, slaughtering, and selling fresh chickens in Northampton. The first defendant (Fowler) was engaged as a sales manager and had instituted a 'van sales operation', namely, selling fresh chickens from itinerant refrigerated vans. The first defendant resigned from the claimant and proceeded to set up his own business of selling fresh chickens from refrigerated vans in the same area. Several employees of the claimant left to join the first defendant's new business. The claimant brought a claim against the first defendant and former employees claiming, inter alia, an injunction and damages for breach of confidence. None of the employees' contracts of employment contained express terms dealing with unauthorized use of confidential information gained during their employment. The allegedly confidential information was 'sales information', which comprised the contact details of customers, the most convenient routes to reach them, the usual orders of customers, the usual delivery days and times, and the prices customers were charged. Goulding J dismissed the claimant's claim and an appeal to the Court of Appeal was dismissed.

Neill LJ (delivering the judgment of the court)**, at pp. 135–9:**

Having considered the cases to which we were referred, we would venture to state these principles:

1. Where the parties are, or have been, linked by a contract of employment, the obligations of the employee are to be determined by the contract between him and his employer: cf. *Vokes Ltd v Heather* (1945) 62 RPC 135, 141.

2. In the absence of any express term, the obligations of the employee in respect of the use and disclosure of information are the subject of implied terms.

3. While the employee remains in the employment of the employer the obligations are included in the implied term which imposes a duty of good faith or fidelity on the employee. For the purposes of the present appeal it is not necessary to consider the precise limits of this implied term, but it may be noted: (a) that the extent of the duty of good faith will vary according to the nature of the contract (see *Vokes Ltd v Heather* 62 RPC 135); (b) that the duty of good faith will be broken if an employee makes or copies a list of the customers of the employer for use after his employment ends or deliberately memorises such a list, even though, except in special circumstances, there is no general restriction on an ex-employee canvassing or doing business with customers of his former employer: see *Robb v Green* [1895] 2 QB 315 and *Wessex Dairies Ltd v Smith* [1935] 2 KB 80.

4. The implied term which imposes an obligation on the employee as to his conduct after the determination of the employment is more restricted in its scope than that which imposes a general duty of good faith. It is clear that the obligation not to use or disclose information may cover secret processes of manufacture such as chemical formulae (*Amber Size and Chemical Co Ltd v Menzel* [1913] 2 Ch 239), or designs or special methods of construction (*Reid & Sigrist Ltd v Moss and Mechanism Ltd* (1932) 49 RPC 461), and other information which is of a sufficiently high degree of confidentiality as to amount to a trade secret. The

obligation does not extend, however, to cover all information which is given to or acquired by the employee while in his employment, and in particular may not cover information which is only 'confidential' in the sense that an unauthorised disclosure of such information to a third party while the employment subsisted would be a clear breach of the duty of good faith. This distinction is clearly set out in the judgment of Cross J in *Printers & Finishers Ltd v Holloway* [1965] 1 WLR 1; [1965] RPC 239 where he had to consider whether an ex-employee should be restrained by injunction from making use of his recollection of the contents of certain written printing instructions which had been made available to him when he was working in his former employers' flock printing factory. In his judgment, delivered on 29 April 1964 (not reported on this point in [1965] 1 WLR 1), he said [1965] RPC 239, 253:

> In this connection one must bear in mind that not all information which is given to a servant in confidence and which it would be a breach of his duty for him to disclose to another person during his employment is a trade secret which he can be prevented from using for his own advantage after the employment is over, even though he has entered into no express covenant with regard to the matter in hand. For example, the printing instructions were handed to Holloway to be used by him during his employment exclusively for the plaintiffs' benefit. It would have been a breach of duty on his part to divulge any of the contents to a stranger while he was employed, but many of these instructions are not really 'trade secrets' at all. Holloway was not, indeed, entitled to take a copy of the instructions away with him; but in so far as the instructions cannot be called 'trade secrets' and he carried them in his head, he is entitled to use them for his own benefit or the benefit of any future employer.

The same distinction is to be found in *E Worsley & Co Ltd v Cooper* [1939] 1 All ER 290 where it was held that the defendant was entitled, after he had ceased to be employed, to make use of his knowledge of the source of the paper supplied to his previous employer. In our view it is quite plain that this knowledge was nevertheless 'confidential' in the sense that it would have been a breach of the duty of good faith for the employee, while the employment subsisted, to have used it for his own purposes or to have disclosed it to a competitor of his employer.

5. In order to determine whether any particular item of information falls within the implied term so as to prevent its use or disclosure by an employee after his employment has ceased, it is necessary to consider all the circumstances of the case. We are satisfied that the following matters are among those to which attention must be paid:

6.

(a) The nature of the employment. Thus employment in a capacity where 'confidential' material is habitually handled may impose a high obligation of confidentiality because the employee can be expected to realise its sensitive nature to a greater extent than if he were employed in a capacity where such material reaches him only occasionally or incidentally.

(b) The nature of the information itself. In our judgment the information will only be protected if it can properly be classed as a trade secret or as material which, while not properly to be described as a trade secret, is in all the circumstances of such a highly confidential nature as to require the same protection as a trade secret *eo nomine*. The restrictive covenant cases demonstrate that a covenant will not be upheld on the basis of the status of the information which might be disclosed by the former employee if he is not restrained, unless it can be regarded as a trade secret or the equivalent of a trade secret: see, for example, *Herbert Morris Ltd v Saxelby* [1916] 1 AC 688, 710 *per* Lord Parker of Waddington and *Littlewoods Organisation Ltd v Harris* [1977] 1 WLR 1472, 1484 *per* Megaw LJ.

We must therefore express our respectful disagreement with the passage in Goulding J's judgment at [1984] ICR 589, 599E, where he suggested that an employer can protect the use of information in his second category, even though it does not include either a trade secret or its equivalent, by means of a restrictive covenant. As Lord Parker of Waddington made clear in *Herbert Morris Ltd v Saxelby* [1916] 1 AC 688, 709, in a passage to which Mr Dehn drew our attention, a restrictive covenant will not be enforced unless the protection sought is reasonably necessary to protect a trade secret or to prevent some personal influence over customers being abused in order to entice them away.

In our view the circumstances in which a restrictive covenant would be appropriate and could be successfully invoked emerge very clearly from the words used by Cross J in *Printers & Finishers Ltd v Holloway* [1965] 1 WLR 1, 6 (in a passage quoted later in his judgment by Goulding J [1984] ICR 589, 601):

> If the managing director is right in thinking that there are features in the plaintiffs' process which can fairly be regarded as trade secrets and which their employees will inevitably carry away with them in their heads, then the proper way for the plaintiffs to protect themselves would be by exacting covenants from their employees restricting their field of activity after they have left their employment, not by asking the court to extend the general equitable doctrine to prevent breaking confidence beyond all reasonable bounds.

It is clearly impossible to provide a list of matters which will qualify as trade secrets or their equivalent. Secret processes of manufacture provide obvious examples, but innumerable other pieces of information are *capable* of being trade secrets, though the secrecy of some information may be only short-lived. In addition, the fact that the circulation of certain information is restricted to a limited number of individuals may throw light on the status of the information and its degree of confidentiality.

(c) Whether the employer impressed on the employee the confidentiality of the information. Thus, though an employer cannot prevent the use or disclosure *merely* by telling the employee that certain information is confidential, the attitude of the employer towards the information provides evidence which may assist in determining whether or not the information can properly be regarded as a trade secret. It is to be observed that in *E Worsley & Co Ltd v Cooper* [1939] 1 All ER 290, 307D, Morton J attached significance to the fact that no warning had been given to the defendant that 'the source from which the paper came was to be treated as confidential'.

(d) Whether the relevant information can be easily isolated from other information which the employee is free to use or disclose. In *Printers & Finishers Ltd v Holloway* [1965] RPC 239, Cross J considered the protection which might be afforded to information which had been memorised by an ex-employee. He put on one side the memorising of a formula or a list of customers or what had been said (obviously in confidence) at a particular meeting, and continued, at p. 256:

> The employee might well not realise that the feature or expedient in question was in fact peculiar to his late employer's process and factory; but even if he did, such knowledge is not readily separable from his general knowledge of the flock printing process and his acquired skill in manipulating a flock printing plant, and I do not think that any man of average intelligence and honesty would think that there was anything improper in his putting his memory of particular features of his late employer's plant at the disposal of his new employer.

For our part we would not regard the separability of the information in question as being conclusive, but the fact that the alleged 'confidential' information is part of a package and that the remainder of the package is not confidential is likely to throw light on whether the information in question is really a trade secret.

These then are the principles of law which we consider to be applicable to a case such as the present one. We would wish to leave open, however, for further examination on some other occasion the question whether additional protection should be afforded to an employer where the former employee is not seeking to earn his living by making use of the body of skill, knowledge and experience which he has acquired in the course of his career, but is merely selling to a third party information which he acquired in confidence in the course of his former employment.

...

But in the present case the following factors appear to us to lead to the clear conclusion that neither the information about prices nor the sales information as a whole had the degree of confidentiality necessary to support the plaintiffs' case. We would list these factors as follows. (1) The sales information contained some material which the plaintiffs conceded was not confidential if looked at in isolation. (2) The information about the prices was not clearly severable from the rest of the sales information. (3) Neither the sales information in general, nor the information about the prices in particular, though of some value to a competitor, could reasonably be regarded as plainly secret or sensitive. (4) The sales information, including the information about prices, was necessarily acquired by the defendants in order that they could do their work. Moreover, as the judge observed in the course of his judgment, each salesman could quickly commit the whole of the sales information relating to his own area to memory. (5) The sales information was generally known among the van drivers who were employees, as were the secretaries, at quite a junior level. This was not a case where the relevant information was restricted to senior management or to confidential staff. (6) There was no evidence that the plaintiffs had ever given any express instructions that the sales information or the information about prices was to be treated as confidential. We are satisfied that, in the light of all the matters set out by the judge in his judgment, neither the sales information as a whole nor the information about prices looked at by itself fell within the class of confidential information which an employee is bound by an implied term of his contract of employment or otherwise not to use or disclose after his employment has come to an end.

The Court of Appeal decision in *Faccenda Chicken* attempts to reconcile the interests of employers in preserving their confidential information with the interests of ex-employees in being able to work freely and to utilize their accumulated experience and knowledge. Do you think the principles articulated by the Court of Appeal achieve an appropriate balance and in a way that has sufficient clarity to be useful? In particular, is it possible to identify with certainty trade secrets, as distinct from confidential information? This is a crucial distinction drawn by the court since apparently an ex-employee's implied duty not to disclose or use confidential information relates only to trade secrets. As well, the court observes that a post-termination restrictive covenant dealing with confidential information will be enforceable only in respect of trade secrets.[105]

[105] See also *FSS Travel and Leisure Systems Ltd v Johnson* [1999] FSR 505, although the test stated is different to that in *Faccenda Chicken*. At [31]–[33] the court states: 'the critical question is whether the employer has trade secrets which can be fairly regarded as his property, as distinct from the skill, experience, knowhow, and general knowledge which can fairly be regarded as the property of the employee to use without restraint for his own benefit or in the service of a competitor. This distinction necessitates examination of all the evidence relating to the nature of the employment, the character of the information, the restrictions imposed on its dissemination, the extent of use in the public domain and the damage likely to be caused by its use and disclosure in competition to the employer.'

FURTHER READING

T. Aplin, L. Bently, P. Johnson, and S. Malynicz, *Gurry on Breach of Confidence* (Oxford: Oxford University Press, 2012), chs 10–12.

P. Goulding (ed.), *Employee Competition: Covenants, Confidentiality and Garden Leave* (2nd edn, Oxford: Oxford University Press, 2011).

9.7 FUTURE OF BREACH OF CONFIDENCE

The English law on breach of confidence may be impacted in future as a result of the adoption on 8 June 2016 of EU Directive 2016/943 on the protection of undisclosed know-how and business information (trade secrets) against their unlawful acquisition, use, or disclosure (Trade Secrets Directive)[106] and its subsequent implementation. The purpose of the Trade Secrets Directive is to address the problems of legal divergences in the protection of trade secrets in Member States. The key divergences relate to the legal mechanism used to regulate trade secrets (criminal or civil law and within civil law, whether unfair competition, tort, contract, or labour law); the definition of trade secrets; whether trade secrets are classified as intellectual property (thus affecting the remedies available); the level of criminal penalties; and the procedural mechanisms for protecting the confidentiality of trade secrets during litigation. Recitals 2 to 4 and 8 of the directive emphasize that removing fragmentation in the internal market will lead to the incentivization of innovation and investment, in particular on a cross-border basis and this, in turn, will bring economic benefits in terms of competitiveness and employment growth in the EU.

The directive harmonizes the protection of trade secrets in terms of both substantive and procedural law. In terms of substantive law, it defines trade secret, trade secret misappropriation, and lawful acts/exception. On the procedural law front, the directive seeks to harmonize limitation periods, confidentiality during court proceedings, and the remedies available for trade secret misappropriation. The obligations for protection of trade secrets are minimum standards, therefore more far-reaching protection can be offered by Member States provided certain substantive and procedural safeguards are met (see Article 1 and recital 10). While these minimum standards resonate with unfair competition law and apparently prohibit property rights (see recitals 1 and 16), they are drafted in sufficiently neutral terms to allow Member States some flexibility in the choice of civil law mechanism used to implement the obligations. There is no attempt to harmonize criminal penalties, thus significant disparities in the existence and level of criminal penalties available for trade secret misuse will continue to exist.

Turning first to outline the harmonization of substantive law, Article 2 of the directive defines a trade secret as information that is secret (i.e. is not generally known among or readily accessible to persons within circles that normally deal with the kind of information in question), has commercial value because it is secret, and has been subject to reasonable steps to preserve secrecy. This is a relatively uncontroversial definition given

---

[106] [2016] OJ L157/1. Art. 20 states that the directive enters into force 20 days after its publication in the Official Journal.

that it mirrors the requirements of Article 39 of the TRIPS Agreement. However, there is a lingering possibility that the definition is broad enough to cover individual claims to commercially valuable private information.[107] Trade secret misappropriation is defined in terms of unlawful acquisition, use, or disclosure and also infringing goods. Unlawful acquisition occurs where, without the consent of the trade secret holder,[108] there is acquisition by unauthorized access to, appropriation, or copy of any materials containing the trade secret or by any other conduct contrary to honest commercial practices (Article 4(2)). Unlawful use or disclosure occurs where it is carried out without the consent of the trade secret holder by a person who has unlawfully acquired the trade secret or in breach of a confidentiality agreement or other duty not to disclose the trade secret; or in breach of a contractual or other duty to limit the use of the trade secret (Article 4(3)). These unlawful acts can extend to third parties where, at the time of acquisition, use, or disclosure, the third party had actual or constructive knowledge that the trade secret was obtained directly or indirectly from another person who was using or disclosing the trade secret unlawfully (Article 4(4)). Article 4(5) prohibits commercially dealing in infringing goods, which according to Article 2(4) are goods whose 'design, characteristics, functioning, manufacturing process or marketing significantly benefits from trade secrets unlawfully acquired, used or disclosed'.

Certain types of acquisition are, however, declared lawful by Article 3 of the directive, in particular independent discovery or creation and reverse engineering. These are important activities to exclude from trade secret protection since they help to foster further innovation and competition and ensure the efficacy of the patent system is not undermined.[109] In addition, Article 5 of the directive specifies that there is no entitlement to remedies for acquisition, use, or disclosure of trade secrets in certain circumstances, including in situations where there is an exercise of the right to freedom of expression, and in order to reveal misconduct, wrongdoing, or other illegal activity that is in the general public interest. These explicit provisions are seen as especially important protections for whistleblowers and journalists.[110]

An important area that appears to be untouched by the directive is that of employees and ex-employees. Recital 14 of the directive emphasizes that the definition of trade secret does not extend to the 'experience and skills gained by employees in the normal course of their employment'. Moreover, Article 1(3) stipulates that, 'Nothing in this Directive shall be understood to offer any ground for restricting the mobility of employees'. In particular, the directive does not offer any basis for: (1) limiting employees' use of information that does not constitute a trade secret; (2) limiting employees' use of skills and experience honestly acquired in the normal course of their employment; and (3) imposing any additional restrictions on employees via their contracts that are not in accordance with EU or national law. Thus, it appears that Member States will be left to regulate post-employment situations, including confidentiality and non-compete clauses. This leaves 'the absence of harmonization on an issue of considerable practical significance'.[111]

[107] See T. Aplin, 'A critical evaluation of the proposed EU Trade Secrets Directive' [2014] IPQ 257, 262–3.
[108] Trade secret holder is defined in Art. 2(2) as 'any natural or legal person lawfully controlling a trade secret'.
[109] T. Aplin, 'Reverse engineering and commercial secrets' (2013) 66 Current Legal Problems 1, 4–6.
[110] J. Lapousterle, C. Geiger, N. Olszak, and L. Desaunettes, 'What protection for trade secrets in the European Union? A comment on the directive proposal' [2016] EIPR 255, 258.
[111] Lapousterle et al., 'What protection for trade secrets in the European Union? A comment on the directive proposal', 259.

Turning next to the procedural aspects of the directive, a key feature is Article 9, which seeks to address the paradox that trade secrets remain valuable and protectable if they are secret and yet court proceedings are inevitably open and public in nature. Thus, a trade secret holder who seeks to litigate will inevitably destroy their trade secret by revealing it during court proceedings. Article 9 therefore obligates Member States to ensure that confidentiality is preserved during court proceedings, while at the same time paying due attention to transparency and open justice. Article 8 sets a limitation period of six years for when proceedings may be brought, but it will be up to Member States to determine when the limitation period begins to run. Finally, Articles 6 to 7 and 10 to 15 deal with the remedies that must be made available where trade secret misappropriation is established. These relate to interim and final measures, along with damages and publication of judicial decisions. An important feature is that courts must assess the proportionality of the remedies that are granted.

Member States must implement the directive by 9 June 2018 (Article 19). In a jurisdiction such as the UK, which relies on the common law action for breach of confidence, it will not be possible simply to rely on existing law. This is for two interrelated reasons. The first is that certain aspects of breach of confidence do not comply with the obligations regarding substantive law in the directive. These include the definition of 'trade secret', what constitutes unlawful acquisition of trade secrets, the limitations in respect of reverse engineering, and the prohibition on infringing goods. By way of contrast, the UK seems largely compliant with the obligations in the directive concerning procedural law. The second reason is that UK compliance would therefore rest on judicial development of the action for breach of confidence and there is no way to guarantee this would occur by the implementation date. Further, such judicial development could be seen as giving direct effect to the directive and thus contrary to the principle stated in *Marleasing SA v La Comercial Internacional de Alimentación SA*.[112] Thus, implementation of the directive will likely require the UK government to introduce specific legislation. The challenge here will be whether the government takes on the ambitious task of codifying the action for breach of confidence in a way that complies with the directive.[113] Alternatively, and more likely to occur, is that the UK will implement the directive along minimalist lines via statutory instrument. But this approach is not without its own problem, namely, whether or not to preserve breach of confidence alongside trade secret protection according to the directive, to the extent that they are not inconsistent.

While the ideal of 'harmonization' might be laudable in the context of trade secrets, it is worth questioning whether the directive is likely to achieve much consistency between Member States' laws. Here, it is important to consider the fact that the directive provides for minimal (not full) harmonization, offers flexibility as to the civil legal mechanisms used for protection, will require several key concepts to be clarified by the CJEU, and omits harmonization of employee mobility and criminal penalties.

---

[112] Case C-106/89 [1990] ECR I-4135, [1992] 1 CMLR 305.

[113] Note that previously the Law Commission has recommended the abolition of breach of confidence and its replacement with a statutory tort of breach of confidence: Law Commission, *Breach of Confidence* (1981), Law Com. No. 110.

FURTHER READING

T. Aplin, 'A critical evaluation of the proposed EU Trade Secrets Directive' [2014] IPQ 257.

Comments of the Max Planck Institute for Innovation and Competition on the Proposal for a Directive on the protection of undisclosed know-how and business information (trade secrets) against their unlawful acquisition, use and disclosure (2014) 45 IIC 953.

V. Falce, 'Trade secrets—looking for (full) harmonization in the innovation Union' (2015) 46 IIC 940.

J. Lapousterle, C. Geiger, N. Olszak, and L. Desaunettes, 'What protection for trade secrets in the European Union? A comment on the directive proposal' [2016] EIPR 255.

N. Sousa, 'What exactly is a trade secret under the proposed directive?' (2014) 9 JIPLP 923.

A. Wennakoski, 'Trade secrets under review: a comparative analysis of the protection of trade secrets in the EU and the US' [2016] EIPR 154.

PRIVACY, PERSONALITY, AND PUBLICITY

10.1 INTRODUCTION

This chapter deals with the protection of privacy, personality, and publicity interests. Conventionally, these interests are included within the broad rubric of intellectual property law. This is because, in the UK, (common law) privacy protection has developed from the law of confidence and, to the extent that there is protection for the commercial exploitation of personality, this has derived from the tort of passing off. Publicity rights, in some jurisdictions, including the US, have been recognized as an aspect of intellectual property law and there has been some suggestion that a right of publicity should be introduced into UK law.

To understand what differentiates these three interests it is useful to offer a hypothetical scenario.

> Jerri Jones is a glamorous English actor who has a distinctive husky voice. She is famous for appearing in a series of spy films playing an undercover agent called Kit. The films have been a massive international success for the production company, S&B Films. S&B Films have licensed Merchandise Inc. to manufacture and sell a line of cosmetics and clothes carrying the 'Kit' name and image. In addition, the actor, Jerri Jones, has appeared as herself in several advertisements for sports cars and jewellery. Recently, she was photographed while sunbathing naked on her luxury yacht. The photographs are about to appear in a national tabloid newspaper. An unrelated company, BrandX, has begun an advertising campaign featuring a Kit lookalike seen driving their latest model of car, with a voiceover impersonating Jerri Jones's distinctive husky tones but without her permission.

There are a number of questions that arise from this scenario. Does Jerri have the right to prevent publication of the photographs in the newspaper? Can BrandX use the Kit character to help promote their cars and, if so, who might object, Jerri Jones, S&B Films, or

Merchandise Inc? Can BrandX appropriate aspects of Jerri's personality, in this instance her distinctive voice, in order to sell their cars? How these questions might be answered is addressed in this chapter. We will first look at the law of privacy and the extent to which individuals can control the use or disclosure of their personal and private information. We will then turn to examine character and personality merchandising and the ways in which the law of registered and unregistered trade marks protects these interests. Finally, we will consider the controversial question of whether individuals can and should be able to prevent the commercial exploitation of their personality and image through a separate publicity right.

10.2 PRIVACY PROTECTION

10.2.1 BACKGROUND

In *Wainwright v Home Office*, a case where visitors to a prison had been strip-searched in a manner inconsistent with prison rules, the House of Lords declared that English law did *not* recognize a tort of invasion of privacy or 'privacy as a principle of law in itself'.[1] Instead, as Lord Hoffmann (who delivered the majority speech) observed, privacy *values* may underlie various common law and statutory remedies. He explained the English approach to privacy protection thus:

> 18. Common law torts include trespass, nuisance, defamation and malicious falsehood; there is the equitable action for breach of confidence and statutory remedies under the Protection from Harassment Act 1997 and the Data Protection Act 1998. There are also extra-legal remedies under Codes of Practice applicable to broadcasters and newspapers. But there are gaps; cases in which the courts have considered that an invasion of privacy deserves a remedy which the existing law does not offer. Sometimes the perceived gap can be filled by judicious development of an existing principle. The law of breach of confidence has in recent years undergone such a process: see in particular the judgment of Lord Phillips of Worth Matravers MR in *Campbell v MGN Ltd* [2003] QB 633. On the other hand, an attempt to create a tort of telephone harassment by a radical change in the basis of the action for private nuisance in *Khorasandjian v Bush* [1993] QB 727 was held by the House of Lords in *Hunter v Canary Wharf Ltd* [1997] AC 655 to be a step too far. The gap was filled by the 1997 [Protection from Harassment] Act.

In *Wainwright* both claimants had been strip-searched during a prison visit. The claimants complained that the location used to conduct the search was not private and that intimate body parts had been touched during the search. Both claimants had had to remove most, if not all, of their clothing. The first instance judge found that requiring the claimants to remove their clothes was a form of trespass to the person and that the distress they had suffered could be compensated. However, the Court of Appeal found that the judge had wrongfully extended the law of trespass in this situation and (except for the award of battery) overturned the awards of damages. The House of Lords upheld the Court of Appeal's decision. Thus, *Wainwright* is an example of where a gap in English law was unable to be filled

---

[1] *Wainwright v Home Office* [2003] UKHL 53, [2004] 2 AC 406, [31].

by judicial development. It is therefore unsurprising that when the Wainwrights brought a complaint against the UK before the European Court of Human Rights (ECtHR), the Court found a violation of their rights under Article 8 of the European Convention on Human Rights (ECHR).[2] Article 8 of the ECHR provides:

1. Everyone has the right to respect for his private and family life, his home and his correspondence.
2. There shall be no interference by a public authority with the exercise of this right except such as in accordance with the law and is necessary in a democratic society in the interests of national security, public safety or the economic well being of the country, for the prevention of disorder or crime, for the protection of health or morals, or for the protection of the rights and freedoms of others.

Another important Convention right and one that, as we shall see, is often balanced against Article 8 is Article 10, the right to freedom of expression.

1. Everyone has the right to freedom of expression. This right shall include freedom to hold opinions and to receive and impart information and ideas without interference by public authority and regardless of frontiers. This article shall not prevent States from requiring the licensing of broadcasting, television or cinema enterprises.
2. The exercise of these freedoms, since it carries with it duties and responsibilities, may be subject to such formalities, conditions, restrictions or penalties as are prescribed by law and are necessary in a democratic society, in the interests of national security, territorial integrity or public safety, for the prevention of disorder or crime, for the protection of health or morals, for the protection of the reputation or the rights of others, for preventing the disclosure of information received in confidence, or for maintaining the authority and impartiality of the judiciary.

The ECHR is an international agreement, dating back to 1950, which allows individuals who allege that their rights have been violated by a state to bring a complaint before the ECtHR. The ECHR has exerted an influence on the development of UK jurisprudence,[3] an influence substantially increased with the adoption of the Human Rights Act 1998 (UK) (HRA). This is because the HRA incorporates key Convention rights into domestic law and makes it unlawful for a public authority (which includes courts) to act in a way that is incompatible with these rights.[4] The HRA has thus been a powerful impetus for courts to develop the action for breach of confidence in order to protect privacy and, as we shall see, the law of confidence has been adapted to protect against misuse of private information.

---

[2] *Wainwright v United Kingdom* App. No.12350/04 (2007) 44 EHRR 40. The applicants were awarded €3,000 each for non-pecuniary damage.

[3] *Campbell v Mirror Group Newspapers Ltd* [2004] 2 AC 457 (HL), [16] (Lord Nicholls): 'The European Convention on Human Rights and the Strasbourg jurisprudence have undoubtedly had a significant influence in this area of the common law for some years.'

[4] See HRA, s. 6. See also the now increasing influence of EU law by virtue of the EU Charter of Fundamental Rights, Arts 7 and 8.

10.2.2 JUDICIAL DEVELOPMENT OF PRIVACY PROTECTION

The case that clearly signalled the absorption of Articles 8 and 10 into the action for breach of confidence is *Campbell v Mirror Group Newspapers Ltd*.[5] Therefore, we turn to examine the decision of the House of Lords in some detail.

Campbell v Mirror Group Newspapers Ltd [2004] 2 AC 457

The case concerned a series of articles published by *The Mirror* newspaper in February 2001. The articles disclosed that the claimant, Naomi Campbell, had a drug addiction (which she had previously denied) and was receiving therapy with Narcotics Anonymous (NA) and gave details of the meeting she was attending. Two of the articles were accompanied by photographs of Ms Campbell, dressed casually, leaving an NA meeting in Chelsea, London. The first of the articles was sympathetic to Ms Campbell, but the later articles were not, in light of the fact that she had commenced proceedings against *The Mirror*. At first instance Morland J held that Ms Campbell had established entitlement to damages for breach of confidence and breach of duty under the Data Protection Act 1998 and awarded her £2,500 in compensatory damages and £1,000 in aggravated damages, for the racist and hurtful remarks contained in the later articles. This was overturned by the Court of Appeal, but upheld by the House of Lords.

Lord Nicholls:

Breach of confidence: misuse of private information

17. The time has come to recognise that the values enshrined in articles 8 and 10 are now part of the cause of action for breach of confidence. As Lord Woolf CJ has said, the courts have been able to achieve this result by absorbing the rights protected by articles 8 and 10 into this cause of action: *A v B plc* [2003] QB 195, 202, para. 4. Further, it should now be recognised that for this purpose these values are of general application. The values embodied in articles 8 and 10 are as much applicable in disputes between individuals or between an individual and a non-governmental body such as a newspaper as they are in disputes between individuals and a public authority.

...

20. I should take this a little further on one point. Article 8(1) recognises the need to respect private and family life. Article 8(2) recognises there are occasions when intrusion into private and family life may be justified. One of these is where the intrusion is necessary for the protection of the rights and freedoms of others. Article 10(1) recognises the importance of freedom of expression. But article 10(2), like article 8(2), recognises there are occasions when protection of the rights of others may make it necessary for freedom of expression to give way. When both these articles are engaged a difficult question of proportionality may arise. This question is distinct from the initial question of whether the published information engaged article 8 at all by being within the sphere of the complainant's private or family life.

21. Accordingly, in deciding what was the ambit of an individual's 'private life' in particular circumstances courts need to be on guard against using as a touchstone a test which brings

[5] [2004] 2 AC 457.

into account considerations which should more properly be considered at the later stage of proportionality. Essentially the touchstone of private life is whether in respect of the disclosed facts the person in question had a reasonable expectation of privacy.

Lord Hope:

86. The language has changed following the coming into operation of the Human Rights Act 1998 and the incorporation into domestic law of article 8 and article 10 of the Convention. We now talk about the right to respect for private life and the countervailing right to freedom of expression. The jurisprudence of the European Court offers important guidance as to how these competing rights ought to be approached and analysed. I doubt whether the result is that the centre of gravity, as my noble and learned friend, Lord Hoffmann, says, has shifted. It seems to me that the balancing exercise to which that guidance is directed is essentially the same exercise, although it is plainly now more carefully focussed and more penetrating. As Lord Woolf CJ said in *A v B plc* [2003] QB 195, 202, para. 4, new breadth and strength is given to the action for breach of confidence by these articles.

...

92. The underlying question in all cases where it is alleged that there has been a breach of the duty of confidence is whether the information that was disclosed was private and not public. There must be some interest of a private nature that the claimant wishes to protect: *A v B plc* [2003] QB 195, 206, para. 11(vii). In some cases, as the Court of Appeal said in that case, the answer to the question whether the information is public or private will be obvious. Where it is not, the broad test is whether disclosure of the information about the individual ('A') would give substantial offence to A, assuming that A was placed in similar circumstances and was a person of ordinary sensibilities.

...

95. I think that the judge was right to regard the details of Miss Campbell's attendance at Narcotics Anonymous as private information which imported a duty of confidence. He said that information relating to Miss Campbell's therapy for drug addiction giving details that it was by regular attendance at Narcotics Anonymous meetings was easily identifiable as private. With reference to the guidance that the Court of Appeal gave in *A v B plc* [2003] QB 195, 206, para. 11(vii), he said that it was obvious that there existed a private interest in this fact that was worthy of protection. The Court of Appeal, on the other hand, seem to have regarded the receipt of therapy from Narcotics Anonymous as less worthy of protection in comparison with treatment for the condition administered by medical practitioners. I would not make that distinction. Views may differ as to what is the best treatment for an addiction. But it is well known that persons who are addicted to the taking of illegal drugs or to alcohol can benefit from meetings at which they discuss and face up to their addiction. The private nature of these meetings encourages addicts to attend them in the belief that they can do so anonymously. The assurance of privacy is an essential part of the exercise. The therapy is at risk of being damaged if the duty of confidence which the participants owe to each other is breached by making details of the therapy, such as where, when and how often it is being undertaken, public. I would hold that these details are obviously private.

96. If the information is obviously private, the situation will be one where the person to whom it relates can reasonably expect his privacy to be respected. So there is normally no need to go on and ask whether it would be highly offensive for it to be published.

Baroness Hale:

137. It should be emphasised that the 'reasonable expectation of privacy' is a threshold test which brings the balancing exercise into play. It is not the end of the story. Once the information is identified as 'private' in this way, the court must balance the claimant's interest in keeping the information private against the countervailing interest of the recipient in publishing it. Very often, it can be expected that the countervailing rights of the recipient will prevail.

[**Lord Carswell** agreed that the information was private for the reasons given by **Lord Hope** and **Baroness Hale**. Although **Lord Nicholls** was in the minority, his statements of principle were consistent with the majority. Where he differed was in the application of those principles to the facts of the case.]

From the above extracts, we can see that breach of confidence is being used as a vehicle for giving effect to Articles 8 and 10 of the ECHR. As well, there is a shift in analytic approach—from the tests used for trade secrets (discussed in Chapter 9) to the balancing of Article 8 against Article 10. What brings Article 8 into play is not whether the information is confidential but rather whether there is a 'reasonable expectation of privacy'. Several subsequent Court of Appeal decisions[6] and the Supreme Court[7] have adopted the test of 'reasonable expectation of privacy' and explained that this will entail a detailed examination of all the circumstances of the case.[8] The relevant factors include:

…the attributes of the claimant, the nature of the activity in which the claimant was engaged, the place at which it was happening, the nature and purpose of the intrusion, the absence of consent and whether it was known or could be inferred, the effect on the claimant and the circumstances in which and the purpose for which the information came into the hands of the publisher.[9]

What do you envisage are the main consequences of asking whether there is a reasonable expectation of privacy, as opposed to asking whether the information is confidential? In particular, will it matter that the information has been published or that the activities concerned have occurred in a public location? We return to address these questions later.

Turning back to *Campbell*, the House of Lords also held that in the case of private information there is no longer a need to show the existence of a confidential relationship.

---

[6] *Douglas v Hello! (No. 3)* [2006] QB 125, 161 (Lord Phillips MR; delivering the judgment of the court); *McKennitt v Ash* [2008] QB 73, [23] (Buxton LJ) (with whom Latham LJ and Longmore LJ agreed); *Associated Newspapers v HRH Prince of Wales* [2007] 3 WLR 222, 276–7 (Lord Phillips MR; delivering the judgment of the court); *Lord Browne of Madingley v Associated Newspapers Ltd* [2007] 3 WLR 289, 298 (Sir Anthony Clarke MR; delivering the judgment of the court); *Murray v Express Newspapers Plc* [2008] ECDR 12, [35] (Sir Anthony Clarke MR; delivering the judgment of the court); *Weller v Associated Newspapers Ltd* [2015] EWCA Civ 1176, [16]–[17] (Lord Dyson MR) (Tomlinson LJ and Bean LJ in agreement).

[7] *In the matter of an application by JR38 for Judicial Review (Northern Ireland)* [2015] UKSC 42, [2015] HRLR 13, [98] (Lord Toulson) (with whom Lord Hodge agreed).

[8] *Lord Browne of Madingley v Associated Newspapers Ltd* [2007] 3 WLR 289, 301; *Murray v Express Newspapers Plc* [2008] ECDR 12, [36]; *Weller v Associated Newspapers Ltd* [2015] EWCA Civ 1176, [16]–[17] (Lord Dyson MR) (Tomlinson LJ and Bean LJ in agreement); and *In the matter of an application by JR38 for Judicial Review (Northern Ireland)* [2015] UKSC 42, [2015] HRLR 13, [98] (Lord Toulson) (with whom Lord Hodge agreed) and [113] (Lord Clarke) (with whom Lord Hodge agreed).

[9] *Murray v Express Newspapers Plc* [2008] ECDR 12, [36] (Sir Anthony Clarke MR; delivering the judgment of the court).

Campbell v Mirror Group Newspapers Ltd [2004] 2 AC 457

Lord Nicholls:

13. The common law or, more precisely, courts of equity have long afforded protection to the wrongful use of private information by means of the cause of action which became known as breach of confidence. A breach of confidence was restrained as a form of unconscionable conduct, akin to a breach of trust. Today this nomenclature is misleading. The breach of confidence label harks back to the time when the cause of action was based on improper use of information disclosed by one person to another in confidence. To attract protection the information had to be of a confidential nature. But the gist of the cause of action was that information of this character had been disclosed by one person to another in circumstances 'importing an obligation of confidence' even though no contract of non-disclosure existed: see the classic exposition by Megarry J in *Coco v A N Clark (Engineers) Ltd* [1969] RPC 41, 47–48. The confidence referred to in the phrase 'breach of confidence' was the confidence arising out of a confidential relationship.

14. This cause of action has now firmly shaken off the limiting constraint of the need for an initial confidential relationship. In doing so it has changed its nature. In this country this development was recognised clearly in the judgment of Lord Goff of Chieveley in *Attorney-General v Guardian Newspapers Ltd (No 2)* [1990] 1 AC 109, 281. Now the law imposes a 'duty of confidence' whenever a person receives information he knows or ought to know is fairly and reasonably to be regarded as confidential. Even this formulation is awkward. The continuing use of the phrase 'duty of confidence' and the description of the information as 'confidential' is not altogether comfortable. Information about an individual's private life would not, in ordinary usage, be called 'confidential'. The more natural description today is that such information is private. The essence of the tort is better encapsulated now as misuse of private information.

Although Lord Nicholls was in the minority, the House was unanimous on important points of principle. Thus, Lord Hope held that a confidential relationship is not required but that a duty will arise where a person knows or ought to know that there is a reasonable expectation of privacy.[10] Baroness Hale cited with approval comments in *Hosking v Runting*[11] that English courts have 'recognised that no pre-existing relationship is required in order to establish a cause of action'.[12] Her ladyship then engaged in a balancing exercise between Articles 8 and 10 of the ECHR, rather than applying the three-limb test of *Coco v Clark*. According to Baroness Hale, the basis upon which the confidential obligation is imposed is that 'the person publishing the information knows or ought to know that there is a reasonable expectation that the information in question will be kept confidential'.[13] Lord Carswell was in agreement.

Campbell emphasizes that, when it comes to protection of personal information or privacy, the 'traditional' action for breach of confidence (as represented by *Coco v Clark*) has been replaced by an 'extended' action or—to use the words of Lord Nicholls—the tort of misuse of private information.[14] Recently, the Court of Appeal in *Google Inc. v Vidal-Hall* has held that misuse of private information is distinct from breach of confidence and tortious (rather

---

[10] *Campbell v Mirror Group Newspapers Ltd* [2004] 2 AC 457, 480.
[11] [2003] 3 NZLR 385. [12] *Campbell v Mirror Group Newspapers Ltd*, 495. [13] At 495.
[14] 'This shift in approach is also highlighted by *obiter dicta* in the House of Lords' decision in *Douglas v Hello! Ltd* sub nom *OBG v Allan* [2008] 1 AC 1. Lord Hoffmann, at [118], commented: 'English law has adapted the action for breach of confidence to provide a remedy for unauthorized disclosure of personal information.'

than equitable) in nature.[15] According to this tort, courts will enquire whether the information is private, i.e. whether the claimant's Article 8 right is engaged, and then balance that right against the Article 10 right of the defendant. How those rights are balanced is an important exercise, one that involves an intense scrutiny of the respective rights, examining whether they are engaged and whether any interference with them pursues a legitimate aim and is proportionate. *Campbell* once again demonstrates this shift in approach.

Campbell v Mirror Group Newspapers Ltd [2004] 2 AC 457

Lord Hope:

[His Lordship stated that the Court of Appeal wrongly held that details of Ms Campbell's therapy were not confidential and thus had failed to carry out the required balancing exercise between Articles 8 and 10.]

Striking the balance

113. ...Any interference with the public interest in disclosure has to be balanced against the interference with the right of the individual to respect for their private life. The decisions that are then taken are open to review by the court. The tests which the court must apply are the familiar ones. They are whether publication of the material pursues a legitimate aim and whether the benefits that will be achieved by its publication are proportionate to the harm that may be done by the interference with the right to privacy....

The article 10 right

...

115. The first question is whether the objective of the restriction on the article 10 right— the protection of Miss Campbell's right under article 8 to respect for her private life—is sufficiently important to justify limiting the fundamental right to freedom of expression which the press assert on behalf of the public. It follows from my conclusion that the details of Miss Campbell's treatment were private that I would answer this question in the affirmative. The second question is whether the means chosen to limit the article 10 right are rational, fair and not arbitrary and impair the right as minimally as is reasonably possible. It is not enough to assert that it would be reasonable to exclude these details from the article. A close examination of the factual justification for the restriction on the freedom of expression is needed if the fundamental right enshrined in article 10 is to remain practical and effective. The restrictions which the court imposes on the article 10 right must be rational, fair and not arbitrary, and they must impair the right no more than is necessary.

116. In my opinion the factors that need to be weighed are, on the one hand, the duty that was recognised in *Jersild v Denmark* (1994) 19 EHRR 1, para. 31 to impart information

Similarly, Lord Nicholls stated, at [255]: 'As the law has developed breach of confidence, or misuse of confidential information, now covers two distinct causes of action, protecting two different interests: privacy, and secret ("confidential") information.' Although Lord Nicholls dissented on the issue of whether *OK!* could recover damages for breach of commercial confidentiality, his statement of general principle is consistent with the comments of Lord Hoffmann (who delivered the leading majority speech).

[15] [2015] EWCA Civ 311, [43] and [51] (Lord Dyson MR and Sharp LJ) (McFarlane LJ in agreement).

and ideas of public interest which the public has a right to receive, and the need that was recognised in *Fressoz and Roire v France* (1999) 31 EHRR 28, para. 54 for the court to leave it to journalists to decide what material needs to be reproduced to ensure credibility; and, on the other hand, the degree of privacy to which Miss Campbell was entitled under the law of confidence as to the details of her therapy. Account should therefore be taken of the respondents' wish to put forward a story that was credible and to present Miss Campbell in a way that commended her for her efforts to overcome her addiction.

117. But it should also be recognised that the right of the public to receive information about the details of her treatment was of a much lower order than the undoubted right to know that she was misleading the public when she said that she did not take drugs. In *Dudgeon v United Kingdom* (1981) 4 EHRR 149, para. 52 the European court said that the more intimate the aspects of private life which are being interfered with, the more serious must be the reasons for doing so before the interference can be legitimate. *Clayton & Tomlinson, The Law of Human Rights* (2000), para. 15.162, point out that the court has distinguished three kinds of expression: political expression, artistic expression and commercial expression, and that it consistently attaches great importance to political expression and applies rather less rigorous principles to expression which is artistic and commercial. According to the court's well-established case law, freedom of expression constitutes one of the essential foundations of a democratic society and one of the basic conditions for its progress and the self-fulfilment of each individual: *Tammer v Estonia* (2001) 37 EHRR 857, para. 59. But there were no political or democratic values at stake here, nor has any pressing social need been identified: contrast *Goodwin v United Kingdom* (1996) 22 EHRR 123, para. 40.

118. As for the other side of the balance, Keene LJ said in *Douglas v Hello! Ltd* [2001] QB 967, 1012, para. 168, that any consideration of article 8 rights must reflect the fact that there are different degrees of privacy. In the present context the potential for disclosure of the information to cause harm is an important factor to be taken into account in the assessment of the extent of the restriction that was needed to protect Miss Campbell's right to privacy.

The article 8 right

119. Looking at the matter from Miss Campbell's point of view and the protection of her article 8 Convention right, publication of details of the treatment which she was undertaking to cure her addiction—that she was attending Narcotics Anonymous, for how long, how frequently and at what times of day she had been attending this therapy, the nature of it and extent of her commitment to the process and the publication of the covertly taken photographs (the third, fourth and fifth of the five elements contained in the article)—had the potential to cause harm to her, for the reasons which I have already given. So I would attach a good deal of weight to this factor.

120. As for the other side of the balance, a person's right to privacy may be limited by the public's interest in knowing about certain traits of her personality and certain aspects of her private life, as L'Heureux-Dubé and Bastarache JJ in the Supreme Court of Canada recognised in *Aubry v Éditions Vice-Versa Inc* [1998] 1 SCR 591, paras. 57–58. But it is not enough to deprive Miss Campbell of her right to privacy that she is a celebrity and that her private life is newsworthy. A margin of appreciation must, of course, be given to the journalist. Weight must be given to this. But to treat these details merely as background was to undervalue the importance that was to be attached to the need, if Miss Campbell was to be protected, to keep these details private. And it is hard to see that there was any compelling need for the public to know the name of the organisation that she was attending for the therapy, or for the

other details of it to be set out. The presentation of the article indicates that this was not fully appreciated when the decision was taken to publish these details. The decision to publish the photographs suggests that greater weight was being given to the wish to publish a story that would attract interest rather than to the wish to maintain its credibility.

121. Had it not been for the publication of the photographs, and looking to the text only, I would have been inclined to regard the balance between these rights as about even. Such is the effect of the margin of appreciation that must, in a doubtful case, be given to the journalist. In that situation the proper conclusion to draw would have been that it had not been shown that the restriction on the article 10 right for which Miss Campbell argues was justified on grounds of proportionality. But the text cannot be separated from the photographs. The words 'Therapy: Naomi outside meeting' underneath the photograph on the front page and the words 'Hugs: Naomi, dressed in jeans and baseball hat, arrives for a lunchtime group meeting this week' underneath the photograph on p. 13 were designed to link what might otherwise have been anonymous and uninformative pictures with the main text. The reader would undoubtedly make that link, and so too would the reasonable person of ordinary sensibilities. The reasonable person of ordinary sensibilities would also regard publication of the covertly taken photographs, and the fact that they were linked with the text in this way, as adding greatly overall to the intrusion which the article as a whole made into her private life.

[**Baroness Hale** delivered a concurring speech; **Lord Carswell** was in agreement. **Lord Nicholls** and **Lord Hoffmann** delivered dissenting opinions.]

Their lordships were divided on the issue of where the balance lay between Ms Campbell's rights under Article 8 and the rights of *The Mirror* under Article 10. A majority concluded that, while the defendant was justified in disclosing the fact of the claimant's addiction, it was not particularly compelling for the public to receive details of her therapy and such disclosure would cause significant harm to the claimant. Whereas the minority took the view that, given it was acceptable to disclose the claimant's drug addiction, publication of the details of her therapy represented a fairly minor intrusion into her private life and was part of the journalistic latitude in reporting the fact of her addiction.[16] Which of these opposing views do you prefer?

Looking again at the above extract, and the discussion of the public interest defence in Chapter 9, would you say that Lord Hope applied this defence or was the focus entirely on Article 10? In your view, is there any difference between the public interest defence and Article 10?

FURTHER READING

T. Aplin, 'Filling the IP gap: privacy and tabloidism' in M. Richardson and S. Ricketson (eds), *Research Handbook on Intellectual Property in Media and Entertainment* (Cheltenham: Edward Elgar, forthcoming 2016).

N. A. Moreham and M. Warby (eds), *Tugendhat and Christie: The Law of Privacy and the Media* (3rd edn, Oxford: Oxford University Press, 2016).

R. Mulheron, 'A potential framework for privacy? A reply to *Hello!*' (2006) 69 MLR 679.

---

[16] *Campbell v Mirror Group Newspapers Ltd*, 468 (Lord Nicholls), 476–7 (Lord Hoffmann).

G. Phillipson, 'Transforming breach of confidence? Towards a common law right of privacy under the Human Rights Act' (2003) 66 MLR 726.

G. Phillipson, 'The "right" of privacy in England and Strasbourg' in A. Kenyon and M. Richardson (eds), *New Dimensions in Privacy Law* (Cambridge: Cambridge University Press, 2006), pp. 184–228.

G. Phillipson and H. Fenwick, 'Breach of confidence as a privacy remedy in the Human Rights Act era' (2000) 63 MLR 660.

P. Stanley, *The Law of Confidentiality: A Restatement* (Oxford: Hart, 2008), Appendix C: Confidence and Privacy.

As we have seen from the above section, *Campbell* undoubtedly signalled a reconfiguration of the law of confidence insofar as it concerns personal or private information. But in so doing, a variety of complex issues have emerged. We now turn to examine some of the most important of these.

10.2.2.1 When is there a reasonable expectation of privacy?

When activities occur in a public location or extensive publication of private information has already occurred there has been some debate about whether a reasonable expectation of privacy arises. In *Campbell*, Baroness Hale remarked in *obiter*:

154. …We have not so far held that the mere fact of covert photography is sufficient to make the information contained in the photograph confidential. The activity photographed must be private. If this had been, and had been presented as, a picture of Naomi Campbell going about her business in a public street, there could have been no complaint. She makes a substantial part of her living out of being photographed looking stunning in designer clothing. Readers will obviously be interested to see how she looks if and when she pops out to the shops for a bottle of milk. There is nothing essentially private about that information nor can it be expected to damage her private life.

Baroness Hale took the view that going about one's ordinary business (as opposed to visiting an NA meeting) in a public location should not engage Article 8 of the ECHR. Yet, a subsequent ECtHR decision suggested otherwise. *Von Hannover v Germany*[17] was the culmination of a ten-year campaign by Princess Caroline against various German magazine publishers to restrain them from publishing (fairly innocuous) photographs of her going about her daily business. The German courts held that as a 'figure of contemporary society' the applicant had to tolerate photographs of herself in a public place, even where she was not engaged in public duties. The exception to this was if she was in a 'secluded place' out of the public eye. However, the notion of 'secluded place' did not extend to activities such as her leaving her home, going shopping, engaging in sporting activities, or being on holiday. The applicant complained to the ECtHR that the lack of adequate state protection of her private life was an infringement of Article 8 of the ECHR. The Court accepted that Article 8 conferred both negative and positive obligations[18] on states and that the claimant's right had

---

[17] (2005) 40 EHRR 1.

[18] Negative obligations are those which require states to refrain from interfering with an individual's Convention rights. Positive obligations refer to states' obligations to protect the rights of individuals,

been infringed. It pointed out that, although the claimant was a public figure, she did not exercise any public or official functions and her private activities were not relevant to any political or public debate. The publication of the photographs did not have the purpose of contributing to any debate of general interest to society, but was solely to satisfy the curiosity of readers. Further, it held that the public 'does not have a legitimate interest in knowing where the applicant is and how she behaves generally in her private life even if she appears in places that cannot always be described as secluded and despite the fact that she is well known to the public'.[19] The Court also referred to the fact that the photographs were often taken 'in a climate of continual harassment that induces in the persons concerned a very strong sense of intrusion into their private life'.[20]

Does *Von Hannover* suggest an extremely broad scope for Article 8? If so, can this be reconciled with the English courts' test of 'reasonable expectation of privacy' and the comments *obiter* of Baroness Hale in *Campbell* extracted above? The potential tension between *Von Hannover* and English authorities was explored in the context of deciding whether a child of a public figure, who was being pushed in a pram along a public street, had a reasonable expectation of privacy.

Murray v Express Newspapers Plc [2008] EWCA Civ 446, [2008] ECDR 12

The case involved innocuous photographs taken on a public street of a child of famous author J. K. Rowling. The colour photograph, which was taken covertly by a photographer, showed the claimant's face in profile, his clothes, size, hair style and colour, and skin colour. The photograph appeared in the *Sunday Express* magazine (published by the first defendant), alongside an article that included quotations from the claimant's mother on her approach to parenting and family life. The claimant issued proceedings against the defendants (the first defendant was a photographic agency which licensed out the use of photographs) for breach of confidence, infringement of his right to privacy, and misuse of private information. At first instance, Patten J struck out the claim based on breach of confidence or invasion of privacy for two reasons. The first was that according to the law (including *Von Hannover*) there remains an area of innocuous conduct in a public place which does not raise a reasonable expectation of privacy. The second reason was that, even if *Von Hannover* conflicted with *Campbell*, he was bound to follow *Campbell* and the New Zealand decision of *Hosking v Runting*,[21] which was cited with approval in *Campbell*, was on all fours with the facts of the case at hand and which denied a privacy claim. An appeal to the Court of Appeal was allowed. In the course of its decision, the court explored the relationship between *Von Hannover* and *Campbell*.

Sir Anthony Clarke (delivering the judgment of the Court):

47. Neither *Campbell* nor *Von Hannover* is a case about a child. There is no authoritative case in England of a child being targeted as David was here.

...

---

particularly against interference by others. For further discussion see N. A. Moreham and M. Warby (eds), *Tugendhat and Christie: The Law of Privacy and the Media* (3rd edn, Oxford: Oxford University Press, 2016), pp. 85–6.

[19] *Von Hannover v Germany* (2005) 40 EHRR 1, 28.   [20] At 25.   [21] [2004] NZCA 34.

55. We recognise that there may well be circumstances in which there will be no reasonable expectation of privacy, even after *Von Hannover*. However, as we see it, all will (as ever) depend upon the facts of the particular case. The judge suggests that a distinction can be drawn between a child (or an adult) engaged in family and sporting activities and something as simple as a walk down a street or a visit to the grocers to buy the milk. This is on the basis that the first type of activity is clearly part of a person's private recreation time intended to be enjoyed in the company of family and friends and that, on the test deployed in *Von Hannover*, publicity of such activities is intrusive and can adversely affect the exercise of such social activities. We agree with the judge that that is indeed the basis of the ECtHR's approach but we do not agree that it is possible to draw a clear distinction in principle between the two kinds of activity. Thus, an expedition to a café of the kind which occurred here seems to us to be at least arguably part of each member of the family's recreation time intended to be enjoyed by them and such that publicity of it is intrusive and such as adversely to affect such activities in the future.

56. We do not share the predisposition identified by the judge in [66] that routine acts such as a visit to a shop or a ride on a bus should not attract any reasonable expectation of privacy. All depends upon the circumstances. The position of an adult may be very different from that of a child. In this appeal we are concerned only with the question whether David, as a small child, had a reasonable expectation of privacy, not with the question whether his parents would have had such an expectation. Moreover, we are concerned with the context of this case, which was not for example a single photograph taken of David which was for some reason subsequently published.

57. It seems to us that, subject to the facts of the particular case, the law should indeed protect children from intrusive media attention, at any rate to the extent of holding that a child has a reasonable expectation that he or she will not be targeted in order to obtain photographs in a public place for publication which the person who took or procured the taking of the photographs knew would be objected to on behalf of the child. That is the context in which the photographs of David were taken.

58. It is important to note that so to hold does not mean that the child will have, as the judge puts it in [66], a guarantee of privacy. To hold that the child has a reasonable expectation of privacy is only the first step. Then comes the balance which must be struck between the child's rights to respect for his or her private life under Art. 8 and the publisher's rights to freedom of expression under Art. 10. This approach does not seem to us to be inconsistent with that in *Campbell*, which was not considering the case of a child.

59. In these circumstances we do not think that it is necessary for us to analyse the decision in *Von Hannover* in any detail, especially since this is not an appeal brought after the trial of the action but an appeal against an order striking the action out. Suffice it to say that, in our opinion, the view we have expressed is consistent with that in *Von Hannover*, to which, as *McKennitt v Ash* makes clear, it is permissible to have regard…

[The court allowed the appeal. It found that there was an arguable case of reasonable expectation of privacy and therefore the judge had wrongly struck out David's claim.]

Does *Murray* satisfactorily reconcile *Von Hannover* and *Campbell* or does it sidestep the issue by focusing on the fact that the claimant was a child? What view would an English court take, do you think, of a situation where an *adult* is surreptitiously photographed whilst going about their ordinary business in a public location? Should it matter whether that person is a public figure or not? The answers to these questions are likely to be influenced by a subsequent decision of the ECtHR in *Von Hannover v Germany (No. 2)* ('*Von Hannover II*').[22] This second complaint was brought by Princess Caroline and her husband as a result of proceedings that they had initiated, following the first *Von Hannover* ruling, seeking an injunction to prevent further publication of photographs taken of them while on a skiing holiday. The applicants were shown walking in St Moritz and taking a chair lift. They had been on holiday while Prince Rainier of Monaco (Princess Caroline's father) was ill. In finding that there had been no violation of Article 8, the Court reiterated certain general principles concerning the notion of private life.

> 95 The Court reiterates that the concept of private life extends to aspects relating to personal identity, such as a person's name, photo, or physical and moral integrity; the guarantee afforded by art.8 of the Convention is primarily intended to ensure the development, without outside interference, of the personality of each individual in his relations with other human beings. There is thus a zone of interaction of a person with others, even in a public context, which may fall within the scope of private life. Publication of a photo may thus intrude upon a person's private life even where that person is a public figure.
>
> 96 Regarding photos, the Court has stated that a person's image constitutes one of the chief attributes of his or her personality, as it reveals the person's unique characteristics and distinguishes the person from his or her peers. The right to the protection of one's image is thus one of the essential components of personal development. It mainly presupposes the individual's right to control the use of that image, including the right to refuse publication thereof.

Does the above extract mean that an individual has a right to control how their image is used? In thinking about the answer to this question, it is important to remember that a balance must be struck between an individual's Article 8 right and a publisher's Article 10 right, so that it will not necessarily be the case that where Article 8 is engaged it is also violated. For example, in *Von Hannover II* the ECtHR dismissed the applicants' complaint because it found that the German Federal Supreme Court had explicitly applied a new approach post-*Von Hannover* and in balancing Articles 8 and 10 had 'attached fundamental importance to the question whether the photos, considered in the light of the accompanying articles, had contributed to a debate of general interest'.[23] The 'debate of general interest' related to Prince Rainier's illness and how his children 'reconciled their obligations of family solidarity with the legitimate needs of their private life, among which was the desire to go on holiday'.[24]

The *Murray* decision also highlights that the reasonable expectation of privacy of children may be evaluated differently to adults. In *Weller v Associated Newspapers Ltd*, the Court of Appeal upheld the first instance decision that publication of photographs of Paul Weller's children (aged 10 months and 16 at the time) taken during a 'family day out' was a misuse of private information. In considering whether the claimants had a reasonable expectation of privacy in relation to the unpixelated images of their faces that were published, the court reiterated that, while the same broad approach must be adopted for adults and children, there are considerations pertinent to children 'which may mean that in a particular case a

---

[22] *Von Hannover v Germany (No. 2)* App. Nos 40660/08 and 60641/08 (2012) 55 EHRR 15.
[23] *Von Hannover II*, [124].
[24] [117]. Note that the German Federal Supreme Court also found that some of the photos and articles accompanying them were not related to an event of contemporary society and did not contribute to a debate of general interest and thus could be restrained from further publication.

child has a reasonable expectation of privacy where an adult does not'.[25] Thus, for very young children who are not sensitive to intrusions to their privacy or able to exercise autonomy, it is appropriate for the court to consider how those responsible for the child's welfare and upbringing have treated the child's privacy.[26] Further, in relation to young children it is usually the parents who exercise decision-making about the nature of the activity and its location. Thus, a 'child's reasonable expectation of privacy must be seen in the light of the way in which his family life is conducted'.[27] The parents' lack of consent to their children being photographed is relevant and, in terms of the impact on the claimant, this cannot be limited to whether the child is aware of the intrusion and greater security concerns may exist in relation to children than in the case of adults.[28] The court concluded that the claimants did have a reasonable expectation of privacy. Although the photographs were taken in a public location, it was a private family outing and no consent had been given to being photographed. The critical factor, however, was that there were children, identified by surname, who had not courted publicity and nor had their parents (who were in the public arena) done so. There was also evidence of a negative impact on the teenage child.[29] When it came to the balancing exercise, the court observed that while a child's right 'is not a trump card in the balancing exercise, the primacy of the best interests of a child means that, where a child's interests would be adversely affected, they must be given considerable weight. It might require very powerful article 10 rights ... to outweigh a child's article 8 rights where publication would be harmful to the child'.[30] The court concluded that the Article 8 interests of the claimants outweighed the Article 10 interests of the defendants since the publication did not contribute to a debate of general interest, the children did not have public profiles nor did they court publicity, and there had been embarrassment on the part of the teenage child.[31]

The Supreme Court *In the matter of an application by JR38 for Judicial Review (Northern Ireland)*[32] has reiterated that while the same test of reasonable expectation of privacy is applicable between adults and children, the status of the claimant as a child is relevant to the way the reasonable expectation of privacy test is to be applied.[33] The court had to determine whether publication in a newspaper of a photograph of a 14-year-old involved in public disorder in Londonderry for the purpose of assisting police in their campaign to reduce sectarian violence, amounted to an infringement of his Article 8 right. The court held that the claimant did not have a reasonable expectation of privacy because of the criminal nature of the activities he was involved in while being photographed and because the purpose of the publication was to identify the claimant.[34] However, Lord Toulson noted that 'the publication of the same photograph for another purpose' might invoke Article 8.[35] Thus, the decision illustrates the fact-sensitive nature of the assessment and that there is no blanket right to privacy for children.

---

[25] *Weller v Associated Newspapers Ltd* [2015] EWCA Civ 1176, [29] (Lord Dyson MR) (Tomlinson LJ and Bean LJ in agreement).

[26] [31] (Lord Dyson MR) (Tomlinson LJ and Bean LJ in agreement).

[27] [33] (Lord Dyson MR) (Tomlinson LJ and Bean LJ in agreement).

[28] [35]–[37] (Lord Dyson MR) (Tomlinson LJ and Bean LJ in agreement).

[29] [59]–[66] (Lord Dyson MR) (Tomlinson LJ and Bean LJ in agreement).

[30] [40] (Lord Dyson MR) (Tomlinson LJ and Bean LJ in agreement).

[31] [72]–[80] (Lord Dyson MR) (Tomlinson LJ and Bean LJ in agreement).   [32] [2015] UKSC 42.

[33] [95] (Lord Toulson) and [113] (Lord Clarke) (Lord Hodge in agreement with both judges).

[34] [98] (Lord Toulson) and [112] (Lord Clarke) (Lord Hodge in agreement with both judges).

[35] [98] (Lord Toulson). See also [112] (Lord Clarke) (Lord Hodge in agreement with both judges).

10.2.2.2 The position of public figures

Many of the English cases alleging misuse of private information have involved high-profile figures, including royalty,[36] footballers,[37] supermodels,[38] movie stars,[39] businessmen,[40] and entertainers.[41] Should it matter if the claimant bringing an action is a public figure or otherwise in the public eye? Does it, or should it, change the level of protection that they receive? The initial trend following the HRA coming into effect was to interpret the 'public interest' defence that exists in breach of confidence very broadly, such that public figures had to expect and accept closer media scrutiny, even in relation to trivial facts. For example, in *A v B plc*,[42] the claimant, simply by virtue of being a professional footballer, was held to be a role model whose off-field behaviour (of having an extra marital affair with a pole dancer) was deemed to be of 'public interest'. In more recent cases, however, the courts have retreated from this approach. As well, while courts have not precisely clarified the relationship between the public interest defence and Article 10 of the ECHR, it appears that 'public interest' is being subsumed within Article 10 considerations. Both of these points are illustrated by the Court of Appeal decision in *McKennitt v Ash*.

McKennitt v Ash [2006] EWCA Civ 1714, [2008] QB 73

In this case, the first defendant (Ash), who had been a close friend and associate of the claimant (McKennitt), a famous folk musician, published a book in which various personal revelations relating to the claimant were disclosed. The claimant brought proceedings based upon breaches of privacy and/or obligations of confidence, seeking a declaration, injunction, and damages. At first instance, Eady J held that the claimant had a reasonable expectation of privacy, such as to engage Article 8 of the ECHR, and this was not outweighed by the Article 10 rights of the first defendant. He granted a declaration and an injunction to restrict further publication of the infringing passages of the book, along with £5,000 damages for hurt feelings and distress. On appeal, Eady J's decision was upheld.

Buxton LJ (with whom Lathan LJ and Longmore LJ agreed):

The public interest: and the first claimant as a public figure

56. One might instinctively think that there was little legitimate public interest in the matters addressed by the book, and certainly no public interest sufficient to outweigh the first

---

[36] *Associated Newspapers v HRH Prince of Wales* [2006] EWCA Civ 1776, [2007] 3 WLR 222 (Prince Charles).

[37] *A v B plc* [2002] EWCA Civ 337, [2003] QB 195 (Gary Flitcroft); *Terry v Persons Unknown* [2010] EWHC 119 (QB), [2010] EMLR 16 (John Terry); *Ferdinand v Mirror Group Newspapers Ltd* [2011] EWHC 2455 (QB) (Rio Ferdinand).

[38] *Campbell v Mirror Group Newspapers Ltd* [2004] 1 AC 457 (HL) (Naomi Campbell).

[39] *Douglas v Hello! Ltd (No. 1)* [2001] QB 967; *Douglas v Hello! Ltd (No. 6)* [2003] EMLR 31 (Ch); *Douglas v Hello! (No. 8)* [2004] EMLR 2 (Ch); *Douglas v Hello! (No. 3)* [2006] QB 125; *Douglas v Hello! Ltd* sub nom *OBG v Allan* [2007] UKHL 21, [2008] 1 AC 1 (Michael Douglas and Catherine Zeta-Jones).

[40] *Lord Browne of Madingley v Associated Newspapers Ltd* [2008] QB 103 (CA) (Lord Browne); *Mosley v News Group Newspapers* [2008] EMLR 20 (Max Mosley); *Hutcheson (formerly KGM) v News Group Newspapers Ltd* [2011] EWCA Civ 808 (Chris Hutcheson).

[41] *McKennitt v Ash* [2008] QB 73 (CA) (Loreena McKennitt); *Ntuli v Donald* [2010] EWCA Civ 1276 (Howard Donald); and *PJS v News Group Newspapers Ltd* [2016] UKSC 26.

[42] [2003] QB 195.

claimant's article 8 right to private life. That is what the judge thought and, as already pointed out, in the absence of error of principle his view will prevail. That conclusion was contested under this head in two respects, which it is necessary to keep separate. First, there was a legitimate public interest in the affairs of the first claimant because she was a public figure, *and for that reason alone.* Second, if a public figure had misbehaved, the allegation in the present case being of hypocrisy, the public had a right to have the record put straight. The parallel for that argument was the case of Ms Campbell, who could not retain privacy for the fact that she was a drug addict because she had lied publicly about her condition.

57. The first of these arguments involves consideration of two recent authorities, already introduced, *Von Hannover v Germany* (2005) 40 EHRR 1 and *A v B plc* [2003] QB 195, to which I must now return.

Von Hannover v Germany

58. There is no doubt that the European Court of Human Rights has restated what were previously thought to be the rights and expectations of public figures with regard to their private lives. The court recognised the important role of the press in dealing with matters of public interest, and the latitude in terms of mode of expression there provided: 40 EHRR 1, para. 58. But a distinction was then drawn between a watchdog role in the democratic process and the reporting of private information about people who, although of interest to the public, were not public figures. The European Court of Human Rights said, at paras. 63–64:

> 63. The court considers that a fundamental distinction needs to be made between reporting facts—even controversial ones—capable of contributing to a debate in a democratic society relating to politicians in the exercise of their functions, for example, and reporting details of the private life of an individual who, moreover, as in this case, does not exercise official functions. While in the former case the press exercises its vital role of 'watchdog' in a democracy by contributing to 'impart[ing] information and ideas on matters of public interest' it does not do so in the latter case.
>
> 64. Similarly, although the public has a right to be informed, which is an essential right in a democratic society that, in certain special circumstances, can even extend to aspects of the private life of public figures, particularly where politicians are concerned, this is not the case here. The situation here does not come within the sphere of any political or public debate because the published photos and accompanying commentaries relate exclusively to details of the applicant's private life.

59. There is more in the same sense. If we follow in this case the guidance given by the English courts, that the content of the law of confidence is now to be found in articles 8 and 10 (see para. 10 above), then it seems inevitable that the first defendant's case must fail. Even assuming that the first claimant is a public figure in the relevant sense (which proposition I suspect the European Court of Human Rights would find surprising), there are no 'special circumstances' apart from the allegation of hypocrisy dealt with in the next section to justify or require the exposure of her private life. But the first defendant argued that English courts could not follow or apply *Von Hannover's* case to the facts of the present case because we were bound by the contrary English authority of *A v B plc* [2003] QB 195. That effectively required the first claimant's private affairs to be exposed to the world, hypocrite or not.

A v B plc

60. The facts have already been set out. The judgment of this court is notable for the detailed guidance that it contains as to how a court should address complaints about invasion

of privacy by public or allegedly public figures. The first defendant placed particular reliance on the court's para. 11(xii):

> Where an individual is a public figure he is entitled to have his privacy respected in the appropriate circumstances. A public figure is entitled to a private life. The individual, however, should recognise that because of his public position he must expect and accept that his actions will be more closely scrutinised by the media. Even trivial facts relating to a public figure can be of great interest to readers and other observers of the media. Conduct which in the case of a private individual would not be the appropriate subject of comment can be the proper subject of comment in the case of a public figure. The public figure may hold a position where higher standards of conduct can be rightly expected by the public. The public figure may be a role model whose conduct could well be emulated by others. He may set the fashion. The higher the profile of the individual concerned the more likely that this will be the position. Whether you have courted publicity or not you may be a legitimate subject of public attention. If you have courted public attention then you have less ground to object to the intrusion which follows. In many of these situations it would be overstating the position to say that there is a public interest in the information being published. It would be more accurate to say that the public have an understandable and so a legitimate interest in being told the information. If this is the situation then it can be appropriately taken into account by a court when deciding on which side of the line a case falls. The courts must not ignore the fact that if newspapers do not publish information which the public are interested in, there will be fewer newspapers published, which will not be in the public interest. The same is true in relation to other parts of the media.

61. The first defendant relied on two parts of this account. First, that 'role models', voluntary or not, have less expectation of privacy. That was reinforced by a later passage in the judgment, at para. 43(vi): 'Footballers are role models for young people and undesirable behaviour on their part can set an unfortunate example. While [the trial judge] was right to say on the evidence which was before him that A had not courted publicity, the fact is that someone holding his position was inevitably a figure in whom a section of the public and the media would be interested.' The first claimant, it was said, was inevitably a figure in whom a section of the public would be, and was, interested. Second, the general interest in supporting the 'media' in the publication of the sort of material that sells newspapers should extend to biographies and literary works generally, such as the book was claimed to be.

62. The width of the rights given to the media by *A v B plc* cannot be reconciled with *Von Hannover's* case. Mr Price said that whether that was right or wrong, we had to apply *A v B plc*, in the light of the rule of precedent laid down by the House of Lords in *Kay v Lambeth London Borough Council* [2006] 2 AC 465, in particular by Lord Bingham of Cornhill, at paras. 43–45. Put shortly, the precedential rules of English domestic law apply to interpretations of Convention jurisprudence. Where, for instance, the Court of Appeal has ruled on the meaning or reach of a particular article of the Convention, a later division of the Court of Appeal cannot depart from that ruling simply on the basis that it is inconsistent with a later, or for that matter an earlier, decision of the European Court of Human Rights.

63. I would respectfully and fully agree with the importance of that rule. The alternative, as an earlier constitution of this court said, is chaos. But I do not think that the rule inhibits us in this case from applying *Von Hannover's* case. If the court in *A v B plc* had indeed ruled definitively on the content and application of article 10 then the position would be different; but that is what the court did not do. Having made the important observation that the content of the domestic law was now to be found in the balance between articles 8 and 10, the court then addressed the balancing exercise effectively in the former English domestic terms of breach of confidence. No Convention authority of any sort was even mentioned...

64. ...[I]t seems clear that *A v B plc* cannot be read as any sort of binding authority on the content of articles 8 and 10. To find that content, therefore, we do have to look to *Von Hannover's* case. The terms of that judgment are very far away from the automatic limits placed on the privacy rights of public figures by *A v B plc*.

65. But, in any event, even if we were to follow *A v B plc*, the guidance that that case gives does not produce the outcome in our case that is sought by the first defendant. First, as to the position of the first claimant, she clearly does not fall within the first category mentioned by Lord Woolf CJ, and 'hold a position where higher standards of conduct can be rightly expected by the public': that is no doubt the preserve of headmasters and clergymen, who according to taste may be joined by politicians, senior civil servants, surgeons and journalists. Second, although on one view the first claimant comes within Lord Woolf CJ's second class, of involuntary role models, I respectfully share the doubts of Lord Phillips MR, set out in para. 63 above, as to the validity of that concept; and it would in any event seem difficult to include in the class a person such as the first claimant, who has made such efforts not to hold herself out as someone whose life is an open book. Third, it is clear that Lord Woolf CJ thought that role models were at risk, or most at risk, of having to put up with the reporting of *disreputable* conduct: such as was the conduct of the claimant before him. The first claimant does not fall into that category; but to make that good I need to go on to the second part of this argument, that exposure is legitimate to demonstrate improper conduct or dishonesty.

66. In so doing I have not overlooked Lord Woolf CJ's second general point, that weight must be given to the commercial interest of newspapers in reporting matter that interests the public. That view has also received criticism, and it seems clear that this court in *Campbell's* case, in the passage cited above, was not entirely happy with it. It is difficult to reconcile with the long-standing view that what interests the public is not necessarily in the public interest, a view most recently expressed by Baroness Hale in *Jameel (Mohammed) v Wall Street Journal Europe Sprl* [2007] 1 AC 359, para. 147:

> The public only have a right to be told if two conditions are fulfilled. First, there must be a real public interest in communicating and receiving the information. This is, as we all know, very different from saying that it is information which interests the public—the most vapid tittle-tattle about the activities of footballers' wives and girlfriends interests large sections of the public but no one could claim any real public interest in our being told all about it.

It is fortunately not necessary to pursue that issue further, because it is merely a general factor that cannot be said to have any significant impact on the present case.

In *McKennitt v Ash*, the Court of Appeal considered at length both *Von Hannover* and *A v B plc*. In what ways do these decisions differ when it comes to assessing the legitimate scrutiny of public figures and how did the court in *McKennitt v Ash* reconcile the tension between them? Which approach do you think is preferable?

In subsequent decisions, courts have been sensitive to whether private information that is published about a public figure contributes to a debate of general interest (as the Strasbourg Court has emphasized)[43] or is simply about satisfying public curiosity.[44] Further, in considering whether there is a public interest in correcting a false image or false information that a public figure has put into the public sphere, courts have emphasized that it is important that an individual has 'set out to present a false

---

[43] See *Von Hannover v Germany* [2005] 40 EHRR 1, [76] and *Springer AG v Germany* [2012] 55 EHRR 6, [90].
[44] *Weller*, [74]–[75]; *Donald v Ntuli* [2010] EWCA Civ 1276, [2011] 1 WLR 294, [19]–[24].

picture'.[45] Thus, it was held that disclosure of extramarital affairs was unjustified because the claimants had presented a public image of a committed relationship (as opposed to a monogamous one).[46] By way of contrast, in assessing the balancing exercise between the Article 8 rights of the claimant and the Article 10 rights of the defendant, the court found that it was in the public interest to publish information about the claimant (who was a child conceived from an extramarital affair) because the father of the child was a well-known politician, who had had previous infidelities, one of which had also resulted in the conception of a child. Therefore, the information about the claimant went to the politician's recklessness and suitability for public office.[47] Also relevant was the fact that the claimant's Article 8 right was accorded less weight because her mother had spoken about the claimant's paternity to the managing director of a major magazine group and had approved a published interview in which speculation about the claimant's paternity was raised.[48]

FURTHER READING

G. Phillipson, 'Judicial reasoning in breach of confidence cases under the Human Rights Act: not taking privacy seriously' [2003] EHRLR 53.

10.2.2.3 The person entitled to bring an action

The person entitled to bring a claim for misuse of private information is the person whose private life is implicated by the disclosure. But it may be that more than one person is implicated by a publication of private information. For example, in the case of adulterous relationships, one can point to Article 8 interests of the adulterer, the lover, and the family of the adulterer, as was the case in *ETK v News Group Newspapers Ltd*.[49] The applicant sought an *ex parte* injunction to restrain the publishers of a tabloid newspaper from disclosing information about an adulterous relationship. Collins J dismissed the application, but on appeal the court found that the judge had erred and granted an injunction. In the Court of Appeal, Ward LJ observed that 'weight must be given not only to the right to respect for the private and family life of the appellant himself, but also to the rights of X [the woman with whom he had had an affair] and, in addition, the rights of the appellant's wife and his children'.[50] The court held that the judge had erred in failing to take into account these other Article 8 interests. X had made clear that she supported the application for an injunction, as did the wife. Also important were the Article 8 interests of the children and the adverse effect that publicity would have on them.[51] There must, however, be evidence of genuine interests.[52]

---

[45] *PJS v News Group Newspapers Ltd* [2016] EWCA Civ 100, [38] (Jackson LJ) (King LJ in agreement).

[46] *PJS v News Group Newspapers Ltd* [2016] EWCA Civ 100, [51]–[53] (Jackson LJ) (King LJ in agreement).

[47] *AAA v Associated Newspapers Ltd* [2013] EWCA Civ 554, [41]–[45] (Lord Dyson MR) (Tomlinson LJ and Ryder LJ in agreement).

[48] *AAA v Associated Newspapers Ltd* [2013] EWCA Civ 554, [25] and [34] (Tomlinson LJ and Ryder LJ in agreement).

[49] [2011] EWCA Civ 439.   [50] [14].

[51] For a similar approach, see *PJS v News Group Newspapers Ltd* [2016] EWCA Civ 100 and [2016] UKSC 26.

[52] See *Ntuli v Donald* [2010] EWCA Civ 1276, [23] (Maurice Kay LJ) where the defendant's reliance on Art. 8 was seen as 'an ex post facto dignification which does not live easily with the evidence of [why she wanted to sell her story to the media]'.

Another issue that arises is whether, once a person has died, the deceased's estate can enforce that obligation of confidence or Article 8 rights. The little authority that exists suggests that a deceased person would still be owed confidentiality obligations or have Article 8 rights.[53] But once a person has died are their dignitary and autonomy interests affected? Or is it their reputation? If the latter, it should be noted that a claim for defamation (which protects reputation) cannot be brought by the deceased's estate. So why should misuse of private information be any different? That said, it could be argued that others closely linked to the deceased (e.g. the spouse of a public figure who died of AIDS) have independent Article 8 interests in preventing disclosure of information about the deceased. In other words, their claim would be based on their *own* privacy interests and not those of the deceased.

FURTHER READING

T. Aplin, L. Bently, P. Johnson, and S Malynicz, *Gurry on Breach of Confidence: The Protection of Confidential Information* (2nd edn, Oxford: Oxford University Press, 2012), ch. 8.

10.2.2.4 The future of privacy protection

We have seen how, following *Campbell*, 'English law has adapted the action for breach of confidence to provide a remedy for unauthorized disclosure of personal information'.[54] But to what extent is it desirable to maintain this form of privacy protection under the umbrella of confidentiality? Some commentators have argued that judicial expansion of breach of confidence to accommodate privacy interests distorts the principles underlying that action.[55] Judicial disquiet along similar lines has also emerged. For example, the Court of Appeal in *Douglas v Hello!* observed:

> We cannot pretend that we find it satisfactory to be required to shoe-horn within the cause of action of breach of confidence claims for publication of unauthorised photographs of a private occasion.[56]

So, would there be advantages to decoupling privacy and breach of confidence completely? In the New Zealand decision of *Hosking v Runting*[57] a majority of the Court of Appeal recognized a tort of interference with privacy, rather than developing the action

---

[53] *Bluck v The Information Commissioner* EA/2006/0090 (17 September 2009) (Information Tribunal); *Lewis v Secretary of State for Health* [2008] EWHC 2196 (QB); and *Editions Plon v France* App. No. 58148/00 (2006) 42 EHRR 36.

[54] *OBG Ltd v Allan* [2007] UKHL 21, [118] (Lord Hoffmann). Baroness Hale and Lord Brown were in agreement with Lord Hoffmann on the breach of confidence issue.

[55] See J. Caldwell, 'Protecting privacy post *Lenah*: should the courts establish a new tort or develop breach of confidence?' (2003) 26 UNSW L. J. 90, 121–2; B. Markesinis et al., 'Concerns and ideas about the developing English law of privacy (and how knowledge of foreign law might be of help)' (2004) 52 American J. of Comparative L. 133, 137; J. Morgan, 'Privacy in the House of Lords, again' (2004) 120 LQR 563; J. Morgan, '*Hello!* again: privacy and breach of confidence' [2005] CLJ 549; R. Mulheron, 'A potential framework for privacy? A reply to *Hello!*' (2006) 69 MLR 679, 686–9; A. Schreiber, 'Confidence crisis, privacy phobia: why invasion of privacy should be independently recognized in English law' [2006] IPQ 161, 170–6; R. Singh and J. Strachan, 'The right to privacy in English law' [2002] EHRLR 129; R. Singh and J. Strachan, 'Privacy postponed' [2003] EHRLR 11, 15.

[56] *Douglas v Hello! (No. 3)*, 150.   [57] *Hosking v Runting* [2005] 1 NZLR 1.

for breach of confidence. In reaching this conclusion, Tipping J (in the majority) made the following comments:

> ... [I]t is more jurisprudentially straightforward and easier of logical analysis to recognise that confidence and privacy, while capable of overlapping, are essentially different concepts. Breach of confidence, being an equitable concept, is conscience-based. Invasion of privacy is a common law wrong which is founded on the harm done to the plaintiff by conduct which can reasonably be regarded as offensive to human values. While it may be possible to achieve the same substantive result by developing the equitable cause of action, *I consider it legally preferable and better for society's understanding of what the Courts are doing to achieve the appropriate substantive outcome under a self-contained and stand-alone common law cause of action to be known as invasion of privacy.*[58]

In Tipping J's view, recognition of a separate tort allows for a better-tailored law, and there is inherent value in the courts explicitly protecting privacy. Do you agree? In considering your views, it is worth remembering that judicial development of breach of confidence to protect privacy has stopped short of protecting against the type of intrusion that was suffered in *Wainwright*. Instead, the action targets the unauthorized *disclosure* or *publication* of private information. Although courts have sometimes expressed sympathy with protecting against certain kinds of 'intrusion',[59] the action for misuse of private information does not prohibit instances of intrusion per se, such as accessing data through phone or computer hacking, secretly photographing a person, or using other forms of surveillance.[60] If the New Zealand experience is anything to go by, decoupling privacy from breach of confidence permits further development and expansion of protection. In *C v Holland*,[61] the New Zealand High Court recognized a tort of intrusion of privacy on the basis that it was entirely compatible with and a logical adjunct to the *Hosking v Runting* tort of wrongful publication of private facts.[62] This new, related tort comprised the following aspects: intentional and unauthorized intrusion; into seclusion (namely intimate personal activity, space, or affairs); involving infringement of a reasonable expectation of privacy that is highly offensive to a reasonable person.[63]

The Court of Appeal decision in *Google Inc. v Vidal-Hall*[64] found that misuse of private information was tortious in nature for the purposes of service of proceedings out of the jurisdiction. The court held that recognition of misuse of private information as a tort rather than as an equitable wrong 'does not create a new cause of action ... it simply gives the correct legal label to one that already exists'.[65] Further, the court observed that, 'there may be broader implications from our conclusions, for example as to remedies, limitation and vicarious liability'.[66] Now that misuse of private information has been untethered from breach of confidence, this may create the potential for later courts to further develop the action in ways that we have seen in jurisdictions such as New Zealand. Alternatively, it may be worth considering whether Parliament should intervene to put protection of privacy on

---

[58] [59] (Tipping J); emphasis supplied.

[59] See T. Aplin, L. Bently, P. Johnson, and S. Malynicz, *Gurry on Breach of Confidence: The Protection of Confidential Information* (2nd edn, Oxford: Oxford University Press, 2012), pp. 274–86, 671, and 680. See especially *Tchenguiz v Imerman* [2010] EWCA Civ 908, [2010] 2 FLR 814, [68] where the Court of Appeal suggested that 'that intentionally obtaining [private] information, secretly and knowing that the claimant reasonably expects it to be private, is itself a breach of confidence'.

[60] See *Tugendhat and Christie*, ch. 10 'Intrusion'.   [61] [2012] NZHC 2155.   [62] [75], [86].

[63] [94].   [64] [2015] EWCA Civ 311.   [65] [43].   [66] [51].

a statutory footing and in doing so extend protection to intrusions into seclusion as well as misuse of private information. Interestingly, this was the recommendation of the Australian Law Reform Commission in its 2014 Report, *Serious Invasions of Privacy in the Digital Era*.[67]

The phone hacking scandal that occurred in Britain should serve as a reminder that, despite judicial developments, privacy protection is still very much a controversial and unresolved issue. Aside from the demise of tabloid newspaper *News of the World*, the scandal prompted the government to establish the Leveson Inquiry (conducted by Lord Justice Leveson) in July 2011.[68] This was the seventh time within 70 years that the government had commissioned investigations into the press.[69] The remit of the Leveson Inquiry was to scrutinize the culture, practices, and ethics of the media and to make recommendations on the future of press regulation. Hundreds of witnesses, including celebrities, public figures, and persons thrust into the public sphere by reason of tragedy, testified before the Inquiry or provided statements. Their repeated refrain was the degree of harassment and intrusion experienced at the hands of the British media. On the other hand, and perhaps unsurprisingly, media representatives argued that an uninhibited and self-regulated press is crucial to the public interest and represents the very embodiment of free expression. The Leveson Report was issued in November 2012. While it recognized that for the most part the British press was to be lauded for its good work in the public interest, there was nevertheless evidence of some serious failings including the prevalence of phone hacking; a willingness to resort to covert methods of surveillance and also harassment; the widespread publication of matters concerning those in the public eye that was not in the public interest; a reckless disregard for accuracy; a failure to take ethical breaches by journalists seriously; and a cultural tendency to reject or resist complaints about their practices. In light of the 'toothless' and ineffective nature of the Press Complaints Commission, the Leveson Report recommended that legislation be introduced to establish a wholly independent self-regulatory body for the press (that features expertise but which also reflects the interests of the wider public), which would develop and enforce codes of conduct with the power to hear complaints and to issue appropriate remedies, including publication of corrections and apologies and financial sanctions. The Report also suggested that the independent body provide an arbitration process whereby civil claims against the press can be brought, which will encourage fair, quick, and inexpensive resolution of disputes. There was much political wrangling on how best to implement the Leveson recommendations. Eventually, however, a cross-party compromise was achieved in the form of a Royal Charter introduced by the Privy Council on 30 October 2013. The Charter creates a Press Recognition Panel, which is an independent body corporate established to approve self-regulatory bodies created by the press and to review and report on these regulatory bodies. The Press Recognition Panel[70] came into existence on 3 November 2014 and was able to receive applications for recognition of regulators from September 2015. The Panel has received one application so far and, in October 2016, approved its first press regulator, IMPRESS,[71] an independent self-regulator that has several small, independent publishers as members. This may be contrasted with the Independent Press Standards Organisation (IPSO),[72] which was established in September 2014 by a majority of the press that opposed the Royal Charter (and following the wind

---

[67] <www.alrc.gov.au/news-media/alrc-releases-report-serious-invasions-privacy-digital-era>.

[68] See <http://webarchive.nationalarchives.gov.uk/20140122145147/http:/www.levesoninquiry.org.uk/>.

[69] See the Royal Commissions in 1947, 1962, and 1973, the Younger Commission on Privacy and two Calcutt Reviews.

[70] <http://pressrecognitionpanel.org.uk/>.   [71] <http://impress.press/>.

[72] <www.ipso.co.uk/IPSO/index.html>.

up of the Press Complaints Commission) and which has not applied for approval from the Press Recognition Panel. As such, the regulation of the UK press arguably remains in an unsatisfactory state.

Judicial development of privacy protection and press regulation still risks being thwarted by the ubiquitous and difficult to control nature of the internet. Where embarrassing information has been widely disseminated in multiple countries via the internet, does it make sense to say that a reasonable expectation of privacy exists or to grant injunctions to prevent further dissemination in England and Wales? In *Mosley v News Group Newspapers Ltd*,[73] footage of the claimant's activities at a sadomasochistic sex party were available on the defendant's website and viewed 1.5 million times. This led to refusal of an interim injunction (because the judge thought it would be futile to grant this relief); however, at trial Eady J held that the claimant's Article 8 right had been violated and was not outweighed by any public interest. Damages of £60,000 were awarded to the claimant.[74] Most recently, in *PJS v News Group Newspapers Ltd*[75] an interim injunction to restrain publication of details of an extramarital affair of a well-known entertainer was upheld by the Supreme Court, even though details had been published in magazines in the US, Canada, and Scotland and on various websites. The Supreme Court overturned the Court of Appeal's decision to discharge the injunction, in part because the court 'did not give due weight to the qualitative difference in intrusiveness and distress likely to be involved in what is now proposed by way of unrestricted publication by the English media'.[76] This latest decision signals that internet leaks may not necessarily destroy the ability of a claimant to obtain an injunction because further and wider publication may aggravate the privacy intrusion that has already occurred.

FURTHER READING

T. Aplin, 'The future of breach of confidence and the protection of privacy' (2007) 7 OUCLJ 137.

T. Aplin, L. Bently, P. Johnson, and S. Malynicz, *Gurry on Breach of Confidence: The Protection of Confidential Information* (2nd edn, Oxford: Oxford University Press, 2012), pp. 274–86.

Australian Law Reform Commission, *Serious Invasions of Privacy in the Digital Era*, Report 123 (2014), <www.alrc.gov.au/publications/serious-invasions-privacy-digital-era-alrc-report-123>.

R. Bagshaw, 'Obstacles on the path to privacy torts' in P. Birks (ed.), *Privacy and Loyalty* (Oxford: Clarendon, 1997), pp. 1–28.

P. Jaffey, 'Privacy, confidentiality, and property' in P. Torremans (ed.), *Copyright and Human Rights* (The Hague: Kluwer Law International, 2004), pp. 447–73.

Leveson Inquiry, <http://webarchive.nationalarchives.gov.uk/20140122145147/http://www.levesoninquiry.org.uk/>.

---

[73] [2008] EWHC 1777 (QB), [2008] EMLR 20.
[74] Note that Mr Mosley later brought a complaint before the ECtHR where he unsuccessfully argued that there was a right for individuals to be notified by media organizations before any publication of private information: see *Mosley v United Kingdom* App. No. 48009/08 (2011) 53 EHRR 30, [2012] EMLR 1.
[75] [2016] UKSC 26.   [76] [35] (Lord Mance; delivering the leading judgment of the majority).

R. Mulheron, 'A potential framework for privacy? A reply to *Hello!*' (2006) 69 MLR 679.

M. Warby, N. Moreham, and I. Christie (eds), *Tugendhat and Christie: The Law of Privacy and the Media* (2nd edn, Oxford: Oxford University Press, 2011), ch. 10.

10.3 PERSONALITY PROTECTION

10.3.1 THE DEFINITION OF CHARACTER AND PERSONALITY MERCHANDISING

According to the World Intellectual Property Organization (WIPO), character merchandising may be defined as 'the use of the essential personality features (name, image, etc.) of fictional characters in the marketing and/or advertising of goods or services'. Personality merchandising, by contrast, according to WIPO:[77]

> involves the use of the essential attributes (name, image, voice and other personality features) of real persons (in other words, the true identity of an individual) in the marketing and/or advertising of goods and services. In general, the real person whose attributes are 'commercialised' is well known to the public at large; this is the reason why this form of merchandising has sometimes been referred to as 'reputation merchandising'. In fact, from a commercial point of view, merchandisers believe that the main reason for a person to buy low-priced mass produced goods (mugs, scarves, badges, T-shirts, etc.) is not because of the product itself but because the name or image of a celebrity appealing to that person is reproduced on the product.

WIPO then goes on to divide personality merchandising between: merchandising where the famous personality's name or image is an 'advertising vehicle' for a product; and where a famous personality endorses a product. Interestingly, in the UK, the term 'character merchandising' has, with some few exceptions, most prominently in relation to product endorsement, been understood by the courts and many legal commentators to encompass both merchandising involving fictional characters and personality merchandising. Furthermore, there is a considerable overlap between the legal means of protecting both character and personality merchandising. Indeed, the legal protection for both, as we shall see, has common roots.

10.3.2 THE LEGAL GROUNDS FOR PROTECTING CHARACTER AND PERSONALITY MERCHANDISING

There is the potential for character and personality merchandising to be protected by different intellectual property rights whether the character is real or imagined. Under UK law, an action for passing off and trade mark registration are the most common routes to protecting character merchandising (including personality merchandising). In this section, we will look at both. But first it is necessary to make a brief comment about copyright and character and personality merchandising.

---

[77] 'Character Merchandising' Report Prepared by the International Bureau of the World Intellectual Property Organization (WIPO), WO/INF/108, 1994, p. 9.

10.3.2.1 Character and personality merchandising and copyright

The limited potential for copyright to protect character and personality merchandising was underlined very early on in *Du Boulay v Du Boulay*,[78] which held that there is no copyright in a name. Subsequent case law in the UK has made it clear that this is the case whether it is the name of a real person or of a fictional character.[79] Furthermore, as was pointed out by Laddie J, in the *Elvis Presley Trade Marks* case,[80] no one owns his own likeness, apart from any copyright, which might subsist in a particular reproduction. And it is also the case that UK courts will almost certainly not find copyright in short phrases that in some instances are identified with particular real or fictional characters: the expression 'shaken not stirred' comes to mind in this regard.[81] Perhaps the only circumstance in which copyright may protect character merchandising is if the defendant reproduces the image of a fictional character without permission from the copyright holder (an issue which we will consider later in this chapter).[82]

10.3.2.2 Passing off and character and personality merchandising

10.3.2.2.1 The relationship between passing off and trade mark protection

Until the passage of the 1994 Trade Marks Act, character merchandising, involving both real and fictional characters, was primarily protected against unfair competition by the law of passing off. The previous trade mark regime had offered little in the way of protection for character merchandising primarily because, under the TMA 1938, it was forbidden for trade mark proprietors to 'traffic' in their marks.[83] As a result, the primary route for protecting character and personality merchandising was through an action for passing off.

10.3.2.2.2 Goodwill and a misrepresentation: the importance of a common field of activity

The typical misrepresentation in character and personality merchandising cases is that the defendant has been licensed to make use of these characters (real or fictional) to promote his own goods. Until relatively recently, for a passing off action in relation to character and personality merchandising to succeed it was necessary for there to be a common field of activity between the claimant and the defendant.[84] For example, in the 'Wombles' case,[85] where the claimant owned copyright in drawings of fictional characters known for their tidiness and the defendant supplied rubbish skips under the name 'Wombles Skips', Walton J found that, in the absence of a common field of activity, the public would be unlikely to assume a licensing connection between the parties. In the 'Abba' case two years later,[86] concerning the popular singing group, Oliver J showed a similar unwillingness to accept that there was a

[78] (1867–9) LR 2 PC 430; see also *Burberrys v J. C. Cording & Co. Ltd* (1909) 26 RPC 693.
[79] *Elvis Presley Trade Marks*, CA; see also *Mirage Studios v Counter-Feat Clothing* [1991] FSR 145.
[80] *Elvis Presley Trade Marks* [1997] RPC 543 (HC).
[81] Although it may be possible to register a short phrase as a trade mark as long as it acts as a badge of origin. See J. Davis and A. Durant, 'To protect or not to protect? The eligibility of commercially used short verbal texts for copyright and trade mark protection' [2011] IPQ 345.
[82] See 10.3.2.2.4.
[83] See the 'Holly Hobbie' case: *American Greetings Corp.'s Application* [1984] 1 WLR 189.
[84] *McCulloch v Lewis A. May (Produce Distributors) Ltd* [1947] 2 All ER 845 ('Uncle Mac'); *Tavener Rutledge Ltd v Trexapalm Ltd* [1975] FSR 479 ('Kojak'); *Wombles Ltd v Wombles Skips Ltd* [1975] RPC 99.
[85] *Wombles Ltd v Wombles Skips Ltd* [1975] RPC 99.   [86] *Lyngstad v Anabas Products* [1977] FSR 62.

wide recognition among the public of merchandising activity by famous personalities. Here the defendants used the name and image of the group, who were not themselves involved in merchandising, on goods such as T-shirts and key rings. However, in this case, the court was concerned less with the absence of a common field of activity, but rather more with the fact that its absence undermined the ability of the claimants to argue that there had been an actionable misrepresentation.

10.3.2.2.3 *The need for a misrepresentation and damage:* Stringfellow

By the time of the decision in the 'Abba' case, the courts in character and personality merchandising cases were beginning to focus on finding an actionable misrepresentation rather than searching for a common field of activity. Indeed, shortly after this decision, Lord Diplock in the 'Advocaat' case[87] confirmed that there could be passing off even though 'the plaintiff and the defendant were not competing traders in the same line of business'. The *Stringfellow* case in 1984 was perhaps the first case concerning character merchandising which explicitly made the break from seeking a common field and instead held that an actionable misrepresentation which would cause damage or the likelihood of damage to the claimant's goodwill was key to a successful action in passing off.

Stringfellow v McCain Foods (GB) Ltd [1984] RPC 501

Peter Stringfellow (S) had run nightclubs for several years, including one in London named 'Stringfellows', using a distinctive butterfly logo accompanied by the name 'Stringfellows' in signature form. 'Disco dancing' took place on a floor of black glass accompanied by flashing lights. By 1983, the club was widely known among a large cross-section of the population as a nightclub and restaurant with a high-class reputation. The defendants made and sold frozen foods and were pioneers in the field of oven-ready chips. They developed a long, thin oven-ready chip called 'Stringfellows' which they claimed was a cross between the names 'Shoestring' and 'Longfellows'. The defendants advertised their product on television against a background of music and disco dancing taking place in a 'suburban' kitchen. The claimant sued for passing off. There was some evidence that people thought S had lent his name to the chips for money. In the High Court, Whitford J found that there was passing off because the club had a reputation, a significant number of the public might be confused, and, because it was a high-class club, its reputation would be damaged if it was associated with oven-ready chips. The defendants appealed. Slade LJ agreed that the club had a wide reputation. He also accepted the choice of name by the defendants was honest. According to Slade LJ, the crucial questions were: (1) whether McCain could be said to have been guilty of any misrepresentation and (2) if so, whether it was a reasonably foreseeable consequence of such misrepresentation that it would cause actual damage to the claimant's business or goodwill.[88] Slade LJ applied Lord Diplock's five-part definition of passing off in 'Advocaat'. In relation to McCain's use of the word 'Stringfellows', he held there was no passing off because by itself such use was unlikely to lead to a reasonable belief amongst the public that S and his club were associated with chips in any way. Slade LJ accepted that the television advert did give rise to some confusion because of the nightclub setting.

---

[87] *Erven Warnink BV v J. Townend & Sons (Hull) Ltd* [1979] AC 731, 742.   [88] At 535.

> **Slade LJ, at p. 538:**
>
> Accordingly, albeit with some misgivings, I would accept that, on the evidence, this form of advertisement did, unwittingly, involve a degree of misrepresentation alleged in the statement of claim, in that its form would lead a number of persons who knew the name of the Club—though I cannot think a large number—into the mistaken belief that the chips were connected in the course of trade with the plaintiffs or that the plaintiffs were collaborating with McCain in marketing them.

S had succeeded in persuading the court that of the three conditions needed for passing off—goodwill, a misrepresentation, and damage—the first two had been proved. But a crucial question remained: had S persuaded the court that as a result of the misrepresentation there would be damage or the likelihood of damage? It was noted by Slade LJ that no evidence of actual damage, such as a fall in numbers visiting the club, had been adduced by the claimant.[89] So the question became: would the misrepresentation lead to a likelihood of damage?

Evidence of three 'experts' in merchandising suggested that with regard 'to modern practices' including franchising, merchandising, sponsorship, and endorsement, the association of the club with a 'hard baked' oven chip, would damage its potential to profit from such activities. Slade LJ noted that there were two questions to address. First, would the claimant now be able to merchandise the mark if there had been no television commercial? Second, did the television advertisement prejudice the claimant's ability to profit from such advertising in the future? Slade LJ gave the following answers:

> As to (i), presumably in view of their fears of tarnishing their image, the plaintiffs would only wish to grant licences (if at all) in connection with goods of a luxury or 'up-market' variety, such as clothes or jewellery. But how many, if any, persons marketing goods of this nature would expect to derive any potential benefit from the use of the name of a nightclub, albeit a celebrated nightclub? The name 'Stringfellows' is not a fancy name. It is a surname which, at least in some parts of the country, is not an uncommon one. Nor is it a name connected with a person, such as a sportsman who has a particular expertise and for the purpose of his job requires particular equipment, the quality of which he can endorse by lending his name. So far as the evidence shows, the plaintiffs possess no relevant copyright (save perhaps their logo) in connection with which they can grant licences. In all the circumstances I do not think it surprising that Mr Stringfellow, for all his business acumen, had never contemplated the exploitation of the name in this manner until the present dispute arose ... In my opinion, the evidence as a whole gives no solid basis for inferring that, but for the television advertisement, the plaintiffs would have been in a position profitably to exploit merchandising rights in the name 'Stringfellows'.
>
> However, even if that conclusion were unjustified, I would still take the view that there is not sufficient evidence that the mere showing of the television advertisement has prejudiced, or is really likely to prejudice, such chances of profitable exploitation of merchandising rights as the plaintiffs may possess. It seems to me that, in regard to this head of alleged potential damage, one is in the field of pure speculation and that this is not enough to ground an action for passing off, particularly against an innocent defendant ...

[89] At 541.

If, however, one has regard to the broader aspects of this claim, there is another side of the coin. The plaintiffs, as a matter of law, can claim no monopoly in the use of the surname Stringfellow, or indeed in the use of the unregistered word 'Stringfellows'. The law does not encourage any such monopoly. McCain or any other persons (albeit with full knowledge of the plaintiffs' prior use) are perfectly free to use that same word in marketing or advertising their goods, provided only that they are not thereby in breach of contract or guilty of passing off, within the principles laid down by the Advocaat case, or of some other tort. Any such use may well lead some uninformed, perhaps unreflective, members of the public to the mistaken belief that there is some connection between the goods in question and the Club, however far apart from that of a high-class nightclub the nature of the goods may be. Experience in the present case has shown that much. Nevertheless, even if it considers that there is a limited risk of confusion of this nature, the court should not, in my opinion, readily infer the likelihood of resulting damage to the plaintiffs, as against an innocent defendant in a completely different line of business. In such a case the onus falling on plaintiffs to show that damage to their business reputation is in truth likely to ensue and to cause them more than a minimal loss is in my opinion a heavy one. I have said nothing about the position which might have arisen in this case if there had been any reason to question the reputability of McCain or of their new product, since these have never been in doubt. As things are, the onus has not in my opinion been discharged.[90]

On these grounds he rejected the claimants' appeal. Once again, we see the UK courts, as in so many other areas of intellectual property law, loath to grant a monopoly where one has not hitherto existed. In this case, Slade LJ seemed to be suggesting that by accepting there had been passing off, the court would effectively be granting the claimant a monopoly in the use of his name 'Stringfellow' for marketing goods and services other than those provided by his nightclub. Does this seem a reasonable judgment today, when we take it for granted that individuals who find fame in one area of commercial endeavour are often quick to exploit it in others?

10.3.2.2.4 *The UK courts recognize character (and personality) merchandising: the case of the 'Ninja Turtles'*

The traditionally cautious approach which the UK courts had shown to the protection of character (and personality) merchandising appeared to change with the decision in the 'Ninja Turtles' case. Although in this case the court was concerned with character merchandising, its judgment was subsequently cited in personality merchandising cases as well.[91]

Mirage Studios v Counter-Feat Clothing Co. Ltd [1991] FSR 145
(the 'Ninja Turtles' case)

An interim injunction was sought by the claimants to restrain the use of four cartoon characters on the grounds that their reproduction constituted either a breach of copyright or passing off. The characters, the Teenage Mutant Ninja Turtles, were at the time

---

[90] At 544–6.　　[91] See the 'Elvis' case at 10.3.2.3.

'a marketing phenomenon',[92] earning hundreds of millions of dollars in the US. They achieved similar success in the UK. The creators of the cartoon had formed a company, Mirage Studios, to exploit the marketing potential of the turtles. The defendants, the Counter-Feat Clothing Co. Ltd (CCL) licensed characters from the owners of copyrights and appointed 'manufacturing agents'. They asked for a licence to merchandise the Ninja Turtles when the phenomenon began, but the licence had already been awarded elsewhere. CCL then sought to merchandise turtles without infringing the rights of the claimants, by commissioning an artist to design humanoid turtles which were not identical to the claimant's own. The claimant produced evidence that there had been confusion with the defendants' T-shirts, which the public believed had been licensed by the claimant. The judgment of Sir Nicolas Browne-Wilkinson V-C addressed the action both in relation to copyright and passing off.

Sir Nicolas Browne-Wilkinson V-C, at p. 148:

Character merchandising is an industry which has grown in sophistication over the comparatively recent past. The owners of the copyright in such cartoon characters as the Mutant Turtles licence their use and the use of the name of these fictitious characters and the reproduction of them on merchandise and goods. The return to the owner of the copyright, the creator of the character, is normally in the form of royalty payments. Those rights are extremely valuable in a case where the success of the underlying cartoon, video and television is as great as it has been in the present case; the royalties run into hundreds of millions of dollars.

The Vice-Chancellor then described how the creators of the Ninja Turtles, 'following a well-known path', had appointed 'worldwide' agents to license the exploitation of the Turtles. At the time of the action, 150 licences had been granted in the UK for the use of the Turtles' name and image. The V-C then employed the principles of *American Cyanamid*[93] to decide whether or not a pre-trial injunction should be granted. He believed that the claimants did have an arguable case in both copyright and passing off. He then considered whether in the absence of a pre-trial injunction, damages would be an adequate remedy if the claimants were to succeed at trial:

At p. 152:

The loss likely to be suffered by the plaintiffs is of two kinds … First, they will lose royalties in the sense that goods which would be or might be manufactured under licence from them will go elsewhere and also the amount of royalties that they can seek to get from those who do take licenses from them is likely to be reduced since the market will not be an exclusive one.

   The second type of damage they will suffer will, it is said, be loss of control over the quality of the garments on which reproductions of the Ninja Turtles and related pictures are used. The evidence is (and I think this is uncontroversial) that the value of a name or characters such as these is linked to maintaining the quality of the goods to which it is attached. If the goods go down-market or are poorly made, that rubs off on the value of the copyright in the character and thereby reduces its value. The loss of royalties head of damage, though possibly difficult to quantify, is certainly capable of quantification. The loss of reputation through bad quality

---

[92] At 147.   [93] *American Cyanamid Co. v Ethicon* [1974] FSR 312 (see 15.5.1).

products is more difficult. Certainly, I have been shown products which do not indicate that the Turtle characters licensed by the defendants are always being applied to very high-class products. It is difficult to know how one would set about at the trial quantifying that.

At p. 154:

The defence put forward, if I may say so with great skill by Miss Vitoria on behalf of the defendant, is primarily a legal one. She says that the plaintiffs have not shown even an arguable case, either in copyright or in passing off. In the event, I do not mean to say much about the claim based on copyright. The difficulties surrounding any claim by the plaintiff based in copyright are primarily two. First, there is the rule in copyright that you can have no copyright in a name, and on that basis it is said that Teenage Mutant Ninja Turtles, or Ninja Turtles, are names and not subject to any copyright. The point seems to me not altogether easy to say whether a descriptive invented name is to be categorised as a name or as a description. The second and more fundamental difficulty in copyright is the saying that 'there is no copyright in ideas'. For myself, I find it difficult to determine what that phrase means in the present context. As I have said, although there are similarities in the graphic reproduction of the defendants' product to those in the plaintiffs' product, they are mainly reproductions of a concept, of the humanoid turtle of an aggressive nature. But whether that permits a claim in copyright or not seems to me to be a very open question; there is certainly an arguable case in copyright. I would not like to say what the final outcome of any case based in copyright would be.

[The V-C concluded that the claimants' case was stronger in relation to passing off. He then applied Lord Diplock's five elements of passing off as set out in the 'Advocaat' case.]

At p. 155:

Applying those requirements to the present case, first, has there been a misrepresentation? The critical evidence in this case is that a substantial number of the buying public now expect and know that where a famous cartoon or television character is reproduced on goods, that reproduction is the result of a licence granted by the owner of the copyright or owner of other rights in that character. Mr Smith, the defendant, accepted that evidence subject to this: he said that was only true where the reproduced matter was an exact reproduction of the character in the cartoon or television show, whereas in his case the defendants' turtles were different. I cannot accept that. If, as the evidence here shows, the public mistake the defendants' turtles for those which might be called genuine plaintiffs' Turtles, once they have made that mistake they will assume that the product in question has been licensed to use the Turtles on it. That is to say, they will connect what they mistakenly think to be the plaintiffs' Turtles with the plaintiffs. To put on the market goods, which the public mistake for the genuine article, necessarily involves a misrepresentation to the public that they are genuine. On the evidence in this case, the belief that the goods are genuine involves a further misrepresentation, namely that they are licensed.

[The V-C then asked whether it was reasonably foreseeable that the defendant's actions would cause injury to the claimants' goodwill.]

At pp. 155–156:

In my judgment, that is the critical question in the present case. What is the plaintiffs' business or goodwill? Mirage Studios are plainly in business as the creators and marketers of cartoons, videos and films of their characters, the Ninja Turtles. But the evidence is quite clear that that is only part of their business: their business also includes the turning to profit of those characters by licensing the reproduction of them on goods sold by other people. A major part of their business income arises from royalties to be received from such licensing enterprise. In relation to the drawings of Ninja Turtles as they appear in cartoons, *etc.,* there is a copyright which can be infringed. If one wishes to take advantage of the Ninja character it is necessary to reproduce the Ninja Turtle and thereby the concept, bizarre and unusual as it is, of the Teenage Mutant Turtle becomes a marketable commodity. It is in that business that the plaintiffs are engaged.

That dual nature of the plaintiffs' business (namely both the creation and exploitation of the cartoons and films themselves and the licensing of the right to use those creations) is in my judgment important. As I have said, if others are able to reproduce or apparently reproduce the Turtles without paying licence royalties to the plaintiffs, they will lose the royalties. Since the public associates the goods with the creator of the characters, the depreciation of the image by fixing the Turtle picture to inferior goods and inferior materials may seriously reduce the value of the licensing right. This damage to an important part of the plaintiffs' business is therefore plainly foreseeable.

The fifth of Lord Diplock's requirements is that foreseen damage actually occurs, or will probably do so. Again, in my judgment that is manifestly clear in the present case.

[The V-C then looked at the relevant case law. He approved the approach taken to character merchandising in Australia in *Children's Television Workshop v Woolworths*[94].]

At p. 157:

In my judgment, the law as developed in Australia is sound. There is no reason why a remedy in passing off should be limited to those who market or sell the goods themselves. If the public is misled in a relevant way as to a feature or quality of the goods as sold, that is sufficient to found a cause of action in passing off brought by those people with whom the public associate that feature or that quality which has been misrepresented.

The V-C then turned to the relevant UK decisions in relation to character merchandising. He noted that the 'Wombles' case differed from the present case, because in the former only the name, which had no copyright protection, had been appropriated by the defendants. By contrast, here the claimants were licensing copyright works. He then differentiated the present case from the 'Kojak' decision,[95] both because the latter had turned on the fact that there was no common field of activity and also because Walton J did not accept that the public was sufficiently aware of the licensing business. Finally, the V-C considered the decision in 'Abba'. Once again, he held that there were crucial differences with the present action because, in the 'Abba' case it was simply the use of the name which had been relied on by the claimant.

At p. 159:

In my judgment the three English cases do not touch on a case such as the present where the plaintiff clearly has copyright in the drawings and is in business on a large scale in this

---

[94] *Children's Television Workshop Inc. v Woolworths (New South Wales) Ltd* [1981] RPC 187, where unauthorized use by defendants of the 'Muppets' name and image on merchandise amounted to passing off, because of public awareness of licensing. See also, *Pacific Dunlop v Hogan* (1989) 87 ALR 14.

[95] *Tavener Rutledge Ltd v Trexapalm Ltd* [1975] FSR 479.

> country in licensing the use of the copyright in those drawings. The defendant is misrepresenting to the public that his drawings are the drawings of the plaintiffs or are licensed by the plaintiffs. I can see no reason why, in those circumstances, the defendants should be allowed to misrepresent his goods in that way. I therefore consider that if the case went to trial, the plaintiffs' case in passing off would succeed.

Following the decision in the 'Ninja Turtles' case, there was a widespread belief among those involved with both character and personality merchandising that the courts had finally recognized their value and were affording them commensurate legal protection. However, there were two assumptions underlying the judgment which suggested this was not necessarily the case. First, what differentiated this action from earlier cases was that it involved the licensing of a specific intellectual property right: copyright. The V-C made it clear that if the case had involved only a name, then the principles in the 'Abba' and 'Wombles' cases would have been applied. The second assumption made by the V-C was that the public was sufficiently aware of character merchandising so that there would be an actionable (and damaging) misrepresentation following the defendant's sale of the T-shirts. The Court of Appeal addressed the 'Ninja Turtles' decision in the *Elvis Presley Trade Marks* case.[96] It made clear that the V-C's judgment stood on the particular facts: first, that the claimants were licensing a copyright work rather than simply a name and, second, that a claim that the public was aware of the practice of licensing, while perhaps true in this case, could not simply be assumed in all situations.

The limits of the 'Ninja Turtles' decision were amply illustrated by the 'Spice Girls' case.[97] This case mirrored the facts of the 'Abba' case, in that the Spice Girls, a pop group, were unsuccessful in preventing the defendant from publishing an 'unofficial' sticker collection which carried the name and photographs of the group. The court did not believe that the public would assume that the pop group had authorized the merchandising of the stickers. Is it surprising that despite the extraordinary growth in the value of character merchandising, which has certainly been acknowledged by the courts in successive judgments, traders may still appropriate others' fame for their own profit without cost? Once we are aware of the limits of the 'Ninja Turtles' decision for character merchandising, we may also understand why this is possible, but we may not approve.[98]

10.3.2.2.5 *Passing off and false endorsement*

We pointed earlier to the fact that the English courts generally elide the distinction between fictional and real personalities when deciding cases involving character and personality merchandising. Exceptionally, Laddie J's decision in *Irvine v Talksport* did draw a clear distinction between the two in cases where the alleged passing off involved an accusation of false endorsement.

Irvine v Talksport Ltd [2002] 1 WLR 2355

Eddie Irvine, the claimant, was a well-known and successful Formula 1 (F1) racing car driver, whose most successful year was 1999. The defendant, Talksport, ran

---

[96] *Elvis Presley Trade Marks* [1999] RPC 567 (CA).
[97] *Halliwell v Panini SpA*, an unreported case mentioned at (1997) 8 Ent. L. R. E94–5.
[98] See e.g. J. Davis, 'The king is dead: long live the king' [2000] CLJ 33.

The University of Law |
Birmingham Centre | Library |
Issued Items

Customer name: Kasongo Mwenso
Customer ID: ***9300

Title: Intellectual property law : text, cases
and materials
ID: B28092
Due: 20180416   235900

Title: Intellectual property
ID: B23981
Due: 20180416   235900

Total items: 2
21/03/2018 21:10
Checked out: 2
Overdue: 0
Hold requests: 0
Ready for pickup: 0

In case of query, please contact:
library-birmingham@law.ac.uk
01483 216041

an eponymous radio station in the UK. In the past it had been known as 'Talk Radio' but in 1999 it decided to concentrate on sport and hence its change of name. In that same year it obtained the rights to live broadcast coverage of the F1 Grand Prix World Championship. It also embarked on a promotional campaign. Part of this campaign involved the production of a number of boxed packs which were sent to 1,000 individuals who were likely advertisers on the station. One of these boxed packs concentrated on F1 racing. It contained, inter alia, a brochure. On the front of the brochure Eddie Irvine was shown holding a radio carrying the words, 'Talk Radio'. In fact, in the original photograph he had been holding a mobile phone, but the photograph had been manipulated by the advertising agency retained by Talksport. Irvine alleged that the distribution of the photograph was an actionable passing off (he did not have any rights in the photograph) and sued for damages, since the defendant had already undertaken not to distribute the photograph further. At the start of his judgment, Laddie J drew a distinction between endorsement, which was the concern of the current action, and other kinds of merchandising.

Laddie J:

9. When someone endorses a product or service he tells the relevant public that he approves of the product or service or is happy to be associated with it. In effect he adds his name as an encouragement to members of the relevant public to buy or use the service or product. Merchandising is rather different. It involves exploiting images, themes or articles which have become famous. To take a topical example, when the recent film, *Star Wars Episode 1* was about to be exhibited, a large number of toys, posters, garments and the like were put on sale, each of which bore an image of or reproduced a character or object in the film. The purpose of this was to make available a large number of products which could be bought by members of the public who found the film enjoyable and wanted a reminder of it. The manufacture and distribution of this type of spin-off product is referred to as merchandising. It is not a necessary feature of merchandising that members of the public will think the products are in any sense endorsed by the film makers or actors in the film. Merchandised products will include some where there is a perception of endorsement and some where there may not be, but in all cases the products are tied into and are a reminder of the film itself. An example of merchandising is the sale of memorabilia relating to the late Diana, Princess of Wales. A porcelain plate bearing her image could hardly be thought of as being endorsed by her, but the enhanced sales which may be achieved by virtue of the presence of the image is a form of merchandising.

In this case, counsel for Mr Irvine argued that as a 'false endorsement case' it fell 'squarely within the modern application of the law of passing off'. Conversely, counsel for the defence relied on the Court of Appeal decision in *Elvis Presley*, to the effect that the claimant was attempting to argue that he had an independent 'character right' that should be protected. This was something which Simon Brown LJ had rejected as a cause of action in the 'Elvis' case.[99]

Laddie J then went on to ask whether the claimant did have a case in passing off stemming from the false endorsement. He began by suggesting that over the years the law of passing off had responded to changes in the nature of trade. Remarkably, given

[99] See 10.3.2.3.

its advanced age, it was agreed by Laddie J and counsel for the claimant that the most recent case of false endorsement in England was the 'Uncle Mac' case,[100] decided in 1947, which foundered on lack of a common field of activity between the claimant and the defendant. Laddie J also referenced the Australian case, *Henderson v Radio Corp.*,[101] where the court had held that there was no need for a common field of activity in cases of false endorsement (in this case the unauthorized use of pictures of ballroom dancers on a record cover). The Australian case, according to Laddie J, illustrated the growing importance of passing off when applied to character merchandising.

Laddie J:

38. ...[T]he law of passing off now is of greater width than as applied by Wynne-Parry J in *McCulloch v May* that if someone acquires a valuable reputation or goodwill, the law of passing off will protect it from unlicensed use by other parties. Such use will frequently be damaging in the direct sense that it will involve selling inferior goods or services under the guise that they are from the claimant. But the action is not restricted to protecting against that sort of damage. The law will vindicate the claimant's exclusive right to the reputation or goodwill. It will not allow others to so use goodwill as to reduce, blur or diminish its exclusivity. It follows that it is not necessary to show that the claimant and the defendant share a common field of activity or that sales of products or services will be diminished either substantially or directly, at least in the short term. Of course there is still a need to demonstrate a misrepresentation because it is that misrepresentation which enables the defendant to make use or take advantage of the claimant's reputation.

39. Not only has the law of passing off expanded over the years, but the commercial environment in which it operates is in a constant state of flux. Even without the evidence given at the trial in this action, the court can take judicial notice of the fact that it is common for famous people to exploit their names and images by way of endorsement. They do it not only in their own field of expertise but, depending on the extent of their fame or notoriety, wider afield also. It is common knowledge that for many sportsmen, for example, income received from endorsing a variety of products and services represent a very substantial part of their total income. The reason large sums are paid for endorsement is because, no matter how irrational it may seem to a lawyer, those in business have reason to believe that the lustre of a famous personality, if attached to their goods or services, will enhance the attractiveness of those goods or services to their target market. In this respect, the endorsee is taking the benefit of the attractive force which is the reputation or goodwill of the famous person.

Laddie J believed that manufacturers and retailers recognized the realities of the marketplace when they paid for well-known personalities to endorse their goods, and in his view the law of passing off should do likewise. He then went on to assert that the three elements needed to support an action in passing off were entirely compatible with a case of false endorsement. Irvine could be said to have a substantial reputation or goodwill because of the popularity of F1 motor racing, the amount of publicity which surrounded it, and, following from that, the considerable extent to which drivers were paid to endorse products. In particular, 1999 had been a highly successful year for Mr Irvine whose professional and personal life had attracted an immense amount of

---

[100] *McCulloch v Lewis A. May (Produce Distributors) Ltd* [1947] 2 All ER 845.
[101] *Henderson v Radio Corp. Pty Ltd* [1969] RPC 218.

press coverage, thus enabling him to earn considerable sums from endorsing products. Laddie J concluded on the first point:

> 57. …that the only reasonable inference is that those who designed this promotion knew of Mr Irvine's fame and wanted it to be attached to the launch of the new sports-related programme.

Moving on to the misrepresentation, Laddie J held that the actions of the defendant created a false message which would be understood by a not insignificant section of its market to mean that its radio programme or station had been endorsed, recommended, or approved of by Mr Irvine, and in particular would 'convey the message to the audience that Talk Radio was so good that it was endorsed and listened to by Mr Irvine'. As for damage, although the defendants argued that the brochure had only gone to 1,000 recipients, the damage to Mr Irvine's reputation might be 'negligible in direct money terms but the potential for long term damage' was considerable. Passing off against the defendant was proved.

10.3.2.2.6 False endorsement and damages

Following the judgment in *Irvine v Talksport*, Laddie J held a further hearing to assess the amount of damages owed by the defendant.[102] Mr Irvine told the court that he had entered into four endorsement agreements in 1999, including one with Tommy Hilfiger. That agreement alone had netted him £75,000. According to Mr Irvine:[103]

> …although I am relatively keen to endorse products, there is and was in 1999 a price below which I would not consider endorsing the product. This is because I would not want it to be known that my endorsement fee was a low figure. Word would soon get around and it could devalue my image and market rate.

Mr Irvine then calculated the cost of an actual endorsement by him for Talksport which took into account both the false endorsement as well as 'the non-fashionable image of Talk Radio' and produced evidence to support his claim. He argued that a 'reasonable company' in the defendant's position would have been prepared to spend by agreement £50.00 per brochure. Laddie J rejected this line of argument. Instead, he held that the correct approach to finding a reasonable royalty or licence fee would be to treat the parties as if they were negotiating at arm's length and to try to find an amount that would have served both their legitimate interests. Even though he accepted that Eddie Irvine 'would not get out of bed' to make such an endorsement, he went on to conclude that 'erring, as it appears to me on the generous side, I would have thought a reasonable figure is £2,000 and I will so order'.[104]

Following the judge's findings, the defendant appealed regarding the finding of liability and the claimant cross-appealed on the issue of damages. The Court of Appeal upheld Laddie J's judgment on passing off, but allowed the claimant's cross-appeal on damages. It agreed that the approach to be followed in assessing damages was to arrive at a reasonable fee for Irvine's endorsement of the defendant's radio station. Furthermore, Laddie J was

---

[102] *Irvine v Talksport Ltd (Damages)* [2002] EWHC 539 (Ch), [2003] EMLR 6.
[103] Quoted in *Irvine v Talksport Ltd* [2003] FSR 35 (CA), 60.
[104] *Irvine v Talksport (Damages)*, 557.

correct to set the level of damages at what the defendants would have to pay 'to do lawfully what was done unlawfully'. However, as the Court of Appeal noted, Laddie J had declined to accept the claimant's evidence as to what that fee should be. Accepting that evidence, the Court of Appeal found that Eddie Irvine would have expected at least £25,000 to endorse a product in 1999 and this should be the level of damages paid by the defendant.

In his judgment Laddie J differentiated cases of false endorsement from the facts in *Elvis Presley*. In relation to the singer, he noted that: 'There could be no question of the performer endorsing anything since he had been dead for many years.'[105] He went on to make a similar point about the marketing of fictional characters, suggesting that they too would not be understood by the public to be endorsing products. This distinction between character merchandising and false endorsement made by Laddie J was recently summarized and approved by Kitchin LJ in the 'Rihanna' case,[106] which concerned the marketing by a large retailer, Topshop, of a T-shirt carrying an image of the singer without her permission. Kitchin LJ noted that:

> 36 ...character merchandising and endorsement are rather different in nature. As its name suggests, character merchandising encompasses a range of activities which share the common feature that they involve the licensing of the names or likenesses of famous characters, whether real or fictional. For example, it may be that there is a relatively simple licence in place, including, possibly, a licence of copyright material. Endorsement, on the other hand, describes one particular kind of relationship between the characters (or their creators) and the goods which bear their names or likenesses, and it implies authorisation and approval.

Do you agree with both Kitchin LJ and Laddie J that only real (and indeed live) people can be the subject of a false endorsement claim? Taking the case of James Bond, but there are many others, we may well assert that although he is a fictional character he does indeed endorse products.[107] Would brand owners pay so handsomely to have their products associated with the fictional spy if they did not believe his qualities would enhance the reputation of their products? We might argue that this investment deserves the same level of protection accorded to real celebrities many of whom achieve and exploit their fame with rather less effort.

FURTHER READING

C. Barton, 'Celebrity image rights: an international comparison' (2003) 5 Washington and Lee L. Rev. 22.

H. Carty, 'Character merchandising and the limits of passing off' (1993) 13 Legal Studies 289.

F. Hoffman, 'The right to publicity in German and English law' [2010] IPQ 325.

---

[105] [46].

[106] *Fenty v Arcadia Group Brands Ltd (No. 2)* [2015] EWCA Civ 3. This case will be discussed in further detail in 10.4 when publicity/image rights are discussed.

[107] For another example, *Hearst Holdings Inc. & Fleischer Studios Inc. v AVELA Inc., Poeticgem Ltd, The Partnership (Trading) Ltd, U Wear Ltd & J. Fox Ltd* [2014] EWHC 439 (Ch) ('Betty Boop') discussed at 10.3.2.3.

S. Maniatis, 'Personality endorsement and character merchandising: a sparkle of unfair competition in English law' in N. Lee, G. Westkamp, A. Kur, and A. Ohly (eds), *Intellectual Property, Unfair Competition and Publicity: Convergences and Development* (Cheltenham: Edward Elgar, 2014), pp. 19–117.

G. Scanlan, 'Personality, endorsement and everything: the modern law of passing off and the myth of the personality right' [2003] EIPR 563.

10.3.2.3 Trade marks, and character and personality merchandising

10.3.2.3.1 Introduction

You may recall that under the TMA 1938 it was not possible to 'traffick' in a registered trade mark. In other words, a trade mark proprietor could not license his registered trade mark which might, for example, comprise a famous name or image, for others to place on goods over which he had no control. It is not surprising that many of those involved in character and personality merchandising looked forward to a definite change of direction following the passage of the TMA 1994, which allowed relatively unconditional licensing of trade marks. Certainly, the new Act eased the position for those marketing fictional characters. Thus, 'Teenage Mutant Ninja Turtles' is now a registered trade mark for a range of goods, including computer games and clothing. But would the protection of personality merchandising also become more certain?

10.3.2.3.2 Elvis Presley Trade Marks: *the High Court*

The first test of the impact of the TMA on personality merchandising was the *Elvis Presley Trade Marks* case.

Elvis Presley Trade Marks [1997] RPC 543 (HC), [1999] RPC 567 (CA)

Elvis Presley Enterprises Inc. ('Enterprises') applied to register three trade marks under the TMA 1938 for toiletries including perfume and antiperspirants. One was a manuscript version of the name 'Elvis A. Presley', which in the proceedings was referred to as the 'signature mark'. One was for the word 'Elvis' and the third for the words 'Elvis Presley'. The application was opposed by Mr Sid Shaw who, for many years, had traded in Elvis memorabilia and who had the registered trade mark 'Elvisly Yours' for a wide range of goods including toiletries. Mr Shaw based his opposition on the assertion that the names 'Elvis' and 'Elvis Presley' lacked the distinctiveness needed for registration. He failed on this argument in the Trade Mark Registry, which held that the three marks were sufficiently distinctive to act as a badge of origin, and he appealed. Although the case was brought under the 1938 Act, any judgment would be relevant to the interpretation of the TMA 1994, since it would be under the terms of the latter Act that, for example, any infringement action would be decided. In the High Court, Laddie J identified the two questions raised by the appeal.

Laddie J, at p. 546:

... (a) [C]an anyone claim the exclusive right under the 1938 Act to the names Elvis and Elvis Presley or the signature as a trade mark for a range of common retail products and, if so, (b) who?

[Laddie J then pointed out that it was not possible for Enterprises to 'own' the names Elvis and Elvis Presley as there is no copyright in a name. He went on:]

At p. 547:

Even if Elvis Presley was still alive, he would not be entitled to stop a fan from naming his son, his dog or goldfish, his car or his house 'Elvis' or 'Elvis Presley' simply by reason of the fact that it was a name given to him at birth by his parents. To stop the use of the whole or part of his name by another he would need to show that as a result of such use, the other person is invading some legally recognised right. This is also reflected in many cases in the law of passing off.

Laddie J then made a similar point about Elvis's likeness, noting that, even during his lifetime, Elvis did not own his appearance. It was open to anyone to make a likeness of Elvis Presley, say as a tattoo or a painting, unless by doing so he or she invaded a legally recognized right, such as copyright. Turning, then, to the two questions posed, Laddie J looked first at the application for the name 'Elvis'. Under the 1938 Act, the mark, to be distinctive and therefore registrable, had to act as a badge of origin either by 'nature' or 'nurture'. He pointed out that:

The more a proposed mark alludes to the character, quality or non-origin attributes of the goods on which it is used or proposed to be used, the lower its inherent distinctiveness.[108]

In this case, counsel for Mr Shaw, Mr Meade, argued that the fact that Elvis had a high level of fame, would not make the mark more distinctive, but less so. For his part, counsel for Enterprises argued that Elvis would certainly have been able to register his name either before he became famous or during his lifetime and the position should be no different just because the singer had died. Laddie J rejected this latter argument. He cited the case *Tarzan Trade Mark*[109] where the author of the Tarzan stories failed in his attempt to register the mark 'Tarzan' for films and other merchandise because by the time of the application 'the word "Tarzan" had passed into the language and had become a household word' and indeed a descriptive word. It followed from the 'Tarzan' decision that the registrability of a mark must be addressed at the time of the application for registration. Instead Laddie J agreed with counsel for Mr Shaw that the word 'Elvis' had very low inherent distinctiveness. Not only was it a well-known given name, it would also be taken by many members of the public to refer back to Elvis Presley memorabilia in general rather than goods from a particular source. He went on:

Just as members of the public will go to see a Tarzan film because it is about Tarzan, so they will purchase Elvis merchandise because it carries the name or likeness of Elvis and not because it comes from a particular source ...[110]

Laddie J also rejected the argument of the applicant's counsel, Mr Prescott, that as the public became more aware of character merchandising they would expect to acquire a

---

[108] At 549. [109] *Tarzan Trade Mark* [1970] FSR 245. [110] At 552.

'genuine' article (i.e. one that resulted from a licence given by the rightsholder in the character to the manufacturer) when they purchased memorabilia. Laddie J disagreed. He noted that Mr Shaw had sold a very large amount of memorabilia, but the applicant had not sought to claim that the public believed the goods originated with themselves.[111] He concluded that there was 'very little distinctiveness in the mark "Elvis"' and that the applications to register both 'Elvis' and 'Elvis Presley' should be rejected.[112] The applicant appealed.

10.3.2.3.3 Elvis Presley Trade Marks: *the Court of Appeal*

The Court of Appeal[113] found for the respondent, Mr Shaw, on much the same grounds as Laddie J in the High Court. Walker LJ gave the leading judgment. He began by confirming that all the products involved in this action were being marketed primarily on the strength of their bearing the name or image of Elvis Presley. He also cited *Tarzan* to the effect that words which once have been distinctive can in time become descriptive. Walker LJ then went on to survey the case law relating to character and personality merchandising both in passing off and registered trade marks, up to and including 'Uncle Mac', 'Kojak', 'Abba', 'Holly Hobbie', and the 'Ninja Turtles'. He suggested that what differentiated the 'Ninja Turtles' case was that the claimant was in the business of not only licensing a name, but also a copyright work (i.e. the drawings of the turtles).

Walker LJ then looked at the arguments of the respective counsel. For Enterprises, Mr Prescott argued: (1) that the 'Tarzan' decision should be restricted to its special facts, i.e. a fictitious character whose name had once been an invented word and was no longer of wide significance; (2) other traders could not legitimately wish to use the names 'Elvis' and 'Elvis Presley'; (3) the law had now evolved to a point where there is a general rule that a trader may not make unauthorized use of the name of a celebrity in order to sell his own goods (he asserted that this principle applied to 'Elvis' who although deceased was of enduring fame); (4) there may be some instances where it would be 'fair dealing' to allow use by others of these marks, such as in biographical material, but 'in those instances—the "product" is really text or information about the celebrity', unlike in this case where the concern is with 'consumable commercial items like soap, toothpaste and perfume'; (5) that it was a matter of 'everyday experience, that reputable traders do not use the name of a living person in connection with their merchandise' without authorization; and finally (6) that the use by others of these marks would not cause confusion with Mr Shaw's mark, because the rights clearly belonged to Enterprises.

The arguments on behalf of Mr Shaw presented by his counsel, Mr Meade, were that: (1) it was a 'bold contention' that, in any instance of the use of a well-known name, either living or dead, fictional or real, the public would assume that the name had been 'franchised'; (2) such an assumption must be proved by real evidence pertaining to that name; (3) Laddie J was right to conclude that the 'Elvis' and 'Elvis Presley' marks had little inherent distinctiveness, especially when applied to memorabilia or as decoration; (4) the singer had become an important part of popular culture whose name and image other traders might legitimately wish to use; (5) that the more famous a 'man becomes, the harder it will be to register his

---

[111] At 554.

[112] He also held that 'Elvis' had not acquired distinctiveness through use in relation to the goods at issue. He took the same view of the signature and held, in addition, that it would conflict with Mr Shaw's own mark which was written in cursive script.

[113] *Elvis Presley Trade Marks* [1999] RPC 567 (CA).

name' if that name is used on memorabilia of Elvis Presley, as the average consumer will be buying such goods because they carry a likeness of the singer rather than as a product from a particular source; (6) that Enterprises could not rely on the fact that it had specific intellectual property rights that they owned which were being infringed (such as copyright); and finally, (7) Enterprises had failed to educate the public that the names 'Elvis' and 'Elvis Presley' were being used by them as a badge of origin.

Walker LJ then canvassed the judgment of Laddie J. He endorsed Laddie J's conclusions.

Walker LJ, at p. 585:

… [T]he public purchase Elvis Presley merchandise not because it comes from a particular source, but because it carries the name or image of Elvis Presley. Indeed the judge came close to finding (although he did not in terms find) that for goods of the sort advertised by Elvisly Yours (or by Enterprises in the United States) the commemoration of the late Elvis Presley is the product, and the article on which his name or image appears (whether a poster, a pennant, a mug or a piece of soap) is little more than a vehicle. I consider that the judge was right to treat all these goods as memorabilia or mementoes, and not to treat some as being in a different class of consumable commercial goods.

As a result, Laddie J had been right to conclude that the marks had 'very low inherent distinctiveness'.

Morritt LJ also supported the findings by Laddie J in respect of the 'Elvis' and 'Elvis Presley' marks. As to the 'Elvis' mark, he suggested that the 'Tarzan' decision should be followed in this case.

Morritt LJ, at pp. 593–4:

I agree with counsel for Mr Shaw that the ['Tarzan'] case is indistinguishable from this. It is true that the goods of which registration is sought, for instance soap, are consumer items. To market those goods under the mark Elvis would obviously seek to turn to account the name and memory of Elvis Presley; but it would seek to do so as descriptive of a popular hero not as distinctive of the connection between the soap and EPEI [Enterprises] as the proprietor of the mark. The soap would be sold as Elvis soap. The character of the soap would be Elvis soap.

As a result, the mark would not act as a badge of origin but rather would be 'a direct reference to the character of the soap'.

With respect to the 'Elvis Presley' mark, Morritt LJ also concluded that it lacked inherent or factual capability to act as a badge of origin. In particular, he noted that 'the fame of Elvis Presley was as a singer. He was not a producer of soap. There is no reason why he or any organization of his should be concerned with toiletries so as to give rise to some perceived connection between his name and the product.'

Morritt LJ, at p. 594:

Counsel for EPEI forcefully contended that such a conclusion would leave the door wide open to unscrupulous traders seeking to cash in on the reputations of others. This is true if, but only if, the mark has become so much a part of the language as to be descriptive of the goods rather than distinctive of their source. But in that event I can see no objection to any trader being entitled to use the description. In the field of memorabilia, which I consider includes consumer items bearing the name or likeness of a famous figure, it must be for that person to ensure by whatever means may be open to him or her that the public associate his or her name with the source of the goods. In the absence of evidence of such association in my view the court should be very slow to infer it.

Like Walker LJ and Morritt LJ, Simon Brown LJ took the view that one could not just assume that the public would be aware of character merchandising, as had been argued by the applicant. According to Simon Brown LJ, whether this was true in each case must turn on its facts. He noted that here there was no connection between toiletries and those attributes for which Elvis Presley was and remained famous; that Elvis memorabilia in the UK had not been primarily marketed by Enterprises; and that, in any event, the public who consumed such items would not assume that the use of the names had been officially licensed.

Simon Brown LJ, at pp. 597–8:

On analysis, as it seems to me, all the English cases upon which Enterprises seeks to rely (Mirage Studios not least) can be seen to have turned essentially upon the need to protect copyright or to prevent passing off (or libel). None creates the broad right for which in effect Mr Prescott contends here, a free standing general right to character exploitation enjoyable exclusively by the celebrity. As Robert Walker LJ has explained, just such a right, a new 'character right' to fill a perceived gap between the law of copyright (there being no copyright in a name) and the law of passing off was considered and rejected by the Whitford Committee in 1977. Thirty years earlier, indeed, when it was contended for as a corollary to passing off law, it had been rejected in *McCulloch v Lewis A. May* [1947] 2 AER 845. I would assume to reject it. In addressing the critical issue of distinctiveness there should be no a priori assumption that only a celebrity or his successors may ever market (or licence the marketing) of his own character. Monopolies should not be so readily created.

In the *Elvis* case, the Court of Appeal had to weigh two persuasive but quite incompatible arguments. The one put by counsel for Mr Shaw was that since the public had contributed to the fame of Elvis Presley (and hence the value inherent in his name), it would be wrong for it to be monopolized by a single undertaking. Or as Jeremy Phillips has written, 'since it is the public who make people celebrities during their lifetimes, it is the public who should be able to enjoy in common the greatest freedom to cherish those celebrities after death'.[114] The other argument, put by counsel for Enterprises, was that since Elvis Presley had accrued such a high degree of fame through his own efforts (and hence the value inherent in his name), it would be wrong if his estate could not profit from it. Which do you think is the more persuasive? We might also ask whether Simon Brown LJ was correct in his assumption that the public that bought Elvis Presley merchandise would not think it had been licensed. Indeed, was the Court of Appeal perhaps underestimating the extent to which the public may seek to buy 'official', rather than often cheaper 'unofficial', merchandise as a way of demonstrating their loyalty to the personality involved?

---

[114] J. Phillips, 'Life after death' [1998] EIPR 201.

10.3.2.3.4 *Trade marks and the registration of famous names following* Elvis

Taken at face value, the *Elvis* decision suggests that the more famous a personality, the less likely he will be able to obtain trade mark protection for his name. Indeed, this point of view was buttressed by the CJEU's decision in the *Picasso* trade mark case.[115] As we have seen, such an outcome is particularly problematic for those involved in character and personality merchandising because the law of passing off will not protect a name as such, except in cases of false endorsement. The decision in the 'Princess Diana' trade mark application appears to confirm that this is a correct understanding of the *Elvis* decision.[116]

Diana, Princess of Wales Trade Mark [2001] ETMR 25

The Trustees of the late Princess Diana's estate applied to register 'Diana, Princess of Wales' as a trade mark to cover a wide range of goods and services. The Registrar refused registration on the grounds that the mark did not fulfil the conditions of section 3 of the TMA in that it lacked distinctive character and had not acquired distinctiveness through use. The Registrar began by clearing up some 'red herrings': 'The first is that whilst she was alive Diana, Princess of Wales owned her name and therefore had an exclusive and unqualified right to the use of it for commercial purposes. No such "personality right" exists under UK law.' The second red herring, according to the Registrar, citing the Court of Appeal in *Elvis Presley*, 'is that a name which is unique to a particular person must by definition have distinctive character as a trade mark. This is not necessarily so'. Turning to the particular facts of this case, the Registrar noted that the evidence for the Estate showed it had licensed the use of Diana's signature on a wide range of products, largely relating to cards and prints, but also on other less obvious products such as margarine. The Estate also produced survey evidence which supported the view that when the public saw the name and signature of Diana on goods they would assume it was related to the Diana Memorial Fund and that the proceeds were meant for charity. The Registrar then turned to the applicable law. In particular, he asked whether the average consumer would see the 'message' sent by these marks as a badge of origin. In other words, were these words acting as a trade mark?

The Registrar:

40. There cannot be any doubt that the late Diana, Princess of Wales was one of the most famous people in the world. I believe that I am entitled to take notice of this and that the name and face of Diana, Princess of Wales has, since her marriage to Prince Charles in 1981, continuously featured on the covers of countless magazines, books and in TV programmes. She was probably one of the most photographed people in the world. None of this use indicated any trade connection between the source of these goods/services and the Princess. The average consumer would be aware of this and that there has long been a trade in this country in souvenirs and mementoes featuring members of the Royal Family without any significance as to the trade source of the goods.

[Noting that her name and signature had not been used as a trade mark before her death, the Registrar concluded:]

---

[115] *Ruiz-Picasso v OHIM (Trade Marks and Designs)* Case C-361/04 P [2006] ECR I-643; see 6.3.3.7.
[116] See also *Jane Austen Trade Mark* [2000] RPC 879.

55. In the light of the use made of the Princess' name whilst she was alive—which could not have been further from a trade mark for products—I do not believe that, at the date of application, the average consumer who was reasonably well informed and circumspect, would have expected all commemorative articles bearing the Princess' name to be commercialised under the control of a single undertaking. The applicants' evidence confirms what one would in any event have suspected, that the average consumer would like some or all of the proceeds of the sale of products bearing the Princess' name to go to charity. It does not establish that the mere appearance of the Princess' name is sufficient to guarantee to the average consumer that all such commemorative products are commercialised under the control of a single undertaking which is responsible for their quality.

[The Registrar concluded:]

61. I believe the answer to this question is straightforward. There is no evidence of any use of the name 'DIANA, PRINCESS OF WALES' as a trade mark.

Following cases such as 'Elvis Presley' and 'Princess Diana', celebrities and their legal representatives might have been forgiven for believing that the law relating to the registrations of famous names had not moved on in the way they had expected with the implementation of the 1994 TMA. However, the practice of the Trade Mark Registry suggests that their gloom is to some extent misplaced. First, the Manual makes clear that a famous name or image on merchandise may be viewed as a badge of origin and hence be protected by trade mark registration, although this will be more difficult for representatives of 'deceased celebrities' and 'defunct groups'. Second, the Registry may take a different approach to registering celebrity names depending upon the type of goods specified in the application. The Registry will almost certainly accept applications for celebrity names for goods which the public would buy as 'official merchandise', which may be a very wide-ranging category. Thus, the Registry has registered the name 'David Beckham' for a variety of goods, including cosmetics, jewellery, clothes, games, and toys, although arguably few consumers will assume that he manufactures or even markets such goods himself. But the Registry will reject applications for those same names on goods, such as posters, where they would not be understood as acting as a badge of origin. In other words, as the Manual puts it, such goods would be seen as 'mere image carriers' and the celebrity name as descriptive. An example of this approach is to be found in Linkin Park's trade mark application.[117] According to Registry practice, the correct approach is to consider whether the name put forward is distinctive of goods or services, in which case it will be registered, or if it is descriptive, pointing out that they are likely to have cause for concern on that score. Linkin Park LLC was the corporate vehicle of the American rock group. It successfully registered its name against a wide range of goods and services, including clothes. However, the group did not succeed in registering 'Linkin Park' for 'printed matter, posters and poster books'. It was held by the Appointed Person that, in relation to these goods, the Registrar had been correct to find that the name, placed on these goods, was purely descriptive and the posters were mere 'image carriers' for the applicant's name. Is the Registry right to view a celebrity name used on posters and other printed matter as descriptive rather than a badge of origin? When seeking to buy official merchandise, will fans really differentiate between, for example, T-shirts and posters? Interestingly,

[117] Trade Marks Manual (UK IPO) (<www.gov.uk/government/publications/manual-of-trade-marks-practice>); *Linkin Park LLC's Application* O/035/05 [2006] ETMR (74) 1017.

in *Hearst Holdings v AVELA*, Birss J came to an opposite conclusion in relation to the use of fictional characters, in this case the famous cartoon character, Betty Boop, on merchandise.

Hearst Holdings Inc. & Fleischer Studios Inc. v AVELA Inc., Poeticgem Ltd, The Partnership (Trading) Ltd, U Wear Ltd & J. Fox Ltd [2014] EWHC 439 (Ch)

Betty Boop is a cartoon character which originated in the US in the 1930s. The claimants have a number of registered trade marks and EUTMs consisting of the words 'BETTY BOOP' and of her image, relating to a variety of goods. The claimants began merchandising Betty Boop in the UK in the 1980s and by 2009 its retail business totalled £24 million. The claimants asserted that they were the only legitimate source of Betty Boop merchandising in the UK and that they had made substantial use of those marks, so that they had acquired a reputation for the purposes of section 10(3) of the TMA. They also claimed to have substantial goodwill in both the name and the image. They alleged that the defendants were liable both for passing off and trade mark infringement in that they had marketed 'unauthorized' Betty Boop merchandise carrying the name or the image or both: unauthorized because the claimants had not authorized their use. AVELA began 'licensing' Betty Boop merchandise in the UK in 2009. The other defendants respectively were: responsible for licensing AVELA's 'rights'; licensees of AVELA; and some supplied 'Betty Boop' merchandise to retailers. Some of the merchandise carried labels stating that it was 'official merchandise' together with the name of the supplier. AVELA asserted that it was a legitimate source of Betty Boop 'imagery' in the UK. It rested its defence, inter alia, on the fact that the source of its Betty Boop images were old movie posters and not the images which were the subject of the trade marks (and in which the claimants claimed copyright). They did not use the words 'BETTY BOOP' but similar words such as BOOP and variations thereon, although some of their retailers did. They also asserted that they were not liable for trade mark infringement because the public did not view the Betty Boop image or name as a badge of origin. For the same reason, they claimed they were not liable for passing off. Furthermore, in their defence to allegations of trade mark infringement, the defendants argued that their use of the marks was descriptive under section 11(1)(b). In reaching his decision, Birss J identified the common problem raised by character merchandising under both trade mark infringement and passing off,[118] which meant that there were 'losers' such Elvis, Princess Diana, and the 'Wombles' among others; and 'winners' such as the 'Teenage Ninja Turtles'.

Birss J:

69. The essential problem in all these cases is one of fact. The question is always concerned with what the relevant sign signifies to the average consumer (or equivalent in a passing off case). When famous names or images are applied to merchandise they are not necessarily being used as indicators of origin of the goods at all. As Richard Arnold QC (as he then was) noted in *LINKIN PARK*, referring back to *TARZAN*, what better way is there to describe a poster depicting the band LINKIN PARK as a 'LINKIN PARK poster'. So if one imagines a consumer asking in a shop for a LINKIN PARK poster, in that context the mark is

---

[118] [68].

being used descriptively and it would be difficult if not impossible for a trader to sell such a poster without calling it a LINKIN PARK poster.

70. An important point lying behind some of these arguments is that unlike copyright, the rights to a trade mark last forever. If the claimants are right in this case then they may be able to prevent anyone (absent a licence) from selling a product like a t-shirt or bag carrying any image of Betty Boop regardless of whether that image infringes their copyright. It could create what is in effect a copyright of unlimited duration. That would be unwelcome if it was the case. I will return to that point below.

71. Finally at this stage it is worth observing that there may well be differences in fact between different kinds of case in this field. As Laddie J. discussed in *Irvine v Talksport*, endorsement can be different from merchandising. Another difference may be between cases concerning real persons and invented characters. For example real people can be photographed by anyone and so the public are used to seeing images of famous people in contexts far removed from endorsement or merchandising. The same may not be the case for invented characters.

In relation to trade marks, Birss J looked first at who were the average consumers involved and identified them as belonging to three classes: licensees or putative licensees; organizations which buy products and sell to the public; and the purchasing public, who would be aware of licensing and merchandising.[119] The claimants argued that given their long period of trading before AVELA entered the market, the general public had come to recognize their merchandise as emanating from a single source and hence acting as a badge of origin. Conversely, the defendants argued that despite the long period of sale, the public did not see the words 'BETTY BOOP' as an indication of origin and that the imagery was viewed by the public as 'origin neutral'. Birss J disagreed and concluded that by 2009 all three groups of average consumers had been educated to view the words 'BETTY BOOP' and the images as trade marks.[120] Nor did he think that the infringement of the marks depended upon a third party making use of only the exact name and or the specific images registered.

101. The reaction of these three classes to Betty Boop as a designation of origin is not confined to particular poses of the character. It is the character Betty Boop herself who is recognised by the average consumers. It is the character who acts as a sign. The character is recognisable in different ways but she is the same character. The words BETTY BOOP have this effect as do pictures of her. The words (and related expressions) and the images of Betty Boop reinforce one another. Often she appears in one of two poses: one sitting with one leg up and the other in the form of the registered device. Nevertheless she is also recognisable in a myriad of other poses. The key visual sign is her head. It is instantly recognisable whether on its own or with a more or less visible body. Usually the name BETTY BOOP appears with at least her head and the recognition is reinforced but either alone is sufficient to convey the message. The fact that one cannot register a character or a concept as a trade mark does not mean that the public do not in fact recognise a character as having origin significance.

...

104. A characteristic of licence driven merchandising is that the Betty Boop products often appear with other trade marks on them. There may be a trade mark which identifies

[119] [73]–[75].   [120] [97].

the retail outlet. That does not prevent the public from recognising Betty Boop merchandise for what it is. The public are aware that character merchandise can be available from numerous outlets but they are also familiar with the idea that it can be licensed from a single ultimate source.

105. None of these conclusions necessarily follow. The appearance of a well known character (real or fictional) on a product may very well not have origin significance. Without many years of education, the public might well regard the appearance of a famous character on a t-shirt or in a poster as conveying no origin information at all. It may be very difficult for a trader to educate the public to see things in any other way but whether or not that has taken place depends on the evidence.

106. There are some forms of merchandise for which it is clear the public do not believe that it derives from a single source. Pictures of famous people by no means necessarily denote trade origin. The evidence showed that there are many sources of pictures of Marilyn Monroe and other famous celebrities. As I said in *Fenty v Arcadia* (at [2]) there is today in England no such thing as a free standing general right by a famous person (or anyone else) to control the reproduction of their image.

107. However Betty Boop is not a real person. There is no law which provides that invented characters have stronger rights than real people in this regard but it does seem to me that it is probably easier to educate the public to believe that goods relating to an invented character derive from a single official source than it might be for a real person, not least because copyright law may give the inventor the ability to control the reproduction of the character for a very long time.

...

110. When the average consumer who is a member of the general public sees something signifying Betty Boop on the front of a product (like a large picture of the character on a t-shirt or the words Betty Boop prominently on a bag) in my judgment the response is multi-faceted. This average consumer will see the image of Betty Boop as being attractive and in that sense aesthetic or decorative. After all, they will not want to buy a product which does not look good. They will also see it as a sign having associations related to the up-to-date image of the character herself which has been generated by the claimants. However in my judgment they will also see Betty Boop as a sign related to trade origin. The effect of the claimants' trading has been to imbue the character with trade mark significance in the public mind. They do not need to look at the swing tag to make the assumption that it is official Betty Boop merchandise any more than they need to look at the swing tag on a t-shirt with Calvin Klein written in large letters across the front to assume that it is from Calvin Klein. Not all merchandising works this way but in my judgment today and at all material times, in the UK (and the rest of Europe), Betty Boop is a sign which can convey that kind of information in the context of the goods in this case.

It followed for Birss J that the claimant's trade marks were acting as a badge of origin. He went on to find infringement under section 10(2) of the TMA 1994 on the basis that offering a merchandise licence for the words 'BETTY BOOP' covering goods identical to those registered (in this case clothing and bags) was the use of identical marks on identical goods. Turning to section 10(2) (Article 9(1)(b)) and the likelihood of confusion, he noted that the comparison was being made between the registered mark 'BETTY BOOP' and the image which was used by the defendants on a T-shirt.

Birss J:

158. As I have also said before, I reject the idea that this image is purely decorative. It is decorative and attractive but not purely so. The average consumer would recognise it as merchandising and take the presence of Betty Boop as an indication that the product was licensed from a source of merchandising licenses associated with that character. Thus the average consumer would regard the presence of Betty Boop on the product as having origin significance. The conceptual similarity between the image and the word mark BETTY BOOP will cause the average consumer to think that the image conveys the same origin information as the words would. Accordingly they will be confused about the trade origin of the goods and so there is a likelihood of confusion in terms of s.10(2)/art.9(1)(b).

By the same reasoning, Birss J held that the public would make a link between the claimants' mark and the defendants' sign for the purposes of section 10(3) (Article 9(2)). He also accepted that the registered marks had a reputation.

176 ... The ideas associated with the character of Betty Boop in the minds of the average consumer today are ideas caused by the claimants' extensive efforts over the years. I have rejected the idea that all an average consumer today would see, when looking at the t-shirt, would be a 1930s cartoon character. They will see a character with modern currency. This association certainly takes advantage of the claimants' investment in Betty Boop because many consumers will be moved to buy the t-shirt as a result of the favourable associations conjured up in their mind by Betty Boop, which associations are the creation of the claimants' extensive work. I do not have to decide if this is sufficient to establish infringement for the purposes of s.10(3)/art.9(1)(c) or whether such a finding would be an unwarranted extension of trade marks beyond their role as designators of origin.

Finally, Birss J did not accept the defendants' argument that they were using the signs descriptively not least because he did not find the defendants' use based on 'honest commercial practices'. His reasoning rested, inter alia, on the fact that the defendants knew of the existence of the claimants' marks, that they marked their own goods 'Official Licensee', which would be liable to cause confusion, and that they were in direct competition with the claimants. Birss J also found the defendants liable for passing off. Even though the defendants placed their own names on the merchandise, the fact that it was also marked 'officially licensed' led to a misrepresentation that it originated from the same source as the claimants'. He also, as we have seen, viewed the defendants' offer to license the products as providing an instrument of deception.[121]

The approach taken in the 'Linkin Park' and 'Princess Diana' cases is compatible with the decision in the earlier 'Spice Girls' case. This suggests that in some areas of character merchandising at least, in particular that concerned with real personalities, trade mark law still offers the same 'uncertain protection' that Lord Bridge believed was available through the law of passing off. Conversely, on the basis of *Hearst v AVELA*, it would appear that there might now be more certain protection for fictional characters through trade mark registration than for famous people. Do you think this development fairly offsets the lesser protection afforded to fictional characters in cases of false endorsement in passing off? Or is there

---

[121] See Chapter 9.

a wider argument that a recognized image or personality right in the UK would ensure there are no such 'winners' and 'losers' but instead a level playing field for the protection of famous people as against fictional characters? We address this question in the following section.

FURTHER READING

S. Bains, 'Personality rights: should the UK grant celebrities a proprietary right in their personality? Part 1' (2007) 18 Ent. L. R. 165; 'Part 2' (2007) 18 Ent. L. R. 205; 'Part 3' (2007) 18 Ent. L. R. 237.

I. Calboli, 'Betty Boop and the return of aesthetic functionality: a bitter medicine against "mutant copyrights"?' [2014] EIPR 80.

10.4 PUBLICITY PROTECTION

10.4.1 THE NATURE OF A RIGHT OF PUBLICITY/IMAGE RIGHT

Unlike the UK, the US has had a reasonably well-established and well-defined right of publicity existing for several decades. It is useful to consider this as a possible model for other jurisdictions. In the following extract, Beverley-Smith gives a general description of what he understands to be the scope and limits of the right of publicity in the US.

H. Beverley-Smith, *The Commercial Appropriation of Personality*
(Cambridge: Cambridge University Press, 2002), pp. 181–3

[The] contours [of the right of publicity] may be sketched, bearing in mind that there are considerable differences between the statutory and common law provisions in different states…

Liability arises where the defendant 'appropriates the commercial value of a person's identity by using, without consent, the person's name, likeness or other indicia of identity for the purposes of trade'. Liability is based on misappropriation rather than misrepresentation, thus proof of deception or consumer confusion is not required. The interest that is protected is the intangible value of the person's identity rather than trading or promotional goodwill. Despite some dicta to the contrary, prior commercial exploitation by the plaintiff does not seem to be a necessary perquisite. Thus a plaintiff who does not exploit his image for the moment, or a plaintiff who does not contemplate exploiting his image at all, will not be precluded from claiming an infringement of his right of publicity…

The unauthorized appropriation must be sufficient to identify the plaintiff, otherwise it cannot be said in any real sense that the plaintiff's identity has been misappropriated, nor his interest violated. In this respect, the right of publicity differs from the law of registered and un-registered trade marks in that there may be liability despite there being no likelihood of confusion as to source or connection by way of endorsement or sponsorship…

A person's identity may be appropriated in various ways and although a plaintiff is most commonly identified by personal name (including former name), nickname or likeness, use of other indicia of identity such as a plaintiff's voice, distinctive catch-phrase or distinctively marked car may give rise to liability. Protection has also been extended to cover more amorphous indicia of identity which might severally combine to identify the plaintiff, such as the plaintiff's distinctive style of dress, hairstyle and pose. Intent to infringe another's right of publicity is not a necessary element of liability at common law and a mistake relating to the plaintiff's consent will not be a defence.

From the earliest cases, it became clear that the right of publicity differed from the right of privacy in that it was a right of property which was freely assignable, rather than a personal right. Thus where the right of publicity is assigned, the assignee has a direct cause of action against a third party infringer, rather than a mere release of liability for invasion of the subject's privacy...

One of the issues that caused greatest trouble for the courts and commentators was defining the duration of the right of publicity and, in particular, determining whether it was descendible. While the right of privacy is a personal right which dies with the plaintiff, the right of publicity, as noted above, is usually described as a property right. Consequently, some argued that it follows that such a property right should be descendible and that the heirs of deceased figures should be allowed to profit from the valuable right that had been enjoyed by their famous ancestors.

From the US case law, we see many examples of where famous individuals have invoked the right of publicity to protect aspects of their image and personality. One such example[122] is *Waits v Frito-Lay Inc.*[123] The plaintiff, Tom Waits, is a famous professional singer, songwriter, and actor, who was described by Chief Justice Boochever as having a 'raspy, gravelly singing voice, described by one fan as "like how you'd sound if you drank a quart of bourbon, smoked a pack of cigarettes and swallowed a pack of razor blades ... Late at night. After not sleeping for three days." '[124] Frito-Lay, which manufactures and sells snack foods, used a close imitation of Waits's voice in a radio advertisement for 'Dorito' taco chips. This amounted to an infringement of his publicity right under Californian common law, i.e. the right to control the commercial use of one's identity, and substantial compensatory damages of $375,000 were awarded. Interestingly, $100,000 of the award related to the fair market value of Waits's services, $75,000 was for injury to his goodwill, professional standing, and future publicity value, and $200,000 was for hurt feelings and distress. This latter award implicitly suggests that economic and dignitary interests are inevitably intertwined.

10.4.2 JUDICIAL PROTECTION OF PUBLICITY INTERESTS

The UK legislature has thus far not intervened to create a right of publicity, nor have UK courts sought to develop or recognize one at common law. That said, it has been suggested that the claimants' success in the *Douglas v Hello!* litigation[125] reflects the protection of publicity interests, more so than privacy. This is supported by two findings in the case. The first relates to the claims by Michael Douglas and Catherine Zeta-Jones. The Court of Appeal recognized that the award of damages at first instance for the labour and expense of editing the photographs that were to be provided to *OK!* magazine was a head of damage that related to the Douglases' commercial exploitation of their wedding and had little

---

[122] Other examples include: *Midler v Ford Motor Co.*, 849 F 2d 460 (9th Cir. 1988); *Carson v Here's Johnny Portable Toilets Inc.*, 698 F 2d. 831 (6th Cir. 1983); and *White v Samsung Electronics Inc.*, 971 F 2d 1395 (9th Cir. 1992), 989 F 2d 1512 (9th Cir. 1993).

[123] 978 F 2d 1093 (9th Cir. 1992).   [124] At 1097.

[125] *Douglas v Hello! Ltd (No. 1)* [2001] QB 967; *Douglas v Hello! Ltd (No. 6)* [2003] EMLR 31 (Ch); *Douglas v Hello! (No. 8)* [2004] EMLR 2 (Ch); *Douglas v Hello! (No. 3)* [2006] QB 125; *Douglas v Hello! Ltd* sub nom *OBG v Allan* [2007] UKHL 21, [2008] 1 AC 1.

to do with interference with their private life.[126] The court saw 'Recognition of the right of a celebrity to make money out of publicizing private information about himself, including his photographs on a private occasion' as breaking new ground.[127] However, the court was not opposed to this development: 'We can see no reason in principle why equity should not protect the opportunity to profit from confidential information about oneself in the same circumstances that it protects the opportunity to profit from confidential information in the nature of a trade secret.'[128] In other words, the court equated private information that is commercially valuable or capable of exploitation with trade secrets and, arguably, in so doing, acknowledged publicity interests. However, it may be questioned how close this is to a right of publicity (such as that in the US) given that a precursor to protection is that information must be private or confidential. For example, how helpful would breach of confidence be to Tom Waits in the situation that was described above?

A second finding in *Douglas v Hello!* gives rise to some concern that it might lead to the creation of an 'image right' which is for the most part co-terminous with a publicity right. In the House of Lords (where only *OK!* appealed), one of the issues was whether the images of the celebrity wedding, over which *OK!* had been given exclusive coverage, could be considered confidential given that *OK!* had published authorized photographs a few hours earlier than the unauthorized photographs published by *Hello!*. (*OK!* had done this in order to prevent a 'scoop' by *Hello!*). The majority of the House of Lords held in favour of *OK!* magazine and allowed its appeal. On the issue of confidentiality, Lord Hoffmann (who delivered the leading speech of the majority) found that confidential information still remained.

Douglas v Hello! Ltd sub nom *OBG v Allan* [2007] UKHL 21, [2008] 1 AC 1

Lord Hoffmann:

122. My Lords, it is certainly the case that once information gets into the public domain, it can no longer be the subject of confidence. Whatever the circumstances in which it was obtained, there is no point in the law providing protection. But whether this is the case or not depends on the nature of the information. Whether there is still a point in enforcing the obligation of confidence depends on the facts. If the purpose of publishing the pictures was simply to convey the information that the Douglases had married, the bride wore a wedding dress and so forth, then the publication of any photographs would have put that information in the public domain. So would a description of the event. In this case, however, the point of the transaction was that each picture would be treated as a separate piece of information which *OK!* would have the exclusive right to publish. The pictures published by *OK!* were put into the public domain and it would have had to rely on the law of copyright, not the law of confidence, to prevent their reproduction. But no other pictures were in the public domain and they did not enter the public domain merely because they resembled other pictures which had.

Lord Brown adopted a similar view to that of Lord Hoffmann, in finding that the secret consisted of 'each and every visual image of the wedding'.[129] What is the result of

---

[126] *Douglas v Hello! (No. 3)* [2006] QB 125, [111].   [127] [113].   [128] [113].
[129] *Douglas v Hello! Ltd* sub nom *OBG v Allan* [2007] UKHL 21, [2008] 1 AC 1, [329].

characterizing each and every photograph of a wedding celebration as distinct confidential information? In his dissenting speech, Lord Walker commented that:

> the confidentiality which the Douglases claimed, and which *OK!* also claims, is of a specialised commercial character, far removed from the sort of intrusion on the privacy of a seriously ill patient which the Court of Appeal considered (but felt unable to remedy) in *Kaye v Robertson* [1991] FSR 62. Their claims come close to claims to a 'character right' protecting a celebrity's name and image such as has consistently been rejected in English law: see *Elvis Presley Trademarks* [1999] RPC 567, 580–582, 597–598, and also Brooke LJ in the interlocutory appeal in this case [2001] QB 967, paras 74 and 75. The present limits of the law of passing off as a protection of a celebrity complaining of 'false endorsement' were thoroughly reviewed by Laddie J in *Irvine v Talksport Ltd* [2002] 1 WLR 2355.[130]

Do you agree with Lord Walker's view that the Douglases' claim was less about privacy and more about controlling the exploitation and dissemination of their image? Consider, in particular, the fact that Douglas and Zeta-Jones had sold *OK!* exclusive coverage of the wedding for $1 million and that, for this reason, *OK!* was also able to bring a claim for breach of confidence and obtain an award of damages.[131] On the other hand, does this sort of protection equate to a US-style publicity right? Would the Douglases have been able to bring an action for breach of confidence in respect of, for example, the use of look-a-like models to promote the Welsh lamb industry? It seems unlikely. Therefore, it is fair to say that breach of confidence, as interpreted and applied in *Douglas v Hello!*, at best may protect *some* publicity interests but in no way approximates a right of publicity. The recent decision of the Court of Appeal in *Fenty v Arcadia*, the 'Rihanna' case, confirms that despite the increasing willingness of the courts to recognize the economic value of merchandising and endorsements, the same may be said of trade marks and passing off.

Fenty v Arcadia Group Brands Ltd (No. 2) [2015] EWCA Civ 3

The claimant, Rihanna, is a world famous pop star. The defendants own and operate a well-known chain of fashion stores called 'Topshop'. In 2012, the defendants started selling a 'fashion T-shirt' both in-store and online which carried Rihanna's image. This particular image was particularly striking, showing her looking at the camera wearing a headscarf. It had been taken at a video shoot for a single from her new album, 'Talk That Talk', and similar images had been used to market the album. The image at issue had been licensed by the photographer to Topshop. This act obviously raised copyright issues, but in these proceedings, Rihanna (and her 'corporate licensing vehicles') sued for passing off, alleging that, while she had not licensed the use of her image, a substantial number of people would mistakenly believe that she had endorsed its use. Among the facts that Birss J in the High Court held to be relevant to his decision were the following: Rihanna has a 'very large endorsement and merchandising' business and has endorsed high-profile goods such as Nike. She has also worked hard to associate herself

---

[130] [285].

[131] According to Lord Hoffmann, [117]: '*OK!* had paid $1 million for the benefit of the obligation of confidence imposed upon all those present at the wedding in respect of any photographs of the wedding. That was quite clear. Unless there is some conceptual or policy reason why they should not have the benefit of that obligation, I cannot see why they were not entitled to enforce it.'

with fashion garments in the eyes of the public and has had agreements with fashion houses to collaborate on designing clothes, for instance with Armani in 2012 which included a T-shirt carrying her image. Much of the clothing she endorses carries a distinctive 'R-slash' logo and/or her name. In 2010 Rihanna had had a brief association with Topshop being the subject of an online competition and she visited their Oxford Street store shortly before the T-shirts went on sale in 2012: a visit which was widely tweeted. Rihanna succeeded in the High Court. Birss J held that the sale of the T-shirt was likely to lead some people to assume that she had licensed or authorized the use of her image. This was so even though there had been nothing on the shirts or their labelling to suggest Rihanna had authorized them and there had be no confusion. He based his decision, inter alia, on the fact that she had become a 'style icon' particularly for young women. He thought customers at Topshop might expect that garments carrying celebrity images would believe they had been licensed. And, in addition, Birss J believed that some fans would be influenced by the competition, by Rihanna's visit to Topshop, or would be likely to associate the image on the T-shirts with the album cover. For these reasons, the judge believed there had been a material misrepresentation and damage would result to Rihanna's goodwill both through loss of sales and loss of control over her reputation in the fashion sphere. Topshop appealed. In the Court of Appeal, Kitchin LJ summarized the four grounds for Topshop's appeal:

25. First, the judge wrongly proceeded on the basis that there was no difference in law between an endorsement case and a merchandising case. Character merchandising generally serves to provide the products concerned with features of shape or get-up which become part of the make-up of the products themselves. It is not the province of the common law to create or confer exclusive rights in particular categories of product.

26. Secondly, the judge properly and correctly acknowledged that the sale of a garment bearing a recognisable image of a famous person does not, in and of itself, amount to passing off. However, the judge fell into error thereafter in failing to proceed on the basis that the law of passing off treats the use on garments of such images as origin neutral. So, Mr Hobbs continues, the claim for passing off in the present case should only have been entertained upon the basis that the market for garments carrying images of Rihanna was, at least in principle, a market which others were lawfully entitled to enter. Further, the injunction granted by the judge is founded upon the proposition that Topshop is answerable for a misrepresentation by omission, that is to say for failing clearly to inform prospective purchasers that the T-shirts were not approved or authorised by Rihanna. Once it is accepted, as it must be, that selling a garment with a recognisable image of a famous person does not, in and of itself, amount to passing off, any claim for misrepresentation by omission should have evaporated.

27. Thirdly, the judge ought to have recognised and accepted that the absence of an image right is a matter of law and not a matter of fact. Further, he ought to have assessed the claim having regard to the perceptions of those persons for whom the presence of the image of Rihanna on the T-shirt was origin neutral, and not the perceptions of those persons who were liable to regard the presence of the image as an indication of authorisation. Indeed, had the judge assessed the issue from the correct perspective he would have been bound to find that the claim as pleaded and pursued disclosed no sustainable basis for a finding of liability.

28. Fourthly, the judge fell into further error in finding Topshop liable for misrepresentation in the way that he did because Rihanna had never properly alleged or developed a case that the particular image in issue was in any way distinctive as a result of any marketing or

promotional activity which she had ever carried out; that there was no admissible evidence that this image was in any way distinctive; and that the evidence upon which the judge relied had no probative value....

In his own judgment, Kitchin LJ began by addressing the question of whether English law recognizes an 'image right'. He stated categorically: 'There is in English law no "image right" or "character right" which allows a celebrity to control the use of his or her name or image.'[132] And he based this assertion on the House of Lords' judgment in *Douglas v Hello! Ltd*.[133] Kitchin LJ then went on to summarize the ways in which a celebrity might nonetheless control his or her image.

33. A celebrity seeking to control the use of his or her image must therefore rely upon some other cause of action such as breach of contract, breach of confidence, infringement of copyright or, as in this case, passing off. However, as Mr Hobbs has properly reminded us, the law of passing off is not designed to protect a person against fair competition. Nor does it protect a person against the sale by others of the same goods or even copied goods. What it protects is goodwill and it prevents one person passing off his goods or services as those of another....

34. It is of course inherent in these propositions that, registered trade marks aside, no-one can claim monopoly rights in a word or a name. Conversely, however, no-one may, by the use of any word or name, or in any other way, represent his goods or services as being the goods or services of another person and so cause that other person injury to his goodwill and so damage him in his business. Further, it is enough that the goods or services are represented as being in some way connected or associated with that other person provided that the connection is a material one in the sense that it has caused or is likely to cause him such damage in his business.

35. The particular kinds of connection and association relevant to the present proceedings are those which arise in cases of character merchandising and endorsement.

Citing *Irvine v Talksport*, Kitchin LJ found with Birss J that there had been passing off on the basis of false endorsement. He went on to state that such a finding would not contradict the finding of the Supreme Court in the *Hello!* case. And he also acknowledged, following *Elvis Presley*, that just because the name or image of a celebrity appears on a product, the public will not assume there has been an endorsement. It followed, according to Kitchin LJ, that:

43. So the claimant in a case of this kind must make good his case on the evidence. He must show that he has a relevant goodwill, that the activities of the defendant amount to a misrepresentation that he has endorsed or approved the goods or services of which he complains, and that these activities have caused or are likely to cause him damage to his goodwill and business.

[Kitchin LJ then went on to consider the case at hand.]

44. With these general principles in mind I turn now to consider Mr Hobbs' submissions and begin with his contention that the judge failed properly to have regard to the distinction between merchandising and endorsement. Mr Hobbs has developed his argument as

---

[132] [29].   [133] [2007] UKHL 21.

follows. Purchasers of T-shirts bearing images of famous pop stars buy them not because they believe that the garments have any material connection with the pop stars at all but simply because they want to wear a garment carrying a picture of their idol. Merchandising therefore carries with it no misrepresentation. Further, even if some members of the public do believe that there is in existence some sort of licensing arrangement with the pop star in question then it is most unlikely to have an effect upon their buying decision.

45. Mr Hobbs has here identified what to my mind are the two critical hurdles which a claimant must overcome in a claim for passing off in a merchandising case. First, it must be shown that application of the name or image to the goods has the consequence that they tell a lie. This requirement, which is closely allied to distinctiveness, will not be satisfied if the name or image denotes nothing about the source of the goods. Secondly, it must be shown that the lie is material. In many merchandising cases, the lie amounts to no more than a false suggestion that the goods are licensed and, as such, it may have no effect upon the buying decision....

However, Kitchin LJ concluded that the judge had been aware of the difference between character merchandising and false endorsement and that he had been correct to find the latter.

47. With all these principles in mind the judge then approached the facts of present case and made his findings. He considered that the use of this image would, in all the circumstances of the case, indicate that the T-shirt had been authorised and approved by Rihanna. Many of her fans regard her endorsement as important for she is their style icon, and they would buy the T-shirt thinking that she had approved and authorised it. In short, the judge found that the sale of this T-shirt bearing this image amounted to a representation that Rihanna had endorsed it. In my judgment the reasoning of the judge discloses no error of principle of the kind for which Mr Hobbs contends.

[Kitchin LJ continued:]

48. I turn now to the second ground of appeal and, in light of the foregoing, I can deal with this quite shortly. Rihanna has always accepted that she has no right in English law to prevent any use of her image. Further and specifically, she acknowledges that the sale of garments bearing recognisable images of her does not, in and of itself, amount to passing off. However, as Mr Martin Howe QC, who appears with Mr Andrew Norris on her behalf, submits, it does not follow that the image itself must be excluded from the matrix of facts which are said to give rise to an overall representation that she has endorsed the goods to which it has been applied. I am entirely satisfied that the proposition that a famous personality has no right to control the use of her image in general does not lead inexorably to the conclusion that the use of a particular image cannot give rise to the mistaken belief by consumers that the goods to which it is applied have been authorised. Here the judge came to the conclusion that the use of this particular image on fashion T-shirts sold by Topshop amounted to a misrepresentation by Topshop that the garments had been approved or authorised by Rihanna. There is no inconsistency between this finding and the proposition that Rihanna has no absolute right to prevent traders selling garments carrying her image. Nor is the judge's approach undermined by the form of injunction which he ultimately granted. It simply recognises that the vice in the impugned activities lay not in the use of Rihanna's image but in using it in such a way as to cause a misrepresentation. As Mr Howe submits and again I accept, Topshop is in effect

> contending not for the absence of an image right, but rather for a positive right to market goods bearing an image even if the use of that image in particular circumstances to particular customers gives rise to a misrepresentation. To accede to that submission would be to sanction a trade which results in the deception of the public.

On the third and fourth grounds of the appeal, Kitchin LJ first held that the judge was correct to assess the misrepresentation from the viewpoints of members of the public who have a particular interest in Rihanna and who shop at Topshop, of whom many would have been aware of the competition and her visit to the store, and hence might have assumed a connection between Rihanna and the T-shirt on sale. Finally, Kitchin LJ held that although aspects of the Birss J's reasoning might be challenged, nonetheless he was right to hold that the fact that the contested image might remind members of the public of the album illustrations was relevant.

Kitchin LJ:

61 ... The judge found on the evidence, as I believe he was entitled to, that the image itself is striking because it is oversized and shows Rihanna's face and shoulders; that Rihanna is looking straight at the camera with her hair tied above her head in a head scarf, in other words that she is in a pose; and that similar images had been used for the recent Talk That Talk album and associated video. It seems to me that, having come this far, the judge was also entitled to go on and make the finding that he did at [69], namely that the relationship between this image and the images for the album and video would be noticed by her fans. Indeed the nature of the image may be thought to have made it very likely indeed that it would be taken to be an authorised publicity shot for what was then her recent musical release ...

62. It follows that the judge was entitled to find that the sale by Topshop of the T-shirt amounted to passing off. I would therefore dismiss the main appeal and refuse permission to appeal against the judgment of 5 July 2013.

The question then arises whether, given the very ad hoc manner in which established rights in signs, goodwill, and confidential information have come to protect some aspects of personality, it would be preferable for a *sui generis*, publicity right to be introduced into UK law. It is one thing, however, to provide indirect protection of publicity via established rights, and another thing to create an independent publicity right. Compelling reasons would need to exist for the latter to be introduced. We turn, therefore, to discuss possible justifications for a right of publicity.

10.4.3 JUSTIFICATIONS FOR A PUBLICITY RIGHT/IMAGE RIGHT

The justifications for a right of publicity mirror the main justifications for intellectual property rights that we explored in Chapter 1, including unjust enrichment, the Lockean labour theory, and economic efficiency. You may wish to turn back to 1.2 in Chapter 1 to revisit these justifications.

Simply stated, the unjust enrichment justification for a publicity right is that celebrities have invested in the development of their image and it would be unfair for others to benefit from this. However, this argument begs the question, *why* is the unauthorized use of a celebrity's image unfair? At this point, Lockean-style arguments are usually invoked, i.e. a celebrity is entitled to the fruits of his or her labour. More specifically, because a celebrity's image, status, and success are the result of their efforts only they should be able to exploit it. But is it correct to adopt such a singular view of whose labour is responsible for celebrity success? Hazel Carty questions this view in the following extract:

H. Carty, 'Advertising, publicity rights and English law' [2004] IPQ 209 at 249–50

... [I]t is not obvious to all commentators (or judges) that celebrity magnetism 'belongs' to the celebrity. Consumers, the media and those who produce and manage the celebrity play a pivotal role in success, leading Madow to comment that it is wrong therefore to have an 'individualistic picture of public image formation ... though this dominates case law'.

...

Indeed, to see the successful image in entertainment or the media as a 'stand alone' phenomenon in many ways misses the point of celebrity as icon. Entertainment or media celebrities are on the whole themselves derivative—the obvious example in recent years being Madonna and her homage to Marilyn Monroe. For Madow the star draws on 'our culture's image bank' and yet tries to 'halt the free circulation of signs and meanings at just the point that suits them'.

...

Again, once celebrity status is 'achieved' does 'common sense' demand that the persona should not be used by others as inspiration for developing ideas or simply to provide fun—i.e. the transformative use of celebrity. In the late 1990s Schweppes ran an advertising campaign using lookalikes of such celebrities as Posh Spice, Sven-Goren Eriksson and Camilla Parker Bowles which was both creative and fun, underlining the fact that a celebrity (as celebrity, rather than as private person) becomes part of 'the public domain' to be used for developing ideas. A more recent example of a fun use of celebrity to catch consumer attention was the advertising campaign run by easyJet featuring the photograph of Major Charles Ingram with the caption 'time to leave the country'. At the time the Major's cheating on the television game show was headline news and the butt of many jokes.

Carty argues that celebrity success cannot be isolated and attributed to one person, but is the result of a more complex interaction. As well, she raises the importance of the 'commons' or 'public domain' and how this may be impoverished by the grant of a publicity right. Do you agree?

In her article, Carty also discusses another popular justification for the right of publicity, the economic justification. She explains that there are three versions of this justification. The first is that a publicity right would encourage or incentivize creative endeavour. Second, such a right would result in a more efficient allocation of the 'resource' of personality or celebrity. Finally, a publicity right can serve to avoid consumer misinformation and confusion. Carty then moves on to interrogate the persuasiveness of these three arguments:

The theory is that by affording property rights the law provides an incentive to creative endeavour. But what evidence is there for such incentive effect? Are we confident that a publicity right results in increased 'innovation' or economic activity? Are property rights necessary to motivate success? Rather, might not publicity or image rights be seen by all those concerned (celebrity and public) as additional benefits—the real incentive to endeavour is the original desire to excel in sport, politics or entertainment generally. Moreover, unlike copyright protection, is it obvious that the public interest is being served by the 'creations' that result we are told from such protection, given that a publicity right encourages not so much the original activity that led to the fame but rather the commercial activity in marketing the resulting image?

What then of allocative efficiency as a justification? Of course it makes sense to ensure the efficient use of scarce resources and to prevent overexploitation, by bestowing property rights on such resources. But as Madow points out here we are not dealing with a non-renewable natural resource like land. Nor, however annoying it is for the individual celebrity concerned, is the cost of free use significant, given, as Fraser points out, 'a fairly plentiful supply of alternative resources exists'.

...

Then there is the final economic justification: the prevention of misinformation. Rather than create rights against misappropriation, this justification focuses on the prevention of harm where there is a clear public interest also served. This is a manifestly worthwhile rationale-combining protection of the celebrity's success with protection of the consumer. It reflects the traditional rationale for trade mark law and the tort of passing off. And indeed the thrust of the demand for publicity or image rights owes far more to an analogy with trade marks than with copyright or patents. However this rationale does not justify a new publicity right and it certainly does not require property rights in the image. Rather it cautions an adherence to the traditional reluctance to expand rights in this area. This rationale sees the role of the law as to prevent a misrepresentation that the celebrity endorses the product with which he is being associated and the consequent misinformation leading to inefficient consumer choice. Harm rather than theft is at the heart of this rationale.[134]

Carty's conclusion is, in effect, that prevention of misinformation is a laudable aim but that this is already served by existing IPRs, namely trade marks and passing off. Do you agree with Carty?

A final justification that emerges from the literature is one based on autonomy and dignity. This has been propounded by Gillian Black, who (unlike Carty) is firmly in favour of introducing a right of publicity into UK law. Black argues that respect for an individual's dignity and autonomy means that they ought to be able to control their persona.

G. Black, 'Exploiting image: making a case for the legal regulation of publicity rights in the UK' [2011] EIPR 413 at 415–16

However, where publicity exploitation makes use of an individual's image and identity—as it invariably does—there is a risk of harm to the individual if that use is unauthorised. Failure to allow individuals to control the use of their image and identity risks infringing their personal autonomy. Autonomy is the notion that individuals should be free to make their own life choices, with as little regulation from external sources as possible, subject to the need for each individual to respect the self-respect and bodily integrity of others. The exercise of autonomy enables each individual to take responsibility for his own life choices and pursuit of the 'good life'. Such is the importance of autonomy in the Western legal tradition that Professor MacCormick has said: 'If there is any fundamental moral value, that of respect for persons as autonomous agents seems the best candidate for that position.' The role of law is, in part, 'to prevent the violation of a citizen's autonomy, dignity and self-esteem'.

---

[134] At 251–2.

The critical importance of image for autonomy has recently been emphasised by a decision of the European Court of Human Rights, *Reklos v Greece*. The action was raised by the parents of a child, claiming a breach of their art.8 right to private and family life. The day after the birth of their son, the applicants (his parents) were offered the opportunity to purchase photographs of him, taken by the professional photographer in the private clinic. The photographs were taken face-on to the baby. Not only had the parents not consented to the taking of these pictures, but they also revealed that the photographer had been into the sterile unit where their son was being treated, despite the fact that access to the unit was restricted to doctors and nurses. The parents complained to the clinic management, but their request that the negatives be handed over was refused. After exhausting their domestic remedies in Greece, they then raised an action under the ECHR.

Although this case is very much a claim under art.8 for invasion of private life (and, critically, there was no attempt to publish or disseminate the photographs), the opinion of the ECtHR is highly relevant.

…

In a key passage, the court stated:

A person's image constitutes one of the chief attributes of his or her personality, as it reveals the person's unique characteristics and distinguishes the person from his peers. The right to the protection of one's image is thus one of the essential components of personal development and presupposes the right to control the use of that image. Whilst in most cases the right to control such uses involves the possibility for an individual to refuse publication of his or her image, it also covers the individual's right to object to the recording, conservation and reproduction of the image by another person. As a person's image is one of the characteristics attached to his or her personality, its effective protection presupposes, in principle and in circumstances such as those of the present case, obtaining the consent of the person concerned at the time the picture is taken and not simply if and when it is published. Otherwise an essential attribute of personality would be retained in the hands of a third party and the person concerned would have no control over any subsequent use of the image.

This is a very strong statement of the importance of an individual's image and its significance for personal development (and thus autonomy), with the corresponding need to ensure that it is protected from unauthorised use.

How does this understanding of autonomy and dignity apply to publicity rights? Central to the exercise of autonomy and dignity are the notions of personal choice and control, and these are the very notions which are jeopardised where there is no right of publicity. Lacking a right of publicity, an individual can attempt to control when and where his image—and his very identity—is used, and by whom, but there is no certainty of success. Autonomy and dignity operate to justify a right for each individual to control the use of his image and identity.

In the above extract Black discusses the ECtHR decision in *Reklos*—a case where photographing a newborn baby whilst in a medical unit without the consent of the parents was held to violate the child's right under Article 8 of the ECHR. To what extent does the control of 'image' in this factual scenario parallel the control of image in the case of a celebrity? Are the autonomy/dignitary interests really the same? Would it matter if the celebrity were seeking not simply to control dissemination of their image but to profit from it as well? Hazel Carty is rather sceptical of the dignitary interests that lie behind a publicity right. She argues that:

…the overall concern [of the publicity right] is to protect the commercial magnetism of the celebrity. Rather than 'personal' dignitary concerns they focus on 'commercial' dignitary concerns. Rather than impacting on the private space of the celebrity they impact on celebrity as brand. In the majority of cases where 'dignitary' issues seem central it is still the commercial interests of the celebrity which are in fact being raised. In such cases the harm to the commercial value of the celebrity image may be alleged to arise from harm to the 'dignity' of the celebrity. At the heart of such objections based on controlling dignitary interests are essentially commercial concerns: the celebrity seeks to control the use of his persona in order to maintain full impact in its further and future commercial use. When such objections are made it is the investment in the celebrity image that is being defended, not privacy.[135]

Do you agree with Carty that dignitary concerns are peripheral in the case of publicity rights or do you prefer Black's view that dignitary interests are prominent and should influence how we construct a right of publicity?

FURTHER READING

H. Beverley-Smith, *The Commercial Appropriation of Personality* (Cambridge: Cambridge University Press, 2002).

H. Beverley-Smith, A. Ohly, and A. Lucas-Schloetter, *Privacy, Property and Personality: Civil Law Perspectives on Commercial Appropriation* (Cambridge: Cambridge University Press, 2005)

G. Black, *Publicity Rights and Image: Exploitation and Legal Control* (Oxford: Hart, 2011).

G. Brüggemeier, A. Colombi Ciacchi, and P. O'Callaghan (eds), *Personality Rights in European Tort Law* (Cambridge: Cambridge University Press, 2010).

H. Carty, 'Advertising, publicity rights and English law' [2004] IPQ 209.

R. J. Coombe, 'Authorizing the celebrity: publicity rights, postmodern politics, and unauthorized genders' (1991–2) 10 Cardozo Arts & Ent. L. J. 365.

D. Gervais and M. L. Holmes, 'Fame, property, and identity: the scope and purpose of the right of publicity' (2015) 25 Fordham Intell. Prop. Media & Ent. L.J. 181.

M. Madow, 'Private ownership of public image: popular culture and publicity rights' (1993) 81 Cal. L .R. 134.

10.5 CONCLUSION

What this chapter has shown is that privacy, personality, and publicity protection in the UK has developed in an ad hoc way which has proved, in many instances, unsatisfactory both to those who think there is insufficient protection and to others who think that there should be less. Thus, on the whole, character and personality merchandisers have been generally disappointed by the limited extent to which the courts have been willing to use either passing off or trade mark law to protect their commercial interests. An example would be the failure to allow 'owners' of fictional characters to sue for false endorsement. Conversely, there is a strong feeling among the press that the judiciary has erred on the side of over-protection of personal privacy (indeed, they have been criticized for creating a limited right of privacy)

---

[135] [2004] IPQ 209, 213.

when it conflicts with the right to freedom of expression. Even very limited moves towards recognizing some aspects of a publicity right, in the case of *Douglas v Hello!*, caused a rift within the House of Lords itself.

At this point it might be useful to return to the example of Jerri Jones, which was offered at the start of this chapter, and the questions that it raised. You may have taken a view not only as to what would be the correct answers to these questions, given the prevailing law, but also whether these would, in your own view, be fair. Thus, it is probable that Jerri Jones would be able to prevent the publication of the sunbathing photographs but not the use by BrandX of her distinctive voice, although here the answer would almost certainly be different in the US. It is unlikely, too, that either S&B Films or Merchandise Ltd could prevent the use by BrandX of a Kit look-a-like to sell their cars since, as we have seen, the courts do not see fictional characters as endorsing products. However, if the public were to identify this look-a-like as Jerri, rather than Kit, then the fact that Jerri has endorsed products in the past will stand her in good stead. Whether you think it wrong that Jerri Jones cannot prevent the exploitation of certain aspects of her personality, such as her voice, may rest upon how you understand the nature of fame. You may take the view that individuals alone should be able to exploit the economic value of their fame or, conversely, you may believe that fame is something which belongs, at least in part, to the society which made the individual famous.

11

PATENTS I:

JUSTIFICATIONS, REGISTRATION, PATENTABLE SUBJECT MATTER, AND INDUSTRIAL APPLICATION

11.1 INTRODUCTION

A patent may be understood as a monopoly right over the commercial exploitation of an invention, granted for a limited time (usually 20 years). Patents may relate to all manner of inventions, including those in the chemical, mechanical engineering, pharmaceutical, biotechnology, and information technology fields. Thus, the medicines we take, the cars we drive, the bicycles we ride, the portable electronic devices or telephones we use, even the food that we consume, are likely to involve a patented product or process somewhere along the line. For some businesses, the difference between owning patents or not can mean the difference between millions, even billions, of pounds. But that is not to say that patent law is entirely the province of big business. It can, and does, have a relevance also to small and medium enterprises. However, one of the struggles for patent law is creating a system that is equally accessible and valuable to all participants.

Patent law grants a territorial right, yet the global significance of patents is without doubt. This has led to international and regional agreements that ensure basic consistencies in the substantive and, to a lesser extent, procedural law relating to patents. The focus of the next three chapters will be on elucidating UK patent law principles. However, it should be remembered that, like so much of intellectual property law today, patent law sits firmly within an international context.

11.2 HISTORY

The following section will provide an overview of the history of UK patent law. This is important, not only because it contextualizes the existing law, but also because it highlights that some of the present-day controversies in patent law are not in fact new.

The UK patent system can be traced back to at least the 14th century, when the Crown granted royal privileges to foreign craftsmen (mainly weavers, salt-makers, and glass-makers) with a view to encouraging them to live in England and practise their trade, thereby transferring skills to the local population. These privileges were granted by a document known as a 'letters patent'[1] and, initially, did not confer any exclusive rights. Further, 'letters patent' were not confined to granting privileges for inventions, but were also used by the Crown to grant land, honours, liberties, and franchises.[2]

In the middle of the 16th century, the practice of granting letters patent to attract superior continental technology was revived on a larger scale, with a key difference being that this time the privileges did confer exclusivity, an idea which seems to have been borrowed from the Venetians.[3] Although the transfer of manufacturing knowledge and skills was the predominant motive for the issue of patents under Elizabeth I, this royal practice was also used to assist in paying off political debts and in raising revenue. These monopolies became a source of discontent because they artificially raised prices, gave patent holders wide powers of enforcement of their rights, and were granted for questionable material. The popular outcry reached such a pitch that in 1601 Elizabeth I agreed to revoke many of the worst patents, by issuing the Proclamation Concerning Monopolies of 1601. This revoked the majority of monopoly grants and, more importantly, allowed matters concerned with such grants to be contested in the common law courts. The next year, Edward Darcy, who had been granted letters patent in the importation, making, and selling of playing cards, attempted to enforce his right against an infringer named Allen. The court held that the monopoly was illegal and the patent was declared invalid.[4]

Elizabeth I's successor, James I, continued to use the patent system in an arbitrary and abusive manner and, as a result, Parliament introduced in 1624 the Statute of Monopolies. This legislation imposed a general prohibition on the grant of patents by the Crown. However, an exception was created by section 6, which stated:

> Provided … that any declaration before mentioned shall not extend to any letters patent and grants of privilege for the term of fourteen years or under … of the sole working or making of any manner of new manufactures within this Realme, to the true and first inventor and inventors of such manufactures which others at the time of making such letters patent and grants shall not use, so as also they be not contrary to the law, or mischievous to the State, by raising prices of commodities at home, or hurt of trade, or generally inconvenient …

[1] Since the Patents Act 1977 (PA 77), letters patent are no longer used to grant patents for inventions in the UK. Rather, the Comptroller-General of Patents, Designs and Trade Marks (i.e. the UK Intellectual Property Office) sends the proprietor a certificate in the prescribed form stating that the patent has been granted to him: see PA 77, s. 24(2); Patents Rules (SI 2007/3291), r. 34.

[2] C. Macleod, *Inventing the Industrial Revolution: The English Patent System 1660–1800* (Cambridge: Cambridge University Press, 1988), p. 10.

[3] The Venetian law of 1474 provided for ten-year exclusive privileges to be granted to inventors of new arts and machines.

[4] *Darcy v Allen* (1602) 77 ER 1260. Questioning the reporting of the case by Coke and thus, in turn, the significance that has been attached to the decision, see M. Fisher, 'The case that launched a thousand writs, or all that is dross? Re-conceiving *Darcy v Allen*: the Case of Monopolies' [2010] IPQ 356.

Section 6 of the 1624 Statute of Monopolies was declaratory of the previous practice and common law.[5] Yet, it is often regarded as laying the foundations of patent law. The tendency to trace patent law back to the 1624 Statute of Monopolies is something that Sherman and Bently warn against, mainly because it encourages us to gloss over the history of the patent system between 1624 to the present day and to treat patent law as predestined and timeless, as opposed to open and historically contingent.[6]

The 17th century 'provided no more than a germ of a functioning patent system'.[7] However, it is interesting to note that in the 17th century, the essential consideration for the grant of the patent was not the filing of a patent specification which sufficiently disclosed the knowledge of the invention, but rather the introduction of the new industry or trade, in other words the putting into practice of the invention.[8]

The requirement that a patent owner provide a written description of the invention did not emerge until the 18th century and was one that grew out of common practice. In the latter half of the 18th century, it effectively became a requirement as courts insisted upon a written description of the invention as 'consideration' for the monopoly granted.[9] An example of such judicial insistence is *Liardet v Johnson*.[10] In this case Liardet brought an action for infringement against Johnson in relation to a patent for a newly invented stucco, or composition, to imitate stone for covering the outside of buildings. Lord Mansfield, in instructing the jury at the end of the trial, emphasized that the specification had to instruct others in how to make the invention. The shifting of the 'consideration' of the patent grant from practising the invention to disclosure of the invention led to a corresponding change in the conception of novelty. In assessing novelty, it was now pertinent also to ask if the trade already knew of the invention through publication.[11]

At the beginning of the 19th century there was deep dissatisfaction with the patent system. Three main complaints emerged:[12] first, that the administrative machinery for securing a patent was excessively unwieldy; second, that the cost of obtaining patents was too high, particularly since separate patents had to be registered for England, Scotland, and Ireland; third, the grounds on which a patent could be declared invalid were too harsh—judges would set aside patents as invalid because of minor errors in the patent specification and yet inventors were not entitled to correct such errors once the specification had been enrolled. In 1829, Thomas Lennard called on Parliament to establish a Select Committee to enquire into the state of patent law. The grievances mentioned above, along with others, were aired before the Select Committee. The main proposal to emerge was the establishment of a scientific commission to examine inventions. It was thought

---

[5] C. Macleod, *Inventing the Industrial Revolution*, pp. 17–19 and J. Pila, 'The common law invention in its original form' [2001] IPQ 209.

[6] B. Sherman and L. Bently, *The Making of Modern Intellectual Property Law* (Cambridge: Cambridge University Press, 1999), pp. 208–9.

[7] W. R. Cornish and D. Llewelyn, *Intellectual Property: Patents, Copyright, Trade Marks and Allied Rights* (6th edn, London: Sweet & Maxwell, 2007) para. 3-06.

[8] See D. Seaborne Davies, 'The early history of the patent specification' (1934) 50 LQR 86, 97, 99–100; and E. W. Hulme, 'On the consideration of the patent grant, past and present' (1897) 13 LQR 313, 313–14.

[9] See E. W. Hulme, 'On the history of patent law in the seventeenth and eighteenth centuries' (1902) 18 LQR 280.

[10] (1778) 62 Eng Rep 1000.   [11] According to Hulme, 'On the history of patent law', 287.

[12] See H. I. Dutton, *The Patent System and Inventive Activity during the Industrial Revolution, 1750–1852* (Manchester: Manchester University Press, 1984), pp. 34–6.

that such an examination process would reduce the number of faulty specifications and the risk of them being set aside by the courts. Unfortunately, the Select Committee's findings were inconclusive and little by way of concrete reform was achieved. Sherman and Bently argue that the Select Committee nonetheless, 'still played an important role in bringing about the emergence of modern patent law: it both operated to expose the confused and uncertain nature of the law and drew together many of the divergent criticisms that existed at the time'.[13]

After the Select Committee, enthusiasm for reform continued. A Bill in 1833 was brought before Parliament by Godson,[14] but failed. This highlighted that although reformers were keen to improve the position of inventors, there was much disagreement about the best way to achieve this.[15] A Bill was introduced in 1835, this time by Lord Brougham. While the 1835 Bill was successful, it brought about modest changes. It was now possible for patentees to amend their specifications to correct minor errors and for patentees to obtain a further seven years' protection upon petitioning the Judicial Committee of the Privy Council.[16] Other minor amendments were achieved by legislation in 1839 and 1844.

Due to other, more pressing, domestic concerns, calls for patent law reform declined during the 1840s. However, interest in patent reform was revived in the late 1840s and early 1850s and culminated in the Patent Law Amendment Act 1852. This Act brought about substantial reform of the patent system. The administration of the system was simplified; an index of patents that could be consulted by the public was introduced; a single patent for the UK replaced the separate patents for England, Scotland, and Ireland; and, perhaps most importantly, the cost of patenting was reduced.[17]

Whereas the first half of the 19th century saw repeated calls and attempts to reform the patent system, the latter half saw calls for its abolition with the controversy reaching its peak between 1850 and 1875.[18] Political economists were key opponents of the patent system and linked the ills of tariff protectionism in trade with those of patent protectionism and the patent monopoly.[19] In order to distance the issue of patent protection from monopoly and free trade issues, the pro-patent lobby sought to justify patents according to natural law and utilitarian rationales. These rationales, which are discussed in the next section on justifications, have a continuing relevance. In the end, the anti-patent movement waned and the pro-patent lobby prevailed. Even so, the attempts to abolish the patent system were critical to a transformation in the legal image of the invention, providing the foundations of modern patent law.[20]

In 1883, the Patents, Designs and Trade Marks Act was passed and gave effect to the Paris Convention for the Protection of Industrial Property 1883 (discussed at 11.4.1.1). There were several important consequences of this Act. First, patent actions were now tried by a single judge. Second, patentees were obliged to include in their specifications at least one claim delineating the scope of their monopoly and judges came to insist that claims mark out the full range of protection for patentees. Finally, the Patent Office began to examine applications, albeit mainly for formal defects and sufficiency of description.

---

[13] Sherman and Bently, *The Making of Modern Intellectual Property Law*, p. 103.
[14] For a discussion see Dutton, *The Patent System and Inventive Activity*, pp. 46–8.
[15] See Dutton, p. 48.   [16] For a discussion see Dutton, pp. 48–51.   [17] Dutton, p. 63.
[18] See F. Machlup and E. Penrose, 'The patent controversy in the nineteenth century' (1950) 10 Journal of Economic History 1, 1–10.
[19] Machlup and Penrose, p. 9.
[20] Sherman and Bently, *The Making of Modern Intellectual Property Law*, pp. 152–7.

In the 20th century, various patent statutes were passed. However, the most important of these were the Patents Act 1902, the Patents Act 1949, and the Patents Act 1977. The Patents Act 1902 saw a change in the examination process. A Select Committee in 1901 (the Fry Committee) had shown that 40 per cent of patents granted were for inventions already described in earlier British patent specifications. Thus, the 1902 Act introduced into the examination process a novelty search, but not a test of obviousness (although this was a ground on which a patent might be revoked). The Patents Act 1949 represented a codification of incremental changes that had occurred via the common law. It also introduced obviousness as a ground of pre-grant opposition and removed the restrictions on patentability of chemical substances that had been introduced in 1919. The Patents Act 1977 (PA 77) was introduced to implement the European Patent Convention 1973 (EPC) and as such represented a landmark change for UK patent law. The PA 77 (as amended) is the law which today regulates patents in the UK.

From the above historical account, it is interesting to note the sorts of concerns that arose during the development of the patent system. These include the detrimental effects of granting a monopoly right, the need for an accessible and efficient patent system, and avoiding the grant of patents for unmeritorious inventions. In reading this and the next chapter, consider the extent to which these are also problematic for modern patent law.

FURTHER READING

W. R. Cornish in *Oxford History of the Laws of England (1820–1914)*, vol. XIII, Part V 'Patents for Inventions' (Oxford: Oxford University Press, 2010), pp. 931–77.

H. I. Dutton, *The Patent System and Inventive Activity during the Industrial Revolution, 1750–1852* (Manchester: Manchester University Press, 1984).

M. Fisher, 'The case that launched a thousand writs, or all that is dross? Re-conceiving *Darcy v Allen*: the Case of Monopolies' [2010] IPQ 356.

E. W. Hulme, 'The history of the patent system under the prerogative and at common law' (1896) 12 LQR 141.

E. W. Hulme, 'On the consideration of the patent grant, past and present' (1897) 13 LQR 313.

E. W. Hulme 'The history of the patent system under the prerogative at common law: a sequel' (1900) 16 LQR 44.

E. W. Hulme, 'On the history of patent law in the seventeenth and eighteenth centuries' (1902) 18 LQR 280.

F. Machlup and E. Penrose, 'The patent controversy in the nineteenth century' (1950) 10 Journal of Economic History 1.

C. Macleod, *Inventing the Industrial Revolution: The English Patent System 1660–1800* (Cambridge: Cambridge University Press, 1988).

J. Pila, 'The common law invention in its original form' [2001] IPQ 209.

D. Seaborne Davies, 'The early history of the patent specification' (1934) 50 LQR 86.

B. Sherman and L. Bently, *The Making of Modern Intellectual Property Law* (Cambridge: Cambridge University Press, 1999).

11.3 JUSTIFICATIONS

Of all the intellectual property rights, a patent grants a true monopoly, insofar as it gives the owner (i.e. a patentee or patent proprietor) an exclusive right to make and sell the invention, even where a third party may have independently developed the same innovation. This will enable the patentee to charge a monopoly price in respect of his or her invention, and is the reason why owning a patent is so valuable. What justifications exist for bestowing this type of privilege on those who invent? As we have seen, in the late 19th century there were fierce opponents of the patent system. To counter this opposition, pro-patent advocates developed four main arguments in support of retaining patent rights, justifications that are often invoked today. The following extract from Machlup and Penrose explores these arguments in detail.

F. Machlup and E. Penrose, 'The patent controversy in the nineteenth century'
(1950) 10 Journal of Economic History 1 at 9–26

The arguments for patents, formulated in these terms and opposed and defended during the controversy of the nineteenth century, are still used today whenever the patent system is debated. Indeed, little, if anything, has been said for or against the patent system in the twentieth century that was not said equally well in the nineteenth.

The Four Main Arguments

It is possible to distinguish four fundamentally different lines of argument to justify the creation of patent rights …

Argument Type One: A man has a natural property right in his own ideas. Their appropriation by others must be condemned as stealing. Society is morally obligated to recognize and protect this property right. Property is in essence exclusive. Hence enforcement of exclusivity in the use of a patented invention is the only appropriate way for society to recognize this right.

Argument Type Two: Justice requires that a man receive, and therefore that society secure to him, reward for his services in proportion as these services are useful to society. Inventors render useful services. The most appropriate way to secure to inventors rewards commensurate with their services is by means of exclusive patent rights in their inventions.

Argument Type Three: Industrial progress is desirable to society. Inventions and their exploitation are necessary to secure industrial progress. Neither invention nor exploitation of invention will be obtained to any adequate extent unless inventors and capitalists have hopes that successful ventures will yield profits which make it worth their while to make their efforts and risk their money. The simplest, cheapest, and most effective way for society to hold out these incentives is to grant exclusive patent rights in inventions.

Argument Type Four: Industrial progress is desirable to society. To secure it at a sustained rate it is necessary that new inventions become generally known as part of the technology of society. In the absence of protection against immediate imitation of novel technological ideas, an inventor will keep his invention secret. The secret will die with him, and society will thereby lose the new art. Hence it is in the interest of society to induce the inventor to disclose his secret for the use of future generations. This can best be done by granting exclusive patent rights to the inventor in return for public disclosure of his invention.

The four types of argument are independent of one another. Any one of them may be upheld if the other three should be rejected. The first two are based on ethical norms, the last two on political expediency. The first is anchored in concepts of natural law, giving the inventor a natural right to protection; the second calls for protection in the name of fairness to secure the inventor his just reward. The third, resting on the assumption that not enough inventions would be made and utilized without adequate inducements, recommends patent protection as the best inducement. The fourth, fearing the loss of inventions through secrecy, recommends patent protection as a means of inducing disclosure and publicity.

The Natural Property Right in Ideas

...

One of the favourite formulations of the property argument by the patent advocates was in terms of man's natural right to the fruits of his labor. The product of one's labor must be recognized as one's property. This form of the argument was challenged by Rodriguez, a Spanish economist, as follows:

Labor, in fact, is not the *title* to it [the invention], but only the rational *method* of acquiring it... Labor results in property when it results in an *exclusive appropriation*; when the product can only belong to him who has done the work; when it would be necessary to take the article or utility created away from its possessor before it can be used by another person.

But, as Chevalier emphasized, 'an idea can belong to an unlimited number of persons; it is indeed the essence of an idea that, once published, it belongs to all the world...'

...

Wirth's position—accepting the theory of property rights in ideas but denying its applicability to technological inventions—was also Chevalier's, who said:

Literary and artistic works have a perfectly decided character of individuality, and on this account they constitute a distinct property, which the law can recognize. In contrast to this, the character of individuality is wanting in real or supposed inventions, which are the object of patents, since what one man made today, another—a hundred others—may make tomorrow.

R. A. Macfie, the most vocal patent abolitionist in England and a severe critic of the theory of natural property rights in inventions, declared that if there were any 'natural rights' in connection with inventions it would be the inventor's 'right to use his own invention'. But just this right, he argued, was frequently denied under the patent system: all too often an inventor would find himself barred from using his own idea because somebody else had obtained a patent on it; this might happen even if his idea were better than the patented one but was considered a version of it.

...

The whole notion of natural rights of property in ideas in general, and in invention in particular, makes sense only to those who recognize 'natural law' and accept private property as part of it. To others, private property in anything is merely an institution given the sanction of positive law for a social purpose; hence it should be confined to areas where the purpose is good.

... During the third quarter of the nineteenth century, chiefly in Germany, the patent opposition was able to weaken the cause of patent protection partly by demolishing its shaky construction as a natural property right. German patent advocates found it expedient to abandon this position and retreat to stronger ones.

The Just Reward for the Inventor

A safer and sounder defense of the claims of inventors was founded on their moral rights to receive reward for services rendered. Many of those who rejected the notion of private property in ideas saw justice in securing a reward to the inventor for his labor and accepted the institution of the patent as the best method of doing it.

…

Other participants in the patent controversy did not deny the inventor's moral right to be rewarded for his work but held that such reward would come without intervention. If an inventor was really ahead of others, the time interval between his use of the invention and its imitation by his competitors would secure him temporary profits or rents sufficient to reward him for his contribution.

…One might recognize that pecuniary rewards for the inventors' efforts were required as a matter of justice…yet one might still reject patent privileges and support a system of cash prizes or bonuses paid to meritorious inventors. This was the conclusion many economists had reached. They were in favour of rewards for inventors but opposed to the patent system.

…

The alternatives most frequently recommended in lieu of patents were bonuses granted to inventors (a) by the government, (b) by professional associations financed through voluntary contributions by private industries, (c) by an intergovernmental agency, or (d) by an international association maintained through contributions from industries of all countries. Proposals along these lines were discussed in the professional journals and conferences almost everywhere.

The proposals for bonus systems of rewarding inventors did not receive great support. The chief objection was that their administration would give rise to partiality, arbitrariness, or even corruption—the dangers of all institutions giving discretionary power to administrators. Bentham had written, many years earlier: 'An exclusive privilege is of all rewards the best proportioned, the most natural, and the least burthesome.' John Stuart Mill clung to this view. He was still convinced that

> an exclusive privilege, of temporary duration is preferable; because it leaves nothing to anyone's discretion; because the reward conferred by it depends upon the invention's being found useful, and the greater the usefulness, the greater the reward; and because it is paid by the very persons to whom the service is rendered, the consumers of the commodity.

This became the standard argument in the defense of the patent system as the most adequate method of securing just rewards to inventors.

…

The Best Incentive to Invent

…

To say that patents are effective incentives to inventive activity is one thing; it is another to contend that they are necessary for inducing an adequate amount of such activity.

…

Even if the need for a special incentive through 'legislative interference' is accepted, the question whether patents are the best or cheapest means to that end arises just as it arose in connection with the method of doing justice to the inventor. There was the same argument, some claiming that money grants were cheaper and more effective incentives than patents.

The counterclaim that patents were the cheapest means of providing effective incentives turned attention to the comparison between the social benefits and social costs of the patent system.

...

To the extent that the stimulus of the patent system is effective, in the sense of causing people to do what they would not do otherwise, its effectiveness may consist chiefly in diverting existing activity into different, perhaps less productive, channels. This is one of the main contentions of the economists opposing the patent system. The diversion may be from ordinary productive pursuits into 'inventing', or from innovation or research activities in one field to the same kind of activities in another field in which the results enjoy patent protection.

The sacrifice of the production that would otherwise have occurred through the alternative uses of the productive resources steered into different channels by the patent incentive must of course be considered a social cost of the patent system. But three other factors were counted among the cost: First, the cost of the bureaucracy administering the patent system: the court personnel, lawyers, agents, and others engaged in prosecuting patent applications and litigations. Second, the economic disadvantages connected with the extension of the monopoly power of certain firms, an extension that often goes far beyond the scope of an individual patent grant. And, third, the social loss involved in the temporary prevention of the use of the most efficient processes by most, if not all, other producers.

It was this social loss that some writers felt was the worst effect of the patent system, and they emphasized the obstacles that the system put in the way of improvement by others of patented inventions...

...

Very often the advocates as well as the opponents of patents discussed the economic effects of the system on the assumption that the inventor was also the owner of the firm using the patent. It was not overlooked, however, that most inventors are either 'employed by a manufacturer or capitalist' or must sell their patents to them for a 'pittance'. This separation and possible conflict of interests between the inventor and exploiter not merely added to the arguments against the 'just-reward' theory but weighed heavily also against the theory that inventive activity requires a special incentive. If the inventors could not hope to reap the fruits of their work, the patent system could hardly be the incentive to their activity that it was represented to be. But another theory could be substituted for the weakened theory of the patent as an incentive to invent: a theory of the patent as an incentive to venture capital for the financing of the development and pioneer exploitation of inventions...

The Best Incentive to Disclose Secrets

...A supplementary or substitute argument in support of patents for inventions was advanced proposing that patents were necessary as incentives to induce inventors to disclose their new inventions instead of keeping them secret. Perhaps there would be enough inventive activity without patents, but could one count on disclosure of inventions so that they would become part of society's general fund of technological knowledge?

The 'incentive-to-disclose' theory of patent protection was often formulated as a social-contract theory... The patent was represented not as a privilege granted by society but as the result of a bargain between society and inventor, a contract in which the inventor agreed to disclose his secret and the state agreed, in exchange, to protect the inventor for a number of years against imitation of his idea. Why should anybody object to such a fair bargain with such a reasonable *quid pro quo*?

But there were objections and rather serious ones. They were based on the following lines of reasoning: (1) If inventors should prefer to keep their ideas secret and if they should succeed in doing so, society would not lose much, if anything, because usually the same or similar ideas are developed simultaneously and independently in several quarters. (2) It is practically impossible to keep inventions secret for any length of time; new products, new tools, and new processes are soon found out by eager competitors. (3) Where an inventor thinks he can succeed in guarding his secret, he will not take out a patent; hence, patent protection does not cause disclosure of concealable inventions but serves only to restrict the use of inventions that could not have been kept secret anyway. (4) Since patents are granted only on inventions developed to a stage at which they can be reduced to practical use, the patent system encourages secrecy in the developmental stage of inventions; without patents, inventors would hurry the publication of their ideas at earlier stages in order to secure recognition and fame, and this would hasten technological progress on all fronts.

The arguments discussed in the above extract from Machlup and Penrose arose in the context of a 19th-century controversy about whether to retain the patent system. For many developed countries, the debate is no longer about the existence of a patent system, but its scope and whether the rationales identified above justify certain features of patent law. For some developing countries, however, the question remains whether patent systems should be introduced at all. This has been particularly controversial in light of the Agreement on Trade Related Aspects of Intellectual Property Rights 1994 (TRIPS Agreement), which is discussed later in the chapter.[21] Commentators have questioned whether the incentive-based arguments used to justify a patent system are indeed applicable to developing countries. The following extract from a Report of the Commission on Intellectual Property Rights illustrates this concern.

Report of the Commission on Intellectual Property Rights, *Integrating Intellectual Property Rights and Developmental Policy* (London, Sept. 2002), pp. 14–15

Patents are one way of addressing…market failure. By conferring temporary market exclusivities, patents allow producers to recoup the costs of investment in R&D and reap a profit, in return for making publicly available the knowledge on which the invention is based. However, someone else can only put that knowledge to potential commercial use with the authorisation of the patentee. The costs of investment in R&D and the return on that investment are met by charging the consumer a price based on the ability to exclude competition.

Protection is therefore a bargain struck by society on the premise that, in its absence, there would be insufficient invention and innovation. The assumption is that in the longer run, consumers will be better off, in spite of the higher costs conferred by monopoly pricing, because the short term losses to consumers are more than offset by the value to them of the

---

[21] At 11.4.1.5.

new inventions created through additional R&D. Economists take the view that the patent system improves dynamic efficiency (by stimulating technical progress) at the cost of static efficiency (arising from the costs associated with monopoly).

This rationale for patent protection is relatively straightforward, but it is dependent on a number of simplifying assumptions that may not be borne out in practice. For instance, the optimal degree of patent protection cannot be accurately defined. If protection is too weak, then the development of technology may be inhibited through insufficient incentives for R&D. If too much protection is conferred, consumers may not benefit, even in the long run, and patentees may generate profits far in excess of the overall costs of R&D. Moreover, further innovation based on the protected technology may be stifled because, for instance, the length of the patent term is too long or the scope of the protection granted is too broad.

The length of the monopoly granted is one determinant of the strength of patent protection. Another is the scope of the patent... Broad patents can tend to discourage subsequent innovation by other researchers in the general area of the patent.

...

The optimal degree of protection (where the social benefits are judged to exceed the social costs) will also vary widely by product and sector and will be linked to variations in demand, market structures, R&D costs and the nature of the innovative process. In practice IPR regimes cannot be tailored so precisely and therefore the level of protection afforded in practice is necessarily a compromise. Striking the wrong compromise—whether too much or too little—may be costly to society, especially in the longer term.

One underlying assumption is that there is a latent supply of innovative capacity in the private sector waiting to be unleashed by the grant of the protection that the IP system provides. That may be so in countries where there is substantial research capacity. But in most developing countries local innovation systems (at least of the kind established in developed countries) are weak. Even where such systems are stronger, there is often more capacity in the public than the private sectors. Thus, in such contexts, the dynamic benefit from IP protection is uncertain. The patent system may provide an incentive but there may be limited local capacity to make use of it. Even when technologies are developed, firms in developing countries can seldom bear the costs of acquisition and maintenance of rights and, above all, of litigation if disputes arise.

Economists are also now very aware of what they call *transaction costs*. Establishing the infrastructure of an IPR regime, and mechanisms for the enforcement of IP rights, is costly both to governments, and private stakeholders. In developing countries, where human and financial resources are scarce, and legal systems not well developed, the opportunity costs of operating the system effectively are high. Those costs include the costs of scrutinising the validity of claims to patent rights (both at the application stage and in the courts) and adjudicating upon actions for infringement. Considerable costs are generated by the inherent uncertainties of litigation. These costs too need to be weighed against the benefits arising from the IP system.

Thus the value of the patent system needs to be assessed in a balanced way, acknowledging that it has both costs and benefits, and that the balance of costs and benefits is likely to differ markedly in diverse circumstances.

Do you agree with the view expressed in the Report that some of the assumptions underlying the 'incentive' rationale for patent protection are not entirely applicable to developing countries? A more sceptical and strident position is taken by commentators, such as Vandana Shiva, who argue that developing countries are being forced to introduce patent systems at the behest of developed countries (via international agreements, such as the TRIPS Agreement) and that the justifications put forward for doing so are untenable.

V. Shiva, *Protect or Plunder?: Understanding Intellectual Property Rights*
(London: Zed Books, 2001), pp. 21–3, 26

The Myth of Stimulating Creativity

The myth that patents contribute to the stimulation of creativity and inventiveness and their absence to lack of creativity and ingenuity is based on an artificial construction of knowledge and innovation—that of knowledge being isolated in time and space, without being connected to the social fabric and contributions from the past. Based on this construct, knowledge is thus seen as capital, a commodity and as a means for exclusive market control.

...

Knowledge, however, by its very nature is a collective, cumulative enterprise. It is based on exchange within a community. It is an expression of human creativity; both individual and collective. Since creativity has diverse expressions, science is a pluralistic enterprise which refers to different 'ways of knowing'. The term 'science' cannot be used to refer only to modern western science. It should include the knowledge systems of diverse cultures in different periods of history. But patents are granted for private intellectual property, built on the fiction of totally individualistic scientific innovation. There is then an intrinsic conflict built into the granting of patents as private rights for individual innovation and creativity and the view of knowledge as a collective endeavour.

...

This interpretation of creativity, as unleashed only when formal regimes of IPR protection are in place, is a total negation of creativity in nature and creativity generated by non-profit motives in both industrial and non-industrial societies. It is a denial of the role of innovation in traditional cultures, as well as in the public domain.

...

Central to the ideology of IPRs is this fallacy...that people are creative only if they can make profits and such profits are guaranteed through IPR protection. This negates the scientific creativity of those not spurred by the search for profits, i.e. the majority of scientists in universities and public research systems. It negates the creativity of traditional societies and the modern scientific community in which the free exchange of ideas is the very condition for creativity, not its antithesis.

...

The Myth of Technology Transfer, Innovation and R&D

The argument frequently promoted for a uniform worldwide IPR system is that such a system will promote investment, research and technology transfer in developing countries. The 'disclosure' clauses in patent laws which are related to medieval incentives for 'revealing the mysteries of the art' are now conveniently projected as necessary for the transferring of knowledge to society. However, the opposite is true. When companies can import products under import monopolies granted by patents, they have no incentive to set up domestic manufacture, or set up local R&D, or transfer technology to local production.

To what extent do you sympathize with the views expressed by Vandana Shiva? Does patent law invoke artificial notions of the way innovation occurs? And is there little likelihood that the introduction of patent systems in developing countries will encourage local investment in research and development?

Aside from whether traditional justifications for patent protection are universal and thus appropriate to developing countries, there is also the issue of whether patents have deleterious effects on indigenous communities. The argument is that a patent system encourages and legitimizes the unauthorized appropriation and commercial exploitation of traditional knowledge, sometimes referred to as 'bio-piracy'. Further, that indigenous communities are not in a position to pursue the benefits that a patent system may offer. These issues were introduced in Chapter 1, in an extract from Daniel Gervais.[22] It is worth turning back to revisit this extract and, in dealing with the relevant patent principles in the next few chapters, considering whether this criticism of the patent system is valid.

FURTHER READING

G. Dutfield, 'Indigenous peoples, bioprospecting and the TRIPs agreement: threats and opportunities' in P. Drahos and M. Blakeney (eds), *IP in Biodiversity and Agriculture: Regulating the Biosphere* (London: Sweet & Maxwell, 2001), pp. 135–49.

E. Kitch, 'The nature and function of the patent system' (1977) 20 Journal of Law and Economics 265.

W. M. Landes and R. A. Posner, 'The economics of patent law' in *The Economic Structure of Intellectual Property Law* (Cambridge, MA: Harvard University Press, 2003), pp. 294–333.

A. Plant, 'The economic theory concerning patents for inventions' in *Selected Economic Essays and Addresses* (London: Routledge, 1974), pp. 35–56.

11.4 SOURCES OF LAW

11.4.1 INTERNATIONAL

A collection of international conventions and treaties exists to regulate patent law and thus it is important to understand the extent of the obligations imposed by these instruments. The main conventions are considered in the following sections.

11.4.1.1 Paris Convention for the Protection of Industrial Property 1883 (Paris Convention)

The Paris Convention, signed in 1883 and revised on several occasions,[23] was the first international convention covering industrial property, i.e. patents, utility models, industrial designs, trade marks, service marks, trade names, indications of source or appellations of origin, and unfair competition.[24] The Convention is administered by the World Intellectual Property Organization (WIPO) and, as at 1 August 2016 194 countries were party to it.[25] The UK has been a party since 7 July 1884.

---

[22] See 1.2.7.

[23] In 1900 (Brussels); 1911 (Washington); 1925 (The Hague); 1934 (London); 1958 (Lisbon); and 1967 (Stockholm) and amended in 1979 (Paris Union).

[24] Paris Convention, Art. 1(2).   [25] See <www.wipo.int/> for details.

A fundamental principle of the Paris Convention is that of national treatment.[26] This means that a Paris Union country cannot discriminate between its nationals and the nationals of other Paris Union countries when it comes to protection of industrial property. In other words, Paris Union countries are obliged to grant nationals of other Paris Union countries the same protection, in respect of industrial property, as they grant to their own nationals. Paris Union countries can, however, subject nationals of other Union countries to the same conditions and formalities that they impose on their own nationals, except for requirements as to domicile or establishment in the country in which protection is claimed.

An important related principle is that of independence of patents. This means that patents applied for in various Paris Union countries by nationals of the Union countries shall be independent of patents obtained for the same invention in other countries, whether members of the Union or not.[27]

Another key principle in the Paris Convention is that of priority, which is relevant to the patent application process. Where a person has duly filed an application for a patent in one of the countries of the Union, that person, or his successor in title, shall enjoy, for the purpose of filing in the other Union countries, a 12-month period of priority, calculated from the date of filing of the first application.[28] The benefit of claiming priority is that the substantive requirements of patentability, such as novelty and inventive step, will be measured against the prior art as it stood at the date of the earlier application. To claim priority based on a previous filing, a person must make a declaration indicating the date of such filing and the country in which it was made and these particulars must be mentioned in the patent specification.[29] Where priority is claimed under the Paris Convention, the duration of the patent obtained will be the same as if that patent had been applied for or granted without the benefit of priority.[30]

The Paris Convention contains very few obligations concerning the substantive law of patents. The major one is that relating to compulsory licences. Article 5A(2) states that each Union country shall have the right to provide for the grant of compulsory licences in their legislation, where this is to prevent abuses which might result from exercise of the exclusive rights conferred by the patent, such as failure to work. Article 5A(4) stipulates that an application for a compulsory licence on the basis of failure to work or insufficient working may not be made until the end of four years from the date of filing of the patent application or three years from the date of the grant of the patent, whichever is later. The compulsory licence shall be refused if the patentee justifies his inaction by legitimate reasons and the form of the compulsory licence must be non-exclusive and non-transferable. Forfeiture of the patent shall only be provided for where the grant of a compulsory licence would not have been sufficient to prevent the said abuses. Proceedings for the forfeiture or revocation of a patent may not occur until the expiration of two years from the grant of the first compulsory licence.[31]

There are two other obligations worthy of note: first, the right of the inventor to be mentioned in the patent;[32] second, that a patent shall not be refused or invalidated on the basis that the sale of the patented product or of a product obtained by means of a patented process is subject to restrictions or limitations resulting from the domestic law.[33]

---

[26] Paris Convention, Art. 2.   [27] Paris Convention, Art. 4*bis*(1).

[28] Paris Convention, Arts 4A(1) and 4C(1)–(2).   [29] Paris Convention, Art. 4D(2).

[30] Paris Convention, Art. 4*bis*(5).   [31] Paris Convention, Art. 5A(3).

[32] Paris Convention, Art. 4*ter*.   [33] Paris Convention, Art. 4*quater*.

11.4.1.2 Patent Cooperation Treaty (PCT)

The PCT, signed at Washington on 19 June 1970 and amended on subsequent occasions,[34] creates a mechanism for making an international patent application. Importantly, it does not establish an international patent, but rather allows for the filing of an international patent application, which in turn enables protection for an invention to be simultaneously sought in any of the Contracting States to the PCT. Under the PCT, an applicant can make an international application and obtain an international search and an international preliminary examination (the international phase), before the patent is forwarded to the patent offices of the designated Contracting States (the national phase). Like the Paris Convention, the PCT is administered by WIPO and as at 1 August 2016 there were 150 Contracting States to the PCT.[35] The UK has been bound by the PCT since 24 January 1978.

Any person who is a resident or national of a Contracting State may file an international application,[36] which must contain the following: a request; a description; one or more claims; one or more drawings (where required); and an abstract.[37] The request must designate the Contracting State or States in which protection for the invention is desired on the basis of the international application. Where the applicant is claiming priority under the Paris Convention, the international application must contain a declaration to this effect.[38] The application is filed at the prescribed Receiving Office,[39] which is either a national office of one of the Contracting States or the International Bureau of WIPO.[40] Provided the prescribed formal requirements have been satisfied, the Receiving Office designates the date of receipt of the international application as the international filing date.[41] The international application shall then have the effect of a regular national application in each designated state as of the international filing date and the international filing date will be considered to be the actual filing date in each designated state.[42] The international application will also be equivalent to a regular national filing within the meaning of the Paris Convention.[43] Thus, it will be possible to claim Paris Convention priority on the basis of a PCT international application.

The next step is the international search conducted by the International Searching Authority,[44] which may be either a national office or an intergovernmental organization.[45] Presently, there are 12 International Searching Authorities: the Patent Offices of the European Patent Organisation, the US, Japan, Sweden, Republic of Korea, Australia, China, Canada, Austria, Spain, Russian Federation, and Finland. The purpose of the international search is to discover relevant prior art.[46] Once the international search report is produced it must be transmitted to the applicant and the International Bureau of WIPO.[47] It must also, along with the international application, be communicated to each designated office.[48] After 18 months from the priority date of the international application, the International Bureau of WIPO publishes the application and the international search report.[49]

Unless the applicant requests an international preliminary examination (which is not obligatory), the international application moves to its national phase. This must occur not later than 30 months from the priority date and occurs by the applicant furnishing a copy of the international application and a translation thereof and paying the national fee (if any) to

---

[34] Amended on 28 September 1979, and modified on 3 February 1984 and 3 October 2001.
[35] See <www.wipo.int/pct/en/pct_contracting_states.html> for details (accessed 1 August 2016).
[36] PCT, Art. 9(1).   [37] PCT, Art. 3(2).   [38] PCT, Art. 8(1).   [39] PCT, Art. 10.
[40] PCT, Art. 2.   [41] PCT, Art. 11(1).   [42] PCT, Art. 11(3).   [43] PCT, Art. 11(4).
[44] PCT, Art. 15.   [45] PCT, Art. 16(1).   [46] PCT, Art. 15(2).   [47] PCT, Art. 18(2).
[48] PCT, Art. 20(1)(a).   [49] PCT, Art. 21(1)–(2)(a).

each designated office.[50] If the applicant fails to do this, then the effect of the international application shall cease in the designated state with the same consequences as the withdrawal of any national application in that state.[51] The designated office will not process or examine the international application prior to the expiration of 30 months from the priority date. However, any designated office may, on the express request of the applicant, process or examine the international application at any time.[52]

For applicants from countries which have adopted Chapter II of the PCT, it is possible to demand an international preliminary examination. By this demand, which is made separately from the international application, the applicant elects the Contracting State or States for which the results of the examination will be used.[53] International preliminary examination is carried out by an International Preliminary Examining Authority[54] and, at present, there are 12 such authorities (the same Patent Offices listed above that are also International Searching Authorities). The purpose of the international preliminary examination is to 'formulate a preliminary and non-binding opinion on the questions whether the claimed invention appears to be novel, to involve an inventive step (to be non-obvious), and to be industrially applicable'.[55] An international preliminary examination report is produced and transmitted to the applicant and the International Bureau of WIPO.[56] The International Bureau in turn communicates the report to each elected office. Provided the election of any Contracting State has been effected within 19 months after the priority date, the national office of that state shall not proceed to the examination and other processing of the international application prior to the expiration of 30 months from the priority date.[57] In other words, for an applicant to take advantage of both the 30-month time delay before the application enters its national phase and the facility for international preliminary examination, the latter must be instigated within 19 months of the priority date.

According to the PCT, there are three main advantages to filing an international application. First, applications in numerous countries may be initiated by a single mechanism. Second, the applicant has 30 months from the priority date in which to decide whether to move to the national phase. This extra time is useful in deciding whether it is worthwhile to obtain a patent in that country and also in delaying the costs associated with pursuing a national patent application (e.g. official fees and translation costs). Third, the international preliminary examination may provide a useful resource for countries that lack an examination system.

According to WIPO, the PCT has been a great success. The number of international applications that are filed annually has grown significantly—from 19,809 in 1990 to 182,377 in 2011 to 214,500 in 2014. The largest number of PCT applications in 2014 came from the US, followed by Japan, European Patent Office, China, Korea, and the UK.[58]

11.4.1.3 Patent Law Treaty (PLT)

The PLT was adopted at Geneva on 1 June 2000 and came into force on 28 April 2005. As at 1 August 2016 it has 37 contracting parties, including the UK. The UK ratified the PLT on 22 December 2005 and the treaty entered into force on 28 April 2005. The PLT is administered by WIPO and aims to harmonize and streamline formal procedures in respect of national

---

[50] PCT, Art. 22.   [51] PCT, Art. 24(1)(iii).   [52] PCT, Art. 23.
[53] PCT, Art. 31(3)–(4)(a).   [54] PCT, Art. 32.   [55] PCT, Art. 33(1).
[56] PCT, Art. 36(1).   [57] PCT, Art. 40.
[58] See WIPO Patent Cooperation Treaty Yearly Review (2015) available at <www.wipo.int/edocs/pubdocs/en/wipo_pub_901_2015.pdf>.

and regional patent applications and patents. It does not seek to regulate substantive patent law.[59] For the most part, the PLT stipulates maximum requirements, which means that a Contracting State may provide more favourable requirements for applicants and owners. These requirements concern, inter alia, the use of PCT Request Forms and the establishment of Model Forms; exceptions from mandatory representation before the relevant patent office; relief in respect of procedural time limits and restrictions on revocation or invalidation of a patent for formal defects; and the implementation of electronic filing. An important minimum requirement relates to the filing date. Article 5 stipulates that a Contracting State will accord a filing date on receipt of three key elements: an indication that the elements received by the Office are intended to be an application; indications that would allow the Office to identify or contact the applicant; and a part which appears to be a description of the invention.

11.4.1.4 Substantive Patent Law Treaty (SPLT)

In November 2000, the WIPO Standing Committee on the Law of Patents initiated discussions on the harmonization of the substantive law of patents. At the fifth session of the Standing Committee, in May 2001, a first draft of the SPLT was considered. Revised drafts were considered and particular issues were explored by subsequent sessions of the WIPO Standing Committee on the Law of Patents. While agreement in principle was reached on several issues, including the scope of the SPLT (e.g. it does not deal with infringement), some issues, such as patentable subject matter, exceptions to patentability, the first-to-file versus first-to-invent rule, the exact scope of the prior art, and the introduction of a grace period were problematic.[60] After a failed joint proposal from the US, Japan, and the EPO to focus on a select few priority items, the negotiations were put on hold in 2006. Since that time, 'the main focus of the work of the SCP [Standing Committee on the Law of Patents] has been on building a technical and legal resource base from which to hold informed discussions in order to develop a work program. Therefore, a series of documents elaborating various aspects of patent law were produced and discussed at the subsequent sessions of the SCP.'[61]

11.4.1.5 Agreement on Trade Related Aspects of Intellectual Property Rights 1994 (TRIPS)

The TRIPS Agreement forms part of the Agreement establishing the World Trade Organization (WTO) and thus binds all WTO members, including the UK and EU which have been WTO members since 1 January 1995.

TRIPS incorporates, inter alia, the key provisions of the Paris Convention,[62] but also goes much further in laying down minimum standards with respect to substantive patent law.[63] Article 27(1) stipulates that patents will be available for inventions, whether products or processes, in all fields of technology, which are new, involve an inventive step, and are capable of industrial application; further, that 'patents shall be available and patent rights enjoyable without discrimination as to the place of invention, the field of technology and whether products are imported or locally produced'. However, TRIPS members may exclude three

[59] PLT, Art. 2(2).
[60] See the documents relating to the Standing Committee at <www.wipo.int/meetings/en/topic.jsp?group_id=61>.
[61] <www.wipo.int/policy/en/scp/>. [62] TRIPS, Art. 2(1).
[63] These minimum standards are set out in TRIPS, Part II, Section 5, Arts 27–34.

types of inventions from patentability: first, inventions whose commercial exploitation would be contrary to *ordre public* or morality;[64] second, diagnostic, therapeutic, and surgical methods for the treatment of humans or animals;[65] finally, plants and animals other than micro-organisms, and essentially biological processes for the production of plants or animals other than non-biological and microbiological processes.[66] Article 27(3)(b) stipulates that this last exclusion be reviewed four years after the date of entry into force of the WTO Agreement. The Ministerial Declaration of the Fourth Ministerial Conference, held at Doha on 9–14 November 2001, instructed the TRIPS Council to consider, while reviewing Article 27(3)(b), the relationship between the TRIPS Agreement and the Convention on Biological Diversity. This work is ongoing.[67]

Article 29(1) provides that members require a patent application to disclose the invention in a manner sufficiently clear and complete for it to be carried out by a person skilled in the art. The exclusive rights conferred by a patent are set out in Article 28. For patented products, this is the right to prevent a person making, using, offering for sale, selling, or importing the product without the owner's consent. For patented processes, this is the right to prevent a person using the process and from using, offering for sale, selling, or importing the product directly obtained by that process. The minimum duration of protection is 20 years from the filing date.[68]

Member states may provide for exceptions, but these must be limited, and not unreasonably conflict with a normal exploitation of the patent and must not unreasonably prejudice the legitimate interests of third parties.[69] Article 31 permits TRIPS members to provide for compulsory licences. Such use may only be permitted where the proposed user has 'made efforts to obtain authorisation from the rightholder on reasonable commercial terms and conditions and that such have not been successful within a reasonable period of time'. This requirement may be waived in situations of national emergency, extreme urgency, or in cases of public non-commercial use. The grant of a compulsory licence is subject to several other conditions, including that the use shall be non-exclusive and non-assignable and predominantly for the supply of the domestic market of the member authorizing such use and that the rightholder is paid adequate remuneration.

The scope of Article 31, and whether it may be invoked to avoid public health crises, such as the HIV/AIDS virus, has been the focus of controversy for some time. In particular, for WTO members with limited or no capacity to manufacture pharmaceuticals, difficulties may arise in seeking to rely on the compulsory licence provision in Article 31. A WTO member who is not able to produce a pharmaceutical will seek to import it from a foreign manufacturer according to the compulsory licence. However, the foreign manufacturer may fall foul of its domestic patent law if a patent for that pharmaceutical is also owned there. This means that a WTO member with insufficient manufacturing ability would be forced to license foreign manufacturers in countries where patent protection is unavailable and these may be very few indeed.[70]

At the Fourth Ministerial Conference held at Doha on 9–14 November 2001, a Declaration on the TRIPS Agreement and Public Health was adopted (the Doha Declaration).[71] This dealt, inter alia, with the right to grant compulsory licences pursuant to Article 31. The Doha Declaration, paragraph 6, instructed the TRIPS Council to find an expeditious solution to

---

[64] TRIPS, Art. 27(2).   [65] TRIPS, Art. 27(3)(a).   [66] TRIPS, Art. 27(3))(b).

[67] See <www.wto.org/english/tratop_e/trips_e/art27_3b_e.htm> for details.

[68] TRIPS, Art. 33.   [69] TRIPS, Art. 30.

[70] P. Rott, 'The Doha Declaration: good news for public health' [2003] IPQ 284, 293.

[71] This may be found at <www.wto.org/english/tratop_e/dda_e/dohaexplained_e.htm>.

the above problem by the end of 2002. A solution was not found, however, until 30 August 2003 when the TRIPS General Council finally issued a decision.[72] The decision created a 'waiver', which facilitates WTO members, in reliance on a compulsory licence, exporting pharmaceutical products to other members with no manufacturing capacity in the pharmaceutical sector.[73] A subsequent decision of 6 December 2005 agreed to amend the TRIPS Agreement along the lines of the 2003 'waiver'. This will become a permanent amendment to the TRIPS Agreement once two-thirds of the WTO's members have ratified the change. They have until 31 December 2017 to do so.[74]

FURTHER READING

M. Blakeney, *Trade Related Aspects of Intellectual Property Rights: A Concise Guide to the TRIPs Agreement* (London: Sweet & Maxwell, 1996).

D. Gervais, *TRIPS Agreement* (3rd edn, London: Sweet & Maxwell, 2008).

S. P. Kumar, 'European border measures and trade in generic pharmaceuticals: issues of TRIPs, Doha Declaration and public health' (2009) 15 Int. TLR 176.

P. Rott, 'The Doha Declaration: good news for public health' [2003] IPQ 284.

C. Tuosto, 'The TRIPs Council decision of August 30, 2003 on the import of pharmaceuticals under compulsory licences' [2004] EIPR 542.

J. Watal, 'From Punta Del Este to Doha and beyond: lessons from the TRIPS negotiating processes' [2011] WIPO J 24.

11.4.1.6 Convention on Biological Diversity (CBD)

The CBD was signed at Rio de Janeiro on 5 June 1992. According to Article 1, its aims are 'the conservation of biological diversity, the sustainable use of its components and the fair and equitable sharing of the benefits arising out of the utilisation of genetic resources, including by access to genetic resources and by appropriate transfer of relevant technologies ... and by appropriate funding'.

Article 15 of the CBD affirms that states have sovereign rights over their natural resources and the authority to determine access to genetic resources. Nonetheless, each Contracting State 'shall endeavour to create conditions to facilitate access to genetic resources for environmentally sound uses by other Contracting Parties'.[75] Access shall be on mutually agreed terms and subject to the prior informed consent of the Contracting State providing such resources.[76] Further, 'each Contracting State shall take legislative, administrative or policy measures, as appropriate ... with the aim of sharing in a fair and equitable way the results of research and development and the benefits arising from the commercial and other utilisation of genetic resources with the Contracting State providing such resources'.[77]

Contracting parties undertake to provide and/or facilitate access for and transfer to other contracting parties of technologies, including biotechnology, that are relevant to the

---

[72] For the decision see <www.wto.org/english/tratop_e/trips_e/implem_para6_e.htm>.

[73] C. Tuosto, 'The TRIPs Council decision of August 30, 2003 on the import of pharmaceuticals under compulsory licences' [2004] EIPR 542.

[74] Amendment of the TRIPS Agreement—Fifth Extension of the Period for the Acceptance by Members of the Protocol Amending the TRIPS Agreement, Decision of 30 November 2015, WT/L/965.

[75] CBD, Art. 15(2).   [76] CBD, Art. 15(4)–(5).   [77] CBD, Art. 15(7).

conservation and sustainable use of biological diversity.[78] Access and transfer of technology shall be provided and/or facilitated under fair and most favourable terms. Where the technology is protected by patents or another intellectual property right, 'such access and transfer shall be provided on terms which recognise and are consistent with the adequate and effective protection of intellectual property rights'.[79] Article 19(2) stipulates that contracting parties, 'shall take all practicable measures to promote and advance priority access on a fair and equitable basis by Contracting Parties, especially developing counties, to the results and benefits arising from biotechnologies based upon genetic resources provided by those Contracting Parties. Such access shall be on mutually agreed terms'.

The role of traditional knowledge in conservation of biological diversity is also covered by the CBD. The preamble recognizes the 'close and traditional dependence of many indigenous and local communities embodying traditional lifestyles on biological resources, and the desirability of sharing equitably benefits arising from the use of traditional knowledge, innovations and practices relevant to the conservation of biological diversity and the sustainable use of its components'. Further, Article 8(j) states that contracting parties shall, as far as possible and as appropriate, respect, preserve, and maintain traditional knowledge.

Professor Michael Blakeney has commented that, 'Reflecting the uncomfortable political deal which was struck in bringing the CBD to conclusion, the language of the Convention is unfortunately vague.'[80] Meanwhile, Peter Drahos has characterized the relationship between the CBD and TRIPS as an opposition of principles, namely, the principle of sustainable development and the principle of economic growth. The TRIPS Agreement does not mention conservation of biodiversity, while the CBD obliges members to ensure that intellectual property rights do not undermine the objectives of the Convention.[81] The relationship between the CBD and TRIPS is a continuing source of tension and thus has been placed on the TRIPS review agenda, in the context of reviewing Article 27(3)(b), which deals with patentability of plant and animal inventions and plant varieties.[82]

FURTHER READING

M. Blakeney, 'Intellectual property aspects of traditional agricultural knowledge' in P. Drahos and M. Blakeney (eds), *IP in Biodiversity and Agriculture: Regulating the Biosphere* (London: Sweet & Maxwell, 2001), pp. 31–52.

P. Drahos, 'The TRIPS Reviews and the CBD' in P. Drahos and M. Blakeney (eds), *IP in Biodiversity and Agriculture: Regulating the Biosphere* (London: Sweet & Maxwell, 2001), pp. 57–67.

N. S. Gopalakrishnan, 'TRIPS and protection of traditional knowledge of genetic resources: new challenges to the patents system' [2005] EIPR 11.

S. R. Harrop, '"Living in harmony with nature?" Outcomes of the 2010 Nagoya conference of the Convention on Biological Diversity' [2011] J. Env. L. 117.

L. M. Warren, 'The Convention on Biological Diversity: will the decisions made at COP10 in Nagoya make it easier to conserve biodiversity?' [2010] Env. L. Rev. 245.

---

[78] CBD, Art. 16(1).   [79] CBD, Art. 16(2).

[80] M. Blakeney, 'Intellectual property aspects of traditional agricultural knowledge' in P. Drahos and M. Blakeney (eds), *IP in Biodiversity and Agriculture: Regulating the Biosphere* (London: Sweet & Maxwell, 2001), pp. 31–52, at p. 40.

[81] P. Drahos, 'The TRIPS Reviews and the CBD' in Drahos and Blakeney, *IP in Biodiversity and Agriculture*, pp. 57–67, at pp. 59–60.

[82] See <www.wto.org/english/tratop_e/trips_e/art27_3b_e.htm>.

11.4.2 REGIONAL

A collection of conventions and EU instruments exists to regulate patent law at the European level and thus it is important to understand the extent of the obligations imposed by them. The main instruments are considered in the following sections.

11.4.2.1 European Patent Convention (EPC)

The EPC was signed in Munich in 1973 and came into operation on 1 June 1978. It is an intergovernmental treaty and *not* an instrument of the EU. The aim of the EPC was to establish a centralized system of obtaining patents in Contracting States. There are at present 38 Contracting States (of which the UK is one).[83]

The EPC does not provide for the granting of a single pan-European patent but rather offers a mechanism for obtaining a bundle of national patents. The EPC established the European Patent Office (EPO), which is the executive arm of the European Patent Organisation, which is an intergovernmental body set up under the EPC and whose members are the EPC Contracting States. Applications for a European patent are made to the Examining Division of the EPO in Munich and must designate the Contracting States in which protection is sought. EPC applications must be in one of three official languages (English, German, or French) and the text of the patent must be in that language. If the application is successful, there is a grant of a European patent for each of the designated Contracting States, which take effect as national patents. It is possible, however, to challenge centrally the grant of a European patent by instigating opposition proceedings in the Opposition Division nine months after grant. The Technical Boards of Appeal hear appeals from the decisions of, inter alia, the examining and opposition divisions of the EPO. Important questions of law may be referred to the Enlarged Board of Appeal either by a Board of Appeal or by the President of the EPO.

11.4.2.2 Revised European Patent Convention (EPC 2000)

A Diplomatic Conference held in Munich in November 2000 produced the Act Revising the Convention on the Grant of European Patents (EPC 2000). This was signed at Munich on 29 November 2000 and extensively amends the EPC. The EPC 2000 entered into force on 13 December 2007 (i.e. two years after the 15th Contracting State—which was Greece—deposited its instrument of ratification). Accompanying it were new implementing regulations, which were adopted by decision of the Administrative Council on 7 December 2006 and last amended on 26 October 2010.[84]

The underlying aim of the EPC 2000 was to modernize the European patent system, in the light of the various political, legal, and technical changes that have occurred since the signing of the EPC in 1973. Thus, the EPC 2000 aims to make the EPO procedures more effective and efficient and to bring the EPC into line with international developments such as TRIPS and the PLT. The following is a summary of the major changes that have come into effect as a result of the EPC 2000.

(1) A Conference of Ministers will be held at least every five years, in order for Contracting States to exercise greater political responsibility over the European Patent Organisation.

---

[83] For details see <www.epo.org/about-us/epo/member-states.html#contracting>.
[84] See <www.epo.org/law-practice/legal-texts/html/epc/2010/e/ma2.html>.

(2) The Administrative Council is now competent to amend the EPC in order to bring it into line with international patent treaties or EU legislation relating to patents.

(3) Several amendments aim to simplify and streamline the patent grant procedure before the EPO. For example, it is possible to file patent applications in any language and a translation into one of the official languages of the EPO is not required until a later date. Further, search and examination occur in the same location, whereas previously search and examination were spread over a number of different locations.

(4) A central procedure before the EPO for amendment of the patent is available, so that proprietors do not have to go through the national patent offices.

(5) The Protocol on the Interpretation of Article 69 of the EPC has been amended to include the doctrine of 'equivalents'.

(6) The content of European applications as filed now form part of the prior art for all EPC Contracting States.

(7) There is the legal basis for special agreements between Contracting States to introduce a central court system for the enforcement of European patents.

At the Diplomatic Conference it was resolved that the exclusion from patentability of computer programs per se should remain, but that this exclusion, along with the patentability of biotechnological inventions, should be revisited at future Diplomatic Conferences.

11.4.2.3 Community Patent Convention (CPC)

The CPC is an intergovernmental treaty that was signed in Luxembourg in 1975 and which aimed to establish a single Community patent obtainable via one central procedure and binding in all Contracting States. It also sought to rationalize patent administration and thus reduce the costs of patenting. Unlike the EPC, the CPC has never come into force since not all signatories have ratified it. (There are, however, substantive provisions from the CPC on infringement in many Contracting States' laws, including the UK.) Rather, there has been a long journey of trying to implement a unitary patent which looks on the brink of finally succeeding as discussed at 11.4.2.6.

11.4.2.4 Supplementary Protection Certification Regulation (SPC Regulation)

The European Community's intervention in the field of patent law has been fairly limited, especially when compared with its activity in the fields of copyright and trade marks. One such intervention is Council Regulation (EEC) No. 1768/92 of 18 June 1992, which created the Supplementary Protection Certificate (SPC) for the benefit of medicinal products for which regulatory approval has been obtained. The purpose behind the SPC is to provide adequate protection to patented medicinal products, whose marketing has been delayed by the need to obtain regulatory approval, in order to encourage pharmaceutical research.[85] This is achieved by granting an SPC, for a maximum duration of five years, at the expiry of

---

[85] SPC Regulation, recital 3. There is also an equivalent SPC for plant protection products: see Council Regulation (EC) No. 1610/96.

the 20-year patent term. The protection granted is strictly confined to the medicinal product for which regulatory approval was obtained.[86]

11.4.2.5 Directive on the legal protection of biotechnological inventions (Biotechnology Directive)

A second, and rather controversial, intervention by the European Community is reflected in the Biotechnology Directive, which sought to harmonize the patent law protection of biotechnological inventions 'in order to maintain and encourage investment in the field of biotechnology'.[87] The path to adoption of the Biotechnology Directive was beset with difficulties. It was first proposed by the European Commission in 1988, but was vetoed by the European Parliament in 1995, due to the intense opposition from the Green Party, animal welfare activists, and environmentalists. The central objection to the proposed directive was that it failed to address adequately the ethical concerns of patenting biotechnological inventions.[88] The European Commission introduced a revised version of the Biotechnology Directive in 1995. After further debate and numerous amendments, the European Council of Ministers eventually adopted the directive in June 1998 and its deadline for implementation was 30 July 2000. The controversy, however, did not end there. Shortly after the adoption of the Biotechnology Directive, the Dutch government brought an action for annulment of the directive before the European Court of Justice. The grounds of the challenge were varied, but mainly procedural in nature.[89] The Opinion of Advocate General Jacobs rejected the arguments for annulment and, in October 2001, the CJEU affirmed the Advocate General's Opinion.[90]

The directive is divided into four chapters. Chapter I harmonizes the rules relating to patentability of biotechnological inventions. For example, Article 3 iterates that inventions concerning biological material are patentable if they are new, involve an inventive step, and are capable of industrial application. However, plant and animal varieties, and essentially biological processes for the production of plants or animals are not patentable.[91] Simple discoveries of the elements of the human body, including the sequence or partial sequence of a gene, cannot constitute a patentable invention.[92] However, Article 5(2) stipulates that 'an element isolated from the human body or otherwise produced by means of a technical process, including the sequence or partial sequence of a gene, may constitute a patentable invention, even if the structure of that element is identical to that of a natural element'. Where the commercial exploitation of an invention would be contrary to *ordre public* or

---

[86] For further discussion of the ambit and application of the SPC Regulation, see *Generics (UK) Ltd v Synaptech Inc.* Case C-427/09 [2012] 1 CMLR 4; *Neurim Pharmaceuticals (1991) Ltd v Comptroller-General of Patents* Case C-130/11 (CJEU Fourth Chamber), 19 July 2012; and *Medeva BV v Comptroller-General of Patents, Designs and Trade Marks* [2012] EWCA Civ 523, [2012] RPC 26. For an example where a bad faith obtaining of an SPC led to a finding of abuse of dominant position see *Astrazeneca AB v European Commission* Case C-457/10 [2013] 4 CMLR 7. For a more recent referral to the CJEU see *GlaxoSmithKline v Comptroller General of Patents* [2013] EWHC 619 (Pat).

[87] Biotechnology Directive, recital 3.

[88] See D. Curley and A. Sharples, 'Patenting biotechnology in Europe: the ethical debate moves on' [2002] EIPR 565.

[89] For a discussion of these grounds see A. Scott, 'The Dutch challenge to the bio-patenting directive' [1999] EIPR 212.

[90] See *Netherlands v European Parliament and Council of the European Union* Case C-377/98 [2001] ECR I-7079.

[91] Biotechnology Directive, Art. 4(1).   [92] Biotechnology Directive, Art. 5(1).

morality, such inventions shall be considered unpatentable.[93] These rules will be discussed in more detail later in this chapter.

Chapter II of the Biotechnology Directive deals with the scope of protection conferred by patents on certain biotechnological inventions. For example, Article 8 states that 'a patent on a biological material possessing specific characteristics as a result of the invention shall extend to any biological material derived from that biological material through propagation or multiplication in an identical or divergent form and possessing those same characteristics'. However, this protection is exhausted where the biological material is placed on the market in the territory of a Member State by the holder of the patent or with his consent.[94] Further, Article 11 contains derogations from the protection set out in Article 8 and 9.

Chapter III provides for compulsory cross-licensing in respect of patents and plant variety rights. In circumstances where a breeder cannot acquire or exploit a plant variety right without infringing a prior patent, he may apply for a compulsory licence for non-exclusive use of the invention protected by a patent. This is subject to payment of an appropriate royalty. Similarly, where the holder of a patent concerning a biotechnological invention cannot exploit it without infringing a prior plant variety right, he may apply for a compulsory licence for non-exclusive use of the plant variety protected by that right, subject to payment of an appropriate royalty. Applicants must show that they have applied unsuccessfully to the holder of the patent or plant variety right to obtain a contractual licence and, further, that the plant variety or invention constitutes significant technical progress of considerable economic interest compared with the invention claimed in the patent or the protected plant variety.

Chapter IV allows the sufficiency requirement under patent law to be satisfied by the deposit of biological material at a recognized depositary institution. This is applicable where an invention involves the use of or concerns biological material which is not available to the public and which cannot be described in a patent application such that a person skilled in the art can work the invention.[95] Article 13 also stipulates that access to the deposited biological material shall be provided through the supply of a sample.

The Biotechnology Directive also includes obligations on the Commission to report to the European Parliament and Council on various matters, including on the development and implications of patent law in the field of biotechnology and genetic engineering.[96] The first such report was issued in 2002 and the latest in 2005.[97]

FURTHER READING

D. Curley and A. Sharples, 'Patenting biotechnology in Europe: the ethical debate moves on' [2002] EIPR 565.

E. R. Gold and A. Gallochat, 'The European Biotech Directive: past as prologue' (2001) 7 European Law Journal 331.

S. Moore, 'Challenge to the Biotechnology Directive' [2002] EIPR 149.

R. N. Weekes, 'Challenging the Biotechnology Directive' (2003) 14 EBL Rev. 325.

---

[93] Biotechnology Directive, Art. 6.   [94] Biotechnology Directive, Art. 10.
[95] Biotechnology Directive, Art. 13(1).   [96] Biotechnology Directive, Art. 16(c).
[97] See Report from the Commission to the European Parliament and the Council, 'Development and implications of patent law in the field of biotechnology and genetic engineering', COM (2005) 312 final.

In recent years, the EU has sought to extend its harmonization efforts in the patent law area to include harmonization of the patentability of computer-related inventions and the introduction of an EU-wide unitary patent and unified patent court. The attempt to harmonize the patentability of computer-related inventions failed after a protracted and controversial legislative process. However, success looks to be forthcoming in the EU's attempt to create a unitary EU patent and to offer a unified patent court.

11.4.2.6 Unified Patent Package

As mentioned at 11.4.2.3, the CPC never came into force. There was another attempt to revive a unitary, Community-wide patent in 1989,[98] but this too failed due to a lack of ratifications by Member States. Eleven years later, a proposal for a Community patent was introduced by the European Commission in 2000,[99] which was aimed at reducing translation costs and creating a centralized court that would hear validity and infringement disputes regarding Community patents. However, negotiations on this proposal stalled within several years. With renewed optimism the European Commission adopted a Communication[100] to improve the patent system in 2007 and to reinvigorate debate on this topic. In subsequent years the European Commission made some headway in creating a proposal for a single EU patent and a unified patent court. There were, however, many twists and turns in the fate of the proposal, driven partly by disputes about which would be the official languages of the unitary patent system and also disagreement on the nature and function of a unified patent court, especially its relationship to the CJEU. The opposition of Spain and Italy to the official languages being limited to French, English, and German (the official languages of the EPO-administered European patent system) was substantial and eventually led to their refusal to cooperate further on the proposals. To circumvent this blockade, a group of Member States triggered a little-used mechanism—that of enhanced cooperation—to continue with the proposals for a unitary patent.[101] This mechanism requires a minimum of nine Member States to cooperate between themselves and move forward with EU legislation. Other Member States soon came on board—all other Member States, in fact, except for Spain and Italy—and developments moved apace. Spain and Italy, however, complained to the CJEU that the new EU patent regime and its implementation by the process of enhanced cooperation was discriminatory and sought an annulment. The CJEU dismissed these challenges,[102] along with two further complaints brought by Spain.[103]

Under the enhanced cooperation procedure, a 'unitary patent package' was developed. It consists of three elements: (1) a regulation creating a European patent with unitary effect (i.e. a unitary patent); (2) a regulation establishing a language regime applicable to the unitary patent; and (3) an international agreement among Member States to set up a single and

---

[98] 89/695/EEC: Agreement relating to Community patents—Done at Luxembourg on 15 December 1989 [1989] OJ L401/1.

[99] Proposal for a Council Regulation on a Community Patent, COM (2000) 412 final.

[100] Communication from the Commission to the European Parliament and the Council, 'Enhancing the Patent System in Europe', COM (2007) 165 final.

[101] See Enhanced cooperation in the area of the creation of unitary patent protection: European Parliament legislative resolution of 15 February 2011 on the draft Council decision authorizing enhanced cooperation in the area of the creation of unitary patent protection [2012] OJ C188E/76.

[102] See *Kingdom of Spain, Italian Republic v Council of the European Union* Joined Cases C-274 and 295/11, Judgment of the Court (Grand Chamber), 16 April 2013 [2013] CMLR 24.

[103] See *Kingdom of Spain v European Parliament and Council of the European Union* Joined Cases C-146 and 147/13, Judgment of the Court (Grand Chamber), 5 May 2015.

specialized patent court (the Unified Patent Court). The first two of these elements have been created by regulations adopted on 17 December 2012,[104] but will not come into effect until the date of entry into force of the Agreement on a Unified Patent Court. In essence, what they create is a European patent with unitary effect. This will be achieved as follows: a European patent granted by the EPO in which participating Member States are designated will lead to a European patent of unitary effect in those Member States (provided it is registered as such) and a European patent (of the old type, i.e. leading to a bundle of national patents) in non-participating Member States and non-Member States.[105] The European patent with unitary effect will enable the proprietor to prevent acts of infringement throughout the territories of the participating Member States.[106] In terms of translation requirements, where the specification of a European patent complies with Article 14(6) of the EPC, i.e. the specification is published in the language of the proceedings before the EPO and includes a translation of the claims into the other two official languages of the EPO, no further translations will be required.[107] When it comes to infringement proceedings, however, the patent proprietor will need to provide at the request and choice of the alleged infringer a full translation of the patent into an official language of either the participating Member State in which the alleged infringement took place or the Member State in which the alleged infringer is domiciled.[108] There are other translation obligations which exist during a transitional period[109] and a method for compensating SMEs, natural persons, universities, non-profit organizations, and public research organizations having their residence or principal place of business within a Member State for translation costs where they file in one of the official languages of the Union that is not an official language of the EPO.[110]

Neither of the two regulations will come into effect until the Agreement on a Unified Patent Court comes into force.[111] The Agreement was signed by 25 Member States on 19 February 2013, however, it will not come into force until there are sufficient ratifications[112] and so far only nine countries have ratified the Agreement.

The Unified Patent Court[113] will have exclusive competence in relation to European patents and European patents with unitary effect (subject to exclusions during a transitional period) and will comprise a Court of First Instance and a Court of Appeal. The Court of First Instance will have a central division as well as local and regional divisions. The central division will be split between Paris, London, and Munich, and the Court of Appeal will be situated in Luxembourg. A patent proprietor will be able to take infringement proceedings in the local or regional division where the infringement occurred, or where the defendant is

[104] See Council Regulation (EU) No. 1260/2012 of 17 December 2012 implementing enhanced cooperation in the area of the creation of unitary patent protection with regard to the applicable translation arrangements [2012] OJ L361/89 and Regulation (EU) No. 1257/2012 of the European Parliament and of the Council of 17 December 2012 implementing enhanced cooperation in the area of the creation of unitary patent protection [2012] OJ L361/1.

[105] See Regulation (EU) No. 1257/2012, Arts 3 and 4.

[106] Regulation (EU) No. 1257/2012, Art. 5.

[107] Council Regulation (EU) No. 1260/2012, Art. 3.

[108] Council Regulation (EU) No. 1260/2012, Art. 4.

[109] Council Regulation (EU) No. 1260/2012, Art. 6—where the language of the proceedings is French or German, a full translation of the specification into English or where the language of the proceedings is English a full translation of the specification into any other official language of the EU.

[110] Council Regulation (EU) No. 1260/2012, Art. 5.

[111] See Council of the EU, Agreement on a Unified Patent Court, 11 January 2013.

[112] 13 ratifications are required including from Germany, the UK, and France. Of these three, only France has ratified thus far.

[113] See <www.unified-patent-court.org/> for details.

resident, or in the central division if the defendant is domiciled outside the EU. Actions for revocation of the patent or a declaration of non-infringement will need to be taken before the central division. Where infringement proceedings are brought and there is a counter-claim for revocation of the patent, the local or regional court may refer the counterclaim to the central division and suspend *or* proceed with the infringement proceedings. So it may be that some local or regional courts decide to bifurcate—i.e. continue with infringement proceedings even where the issue of validity of the patent is still pending—while others do not. The court will appoint, through a process of application, both legally qualified and tech-nically qualified judges who are nationals of a Contracting Member State. The Preparatory Committee is currently overseeing the work needed to ensure that the UPC is established. It has thus far adopted rules of procedure, rules on court fees and recoverable costs, and initiated the process for recruiting judges. It is hoped that the court will be able to start operations in early 2017.

FURTHER READING

C. M. Pehlivan, 'The creation of a single European patent system: from dream to (almost) reality' [2012] EIPR 453.

11.4.3 NATIONAL

11.4.3.1 Patents Act 1977 (PA 77)

The PA 77 established the UK Patent Office (now known as the UK Intellectual Property Office (UK IPO)), its procedure, and the substantive law of patents in the UK. The Patents Rules 2007[114] are the main piece of secondary legislation made under the PA 77 and they regulate the business and procedure of the UK IPO.

The PA 77 saw the UK's entry into the EPC. As such, it brought about numerous substan-tive and procedural changes to UK patent law. Section 130(7) of the PA 77 states that certain provisions of the Act 'are so framed as to have, as nearly as practicable, the same effects in the United Kingdom as the corresponding provisions of the European Patent Convention'.[115] UK courts must therefore have regard to this legislative intention when interpreting these provisions. The importance of avoiding divergent interpretations between the EPO and the UK, together with the considerable persuasive authority of decisions of the Boards of Appeal and Enlarged Board of Appeal of the EPO, has been stressed on several occasions.[116] Most recently, the Supreme Court in *Human Genome Sciences v Eli Lilly & Co.*[117] made the

---

[114] SI 2007/3291.

[115] Jacob LJ, referring to PA 77, ss. 125 and 130, has commented that: 'To this day I remain baffled, nay flabbergasted, by this convoluted and roundabout way of implementing the relevant provisions of the trea-ties'; see *Schütz v Werit* [2011] EWCA Civ 303, [2011] FSR 19, [39]. For similar criticism see *Grimme v Scott* [2010] EWCA Civ 110, [88].

[116] See *Gale's Application* [1991] RPC 305, 322–3 (Nicholls LJ), cited with approval in *Re Fujitsu Ltd's Application* [1997] RPC 608, 611 (Aldous LJ); *Merrell Dow v Norton* [1996] RPC 76, 82 (Lord Hoffmann); *Biogen v Medeva* [1997] RPC 1, 34 (Lord Hoffmann); *Generics (UK) Ltd v H Lundbeck A/S* [2009] UKHL 12, [2009] RPC 13, [35] (Lord Walker), [46] (Lord Mance), and [86] (Lord Neuberger); *Conor Medsystems Inc. v Angiotech Pharmaceuticals Inc.* [2008] UKHL 49, [3] (Lord Hoffmann); and *Human Genome Sciences v Eli Lilly Co.* [2010] RPC 14 (CA), [6]–[41]; [2011] UKSC 51, [83]–[87] (Lord Neuberger) (delivering the leading judgment of the Supreme Court).

[117] [2011] UKSC 51.

following observations about the way in which English courts should treat decisions of the Boards of Appeal of the EPO:

Lord Neuberger (delivering the leading judgment):

83. Where the EPO decides that a patent, or a claim in a patent, is invalid, then that is the end of the issue (subject, of course, to the patentee or applicant appealing to the Board) in relation to all countries which are signatories to the EPC. Where, however, the EPO decides that a patent, or a particular claim, is valid, then, as this case shows, it is still open to a national court to decide that the patent, or claim, is invalid within its territorial jurisdiction. In all cases, however, the EPO and each national court are, of course, applying the principles contained in the EPC. It is plainly appropriate in principle, and highly desirable in practice, that all these tribunals interpret the provisions of the EPC in the same way.

84. In a number of recent decisions of the House of Lords, attention has been drawn to 'the importance of UK patent law aligning itself, so far as possible, with the jurisprudence of the EPO (and especially decisions of its Enlarged Boards of Appeal)', to quote Lord Walker in *Generics (UK) Ltd v H Lundbeck A/S* [2009] UKHL 12; [2009] RPC 13, para 35. It is encouraging that the same approach is being adopted in Germany by the Bundesgerictshof [sic]—see *Case Xa ZR* 130/07 (10 September 2009), para 33.

85. However, as Lord Walker went on to explain in *Generics* [2009] RPC 13, para 35, 'National courts may reach different conclusions as to the evaluation of the evidence in the light of the relevant principles' even though 'the principles themselves should be the same, stemming as they do from the EPC'. Thus, the EPO (or another national court) and a national court may come to different conclusions because they have different evidence or arguments, or because they assess the same competing arguments and factual or expert evidence differently, or, particularly in a borderline case, because they form different judgments on the same view of the expert and factual evidence.

86. As Lord Hoffmann said in *Conor Medsystems Inc v Angiotech Pharmaceuticals Inc* [2008] UKHL 49, [2008] RPC 28, para 3:

A European patent takes effect as a bundle of national patents over which the national courts have jurisdiction. It is therefore inevitable that they will occasionally give inconsistent decisions about the same patent. Sometimes this is because the evidence is different. In most continental jurisdictions, including the [EPO], cross-examination is limited or unknown. Sometimes one is dealing with questions of degree over which judges may legitimately differ. Obviousness is often in this category. But when the question is one of principle, it is desirable that so far as possible there should be uniformity in the way the national courts and the EPO interpret the [EPC].

87. Further, while national courts should normally follow the established jurisprudence of the EPO, that does not mean that we should regard the reasoning in each decision of the Board as effectively binding on us. There will no doubt sometimes be a Board decision which a national court considers may take the law in an inappropriate direction, misapplies previous EPO jurisprudence, or fails to take a relevant argument into account. In such cases, the national court may well think it right not to apply the reasoning in the particular decision. While consistency of approach is important, there has to be room for dialogue between a national court and the EPO (as well as between national courts themselves). Nonetheless, where the Board has adopted a consistent approach to an issue in a number of decisions, it would require very unusual facts to justify a national court not following that approach.

As we will see throughout the course of these chapters, there have been various points of divergence between the UK and the EPO on particular patent principles. In examining these principles you should consider how far convergence has been achieved and whether this is likely to be enhanced by the introduction of a Unified Patent Court.

11.4.3.2 Patents Act 2004 (PA 2004)

The PA 2004 was enacted primarily with a view to implementing the EPC 2000, but also with the aim of generally modernizing the PA 77. The PA 2004 has now come into force[118] and, consequently, the PA 77 has been amended in a variety of ways. Broadly speaking, the changes that it brought about can be divided into four areas: (1) changes necessary to give effect to the EPC 2000; (2) changes related to or consequential upon EPC 2000 revisions but not required for its implementation; (3) changes related to enforcement and post-grant issues; and (4) general modernization of the PA 77. Where relevant, the changes brought about by the PA 2004 will be discussed later in the chapter in relation to specific topics.

11.5 OBTAINING A PATENT

11.5.1 PRELIMINARY QUESTIONS

In deciding whether to apply for a patent, a company or individual will take into account various considerations. These include the relative advantages and disadvantages of patent protection as compared with other forms of protection, such as the law of confidence or contract law, and the strategic or commercial value of owning a patent.

Briefly, there are two key advantages to relying on patent law, as opposed to the law of confidence or contract law, to protect one's invention. First, patent law confers a property right, i.e. a right enforceable *in rem* rather than *in personam*. Thus, a patent owner can exercise her exclusive monopoly right against third parties and is not restricted to enforcing her right against the party/parties to the contract or to the person who is under an obligation to keep the commercial information secret. The second advantage of relying on patent law is that it protects those inventions that do not lend themselves to secrecy. The law of confidence (which relies upon the invention not being in the public domain) is not useful when an invention can be easily discovered from studying a product incorporating the invention that has been released onto the market.

There are, however, certain disadvantages associated with patenting an invention, as opposed to relying on contract or confidentiality. First, there is the bureaucratic process of registering a patent, which is both time-consuming and costly. Second, the *quid pro quo* for obtaining a patent is disclosing the invention to the rest of the world. If a person wishes to keep their invention entirely secret from their competitors this disclosure will be

---

[118] The Patents Act 2004 (Commencement No. 1 and Consequential and Transitional Provisions) Order 2004 (SI 2004/2177) came into force on 22 September 2004; the Patents Act 2004 (Commencement No. 2 and Consequential, etc. and Transitional Provisions) Order 2004 (SI 2004/3205) came into force on 1 January 2005; the Patents Act 2004 (Commencement No. 3 and Transitional Provisions) Order 2005 (SI 2005/2471) came into force on 1 October 2005; the Patents Act 2004 (Commencement No. 4 and Transitional Provisions) Order 2007 (SI 2007/3396) came into force on 13 December 2007.

counterproductive, and it may be preferable to rely on the law of confidence. Finally, patent protection lasts for 20 years whereas protection may be longer under contract (depending on the terms of the contract) or the law of confidence (depending on whether the information is still secret).

The strategic or commercial value of owning a patent will also be a relevant consideration. Aside from the obvious value in having an exclusive monopoly right to make or use the invention, there are other consequential benefits. For example, obtaining a patent will allow the owner to value that asset more easily from an accounting point of view. Further, a patent operates as a visible public identification of one's intellectual property rights and this may serve as a disincentive to others to produce competing products for fear of possible infringement. Finally, owning a patent may be strategically valuable when it comes to negotiating with other patent owners in the same field to obtain licences to use their patented technology.

Having decided to apply for a patent, rather than rely on contract law or the law of confidence, the applicant will need to ask further questions, such as: in which countries do I want a patent and how much am I prepared to spend on patent protection? The latter question is tied to the first since the more countries in which patent protection is sought, the higher will be the costs of obtaining and maintaining protection. As we will see from the discussion below, there are three possible routes to obtaining patent protection. The first is to apply for a national patent, for example apply to the UK IPO for a UK patent or to the US Patent Office for a US patent. The second is to apply to the EPO for a European patent, designating the Contracting States in which protection is sought (e.g. UK and Germany). The third is to make a PCT application designating the Contracting States in which protection is sought (e.g. UK, Germany, and the US). As was stressed in 11.4.1.2, this does not lead to an international or global patent. Rather, it allows for an international patent application, which enables protection for an invention to be simultaneously sought in any of the PCT Contracting States.

11.5.2 REGISTRATION PROCESS

This section will provide a general overview of the registration process and its function. We begin with a brief discussion of the value of a registration system before turning to describe the application process.

What is the value of having a registration system for patents? Several benefits may be pointed out. First, operating a central register allows competitors and other third parties to search for patents that might impact upon their commercial decisions and activities, thus minimizing the risk of inadvertent infringement. Second, it assists third parties in ascertaining the ambit of the patented invention, which in turn may help them to invent around the patent. Finally, the successful applicant can feel reasonably secure of the validity of the patent granted to them, because their application has gone through an examination process. This last point, however, depends on the rigour or quality of the examination process. Further, it is still possible for third parties to challenge the validity of the granted patent, right up until its expiry.

As mentioned above, there are three possible application routes: national, via the EPO, and via the PCT. The following is an overview of the application process via the national and EPO routes. The PCT application process is not discussed here since it was dealt with at 11.4.1.2.

11.5.2.1 Filing an application

Any person may make an application;[119] however, the person entitled to the grant of a patent is generally speaking the inventor.[120] An application for a UK patent should be made to the UK IPO and, for a European patent, to the EPO designating the particular Contracting States in which patent protection is sought.[121] For a European patent application, the application may proceed in any of the official languages, i.e. English, French, or German.[122]

Filing an application is important because it establishes the 'priority date' of the application, i.e. the date at which the validity requirements (of novelty, inventive step, etc.) for a patent will be assessed. The general rule is that the filing date is the priority date *unless* an applicant is claiming 'Convention priority'. Convention priority refers to where the applicant has filed, within the previous 12 months, an earlier application in a Paris Convention country. The result is that the priority date is treated as the date of filing of the earlier application. To claim Convention priority, the applicant must file a declaration of priority at the time of filing the application.[123]

To make a full application, the following elements must be included: a request for the grant of a patent; a specification containing a description of the invention, a claim or claims, and any drawing referred to in the description or any claim; and an abstract.[124]

It is possible, prior to making a full application, to file an early 'informal' application. This occurs where a person files documents indicating that a patent is sought, information identifying the applicant, and a description of the invention.[125] The applicant then has 12 months in which to file the remaining documents—i.e. the abstract and claims. The advantage of early filing is that it establishes a priority date and also gives the applicant 12 months in which to decide whether to pursue a patent. Importantly, however, the later documentation must be 'supported' by the earlier application.

11.5.2.2 Preliminary examination and search

The next step is that the applicant should request, within 12 months of the date of filing, a preliminary examination and search.[126] The preliminary examination involves the examiner or, for the EPO, the Receiving Section, determining whether the application has complied with certain formal requirements. These are that: (1) the application contains the relevant documents; (2) the fees have been paid; (3) the inventors have been identified; and (4) for the EPO, the application designates the Contracting States in which patents are sought. The applicant receives a preliminary examination report, which will list any problems and allow an applicant to respond to them.

A limited search is then conducted by the examiner or, at the EPO, the Search Division.[127] The search will identify relevant prior art (i.e. documents published before the priority date that contain similar inventions to the one applied for), which will be used at the substantive examination stage. The applicant receives an Examiner's Report or, from the EPO, a European Search Report.

---

[119] PA 77, s. 7(1); EPC, Art. 58.   [120] PA 77, s. 7(2)(a); EPC, Art. 60.   [121] EPC, Art. 79.
[122] EPC, Art. 14(1).   [123] PA 77, s. 5(2); Patents Rules, r. 6(1); EPC, Art. 88(1).
[124] PA 77, s. 14(2); EPC, Art. 78.   [125] PA 77, s. 15; EPC, Art. 80.
[126] PA 77, s. 17; EPC, Art. 90.   [127] PA 77, s. 17(1)–(2); EPC, Art. 92.

Finally, at this stage, the application will be examined to ensure that it relates to one invention or to a group of inventions so linked as to form a single inventive concept.[128]

This requirement is important because two patents should not be obtained for the cost of one and also it simplifies the classification and search of patent specifications.[129] Where the application relates to more than one invention, the applicant can divide it into multiple new applications, but still rely on the priority date of the original application.

11.5.2.3 Publication of patent application

The patent application, including any amended claims, is published 18 months from the date of filing or, in the case of the EPO and where Convention priority has been claimed, from the priority date.[130] The examiner's report or European search report is also published, as an annex to the application.

Publication has three significant consequences. First, it prevents the applicant from relying on the law of confidentiality to protect their invention. Second, if the patent is granted, the date of publication is the date from which the patentee is able to claim for damages for any infringement of the patent.[131] For a European patent application, an applicant will need to translate the claims into the languages of the designated Contracting States if they want to obtain protection from the publication date to the date of grant.[132] Finally, following publication of an application it is possible for third parties to submit observations as to whether the invention is patentable.[133] The observations must be filed in writing and include appropriate reasons. The comptroller of the UK IPO must consider the observations whereas the EPO need only communicate those observations to the applicant, who may comment on them. The person submitting observations does not become a party to proceedings.

11.5.2.4 Substantive examination

Within six months of the date of publication of the application, or at the EPO the publication of the Search Report, the applicant must request a substantive examination.[134] The purpose of the substantive examination is for the examiner to consider whether the requirements of the PA 77 or EPC have been satisfied,[135] and in particular, to assess whether the invention does not consist of subject matter excluded from patentability, and is novel, inventive, and capable of industrial application. The examiner also considers whether the claims are clear and concise and supported by the description, and whether the specification discloses the invention in a manner which is clear and complete enough for the invention to be performed by a person skilled in the art.

The examiner issues a report in which any objections are raised. It is then up to the applicant to persuade the examiner that the objections are unfounded or to amend the application so as to comply with the requirements.[136]

If the examiner is satisfied with the application, the patent will be granted.[137] If the objections raised by the examiner have not been resolved, the applicant may have a hearing

---

[128] PA 77, s. 14(5)(d) and (6); PA 77, s. 17(6); EPC, Art. 82.
[129] Cornish and Llewelyn, *Intellectual Property*, paras 4–15.   [130] PA 77, s. 16; EPC, Art. 93.
[131] PA 77, s. 69; EPC, Art. 67.   [132] EPC, Art. 67(3).   [133] PA 77, s. 21; EPC, Art. 115.
[134] PA 77, s. 18(1); EPC, Art. 94.   [135] PA 77, s. 18(2); EPC, Art. 94(1).
[136] PA 77, s. 18(3); EPC, Art. 96.   [137] PA 77, s. 18(4); EPC, Art. 97(2).

before the Senior Examiner in the UK or the full Examining Division of the EPO. From there it is possible to appeal to the UK Patents Court or the Technical Board of Appeal of the EPO.[138]

11.5.2.5 Grant of the patent

The patent will be granted where the UK IPO or EPO is satisfied that all the necessary requirements have been satisfied. If they are not, the application will be refused. A notice that the patent has been granted must be published in the UK IPO Official Journal or the European Patent Bulletin.[139] It is from this date that the patent takes effect and protection lasts for up to 20 years from the date of filing, provided the requisite renewal fees are paid.[140]

Once a European patent is granted and takes effect, it transforms into a bundle of national patents corresponding to the designated Contracting States. For example, a European patent designating the UK, as from the publication of its grant in the European Patent Bulletin, will be treated as a patent under the PA 77, as if it had been granted by the UK IPO.[141] Upon grant, the patent claims must be translated into the other official languages of the EPC.[142] In addition, Contracting States may require the whole specification to be translated into the language of that Contracting State within three months of grant.[143] However, Contracting States that have ratified or acceded to the London Agreement (the UK being one)[144] may waive entirely or partially the requirement for translations of European patents.[145]

11.5.2.6 Revocation

Although the UK IPO and EPO operate a reasonably stringent examination process, it is not comprehensive and therefore cannot be treated as conclusive. Thus, it is possible for the validity of a patent to be challenged following its grant upon the following grounds.[146]

(1) The invention is not a patentable invention.

(2) The patent was granted to the wrong person, i.e. the person who was not entitled to the patent.

(3) The patent specification does not disclose the invention clearly and completely enough for it to be performed by a person skilled in the art.

---

[138] PA 77, s. 97(1); EPC, Arts 106 and 110.   [139] PA 77, s. 24(1); EPC, Art. 97(4).

[140] PA 77, s. 25; EPC, Art. 63(1).   [141] PA 77, s. 77(1).

[142] EPC, r. 71(3) and (7).   [143] EPC, Art. 65.

[144] Agreement on the application of Art. 65 of the Convention on the Grant of European Patents, 17 October 2000 ([2001] OJ EPO 549). The UK ratified the London Agreement on 15 August 2005 and it entered into force on 1 May 2008.

[145] A state which has an official language in common with one of the official languages of the EPO shall dispense entirely with the translation requirements, whereas a state which does not have an official language in common with one of the official languages of the EPO will dispense with the translation requirements if the European patent has been granted in the official language of the EPO prescribed by that state, or translated into that language and supplied under the conditions provided for in Art. 65(1) of the EPC. These states may, however, require a translation for claims into one of their official languages.

[146] PA 77, s. 72; EPC, Art. 138.

(4) The matter disclosed in the specification extends beyond that disclosed in the patent application as filed.

(5) The protection conferred by the patent has been extended by an amendment which should not have been allowed.

In the UK, the court or comptroller may revoke a patent on any of the above grounds, on the application of any person.[147] In addition, the comptroller may on his own initiative revoke the patent.[148]

In the EPO, once a European patent is granted it transforms into a bundle of national patents. Thus, it can be revoked according to the provisions set out in the relevant national law. However, it is possible centrally to challenge the validity of a European patent through a process called 'opposition'. Any person, within nine months of the grant of the patent, may give notice to the EPO of opposition to the European patent granted.[149] The grounds of opposition are:

(1) The invention is not a patentable invention.

(2) The patent specification does not disclose the invention clearly and completely enough for it to be performed by a person skilled in the art.

(3) The matter disclosed in the specification extends beyond that disclosed in the patent application as filed.[150]

The Opposition Division examines the grounds of opposition and the patent proprietor is given the opportunity to contest the opposition, make observations, and/or make amendments. The Opposition Division will decide whether or not the European patent should be revoked, maintained, or maintained in an amended form.[151]

Opposition proceedings arguably provide a cheaper and more convenient way of initiating a single attack, as compared with instigating revocation proceedings in each of the Contracting States where the patent was granted. However, experience has shown that opposition proceedings can often take many years. The availability of opposition proceedings in the EPO, along with revocation proceedings in a Contracting State, give rise to the possibility that parallel proceedings may occur. In such circumstances, the national court may stay revocation proceedings until the outcome of the opposition proceedings is determined. The UK Court of Appeal in *Glaxo Group Ltd v Genentech Inc.*[152] held that the Patents Court has a wide discretion whether to stay proceedings, having regard to the balance of justice between the parties. Further, it held that no presumption exists that the duplication of proceedings in it and the EPO is, by itself, a ground for stay of proceedings in the Patents Court. Considerations that affect the balance of justice include the additional costs in the duplication of proceedings and the order in which the proceedings were commenced. However, the factor that usually will carry most weight is if commercial certainty will be achieved at a considerably earlier date in one forum rather than the other.[153] As the Court of Appeal explained:[154]

> The length of the stay of proceedings, if granted, is, in general, the most significant factor in the discretion. Both the parties' legitimate interests and the public interest are in dispelling the uncertainty surrounding the validity of the monopoly rights conferred by the grant of

---

[147] PA 77, s. 72.   [148] PA 77, s. 73.   [149] EPC, Art. 99.   [150] EPC, Art. 100.
[151] EPC, Arts 101–2.   [152] [2008] FSR 18.   [153] [79]–[88].   [154] [84].

> a patent and the existence or non-existence of the exclusive proprietary rights on a public register ... If the likelihood is that proceedings in the Patents Court would achieve this resolution significantly sooner than the proceedings in the EPO, it would normally be a proper exercise of discretion to decline to stay the Patents Court proceedings.

Aside from the possibility of parallel opposition and revocation proceedings, another potential conflict may arise where a person initiates opposition proceedings in the EPO, but before these have been concluded the patent proprietor successfully sues for patent infringement in the UK Patents Court. This is indeed what occurred in *Unilin Beheer BV v Berry Floor*[155] where the patent had been declared valid and infringed by the defendants. The defendants sought a stay of proceedings for an account of profits, on the basis that their opposition proceedings in the EPO were still pending and might eventually succeed. The Court of Appeal held that the defendants were estopped from challenging the claimant's entitlement to an account of profits, whatever the ultimate result in the EPO. This outcome was an inevitable consequence of the EPC permitting opposition nine months after the date of grant of the patent, along with proceedings in the national courts. As Jacob LJ stated: 'No one pretends that the compromise is satisfactory—it was a fudge at the time and remains so. Unless and until sensible judicial arrangements are put in place, the litigation of European patents in various national courts and the EPO will remain a messy, expensive and prolix business.'[156] It is doubtful whether the proposed Unified Patent Court (discussed at 11.4.2.6) is the sensible judicial arrangement that Jacob LJ was hoping for.

11.5.2.7 Amendment

During the application process, it is possible for an applicant to amend their application in order to address objections that have been raised during the preliminary and substantive examination stages.[157] There is also a general power to amend the patent application at any time before a patent is granted.[158]

Once a UK patent is granted, it is possible for the owner to amend the patent, although this is at the discretion of the comptroller or court (whichever is applicable).[159] Under the EPC, amendment of a patent can only occur in opposition proceedings, otherwise it is a matter for national law.[160]

11.5.2.8 Correction of errors

Errors of translation or transcription or clerical mistakes in a patent specification may be corrected, upon request to the comptroller or the EPO.[161] The correction must be obvious in the sense that it is immediately evident that nothing else would have been intended other than what is suggested as the correction.[162]

---

[155] [2007] FSR 25.   [156] [17]. Arden LJ and Mummery LJ were in agreement.
[157] PA 77, ss. 15A(6) and 18(3); EPC, Art. 123(1), r. 86.
[158] PA 77, s. 19(1); EPC, Art. 123(1), r. 86.   [159] PA 77, ss. 27(1) and 75.
[160] EPC, Arts. 102(3) and 123, r. 57a.   [161] PA 77, s. 117(1); EPC, r. 88.
[162] Patents Rules, r. 50; EPC, r. 88.

11.5.3 PATENT SPECIFICATION

A crucial document in the application process, and indeed also in relying upon a granted patent, is the patent specification. In the UK and EPO systems the specification comprises two main parts: the *description* (which may be accompanied by diagrams) and the *claims*. Pages from a sample patent specification are extracted below in order to give a better sense of this document.

The front page or title page is the least important part of the specification. Nevertheless, it contains some significant information. The first is the date of filing (in this example, 7 April 1992), which will serve as the priority date, unless the applicant is claiming Convention priority. However, it seems that the applicant is not claiming priority from an earlier application since, if she had been, this would have been listed on the title page as 'priority data'. The names of the applicant and inventor are also listed on the title page. In this example, Mandy Nicola Haberman is both the applicant and the inventor and, as such, will be entitled to grant of the patent if the application is successful. The date of publication of the application is listed as 20 October 1993. As was mentioned above, the significance of publication is that, once the patent is granted, the patentee will be able to sue for any infringing acts that occur after this date. Finally, the title page contains the *abstract* listed under 'Drinking vessel suitable for use as a trainer cup'. The abstract is one of the documents required in order to make a full application. It is a brief summary of the important technical features of the invention and is a crucial element in facilitating searches of the patent register and alerting third parties to the existence of the application. Importantly, the abstract is only a source of technical information and does not form part of the state of the art.[163]

The subsequent pages contain *drawings* of the invention; these must be included in making an application where they are referred to in either the claims or the description. Along with the description, the drawings may be used to interpret the claims.

Next there is the *description* of the invention, which is also a necessary part of filing an application. The purpose of the description is to teach the notional skilled person in the relevant technological field (i.e. the person skilled in the art) about the invention. The specification must disclose the invention in a manner which is clear and complete enough for the person skilled in the art to perform the invention,[164] and the description is a key means of making such disclosure. The description will usually set out the background to the invention, summarizing any relevant prior art, and set out the technical problem which the invention seeks to solve. For example, in the patent application extract the background is that drinking cups for toddlers, known as trainer cups, are crucial in the developmental stage of children learning to drink from normal cups. However, the description tells us that existing trainer cups are prone to spillage when shaken or knocked over. In the field of baby feeding bottles, it is said that the use of certain 'valve means' has been helpful in interrupting the flow of liquid, but that such 'valve means' have not yet been used in relation to trainer cups. The invention, as described, is a trainer cup which uses 'valve means adapted to prevent flow of liquid from the interior of the container through the mouthpiece unless a predetermined level of lip pressure and suction is applied to the mouthpiece'. The valve means is then described in more detail with reference to the drawings.

---

[163] PA 77, s. 14(7); EPC, Art. 85.   [164] PA 77, s. 14(3); EPC, Art. 83.

(12) **UK Patent Application** (19) **GB** (11) **2 266 045** (13) **A**

(43) Date of A publication **20.10.1993**

(21) Application No 9207766.8

(22) Date of filing 07.04.1992

(71) Applicant
Mandy Nicola Haberman
Dove Cottage, 44 Watford Road, Radlett,
Hertfordshire, WD7 8LR, United Kingdom

(72) Inventor
Mandy Nicola Haberman

(74) Agent and/or Address for Service
Lloyd Wise, Tregear & Co
Norman House, 105-109 Strand, London, WC2R 0AE,
United Kingdom

(51) INT CL⁵
A47G 19/22

(52) UK CL (Edition L)
A4A ALN
A5X X5E
U1S S1787 S2409

(56) Documents cited
GB 2169210 A | US 5050758 A | US 4946062 A
US 4782975 A | US 4441624 A | US 4245752 A
US 4190174 A | US 4184604 A

(58) Field of search
UK CL (Edition K) A4A ALC ALN ALQ ALX AN ASA
ASB ASX, A5X X5E X5X
INT CL⁵ A47G, A61J
Online database: WPI

(54) **Drinking vessel suitable for use as a trainer cup**

(57) A drinking vessel suitable for use as a trainer cup or cup for the elderly comprises an open-mouthed generally cup-shaped container (2) and a lid (5) for covering the open mouth of the container (2). The lid (5) has an associated mouthpiece (6). Valve means (10) are provided to prevent flow of liquid from the interior of the container (2) through the mouthpiece (6) unless a predetermined level of lip pressure and suction is applied to the mouthpiece (6). Other embodiments of the valve mechanism are described (see Figures 4, 10, 13 and 15).

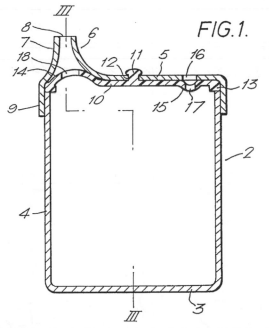

FIG.1.

At least one drawing originally filed was informal and the print reproduced here is taken from a later filed formal copy.

GB 2 266 045 A

1/6

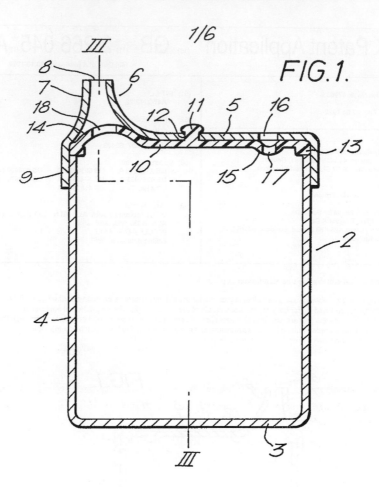

FIG.1.

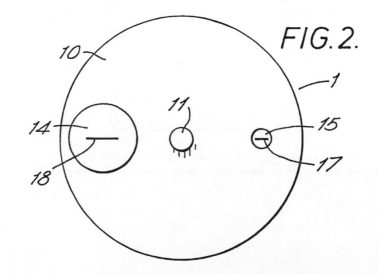

FIG.2.

2266045

1

DRINKING VESSEL SUITABLE FOR USE
AS A TRAINER CUP OR THE LIKE

This invention relates to drinking vessels and more particularly to drinking vessels suitable for use as a trainer cup or the like.

Trainer cups (that is a cup or mug provided with a lid having a mouthpiece - usually a spout - associated therewith) are well known and have been designed to bridge the gap between use of a baby's feeding bottle and use of a normal cup or glass by a young child. Such a trainer cup will often be a child's first step in learning to feed itself. As this period in a child's development will usually coincide with the cutting of its first teeth, quite apart from the child's inherent difficulty in handling what is new to it which may lead to the cup inadvertently being knocked over, the irritability characteristic of teething allied with the natural exuberance of young children tends to exacerbate what is frequently a noisy and messy experience.

The existence of the lid may reduce or at least delay the effect of knocking the cup over, but will not deter a child from shaking the cup violently up and down. Neither will the lid delay spillage for very long if the cup is knocked over. Notwithstanding that trainer cups of this kind have been known for a very lengthy period of time, I am unaware of any practical arrangement for overcoming these self-evident problems.

In the somewhat different field of babies feeding bottles, I have myself designed arrangements in which a valve interrupts the flow of fluid from the interior of the bottle through a teat or other mouthpiece (see for example my Patent Specifications Nos: 2 131 301 and

2

2 169 210). Bottles to my design have achieved some commercial success particularly in the rather specialised field of feeding of babies with_sucking problems. Other arrangements proposing valved feeding bottles such as US Patents 4 135 513, 3 704 803 and 4 339 046 and UK Patents 460 274 and 1 253 398 have been proposed in the patent literature but I am not aware that any of these proposals have proved of practical utility. I am not aware of any of them having been marketed. Nevertheless, it is clear that there have been a series of proposals by different workers for the valving of babies feeding bottles. Notwithstanding this, I am not aware of any previous proposal for valving training cups or the like. As will become clear from the detailed description hereinbelow of a presently preferred embodiment of training cup or the like constructed in accordance with my present invention, the present invention enables the production of practical embodiments of trainer cups which neatly and effectively overcome the problems of accidental spillage or of child-generated deliberate attempts at spilling the contents of the trainer cup. Moreover, my practical embodiment achieves this desirable end, never previously achieved, so far as I am aware, in a simple, neat construction which is cheap and simple to manufacture and facilitates easy cleaning. It has no moving parts.

In broad terms, my invention in its broadest context provides a drinking vessel suitable for use as a trainer cup or the like, comprising: an open-mouthed generally cup-shaped container; and a lid for the open mouth of said container, the lid having a mouthpiece associated therewith; the vessel being provided with valve means adapted to prevent flow of liquid from the interior of the container through the mouthpiece unless a predetermined level of lip pressure and suction is applied to the mouthpiece.

3

The valve may be a separate valve member located in use between the container and the lid. Alternatively the valve may be integrally formed with the lid.

Suitably the lid is apertured to allow for the ingress of air to make up for the liquid sucked via the valve through the mouthpiece. To prevent the possibility of liquid issuing through this aperture, that is also suitably provided with a valve, preferably a non-return valve allowing flow of air from the exterior into the container but preventing flow of liquid from the interior of the container outwardly through the aperture.

Conveniently the two valves are provided by a single valve member which may be attached to the lid. The valve member may comprise a single piece of latex, silicone rubber, plastics or other suitable flexible material integrally moulded with two valves, one adapted to underlie the lid in the region of the mouthpiece and the other underlying the aperture. The two valves may comprise dome-shaped regions, the larger underlying the lid in the region of the mouthpiece and being concave towards the interior of the container, and the smaller underlying the aperture and being convex towards the interior. These dome-shaped regions are provided with a simple slit or cross-cut which in effect is self-closing, in each case the slit or cross-cut allowing flow from the concave to the convex side but not in the reverse direction. Other valve formations (e.g., a so-called "duck-bill" or a flap valve) are feasible. The valve member may be held in place between the lid and a valve member support plate.

In an alternative arrangement in which the valve is integrally formed with the lid, the lid itself may be made of a material listed above as a candidate for the separate valve member. The exit valve may comprise several dome-

12

CLAIMS

1. A drinking vessel suitable for use as a trainer cup or the like, comprising: an open-mouthed generally cup-shaped container; and a lid for the open mouth of said container, the lid having a mouthpiece associated therewith; the vessel being provided with valve means adapted to prevent flow of liquid from the interior of the container through the mouthpiece unless a predetermined level of lip pressure and suction is applied to the mouthpiece.

2. A drinking vessel according to Claim 1, wherein said valve means is a separate valve member located in use between the container and the lid.

3. A drinking vessel according to Claim 1, wherein said valve means is integral with the lid.

4. A drinking vessel according to Claims 1 or 3, wherein the valve means is at the extreme end of the mouthpiece.

5. A drinking vessel according to any preceding claim, wherein the lid is provided with an aperture to allow for the ingress of air.

6. A drinking vessel according to Claim 5, wherein said vessel is provided with additional valve means to prevent flow of liquid from the interior of the container through said aperture.

7. A drinking vessel according to both Claim 2 and Claim 6, wherein both said valve means are provided on the same said valve member located in use between the lid and the container.

Another important aspect of the application is the *claims*. Whereas the purpose of the description is to teach the reader about the invention and ensure that it is of some practical use, the purpose of the claims is to define the scope of the patent owner's monopoly. As such, the claims have a key role in determining whether or not a patent is valid and infringed and difficult questions of interpretation of the language of the claims may arise. Usually, the claims are arranged hierarchically, with the broadest or principal claim listed first and the narrower or subsidiary claims listed subsequently. The advantage of doing this is that, if the principal claim is rejected or declared invalid, the patentee can still rely on the narrower claims. The types of the claims that may be encountered are various, but it is important to appreciate two key types of claims—product claims and process claims. Product claims are to inventions concerning products, articles, machines, compounds, or substances. Process claims are to inventions relating to processes, methods, or uses.

As should be apparent from the excerpted patent application and discussion above, the patent specification is a highly technical document which requires specialist knowledge and expert drafting skills. For this reason, they are often drafted with the assistance of experts, called patent agents (in the UK) or European patent agents (for the EPC). These persons normally have knowledge of the patent administration process, patent law, and a particular branch of science.

11.6 PATENTABLE SUBJECT MATTER

11.6.1 INTRODUCTION

Article 52(1) of the EPC and section 1(1) of the PA 77 state that a patent may be granted for an *invention* which is new, involves an inventive step, and is capable of industrial application.[165] Each of these requirements will be examined in detail in later sections.[166] Section 1(1)(d) of the PA 77 also requires that the grant of a patent is not excluded by subsections (2) and (3) or section 4A. Section 1(3) excludes inventions which are contrary to public policy or morality, while section 4A excludes methods of medical and veterinary treatment. Both of these exclusions are discussed later in this chapter.[167]

Notably, section 1(2) of the PA 77 declares that certain things are *not inventions*, including:

(a) a discovery, scientific theory or mathematical method;

(b) a literary, dramatic, musical or artistic work or any other aesthetic creation whatsoever;

(c) a scheme, rule, or method for performing a mental act, playing a game or doing business, or a program for a computer;

(d) the presentation of information,

but only to the extent that a patent or patent application relates to that thing *as such*.[168]

Prior to the PA 77, inventions were defined positively as a 'manner of new manufacture'—a test which had its origins in section 6 of the Statute of Monopolies 1624.[169] However, sections

---

[165] For European patents see EPC, Art. 52(1).

[166] See 11.8 for industrial application, 12.1 for novelty, and 12.2 for inventive step.

[167] See 11.9 for methods of medical and veterinary treatment and 11.7.7 for the public order and morality exclusion.

[168] The EPC equivalent is to be found in Art. 52(2)–(3).   [169] Discussed at 11.2.

1(1)(d) and 1(2) of the PA 77 reflect a new approach to defining inventions, which accords with Article 52(2)–(3) of the EPC, namely to define them in a negative sense. The issue of whether there is a residual positive requirement or concept of invention has been left open.[170]

FURTHER READING

J. Pila, 'Article 52(2) of the Convention on the Grant of European Patents: what did the framers intend? A study of the *travaux préparatoires*' (2005) 36 IIC 755.

J. Pila, 'On the European requirement for an invention' (2010) 41 IIC 906.

11.6.2 APPLYING SECTION 1(2) OF THE PA 77/ARTICLE 52(2)–(3) OF THE EPC

As mentioned above, UK patent law had previously defined 'invention' positively as a 'manner of new manufacture'. Under the PA 77 and EPC, however, the approach is to define 'invention' negatively, stipulating certain categories of subject matter that are *not* inventions. Is there an explanation for why these particular categories are excluded? Do they share a common objection or can the exclusion of each category be justified for different reasons? In *Aerotel*, the Court of Appeal explored these questions.

Aerotel Ltd v Telco Holdings Ltd [2007] RPC 7

The facts are discussed at 11.6.5.3.

Jacob LJ (giving the judgment of the court):

8. The provisions about what are not to be 'regarded as inventions' are not easy. Over the years there has been and continues to be much debate about them and about decisions on them given by national courts and the Boards of Appeal of the EPO. They form the basis of a distinct industry of conferences and are the foundation of a plethora of academic theses and publications. There has also been much political debate too: some urging removal or reduction of the categories, others their retention or enlargement. With the political debate we have no concern—it is our job to interpret them as they stand.

9. As the decisions show this is not an easy task. There are several reasons for this:

i)   In the first place there is no evident underlying purpose lying behind the provisions as a group—a purpose to guide the construction. The categories are there, but there is nothing to tell you one way or the other whether they should be read widely or narrowly.

ii) One cannot form an overall approach to the categories. They form a disparate group—no common, overarching concept, for example, links rules for playing games with computer programs or either of these with methods for doing business or aesthetic creations.

---

[170] See comments *obiter* of Lord Hoffmann in *Biogen Inc. v Medeva Plc* [1997] RPC 1, 41–2, and those of Lord Mustill at 31–2. Contrast the view taken in J. Pila, 'On the European requirement for an invention' (2010) 41 IIC 906. Dr Pila argues for a positive conception of invention that 'requires a human action on the physical world producing an objectively discernible (material) result directed to advancing the industrial arts' (at 914) which would, in effect, make the patentability exclusions unnecessary.

iii) Some categories are given protection by other intellectual property laws. Most importantly, of course, aesthetic creations and computer programs have protection under the law of copyright. So the legislator may well have formed the view that additional protection by way of patentability was unnecessary or less appropriate.

iv) Further, some categories are so abstract that they are unnecessary or meaningless. For instance a scientific theory as such is excluded. But how could a scientific theory ever be the subject of a patent claim in the first place? Einstein's special theory of relativity was new and non-obvious but it was inherently incapable of being patented. A patent after all is to a legal monopoly over some commercial activity carried out by human beings such as making or dealing in goods or carrying out a process. A scientific theory is not activity at all. It simply is not the sort of thing which could be made the subject of a legal monopoly.

Nor can the presence of the exclusion be explained on the narrower basis that it was intended to exclude woolly and general claims such as 'Any application of $E = mc^2$'. For such a claim would be bad for the more conventional reason that it does not disclose the invention 'in a manner sufficiently clear and complete for it to be carried out by a person skilled in the art' (Arts 83 and 100(b)).

v) There is or may be overlap between some of the exclusions themselves and between them [and] the overall requirement that an invention be 'susceptible of industrial application'. The overall requirement is, perhaps surprisingly, hardly ever mentioned in the debate about the categories of 'non-invention' (no-one relied upon it before us) but it is clearly a factor lying behind some of the debate.

…

11. So, one asks, what help can be had from the *travaux preparatoires* to the EPC? The answer is not a lot. The debates amongst the framers of the Convention which lead to the excluded categories were the subject of two fascinating and valuable articles in 2005 by Dr Justine Pila of the Oxford University Intellectual Property Research Centre ('Dispute over the meaning of "invention" in Art. 52(2) EPC—The patentability of computer-implemented inventions in Europe' 36 IIC 173; 'Art. 52(2) of the Convention on the Grant of European Patents: What did the framers intend?' 36 IIC 755). She shows that the *travaux* provide no direct assistance to any of the categories we have to consider. 'Only a bull's-eye counts' (per Lord Steyn in *Effort Shipping Co Ltd v Linden Management SA* [1988] AC 605 at 625) and there are no bull's-eyes in the *travaux* for present purposes. What does emerge is that the various categories are the result of various compromises and distinct discussions about each of them. So one can at least find confirmation that no overarching principle was intended. What was done was to formulate the language of each of the categories independently of one another, add the 'as such' rider to all of them and leave it to the EPO and European patent judges to work out the detail.

12. Perhaps one other thing emerges—by its absence. There is no indication of any intention as to how the categories should be construed—either restrictively or widely. In EU law exceptions to a general principle are generally interpreted restrictively, see, e.g. per La Pergola A-G at [8] in Case C-12/98 *Amengual Far v Amengual Far* [2002] STC 382 (a VAT case): 'This criterion has been consistently followed in the case law of this court.' The EPO Boards of Appeal have applied that principle to the interpretation of Art. 53. See, e.g. *HARVARD/Oncomouse* (1990) T 0019/90 [1990] OJ EPO 376, T 356/93 *Plant Genetic Systems/Glutamine Synthetase Inhibitors* (1995) [1995] OJ EPO 545; [1995] EPOR 357. But Art. 53 is not the

same as Art. 52(2). It is expressly entitled 'Exceptions to patentability'. The exceptions are clearly specified as such and the exception principle of construction can and does apply to them. But Art. 52(2), by contrast, is not expressed as an exception to patentability—it sets out positive categories of things which are not to be regarded as inventions.

What are the difficulties, according to *Aerotel*, of interpreting section 1(2) of the PA 77? Further, is the correct approach for courts to interpret each category of excluded subject matter according to its particular underlying purpose and legislative background?

In assessing whether an invention falls foul of section 1(2) of the PA 77, courts will look at the invention as a *whole*, even where it is a mix of patentable and non-patentable elements. However, this can create difficulties around establishing whether the invention as claimed falls within the excluded categories of subject matter. To assist in determining whether the invention falls within the exclusions, courts have developed the test of 'technical effect', 'technical contribution', or 'technical character'. If the invention has a technical effect, or makes a technical contribution or features a technical character, the logic is that it must fall outside section 1(2) of the PA 77 or Article 52(2)–(3) of the EPC because these provisions are concerned with categories of subject matter that are non-technical in nature. Brad Sherman describes the advantage of this test:

One of the main advantages of this way of approaching Article 52(2) is that by shifting attention towards the idea of 'technical character', the Board of Appeal is able to avoid having to formulate a workable definition of 'computer program', a task which is not only technically problematic but also one that changes in technology are likely to render obsolete. Indeed one of the major problems with specific formulations such as Article 52(2) is that because they are drafted in the light of contemporary technology they are prone to obsolescence or, at least, convoluted interpretations. Whatever advantages this approach to Article 52 may have, it still leaves the Board of Appeal with two further questions: first, the need to characterise the invention; second, the task of having to formulate and understand what is meant by the term 'technical' ...[171]

Examining the invention as a whole and asking whether it produces a 'technical effect' or 'technical contribution' was first introduced by the Technical Board of Appeal in *Vicom/Computer-related invention*.[172] This case involved a European patent application for a method of digitally processing images using a device called an operator matrix, which aimed at producing enhanced images. The Examining Division rejected the application on the ground that it was for a mathematical method and/or a computer program as such. The applicants appealed to the Technical Board of Appeal, arguing that the invention conferred a technical benefit, in the form of a substantial increase in processing speed compared with the prior art and, further, that digital image processing was not an abstract process, 'but the physical manipulation of electrical signals representing the picture in accordance with the procedures defined in the claims'. As such, the invention reflected a new and valuable contribution which was not excluded by Article 52(2)–(3) of the EPC.

[171] B. Sherman, 'The patentability of computer-related inventions in the United Kingdom and the European Patent Office' [1991] EIPR 85, 87–8.
[172] T208/84 [1987] EPOR 74.

The Technical Board of Appeal set aside the decision of the Examining Division, stating that:

> Generally speaking, an invention which would be patentable in accordance with conventional patentability criteria should not be excluded from protection by the mere fact that for its implementation modern technical means in the form of a computer program are used. Decisive is what technical contribution the invention as defined in the claim when considered as a whole makes to the known art.[173]

The Board also commented that where the method is 'carried out on a physical entity (which may be a material object but equally an image stored as an electric signal) by some technical means implementing the method and provides as its result a certain change in that entity',[174] this could amount to a technical result. In your view, is this guidance from the Board as to what constitutes a 'technical result' or 'technical contribution' helpful?

In a subsequent case, *Koch & Sterzel/X-Ray Apparatus*,[175] the approach in *Vicom* was challenged. However, the Technical Board of Appeal reiterated the 'technical effect' test for determining whether the invention as a whole falls foul of the excluded subject matter in Article 52(2)–(3) of the EPC. Shortly after *Vicom* and *Koch & Sterzel*, the UK Court of Appeal had an opportunity to consider how to approach section 1(2) of the PA 77.

Merrill Lynch Inc.'s Application [1989] RPC 561

The invention related to an improved data processing system for implementing an automated trading market for securities. The principal examiner held that the invention was unpatentable pursuant to section 1(2) of the PA 77. The applicants appealed and the appeal was dismissed by Falconer J in the Patents Court. Falconer J held that the principal examiner had correctly construed the qualification in section 1(2). In the Court of Appeal, the appeal was dismissed. The approach of Falconer J was not followed, but rather the approach in *Vicom*.

Fox LJ (with whom Stocker and Taylor LJJ agreed), at p. 569:

The position seems to me to be this. *Genentech* decides that the reasoning of Falconer J is wrong. On the other hand, it seems to me to be clear, for the reasons indicated by Dillon LJ, that it cannot be permissible to patent an item excluded by section 1(2) under the guise of an article which contains that item—that is to say, in the case of a computer program, the patenting of a conventional computer containing that program. Something further is necessary. The nature of that addition is, I think, to be found in the *Vicom* case where it is stated: 'Decisive is what technical contribution the invention makes to the known art.' There must, I think, be some technical advance on the prior art in the form of a new result (e.g., a substantial increase in processing speed as in *Vicom*).

Now let it be supposed that claim 1 can be regarded as producing a new result in the form of a technical contribution to the prior art. That result, whatever the technical advance may be, is simply the production of a trading system. It is a data-processing system for doing a specific business, that is to say, making a trading market in securities. The end result,

---

173 [16].   174 [5].   175 T26/86 [1988] EPOR 72.

therefore, is simply 'a method of doing business', and is excluded by section 1(2)(c). The fact that the method of doing business may be an improvement on previous methods of doing business does not seem to me to be material. The prohibition in section 1(2)(c) is generic; qualitative considerations do not enter into the matter. The section draws no distinction between the method by which the mode of doing business is achieved. If what is produced in the end is itself an item excluded from patentability by section 1(2), the matter can go no further. Claim 1, after all, is directed to 'a data processing system for making a trading market'. That is simply a method of doing business. A data processing system operating to produce a novel technical result would normally be patentable. But it cannot, it seems to me, be patentable if the result itself is a prohibited item under section 1(2). In the present case it is such a prohibited item.

Although the *Vicom* approach was followed in *Merrill Lynch*, the Court of Appeal added the 'rider' that where the technical contribution relates to excluded subject matter (e.g. is a method of doing business) it will still be excluded. In other words, the technical contribution must not reside in the excluded subject matter. Although the applicability of the 'rider' to the 'technical effect' approach was subsequently questioned,[176] it has since been reiterated in *Aerotel* (see 11.6.5.3).

Implicit in the 'technical effect' or 'technical contribution' approach is that the court looks to what is *new* and/or *inventive* about the invention (i.e. the contribution) to judge whether it is technical in nature. In *PBS Partnership/Pension Benefit Systems*,[177] the Technical Board of Appeal rejected this approach because, inter alia, it confused the requirements of 'invention', 'novelty', and 'inventive step'. Instead, the Board held that:

a computer system suitably programmed for use in a particular field, even if that is the field of business and economy, has the character of a concrete apparatus in the sense of a physical entity, man-made for a utilitarian purpose and is thus an invention within the meaning of Article 52(1) EPC.[178]

Thus, the invention had a technical character by virtue of being embodied in physical apparatus, i.e. computer hardware, and was held *not* to be excluded subject matter. The approach in *Pension Benefit Systems* has thus been referred to as the 'any hardware' approach.[179] Later decisions of the Technical Board of Appeal (in *Hitachi/Auction Method*[180] and *Microsoft/Clipboard Formats I*[181]) have also rejected the 'technical effect' approach to Article 52(2)–(3) of the EPC in favour of the 'any hardware' approach. These decisions, along with *Pension Benefit Systems*, are discussed in more detail at 11.6.5.2.

The divergence of approaches in the jurisprudence of the Technical Boards of Appeal has put the UK in an awkward position when it comes to pursuing uniformity with the EPO. In *Aerotel*, the Court of Appeal declined to follow the EPO approach to Article 52(2)–(3) of the EPC, as reflected in *Pension Benefit Systems*,[182] *Hitachi*,[183] and *Microsoft/Clipboard Formats I*.[184] The court stated:[185]

---

[176] As a result of a comment by Aldous LJ in *Fujitsu* [1997] RPC 608, 614.

[177] T931/95 [2002] OJ EPO 441. Discussed further at 11.6.5.2.   [178] At 530.

[179] *Aerotel*, [26]: 'ask whether the claim involves the use of or is to a piece of physical hardware, however mundane'.

[180] T258/03 [2004] EPOR 55.   [181] T424/03 [2006] EPOR 39.   [182] T931/95.

[183] T258/04.   [184] T424/03.   [185] [2007] RPC 7, [29].

> We are conscious of the need to place great weight on the decisions of the Boards of Appeal, but, given the present state of conflict between the old (*Vicom* etc) and the new (*Hitachi* etc) approaches, quite apart from the fact that there are three distinct new approaches each to some extent in conflict with the other two, it would be premature to do so. If and when an Enlarged Board rules on the question, this Court may have to re-consider its approach ... All we decide now is that we do not follow any of the trio. The fact that the BGH has already declined to follow *Pension Benefits* reinforces this view—doing so will not lead to European consistency.

Instead, the Court of Appeal reiterated that the approach was as follows:

> (1) properly construe the claim;
>
> (2) identify the actual contribution;
>
> (3) ask whether it falls solely within the excluded subject matter;
>
> (4) check whether the actual or alleged contribution is actually technical in nature.

Subsequent to *Aerotel*, a reference to the Enlarged Board of Appeal was crankily refused in *Duns Licensing Associates*,[186] the Technical Board of Appeal commenting that the court's approach in *Aerotel* (discussed further at 11.6.5.3) was 'not consistent with a good faith interpretation' of the EPC. In its subsequent decision in *Symbian Ltd*,[187] the Court of Appeal sought to be more diplomatic, but still refused to adopt the 'any hardware' approach (discussed further at 11.6.5.2). When a reference to the Enlarged Board of Appeal finally occurred in *Programs for computers*,[188] as a result of a reference by the President of the EPO under Article 112(1)(b) of the EPC, disappointingly the Board ruled that while the questions concerned points of law of fundamental importance there were not diverging decisions of the Boards of Appeal and so the reference was not admissible.[189] However, in the course of explaining why there are no diverging decisions, the Enlarged Board of Appeal in effect endorsed the 'any hardware' approach.

To what extent do these approaches differ and will this have an impact in practice? Deputy Judge Peter Prescott QC in *CFPH LLC's Application*[190] explored this very question and made the following observations:

> 44. Let me first outline the practice of the UK Patent Office. They look at the applicant's claim, and ask themselves: what is his 'technical contribution'? If there is none—as in my tax-planning example—they reject the application. They hold that is not an 'invention'. If there is some 'technical contribution', they still have to decide whether to reject it for being old, or obvious. It is an 'invention', but it may be an old invention, or an obvious one.

---

[186] T154/04 [2007] EPOR 38.

[187] [2008] EWCA Civ 1066, [2009] RPC 1. For a further discussion see 11.6.3.2.

[188] G3/08 [2010] EPOR 36 (EBA).

[189] This has been robustly criticized by J. Pila, 'Software patents, separation of powers and failed syllogisms: a cornucopia from the Enlarged Board of Appeal of the European Patent Office' [2011] CLJ 203.

[190] [2006] RPC 5.

45. Now let me outline the practice of the European Patent Office. They look at the applicant's claim, and ask themselves: does it have any 'technical features'? If there are no 'technical features' at all they reject the application, for not being an 'invention'. But they consider it is an invention if there is any 'technical feature' at all. They take it very far. Even paper, or ink, can count as a technical feature. I suppose a detective story, written on paper with ink, would pass that part of their test. What they then go on to do is to ask themselves, 'Yes, but is it old, or obvious?' And in deciding if it is old or obvious, they *ignore* anything that is not a 'technical feature'.

46. In short, the difference between the two approaches is that the EPO filters out excluded subject-matter at the stage of considering obviousness—at the last stage—while the UK Patent Office does so at the first stage (when considering excluded subject-matter). Or to put it a little more precisely, what the UK Patent Office does is to consider the exclusion under the description 'novelty', but the EPO does so under the description 'inventive step'.

Does It Matter?

47. Do both approaches lead to the same end-result in practice? I asked counsel if they could come up with a clear concrete example, real or imaginary, where it made all the difference, but they were not able to think of one. Not a convincing one, anyway.

48. So why is it that the difference may matter all the same? It is because, as Renan and Lord Hoffmann said in other contexts, *la verité est dans une nuance*. Even if the two approaches are the same functionally they may, conceivably, produce different results when it comes to matters of evaluation. That is because cases have to be decided by human beings; but the human mind is affected by the context in which a question is posed. And technological invention cannot reliably be divorced from business context.

Would it be fair to say that the UK takes the 'invention' requirement more seriously than the EPO? On the other hand, if the EPO considers only *technical* contributions when assessing inventive step, is it not the case that inventions simply get refused at a later stage of the examination process? As we shall see in Chapter 12, the requirement of inventiveness must be considered in relation to the prior art (and so the relevant prior art must be identified). Whereas, the question of whether there is an excluded invention can be determined without regard to the prior art. Will this make it possible to reach different outcomes? It is important to bear these questions in mind in the discussion that ensues about particular categories of excluded subject matter. We turn now to examine in more detail the exclusions for computer programs, methods for performing mental acts, and methods of doing business.

11.6.3 COMPUTER PROGRAMS AND PATENT PROTECTION

11.6.3.1 Introduction

Patent law, on the face of it, has very little to offer when it comes to protection of computer programs. This is because Article 52(2)–(3) of the EPC and section 1(2) of the PA 77 exclude 'computer programs as such' from being inventions. The policy reasons for this prohibition are neatly summarized in the following extract.

CFPH LLC's Application [2006] RPC 5

Deputy Judge Peter Prescott QC:

35. ... The reason why computer programs, as such, are not allowed to be patented is quite different. Although it is hotly disputed now by some special interest groups, the truth is, or ought to be, well known. It is because at the time the EPC was under consideration it was felt in the computer industry that such patents were not really needed, were too cumbersome (it was felt that searching the prior art would be a big problem), and would do more harm than good. I shall not go into details here but it is worth noting that the software industry in America developed at an astonishing pace when no patent protection was available. Copyright law protects computer programs against copying. A patent on a computer program would stop others from using it even though there had been no copying at all. So there would have to be infringement searches. Furthermore you cannot have a sensible patent system unless there exists a proper body of prior art that can be searched. Not only are most computer programs supplied in binary form—unintelligible to humans—but most of the time it is actually illegal to convert them into human-readable form. A patent system where it is illegal to search most of the prior art is something of an absurdity.

11.6.3.2 UK approach

Importantly, it is computer programs *as such* that are excluded from patentability. Thus, even though an invention may include a computer program, if it does not claim a computer program *as such* it will be patentable. As we shall see from the following case, UK courts have determined this issue by using the test of 'technical effect' or 'technical contribution'.

Fujitsu Ltd's Application [1997] RPC 608

The application related to a method and apparatus for modelling a synthetic crystal structure for designing inorganic materials. It involved a computer programmed so that an operator could select an atom, a lattice vector, and a crystal face in each of two crystal structures displayed on the computer. The computer then converted data representing the physical layouts of the two crystal structures into data representing the crystal structure that would have been obtained by combining the original two structures in that way. The resulting data was then displayed to give an image of the resulting combined structure. Conventionally, the modelling of such structures occurred by assembling plastic models.

The examiner objected that the application was a method for performing a mental act or a program for a computer as such. The Hearing Officer rejected the application on the same basis. On appeal to the Patents Court, Laddie J held that, in form at least, the claims were not to programs as such, but that they did relate to a method for performing a mental act as such. In the Court of Appeal, the appeal was dismissed.

Aldous LJ (with whom Roch and Leggatt LJJ agreed), **at pp. 614–19:**

The law

Section 1(2)(c) of the Act has been considered by this court in *Merrill Lynch's Application* [1989] RPC 561 and in *Gale's Application.* In both those cases the court drew attention to the proviso to section 1(2) which states that the 'things', referred to in the subsection, should only be excluded 'to the extent that a patent or an application for a patent relates to that thing as such'.

In *Merrill Lynch* the applicants submitted that the question for the court was to decide whether the subject matter of the claim was a computer program. If it was, it was not patentable. If it was not, then the invention was not excluded from patentability by section 1(2). Thus it was said that a piece of machinery (a computer) which follows the instructions of a computer program was patentable, although the program itself would be excluded from patentability by the section. That was rejected by the Court of Appeal. Fox LJ said at page 569:

> It seems to me to be clear, ... that it cannot be permissible to patent an item excluded by section 1(2) under the guise of an article which contains that item—that is to say, in the case of a computer program, the patenting of a conventional computer containing that program. Something further is necessary. The nature of that addition is, I think, to be found in the *Vicom* case where it is stated: 'Decisive is what technical contribution the invention makes to the known art.' There must, I think, be some technical advance on the prior art in the form of a new result (eg. a substantial increase in processing speed as in *Vicom*).

By that statement Fox LJ was making it clear that it was not sufficient to look at the words of the claimed monopoly. The decision as to what was patentable depended upon substance not form. He also went on to point out the importance of considering whether the invention made a technical contribution, despite the fact that neither the statute nor Article 52 of the Convention lays down that the matter, which would result in the invention not relating to the thing as such, must provide a technical contribution. It would therefore seem that as a matter of words, if for instance the patent was not confined to a computer program, then it could not be excluded under subsection (2), as to an extent the patent would not relate to the computer program as such. However it is and always has been a principle of patent law that mere discoveries or ideas are not patentable, but those discoveries and ideas which have a technical aspect or make a technical contribution are. Thus the concept that what is needed to make an excluded thing patentable is a technical contribution is not surprising. That was the basis for the decision of the Board in *Vicom*. It has been accepted by this court and by the EPO and has been applied since 1987. It is a concept at the heart of patent law.

...

The reasoning in *Vicom* as to what was the technical contribution is not easy to ascertain. However, I do not read the decision as concluding that all claims to processing real images are patentable and I can see no reason why, if they are, the same reasoning should not apply to all useful images. As I read the decision, the Board saw a technical contribution, namely the generation of the enhanced picture. As the Principal Examiner pointed out:

> the numbers which are mathematically processed in *Vicom* do not merely determine the intellectual content of the images which are displayed, but are also the technical means

which cause the display to operate to a technical level. Thus in *Vicom* manipulating numbers in the manner described affects the technical quality of the image. So in *Vicom*, the invention concerned the technical representation, or technical control of what is displayed and not the information content of what is displayed.

In my view *Vicom* does not support the submission that claims to processing of real images are allowable. The technical contribution was not the fact that an image was being produced. It was the way the enhanced image was produced

In *Gale* this court had to consider a patent application for a ROM programmed to carry out a method of calculating a square root of a number. Nicholls LJ who gave the leading judgment described the working of a computer and said:

> In principle, the instructions in a computer program do no more than prescribe a particular manner of operation for which it was constructed. Thus writing a fresh set of instructions for use in a computer in particular circumstances or for particular purposes cannot in itself be regarded as inventive.

He went on to point out that, to be used in a computer, a series of instructions had to be recorded in some physical form perhaps on a disc in a ROM. He said that if the instructions *qua* instructions were not patentable, they were not patentable merely because they were recorded on or in a known piece of apparatus. The disc on ROM was 'merely the vehicle used for carrying' the instruction.

> … the physical differences are not material for patent purposes, because they constitute no more than the use of a compact disc for its intended purpose. Likewise with a disc or ROM which records or reproduces a new set of instructions, if those instructions are recorded on a conventional disc, or are stored in a ROM using conventional methods. To decide otherwise would be to exalt form over substance.

He went on to conclude that the application before him did not contain a technical contribution and therefore was a computer program which was excluded from patentability.

I, like Nicholls LJ, have difficulty in identifying clearly the boundary line between what is and what is not a technical contribution. In *Vicom* it seems that the Board concluded that the enhancement of the images produced amounted to a technical contribution. No such contribution existed in *Gale's Application* which related to a ROM programmed to enable a computer to carry out a mathematical calculation or in *Merrill Lynch* which had claims to a data processing system for making a trading market in securities. Each case has to be decided upon its own facts.

…

There is only one invention. The fact that it is claimed as a method, a way of manufacture or an apparatus having appropriate features is irrelevant. Further there is no dispute as to what the invention is. In summary it uses a computer program so that an operator can select an atom, a lattice vector and a crystal face in each of two crystal structures displayed. The computer, upon instruction and using the program, then converts data representing the physical layouts of the two crystal structures into data representing the physical layout of the structure that is obtained by combining the original two structures in such a way that the selected atoms, the selected lattice vectors and the selected faces are superposed. The resulting data are then displayed to give a picture of the resulting combined structure. Clearly the whole operation revolves around the computer program and the question for decision is whether there is a technical contribution so that it cannot be said that the invention consists of a computer program as such.

> ...
>
> I believe that the application is for a computer program as such. I agree in general with the reasons of the Principal Examiner which I have quoted. In *Vicom* the technical contribution was provided by the generation of the enhanced display. In the present case the combined structure is the result of the directions given by the operator and use of the program. The computer is conventional as is the display unit. The two displays of crystal structures are produced by the operator. The operator then provides the appropriate way of superposition and the program does the rest. The resulting display is the combined structure shown pictorially in a form that would in the past have been produced as a model. The only advance is the computer program which enables the combined structure to be portrayed quicker.
>
> I conclude that the application does not relate to a patentable invention as it is excluded by section 1(2)(c) as being a program for a computer as such.

Although Aldous LJ followed the approach set out in *Vicom/Computer Related Invention*[191] and *Merrill Lynch's Application*,[192] he commented on the difficulty of identifying a 'technical contribution'. He distinguished *Vicom* on its facts, stating that the technical contribution in that case was the generation of an enhanced display, whereas, in *Fujitsu*, the only real contribution was the computer program (enabling images to be displayed faster) and this was excluded subject matter. The Court of Appeal in *Symbian Ltd v Comptroller of Patents*[193] has commented 'while the test applied by the court in *Fujitsu* was ostensibly consistent with that in *Vicom* and *Gale*, the outcome is a little hard to reconcile with the view taken in those two cases to the question of what constitutes a "technical" contribution'.[194] Would you agree? If so, does that mean the decision in *Fujitsu* was incorrect? The Court of Appeal in *Symbian* suggests not, on the basis of the alternative ground that the alleged invention was a 'method for performing a mental act'.

11.6.3.3 Divergence with the EPO

As was discussed at 11.6.2, the current EPO approach to determining whether there is a patentable invention differs from that adopted in the UK. Although both the UK IPO and the EPO take the approach that if subject matter exhibits a technical contribution or effect then it is not a computer program *as such*, they differ as to what constitutes a *technical* contribution or effect. The EPO, following the Board of Appeal decisions in *Pension Benefit System Partnership*,[195] *Hitachi/Auction Method*,[196] and *Microsoft/Clipboard formats I*,[197] does not treat subject matter as excluded where it has technical features and these are interpreted very broadly to include hardware of most kinds (e.g. storing a computer program on a carrier or a computer). In other words, the EPO takes a formalistic approach to Article 52(2)–(3) and leaves it to the inventive step stage to filter out excluded subject matter. In the UK, however, the approach in *Vicom, Merrill Lynch*, and *Fujitsu* is followed and the question is whether there is a technical contribution. If no technical contribution exists, then the subject matter is not an invention and the enquiry goes no further (into novelty or inventive step).

The divergence between the EPO and UK approaches is clearly undesirable. However, the UK Court of Appeal indicated in *Aerotel Ltd v Telco Holdings Ltd*[198] that it would not reconsider its approach until the Enlarged Board of Appeal ruled on the question. For a

---

[191] T208/84 [1987] OJ EPO 14.   [192] [1989] RPC 561.   [193] [2008] EWCA Civ 1066.
[194] [42].   [195] T931/95 [2002] EPOR 52.   [196] T258/03 [2004] EPOR 55.
[197] T424/03 [2006] EPOR 39.   [198] [2007] RPC 7.

detailed discussion of that approach see 11.6.5.3. The Court of Appeal reiterated this view in *Symbian Ltd v Comptroller of Patents*.[199] The court held that it would not adopt the EPO approach for several reasons: (1) there was no decision of the Enlarged Board on this issue; (2) the decisions of the Boards of Appeal are not consistent; (3) the approach of the EPO may lead to the computer exclusion losing its meaning; (4) other jurisdictions, notably Germany, have expressed concerns about the EPO approach to the computer programs 'as such' exclusion; and (5) if the Court of Appeal 'is seen to depart too readily from its previous, carefully considered, approach, it would risk throwing the law into disarray'.[200] The Court of Appeal, however, reiterated the 'strong desirability of the approaches and principles in the two offices marching together as far as possible' and that this meant the 'need for a two-way dialogue between national tribunals and the EPO, coupled with a degree of mutual compromise'.[201]

Many hoped that the EPO position would be clarified as a result of the reference made to the Enlarged Board of Appeal in *Programs for computers*.[202] However, as already noted, the Board declared the reference inadmissible because it held there were not different decisions of the Technical Boards of Appeal on the questions referred. According to the Enlarged Board, it was clear from the case law that 'a claim in the area of computer programs can avoid exclusion under Article 52(2)(c) and (3) of the EPC merely by explicitly mentioning the use of a computer or a computer-readable storage medium'.[203] Apparently, this did not render Article 52(2) and (3) redundant:

> However, this does not mean that the list of subject matters in Article 52(2) EPC…has no effect on such claims. An elaborate system for taking that effect into account in the assessment of whether there is an inventive step has been developed, as laid out in T154/04, *Duns*, … the list of 'non-inventions' in Article 52(2) EPC can play a very important role in determining whether claimed subject matter is inventive.[204]

Do you agree with the Enlarged Board of Appeal's view?

Meanwhile, English courts—bound as they are by the Court of Appeal decisions in *Aerotel* and *Symbian*—have sought to further explicate when there is a technical effect. For example, in *AT&T Knowledge Ventures*[205] Lewison J (as he then was) held as follows:

> 39. It seems to me, therefore, that Lord Neuberger's reconciliation of the approach in *Aerotel* (by which the Court of Appeal in *Symbian* held itself bound, and by which I am undoubtedly bound) continues to require our courts to exclude as an irrelevant 'technical effect' a technical effect that lies solely in excluded matter.
>
> 40. As Lord Neuberger pointed out, it is impossible to define the meaning of 'technical effect' in this context, but it seems to me that useful signposts to a relevant technical effect are:
>
> i) whether the claimed technical effect has a technical effect on a process which is carried on outside the computer;
>
> ii) whether the claimed technical effect operates at the level of the architecture of the computer; that is to say whether the effect is produced irrespective of the data being processed or the applications being run;

---

[199] [2008] EWCA Civ 1066.   [200] [46].   [201] [61].   [202] G3/08 [2010] EPOR 36.
[203] At 10.13.   [204] [2010] EPOR 36, [81].   [205] [2009] EWHC 343 (Pat), [2009] FSR 19.

> iii) whether the claimed technical effect results in the computer being made to operate in a new way;
>
> iv) whether there is an increase in the speed or reliability of the computer;
>
> v) whether the perceived problem is overcome by the claimed invention as opposed to merely being circumvented.
>
> 41. If there is a technical effect in this sense, it is still necessary to consider whether the claimed technical effect lies solely in excluded matter.

The Court of Appeal in *HTC Europe Co. Ltd v Apple Inc.*[206] agreed that the above were useful signposts, but emphasized that they should not be seen as determinative or prescriptive.[207] Further, that the fourth signpost could be adjusted to refer to where a program 'makes a computer a better computer in the sense of running more efficiently and effectively as a computer'.[208] The court also indicated that, for the reasons expressed in *Symbian*, 'it remains appropriate (though not strictly necessary) to follow the four stage structured approach adopted in *Aerotel*'.[209] This was despite the fact that the court saw the *Aerotel* and EPO approaches as arriving at the same conclusion. According to Kitchin LJ: 'On the *Aerotel* approach a claimed invention whose only contribution is not technical or lies in an excluded field falls to be rejected under Art 52 under steps (iii) and (iv), whereas on the *Duns* approach such an invention falls to be rejected under Art 56 because such a contribution must be cut out of the assessment of inventive step.'[210] In light of this decision, it seems that, absent a Supreme Court decision on the issue, the UK is unlikely to follow the EPO approach to computer programs as such.[211]

11.6.3.4   Reform

The 'computer programs as such' exclusion has been the focus of reform efforts. At the Diplomatic Conference to revise the EPC, held in Munich in November 2000, it was proposed to delete this exclusion from Article 52(2)(c). The reason was that the exception had become de facto obsolete, given Board of Appeal decisions holding that computer programs that produced a technical effect were patentable subject matter. However, delegates to the Diplomatic Conference voted against the proposal and the exclusion remains.

Subsequently, the debate about how best to regulate inventions involving computer programs shifted to the European Commission and Parliament. The European Commission, believing that the legal situation concerning patenting of computer-related inventions was ambiguous and uncertain, and that the approaches of Member States were divergent, presented a Proposed Directive on the patentability of computer-implemented inventions in February 2002.[212] The Proposed Directive sought to harmonize the rules relating to patentability of computer-implemented inventions. A key feature was retaining the requirement

---

[206] [2013] EWCA Civ 451, [2013] RPC 30.   [207] [51] (Kitchin LJ) and [149] (Lewison LJ).
[208] [51] (Kitchin LJ) and see also [150] (Lewison LJ).
[209] [44] (Kitchin LJ) (delivering the leading judgment).   [210] [41].
[211] Currently, Practice Note 'Patents Act 1977: Patentability of computer programs', 8 December 2008, applies subject to its updating of Practice Note 'Patents Act 1977: Patentability of Mental Acts', 17 October 2011.
[212] COM (2002) 92 final.

of 'technical contribution' and ensuring that it was included in the patent legislation of Member States in relation to computer-implemented inventions.

Although the proposed reforms were fairly minimal, largely seeking to codify the EPO practice at the time, the Proposed Directive proved controversial and ran into difficulties during its legislative passage. On 24 September 2003, the European Parliament voted for preliminary approval to an amended version of the Proposed Directive. On 7 March 2005, the Council, by a qualified majority, adopted a common position. However, the European Parliament rejected the Common Position on 7 July 2005, thus bringing the legislative procedure to an end. As such, the patentability of computer-related inventions remains governed by the national law of Member States and the EPC.

It is clear that computer programs are patentable subject matter, provided a relevant technical effect or contribution can be shown. But the likelihood of establishing that technical effect will differ depending on whether one is applying via the EPO or the UK IPO.

Of course, even if the invention is characterized as protectable subject matter, the hurdles of novelty and inventive step must still be surmounted and this may be difficult given the incremental developments that tend to occur in the information technology field. Certainly, we need to ask whether it makes sense to retain the 'computer programs as such' exclusion. If so, which approach is preferable—that of the EPO or the UK IPO, or should we adopt a different approach, such as the one taken in the US (and discussed below)? Further, how important is it that the same approach be used in all Member States and should this be achieved through harmonization?

FURTHER READING

R. M. Ballardini, 'Software patents in Europe: the technical requirement dilemma' (2008) 3 JIPLP 563.

D. Booton and P. Mole, 'The action freezes? The Draft Directive on the patentability of computer implemented inventions' [2002] IPQ 289.

P. Leith, *Software and Patents in Europe* (Cambridge: Cambridge University Press, 2007).

J. Pila, 'Dispute over the meaning of "invention" in Article 52(2) EPC: the patentability of computer-implemented inventions in Europe' (2005) 36 IIC 173.

J. Pila, 'Software patents, separation of powers and failed syllogisms: a cornucopia from the Enlarged Board of Appeal of the European Patent Office' [2011] CLJ 203.

11.6.4 METHOD FOR PERFORMING A MENTAL ACT

The reason for incorporating this exclusion into Article 52(2)–(3) is not apparent from the *travaux préparatoires* of the EPC. This may explain why both narrow and broad interpretations of this exclusion have emerged in EPO and UK jurisprudence. It is also worth noting that the exclusion for a method for performing a mental act is closely related to the exclusion concerning computer programs. This is because computer-related inventions may represent an automated, and therefore more efficient, way of carrying out a mental process.

In the UK, the *Fujitsu* decision highlights the close relationship between the exclusions relating to a computer program and a method for performing a mental act.

Fujitsu Ltd's Application [1996] RPC 511

See 11.6.3.2 for the facts.

Laddie J, at pp. 532–3:

In this case, Fujitsu's application leaves it to the operator to select what data to work on, how to work on it, how to assess the results and which, if any, results to use. The process is abstract and the result of use of it is undefined. What is produced is not an inevitable result of taking a number of defined steps but is determined by the personal skill and assessment of the operator. As such it consists in substance of a scheme or method for performing a mental act and is unpatentable.

...

I should mention that both before me and before Mr Haselden, particular emphasis was placed on the fact that the steps to be carried out with the assistance of the programmed computer matched steps which, prior to Fujitsu's development, were done manually by workers in this field. For example physical models of crystals were built and manipulated to help visualise new hybrid structures. However the fact that a new process is the electronic equivalent of what has been done manually before goes primarily to the issue of novelty (a matter not before me) not the question of whether the application falls within section 1(2). I would have come to the same conclusion that this invention was not patentable even if all the steps set out in the claims had been novel.

In the Court of Appeal, the basis for rejecting the application was that it was a computer program as such.[213] On the issue of whether the claim was a method of performing a mental act as such, the appellant argued that the words in section 1(2)(c) of the PA 77 should be construed as covering methods which the human mind *actually* carries out and not the sort of acts which a human mind could carry out. Aldous LJ concluded that there was no need to decide this issue. Nevertheless, he commented *obiter* that this 'narrow construction' of the exclusion should be rejected:

There are good reasons to reject the narrow construction. First, a decision as to whether an invention is patentable as consisting of a method of performing a mental act as such should be capable of determination without recourse to evidence as to how the human mind actually works. If it were to the contrary, the section would pose an extremely difficult problem. Second, the narrow interpretation appears to introduce a consideration of novelty which is covered in section 1(1)(a). Third, the words used as 'a mental act' suggest any mental act whether done before or not.[214]

Do you agree with the view expressed by Aldous LJ and his reasons for reaching it? Interestingly, in *Aerotel*, the Court of Appeal commented *obiter* that 'we are by no means convinced that Aldous LJ's provisional view is correct. There is no particular reason to suppose that "mental act" was intended to exclude things wider than, for instance, methods of doing mental arithmetic ... or remembering things.'[215] Most recently, this issue was considered at length by HHJ Birss QC in *Halliburton*.

---

[213] See 11.6.3.1.   [214] *Fujitsu Ltd's Application* [1997] RPC 608, 620.   [215] *Aerotel*, [97].

Halliburton [2011] EWHC 2508 (Pat), [2012] RPC 12

The case involved a patent application for an invention which sought to improve the design of drill bits used in oil drilling. The invention used computer simulation of the interaction of the drill bit with the material being drilled in order to optimize various design features of the drill bits, thus eliminating field testing. The applications had been refused for being a method of performing a mental act or for being a computer program as such.

Judge Birss

42. There are essentially two possible interpretations of this exclusion, a wide one and a narrow one. The wide construction is that a method is 'a scheme, rule or method for performing a mental act' if it is capable of being performed mentally regardless of whether, as claimed, it is in fact performed mentally. Read this way the exclusion excludes methods of the type performed mentally regardless of how they are claimed. So a claim to a computer programmed to carry out a method of performing a calculation (say a square root), would not only be caught by the computer program and mathematical method exclusions but would also be excluded by the mental act exclusion because calculations are the kind of thing which are capable of being performed mentally. On the wide construction this conclusion follows even though, as claimed in this example, the invention clearly does not cover performing the calculation mentally at all because the claim is limited to using a computer. This wide construction is the one which Aldous L.J. favoured provisionally in Fujitsu (see p.619 line 10 to p.621 line 30).

43. The narrow construction is that the exclusion only excludes acts carried out mentally. On the narrow construction a claim to a calculation carried out on a computer could never be caught by the mental act exclusion because the claim does not encompass carrying out the calculation mentally. The fact that calculations in general are the kinds of thing which are capable of being performed as mental acts is irrelevant. This narrow interpretation is the one favoured by Jacob L.J. in Aerotel, doubting the views of Aldous L.J. on this point in Fujitsu.

...

44. In this case Mr Thorpe applied the wide construction. If the wide construction is right then the '735 claim is excluded from patentability...

51. In any event, after Aerotel (which, insofar as Pumfrey J. had taken a wide view of mental act in Halliburton v Smith, had doubted it was correct) Pumfrey J. returned to the mental act issue in his judgment in Cappellini's/Bloomberg's Application [2007] F.S.R. 26. At paras.7 and 8 he said as follows:

7. It is plain that the Court of Appeal in Aerotel thought that the 'mental act' exclusion was a narrow one. The rival views are summarised in the appendix to the judgment at [94]–[98]. In summary, the rival contentions are that of Aldous L.J. in Fujitsu ('Methods of performing mental acts, which means methods of the type performed mentally, are unpatentable, unless some concept of technical contribution is present') and that of the Court of Appeal in Aerotel: 'There is no particular reason to suppose that "mental act" was intended to exclude things wider than, for example, methods of doing mental arithmetic (every now and then someone comes up with a trick for this, for instance Trachtenberg's system) or remembering things (e.g., in its day, Pelmanism).'

8. As a matter of precedent, I am free to choose between these alternatives, while acknowledging that the second comes with a clearly expressed doubt as to the correctness

of the first. As a practical matter, I doubt whether the difference will normally be of concern. The views of the Court of Appeal in *Aerotel* make it quite clear that, like most other problems that arise with a patent, the question of patentable subject matter is essentially a question of the scope of the claim. If the claim covers a method of arriving at a particular result by the exercise of rational processes alone, then it is, in my view, a claim to a 'scheme, rule or method for performing a mental act'. I adhere to the view that I expressed in *Halliburton v Smith* [2005] EWHC 1623 (Pat), [2006] R.P.C. 2. That case was a case of a claim to a method of design, in which certain calculations were to be carried out recursively, modifying the results each time until a particular criterion was satisfied. Obviously, such a method was particularly susceptible to performance by a computer, but as a matter of principle the claim was not so limited. Nor was the claim limited to the employment of such a method in the production of a physical article. It would have been infringed had the person employing the method stopped at the end of the necessary calculations. Such a case, in my view, can be saved by limiting it to a method of manufacture of the resulting article. I do not think it can then be objectionable. But standing alone, I would respectfully suggest that an algorithm capable of being performed by a human being mentally, and complete (so far as the claim is concerned) when the algorithm terminates, is, as a matter of literal meaning, a scheme … for performing a mental act. If the physical article resulting from this design process becomes a feature of the claim, it cannot, in my judgment, be objectionable. But it is objectionable, in my view, unless 'tethered' to that result. I do not, of course, say that every result must be a physical article before the claim is allowable. But if I revert for a moment to the four-stage test, there is no contribution lying outside excluded matter until the claim also covers the physical result of performing the claimed algorithm.

52. Mr Mitcheson submitted that the reference in para.8 above to an '*algorithm capable of being performed by a human being mentally*' meant that Pumfrey J. was maintaining the wide construction of the mental act exclusion. I do not agree. For an algorithm to be a scheme for performing a mental act Pumfrey J. required two things, first the algorithm must be capable of being performed mentally and second it must be complete when the algorithm terminates so far as the claim is concerned. The second condition is a reference to the judge's earlier point that a claim in the objectionable form was not limited to being performed by a computer and, without amendment, would have been infringed had the person employing the method stopped at the end of the necessary calculations. Such a claim could be cured by an appropriate amendment to make sure that it could not be infringed by a person working alone. Therefore in this passage Pumfrey J. was certainly not adopting the wide construction of the mental act exclusion. It seems to me he was adopting a narrow one.

53. The mental act exclusion came up again in *Kapur* [2008] EWHC 649 (Pat) before Floyd J. In this judgment Floyd J. again reviewed the same line of authorities (now up to and including *Cappellini*) and held that the narrow view of the mental act exclusion was the right one. Floyd J. said:

20. In my judgment the narrow view of the exclusion is the correct one. More specifically I think the correct view is that, provided the claim cannot be infringed by mental acts as such, its subject matter is not caught by the exclusion. It seems to me that if this were not so the scope of the exclusion would be unacceptably broad, as well as being uncertain in scope. It follows that the exclusion will not apply if there are appropriate non-mental limitations in the claim. In those circumstances it will not be possible to infringe the claim by mental acts alone, and the invention will not comprise a method for performing a mental act.

54. There is no question that this is part of the *ratio* of Floyd J.'s judgment since it was a crucial part of his reasoning which led to the overturning of the decision of the hearing officer on the point (see para.37) and the basis for this part of the case being remitted back to the Comptroller (paras.38 and 39). Regrettably this clear judgment does not appear to have been drawn to Mr Thorpe's attention in the present case.

55. The final case to consider in this line is *Symbian* [2009] R.P.C. 1 (Court of Appeal). The Court was not concerned with the ambit of the mental act exclusion but it was mentioned in relation to *Fujitsu*. Lord Neuberger (giving the judgment of the court) indicated that the court had some difficulty reconciling the outcome of the *Fujitsu* case in relation to what constitutes a technical contribution with earlier decisions but stated that '*the actual decision in* Fujitsu *may well have been justified on the alternative ground tentatively relied on by Aldous L.J., namely that the alleged invention was a "method for performing mental acts"* ' (para.42).

56. Now the Court of Appeal were not considering the ambit of the mental act exclusion at all in *Symbian* and the sentence I have quoted is all that is said on the topic. However it would be disingenuous not to face up to the fact that Lord Neuberger's suggestion only works if the wide approach to the mental act exclusion is taken, as was tentatively proposed by Aldous L.J. in *Fujitsu* itself, but which has been doubted in later cases. That is because in *Fujitsu* at least some of the claims could not be infringed by mental acts alone (see claims 9 and 10 at p.613 of the report). Indeed claim 9 of *Fujitsu* is a claim 'tethered' to a manufacturing step (compare *Hallibuton* [sic] *v Smith*). Does this sentence in *Symbian* mean that the judgment of Floyd J. in *Kapur* has been overruled or even seriously doubted or that the reasoning subsequent to *Fujitsu* on mental acts in *Aerotel* and *Cappellini* has been undermined? In my judgment it does not. The ambit of the mental act exclusion was just not before the Court of Appeal in *Symbian*. They were not focused upon it and its scope was not a necessary part of the court's reasoning.

57. So the balance of authority in England is in favour of the narrow approach to the mental act exclusion. I will only add that, if the matter were free from authority, I would favour the narrow interpretation on its own merits. The wide construction seems to me to be uncertain in scope and I am not aware of any good reason why the exclusion needs to be interpreted widely. On the other hand I can see a logic behind the narrow interpretation, preventing patents being granted which could be infringed by a purely mental process. Allowing for the possibility of patent infringement by thought alone seems to me to be undesirable.

Do you agree with Judge Birss that a narrow interpretation of this exclusion is to be preferred? Applying the *Aerotel* four-step approach and a narrow construction of the exclusion for methods of performing a mental act, the judge concluded that the Hearing Officer had been wrong to apply this exclusion and that it made a technical contribution to the art.[216] It should be noted that after this decision the UK IPO issued a Practice Note indicating that it would now apply the narrow view of the mental act exclusion, such that '[i]n future, claims which specify that the invention is implemented using a computer will not be considered to be excluded from patentability as a mental act'.[217]

---

[216] [65]–[77].
[217] Practice Note 'Patents Act 1977: Patentability of Mental Acts', 17 October 2011 reported in [2012] Bus. L. R. 1264.

11.6.5 METHOD FOR DOING BUSINESS

11.6.5.1 Rationale

It was uncontroversial that methods for doing business would form part of the excluded subject matter when it came to drafting Article 52(2)–(3) of the EPC.[218] This is because historically business schemes had been unpatentable in the UK and other Contracting States to the EPC. The reason for this could have been that methods for doing business were considered inherently unsuitable to patents. Alternatively, it could have been because patents were thought unnecessary in this field, given that commercial innovation had flourished in the absence of patents.[219]

The development of information technologies, including software and the internet, has facilitated new types of innovation in the business sphere and this has placed the 'business methods as such' exclusion under pressure. Moreover, in the US, business methods are not unpatentable per se[220] and this also created pressure for the EPO and the UK (along with other jurisdictions) to allow patents for methods of doing business.

In this area we must ask whether the patenting of business methods can be justified. Is it the case that an incentive, in the form of patent protection, is needed to encourage business innovation? Would the grant of patents for business methods (particularly ones of dubious merit) unduly restrict the activities of competitors and stifle further innovation? On the other hand, if patents are viewed as a means of rewarding innovation, should a business innovation be excluded if it satisfies the requirements of novelty and inventive step? In this respect, it is important to note that Article 27 of TRIPS provides that patents should be available in all fields of technology. In the extract below, the authors explore the key arguments in favour of, and against, business method patents.

J. McNamara and L. Cradduck, 'Can we protect how we do what we do? A consideration of business methods patents in Australia and Europe'
(2008) 16 IJL & IT 96 at 113–16

4.1.1 Philosophical Objections

Business method patents are claimed to be a 'soft' area of intellectual property where the usefulness of patents as a tool is questioned. It is argued that patents over *business methods* are not justified on an economic basis because the implementation of *business methods* merely involves market risk as opposed to technological risk as all enterprises implementing a new product take market risk. The developer of any new product faces the risk that the product will not achieve market acceptance and developers of *business methods* should not receive any special shelter from this risk.

---

[218] See J. Pila, 'Article 52(2) of the Convention on the Grant of European Patents: what did the framers intend? A study of the *travaux préparatoires*' (2005) 36 IIC 755.

[219] See *CFPH LLC's Application* [2006] RPC 5, [41].

[220] Initially, *State Street Bank & Trust Co. v Signature Financial Group, Inc.*, 149 F 3d 1368 (Fed. Cir. 1993) sent a positive signal for patentability of business methods provided they produced a 'useful, concrete and tangible result'. The US position now appears more cautious after the Supreme Court decision in *Bilski v Kappos*, 130 S Ct 3218 (2010), but the Court did reject the argument that business methods are categorically excluded from patentable subject matter.

Other commentators expressed concern that by enabling the registration of *business method patents* the way has been '*…paved…for patenting developments in the liberal arts, social sciences, the law, and other indeterminate areas of human activity*'.

An argument that patents generally do not encourage innovation, but are merely wealth creation or protection devices (not necessarily to the benefit of the true inventors) also has been raised. Detailed consideration of this argument is beyond the scope of this paper, however, it is noted that it may be particularly apposite for *business method patents* because monopolies in *business methods* may lead to far greater stifling of competition than in other more technical fields.

As some commentators have suggested, the underlying questions to be asked in respect of *business method patents* are—'*Do these methods serve the purpose of patent law? Do they promote innovation?*' Without international harmonisation however it is submitted that internationally these questions are difficult to answer as the underlying premise of patent law varies from jurisdiction to jurisdiction.

4.1.2 Lack of rigour in granting business method patents

The lack of a prior art database and the inexperience of patent examiners in business fields means that it can be difficult for patent examiners to assess whether the alleged innovation is actually new. As a result it is argued that many *business method patents* have been granted that, if tested in the courts, would be found to be invalid. If too many *business method patents* are ultimately found to be invalid, the integrity of the patent system will be undermined. In addition, businesses may be uncertain as to whether they are infringing patent rights because *business methods* are difficult to define in patent claims.

4.1.3 Effects on Competition

During the ACIP Review, the Australian Consumers' Association raised concerns with the compliance costs that *business method patents* impose on small to medium enterprises ('SMEs'). They identified that firstly, the payment of royalty fees is an added expense to be passed on to the consumers; and secondly, that protection of intellectual property diverts SMEs from their core activity, resulting in a less efficient industry.

Expensive and protracted patent disputes may be a significant threat to the development of e-commerce. While *business method patents* may be challenged on the grounds of lack of novelty or obviousness, the cost of such a challenge may be prohibitive for SMEs. Patents therefore may be used as a tool to stifle legitimate competition. Worse still '*…knowledge that was…freely exchanged between researchers will…be tied…posing a big danger to innovation*'.

It is possible that patents may be used by SMEs to protect their own business assets, which is to their advantage. Overall however, as patents are traditionally used by big business to stifle competition, it is argued that small businesses cannot afford to obtain and maintain a sufficient number of patents to obtain bargaining leverage.

4.2 In Defence of Business Method Patents

Submissions to the ACIP Review suggested various ways of ensuring that *business methods* are not patentable, including by imposing a requirement that a patentable advance must be technology rather than merely use technology. Such a requirement is not justifiable and would discriminate against innovations in the business as opposed to scientific fields. In any event, many scientific patents simply use technology rather than advance it. Also, it is suggested that discrimination between scientific methods and *business methods* would cause confusion in patent law.

Other submissions were concerned not to deny the patentability of *business methods* but rather to ensure that *business method patents* that are granted are properly examined to ensure that they are novel and involve an inventive step. The majority of submissions to the ACIP Review supported the patentability of *business method patents*. Other commentators support *business method patents* on the grounds that they '...*in fact encourage innovation ...and therefore serve consumer interest by enhancing choice...*'

To exclude *business methods* from patentability would be in breach of Australia's obligations under TRIPS which requires *business methods* to be patentable. The field of technology requirement in Article 27(1) of TRIPS is meant to be expansive, i.e. it indicates that patents are to be granted in all fields of technology (unless the specific exclusions in Art 27(2) and (3) apply), rather than limiting. It is submitted that as the European exception predates TRIPS, it is not justified and cannot be sustained. Further, even if a *business method* exception is allowable under TRIPS, *business methods* are patentable in the US and, except in narrow circumstances, in the EU. Accordingly, Australia should not implement an exception in relation to *business methods* that would be contrary to its TRIPS obligations.

Intellectual property protection is crucial to the growth of Australia's information and communications technology sector. Without patent protection, there would be little incentive for businesses to continue to develop their business ideas, as those ideas could simply be exploited by others with whom the developer must share their idea in order to develop their business. Barriers to entry for Internet based businesses are relatively few and lack of patent protection for new business innovations would be an unfair advantage to the imitator over the innovator. However, if Australia did implement an exception that was out of step with our ICT trading partners it would be damaging to our ICT industry.

Supporters of *business method patents* argue that problems that have arisen with some *business method patents* are because the patents granted were not novel or inventive. A particular problem arises where known business ideas are applied in a new medium such as the Internet. Accordingly, most of the recommendations made for change by those who support *business method patents* in principle relate to closer examination of patents by IP Australia. It is clear however that business believes that to ignore *business methods* would be to be '...*left behind*'.[221]

Having considered the arguments raised in the above extract, do you consider there to be sound, principled objections to allowing patents for methods of doing business or is the problem essentially how to effectively examine business method patents so that unmeritorious ones do not make it onto the Register? If the latter, is this a problem that can be adequately addressed?

We turn next to consider the different ways in which the EPO and the UK approach the 'method for doing business *as such*' exclusion.

---

221 Original references and footnotes omitted.

FURTHER READING

V. M. Janich, 'Sui generis rights for business methods' (2004) 35 IIC 376.

A. Kalpakidou, 'Business method patents: should they survive in Europe?' (2005) 13 IJL & IT 243.

R. Stern, 'Being within the useful arts as a further constitutional requirement for US patent-eligibility' [2009] EIPR 6.

X. Yu and Y. Zhang, 'The patent protection for business method inventions in China' [2008] EIPR 412.

11.6.5.2 EPO approach

In this field the EPO first adopted the 'technical effect' approach that it had enunciated in *Vicom* and subsequent cases.[222] However, in *Pension Benefit Systems*, the Technical Board of Appeal applied the 'any hardware' approach, at least in relation to apparatus claims.

PBS Partnership/Pension Benefit Systems T931/95 [2002] OJ EPO 441, [2002] EPOR 522

Claim 1 of the European patent application related to a method of controlling a pension-benefits programme, comprising the successive steps of providing employee personal and employment information to data-processing means; determining the average age of all enrolled employees by average-age computing means; determining the periodic cost of life insurance for all enrolled employees by life-insurance-cost computing means; and estimating all administrative, legal, trustee, and government premium yearly expenses for said subscriber employer by administrative-cost computing means, the method producing for the employer information as to his relevant financial liability. Claim 5 was to an apparatus for controlling a pension benefits system comprising a data-processing means and a processor which includes average-age computing means; life-insurance-cost computing means; and administrative-cost computing means.

The application was rejected as being non-patentable under Article 52(2)–(3) of the EPC since the subject matter, considered as a whole, related to a method for doing business and lacked any technical character or contribution. The applicant appealed to the Technical Board of Appeal.

Technical Board of Appeal, at pp. 528, 530:

[The Board began by reiterating that 'technical character' is an implicit requirement of patentability under Article 52 of the EPC. It turned first to consider the method claim:]

Claim 1 of the main request is, apart from various computing means mentioned in that claim, directed to a 'method for controlling a pension benefits program by administering at least one subscriber employer account'. All the features of this claim are steps of

---

[222] *Petterson/Queuing System* T1002/92 [1996] EPOR 1.

processing and producing information having purely administrative, actuarial and/or financial character. Processing and producing such information are typical steps of business and economic methods.

Thus the invention as claimed does not go beyond a method of doing business as such and, therefore, is excluded from patentability under Article 52(2)(c) in combination with Article 52(3) EPC; the claim does not define an invention within the meaning of Article 52(1)EPC.

The appellant referred to the data processing and computing means defined in the method claim, arguing that the use of such means conferred technical character to the method claimed. However, the individual steps defining the claimed method amount to no more than the general teaching to use data processing means for processing or providing information of purely administrative, actuarial and/or financial character, the purpose of each single step and of the method as a whole being a purely economic one.

The feature of using technical means for a purely non-technical purpose and/or for processing purely non-technical information does not necessarily confer technical character to any such individual steps of use or to the method as a whole: in fact, any activity in the non-technical branches of human culture involves physical entities and uses, to a greater or lesser extent, technical means.

Arguments or facts which indicate that the individual steps of the method or the method itself solve any particular technical problem or achieve any technical effect, are not derivable from the patent application and have not been submitted to the board.

The board notes that the mere occurrence of technical features in a claim does thus not turn the subject-matter of the claim into an invention within the meaning of Article 52(1). Such an approach would be too formalistic and would not take due account of the term 'invention'.

[The Technical Board then went on to consider the apparatus claim:]

In the board's view a computer system suitably programmed for use in a particular field, even if that is the field of business and economy, has the character of a concrete apparatus in the sense of a physical entity, man-made for a utilitarian purpose and is thus an invention within the meaning of Article 52(1) EPC.

This distinction with regard to patentability between a method for doing business and an apparatus suited to perform such a method is justified in the light of the wording of Article 52(2)(c) EPC, according to which 'schemes, rules and methods' are non-patentable categories in the field of economy and business, but the category of 'apparatus' in the sense of 'physical entity' or 'product' is not mentioned in Article 52(2) EPC.

This means that, if a claim is directed to such an entity, the formal category of such a claim does in fact imply physical features of the claimed subject-matter which may qualify as technical features of the invention concerned and thus be relevant for its patentability.

Did the Technical Board of Appeal approach the method claim differently to the apparatus claim? If so, how? As mentioned previously, the 'technical contribution' test was jettisoned when the Board considered the apparatus claim because it considered that this confused the requirement of 'invention' with the requirements of novelty and inventive step. But why then did the Board apply this test to the method claim?

Although the apparatus claim in *Pension Benefit Systems* was not excluded under Article 52(2)–(3) of the EPC, the Technical Board of Appeal found that it lacked an inventive step. This is because inventive step had to involve technical subject matter and here the improvement on the prior art was non-technical in nature: 'the improvement envisaged by the invention according to the application is an essentially economic one, i.e. lies in the field of economy, which, therefore, cannot contribute to inventive step'.[223] Any technical contribution lay in the programming of a computer system for carrying out the invention; however, that programming and information processing would have been well known and therefore obvious, according to a person skilled in the art (software developer or application programmer).

A later decision of the Technical Board of Appeal entirely rejected the 'technical effect' or 'technical contribution' approach to Article 52(2)–(3) of the EPC, in favour of the 'any hardware' approach. In *Hitachi/Auction Method*,[224] the European patent application claimed an automatic auction method executed in a server computer. It comprised the following series of steps: information about a product to be auctioned is transmitted to bidders; bidders then enter a desired price and a maximum price; the auction price is started high and then lowered until it corresponds with a bid (i.e. desired price); and if it corresponds with more than one bid then the auction price proceeds upwards until there is a single highest bidder (taken from the maximum price). The application also claimed a 'computerised auction apparatus for performing an automatic auction via a network'.

The Examining Division refused the application on the grounds, inter alia, that the method and corresponding apparatus claim fell foul of Article 52(2)–(3) of the EPC for being a method of doing business. On appeal, the Technical Board of Appeal held that Article 52(2)–(3) of the EPC did not exclude the apparatus claim since it comprised technical features such as a 'server computer', 'client computers', and a 'network'. This conclusion was said to be in conformity with *Pension Benefit Systems*.

On the question of the method claim, however, the Board departed from its earlier decision in *Pension Benefit Systems*, finding that the justification for rejecting the 'technical effect' approach for apparatus claims was equally applicable to method claims:

in order to be consistent with the finding that the so-called 'contribution approach', which involves assessing different patentability requirements such as novelty or inventive step, is inappropriate for judging whether claimed subject matter is an invention within the meaning of Art. 52(2) EPC, there should be no need to further qualify the relevance of technical aspects of a method claim in order to determine the technical character of the method.[225]

[The Board added that it was:]

... not convinced that the wording of Art. 52(2)(c) EPC, according to which 'schemes, rules and methods for performing mental acts, playing games or doing business' shall not be regarded as inventions within the meaning of Art. 52(1) EPC, imposes a different treatment of claims directed to activities and claims directed to entities for carrying out these activities. What matters having regard to the concept of 'invention' within the meaning of Art. 52(1) EPC is the presence of technical character which may be implied by the physical features of an entity or the nature of an activity, or may be conferred to a non-technical activity by the use of technical means. In particular, the Board holds that the latter cannot be considered to be a non-invention 'as such' within the meaning of Arts. 52(2) and (3) EPC. Hence, in the Board's view, activities falling within the notion of non-invention 'as such' would typically represent purely abstract concepts devoid of any technical implications.

The Board is aware that its comparatively broad interpretation of the term 'invention' in Art. 52(1) EPC will include activities which are so familiar that their technical character tends

---

[223] At 532.   [224] T258/03 [2004] EPOR 55.   [225] At 4.3.

to be overlooked, such as the act of writing using pen and paper. Needless to say, however, this does not imply that all methods involving the use of technical means are patentable. They still have to be new, represent a non-obvious technical solution to a technical problem, and be susceptible of industrial application.[226]

Thus, in *Hitachi* the Technical Board of Appeal adopted the 'any hardware' approach for *both* apparatus and method claims and recognized that a broad interpretation should be given to 'invention'.[227] Do you agree with the Board's view that the same approach must be applied regardless of whether apparatus or method claims are involved? Further, did the Board adopt too generous a view of what can confer 'technical character', i.e. any hardware? Does a generous interpretation matter given that an invention must still satisfy the other validity requirements?

In *Microsoft/Clipboard Formats I*,[228] the approach in *Hitachi* was taken even further in that a computer program stored on a carrier (e.g. a disk) was held to feature technical character. In other words, the technical character was provided by the mere fact that the claim related to a computer-readable medium.

11.6.5.3 UK approach

The UK courts have thus far refused to follow *Pension Benefit Systems*, *Hitachi*, or *Microsoft* as the Court of Appeal decision in *Aerotel* illustrates.

Aerotel Ltd v Telco Holdings Ltd [2007] RPC 7

The case concerned two appeals—the 'Aerotel' appeal and the 'Macrossan' appeal. In the first appeal, Aerotel were appealing the decision of Lewison J to grant summary judgment for revocation of their patent. The invention related to a new method of making telephone calls and a new apparatus for making such calls. The essence of the invention was the use of an extra piece of equipment, called a 'special exchange'. The caller would have an account with the owner of that special exchange and deposit credit with him. The caller also had a code and, to make a call, the caller would dial the number of the special exchange, input the code, and then the caller's number. If the code was verified and there was enough credit the call was connected.

In the second appeal, an application for a UK patent had been made in relation to an automated method of acquiring the documents necessary to incorporate a company. It involved the user sitting at a computer and communicating with a remote server, answering questions. By posing questions, enough information was gleaned from the user's answers to produce the required documents. This application had been rejected by the Patent Office on the ground that the subject matter was unpatentable. The objection was upheld and an appeal to Mann J dismissed.

---

[226] At 4.5 and 4.6.
[227] The divergence in approach to method claims in *Pension Benefit Systems* and *Hitachi* has yet to be reconciled by the EPO, since the EPO Guidelines still reflect the *Pension Benefit Systems* approach (see Ch. IV, Part C, para. 2.3.6).
[228] T424/03 [2006] EPOR 39.

Jacob LJ (delivering the judgment of the court):

38. The fact is that this court is bound by its own precedent: that decided in *Merill Lynch*, *Gale* and *Fujitsu*—the technical effect approach with the rider. We think we must apply it as we understand it, namely as set out above. That we will proceed to do.

39. However before doing so we must consider the approach which the Comptroller, through Mr Birss, urges upon us. We must in particular consider whether it is consistent with that which has already been decided.

40. The approach is in 4 steps:

(1) properly construe the claim;

(2) identify the actual contribution;

(3) ask whether it falls solely within the excluded subject matter;

(4) check whether the actual or alleged contribution is actually technical in nature.

41. The Comptroller submits that this approach is structured and thus helpful to the public and examiner alike and is consistent with the principles enunciated in *Merrill Lynch*. He further submits:

> A structured approach needs to be workable across the whole field of Section 1(2). This is important because although the policy behind different exclusions is not uniform, the structure of the legislation requires that they ought to work the same way. A structured approach will also allow the examiners and hearing officers applying this area of law to follow a consistent scheme and will allow the public to see how a decision has been arrived at. A problem the Comptroller is often confronted with is reliance by applicants on broad observations from earlier decisions which work well in the particular circumstances in which they were made but break down when applied elsewhere. (Mr Birss' skeleton argument).

We think this structured approach is indeed consistent with what has been decided by this court. It is a re-formulation in a different order of the *Merill Lynch* test.

42. No-one could quarrel with the first step—construction. You first have to decide what the monopoly is before going on the question of whether it is excluded. Any test must involve this first step.

43. The second step—identify the contribution—is said to be more problematical. How do you assess the contribution? Mr Birss submits the test is workable—it is an exercise in judgment probably involving the problem said to be solved, how the invention works, what its advantages are. What has the inventor really added to human knowledge perhaps best sums up the exercise. The formulation involves looking at substance not form—which is surely what the legislator intended.

44. Mr Birss added the words 'or alleged contribution' in his formulation of the second step. That will do at the application stage—where the Office must generally perforce accept what the inventor says is his contribution. It cannot actually be conclusive, however. If an inventor claims a computer when programmed with his new program, it will not assist him if he alleges wrongly that he has invented the computer itself, even if he specifies all the detailed elements of a computer in his claim. In the end the test must be what contribution has actually been made, not what the inventor says he has made.

45. The third step—is the contribution solely of excluded matter?—is merely an expression of the 'as such' qualification of Art. 52(3). During the course of argument Mr Birss accepted a re-formulation of the third step: Ask whether the contribution thus identified

consists of excluded subject matter as such? We think either formulation will do—they mean the same thing.

46. The fourth step—check whether the contribution is 'technical'—may not be necessary because the third step should have covered that. It is a necessary check however if one is to follow *Merrill Lynch* as we must.

Applying the 'technical effect' structured approach to the Aerotel invention, the court held that the contribution was a new system. Although it used conventional computers, the key to it was a new physical combination of hardware and, as such, there was more than just a method of doing business as such. Finally, the system was clearly technical in nature.[229]

In relation to the Macrossan application, the court dismissed the appeal on the basis that this was a method of doing business, or a computer program, as such. The contribution was an interactive system which would do the job otherwise done by a solicitor or company-formation agent. This method was for the very business of advising upon and creating appropriate company-formation documents. Further, there was nothing technical about the contribution beyond the mere fact of the running of a computer program.[230]

In looking at the Boards of Appeal and UK decisions we again see that the main divergence is that the EPO will consider 'technical character' to be satisfied easily by the presence of any technical feature (such as mention of hardware) and consider excluded subject matter (such as whether it is a method of doing business) at the inventive step stage. The UK approach, on the other hand, is to scrutinize more carefully, at the invention stage, whether there is a technical contribution. If the only contribution is that which falls within excluded subject matter then the patent fails at that stage without going on to consider novelty or inventive step. As we have asked before, how significant do you consider this divergence to be and should the UK fall into line with the EPO?

11.6.5.4 US approach

It is useful briefly to compare how the US has grappled with the difficult issue of patentability of business methods. Section 101 of the Patents Act (Title 35 of the US Code) defines patentable subject matter as 'any new and useful process, machine, manufacture, or composition of matter, or any new and useful improvement thereof'. The US Supreme Court has also identified unpatentable subject matter as including 'laws of nature, natural phenomena and abstract ideas'.[231] In *State Street Bank & Trust Co. v Signature Financial Group Inc.* the Federal Court indicated that an invention was a patentable 'process' under section 101 where it produced a 'useful, concrete and tangible result'[232] and held that the business method did produce such a result and thus was patentable. The invention was a data processing system that implemented an investment structure 'whereby mutual funds (Spokes) pool their assets in an investment portfolio (Hub) organized as a partnership. This investment configuration provides the administrator of a mutual fund with the advantageous combination of economies of scale in administering investments coupled with the tax advantages of a partnership.'[233]

---

[229] [51]–[54].   [230] [63]–[72].   [231] *Diamond v Diehr*, 450 US 175, 185 (1981).
[232] 149 F 3d 1368, 1373 (Fed. Cir. 1993).   [233] At 1370.

The US Supreme Court subsequently had an opportunity to consider business method patents in *Bilski v Kappos*.[234] This case concerned a patent application that claimed a method for instructing buyers and sellers on how to hedge against the risk of price fluctuations in the energy market. The US Court of Appeals for the Federal Circuit rejected the test articulated in *State Street Bank* and held that the *sole* test for determining patentability under section 101 of the US Patents Act was the 'machine-or-transformation test', i.e. whether a claimed process was 'tied to a particular machine or apparatus' or 'transforms a particular article into a different state or thing'.[235] Further, the court held that the patent application did not satisfy this test and so was unpatentable subject matter. In light of this decision, it was thought that fewer business methods patents would be patentable under US law. On appeal, however, the US Supreme Court rejected the 'machine-or-transformation' test as the sole test for determining what constitutes a patentable process under section 101, rather it was considered 'a useful and important clue, an investigative tool'.[236] The Supreme Court also held that business methods were not categorically excluded by section 101, but noted the concerns relating to business method patents:

> The Information Age empowers people with new capacities to perform statistical analyses and mathematical calculations with a speed and sophistication that enable the design of protocols for more efficient performance of a vast number of business tasks. If a high enough bar is not set when considering patent applications of this sort, patent examiners and courts could be flooded with claims that would put a chill on creative endeavour and dynamic change.[237]

Importantly, the Court held that the way to cater for these concerns was to utilize the judicially created exclusion for abstract ideas and to apply the patent requirements of novelty, inventiveness, and adequate description.[238] Applying this approach, the Court held that the patent application did not contain a patentable process because '[t]hese claims attempt to patent the use of the abstract idea of hedging risk in the energy market and then instruct the use of well-known random analysis techniques to help establish some of the inputs into the equation'.[239]

The US Supreme Court revisited this issue in *Alice Corp. Pty Ltd v CLS Bank Intern*.[240] In this case, the respondents had sought a declaration that the plaintiff's patents, which related to a scheme for mitigating settlement risk in financial transactions by using a computer system as a third party intermediary, were invalid. The Supreme Court affirmed the lower court decisions that the claims were to unpatentable subject matter. In doing so, the Court first sought to identify whether the claims were to a patent-ineligible concept and concluded that, in light of *Bilski* in particular, they were: they related to the abstract idea of intermediated settlement.[241] Further, applying their decision in *Mayo Collaborative Services v Prometheus Laboratories Inc.*,[242] the Court held that there was no inventive concept sufficient to transform the abstract idea into a patent eligible application. In this respect, it did not suffice that the claims referred to generic computer implementation: instead, what was required were claims purporting to improve the functioning of the computer itself or another technological field.[243]

---

[234] 130 S Ct 3218 (2010).   [235] *In re Bilski* 545 F 3d 943, 954 and 959–60 (Fed. Cir. 2008).
[236] *Bilski v Kappos* 130 S Ct 3218, 3227 (2010).   [237] At 3229.   [238] At 3229.
[239] At 3231.   [240] 134 S Ct 2347 (2014).   [241] At 2335–6.   [242] 132 S Ct 1289 (2012).
[243] 134 S Ct 2347, 2357–9 (2014).

Stepping back from this US case law, we can see an approach to patentable subject matter (including business methods) that differs from European and UK patent law. There are no specific statutory exclusions for certain types of subject matter; however, the Supreme Court has interpreted 'any new and useful process, machine, manufacture, or composition of matter' as precluding laws of nature, natural phenomena, and abstract ideas. According to these limiting principles, software and business method patents could be, but are not necessarily, excluded from eligibility for patent protection. However, the Court is clear that obvious use of computer implementation is not going to transform an abstract idea into patentable subject matter. Rather, what is needed is an inventive concept that might relate to improving the functioning of a computer or other technology. Although there is a different legal framework and set of judicial decisions, do you think that the US approach to software and business method patents shows any similarity to the approaches in the UK or EPO?

11.7 BIOTECHNOLOGICAL INVENTIONS

11.7.1 INTRODUCTION

In this section we consider exclusions from patentability that are particularly relevant to biotechnological inventions. These are discoveries as such: plant and animal varieties and non-microbiological processes for their production; and inventions which are contrary to *ordre public* or morality. It should be stressed that these exclusions are not confined to biotechnological inventions. Nevertheless, it is fair to say that they have assumed increased significance in the light of modern biotechnological research. Indeed, the Biotechnology Directive sought to harmonize the approach to these exclusions.[244]

FURTHER READING

P. W. Grubb and P. R. Thomsen, *Patents for Chemicals, Pharmaceuticals and Biotechnology: Fundamentals of Global Law, Practice and Strategy* (5th edn, Oxford: Oxford University Press, 2010), chs 14 and 15.

11.7.2 DISCOVERIES

According to section 1(2) of the PA 77 and also Article 52(2)–(3) of the EPC, a discovery as such is not an invention. In the context of biotechnological research, it has been argued that identification of a gene[245] is simply a discovery because the gene already exists in nature. By way of response, it has been argued that the invention is not the naturally occurring gene but rather an isolated form of that gene and thus it has technical character. The following decision of the Technical Board of Appeal illustrates the approach the EPO has taken to these arguments.

---

[244] Discussed at 11.4.2.5.

[245] A gene is a discrete segment of DNA molecules that contains the information necessary for producing specific proteins.

Howard Florey/Relaxin [1995] EPOR 541

The patent granted related to a process for obtaining H2-relaxin and the complementary DNA sequence coding for H2-relaxin. H2-relaxin is a naturally occurring hormone in the human ovaries that relaxes the uterus during childbirth. The complementary DNA sequence coding for this hormone had been isolated from ovarian tissue removed in the treatment of an ectopic pregnancy. The Green Party opposed the grant of the patent on several grounds, including that it was a discovery and thus not patentable under Article 52(2)(a) of the EPC. The Opposition Division of the EPO rejected this argument.

> 5.1 …This argument ignores the long-standing practice of the European Patent Office concerning the patentability of natural substances. As explained in the Guidelines, C-IV, 2.3, to find a substance freely occurring in nature is mere discovery and therefore unpatentable. However, if a substance found in nature has first to be isolated from its surroundings and a process for obtaining it is developed, that process is patentable. Moreover, if this substance can be properly characterised by its structure and it is new in the absolute sense of having no previously recognised existence, then the substance *per se* may be patentable.
>
> 5.2 The above guideline is highly appropriate in the present case. Human H2-relaxin had no previously recognised existence. The proprietor has developed a process for obtaining H2-relaxin and the DNA encoding it, has characterised these products by their chemical structure and has found a use for the protein. The products are therefore patentable under Article 52(2) EPC.

The logic reflected in the above passage—that isolating a substance found in nature gives it sufficient technical character to avoid being a mere discovery—was adopted in Articles 3 and 5 of the Biotechnology Directive.[246] Thus, Article 3(2) provides:

> (2) Biological material which is isolated from its natural environment or produced by means of a technical process may be the subject of an invention even if it previously occurred in nature.

Similarly, in the context of the human body, Article 5 of the Biotechnology Directive provides:

> (1) The human body, at the various stages of its formation and development, and the simple discovery of one of its elements, including the sequence or partial sequence of a gene cannot constitute patentable inventions.
>
> (2) An element isolated from the human body or otherwise produced by means of a technical process, including the sequence or partial sequence of a gene, may constitute a patentable invention, even if that element is identical to that of a natural element.

Do you find convincing the view that technical character is conferred either via the process of isolating a gene sequence or because an artificial molecule of that gene sequence has been

---

[246] Which have been implemented in the PA 77, Sch. A2.

created? Does such a view give proper weight to the exclusion of discoveries *as such*? Here it is interesting to note that the US Supreme Court in *Association for Molecular Pathology v Myriad Genetics* held, in a unanimous decision that claims to isolated DNA are not patentable, whereas claims to complementary DNA are patentable.[247]

FURTHER READING

R. C. Dreyfuss, 'Implications of the DNA patenting dispute: a US response to Dianne Nicol' (2012) 22 J. L. Inf. & Sci. 1.

Nuffield Council, *Discussion Paper on The Ethics of Patenting DNA* (July 2002), pp. 27–8.

T. L. Russell, 'Unlocking the genome: the legal case against genetic diagnostic patents' (2012) 16 Marq. Intell. Prop. L. Rev. 81.

E. Van Zimmerman and G. Van Overwalle, 'A paper tiger? Compulsory licensing regimes for public health in Europe' (2011) 42 IIC 4.

11.7.3 PLANT VARIETIES

Article 53(b) of the EPC provides that a European patent shall not be granted in respect of plant varieties or essentially biological processes for the production of plants.[248] The origin of this exclusion may be explained in the light of *sui generis* plant breeder's protection that had been established in accordance with the International Convention for the Protection of New Varieties of Plants 1961 (UPOV Convention). It was desired that plant breeders be prevented from obtaining dual protection under both plant breeder's legislation and patent law. To that end, a prohibition on double protection was included in Article 2(1) of the UPOV Convention (although subsequently deleted when the Convention was revised in 1991). Article 53(b) of the EPC was included to give effect to this aim.[249]

The concept of 'plant variety' is not defined in the EPC and there is no generally recognized taxonomic definition of 'variety' as there is for 'species' and 'genus'. The concept of 'plant variety' was considered by the Boards of Appeal of the EPO on a few occasions[250] and subsequently harmonized by the Biotechnology Directive. Article 2(3) of the Biotechnology Directive defines 'plant variety' according to Article 5 of Regulation (EC) No. 2100/94 on Community plant variety rights, which states that 'plant variety':

shall be taken to mean a plant grouping within a single botanical taxon of the lowest known rank, which grouping … can be:

– defined by the expression of the characteristics that results from a given genotype or combination of genotypes,

---

[247] *Association for Molecular Pathology v US Patent and Trademark Office* No. 12-398 (June 13, 2013).

[248] Prior to the implementation of the Biotechnology Directive, this exclusion was contained in PA 77, s. 1(3)(b). It is now contained in PA 77, para. 3(f) of Sch. A2.

[249] For a more detailed discussion of the historical background to Art. 53(b) see the decision of the Enlarged Board of Appeal in *Novartis/Transgenic plant* [2000] EPOR 303, 315–18.

[250] Including *Ciba Geigy/Propagating material* T49/83 [1979–85] EPOR C758; *Lubrizol/Hybrid plants* T320/87 [1990] EPOR 173; *Plant Genetic Systems/Glutamine synthetase inhibitors* T356/93 [1995] EPOR 357.

> – distinguished from any other plant grouping by the expression of at least one of the said characteristics, and
>
> – considered as a unit with regard to its suitability for being propagated unchanged.

This definition has been implemented into UK law as paragraph 11 of Schedule A2 to the PA 77.

The first case involving a genetically engineered plant to come before the Technical Board of Appeal was *Plant Genetic Systems/Glutamine synthetase inhibitors*.[251]

It concerned a European patent relating to plants and plant cells that possessed a foreign gene which made them resistant to a type of herbicide. This allowed farmers to spray their crops with the herbicide safe in the knowledge that it would only affect the unmodified weeds. The claims related to processes for producing the modified plants and plant cells and also to the modified plants and plant cells themselves. In opposition proceedings it was contended, inter alia, that the claims were not patentable according to Article 53(b) of the EPC. The Technical Board of Appeal held that the claim relating to modified plant cells was not excluded as a 'plant variety'. However, the claim relating to modified plants *was* held to fall within the 'plant variety' exclusion. This was so even though the claim was not drafted in terms of a variety description (because there was no reference to a single botanical taxon of the lowest-known rank). Rather, the claim was in general directed to a plant which possessed, integrated in its genome in a stable manner, a heterologous DNA containing a foreign nucleotide sequence encoding a protein having a non-variety-specific enzymatic activity capable of neutralizing or inactivating a glutamine synthetase inhibitor. The working examples of the patent, however, showed that the practical forms of realization of the invention according to this claim were genetically transformed plant varieties. Thus, since the claim *encompassed* plant varieties (even though it was not drafted in terms of a variety description), it was held to fall within the plant variety exclusion in Article 53(b). The Technical Board of Appeal reasoned that this had to be the case otherwise the Article 53(b) exclusion could be evaded too easily.

This aspect of the *Plant Genetic Systems* decision was particularly controversial because it meant that, in most cases, plants produced as a result of genetic engineering would be unpatentable. A referral of the case to the Enlarged Board by Appeal by the President of the EPO was rejected and it was not until the *Novartis* decision (considered below) that the Enlarged Board of Appeal overruled the approach taken in *Plant Genetic Systems*. Prior to *Novartis*, however, the Biotechnology Directive had been adopted and addressed this particular issue in Article 4. Specifically, Article 4 states:

> 1. The following shall not be patentable:
>
>   (a) plant and animal varieties;
>
>   …
>
> 2. Inventions which concern plants or animals shall be patentable if the technical feasibility of the invention is not confined to a particular plant or animal variety.

---

[251] T356/93 [1995] EPOR 357.

Article 4(1) of the Biotechnology Directive corresponds to Article 53(b) of the EPC. However, Article 4(2) allows claims to plants which embrace more than one variety. This is made clear from recital 31, which states:

> Whereas a plant grouping which is characterised by a particular gene (and not its whole genome) is not covered by the protection of new varieties and is therefore not excluded from patentability even if it comprises new varieties of plants.

As a result of Article 4(2) of the Biotechnology Directive, a discrepancy existed between the approach taken in the directive and that taken in *Plant Genetic Systems*. This discrepancy was, however, resolved by the Enlarged Board of Appeal in *Novartis*.

Novartis/Transgenic plant G01/98 [2000] EPOR 303

The European patent application in suit contained claims to genetically modified plants, and methods for producing such plants, comprising in their genomes specific recombinant DNA sequences, the expression of which resulted in the plants becoming pathogen-resistant (i.e. resistant to fungi). The Examining Division refused the application on the basis that several of the claims did not satisfy Article 53(b) of the EPC. It followed *Plant Genetic Systems* on the issue of whether a claim to genetically engineered plants and seeds generally, but which encompassed plant varieties, was not allowable under Article 53(b). On appeal, the Technical Board of Appeal decided to refer questions to the Enlarged Board of Appeal.[252] The Enlarged Board emphasized that the claimed invention neither expressly nor implicitly encompassed a plant variety and went on to consider whether a claim that encompassed a plant variety, but was not to a plant variety per se, was caught by Article 53(b) of the EPC.

Enlarged Board of Appeal:

3.3.1 …[W]hereas the exclusion for processes is related to the production of plants, the exclusion for products is related to plant varieties. The use of the more specific term 'variety' within the same half-sentence of the provision relating to products is supposed to have some meaning. If it was the intention to exclude plants as a group embracing in general varieties as products, the provision would use the more general term plants as used for the processes.

The Enlarged Board then examined in detail the history of Article 53(b) of the EPC and its origins in Article 2(b) of the Strasbourg Patent Convention, which in turn sought to implement the ban on dual protection in the UPOV Convention. Thus, the intention was that the exclusion in the EPC should correspond to the availability of protection in the UPOV Convention. It continued:

3.8 …Whereas in the case of a plant variety, the breeder has to develop a plant grouping fulfilling in particular the requirements of homogeneity and stability, this is not the case

---

[252] See *Novartis/Transgenic plant* T1054/96 [1999] EPOR 123 for the referring decision of the TBA.

with a typical genetic engineering invention in a claim such as that referred to in question 2. The inventor in the latter case aims at providing tools whereby a desired property can be bestowed on plants by inserting a gene into the genome of those plants. Providing these tools is a step which precedes the further step of introducing the gene into a specific plant. Nevertheless, it is the contribution of the inventor in the genetic field which makes it possible to take the second step and insert the gene into the genome of any appropriate plant or plant variety. Choosing a suitable plant for this purpose and arriving at a specific, marketable product, which will mostly be a plant variety, is a matter of routine breeding steps which may be rewarded by a plant breeders' right. The inventor in the genetic engineering field would not obtain appropriate protection if he were restricted to specific varieties for two reasons: first, the development of specific varieties will often not be in his field of activity and, secondly he would always be limited to a few varieties even though he had provided the means for inserting the gene into all appropriate plants.

...

3.10 In summary, according to Article 53(b) EPC, a patent is 'in respect of plant varieties' and shall not be granted if the claimed subject-matter is directed to plant varieties. In the absence of the identification of a specific plant variety in a product claim, the subject-matter of the claimed invention is not directed to a plant variety or varieties within the meaning of Article 53(b) EPC. This is why it is, contrary to the conclusions of the referring Board, in agreement with the rules of logic that a patent shall not be granted for a single plant variety but can be granted if varieties may fall within the scope of its claims. The conclusion of the referring Board is based on the premise that a claim is necessarily 'in respect of' a certain subject if it may comprise this subject. For Article 53(b) EPC, this interpretation is, as set out above, at odds with the purpose of the provision. It disregards the fact that Article 53(b) EPC defines the borderline between patent protection and plant variety protection. The extent of the exclusion for patents is the obverse of the availability of plant variety rights. The latter are only granted to specific plant varieties and not for technical teachings which can be implemented in an indefinite number of plant varieties... It is not sufficient for the exclusion of Article 53(b) EPC to apply that one or more plant varieties are embraced or may be embraced by the claims.

Was the Enlarged Board's narrow construction of Article 53(b) of the EPC heavily influenced by the purpose of that provision to prohibit dual protection under plant variety rights and patent law? If so, why is it that an invention relating to a genetically engineered plant, but not specifically claiming a plant variety, would not be adequately protected by plant variety rights?

Should the decision of the Enlarged Board of Appeal in *Novartis* be welcomed on the grounds that it engenders consistency between Article 53(b) of the EPC and the Biotechnology Directive? If so, do any residual difficulties remain, such as attempts by patent applicants to avoid the Article 53(b) exclusion by the way in which they draft their claims? Finally, as has been suggested by Margaret Llewelyn, would it make sense to delete the exclusion altogether? Or, alternatively, to extend the exclusion to cover all plant material, thus leaving plant variety rights, and not patent law, to govern this type of subject matter?[253]

[253] M. Llewelyn, 'The patentability of biological material: Continuing contradiction and confusion' [2000] EIPR 191.

> **FURTHER READING**
>
> S. Bostyn, 'The patentability of genetic information carriers' [1999] IPQ 1.
>
> M. Llewelyn, 'The patentability of biological material: continuing contradiction and confusion' [2000] EIPR 191.

11.7.4 ANIMAL VARIETIES

Article 53(b) of the EPC provides that a European patent shall not be granted in respect of animal varieties or any essentially biological processes for the production of animals.[254] The scope of this exclusion has been considered on several occasions by the EPO in relation to the *Harvard/Onco-mouse* patent.

A European patent application was filed on 24 June 1985 by the President and Fellows of Harvard College in respect of the (now infamous) onco-mouse. The patent application claimed a method for producing a transgenic[255] non-human mammalian animal having an increased likelihood of developing cancer, which would prove useful in cancer research. The method involved introducing an activated oncogene into a non-human mammalian animal. The application also claimed the transgenic non-human mammalian animals produced by this method, in particular transgenic rodents. The Examining Division of the EPO refused the application on the basis that the claims fell foul of Article 53(b).[256] The Examining Division took the view that Article 53(b), as it relates to animal varieties, should not be interpreted restrictively as had been done for plant varieties. This was because the plant-variety exclusion existed to avoid double protection (of patents and plant varieties) and a similar situation did not exist in relation to animal varieties. The Examining Division therefore interpreted Article 53(b) 'to refer not only to these cases where a specifically designated variety is claimed but also to cases where varieties are covered by a claim'.[257] Since the claims covered an animal variety they were excluded by Article 53(b) of the EPC.

On appeal, the Technical Board of Appeal set aside the decision and remitted the case back to the Examining Division for the reasons expressed below.

Harvard/Onco-mouse T 19/90 [1990] OJ EPO 476, [1990] EPOR 501

Technical Board of Appeal:

4.2 As pointed out by the Examining Division, the three texts of Article 53(b) EPC differ in terminology as to the non-patentable area. In particular, the German term 'Tierarten' is broader than the English 'animal varieties' and the French 'races animales'.

4.3 Article 177(1) EPC lays down that the English, French and German texts of the EPC are all equally authentic. In the present case, there is obviously a need to establish their common meaning through interpretation of the Convention in order to determine to what extent animals are excluded from patentability under Article 53(b), first half-sentence, EPC.

---

[254] Prior to the implementation of the Biotechnology Directive, this exclusion was contained in PA 77, s. 1(3)(b). It is now contained in PA 77, para. 3(f) of Sch. A2.

[255] i.e. genetically modified.

[256] *Harvard/Onco-mouse Application* No. 85 304 490.7 [1990] EPOR 4.   [257] At 7.1.2.

4.4 In the Decision under appeal the Examining Division interpreted Article 53(b) EPC as excluding not only certain groups of animals from patentability but, in fact, animals as such. The Board is unable to accept this interpretation.

4.5 Firstly, the Examining Division did not take duly into account that Article 53(b) EPC is an exception, for certain kinds of inventions, to the general rule under Article 52(1) EPC that European patents 'shall be' granted for all inventions which are susceptible of industrial application, which are new and which involve an inventive step. Any such exception must, as repeatedly pointed out by the Boards of Appeal, be narrowly construed (cf. in particular T320/87, point 6, OJ EPO 1990, 76). The Examining Division has given no convincing reasons for deviating in this particular case from this principle of interpretation, nor are any such reasons apparent to the Board.

4.6 The possibility that the reference to certain categories of animals rather than to animals as such was simply a mistake by the legislators can be ruled out. Nothing in the legislative history of either the EPC or the Strasbourg Convention of 27 November 1963 on the Unification of Certain Points of Substantive Law on Patents for Invention, whose Article 2(b) was taken over and incorporated into Article 53(b) EPC, supports such an assumption. On the contrary, a clear indication that the terms 'animal varieties', 'races animales' and 'Tierarten' were not intended to cover animals as such is the wording of Article 53(b) EPC itself. The very same provision also contains, as appears from paragraph 4.1 above, a reference to 'animals' (in general). In using the different terms 'animal varieties' ('races animales', 'Tierarten') and 'animals' ('animaux', 'Tiere') in this way, the legislators cannot have meant 'animals' in both cases.

4.7 In contrast to the exclusion of 'plant varieties' from patentability under Article 53(b) EPC (cf. T320/87—see above), the preparatory documents to this provision are completely silent as to the purpose of excluding 'animal varieties' from patentability. However, the purpose of a law (*ratio legis*) is not merely a matter of the actual intention of the legislators at the time when the law was adopted, but also of their presumed intention in the light of changes in circumstances which have taken place since then. It is now the task of the European Patent Office to find a solution to the problem of the interpretation of Article 53(b) EPC with regard to the concept of 'animal varieties', providing a proper balance between the interest of inventors in this field in obtaining reasonable protection for their efforts and society's interest in excluding certain categories of animals from patent protection. In this context it should, *inter alia*, be borne in mind that for animals—unlike plant varieties—no other industrial property right is available for the time being.

4.8 To sum up, the Board concludes that the Examining Division was wrong in refusing the present application on the ground that Article 53(b) EPC excludes the patenting of animals as such. The proper issue to be considered is, therefore, whether or not the subject-matter of the application is an 'animal variety' ('race animale', 'Tierart') within the meaning of Article 53(b) EPC. On this point the contested decision is for obvious reasons entirely silent. In view of the importance of this matter and the desirability of having it considered by at least two instances, the Board will exercise its powers under Article 111(1) EPC to remit the case to the department of first instance for further prosecution. It should also be noted that a number of questions outlined below and not yet dealt with by the Examining Division now need to be considered.

In its resumed examination with regard to Article 53(b) EPC, the Examining Division must, as indicated above, first consider whether the subject-matter of the present application constitutes an 'animal variety', 'race animale' or 'Tierart' within the meaning of that provision. If it comes to the conclusion that the subject-matter is not covered by any of these three terms, then Article 53(b) EPC constitutes no bar to patentability. If, however, it considers that any of these terms applies, then refusal of the application would only be justified if that specific term represents the proper interpretation of Article 53(b) (see point 4.3 above). This would also presuppose that Article 53(b) EPC can be applied at all in respect of animals which are genetically manipulated, given that neither the drafters of the Strasbourg Convention nor those of the EPC could envisage this possibility.

What were the main reasons given by the Technical Board of Appeal for rejecting the argument that Article 53(b) of the EPC excludes the patenting of animals as such?

The case was remitted back to the Examining Division, which considered whether the application constituted an 'animal variety', '*race animale*', or '*Tierart*' within the meaning of Article 53(b) of the EPC. The Examining Division[258] held that the exact scope of 'animal variety' was not clear given the differing wording in the three official languages of the EPC. Nevertheless, it concluded that rodents constituted a taxonomic classification unit much higher than species and thus it was unnecessary to determine whether Article 53(b) of the EPC referred to species or sub-unit of a species. The patent was granted in favour of the applicants on 15 May 1992.

After grant, 17 oppositions were filed against the patent on a variety of grounds, including that the patent was contrary to Article 53(b) of the EPC. In the meantime, the Biotechnology Directive had been adopted. Between the time when the oppositions were filed and the opposition proceedings were decided, the Administrative Council of the EPO had implemented the relevant provisions of the Biotechnology Directive by adding rules 23b–e of the EPC to Part II of the Implementing Regulations.[259] Relevantly, Article 4(1)(a) of the Biotechnology Directive states that animal varieties shall not be patentable. However, Article 4(2) provides that 'Inventions which concern ... animals shall be patentable if the technical feasibility of the invention is not confined to a particular ... animal variety.'

The Opposition Division considered whether new rules 23b–e of the EPC, implementing the Biotechnology Directive, was applicable to the opposition proceedings in hand.[260] It held that '[a]s a general rule, in the absence of transitional provisions, administrative and judicial bodies have to apply the law as it stands at the date when a decision is taken' and that this applied to pending patent cases, whether in examination or in opposition. Only in exceptional circumstances would this not be the case.[261] Given that the new rules 23b–e of the EPC did not constitute a major departure from the previous law, but merely interpreted relevant provisions of the EPC, there was no need to restrict the applicability of the new rules.

The Opposition Division went on to consider patentability of animals under Article 53(b) of the EPC as it relates to animal varieties. It followed the earlier Technical Board of Appeal decision in *Onco-mouse*. It also referred to the decision of the Enlarged Board in *Novartis* and stated that the holding could be transferred to the interpretation of the exclusion of animal varieties. More specifically, it held that claims to animals that encompassed an animal variety or varieties would not be caught by the exclusion, but only claims directed to an animal variety or varieties per se. On the facts, the Opposition Division held that the invention as claimed was applicable to more than just varieties of mice and thus Article 53(b) of the EPC was not a bar to patentability.

[258] *Harvard/Onco-mouse Application* No. 85 304 490.7 [1991] EPOR 525.
[259] These Rules entered into force on 1 September 1999.
[260] In its Decision [2003] 10 OJ EPO 473.   [261] Decision, para. 9.7.2.

11.7.5 ESSENTIALLY BIOLOGICAL PROCESSES FOR THE PRODUCTION OF PLANTS AND ANIMALS

Article 53(b) of the EPC, in addition to excluding animal and plant varieties from patentability, also excludes essentially biological processes for the production of plants or animals. This exclusion was reiterated in Article 4(1)(b) of the Biotechnology Directive. The exclusion is limited to *processes* where those processes are *essentially* biological. This, of course, begs the question: when is a process *essentially* biological in nature?

Article 2(2) of the Biotechnology Directive, as adopted, states that, 'a process for the production of plants or animals is essentially biological if it consists entirely of nature phenomena such as crossing or selection'.[262] The meaning of this exclusion was considered by the Enlarged Board of Appeal in the following ruling.

Essentially Biological Processes G2/07 and G1/08 [2011] EPOR 27

Two Technical Board of Appeal decisions, *Plant Bioscience/Broccoli*[263] and *State of Israel/Tomatoes*,[264] referred questions to the Enlarged Board of Appeal on the meaning of the exclusion from patentability of essentially biological processes for the production of plants or animals. There were primarily two reasons necessitating a reference. First, although the Enlarged Board of Appeal had ruled on the scope of the plant varieties exclusion in *Novartis* (G1/98; discussed earlier) it left unanswered how to determine whether a process is 'essentially biological'. This was despite the fact that the Technical Board of Appeal in *Novartis* (T320/87) had identified several possible relevant factors or approaches. Second, Article 2(2) of the Biotechnology Directive, which had been implemented as rule 23(b)(5) of the EPC 1973 and rule 26(5) of the EPC 2000, stipulates 'a process for the production of plants or animals is essentially biological if it consists entirely of natural phenomena, such as crossing or selection'. The referring Technical Boards of Appeal noted that this was a confusing, indeed contradictory, statement because it suggests that crossing and selection, which involve human (technical) intervention, are examples of natural phenomena. We turn now to consider the Enlarged Board's reasoning and conclusions. It began first by considering the legislative history of Article 2(2) of the Biotechnology Directive and concluded that it did not assist in determining what that provision was intended to mean. The inherent 'self contradictory' nature of the provision could not be clarified. As such:

> 95. ...[T]he consequence of the self-contradictory wording of art.2(2) Biotech Directive having been transposed verbatim into r.26(5) EPC is, regrettably, that r.26(5) EPC does not give any useful guidance on how to interpret the term 'essentially biological process for the production of plants' in art.53(b) EPC and therefore that term must be interpreted on its own authority. This is for the Enlarged Board to do.

> [The Enlarged Board therefore turned to focus on Article 53(b) of the EPC. It noted that because of the difference in language between plant varieties and plants, the exclusion could not be read as only applying where the result of an essentially biological process is a plant variety. The Board then turned to dismiss possible approaches to the exclusion.]

---

[262] This has been implemented in PA 77, para. 11 of Sch. A2.

[263] T83/05 [2008] EPOR 14.

[264] T1242/06 [2008] EPOR 26.

The article 52(4) EPC 1973 analogy

107. The first approach would be analogous to that used under art.52(4) EPC 1973 in relation to methods of treatment by surgery and therapy and would result in the inclusion in a claimed process of a step of an essentially biological nature not being allowable. However, it already follows from the wording of the exclusion, which requires the claimed process, i.e. the process as a whole, to have a biological 'essence' (whatever that may mean precisely), that the mere presence of one biological feature in a process cannot automatically confer an essentially biological character on the process as a whole.

The computer-related inventions approach

108. The same applies to the converse approach. That second approach would be to require, in order for the process to escape the prohibition of art.53(b) EPC, at least one clearly identified 'non-biological' process step, while allowing any number of additional 'essentially biological steps', which would be carried into allowability by the 'non-biological' process step. In the present proceedings the argument was also based on the proposal that an analogy should be drawn with the principles developed for determining the technical character of certain computer-implemented inventions....

110. It can, however, already be concluded from the difference in the wording of art.52(2) EPC from that of art.53(b) EPC that the suggested comparison does not hold good.

111. According to art.52(3) EPC, para.2 shall exclude the patentability of the subject-matter or activities referred to therein only to the extent to which a European patent application or European patent relates to such subject-matter or activities as such. This is interpreted in the jurisprudence as meaning that 'any technical means' makes the claimed subject-matter escape the exclusion under art.52(2) EPC (see G3/08, loc. cit.).

112. By contrast, for the exclusion under art.53(b) EPC to apply, it suffices that the claimed process be essentially biological. However narrowly one might wish to construe the reference to some kind of 'essentiality', any possibility of interpreting the exclusion in the sense that any technical feature, irrespective of its importance for an otherwise biological process for the production of plants, makes the process escape the exclusion under art.53(b) EPC, is thereby also ruled out from the outset.

The T320/87 approach

Criteria linked to the state of the art

113. In Decision T320/87 (supra) several criteria were used for assessing whether the claimed invention is essentially biological or not (see 3.2.1 above). Some of these are defined in such a way that determining whether they are fulfilled depends on the state of the art to be taken into account in the individual case. This applies to the questions whether the totality and sequence of the specified operations do or do not correspond to the classical breeders' processes, whether they occur in nature or whether a technical feature in the claim is trivial or alters the character of a known process in a fundamental way or whether the essence of the claimed invention lies in it, to the extent that the essence of the invention is determined on the basis of the objective problem solved.

114. Basically, any approach that makes the decision on whether a claimed process for the production of plants is essentially biological and therefore excluded from patentability, or technical and therefore patentable, dependent on criteria which are determined by reference

to the state of art is flawed because it conflates the considerations which are relevant for patentability with those relevant for novelty and inventive step.

115. Furthermore, such an approach is detrimental to legal certainty, since the qualification of a process as being patentable subject-matter or, on the contrary, excluded from patentability could then change with every new state of the art that comes to be considered in the various procedural stages which an application and a patent granted on it may run through during the whole lifetime of the patent.

116. There is, furthermore, simply no logic in saying that the decision whether a process is technical or essentially biological depends on what was already known or used in the art or on how far the claimed subject-matter went beyond that.

...

Human intervention

124. In Decision T320/87 (supra) the board held that a further criterion for delimiting unpatentable essentially biological processes from patentable processes was the totality of human intervention in the process and its impact on the result achieved...

133. As the essentially biological processes for the production of plants are excluded from patentability by art.53(b) EPC even though they are inventions and are as such characterised by human intervention, the board in T320/87 (supra) was fundamentally correct in its starting point that not just any kind of human intervention can suffice to make an invention in this field escape the exclusion.

134. In order to determine more precisely how the excluded kinds of processes involving human intervention are properly to be delimited from the patentable ones, it is necessary to consider the purpose of the exclusion...

Conclusions

146. As is apparent from the above, the first Preliminary Draft Convention of the EC Working Group of March 14, 1961 already contained an exception from patentability for 'inventions relating to the production of or a process for producing a new plant variety...'. Although the explanations given with regard to plants are rather rudimentary, they nevertheless contain some indication that at that point in time the legislator was concerned with excluding from patentability the processes applied by plant breeders in connection with the creation of new plant varieties, for which a special property right was going to be introduced under the UPOV Convention. It must be concluded that the legislator's intention was to exclude from patentability the kind of plant breeding processes which were the conventional methods for the breeding of plant varieties of that time. These conventional methods included in particular those (relevant for the present referrals) based on the sexual crossing of plants (i.e. of their whole genomes) deemed suitable for the purpose pursued and on the subsequent selection of the plants having the desired trait(s). The application of technical means or other forms of human intervention in such processes which helped to perform them was already common. Nevertheless, the said processes were characterised by the fact that the traits of the plants resulting from the crossing were determined by the underlying natural phenomenon of meiosis. This phenomenon determined the genetic make-up of the plants produced, and the breeding result was achieved by the breeder's selection of plants having the desired trait(s). That these were processes to be excluded also follows from the fact that processes changing the genome of plants by technical means such as irradiation are cited as examples of patentable technical processes.

147. A further teaching is also clearly discernible from the explanations given in the memorandum of the Secretariat of the Committee of Experts for agreeing to the replacement of the words 'purely biological' by the version still valid today: The exchange of the word 'purely' for 'essentially' was deliberate and reflects the legislative intention that the mere fact of using a technical device in a breeding process should not be sufficient to give the process as such a technical character and should not have the effect that such process is no longer excluded from patentability. The example mentioned at this early stage of development in technologies in the realm of biology, of the use of a special greenhouse for growing a plant, shows that the legislator did not wish breeding processes to be patented in which the technical measures used are only means serving to bring about processes for the production of plants which are otherwise based on biological forces. This is made abundantly clear by the additional remark in the explanatory notes that such technical devices may perfectly well be patented in themselves but not so the biological process in which they are used.

...

149. This is an important point which cannot be ignored for the interpretation of art.53(b) EPC today. Certainly, in the meantime the technical means available to influence crossing and selection procedures have increased enormously and become much more sophisticated. Furthermore, modern technical means may allow crossing and selection procedures which would otherwise not be possible or at least not realistic or economically viable. However, the clear intention of the legislator behind replacing the word 'purely' by 'essentially' can even today not be simply ignored, given that the wording of this provision has remained unchanged over time and that not one of the various legislators has apparently seen a need to revise that text. No doubt one could argue that with such an old law as the exclusion has now become, what the original legislator wished to provide is no longer of such great significance. Be that as it may, the Enlarged Board is unable to see why the legislator's decision to provide appropriate patent protection for 'secondary' features such as technical devices or means (today e.g. markers) by allowing them to be patented in themselves but not to extend protection to the biological process in which they are used, would no longer be justified today, merely because today many more such technical possibilities exist.

150. On the contrary, given that there is a certain tendency to ever broaden the technical field covered by a patent by drafting claims directed to all envisaged contexts in which the invention might potentially be used, the fact that the legislator did not want such an extension of protection in the field considered here is still a valid consideration to be respected. Hence, it must be concluded that the provision of a technical step, be it explicit or implicit, in a process which is based on the sexual crossing of plants and on subsequent selection does not cause the claimed invention to escape the exclusion if that technical step only serves to perform the process steps of the breeding process.

...

153. Hence, in more general terms, the conclusion to be drawn is that a process for the production of plants which is based on the sexual crossing of whole genomes and on the subsequent selection of plants, in which human intervention, including the provision of a technical means, serves to enable or assist the performance of the process steps, remains excluded from patentability as being essentially biological within the meaning of art.53(b) EPC.

154. However, if a process of sexual crossing and selection includes within it an additional step of a technical nature, which step by itself introduces a trait into the genome or modifies a trait in the genome of the plant produced, so that the introduction or modification of that trait is not the result of the mixing of the genes of the plants chosen for sexual crossing, then that process leaves the realm of the plant breeding, which the legislator wanted to exclude from patentability. Therefore, such a process is not excluded from patentability under art.53(b) EPC but qualifies as a potentially patentable technical teaching.

Looking particularly at the last three paragraphs extracted above, can you identify how the Enlarged Board of Appeal interpreted Article 53(b) of the EPC as it relates to 'essentially biological processes'? How does this approach differ from the way in which other exclusions from patentability are interpreted, and why were these interpretations rejected by the Enlarged Board?

The claims to patented inventions in both the *Tomatoes* and *Broccoli* cases were amended in such a manner as to be product-by-process claims. An issue therefore arose as to whether these *product* claims would fall foul of the exclusion for 'essentially biological *processes*', given that the products could only be produced by an essentially biological process. In essence the question was: should a product-by-(essentially biological)-process claim be permitted or was this a skilful avoidance of the patentability exclusion? The Technical Board of Appeal referred both cases to the Enlarged Board of Appeal and the referrals were consolidated (and known as *Tomatoes II*[265] and *Broccoli II*[266]). The Enlarged Board of Appeal issued its decision on 25 March 2015.[267] First of all, the Enlarged Board found that the referrals were admissible in order to ensure a uniform application of the law. Second, it held that: 'Even if the product, i.e. the plant or plant material such as a fruit or plant parts, can only be obtained by essentially biological processes with no other methods either disclosed in the patent application or otherwise known, the process exclusion in Article 53(b) EPC does not extend to product claims and product-by-process claims.'[268] In reaching this conclusion, the Enlarged Board relied on literal and purposive interpretations and the *travaux préparatoires* to Article 53(b) of the EPC and indicated that if the exclusion for essentially biological processes was intended to cover products, then the legislator would have indicated so, particularly in the revised EPC 2000. The Enlarged Board was also not persuaded that allowing such claims would amount to skilful circumvention of the exclusion, in large part because a patentee would still have to meet the formal and substantive criteria for patentability. Do you agree with the narrow construction of Article 53(b) of the EPC adopted by of the Enlarged Board? Is it a boon for the biotechnology industry?

11.7.6 MICROBIOLOGICAL PROCESSES FOR THE PRODUCTION OF PLANTS AND ANIMALS

Notably, Article 53(b) of the EPC contains a qualification to the exclusion for plant or animal varieties or essentially biological processes for the production of plants or animals. This is where the process is a microbiological process or the product thereof.

---

[265] G1/98.   [266] G2/07.
[267] *Essentially biological processes* G2/12 and G2/13 [2015] EPOR 28.   [268] [90].

Prior to the Biotechnology Directive, the issue arose whether technical processes *including* a microbiological step could be equated with microbiological processes. In *Plant Genetic Systems*, the Technical Board of Appeal opined that the process had to be judged as a whole and that, where it was really a technical process that included a microbiological step, it would not constitute a microbiological process.

Subsequently, the Biotechnology Directive was adopted. Article 4(3) of the Biotechnology Directive states that the exclusion in Article 4(1) (for plant or animal varieties and essentially biological processes), 'shall be without prejudice to the patentability of inventions which concern a microbiological or other technical process or a product obtained by means of such a process'. Article 2 of the Biotechnology Directive defines 'microbiological process' as 'any process involving or performed upon or resulting in microbiological material'. Given that Article 4(3) refers to microbiological *or other technical processes*, it seems that technical processes which include a microbiological step (e.g. manipulation of micro-organisms by genetic engineering or fusion techniques) will be covered by the qualification and thus held not to fall foul of the exclusion set out in Article 4(1). However, it is worth remembering that product claims for plant or animal varieties cannot be allowed, even if the variety is produced by means of a microbiological process. This is because the exception to patentability in Article 53(b) relating to plant or animal varieties applies *irrespective* of the way in which they are produced.

11.7.7 *ORDRE PUBLIC* AND MORALITY

11.7.7.1 Pre-Biotechnology Directive

Since the Statute of Monopolies 1624, it has been a principle of UK patent law that inventions which are contrary to law or morality are excluded from protection. Prior to UK implementation of the Biotechnology Directive, the *ordre public* and morality exclusion was contained in section 1(3)(a) of the PA 77. This section provided that a patent 'shall not be granted … for an invention the publication or exploitation of which would be generally expected to encourage offensive, immoral or anti-social behaviour'. Section 1(4) of the PA 77 then went on to qualify that behaviour would not be offensive, immoral, or anti-social simply because it was illegal in the UK. These provisions were intended to give effect to the comparable exemption in Article 53(a) of the EPC which states that European patents shall not be granted in respect of:

> inventions the publication or exploitation of which would be contrary to 'ordre public' or morality, provided that the exploitation shall not be deemed to be so merely because it is prohibited by law or regulation in some or all of the Contracting States.[269]

With the advent of biotechnological research and subsequent attempts to patent genetically engineered inventions, this exclusion has been invoked with reasonable frequency and its scope interpreted on a number of occasions.

The first such occasion was in the *Onco-mouse* decision. As already discussed above, the application claimed a non-human mammal (such as a mouse), into which an oncogene had

---

[269] Note that the wording of Art. 53(a) has changed as a result of the EPC 2000. It now refers to 'inventions the commercial exploitation of which would be contrary to "ordre public" or morality'.

been inserted which would make it susceptible to cancer. The Examining Division considered that patent law was an inappropriate legislative tool for assessing the ethical and environmental considerations associated with the patenting of genetically modified animals and thus did not refuse the application on the basis of Article 53(a) of the EPC.[270] On appeal, the Technical Board of Appeal directed the Examining Division to apply this exclusion for the reasons expressed in the following passage:[271]

> The Board considers, however, that precisely in a case of this kind there are compelling reasons to consider the implications of Article 53(a) EPC in relation to the question of patentability. The genetic manipulation of mammalian animals is undeniably problematical in various respects, particularly where activated oncogenes are inserted to make an animal abnormally sensitive to carcinogenic substances and stimuli and consequently prone to develop tumours, which necessarily cause suffering. There is also a danger that genetically manipulated animals, if released into the environment, might entail unforeseeable and irreversible adverse effects. Misgivings and fears of this kind have been expressed by a number of persons who have filed observations with the Board under Article 115 EPC. Considerations of precisely this kind have also led a number of Contracting States to impose legislative control on genetic engineering. The decision as to whether or not Article 53(a) EPC is a bar to patenting the present invention would seem to depend mainly on a careful weighing up of the suffering of animals and possible risks to the environment on the one hand, and the invention's usefulness to mankind on the other. It is the task of the department of first instance to consider these matters in the context of its resumed examination of the case.

Do you agree with the view of the Technical Board of Appeal that Article 53(a) of the EPC should be considered in relation to inventions involving genetically modified animals or with the view of the Examining Division that the EPO is an inappropriate forum in which to assess such ethical issues? Further, would you describe the Technical Board's approach to Article 53(a) as utilitarian? If so, is this an appropriate ethical framework by which to determine whether certain kinds of invention should be patentable?

The case was later remitted back to the Examining Division, which sought to weigh up the risks and benefits to mankind of the onco-mouse.[272] The Examining Division found that the invention's usefulness to mankind could not be doubted, given that cancer is a frequent cause of death and suffering in many countries. Further, the use of genetically engineered rodents in cancer research was likely to involve fewer animals than was the case with conventional research and thus contribute 'to a reduction of the overall extent of animal suffering'. There was also evidence to suggest that animal testing was indispensable to cancer research. The Examining Division did not consider that the invention would pose risks to the environment, given that it would be used in controlled laboratory conditions by qualified staff. Further, it commented that exclusion from patentability could not be justified 'merely because a technology is dangerous' and that the regulation of dangerous activity was the task of specialist government authorities and not that of the EPO. Thus, the Examining Division concluded that the invention could not be considered as contrary to public order or morality.

[270] *Harvard/Onco-mouse* [1990] EPOR 4, para. 10.3.
[271] *Harvard/Onco-mouse* T19/90 [1990] EPOR 501, 513.
[272] *Harvard/Onco-mouse* [1991] EPOR 525, 527–8.

Did the Examining Division's assessment of whether the invention fell foul of Article 53(a) of the EPC take into account general objections in principle to the patenting of transgenic animals or were the moral considerations limited to the special circumstances of the case? If the latter, does this reflect a failure to engage in a comprehensive moral assessment?[273]

Transgenic plants have also been subjected to scrutiny according to Article 53(a) of the EPC, as illustrated by *Plant Genetic Systems.*[274] In this case, which involved transgenic plants and plant cells resistant to herbicide, the Technical Board of Appeal did not adopt a balancing exercise of advantages and disadvantages of the invention. This was because no sufficient evidence of actual disadvantages had been adduced and the 'balancing' approach was seen as just one possible way of assessing patentability according to Article 53(a).[275] The Board began by articulating the scope of the concepts of *ordre public* and morality under Article 53(a) of the EPC:

> It is generally accepted that the concept of 'ordre public' covers the protection of public security and the physical integrity of individuals as part of society. This concept encompasses also the protection of the environment. Accordingly, under Article 53(a) EPC, inventions the exploitation of which is likely to breach public peace or social order (for example, through acts of terrorism) or seriously to prejudice the environment are to be excluded from patentability as being contrary to 'ordre public'.
>
> The concept of morality is related to the belief that some behaviour is right and acceptable whereas other behaviour is wrong, this belief being founded on the totality of the accepted norms which are deeply rooted in a particular culture. For the purposes of the EPC, the culture in question is the culture inherent in European society and civilisation. Accordingly, under Article 53(a) EPC, inventions the exploitation of which is *not* in conformity with the conventionally-accepted standards of conduct pertaining to this culture are to be excluded from patentability as being contrary to morality.
>
> The second half-sentence of Article 53(a) EPC contains the qualification 'that the exploitation shall not be deemed to be so contrary merely because it is prohibited by law or regulation in some or all of the Contracting States'. This qualification makes clear that the assessment of whether or not a particular subject-matter is to be considered contrary to either 'ordre public' or morality is not dependent on any national laws or regulations. Conversely and by the same token, the Board is of the opinion that a particular subject-matter shall not automatically be regarded as complying with the requirements of Article 53(a) EPC merely because its exploitation is permitted in some or all of the Contracting States. Thus, approval or disapproval of the exploitation by national law(s) or regulation(s) does not constitute per se a sufficient criterion for the purposes of examination under Article 53(a) EPC.[276]

How useful is the above guidance of the Technical Board? Importantly, what sort of evidence will go to establish whether an invention is contrary to *ordre public* or morality?

To support their objections under Article 53(a) of the EPC, the opponents in *Plant Genetic Systems* sought to rely on survey and opinion poll evidence as probative of public opinion. For example, they submitted a survey conducted among Swedish farmers, according to which a large majority were opposed to genetic engineering; and an opinion poll carried

---

[273] A. Warren, 'A mouse in sheep's clothing: the challenge to the patent morality criterion posed by "Dolly"' [1998] EIPR 445, 447–8 suggests that it does.

[274] *Plant Genetic Systems/Glutamine synthetase inhibitors (Opposition by Greenpeace)* T356/93 [1995] EPOR 357.

[275] At 373.   [276] At 366–7.

out in Switzerland, according to which the majority of those surveyed were opposed to patenting animals and plants. The Technical Board of Appeal rejected this evidence for the following reasons:[277]

> The results of surveys or opinion polls can scarcely be considered decisive per se when assessing patentability of a given subject-matter with regard to the requirements of Article 53(a) EPC, for the following reasons:
>
> — Surveys and opinion polls do not necessarily reflect 'ordre public' concerns or moral norms that are deeply rooted in European culture.
>
> — The results of surveys and opinion polls can fluctuate in an unforeseeable manner within short time periods and can be very easily influenced and controlled, depending on a number of factors, including the type of questions posed, the choice and the size of the representative sample, and so on.
>
> — Surveys of particular groups of people (for example, farmers) tend to reflect their specific interests and/or their biased beliefs.
>
> — As stated above, the question whether Article 53(a) EPC constitutes a bar to patentability is to be considered in each particular case on its merits. Consequently, if surveys and opinion polls were to be relied on, they would have to be made ad hoc on the basis of specific questions in relation to the particular subject-matter claimed. For obvious reasons, such a procedure is scarcely feasible.
>
> — Like national law(s) and regulation(s) approving or disapproving the exploitation of an invention . . ., a survey or an opinion poll showing that a particular group of people or the majority of the population of some or all of the Contracting States opposes the granting of a patent for a specified subject-matter, cannot serve as a sufficient criterion for establishing that the said subject-matter is contrary to 'ordre public' or morality.

Was the Technical Board ruling out completely the use of surveys or opinion polls? If so, what sort of evidence can be relied upon when it comes to mounting a challenge on the grounds that an invention is contrary to *ordre public* or morality?

In *Plant Genetic Systems* the Technical Board of Appeal concluded that the invention was neither contrary to morality or *ordre public*. On the morality point, the Board held that the claimed subject matter did not relate to a misuse or destructive use of plant biotechnology because it concerned activities or products which could not be considered wrong in the light of conventionally accepted standards of conduct of European culture.[278] A factor which seemed to influence the Board's decision was that plant biotechnology was similar in its goals to traditional selective breeding.[279] With regards to *ordre public*, the Board held that there must be evidence sufficiently substantiating that the patent would seriously prejudice the environment and that no such conclusive evidence had been presented. Evidence of possible, but not yet conclusively documented, hazards was insufficient.[280]

Again, the question must be asked, what type of evidence *will* be accepted in order conclusively to show serious prejudice to the environment or that an invention offends the norms of European culture? In *Howard Florey/Relaxin*[281] the opponents requested that the EPO carry out a referendum, in order to determine whether the process for obtaining the hormone H2-relaxin and the complementary DNA sequence coding for H2-relaxin, was contrary to

[277] At 368–9.   [278] At 370.   [279] At 369–70.   [280] At 372.   [281] [1995] EPOR 541.

morality. The Opposition Division refused this request on the basis that the opponent had the burden of proof and it was thus their responsibility to adduce such evidence. Further, the Opposition Division doubted the weight of such evidence, commenting that it would be 'only in those very limited cases in which there appears to be an overwhelming consensus that the exploitation or publication of an invention would be immoral may an invention be excluded from patentability under Article 53(a)'.[282] In your view, is it fair to place such a heavy, and apparently vague, evidential burden on opponents of granted patents?

FURTHER READING

L. Bently and B. Sherman, 'The question of patenting life' in L. Bently and S. Maniatis (eds), *Intellectual Property and Ethics* (London: Sweet & Maxwell, 1998), pp. 111–25.

P. Drahos, 'Biotechnology patents, markets and morality' [1999] EIPR 441.

M. Llewelyn, 'Article 53 revisited' [1995] EIPR 506.

Nuffield Council on Bioethics, *Report on Human Tissue: Ethical and Legal Issues* (April 1995), pp. 97–8.

11.7.7.2 Post-Biotechnology Directive

Article 6 of the Biotechnology Directive sought to clarify the application of the *ordre public* and morality exclusion to biotechnological inventions. Article 6(1) provides:

> Inventions shall be considered unpatentable where their commercial exploitation would be contrary to ordre public or morality; however, exploitation shall not be deemed to be so contrary merely because it is prohibited by law or regulation.

Section 1 of the PA 77 was amended to be consistent with Article 6 of the Biotechnology Directive. Thus, section 1(3) of the PA 77 now provides:

> A patent shall not be granted for an invention the commercial exploitation of which would be contrary to public policy or morality.[283]

Article 6(2) of the Biotechnology Directive sets out an illustrative list of inventions which are deemed unpatentable under Article 6(1):

> (a) processes for cloning human beings;
>
> (b) processes for modifying the germ line genetic identity of human beings;
>
> (c) uses of human embryos for industrial or commercial purposes;
>
> (d) processes for modifying the genetic identity of animals which are likely to cause them suffering without any substantial medical benefit to man or animal, and also animals resulting from such processes.

---

[282] *Howard Florey/Relaxin* [1995] EPOR 541, para. 6.5.

[283] As a result of EPC 2000, Art. 53(a) of the EPC was also amended to be consistent with Art. 6(1) of the Biotechnology Directive.

Article 6(2) of the Biotechnology Directive has been incorporated into the PA 77 as paragraph 3(f) of Schedule A2 and into the EPC as part of its Implementing Regulations. Previously it was rule 23(d) of the Implementing Regulations, but is now rule 28 of the Implementing Regulations to the EPC 2000.

In the action for annulment of the Biotechnology Directive[284] the applicant pleaded that the directive exacerbated the legal ambiguities identified in the recitals, and thus was in breach of the principle of legal certainty. In particular, the applicant argued that Article 6 gave national authorities too much discretion in applying concepts expressed in general and ambiguous terms. The ECJ rejected this argument. It held that while Article 6 gave national authorities a wide scope for manoeuvre in applying the exclusion, this was necessary in order to take into account the particular difficulties that may arise from a patent in the social and cultural context of each Member State. Further, the type of provision reflected in Article 6 was well known in patent law. Finally, the provision was not discretionary because it was limited by well-known concepts of *ordre public* and morality and because it gave four examples of processes or uses which are not patentable. 'Thus, the Community legislature gives guidelines for applying the concepts at issue which do not otherwise exist in the general law on patents.'[285]

Do you agree that Article 6(2) of the Biotechnology Directive provides clear and useful guidance on the scope of the *ordre public* and morality exclusion? What ambiguities and controversies could arise in relation to the illustrative list contained in Article 6(2)?

FURTHER READING

S. Bostyn, 'The patentability of genetic information carriers' [1999] IPQ 1.

Two aspects of Article 6(2) of the Biotechnology Directive that have caused particular difficulties of interpretation are sub-paragraphs (c) (uses of human embryos for industrial or commercial purposes) and (d) (processes for modifying the genetic identity of animals, etc.).

Article 6(2)(c) of the Biotechnology Directive, which prohibits as contrary to *ordre public* or morality uses of human embryos for industrial or commercial purposes, has been the subject of interpretation by the Enlarged Board of Appeal in *WARF/Thomson stem cell application*.[286]

WARF/Thomson stem cell application G2/06 [2009] EPOR 15

Wisconsin Alumni Research Foundation (WARF) filed a European patent application for an invention by James Thomson which claimed the cultures of human embryonic stem cells. The application was refused by the Examining Division as contrary to rule 28(c) of the EPC (formerly rule 23(d)(c)) because, in order to generate the human embryonic stem-cell cultures, human embryos were used as starting material. The Technical Board of Appeal decided to refer questions to the Enlarged Board. Question 1 asked whether rule 28(c) of the EPC (formerly rule 23(d)(c)) applied to an application filed

---

[284] *Netherlands v European Parliament and Council of the European Union* Case C-377/98 [2001] ECR I-7079.
[285] [39].   [286] G2/06 [2009] EPOR 15.

before the entry into force of the rule. If yes, question 2 asked whether the rule forbade claims directed to products (here human embryonic stem cells) which at the date of filing could only be prepared by a method that necessarily involved the destruction of human embryos. Question 3 asked whether Article 53(a) of the EPC in any event forbade the patenting of such claims. Question 4 asked whether it was relevant to rule 23(d)(c) or Article 53(a) of the EPC that, after the filing date, the same products could be obtained without having to use a method that necessarily involved the destruction of human embryos.

Enlarged Board of Appeal:

[On question 1, the Board indicated that the EPC provisions implementing the Biotechnology Directive had been introduced without any transitional provisions.]

13. ...[This] can only be taken as meaning that this detailed guidance on what was patentable and unpatentable was to be applied as a whole to all then pending applications.

14. In view of the above, the answer to referred Question 1 must be that Rule 28(c) (formerly 23d(c)) EPC applies to all pending applications, even those filed before the entry into force of the rule. As the Appellant itself agrees with this answer, as does the President of the EPO and the vast majority of the *amicus curiae* briefs, nothing more need be said.

[On question 2, the appellant contended that embryos referred to embryos 14 days or older, which were not involved in the method that produced the human embryonic stem cells.]

20. Neither the EU legislator nor the EPC legislator have chosen to define the term 'embryo', as used in the Directive or now in Rule 28 (formerly 23d) EPC. This contrasts with the German law ... where embryo is defined as including a fertilized egg, or the UK law ... where embryo includes the two cell zygote and an egg in the process of fertilisation. The EU and the EPC legislators must presumably have been aware of the definitions used in national laws on regulating embryos, and yet chose to leave the term undefined. Given the purpose to protect human dignity and prevent the commercialization of embryos, the Enlarged Board can only presume that 'embryo' was not to be given any restrictive meaning in Rule 28 (formerly 23d) EPC, as to do so would undermine the intention of the legislator, and that what is an embryo is a question of fact in the context of any particular patent application. [The appellant also contended that use of human embryos must be claimed.]

21. However, this Rule (as well as the corresponding provision of the Directive) does not mention claims, but refers to 'invention' in the context of its exploitation. What needs to be looked at is not just the explicit wording of the claims but the technical teaching of the application as a whole as to how the invention is to be performed. Before human embryonic stem cell cultures can be used they have to be made. Since in the case referred to the Enlarged Board the only teaching of how to perform the invention to make human embryonic stem cell cultures is the use (involving their destruction) of human embryos, this invention falls under the prohibition of Rule 28(c) (formerly 23d(c)) EPC ... To restrict the application of Rule 28(c) (formerly 23d(c)) EPC to what an applicant chooses explicitly to put in his claim would have the undesirable consequence of making avoidance of the patenting prohibition merely a matter of clever and skilful drafting of such claim. [The appellant also argued that the use of human embryos to make the stem cell cultures was not for industrial or commercial purposes.]

25. A claimed new and inventive product must first be made before it can be used. Such making is the ordinary way commercially to exploit the claimed invention and falls within the monopoly granted, as someone having a patent application with a claim directed to this product has on the grant of the patent the right to exclude others from making or using such product. Making the claimed product remains commercial or industrial exploitation of the invention even where there is an intention to use that product for further research. On the facts which this Board must assume in answering the referred Question 2, making the claimed product involves the destruction of human embryos. This use involving destruction is thus an integral and essential part of the industrial and commercial exploitation of the claimed invention, and thus violates the prohibition of Rule 28(c) (formerly 23d(c)) EPC.

Question 3 did not need answering in light of the answer to question 2. In relation to question 4, the Enlarged Board concluded that technical developments which became available after the filing date could not be taken into consideration.

Do you agree with the Enlarged Board's interpretation of rule 28(c) of the EPC? In particular, that the question of what is a human embryo is a question of fact? Further, that if the only teaching of how to perform the invention involves the destruction of human embryos, the provision applies, even if subsequent workings of the invention did not involve such destruction?

The issues raised in the *WARF* decision were ventilated again in a later case, this time before the CJEU (Grand Chamber) in respect of Article 6(2)(c) of the Biotechnology Directive. This was the first time that the CJEU had ventured into the area of patent law.

Brüstle v Greenpeace Case C-34/10 [2012] 1 CMLR 41

The case involved a German patent relating to isolated and purified neural precursor cells, processes for their production from embryonic stem cells, and use of neural precursor cells for the treatment of neural defects. The patent was seeking to resolve the technical problem of producing an almost unlimited supply of isolated and purified precursor cells having neural properties (because it was not possible to have unlimited, ethical use of cerebral tissue from human embryos). The Bundesgerichtshof (German Federal Supreme Court) referred several questions on Article 6(2)(c) of the Biotechnology Directive to the CJEU for a ruling. These concerned: (1) the interpretation of the concept of 'human embryos'; (2) whether 'uses of human embryos for industrial and commercial purposes' covered the use of human embryos for the purposes of scientific research; and (3) whether an invention was unpatentable where the use of human embryos did not form part of the technical teaching of the patent but was a necessary precondition for the application of that teaching.

On the first question, the CJEU held that although the Biotechnology Directive did not define 'human embryo' it was nevertheless 'an autonomous concept of EU' which had to be interpreted uniformly throughout the EU.[287] This was a conclusion supported by the object of the directive, namely to harmonize the rules for legal protection of biotechnological inventions.[288] The Court went on to consider the definition of 'human embryo':

[287] [26].   [288] [27].

30 As regards the meaning to be given to the concept of 'human embryo' set out in art.6(2)(c) of the Directive, it should be pointed out that, although, the definition of human embryo is a very sensitive social issue in many Member States, marked by their multiple traditions and value systems, the Court is not called upon, by the present order for reference, to broach questions of a medical or ethical nature, but must restrict itself to a legal interpretation of the relevant provisions of the Directive (see, to that effect, *Mayr v Bäckerei und Konditorei Gerhard Flöckner OHG* (C-506/06) [2008] E.C.R. I-1017; [2008] 2 C.M.L.R. 27 at [38]).

…

34 The context and aim of the Directive thus show that the EU legislature intended to exclude any possibility of patentability where respect for human dignity could thereby be affected. It follows that the concept of 'human embryo' within the meaning of art.6(2)(c) of the Directive must be understood in a wide sense.

35 Accordingly, any human ovum must, as soon as fertilised, be regarded as a 'human embryo' within the meaning and for the purposes of the application of art.6(2)(c) of the Directive, since that fertilisation is such as to commence the process of development of a human being.

36 That classification must also apply to a non-fertilised human ovum into which the cell nucleus from a mature human cell has been transplanted and a non-fertilised human ovum whose division and further development have been stimulated by parthenogenesis. Although those organisms have not, strictly speaking, been the object of fertilisation, due to the effect of the technique used to obtain them they are, as is apparent from the written observations presented to the Court, capable of commencing the process of development of a human being just as an embryo created by fertilisation of an ovum can do so.

37 As regards stem cells obtained from a human embryo at the blastocyst stage, it is for the referring court to ascertain, in the light of scientific developments, whether they are capable of commencing the process of development of a human being and, therefore, are included within the concept of 'human embryo' within the meaning and for the purposes of the application of art.6(2)(c) of the Directive.

[The CJEU then considered the second question.]

41 With regard, therefore, solely to the determination of whether the exclusion from patentability concerning the use of human embryos for industrial or commercial purposes also covers the use of human embryos for purposes of scientific research or whether scientific research entailing the use of human embryos can access the protection of patent law, clearly the grant of a patent implies, in principle, its industrial or commercial application.

42 That interpretation is supported by recital 14 in the preamble to the Directive. By stating that a patent for invention 'entitles [its holder] to prohibit third parties from exploiting it for industrial and commercial purposes', it indicates that the rights attaching to a patent are, in principle, connected with acts of an industrial or commercial nature.

43 Although the aim of scientific research must be distinguished from industrial or commercial purposes, the use of human embryos for the purposes of research which constitutes the subject-matter of a patent application cannot be separated from the patent itself and the rights attaching to it.

[The CJEU went on to observe at [44]–[45] that recital 42 supported this conclusion, as did the Enlarged Board of Appeal ruling in *WARF*. Thus, the Court concluded:]

46 The answer to the second question is therefore that the exclusion from patentability concerning the use of human embryos for industrial or commercial purposes in art.6(2)(c) of the Directive also covers use for purposes of scientific research, only use for therapeutic or diagnostic purposes which are applied to the human embryo and are useful to it being patentable.

[The CJEU then turned to consider the third and final question.]

49 Accordingly, on the same grounds as those set out in [32]–[35] above, an invention must be regarded as unpatentable, even if the claims of the patent do not concern the use of human embryos, where the implementation of the invention requires the destruction of human embryos. In that case too, the view must be taken that there is use of human embryos within the meaning of art.6(2)(c) of the Directive. The fact that destruction may occur at a stage long before the implementation of the invention, as in the case of the production of embryonic stem cells from a lineage of stem cells the mere production of which implied the destruction of human embryos is, in that regard, irrelevant.

50 Not to include in the scope of the exclusion from patentability set out in art.6(2)(c) of the Directive technical teaching claimed, on the ground that it does not refer to the use, implying their prior destruction, of human embryos would make the provision concerned redundant by allowing a patent applicant to avoid its application by skilful drafting of the claim.

The CJEU again noted that this conclusion was consistent with the Enlarged Board of Appeal ruling in *WARF*. Do you think the Court got the answer to this question right? Here it is important to bear in mind that the exclusion prohibits patents for use of human embryos as being immoral *not* patents which involve inventions that have derived from research on human embryos at some distant point in the past.

After having considered the *WARF* and *Brüstle* decisions how would you describe the respective approaches of the Enlarged Board of Appeal and CJEU to the meaning of 'human embryo'? Do you think the CJEU was being disingenuous in claiming that it was simply answering a legal—as opposed to medical or ethical—question? And was it appropriate for the Court to adopt a broad interpretation of 'human embryo'? This aspect of the Court's ruling has been criticized as follows:

In essence, the ECJ has held that 'human dignity' (and we are not given much instruction on what this concept means because it was hardly discussed) should be extended to entities that in no way resemble human beings, or even fertilised human embryos awaiting implantation into a female uterus. It made a finding of equality between fully formed humans and individual somatic cells in (or from) the human body. This rather bold finding is made all the more bold (and troubling) by the absence of any prefacing value-based or morally cognisant deliberation. The decision evinced no deep understanding of the meaning or purpose of the important socio-moral concept that is human dignity, nor of its scope or deployment in other socio-legal settings which might influence science and commercialisation (and vice versa). It did not apparently take into account how the concept of human dignity referenced in the Biotech Directive might colour its evaluation by supporting the development of treatments from hESC [human embryonic stem cells] to positively aid the human dignity of those suffering from long-term illnesses, and how this should or could be balanced. It did not address itself to any *other* values that might be important to the field (or to their definition), nor did it seem to recognise any of the jurisdictions within Europe that consider the destruction of

> spare embryos and/or embryos specifically created for research to be morally and legally permissible. Finally, it failed to acknowledge the ECtHR jurisprudence on the level of protection warranted to pre-natal entities under human rights law.[289]

Finally, what do you think the impact of the rulings on questions 2 and 3 might be? Will there be a reluctance to invest in research into human embryonic stem cell research in Europe as a result? In considering this question it is important to note that technology has moved on since the Brüstle patent such that pluripotent stem cells no longer have to derive from destroyed embryos and, further, that the absence of patent protection does not preclude research in a particular field.

The CJEU (Grand Chamber) had another opportunity to interpret Article 6(2)(c) of the Biotechnology Directive in its ruling in *International Stem Cell Corp. v Comptroller General of Patents*.[290] In this case, there had been an appeal to the Patents Court from the decision of the hearing officer, whereby two patent applications had been rejected as contrary to morality because they were uses of human embryos for industrial or commercial purposes. The following question was referred by Deputy Judge Henry Carry QC (as he then was): 'Are unfertilised human ova whose division and further development have been stimulated by parthenogenesis, and which, in contrast to fertilised ova, contain only pluripotent cells and are incapable of developing into human beings, included in the term "human embryos" in Article 6(2)(c) of Directive 98/44/EC on the legal protection of biotechnological inventions?'[291] If you re-read paragraphs 35 and 36 of the *Brüstle* decision extracted above, it should become apparent why the answer to this question was not *acte clair*. This lack of clarity is also nicely explained by Advocate General Cruz Villalón in his Opinion:

> 69. How is one to understand the term 'capable of commencing the process of development of a human being' [in *Brüstle*]? At first sight it could seem ambiguous, emphasising either the parallelism of the first developmental steps, i.e. whether an organism engages in a process of cell division and differentiation similar to that of a fertilised ovum, or emphasising the fact that the organism has the inherent capacity of developing into a human being.

Deputy Judge Carr indicated his preliminary view of the referred question, namely, that if non-fertilized human ova, whose division and further development have been stimulated by parthenogenesis,[292] are incapable of leading to a human being then it should not be excluded from patentability as a human embryo. This view, he believed, achieved a balance between the aim of encouraging research in the field of biotechnology and 'the need to

---

[289] S. H. E. Harmon, G. Laurie, and A. Courtney, 'Dignity, plurality and patentability: the unfinished story of *Brüstle v Greenpeace*' [2013] E. L. Rev. 92, 97.

[290] Case C-364/13 [2015] RPC 19.

[291] [2013] EWHC 807 (Ch), [2014] RPC 2.

[292] The judge explained at [16] that 'Parthenogenesis refers to the initiation of embryogenesis without fertilisation by activation of an oocyte in the absence of sperm. Such activation can be induced with a variety of chemical and electrical techniques. The activated oocyte (referred to as a parthenote) contains a single or double set of maternally derived chromosomes but does not contain any paternal DNA' and at [17] 'A parthenote ... cannot develop to term because of the absence of any paternal DNA'.

respect the fundamental principles safeguarding the dignity and integrity of the person'.[293] The Advocate General opined that the Court in *Brüstle* was referring to the inherent capacity of an unfertilized ovum to develop into a human being[294] and the CJEU adopted this view.[295] It ruled that the key question was whether 'human parthenotes, such as those which are the subject of the applications for registration in the case in the main proceedings, have the inherent capacity of developing into a human being' and that this needs to be judged 'in the light of current scientific knowledge'.[296]

FURTHER READING

E. Bonadio, 'Biotech patents and morality after *Brüstle*' [2012] EIPR 433.

S. Burke, 'Interpretive clarification of the concept of "human embryo" in the context of the Biotechnology Directive and the implications for patentability: *Brüstle v Greenpeace eV* (C-34/10)' [2012] EIPR 346.

P. England, 'Where now for stem cell patents?' (2012) 7 JIPLP 738.

S. H. E. Harmon, G. Laurie, and A. Courtney, 'Dignity, plurality and patentability: the unfinished story of *Brüstle v Greenpeace*' (2013) 38 E .L. Rev. 92.

M. Ines Schuster, 'The Court of Justice of the European Union's ruling on the patentability of human embryonic stem-cell-related inventions (case C-34/10)' (2012) 43 IIC 626.

A. Nordberg and T. Minssen, 'A "ray of hope" for European stem cell patents or "out of the smog and into the fog"? An analysis of recent European case law and how it compares to the US' (2016) 47 IIC 138.

S. Sterckx, 'The European Patent Convention and the (non) patentability of human embryonic stem cells: the *WARF* case' [2008] IPQ 478.

The scope of Article 6(2)(d) of the Biotechnology Directive reared its head in the *Onco-mouse* proceedings. Earlier it was discussed how the Examining Division did not deny granting a patent in *Onco-mouse* on the basis of Article 53(a) of the EPC. This was because the benefits to mankind outweighed any risks. However, after the patent was granted 17 parties filed opposition proceedings on various grounds, including that the patent was contrary to Article 53(a) of the EPC. By the time of the decision of the Opposition Division, Article 6(2)(d) of the Biotechnology Directive had been implemented as rule 23(d)(d) of the Implementing Regulations to the EPC. At this point, you should refer back to this provision to see how it differs, if at all, from the utilitarian approach adopted by the Examining Division in *Onco-mouse*.

The Opposition Division in *Onco-mouse* considered both Article 53(a) of the EPC and rule 23(d)(d). In terms of its approach to Article 53(a) of the EPC, it followed the Technical Board of Appeal's decision in *Plant Genetic Systems*.

---

[293] [2013] EWHC 807 (Ch), [2014] RPC 2, [58].
[294] Case C-364/13 [2015] RPC 19, [70]–[73] of the Advocate General's Opinion.
[295] [36]–[38] of the ruling of the Grand Chamber.
[296] [36] and [38] of the ruling of the Grand Chamber.

For the purposes of Article 53(a) EPC, 'ordre public' and morality have to be assessed primarily by looking at laws or regulations which are common to most of the European countries because these laws and regulations are the best indicator about what is considered right or wrong in European society. In so far as such laws or regulations concerning the relevant issue exist, it appears neither necessary nor appropriate to rely on other possible means of assessment such as public opinion polls which were relied upon or requested by several Opponents.

In applying the above principles to the assessment of 'ordre public' and morality under Article 53(a) EPC for an invention which is concerned with test animals in medicinal research, statutory law regulating the use of such animals for testing is highly indicative because it shows whether the exploitation of the invention is de facto prohibited or not. The use of animals for experimental or other scientific purposes is allowed under certain conditions in most if not all of the states being party to the EPC... It is therefore concluded that patenting of those animals of the present invention being useful as test animals in the sense of this Directive complies with the principle requirement of morality because the exploitation of the invention is explicitly allowed.[297]

Insofar as the Opposition Division rejected the use of public opinion polls, is this in line with *Plant Genetic Systems*? To the extent that the Opposition Division also relied upon compliance with European laws and regulations to indicate that the invention was not excluded by Article 53(a) of the EPC, is this also consistent with *Plant Genetic Systems*?

The Opposition Division then considered the relevance of rule 23(d)(d). It held that it superseded the balancing approach in the first *Onco-mouse* decision. Further, that it should be applied as a second round in the assessment of patentability. The Opposition Division also dealt with when the questions of 'suffering' and 'substantial medical benefit to man or animal' would have to be assessed. The assessment of suffering would occur *after* the filing date, whereas substantial medical benefit would be assessed *at* the filing date, without taking into account later evidence as to actual outcome of the exploitation. Further, the question would be whether at the filing date the inventor had a bona fide reason to believe that his invention would have a substantial medical benefit. The Opposition Division concluded:

In the present case, it cannot be denied that the animals of the invention were made for a good cause, namely, progress in cancer research. In view of the new approach the inventor took vis-à-vis the problem of medical cancer testing at the time, there were bona fide reasons at the effective date to expect a substantial medical benefit. Rule 23(d)(d) EPC is therefore no bar to patentability of those animals covered by the patent which were found to be allowable under Article 53(a) EPC above.[298]

The approach of the Opposition Division of applying rule 23(d)(d) as a second round in the assessment of patentability is curious since it is meant to reflect instances when Article 53(a) of the EPC is contravened. Arguably, the better approach is to begin by applying the illustrative list in Article 6(2) of the Biotechnology Directive/rule 23(d) of the EPC, and then to consider Article 53(a) of the EPC.

---

[297] *Onco-mouse* [2003] OJ EPO 473, 502–3.   [298] At 504.

FURTHER READING

D. Thomas and G. A. Richards, 'The importance of the morality exception under the European Patent Convention: the *Onco-mouse* case continues' [2004] EIPR 97.

11.7.7.3 Conclusion

Having considered the scope of Article 53(a) of the EPC and the guidance sought to be provided by Article 6(2) of the Biotechnology Directive, as implemented in rule 28 of the EPC, do you consider that it is appropriate for patent law to exclude inventions the commercial exploitation of which are contrary to *ordre public* or morality? If so, is the EPO approach to this assessment satisfactory? If not, what alternatives could be pursued?

11.8 INDUSTRIAL APPLICATION

For an invention to be patentable it must be capable of industrial application[299] and an invention will be capable or susceptible of industrial application 'if it can be made or used in any kind of industry, including agriculture'.[300] This requirement ensures that patents are not granted for abstract creations and emphasizes that inventions should have a practical or concrete application.[301]

Generally speaking, most inventions will be capable of industrial application. However, in the case of biotechnological inventions this requirement may prove difficult to satisfy where the function of substances (such as a protein or DNA sequence) that have been identified and isolated is unknown. For example, in *Chiron Corp. v Murex Diagnostics Ltd*,[302] the patent in suit claimed an almost infinite number of polypeptides[303] of the Hepatitis C virus, which were useless for any known purpose. The proprietor of the patent sued the defendants, who manufactured and sold kits to test for the Hepatitis C virus, for infringement and the defendants alleged that the patent was invalid on the grounds, inter alia, that the invention was not capable of industrial application. This argument was rejected at first instance, but accepted on appeal. Morritt LJ explained:

> We accept that the polypeptides claimed in the second part of claim 11 can be made, for as will become apparent from the section of our judgment dealing with insufficiency, it is a routine task to see whether one polynucleotide will hybridise with another. But the sections require that the invention can be made or used 'in any kind of industry' so as to be 'capable' or 'susceptible of industrial application'. The connotation is that of trade or manufacture in its widest sense and whether or not for profit. But industry does not exist in that sense to make or use that which is useless for any known purpose.[304]

---

[299] PA 77, s. 1(1)(c); EPC, Art. 52(1).   [300] PA 77, s. 4(1); EPC, Art. 57.
[301] *Max-Planck/BDP1 Phosphatase* T870/04 [2006] EPOR 14, [20].
[302] [1996] RPC 535.
[303] Polypeptides are amino acids joined together by peptide bonds, and amino acids are constituent units of proteins.
[304] *Chiron Corp. v Murex Diagnostics Ltd* [1996] RPC 535, 607.

In a more recent decision, the UK Supreme Court had occasion to consider the requirement of industrial application in Article 57 of the EPC and section 4 of the PA 77.

Human Genome Sciences v Eli Lilly & Co. [2011] UKSC 51, [2012] RPC 6

A European patent (UK) had been granted to Human Genome Sciences (HGS) for a novel human protein called neutrokine-α and its encoding nucleotides, amino acid sequence, and certain antibodies. Neutrokine-α was a previously unknown member of the TNF ligand superfamily, which are proteins which act as inter-cellular mediators in inflammation and other immune responses. A superfamily of proteins is a group of proteins which have shared structural characteristics and which will have similar or common functions but may also include members with unique or different functions. The European patent (UK) specification described the invention as potentially useful for the diagnosis, prevention, or treatment of a wide and disparate variety of disorders of the immune system. However, no data was disclosed to support any of these suggestions. Eli Lilly brought opposition proceedings against the European patent (UK). The Opposition Division held the patent invalid for lack of industrial application under Article 57 of the EPC. This decision was, however, overturned by the Technical Board of Appeal. Meanwhile, Eli Lilly brought parallel proceedings for revocation of the patent in the UK. Before the Board's decision was handed down, Kitchin J at first instance held, inter alia, that the patent lacked industrial application. In light of the common general knowledge, the person skilled in the art would have concluded that the functions of neutrokine-α 'were, at best, a matter of expectation and then at far too high a level of generality to constitute a sound or concrete basis for anything except a research project'.[305] This decision was upheld by the Court of Appeal, despite the contrary conclusion that had been reached by the Technical Board of Appeal. Jacob LJ, delivering the leading judgment in the Court of Appeal held that although enough information was conveyed to make it plausible that neutrokine-α was a member of the TNF ligand superfamily, the biological effects and activities of that family were so poorly understood that any actual use was too speculative and that further investigations would be needed. HGS then appealed to the Supreme Court. The Supreme Court considered that the question for decision was whether Kitchin J and the Court of Appeal had followed the principles laid down by the Board's jurisprudence (which they had ostensibly sought to do in their respective judgments). As we shall see from the following extracts, not only did the Supreme Court show deference to the jurisprudence of the Technical Board of Appeal of the EPO, it also took into account the wider policy context.

Lord Neuberger (with whom Lord Walker, Lord Clarke, and Lord Collins agreed):

97. The requirements of clarity and certainty in this area of law are emphasised by the BIA [an intervening party]. As its submissions also explain, after the discovery of a naturally occurring molecule, particularly a protein and its encoding gene, a large amount of research and development is required before there can be any therapeutic benefit. It is therefore important for bioscience companies to be able to decide at what stage to file for patent protection...

[305] [2008] RPC 29, [234].

98. Similarly, funding for research and development on the potential therapeutic value of a newly discovered and characterised protein or its antibodies is dependent on the funders being reasonably confident that the patent (or patent application) concerned will be reasonably safe from attack (or likely to be granted). It is also relevant that bioscience companies attract investment by reference to their patent portfolios, which gives rise to the same need for certainty.

99. As the BIA suggests, it is worth remembering the purpose of the patent system, namely to provide a temporary monopoly as an incentive to innovation, while at the same time facilitating the early dissemination of any such innovation through an early application for a patent, and its subsequent publication. Although this is true in any sector, it has particular force in the pharmaceutical field, where even many of those who are sceptical about the value of intellectual property rights accept that there is a public interest in, and a commercial need for, patent protection.

100. For obvious reasons, the BIA has not set out to support either of the two parties to this appeal in its trenchant written submissions in these proceedings. However, it does suggest that if we agree with the reasoning of the Court of Appeal there is at least a risk that it will 'make it appreciably harder for patentees to satisfy the requirement of industrial applicability in future cases.' If that were so, it is suggested that this 'would cause UK bioscience companies great difficulty in attracting investment at an early stage in the research and development process'.

101. This consequence is said to arise from the reasoning of the Court of Appeal (and hence of Kitchin J), on the basis that there will normally be a need to conduct tests to provide experimental data to establish to the standard they require that a protein (or its antagonists) have therapeutic use. This in turn is said to lead to two problems. First, such tests will or may involve clinical work, which, as I understand it, would be hard to keep confidential, especially in the age of the internet. Secondly, such tests would often be expensive to run, and, as already mentioned, funding would be hard to obtain for a project of this sort which had no protection in the form of a patent application.

102. Having said this, the BIA accepts that it would be wrong in principle to enable applications for patents to be made when the applicant can reveal no more than 'a vague indication of possible objectives that might or might not be achievable by carrying out further research'. After all, as the BIA also states, the purpose of the patents system is not 'to reserve an unexplored field of research for the applicant nor to give the patentee unjustified control over others who are actively investigating in that area and who might eventually find ways actually to exploit it.'

[After considering these wider policy considerations, Lord Neuberger went on to summarize the principles emerging from the Board of Appeal's jurisprudence.]

107. The essence of the Board's approach in relation to the requirements of Article 57 in relation to biological material may, I think, be summarised in the following points:

The general principles are:

(i) The patent must disclose 'a practical application' and 'some profitable use' for the claimed substance, so that the ensuing monopoly 'can be expected [to lead to] some … commercial benefit' (T 0870/04, para 4, T 0898/05, paras 2 and 4);

(ii) A 'concrete benefit', namely the invention's 'use … in industrial practice' must be 'derivable directly from the description', coupled with common general knowledge (T 0898/05, para 6, T 0604/04, para 15);

(iii) A merely 'speculative' use will not suffice, so 'a vague and speculative indication of possible objectives that might or might not be achievable' will not do (T 0870/04, para 21 and T 0898/05, paras 6 and 21);

(iv) The patent and common general knowledge must enable the skilled person 'to reproduce' or 'exploit' the claimed invention without 'undue burden', or having to carry out 'a research programme' (T 0604/04, para 22, T 0898/05, para 6);

Where a patent discloses a new protein and its encoding gene:

(v) The patent, when taken with common general knowledge, must demonstrate 'a real as opposed to a purely theoretical possibility of exploitation' (T 0604/04, para 15, T 0898/05, paras 6, 22 and 31);

(vi) Merely identifying the structure of a protein, without attributing to it a 'clear role', or 'suggest[ing]' any 'practical use' for it, or suggesting 'a vague and speculative indication of possible objectives that might be achieved', is not enough (T 0870/04, paras 6–7, 11, and 21; T 0898/05, paras 7, 10 and 31);

(vii) The absence of any experimental or wet lab evidence of activity of the claimed protein is not fatal (T 0898/05, paras 21 and 31, T 1452/06, para 5);

(viii) A 'plausible' or 'reasonably credible' claimed use, or an 'educated guess', can suffice (T 1329/04, paras 6 and 11, T 0640/04, para 6, T 0898/05, paras 8, 21, 27 and 31, T 1452/06, para 6, T 1165/06 para 25);

(ix) Such plausibility can be assisted by being confirmed by 'later evidence', although later evidence on its own will not do (T 1329/04, para 12, T 0898/05, para 24, T 1452/06, para 6, T 1165/06, para 25);

(x) The requirements of a plausible and specific possibility of exploitation can be at the biochemical, the cellular or the biological level (T 0898/05, paras 29–30);

Where the protein is said to be a family or superfamily member:

(xi) If all known members have a 'role in the proliferation, differentiation and/or activation of immune cells' or 'function in controlling physiology, development and differentiation of mammalian cells', assigning a similar role to the protein may suffice (T 1329/04, para. 13; T 0898/85, para. 21; T 1165/06, paras 14 and 16, and T 0870/04, para 12);

(xii) So 'the problem to be solved' in such a case can be 'isolating a further member of the [family]' (T 1329/04, para 4, T 0604/04, para 22, T 1165/06, paras 14 and 16);

(xiii) If the disclosure is 'important to the pharmaceutical industry', the disclosure of the sequences of the protein and its gene may suffice, even though its role has not 'been clearly defined' (T 0604/04, para 18);

(xiv) The position may be different if there is evidence, either in the patent or elsewhere, which calls the claimed role or membership of the family into question (T 0898/05 para 24, T 1452/06, para 5);

(xv) The position may also be different if the known members have different activities, although they need not always be 'precisely interchangeable in terms of their biological action', and it may be acceptable if 'most' of them have a common role (T 0870/04, para 12, T 0604/04, para 16, T 0898/05, para 27).

108. As already explained, Kitchin J concluded that (a) the Patent discloses Neutrokine-α as a new member of the TNF ligand superfamily; (b) all known members of the superfamily had pleiotropic effects, (c) there were some features which all those known members

shared, such as expression by T-cells and a role in the regulation of T-cell proliferation and T-cell mediated responses; (d) however, there were other features which some family members had, but others did not; (e) it would be anticipated that the activities of Neutrokine-α 'might relate to T-cells and, in particular, be expressed on T-cells and be a co-stimulant of B-cell production; that it might play a role in the immune response and in the control of tumours and malignant disease; that it might have an effect on B-cell proliferation'; (f) subsequent research has confirmed that was indeed the case; (g) there was a search for new members of the family as they were of interest to the pharmaceutical industry.

109. In those circumstances, it seems to me that, subject to dealing with a number of specific arguments to the contrary, the disclosure of the existence and structure of Neutrokine-α and its gene sequence, and its membership of the TNF ligand superfamily should have been sufficient, taking into account the common general knowledge, to satisfy the requirements of Article 57, in the light of the principles which I have attempted to summarise in para 107 above. Points (viii), (ix) and (x) appear to apply so far as the plausibility of at least some of the claims are concerned, and points (xi), (xii) and (xiii) all appear to be satisfied, given the evidence in relation to the TNF ligand superfamily (and point (xiv) cannot be invoked by Eli Lilly).

110. Like Lord Hope, I derive considerable assistance from the approach set out at T0018/09, para 22, which appears to me to be entirely consistent with the Board's earlier jurisprudence (as summarised in para 107 above), and the application in the ensuing four paragraphs, of that approach to the Board's view of what constituted the centrally relevant facts, which (subject to the arguments considered in the next section of this judgment) do not appear to me to be inconsistent with the findings made by Kitchin J.

111. As Lord Hope says at para 152 below, the Board's conclusion was effectively this, that the disclosure of what was accepted to be a new member of the TNF ligand superfamily (coupled with details of its tissue distribution) satisfied Article 57, because all known members were expressed on T-cells and were able to co-stimulate T-cell proliferation, and therefore Neutrokine-α would be expected to have a similar function. This conclusion was supported, or reinforced, by the statement that Neutrokine-α was expressed in B-cell and T-cell lymphomas (referred to in T 0018/09, para 30), and indeed by the interest and effort in the pharmaceutical industry in finding a new member of the superfamily (as explained by Kitchin J at [2008] RPC 29, paras 72–74).

[Lord Neuberger then went on to dismiss the arguments that were raised in favour of the conclusions reached by Kitchin J and the Court of Appeal.]

The arguments in support of the conclusion reached below

112. The first argument to the contrary is based on the fact that the members of the TNF ligand superfamily were known to have pleiotropic effects. On behalf of Eli Lilly, Mr Waugh QC therefore relies on point (xv) i.e. that the claim to a new member of a superfamily is not good enough because the known members of the family have different activities. In my opinion, that point does not apply in a case where all known members of the superfamily also manifest to a significant degree common activities which are, of themselves, enough to bring the patent within the ambit of points (xi), (xii) and (xiii).

113. Given that the fact that all known family members have sufficient common features to satisfy those points can justify a patent for a new member, it would seem somewhat bizarre if the fact that they had additional, but differing, qualities, should preclude the grant of such a patent. The disclosure of a new member would not only be of greater potential value

than if the additional qualities did not exist, but the reason for the grant of the patent is the perceived value of a new member because of the common features of all known members, a feature which is unaffected by the additional qualities.

...

116. A second argument raised against validity is the unsatisfactory drafting of the Patent (mentioned by the Court of Appeal at [2010] RPC 14, para 148). If the Judge had found that the drafting of the specification of the Patent was so confusing and potentially misleading that the skilled reader would have been put off the scent in relation to what would otherwise have been appreciated from common general knowledge and reading the literature as to the potential and plausible uses to which the disclosure could be put, that may well have been a problem for HGS's case. However, although the Judge was (in my view, rightly) critical about the drafting of the specification, he did not anywhere in his full and careful judgment say, or even suggest, that its wide-ranging prolix contents would have actually diverted the notional addressees, the appropriately skilled persons, from what they would otherwise have understood the Patent to be revealing, in the light of what was appreciated about the properties of the known members of the TNF ligand superfamily. Indeed, Mr Thorley QC, for HGS, identified passages in the evidence of Professor Saklatvala, which would have made such a finding difficult to justify.

117. Mr Waugh's submission that the extravagant and wordy claims of the specification should count against HGS as a matter of policy has some attraction. However, I refer again to the Board's comments at T 0018/09, para 27, cited in para 6 above. The drafting of a patent is a ticklish business, no doubt particularly in some types of case, of which biological patents may well be an example, not least because it is a fast developing field, with substantial commercial and scientific pressures.

118. In the end, the question is whether the drafting of the Patent would actually have diverted the notional addressees from what their search of the literature, coupled with common general knowledge, would otherwise have led them to understand represented the teaching of the Patent. The Board held that it would not have done so—see at T 0018/09, para 26. Given (a) the fact that the Judge made no express finding that there would have been such a diversion, (b) the evidence of Professor Saklatvala suggested that there would have been no such diversion, and (c) the way in which the Judge expressed himself at [2008] RPC 29, paras 232 and 234 (quoted respectively at paras 70 and 75 above), I would infer that Kitchin J did not think differently. That is unsurprising, given the fact that there was fairly intense interest in the TNF ligand superfamily as the Judge held at [2008] RPC 29, paras 72 and 74 (quoted at para 26 above), and the fact that there is nothing in the description which positively points away from what was known about the family.

119. A third argument is based on the Judge's remarks at [2008] RPC 29, paras 176 and 234, that the disclosure in the Patent as to the uses of Neutrokine-α, even when taken together with common general knowledge, was no more than 'speculative' and did not give rise to an 'immediate concrete benefit'—i.e. invoking on points (ii) and (iii). This argument (which was also relied on by the Court of Appeal—see at [2010] RPC 14, para 132) proceeds on the implicit assumption that the disclosure of the Patent as summarised in para 108 above is not sufficient in itself to satisfy the requirements of Article 57.

120. However, if, as I consider, the effect of the Board's jurisprudence is that the sort of disclosure summarised in para 108 above does justify patentability, then the fact that the 'plausible' predictions for the use of the invention could also be said to involve speculation takes matters no further. If the known activities of the TNF ligand superfamily were enough to justify

patentability for the disclosure of a novel molecule (and its encoding gene) which was plausibly identified as a member of that family, the fact that further work was required to see whether the disclosure actually had therapeutic benefits does not, at least without more, undermine the validity of a patent. In other words, in agreement with Lord Hope, I think that the approach of the Board in this case, in particular at T 0018/09, paras 22–30, appears more in line with the previous EPO jurisprudence than the approach of Kitchin J and the Court of Appeal.

121. The Court of Appeal made much of the Board's statement that a patent should yield an 'immediate concrete benefit' (see at [2010] RPC 14, paras 146, 149, 155 and 156). I certainly accept that, in some cases, different tribunals can and will legitimately come to different views as to whether a particular claimed invention can satisfy the requirement of providing an 'immediate concrete benefit'. However, I am not persuaded that such an argument is open to Eli Lilly in this case. In my view, the Court of Appeal's approach, like that of the Judge, was implicitly predicated on the mistaken basis that it was not enough for the Patent to satisfy the requirements of points (xi) to (xiii).

122. Further, at least in the context of the present case, I do not consider that the Courts below gave proper weight to points (viii), (ix) and (x). In particular, in my judgment, the Court of Appeal did not approach the concept of plausibility consistently with the jurisprudence of the Board. That is well demonstrated by Jacob LJ's observation at [2010] RPC 14, para 112, that '[i]t is not good enough to say this protein or any antibody to it probably has a pharmaceutical use. Such a statement is indeed plausible, but is of no real practical use. You are left to find out what that use is.' If the statement 'is indeed plausible', then, in the absence of any reason to the contrary, it at least *prima facie* satisfies the requirements of Article 57 according to the Board.

123. I appreciate that the dividing line between 'plausibility' and 'educated guess', as against 'speculation', just like the contrast between 'a real as opposed to a purely theoretical possibility of exploitation', can be difficult to discern in terms of language and application, and is a point on which tribunals could often differ. (I might add that the notion that the dividing line is not very satisfactory is illustrated by the fact that, at one point in his evidence, Professor Saklatvala effectively equiparated speculation with an educated guess.) However, as a result of the decisions discussed above, the Board's approach to patents such as that in this case is, I believe, tolerably clear.

124. I also consider that the Judge did not give sufficient weight to point (x), in that he concentrated on the absence of firm evidence of specific therapeutic roles, as opposed to the other roles of Neutrokine-α. This is well demonstrated by his reliance in what is perhaps the crucial paragraph of his judgment, [2008] RPC 29, para 234, on the fact that '[n]either the Patent nor the common general knowledge identified any disease or condition which Neutrokine-α could be used to diagnose or treat'. He did not, in this context, take into account the roles at other levels which could be attributed to Neutrokine-α as a result of its membership of the TNF ligand superfamily and their known activities. (The same point may be made about Jacob LJ's judgment at [2010] RPC 14, paras 112 and 119, quoted by Lord Hope at para 150 below).

125. Eli Lilly also relied on the Judge's finding at [2008] RPC 29, para 234 that the precise uses to which Neutrokine-α could be put would, on the basis of the disclosure in the Patent, involve 'a research project', effectively raising point (iv). Although the Court of Appeal also relied on this point (see at [2010] RPC 14, para 149), it does not appear to me to be maintainable, essentially for the reason given in the immediately preceding paragraphs of this judgment.

126. I draw support for this conclusion from the Board's third reason for rejecting a similar argument raised by Eli Lilly in the EPO, namely that 'the skilled person would not have been able to reproduce [the activities of Neutrokine-α as described in the Patent] without the undue burden of undertaking a research programme'. The Board said that the disclosure of the Patent 'may represent a valid basis for a possible industrial application. In particular, the inhibition of co- stimulation and/or proliferation of lymphocytes might be *prima facie* of relevance for certain immune diseases'—in T0018/09, para 29. If a patent advances an appropriately plausible function for the claimed protein, then the question of undue burden has to be considered in relation to the making of the protein, as the Board's observation at T 0604/04, para 22 that 'the patent specification provides adequate experimental instructions for the skilled person to be able to reproduce without undue burden the [claimed] polypeptides' shows.

...

129. Accordingly, I would allow HGS's appeal on the issue as to whether the Patent satisfied the requirements of Article 57, and hold that it does. As explained, I have reached this conclusion by applying my understanding of the jurisprudence of the Board to the facts found by Kitchin J. However, particularly as I have stated in para 105 above that there is good sense in the contrary conclusion reached by the Judge and the Court of Appeal, it is right to emphasise that there is also good sense in the result which, at least in my view, is mandated by the Board's approach to the law in this field.

130. Just as it would be undesirable to let someone have a monopoly over a particular biological molecule too early, because it risks closing down competition, so it would be wrong to set the hurdle for patentability too high, essentially for the reasons advanced by the BIA and discussed in paras 97–100 above. Quite where the line should be drawn in the light of commercial reality and the public interest can no doubt be a matter of different opinions and debate. However, in this case, apart from the fairly general submissions of the parties and of the BIA, we have not had any submissions on such wider policy considerations.

Lord Hope delivered a concurring judgment with which Lord Walker, Lord Clarke, and Lord Collins agreed. Lord Hope noted that Jacob LJ had attributed the difference in conclusions reached by the Court of Appeal and Technical Board of Appeal to the fact that the latter was working on different evidence and was using different procedure.[306] However, he went on to find that in fact Kitchin J and the Court of Appeal had applied a different test to that applied by the Technical Board of Appeal.

150. In para 102 of his judgment in the Court of Appeal, however, having reviewed the EPO case law, Jacob LJ said:

It is clear from these authorities that discovering a nucleotide sequence encoding for a human protein and being able to show that the protein concerned has some common homology with known proteins (ie is a member of a family) may satisfy article 57. But whether it does or not is case dependent and in particular depends upon how well established the functions of the other members of the family are. To say, 'my new protein is similar to a known family of proteins' is not all that helpful in indicating a possible use if the function of that family is itself poorly understood at best.

[306] [145].

In para 112, having said that to be 'plausible' a statement must be sufficiently precise, he added:

> It is not good enough to say this protein or any antibody to it probably has a pharmaceutical use. Such a statement is indeed plausible, but is of no real practical use. You are left to find out what that use is.

In para 119, having summarised the findings and conclusions of Kitchin J, he said:

> So the Judge addressed the crucial question: is it enough to make the invention 'susceptible of industrial application' to tell the skilled reader that Neutrokine-α is 'structurally similar to TNF and related cytokines and is believed to have similar biological effects and activities'? That depends on what was known about the biological effects and activities of the known members of the superfamily. Each of the postulated uses of Neutrokine-α or its antagonists was possible in the sense that one could not rule that out as a matter of science based on what was known about other superfamily members. So in one sense each was 'plausible', even though all of them collectively were not and indeed some contradicted others so both could not be true. But that is miles away from being able to say that any particular use was plausible in the sense of being taken, by the reader, to be reasonably so. In reality one was faced with a research programme to see which, if any, of the possible uses of the Neutrokine-α or its antagonists was real.

151. I think that there are indications in these passages that the standard which Jacob LJ was setting for susceptibility to industrial application was a more exacting one than that used by the TBA. He appears to have been looking for a description that showed that a particular use for the product had actually been demonstrated rather than that the product had plausibly been shown to be 'usable'.

152. In para 23 of the reasons for its decision in the present case the TBA noted that, as known in the art and acknowledged in the Patent, a feature common to all members of this particular superfamily without exception was the expression on activated T cells and the ability to co-stimulate T cell proliferation. It followed, in view of the assignment of Neutrokine-α to the family, that the skilled person would expect it to display that common feature. Asking itself whether there was anything in the patent specification which contradicted that expectation, the Board found that the technical data in the patent specification, far from contradicting the ability of Neutrokine-α to co-stimulate T-cell proliferation, actually supported it. That information could not be taken as a mere theoretical or purely hypothetical assumption.

153. In para 26 the TBA said that a skilled person, when reading the patent specification, would distinguish the positive technical information from the contradictory and broad statements to which Eli Lilly had drawn its attention:

> This is because the skilled person realises that the description of the structure of Neutrokine-α, its structural assignment of the family of TNF ligands, and the reports about its tissue distribution and activity on leucocytes, are the first essential steps at the onset of research work on the newly found TNF ligand superfamily member. In view of the known broad range of possible activities of such a molecule, the skilled person is aware of the fact that the full elucidation of all properties requires further investigations which will gradually reveal them. In this context, the skilled person regards the long listing of possible actions of Neutrokine-α and of medical conditions in which it might take part as the enumeration or generalisation of the properties of the members of the TNF ligand superfamily. This is seen as the frame in which the newly found molecule has to be placed as one could prima facie have a reasonable expectation that most of them could in fact be present.

154. This is in sharp contrast to Jacob LJ's comment in [2010] RPC 14, para 145 that the Patent, even in relation to T-cell activity, was just too speculative to provide anything of practical value other than information upon which a research programme could be based. Referring to the first sentence of the passage which I have just quoted, he then said that 'a first step at the onset of research work' was hardly enough to provide 'an immediate and concrete benefit': para 149. The phrase 'immediate concrete benefit'—the 'and' which Jacob LJ inserted into this phrase is his own word—comes from para 6 of the TBA's reasons for its decision in *ZymoGenetics*; see also para 21 of its reasons in the present case. Here again there is an indication that Jacob LJ was applying a different test from that applied by the TBA. The immediate concrete benefit that he was looking for was something more than that there was a reasonable expectation that the molecule would be usable for the purposes of research work.

155. In para 27 the TBA said that, despite its long list of conditions and activities, the description of the Patent delivered sufficient technical information (namely the effect of Neutrokine-α on T-cells and the tissue distribution of Neutrokine-α mRNA) to satisfy the requirement of disclosing the nature and purpose of the invention and how it could be used in industrial practice. In para 29 it rejected Eli Lilly's arguments that, in view of the technical difficulties involved in measuring the co-stimulation of T cells by Neutrokine-α and the absence of any detailed experimental information on the activities of Neutrokine-α listed in the Patent, the skilled person would not have been able to reproduce them without the undue burden of undertaking a research programme and that no industrial application could be directly derived from a mere co-stimulation of T-cells. It pointed out that there was a convincing body of post-published evidence showing that, using standard assays, Neutrokine-α activity was indeed present on T-cells, that the reference in the Patent to the presence of Neutrokine-α activity in lymphocytes would prompt the skilled person to look for that activity in all types of lymphocytes, including B lymphocytes as well as T lymphocytes. Contrary to Eli Lilly's view, it held that these activities might represent a valid basis for a possible industrial application. The industrial application that it had in mind was the use of the molecule for research, which it must be taken to have regarded in itself as an industrial activity.

...

165. For these reasons I cannot agree with Jacob LJ that the differences between the conclusions reached by the judge and the TBA are attributable to the fact the Board was working on different evidence and was using a different procedure. It seems to me that they are attributable to differences of principle about the amount of information that was needed to show that the invention was susceptible of industrial application. The test to be applied to determine this issue is a question of law, not one of fact. As Jacob LJ observed, our practice is to follow any principle of law clearly laid down by the TBA: [2010] RPC 14, para 39.

166. It is a strong thing to disagree with the concurrent findings of judges with such experience in this field. But our decision in this appeal does not depend on a re-evaluation of the evidence. It turns on the principle of law which I find clearly set out by the TBA in the passages to which I have referred. In my opinion that principle leads inevitably to the conclusion that HGS's appeal on the article 57 issue must be allowed and the decision of Kitchin J that the claimed inventions were not susceptible of industrial application at the date of the Patent set aside.

In your view, was the Supreme Court correct to conclude that Kitchin J and the Court of Appeal had applied the wrong standard of test for industrial applicability? Did the Supreme

Court pay enough attention to the fact that EPO jurisprudence talks about industrial application not being vague and resulting in an 'immediate and concrete benefit'? According to the Supreme Court, it seems sufficient that 'there was a reasonable expectation that the molecule would be usable for the purposes of research work' (Lord Hope, above). In other words, it is enough if a protein is shown plausibly to be a useful focus for further research. Does the Supreme Court's approach consider how this test of industrial application might advantage some players over others in the biotechnology field? Odell-West is critical of the Supreme Court's decision in this respect:

> The patent system must be seen to operate in the public interest. Whether it serves public policy to support the patenting of early-stage research in the biosciences or whether health care research will be 'stultified' merits sober consideration. That their Lordships did not give any weight when articulating policy to the possible upstream (and downstream) effects of patenting at an early stage was regrettable, this being an issue that has dominated the bioscience patent literature since Heller and Eisenberg's anticommons hypothesis was published in 1998. If it is correct that an anticommons tragedy in bioscience does in fact exist, the policy promoting early-research patenting promulgated by the Supreme Court is likely to exacerbate it. The early-research patent policy has been achieved by eroding the requirement to show industrial applicability to such an extent that patents may be granted over genes and proteins that offer little more than sequence data with an educated guess about function (or indeed any practical use at all). Widespread uncertainty across Europe about patent validity generally in the sector will increasingly shift the remit of granting offices to maintain the quality of patents on to industry itself to regulate through litigation. Young, innovative firms, strategically important to the United Kingdom's innovation performance, are least capable of absorbing such costs.[307]

FURTHER READING

T. Minssen and D. Nilsson, 'The industrial application requirement for biotech inventions in light of recent EPO & US case law: a plausible approach or a mere "hunting license"?' [2012] EIPR 689.

A. Odell-West, 'Has the commodore steered the fleet onto the rocks? Biotechnology and the requirement for industrial applicability' [2013] IPQ 279.

A. Sharples, 'Industrial applicability, patents and the Supreme Court: *Human Genome Sciences Inc v Eli Lilly and Co*' [2012] EIPR 284.

N.-L. Wee Loon, 'Patenting of genes: a closer look at the concepts of utility and industrial applicability' (2002) 33 IIC 393.

11.9 METHODS OF MEDICAL AND VETERINARY TREATMENT

Until recently, methods of medical and veterinary treatment were regarded as unpatentable on the ground that they were not associated with trade or manufacture and thus were not

---

[307] A. Odell-West, 'Has the commodore steered the fleet onto the rocks? Biotechnology and the requirement for industrial applicability' [2013] IPQ 279, 302.

capable of industrial application.[308] Subsequently, however, this was thought to be a legal fiction which masked the real policy and public-health considerations underpinning the exclusion.[309] Thus, the EPC 2000 retained the exclusion for methods of medical and veterinary treatment, but as a stand-alone provision in Article 53 of the EPC (deleting Article 52(4)). Section 4(2) of the PA 77 was deleted and replaced by section 4A, which provides:

(1) A patent shall not be granted for the invention of—

    (a) a method of treatment of the human or animal body by surgery or therapy, or

    (b) a method of diagnosis practised on the human or animal body.

(2) Subsection (1) above does not apply to an invention consisting of a substance or composition for use in any such method.

The public-policy justification for this exclusion has been described by the Enlarged Board of Appeal as allowing freedom to medical and veterinary practitioners to 'take the actions they consider suited to diagnose illnesses by means of investigative methods' without being inhibited by patents or the fear of infringing them.[310] Not everyone, however, agrees with this rationale, as the following extract indicates.

S. Bostyn, 'No cure without pay? Referral to the Enlarged Board of Appeal concerning the patentability of diagnostic methods' [2005] EIPR 412 at 415

The rationale of Art. 52(4) EPC, as it has been expressed by the Technical Boards of Appeal, and also in national case law, has been that medical personnel should not be hindered in performing their medical (health care) activities. It can be doubted whether this rationale is still of value today. All features of medicine are patentable, except for medical treatment and diagnostic methods. It is difficult to understand why a method of diagnosis on the human body should be excluded from patentability, while the products used therein, and the products used for the treatment are perfectly patentable. It cannot be readily seen why, from an ethical point of view, there would be more reasons to deny patent protection for medical treatment methods than there would be for patenting medical products and medicaments. The latter categories are not contested, however. It seems that relics from the past, from times when the judiciary and the legislator had difficulties in dealing with these types of problems, have succeeded in surviving the stone-ages of patent law. Maybe it is time to lay this ill-conceived exclusion to rest. The consequences of this exclusion on doubtful grounds are to be felt in all fields of medical technology, including treatment and diagnosis. The consequences are probably more severe for medical treatment methods than they are for diagnostic methods.

Other commentators, however, fiercely defend the method of medical and veterinary treatment exclusion. For example, Alexandra Sims[311] argues that patents for methods of treatment

---

[308] See previous PA 77, s. 4(2), and EPC, Art. 52(4) (now repealed).

[309] *Diagnostic Methods* G1/04 [2006] EPOR 15, [7]; *Medi-Physics/Treatment by surgery* G1/07 [2010] EPOR 25, [34].

[310] *Diagnostic Methods* G1/04 [2006] EPOR 15, [7]; *Medi-Physics/Treatment by surgery* G1/07 [2010] EPOR 25, [36].

[311] A. Sims, 'The case against patenting methods of medical treatment' [2007] EIPR 43.

of this kind are unnecessary because, unlike pharmaceuticals, they do not involve the same vast expenditure to develop. Further, she doubts whether patenting such methods would lead to disclosure of important technical knowledge because there is no requirement in patent law to disclose the best method for performing the invention and medical practitioners already operate within a culture of sharing. Sims is also sceptical that patents would encourage more innovation with respect to methods of medical treatment since there are other types of incentives within the medical community, such as recognition, promotion, prizes, and publication in prestigious journals. In fact, she suggests that patents might stifle innovation in this field, rather than promote it, as well as increase the cost to society of providing medical care and, thus, in turn reduce patient access to such care.

Of the two positions described above which would you favour? In considering this issue, it is worth noting that newly discovered pharmaceutical substances are patentable and, as we shall see at 12.1, known pharmaceutical substances that are used for different therapeutic purposes along with known substances that feature a novel dosage regime. Given the scope of protection that is available to pharmaceuticals, one might query whether it is justified to exclude methods of medical and veterinary treatment from patentability. One might also ask whether, in light of the narrow construction of this exclusion and the generous approach to novelty for pharmaceutical substances, this exclusion still serves a useful purpose. Finally, we might consider whether an exclusion from patentability is the best means of achieving the aim of enabling medical and veterinary practitioners freedom to practise. Instead, as Professor Bently has suggested,[312] European and UK patent law could allow patents for methods of medical and veterinary treatment but create an exception to infringement in favour of medical professionals in the performance of their duties, as exists in the US.[313]

We turn now to consider the ways in which the exclusions for methods of medical and veterinary treatment have been interpreted.

11.9.1 TREATMENT BY SURGERY

'Treatment... by surgery' does not include methods that ultimately lead to the death of the living beings under treatment. For example, in *Shell/Blood Flow*[314] the application related to a method for measuring blood-flow to a specific tissue in an animal; however, it ultimately led to the animal being killed. On this basis, the Technical Board of Appeal set aside the

---

[312] L. Bently, 'Exclusions from patentability and exceptions to patentees' rights: taking exceptions seriously' (2011) 64 Current Legal Problems 315.

[313] See US Patent Act, s. 287(c)(1): 'With respect to a medical practitioner's performance of a medical activity that constitutes an infringement under section 271 (a) or (b) of this title, [no remedy should be available] against the medical practitioner or against a related health care entity with respect to such medical activity. (2) ... (A) the term "medical activity" means the performance of a medical or surgical procedure on a body, but shall not include (i) the use of a patented machine, manufacture, or composition of matter in violation of such patent, (ii) the practice of a patented use of a composition of matter in violation of such patent, or (iii) the practice of a process in violation of a biotechnology patent. (B) the term "medical practitioner" means any natural person who is licensed by a State to provide the medical activity described in subsection (c) (1) or who is acting under the direction of such person in the performance of the medical activity. (C) the term "related health care entity" shall mean an entity with which a medical practitioner has a professional affiliation under which the medical practitioner performs the medical activity, including but not limited to a nursing home, hospital, university, medical school, health maintenance organization, group medical practice, or a medical clinic.'

[314] T182/90 [1994] EPOR 320.

Examining Division's decision that this was excluded as a method of surgical treatment. It commented that 'methods consciously ending in the laboratory animal's death ... are not in their nature methods of surgical treatment, even if some of the steps they involve may have a surgical character'.[315]

The scope of this exclusion has been ruled upon by the Enlarged Board of Appeal in the following decision.

Medi-Physics/Treatment by surgery G1/07 [2010] EPOR 25

The patent involved a method for magnetic resonance imaging (MRI) the pulmonary and/or cardiac vasculature using dissolved-phase polarized Xe. The imaging method could precede surgery or a drug therapy for treating pulmonary or cardiac vasculature problems. One of the steps of the method was delivering the polarized Xe, either by inhalation or via an injection into the heart. The referring decision from the Technical Board of Appeal held that in light of *Diagnostic Methods*[316] (discussed at 11.9.3) this was not an excluded diagnostic method because the information gathered related to the examination phase only. Further, the TBA was unsure whether the method could be regarded as a treatment by surgery because, although an injection of polarized Xe into the heart represented a substantial physical intervention on the body which entailed health risks and required professional medical expertise, it was not itself aimed at maintaining life and health. Finally, the Board noted that the definitions of surgery differed in the decisions of the Boards of Appeal, and its clarification was an important point of law. As a result, several questions were in fact referred to the Enlarged Board of Appeal for a ruling. Of particular importance was the first question, namely:

> 1. Is a claimed imaging method for a diagnostic purpose (examination phase within the meaning given in G1/04 *Diagnostic methods* [2006] E.P.O.R. 15), which comprises or encompasses a step consisting in a physical intervention practised on the human or animal body (in the present case, an injection of a contrast agent into the heart), to be excluded from patent protection as a 'method for treatment of the human or animal body by surgery' pursuant to art.52(4) EPC if such step does not per se aim at maintaining life and health?

In addressing this question, the Enlarged Board of Appeal began by noting that there was no general principle of narrow interpretation of exclusions from patentability.[317] Further, the Board concluded that multi-step methods which *comprise or encompass* a therapeutic or surgical step are excluded because: (1) unlike Article 52(4) there is no reference to 'as such'; (2) support could be drawn for this conclusion from the Enlarged Board of Appeal's decision in G1/04; and (3) this interpretation gave full effect to the purpose of the exclusion, namely, to allow medical practitioners the freedom to use the best available treatments to the benefit of their patients.[318] The Board went on to consider if the exclusion for treatments by surgery was limited to surgery for a therapeutic purpose only. It held that it was not so limited:

---

[315] *Shell/Blood Flow*, 324.   [316] G1/04 [2006] EPOR 15.   [317] [94].   [318] [104]–[107].

147 Summarising the above, neither the legal history nor the object and purpose (*ratio legis*) of the exclusions from patentability in art.53(c) EPC justify a limitation of the term 'treatment by surgery' to curative surgery, contrary to what the ordinary meaning of the word 'surgery' implies and contrary to the fact that art.53(c) EPC defines three separate alternative exclusions thereby suggesting that these are not merely identical in scope. Hence, the Enlarged Board concludes that the meaning of the term 'treatment by surgery' is not to be interpreted as being confined to surgical methods pursuing a therapeutic purpose.

[The Board then sought to examine in depth which interventions would be caught as 'treatment by surgery'. It began by considering whether a medical practitioner necessarily had to be involved.]

3.4 The scope of interventions being 'treatment by surgery'

3.4.1 Necessary involvement of a practitioner?

148 This question has been comprehensively dealt with and answered by the Enlarged Board in opinion G1/04, point 6.3 of the reasons, and the Enlarged Board will not go into detail again in the present context. Whether or not a method is excluded from patentability under art.53(c) EPC cannot depend on the person carrying it out. The findings of the Enlarged Board in point 6.3 of the Reasons relate to diagnostic methods, but they quite generally deal with the exclusion from patentability under art.52(4) EPC 1973 and are thus equally valid with respect to the other exclusion conditions contained in today's art.53(c) EPC. That the drafters of the EPC, historically, have discussed the problem they perceived in relation to the medical and veterinary practitioners cannot be a reason for not adapting the application of the exclusion to the changing reality in the field of the medical and veterinary profession caused by the technological advances altering how and by whom health care is administered, as the Enlarged Board has explained in its opinion G1/04 in point 6.3 of the Reasons.

Do you agree with the Board's view that the exclusion for treatment by surgery on the human or animal body cannot be determined according to the character of the person carrying out the intervention?

The Board next considered the construction that had been given to 'treatment by surgery' in some Technical Board of Appeal decisions. These decisions found that the exclusion covered 'any non-insignificant intervention performed on the structure of an organism by conservative (closed, non-invasive) procedures such as repositioning or by operative (invasive) procedures using instruments including endoscopy, puncture, injection, excision, opening of the bodily cavities and catheterization'.[319] As we will see from the following passages, the Board held that this broad construction was not justified.

Is such broad construction still justified?

150 This broad view of what should be regarded as surgical activities excluded from patentability has in the Enlarged Board's view rightly been criticised by the appellant as being or having become overly broad when considering today's technical reality. The advances in safety and the now routine character of certain, albeit invasive techniques, at least when

---

[319] [149].

performed on uncritical parts of the body, have entailed that many such techniques are nowadays generally carried out in a non-medical, commercial environment like in cosmetic salons and in beauty parlours and it appears, hence, hardly still justified to exclude such methods from patentability. This applies as a rule to treatments such as tattooing, piercing, hair removal by optical radiation, micro abrasion of the skin.

151 If so, that can also not be ignored when it comes to the application of routine interventions in the medical field.

152 Today, numerous and advanced technologies do exist in the medical field concerning the use of devices which in order to operate must in some way be connected to the patient. Methods for retrieving patient data useful for diagnosis may require administering an agent to the patient, potentially by an invasive step like by injection, in order to yield results—or at least they yield better results when using such a step.

153 Considering this technical reality, excluding from patentability also such methods as make use of in principle safe routine techniques, even when of invasive nature, appears to go beyond the purpose of the exclusion of treatments by surgery from patentability in the interest of public health.

154 Insofar as the definition given in opinion G1/04 that ' "any physical intervention" on the human or animal body...' is a method of surgery within the meaning of art.52(4) EPC 1973 (point 6.2.1 of the Reasons) appears too broad.

Elements of a narrower understanding

155 Hence, a narrower understanding of what constitutes by its nature a 'treatment by surgery' within the meaning of art.53(c) EPC is required. It must allow the purpose of the exclusion to be effective but it must also not go beyond it. The exclusion serves the purpose of, in the interests of public health and of patients, specifically freeing the medical profession from constraints which would be imposed on them by patents granted on methods for surgical or therapeutic treatment, thus any definition of the term 'treatment by surgery' must cover the kind of interventions which represent the core of the medical profession's activities, i.e. the kind of interventions for which their members are specifically trained and for which they assume a particular responsibility. These are the physical interventions on the body which require professional medical skills to be carried out and which involve health risks even when carried out with the required medical professional care and expertise. It is in this area that the *ratio legis* of the provision to free the medical profession from constraints by patents comes into play. Such a narrower understanding rules out from the scope of the application of the exclusion clause uncritical methods involving only a minor intervention and no substantial health risks, when carried out with the required care and skill, while still adequately protecting the medical profession.

...

Scope of definition given in this decision

157 Clearly, it is not possible for the Enlarged Board in the context of the present referral when trying to redefine the meaning of the term 'treatment by surgery' to give a definition which would, once and for all, also delimit the exact boundaries of such a new concept with respect to the whole comprehensive body of technical situations which might be concerned by it.

158 Assuming such a task would go far beyond the scope of present referred question 1. The set of circumstances underlying the referral has been determined in the referring decision as encompassing an invasive step representing a substantial physical intervention on the body which requires professional medical expertise to be carried out and which entails a health risk. Hence, what the Enlarged Board must do in answering question 1, is to define the scope of the term 'treatment by surgery' to an extent which allows the referring Board to decide whether or not the step claimed in the application-in-suit falls under that definition.

159 This will also indicate the direction in which further practice and jurisprudence should develop. The required new direction is that the exclusion from patentability should not be applied to methods in respect of which the interests of public health, of protection of patients and as a counterpart to that of the freedom of the medical profession to apply the treatment of choice to their patients does not call for their exclusion from patentability.

160 The first instance bodies and the boards of appeal are much better suited to define the boundaries of a more narrowly construed concept of 'treatment by surgery' in situations other than the one underlying the present referral, based on the technical reality of the individual cases under consideration.

161 This includes that the required medical expertise and the health risk involved may not be the only criteria which may be used to determine that a claimed method actually is a 'treatment by surgery' within the meaning of art.53(c) EPC. The referring decision and the president have mentioned the degree of invasiveness or the complexity of the operation performed but these do not appear to be issues in the case underlying the referring decision. At least, the referring decision contains no statement of fact establishing the presence of such circumstances which the Enlarged Board would have to consider when determining the scope of its answer given. Although it appears likely that interventions involving a high degree of complexity and/or a high degree of invasiveness would normally also be such as to require professional medical expertise and entail health risks even when carried out with the required care and expertise, the Enlarged Board does not wish to rule out from the outset that, depending on the circumstances of the individual case under consideration, other criteria could not also determine that a physical intervention on the human or animal body is a 'treatment by surgery' within the meaning of art.53(c) EPC.

Variability of concept of 'surgery' in the medical sense

162 Another reason why the Enlarged Board cannot, in the context of the present referral, give an authoritative once and for all definition of what the term 'treatment by surgery' may comprise is that in the ever changing technical and medical reality the term 'surgery' itself does not appear to have a once and for all fixed meaning, either. There appears to be no general common concept for the acts which are commonly regarded as surgical in the medical sense. Rather, it appears that what is to be understood by 'surgery' in the medical sense is to a large extent a matter of convention. Thus, in order to be surgical, it is not necessary that the intervention be invasive or that tissues be penetrated (T5/04, unreported, of January 17, 2006, point 2 of the Reasons). Repositioning body limbs or manipulating a body part is traditionally considered surgical. The mere catheterisation or the insertion of components of a device into the body is already regarded as prohibited as being a surgical step even if it does not require the penetration of tissues (T5/04). All this implies that the scope of what is surgery may change with time and with new technical developments emerging, as was already acknowledged in decision T182/90, point 2.4 of the Reasons.

Do you agree with the Enlarged Board of Appeal's reasons for rejecting a broad construction of the treatment by surgery exclusion? In stipulating a narrower construction for the exclusion, the Enlarged Board of Appeal avoided a definitive interpretation. This was for several reasons: (1) because it would have gone beyond the scope of the referral that had been made to it; (2) it was impossible to stipulate a comprehensive definition for the vast number of methods that potentially involved surgical steps; (3) first instance bodies would be better placed to develop the boundaries of a more narrowly construed concept of 'treatment by surgery'; and (4) understandings of surgery are variable and may change over time. The overarching consideration for subsequent interpretation of the exclusion would be whether or not it was consistent with the rationale of the provision. Do you agree that this was the right approach for the Enlarged Board of Appeal to take? Limiting itself to the particular referral (and its facts), the Enlarged Board of Appeal concluded that the particular method of treatment, which concerned an invasive step (an injection into the heart) and represented a substantial physical intervention on the body which required professional medical expertise and which entailed a substantial health risk even when carried out by these professionals, was excluded from patentability as a method of treatment of the human or animal body by surgery pursuant to Article 53(c) of the EPC.

11.9.2 TREATMENT BY THERAPY

The scope of 'treatment ... by therapy' has been interpreted in the following Board of Appeal decision.

Salminen/Pigs III T58/87 [1989] EPOR 125

The case involved a patent for a method for preventing piglets from suffocating under the dam (i.e. mother) in a brooding pen. Newborn piglets have a tendency to creep under the dam whilst standing up, in order to feed, and they risk being suffocated when the dam lies down. The method thus involved using a sensor to detect when the dam was standing and lying down and, when the dam was standing up, triggering unpleasant conditions for the piglets by blowing hot air under the dam. The appellant opposed the grant of the patent on the basis, inter alia, that it was not capable of industrial application pursuant to Article 52(4) of the EPC. The Board dismissed the appeal, indicating the scope of 'therapy' in Article 52(4), and finding that the method did not constitute a therapeutic method.

Technical Board of Appeal, at pp. 127–8:

2.1 The Board agrees in that the word 'therapy'

— covers any non-surgical treatment which is designed to cure, alleviate, remove or lessen the symptom of, or prevent or reduce the possibility of contracting any malfunction of the animal body (cf. *Patent Law of Europe and the United Kingdom* by A. M. Walton, H. I. L. Laddie, J. P. Baldwin and D. J. T. Kitchin, 1983, page II [684]), and also

— relates to the treatment of a disease in general or to a curative treatment in the narrow sense as well as the alleviation of the symptoms of pain and suffering (cf. *Chambers Twentieth Century Dictionary*, 1399, 'Therapy'; *The Oxford English Dictionary*, Vol. XI, 280, 'Therapy'; and, for example, T144/83 (Point 3); OJ, EPO 1986, 301).

> 2.3 The behaviour of newborn piglets to creep under the dam standing up to eat and drink either during or after farrowing cannot be fairly regarded as a malfunction of piglets whose instinct is not adequately developed. Furthermore, as far as the language of Claim 1 is concerned, it clearly covers a method for protection of piglets from the disadvantageous consequences of this behaviour, such as suffocating under the dam, by blowing air under the standing dam thus creating unpleasant conditions for the piglets. This cannot reasonably be called a treatment by therapy, which is practised on the bodies of piglets, within the meaning of Article 52(4) EPC. As the Opposition Division rightly considered, the invention is concerned with preventing accidents, analogous to a method of preventing a worker from trapping his hand in machinery.
>
> 2.4 Consequently, the Claims 1 and 2 comply with the requirements of Article 57 EPC.

On what basis did the Technical Board of Appeal find that the invention was *not* a method of treatment by therapy? Therapeutic treatment will often be linked to that which is targeting disease. Here it is interesting to note that pregnancy is not regarded as a disease and therefore inventions relating to contraceptive methods are not caught by the exclusion.[320] However, substances aimed at preventing the unwanted side effects of oral contraception have been held to fall within the exclusion,[321] as have nutritional compositions aimed at improving gastrointestinal health.[322]

Where a method of treatment is claimed that provides both therapeutic and cosmetic benefits this will still be caught by the exclusion. For example, in *ICI/Cleaning Plaque (Opposition by Blendax)*[323] the patent in question was a method of using water-soluble lanthanum salts as an agent for cleaning plaque and/or stains from human teeth. The Technical Board of Appeal held that this was directed both to therapeutic benefits (i.e. reducing plaque) and cosmetic benefits (the teeth looking cleaner). This was distinguished from *Du Pont/Appetite Suppressant*,[324] where the claim was clearly directed to a method of treatment of the human body for cosmetic purposes only (i.e. weight loss).

11.9.3 DIAGNOSTIC METHODS

The Enlarged Board of Appeal has ruled upon the scope of the exclusion for methods of diagnosis practised on the human or animal body.

Diagnostic Methods G1/04 [2006] EPOR 15

The reference to the Enlarged Board on the scope of the exclusion for 'diagnosis practised on the human or animal body' arose out of two conflicting decisions in the area. In one decision, *Bruker/Non-invasive Measurement*,[325] the Technical Board of Appeal held that the exclusion applied only to those diagnostic methods the results of which immediately made it possible to decide on a particular course of medical treatment. However,

---

[320] *British Technology Group/Contraceptive Method* T74/93 [1995] EPOR 279.
[321] *Bayer Schering Pharma AG/Composition for contraception* T1635/09 [2012] EPOR 23.
[322] *Nestec/High fibre high calorie liquid or powdered nutritional composition* T1002/09 [2010] EPOR 42.
[323] T290/86 [1991] EPOR 157.   [324] T144/83 [1987] EPOR 6.   [325] T385/86 [1988] EPOR 357.

in *Cygnus/Diagnostic Method*,[326] the Technical Board of Appeal held that the exclusion applied to all methods practised on the human or animal body which relate to diagnosis or which are of value for the purposes of diagnosis.

Enlarged Board of Appeal:

6.1 As a starting point, Article 52(4) EPC mentions 'diagnostic methods practised on the human or animal body'. The provision does not make reference to particular steps pertaining to such methods, nor does it contain a wording such as 'relating to diagnosis' or 'of value for diagnostic purposes'. Thus, the text of the provision itself already gives an indication towards a narrow interpretation in the sense that, in order to be excluded from patentability, the method is to include all steps relating to it. Furthermore, if the aim of the exclusion of such methods is to prevent medical or veterinary practitioners being inhibited by patents from taking the actions they consider appropriate to diagnose illnesses (*cf.* point 4 above), it will indeed be necessary to define the persons that are considered to be such practitioners. However, it is difficult, if not altogether impossible, to give such a definition on a European level within the framework of the EPC. From this it follows that, for reasons of legal certainty, which is of paramount importance, the European patent grant procedure may not be rendered dependent on the involvement of such practitioners. Since a comprehensive protection of medical and veterinary practitioners may be achieved by other means if deemed necessary, in particular by enacting legal provisions on the national level of the Contracting States of the EPC, introducing a right to use the methods in question, a narrow interpretation of the scope of the exclusion from patentability referred to above is therefore equitable. On the national level, it will also be more appropriate to define what a medical or veterinary practitioner is. Moreover, such a narrow interpretation is also justified by the fact that recent developments in the field of diagnostics for curative purposes render these methods more and more complex and technically sophisticated so that it is becoming increasingly difficult for medical or veterinary practitioners to have the means to carry them out. In this respect, they will hardly be hampered in their work by the existence of patents related to such methods. It is therefore difficult to see why applicants and inventors in the field of diagnostics should be deprived of a comprehensive patent protection.

...

6.2.2 The method steps to be carried out prior to making a diagnosis as an intellectual exercise (*cf.* point 5.2 above) are related to examination, data gathering and comparison (*cf.* point 5 above). If only one of the preceding steps which are constitutive for making such a diagnosis is lacking, there is no diagnostic method, but at best a method of data acquisition or data processing that can be used in a diagnostic method (*cf.* T385/86, point 3.3 of the Reasons). It follows that, whilst the surgical or therapeutic nature of a method claim can be achieved by a single method step (*cf.* point 6.2.1 above), several method steps are required to define a diagnostic method within the meaning of Article 52(4) EPC due to the inherent and inescapable multi-step nature of such a method (*cf.* point 5 above). Consequently, the restrictive interpretation of the patent exemption for diagnostic methods adopted by decision T385/86 does not amount to setting a different standard for diagnostic methods than that established for methods of surgery or therapy, as has been asserted in decision T964/99, point 3.6 of the Reasons.

---

[326] T964/99 [2002] EPOR 26.

The Enlarged Board of Appeal preferred the narrower interpretation of the exclusion, as reflected in *Bruker*. As such, diagnostic methods practised on the animal or human body are only excluded 'if all of the preceding steps which are constitutive for making a diagnosis as an intellectual exercise ... are performed on a living human or animal body'.[327] Those steps are: '(i) the examination phase involving the collection of data; (ii) the comparison of these data with standard values; (iii) the finding of any significant deviation, i.e. a symptom, during the comparison; and (iv) the attribution of the deviation to a particular clinical picture, i.e. the deductive medical or veterinary decision phase'.[328] This means that inventions that only yield intermediate results will not be caught by this exclusion.[329]

Do you agree with the reasons expressed by the Enlarged Board as to why the exclusion relating to diagnostic methods had to be construed more narrowly than that relating to methods of surgical or therapeutic treatment?

FURTHER READING

L. Bently, 'Exclusions from patentability and exceptions to patentees' rights: taking exceptions seriously' (2011) 64 Current Legal Problems 315.

A. Nordberg, 'Patentability of methods of human enhancement' (2015) 10 JIPLP 19.

E. Ventose, 'Making sense of the decision of the Enlarged Board of Appeal in *Cygnus/ Diagnostic Method*' [2008] EIPR 145.

E. Ventose, 'Patent protection for therapeutic methods under the European Patent Convention' [2010] EIPR 120.

E. Ventose, *Medical Patent Law: The Challenges of Medical Treatment* (Cheltenham: Edward Elgar, 2011).

E. Ventose, *Patenting Medical and Genetic Diagnostic Methods* (Cheltenham: Edward Elgar, 2013).

---

[327] *Diagnostic Methods*, [6] at p. 172.   [328] [5] at pp. 171–2.
[329] As in *Koninklijke Philips Electronics NV/Medical Diagnostic imaging* T9/04 [2007] EPOR 10.

PATENTS II:

NOVELTY, INVENTIVE STEP, SUFFICIENCY, AND SUPPORT

12.1 NOVELTY

12.1.1 INTRODUCTION

A crucial requirement for patentability is that the invention is *new*[1] or, in other words, is not anticipated. An invention is new if it does not already form part of the state of the art and the 'state of the art' is defined broadly to include all matter that is available to the public before the priority date of the invention.[2]

The rationale behind the novelty requirement is twofold: first, to ensure that patents are not used to prevent people doing what they did before the patent was granted (the 'right to work' rationale); second, to make certain that a patent is being given in relation to technical information that is not otherwise accessible to the public (the 'information disclosure' rationale).

12.1.2 THE STATE OF THE ART

12.1.2.1 General rule

Given that an invention will not be new if it forms part of the state of the art (also known as the prior art), it is important to ascertain what comprises this body of knowledge. According to section 2(2) of the PA 77:

> The state of the art in the case of an invention shall be taken to comprise all matter (whether a product, process, information about either, or anything else) which has at any time before the priority date of that invention been made available to the public (whether in the United Kingdom or elsewhere) by written or oral description, by use or in any other way.[3]

---

[1] PA 77, s. 1(1); EPC, Art. 52(1).   [2] PA 77, s. 2; EPC, Art. 54.
[3] For the EPC equivalent see Art. 54(2).

As is apparent from this definition, the *priority date* is essential to establishing the prior art. The priority date is usually the date on which the application was filed; however, it may be an earlier date where the applicant is claiming Convention priority.[4]

The state of the art comprises all matter made available to the public before the priority date *whether in the UK or elsewhere*. In other words, the prior art is not territorially restricted and can comprise material that is available anywhere in the world (referred to as 'absolute' novelty). Thus, a document published in the US or Brazil, or a prior use in India, for example, could anticipate the invention. This is in contrast to the position under earlier UK patent law where the prior publication or use had to occur *within* the UK (referred to as 'local' novelty). It is also stricter than a 'relative' novelty approach according to which acts of prior use are limited to those occurring within a particular territory, but prior documentary disclosures are territorially unrestricted.[5] What is the purpose, do you think, of adopting an absolute, as opposed to local or relative, approach to novelty and is it preferable?

It is not required that the material has been disseminated at large in order for it to form part of the state of the art. For example, it suffices that a document is placed in a library or other place in the UK for consultation as of right by any person (with or without paying a fee).[6] Further, giving away or selling a single item will be sufficient for it to form part of the prior art,[7] as will limited use in a remote area.[8] In this context, it is worth considering whether digital networks potentially expand the scope of the prior art. In *Philips*,[9] the Technical Board of Appeal considered the circumstances in which publications accessible via the internet are 'made available to the public' such that they form part of the prior art. The Board rejected the view that the mere existence of a document or publication on the internet meant that it had become publicly available. While the Board recognized that publications may be theoretically accessible via the internet, it also observed that they may not be practically so, due to being held in obscure locations or being hard to find. Therefore, the Board found that the mere fact material is online is not sufficient for it to have been 'made available to the public': what needs to be shown is that there is 'direct and unambiguous access' to the material by 'known means and methods'.[10] The Board indicated that this test would be satisfied where a document stored on the internet and accessible via a specific URL could be found using a search engine by using keywords relating to the essential content of the document and was accessible at that URL for long enough for a member of the public to have direct and unambiguous access to it.[11] In another *Philips* decision,[12] the Technical Board of Appeal held that information sent via email does not form part of the prior art simply because an individual or an Internet Service Provider might have intercepted it.

The form of disclosure to the public is unrestricted since section 2(2) of the PA 77 refers to matter made available to the public 'by written or oral description, by use or in any other way'. Thus, the prior art may include material such as patent applications or specifications, journal articles, photographs, conference presentations, conversations, product samples, prototypes, or sales.

---

[4] See 11.5.2.1.   [5] As is the case in the US and Australia, for example.
[6] PA 77, s. 130(1).   [7] *Fomento v Mentmore* [1956] RPC 87.
[8] See *Windsurfing International Inc. v Tabur Marine (Great Britain) Ltd* [1985] RPC 59.
[9] *Philips/Public availability of documents on the World Wide Web* T1533/06 (12 March 2012).
[10] Reason 6.5.4.   [11] Reason 6.7.3.
[12] *Philips/Public availability of an email transmitted via the Internet* T2/09 (12 March 2012).

It is worth noting that section 2(2) does not distinguish between whether the matter has been made available to the public by the inventor or by a third party. Thus, it is possible for the inventor to anticipate his or her own invention by disclosing it before he or she applies for a patent. It is therefore unwise for an inventor to discuss his or her invention, or to show it to anyone, unless done under strict conditions of confidentiality. Even so, there is the risk that the person to whom the inventor has confided may breach that obligation of confidence. If that happens, as we shall see below, such disclosures may be excluded from the prior art if they occur six months prior to the filing date. In several jurisdictions, such as the US, 'grace periods' are used to mitigate the harshness of a bright-line novelty rule.[13] A grace period refers to where publications by the inventor occurring during a limited time before the date of filing are excluded from the state of the art. In your view, should inventors in the UK and under the EPC be able to rely on a grace period? In this respect, it is worth considering the types of inventors that a grace period is likely to favour and the inevitable complication that will arise when it comes to the novelty assessment.

12.1.2.2 Material deemed excluded from the state of the art

According to section 2(4) of the PA 77, certain disclosures shall be disregarded in determining novelty, i.e. they will be excluded from the prior art where they occur during the six months prior to the date of filing of the patent application. It is important to note that the six months is judged *not* from the priority date but from the *date of filing*.[14] This may be significant where, due to Convention priority, the date of filing and the priority date differ.

The disclosures that will be disregarded relate to two situations. The first is where the information was obtained unlawfully or in breach of confidence either from the inventor or from any third party who had obtained it in confidence from the inventor.[15] The second situation is where the disclosure was due to, or made in consequence of, the inventor displaying the invention at an 'international exhibition', as prescribed by the Convention on International Exhibitions 1928.[16] The applicant must, on filing the application, state that the invention has been so displayed.[17] According to the Convention, an 'international exhibition' is one that is non-commercial, with a duration of more than three weeks, and which is officially organized by a nation and to which other nations are invited.[18] The frequency and quality of international exhibitions so defined is regulated by the Bureau International des Expositions.[19]

12.1.2.3 Material deemed included in the state of the art

Importantly, certain matter is deemed to form part of the state of the art *even though it is published after the priority date*. Section 2(3) of the PA 77 provides that the state of the art includes matter contained in other patent applications where that other application is published on or after the priority date of the invention. This is provided the priority date of the

---

[13] For further discussion see W. Xiaoli, 'The patent novelty grace period in China in comparative perspective' (2009) 40 IIC 182.

[14] *University Patents/Herpes Simplex Virus* [2001] EPOR 33.

[15] PA 77, s. 2(4)(a)–(b); EPC, Art. 55(1)(a).   [16] PA 77, s. 130; EPC, Art. 55(1)(b).

[17] PA 77, s. 2(4)(c); EPC, Art. 55(1)(b).

[18] See the Convention on International Exhibitions 1928, Arts 1–2.

[19] See <www.bie-paris.org/>.

other application predates that of the invention and that the matter was contained in the other application, both as filed and as published.[20]

The reason for this provision, and its scope, was considered in *Woolard's Application*.[21] In this case the applicant had filed an application on 1 December 1995. He decided to withdraw this application and his patent agents wrote to the Patent Office abandoning the 1995 application. This letter was received by the Patent Office on 12 May 1997 and became effective on that date; however, the application was nevertheless published on 4 June 1997. The applicant later filed a fresh application on 3 June 1997 but this was refused on the ground of lack of novelty due to the earlier application that he had filed and which formed part of the state of the art by virtue of section 2(3) of the PA 77. The applicant's appeal was allowed. Laddie J held that the purpose of section 2(3) was to 'avoid the potential co-existence of two patents for the same subject matter'[22] and, as such, the two applications need to be made in the same country. Further, he held that if the earlier application is withdrawn before it is published it should not be treated as prior art for any purpose.[23]

12.1.3 INTERPRETING THE PRIOR ART

The prior art is interpreted according to the perspective of a notional person, known as the person skilled in the art. For more details of the characteristics of this person see the discussion under inventive step at 12.2.

12.1.3.1 Documents

A person skilled in the art will interpret a document forming part of the prior art 'as at the date of its publication, having regard to the relevant surrounding circumstances which then existed, and without regard to subsequent events'.[24] This may be contrasted with other forms of prior art, which will be interpreted as at the date of priority. This special rule for documentary disclosure thus seems somewhat out of place and the justifications for it are not entirely clear.

Importantly, it is not possible for documents to be combined or read together, i.e. to 'mosaic' documents, except in limited circumstances. Thus, in *ICI/Latex Composition*,[25] the Technical Board of Appeal held that the abstract of a document, which conveyed conflicting data to that contained in the original document, had to be interpreted by reference to the original document, so that the data stipulated in the original document prevailed. Similarly, in *Scanditronix/Radiation Beam Collimation*[26] the Technical Board of Appeal emphasized that:

> the technical disclosure in a prior art document should be considered in its entirety, as it would be done by a person skilled in the art. It is not justified arbitrarily to isolate parts of such document from their context in order to derive therefrom a technical information, which would be distinct from or even in contradiction with the integral teaching of the document.[27]

---

[20] For the equivalent EPC provision see Art. 54(3). Note that prior to the EPC 2000, later published European patent applications having earlier priority or filing dates were only considered part of the state of the art to the extent that the same Contracting States were designated in the earlier and later applications. This restriction has been dropped as a consequence of the EPC 2000 coming into effect.

[21] [2002] RPC 39.   [22] [17], p. 772.   [23] [17], p. 772.

[24] *General Tire & Rubber v Firestone Tyre & Rubber* [1971] FSR 417, 443.

[25] T77/87 [1989] EPOR 246.   [26] [1990] EPOR 352.   [27] At 358.

12.1.3.2 Products and prior use

Determining what information a product, substance, or prior use contributes to the prior art depends on what information a person skilled in the art can derive from that product or prior use. This includes information that can be ascertained from analysing the substance or product, even if there is no motivation for doing so. This is highlighted by the following extract from the Enlarged Board of Appeal decision in *Availability to the Public*.[28]

> 1.4 An essential purpose of any technical teaching is to enable the person skilled in the art to manufacture or use a given product by applying such teaching. Where such teaching results from a product put on the market, the person skilled in the art will have to rely on his general technical knowledge to gather all information enabling him to prepare the said product. Where it is possible for the skilled person to discover the composition or the internal structure of the product *and to reproduce it without undue burden*, then both the product and its composition or internal structure become state of the art.
>
> ...
>
> 2. There is no support in the EPC for the additional requirement referred to by Board 3.3.3 in Case T93/89 (cf. point II above) that the public should have particular reasons for analysing a product put on the market, in order to identify its composition or internal structure. According to Article 54(2) EPC the state of the art shall be held to comprise everything made available to the public. It is the fact that direct and unambiguous access to some particular information is possible, which makes the latter available, whether or not there is any reason for looking for it.

12.1.4 DETERMINING WHETHER THE INVENTION IS NEW

Under the old law (Patents Act 1949), the courts placed particular emphasis on the 'right to work' rationale of novelty. They did this by using what was known as a 'reverse infringement' test for novelty. More specifically, if a prior use would have constituted an infringement if it had occurred *after* the priority date, then it was treated as an anticipation of the invention if it occurred *before* the priority date. As such, prior use of an invention, whether it was secret, inherent, or unknown at the time, would anticipate. The new law, as reflected in the PA 77, takes a different approach to novelty, which is aptly illustrated by the House of Lords decision in *Merrell Dow Pharmaceuticals Inc. v Norton*.

Merrell Dow Pharmaceuticals Inc. v Norton [1996] RPC 76

Merrell Dow (MD) obtained a patent in the UK in 1972 for an antihistamine drug called terfenadine. MD later conducted research into the way in which the drug actually worked. They discovered that the drug passed through the stomach to be absorbed in the small intestine and was then 99.5 per cent metabolized in the liver, which explained why the drug did not produce any side effects such as drowsiness. In 1980, MD obtained a second patent, this time in respect of the acid metabolite which was formed in the

---

[28] [1993] OJ EPO 277.

liver. After the first patent expired, pharmaceutical companies began manufacturing and selling terfenadine. MD brought an action for infringement of the second patent against the defendant. It claimed that the defendant was a contributory infringer under section 60(2) of the PA 77 by virtue of knowingly supplying consumers with the means for putting the invention in the second patent (i.e. the acid metabolite) into effect.

The defendant applied to strike out the infringement action as disclosing no cause of action. Aldous J dismissed the action on the basis of lack of novelty and the Court of Appeal affirmed his decision on this ground. On appeal to the House of Lords, the appeal was dismissed.

Lord Hoffmann (delivering the leading speech), **at pp. 85–91:**

8. Anticipation by Use

…

It is important to notice that anticipation by use relies solely upon the fact that the volunteers in the clinical trials took terfenadine and therefore made the acid metabolite. There is no suggestion in the Agreed Statement of Facts and Issues that the volunteers were also at liberty to analyse the terfenadine to discover its composition. If it was open to them to have done so, they would have been in the same position as if they had read the terfenadine specification and the arguments for anticipation by use would have been the same as for anticipation by disclosure.

…

(a) The Old Law

I think that there can be no doubt that under the Patents Act 1949, uninformative use of the kind I have described would have invalidated the patent. One of the grounds for revocation in section 32(1) was (e): 'the invention … is not new having regard to what was *known or used*, before the priority date of the claim, in the United Kingdom'. [Emphasis added] Ground 32(1)(i) was that before the priority date the invention was 'secretly used' in the United Kingdom. In *Bristol-Myers Co (Johnson's) Application* [1975] RPC 127 this House decided that use included secret or otherwise uninformative use. (I distinguish between secret and uninformative use because the House decided by a majority that 'secret' meant that information about the invention had been deliberately concealed. It did not include a case in which the manufacturer was also unaware of the relevant facts.) Bristol-Myers had applied for a patent with a product claim for an ampicillin compound which was found to be more stable than alternative forms. Beechams were able to show, from samples providentially retained, that before the priority date they had made some quantities of that particular compound, although at the time they did not know or care which ampicillin compound it was and were unaware of the advantages discovered by Bristol-Myers. Furthermore, they had marketed the ampicillin in a form which made it impossible to discover what the original compound had been. Thus the anticipation upon which Beechams relied conveyed no relevant information about the product to the general public. The compound in the hands of the reasonably skilled member of the public told him nothing about its distinctive chemical form or how he could make it or what the advantages of that form would be. Nevertheless, the compound was anticipated by use.

The reasoning of the House was founded upon two principles of the old United Kingdom patent law. The first, to which I have already referred, was that the Crown could not grant a patent which would enable the patentee to stop another trader from doing what he had done before. It did not matter that he had been doing it secretly or otherwise uninformatively. The second was that the test for anticipation before the priority date was in this respect co-extensive with the test for infringement afterwards. If the use would have been an infringement afterwards, it must have been an anticipation before. For the purpose of infringement, it was not necessary that the defendant should have realised that he was doing an infringing act. Such knowledge was therefore equally unnecessary for anticipation.

(b) The New Law

… This provision [Art. 54 EPC] makes it clear that to be part of the state of the art, *the invention* must have been made available to the public. An invention is a piece of information. Making matter available to the public within the meaning of section 2(2) therefore requires the communication of information. The use of a product makes the invention part of the state of the art only so far as that use makes available the necessary information.

The 1977 Act therefore introduced a substantial qualification into the old principle that a patent cannot be used to stop someone doing what he has done before. If the previous use was secret or uninformative, then subject to section 64, it can. Likewise, a gap has opened between the tests for infringement and anticipation. Acts done secretly or without knowledge of the relevant facts, which would amount to infringements after the grant of the patent, will not count as anticipations before.

This construction of section 2(2) is supported by a number of authorities both in the courts of this country and the EPO. I shall refer to only two. In *PLG Research Ltd. v. Ardon International Ltd* [1993] FSR 197, 225, Aldous J. said:

> Mr Thorley submitted that if a product had been made available to the public, it was not possible thereafter to patent the product whether claimed as a product claim or a product-by-process claim. That submission is too broad. Under the 1977 Act, patents may be granted for an invention covering a product that has been put on the market provided the product does not provide an enabling disclosure of the invention claimed. In most cases, prior sale of the product will make available information as to its contents and its method of manufacture, but it is possible to imagine circumstances where that will not happen. In such cases a subsequent patent may be obtained and the only safeguard given to the public is section 64 of the Act.

And in *MOBIL/Friction reducing additive Decision* G02/88 [1990] EPOR 73 the Enlarged Board of Appeal of the EPO said (at page 88):

> [T]he Enlarged Board would emphasise that under Article 54(2) EPC the question to be decided is what has been 'made available' to the public: the question is not what may have been 'inherent' in what was made available (by a prior written description, or in what has previously been used (prior use), for example). Under the EPC, a hidden or secret use, because it has not been made available to the public, is not a ground of objection to [the] validity of a European patent. In this respect, the provisions of the EPC may differ from the previous national laws of some Contracting States, and even from the current national laws of some non-Contracting States. Thus, the question of 'inherency' does not arise as such under Article 54. Any vested right derived from prior use of an invention is a matter for national law …

Mr Thorley is therefore right in saying that his claim cannot be dismissed simply on the ground that making the acid metabolite is something which has been done before. To that extent, the intuitive response is wrong.

9. Anticipation by disclosure

I turn therefore to the ground upon which the respondents succeeded before Aldous J and the Court of Appeal, namely that the disclosure in the terfenadine specification had made the invention part of the state of the art. This is different from the argument on anticipation by use because it relies not upon the mere use of the product by members of the public but upon the communication of information. The question is whether the specification conveyed sufficient information to enable the skilled reader to work the invention.

Mr Thorley says that no one can know about something which he does not know exists. It follows that if he does not know that the product exists, he cannot know how to work an invention for making that product in any form. The prior art contained in the terfenadine specification gave no indication that it would have the effect of creating the acid metabolite in the human body. Therefore it did not contain sufficient information to enable the skilled reader to make the substance in that or any other form. It did not make the acid metabolite available to the public.

What does Mr Thorley mean when he says that no one knew that the acid metabolite existed? What Merrell Dow's research revealed was that something was created in the liver which could be given a chemical description. But the same thing may be known under one description and not known under another.

...

My Lords, I think that on this point the Patents Act 1977 is perfectly clear. Section 2(2) does not purport to confine the state of the art about products to knowledge of their chemical composition. It is the *invention* which must be new and which must therefore not be part of the state of the art. It is therefore part of the state of the art if the information which has been disclosed enables the public to know the product under a description sufficient to work the invention.

For most of the purposes of a product claim, knowledge of its chemical composition will be necessary to enable the public to work the invention. It is something they will need to know in order to be able to make it. So in *Availability to the Public Decision* G01/92 [1993] EPOR 241 the President of the EPO referred to the Enlarged Board of Appeal the question of the circumstances in which making a product available to the public would count as making available its chemical composition. The Board answered that the composition or internal structure of a product becomes part of the state of the art if it is possible for a skilled person to discover it and reproduce it without undue burden. Mr Thorley took this case to mean that in no context can a product be part of the state of the art unless its chemical composition is readily discoverable. But that is not what the case says. The Board was asked about the circumstances in which the chemical composition of a product becomes part of the state of the art. It was not asked about the circumstances in which knowing its chemical composition was necessary for the purpose of treating the product as part of the state of the art.

Other decisions of the EPO seem to me to make it clear that, at least for some purposes, products need not be known under their chemical description in order to be part of the state of the art. In *BAYER/Diastereomers Decision* T12/81 [1979–85] EPOR Vol. B. 308, 312, the Technical Board of Appeal said:

[T]he concept of novelty must not be given such a narrow interpretation that only what has already been described in the same terms is prejudicial to it. The purpose of Art. 54(1) EPC is to prevent the state of the art being patented again. Art. 54(2) EPC defines the state of the art as comprising everything made available to the public before the date of filing in any way, including by written description. There are many ways of describing a substance in chemistry and this is usually done by giving its precise scientific designation. But the latter is not always available on the date of filing … [It] is the practice of a number of patent offices to accept the process parameter, in the form of a product-by-process claim, for closer characterisation of inventions relating to chemical substances. To the Board's knowledge this is also the practice at the European Patent Office. If inventions relating to chemical substances defined by claims of this kind are patented, it necessarily follows that the resulting patent documents, once they enter the state of the art, will be prejudicial to the novelty of applications claiming the same substance although in a different and perhaps more closely defined form.

In other words, if the recipe which inevitably produces the substance is part of the state of the art, so is the substance as made by that recipe. *CPC/Flavour Concentrates Decision* T303/86 [1989] 2 EPOR 95 was a case about actual recipes for cooking. The application was to patent a process for making flavour concentrates from vegetable or animal substances by extraction with fat solvents under pressure in the presence of water. The claim specified certain parameters for the ratio between the vapour pressure of the water in the meat or vegetables and the vapour pressure of the free water. Opposition was based upon two cookbook recipes for pressure-frying chickens and making stews which in non-technical terms disclosed processes having the same effect. The Technical Board of Appeal said (at page 98):

> It is sufficient to destroy the novelty of the claimed process that this process and the known process are identical with respect to starting material and reaction conditions since processes identical in these features must inevitably yield identical products.

Furthermore, it did not matter that the cook did not realise that he was not only frying a chicken, but also making a 'flavour concentrate' in the surplus oil. It was enough, as the Board said, that 'some flavour of the fried chicken is extracted into the oil during the frying process even if this is not the desired result of that process'.

Mr Thorley said that *CPC/Flavour Concentrates* can be explained on the ground that the flavour concentrates as made according to the cooking recipes could have been analysed and chemically identified. Perhaps they could. But this was not the ground for the Board's decision. It proceeded on the basis that for the purpose of being part of the state of the art, a process for making flavour concentrates was sufficiently described by a recipe for cooking food which did not expressly refer to the flavour concentrates but would inevitably have the effect of making them.

In this case, knowledge of the acid metabolite was in my view made available to the public by the terfenadine specification under the description 'a part of the chemical reaction in the human body produced by the ingestion of terfenadine and having an anti-histamine effect'. Was this description sufficient to make the product part of the state of the art? For many purposes, obviously not. It would not enable anyone to work the invention in the form of isolating or synthesising the acid metabolite. But for the purpose of working the invention by making the acid metabolite in the body by ingesting terfenadine, I think it plainly was. It enabled the public to work the invention by making the acid metabolite in their livers. The fact that they would not have been able to describe the chemical reaction in these terms does mean that they were not working the invention. Whether or not a person is working a product invention is an objective fact independent of what he knows or thinks about what he is doing …

It may be helpful at this point to highlight the similarities and the distinctions between the case for anticipation by use, which I have rejected, and the case for anticipation by disclosure, which I have accepted. In both cases no one was aware that the acid metabolite was being made. In the case of anticipation by use, however, the acts relied upon conveyed no information which would have enabled anyone to work the invention, i.e. to make the acid metabolite. The anticipation in this form relies solely upon the fact that the acid metabolite was made, as the anticipation in *Bristol-Myers Co (Johnson's) Application* relied solely upon the fact that ampicillin trihydrate had been made and sold to the public. It disavows any reliance upon extraneous information, such as the formula for making terfenadine and the instructions to take it for its anti-histamine effect. Anticipation by disclosure, on the other hand, relies upon the communication to the public of information which enables it to do an act having the inevitable consequence of making the acid metabolite. The terfenadine specification teaches that the ingestion of terfenadine will produce a chemical reaction in the body and for the purposes of working the invention in this form, this is a sufficient description of the making of the acid metabolite. Under the description the acid metabolite was part of the state of the art.

What is the shift in approach to novelty that has occurred under the new law according to *Merrell Dow*? Would you say that there is now more emphasis placed on the 'information disclosure' rationale than the 'right to work' rationale? Why is it that the patent for the acid metabolite was anticipated by the patent specification for terfenadine but *not* by the prior use of the antihistamine ingested by clinical volunteers? Is the distinction made between the two types of prior art convincing? In this respect, it is important to note the limited basis upon which anticipation by use in *Merrell Dow* was alleged, namely, the ingestion of a substance which did not actually contain the acid metabolite, but which produced it in the body, and the fact that the clinical volunteers were not at liberty to analyse the terfenadine pills. This may be contrasted with the case of *Evans Medical Ltd's Patent*[29] where the patent in suit was for a particular protein, pertactin, which helped immunize against the whooping cough. Laddie J held that the patent was invalid for lack of novelty because, before the priority date, a whooping cough vaccine had been used in Japan which, unknown to the person skilled in the art, contained the protein pertactin. Laddie J distinguished *Merrell Dow* on the ground that, unlike the terfenadine pills ingested by the clinical volunteers, the vaccine was open to anyone to analyse it and thus the information within it (i.e. the protein) formed part of the prior art.

In *Merrell Dow* Lord Hoffmann refers to an invention lacking novelty where there exists information available to the public that would enable the working of the invention. Another way of describing this requirement is as 'enabling disclosure'. However, as we shall see from the decision below, the House of Lords has subsequently insisted that 'enabling disclosure' in fact reflects two distinct, but related, requirements of 'disclosure' and 'enablement'.

Synthon BV v SmithKline Beecham Plc (No. 2) [2006] RPC 10

Paroxetine is a chemical compound that has been successfully marketed in the form of its hydrochloride hemihydrate salt as a treatment for depression. The patent in suit in an application for revocation related to a different paroxetine salt, i.e. paroxetine methanesulfonate (PMS) in a particular crystalline form, which had properties making it more suitable for pharmaceutical use. The applicant for revocation, Synthon, had filed an application for a patent which claimed a broad class of sulfonic acid salts including PMS. The specification identified PMS as a compound which had good stability and high

[29] [1998] RPC 517.

solubility and described how to make PMS in crystalline form. SmithKline Beecham, before the Synthon application was published, filed a patent application which claimed PMS in a particular crystalline form. Both patents were granted. However, Synthon subsequently sought to revoke the SmithKline patent, on the ground that the crystalline form of PMS described in the claims was not new. Synthon argued that its application formed part of the state of the art, pursuant to section 2(3) of the PA 77 and thus anticipated the SmithKline patent. The first instance judge, Jacob J, held that the SmithKline patent lacked novelty but the Court of Appeal upheld the validity of the patent. On appeal, the House of Lords allowed the appeal, restoring the order of the judge.

Lord Hoffmann (delivering the leading speech):

The law

19. Before I discuss what the Court of Appeal made of these findings, I must say something about the law. I have said that there are two requirements for anticipation: prior disclosure and enablement.

(a) Disclosure

20. The concept of what I have called disclosure has been explained in two judgments of unquestionable authority. The first is Lord Westbury LC in *Hill v Evans* (1862) 31 LJ Ch (NS) 457, 463:

> I apprehend the principle is correctly thus expressed: the antecedent statement must be such that a person of ordinary knowledge of the subject would at once perceive, understand and be able practically to apply the discovery without the necessity of making further experiments and gaining further information before the invention can be made useful. If something remains to be ascertained which is necessary for the useful application of the discovery, that affords sufficient room for another valid patent.

21. The second authoritative passage is in the judgment of the Court of Appeal (Sachs, Buckley and Orr LJJ) in *General Tire and Rubber Co v Firestone Tyre and Rubber Co Ltd* [1972] RPC 457, 485–6:

> To determine whether a patentee's claim has been anticipated by an earlier publication it is necessary to compare the earlier publication with the patentee's claim…If the earlier publication…discloses the same device as the device which the patentee by his claim…asserts that he has invented, the patentee's claim has been anticipated, but not otherwise…
>
> When the prior inventor's publication and the patentee's claim have respectively been construed by the court in the light of all properly admissible evidence as to technical matters, the meaning of words and expressions used in the art and so forth, the question whether the patentee's claim is new…falls to be decided as a question of fact. If the prior inventor's publication contains a clear description of, or clear instructions to do or make, something that would infringe the patentee's claim if carried out after the grant of the patentee's patent, the patentee's claim will have been shown to lack the necessary novelty…The prior inventor, however, and the patentee may have approached the same device from different starting points and may for this reason, or it may be for other reasons, have so described their devices that it cannot be immediately discerned from a reading of the language which they have respectively used that they have discovered in truth the same device; but if carrying out the directions contained in the prior inventor's publication will inevitably result in something being made or done which, if the patentee's claim were valid, would constitute

an infringement of the patentee's claim, this circumstance demonstrates that the patentee's claim has in fact been anticipated.

If, on the other hand, the prior publication contains a direction which is capable of being carried out in a manner which would infringe the patentee's claim, but would be at least as likely to be carried out in a way which would not do so, the patentee's claim will not have been anticipated, although it may fail on the ground of obviousness. To anticipate the patentee's claim the prior publication must contain clear and unmistakeable directions to do what the patentee claims to have invented ... A signpost, however clear, upon the road to the patentee's invention will not suffice. The prior inventor must be clearly shown to have planted his flag at the precise destination before the patentee.

22. If I may summarise the effect of these two well-known statements, the matter relied upon as prior art must disclose subject-matter which, if performed, would necessarily result in an infringement of the patent. That may be because the prior art discloses the same invention. In that case there will be no question that performance of the earlier invention would infringe and usually it will be apparent to someone who is aware of both the prior art and the patent that it will do so. But patent infringement does not require that one should be aware that one is infringing: 'whether or not a person is working [an] ... invention is an objective fact independent of what he knows or thinks about what he is doing': *Merrell Dow Pharmaceuticals Inc v H N Norton & Co Ltd* [1996] RPC 76, 90. It follows that, whether or not it would be apparent to anyone at the time, whenever subject-matter described in the prior disclosure is capable of being performed and is such that, if performed, it must result in the patent being infringed, the disclosure condition is satisfied. The flag has been planted, even though the author or maker of the prior art was not aware that he was doing so.

23. Thus, in *Merrell Dow*, the ingestion of terfenadine by hay-fever sufferers, which was the subject of prior disclosure, necessarily entailed the making of the patented acid metabolite in their livers. It was therefore an anticipation of the acid metabolite, even though no one was aware that it was being made or even that it existed. But the infringement must be not merely a possible or even likely consequence of performing the invention disclosed by the prior disclosure. It must be necessarily entailed. If there is more than one possible consequence, one cannot say that performing the disclosed invention will infringe. The flag has not been planted on the patented invention, although a person performing the invention disclosed by the prior art may carry it there by accident or (if he is aware of the patented invention) by design. Indeed, it may be obvious to do so. But the prior disclosure must be construed as it would have been understood by the skilled person at the date of the disclosure and not in the light of the subsequent patent. As the Technical Board of Appeal said in T-396/89 *UNION CARBIDE/high tear strength polymers* [1992] EPOR 312 at [4.4]:

It may be easy, given a knowledge of a later invention, to select from the general teachings of a prior art document certain conditions, and apply them to an example in that document, so as to produce an end result having all the features of the later claim. However, success in so doing does not prove that the result was inevitable. All that it demonstrates is that, given knowledge of the later invention, the earlier teaching is capable of being adapted to give the same result. Such an adaptation cannot be used to attack the novelty of a later patent.

24. Although it is sometimes said that there are two forms of anticipatory disclosure: a disclosure of the patented invention itself and a disclosure of an invention which, if performed, would necessarily infringe the patented invention (see, for example, Laddie J in *Inhale Therapeutic Systems Inc v Quadrant Healthcare Plc* [2002] RPC 21 at [43]) they are both

aspects of a single principle, namely that anticipation requires prior disclosure of subject-matter which, when performed, must necessarily infringe the patented invention.

25. As I have indicated by reference to the quotation from *UNION CARBIDE*, it is this requirement that performance of an invention disclosed in the prior art must necessarily infringe the patent which distinguishes novelty from obviousness. If performance of an invention disclosed by the prior art would not infringe the patent but the prior art would make it obvious to a skilled person how he might make adaptations which resulted in an infringing invention, then the patent may be invalid for lack of an inventive step but not for lack of novelty. In the present case, the Synthon application is deemed to form part of the state of the art for the purposes of novelty (s. 2(3)) but not for the purpose of obviousness (s. 3). As Synthon rely solely upon s. 2(3) matter as prior art, they do not rely and cannot succeed on obviousness.

(b) Enablement

26. Enablement means that the ordinary skilled person would have been able to perform the invention which satisfies the requirement of disclosure. This requirement applies whether the disclosure is in matter which forms part of the state of the art by virtue of s. 2(2) or, as in this case, s. 2(3). The latter point was settled by the decision of this House in *Asahi Kasei Kogyo KK's Application* [1991] RPC 485.

27. *Asahi's* case was decided on the assumed facts that there had been a prior disclosure of the same invention (a particular polypeptide) but that neither the disclosed information nor common general knowledge would have enabled the skilled man to make it. The House therefore did not have to consider the test for deciding what degree of knowledge, skill and perseverance the skilled man was assumed to have. But the concept of enablement is used in other contexts in the law of patents (see *Biogen Inc v Medeva Plc* [1997] RPC 1, 47) and in particular as a ground for the revocation of a patent under s. 72(1)(c): 'the specification of the patent does not disclose the invention clearly enough and completely enough for it to be performed by a person skilled in the art'. The question of what will satisfy this test has been discussed in a number of cases. For example, in *Valensi v British Radio Corp* [1973] RPC 337, 377 Buckley LJ said:

> the hypothetical addressee is not a person of exceptional skill and knowledge, that he is not to be expected to exercise any invention nor any prolonged research, inquiry or experiment. He must, however, be prepared to display a reasonable degree of skill and common knowledge of the art in making trials and to correct obvious errors in the specification if a means of correcting them can readily be found.

There is also a valuable and more extended discussion in the judgment of Lloyd LJ in *Mentor Corp v Hollister Incorporated* [1993] RPC 7. In the present case the Court of Appeal was reluctant to say that the test of enablement of a prior disclosure for the purpose of anticipation was the same as the test of enablement of the patent itself for the purpose of sufficiency. But I can think of no reason why there should be any difference and the Technical Board of Appeal has more than once held that the tests are the same: see T-206/83 *ICI/Pyridine Herbicides* [1986] 5 EPOR 232, [2]; *COLLABORATIVE/Preprorennin* [1990] EPOR 361, [15]. In my opinion, therefore, the authorities on s. 72(1)(c) are equally applicable to enablement for the purposes of ss. 2(2) and (3). There may however be differences in the application of this test to the facts; for example, because in the case of sufficiency the skilled person is attempting to perform a claimed invention and has that goal in mind, whereas in the case of prior art the subject-matter may have disclosed the invention but not identified it as such. But no such question arises in this case, in which the application plainly identified crystalline PMS as an embodiment of the invention.

(c) Keeping the concepts distinct

28. It is very important to keep in mind that disclosure and enablement are distinct concepts, each of which has to be satisfied and each of which has its own rules. As Laddie J said in relation to sufficiency in *University of Southampton's Applications* [2005] RPC 11, [46]:

> In my view, devising an invention and providing enabling disclosure are two quite different things. Although both may be necessary to secure valid protection, as section 14 of the Act shows, they relate to different aspects of the law of patents. It is very possible to make a good invention but to lose one's patent for failure to make an enabling disclosure. The requirement to include an enabling disclosure is concerned with teaching the public how the invention works, not with devising the invention in the first place.

29. For a similar point, see Jacob J in *Beloit Technologies Inc v Valmet Paper Machinery Inc* [1995] RPC 705, 739. Of course the same disclosure may satisfy both requirements. The prior art description may be sufficient in itself to enable the ordinary skilled man, armed with common general knowledge of the art, to perform the subject-matter of the invention. Indeed, when the prior art is a product, the product itself, though dumb, may be enabling if it is 'available to the public' and a person skilled in the art can discover its composition or internal structure and reproduce it without undue burden: see the decision of the Enlarged Board of Appeal in GO1/92 *Availability to the Public* [1993] EPOR 241, GO1/92 [1.4].

30. Nevertheless, in deciding whether there has been anticipation, there is a serious risk of confusion if the two requirements are not kept distinct. For example, I have explained that for the purpose of disclosure, the prior art must disclose an invention which, if performed, would necessarily infringe the patent. It is not enough to say that, given the prior art, the person skilled in the art would, without undue burden, be able to come up with an invention which infringed the patent. But once the very subject-matter of the invention has been disclosed by the prior art and the question is whether it was enabled, the person skilled in the art is assumed to be willing to make trial and error experiments to get it to work. If, therefore, one asks whether some degree of experimentation is to be assumed, it is very important to know whether one is talking about disclosure or about enablement.

31. An example of laying oneself open to misunderstanding in this way is the famous statement by Lord Westbury LC in *Hill v Evans* (1862) 31 LJ Ch (NS) 457, 463, which I have quoted above. Lord Westbury said that the person skilled in the art must be able practically to apply the discovery 'without the necessity of making further experiments and gaining further information before the invention can be made useful'. Was he referring to disclosure or enablement? I rather think he meant disclosure and was saying the same as the Court of Appeal did later in *General Tire* when it said that the prior disclosure must have planted the flag on the invention. On the other hand, by speaking of the man skilled in the art being 'able practically to apply the discovery' he certainly gave the impression that he was talking about enablement, and was so understood by Lord Reid in *C Van der Lely NV v Bamfords Ltd* [1963] RPC 61, 71, when he said, correctly in relation to enablement:

> Lord Westbury must have meant experiments with a view to discovering something not disclosed. He cannot have meant to refer to the ordinary methods of trial and error which involve no inventive step and are generally necessary in applying any discovery to produce a practical result.

32. Likewise, the role of the person skilled in the art is different in relation to disclosure and enablement. In the case of disclosure, when the matter relied upon as prior art consists (as in this case) of a written description, the skilled person is taken to be trying to understand what the author of the description meant. His common general knowledge forms the background to an exercise in construction of the kind recently discussed by this House in *Kirin-Amgen Inc v Hoechst Marion Roussel Ltd* [2005] RPC 9. And of course the patent itself must be construed on similar principles. But once the meanings of the prior disclosure and the patent have been determined, the disclosure is either of an invention which, if performed, would infringe the patent, or it is not. The person skilled in the art has no further part to play. For the purpose of enablement, however, the question is no longer what the skilled person would think the disclosure meant but whether he would be able to work the invention which the court has held it to disclose.

33. There is also a danger of confusion in a case like *Merrell Dow Pharmaceuticals Inc v H N Norton & Co Ltd* [1996] RPC 76, in which the subject-matter disclosed in the prior art is not the same as the claimed invention but will, if performed, necessarily infringe. To satisfy the requirement of disclosure, it must be shown that there will necessarily be infringement of the patented invention. But the invention which must be enabled is the one disclosed by the prior art. It makes no sense to inquire as to whether the prior disclosure enables the skilled person to perform the patented invention, since ex hypothesi in such a case the skilled person will not even realise that he is doing so. Thus in *Merrell Dow* the question of enablement turned on whether the disclosure enabled the skilled man to make terfenadine and feed it to hay-fever sufferers, not on whether it enabled him to make the acid metabolite.

In what ways do the 'disclosure' and 'enablement' requirements differ and why is it important to treat them as distinct? Here, it is worth noting Lord Walker's comments (in a concurring speech) that the practical importance of keeping the enquiries distinct may depend on whether low-tech or high-tech inventions are involved. For low-tech inventions 'the simple disclosure of the invention will probably be enough to enable the skilled person to perform it', but this is unlikely to be the case for high-tech inventions.[30]

How did the requirements of 'disclosure' and 'enablement' apply to the facts of *Synthon*? To establish disclosure, Synthon relied on the fact that their patent application had disclosed PMS in crystalline form. The problem was that the crystalline form disclosed in their application was different to the crystalline form disclosed in SmithKline's application. To address this problem, Synthon established at trial that the crystalline form of PMS was in fact monomorphic, rather than polymorphic. In other words, that PMS had only one crystalline form, rather than several crystalline forms, so that performance of their invention would inevitably have infringed the SmithKline patent. In seeking to establish enablement, the difficulty for Synthon was that the method described in their application, when performed, did not produce seeding crystals. However, they argued that a person skilled in the art would engage in reasonable trial and error and subsequently be able to crystallize the PMS. Jacob J (as he then was) accepted these arguments at first instance. They were also accepted by the House of Lords, which held that the Court of Appeal had fallen into error by confusing the requirements of disclosure and enablement.

In stating in *Synthon* that 'the matter relied upon as prior art must disclose subject matter which, if performed, would necessarily result in an infringement of the patent', was Lord Hoffmann retreating from the approach taken in *Merrell Dow* where the reverse-infringement test was apparently rejected for the purpose of assessing whether secret or

[30] *Synthon*, [64].

uninformative use anticipated the invention? Further, in *Merrell Dow* Lord Hoffmann held, in relation to anticipation by prior use, that 'the acts relied upon conveyed no information which would have enabled anyone to work the invention, i.e. to make the acid metabolite'.[31] In the light of *Synthon*, can this objection be characterized as one of lack of disclosure or lack of enablement? Here it is interesting to note that Lord Hoffmann in *Synthon* commented that the disclosure requirement in *Merrell Dow* had been satisfied because the patent specification for terfenadine disclosed the ingestion of the antihistamine and this 'necessarily entailed the making of the patented acid metabolite in their livers'. There was also enablement because the specification enabled the skilled person to make terfenadine and feed it to hay-fever sufferers. Given this was Lord Hoffmann's view of anticipation via the patent specification, do you think prior use in *Merrell Dow* failed for lack of disclosure or lack of enablement? In other words, was the difficulty identified in *Merrell Dow* with secret, inherent, or unknown use one relating to disclosure or enablement?

FURTHER READING

P. England, 'Novelty and sufficiency in a single, pan-European standard' [2010] EIPR 467.

C. Floyd, 'Novelty under the Patents Act 1977: the state of the art after *Merrell Dow*' [1996] EIPR 480.

12.1.5 NOVELTY IN RELATION TO PHARMACEUTICALS

Although new pharmaceutical substances or drugs may be patentable, the pharmaceutical industry has directed much of its research not towards the creation of new substances or drugs but to discovering new uses or new benefits of known ones. It seems there are two main explanations for this trend. First, the difficulty of coming up with truly new substances and, second, the ability to satisfy regulatory approval more easily if there is new use of an already existing substance, for which approval has already been obtained. The difficulty, however, with patenting a new use of a known substance is that it risks being caught by the method of medical treatment exclusion that was discussed at 11.9. As the Enlarged Board of Appeal in *Eisai/Second Medical Indication*[32] explained, this is because:

> a claim directed to the 'use of a substance or composition for the treatment of human or animal body by therapy' was in no way different in essential content from a claim directed to 'a method of treatment of the human or animal body by therapy with the substance or composition'. The difference between the two claims is one of form only and the second form of claim is plainly in conflict with Article 52(4) EPC [now Article 53(c) of the EPC].

The solution to the difficulty was to include Article 54(5) of the EPC, which provided:

> The provisions of paragraphs 1 to 4 shall not exclude the patentability of any substance or composition, comprised in the state of the art, for use in a method referred to in Article 52, paragraph 4, provided that its use for any method referred to in that paragraph is not comprised in the state of the art.

---

[31] *Merrell Dow*, p. 91. [32] G05/83 [1979–85] EPOR B241, [13].

Following the coming into force of the EPC 2000, however, the relevant provisions of Article 54 of the EPC now read:

(4) Paragraphs 2 and 3 shall not exclude the patentability of any substance or composition, comprised in the state of the art, for use in a method referred to in Article 53(c), provided that its use for any such method is not comprised in the state of the art.

(5) Paragraphs 2 and 3 shall also not exclude the patentability of any substance or composition referred to in paragraph 4 for any specific use in a method referred to in Article 53(c), provided that such use is not comprised in the state of the art.

In the PA 77 the equivalent provision to the previous Article 54(5) of the EPC was section 2(6). Now the corresponding provisions to the new Article 54(4)–(5) of the EPC are reflected in section 4A(3)–(4) of the PA 77. The effect of the old Article 54(5) of the EPC was considered at length by the Enlarged Board of Appeal in *Eisai*.

Eisai/Second Medical Indication G05/83 [1979–85] EPOR B241

In the course of examining seven separate appeals against refusals of European patent applications, the Technical Board of Appeal referred to the Enlarged Board of Appeal a question of law regarding medical use claims. It is worth noting that the Enlarged Board of Appeal refers in its decision to the old provision excluding methods of medical treatment (Article 52(4) of the EPC), which was expressed in terms of lack of industrial application.

Enlarged Board of Appeal:

15. Furthermore, Article 54(5) EPC provides that the general rules of law relating to novelty (Article 54(1) to (4) EPC) shall not exclude the patentability of any substance or compositions, comprised in the state of the art, for use in a method referred to in Article 52(4) EPC, provided that its use for any such method is not comprised in the state of the art. Thus the inventor of a 'first medical indication' can obtain purpose-limited product protection for a known substance or composition, without having to restrict himself to the substance or composition when in a form technically adapted to a specified therapeutic purpose. The appropriate protection for him is, therefore, in its broadest form, a purpose-limited product claim. No problem arises over its susceptibility of industrial application, within the meaning of Article 57 EPC.

16. Claims directed to the use of a substance or composition for the preparation of a pharmaceutical product are equally clearly directed to inventions which are susceptible of industrial application, within the meaning of Article 57 EPC.

In the above extract, the Enlarged Board of Appeal referred to the exception to novelty for pharmaceutical substances created by Article 54(5) of the EPC, namely, that use of an existing substance in a method of medical treatment satisfies the novelty requirement. However, this is provided that use of the substance for any such method is not already known and also that the invention is claimed as a purpose-limited product.

This latter requirement is necessary to avoid the prohibition on patenting of methods of medical treatment.

The Enlarged Board of Appeal also had to consider the situation where subsequent or second medical uses are discovered for known substances. This type of invention had been claimed in the Swiss Intellectual Property Office as follows: the 'use of a substance or composition for the manufacture of a medicament for a specified (new) therapeutic application'. The Enlarged Board of Appeal then considered the patentability of these 'Swiss-type' claims:

19. As indicated in the Enlarged Board of Appeal's communication dated 31 July 1984, having regard to the statement of practice of the Swiss Federal Intellectual Property Office, the Enlarged Board has also given careful consideration to the possibility of protecting second (and subsequent) medical indications by means of a claim directed to the use of a substance or composition for the manufacture of a medicament for a specified (new) therapeutic application. Such claims do not conflict with Article 52(4) EPC or Article 57 EPC but there may be a problem concerning the novelty of the invention.

20. Where the medicament itself is novel in the sense of having novel technical features, for example, a new formulation, dosage or synergistic combination, the ordinary requirements of Article 54(1) to (4) EPC will be met and there will in principle be no difficulty over the question of novelty, whether the claim be directed to the medicament *per se* or to the use of the active ingredient to prepare the medicament. The critical case is, however, that in which the medicament resulting from the claimed use is not in any way different from a known medicament.

21. As is rightly recognised by the Federal Court of Justice, Article 52(1) EPC expresses a general principle of patentability for inventions which are industrially applicable, new and inventive and it is clear that in all fields of industrial activity other than those of making products for use in surgery, therapy and diagnostic methods, a new use for a known product can be fully protected as such by claims directed to that use.

This is in fact the appropriate form of protection in such cases as the new and non-obvious use of the known product constitutes the invention and it is the clear intention of the European Patent Convention that a patent be granted for the invention to which a European patent application relates (cf. Articles 52(1), 69, 84 and Rule 29 EPC read together). Article 54(5) EPC provides an exception to this general rule, however, so far as the first use of medicaments is concerned, in respect of which the normal type of use claim is prohibited by Article 52(4) EPC. In effect, in this case the required novelty for the medicament which forms the subject-matter of the claim is derived from the new pharmaceutical use.

It seems justifiable by analogy to derive the novelty for the process which forms the subject-matter of the type of use claim now being considered from the new therapeutic use of the medicament and this irrespective of the fact whether any pharmaceutical use of the medicament was already known or not. It is to be clearly understood that the application of this special approach to the derivation of novelty can only be applied to claims to the use of substances or compositions intended for use in a method referred to in Article 52(4) EPC.

22. The intention of Article 52(4) EPC, again as recognised by the Federal Court of Justice, is only to free from restraint non-commercial and non-industrial medical and veterinary activities. To prevent the exclusion from going beyond its proper limits, it seems appropriate to take a special view of the concept of the 'state of the art' defined in Article 54(2) EPC. Article 54(5) EPC alone provides only a partial compensation for the restriction of patent rights in the industrial

and commercial field resulting from Article 52(4) EPC, first sentence. It should be added that the Enlarged Board does not deduce from the special provision of Article 54(5) EPC that there was any intention to exclude second (and further) medical indications from patent protection other than by a purpose-limited product claim. The rule of interpretation that if one thing is expressed the alternative is excluded (*expressio unius (est) exclusio alterius*), is a rule to be applied with very great caution as it can lead to injustice. No intention to exclude second (and further) medical indications generally from patent protection can be deduced from the terms of the European Patent Convention; nor can it be deduced from the legislative history of the articles in question. On this last point, after conducting its own independent studies of the preparatory documents, the Enlarged Board finds itself also in accord with the conclusion of the Federal Court of Justice.

23. For these reasons, the Enlarged Board considers that it is legitimate in principle to allow claims directed to the use of a substance or composition for the manufacture of a medicament for a specified new and inventive therapeutic application, even in a case in which the process of manufacture as such does not differ from known processes using the same active ingredient.

As is apparent from the above extract, the Enlarged Board of Appeal considered that with Swiss-form claims novelty arose by virtue of the new therapeutic or pharmaceutical use and this was the case even if other therapeutic uses had already been discovered. The justification for this special approach to novelty was the terms of Article 54(5) of the EPC and the fact that it ensured that the exclusion in Article 52(4) of the EPC did not go beyond its proper limits.

The *Eisai* approach to novelty of Swiss-type claims to second medical uses of known substances was followed by the English courts in *John Wyeth's Application; Schering AG's Application*,[33] largely because of the desirability of achieving conformity with the EPO. The correctness of *Eisai* and *John Wyeth's Application*, along with the circumstances when a second medical use of a known substance may be regarded as novel, were considered by the Court of Appeal in the following two cases.

Bristol-Myers Squibb Co. v Baker Norton Pharmaceuticals [2001] RPC 1

The patent in dispute was for a particular regime covering the dosage and infusion duration of the known anti-cancer drug taxol. One inevitable side effect of the use of taxol is that it leads to a fall in the patient's white blood cell count (which is known as 'neutropenia'). Claim 1 of Bristol-Myer's patent, which was in Swiss form, sought protection for:

Use of taxol and sufficient medications to prevent severe anaphylactic reactions, for manufacturing a medicamentation for simultaneous, separate, or sequential application for the administration of from 135mg/m2 up to 175mg/m2 taxol over a period of about 3 hours or less as a means for treating cancer and simultaneously reducing neutropenia.

Bristol-Myers claimed that the novelty of their invention lay in the discovery of a regime of dosage/infusion of taxol that reduced the side effect of neutropenia, without losing any of the benefits of the taxol. In addition, a shorter dosage time meant that the supply

[33] [1985] RPC 545.

of taxol could be extended and it would minimize patient discomfort and expense. In an action for infringement with a counterclaim for revocation of the patent, the defendants alleged, inter alia, that the claim was merely to a method of medical treatment and thus unpatentable under Article 52(4) of the EPC and that the patent lacked novelty. In support of the latter claim, the defendants relied upon a public lecture (the Winograd lecture) given before the priority date, in which the initial stages of a clinical study comparing 24-hour continuous infusion with short, three-hour continuous infusion with different dosages were revealed. The lecture indicated that three-hour infusion was as feasible and safe as 24-hour infusion, but did not indicate that neutropenia was less. At first instance, Jacob J (as he then was) found that the claim was not to a method of medical treatment, but that it lacked novelty. There was an appeal to the Court of Appeal.

Aldous LJ:

34. The appellants accept that taxol had by the priority date been made available to the public as an effective treatment for cancer when administered over a period of 24 hours. Their case for novelty depended upon the last part of claim 1, namely that the medicament was for administration at the claimed dosage over about three hours as a means for treating cancer and simultaneously reducing neutropenia. Thus the claim in broad terms was for the use of two known products to produce a medicament with the novelty relied on being provided by the alleged new application. The appellants submitted that such a claim was novel according to the principles laid down by the Enlarged Board in the *Eisai* case which concluded in paragraph 23 of their reasons:

> the Enlarged Board considers that it is legitimate in principle to allow claims directed to the use of a substance or composition for the manufacture of a medicament for a specified new and inventive therapeutic application, even in a case in which the process of manufacture as such does not differ from the known processes using the same active ingredient.

35. A claim of the type considered to be legitimate by the Enlarged Board has become known as a 'Swiss-type' claim.

36. The conclusion reached in *Eisai* was at the time and has since been the subject of considerable discussion amongst patent lawyers. Its importance was recognised by Whitford J and Falconer J who sat en banc to decide whether it should be followed in this country. They held in *John Wyeth and Brothers Ltd's Application* and *Schering AG's Application* [1985] RPC 545 that it should be ... Having referred in detail to the reasoning of the Enlarged Board in *Eisai*, they held at page 567:

> That approach to the novelty of the Swiss type of use claim directed to a second, or subsequent, therapeutic use is equally possible under the corresponding provisions of the 1977 Act and, not withstanding the opinion expressed earlier as to the better view of the patentability of such a Swiss type claim under the material provisions of the Act considered without regard to the position, as it has developed under the corresponding provisions of the EPC, having regard to the desirability of achieving conformity, the same approach should be adopted to the novelty of Swiss-type of claim now under consideration under the material provisions of the Act.

37. The patent judges in the *John Wyeth* case correctly summarised the approach of the Enlarged Board and I believe that they came to the right conclusion in the cases before them ...

44. Mr Waugh submitted that claim 1 contained two novel features over the Winograd lecture. First, there was no disclosure that taxol was suitable for treating cancer when infused in the claimed amount over a period of three hours. Secondly, that there was no disclosure of reduction of neutropenia.

45. In my view the judge was right to reject the first submission. The claim requires the medicament to be suitable for treating cancer. Anybody listening to the lecture would have realised that the three-hour arm of the trial had not shown adverse hypersensitivity and was safe and that a response had been shown which Dr Winograd categorised as in the ballpark of what had been published up to now. No doubt it would have been sensible to await the conclusion of the trials, but the lecture disclosed that taxol was suitable for trying to treat cancer using a three-hour treatment.

46. The second submission depends upon the discovery that less neutropenia occurred during the three-hour infusion than during a 24-hour infusion. That was not mentioned in the lecture, but it was, as I have already pointed out, a discovery not a second therapeutic use as considered in *Eisai*. Further it is an inevitable consequence of the three-hour, 135mg/m2 infusion, described in the lecture and as such cannot impart novelty to the claim. As the judge held, the public could, using the information in the lecture, carry out the disclosed and claimed three-hour infusion with premedication without the need of any information from the patent. Such a person would inevitably monitor the patient's blood and would inevitably find the extent of neutropenia that occurred. The lecture contained clear and unmistakable directions to carry out such a three-hour infusion and the result would inevitably be that which was claimed. The information given in the lecture enabled the public to carry out an act which would have the inevitable consequence of less neutropenia. That conclusion is consistent with the attitude expressed by the Technical Boards in *Dow Chemical Company* T.90/0958 and *American Cyanamid* T.93/0279. In my view the judge came to the right conclusion. Claim 1 lacks novelty.

...

48. It is not necessary to come to any concluded view as to whether Mr Thorley's submissions as to the correctness of *Eisai* were right and I decline to do so. However, it is relevant to point out that *Eisai* has been applied by the EPO since at least 1985 and was accepted as correctly stating the law in 1985 by the Patents Court in the *John Wyeth* case. It has also, I believe, been applied by the members of the EPC, except perhaps France. There are therefore strong reasons for maintaining the view expressed by the patent judges in the *John Wyeth* case.

...

63. In my view the form of claim 1 does not disguise its effect. The invention was the discovery that by changing the treatment from a 24-hour infusion to three hours a similar effect was obtained with less neutropenia. That was a discovery that a change in the method of treatment provided the result. The claim is an unsuccessful attempt to monopolise the new method of treatment by drafting it along the lines of the Swiss-type claim. When analysed it is directed step-by-step to the treatment. The premedication is chosen by the doctor, and administered prior to the taxol according to the directions of the doctor. The amount of taxol is selected by the doctor as is the time of administration. The actual medicament that is said to be suitable for treatment is produced in the patient under supervision of the medical team. It is not part of a manufacture. In my view Mr Thorley is correct. The invention made and claimed was a method of treatment precluded from patentability by section 4(2) (Article 52(4)). That is emphasised by the way the allegations of infringement were pleaded.

Buxton LJ:

82. The conclusion that we ought to adopt the approach of the Board in *Eisai* requires us to look closely at what *Eisai* in fact decided; and in particular at what was meant by in *Eisai* by new 'pharmaceutical' use; new 'therapeutic' use; and new 'therapeutic application': all of these expressions appearing to carry the same meaning.

83. It is important in this enquiry to remember the emphasis placed by the Board on justification by analogy from cases of first medical use. Recognition of first medical use as a subject of patentability necessarily entails the use of the substance for new and completely different purposes from that in relation to which it is already known. If the Board's analogy is to hold, therefore, the relationship between the first and the second medical use must be of the same nature: the second medical use must be for an end-purpose distinctively different from the first, albeit also medical, purpose for which the substance was used. That not only follows from the structure of the Board's argument, but also from the need to respect the exclusion of methods for treatment from patentability. If the novelty can lie in the nature of use, rather than in the end-result at which that use aims, then it is indeed the method of treatment on which patentability rests.

...

88. Judged by the test just set out, I cannot agree that the patent in suit claims an invention that is new in the terms of Article 54 of the EPC as it was understood in *Eisai*. The inventive step is to find that in the use of taxol for the treatment of cancer three-hour infusion, when compared with longer infusion, achieves antineoplastic effect with reduced myelosuppression. That is an improvement in the method of administering an existing treatment; it is not a new therapeutic purpose. The judge was right to hold, at paragraph 66, that

> This is not a case of a second or other medical use. It is a case of mere discovery about an old use.
>   The invention is therefore not patentable....

93. ... As my Lord has described, the mixing is of amounts and types of premedication, and of amounts of taxol, all determined by the doctor in relation to the specific patient. It is in reality not a self-standing operation, but subordinate and incidental to the doctor's treatment of the patient. True it is that, in treating the patient, the doctor will, or at least may, administer the drugs according to the guidance contained in the patent. But that merely underlines that what the patent teaches is not how to manufacture a drug for use in the treatment of the patient, which would be in form at least a Swiss-type claim, but how to treat the patient: which is the teaching that the Swiss-type claim is designed to avoid.

94. The invention in the patent in suit is, therefore, of a method of medical treatment, which is not patentable.

Holman J (agreed with both Aldous LJ and Buxton LJ and added):

107. I respectfully disagree with the view of the judge that this patent was not a claim to a method of treatment of the human body by therapy. In my view it clearly was ... It is clear that the clinician must make a decision as to, and prescribe, the actual quantities of premedication to be given to, and taxol to be infused into the particular patient and as to the period of infusion ...

...

> 111. In the present case, however, the drug, taxol, is exactly the same; the method of administration, by injection and infusion, is exactly the same; and the therapeutic application or purpose, namely the attempt to treat cancer, is exactly the same. The only difference is the discovery that if the drug is infused over a shorter period an undesirable side-effect, neutropenia, is less than it otherwise would be, while the therapeutic effect remains. No 'previously unrecognised advantageous properties in [the] chemical compound' have been discovered. All that has been discovered (important though that discovery is) is that if the compound is administered over a shorter period, one of its disadvantageous side-effects will be less than it otherwise would be.

How would you describe the ratio of *Bristol-Myers v Norton*? Is it that the claim was in effect a method of medical treatment, given the interventions and steps that would have to be taken by medical staff to implement the invention? Or is it that the Swiss-form claim lacked novelty because it did not disclose a new and distinct therapeutic purpose but simply disclosed that an old use would reduce the side effects associated with taxol? Alternatively, is the ratio that the invention lacked novelty because the Winograd lecture contained clear and unmistakeable directions to carry out the new infusion regime and an inevitable consequence of doing so would have been to reduce neutropenia? The exact ratio of *Bristol-Myers v Norton* was crucial to a later decision of the Court of Appeal, in which it considered the novelty of a new dosage regime.

Actavis UK Ltd v Merck & Co. Inc. [2008] EWCA Civ 444, [2008] RPC 26

Merck had obtained a patent in respect of the following:

> The use of [finasteride] for the preparation of a medicament for oral administration useful for the treatment of androgenic alopecia in a person and wherein the dosage amount is about 0.05 to 1.0mg. (Claim 1)

The substance finasteride was known and as at the priority date it was also known that it could be used to treat androgenic alopecia (i.e. male pattern baldness). Nevertheless, Merck claimed that the particular dosage regime was new. Warren J rejected this argument at first instance, holding that claim 1 was invalid for lack of novelty. On appeal, the Court of Appeal considered whether a new dosage regime could be novel according to *Eisai* and subsequent Board of Appeal authority and whether *Bristol-Myers v Norton* precluded a finding of novelty.

> **Jacob LJ** (delivering the judgment of the court):
>
> 22. Next the Board [in *Eisai*] puts on one side cases where it sees no novelty objection:
>
> [20] Where the medicament itself is novel in the sense of having novel technical features—e.g. a new formulation, dosage or synergistic combination—the ordinary requirements of Article 54(1) to (4) EPC will be met and there will in principle be no difficulty over the question of novelty, whether the claim be directed to the medicament *per se* or to the use of the active ingredient to prepare the medicament.

23. In the course of argument Rimer LJ noted that the Board considered that a new *dosage* form would be enough to confer novelty. Mr Prescott seized upon that, submitting that the Board clearly contemplated that a new dosage—even for treating a disease previously treated with the same substance in a different dosage was regarded as novel. We agree. A claim to a pill containing a 1mg dose of finasteride would be a claim to a new thing. No-one had made or proposed such a thing, so why should it not be novel? Whether it would be obvious is a quite different matter. Since the patent in fact has no claim to a pill with a 1 mg dose is not necessary to pursue this further, though in view of our conclusion on obviousness it may be that such a claim would have stood as valid on its own.

[Referring to Swiss-form claims:]

28. Does this mean only treatment of a different disease ('second medical indication' in a narrow sense), or does it also extend to a different method of using a compound for treatment of a particular disease when it was already known for use in treating that disease but by a different method?

29. We think that the latter should be the answer is fairly clear from policy. The Enlarged Board clearly had policy in mind for it went on to say:

[22] The intention of Article 52(4) EPC…is only to free from restraint non-commercial and non-industrial medical and veterinary activities.

So the method of treatment exception to patentability should be construed restrictively When Mr Thorley was asked what policy reason there should be for on the one hand allowing Swiss form second medical treatment claims for different diseases but not allowing them for the same disease, the only answer he could devise was that the treatment might cost more. Why, he said, should you have to pay more for a 1mg pill than for an out of patent 5mg pill? The reason is obvious—the 1mg pill has only come about because of expensive unpredictable research. Patented things often cost more. And the reason is because the monopoly has been given as result of the research which led to it. Research into new and better dosage regimes is clearly desirable—and there is simply no policy reason why, if a novel non-obvious regime is invented, there should not be an appropriate patent reward. Such a reward cannot extend to covering the actual treatment but a Swiss form claim which specifies the new, inventive, regime is entirely in accordance with policy.

…

31. Accordingly on the basis of *Eisai* alone we would hold that Swiss form claims are allowable where the novelty is conferred by a new dosage regime or other form of administration of a substance.

32. So holding is far from saying that in general just specifying a new dosage regime in a Swiss form claim can give rise to a valid patent. On the contrary nearly always such dosage regimes will be obvious—it is standard practice to investigate appropriate dosage regimes. Only in an unusual case such as the present (where, see below, treatment for the condition with the substance had ceased to be worth investigating with any dosage regime) could specifying a dosage regime as part of the therapeutic use confer validity on an otherwise invalid claim.

33. The EPO takes the same view about the effect of *Eisai* as us. For there is now clear Board of Appeal authority holding, as we do, that it follows from *Eisai* that a novel dosage regime can confer novelty to a Swiss form claim. In *Genentech/method of administration of*

IFG-I, T1020/03 [2006] EPOR 9 a Legal Board of Appeal specifically so held in an unusually detailed and carefully crafted reasoned opinion. It said:

[72] ...the Board interprets decision G 5/83 [*Eisai*] allowing Swiss form claims directed to the use of a composition for manufacture of a medicament for a specified new and inventive therapeutic application, where the novelty of the application might lie only in the dose to be used or the manner of application. This Board allowed such a claim, where only the manner of application was new, already eleven years ago in T 0051/93 of 8 June 1994. The discussion in decision G 0005/83 concerning further medical indications did indeed refer to use for treating a new illness. But the Board regards this significant only of the fact that most further medical use claims will refer to a new illness, as in that case novelty and inventive step are more likely to exist than in the case of a minor modification of the treatment known for an existing illness. The logic of decision G 0005/83 allowing claims to further medical uses of known compositions, seems equally applicable to any use of such known composition for a new and inventive treatment which cannot be claimed as such because of Article 54(4) EPC first sentence.

34. *Genentech* was hardly a new departure in some respects, even though it disapproved certain earlier decisions. The quoted passage refers to T0051/93, an important case not cited in *BMS*. It was about a claim to 'use of X for the manufacture of a medicament for use in the treatment by subcutaneous administration of [an identified disorder]'. The prior art disclosed the use of X *for the same disorder* but by intramuscular administration. The difference in the method of treatment was enough to confer novelty because the purpose of manufacture was different. There cannot be any sensible difference between different dosage regimes and different methods of administration: either they confer novelty or they do not. The EPO has decided both do.

The court referred also to the fact that Germany and New Zealand permitted Swiss-form claims whose novelty depends on a new treatment by a different dosage regime or method of administration. The court went on to conclude that, subject to the binding effect, if any, of *Bristol-Myers v Norton*, it would follow the EPO and hold that a new dosage regime is enough to confer novelty on a Swiss-form claim.

The court then turned to analyse the Court of Appeal decision in *Bristol-Myers v Norton* and concluded that the ratio was that the claim was essentially to a method of medical treatment and *not* that a Swiss-form claim lacks novelty if the only difference between it and the prior art is a new dosage regime for a known medical condition. The court went on to consider the conclusions of Warren J at first instance:

74. The Judge held the claim lacked novelty and was for a method of treatment. In both cases he considered that *BMS* required him so to do. As to novelty for the reasons we have given we think he was wrong because there is no clear *ratio* of *BMS* on the point.

75. As to the method of treatment point, the Judge dealt with it briefly. He accepted Mr Thorley's submission that the dosing regime was a matter of choice for the doctor and that as far as the prior art was concerned it would make no difference whether the patient was given five 1 mg tablets a day or one 5mg tablets per day. But that is not enough in our view to mean that the claim is in substance to a method of treatment. There is nowhere

near the degree of involvement of medical personnel which turned the case in *BMS*. In its essence the claim here is to the use of finasteride for the preparation of a medicament of the specified dosages. It is not aimed at and does not touch the doctor— it is directed at the manufacturer. Putting it another way, even if *BMS* is right on this point, it cannot be extended to cover every case where novelty depends on a specified dosage regime. After all every prescription medicine must be prescribed—that does not mean they are all for methods of treatment.

76. Accordingly we think the Judge was wrong on both aspects. We should record in fairness that he did not have the benefit of the sustained argument we have had before us on these points.

...

84. Since we are satisfied that there is no clear *ratio* of *BMS* governing this case, we are free therefore to hold, and do hold, that we should follow *Genentech* and, subject to the cross-appeal on obviousness, allow the appeal.

The court then considered what the position would be if it were wrong and *Bristol-Myers v Norton* did in fact contain a clear ratio precluding the novelty of new dosage regimes. Rather surprisingly, it created a further exception to the rule in *Young v Bristol Aeroplane Co.*[34] that the Court of Appeal is bound to follow previous decisions of its own.

107. So we hold that there ought to be, and is, a specialist and very limited exception to the rule in *Young v The Bristol Aeroplane Company*. Spelling it out it is that this court is free but not bound to depart from the *ratio decidendi* of its own earlier decision if it is satisfied that the EPO Boards of Appeal have formed a settled view of European Patent law which is inconsistent with that earlier decision. Generally this court will follow such a settled view.

The decision of the Enlarged Board of Appeal in *Eisai* and the Legal Board of Appeal in *Genentech* supports a Swiss-form claim having novelty where it contains a new dosage regime. But do you agree with the Court of Appeal that this approach makes sense from a policy perspective? Will it lead to a flood of patents for known pharmaceuticals but in different dosages? Further, do you agree with the court's interpretation of the ratio of *Bristol-Myers v Norton*? Finally, is it desirable for the UK Court of Appeal to be able to depart from its own precedent in circumstances where the Boards of Appeal of the EPO have expressed a settled view that is inconsistent with that previously taken by the court?

The dispute in *Actavis v Merck* concerned the law in force before the EPC 2000 came into effect.[35] The Enlarged Board of Appeal has since considered the position under the revised EPC in *Abbott Respiratory/Dosage Regime*.[36]

---

[34] [1944] KB 718.
[35] Following the EPC 2000 the semantic difficulties associated with the Swiss-form claim may be avoided by formulating claims as 'compound X for use in treating disease Y'. See new Art. 54(5) of the EPC, and P. W. Grubb and P. R. Thomsen, *Patents for Chemicals, Pharmaceuticals, and Biotechnology: Fundamentals of Global Law, Practice, and Strategy* (5th edn, Oxford: Oxford University Press, 2010), p. 262.
[36] G2/08 [2010] EPOR 26.

Abbott Respiratory/Dosage Regime G2/08 [2010] EPOR 26

The patent related to the use of nicotinic acid for the manufacture of a sustained release medicament in a particular dosage for use in the treatment by oral administration once per day prior to sleep, of hyperlipidaemia (excess fat in the blood). The Board considered the three questions that were extracted above, beginning with the first question.

82 5.8 As regards new art.54(4) EPC which corresponds to the former art.54(5) EPC 1973, no fundamental change was intended. These provisions relate to the so-called first medical indication of a per se already known substance or composition.

83 In other words either a product for use in a method under art.53(c) EPC is new per se and can constitute the subject-matter of a product claim under art.53(c), second sentence, EPC, or a product (substance or composition) is already known per se but can nevertheless be granted patent protection provided, under art.54(4) EPC, said product has not yet been used in a method under art.53(c), first sentence, EPC....

[The Board then turned to consider the new Article 54(5) EPC.]

86 5.9 In contrast to the absence of any provision on this in the EPC 1973, art.54(5) EPC now expressly allows further patent protection of substances or compositions already known as medicines provided their use in a method under art.53(c) EPC be specific and not comprised in the state of the art.

87 Thus, under the new law the lacuna in the former provisions, which had been filled in a praetorian way by the Enlarged Board of Appeal with decision G5/83 and the case law based on that decision, no longer exists....

99 5.10 Reformulated, the first question corresponds in fact to the following:
Is a new use, deserving patent protection, of a per se known medicament, necessarily restricted to a disease not yet treated by said composition?

100 5.10.1 This question was mainly although not unanimously answered in the negative by the Boards of Appeal under the old law, EPC 1973, provided the invention was claimed in the so-called Swiss-type format, adopted by the Enlarged Board of Appeal in its decision G5/83 [ie *Eisai*]. That decision of the Enlarged Board of Appeal had filled a gap in the legal provisions and allowed claims concerning a second therapeutic indication of a known product, although not specifying whether such a second use could be something else than the treatment of another disease.

101 5.10.2 Under the new law, EPC 2000, the lacuna in the old provisions which had been closed in a praetorian way by decision G5/83 and the subsequent case law of the boards of appeal, no longer exists. art. [sic] 54(5) EPC now provides for patent protection of a known substance or composition for 'any specific use' of the said product in a method of therapy provided this use is not comprised in the state of the art and is inventive.

102 5.10.3 The Enlarged Board comes to the conclusion that there can be only one sensible way of construing the requirement underlying the specificity of the use, namely merely by contrast to the generic broad protection conferred by the first claimed medical application of a substance or composition, which is in principle not confined to a particular indication. Thus, the new use within the meaning of art.54(5) EPC need not be the treatment of another disease.

103 5.10.4 This is confirmed by the preparatory documents, which normally witness the intention of the legislator and constitute an ancillary means of interpretation of dispositions of law at least when it comes to their *ratio legis*....

108 5.10.5 From the very wording of decision G5/83, point 21 of the Reasons, the Enlarged Board of Appeal cannot deduce that said ruling was to be restricted to a new indication in the sense of a new disease.

109 The same holds true for point 23 of the Reasons, reflected in point 2 of the Order of decision G5/83. Both points mention 'a specified new and inventive therapeutic application' which does not necessarily correspond to a new indication being restricted to a 'new disease'.

110 5.10.6 This is illustrated by the case law of the Boards of Appeal subsequent to decision G5/83. In this respect the Enlarged Board of Appeal considers that there is no reason to restrict the intention of the legislator that 'the case law evolved by the EPO Enlarged Board of Appeal should be enshrined in the Convention' (see point 5.10.4 above) to the sole teaching of decision G5/83. In fact the legislator can reasonably be deemed to have been aware of and have wished to include this later jurisprudence; in this respect, the terms 'case law evolved' also make more sense.

111 5.10.7 Under the EPC 1973 a well-established case law already acknowledged patentability of substances and compositions known in the prior art for use in the treatment by therapy of a particular disease, even if they were directed to the treatment of the same illness, provided this treatment was new and inventive.

112 To cite merely a few see, e.g.:

(A) (T19/86), [1989] OJ EPO 24T893/90 of July 22, 1993, unreported, T233/96 of May 4, 2000, unreported, all relating to a novel group of subjects treated;

(B) T51/93, of June 8, 1994, unreported T138/95 of October 12, 1999, unreported both relating to a new route or mode of administration;

(C) ICI/Cleaning plaque (T290/86) [1991] E.P.O.R. 157; [1992] OJ EPO 414, ORTHO PHARMACEUTICAL/Prevention of skin atrophy (T254/93) [1999] E.P.O.R. 1; [1998] OJ EPO 285, relating to a different technical effect and leading to a truly new application as set out in T1020/03, [2007] OJ EPO 204.

113 5.10.8 The Enlarged Board of Appeal comes to the conclusion that, since the legislator wished to maintain the status quo, as regards the availability of patent protection for further therapeutic uses, and insofar intended no change due to the introduction of the current provisions of art.54(5) EPC, the principles established by this case law still hold true.

114 5.10.9 Therefore, the first sentence of art.53(c) EPC, prohibiting patent protection of methods for treatment by therapy, is to be read and understood together with the provisions of its second sentence and with those of arts 54(4) and art.54(5) EPC respectively so that far from being mutually exclusive they are complementary.

115 By virtue of a legal fiction arts 54(4) and art.54(5) EPC acknowledge the notional novelty of substances or compositions even when they are as such already comprised in the state of the art, provided they are claimed for a new use in a method which art.53(c) EPC excludes as such from patent protection.

116 In such cases the notional novelty and following it the non-obviousness, if any, is not derived from the substance or composition as such but from the purpose the claimed substance or composition is related to, namely from its intended therapeutic use.

117 Such use can be either a new indication *stricto sensu* (in the sense of a disease not yet treated by the claimed substance or composition), or one or more steps pertaining by their nature to a therapeutic method which may not be claimed as such.

118 Article 54(5) EPC, however, refers to '*any* specific use' [emphasis supplied]. On the basis of that wording in conjunction with the declared intention of the legislator to maintain the status quo of protection evolved in the case law of the boards of appeal under decision G5/83, the Enlarged Board holds that said use cannot be *ex officio* limited to a new indication *stricto sensu*.

...

6. Answer to the second referred question

120 6.1 The term 'dosage regime' may cover different acceptations that are normally reflected by corresponding features in the wording of the claim. However, the Enlarged Board of Appeal considers that there is no need to define the term more precisely here. Having regard to its findings with respect to the first question and considering in particular that, since art.54(5) EPC may be used in cases of the treatment of the same illness, the 'specific use' in the sense of that provision may reside in something else than the treatment of a different illness, the Enlarged Board of Appeal holds that there is no reason to give to a feature consisting in a new dosage regime of a known medicament a different treatment than the one given to any other specific use acknowledged in the case law (see point 5.10.7).

121 6.2 Therefore, the second question also has to be answered in the affirmative.

...

7. Answer to the third question

130 7.1 Consequence of the new law in respect of so-called Swiss-type claims.

131 7.1.1 Claim 1 submitted to the referring Board of Appeal for consideration is drafted in the so-called Swiss-type format. It has been established practice under the EPC 1973 that a patent related to a further medical application of a known medicament could only be granted for a claim directed to the use of a substance or composition for the manufacture of a medicament for a specified therapeutic application (cf. G5/83, point 2 of the Order).

132 Since the medicament per se was not new the subject-matter of such a claim was rendered novel by its new therapeutic application (cf. G5/83, points 20 and 21 of the Reasons). This praetorian approach was a 'special approach to the derivation of novelty' (cf. point 21 of G5/83) and therefore constituted a narrow exception to the principles governing the novelty requirements which was not intended to be applied in other fields of technology.

133 That praetorian ruling found its cause in the fact that a claim directed to the use of the substance or composition for the treatment of the human body by therapy had to be regarded as a step of treatment (see point 18, *in fine* of G5/83). A claim of that kind was forbidden. On the other hand only the first medical indication of a known composition in the form of a medicament was by virtue of art.54(5) EPC 1973 (art.54(4) EPC 2000) entitled to be drafted in the form of a purpose-related product claim. And since the intention of the legislator was clearly not to exclude second therapeutic indications of a known medicament from the field of patentability the so-called Swiss-type claim constituted the adequate but exceptional solution.

134 7.1.2 Article 54(5) EPC now permits purpose-related product protection for any further specific use of a known medicament in a method of therapy. Therefore, as mentioned in the preparatory document (MR/24/00, point 139) the loophole existing in the provisions of the EPC 1973 was closed.

135 In other words *'cessante ratione legis, cessat et ipsa lex'*, when the reason of the law ceases, the law itself ceases.

...

137 7.1.3 Moreover, Swiss-type claims could be (and have been) considered objectionable as regards the question as to whether they fulfil the patentability requirements, due to the absence of any functional relationship of the features (belonging to therapy) conferring novelty and inventiveness, if any, and the claimed manufacturing process. Therefore, where the subject matter of a claim is rendered novel only by a new therapeutic use of a medicament, such claim may no longer have the format of a so called Swiss-type claim as instituted by decision G5/83.

138 7.1.4 The Enlarged Board of Appeal is aware of the fact that patents have been granted and many applications are still pending seeking patent protection for claims of this type. In order to ensure legal certainty and to protect legitimate interests of applicants, the abolition of this possibility by the interpretation of the new law given by the Enlarged Board in this decision shall therefore have no retroactive effect, and an appropriate time limit of three months after publication of the present decision in the *Official Journal of the EPO* is set in order for future applications to comply with this new situation. In this respect the relevant date for future applications is their date of filing or, if priority has been claimed, their priority date.

The Enlarged Board of Appeal's ruling confirms that the new Article 54(4) and (5) of the EPC 2000 was not intended to change what is patentable but simply to close a legislative gap. The Enlarged Board ruled that according to Article 54(5) of the EPC, known pharmaceutical substances may be novel where they are used in the treatment of a particular disease. The novelty of such use can relate to use of a known pharmaceutical substance for a new therapeutic purpose or, where there is the same therapeutic purpose, from 'steps pertaining by their nature to therapeutic method', such as a new formulation or dosage regime.[37] However, the Enlarged Board departed from *Eisai* insofar as it rejected the prospective use of 'Swiss-type' claims. The Board found that 'Swiss-type' claims had been judicially developed in order to deal with the lack of an explicit recognition in the EPC 1973 that second therapeutic uses of a known medicament were permitted. But with the introduction of Article 54(5) in the EPC 2000 this legislative gap had been closed and so the need to rely on Swiss-type claims had also disappeared.

What then is the effect of prohibiting 'Swiss-type' claims?[38] At a basic level it means that claims for second medical use must be formulated in the following manner: 'substance X for

[37] Note that although the Enlarged Board refers only to 'therapeutic' methods or uses, second medical use claims may also extend to use of known substances or compositions in any method falling within the exclusion of s. 4A(1), so including diagnostic or surgical methods as well: see UK IPO, *Examination Guidelines for Patent Applications relating to Medical Inventions in the Intellectual Property Office* (May 2013), para. 105.

[38] Note that the Enlarged Board of Appeal indicated that their decision on Swiss-type claims would not have retrospective effect and only take effect three months after the publication of their decision in the Official Journal of the EPO. Thus, the EPO now rejects Swiss-type claims in applications with an earliest priority date of 29 January 2011 or later. The UK IPO issued a Practice Note on 26 May 2010 indicating that it would no longer allow claims in the Swiss-type format.

use in the treatment of disease Y'. This is a purpose-limited product claim and differs from the following formulation: 'The use of substance X in the treatment of disease Y', which is a method or process claim and would be prohibited as an unpatentable method of medical treatment under Article 53 of the EPC/section 4A(1) of the PA 77. The new form of second medical use claims are simpler and clearer than Swiss-type claims, not least because under the latter there was no functional relationship between the method of manufacturing a medicament and the intended use of the medicament. It also seems that the scope of the new form of second medical use claim will be broader than the old Swiss-type form, not least because the former is a purpose-limited *product* claim whereas the latter is a purpose-limited *process* claim.[39] However, the precise differences in scope of protection have not been fully explored. Further, there is the important issue of how second medical use claims may be infringed given that they are purpose-limited product claims and the fact that direct infringement does not require intention or knowledge, but simply the carrying out of the infringing act. In *Actavis v Merck*, the Court of Appeal suggested that this had not caused problems, 'because manufacturers, particularly those for prescription medicine and probably many others, have to provide detailed instructions and information about the use(s) and dosage(s) of their products. So in practice you can tell whether someone has used X for the manufacture of a medicament for the treatment of Y.'[40] However, problems have arisen when it comes to infringement as the litigation in *Warner-Lambert v Actavis* illustrates.[41] In this case, the defendant marketed a known drug, pregabalin, under the brand name 'Lecaent', for treating generalized anxiety disorder. The claimant owned a second medical use patent, which claimed use of pregabalin for the preparation of a pharmaceutical composition for treating pain,[42] and which it marketed under the brand name 'Lyrica'. In this situation, the court had to assess whether patent infringement occurred where doctors prescribed pregabalin generically rather than by brand name and a pharmacist dispensed 'Lecaent' instead of 'Lyrica' for the purpose of treating pain. An issue was whether the court has to look at the subjective intention of the use of pregabalin despite the fact that directly infringing activities do not require knowledge or intention. This issue is further explored at 13.1.3.8.

FURTHER READING

S. Bostyn, 'Personalised medicine, medical indication patents and patent infringement: emergency treatment required' [2016] IPQ 151.

J. Cockbain and S. Sterckx, 'Is the Enlarged Board of Appeal of the European Patent Office authorized to extend the bounds of the patentable? The G5/83 *Second Medical Indication/Eisai* and G2/08 *Dosage Regime/Abbott Respiratory* cases' (2011) 42 IIC 257.

12.1.6 NOVELTY OF PURPOSE

It has long been the case that new things, as well as new uses of an old thing, are patentable. But is a claim to an old substance used in an old way but for a new purpose patentable? This might seem very plausible in the light of what has been discussed in the previous section. However, this question is different insofar as it deals with novelty of purpose generally, as opposed to on the restricted basis of use of an existing pharmaceutical substance for a new

---

[39] *Board of Regents, University of Texas System/Cancer Treatment* T1780/12 [2014] EPOR 28, [39].
[40] *Actavis UK Ltd v Merck & Co. Inc.* [2008] EWCA Civ 444, [2008] RPC 26, [10].
[41] *Warner-Lambert v Actavis* [2015] RPC 25 (CA).
[42] The patent claims were in the old Swiss-type form.

therapeutic purpose, which is justified by specific statutory provisions. Whether novelty of purpose is permissible beyond the pharmaceutical sphere was considered by the Enlarged Board of Appeal in the following case.

Mobil/Friction Reducing Additive G2/88 [1990] EPOR 73

The patent application related to a compound for use as an additive for lubricating oils. The purpose of the additive was to reduce friction between sliding surfaces in an engine. However, a prior US patent disclosed the same compound as an additive for motor oils, except with the purpose of reducing rust formation. Mobil amended their patent to claim the use of the compound as a 'friction-reducing additive'. Several questions of law were referred to the Enlarged Board of Appeal, including whether novelty can exist where there is a known use of a known compound but for a new purpose.

Enlarged Board of Appeal:

6.1 ... The question of law which was referred to the Enlarged Board in G05/83 [*Eisai*] arose essentially because of the particular exclusion from patentability in relation to 'methods of treatment of the human or animal body' set out in the first sentence of Article 54(5) EPC, and the exception to that exclusion set out in Article 54(5) EPC. The reasoning in G05/83 is therefore primarily directed to answering a question of law concerning the allowability of claims whose subject-matter is a particular kind of medical or veterinary invention. The *ratio decidendi* of that decision is essentially confined to the proper interpretation of Articles 52(4) and 54(5) EPC in their context.

...

In contrast, the question of law which has been referred to the Enlarged Board in the present case is not related to medical inventions but is of a general nature, being primarily concerned with the question of interpretation of Article 54(1) and (2) EPC.

6.2 Question (iii) assumes that the only novel feature in the claim under consideration is the purpose for which the compound is to be used. However, in so far as the question of interpretation of Article 54(1) and (2) EPC and the question of the allowable scope of protection (if any) of inventions concerning a further non-medical use are matters of general importance, it will be appropriate for this Board to consider the question raised more generally, and in particular to consider other possible constructions for such use claims.

[We can see that the Enlarged Board of Appeal refused to draw analogies with *Eisai* on the basis that this decision was concerned with a specific question of law, namely, the proper interpretation of Article 54(5) of the EPC, whereas the question of law in the present case was of a general nature. The Board went on to consider this question:]

7.1 ... In relation to a claim to a use of a known entity for a new purpose, the initial question is again: what are the technical features of the claimed invention? If the new purpose is achieved by a 'means of realisation' which is already within the state of the art in association with the known entity, and if the only technical features in the claim are the (known) entity in association with the (old) means of realisation, then the claim includes no novel technical feature. In such a case, the only 'novelty' in the claimed invention lies in the mind of the person carrying out the claimed invention, and is therefore subjective rather than objective, and not relevant to the considerations that are required when determining novelty under Article 54(1) and (2) EPC.

7.2 It follows that in the Enlarged Board's judgment, in relation to a claim to a new use of a known compound (the new purpose of such use being the only potentially novel feature), if on its proper construction the claim contains no technical feature which reflects such new use, and the wording of the claim which refers to such new use is merely mental in nature and does not define a technical feature, then the claim contains no novel technical feature and is invalid under Article 54(1) and (2) EPC (because the only technical features in the claim are known).

[At this point, one might be forgiven for thinking that the Enlarged Board was about to conclude that the patent in question lacked novelty. However, the Board went on to hold that the *fact* that the substance achieved the new purpose would result in an objective technical feature of the invention, not residing in the mind of the user.]

10.3 The answer to question (iii) may therefore be summarised as follows: with respect to a claim to a new use of a known compound, such new use may reflect a newly discovered technical effect described in the patent. The attaining of such a technical effect should then be considered as a functional technical feature of the claim (for example, the achievement in a particular context of that technical effect). If that technical feature has not been previously made available to the public by any of the means as set out in Article 54(2) EPC, then the claimed invention is novel, even though such technical effect may have inherently taken place in the course of carrying out what has previously been made available to the public.

The same conclusion was reached by the Enlarged Board of Appeal in *Bayer/Plant Growth Regulating Agent* G06/88.[43] Here the patent application was directed to the use of a compound as a fungicide, whereas the prior art described the use of the same compound as an agent for influencing plant growth. The claim in question was held to include a functional technical feature, namely, 'that the named compounds, when used in accordance with the described means of realisation, in fact achieve the effect (that is, perform the function) of controlling fungus'.[44] Do you agree with the conclusions reached by the Enlarged Board of Appeal in these two decisions?

In the UK, concerns have been expressed about the approach in *Mobil Oil* and *Bayer*. For example, Lord Hoffmann in *Merrell Dow v Norton*[45] commented *obiter*:

I think it is fair to say that, in the United Kingdom at least, this aspect of the Enlarged Board's decision has been criticised on the ground that a patent for an old product used in an old way for a new purpose makes it difficult to apply the traditional United Kingdom doctrine of infringement. Liability for infringement is, as I have said, absolute. It depends upon whether the act in question falls within the claims and pays no attention to the alleged infringer's state of mind. But this doctrine may be difficult to apply to a patent for the use of a known substance in a known way for a new purpose. How does one tell whether the person putting the additive into his engine is legitimately using it to inhibit rust or infringing by using it to reduce friction? In this appeal, however, we are not concerned with this aspect of the case.

The difficulties which novelty of purpose claims pose for determining infringement were most likely not in the forefront of the minds of the members of the Enlarged Board of Appeal because the EPO is concerned only with issues of validity.[46] However, the difficulty identified

---

[43] [1990] EPOR 257. [44] [7]. [45] [1996] RPC 76, 92.
[46] In *Bristol-Myers Squibb Co. v Baker Norton Pharmaceuticals Inc.* [1999] RPC 253, 272, Jacob J (as he then was) commented at first instance that it is not helpful for the EPO 'to take a view on validity (particularly novelty) which simply leaves intractable problems for an infringement court'.

by Lord Hoffmann is particularly real for English courts because they deal with *both* validity and infringement. As has already been noted in the previous section and is discussed further at 13.1.3.8, similar difficulties arise in the context of second medical use claims, i.e. patents for known pharmaceuticals used for a particular therapeutic purpose.

12.1.7 SELECTION PATENTS

We have seen that, in relation to pharmaceutical substances, there is a statutory exception for novelty that has been broadly interpreted by UK courts and also the Enlarged Board of Appeal. The area of selection patents has traditionally been considered as another (judge-made) exception to the novelty requirement, although recent jurisprudence suggests otherwise.[47]

The concept of selection patents arose in response to the problem caused by patenting compounds. More specifically, an earlier disclosure might have referred to an extremely broad class of compounds (i.e. a generic disclosure), yet later it may have been discovered that an individual compound within that class had a particular quality or advantage that was not previously known. Did the earlier generic disclosure (which would have included that individual compound) anticipate the individual compound? In *IG Farbenindustrie's Patent*,[48] Maugham J held that where the individual compounds had not been previously made, the patent might be valid if the following three requirements were satisfied:

> First, a selection patent to be valid must be based on some substantial advantage to be secured by the use of the selected members (the phrase will be understood to include the case of a substantial disadvantage to be thereby avoided). Secondly, the whole of the selected members must possess the advantage in question. Thirdly, the selection must be in respect of a quality of a special character which can fairly be said to be peculiar to the selected group.[49]

This decision was followed and the notion of selection patents further explored by the House of Lords in *EI du Pont de Nemours & Co's (Witsiepe's) Application*.

EI du Pont de Nemours & Co.'s (Witsiepe's) Application [1982] FSR 303

Du Pont sought a patent under the Patents Act 1949 for co-polyesters made of three ingredients: (1) terephthalic acid, (2) polyalkylene oxide, and (3) 1,4-butanediol. These co-polyesters were described as especially effective in injection moulding because of their improved hardening rates. Du Pont's application was opposed on the basis, inter alia, of anticipation by an earlier patent specification published in 1952. The published specification claimed a class of co-polyesters that had an enhanced absorptive capacity for water, thus enabling them to be more readily dyed in the form of fibres for textiles. The specification mentioned the first two ingredients of the applicant's invention, together with a series of nine glycols defined by a general formula, of which 1,4-butanediol was named as one. However, the working examples described the use only of the first member of the series, namely, ethylene glycol. It was argued that the earlier

---

[47] *Dr Reddy's Laboratories (UK) Ltd v Eli Lilly and Co. Ltd* [2009] EWCA 1362, [2010] RPC 9.
[48] (1930) 47 RPC 289.   [49] At 322–3.

patent specification gave sufficient directions to enable a chemist to make any of the indicated nine co-polyesters and that each and all of these was therefore available to the public and anticipated Du Pont's invention. The Hearing Officer accepted this objection, but was reversed by Whitford J in the Patents Court. The Court of Appeal upheld Whitford J's judgment and an appeal to the House of Lords was dismissed.

Lord Wilberforce (delivering the leading speech), at pp. 309–12:

In order to consider whether [the opponent's] argument is correct, or whether it is too simplistic, it is necessary to look more closely at the process by which an invention is disclosed in a document, and the nature of the identification required. There are several principles here involved. First, it may be true to say as a general rule that where an invention for a substance is specifically disclosed, with a claim for particular advantages, or where a substance is already known, a discovery that the disclosed or known substance has some advantage or useful quality not previously recognised does not give a right to a patent. The difficulty arises when disclosure is made of a group or class of substances for which some advantage is claimed, and later it is found that one or more of this group or class possesses special advantages not belonging to the rest of the group or class, and not previously identified. This situation arises particularly in relation to inventions in the chemical field, particularly where molecular combinations are involved. In many fields, of which those concerned with polymeric chains are a good example, the number of combinations of chains, sub-chains, rings, individual molecules, may be very large. When a researcher is able to discover that a particular combination produces advantageous results he will most probably be able to assert, and will assert in the specification of his invention, that the same qualities will be produced by a number of variants or homologues described by a formula, or formulae. Moreover, having described how to produce the particular combination, he may well be able to assert, with truth, that productions of any of the combinations can be made by any skilled chemist, following the indications he has given. Is, then, the mere fact that he has disclosed or published in general terms the possibility of these combinations, in such a way that they can be made, a disclosure or publication of unrecognised advantages which may be found to be possessed by one or some of them?

The law regarding selection patents has been developed to deal with this problem. It has done so in the direction of recognising two objectives, first to protect the original inventor, as regards the invention which he has made, but secondly, to encourage other researchers in the field to use their inventive powers so as to discover fresh advantages and to treat the discovery of such advantages as inherent in selected members of the group or class as a patentable invention. The modern statement of this part of the law as regards chemical patents is the judgment of Maugham J in *I G Farbenindustrie A.G.'s Patents* (1930) 47 RPC 289, a case concerned with chemical combinations for the production of dyes.

…

In the first place, in order to leave open a field for selection by a subsequent inventor, it does not matter whether the original field is described by formula or by enumeration. A skilled chemist could, in most cases, quite easily transform the one into the other and the rights of the subsequent inventor cannot depend upon the notation used. In the present case, the I.C.I. specification uses both a formula, and, to some extent, an enumeration: it does not matter to which one directs attention.

Secondly, the size of the initial group or class is not in itself decisive as to a question of prior publication of an invention related to a selected member or members. A selection patent might be claimed for one or several out of a class of 10 million (*cf. I G Farbenindustrie A.G.'s*

Patents v.s. p. 321) or for one out of two (*cf.* the selection of one of two epimers of a synthetic penicillin combination). The size of the class may be relevant to a question of obviousness, and that question in turn may depend, in part, upon whether the later invention relates to the same field as that occupied by the prior invention, or to a different field. If an ordinary uninventive man would not be likely to look for the advantages he desires to produce in the area occupied by the prior invention, a decision to do so may well amount to the beginning of an inventive step. Here, to look for a product possessing special thermoplastic and elastomeric qualities in a 20-year old patent concerned with producing dyable fibres involves, *prima facie*, an inventive approach.

Thirdly, disclosing a prior invention does not amount to prior publication of a later invention if the former merely points the way which might lead to the latter.

…

It is the absence of the discovery of the special advantages, as well as the fact of non-making, that makes it possible for such persons to make an invention related to a member of the class.

Applying the law as I have endeavoured to state it, I have no doubt that the invention made by Du Pont was not disclosed or published by I.C.I. The latter merely indicated that the use, with other ingredients, of one preferred glycol would produce a compound with particular qualities, suggesting at the same time that use of any one of the other eight glycols would produce the same result. There was no statement that any of these others had in fact been used or that the product resulting therefrom had been found to have any particular advantages. That left it open to Du Pont to select one of them, to exercise upon it inventive research, and to discover that the product so made had valuable properties in a different field. I do not therefore understand how it can be claimed that this product, with its advantages, had been anticipated by I.C.I.

The approach to so-called 'selection patents' articulated in *Du Pont* applied to pre-1977 patent law. With the introduction of the PA 1977 to implement the EPC 1973 the question arose whether this approach would remain relevant or simply be treated as a quirk of the old law. In *Dr Reddy's Laboratories (UK) Ltd v Eli Lilly and Co. Ltd*, the Court of Appeal had occasion to consider the requirements for dealing with selection patents set out in *IG Farbenindustrie's Patents* and *Du Pont* and their relevance.

Dr Reddy's Laboratories (UK) Ltd v Eli Lilly and Co. Ltd [2009] EWCA Civ 1362, [2010] RPC 9

The claimant (appellant) had sought revocation of the defendant's (respondent's) European patent (UK) on the grounds of lack of novelty, inventive step, and insufficiency. The defendant's patent related to olanzapine, a popularly used anti-psychotic agent used in treating schizophrenia. One of the pieces of prior art relied upon was UK provisional specification 1,533,235 ('the 235 provisional'). This claimed a wide class of thieno-benzodiazepines as 'having useful central nervous system activity'. The class was defined according to a general formula. Formula I of this included at least 1,019 compounds and the preferred 'narrower' class comprised 86,000 compounds. Olanzapine was one of the compounds within formula I and the preferred class but was not mentioned specifically. The claimant contended that, on this basis, olanzapine lacked novelty and inventiveness and further, that so-called 'selection patent' requirements had not been satisfied here.

These challenges to validity (along with the insufficiency challenge) were rejected at first instance and the appeal to the Court of Appeal was dismissed.

Jacob LJ (Richards LJ in agreement):

Lack of Novelty over 235

23. Olanzapine is one of the 1019 compounds of formula (I) and one of the 86,000 compounds of the 'preferred' class. It is not mentioned specifically.

24. DRL contends that nonetheless this specific compound lacks novelty—that in the language of EPC Art.54 it formed 'part of the state of the art' having been 'made available to the public by means of a written … description.' The contention amounts to this: that every chemical class disclosure discloses each and every member of the class. It would, it seems, even apply if the formula had simply been written down without any suggested utility.

25. I reject the contention for two reasons: firstly as a matter of *a priori* reasoning and secondly because it is inconsistent with settled EPO Board of Appeal case law.

26. First then, the *a priori* considerations apart from case-law. An old question and answer runs as a follows: 'Where does a wise man hide a leaf? In a forest.' It is, at least faintly, ridiculous to say that a particular leaf has been made available to you by telling you that it is in Sherwood Forest. Once identified, you can of course see it. But if not identified you know only the generality: that Sherwood Forest has millions of leaves.

27. The contention has no logical stopping place. If there is disclosure of olanzapine here, why would one not regard an even more general disclosure as a disclosure of it. Suppose the prior art had merely been of '3-ringed organic compounds'? Such a description would encompass much much bigger numbers than the 1019 of formula I. Yet the logic of the argument would be the same—that there is a disclosure of each and every member of the class.

28. I would add that I would regard the listing out of a great number of compounds as opposed to the use of a Markush formula in the same way. To say a particular book is identified by saying 'the books in the Bodleian' is no different from saying it is identified by providing access to the catalogue of the Bodleian.

29. Similarly it makes no sense to say that a generalised prior description discloses a specific matter falling within in [sic]. The judge's example illustrates the point. A prior disclosure of 'fixing means' is not a disclosure of a particular fixing means e.g. welding or riveting even though you could list out a whole number of ways of fixing things together which would include these means.

30. Thus logic dictates rejection of the argument that a disclosure of a large class is a disclosure of each and every member of it. So also does EPO case-law. Mr Carr accepted that was so, so I can take the matter quite shortly, going to just one case, *Hoescht/Enantiomers* T 0296/87, 30 August 1988, which effectively sums up earlier cases. It said:

6.1 Here the Board is guided by the conclusions it reached in its 'Spiro compounds' decision T 181/82 (OJ EPO 1984, 401) concerning the novelty of chemical entities within a group of substances of known formula. With regard to products of the reaction of specific spiro compounds with a (C1-C4)-alkyl bromide defined as a group, the Board drew a sharp distinction between the purely intellectual content of an item of information and the material disclosed in the sense of a specific teaching with regard to technical action. Only a technical teaching of this kind can be prejudicial to novelty. If any such teaching is to apply in the case of a chemical substance, an individualised description is needed.

So what one must look for by way of an anticipation is an 'individualised description' of the later claimed compound or class of compounds. This case is miles from that. It is noteworthy that the Board's application of that principle in that case to enantiomers was specifically followed by this Court in *Generics (UK) Ltd v H. Lundbeck A/S* [2008] EWCA Civ 311; [2008] R.P.C. 19 *per* Lord Hoffmann at [9].

31. It is not necessary here to go into what is sufficient to amount to an 'individualised description.' Obviously the question may partly be one of degree, but other considerations may come in too, for instance the specificity of any indicated purpose for making the compounds. A mere woolly indication of the possible use of the prior class may require less specificity than a precise one.

32. This view of the law accords with the decision of the House of Lords in *SmithKline Beecham plc's (Paroxetine Methanesulfonate) Patent* [2006] R.P.C. 10. Lord Hoffmann said:

> [22] If I may summarise the effect of these two well-known statements, the matter relied upon as prior art must disclose subject-matter which, if performed, would necessarily result in an infringement of the patent. That may be because the prior art discloses the same invention. In that case there will be no question that performance of the earlier invention would infringe and usually it will be apparent to someone who is aware of both the prior art and the patent that it will do so.

Where you have a patent for a particular chemical compound and a prior art general disclosure, performance of the general disclosure (which means no more than using anything within it) does not necessarily result in infringement of the patent. In this case, for instance, you can 'perform' 235 in any of 1019 ways—only one of them would result in infringement of the later patent.

33. Accordingly I would reject the anticipation attack. In so doing I am glad to find that the approach I adopt is not only the same as that in the EPO but also the same as that in Germany. It was well-articulated in the case involving the German equivalent of the patent in suit, *STADApharm No.1-2W 47/07* (29 May 2008)...

[Jacob LJ went on to discuss obviousness.]

Obviousness over 235

...

35. The 'individualised description' approach was *not* part of the UK approach to anticipation under the pre-EPC law. On the contrary the general rule was that 'disclosure of the class prima facie deprives its members of novelty' and 'prima facie a general disclosure of a class is a disclosure of all members of the class, however obscure and whatever the consequences.' (Blanco White Q.C., *Patents for Inventions* 4th Edn. (1974) p.120 fn.60, fn. 62. and p.121.

36. This is of great significance to understanding the previous law of 'selection patents.' To avoid a finding of anticipation a patent for a compound or sub-class had to disclose something special about the compound or sub-class, which led to the rules about so-called 'selection patents'. Those rules were famously formulated by Maugham J. in *I.G. Farbenindustrie's Patents* (1930) 47 R.P.C. 289 at p.322–3...

...

They were actually formulated under the common law, which did not draw a distinction between lack of novelty and obviousness, both of which fell under the general umbrella 'lack of subject-matter.' The rules were carried over by the judges into the newly codified law in

1932 and remained, almost as a special sub-branch of patentability, as part of English law until the 'new law of patents' (a recital to the Patents Act 1977) came in.

37. The rule was last considered as part of the pre-1977 law by the House of Lords in E.I. *Du Pont's de Nemours & Co (Witsiepe's) Application Patent* [1982] F.S.R. 303. We had much debate before us analysing what Lords Wilberforce and Simon had to say about the position and the differences between them. Interesting though it was, in the end I did not find it helpful. It is most unlikely that the courts of any of the other 33 members of the European Patent Union would pay the slightest attention to English pre-1977 jurisprudence even of the highest court (why should they?). The EPO does not use the IG rules. They form no part of the EPO Guidelines for Examination and no Board of Appeal decision was cited which applied them. So I think the best thing to do is to regard them as part of legal history, not as part of the living law.

38. In so saying I am conscious that this court referred to the IG rules in *Hallen Co v Brabantia UK Ltd* [1989] R.P.C. 307, a case which was indeed under the 1977 Act. But I do not regarding it as deciding that the rules were part of the post-1977 law—that was never argued. The case involved no more than an attempt by the patentee to justify its patent by reference to the IG rules and an answer by the defendant that the patent did not comply with them because there was no disclosure of the alleged special advantage.

39. I would only add this about the IG rules. If one thinks about them, it is difficult to see how, realistically, they could be complied with unless the patentee carried out an enormous range of experiments. How can you show your class (or compound) has a 'substantial advantage' over the prior class without experimenting with at least quite a lot of the class—enough to make a sound prediction at the very least? Or how can you show that the quality which makes your selected class is peculiar to that class? If you put in your thumb and pull out a plum, how are you to say that there are no other plums in the pudding?

40. So I think the better approach is to see what the EPO Boards do when a patented product or class of products falls within a greater class. They deploy the objection of obviousness where the patentee has in truth made no real technical advance …

44. What then does the EPO do? The answer is essentially this: that it regards what can fairly be regarded as a mere arbitrary selection from a class as obvious. If there is no more than an arbitrary selection then there is simply no technical contribution provided by the patentee.

Lord Neuberger of Abbotsbury MR (Richards LJ in agreement):

103. In the present instance, it seems to me that there is no good reason for not following the Board's approach. Although *IG Farbenindustrie* (1930) 47 R.P.C. 289 is a decision which has often been cited and relied on in this jurisdiction, and *Witsiepe* [1982] F.S.R. 303 is a decision of the House of Lords, they were both concerned with patent validity under a different regime, namely the common law or the Patents Act 1949, i.e. purely domestic law relating to domestic patents. The 1977 Act, as already mentioned, was expressly enacted to create a 'new' regime for patents, and it was avowedly intended to be interpreted in accordance with the EPC. (It is only right to add that this does not mean that it is now appropriate to ignore cases decided under earlier legislation when considering issues under the 1977 Act: the wisdom and experience of previous judges in the field of patent law is of great value when it comes to considering problems thrown up today in the same field. The fact that the 1977 Act has introduced a 'new' law of patents which is, to a substantial degree, intended to align our law with certain international Conventions does not mean that our courts should need to reinvent the wheel.)

104. Further, as I have tried to show, and as Jacob L.J.'s analysis in paras.44 to 50 demonstrates, the Board's approach in cases such as these is consistent and clear, and it is based on its general approach to patent validity on novelty and obviousness. There is nothing in the 1977 Act (any more than there was in the 1949 Act, it is fair to say) which recognises, or even implies, a special approach to, or even the existence of, selection patents as a special category of patent, which require a different approach when determining validity from other patents.

In applying these principles to the facts of the case, the Court of Appeal concluded that the defendant's patent was both novel and inventive. It was contrary to common sense to say that the general disclosure of provisional 235 disclosed olanzapine. Further, the selection of olanzapine was not arbitrary and the single selected compound had technical applications which represented a contribution to the art. In what ways does the Court of Appeal's approach differ from the approach stated in *IG Farbenindustrie* and *Du Pont*? Does it seem like an approach more consistent with the general principles of novelty as discussed and inventive step (discussed at 12.2)?

12.2 INVENTIVE STEP

12.2.1 INTRODUCTION

To be patentable, an invention must feature an inventive step. According to section 3 of the PA 77, an invention will involve an inventive step 'if it is not obvious to a person skilled in the art, having regard to any matter which forms part of the state of the art'. Failure to satisfy this requirement is variously described as 'lack of inventive step', 'lack of inventiveness', or 'obviousness'. An invention that surmounts this hurdle is described as 'inventive' or 'non-obvious'.

The requirement of inventive step in the UK emerged from case law at the end of the 19th century. It was put on a statutory footing (as a ground for revocation of a patent) in 1932 and as a ground for opposing the award of a patent in 1949. The requirement of inventive step was included in the PA 77 in terms similar to the equivalent provision in the EPC (Article 56).[50] An obviousness objection can be raised during examination or, after the patent is granted, in opposition proceedings in the EPO or in revocation proceedings (either in the UK IPO or before a court).

Whereas novelty is a quantitative requirement—is the invention new, inventive step is qualitative in nature—is the invention obvious?[51] More specifically, the requirement of inventive step ensures that patents are granted for meritorious inventions, as opposed to obvious extensions and modifications of the prior art.[52] As stated in *PLG Research v Ardon International*, the 'philosophy behind the doctrine of obviousness is that the public should not be prevented from doing anything which was merely an obvious extension or workshop

---

[50] For further details of the history of this requirement see: F.-K. Beier, 'The inventive step in its historical development' (1986) 17 IIC 301; S. Gratwick, 'Having regard to what was known and used' (1972) 88 LQR 341; J. Bochnovic, *The Inventive Step: Its Evolution in Canada, the United Kingdom and the United States* (Munich: Max Planck, 1982).

[51] *Molnlycke AB v Proctor & Gamble Ltd* [1994] RPC 49, 112.

[52] A. Griffiths, '*Windsurfing* and the inventive step' [1999] IPQ 160, 163–4.

variation of what was already known at the priority date'.[53] Thus, while novelty is concerned with prior art acting as a 'flagpost', the inventive step enquiry considers prior art in terms of 'signposts', as the following statement from *General Tire* highlights: 'If, on the other hand, the prior publication contains a direction which is capable of being carried out in a manner which would infringe the patentee's claim, but would be at least as likely to be carried out in a way which would not do so, the patentee's claim will not have been anticipated, *although it may fail on the ground of obviousness.*'[54]

Inventive step is a question of fact and, as such, precedents have limited value in relation to this enquiry (aside from setting out the relevant principles of law) and it will be difficult to predict the outcome of a challenge based on obviousness.[55] Further, appeal courts will be reluctant to overturn decisions of lower courts on this issue.[56] Novelty is also a question of fact, but because of its quantitative focus it is much less evaluative and unpredictable than inventive step.

12.2.2 STATE OF THE ART

The inventive step enquiry asks whether the invention is obvious to a person skilled in the art, having regard to what forms part of the state of the art. What comprises the prior art is essentially the same as for novelty, but with two key differences. First, matters specified in section 2(3) of the PA 77, i.e. earlier unpublished patent applications, are excluded from the prior art for the purpose of obviousness. Presumably this is because the aim of section 2(3) is to avoid double patenting and, as this function is carried out at the novelty stage, it is unnecessary to apply this principle at the stage of inventive step. Second, it is possible to combine together different pieces of prior art, i.e. to 'mosaic' prior art, where it is obvious to do so (e.g. where there are cross-references).

The person skilled in the art is expected only to have scrutinized the information available in their own or closely related fields.[57] We turn now to consider the characteristics of this hypothetical person.

12.2.3 PERSON SKILLED IN THE ART

Central to the inventive step enquiry is the person skilled in the art, variously referred to as the hypothetical skilled addressee or notional skilled addressee. The attributes of this hypothetical person have been expounded in numerous cases and are helpfully summarized below by Laddie J.

Pfizer Ltd's Patent [2001] FSR 16

Laddie J, at pp. 226–7:

62. … The question of obviousness has to be assessed through the eyes of the skilled but non-inventive man in the art. This is not a real person. He is a legal creation. He is supposed to offer an objective test of whether a particular development can be protected by a patent.

---

[53] [1999] FSR 116, 136.
[54] *General Tire & Rubber Co. Ltd v Firestone Tyre & Rubber Co. Ltd (No. 1)* [1971] FSR 417, 444.
[55] *Molnlycke AB v Proctor & Gamble Ltd* [1994] RPC 49, 114.
[56] *Biogen v Medeva* [1997] RPC 1, 45.   [57] See *John Manville Corp.'s Patent* [1967] RPC 327.

He is deemed to have looked at and read publicly available documents and to know of public uses in the prior art. He understands all languages and dialects. He never misses the obvious nor stumbles on the inventive. He has no private idiosyncratic preferences or dislikes. He never thinks laterally. He differs from all real people in one or more of these characteristics. A real worker in the field may never look at a piece of prior art—for example he may never look at the contents of a particular public library—or he may be put off because it is in a language he does not know. But the notional addressee is taken to have done so. This is a reflection of part of the policy underlying the law of obviousness. Anything which is obvious over what is available to the public cannot subsequently be the subject of valid patent protection even if, in practice, few would have bothered looking through the prior art or would have found the particular items relied on. Patents are not granted for the discovery and wider dissemination of public material and what is obvious over it, but only for making new inventions. A worker who finds, is given or stumbles upon any piece of public prior art must realise that that art and anything obvious over it cannot be monopolised by him and he is reassured that it cannot be monopolised by anyone else.

63. Of particular importance in this case, in view of the way that the issue has been developed by the parties, is the difference between the plodding unerring perceptiveness of all things obvious to the notional skilled man and the personal characteristics of real workers in the field. As noted above, the notional skilled man never misses the obvious nor sees the inventive. In this respect he is quite unlike most real people. The difference has a direct impact on the assessment of the evidence put before the court. If a genius in a field misses a particular development over a piece of prior art, it could be because he missed the obvious, as clever people sometimes do, or because it was inventive. Similarly credible evidence from him that he saw or would have seen the development may be attributable to the fact that it is obvious or that it was inventive and he is clever enough to have seen it. So evidence from him does not *prove* that the development is obvious or not. It may be valuable in that it will help the court to understand the technology and how it could or might lead to the development. Similarly evidence from an uninspiring worker in the field that he did think of a particular development does not prove obviousness either. He may just have had a rare moment of perceptiveness. This difference between the legal creation and the real worker in the field is particularly marked where there is more than one route to a desired goal. The hypothetical worker will see them all. A particular real individual at the time might not. Furthermore, a real worker in the field might, as a result of personal training, experience or taste, favour one route more than another. Furthermore, evidence from people in the art as to what they would or would not have done or thought if a particular piece of prior art had, contrary to the fact, been drawn to their attention at the priority date is, necessarily, more suspect. Caution must also be exercised where the evidence is being given by a worker who was not in the relevant field at the priority date but has tried to imagine what his reaction would have been had he been so.

64. This does not mean that evidence from those in the art at the relevant time is irrelevant. It is not. As I have said, it may help the court to assess the possible lines of analysis and deductions that the notional addressee might follow. Furthermore, sometimes it may be very persuasive. If it can be shown that a number of ordinary workers in the relevant field at the relevant time who were looking for the same goal and had the same prior art, missed what has been patented then that may be telling evidence of non-obviousness.

Why is it that obviousness is evaluated according to a hypothetical person, as opposed to an expert in the particular field of the invention or an ordinary user of the invention, and what does this indicate about the level of inventiveness required by patent law? Where research in a field is normally conducted by a team, it may be that a notional team of researchers will replace the notional individual skilled in the art. See, for example, Mustill LJ's comments in *Genentech's Patent*:

> The successful pursuit of Genentech's research required the deployment of techniques in more than one field: for example, protein sequencing, handling mRNA, building a library, making a probe. I am satisfied on the evidence that there was nobody who united in himself (or herself) all the knowledge and practical skills in each field to a sufficient extent to carry out any kindred project, even if assumed to be non-inventive, on his own. This fact has two corollaries, neither of which I understood to be in dispute. First, that the hypothetical person is a team of persons. Second, that since the search embraced a series of arts, the obviousness of any particular contribution to the ultimate success must be adjudged by reference individually to the hypothetical members of the team, attributing to each the appropriate degree of skill.[58]

The person skilled in the art is also imputed with the *common general knowledge* of the particular art or technical field in question. The common general knowledge is an important source of information in its own right and also forms the basis from which the hypothetical addressee will consider the prior art. It must be stressed that common general knowledge does not equate to the prior art or what is public knowledge. Rather, 'it is part of the mental equipment necessary for competency in that art or science concerned'.[59] What may comprise this body of knowledge was helpfully summarized by the Court of Appeal in the case below.

Beloit Technologies Inc. v Valmet Paper Machinery Inc. [1997] RPC 489

Aldous LJ (with whom Schiemann and Hirst LJJ agreed), **at pp. 494–5:**

It has never been easy to differentiate between common general knowledge and that which is known by some. It has become particularly difficult with the modern ability to circulate and retrieve information. Employees of some companies, with the use of libraries and patent departments, will become aware of information soon after it is published in a whole variety of documents; whereas others, without such advantages, may never do so until that information is accepted generally and put into practice. The notional skilled addressee is the ordinary man who may not have the advantages that some employees of large companies may have. The information in a patent specification is addressed to such a man and must contain sufficient details for him to understand and apply the invention. It will only lack an inventive step if it is obvious to such a man.

It follows that evidence that a fact is known or even well-known to a witness does not establish that that fact forms part of the common general knowledge. Neither does it follow that it will form part of the common general knowledge if it is recorded in a document. As

---

[58] *Genentech's Patent* [1989] RPC 147 (CA), 278 (LJ Mustill); see also *Boehringer Mannheim v Genzyme* [1993] FSR 716, 726.
[59] R. Miller, G. Burkill, Hon. Judge Birss, and D. Campbell, *Terrell on the Law of Patents* (17th edn, London: Sweet & Maxwell, 2010), 8–24.

stated by the Court of Appeal in *General Tire & Rubber Co v Firestone Tyre & Rubber Co Ltd* [1972] RPC 457, at page 482, line 33:

The two classes of documents which call for consideration in relation to *common general* knowledge in the instant case were individual patent specifications and 'widely read publications'.

As to the former, it is clear that individual patent specifications and their contents do not normally form part of the relevant *common general* knowledge, though there may be specifications which are so well known amongst those versed in the art that upon evidence of that state of affairs they form part of such knowledge, and also there may occasionally be particular industries (such as that of colour photography) in which the evidence may show that all specifications form part of the relevant knowledge.

As regards scientific papers generally, it was said by Luxmoore, J in *British Acoustic Films* (53 RPC 221 at 250):

In my judgment it is not sufficient to prove common general knowledge that a particular disclosure is made in an article, or series of articles, in a scientific journal, no matter how wide the circulation of that journal may be, in the absence of any evidence that the disclosure is accepted generally by those who are engaged in the art to which the disclosure relates. A piece of particular knowledge as disclosed in a scientific paper does not become common general knowledge merely because it is widely read, and still less because it is widely circulated. Such a piece of knowledge only becomes general knowledge when it is generally known and accepted without question by the bulk of those who are engaged in the particular art; in other words, when it becomes part of their common stock of knowledge relating to the art.

And a little later, distinguishing between what has been written and what has been used, he said:

It is certainly difficult to appreciate how the use of something which has in fact never been used in a particular art can ever be held to be common general knowledge in the art.

Those passages have often been quoted, and there has not been cited to us any case in which they have been criticised. We accept them as correctly stating in general the law on this point, though reserving for further consideration whether the words 'accepted without question' may not be putting the position rather high: for the purposes of this case we are disposed, without wishing to put forward any full definition, to substitute the words 'generally regarded as a good basis for further action'.

How does the common general knowledge of a person skilled in the art differ from the state of the art? What sorts of things might you expect to see included in the latter that would not be included in the former?

The person skilled in the art asks whether the invention is technically or practically obvious, as opposed to whether it is commercially worthwhile or obvious to pursue.[60] As we shall see, this means that evidence of the commercial success of an invention is not essential to proving its inventiveness and, indeed, is very cautiously approached when it comes to this enquiry. Even so, courts have taken commercial considerations into account when determining the mindset of a person skilled in the art. For example, in *Dyson Appliances*

---

[60] *Hallen Co. v Brabantia (UK) Ltd* [1991] RPC 195, 213 (Slade LJ).

Ltd v Hoover Ltd[61] the Court of Appeal held that the trial judge had been correct to take into account, as part of the mindset of the person skilled in the art, commercial considerations that made it extremely unlikely that a particular line of enquiry would be pursued. More specifically, the invention related to a vacuum cleaner which operated by virtue of cylindrical and conical cyclone units, such that the dirt could be emptied directly from the units and filter bags were not required. The trial judge had imputed to the notional addressee an aversion to cyclone units and an addiction to the use of filter bags, on the basis that the vacuum cleaner industry was steeped in usage of the latter. The fact that this prejudice of the field was commercially influenced did not matter. As Sedley LJ commented:[62]

> it remains the case that the perceived limits of technical practicability are a matter of mindset, and that mindset is characteristically affected by awareness of need, of which commercial potential is both a function and an index.
>
> ...
>
> If then the intellectual horizon of practical research and innovation is in part set by the economic milieu, commercial realities cannot necessarily be divorced from the kinds of practical outcome which might occur to the law's skilled addressee as potentially worthwhile.
>
> ...
>
> The vacuum-cleaner industry was functionally deaf and blind to any technology which did not involve a replaceable bag. The fact that the handicap was entirely economically determined made it, if anything, more entrenched. The industrial perception of need was consequently, in the judge's happy coinage, bagridden. It is entirely in accordance with what we know about innovation that this commercial mindset will have played a part in setting the notional skilled addressee's mental horizon, making a true inventor of the individual who was able to lift his eyes above the horizon and see a bag-free machine.

How does taking commercial realities into account as part of the mindset of the person skilled in the art differ from asking whether an invention is commercially worthwhile or obvious?

12.2.4 UK APPROACH

The way in which UK courts have approached the obviousness inquiry was established by the Court of Appeal in *Windsurfing v Tabur*, and later restated by the Court of Appeal in *Pozzoli*.

12.2.4.1 *Windsurfing v Tabur*

Windsurfing International v Tabur Marine [1985] RPC 59

The patent in suit related to the basic equipment employed in windsurfing. It comprised a surfboard with a spar attached. The spar was connected to the surfboard by a joint

---

[61] [2002] RPC 22. [62] [87]–[89]. See also [56]–[57] (Aldous LJ) and [95] (Arden LJ).

having three axes of rotation. A triangular sail was attached to the spar by a pair of arcuate (i.e. wishbone) booms, which were also used as a handle to steer and manipulate the sail. The inventive concept was the 'free sail concept', i.e. the unstayed spar which was free to move in any direction under the direct control of the user.

The claimants commenced infringement proceedings under the Patents Act 1949 against the defendants, who in turn counterclaimed, contesting the validity of the patent on the grounds of, inter alia, novelty and obviousness. The claim of obviousness was based primarily on prior publication of an article written for an American periodical, which was reproduced in the UK in October 1966 in a publication produced by the Amateur Yacht Research Society (the Darby article). The article described essentially the same basic concept as the claimant's invention, namely, the use of an unstayed sail, which is used to steer the vehicle and which can be jettisoned in case of trouble. However, the sailboard described in the article used a square sail, and the unstayed spar was attached by a socket from which it could be removed, not by a movable joint. The article described how to build the sail and board, with diagrammatical illustrations. The defendants also relied on the prior use of a 12-year-old child (Chilvers), who had made a sailboard similar to the patent in suit, except that it employed straight booms, rather than arcuate booms. The prior use had occurred at an inlet at Hayling Island on summer weekends during 1958.

Oliver LJ (delivering the judgment of the court), **at pp. 73–4:**

There are, we think, four steps which require to be taken in answering the jury question. The first is to identify the inventive concept embodied in the patent in suit. Thereafter, the court has to assume the mantle of the normally skilled but unimaginative addressee in the art at the priority date and to impute to him what was, at that date, common general knowledge in the art in question. The third step is to identify what, if any, differences exist between the matter cited as being 'known or used' and the alleged invention. Finally, the court has to ask itself whether, viewed without any knowledge of the alleged invention, those differences constitute steps which would have been obvious to the skilled man or whether they require any degree of invention. As regards the first step, we respectfully agree with the learned judge that the inventive concept of the patent is the free-sail concept. It is that which constitutes the essential difference between the patent in suit and other conventional vehicles propelled by sail. Going back, then, to the priority date, anyone familiar with sailing and sailing craft would then have known, as part of his general knowledge, the difference between square sail and Bermuda rigs and the disadvantages as regards manoeuvrability presented by the former. He would also have been familiar with twin booms arcuate in shape known as 'wishbone' booms which, though not in wide use in the 1960s, were well known to anyone interested in constructing light craft. Darby's article was addressed initially to the knowledgeable handyman for whom the American journal *Popular Science Monthly* (in which it first appeared) was designed and, so far as the publication in this country was concerned, was directed to members of a society dedicated to amateur research into yachts. It in fact disclosed, and disclosed to persons knowledgeable in the art, the self-same inventive step claimed by the patent in suit, the only difference of any substance being the use of the kite rig held by the crossed spar and boom instead of a Bermuda rig with a wishbone boom. We agree, of course, that one must not assume that the skilled man, casting his experienced eye over Darby, would at once be fired with the knowledge that here was something which had a great commercial future which he must bend every effort to develop and improve, but he must at least be assumed to appreciate and understand the free-sail concept taught by Darby and to consider, in the light of his knowledge and experience, whether it will work and how it will work. In the light of the evidence, it seems to us inescapable that anyone skilled in the art and contemplating Darby's article in 1966 would immediately recognise, as the witnesses did, that the kite rig suggested for this very simple and elementary device would suffer from the disadvantages that it would perform poorly upwind and would require to be manipulated from the lee side of the sail. It does not, in our judgment, require the attribution to the skilled addressee of any inventive faculty to say that, if he applied his mind to it at all, it would be immediately obvious to him that these disadvantages would disappear if the rig were changed to Bermuda, a change which, as would also be obvious to him, required the sail to be stretched by means of a wishbone boom. It may well be that nobody in the United Kingdom at that time would have considered that there was a commercial future in this interesting beach novelty, but that is not as we conceive the question which has to be answered. One has, in our judgment, to postulate a person who comes to Darby knowing of the advantages of a Bermuda rig over a square rig and who is at least sufficiently interested to read the article and consider how the vehicle described would work on the water. All the evidence suggests that such a person would immediately see, by application of his own general knowledge, the adoption of a Bermuda rig as an obvious way of improving the performance of the Darby vehicle.

Obviousness based on prior publication—i.e. the Darby article—was enough to dispose of the appeal. However, the court went on to consider the obviousness challenge based on prior use of the Chilvers sailboard. It held that, although the use was of a short duration and had only a limited audience, it nonetheless formed part of the prior art and, further, that a person skilled in the art, on seeing the Chilvers sailboard, would have at once considered it obvious to replace the unconventional straight boom with an arcuate boom.

Although *Windsurfing v Tabur* was decided in relation to the Patents Act 1949, the structured approach to obviousness that it sets out has been followed in subsequent Court of Appeal decisions concerning the PA 77.[63] While the House of Lords has not expressly followed *Windsurfing v Tabur*, neither has it disapproved of the approach taken in that case.[64]

The Court of Appeal in *Pozzoli SPA v BDMO SA*[65] has restated the four-step *Windsurfing* approach as follows:

1. (a) Identify the notional 'person skilled in the art';

   (b) Identify the relevant common general knowledge of that person;

2. Identify the inventive concept of the claim in question or if that cannot readily be done, construe it;

3. Identify what, if any, differences exist between the matter cited as forming part of the 'state of the art' and the inventive concept of the claim or the claim as construed;

4. Viewed without any knowledge of the alleged invention as claimed, do those differences constitute steps which would have been obvious to the person skilled in the art or do they require any degree of invention?

---

[63] See e.g. Court of Appeal decisions in *Molnlycke AB v Proctor & Gamble Ltd* [1994] RPC 49; *Wheatley (Davina) v Drillsafe Ltd* [2001] RPC 133; and *Dyson Appliances Ltd v Hoover Ltd* [2002] RPC 22.

[64] See *Biogen v Medeva* [1997] RPC 1 and *Sabaf SpA v MFI Furniture Centres Ltd* [2005] RPC 10.

[65] [2007] FSR 37, 23 (Jacob LJ) (Keene and Mummery LJJ in agreement).

The difference between the *Windsurfing* four-step approach and the restatement in *Pozzoli* is marginal. Basically, the order of the first two questions in *Windsurfing* has been switched, so that the first step involves identifying the person skilled in the art and imputing to him the common general knowledge in the field, rather than identifying the inventive concept. Jacob LJ explained that the reason for the switch was that the inventive concept could only be understood through the eyes of the skilled addressee.[66] However, one might equally suggest that the person skilled in the art can only be identified once the inventive concept has been identified. In the second step Jacob LJ has also sought to emphasize that the inventive concept is not some generalized concept to be derived from the patent specification as a whole, but that which is reflected in the patent claim(s). Finally, the third step refers to the 'state of the art' rather than what was 'known or used' in order to make it consistent with the EPC and PA 77.

In this case the claimant was the proprietor of a European patent (UK) for a container suitable for storing a plurality of discs, in particular compact discs. The prior art included compact disc containers that featured tray-like holders with side-by-side recesses; however, the dimensions of these containers meant they were often too tall to be accommodated by an average bookshelf. The patentee's invention was a container in which the discs were offset and raised above one another. When the claimant sued the defendants for infringement, the defendants counterclaimed that the patent was invalid for lack of inventive step. The Court of Appeal upheld the first instance decision of obviousness. The court identified the person skilled in the art as a person who might wish to package discs; that this person would as part of their common general knowledge be aware of common forms of packaging CDs and not have a prejudice against overlapping discs; that the inventive concept was overlapping discs, spaced apart via a step-like arrangement; and that when compared with the prior art it was obvious to overlap the discs if you wanted to reduce the height of the container.

FURTHER READING

G. Grant and D. Dibbins, ' "Inventive concept": is it a good idea?' [2005] EIPR 170.

S. Gratwick, 'Having regard to what was known and used: revisited' (1986) 102 LQR 403.

A. Griffiths, '*Windsurfing* and the inventive step' [1999] IPQ 160.

12.2.4.2 The importance of identifying the inventive concept: the approach to collocation

What is the situation where the alleged inventiveness comes from combining known features? Previously, courts have applied the so-called 'law of collocation' as set out by Lord Tomlin in *British Celanese Ltd v Courtaulds Ltd*:[67]

> a mere placing side by side of old integers so that each performs its own proper function independently of any of the others is not a patentable combination, but that where the old integers when placed together have some working inter-relation producing a new or improved result then there is patentable subject-matter in the idea of a working interrelation brought about by the collocation of the integers.

---

[66] *Pozzoli SPA v BDMO SA*, [15].   [67] (1935) 52 RPC 171, 193.

Guidance on this issue is also to be found in the EPO Guidelines for Substantive Examination (December 2003 edition) in Chapter IV:

> 9.5 Combination vs. juxtaposition or aggregation. The invention claimed must normally be considered as a whole. When a claim consists of a 'combination of features', it is not correct to argue that the separate features of the combination taken by themselves are known or obvious and that 'therefore' the whole subject-matter claimed is obvious. However, where the claim is merely an 'aggregation or juxtaposition of features' and not a true combination, it is enough to show that the individual features are obvious to prove that the aggregation of features does not involve an inventive step. A set of technical features is regarded as a combination of features if the functional interaction between the features achieves a combined technical effect which is different from, e.g. greater than, the sum of the technical effects of the individual features. In other words, the interactions of the individual features must produce a synergistic effect. If no such synergistic effect exists, there is no more than a mere aggregation of features.

The House of Lords in *Sabaf SpA v MFI Furniture Centres Ltd*[68] clarified that there is no law of collocation in the sense of some kind of qualification to the test of inventive step stated in the PA 77. In other words, where the invention involves a combination of elements the proper test to apply is that contained in section 3. However, Lord Hoffmann (who delivered the leading speech) noted that in determining the invention, the court must decide whether it is dealing with a single inventive concept or a collocation of separate inventions. He added:

> If the two integers interact upon each other, if there is synergy between them, they constitute a single invention having a combined effect and one applies s. 3 to the idea of combining them. If each integer 'performs its own proper function independently of any of the others', then each is for the purposes of s. 3 a separate invention and it has to be applied to each one separately. That, in my opinion, is what Laddie J meant by the law of collocation.

Thus, where several known integers are combined, the court must determine whether this reflects a single invention or separate inventions and apply the test of inventive step accordingly. In other words, properly identifying the inventive concept is crucial. Lord Hoffmann held that Laddie J had adopted this approach and, having determined that two separate inventions were involved, had found that there were pieces of prior art that rendered each of the inventions obvious.[69]

The approach to inventiveness of a collocation of elements in *Sabaf* makes sense, although it is puzzling why a claim would in fact feature two or more separate inventions given the procedural requirement in section 14(5)(d) of the PA 77 that a claim shall 'relate to one invention or to a group of inventions which are so linked as to form a single inventive concept'. Could it be that examiners sometimes fall into error in this respect or that the courts subsequently take a different view to that adopted by the examiner?

FURTHER READING

M. Wilkinson, 'Patents: inventive step—collocation, validity and infringement' [2005] EIPR N47.

---

[68] [2005] RPC 10.   [69] [27].

12.2.4.3 The importance of identifying the inventive concept and its relationship to sufficiency

The House of Lords in *Conor Medsystems Inc. v Angiotech Pharmaceuticals Inc.*[70] has emphasized that inventive step and sufficiency (discussed at 12.3) are separate enquiries that should not be conflated. In this case, Angiotech and the University of British Columbia had obtained a European patent (UK) for a stent coated with taxol for treating restenosis. Stents are tubular metal scaffolds inserted into an artery to keep it open. When stents are inserted, there is often injury to the inner layer of the artery, which in turn produces an exaggerated healing response that tends to constrict the artery (known as restenosis). The patentees discovered that a known cancer-treating drug, taxol, had properties which could be used to inhibit or prevent tissue growth in restenosis and thus claimed taxol-coated stents. At trial, counsel for Conor Medsystems argued that the inventive step was not the taxol-coated stent but rather the *idea* of trying to treat or prevent restenosis by coating a stent with taxol. As such, the invention was obvious because it was known that taxol was worth a try. Further, it was unnecessary to show that it was obvious actually to use a taxol-coated stent to treat restenosis because the patent did not teach that it would work.

Lord Hoffmann, delivering the leading speech in the House of Lords, regarded Conor's argument 'as an illegitimate amalgam of the requirements of inventiveness (Article 56 of the EPC) and either sufficiency (Article 83) or support (Article 84) or both'[71] and that 'the invention is the product specified in the claim' as opposed to 'some vague paraphrase based upon the extent of his disclosure in the description'.[72] His lordship held that if the patent specification had not taught that a taxol-coated stent would treat or prevent restenosis, the patent would have been insufficient.[73] But once 'a specification passes the threshold test of disclosing enough to make the invention plausible' there was no reason to apply a different test of obviousness. Thus, the question was whether it was obvious that a taxol-coated stent would treat restenosis as opposed to whether it was obvious that taxol (among many other products) might have this effect.[74]

FURTHER READING

A. Carter, '*Conor Medsystems Inc v Angiotech Pharmaceuticals Inc*: House of Lords judgment clarifying the assessment of "inventive step"' [2008] EIPR 129.

12.2.4.4 'Obvious-to-try': *Conor v Angiotech*

Although the UK approach to obviousness is that set out in *Windsurfing v Tabur* as restated in *Pozzoli*, UK courts have nevertheless developed certain 'sub-tests' that may be applicable in appropriate circumstances. One such 'sub-test' is the 'obvious-to-try' test. This 'sub-test' may be particularly applicable where at the priority date the inventor had several technical options that could have been pursued in order to arrive at his invention. In *Conor v Angiotech*, the House of Lords held that the refusal of the Court of Appeal to apply the 'obvious-to-try' sub-test to the patent in suit was erroneous.

---

[70] [2008] UKHL 49, [2008] RPC 28.   [71] [17].   [72] [18].   [73] [27] and [37].   [74] [28].

Conor Medsystems Inc. v Angiotech Pharmaceuticals Inc. [2008] UKHL 49, [2008] RPC 28

The facts were discussed at 12.2.4.3.

Lord Hoffmann (delivering the leading speech):

42. In the Court of Appeal, Jacob LJ dealt comprehensively with the question of when an invention could be considered obvious on the ground that it was obvious to try. He correctly summarised the authorities, starting with the judgment of Diplock LJ in *Johns-Manville Corporation's Patent* [1967] RPC 479, by saying that the notion of something being obvious to try was useful only in a case in which there was a fair expectation of success. How much of an expectation would be needed depended upon the particular facts of the case. As Kitchin J said in *Generics (UK) Ltd v H Lundbeck A/S* [2007] RPC 32, para 72:

> The question of obviousness must be considered on the facts of each case. The court must consider the weight to be attached to any particular factor in the light of all the relevant circumstances. These may include such matters as the motive to find a solution to the problem the patent addresses, the number and extent of the possible avenues of research, the effort involved in pursuing them and the expectation of success.

43. But Jacob LJ rejected this approach (at paragraph 48) on the grounds that 'this is not an "obvious to try" case of the Johns-Manville type' because 'the patent has not in any way demonstrated that taxol actually works to prevent restenosis'. I agree with the Dutch court that patent law does not require such a demonstration. It was not a sufficient reason for not applying the ordinary principles of obviousness to the claimed invention. I would therefore allow the appeal.

Apparent from the above extract is the point referred to in the previous section, namely, that the issues of obviousness and sufficiency should be treated separately. Further, when it came to obviousness it was appropriate to ask whether a person skilled in the art would have a fair expectation of success sufficient to induce him to incorporate taxol in a drug-eluting stent. Lord Hoffmann concluded that if Pumfrey J had applied this test at first instance the patent would have been found to be inventive.[75] The Court of Appeal in *TEVA UK Ltd v LEO Pharma A/S*[76] reiterated that the 'obvious to try' test was useful in situations where there was a fair expectation of success. The patented invention was for an ointment comprising two active ingredients (calcipotriol and betamethasone) and a commercially available solvent suitable for treating an inflammatory skin disease, psoriasis. It was well established before the priority date that each active ingredient was suitable for use in separate psoriasis ointments, to be used successively, and there had been a long-felt need for an ointment that contained both active ingredients. However, it was not possible to combine the active ingredients because they became unstable when used with an aqueous solvent. The court found that while a person skilled in the art would appreciate that the solution to this problem was the combination of active ingredients with a non-aqueous non-toxic solvent, it could not be said 'that a formulator would have anything like a strong expectation that any particular

---

[75] [40]–[41]. See further *Generics (UK) Ltd v Daiichi Pharmaceutical Co. Ltd* [2009] EWCA Civ 646, [2009] RPC 23, [22].

[76] [2015] EWCA Civ 779.

non-aqueous non-toxic solvent would work … On the contrary he would have to undergo a research project.'[77] In other words, there was no sufficient expectation of success that the particular non-aqueous non-toxic solvent used in the patented invention would work.

FURTHER READING

P. England, 'Obvious to try, one year on' (2009) 4 JIPLP 114.

12.2.5 THE EPO APPROACH

12.2.5.1 'Problem-and-solution' analysis

The EPO has adopted a different approach to assessing 'inventive step' than the UK courts. This 'problem and solution' approach was first espoused in *Bayer/Carbonless Copying Paper*.[78]

The case involved a chemical invention, namely, microcapsules for carbonless copying paper which contained something called dyestuff-intermediate. The Examining Division refused the European patent application for lack of inventive step. This was because a German unexamined application disclosed the manufacture of carbonless copying papers containing the micro-encapsulated dyestuff solution. However, this paper was not impermeable to water, which meant that the paper had problems with storage stability, which in turn affected its duplicating capacity. In their appeal to the Technical Board, the applicant narrowed its claims to refer to the use of a more precise chemical element (which was water-repelling) to create special walls on the microcapsule containing the dyestuff-intermediate.

The Technical Board of Appeal allowed the appeal. It found that the applicant had defined the problem, vis-à-vis the nearest prior art as not just preparing other copying papers but improved copying papers. In order to solve the problem of storage stability, the applicant proposed to encapsulate the dyestuff-intermediate as a solution within capsule walls made up of the more precisely described chemical element. It was known from the German application that in principle a range of chemical elements could be used for the capsule walls. But, from the point of view of the problem of preparing copying paper that had improved storage stability, it did not indicate the more precisely prescribed chemical element. Thus, a person skilled in the art who had tried to improve copying papers would not, on the basis of the prior art cited, have arrived at the solution claimed in the application.

12.2.5.2 Criticisms

The problem-and-solution approach to inventive step has been widely accepted by the EPO. Even so, it was criticized by the Technical Board of Appeal in *Alcan/Aluminium Alloys Case*[79] for several reasons. First, the approach is inherently based on hindsight because it relies on the results of a search made with actual knowledge of the invention. Second, it is difficult to apply the approach to fields where new ground is broken, and thus no close prior art exists from which to formulate the problem. Third, it can lead to formulations of unrealistic and artificial technical problems, especially where there is no close prior art (or no problem in mind). Fourth, the benefit of the approach is said to be its 'objectiveness'. However, the problem-and-solution analysis does not remove the element of judgment inherent in the

---

[77] [21].   [78] [1981] OJ EPO 206.   [79] T465/92 [1995] EPOR 501.

assessment of inventiveness, but rather displaces it from the task set by the EPC to another task, which is inessential to Article 56 of the EPC.

Despite *Alcan*, the EPO and Technical Board of Appeal have continued to use the problem-and-solution approach, which involves asking whether the solution to a problem that an invention provides would have been obvious. The differences between the problem-and-solution approach and the UK *Windsurfing/Pozzoli* test, along with the strengths and weaknesses of the former, were helpfully explored by Jacob LJ in the following case.

Actavis UK Ltd v Novartis AG [2010] EWCA Civ 82, [2010] FSR 18

25. Another approach, often used in the EPO both for examination and opposition is the 'problem and solution approach' (PSA). It is conveniently described in the EPO's Guidelines for Substantive Examination (the Guidelines):

11.7 Problem-and-solution approach In practice, in order to assess inventive step in an objective and predictable manner, the examiner should normally apply the so-called 'problem-and-solution approach'. In the problem-and-solution approach, there are three main stages:

   (i) determining the 'closest prior art',

   (ii) establishing the 'objective technical problem' to be solved, and

   (iii) considering whether or not the claimed invention, starting from the closest prior art and the objective technical problem, would have been obvious to the skilled person.

26. I have a few comments about the PSA. First, and most important, is to emphasise that no-one suggests or has ever suggested that it is the only way to go about considering obviousness. The Guidelines say no more than that the examiner should 'normally' apply it. That makes sense for an examining office which needs a common structured approach. When it comes to a national court making a full multifactorial assessment of all relevant factors (which may include so-called 'secondary indicia' such as commercial success, especially if there has been a long-felt want) it may perhaps be used less often—particularly where there is significant room for argument about what the 'objective technical problem' is. In this case, however, as will be seen, I think the approach is indeed useful.

27. My second comment is about stage 1—identify the closest piece of prior art. It is not related to the remaining steps. It is about where they start from. Generally it is an immensely practical way of dealing with the fact that practitioners before the Office seem to think they can improve opposition attacks by the citation of a very large number of pieces of prior art. Currently there is nothing in the procedural rules (for instance a fee or costs sanction) to prevent this. Nor, in many cases, have practitioners themselves developed a culture of identifying their best piece or pieces (perhaps two or three maximum) of prior art. What is the Office to do when faced with a profligate number of citations? Laboriously consider the question of obviousness over each, one by one? Even though there may be 50 or more? That would be intolerable besides leading to even worse delays than there are now. So step 1 is essentially Office protective. It is an attempt to identify the best obviousness attack. The logic is simple: if that succeeds it does not matter if there are other attacks which might also succeed. And if it fails, other, weaker attacks would also do so.

28. So step 1 is a useful tool when there are many citations. It can have its difficulties—for instance deciding which piece of prior art is the closest can lead to something of a satellite dispute. You could argue, for instance, about whether you use a mechanical approach

of just identifying which citation has the highest number of elements corresponding to elements in the claim, or use a more holistic approach of asking which is conceptually or technically closest.

29. It will be noticed that there is nothing like PSA step 1 in the *Pozzoli/Windsurfing* approach. The reason is essentially this: that practitioners before the English Patents Court have learned to confine themselves to their best cases, especially by the time of trial. English patent judges are simply not faced with profligate citations. And indeed if a party attempted to indulge in profligate citation it would be likely to find that when the case-management stage of the case was reached, it would be made to identify its best case, or few best cases. Moreover wasteful conduct, which would generally include profligate citation of prior art, is likely to be met with adverse costs orders.

30. I turn to the next step—establishing the 'objective technical problem'. The Guidelines say this:

In the context of the problem-and-solution approach, the technical problem means the aim and task of modifying or adapting the closest prior art to provide the technical effects that the invention provides over the closest prior art. The technical problem thus defined is often referred to as the '*objective technical problem*'.

The objective technical problem derived in this way may not be what the applicant presented as 'the problem' in his application. The later may require reformulation, since the objective technical problem is based on objectively established facts, in particular appearing in the prior art revealed in the course of the proceedings, which may be different from the prior art of which the applicant was actually aware at the time the application was filed. In particular, the prior art cited in the search report may put the invention in an entirely different perspective from that apparent from reading the application only.

31. There is recognition here of that fact that in many cases the patentee did not start from the closest piece of prior art identified by step 1. He may have thought he was solving some larger or different problem. He may not have known of this piece of prior art.

32. The 'reformulation' referred to thus involves the court or tribunal artificially creating a problem supposed to be solved by the invention. It is perhaps here that there can be real difficulties: for so much may depend on that reformulation however objectively one attempts the reformulation.

33. The Guidelines grapple with those difficulties.

It is noted that the objective technical problem must be so formulated as not to contain pointers to the technical solution, since including part of a technical solution offered by an invention in the statement of the problem must, when the state of the art is assessed in terms of that problem, necessarily result in an ex post facto view being taken on inventive activity (T 229/85, OJ 6/1987, 237).

The expression 'technical problem' should be interpreted broadly; it does not necessarily imply that the technical solution is a technical improvement over the prior art. Thus the problem could be simply to seek an alternative to a known device or process providing the same or similar effects or which is more cost-effective.

34. For myself, I think the re-formulation—which really means retrospective construction—of a problem is perhaps the weakest part of the PSA. It will be noted that with the *Pozzoli/Windsurfing* approach, once one has finished the orienting step 3, the question is simply left open: is the invention obvious? There is no attempt to force the question into a problem/solution.

35. Moreover the PSA does not really cope well with cases where the invention involves perceiving that there is a problem, or in appreciating that a known problem, perhaps 'put up with' for years, can be solved. Take for instance the 'Anywayup Cup' case, *Haberman v Jackel International Ltd* [1999] F.S.R. 683. The invention was a baby's drinker cup fitted with a known kind of valve to prevent it leaking. Babies' drinker cups had been known for years. Parents all over the world had put up with the fact that if they were dropped they leaked. No one had thought to solve the problem. So when the patentee had the technically trivial idea of putting in a valve, there was an immediate success. The invention was held non-obvious, a conclusion with which most parents would agree. Yet fitting reasoning to uphold the patent into a PSA approach would not really work. For by identifying the problem as leakage and suggesting it can be solved, one is halfway to the answer—put in a valve.

36. Another aspect of obviousness which is not readily answered by the PSA is illustrated by the five-and-a-quarter inch plate paradox. This runs like this. Suppose the patent claim is for a plate of diameter five-and-a-quarter inches. And suppose no one can find a plate of that particular diameter in the prior art. Then (a) it is novel and (b) it is non-obvious for there is no particular reason to choose that diameter. The conclusion, that the plate is patentable, is so absurd that it cannot be so.

37. What then is the answer to the paradox? It is this: the five-and-a-quarter inch limitation is purely arbitrary and non-technical. It solves no problem and advances the art not at all. It is not inventive. And although 'inventive step' is defined as being one which is not obvious, one must always remember the purpose of that definition—to define what is inventive. That which is not inventive by any criteria is not made so by the definition. Trivial limitations, such as specifying the plate diameter, or painting a known machine blue for no technical reason are treated as obvious because they are not inventive.

38. The PSA does not assist in providing an answer to the paradox. This is for the simple reason that there is no problem and so no solution to it.

39. Having said that the PSA has its limitations I hasten to add this: the PSA is apt to work very well when there is no need to reformulate the problem. This, as will be seen, is such a case. And it also generally works where, although there needs to be a reformulation, the reformulation is not controversial.

40. The last step of the PSA, asking whether the invention is obvious starting from the closest prior art and the objective technical problem corresponds to *Pozzoli/Windsurfing* step 4, though the latter is not limited to any 'objective technical problem'. As I have said it leaves the question unconstrained by any necessary requirement to identify a problem.

On the approach to inventive step, how important is it for the UK also to adopt the problem-and-solution approach? Or is it fine for the UK to continue using the *Windsurfing/Pozzoli* test for obviousness? This depends on the extent to which the tests are in fact different. In *Generics (UK) Ltd v Daiichi Pharmaceutical Co. Ltd*,[80] Jacob LJ observed on this issue:

19. Some have seen this [*Windsurfing/Pozzoli* test] as a peculiarly English test. But I do not think it is. It is no more than a structure by which the question, obvious or not, is to be approached. The first three steps do no more than put the court in the right state to answer that question. They are necessary inherent preliminary matters to be determined before one

---

[80] [2009] EWCA Civ 646, [2009] RPC 23.

can properly set about answering the fourth question. Implicitly I think all courts (and patent offices) do and must do the same. The approach in the *Windsurfing/Pozzoli* way merely makes explicit that which is implicit. The value of doing this is that it makes one focus on each key element properly—just what are the attributes and knowledge of the notional skilled person, what exactly are the differences between the prior art and the invention and so on? In this case for instance it helps direct attention at the common general knowledge of the notional person skilled in the art—see below.

20. Some have suggested that *Pozzoli/Windsurfing* is different from the EPO's problem/solution approach. It is not. The problem/solution approach only applies at stage four. The first three stages must be carried out at least implicitly as much for the problem/solution approach as for any other.

Do you share Jacob LJ's views about the respective EPO and UK approaches to obviousness?

FURTHER READING

P. G. Cole, 'Inventive step: meaning of the EPO problem and solution approach, and implications for the United Kingdom: Part 1' [1998] EIPR 214.

P. G. Cole, 'Inventive step: meaning of the EPO problem and solution approach, and implications for the United Kingdom: Part 2' [1998] EIPR 267.

P. England, 'Towards a single pan-European standard—common concepts in UK and "continental European" patent law: Part 2: obviousness' [2010] EIPR 259.

P. England and S. Parker, 'Obviousness in the new European order' (2012) 7 JIPLP 805.

12.2.6 EVIDENCE OF INVENTIVE STEP

12.2.6.1 Primary evidence

Parties will call evidence from experts in the particular field about whether or not an invention was obvious. This is primary evidence and all other evidence is secondary in nature.[81] As already mentioned, the views of experts cannot be equated to those of the person skilled in the art. Nonetheless, courts will find expert evidence helpful in assessing the possible lines of analysis and research avenues a notional addressee might follow.

12.2.6.2 Secondary evidence

Secondary evidence is an aid to assessing primary evidence. It includes evidence concerning the commercial success of the invention, the failure of others to find a solution to the problem which the invention solves, and whether there has been a long-felt want for that particular invention. UK courts have been sensitive to the pitfalls of relying on secondary evidence and thus cautious about when it is relied upon.[82] What do you consider the pitfalls of secondary evidence to be?

---

[81] *Hoechst Celanese Corp. v BP Chemicals Ltd* [1997] FSR 547, 563; *Molnlycke AB v Proctor & Gamble Ltd* [1994] RPC 49, 113.

[82] e.g. see *Hoechst Celanese Corp. v BP Chemicals Ltd* [1997] FSR 547, 563; *Molnlycke AB v Proctor & Gamble Ltd* [1994] RPC 49, 113.

In the following case, Laddie J explored the way in which courts should approach secondary evidence, particularly that relating to commercial success.

Haberman v Jackel International Ltd [1999] FSR 683

The case involved a UK patent for a trainer cup, the specification for which was discussed at 11.5.3. A trainer cup is a feeding device for use by toddlers to help wean them off the mother's nipple or a feeding bottle, and to transfer to using a normal cup. A key difference between trainer cups and feeding bottles is that a feeding bottle uses a synthetic nipple-like teat, whereas a training cup uses a spout made out of soft or flexible material. The inventor of the patent in suit, Mrs Haberman, had observed that children were prone to knocking over their trainer cups, or shaking them violently, and that the contents of the cup would leak out as a result. She subsequently developed a trainer cup involving a conventional design, except for the use of a slit valve in the spout, which ensured that there was no leakage of fluid between sips. After obtaining a patent, Mrs Haberman granted an exclusive licence for the UK to V&A Marketing Ltd. The trainer cup, marketed as the Anywayup Cup, was immensely successful. Sales commenced in March 1996 and by the end of the year 20,000 cups were being sold per month. Twelve months after the launch, the cups were selling at 685,000 per annum and in the first nine months of 1998 sales had reached nearly 2 million cups. Both parties sued the defendant for infringement of the patent and the defendant counterclaimed for revocation of the patent on the ground, inter alia, of obviousness.

Laddie J, at pp. 699–701:

In most cases this type of evidence is of little or no value because it does no more than show that a particular item or process which employs the patented development has sold well. The mere existence of large sales says nothing about what problems were being tackled by those in the art nor, without more, does it demonstrate that success in the market place has anything to do with the patented development nor whether it was or was not the obvious thing to do. After all, it is sometimes possible to make large profits by selling an obvious product well. But in some circumstances commercial success can throw light on the approach and thought processes which pervade the industry as a whole. The plaintiffs rely on commercial success here. To be of value in helping to determine whether a development is obvious or not it seems to me that the following matters are relevant:

(a) What was the problem which the patented development addressed? ...

(b) How long had that problem existed?

(c) How significant was the problem seen to be? A problem which was viewed in the trade as trivial might not have generated much in the way of efforts to find a solution. So an extended period during which no solution was proposed (or proposed as a commercial proposition) would throw little light on whether, technically, it was obvious ... On the other hand evidence which suggests that those in the art were aware of the problem and had been trying to find a solution will assist the patentee.

(d) How widely known was the problem and how many were likely to be seeking a solution? Where the problem was widely known to many in the relevant art, the greater the prospect of it being solved quickly.

(e) What prior art would have been likely to be known to all or most of those who would have been expected to be involved in finding a solution? A development may be obvious over a piece of esoteric prior art of which most in the trade would have been ignorant. If that is so, commercial success over other, less relevant, prior art will have much reduced significance.

(f) What other solutions were put forward in the period leading up to the publication of the patentee's development? This overlaps with other factors. For example, it illustrates that others in the art were aware of the problem and were seeking a solution. But it is also of relevance in that it may indicate that the patentee's development was not what would have occurred to the relevant workers. This factor must be treated with care. As has been said on more than one occasion, there may be more than one obvious route round a technical problem. The existence of alternatives does not prevent each or [sic] them from being obvious. On the other hand where the patentee's development would have been expected to be at the forefront of solutions to be found yet it was not and other, more expensive or complex or less satisfactory, solutions were employed instead, then this may suggest that the *ex post facto* assessment that the solution was at the forefront of possibilities is wrong.

(g) To what extent were there factors which would have held back the exploitation of the solution even if it was technically obvious? For example, it may be that the materials or equipment necessary to exploit the solution were only available belatedly or their cost was so high as to act as a commercial deterrent. On the other hand if the necessary materials and apparatus were readily available at reasonable cost, a lengthy period during which the solution was not proposed is a factor which is consistent with lack of obviousness.

(h) How well has the patentee's development been received? Once the product or process was put into commercial operation, to what extent was it a commercial success. In looking at this, it is legitimate to have regard not only to the success indicated by exploitation by the patentee and his licensees but also the commercial success achieved by infringers. Furthermore, the number of infringers may reflect on some of the other factors set out above. For example, if there are a large number of infringers it may be some indication of the number of members of the trade who were likely to be looking for alternative or improved products…

(i) To what extent can it be shown that the whole or much of the commercial success is due to the technical merits of the development, i.e. because it solves the problem? Success which is largely attributable to other factors, such as the commercial power of the patentee or his license, extensive advertising focusing on features which have nothing to do with the development, branding or other technical features of the product or process, says nothing about the value of the intention.

I do not suggest that this list is exhaustive. But it does represent factors which taken together may point towards or away from inventiveness. Most of them have been addressed in this case.

[Laddie J went on to consider these factors in relation to the evidence and concluded that the patent disclosed an inventive step.]

At pp. 701–2:

There is no dispute that the problem which Mrs Haberman's patent seeks to solve, namely the leakage of fluids from feeding containers, has existed for a very long time. Nor is there any doubt that it was seen to be significant… The industry as a whole appears to have wanted to produce spill-proof trainer cups.

…

The variety of solutions put forward to meet the leakage problem is impressive not only in number but because they all appear to suffer from significant disadvantages when compared with Mrs Haberman's design… if one looks at what was on the market before April 1992 the multitude of difficult and partially ineffective designs is apparent. Although the objective of making a leak-proof cup was known, by and large it had not been achieved. There were numerous designs of products which could be rendered leak proof by parental intervention. But in all these cases the parent turned the cup on or off.

…

These efforts should be set against the simplicity of what Mrs Haberman suggested. All the raw materials were readily available. The simplest of valves, used frequently in the same trade, could be used to make a product which had all the virtues which anyone designing a product would want to achieve. The advantages of the use of such a design would have been immediately apparent, once it was thought of. There was nothing which was holding anyone back.

It is against this background that the claim to commercial success has to be gauged… Mrs Haberman's product was cheap, simple, effective and a remarkable commercial success.

…

The point to be made about this evidence is that the only selling feature relied upon was that the product was leak resistant. I have already noted that its appearance was dull and unexceptional. In other words it was only the effect of Mrs Haberman's design which was used to promote the Anywayup cup and it was only that which achieved the sales.

To what extent was Laddie J in *Haberman v Jackel* sensitive to the fact that commercial success may be attributable to factors other than the technical merits of the invention? Further, how does evidence of the failure of others and long-felt want interact with evidence of commercial success? Is it fair to say the latter type of evidence is only meaningful where in fact there has been a long-felt want and others, working from the same or similar prior art, have failed? Finally, do you agree with the conclusion reached by Laddie J about the inventiveness of the Anywayup trainer cup?

FURTHER READING

R. P. Merges, 'Commercial success and patent standards: economic perspectives on innovation' (1988) 76 Cal. L. R. 803.

12.3 SUFFICIENCY AND SUPPORT

12.3.1 INTRODUCTION

In addition to showing that an invention is patentable subject matter, new, inventive, and capable of industrial application, an applicant must satisfy certain disclosure requirements. Section 14(3) of the PA 77 provides that the *specification* of an application must disclose the invention in a manner that is clear and complete enough for it to be performed by the person skilled in the art.[83] This requirement is known as *sufficiency* of disclosure. In addition, section 14(5)(c) of the PA 77 provides that the *claims* must be clear and concise and supported by the description.[84] This requirement is known as the claims being *supported* by the description.

Each of these requirements is distinct, but interrelated. They are distinct insofar as they have differing purposes. Sufficiency of disclosure is aimed at ensuring that the consideration for granting the patent is extracted, i.e. ensuring that practical information about working the invention is disclosed to the public, whereas the requirement of the description supporting the claims is seeking to ensure that the patentee is not claiming a monopoly that is wider than the invention they have disclosed. The requirements are interrelated insofar as lack of sufficiency is explicitly a basis upon which a patent may be revoked;[85] however, lack of support is not. Even so, it has been held that failure to comply with the requirement of claims being supported by the description *is* a ground on which a patent can be revoked. In *Biogen v Medeva*[86] Lord Hoffmann, who delivered the leading speech of the House of Lords, held that the substantive effect of section 14(5)(c) of the PA 77 (i.e. sufficiency of disclosure) is that the description should constitute an 'enabling disclosure' and given that section 72(1)(c) of the PA 77 gives effect to this requirement, it must also include lack of support as a ground for revocation. The logic is that a description would not support claims for the purpose of section 14(5)(c) unless the specification contained sufficient material to constitute an enabling disclosure under section 14(3).

The interrelationship between section 14(3) and (5)(a) was explored again by the House of Lords in *Generics (UK) Ltd v H. Lundbeck A/S.*[87] The House confirmed the view taken in *Biogen v Medeva*, namely, that the requirements are closely connected, albeit that 'section 14(3) relates to the specification as a whole, whereas section 14(5)(c) relates to the claims which define the monopoly sought by the inventor' and the provisions 'operate together … to spell out the need for an "enabling disclosure" '.[88]

To summarize, the courts have solved the absence of lack of support as an explicit ground of revocation through linking the requirements of sufficiency and support and relying upon section 72(1)(c) of the PA 77 to encompass both. Another consequence of considering sufficiency and support as interrelated requirements is that courts have interpreted the concept of insufficiency in a more expansive way. As Arnold J described in *Sandvik Intellectual Property AB v Kennametal UK Ltd*,[89] there are three categories of insufficiency: classical insufficiency, ambiguity, and excessive claim breadth. We turn now to consider these.

12.3.2 SUFFICIENCY

12.3.2.1 Classical insufficiency

'Classical' insufficiency is concerned with where the person skilled in the art is unable to work the invention in light of the instructions in the specification and the common general knowledge. The Court of Appeal decision in *Mentor v Hollister* elucidates this conception of sufficiency.

---

[83] See also EPC, Art. 83.   [84] See also EPC, Art. 84.   [85] See PA 77, s. 72(1).
[86] *Biogen Inc. v Medeva Plc* [1997] RPC 1.   [87] [2009] UKHL 12, [2009] RPC 13.
[88] [19]–[20] (Lord Walker).   [89] [2011] EWHC 3311 (Pat), [2012] RPC 23, [106]–[124].

Mentor v Hollister [1993] RPC 7

Mentor had patented a new type of male incontinence device, which they marketed as the Freedom Catheter. The invention incorporated a layer of adhesive in a rolled-up sheath of latex rubber, such that when the sheath was unrolled the adhesive would be released onto the inside of the sheath and come into contact with the skin. This in turn created a leak-proof seal. At the other end of the sheath there was a tube leading to a bag for the collection of urine. The claimant's device achieved substantial commercial success in the UK and elsewhere. Hollister copied the device and, when sued for infringement, counterclaimed that the patent was invalid on the ground that it lacked sufficiency. More specifically, Hollister argued that the specification did not disclose the invention clearly and completely enough for it to be performed by a person skilled in the art because it failed to disclose which adhesive would be suitable for making the device, nor how to select a latex rubber to release the adhesive as the sheath was unrolled. The first instance judge found that the patent was valid. The defendant's appeal was dismissed.

Lloyd LJ (with whom Stuart-Smith and Scott LJJ agreed), at pp. 10–13:

…Disclosure of an invention does not have to be complete in every detail, so that anyone, whether skilled or not, can perform it. Since the specification is addressed to the skilled man, it is sufficient if the addressee can understand the invention as described, and can then perform it. In performing the invention the skilled man does not have to be told what is self-evident, or what is part of common general knowledge, that is to say, what is known to persons versed in the art. But then comes the difficulty. How much else may the skilled man be expected to do for himself? Is he to be able to produce what Mr Thorley called a workable prototype of the invention at his first attempt? Or may he be required to carry out further research or at least make some further enquiries before achieving success? And how does one draw the line between production of the so-called workable prototype and the subsequent development or 'optimisation' of the commercial product?

…

The parameters within which the skilled man is entitled to look for instruction were authoritatively stated by Cotton LJ in *Edison & Swan v Holland*, supra at page 277, and have often been repeated and paraphrased. On the one hand the addressee must be able to perform the invention without any further inventive step on his part. On the other hand it is not required that he should be able to perform the invention without any trial or experiment at all, in particular where the subject matter is new or especially delicate. Lindley LJ, at page 282, put the matter with somewhat different emphasis. He acknowledged that practice might be necessary, but added that he felt great difficulty in defining the amount of practice which might be required without affecting the validity of the patent. Nevertheless he was clear that practice was one thing; experiment and trial was another.

…

But if a working definition is required then one cannot do better than that proposed by Buckley LJ in giving the judgment of the Court of Appeal in *Valensi v British Radio Corporation* [1973] RPC 377. After referring to a number of earlier authorities, including *Edison & Swan v Holland*, he said:

We think that the effect of these cases as a whole is to show that the hypothetical addressee is not a person of exceptional skill and knowledge, that he is not to be expected to exercise

> any invention nor any prolonged research, inquiry or experiment. He must, however, be pre-
> pared to display a reasonable degree of skill and common knowledge of the art in making
> trials and to correct *obvious* errors in the specification if a means of correcting them can
> readily be found.

Then a little later:

> Further, we are of the opinion that it is not only inventive steps that cannot be required of the
> addressee. While the addressee must be taken as a person with a will to make the instruc-
> tions work, he is not to be called upon to make a prolonged study of matters which present
> some initial difficulty: and, in particular, if there are actual errors in the specification—if
> the apparatus really will not work without departing from what is described—then, unless
> both the existence of the error and the way to correct it can quickly be discovered by
> an addressee of the degree of skill and knowledge which we envisage, the description
> is insufficient.

In that case there was a mistake in the specification. But Buckley LJ's language is equally apt
to cover an omission. Aldous J held that the *Valensi* test is as apposite under the 1977 Act as
it was under the 1949 Act. I agree.

The court found that the judge had not erred in principle and that, on the facts, there was
no lack of sufficiency. Although several tests had been performed in order to produce a
workable prototype of the invention, this was routine trial and error and did not involve
prolonged experimentation.

In a later decision, *Novartis AG v Johnson & Johnson Medical Ltd*,[90] the Court of Appeal
cited with approval *Mentor v Hollister* and also referred to authority from the EPO
Technical Boards of Appeal,[91] and summarized the test for (classical) sufficiency thus: 'Can
the skilled person readily perform the invention over the whole area claimed without
undue burden and without needing inventive skill?'[92] Do you agree that sufficiency of disclosure should mean that a person skilled in the art is neither required to exercise inventiveness nor to carry out prolonged research or experimentation, even if that research is
straightforward (i.e. non-inventive) in nature? Should there be an additional aspect to the
sufficiency requirement, namely that the specification discloses the *best* mode of performing the invention? This used to be the case under the Patents Act 1949,[93] but is no longer so
under the PA 77.

12.3.2.2 Ambiguity and excessive claim breadth

Insufficiency arising from ambiguity is where the claim is so unclear that it is impossible for the person skilled in the art to know what falls within it. Whereas insufficiency
for excessive claim breadth deals with those situations where the breadth of the claim
goes beyond the technical contribution to the art made by the invention. It is this latter
category of insufficiency that has been the subject of two House of Lords' decisions.
The first decision was *Biogen v Medeva*,[94] where the principal claim of the patent in

---

[90] [2010] EWCA Civ 1039, [2011] ECC 10.
[91] *Detergents/UNILEVER* T0435/91 and *Plant gene expression/MYOCGEN* T-0494/92.
[92] [74].   [93] See PA 1949, s. 32(1)(h).   [94] [1997] RPC 1.

suit was for an artificially constructed molecule of DNA carrying a genetic code which, when introduced into a suitable host cell, would cause that cell to make antigens of the virus Hepatitis B (HBV). At the application date, the inventiveness of this invention lay in the fact that it permitted an artificially constructed molecule of DNA to be constructed *before* the sequencing of DNA was known. The invention involved taking fragments of DNA (cut with the use of restriction enzymes) and using standard plasmids to create a recombinant molecule inserted into a host bacterium that would produce HBV antigens.

The patent in suit generalized this invention in two ways: in terms of the result achieved and the method that had been used. It claimed *any* recombinant DNA molecule which expressed the genes of any HBV antigen in any host cell, and *any* method of manufacture that would achieve the necessary expression. Lord Hoffmann commented *obiter* that the reasoning that led to lack of support (discussed at 12.3.3) also led to lack of sufficiency.[95] Thus, the disclosure in the specification (which was of *one* particular method of creating a particular recombinant DNA molecule) was not clear and complete enough to enable a person skilled in the art to work the broad monopoly that was claimed (i.e. *any* recombinant DNA molecule which expressed the genes of any HBV antigen in any host cell or *any* method of creating such a molecule). To amount to sufficient disclosure, the specification would have had to disclose a general principle for the making of recombinant DNA capable of producing HBV antigens.

In a subsequent decision, *American Home Products Corp. v Novartis Pharmaceuticals UK Ltd*,[96] the Court of Appeal had occasion to consider sufficiency in relation to a biotechnological invention and sought to apply the *Biogen* principles. The claimants in the case held a second medical-use patent for a product called rapamycin, which was useful in suppressing transplant rejection (and which had previously been used for its antifungal and anti-tumour properties). Novartis also produced an immunosuppressant, referred to as SDZ RAD, which is a derivative of rapamycin. They were sued for infringement by the claimants who argued that the patent claim covered both rapamycin *and* its derivatives. The defendants counterclaimed, alleging that, if the patent claim was construed in that way, the patent was invalid for insufficiency. This was because the specification disclosed only the beneficial property of rapamycin and not a beneficial property of a *class* of products (i.e. rapamycin and its derivatives). Laddie J at first instance held that the patent was valid and infringed.

On appeal, Aldous LJ (with whom Sedley and Simon Brown LJJ agreed) held that the principles relating to sufficiency had been settled by *Biogen v Medeva*. Applying those principles, he concluded that a person skilled in the art, looking at the patent specification, would not have been able to predict *which* rapamycin derivatives would have beneficial immunosuppressant qualities. Instead, it would require the person skilled in the art to engage in prolonged tests in order to ascertain if the derivative did have the appropriate qualities. Thus, the patent specification did not provide an enabling disclosure across the breadth of the claim, but only a starting point for further research.[97]

In your view, does *American Home Products* illustrate insufficiency for excessive claim breadth or on 'classical' grounds?

Most recently, the House of Lords has clarified the nature and scope of insufficiency based on excessive claim breadth.

---

[95] At 53.   [96] [2001] RPC 8.   [97] [40]–[44].

Generics (UK) Ltd v H Lundbeck A/S [2009] UKHL 12, [2009] RPC 13

Lundbeck had previously held a patent for an organic compound, citalopram, which operates as an anti-depressant. After the patent expired its competitors began marketing citalopram. Citalopram is a racemate, meaning that it is a combination of two types of molecules, called enantiomers, each being a mirror image of each other. It was not known which of the (+) and (–) enantiomers of citalopram was responsible for its anti-depressant quality. Lundbeck devised a novel and inventive means of separating the (+) and (–) enantiomers and discovered that it was the (+) enantiomer that had the desired effect. They then applied for and obtained a European patent (UK) for the (+) enantiomer, known as escitalopram.

The generic pharmaceutical companies, Generics (UK) Ltd, Arrow Generics Ltd, Teva UK Ltd, and Teva Pharmaceutical Industries Ltd, brought an action for revocation of the Lundbeck patent, claiming that it lacked novelty, inventive step, and sufficiency. The attacks based on lack of novelty and obviousness failed at first instance. However, Kitchin J held that claims 1 and 3 were invalid for insufficiency. Claim 1 was to the (+) enantiomer itself and claim 3 was to a pharmaceutical composition comprising as an active ingredient the (+) enantiomer. Kitchin J based his conclusion on insufficiency on the House of Lords decision in *Biogen*.

On the issue of insufficiency, the Court of Appeal took a different view. It concluded that the claim was to a patented product, the enantiomer of the anti-depressant drug citalopram, and not to a class of products, as was the case in *Biogen*. As such, there was sufficiency of disclosure given that the patent specification disclosed at least one way of making the enantiomer. Jacob LJ noted that product claims provide extensive protection in at least two ways.[98] The first is that product claims are infringed whenever the product is made even if it is made by a method which is inventive and quite different from the patentee's route. Second, a product claim will provide a monopoly to the patentee over all uses of the product, even those which he has not discovered. Nevertheless, the court concluded that this was the nature of product claims and Parliament had seen fit to allow them.[99]

Generics (UK) Ltd et al. appealed to the House of Lords, but the appeal was dismissed.

Lord Neuberger (with whom Lord Phillips and Lord Scott agreed; Lord Walker and Lord Mance delivered concurring opinions):

74. Of course, sections 1 and 14 are concerned with the grant of patents, whereas it is section 72 (reflecting art 100 of the EPC) which is concerned with the revocation of patents, and which is therefore the section directly in point on this appeal. Section 72(1) provides that a patent can 'only' be revoked on certain specified grounds. These grounds include '(a) the invention is not a patentable invention', and '(c) the specification…does not disclose the invention clearly enough and completely enough for it to be performed by a person skilled in the art'. Section 72(1)(a) reflects section 1(1) though it may also go further. Section 72(1)(c) appears only to reflect section 14(3), but, as explained by Lord Hoffmann in *Biogen* [1997] RPC 1, 47, it also extends to what is covered by section 14(5)(c).

---

[98] *H. Lundbeck A/S v Generics (UK) Ltd* [2008] RPC 437, [54]–[55] (Jacob LJ).
[99] [46] (Lord Hoffmann) and [57] (Jacob LJ).

The reasoning of the courts below

75. In a sense, it was at this point that the reasoning of the Court of Appeal in this case ended. At [2008] RPC 19, para 36, Lord Hoffmann said that '[w]hen a product claim satisfies the requirements of section 1 of the 1977 Act, the technical contribution to the art is the *product* and not the process by which it was made, even if that process was the only inventive step'. Accordingly, as sections 1 and 14 appeared to be satisfied by the patent, he concluded that the claim to escitalopram was valid.

76. To the same effect, Jacob LJ said at [2008] RPC 19, para 52, that, as at June 1988, the pure (+)-enantiomer, as a product, was 'novel and non-obvious', and if 'one asks the straightforward question "Does the patent enable the skilled man to make it?" the answer is an equally straightforward "Yes". So, in the language of art 83, the patent "discloses the invention in a manner sufficiently clear and complete for it to be carried out." '

77. The different view formed by Kitchin J was not based on any disagreement with this approach as far as it goes, but on reasoning which is helpfully summarised in his judgment at [2007] RPC 32, paras 264 and 265. He described the obtaining of the purified enantiomers as 'an obviously desirable goal', and said that, accordingly, the 'inventive step' was 'not deciding to separate the enantiomers ... but finding a way it could be done'. He went on to say that the technical contribution made by the Patent was not to find a new product, but to find a way of making a product, namely a single enantiomer of citalopram, through the medium of isolating the diol intermediate.

78. Accordingly, the Judge concluded that, as the specification disclosed that the respondent had found only one way to make the (+)-enantiomer, it would be a monopoly disproportionate to the technical contribution if the Patent effectively covered all ways of making the enantiomer, which would be the effect of the product claim. The principle he relied on was succinctly encapsulated in a short sentence virtually at the end of his judgment, namely 'The first person to find a way of achieving an obviously desirable goal is not permitted to monopolise every other way of doing so.'

79. The sole authority upon which Kitchin J relied in support of this analysis was the speech of Lord Hoffmann in *Biogen* [1997] RPC 1. I propose first to consider whether his conclusion is justified on the basis of any principle or authority other than what was said in this House in *Biogen* [1997] RPC 1, and then to address the reasoning in *Biogen* [1997] RPC 1.

The insufficiency argument apart from *Biogen* [1997] RPC 1

80. The starting point must, of course, be the 1977 Act and the EPC. I have already identified and discussed the centrally relevant provisions of the 1977 Act, namely section 72(1)(a) and (c), which reflect art 100 of the EPC and refer back to sections 1(1), 14(3), and 14(5), which in turn reflect arts. 52, 83, and 84 of the EPC. It is hard to discern any statutory provision (or, by the same token, any provision in the EPC) to support the proposition that, once it has been established that a product claimed in a patent is novel and non-obvious, and the specification sufficiently explains to the person skilled in the art how to make it, the claim can nonetheless be rejected because there may be other ways of making the product which owe nothing to the teaching of the patent.

81. Mr Simon Thorley QC, for the appellants, relied on section 14(5)(c): he said that where, as in this case, a product was a known *desideratum*, the first person to make it could rely on his way of making it as 'support' for a claim for that process, but not for a claim for the product, as the single process did not support a claim for the product. I think that that argument ascribes an effect to section 14(5)(c) which it does not have. In *Asahi Kasei Kogyo*

KK's Application [1991] RPC 485, 536, Lord Oliver of Aylmerton explained that 'a description would not "support" the claims for the purpose of subsection (5)(c) unless it contained sufficient material to enable the specification to constitute the enabling disclosure which subsection (3) required' (to quote Lord Hoffmann's summary in *Biogen* [1997] RPC 1, 47). That brings one straight back to section 14(3), and, as already mentioned, the specification of the Patent clearly sets out the diol method of manufacturing escitalopram, and therefore it plainly satisfies section 14(3).

...

84. Subject, at any rate, to *Biogen* [1997] RPC 1 (and some cases purportedly following it), your Lordships have not been referred to any decided case in this jurisdiction which calls into question the approach of Lord Hoffmann and Jacob LJ in this case, as summarised in paras 74 and 75 above.

...

86. While, as my noble and learned friend Lord Mance says, no real help in this case can be obtained from judicial decisions in countries which are not signatories to the EPC, quite different considerations apply to decisions of the Board. Your Lordships' House has frequently emphasised that the principles of patent law adopted by courts in this jurisdiction should, if at all possible, be the same as those adopted by the Board—see for instance *Merell Dow Pharmaceuticals Inc v H N Norton & Co Ltd* [1996] RPC 76, 82, *Kirin-Amgen Inc v Hoechst Marion Roussel Ltd* [2004] UKHL 46, [2005] RPC 9, para 101, and *Conor Medsystems Inc v Angiotech Pharmaceuticals Inc* [2008] UKHL 49, [2008] 4 All ER 621, para 3.

87. In that connection, the approach of the Board has been consistently along the same lines as that of the Court of Appeal in this case. Thus, in T595/90 *Grain-orientated silicon sheet/Kawasaki* [1994] OJEPO 695, 703, the Board said:

[A] product which can be envisaged as such with all characteristics determining its identity together with its properties in use, i.e. an otherwise obvious entity, may become nevertheless non-obvious and claimable as such if there is no known way or applicable (analogy) method in the art to make it and the claimed methods for its preparation are therefore the first to achieve this in an inventive manner.

(See also the decisions cited by Lord Hoffmann at [2008] RPC 19, paras 38 and 39.)

88. Indeed, specifically in relation to the type of question arising in this case, the Board has held on more than one occasion that the fact that 'the two enantiomers ... actually exist unseparated in the racemate ... [and generally] can also be separated ...' are 'considerations [which] are immaterial to the question of novelty ... and will be more usefully applied to the examination as to inventive step' (quoted from T0296/87, *Hoechst*, 30 August 1988, para 6.5, and see also, for example, T1046/97, *Enantiomer/Zeneca*, 2 December 1999, para 2.1.1.4). That would suggest that Kitchin J's conclusion on novelty was correct and that he rightly addressed the issue of obviousness, but that, having decided those issues in favour of the respondent, he should have upheld the claim to escitalopram.

89. It is true that in none of these decisions of the Board was any consideration given to whether the product claim failed on the ground of insufficiency for the reason given by Kitchin J in this case at [2007] RPC 32, paras 264 to 265. However, the argument based on obviousness considered by the Board is very similar to the insufficiency reason given by Kitchin J. It also seems to me that, in the light of the expertise and experience of the members of the Board, and the number of decisions where the insufficiency reason could have been raised, it is fanciful to suggest that, if the reason had been arguable, it would not have been raised before or by the Board by now. As mentioned below, much of the reasoning in

Biogen [1997] RPC 1 was based on decisions of the Board, and members of the Board appear to be well aware of their previous decisions, and, at least in general, anxious to have a consistent approach. Further, the decision in *Biogen* [1997] RPC 1 was well known in the world of patents, and it did not cause the Board to change its view on the issue of product claims, as is demonstrated by the reasoning in *Enantiomer/Zeneca* in relation to enantiomers, and, more generally, in T1195/00 *Alcan International Ltd*, 24 May 2004.

90. In the light of this discussion, it appears clear to me that, unless precluded by the reasoning in *Biogen* [1997] RPC 1, on which Kitchin J primarily relied in his decision and on which Mr Thorley primarily relies in his argument, the product claim in the present case is valid. I appreciate that this means that, by finding one method of making a product, a person can obtain a monopoly for that product. However, that applies to any product claim. Further, where (as here) the product is a known *desideratum*, it can be said (as Lord Walker pointed out) that the invention is all the more creditable, as it is likely that there has been more competition than where the product has not been thought of. The role of fortuity in patent law cannot be doubted: it is inevitable, as in almost any area of life. Luck as well as skill often determines, for instance, who is first to file, whether a better product or process is soon discovered, or whether an invention turns out to be valuable. Further, while the law must be principled, it must also be clear and consistent.

The insufficiency argument based on *Biogen* [1997] RPC 1

91. As I have mentioned, the principal plank in the appellants' argument is the opinion of Lord Hoffmann in *Biogen* [1997] RPC 1, no doubt for the reasons just discussed. Mr Thorley was able to point to a number of observations in that opinion which, at least if read on their own, might at first sight be said to support his contention that, given that the (+)-enantiomer was known to be a desirable goal, the only technical contribution of the Patent was the diol method of making the enantiomer, and accordingly it is that process, and not the enantiomer, which should have been claimed.

92. Of the seven passages in the speech of Lord Hoffmann Mr Thorley particularly relied on, I shall limit myself to three, although the observations which follow apply equally to the other passages. At [1997] RPC 1, 48, Lord Hoffmann said that 'if the claims include a number of discrete methods or products, the patentee must enable the invention to be performed in respect of each of them'. But in this case the claim is to a single product, and it is clear that the product is enabled by the disclosure in the Patent.

93. At [1997] RPC 1, 50, there is this: '[The issue] is not whether the claimed invention could deliver the goods, but whether the claims cover other ways in which they might be delivered: ways which owe nothing to the teaching of the patent or any principle which it disclosed'. This is perhaps the most important of the three passages for present purposes. The vital point is that Lord Hoffmann was not dealing with a simple product claim, as is involved in this Patent. As he explained at [1997] RPC 1, 40, the claim in that case was 'to a product, a molecule identified partly by the way in which it has been made … and partly by what it does'. In that case, the patentee could claim neither the product (a DNA fragment of the so-called Dane particle), as it had already been made (see per Aldous J at first instance at [1995] RPC 25, 57), nor the process (recombinant DNA technology enabling expression in a cell), as it had already been invented (see at [1995] RPC 25, 58 and 65). Nor could he identify the product in any other way, as it had not been mapped or sequenced (see e.g. at [1995] RPC 25, 65).

94. Accordingly, the invention claimed in *Biogen* [1997] RPC 1 was, as it were, the notion of subjecting the product (the unsequenced DNA fragment from the Dane particle) to the

process (recombinant DNA technology) in order for it to be expressed to produce HBV antigens. It was therefore at least as much as a process claim as a product claim. In those circumstances, one can well see why the claim was held to be insufficient. The patent disclosed one way in which the DNA fragments could produce HBV antigens, but the claim 'cover[ed] other ways in which they might be delivered, ways which owed nothing to the teaching of the patent or any principle which it disclosed'—[1997] RPC 1, 50. Accordingly, the claim was very different from a simple product claim as in the present case. This analysis of the facts in *Biogen* [1997] RPC 1 also explains why Lord Hoffmann said at pp. 51–52 that 'the excessive breadth' of the patent in that case was due 'to the fact that the same results could be produced by different means' from that disclosed by the patent.

95. Finally, at [1997] RPC 1, 54, Lord Hoffmann emphasised that 'the extent of the monopoly claimed [should not] exceed ... the technical contribution to the art made by the invention as described in the specification'. As already explained, in the context of a simple product claim such as the present (especially where the claim is to a single chemical product), the technical contribution is (at least in the absence of special factors) the product itself. As I have suggested, the technical contribution can often be equated with non-obvious novelty—what is new to the art and not obvious is really another way of identifying the technical contribution.

96. The notion that Lord Hoffmann was not seeking to depart from the established approach of the Board is supported by the weight he placed on the reasoning in its decisions, especially *Genentech/Polypeptide expression* [1989] OJEPO 275 and T409/91 *EXXON/Fuel Oils* to which I have referred—see at [1997] RPC 1, 48–53. The fact that he took a different view from the Board on the patent in suit does not detract from this point: he was considering an argument which had not been raised in the opposition proceedings—see section 12 of his judgment at [1997] RPC 1, 52–53. Indeed, at the end of that section Lord Hoffmann was at pains to point out that there was no 'divergence between the jurisprudence of this court and that of the EPO'.

97. It is perhaps worth referring to one passage in the Board's decision in T409/91 *EXXON/Fuel Oils*, which was relied on by Mr Thorley, and was quoted in *Biogen* [1997] RPC 1, 49. The quotation, taken from para 3.3 of the decision, concludes with the statement that there is a 'general legal principle that the extent of the patent monopoly, as defined by the claims, should correspond to the *technical contribution* to the art in order for it to be supported, or justified'. However, the passage continues:

This means that the definitions in the claims should essentially correspond to the scope of the invention as disclosed in the description. In other words ... the claims should not extend to subject-matter which, after reading the description, would still not be at the disposal of the person skilled in the art.

98. Thus, it is clear that, in that paragraph the Board was discussing insufficiency and support in the normal sense, and there is nothing to suggest that, in the case of a product claim, once it is decided that the product is novel, the technical contribution may not be the product itself, if it is a known *desideratum*.

99. In my opinion, therefore, in agreement with the Court of Appeal, the opinion of Lord Hoffmann in *Biogen* [1997] RPC 1, though a *tour de force* as Lord Walker says, is of no assistance to the appellants in this case. It applied in the light of the very unusual nature of the claim in that case. Far from being a straightforward product claim (as in this case) or even a product-by-process claim (as discussed in *Kirin-Amgen* [2005] RPC 9, paras 86–91 and 101), the claim was to a product identified in part by how it was made and in part by what it did—almost a process-by-product-by-process claim.

In the above extract, Lord Neuberger emphasizes the importance of UK courts taking an approach consistent with the EPO. How significant were the EPO Board of Appeal decisions to Lord Neuberger's reasoning in the case? What was the main distinction made between *Biogen* and the Lundbeck patent?

At first instance, Kitchin J's concern was that Lundbeck had acquired a patent for a product (as opposed to merely a process for obtaining escitalopram) and that this would give it the exclusive right to, inter alia, make the product and to prevent others from doing so, even if they made escitalopram by a different method to the one developed by Lundbeck. The Court of Appeal and House of Lords took the view that this was simply a consequence of having product claims. Does this seem like a fair outcome? Should Parliament provide for a different scope of protection for patented products depending on the type of technical contribution that has been made?

FURTHER READING

A. Batteson and I. Karet, '*Lundbeck v Generics*: "*Biogen* insufficiency" explained' [2009] EIPR 51.

D. Brennan, '*Biogen* sufficiency reconsidered' [2009] IPQ 476.

M. Fisher, 'Extracting the price of a patent: enablement and written description' [2012] IPQ 262.

J. Pila, 'Chemical product patents and *Biogen* insufficiency before the House of Lords' (2009) 125 LQR 573.

12.3.3 SUPPORT

The leading case on when claims will be supported by the description is *Biogen v Medeva*.

Biogen v Medeva [1997] RPC 1

The facts were described at 12.3.2.2. The issue of lack of support arose because Biogen were claiming an earlier priority date, by virtue of an earlier application.[100] As such, they needed to show that the patent claim was supported by matter disclosed in the earlier application. The earlier priority date was crucial because otherwise their invention would have lacked inventive step.

Lord Hoffmann (delivering the leading speech), **at pp. 51–2:**

As I have said, I accept the judge's findings that the method was shown to be capable of making both antigens and I am willing to accept that it would work in any otherwise suitable host cell. Does this contribution justify a claim to a monopoly of *any* recombinant method of making the antigens? In my view it does not. The claimed invention is too broad. Its excessive breadth is due, not to the inability of the teaching to produce all the promised results, but to the fact that the same results could be produced by different

---

[100] See PA 77, s. 5(2)(a).

means. Professor Murray had won a brilliant Napoleonic victory in cutting through the uncertainties which existed in his day to achieve the desired result. But his success did not in my view establish any new principle which his successors had to follow if they were to achieve the same results. The inventive step, as I have said, was the idea of trying to express unsequenced eukaryotic DNA in a prokaryotic host. Biogen 1 discloses that the way to do it is to choose the restriction enzymes likely to cleave the Dane particle DNA into the largest fragments. This, if anything, was the original element in what Professor Murray did. But once the DNA had been sequenced, no one would choose restriction enzymes on this basis. They would choose those which digested the sites closest to the relevant gene or the part of the gene which expressed an antigenic fragment of the polypeptide. The metaphor used by one of the witnesses was that before the genome had been sequenced everyone was working in the dark. Professor Murray invented a way of working with the genome in the dark. But he did not switch on the light and once the light was on his method was no longer needed. Nor, once they could use vectors for mammalian cells, would they be concerned with the same problem of introns which had so exercised those skilled in the art in 1978. Of course there might be other problems, but Biogen 1 did not teach how to solve them. The respondents Medeva, who use restriction enzymes based on knowledge of the HBV genome and mammalian host cells, owe nothing to Professor Murray's invention.

It is said that what Professor Murray showed by his invention was that it could be done. HBV antigens could be produced by expressing Dane particle DNA in a host cell. Those who followed, even by different routes, could have greater confidence by reason of his success. I do not think that this is enough to justify a monopoly of the whole field. I suppose it could be said that Samuel Morse had shown that electric telegraphy could be done. The Wright Brothers showed that heavier-than-air flight was possible, but that did not entitle them to a monopoly of heavier-than-air flying machines. It is inevitable in a young science, like electricity in the early nineteenth century or flying at the turn of the last century or recombinant DNA technology in the 1970s, that dramatically new things will be done for the first time. The technical contribution made in such cases deserves to be recognised. But care is needed not to stifle further research and healthy competition by allowing the first person who has found a way of achieving an obviously desirable goal to monopolise every other way of doing so. (See Merges and Nelson, 'On the complex economics of patent scope' (1990) 90 Columbia LR 839.)

I would therefore hold that Biogen 1 did not support the invention as claimed in the European Patent and that it is therefore not entitled to the priority date of Biogen 1. As it is conceded that the invention was obvious when the patent application was filed, it is invalid.

[His lordship also gave two examples of where the description would not support the claims:]

The patent may claim results which it does not enable, such as making a wide class of products when it enables only one of those products and discloses no principle which would enable others to be made. Or it may claim every way of achieving a result when it enables only one way and it is possible to envisage other ways of achieving that result which make no use of the invention.

As *Biogen* demonstrates, this type of lack of support may arise particularly in situations where new areas of technology are emerging and the patent obtained is one of the first in the field. Do you think that it is important, as Lord Hoffmann said, to ensure that further research and healthy competition are not stifled? Or does this approach to the requirement of support act as a disincentive for those who engage in ground-breaking areas of research?

Where there is a lack of support of the type indicated in *Biogen*, will the specification invariably lack sufficiency? If so, does *Biogen* risk conflating the requirements of support and sufficiency or does it merely highlight how closely connected are the requirements?

FURTHER READING

M. Spence, 'Patents and biotechnology' (1997) 113 LQR 368.

13

PATENTS III:

INFRINGEMENT, EXCEPTIONS,
AND ENTITLEMENT

13.1 INFRINGEMENT

13.1.1 INTRODUCTION

Broadly speaking, assessing whether or not a patent has been infringed involves a three-stage enquiry. First, the patent claims must be construed to see whether the defendant's activities fall within the scope of the monopoly. Second, it is necessary to identify the infringing acts which the defendant is alleged to have carried out. Third, the applicability of exceptions to infringement must be considered. Each of these topics will be discussed in turn.

Before we do so, however, it is worth noting a practical consequence of commencing an action for infringement. Not only is litigation an expensive process, but perhaps more importantly, it also makes one's patent vulnerable to an invalidity challenge. This is because a defendant will usually counterclaim, arguing that even if they have infringed the patent it is in fact invalid. Moreover, in contesting the validity of the patent, particularly on the grounds of novelty or sufficiency, the defendant will force the patent proprietor to put forward an interpretation of the scope of the claims that is not overreaching for the purposes of infringement. This is because UK courts adopt a consistent interpretation of the claims for both validity and infringement purposes and if a proprietor advances too wide a construction of the claims this will increase the risk of his patent being anticipated by the prior art or lacking sufficiency.[1]

13.1.2 CONSTRUCTION OF THE CLAIMS

The claims are a crucial feature of the patent specification for the reasons expressed in the following extract.

[1] See the discussion of the 'Rapamycin' case at 12.3.2.2 to illustrate this point.

D. Chisum, 'Common law and civil law approaches to patent claim interpretation' in D. Vaver and L. Bently (eds), *Intellectual Property in the New Millennium* (Cambridge: Cambridge University Press, 2004), p. 97

Whether patent law ought to require a written claim to an invention is debatable, but the requirement is conventionally accepted as sound. Under the conventional view, the claiming requirement serves two purposes. First, the claim defines the invention for purposes of determining patentability, during both examination by a patent office and judicial assessment. Second, the claim provides notice to the public, usually, a business entity seeking to avoid a patent, of what the patent covers. The notice supposedly provided by a written claim enables the entity not only to determine whether to engage in potentially infringing conduct but also how to develop alternative technology ('design around').

But words are only words, and a claiming requirement can fully serve its intended purposes only if there is reasonably predictable certainty as to how the words of a claim will be interpreted by critical decision-makers. Thus arises a central problem for every patent system that requires a verbal definition of a protected invention: how to achieve consistency in the interpretation of the claims in patents.

Thus, claims are important because they help define the invention and because they provide notice to the public of the scope of the monopoly that the patentee has been granted. This dual role of claims developed relatively recently, from the early 20th century onwards,[2] and makes it imperative that they can be interpreted with reasonable predictability. Traditionally, however, the UK and Germany have adopted divergent approaches to the interpretation of claims, which posed difficulties when it came to drafting the EPC, as the following extract from Chisum explains.[3]

The framers of European patent law harmonization were faced with a specific national conflict (or at least the perception of a conflict) on judicial patent claim interpretation: Germany versus the United Kingdom. The former has a civil law tradition; the latter a common law tradition. Resolution of the conflict was essential: the two countries had the largest volume of litigation over patent infringement in Europe. On the one hand, German courts were deemed to view the language of a patent claim as a guide to determining what the patented invention is—only a guide, the invention and whether it has been misappropriated by an accused infringer being determined by a plenary consideration of the patent's disclosure and the relationship between the invention and the prior art. On the other hand, United Kingdom courts were deemed to view patent claim language as the exclusive and restricting definition of the invention. For example, if a patent claim required that a component be 'vertical', the German courts would assess the reason for the 'vertical' limitation—did the nature of the invention as an advance over the prior art require strict verticality or merely substantial verticality that would perform the function of the invention?—and deem the patent to cover any structure or method that appropriated the invention. This approach, in theory, assured a fair scope of protection for patent owners: allowing a slight variation from the literal requirement of 'vertical' might authorize appropriation of the invention's essence. The United Kingdom courts would define 'vertical' and deem the patent to cover only structures or methods that met

---

[2] D. J. Brennan, 'The evolution of English patent claims as property definers' [2005] IPQ 361.
[3] At p. 98.

the definition. This approach, in theory, assured certainty and predictability of the scope of patent protection.

Professor William Cornish, in his characteristic lucid manner, described the conflict as between 'fence post' claiming and 'sign post' claiming.

Under the German 'sign post' approach to claim interpretation, there were different layers of protection: the core direct subject matter of the invention, the subject matter of the invention (as supplemented by the technical teaching), and the general inventive idea deducible by the person skilled in the art without any inventive effort. According to Dr Matthew Fisher:

The combined effect of these layers of protection was that the wording of the claims, which would in the UK have been considered more or less precise boundaries of protection, occupied a position of far more flexibility within the German construct for determination of scope. The outer layer of the patent's influence therefore extended beyond the inventor's choice of descriptive words, to cover equivalents that were not immediately apparent from the claims but which were nevertheless deducible by the average person skilled in the art.[4]

The UK 'literal' or 'fence post' approach to interpretation of claims was driven by the desire for certainty. As Lord Russell in *EMI v Lissen*[5] commented:

The function of the claims is to define clearly and with precision the monopoly claimed, so that others may know the exact boundaries of the area within which they will be trespassers. Their primary object is to limit and not to extend the monopoly. What is not claimed is disclaimed. The claims must undoubtedly be read as part of the entire document, and not as a separate document; but the forbidden field must be found in the language of the claims and not elsewhere.

According to the 'fence post' approach, infringement would not occur where some of the integers of the claim were omitted or replaced by mechanical equivalents. However, the courts later developed the doctrine of 'pith and marrow' to deal with situations where there were colourable or immaterial variations of the claimed invention, in other words where an obvious equivalent was substituted for an inessential integer in the claim.[6] Where that occurred, a person could still infringe because he had taken the substance or 'pith and marrow' of the invention. This approach has been described by some as the UK's attempt to protect equivalents and as illustrative of the fact that the UK never adopted a strict 'fence post' approach to claim construction.[7]

Dr Fisher has suggested that the different approaches to claim construction in Germany and the UK may be explained by different underlying rationales for patent protection. He explains that in Germany the emphasis is on rewarding the patentee for their inventive contribution and as such 'the claims still form the essential basis for the determination of scope, but the key investigation is focussed more firmly on the technical teaching of the patent'.[8]

---

[4] M. Fisher, 'New protocol, same old story? Patent claim construction in 2007; looking back with a view to the future' [2008] IPQ 133, 147–8.

[5] *Electrical and Musical Industries Ltd v Lissen Ltd* (1939) 56 RPC 23, 39 (Lord Russell).

[6] *Marconi v British Radio Telegraph and Telephone Co. Ltd* (1911) 28 RPC 181, 217; *Van der Lely v Bamfords* [1963] RPC 61.

[7] H. Laddie, '*Kirin Amgen*—the end of equivalence in England?' (2009) 40 IIC 3.

[8] Fisher, 'New protocol, same old story?', 155.

Whereas, in the UK, one has to take into account the historical antipathy to monopolies (as illustrated by the Statute of Monopolies 1624). As Dr Fisher explains:

> the patent is an exception to an otherwise outright prohibition upon monopoly; as such, the temporally limited patent grant operates, first and foremost, as an incentive to invest in the creation of new and innovative technology [and] the reward of the patentee is relegated to a position of secondary importance because of the potential blocking effect a broad patent would have on the furtherance of the system's primary goal.[9]

When the EPC was being drafted, it was vital to achieve a harmonized approach to claim construction, but the question arose which approach—sign post or fence post—would prevail. In the end, a diplomatic compromise between the two traditions was reached. Article 69 of the EPC 1973 set out the main norm for determination of patent scope:

> The extent of the protection conferred by a European patent or a European patent application shall be determined by the terms of the claims. Nevertheless, the description and drawings shall be used to interpret the claims.

In addition, a Protocol to Article 69 of the EPC 1973 was also inserted:

> Article 69 should *not be interpreted* in the sense that the extent of the protection conferred by a European patent is to be understood as that defined *by the strict, literal meaning* of the wording used in the claims, the description and the drawings being employed only for the purpose of resolving an ambiguity found in the claims. *Neither* should it be *interpreted* in the sense that the *claims serve only as a guideline* and that the actual protection conferred may extend to what, from a consideration of the description and drawings by a person skilled in the art, the patentee has contemplated. On the contrary, it is to be *interpreted* as defining a position *between these extremes* which combines a *fair protection* for the patentee with a *reasonable degree of certainty* for third parties.[10]

Both Article 69 and the Protocol were given effect in UK law via section 125 of the PA 77. Following the EPC 2000, Article 69 was amended to remove the words 'terms of the claims' to simply 'the claims' and the Protocol to Article 69 was amended to include the above provision as Article 1 and to introduce a new provision, Article 2, dealing with equivalents. Article 2 of the Protocol, which will be discussed later at 13.1.2.3,[11] states:

> For the purpose of determining the extent of protection conferred by a European patent, due account shall be taken of any element which is equivalent to an element specified in the claims.

As previously mentioned, the purpose of the Protocol to Article 69 of the EPC was to achieve a convergence in claim interpretation in EPC Contracting States. In reading the following sections, it is important to ask: to what extent has the Protocol succeeded in its aim?

---

[9] Fisher, 'New protocol, same old story?', 154.   [10] Emphasis supplied.
[11] For a brief history of Art. 69 and the Protocol under the EPC 1973 and EPC 2000 see Fisher, 'New protocol, same old story?', 133–43.

13.1.2.1 *Catnic*

As has been mentioned, the Protocol to Article 69 sought to move UK courts away from a 'literal' or 'fence post' approach to construction of the patent claims. In fact, however, this shift had already begun to occur, as shown by the landmark House of Lords decision in *Catnic*.

Catnic v Hill and Smith [1982] RPC 183

The claimant's invention was a steel lintel for use in spanning the spaces above window and door openings. Part of the reason for the claimant's success was that previous, solid, much heavier lintels had been used (i.e. timber and heavy gauge metal girders). With the claimant's invention the necessary strength and rigidity was obtained, but with lightness, economy of material, and ease of handling. The invention had a vertical back plate and an angled front plate. Specifically, the claims referred to 'a second rigid support member extending vertically from or near the rear edge of the first horizontal plate or part'. The defendants produced a lintel that had a back plate that was inclined to a slight angle of six degrees from the vertical. This was done to avoid infringement of the claimant's patent and in response to customer feedback. The claimant sued for infringement under the Patents Act 1949. At first instance, Whitford J held that although the defendant's lintel did not 'extend vertically' and thus was not a literal (or textual) infringement of the claims, the defendants had taken all the essential features of a number of the claims and thus the defendants' lintels constituted an infringement. On appeal, the Court of Appeal held that there had been no literal infringement of the claims; further the court held that it was an essential feature of the claims that the rear support member should 'extend vertically', and accordingly there could be no infringement of the 'pith and marrow' of the invention. The claimant appealed to the House of Lords.

Lord Diplock (with whom the other law lords agreed), **at pp. 242–3:**

My Lords, in their closely reasoned written cases in this House and in the oral argument, both parties to this appeal have tended to treat 'textual infringement' and infringement of the 'pith and marrow' of an invention as if they were separate causes of action, the existence of the former to be determined as a matter of construction only and of the latter upon some broader principle of colourable evasion. There is, in my view, no such dichotomy; there is but a single cause of action and to treat it otherwise, particularly in cases like that which is the subject of the instant appeal, is liable to lead to confusion.

The expression 'no textual infringement' has been borrowed from the speeches in this House in the hay-rake case, *Van der Lely v Bamfords*, where it was used by several of their Lordships as a convenient way of saying that the word 'hindmost' as descriptive of rake wheels to be dismounted could not as a matter of linguistics mean 'foremost': but this did not exhaust the question of construction of the specification that was determinative of whether there had been an infringement of the claim or not. It left open the question whether the patentee had made his reference to the 'hindmost' (rather than any other wheels) as those to be dismounted, an essential feature of the monopoly that he claimed. It was on this question that there was a division of opinion in this House and in the Court of Appeal in the hay-rake case.

My Lords, a patent specification is a unilateral statement by the patentee, in words of his own choosing, addressed to those likely to have a practical interest in the subject matter of his invention (i.e. 'skilled in the art'), by which he informs them what he claims to be the essential features of the new product or process for which the letters patent grant him a monopoly. It is those novel features only that he claims to be essential that constitute the so-called 'pith and marrow' of the claim. A patent specification should be given a purposive construction rather than a purely literal one derived from applying to it the kind of meticulous verbal analysis in which lawyers are too often tempted by their training to indulge. The question in each case is: whether persons with practical knowledge and experience of the kind of work in which the invention was intended to be used, would understand that strict compliance with a particular descriptive word or phrase appearing in a claim was intended by the patentee to be an essential requirement of the invention so that *any* variant would fall outside the monopoly claimed, even though it could have no material effect upon the way the invention worked.

The question, of course, does not arise where the variant would in fact have a material effect upon the way the invention worked. Nor does it arise unless at the date of publication of the specification it would be obvious to the informed reader that this was so. Where it is not obvious, in the light of then-existing knowledge, the reader is entitled to assume that the patentee thought at the time of the specification that he had good reason for limiting his monopoly so strictly and had intended to do so, even though subsequent work by him or others in the field of the invention might show the limitation to have been unnecessary. It is to be answered in the negative only when it would be apparent to any reader skilled in the art that a particular descriptive word or phrase used in a claim cannot have been intended by a patentee, who was also skilled in the art, to exclude minor variants which, to the knowledge of both him and the readers to whom the patent was addressed, could have no material effect upon the way in which the invention worked.

...

...Put in a nutshell the question to be answered is: Would the specification make it obvious to a builder familiar with ordinary building operations that the description of a lintel in the form of a weight-bearing box girder of which the back plate was referred to as 'extending vertically' from one of the two horizontal plates to join the other, could *not* have been intended to exclude lintels in which the back plate although not positioned at precisely 90 degrees to both horizontal plates was close enough to 90 degrees to make no material difference to the way the lintel worked when used in building operations? No plausible reason has been advanced why any rational patentee should want to place so narrow a limitation on his invention. On the contrary, to do so would render his monopoly for practical purposes worthless, since any imitator could avoid it and take all the benefit of the invention by the simple expedient of positioning the back plate a degree or two from the exact vertical.

It may be that when used by a geometer addressing himself to fellow geometers, such expressions descriptive of relative position as 'horizontal', 'parallel', 'vertical' and 'vertically' are to be understood as words of precision only; but when used in a description of a manufactured product intended to perform the practical function of a weight-bearing box girder in supporting courses of brickwork over window and door spaces in buildings, it seems to me that the expression 'extending vertically' as descriptive of the position of what in use will be the upright member of a trapezoid-shaped box girder, is perfectly capable of meaning positioned near enough to the exact geometrical vertical to enable it in actual use to perform satisfactorily all the functions that it could perform if it were precisely vertical; and having regard to those considerations to which I have just referred that is the sense in which in my opinion 'extending vertically' would be understood by a builder familiar with ordinary building operation. Or, putting the same thing in another way, it would be obvious to him that the patentee did not intend to make exact verticality in the positioning of the back plate an essential feature of the invention claimed.

My Lords, if one analyses line by line the ways in which the various expressions are used in the specification, one can find pointers either way as to whether in particular lines various adjectives and adverbs descriptive of relative position are used as words of precision or not. Some of these are discussed in the judgments of the majority of the Court of Appeal who found the pointers in favour of precision stronger than those to the contrary, of which one example is the description of the two 'horizontal' plates as being only *substantially* parallel'. For my part I find the result of such analysis inconclusive and of little weight as compared with the broad considerations to which I have referred and which are a consequence of giving as I think one should, a purposive construction to the specification.

It follows that I have reached the same conclusion as the trial judge and Sir David Cairns, although not by the route of drawing a distinction between 'textual infringement' and infringement of the 'pith and marrow' of the invention. Accordingly I would allow the appeal.

Did Lord Diplock in *Catnic* reject the previous tests of 'literal construction' and 'pith and marrow', in favour of a purposive construction of the claims? What does purposive construction entail and do you agree that this approach is preferable?

13.1.2.2 *Improver*

As *Catnic* was a decision under the Patents Act 1949, the issue subsequently arose whether the *Catnic* 'purposive construction' test was consistent with the Protocol to Article 69 of the EPC, as implemented by section 125 of the PA 77. This issue was considered in *Improver*.

***Improver Corp. v Remington Consumer Products Ltd* [1990] FSR 181**

The claimants' European patent (UK) was for an electrical device for plucking hairs from the body. Its principal element consisted of a helical spring bent to the form of an arc which was rotated at a high speed. Because of the arcuate form, on the convex side the spring would open out, while on the concave side it would close together. Hairs would accordingly be captured and then plucked with the rotation of the spring. The result was less painful than waxing and more long-lasting than shaving. The claimants' device, the 'Epilady', was a great commercial success. The defendants' device was designed as a less painful alternative to 'Epilady'. In place of a helical spring it had a tube of synthetic rubber, partly cut through by slits. When rotated, hair was drawn into the slits and then plucked, as the slits squeezed together. It was marketed as 'Smooth and Silky' with additional tubes for replacement after some seven hours' use. The claimants sued for infringement of their patent.

Hoffmann J (as he then was)**, at pp. 188–90:**

[Hoffmann J began by setting out the general principles of construction with reference to *Catnic*:]

The proper approach to the interpretation of patents registered under the Patents Act 1949 was explained by Lord Diplock in *Catnic Components Ltd v Hill & Smith Ltd* [1982]

RPC 183, 242. The language should be given a 'purposive' and not necessarily a literal construction. If the issue was whether a feature embodied in an alleged infringement which fell outside the primary, literal or a contextual meaning of a descriptive word or phrase in the claim ('a variant') was nevertheless within its language as properly interpreted, the court should ask itself the following three questions:

(1) Does the variant have a material effect upon the way the invention works? If yes, the variant is outside the claim. If no—

(2) Would this (i.e. that the variant had no material effect) have been obvious at the date of publication of the patent to a reader skilled in the art. If no, the variant is outside the claim. If yes—

(3) Would the reader skilled in the art nevertheless have understood from the language of the claim that the patentee intended that strict compliance with the primary meaning was an essential requirement of the invention. If yes, the variant is outside the claim.

On the other hand, a negative answer to the last question would lead to the conclusion that the patentee was intending the word or phrase to have not a literal but a figurative meaning (the figure being a form of synecdoche or metonymy) denoting a class of things which included the variant and the literal meaning, the latter being perhaps the most perfect, best-known or striking example of the class.

Thus in *Catnic* itself the claim of a patent for a lintel of box construction required that the upper plate be supported upon the lower plate by two rigid supports, one in the front and the other 'extending vertically' from the one plate to the other at the rear. The defendant's lintel had a rear support which was inclined 6° or 8° from the vertical. The House of Lords decided that this variation had no material effect upon the load-bearing capacity of the lintel or the way it worked and that this would have been obvious to the skilled builder at the date of publication of the patent. It also decided that the skilled reader would not have understood from the language of the claim that the patentee was insisting upon precisely 90° as an essential requirement of his invention. The conclusion was that 'extending vertically' meant 'extending with the range of angles which give substantially the maximum load-bearing capacity and of which 90° is the perfect example'.

In the end, therefore, the question is always whether the alleged infringement is covered by the language of the claim. This, I think, is what Lord Diplock meant in *Catnic* when he said that there was no dichotomy between 'textual infringement' and infringement of the 'pith and marrow' of the patent and why I respectfully think that Fox LJ put the question with great precision in *Anchor Building Products Ltd v Redland Roof Tiles Ltd* (CA), unreported, 23 November 1988, transcript at p. 18. when he said the question was whether the absence of a feature mentioned in the claim was 'an immaterial variant which a person skilled in the trade would have regarded as being *within the ambit of the language*' (My emphasis). It is worth noticing that Lord Diplock's first two questions, although they cannot sensibly be answered without reference to the patent, do not primarily involve questions of construction: whether the variant would make a material difference to the way the invention worked and whether this would have been obvious to the skilled reader are questions of fact. The answers are used to provide the factual background against which the specification must be construed. It is the third question which raises the question of construction and Lord Diplock's formulation makes it clear that on this question the answers to the first two questions are not conclusive. Even a purposive construction of the language of the patent may lead to the conclusion that although the variant made no material difference and this would have been obvious at the time, the patentee for some reason was confining his claim to the primary meaning and excluding the variant. If this were not the case, there would be no point in asking the third question at all.

[Hoffmann J observed that, even though *Catnic* was a decision according to the Patents Act 1949, subsequent courts had regarded Lord Diplock's speech as indicating the same approach to construction as that laid down in the Protocol. Thus, he regarded *Catnic* as binding authority and went on to apply the *Catnic* test, as reformulated into three questions.]

At pp. 192–7:

(1) Does the variant have a material effect on the way the invention works?

The answer to this question depends upon the level of generality at which one describes the way the invention works.

...

...It seems to me that the right approach is to describe the working of the invention at the level of generality with which it is described in the claim of the patent. As I have said, Dr Laming agreed that there was no difference between the descriptions in Mr Gross's patent and the patent in suit of the way the inventions worked. The differences lay entirely in the descriptions of the hardware. In my judgment, at the appropriate level of description, the rubber rod works in the same way as the helical spring and the differences I have mentioned, so far as they exist, are not material.

(2) Would it have been obvious to a man skilled in the art that the variant would work in the same way?

...

In my view the question supposes that the skilled man is told of both the invention and the variant and asked whether the variant would obviously work in the same way.

...

Dr Laming and Dr Sharp, the eminent engineer called as an expert by the plaintiff, agreed that it would have been obvious to the skilled man that the attributes which enabled the helical spring to function in the way described in the specification were that it was capable of rotating, capable of transmitting torque along its length to resist the forces involved in plucking hairs, *bendy* (to form an arc) and *slitty* (to entrap hairs by the opening and closing effect of rotation). They also agreed that it would have been obvious that any rod which had these qualities in sufficient degree and did not have other defects such as overheating or falling to bits would in principle work in the same way and that the rubber rod plainly belonged to that class. On this evidence the second question must in my judgment be answered yes. I express no view on whether the rubber rod was also an inventive step.

...

(3) Would the skilled reader nevertheless have understood that the patentee intended to confine his claim to the primary meaning of a helical spring?

This brings one to the question of construction. Since the question is what the skilled reader would have understood, I set out the views of the rival experts.

...

In my judgment the difference between the experts depends upon how one construes the equivalents clause. The first part of the clause merely says that the description should not be used to restrict the meaning of the language used in the claims. That is not the question here. What matters is the final words: '*and all variations which come within the meaning and range of equivalency of the claims are therefore intended to be embraced therein*'. If this means: 'whatever contrary impression the skilled man may be given by the language of the claims read in the context of the rest of the description, all references in the claims to hardware are deemed to include any other hardware which would in any circumstances function in the same way' then I think Dr Sharpe must be right. In my judgment, however, the clause does not have so wide an effect. The words I have quoted say that the variation must still come within the *meaning* of the claims and the reference to 'range of equivalency' means in my judgment no more than 'don't forget that the claims must be interpreted in accordance with *Catnic* and the Protocol'.

Thus interpreted, I do not think that 'helical spring' can reasonably be given a wide generic construction and I accept Dr Laming's reasons for thinking that a skilled man would not understand it in this sense. This is not a case like *Catnic* in which the angle of the support member can be regarded as an approximation to the vertical. The rubber rod is not an approximation to a helical spring. It is a different thing which can in limited circumstances work in the same way. Nor can the spring be regarded as an 'inessential' or the change from metal spring to rubber rod as a minor variant. In *Catnic* Lord Diplock asked rhetorically whether there was any reason why the patentee should wish to restrict his invention to a support angled at precisely 90°, thereby making avoidance easy. In this case I think that a similar question would receive a ready answer. It would be obvious that the rubber had problems of hysteresis which might be very difficult to overcome. The plaintiff's inventors had done no work on rubber rods. Certainly the rubber rod cannot be used in the loop configuration which is the plaintiff's preferred embodiment. On the other hand, drafting the claim in wide generic terms to cover alternatives like the rubber rod might be unacceptable to the patent office. I do not think that the hypothetical skilled man is also assumed to be skilled in patent law and he would in my judgment be entitled to think that patentee had good reasons for limiting himself, as he obviously appeared to have done, to a helical coil. To derive a different meaning solely from the equivalents clause would in my view be denying third parties that reasonable degree of certainty to which they are entitled under the Protocol.

Hoffmann J reformulated the *Catnic* test into three questions, known as the *Improver* questions. These were subsequently renamed the Protocol questions on the basis that they were consistent with the Protocol to Article 69 of the EPC.[12] In your view, do the *Improver* questions accurately reflect Lord Diplock's speech in *Catnic*?

The patent in *Improver* contained an equivalents clause. How did Hoffmann J treat this clause in the context of construing the claims? Here it is worth noting that Lord Hoffmann (as he then became) returned to this issue in *Kirin-Amgen*, discussed at 13.1.2.3.

Finally, the European patent in *Improver* was litigated in several European states where, in Germany at least, the defendants' device was found to be an infringement. The German court took the view that the person skilled in the art would realize that the claimants had chosen a helical coil spring because it was an elastic cylindrical body that could be rotated quickly in an arcuate shape, with gaps at the convex side and clamping on the concave side (to allow the hair to be captured and plucked). According to Dr Fisher, 'This broad, functional construction of the claim language lies in stark contrast to the formalistic interpretation advanced by Hoffmann J.'[13] Dr Fisher argues that 'The underlying thought process

---

[12] See *Wheatly v Drillsafe* [2001] RPC 133, 142 (Aldous LJ).
[13] Fisher, 'New protocol, same old story?', 156.

apparent from the case appears to be that if the patentee had wished for broader, more functional, protection then they should have chosen broader, more functional, wording. By concentrating on the claim in this manner, conventions of language dictate that "coiled helical spring" means just that and no more.'[14]

The German court's decision was drawn to the attention of Hoffmann J, who took the view that his colleagues in Germany were adopting an interpretation 'closer to treating the language of the claims as a "guideline" than the median course required by the Protocol'.[15] Given the different outcomes in the *Improver* litigation in different Contracting States, does this suggest that the Protocol is not enough to unify the distinct and long-standing traditions to infringement reflected in the UK and Germany?[16]

13.1.2.3 *Kirin-Amgen*

Subsequent decisions of the Court of Appeal affirmed that the *Catnic* test and the *Improver* questions (later known as the Protocol questions) were consistent with the Protocol to Article 69 of the EPC.[17] However, it was not until *Kirin-Amgen Inc. v Hoechst Marion* that the House of Lords had an opportunity to consider this issue.

Kirin-Amgen Inc. v Hoechst Marion [2004] UKHL 46, [2005] RPC 9

Kirin-Amgen ('Amgen') sued Transkaryotic Therapies Inc. ('TKT') for infringement of its European patent (UK) relating to the production of erythropoietin (EPO) by recombinant DNA technology. EPO is a hormone made in the kidney which stimulates the production of red blood cells by the bone marrow. Amgen's method of making EPO artificially for use as a drug was a significant advance in the treatment of anaemia, particularly when associated with kidney failure. Amgen's method involved an exogenous DNA sequence coding for EPO which had been introduced into a host cell. TKT had also developed a method for making EPO, but used a different process, called 'gene activation'. This involved an endogenous DNA sequence coding for EPO naturally present in a human cell, into which an exogenous upstream control sequence had been inserted, thereby 'activating' the production of DNA. On the issue of infringement, the key question was construction of the claims. Would a person skilled in the art understand 'host cell' to mean a cell which is host to the DNA sequence which coded for EPO? Or would a person skilled in the art understand 'host cell' to include a cell in which the DNA sequence coding for EPO is endogenous, provided the cell is host to some exogenous DNA? At first instance, Neuberger J held, inter alia, that claim 19 was invalid for insufficiency and that claim 26 was valid and infringed. However, the Court of Appeal found both claims to be valid, but that TKT had not infringed. Both sides appealed.

---

[14] Fisher, 'New protocol, same old story?', 157.

[15] *Improver*, 198.

[16] See further B. Sherman, 'Patent claim interpretation: the impact of the protocol on interpretation' (1991) 54 MLR 499.

[17] See e.g. *Kastner v Rizla* [1995] RPC 585; *Union Carbide Corp. v BP Chemicals Ltd* [1999] RPC 409; *Wheatly v Drillsafe* [2001] RPC 133.

Lord Hoffmann (delivering the leading speech):

[Lord Hoffmann took the opportunity to review the history and background of Article 69 of the EPC and the Protocol, before moving on to consider whether *Catnic* was consistent with the Protocol.]

Is *Catnic* consistent with the Protocol?

47. The Protocol, as I have said, is a Protocol for the construction of art. 69 and does not expressly lay down any principle for the construction of claims. It does say what principle should not be followed, namely the old English literalism, but otherwise it says only that one should not go outside the claims. It does however say that the object is to combine a fair protection for the patentee with a reasonable degree of certainty for third parties. How is this to be achieved? The claims must be construed in a way which attempts, so far as is possible in an imperfect world, not to disappoint the reasonable expectations of either side. What principle of interpretation would give fair protection to the patentee? Surely, a principle which would give him the full extent of the monopoly which the person skilled in the art would think he was intending to claim. And what principle would provide a reasonable degree of protection for third parties? Surely again, a principle which would not give the patentee more than the full extent of the monopoly which the person skilled in the art would think that he was intending to claim. Indeed, any other principle would also be unfair to the patentee, because it would unreasonably expose the patent to claims of invalidity on grounds of anticipation or insufficiency.

48. The *Catnic* principle of construction is, therefore, in my opinion, precisely in accordance with the Protocol. It is intended to give the patentee the full extent, but not more than the full extent, of the monopoly which a reasonable person skilled in the art, reading the claims in context, would think he was intending to claim.

Can we say with certainty that the purposive construction approach in *Catnic* is consistent with the Protocol to Article 69? What about the Protocol questions?

Lord Hoffmann also considered the role of 'equivalents' under the EPC and PA 77. He began by explaining the doctrine of equivalents and that it does not form part of the EPC.

The doctrine of equivalents

36. At the time when the rules about natural and ordinary meanings were more or less rigidly applied, the United Kingdom and American courts showed understandable anxiety about applying a construction which allowed someone to avoid infringement by making an 'immaterial variation' in the invention as described in the claims. In England, this led to the development of a doctrine of infringement by use of the 'pith and marrow' of the invention (a phrase invented by Lord Cairns in *Clark v Adie* (1877) 2 App Cas 315, 320) as opposed to a 'textual infringement'. The pith and marrow doctrine was always a bit vague ('necessary to prevent sharp practice' said Lord Reid in *C Van Der Lely NV v Bamfords Ltd* [1963] RPC 61, 77) and it was unclear whether the courts regarded it as a principle of construction or an extension of protection outside the claims.

37. In the United States, where a similar principle is called the 'doctrine of equivalents', it is frankly acknowledged that it allows the patentee to extend his monopoly beyond the claims. In the leading case of *Graver Tank & Manufacturing Co Inc v Linde Air Products Co* 339 US 605, 607 (1950), Jackson J said that the American courts had recognised:

> that to permit imitation of a patented invention which does not copy every literal detail would be to convert the protection of the patent grant into a hollow and useless thing. Such a limitation

would leave room for—indeed encourage—the unscrupulous copyist to make unimportant and insubstantial changes and substitutions in the patent which, though adding nothing, would be enough to take the copied matter outside the claim, and hence outside the reach of law.

…

41. There is often discussion about whether we have a European doctrine of equivalents and, if not, whether we should. It seems to me that both the doctrine of equivalents in the United States and the pith and marrow doctrine in the United Kingdom were born of despair. The courts felt unable to escape from interpretations which 'unsparing logic' appeared to require and which prevented them from according the patentee the full extent of the monopoly which the person skilled in the art would reasonably have thought he was claiming. The background was the tendency to literalism which then characterised the approach of the courts to the interpretation of documents generally and the fact that patents are likely to attract the skills of lawyers seeking to exploit literalism to find loopholes in the monopoly they create. (Similar skills are devoted to revenue statutes.)

42. If literalism stands in the way of construing patent claims so as to give fair protection to the patentee, there are two things that you can do. One is to adhere to literalism in construing the claims and evolve a doctrine which supplements the claims by extending protection to equivalents. That is what the Americans have done. The other is to abandon literalism. That is what the House of Lords did in the *Catnic* case, where Lord Diplock said (at [1982] RPC 183, 242):

> Both parties to this appeal have tended to treat 'textual infringement' and infringement of the 'pith and marrow' of an invention as if they were separate causes of action, the existence of the former to be determined as a matter of construction only and of the latter upon some broader principle of colourable evasion. There is, in my view, no such dichotomy; there is but a single cause of action and to treat it otherwise … is liable to lead to confusion.

43. The solution, said Lord Diplock, was to adopt a principle of construction which actually gave effect to what the person skilled in the art would have understood the patentee to be claiming.

44. Since the *Catnic* case we have art. 69 which, as it seems to me, firmly shuts the door on any doctrine which extends protection outside the claims. I cannot say that I am sorry because the *Festo* litigation suggests, with all respect to the courts of the United States, that American patent litigants pay dearly for results which are no more just or predictable than could be achieved by simply reading the claims.

[Lord Hoffmann goes on to explain that while there is no doctrine of equivalents in the EPC, equivalence *is* a relevant factor in the construction of claims and to discuss how the Protocol questions operate as guidelines for applying the principle of purposive construction to equivalents.]

Equivalents as a guide to construction

49. Although art. 69 prevents equivalence from extending protection outside the claims, there is no reason why it cannot be an important part of the background of facts known to the skilled man which would affect what he understood the claims to mean. That is no more than common sense. It is also expressly provided by the new art. 2 added to the Protocol by the Munich Act revising the EPC, dated November 29, 2000 (but which has not yet come into force):

> For the purpose of determining the extent of protection conferred by a European patent, due account shall be taken of any element which is equivalent to an element specified in the claims.

50. In the *Catnic* case [1982] RPC 183, 243 Lord Diplock offered some observations on the relevance of equivalence to the question of construction:

> The question in each case is: whether persons with practical knowledge and experience of the kind of work in which the invention was intended to be used, would understand that strict compliance with a particular descriptive word or phrase appearing in a claim was intended by the patentee to be an essential requirement of the invention so that any variant would fall outside the monopoly claimed, even though it could have no material effect upon the way the invention worked.

The question, of course, does not arise where the variant would in fact have a material effect upon the way the invention worked. Nor does it arise unless at the date of publication of the specification it would be obvious to the informed reader that this was so. Where it is not obvious, in the light of then-existing knowledge, the reader is entitled to assume that the patentee thought at the time of the specification that he had good reason for limiting his monopoly so strictly and had intended to do so, even though subsequent work by him or others in the field of the invention might show the limitation to have been unnecessary. It is to be answered in the negative only when it would be apparent to any reader skilled in the art that a particular descriptive word or phrase used in a claim cannot have been intended by a patentee, who was also skilled in the art, to exclude minor variants which, to the knowledge of both him and the readers to whom the patent was addressed, could have no material effect upon the way in which the invention worked.

51. In *Improver Corp v Remington Products Ltd* [1990] FSR 181, 189, I tried to summarise this guidance:

> If the issue was whether a feature embodied in an alleged infringement which fell outside the primary, literal or a contextual meaning of a descriptive word or phrase in the claim ('a variant') was nevertheless within its language as properly interpreted, the court should ask itself the following three questions:
>
> (1) Does the variant have a material effect upon the way the invention works? If yes, the variant is outside the claim. If no?
>
> (2) Would this (ie that the variant had no material effect) have been obvious at the date of publication of the patent to a reader skilled in the art? If no, the variant is outside the claim. If yes?
>
> (3) Would the reader skilled in the art nevertheless have understood from the language of the claim that the patentee intended that strict compliance with the primary meaning was an essential requirement of the invention? If yes, the variant is outside the claim.

On the other hand, a negative answer to the last question would lead to the conclusion that the patentee was intending the word or phrase to have not a literal but a figurative meaning (the figure being a form of synecdoche or metonymy) denoting a class of things which include the variant and the literal meaning, the latter being perhaps the most perfect, best-known or striking example of the class.

52. These questions, which the Court of Appeal in *Wheatley v Drillsafe Ltd* [2001] RPC 133, 142 dubbed 'the Protocol questions' have been used by English courts for the past 15 years as a framework for deciding whether equivalents fall within the scope of the claims. On the whole, the judges appear to have been comfortable with the results, although some of the cases have exposed the limitations of the method. When speaking of the '*Catnic* principle' it is important to distinguish between, on the one hand, the principle of purposive construction which I have said gives effect to the requirements of the Protocol, and on the other

hand, the guidelines for applying that principle to equivalents, which are encapsulated in the Protocol questions. The former is the bedrock of patent construction, universally applicable. The latter are only guidelines, more useful in some cases than in others.

Having read the above passages from Lord Hoffmann's speech, how would you describe the difference between the *Catnic* principle of purposive construction and the Protocol questions?

The key issue of construction in *Kirin-Amgen* was whether a person skilled in the art would understand 'host cell' to mean a cell which is host to the DNA sequence which coded for EPO or whether it included an EPO sequence endogenous to the cell, provided the cell hosted some exogenous DNA. Lord Hoffmann held that, in light of the evidence of expert witnesses and the language of the specification, Neuberger J at first instance had construed the claims correctly to mean the former.[18] However, his lordship held that the first instance judge had erred in classifying his construction as 'literal' and then moving on to apply the Protocol questions.

The judge's application of the Protocol questions

63. ...The judge's construction could not possibly be described as acontextual. It was entirely dependent on context and reflected the evidence of how the claim would have been understood by men skilled in the art.

...

66. ...[T]he present case illustrates the difficulty of applying the Protocol questions when no such question arises. No one suggests that 'an exogenous DNA sequence coding for EPO' can have some looser meaning which includes 'an endogenous DNA sequence coding for EPO'. The question is rather whether the person skilled in the art would understand the invention as operating at a level of generality which makes it irrelevant whether the DNA which codes for EPO is exogenous or not. That is a difficult question to put through the mangle of the Protocol questions because the answer depends entirely upon what you think the invention is. Once you have decided that question, the Protocol questions answer themselves.

...

69. ...The determination of the extent of protection conferred by a European patent is an examination in which there is only one compulsory question, namely that set by art. 69 and its Protocol: what would a person skilled in the art have understood the patentee to have used the language of the claim to mean? Everything else, including the Protocol questions, is only guidance to a judge trying to answer that question. But there is no point in going through the motions of answering the Protocol questions when you cannot sensibly do so until you have construed the claim. In such a case—and the present is in my opinion such a case—they simply provide a formal justification for a conclusion which has already been reached on other grounds.

70. I agree with the Court of Appeal that the invention should normally be taken as having been claimed at the same level of generality as that at which it is defined in the claims. It would be unusual for the person skilled in the art to understand a specification to be claiming an invention at a higher level of generality than that chosen by the patentee.

---

[18] *Kirin-Amgen*, [54]–[58].

That means that once the judge had construed the claims as he did, he had answered the question of infringement. It could only cause confusion to try to answer the Protocol questions as well.

71. No doubt there will be patent lawyers who are dismayed at the notion that the Protocol questions do not provide an answer in every case. They may feel cast adrift on a sea of interpretative uncertainty. But that is the fate of all who have to understand what people mean by using language. The Protocol questions are useful in many cases, but they are not a substitute for trying to understand what the person skilled in the art would have understood the patentee to mean by the language of the claims.

Why was the trial judge's reliance on the Protocol questions held to be erroneous? Given that the Protocol questions will always be secondary to the *Catnic* principle of purposive construction, when does it make sense to utilize them? Here it is interesting to note that post-*Kirin-Amgen* courts have been unwilling to apply the Protocol questions. Instead, they have either applied the general principles set out in *Kirin-Amgen*[19] or relied upon a 'practical working guide' based on the decision, as set out by the Court of Appeal, in *Mayne Pharma v Pharmacia Italia*[20] and extracted below.

Jacob LJ (Hooper LJ and Dame Elizabeth Butler-Sloss P in agreement):

5. To decide upon that meaning one must construe the claim in context. I summarised the principles in paragraph 41 of my judgment in *Technip SA's Patent* [2004] RPC 919. The House of Lords in *Kirin-Amgen* [2004] UKHL 46, through Lord Hoffmann's speech, has approved those principles (save for one minor matter) and provided a much fuller justification for them than did I. As a practical working guide, it will generally be sufficient to use my summary as approved. I repeat it here, but stripped down to bare essentials:

(a) The first, overarching principle, is that contained in Art 69 itself.

(b) Art 69 says that the extent of protection is determined *by the terms of the claims*. It goes on to say that the description and drawings shall be used to interpret the claims. In short the claims are to be construed in context.

(c) It follows that the claims are to be construed purposively—the inventor's purpose being ascertained from the description and drawings.

(d) It further follows that the claims must not be construed as if they stood alone—the drawings and description only being used to resolve any ambiguity. Purpose is vital to the construction of claims.

(f) Nonetheless purpose is not the be-all and end-all. One is still at the end of the day concerned with the meaning of the language used. Hence the other extreme of the Protocol—a mere guideline—is also ruled out by Art 69 itself. It is the terms of the claims which delineate the patentee's territory.

(g) It follows that if the patentee has included what is obviously a deliberate limitation in his claims, it must have a meaning. One cannot disregard obviously intentional elements.

---

[19] *Merz Pharma GmbH v Allergan Inc.* [2006] EWHC 2686 (Pat); *Corus UK Ltd v Qual-Chem Ltd* [2008] EWCA Civ 1177, [30] (Jacob LJ) (Scott Baker and Pill LJJ in agreement); *Grimme v Scott* [2010] EWCA Civ 1110, [2011] FSR 7, [9].

[20] [2005] EWCA Civ 137, [5] (Jacob LJ).

(h) It also follows that where a patentee has used a word or phrase which, acontextually, might have a particular meaning (narrow or wide) it does not necessarily have that meaning in context.

(i) It further follows that there is no general 'doctrine of equivalents'.

(j) On the other hand purposive construction can lead to the conclusion that a technically trivial or minor difference between an element of a claim and the corresponding element of the alleged infringement nonetheless falls within the meaning of the element when read purposively. This is not because there is a doctrine of equivalents: it is because that is the fair way to read the claim in context.

(k) Finally purposive construction leads one to eschew what Lord Diplock in *Catnic* called (at p.243): 'the kind of meticulous verbal analysis which lawyers are too often tempted by their training to indulge.'

The Court of Appeal has followed this summary of the relevant principles of claim construction in *Virgin Atlantic Airways Ltd v Premium Aircraft Interiors UK Ltd*[21] and *Occlutech GmbH v AGA Medical Corp.*[22] While this list may be seen as 'relatively uncontentious'[23] the statement that 'there is no general "doctrine of equivalents"' is not so. Some commentators have argued that the courts have failed seriously to consider 'whether the new Protocol was intended to bring about a fundamental change in the prevailing interpretative regime'[24]. Further, that Lord Hoffmann painted an unfair picture of the doctrine of equivalence, which (incorrectly) assumes that protection for equivalents automatically means that the scope of the claims is unbounded.[25] Others have taken the view that the UK position on equivalence, namely, that it merely forms 'an important part of the background of facts known to the skilled man which would affect what he understood the claims to mean' masks important aspects of equivalence that need to be addressed and discussed at a pan-European level.[26] In other words, we have yet to achieve a uniform approach to claim construction between EPC Contracting States.

There is lingering suspicion among some commentators that the purposive construction approach adopted in *Kirin-Amgen* and subsequently applied by the Court of Appeal and lower courts is flawed—or at least not compliant with Article 69 and Articles 1 and 2 of the Protocol. The late Sir Hugh Laddie has branded the House of Lords' approach in *Kirin-Amgen* as a conservative one, which limits the patent's scope to the language of the claims and pursues a futile objective of seeking to achieve maximum certainty for the benefit of third parties. According to Laddie, this 'does not accord with the legislative intent behind Art 69 and the Protocol'.[27] Dr Matthew Fisher argues that purposive construction has an,

[21] [2009] EWCA Civ 1062, [2010] RPC 8, [5].

[22] [2010] EWCA Civ 702, [23] (Patten LJ) (Pill LJ and Sir Paul Kennedy in agreement).

[23] M. Fisher, 'A case-study in literalism? Dissecting the English approach to patent claim construction in light of *Occlutech v AGA Medical*' [2011] IPQ 283, 295.

[24] Fisher, 'A case-study in literalism?'. See also H. Laddie, '*Kirin Amgen*—the end of equivalence in England?' (2009) 40 IIC 3, [67].

[25] M. Fisher, *Fundamentals of Patent Law: Interpretation and Scope of Protection* (Oxford: Hart, 2007), pp. 363, 373.

[26] N. Hölder, 'Exogenous equals endogenous? Claim construction after the *Amgen* decision' (2006) 37 IIC 662, 669.

[27] Laddie, '*Kirin Amgen*—the end of equivalence in England?', [78]–[79].

'unarticulated predilection towards literalism'[28] as demonstrated by the Court of Appeal's emphasis in *Occlutech* on the use of ordinary dictionary meanings. With the emergence of the Unified Patent Court, the objective of applying a consistent approach to claim construction and equivalence will become even more important and these principles are bound to attract more attention—as well as debate—in the future.

FURTHER READING

P. England, 'Towards a single pan-European standard—common concepts in UK and "continental European" patent law: Part 1: scope of patent protection and inventive concept' [2010] EIPR 195.

M. Fisher, *Fundamentals of Patent Law: Interpretation and Scope of Protection* (Oxford: Hart, 2007), chs 1, 9, and 10.

M. Fisher, 'New Protocol, same old story? Patent claim construction in 2007; looking back with a view to the future' [2008] IPQ 133.

N. Hölder, 'Exogenous equals endogenous? Claim construction after the *Amgen* decision' (2006) 37 IIC 662.

H. Laddie, '*Kirin Amgen*—the end of equivalence in England?' (2009) 40 IIC 3.

B. Sherman, 'Patent claim interpretation: the impact of the protocol on interpretation' (1991) 54 MLR 499.

C. Von Drathen, 'Patent scope in English and German law under the European Patent Convention 1973 and 2000' (2008) 39 IIC 384.

13.1.2.4 Relevance of prosecution history to construction

Can the documents, in particular the correspondence between patent applicants and the examiner which are generated during the examination process, be used by courts as an aid to construction of the patent as granted? In the UK, the answer is generally no,[29] although there have been exceptional cases where this has happened. For example, in *Furr v Truline (Building Products) Ltd*[30] the judge relied upon documents evidencing the prosecution history. However, these were submitted by the patentee to support a narrow construction of the patent claim and thus could be seen as an admission against interest.[31] Another example is *Rohm & Haas v Collag Ltd*[32] where the Court of Appeal accepted that a letter between the patentee and the EPO 'could be of assistance in resolving some puzzling features of the specification'.[33]

The resistance of the UK courts to admitting evidence relating to the prosecution history may be contrasted with the approach taken in the US, where courts regularly consider such evidence, alongside the language of the claim and the specification. The reasons for doing so are explored below.

---

[28] M. Fisher, 'A case-study in literalism? Dissecting the English approach to patent claim construction in light of *Occlutech v AGA Medical*' [2011] IPQ 283, 303.

[29] See *Bristol-Myers Squibb Co. v Baker Norton Pharmaceuticals Inc.* [1999] RPC 253, 274–5; *Taylor v Ishida (Europe) Ltd* [2001] EWCA Civ 1092.

[30] [1985] FSR 553.

[31] N. Fox, 'Divided by a common language: a comparison of patent claim interpretation in the English and American courts' [2004] EIPR 528, 532.

[32] [2002] FSR 28.   [33] *Rohm & Haas v Collag Ltd*, 457–8.

N. Fox, 'Divided by a common language: a comparison of patent claim interpretation in the English and American courts' [2004] EIPR 528 at 531

In the United States, although comments in the prosecution file will not be taken to override the content of the claims or the description, the prosecution file is considered to be 'intrinsic' evidence and is favoured over 'extrinsic' evidence. It is easy to understand why prosecution history should be given this favoured status as it is the prosecution history that enables the court to interpret a claim in a manner matching the construction which caused a claim to be granted. This should ensure that any patent will be valid over the prior art considered by the USPTO during prosecution and hence will complement the liberal interpretation which is most likely to maintain an inventor's rights.

Additionally, the content of 'intrinsic' evidence is ultimately under the control of the patentee. It is the patentee who drafts the specification and formulates the wording of the claims. It is also the patentee who is responsible for making claim amendments and for presenting arguments to persuade the USPTO to allow a patent to be granted. If during the course of patent prosecution a patentee wishes to argue in favour of broader protection, that option is open to him. In contrast, if a patentee argues that certain wording should be narrowly construed, reference to the prosecution file will ensure that the same wording is consistently construed when the scope of a patent is considered in the context of a potential infringement. Since all these matters are under the control of the patentee, statements and amendments made during a prosecution can reasonably be taken to reflect the patentee's view as to the extent of the patentee's invention.

It is principally these arguments in favour of consistency and fairness that justify the status of prosecution history in US claim interpretation. The wording of the claims and specification as granted reflect the scope of monopoly that the USPTO considered acceptable. The prosecution file is then a record of both the reasons why the granted claims were considered acceptable and a history of rejected wording which was not considered acceptable. Admitting the prosecution history as evidence therefore achieves the dual aims of trying to maintain an inventor's rights while limiting those rights to the true extent of a claimed invention.

Are the reasons for considering prosecution history when it comes to interpreting the patent claims in the US equally as applicable in the UK? What would be the obstacles or disadvantages to UK courts taking this approach? Jacob J (as he then was) discussed some of these in *obiter* in *Bristol-Myers Squibb Co. v Baker Norton Pharmaceuticals Inc.*

Bristol-Myers Squibb Co. v Baker Norton Pharmaceuticals Inc. [1999] RPC 253

See 12.1.5 for the facts.

Jacob J, at pp. 274–5:

Now there are several points to be made about a claim construction argument based on the prosecution history. First, whether that history can, and if so how, be used as an aid to construction would not be governed by national rules of construction. Claim construction is no longer a matter for national law but is governed by Article 69 and the Protocol. Thus, by way of example, specific English law notions of estoppel, cannot, as such, be used to construe the claim. Preventing him from asserting such a wide construction may be different—a specific English law defence. Second, there is an obvious important practical difference between merely referring to the specification as originally filed as an aid to construction and referring to detailed matter (e.g. contentions in correspondence or evidence) as contained in the EPO file. The specification as filed is a published document (the 'A' specification) and is referred to in the specification as granted. The intermediate processing correspondence with the examiner is different in volume and character, not least because it is not normally translated. Thirdly, there is another obvious difference between using the prosecution history to *widen* the claim and using that history to *narrow* it. It would be unfair on the public if material they would not normally look at could serve as a basis for supporting a wide construction of the claim. But there is not the same sort of unfairness if a patentee having contended for a narrow construction of his claim during prosecution is held to that construction later (cf. *Furr v Truline (Building Products) Ltd* [1985] FSR 553, an English case). Fourthly there is a difference between merely resolving a puzzle in the specification (though not the claim) by reference to the specification as filed and using the specification as filed as an aid to construction of the claim itself . . . All these are matters to be considered, perhaps by the Enlarged Board of Appeal or, if current proposals were to proceed, by a European Patent Court.

Having considered the comments of Jacob J in *Bristol-Myers*, do you regard the UK position on prosecution history as justifiable? The Court of Appeal held recently in *Actavis v Eli Lilly* that reference to the prosecution history was unhelpful, at [2015] EWCA Civ 555, [58–59].

13.1.3 INFRINGING ACTS

Once the claims have been properly construed and it is established that a person is doing something which falls within their scope, the next issue to consider is whether one of the exclusive acts has been carried out. The exclusive acts are stipulated in section 60 of the PA 77 and divide into acts of direct infringement and those of contributory (or indirect) infringement. Importantly, section 60 of the PA 77 should be interpreted consistently with Article 25 of the Community Patent Convention (CPC).[34] The following sections will examine the scope of acts amounting to direct infringement; contributory infringement will be considered in a later section.

13.1.3.1 Introduction

To directly infringe a patent, a person must carry out one of the prescribed exclusive acts *in the UK* in relation to the invention *without the consent* of the proprietor of the patent.[35] In other words, acts of infringement are territorially limited and if the proprietor has granted a licence to carry out the particular exclusive acts liability will not ensue.

For product inventions, the exclusive acts are to make, dispose of, offer to dispose of, use, or import the product or keep it whether for disposal or otherwise.[36] For process inventions, the exclusive acts are to dispose of, offer to dispose of, use, or import any product *obtained directly* by means of that process or keep any such product whether for disposal or otherwise.[37] In addition, where the invention is a process, it is an infringement for a person to use the process or offer it for use in the UK when he knows, or it is obvious to a reasonable person in the

---

[34] PA 77, s. 130(7).   [35] PA 77, s. 60(1).   [36] PA 77, s. 60(1)(a).   [37] PA 77, s. 60(1)(c).

circumstances, that its use there without the consent of the proprietor would be an infringement of the patent.[38] This is the only act of direct infringement that involves an element of knowledge. The following sections will discuss the scope of these exclusive acts.

13.1.3.2 Right to make the patented product

The most fundamental exclusive act for product inventions is making the patented product. The main issue that has arisen is whether repairing a patented product amounts to making it. The following House of Lords' decision has provided helpful clarification on this issue.

United Wire Ltd v Screen Repair Services [2001] RPC 24

The case involved an action for infringement of two UK patents. The inventions related to improvements to sifting screens used to recycle drilling fluid in the offshore drilling industry. When drilling fluid is pumped down the shaft and brought back to the surface, it contains quantities of foreign solids which must be filtered out. The fluid is filtered by being passed through mesh screens vibrating at high speed in a vibrating sifting machine. The claimant's patented inventions were 'screens' and consisted of a frame to which meshes were bonded or adhesively secured at the edge so as to be different tensions. The meshes of the screens had a relatively short life, but the frames to which they were bonded often remained serviceable. The claimant enjoyed a captive and profitable aftermarket in selling replacement screens. The defendants sought to break into this market by selling reconditioned screens made from the claimant's own frames. The defendants would acquire the frames from the claimant's customers, strip them down to the bare metal, recoat them with adhesive polyethylene, and attach the two layers of mesh (coarse and fine) with differential tensions. The screens were then sold on to the customers, who received a credit for supplying the frames.

The defendants argued, inter alia, that the repaired screens did not infringe because they 'repaired' a screen, rather than 'made' it within the meaning of section 60(1)(a) of the PA 77. This succeeded at first instance, but the Court of Appeal allowed an appeal on this issue. The Court of Appeal held that the trial judge had erred in focusing on whether or not the actions were in fact repair: the issue was whether the acts amounted to a manufacture of the product, taking into the account the nature of the repair claimed. The defendants appealed, but this was dismissed by the House of Lords.

Lord Hoffmann (with whom the other law lords agreed):

65. The defendants say that although the product which they sell is a screen in accordance with the invention, they do not infringe because they do no more than repair screens which have been marketed with the consent of the plaintiffs. The grounds upon which this is said not to constitute an infringement is put in various ways. First, it is said that, in marketing the screens, the plaintiffs impliedly licence anyone who acquires a screen to prolong its life by repair. Secondly, it is said that the marketing of the screens constitutes an exhaustion of any rights which a repair might infringe. Thirdly, it is said that a person who repairs a screen does not

---

[38] PA 77, s. 60(1)(b).

'make' that screen within the meaning of the definition of an infringement in section 60(1)(a) of the Patents Act 1977.

...

68. My Lords, the point is a very short one and in my opinion the Court of Appeal was right. The concept of an implied licence to do various acts in relation to a patented product is well established in the authorities. Its proper function is to explain why, notwithstanding the apparent breadth of the patentee's rights, a person who has acquired the product with the consent of the patentee may use or dispose of it in any way he pleases. The traditional Royal Command in the grant of a patent forebade others not only to 'make' but also to 'use, exercise or vend' the invention. Similarly, s. 60(1)(a) provides that a person infringes a patent for a product not only if he 'makes' it but also if, without the consent of the proprietor, he 'disposes of, offers to dispose of, uses or imports the product or keeps it whether for disposal or otherwise'. Put shortly, the problem is to explain why, for example, a patentee cannot complain when someone to whom he had sold the patented product then, without any further consent, uses it or disposes of it to someone else. The answer given by Lord Hatherley LC in the leading case of *Betts v Willmott* (1871) LR 6 Ch App 239, 245 (which concerned the resale of a patented product) was that he did so by virtue of an implied licence:

> I apprehend that, inasmuch as [the patentee] has the right of vending the goods in France or Belgium or England, or in any other quarter of the globe, he transfers with the goods necessarily the licence to use them wherever the purchaser pleases. When a man has purchased an article he expects to have the control of it, and there must be some clear and explicit agreement to the contrary to justify the vendor in saying that he has not given the purchaser his licence to sell the article, or to use it wherever he pleases as against himself.

69. An alternative explanation, adopted in European patent systems, is that of exhaustion of rights. The patentee's rights in respect of the product are exhausted by the first sale: see *Merck & Co Inc v Primecrown Ltd* [1997] 1 CMLR 83 at page 119. The difference in the two theories is that an implied licence may be excluded by express contrary agreement or made subject to conditions while the exhaustion doctrine leaves no patent rights to be enforced.

70. Where however it is alleged that the defendant has infringed by *making* the patented product, the concepts of an implied licence or exhaustion of rights can have no part to play. The sale of a patented article cannot confer an implied licence to make another or exhaust the right of the patentee to prevent others from being made. A repair of the patented product is by definition an act which does not amount to making it: as Lord Halsbury LC said of the old law in *Sirdar Rubber Co Ltd v Wallington, Weston & Co* (1907) 24 RPC 539 at page 543:

> you may prolong the life of a licensed article but you must not make a new one under the cover of repair.

71. Repair is one of the concepts (like modifying or adapting) which shares a boundary with 'making' but does not trespass upon its territory. I therefore agree with the Court of Appeal that in an action for infringement by making, the notion of an implied licence to repair is superfluous and possibly even confusing. It distracts attention from the question raised by section 60(1)(a), which is whether the defendant has made the patented product. As a matter of ordinary language, the notions of making and repair may well overlap. But for the purposes of the statute, they are mutually exclusive. The owner's right to repair is not an independent right conferred upon him by licence, express or implied. It is a residual right, forming part of the right to do whatever does not amount to making the product.

...

> 73. …[I]n this case the Court of Appeal was in my opinion entitled to substitute its own evaluation because I think, with great respect to the judge, that he did not correctly identify the patented product. He said that the frame was an important part of the assembly and that the defendants had prolonged 'the screen's useful life'. It is quite true that the defendants pro-longed the useful life of the *frame*. It would otherwise presumably have been scrapped. But the *screen* was the combination of frame and meshes pre-tensioned by attachment with adhesive according to the invention. That product ceased to exist when the meshes were removed and the frame stripped down to the bare metal. What remained at that stage was merely an impor-tant component, a skeleton or chassis, from which a new screen could be made.

According to *United Wire*, is there ever any point in asking whether a product has been repaired as opposed to made? Also, what is the relationship between the right to make a patented product and the concepts of implied licence and exhaustion of rights? To which acts would an implied licence or the doctrine of exhaustion of rights apply?

The House of Lords' decision in *United Wire* was recently revisited in *Schütz v Werit*.[39] The claimant in this case was the exclusive licensee of a European patent (UK) for an intermediate bulk container (IBC) which comprised an outer protective cage and a removable inner bottle that could store a large volume of liquid. As IBCs are used to transport a wide range of liquids they have to be leak-proof, sturdy enough to withstand the tough conditions of transport, and be able to be stacked. Often the inner bottles become damaged or are no longer able to be used because they are contaminated. Thus, a practice of 'rebottling' or 'cross bottling' emerged, whereby the old bottle is removed, the outer cage repaired, and a new bottle fitted within the cage. In this case, Werit sold bottles for IBCs to Delta, who in turn purchased old Schütz IBCs, removed their bottles, repaired the cages, and inserted the new bottles bought from Werit and offered the 'rebottled' IBCs for sale. The claimant brought proceedings against Werit. It argued that Delta infringed their patent by making the patented product and that Werit was therefore a contributory infringer by supplying an essential element of the invention for putting it into effect. The crucial legal issue was whether Delta's activities amounted to *making* Schütz's patented product.

At first instance Lloyd J distinguished the House of Lords' decision in *United Wire* and concluded that Delta's activity was *not* making the patented product because when the bottle was removed, what remained (i.e. the cage) was the whole inventive concept.[40] The Court of Appeal (Jacob LJ delivering the leading judgment)[41] dismissed the defendants' argument that the House of Lords in *United Wire* applied a 'whole inventive concept' test for determining whether there was a making of a patented product (i.e. to ask whether, when the part was removed, what was left behind embodied the whole inventive concept of the claim). The Court of Appeal examined carefully the decision in *United Wire* and concluded that it endorsed the 'making' test and excluded any additional 'whole inventive concept' test.[42] Further, that it would be unwise to adopt a 'whole inventive concept' test because it would be uncertain in its application.[43] Finally, in response to the defendants' concerns that Schütz would have, in effect, a monopoly in replacing bottles for its cages, the court doubted whether freedom of competition was really at stake here and that, in any case, this was an 'essentially economic concern … not really an apt matter for patent law'.[44]

---

[39] [2010] EWHC 660 (Pat), [2010] FSR 22; [2011] EWCA Civ 303, [2011] FSR 19; [2013] UKSC 16, [2013] 2 All ER 177.

[40] [2010] EWHC 660 (Pat), [2010] FSR 22, [181], [197], and [206].

[41] [2011] EWCA Civ 303, [2011] FSR 19.   [42] See [47]–[69].   [43] [72].   [44] [79]–[80].

On appeal, the Supreme Court found in favour of Werit, i.e. replacing the bottle in the IBC did *not* involve making the patented product and so they were not contributory infringers by virtue of selling bottles to Delta. Lord Neuberger (delivering the leading judgment)[45] held that both Lloyd J and the Court of Appeal had adopted the incorrect approach to determining the question of whether a particular activity involves 'making' a patented product. According to his lordship, Lloyd J had 'oversimplified the position' and the Court of Appeal 'were too ready to accept that the outcome of this case was governed by *United Wire*'.[46] The conclusions of the Supreme Court are neatly summarized in the following paragraph.

> 78. Deciding whether a particular activity involves 'making' the patented article involves, as Lord Bingham [in *United Wire*] said, an exercise in judgment or, in Lord Hoffmann's words [in *United Wire*], it is a matter of fact and degree. In some such cases, one can say that the answer is clear; in other cases, one can identify a single clinching factor. However, in this case, it appears to me that it is a classic example of identifying the various factors which apply on the particular facts, and, after weighing them all up, concluding, as a matter of judgment, whether the alleged infringer does or does not 'make' the patented article. In the present case, given that (a) the bottle (i) is a freestanding, replaceable component of the patented article, (ii) has no connection with the claimed inventive concept, (iii) has a much shorter life expectancy than the other, inventive, component, (iv) cannot be described as the main component of the article, and (b) apart from replacing it, Delta does no additional work to the article beyond routine repairs, I am of the view that, in carrying out this work, Delta does not 'make' the patented article.

A particularly interesting factor that the Supreme Court took into account was the much shorter life expectancy of the bottle as compared with the cage, which the court indicated would lead to the legitimate expectation that it could be replaced and thus was a subsidiary part of the article.[47] Is this a factor that indirectly takes into account the competition considerations that were dismissed by the Court of Appeal? Is the 'fact and degree' approach adopted by the Supreme Court likely to provide clarity and certainty to patentees and third parties?

In *Nestec SA v Dualit Ltd*,[48] Arnold J applied the House of Lords' decision in *United Wire* and the Supreme Court decision in *Schütz v Werit* to assess whether an owner of a Nestec 'Nespresso' coffee machine who purchased Dualit's compatible NX coffee capsules (rather than Nespresso capsules) was 'making' the patented system. The patented system was an extraction system comprising a device for the extraction of a capsule and a capsule that can be extracted in the device. (Note that there had been a European patent for the Nespresso capsules that had expired in 2011.) The patent was found to be invalid; however, Arnold J went on to consider infringement. The issue was one of indirect infringement under section 60(2) of the PA 77 (discussed at 13.1.3.7). As part of this assessment, Arnold J had to consider whether the NX capsules constituted a 'means suitable for putting the invention into effect' and this depended on whether the person purchasing an NX capsule for use with a Nespresso machine was 'making' the patented system. Arnold J held (in *obiter*) that, owners of Nespresso machines did not 'make' the patented system when

---

[45] With whom Lord Walker, Lady Hale, Lord Mance, and Lord Kerr agreed.
[46] [2013] UKSC 16, [2013] 2 All ER 177, [56] and [57].   [47] [65]–[66].
[48] [2013] EWHC 923 (Pat), [2013] RPC 32.

they purchased Dualit NX capsules.[49] First, the capsule was seen as an entirely subsidiary part of the system—capsules were considerably cheaper than the machines and discarded once used and did not affect the value or performance of the coffee machines. Second, the machines and capsules had an independent commercial existence insofar as they were sold separately. Third, the capsules were consumables and purchasers of machines would assume that the capsules could be bought from whatever source they pleased. Fourth, the capsule did not embody the inventive concept of the patent. Although the flange of the capsule was relevant to the way the capsule worked, the invention was really about the way in which the machine operated. Finally, Arnold J commented that: 'it is manifest that the owner of the machine is not even doing anything which would ordinarily be described as repairing a product, let alone making one. The only reason why Nestec is even able to argue that the owner is "making" something is that the claim is directed to a "system" which consists of a collocation of two entirely separate, but conceptually related products (namely the machine and the capsule).'[50]

Interestingly, Arnold J also considered that purchasers of Nespresso machines were impliedly licensed to obtain and use capsules with the machine or, alternatively, that, via sale of the Nespresso machines, Nestec had exhausted their rights to restrict purchasers' freedom to use their coffee machines in accordance with their normal function. On the face of it, this finding would seem contrary to Lord Hoffmann's statement in *United Wire* that where 'it is alleged that the defendant has infringed by *making* the patented product, the concepts of an implied licence or exhaustion of rights can have no part to play'.[51]

13.1.3.3 Right to dispose of or offer to dispose of the product

The right to dispose of the product includes the right to sell (or vend) the product. As such, an offer to dispose of a product includes an offer of sale. Importantly, the sale or offer of sale must occur within the UK. *Kalman v PCL Packaging*[52] illustrates these points. In this case the second defendant was a corporation operating in the US, with no place of business in the UK and no regular trading activities outside the US. The second defendant had sold and delivered to the first defendant two allegedly infringing articles within the US. Falconer J held that the second defendant had not disposed of the products within the UK, given that the allegedly infringing articles had been sold in the US. Neither had it offered to dispose of an infringing product, since this would have required an offer *made in the UK* to dispose of filters *within* the UK. While the second defendant had arguably made an offer in the UK, it was not an offer to dispose of the filters within the UK.

In *Gerber v Lectra*[53] Jacob J (as he then was) emphasized the importance of interpreting section 60 of the PA 77 consistently with the corresponding provision in Article 25 of the CPC, which states that the exclusive acts of the patent proprietor are 'making, offering, putting on the market, or using a product which is the subject-matter of the patent, or importing or stocking the product for these purposes'. The issue in this case was what amounted to 'an offer to dispose of' under section 60(1) of the PA 77 and whether this was limited to contractual offers. Jacob J held that offers to dispose of were not limited to contractual offers: 'A party who approaches potential customers individually or by

---

[49] [200]–[205].   [50] [204].   [51] *United Wire*, [70].   [52] [1982] FSR 406.
[53] [1995] RPC 383. On appeal the first instance decision was reversed in part, but not on the interpretation of 'offer to dispose of': [1997] RPC 443.

advertisement saying he is willing to supply a machine, terms to be agreed, is offering it or putting it on the market.'[54]

13.1.3.4 Right to keep the product whether for disposal or otherwise

In relation to the PA 77, it was unclear whether passively storing a patented product, or the product directly obtained from a patented process, would constitute keeping the product for disposal or otherwise. Oliver J considered this issue in *SKF v Harbottle*.[55] In this case, British Airways were in the process of transporting, at the request of the first defendant, an antihistamine drug called cimetidine from Italy to Nigeria. The quantity of drugs had not been cleared through customs and was stored at their bonded warehouse. The claimants, who held a UK patent covering the drug cimetidine, brought an infringement action against the importer of the drug, Harbottle. British Airways was joined as a co-defendant and was thereby restrained from disposing of the drug. The claimants claimed that British Airways had infringed their right to keep the product.

Oliver J declined to arrive at a definitive meaning of 'keep'. However, he held that the act of passively storing a patented drug in a warehouse in London could *not* be construed as 'keeping of a product' within the meaning of section 60(1) of the PA 77. In coming to this conclusion, he noted the lack of positive language to effect such a significant change. Prior to the PA 77, a carrier or warehouseman who did no more than innocently carry or store infringing goods for a consignor/consignee was not liable as an infringer. Oliver J reasoned:

> But if it had been the intention of Parliament to bring within the category of infringers a new and extensive class of persons who by the very nature of their trade or calling would be unlikely to have any knowledge, either actual or potential, of any patent protection affecting the goods which were only transitorily in their control, one would have expected so revolutionary a change in the common law to be effected by a pronouncement of a less Delphic nature.[56]

In addition, Oliver J was influenced by the 'very much more limited' terms employed in Article 29(a) of the CPC, which refers to 'stocking' of the patented product, and the fact that, as has already been mentioned, the intention of the framers of the PA 77 was to give effect to the provisions of the CPC.[57] Thus, 'keep' implied 'keeping in stock' rather than acting as a custodian.[58]

This interpretation was followed by the Court of Appeal in *McDonald v Graham*.[59] This case concerned a patent relating to 'folded sheet material' which, when folded, resembled a plastic credit card, but when opened out was a sheet of printed material intended for publicity purposes. The defendant sought to become involved in marketing the patented product and, to that end, organized promotional samples of the product. The relationship between the claimant and the defendant deteriorated and the claimants brought an action for infringement, alleging that the defendant had not destroyed the promotional samples,

---

[54] *Gerber*, 412.   [55] [1980] RPC 363.   [56] At 371.   [57] See PA 77, s. 130 (7).
[58] *SKF v Harbottle*, 363, 373.   [59] [1994] RPC 407.

but had kept and subsequently used the cards for the purposes of his business. The Court of Appeal held that the evidence demonstrated that the defendant was keeping the product, 'in the sense of keeping them in stock for the purposes of his business in order to make use of them as and when it would be beneficial to him to do so'.[60]

13.1.3.5 Right to import the product

According to the House of Lords' decision in *Sabaf SpA v MFI Furniture Centres Ltd*,[61] where goods have been sold outside the UK, arranging transport of the goods from outside the UK to the UK does not constitute importation.

13.1.3.6 Direct infringement of a patented process

Section 60(1)(c) of the PA 77 stipulates that a person will infringe a *process* patent if they dispose of, offer to dispose of, use, or import any product *obtained directly* by means of that process or keep any such product whether for disposal or otherwise. The stipulation that the product must be obtained *directly* from the patented process is a way of ensuring that the scope of the monopoly is kept within justifiable limits. If it did not exist, the provision might cover those products which were only tangentially or partly derivative from the patented process.

The Court of Appeal in *Pioneer Electronics Capital Inc. v Warner Music*[62] shed light on when a product is obtained directly from a process. The case concerned European patents (UK) for methods for making optical discs. The defendants applied to strike out the writs and statements of claim. This application succeeded before Aldous J (as he then was), who held that the products complained of could not be said to have been obtained directly by means of the patented processes. The claimants appealed. Nourse LJ (with whom Leggatt and Schiemann LJJ agreed) turned to German authorities in particular to interpret section 60(1)(c) of the PA 77. This was because there were no relevant UK authorities and section 130(7) of the PA 77 requires that section 60(1)(c) be interpreted in conformity with the corresponding provisions of the EPC and CPC. From German jurisprudence, Nourse LJ extracted the principle:[63]

> that the product obtained directly by means of a patented process is the product with which the process ends; it does not cease to be the product so obtained if it is subjected to further processing which does not cause it to lose its identity, there being no such loss where it retains its essential characteristics.

Nourse LJ was of the view that authorities from other European countries did not differ from the German approach and that the 'loss of identity test' could be taken to reflect the test adopted by European law. The question of whether a product had retained its essential characteristics such that it had not lost its identity and could be said to be directly obtained from the patented process was a question of fact and degree. Do you agree that a test of 'loss of identity' is an appropriate way in which to measure whether a product has been obtained directly from a patented process?

---

[60] At 431 (Ralph Gibson LJ).   [61] [2004] UKHL 45, [2005] RPC 10, [40] (Lord Hoffmann).
[62] [1997] RPC 757.   [63] At 771.

On the facts of this case, however, it was clear that the product had not retained its identity. Nourse LJ held:

> It is not correct to say that the finished discs are identical copies of the masters. As the judge said, the finished disc differs in material from the master and is the result of three further stages of production. From each of those stages emerges a new and different product which is a necessary instrument in the production of the finished disc. Neither the master nor any of the intermediate products is capable of performing the same function as the finished disc, in illustration of which it is only necessary to observe that none of them can be put into the compact disc player and played in the home.[64]

13.1.3.7 Indirect or contributory infringement

Section 60(2) of the PA 77 creates a form of indirect or contributory infringement. This subsection provides:

> Subject to the following provisions of this section, a person (other than the proprietor of the patent) also infringes a patent for an invention if, while the patent is in force and without the consent of the proprietor, he supplies or offers to supply in the United Kingdom a person other than a licensee or other person entitled to work the invention with any of the means, relating to an essential element of the invention, for putting the invention into effect when he knows, or it is obvious to a reasonable person in the circumstances, that those means are suitable for putting, and are intended to put, the invention into effect in the United Kingdom.

Section 60(2) of the PA 77 was intended to have the same meaning as the corresponding provisions in the CPC.[65] Thus, section 60(2) should have the same meaning as the CPC as revised in 1989.[66] In short, to establish indirect infringement, one must show that:

(1) without the consent of the proprietor of the patent, a person supplies or offers to supply means relating to an *essential element* of the invention; and

(2) there must be *actual or constructive knowledge* on the part of the supplier, both that the means are 'suitable' for and are 'intended' to be used in putting the invention into effect.

The territorial limitation applies both to where the supply or offer to supply is made *and* also to where the invention is put into effect. In other words, if a person were to supply an essential element of a patented invention in the UK, but the invention was put into effect outside the UK (say, in Italy), this provision would not be infringed. It is also important to note that according to section 60(3) of the PA 77, supply or offer of a *staple commercial product* will not constitute an indirect infringement under section 60(2), unless the supply or offer is made for the purpose of inducing a direct infringement under section 60(1). What is a 'staple commercial product' is undefined in the PA 77 and has had limited judicial interpretation. What is apparent from the case law is that it is probably 'a commodity or raw material'[67] or 'ordinarily... one which is supplied commercially for a variety of uses'.[68]

---

[64] At 764–5.   [65] PA 77, s. 130(7).
[66] *Grimme v Scott* [2010] EWCA Civ 1110, [2011] FSR 7, [84]–[85].
[67] *Pavel v Sony Corp.*, unreported, 13 January 1993, [6.4] (HHJ Ford).
[68] *Nestec SA v Dualit Ltd* [2013] EWHC 923, [2013] RPC 32, [182].

The scope of section 60(2) was considered for the first time by the Court of Appeal in *Grimme v Scott*.

Grimme v Scott [2010] EWCA Civ 1110, [2011] FSR 7

The claimant sued the defendant for infringement of its European patent (UK) for a machine for separating potatoes from extraneous matter such as weeds, earth, stones, and haulm. The defendant denied infringement and also counterclaimed for invalidity of the patent. All that concerns us here, however, is the infringement claim. The first instance judge held that the defendant had both directly and indirectly infringed particular claims of the patent (that were held to be valid). Direct infringement had occurred by the sale and offering for sale of the defendant's potato separator machine when fitted with two pairs of elastomeric (i.e. rubber) rollers (such machine falling within the scope of the patent claims). The same machine when sold with steel clod rollers did not fall within the scope of the patent claims. However, because the machine was designed to be interchangeable so that rubber rollers could be substituted, the judge held their supply did amount to indirect infringement within the meaning of the section 60(2) provision on indirect infringement. The defendant appealed these findings of infringement. The Court of Appeal held that the defendant's machine sold with rubber rollers fell within the scope of the claimant's valid patent. It then turned to consider the indirect or contributory infringement provision and its applicability to the defendant's machine sold with steel clod rollers.

Jacob and Etherton LJJ (Sir David Keene in agreement):

[Their lordships began by discussing the distinctive features of this provision and the fact that establishing contributory infringement did not depend on establishing actual direct infringement.]

87. The type of infringement described in art.26 and s.60(2) is commonly referred to as 'indirect' or 'contributory' infringement, by way of contrast with 'direct' infringement contrary to s.60(1) and art.25.

88. Section 60(2) creates a statutory tort, but it does not spring from any previous notional or common law tort. Its distinctive features, by way of contrast with common law tortious claims, are that the tort is actionable (1) even though what is supplied is capable of perfectly lawful, non-infringing use, (2) even though what is supplied never has been and may never in fact be used in a way directly infringing the patent in suit, (3) without any damage being suffered by the patentee, and (4) at the moment of supply, irrespective of anything that may or may not occur afterwards.

89. This marks a distinct contrast with the common law principle that it is not infringement merely to sell an ingredient to another with the knowledge that the purchaser will use it to infringe (*Belegging-en-Exploitatiemaatschapij Lavender BV v Witten Industrial Diamonds Ltd* [1979] F.S.R. 59), the refusal of the courts, before the 1977 Act, to order the delivery up of items which could be used in a non-infringing way (*Electrical and Musical Industries Ltd v Lissen Ltd* (1937) 54 R.P.C. 5), and the need to show damage for the 'so-called' economic torts—such as inducing breach of contract, causing loss by unlawful means and conspiracy (see generally *Clerk & Lindsell on Torts*, 19th edn (London: Sweet & Maxwell, 2005), Ch.25).

90. It also makes the description 'contributory' as opposed to 'indirect' infringement something of a misnomer. If and to the extent that Mr Scott's case is that there can be no infringement under s.60(2) unless there is actual direct infringement, it is plainly wrong. In this connection it is particularly important to observe that there can even be infringement by 'offering' to sell an essential means—at the time of the offer there is unlikely to be any particular end user in mind.

[Their lordships next considered the argument that section 60(2) was applicable only to component elements and not a complete, non-infringing machine. The defendant submitted that the policy of the provision could not have been to prevent the supply of entire non-infringement machines or apparatus simply because they were obvious modifications that could be made such that the machine became infringing.]

102. ... On the facts of the present case, there is no obscurity in the meaning and application of the expression 'means, relating to an essential element of the invention, for putting the invention into effect'. Grimme's invention is 'put into effect' when the Evolution [i.e. defendant's] machine is fitted with rubber rollers. The supply of a steel-rollered machine, which is designed and indeed promoted to enable the steel rollers to be changed for rubber rollers, is plainly the supply of the means by which that can be achieved, and is the supply of a means essential for that purpose. The fact that a steel-rollered Evolution machine, so long as it remains steel-rollered, does not infringe and is capable of lawful use as a complete machine in that state is irrelevant. The section is clearly intended to apply to, among other things, products which are perfectly capable of being used in a manner which will not constitute a direct infringement within s.60(1). The requirements as to suitability and knowledge of intended use limit the scope of the statutory tort in relation to such products, not whether the product itself is capable of lawful use without alteration, addition or adaptation.

103. Moreover we can see no rational basis for the 'whole machine' point. Why should a device to which a part can be readily added to make it fall within the claim be a 'means essential' but a device from which a part can readily be removed or replaced to make it fall within the claim not be such a means?

104. Accordingly we reject this point.

[Their lordships then went on to consider 'the more difficult problem' of the knowledge requirement—i.e. that the supplier 'knows...that those means...are intended to put the invention into effect' (at [105]).]

108. First then the person who must have the intention. One can rule out the supplier himself. The required intention is to put the invention into effect. That the supplier himself does not intend to do. The question is what the supplier knows or ought to know about the intention of the person who is in a position to put the invention into effect—the person at the end of the supply chain. Arnold J. put it pithily in *KCI Licensing Inc v Smith & Nephew Ltd* [2010] EWHC 1487 (Pat); [2010] FSR 31 at [200]:

> It is implicit in this reasoning [i.e. that of Lewison J. in *Cranway Ltd v Playtech Ltd* [2009] EWHC 1588 (Pat); [2010] FSR 3] that the relevant intention is not that of the supplier. In my judgment this is correct. S.60(2) makes it clear that there can be infringement not merely if the supplier knows that the means are intended to put the invention into effect, but also if that would be obvious to a reasonable person in the circumstances. That is inconsistent with a requirement of intention on the part of the supplier. Thus the relevant intention must be that of the person supplied.

109. Next, must the required intention be that of the person directly supplied by the alleged infringer? Lewison J. took that view in *Cranway* [2010] FSR 3, saying at [156]:

Whether means are *suitable* for putting an invention into effect must be a purely objective test. But whether they are *intended* to put an invention into effect cannot be wholly objective. Only human beings can have intentions, although their intentions may be attributed to other legal persons, according to rules of attribution. Thus this limb of the test must depend on the subjective intention of someone. A supplier of essential means might reasonably be supposed to know what the intention of his immediate counter-party is. But it would be a far stronger thing to expect him to discern the intention of a person far down the supply chain. Moreover, at the time of the supplier's supply of the essential means the person who ultimately forms the intention to use the means to put the invention into effect may not be ascertainable and he may not have formed that intention. It thus seems to me to be more likely that s.60(2) was directed to a supply of essential means to a direct infringer rather than to another secondary infringer ...

110. We do not agree for two reasons. First, if that view were right, a party who only supplied essential means to middlemen could never fall within the provision. It cannot have been intended that the legislation would not catch a primary supplier to the ultimate market even if he very well knew that the ultimate users would adapt the means so as to infringe.

111. Secondly, the reasoning presupposes an actual, already formed, intention in the user. We do not think that is necessary (see below).

112. What then of the 'inherently probable' view? This was essentially that for which Mr Chacksfield argued. He submitted that it was enough if the supplier knew (or it was obvious in the circumstances) at the time of his offer to supply or supply that *some* (disregarding freak use) ultimate users would intend to use, adapt or alter the 'means essential' so as to infringe.

113. Against this view it can be said that art.26 requires that the alleged infringer must know (or it must be obvious etc) that the means *are* intended to put the invention into affect. The present tense is used. So it can be said that a future intention—even a probable future intention—is not enough.

114. Notwithstanding the force of that linguistic point, we conclude that the 'inherently probable' view is indeed the correct construction of the provision. We do so for a number of reasons.

115. First, it is the only way to make sense of the fact that the provision not only covers the case where the alleged infringer supplies the means but also the case where he offers to supply it. When a person makes an 'offer' the offeree cannot yet have formed a settled intention to put the invention into effect. This consideration played a significant part in the German cases (see below) and we consider rightly so.

116. Secondly, it was essentially the reasoning of Jacob J. in *Chapman*. He said:

It is sufficient if it is shown that the invention will be put into effect by some users. One would only disregard maverick or unlikely uses of the thing.

117. That must, of course, be established in the usual way on a balance of probabilities. It is more accurate, therefore, to state the test in terms of what probably will be intended and what probably will be the use to which the means will be put. This chimes with the German cases (below).

118. Thirdly, it is consistent with '*moyens sont...destinés à cette mise en oeuvre*' in the French version of art.26.1 and also '*bestimmt*' in the German version. Both versions convey

the notion of what will happen ultimately rather than a need to look for the intention of a presently identifiable user.

119. Fourthly, the linguistic point does not make any sense looking at art.26 and s.60(2) purposively. Those provisions are clearly aimed at people who supply things which will be used to infringe—people who put into circulation 'means essential' in circumstances when they know or ought to know that infringement will be the result because the ultimate users will intend to do acts amounting to infringement.

120. Fifthly, that is the effect of the German cases, which, as we have said, should be followed unless we think they are wrong—which we do not.

121. Sixthly, it is the effect of the Dutch case *Grimme v Steenwoorden Constructie*, April 20, 2010. We need say no more about this case because the view was taken in *kort geding* (provisional) proceedings only, and the German cases contain a much fuller analysis of the provision.

122. It is to the German cases we now turn. We were shown six. Of these the most recent (in 2006/7) were all from the Supreme Court (BGH as it is generally called) and are clearly the most authoritative. They were *Deckenheizung* [BGH X ZR 153/03], June 13, 2006; *Haubenstretchautomat* [BGH X ZR 173/02], January 9, 2007; and *Pipettensystem* [BGH X ZR 38/06], February 27, 2007. The three earlier cases are *Luftheizgerät* [BGH X ZR 176/98], October 10, 2000; *DI B.V.* [2004] ENPR 194 of March 25, 1999 (*Oberlandsgericht*, Düsseldorf); and *Antriebsscheibenaufzug* [BGH X ZR 247/02], June 7, 2005.

123. The leading case is *Deckenheizung*. The patent claimed a room ceiling comprising inter alia metal plates and flexible heating/cooling pipes positioned thereon. The patent claim required that the pipes had to be placed 'loosely' on the metal plates. The defendant sold cooling mats which could be placed loosely into such a roof, although with instructions suggesting that they be incorporated into metal cassettes (and therefore not 'loose'). On the facts, however, in about 20 per cent of cases ultimate users placed the mats loosely.

124. Contributory infringement was held established. Necessarily such a conclusion is inconsistent with any requirement that the intention of the individual ultimate user must be known to the defendant at the moment of the alleged infringement. The BGH said this:

[22] …According to established statute of the senate, the intention of using the protected invention is a circumstance that is within the sphere of the buyer (*Antriebsscheibenaufzug*). However, the condition of indirect patent infringement is not met only when the buyer had already actually decided to use the devices in a patent-infringing manner and the vendor or supplied knew it. Rather, it is met when an intent to use the devices for patent-infringing uses is obvious to a third party based on the circumstances as a legal condition, in other words it must be obvious to the vendor or to suppliers of the devices suitable for use according to the patent. This is meant to facilitate verification of indirect patent infringement. This allows one to consider the condition as being in place when, from the point of view of a third party [the supplier] objectively considering the circumstances, a sufficiently certain expectation exists that the buyer will intend to use the offered or delivered devices for patent-infringing purposes.

125. Whilst it is the intention of the buyer (this must mean ultimate buyer) which matters, a future intention of a future buyer is enough if that is what one would expect in all the circumstances. The BGH went on to explain this more:

[23] The subject matter of the infringing behaviour according to § 10 of the PatG (corresponding to Art. 26) is not participation in the violation by the buyer of the obligations to

which it is subject according to patent law, but an actual infringing action by a third party. Accordingly, the senate came to the decision more than once that it is not necessary for direct infringement of the patent by the buyer—either attempted or successful—to occur for an indirect patent infringement to occur, but rather it is sufficient merely for an offer or delivery of suitable devices to have occurred provided that the subjective prerequisites of its intention for use according to the patent are met (citations omitted). In particular, in a legal, unsolicited first offer, an intention for the buyer to use the devices according to the patent will in general not exist in the form of a decision that has already been made. It will also consequently often be lacking objectively, and in any case will appear debatable according to the pertinent state of knowledge of the vendor. According to the nature of this intention as a condition which threatens a patent (citations omitted), the purpose of §10 of the PatG is, in this case as well, to protect the patentee from an impending infringement of its rights. Therefore, the regulation must take effect when it is sufficiently safe to expect, from the point of view of a third party, that the buyer will use the delivered devices in a manner according to the patent.

126. The reasoning based on the fact that provision covers 'offering for sale' is a point we noted earlier. It seems unassailable.

127. The BGH went on to flesh out its reasoning further. It in particular considered the position where the alleged contributory infringer has proposed the infringing use (as in the case of Mr Scott). It said:

24. The features outlined in the law for fleshing out the subjective condition (if one knows or if it is obvious according to the circumstances) thus provide the possibility of establishing the required state of knowledge of the vendor or supplier of the impending infringement of the rights of the patentee through two alternative routes. Either a third party knows that the buyer has intended to use the devices according to the patent, or such an intent is obvious to expect according to the circumstances of the individual case, such as because they are self-evident. Knowledge and obviousness are thus two ways to establish the required high degree of expectation of use of the devices according to the patent. In this light, the necessary high degree of expectation usually exists in particular when the vendor or supplier had itself proposed such use.

128. The last sentence is particularly apposite to the present case. Mr Scott sought to enhance his sales by pointing out that users could adapt the device for less stringent conditions by a simple modification. He sold the means for that too. We do not think it matters that he now says only a few users do make the change (and for the reasons we have indicated we do not think that is at present established). Mr Scott knew that users would intend to make their devices infringing if it suited them and positively encouraged that intention.

129. The BGH took the same approach in *Haubenstretchautomat* and *Luftheizgerät*. In *Haubenstretchautomat* the test was expressed as: 'the [third party] expected...with sufficient certainty that...['] (para.35); and 'the impending infringement...is so clearly apparent that...' (para.36). The BGH in that case said that the test was likely to be satisfied 'if the supplier indicates or even recommends the possibility of use according to a patent in an owner's manual, operating instructions or similar' (para.37).

130. In *Luftheizgerät* the test was expressed as: 'a high degree of foreseeability in respect of...the intention' (p.16). The BGH said that: 'If the supplier recommends a particular use to the person supplied, experience suggests that the person supplied will...put the device to such use, and that the supplier knows this' (p.15).

131. Although the test is expressed in *Deckenheizung*, *Haubenstretchautomat* and *Luftheizgerät* in slightly different language, they are all to the same effect, and are consistent

with what Jacob J. said in *Chapman*. In short, the knowledge and intention requirements of art.26 and s.60(2) are satisfied if, at the time of supply or offer of supply, the supplier knows, or it is obvious in the circumstances, that ultimate users will intend to put the invention into effect. That is to be proved on the usual standard of balance of probabilities. It is not enough merely that the means are suitable for putting the intention into effect (for that is a separate requirement), but it is likely to be the case where the supplier proposes or recommends or even indicates the possibility of such use in his promotional material.

132. Accordingly, for all these reasons we affirm the judge's decision as to contributory infringement.

The Court of Appeal held that the person who has the intention to put the invention into effect is not the supplier and indeed need not be the person directly supplied by the alleged (contributory) infringer (but could be the ultimate user of the essential element). Further, it is enough if the supplier knows, or it is obvious in the circumstances (i.e. constructive knowledge), that ultimate users will intend to put the invention into effect. In reaching this conclusion, the court was significantly influenced by appellate authorities from other EPC Contracting States, in particular Germany. Do you agree that an English appellate court should treat these authorities as highly persuasive? According to the court, the number of users who actually put the invention into effect is not relevant to liability; however, would this be relevant to the question of remedies instead? On this point, Jacob LJ and Etherton LJ observed as follows:

137. That raises the difficult question of how quantum (of damages or profits) is to be assessed. It would seem to depend on the degree to which ultimate users adapt or intend to adapt the device so as to infringe. One could simply apply the proportion which is adapted to infringe as the proportion of the defendants' sales which should be treated as infringing. Another view might be that the real question depends on how much the defendant augmented his sales by virtue of his contributory infringement. That would be difficult to assess, but one might as working rule start with the same proportion.

Amongst other issues, *Grimme v Scott* highlights that supply of a means relating to an essential element of the invention does not require the supply of something which could be used without alteration by the buyer. This was reiterated in *Actavis v Eli Lilly*[69] where the Court of Appeal found that supply of pemetrexed dipotassium was supply of the means relating to an essential element of the invention, in this case pemetrexed disodium, because pemetrexed dipotassium was generally reconstituted in saline before administration such that it became pemetrexed disodium.

13.1.3.8 Second medical use inventions

At 12.1.5 the special rules on novelty for pharmaceuticals were discussed, in particular where there is a second medical use of known pharmaceuticals. As was mentioned, difficulties arise in relation to infringement of second medical use inventions and this is aptly highlighted by the litigation in *Warner-Lambert v Actavis*.[70] The facts have already been outlined at 12.1.5. Suffice to add here that the claimant argued there was threatened direct

---

[69] [2015] EWCA Civ 555, [2015] Bus. L. R. 1068.   [70] [2015] RPC 25 (CA).

and indirect infringement by the defendant. The patent was in the Swiss-form claim and, as such, was a purpose-limited process claim. Thus, the claimants argued that section 60(1)(c) was applicable. More specifically, that the defendant's product, Lecaent, was the product of a patented process (the manufacture of pregabalin for the treatment of neuropathic pain) and infringement occurred when that product was disposed of by the defendant. In addition, the claimants argued that section 60(2) on indirect infringement was applicable insofar as the supply or offer to supply of Lecaent was a means relating to an essential element of the claimant's invention. At first instance, Arnold J refused a claim for interim relief and also struck out part of the claimant's case. On appeal, the Court of Appeal dismissed the appeal against Arnold J's decision to refuse injunctive relief, but allowed it in terms of the strike-out claim. As such, both issues of direct and indirect infringement went to trial, which was heard before Arnold J.[71]

Because novelty in Swiss-form claims is conferred by the purpose-limited nature of the claims (in this case, the manufacture of pregabalin for the treatment of neuropathic pain), this creates a mental element. But what is the nature of this mental element? The approach of the Court of Appeal is examined in the following extract from Arnold J's judgment.

Generics (UK) Ltd (t/a Mylan) v Warner-Lambert Co. LLC [2015] EWHC 2548 (Pat), [2016] RPC 3

606. The issue as to the nature of mental element in Swiss form claims was considered in detail by Floyd LJ in *Warner-Lambert* CA. As he said at [99], it is 'a very difficult question'. For reasons that will appear, it is necessary for me to consider his judgment at some length.

607. Floyd LJ started at [113] by observing that the issue was a question of construction of the claim. Like any such question, the task for the court was to determine what the skilled reader of the patent would understand the patentee to be using the language of the claim to mean. Next, he pointed out at [115]–[117] that it was important to distinguish between the technical subject matter of the claim and the rights which a patent gave the owner of the patent as a matter of national law.

608. He proceeded to analyse the technical subject matter of the claim as follows:

118 ...The skilled person would understand that the technical features of the present claim extend beyond making pregabalin, yet fall short of including the step of actually using pregabalin for treating pain. Instead it includes a feature concerned with the ultimate purpose of the product manufactured, namely the intentional treatment of pain. I would describe the subject matter of the claim, therefore, as making pregabalin for patients to whom it will be intentionally administered for treating pain. Making pregabalin for patients to whom it is to be administered for the non-patented indications is not within the technical subject matter of the claim. Only the former category of manufacture makes use of the technical contribution of the patentee.

119. I think the skilled person would understand the technical subject matter of the claim in the way I have indicated because he or she would first understand that it was necessary for the claim to include a manufacturing step to ensure that the claim does not touch the doctor, and fall foul of the method of treatment exclusion. However the skilled person would understand that any manufacturing step is adequate for this purpose, as the doctor does not manufacture the medicament.

[71] *Generics (UK) Ltd (t/a Mylan) v Warner-Lambert Co. LLC* [2015] EWHC 2548 (Pat), [2016] RPC 3.

120. The skilled person would understand that the claim in question owes its novelty to the discovery of the new therapeutic use of the medicament....

121. Thus the skilled person would understand that the technical subject matter of the claim was concerned with the ultimate end use of the medicament, from which it derived its novelty. The therapeutic treatment is of course new because, and only because, it is carried out with the intention of producing the new therapeutic effect. The prior use of the compound may have in fact produced the effect, for example if a patient taking it for GAD or epilepsy was at the time experiencing pain as well. This demonstrates, to my mind, that it is the intention for which the compound is administered which is at the heart of the invention.

609. He then turned to consider the meaning of the word 'for', and observed at [122]:

Against that background the skilled person would understand the word 'for' in the claim to be providing a link between the act of manufacture using pregabalin and the ultimate intentional use of the drug by the end user to treat pain. The critical issue for me to decide is what is sufficient to constitute that link. An extreme view might be that if the drug is in fact used for the patented indication then it has been made 'for' that indication, whatever the manufacturer's intention might be. [Counsel for Pfizer] did not contend for that construction. I think he was right not to do so. It would mean that a manufacturer could not tell whether he had made use of the subject matter until after, and perhaps a long time after, he had disposed of the product. The realistic candidates are therefore (a) foreseeability that the drug will intentionally be used for the patented indication and (b) a subjective intention to that effect.

610. He rejected Actavis' argument that intention was required for reasons he expressed as follows:

123. [Counsel for Actavis] is right that the skilled person would understand the purpose of the Swiss form of claim to be that of avoiding the twin perils of lack of novelty and lack of patentable subject matter. However, as this court made clear in *Actavis v Merck*, the objection of lack of patentable subject matter is overcome by the fact that the claim is a manufacturing process claim. The skilled person would thus appreciate that there is no reason to imply a narrow or strict mental element in order ensure that this peril is avoided.

124. If [counsel for Actavis] were correct that a subjective mental element on the part of the manufacturer were necessary in order to provide the claim with novelty, there would be powerful reasons for adopting it. However, I do not see how that can in fact be so. If a product is 'for' a particular therapeutic indication if it is reasonably foreseeable that it will be used intentionally for the treatment of pain, then it will not be rendered lacking in novelty by showing that products in the prior art had been manufactured in circumstances when it was not possible to foresee such a result.

125. Mr Speck's point is a slightly different one, namely that no-one should be prevented by the grant of a patent from doing that which they did, or could have done, before. He called this the 'golden thread' of English patent law. That principle is not, however, an entirely reliable one. It was relied on in *Merrell Dow*...to suggest that the patent was invalid because it would have the effect of restraining the continuance of the prior use. The principle was ineffective there because the old use itself was 'uninformative'. At pages 86–87 Lord Hoffmann recognised that a gap had opened up under the 1977 Act between anticipation and infringement. The present case is another situation in which one cannot rely on the principle, because the subject matter of the invention is concerned with the purpose of acts which are in themselves no different from those which were done before. In any case it is not correct that the patent can prevent that which was done before. It was not possible before the patent was granted to foresee that the product would intentionally be used for treating pain.

611. Having noted at [126] that the test he had proposed had 'structural similarities' to that under section 60(2), and expressed the view that a requirement of intention would 'rob Swiss claims of much of their enforceability', he went on:

127. I can therefore see no reason why the skilled person would conclude that the word 'for' implied subjective intent. He would understand that the manufacturer who knows (and for this purpose constructive knowledge is enough) or could reasonably foresee that some of his drug will intentionally be used for pain is making use of the patentee's inventive contribution, in the same way as a manufacturer who actively desires that result. In my judgment, therefore, the skilled person would understand that the patentee was using the word 'for' in the claim to require that the manufacturer knows (in the above sense) or can reasonably foresee the ultimate intentional use for pain, not that he have that specific intention or desire himself.

128. In reaching his conclusion that it was the manufacturer's intention that was determinative, the judge relied on what Jacob LJ said in *Actavis v Merck* at [75], namely that claims in Swiss form were aimed at the manufacturer and did not touch the doctor. I think the judge may have read too much in to this passage. Jacob LJ was there considering whether the claim was a disguised claim to a method of treatment. The inclusion of a manufacturing step ensures that it is not. Jacob LJ was not addressing the nature of the mental element in the claim. It is, I think, important to bear in mind that there are two mental elements involved: the question is what the manufacturer knows or foresees about the intentional use of the drug by the end user which counts.

612. Floyd LJ then turned to the question of the rights conferred on the owner of the patent by national law. Having noted that liability under section 60(1)(b) was strict, he continued at [129]:

How does one tell whether a manufacturer is using the manufacturing process of the claim, and therefore rendering himself liable for patent infringement? The answer must be when he manufactures pregabalin when he knows or foresees that users will intentionally administer it for pain.

[The passages from Floyd LJ's judgment cited by Arnold J indicate that it is not required to provide subjective intent, but that what must be shown is that a manufacturer knows or could reasonably foresee that his drug will intentionally be used for pain. However, this is potentially a very low standard and one that will be easy to satisfy. It is therefore not surprising that Arnold J went on to express some doubts as to the correctness of this legal test.]

627. This leaves what seems to me to be perhaps the most persuasive argument advanced by counsel for Actavis and counsel for the Secretary of State, which is that Floyd LJ's interpretation does not achieve its intended effect. As they pointed out, Floyd LJ expressly accepted at [118] that '[m]aking pregablin for patients to whom it is to be administered for the non-patented indications is not within the technical subject matter of the claim'. Accordingly, this cannot be an infringing act. Counsel submitted that Floyd LJ's construction apparently had the consequence that, if it was foreseeable to an unlicensed manufacturer of pregabalin that '*some* of his drug' (as Floyd LJ put it at [127], emphasis added) would be intentionally administered for the treatment of pain, then all of that manufacturer's acts of manufacture of pregabalin would be infringing acts even though it was foreseeable that the remainder of its pregabalin would be administered for the treatment of non-patented indications...Furthermore, this would be so even if it was foreseeable that the majority (possibly even the vast majority, depending on what was meant by 'some') of the pregabalin made by that manufacturer would be administered for the treatment of the non-patented indications and even if the majority (possibly the vast majority) was in fact administered for the treatment of those indications. Still further, all of the pregabalin would be infringing product, and thus anyone who subsequently dealt in it

would also infringe on a strict liability basis. Counsel for Actavis submitted that this outcome would be worse for the manufacturer than the 'extreme view' which Floyd LJ rejected at [122], because at least the 'extreme view' meant that only the proportion of pregabalin which was in fact administered for the treatment of pain would be infringing.

628. I think it is reasonably clear from Floyd LJ's judgment that he did not intend his interpretation to have this consequence. The only indication I can see as to how he thought it was to be avoided, however, comes when he discusses the question of remedies. As noted above, he suggested that any 'potential unfairness' of his interpretation in the first of the two 'hard cases' he considered could be mitigated by restricting the scope of the injunction so that it did not prevent the sale of the product. This suggests that he considered that the injunction might somehow be tailored so as only to prohibit manufacture of pregabalin which it was foreseeable would be intentionally administered to treat pain, and not pregabalin which it was foreseeable would be administered for non-patented indications, although his statement that it might be unjust to grant an injunction at all indicates that he appreciated that this could be very difficult. Similarly, it appears that he envisaged that the financial remedy would only apply to pregabalin which it was foreseeable would be intentionally administered to treat pain, presumably on a statistical basis.

629. The problem with this is that, on any view, a manufacturer in the position of Actavis cannot foresee which pack of pregabalin will be administered for which indication.

[Arnold J went on to apply the Court of Appeal's interpretation to the facts. He noted that intentional administration of pregabalin for the treatment of pain was at heart of the invention and then considered how that intention could be fulfilled.]

636. Counsel for Actavis submitted that the relevant intention was that of the prescribing doctor. I agree that the intention of the doctor is highly relevant, if not exclusively so. Floyd LJ expressly referred to 'the doctor' at [119], and at [121] he made the point that the novelty of the claim derives from 'the intention of producing the new therapeutic effect'. It is the prescribing doctor who intends to produce the new therapeutic effect (here treating pain) because it is the doctor who has the requisite medical knowledge (derived from the SmPC for Lyrica, and hence from the clinical trials carried out by Pfizer to substantiate the claim made in the Patent of efficacy for neuropathic pain, or from the doctor's appreciation that pregabalin may also be effective for treating other kinds of pain if prescribed off-label, as is also claimed in the Patent).

637. Counsel for Actavis also submitted that it was not sufficient that the prescribing doctor intended pregabalin from any source to be administered for the treatment of pain. I agree with this. Floyd LJ expressly referred at [127] to the manufacturer foreseeing that 'some of *his* drug will intentionally be used for pain [emphasis added]'. Furthermore, it would make no sense for it to be sufficient that the doctor intended pregabalin from any source to be administered for pain. Infringement must depend on what the manufacturer can foresee happening with the pregabalin it manufactures, not pregabalin made by others. Moreover, statistically, it would be probable that pregabalin from any source would be made by Pfizer and hence non-infringing on any view.

638. What about the pharmacist? Floyd LJ does not expressly refer to the pharmacist in his analysis, but as counsel for Pfizer pointed out, his language in [122]–[129] is quite general, referring, for example, to 'intentional use for pain'. After considerable hesitation, I have concluded that, on Floyd LJ's reasoning, the intention of the pharmacist is also relevant. In general, of course, the pharmacist will simply intend to dispense the drug which the doctor has prescribed for the purpose of treating whatever indication the doctor has prescribed that

drug for. Moreover, in general, the pharmacist will not know what that indication is. In those circumstances the pharmacist's intention adds nothing to that of the doctor. Even if the doctor prescribes generic pregabalin for treating pain and the pharmacist dispenses the generic manufacturer's product, neither the doctor nor the pharmacist nor the two in combination will have *intended* that *that* product be administered for the treatment of pain. But what if the pharmacist knows that the doctor has prescribed generic pregabalin for treating pain and the pharmacist dispenses the generic manufacturer's product? In those circumstances it seems to me that it can be said that the result is intentional administration of the generic manufacturer's product to treat pain.

639. As for the patient, notwithstanding Floyd LJ's reference in [128] to 'the end user', I cannot see that the patient's intention is relevant. The patient is the one who is being treated. In general the patient intends to take whatever drug the doctor has prescribed for whatever condition the doctor has prescribed it for. Usually the patient will not have any medical knowledge about the efficacy of that drug for that condition. Moreover, the patient will rely on the pharmacist to dispense the correct drug, and in general the patient will not have any choice as to the source of that drug. Indeed, many patients will be oblivious to the source of the drug.

Do you agree with how Arnold J has interpreted the intentional element? Does it make infringement harder to establish? According to Bostyn it does, who argues that 'the intentional element would only be proven and hence there could only be infringement if the physician had prescribed a specific generic drug from a specific manufacturer and/or the pharmacist had dispensed as a consequence of that prescription also a generic drug from that specific manufacturer. As that is unlikely to ever happen, I think it shuts the door quite firmly on infringement.'[72]

When it came to the issue of indirect infringement, which the Court of Appeal held was arguable, Arnold J dismissed the claimant's arguments fairly swiftly.

684. The fundamental difficulty with Pfizer's claim under section 60(2) remains, as it has always done, that claims 1 and 3 of the Patent are claims to processes of manufacture, but there is no act of manufacture by any party downstream from Actavis, nor even the prospect of such an act. This is so even if manufacturing (or 'preparation', to use the word in the claims) for this purpose includes packaging with appropriate instructions. In particular, there is no act of manufacture by pharmacists, nor any prospect of such an act. It follows that, although there is no difficulty in concluding that Lecaent's active ingredient is 'means, relating to an essential element of the invention, for putting the invention into effect', Lecaent is not suitable for putting, or intended to put, the invention into effect: either the invention has already been put into effect by the time that Lecaent leaves Actavis' hands or it is not put into effect at all. Accordingly, I conclude that Actavis have not infringed claims 1 and 3 of the Patent pursuant to section 60(2).

Despite this clear finding by Arnold J, commentators have suggested that indirect infringement of second medical use patents could be established.[73]

---

[72] S. J. R. Bostyn, 'Personalised medicine, medical indication patents and patent infringement: emergency treatment required' [2016] IPQ 151, 169. See now *Warner-Lambert v Actavis* [2016] EWCA Civ 1006.
[73] Bostyn, 'Personalised medicine', 184.

The interpretative gymnastics and uncertainties involved when it comes to scope of protection for second medical use claims is unsatisfactory, not least because it potentially limits the therapeutic freedom of medical practitioners and pharmacists. This has led to suggestions for reform, including an exception to infringement for the benefit of medical practitioners and pharmacists, repeal of the exclusion for methods of medical treatment (which precipitated the need for first and second medical use claims), and repeal of the special novelty rules for pharmaceuticals.[74] Would you agree that reform in this area is needed and, if so, along what lines?

13.2 EXCEPTIONS TO INFRINGEMENT

There are a limited number of exceptions to patent infringement. The following section will focus on three key exceptions within the PA 77: acts done for experimental purposes ('experimental use'); acts done for private and non-commercial purposes ('private use'); and the right to continue use begun before the priority date ('prior use').

13.2.1 EXPERIMENTAL USE

We have seen that one of the justifications for the patent system is that it encourages disclosure of inventions[75] and this, in turn, benefits society because others can learn from and build upon existing innovations. We have also seen that the requirements of novelty and sufficiency emphasize the disclosure rationale of patent law. However, if patent proprietors have the exclusive right to make a patented product or products directly resulting from a patented process, does this mean that third parties will have to wait until the 20-year grant expires before they can utilize the knowledge disclosed in the specification? To the extent that their activities fall within the scope of the claims, this will constitute infringement. But should a person be liable where they are conducting research or experiments in order to understand how the invention works or to develop ways of improving it or to acquire knowledge that will be beneficial to other technological areas? Professor Cornish has succinctly noted the tension that arises:

> If they may engage in such experiments as they please, the initial incentive of the patent may to a degree be diminished. But if they may not, the original patentee may control the further progress of a particular technology for the duration of his exclusive right.[76]

Section 60(5)(b) of the PA 77 seeks to balance the competing interests of the patentee and third parties by exempting from infringement acts done for experimental purposes relating to the subject matter of the invention. The origin of this exception is Article 27(b) of the CPC.[77] Although it was intended to exclude only academic or non-commercial research from infringement, the terms of Article 27(b) of the CPC did not make this distinction.[78]

---

[74] See Bostyn, 'Personalised medicine' and also *Warner-Lambert Co. LLC v Actavis Group PTC EHF* [2015] EWCA Civ 556, [2015] RPC 25, [55] (Floyd LJ).

[75] See 11.3.

[76] W. R. Cornish, 'Experimental use of patented inventions in the EC states' (1998) 29 IIC 735.

[77] See PA 77, s. 130(7).

[78] Cornish, 'Experimental use of patented inventions in the EC states', 736.

As we shall see, the courts have interpreted the exception generously, in a manner that does not restrict it to purely non-commercial or academic research.

Monsanto Co. v Stauffer Chemical Co. [1985] RPC 515

The claimants were proprietors of a patent relating to herbicides for agricultural use and marketed a herbicide under the trade mark 'Roundup'. The defendants devised their own herbicide which performed substantially the same function as the claimants' herbicide, which they marketed under the trade mark 'Touchdown'. The claimants brought an action for infringement against the defendants and obtained interlocutory relief restraining the defendants from further using or selling their allegedly infringing product. The defendants applied to modify the injunction to permit them to undertake certain experimental uses. Falconer J dismissed the application and the defendants appealed.

Dillon LJ (with whom Watkins LJ and Sir Denys Buckley agreed), **at pp. 537–9:**

Section 60 was, as section 130(7) shows, enacted to bring UK patent law into line with the corresponding provisions of the Community Patent Convention and I have no reason to suppose that the signatories of that Convention were concerning themselves with the minutiae of earlier UK patent law. Beyond that, however, the word 'experiment' is an ordinary word in the English language and has never been a term of art in UK patent law.

Mr Gratwick further submits that the words 'for experimental purposes' are limited to experiments in the privacy of a laboratory or glasshouse. I cannot, however, see why that should be so. What may legitimately be the subject of experiment may perhaps depend upon the nature of the product but, with herbicides or compositions to stimulate plant growth, it must surely be a legitimate area for experiment to see if results obtained in the laboratory or glasshouse can also be achieved in natural conditions in the open air where the product will have to be used.

Mr Gratwick urges that the words in section 60(5)(b) 'relating to the subject-matter of the invention' ought to be narrowly construed so as to exclude experiments directed to the commercial exploitation of the invention. For my part, however, I find it difficult to draw any such hard and fast line. The distinction between the wording of sub-head (a) and the wording of sub-head (b) in section 60(5) indicates that experimental purposes in sub-head (b) may yet have a commercial end in view, as do all the activities of companies such as the parties to this dispute. I would regard the sort of experimental activity which was considered by the Supreme Court of Canada in *Micro-Chemicals Ltd v Smith Kline and French Inter-American Ltd* (1971) 25 DLR 79 at the top of page 89, viz. a limited experiment to establish whether the experimenter could manufacture a quality product commercially in accordance with the specification of a patent, as being covered by the words 'for experimental purposes relating to the subject-matter of the invention'.

The defendants' farm in Essex is described in the evidence as a research farm, and that makes sense in the context of all that is disclosed on the evidence about the defendants' activities. Accordingly, I would modify the injunction by providing that it shall not extend to acts done for experimental purposes relating to the subject-matter of the invention in laboratories or glasshouses in the United Kingdom or on the defendants' farm in Essex.

The second category of field trials for which the defendants seek a relaxation covers trials to be carried out by the second defendant's personnel on land rented by the second defendant on other farms. What the defendants want to do, by arrangement with farmers in different parts of the country, is to use TOUCHDOWN on different crops, and at different stages of the year, and at different concentrations, on small areas, of perhaps a couple of acres each, on some 20 or 25 farms in different parts of the country and to tabulate the results. They submit with obvious force that, if it is necessary to experiment to see if what is successful in the laboratory or glasshouse works successfully out of doors, it is necessary that the experiments should be carried out in different soil conditions and in different climatic conditions. What works in California will not necessarily work in England and what works on their farm in Essex may not necessarily work in Wales or Cumbria.

The real problem here, however, is whether, in the light of all they have already done which culminated in the commercial launch of TOUCHDOWN in August 1983, what they want to do now by these field trials can fairly be classified as experimental, or is in truth merely a matter of amassing statistics to further the commercial exploitation, after 22 October 1987, of a product whose qualities they already know. It is therefore necessary to look at some of the evidence.

[After reviewing the evidence, Dillon LJ concluded:]

Trials carried out in order to discover something unknown or to test a hypothesis or even in order to find out whether something which is known to work in specific conditions, e.g. of soil or weather, will work in different conditions can fairly, in my judgment, be regarded as experiments. But trials carried out in order to demonstrate to a third party that a product works or, in order to amass information to satisfy a third party, whether a customer or a body such as the PSPS or ACAS, that the product works as its maker claims are not, in my judgment, to be regarded as acts done 'for experimental purposes'. The purposes for which tests or trials are carried out may in some cases be mixed and may in some cases be difficult to discern; indeed, in the present case, if fuller evidence is given at the trial, a different result may then be reached. On the affidavit evidence before this court, it is not clear to me what the defendants are still wanting to find out about TOUCHDOWN. On that, evidence, if I ask, in relation to the defendant's proposed field trials of category (2) to be carried out by the second defendant's personnel on land rented on other farms, the broad question whether those trials would be carried out, or done, for experimental purposes, my answer is that they would not; they would be carried out in order to obtain the approval of the PSPS and ACAS.

I therefore agree with Falconer J that the injunction should not be modified to permit the defendants to carry out field trials of category (2).

By the same reasoning, the injunction should not be modified to permit the defendants to carry out field trials of category (3), trials to be carried out on their own lands, albeit for the defendants, by ACAS, the Forestry Commission, certain Water Authorities and others.

It is worth noting that courts in other European states, notably Germany and the Netherlands, have adopted a similar approach to that taken by the Court of Appeal in *Monsanto*.[79] Do you agree that it makes sense to permit experiments where there is a commercial end in view? Or should the exception be confined to activities that are strictly non-commercial? Why is it, do you think, that trials carried out to amass information in order to obtain regulatory approval do not fall within the scope of the exception?

As well as establishing an experimental purpose, a defendant must show that the purpose relates to the *subject matter of the invention*. The meaning of this requirement was explored in the following case.

---

[79] See Cornish, 'Experimental use of patented inventions in the EC states'.

SKF v Evans [1989] FSR 513

The claimants, Smith Kline & French, were proprietors of three patents relating to the drug cimetidine. The patents were described as the generic patent, the master patent, and the polymorph patent. SK&F applied to the Patent Comptroller to amend the polymorph patent. The defendant, Evans, opposed this application to amend and, to support their case, carried out an experiment which SK&F alleged infringed all three patents. SK&F applied for summary judgment against Evans and Evans sought to strike out the action. Evans did not dispute that they had used over 30kg of cimetidine and had proceeded to make it into tablets and that they had done an act falling within section 60(1)(a) of the PA 77. However, they argued, inter alia, that their acts were exempted as experimental use.

Aldous J:

Section 60(5)(b) not only requires the act to be done for experimental purposes, but also that the purposes relate to the subject matter of the invention. The invention referred to appears to me to be an invention of the patent in respect of which infringement is alleged. In the present case there are three patents, and SK&F contend that even if the acts were done for experimental purposes, they did not relate to the subject matter of the generic or master patents. They only related to the subject matter of the polymorph patent. This requires a determination of the meaning of the words 'purposes relating to the subject matter of the invention'.

First it should be noted that the words 'the invention' are used, and not 'an invention'. Secondly, section 130(7) states that section 60 of the Patents Act 1977 was framed as to have as nearly as practical the same effect in the United Kingdom as the corresponding provisions of *inter alia* the Community Patent Convention has in other Convention countries. Articles 29 and 31 of the CPC suggest that the subject-matter of an invention is to be found in the claims of the patent. Thus I believe that if an act is to fall within subsection (5)(b) it must be done for purposes relating to the subject-matter of the invention found in the claims of the patent alleged to be infringed.

So far so good, but the real difficulty arises as to what nexus is required by the words 'relating to'. Can it be an indirect relationship, or must it be a direct relationship? The difficulty is best illustrated by an example which was canvassed before me in argument. Supposing a company seeking to investigate a chemical patent either for the purposes of challenging its validity or for the purposes of improving upon the invention of that patent, carries out the process of the patent using a reagent which is made and marketed by a third party who has patented that reagent. In such circumstances can the experimenter, relying on subsection (5)(b), manufacture the reagent without the consent of the patentee of the reagent patent, thereby depriving him of the sale. In my view he cannot. I believe that in the circumstances outlined the experimental purposes relate to the chemical patent and not to the reagent patent. A contrary conclusion would, in practice, deprive the words 'relating to the subject-matter of the invention' of any meaning as subsection (5)(b) would apply in all cases where experiments were carried out which involve the use of an invention. Such an act would be protected as it would inevitably involve and therefore relate to the subject-matter of the invention.

Further, the words I have quoted suggest that some acts done for experimental purposes do not have the required relationship. It therefore seems to me that the relationship must be a real and direct one. I am therefore of the view that section 60(5)(b) covers acts done for experimental purposes including experiments with a commercial end in view, but the purposes must relate to the claimed subject-matter of the patent in suit in the sense of having a real and direct connection with that subject-matter.

It is clear that Evans carried out their experiment for the purposes of the amendment proceedings. In so doing they carried out an example of the master patent with a view of challenging the polymorph patent. They do not contend that the experiment was carried out to invalidate the generic patent, but say that all three patents relate to the same subject matter and therefore subsection (5)(b) applies. However, this disregards the fact that each of the patents relates to a separate invention. Thus upon my view of the correct construction of subsection (5)(b), I believe that this subsection does not provide a defence to infringement of at least the generic patent. However I believe that the relationship between the experiment and the master patent is sufficiently direct as to be covered by the subsection.

Why is it important that the experimental purpose relates to the subject matter of the invention in the claims of the patent allegedly infringed, and that the relationship is a real and direct one?

Finally, it should be noted that the experimental use exception does not apply to acts of indirect infringement.[80] Commentators have queried 'why there should be such a limitation on supplying for the purpose of permitting others to perform excepted experiments'.[81] However, Professor Cornish has argued that this has not arisen as a problem in the cases because the defendant who procures the experiment is usually liable directly and not indirectly and is thus able to rely on the exception.[82]

FURTHER READING

F. Bor, 'Exemptions to patent infringement applied to biotechnology research tools' [2006] EIPR 5.

T. Cook, 'Responding to concerns about the scope of the defence from patent infringement for acts done for experimental purposes relating to the subject matter of the invention' [2006] IPQ 193.

W. R. Cornish, 'Experimental use of patented inventions in the EC states' (1998) 29 IIC 735.

R. Eisenberg, 'Patents and the progress of science: exclusive rights and experimental use' (1989) 56 U. Chicago L. R. 1017.

13.2.2 PRIVATE USE

Acts which are done privately, and for purposes that are not commercial, are exempt from infringement pursuant to section 60(5)(a) of the PA 77. The scope of this exception was first considered in *SKF v Evans*.

---

[80] See PA 77, s. 60(6).
[81] Cornish, 'Experimental use of patented inventions in the EC states', 751.
[82] Cornish, 'Experimental use of patented inventions in the EC states', 751–2.

SKF v Evans [1989] FSR 513

For the facts see 13.2.1. SKF alleged that Evans had infringed all three of their patents and applied for summary judgment. Evans sought to rely on the defence for private and non-commercial use.

Aldous J, at pp. 517–18:

The first matter that needs to be established is that the act is done privately. As this subsection goes on to exclude acts done for commercial purposes the word 'privately' includes commercial and non-commercial situations. This word is not, in my view, synonymous with 'secret' or 'confidential' and would include acts which were secret or confidential or were not. This word appears to me to be used as the opposite of 'publicly' and to be used in the sense of denoting that the act was done for the person's own use. This construction of the word 'privately' is consistent with the rest of the subsection which provides that even if the acts are done privately in the sense of for the person's own use, there will be infringement if the acts are done for commercial purposes.

As I have said, the subsection excludes acts which, even if done privately, are done for purposes which are not commercial. The court is therefore required to consider the purpose of the alleged infringing act and then decide whether that purpose was commercial or not. The word 'commercial' does not need explanation and clearly includes any commercial purpose. The more difficult question is whether acts done primarily for purposes which are not commercial, but do have a commercial benefit, are infringing acts. For instance, in the present case Evans contend that the only purpose of their experiment was private, but accept that in carrying out those experiments they may have acquired information which would be of commercial use to them. I believe that in such circumstances the court is required to consider what the purposes of the acts were. It is a subjective test and if, on the evidence, the court should find that there was a dual purpose, then in those circumstances there would be infringement. If, however, all the purposes were not commercial, the fact that knowledge gained could and might be of commercial benefit would not preclude the act from falling within section 60(5)(a) and therefore be an act which was not an infringement.

In the present case it is accepted that the experiment carried out by Evans was done privately. The dispute turns on whether it was done for purposes which were commercial. Evans says that the only purpose of the experiment was to produce evidence for the amendment proceedings but, as I have said, accept that in carrying out the experiment it can be assumed that they acquired information which would be useful in commercial production.

If they are right on the facts, then I believe that the acts alleged fall within section 60(5)(a). Experiments done for legal proceedings in the High Court or in the Patent Office are not, in my view, done for a commercial purpose. However, SK&F say that from the nature of the experiment it is clear that Evans had a dual purpose, namely to provide evidence for the amendment proceedings and to obtain commercial experience. If they are right as a matter of fact then it seems to me that section 60(5)(a) does not apply.

Under Order 14 summary judgment should only be given if the plaintiff can prove his claim clearly and the defendant is unable to set up a *bona fide* defence. Leave to defend must be given unless it is clear that there is no real substantial question to be tried. In the present case I consider that there is a substantial issue to be tried, namely whether the alleged infringing acts were done for the sole purpose of the amendment proceedings, or whether there was a dual purpose, one of which was a commercial purpose.

Does it make sense that 'private' use is the opposite of 'public', but yet this does not necessarily mean 'secret' or 'confidential'? If the use has both commercial and non-commercial purposes, will it still come within the exception? Finally, is the distinction between a commercial purpose and a purpose which is non-commercial but which may have a commercial benefit an easy one to draw?

13.2.3 PRIOR USE

According to *Merrell Dow v Norton*, secret, inherent, or uninformative use before the priority date does not amount to anticipation since the invention must have been 'made available to the public'.[83] As a result of this shift in approach to novelty, third parties may infringe a patent if they continue to carry out such activities. In recognition of the 'right to work' principle, namely, that it would be unfair if patents were used to prevent persons from carrying out activities that they were doing before the priority date, section 64 of the PA 77 gives prior users a personal defence. Section 64(1) provides:

> Where a patent is granted for an invention, a person who in the United Kingdom before the priority date of the invention—
>
> (a) does in good faith an act which would constitute an infringement of the patent if it were in force, or
>
> (b) makes in good faith effective and serious preparations to do such an act,
>
> has the right to continue to do the act or, as the case may be, to do the act, notwithstanding the grant of the patent; but this right does not extend to granting a licence to another person to do the act.

In the following case, Jacob J (as he then was) commented *obiter* on the scope of the prior use defence.

Lubrizol Corp. v Esso Petroleum Co. Ltd [1997] RPC 195

The patent in suit was granted under the PA 1949 and related to lubricant oil containing a particular additive produced by reacting an amine or other active compound with a defined succinic acylating agent. In an action for infringement, the defendants challenged the validity of the patent on grounds of ambiguity and lack of novelty. They also sought to rely on section 64 of the PA 77 in relation to acts of infringement occurring after 1977. Jacob J found the patent bad for ambiguity and lack of novelty under the PA 1949. In *obiter*, he commented on the scope of section 64 of the PA 77 and found that it did not apply to the defendants.

Jacob J, at pp. 215–16:

In earlier proceedings in the present case, *Lubrizol Corp v Esso Petroleum Co Ltd (No 1)* [1992] RPC 281 at page 285, Laddie J disagreed with this, also *obiter*

> I think it is only right to say that I have some doubts, with great respect to Aldous J, as to whether *Helitune* is correct. The act which the alleged infringer is entitled to continue to

---

[83] See 12.1.4.

> conduct by virtue of section 64(2) is the act which he was committing before the priority date. It is that specific act of commerce which he is entitled to continue. I have difficulty in accepting that by, for example, manufacturing product A before the priority date, he was thereby given a right to manufacture any product after the priority date. In my view, section 64 is intended to safeguard the existing commercial activity of a person in the United Kingdom which is overtaken by the subsequent grant of a patent. It is not meant to be a charter allowing him to expand into other products and other processes.
>
> I agree with Laddie J for all the reasons he gave in his decision, and because I do not think the actual language of section 64 is appropriate were Aldous J correct. It is *the doing of that act* which is protected, not *any act which would otherwise be an infringement*.
>
> However there was a slight gloss. I think Laddie J's reference to 'existing commercial activity'—the protected 'act' of the section—means an activity which is substantially the same as the prior act or act for which substantial and effective preparations were made. In deciding whether the activity is substantially the same all the circumstances must be considered. Both technical and commercial matters must be taken into account. That is important in a case such as the present where there are inherent minor variations in starting materials or the like. If the protected act has to be *exactly* the same (whatever that may mean) as the prior act then the protection given by the section would be illusory. The section is intended to give a practical protection to enable a man to continue doing what in substance he was doing before. In so holding I reject Mr Young's suggestion that the nature of the protected act depends in some way on the claims of the patent specification. I cannot see how that can be: an act is protected or not depending on what it was, not on the somewhat adventitious manner in which the patentee may have chosen to cast his monopoly.

Jacob J concluded that the defence did not apply since preliminary planning did not constitute 'effective and serious preparations' to do an act.

Based on the terms of section 64 of the PA 77 and *Lubrizol*, the following should be noted about the prior use exception.

(1) It only applies where the prior acts were committed in the UK and the acts were carried out in good faith.

(2) The defendant must have done acts or made 'serious and effective preparations' before the priority date of the patent to do an act which would be infringing if it was carried out after the grant of the patent.

(3) The defence allows a prior user to do an act which is the *same* or *substantially* the same as the prior act or act for which substantial and effective preparations were made. Substantial and effective preparations to do an act do not include acts of preliminary planning.

(4) The continued use must be by the same person. However, where the act or preparations were done in the course of business, the prior user has the right to authorize the doing of the act by their partners for the time of the business: section 64(2) of the PA 77. The defence does not extend to granting a licence to another to do the act.

Does the prior use defence give sufficient weight to the 'right to work' rationale that was previously protected by allowing secret or uninformative prior use to anticipate an invention? Further, does the defence provide any protection against those inventions, such as in *Mobil Oil*, where novelty is established by a new purpose?

13.3 ENTITLEMENT

13.3.1 INTRODUCTION

Although any person may apply for a patent,[84] only certain persons are entitled to the grant of a patent. These are: (1) the inventor or joint inventors;[85] (2) the employer of the inventor when the invention is made in the course of employment; or (3) a person who by virtue of any foreign law, treaty, or international convention is entitled to the grant.[86] In addition, a patent may be granted to any successor in title of any of these persons.[87] The person entitled to the grant of a patent will be the first owner, i.e. proprietor, of the patent. The proprietor may then assign, license, or mortgage the patent[88] and is able to sue for infringement.[89]

Where there are joint proprietors, each has an equal, undivided share in the patent (unless otherwise agreed) and a co-proprietor may carry out any of the exclusive acts for his own benefit *without* the consent of the other co-proprietor(s) and without having to compensate them.[90] However, consent must be obtained from the other co-proprietor(s) in order to assign the patent, mortgage a share in the patent, or to grant a licence.[91] Where a deadlock between co-proprietors arises, the Comptroller has jurisdiction to grant or to order a co-proprietor to grant a licence to third parties.[92]

13.3.2 DETERMINING ENTITLEMENT

It is possible to have the question of entitlement determined *before* or *after* the grant of a patent for an invention. Section 8(1)(a) of the PA 77 provides that at any time *before* a patent has been granted (whether or not an application has been made for it):

> (a) any person may refer to the comptroller the question whether he is entitled to be granted a patent for the invention (either alone or with any other person) or has or would have any right in or under any patent so granted or any application for such a patent; or
>
> (b) any of two or more co-proprietors of an application for a patent for that invention may so refer the question whether any right in or under the application should be transferred or granted to any other person;
>
> and the comptroller shall determine the question and may make such order as he thinks fit to give effect to the determination.

After a patent has been granted, section 37(1) of the PA 77 states that any person having or claiming a proprietary interest in or under the patent may refer to the Comptroller the question:

---

[84] PA 77, s. 7(1)(a).   [85] PA 77, s. 7(2)(a).   [86] PA 77, s. 7(2)(b).   [87] PA 77, s. 7(2)(b).

[88] PA 77, s. 30. Note that according to s. 30(6) of the PA 77, assignments and mortgages must be in writing signed by or on behalf of the assignor or mortgagor.

[89] PA 77, s. 61. Note that exclusive licensees are also entitled to sue for infringement: PA 77, s. 30(7).

[90] PA 77, s. 36(1)–(2).

[91] PA 77, s. 36(3). In support of such rules for joint proprietors see R. P. Merges and L. A. Locke, 'Co-ownership of patents: a comparative and economic view' (1990) 72 J. Pat. & Trademark Off. Soc. 586, 592–6.

[92] *Hughes v Paxman* [2007] RPC 2. This discretion must be exercised rationally, fairly, and proportionately and must have regard to all the circumstances of the case.

(a) who is or are the true proprietor or proprietors of the patent;

(b) whether the patent should have been granted to the person or persons to whom it was granted; or

(c) whether any right in or under the patent should be transferred or granted to any other person or persons;

and the comptroller shall determine the question and make such order as he thinks fit to give effect to the determination.

Importantly, the reference must be made before the end of two years after the date of grant of the patent.[93] Where the reference initially claims joint entitlement, but then is amended to claim sole entitlement, this does not constitute a new reference and, provided the initial reference was made within the limitation period, the fact that the amendment occurred after the limitation period will not bar the claim.[94]

13.3.3 DETERMINING THE INVENTOR

It is important to determine the inventor or joint inventors since they are the persons who are generally entitled to the grant of a patent. Further, the inventor or joint inventors must be identified in any published application for a patent or in any patent granted for an invention, unless they have waived their right to be so mentioned.[95]

The courts have developed a basic, two-step approach to identifying the inventor(s). First, it is necessary to identify the inventive concept and then, second, to determine who was responsible for the inventive concept.[96]

In terms of the first step, identifying the inventive concept, courts have considered how this should be approached when there is a patent *application*, as opposed to a granted patent. More specifically, courts have considered whether the patentability of the invention should be taken into account. It seems that, in general, the patentability or validity of the invention should be ignored.[97] However, the Court of Appeal in *Markem Corp. v Zipher Ltd*[98] held that:

[i]f the patent or part of it is clearly and unarguably invalid, then we see no reason why as a matter of convenience, the Comptroller should not take it into account in exercising his wide discretion. The sooner an obviously invalid monopoly is removed, the better from the public point of view. But we emphasise that the attack on validity should be clear and unarguable.[99]

---

[93] PA 77, s. 37(5).

[94] *Rhone-Poulenc Rorer International Holdings Inc. v Yeda Research and Development Co. Ltd* [2007] UKHL 43.

[95] See PA 77, ss. 13(1) and 24(3).

[96] See *Henry Bros v Ministry of Defence* [1999] RPC 442, 448 (Robert Walker LJ); *Collag Corp. v Merck & Co. Inc.* [2003] FSR 16, 291 (Pumfrey J); *Minnesota Mining and Manufacturing Co.'s International Patent Application* [2003] RPC 28, 555–6 (Mr Peter Hayward); *University of Southampton's Applications* [2006] RPC 21, 575 (Jacob LJ) (with whom Wilson and Ward LJJ agreed); *Rhone-Poulenc Rorer International Holdings Inc. v Yeda Research and Development Co. Ltd* [2007] UKHL 43, [20] (Lord Hoffmann).

[97] *Minnesota Mining and Manufacturing Co.'s International Patent Application* [2003] RPC 28, [32] and [44] (Mr Peter Hayward).

[98] [2005] RPC 31.   [99] At 796, [88] (Jacob LJ) (Mummery and Kennedy LJJ in agreement).

In identifying the inventive concept, the Court of Appeal in *Markem v Zipher* emphasized that in determining entitlement (in this case under section 8 of the PA 77) the court is not restricted to the claims. This is because section 8 applies to situations where there may not even be a patent application and because patent applications are not required to have claims. Jacob LJ held that:

> s. 8 is referring essentially to information in the specification rather than the form of the claims . . . s. 8 calls for identification of information and the rights in it. Who contributed what and what rights if any they had in it lies in the heart of the inquiry, not what monopolies were actually claimed. . . . What one is normally looking for is 'the heart' of the invention.[100]

In relation to the second step, determining who is responsible for, or who devised, the inventive concept, the PA 77 provides little guidance. Section 7(3) of the PA 77 defines 'inventor' in relation to an invention to mean the 'actual deviser of the invention' and 'joint inventor' is to be construed accordingly.

In the following case, one of the issues was whether there was a sole inventor or joint inventors.

Staeng Ltd's Patent [1996] RPC 183

A Mr Neely applied to the Comptroller to be named as the sole inventor and proprietor of UK and European patents which had been granted in favour of Staeng and which named one of their employees, a Mr Robertson, as inventor. The invention in question concerned securing electric-cable sheathing to the body portion of a 'connector backshell adaptor'. Mr Neely worked for Hellermann, whose business was primarily aimed at the provision of cable markers and heat-shrink products for use in the cable industry. Staeng's business was designing and developing cable harnesses and backshell adaptors. The two companies worked in close collaboration in the development of connector kits and the invention had arisen from this collaboration.

> **Dr P. Ferdinando** (Superintending Examiner)**, at pp. 188–90:**
>
> As part of the usual collaboration between the two companies Mr Robertson visited Mr Neely at Hellermann's Plymouth premises in May 1987, as was apparently his common practice. At some point in the discussion Mr Robertson showed Mr Neely a backshell adaptor which Staeng had been developing.
>
> . . .
>
> Mr Robertson asked Mr Neely if he could think of an alternative way of holding the cable screen to the adaptor without the use of specialised machinery. The question was apparently posed very casually. As Mr Robertson put it, it was along the lines of 'wouldn't it be nice if there was a better way . . .' or 'is there a better way . . .' or 'there must be a better way . . .' of securing the braid to the adaptor.

---

[100] At 798, [101] and [102]. This approach was followed in *University of Southampton's Applications* [2006] RPC 21, 575 (Jacob LJ) (Wilson and Ward LJJ in agreement).

Both men agree that Mr Neely suggested the use of a constant tension spring, as he had seen one only a short time earlier being used to attach an earth strap for a power cable to the cable armour. He went to the office of a Mr Isaac, who was investigating the use of springs in this context, and obtained a few sample springs to try in place on top of the braid over the groove in the body of the adaptor which Mr Robertson had produced. They appeared to work well, Mr Neely being especially surprised that the spring was not dislodged when the cable braid was tugged. Both Mr Robertson and Mr Neely together then tested the electrical resistance between the braid and adaptor of the assembly and found it to be more than satisfactory.

...

Section 7 of the Patents Act 1977 defines the inventor as 'the actual deviser of the invention', and states that 'joint inventor shall be construed accordingly'. The evidence leaves me in no doubt that, as is now conceded on behalf of Staeng, Mr Neely contributed to the invention the idea of using a spring coiled around the body of the adaptor over the sheathing to secure the latter to the former, and that to this extent at least, as accepted by Mr Wilson, I find that he was the actual deviser, and as such the inventor, or [sic] the invention the subject matter of both GB049 and EP266.

Mr Neely's claim, however, goes further than this, since he claims to have been the *sole* inventor, and seeks to *replace* Mr Robertson in this respect.

...

...[T]he onus lies with Mr Neely to establish his claim to sole inventorship.

I conclude on this limited basis that Mr Neely has failed to establish that Mr Robertson has no right to continue to be named as an inventor. It seems clear on the evidence that Mr Neely did not come up with the idea of using a spring unprompted, and, indeed, that he is unlikely to have done so had Mr Robertson not spoken to him about the problem in the first place. Mr Neely himself has said on several occasions that he was not skilled in the art of backshell adaptor construction. His background experience was in the field of cable markers and heatshrink products. Mr Robertson alerted Mr Neely to the notion that the method of attaching cable braids to backshell adaptors which Staeng had been using until then might in some way be improved. Mr Robertson posed the question, and Mr Neely came up with a suggested solution. Tests on that solution surpassed their expectations. In these circumstances, and especially in view of the onus upon Mr Neely to persuade me to alter Mr Robertson's present status as inventor, I find that Mr Neely and Mr Robertson jointly invented the invention which is the subject of GB049 and EP266.

Do you agree that Mr Robertson was partly responsible for the inventive concept, such as to make him a joint inventor? Relevant here is section 43(3) of the PA 77 which states that, 'references to the making of an invention by an employee...do not include references to his merely contributing advice or other assistance in the making of an invention by another employee'. Could the question posed by Mr Robertson about whether there was an improved way of securing cable braids to backshell adaptors be characterized as little more than advice? Or was Mr Robertson's contribution that he identified a problem to be solved? But can this be inventive if all he did was articulate a known problem that was regularly encountered in the field?[101]

The *Staeng* decision highlights that the burden of proof lies on the person claiming joint or sole inventorship. This has been emphasized by the House of Lords in *Rhone-Poulenc*

---

[101] See P. Chandler, 'Employees' inventions: inventorship and ownership' [1997] EIPR 262, 262–3.

Rorer International Holdings Inc. v Yeda Research and Development Co. Ltd[102] where Lord Hoffmann stated:

> The effect of section 7(4) is that a person who seeks to be added as a joint inventor bears the burden of proving that he contributed to the inventive concept underlying the claimed invention and a person who seeks to be substituted as sole inventor bears the additional burden of proving that the inventor named in the patent did not contribute to the inventive concept.[103]

The following case is an example of where this burden of proof was discharged and sole inventorship established on the basis of suggesting an idea.

University of Southampton's Applications [2006] EWCA Civ 145, [2006] RPC 21

The University of Southampton (along with the second and third respondents) filed a patent application for a method for controlling pests by trapping or killing them by exposing the pest to a composition consisting of magnetic particles. The second respondent, Professor Howse, had been contacted by Mr Metcalfe of IDA (the appellants) who had read about another of Professor Howse's inventions for pest control which involved the use of electrostatic talcum powder. Mr Metcalfe suggested to Professor Howse the idea of using magnetic powders instead, their advantages over electrostatic powder being that they would not lose their stickiness over time. Professor Howse pursued Mr Metcalfe's suggestion and through routine trial and experimentation learned that magnetic particles worked successfully. IDA brought a reference under section 8 of the PA 77 and the Hearing Officer found that it was entitled to ownership of the patent. On appeal, Laddie J in the Patents Court held that IDA and the University of Southampton were jointly entitled. IDA then appealed to the Court of Appeal.

Jacob LJ (with whom Wilson and Ward LJJ agreed):

[Jacob LJ began by stating the general principles in this area:]

23. In *Henry Brothers (Magherafelt) Ltd v Ministry of Defence and Northern Ireland Office* [1997] RPC 693 at 706 I said:

> One must seek to identify who in substance made the combination. Who was responsible for the inventive concept, namely the combination?

24. The Court of Appeal in [1999] RPC 442 agreed with this approach, although on the facts did not accept there was a combination. See *per* Robert Walker LJ at 449. Moreover, in *Markem* it was held that:

> S.8 is referring essentially to information in the specification rather than the form of the claims...s.8 calls for identification of information and the rights in it. Who contributed what and what rights, if any, lies in the heart of the inquiry, not what monopolies were actually claimed, [101].

---

[102] [2007] UKHL 43, [2008] RPC 1.   [103] [21].

25. Later we said:

What one is normally looking for is 'the heart' of the invention. There may be more than one 'heart' but each claim is not to be considered as a separate 'heart' on its own, [102].

[Jacob LJ then went on to consider the application of these principles to the facts:]

31. The parallel with Claim 1 of Professor Howse's 1994 patent is exact. In 1994 the exposure was 'to particles carrying an electrostatic charge'; in the patent in suit the exposure is 'to a composition comprising particles containing or consisting of at least one magnetic material'. In short: magnetic particles for electrostatic particles. To my mind, that is the sole key to the information in the patent in suit. That key was provided solely by Mr Metcalfe. Putting it another way, insofar as there is anything inventive in the patent, it was provided only by him.

32. It is true that he did not know whether his idea would work and it is true that he had not realised that if it did work it would be by adhesion to the legs of the insects, or that because of that insects could be made to pick up insecticide (what Laddie J called the 'sticky poison concept'). Neither of these matters prevents Mr Metcalfe from being the sole devisor of the invention. For neither of these matters involve the contribution of anything inventive to his idea. So far as finding out whether or not his idea worked that was a matter of simple and routine experimentation—mere verification.

33. So far as the sticky poison concept is concerned that would follow by adding that which any ordinary skilled worker in the field of insect killing would have known. All that Professor Howse added to Mr Metcalfe's idea is the common general knowledge of those in the art. There was nothing inventive about it and I do not see how Professor Howse could fairly be described as an inventor. The 'heart' was Mr Metcalfe's idea and his alone.

...

38. Next, it should be noted that this is a case where what was needed to get a patent was only disclosure of an idea. Disclosure of a means of enablement was not necessary: given the idea, the skilled man could readily practice the invention, as the graduate students did ...

39. In the context of entitlement to a patent a mere, *non-enabling* idea, is probably not enough to give the patent for it to solely the devisor. Those who contribute enough information by way of *necessary* enablement to make the idea patentable would count as 'actual devisors', having turned what was 'airy-fairy' into that which is practical (see the discussion about the co-inventors in *Markem* at [36]–[37]). On the other hand those who contribute no more than essentially unnecessary detail cannot on any view count as 'actual devisors' as Laddie J rightly said: see his [45].

What was the inventive concept in *University of Southampton's Applications* and why did it not include the sticky poison concept? Further, why did disclosure of an idea amount to an inventive contribution in this case? Will disclosure of an idea usually be enough to make a person an inventor or joint inventor?

The House of Lords in *Rhone-Poulenc Rorer International Holdings Inc. v Yeda Research and Development Co. Ltd*[104] held that the key question under section 7(2)(a) of the PA 77 is always who is the inventor or joint inventors and there is no additional requirement that a person must show that a proprietor is not entitled to a patent because he or she obtained it as

---

[104] [2007] UKHL 43, [2008] RPC 1.

a result of breach of confidence.[105] Thus, if person A discloses in confidence an invention to person B and person B then makes an unauthorized use of that information and patents the invention, all that person A has to establish is that he was in fact the inventor. It is not necessary for person A also to show that person B was granted the patent as a result of a breach of confidence. What about the situation where person A discloses information to person B that is *not* an invention, but which enables person B to come up with an invention? In this situation, Lord Walker in *Yeda Research* suggested in *obiter* that this may give person A the right to claim an injunction or damages, or an account of profits, but not to claim entitlement to the invention.[106]

13.3.4 EMPLOYEE INVENTORS

Article 60 of the EPC provides that the right to a European patent shall belong to the inventor or his successor in title. However, the EPC does *not* regulate the position of employee inventors. Instead, this is governed by the law of the Contracting State in which the employee is mainly employed or, if that cannot be determined, the law of the state in which the employer has his place of business to which the employee is attached. To ensure that the EPO does not have to investigate entitlement, Article 60(3) of the EPC provides that the applicant shall be deemed to be entitled to exercise the right to the European patent.

In the UK, the position of employee inventors is governed by sections 39 to 43 of the PA 77. Previously, this area was developed and regulated by the common law.[107] Although guidance may be obtained from pre-77 cases, the PA 77 has superseded the previous common law and it is the language of the relevant statutory provisions that must be interpreted and applied.[108]

According to section 39 of the PA 77, an invention made by an employee mainly employed in the UK shall belong to his employer in two situations. The first is where the invention is made *in the course of normal duties* or *specifically assigned duties* and an invention might *reasonably be expected to result* from the carrying out of his duties.[109] The second situation is where the invention is made in the *course of the employee's duties* and, because of the nature of his duties and associated responsibilities, the *employee has a special obligation* to further the interests of his employer's undertaking.[110] Otherwise, an invention made by an employee will belong to the employee.[111] Importantly, section 42 of the PA 77 makes unenforceable any term in a contract between employee and employer or an employee and a third party (at the request of the employer) which diminishes the employee's rights in inventions made by him. Thus, it would not be possible to include a term in a contract of employment legally requiring the employee to assign to the employer all inventions which he may make, since the only inventions which belong to an employer are those set out in section 39.

---

[105] [18]–[24] (Lord Hoffmann delivering the leading speech) and [62] (Lord Walker).

[106] [62] (Lord Walker).

[107] As reflected in cases such as *Worthington Pumping Engine Co. v Moore* (1903) 20 RPC 41; *Patchett v Stirling Engineering Co. Ltd* (1955) 72 RPC 50; *British Syphon Co. Ltd v Homewood* [1956] RPC 225; and *Electrolux Ltd v Hudson* [1977] FSR 312.

[108] *Harris' Patent* [1985] RPC 19, 28 (Falconer J); *Liffe v Pinkava* [2007] RPC 30, [57] (Morritt V-C) and [92] (Jacob LJ).

[109] PA 77, s. 39(1)(a).   [110] PA 77, s. 39(1)(b).   [111] PA 77, s. 39(2).

Where an employer owns an employee invention pursuant to section 39 of the PA 77, there is no question of the employee retaining beneficial ownership as against the employer. As held by Pumfrey J in *French v Mason*:[112]

> Where the section speaks of the invention being 'taken to belong to his employer for the purposes of this Act and for all other purposes' it is in my view plainly talking about ownership in a sense which is not technical, and which does not distinguish between legal and equitable ownership. It is talking of the ownership which permits the owner to deal with the patent and to work under it.

We turn to consider the first limb of section 39.

13.3.4.1 In the course of normal duties or specifically assigned duties: section 39(1)(a)

Harris' Patent [1985] RPC 19

The patent in suit concerned a slide valve for controlling the flow of material, in particular powdery and erosive material such as coal dust, through a duct into which the valve plate is slid to stop the flow and from which it is withdrawn to permit the flow. The invention was thought to be an improvement on known slide valves—i.e. 'Wey' valves (so-called after the inventor Joseph Wey)—in that it reduced problems of jamming of the valve plate and erosion of seals.

Reiss Engineering sold Wey valves and provided an after-sales service. Harris was employed as a manager of the Wey valve department and made the invention whilst he was working for them (after he received notice of his redundancy but prior to his departure) and filed a patent application. Reiss Engineering sought an order under section 8 of the PA 77 that the patent application should proceed in their name; however, as the patent had been granted, the matter came to be decided pursuant to section 37 of the PA 77. This was an appeal from the decision of the superintending examiner, who found that Harris was the inventor and proprietor of the patent.

Falconer J, at pp. 29, 31–2:

As to the second requirement in the paragraph, that is to say, whether the circumstances were such that an invention might reasonably be expected to result from his carrying out those duties, Miss Vitoria submitted that the circumstances referred to in paragraph (a) must be the circumstances in which the invention was made; and it seems to me that submission must be right. Mr Pumfrey, in the course of his argument, pointed out that the wording of the paragraph was '*an* invention might reasonably be expected to result' and not '*the* invention might' and so on. But plainly, the wording 'an invention' cannot mean any invention whatsoever; it is governed by the qualification that it has to be an invention that 'might reasonably be expected to result from the carrying out of his duties' by the employee. That wording

---

[112] [1999] FSR 597, 604.

applies equally to the second alternative in paragraph (a), that of 'specifically assigned' duties falling outside the employee's normal duties; and, therefore, in my judgment the wording 'an invention might reasonably be expected to result from the carrying out of his duties' must be referring to an invention which achieves, or contributes to achieving, whatever was the aim or object to which the employee's efforts in carrying out his duties were directed, in the case of alternative (i) of paragraph (a) his normal duties being performed at the time; in the case of alternative (ii) of paragraph (a) the specifically assigned duties, that is to say, such an invention as that made, though not necessarily the precise invention actually made and in question.

Thus, it seems the court must ask whether an invention *of the type that was made* would have been expected to result from the carrying out of the employee's normal duties or specifically assigned duties.

Falconer J went on to consider the business of Reiss Engineering in order to ascertain Mr Harris's normal duties at the material time.

Reiss Engineering did not themselves manufacture valves until after Mr Harris left their employ. It is also to be noted that Reiss Engineering sold only valves made by Sistag or to Sistag drawings. Reiss Engineering had no research laboratory or primary design office and only one of its two draughtsmen was employed in their valve division...In promoting the sale of their valves, Reiss Engineering, of course, advised customers and made recommendations as to the type of valve to use and as to what body material and seal material would be supplied for the customer's particular application. They were concerned to see satisfactory installation of any valve they sold and provided after-sale service. But during the period when Mr Harris was employed by them Reiss Engineering never themselves designed a valve or an improvement or a modification to a valve...It is quite clear from the evidence that, when a problem developed with a valve they had sold to a customer, the practice was that Reiss Engineering would investigate and report on the problem to Sistag, but it was for Sistag to deal with any such problem and find a solution.

...

...There is, it seems to me, great force in Miss Vitoria's submission that, as Reiss Engineering never took it upon themselves to solve design problems in the valves but restricted their role in regard to such problems to reporting any such problem to Sistag for Sistag to consider and solve, it cannot have been part of Mr Harris's normal duties to provide solutions to problems relating to the design of the valves; there was no reason why they should, and no evidence that they did, impose on Mr Harris, their employee, as part of his normal duties, an obligation they never assumed themselves. His duty in regard to any such problems was to report them for transmission to Sistag for Sistag's consideration and solution.

Falconer J concluded that the invention was not made in the course of Mr Harris's normal duties, nor were the circumstances such that such an invention might reasonably be expected to have resulted from carrying out his normal duties.

In *Harris* no contract of employment had been put before the superintending examiner. As such, Harris's duties were determined by looking at the nature of the various tasks that he undertook whilst employed by Reiss Engineering. But what is the position where a written contract of employment exists? Will this be determinative of what constitutes an employee's normal duties? This issue was considered in *Greater Glasgow Health*

Board's Application.[113] In this case, Dr Montgomery was the sole inventor of an optical spacing device for use with an indirect ophthalmoscope, which allowed for more effective measuring of the retina to be carried out. At the time of making the invention, Dr Montgomery was employed by the Greater Glasgow Health Board (GGHB) as a registrar in the Department of Ophthalmology. GGHB filed a PCT application in respect of the invention and a reference under section 12 of the PA 77 was made. The superintending examiner found that the invention in the application in suit was made in the course of Dr Montgomery's normal duties in circumstances such that an invention might reasonably have been expected to result from the carrying out of those duties. As such, it was owned by GGHB pursuant to section 39(1)(a) of the PA 77. An appeal from the examiner's decision was allowed by Laddie J. In assessing the 'normal duties' of Dr Montgomery, Laddie J thought it instructive to look not only at the contract of employment, which indicated that the doctor had clinical responsibilities, teaching duties, and an expectation to avail himself of the research facilities, but also to look at the *duties actually carried out by the employee.* In looking at what Dr Montgomery actually did, Laddie J found that research and invention were not in fact part of his normal duties. Rather, he was mainly involved in clinical treatment, with some involvement in teaching.[114]

The Court of Appeal in *Liffe v Pinkava*[115] has reiterated that the court must look at what the employee actually does, as well as his or her contract of employment. As such, it is possible for the normal duties of an employee to exceed those stipulated in the employment contract, as was the case in *Liffe v Pinkava.*

We turn now to consider the second limb of section 39 of the PA 77.

13.3.4.2 In the course of duties where the employee has a special obligation: section 39(1)(b)

Where the employee's status within the employer's business creates a special obligation to further the interests of the employer, the invention will be owned by the employer. Section 39(1)(b) has only been considered in *Harris's Patent* and also, in *obiter*, in *Staeng's Patent*. In *Harris*, the employee was held not to owe his employer a special obligation, whereas an opposite conclusion was reached in *Staeng's Patent*. The reasons for these differing conclusions are dealt with in the following extract.

Staeng Ltd's Patent [1996] RPC 183

For the facts see 13.3.3.

Dr P. Ferdinando, at pp. 200–3:

Although my findings under section 39(1)(a) make it strictly unnecessary for met [sic] to decide whether Mr Neely's employers are also entitled to the invention by virtue of section 39(1)(b), much time was occupied at the hearing on the issue of the seniority of Mr Neely's

---

[113] [1996] RPC 207.   [114] At 221–3.
[115] [2007] RPC 30, [58] (Morritt V-C, with whom Longmore and Jacob LJJ agreed).

status within Hellermann, with a view, as I understood it, to persuading me that he either did or did not have the special obligation to further the interests of his employers' undertaking required under section 39(1)(b). I will therefore address this question.

Following *Harris*, I note that there are two conditions to be fulfilled under section 39(1)(b). The first is that the invention was made in the course of the duties of the employee. Since I have already found that the invention in suit met the narrower condition of section 39(1)(a) of having been made as part of Mr Neely's *normal* duties, it follows that it also meets the broader first condition of 39(1)(b).

The second condition is that, at the time of making the invention, because of the nature of his duties and the special responsibilities arising from their nature, the employee had a special obligation to further the interests of the employers' undertaking.

In *Harris* it was held that the extent of an employee's obligation to further the interest of his employer's undertaking was dependent on his status and the duties and responsibilities associated with that status. In *Harris*' case he only had to sell Wey valves and ensure after-sales service; his powers as a manager did not extend to hiring or firing staff or agreeing holiday dates and he did not attend board meetings even when his own department was under discussion. His status was not such that his obligations would take him within the confines of section 39(1)(b).

...Mr Neely was employed under contract directly by the holding company, rather than by Hellermann, and such contracts were reserved for senior executives. Mr Neely's was a 'Category V(1)' contract, which again was reserved for Directors and other senior executives within the various divisions of Bowthorpe...There were then five senior executives, including Mr Neely as Business Development Manager...Mr Neely was to receive a bonus of 1% of the subsidiary company or division's annual trading profit above a certain level. This was presumably in addition to the basic salary, set at £22,000 per annum when Mr Neely took up employment.

...

I am satisfied that, within the framework of Hellermann at the time of Mr Neely's employment there, he enjoyed a position of high status and responsibility. His involvement in the profit bonus scheme and his direct employment by the parent company identified him specifically as a senior executive, and he was plainly perceived as such by his colleagues...In particular it is clear that he operated at a significantly more senior level than did Harris within his employer company. Harris' duties were confined solely to sales. He was described as a 'trouble-shooter' to deal with problems that customers experienced with their installations, not by solving their problems directly but by passing them on to another company for solution. He thus had no opportunity for developing his employer's product, whereas Mr Neely was charged with the need to identify new products; his job title—Product Development Manager—encapsulated that intention. Moreover, Mr Neely was given the highly responsible task of streamlining and restructuring the Hellermann product range, and had sufficient authority to achieve a major reform in this respect within a short time of joining the company. Harris did not attend board meetings, whereas Mr Neely was involved in the sort of meetings and engaged in the sort of discussion that were also the province of directors. Although there were constraints on Mr Neely's ability to hire and fire and to spend, his powers clearly exceeded those of Harris in this respect.

...

In all these circumstances it is clear to me, therefore, that the invention was made by Mr Neely under the second condition set out in the section 39(1)(b), namely in which the

> nature of his duties and the particular responsibilities arising from them were such that he had a special obligation to further the interests of his employer's undertaking.
>
> I therefore find that, under both sections 39(1)(a) and (b) as between Mr Neely and his employers, the invention in suit must be taken to belong to his employers for all purposes.

Which factors contributed to Mr Neely owing a special obligation to his employer and how did his situation differ from the employee in *Harris*?

13.3.5 COMPENSATION FOR EMPLOYEE INVENTIONS

Section 40 of the PA 77 introduced a statutory right of compensation to employee inventors in two instances. The first instance is set out in section 40(1) of the PA 77. This section provides that compensation is payable where the patent is owned by the employer[116] and it can be shown that 'having regard among other things to the size and nature of the employer's undertaking, the invention or the patent for it (or the combination of both) is of outstanding benefit to the employer and by reason of those facts it is just that the employee should be awarded compensation to be paid by the employer.'[117] It should be noted that the language of this section was amended[118] and previously referred only to the *patent* being of outstanding benefit to the employer.

The second instance is set out in section 40(2) of the PA 77 and applies where the employee invention has been assigned or exclusively licensed to the employer and it can be shown that the benefit received by the employee from the assignment or exclusive licence was inadequate in relation to the benefit derived by the employer from the patent and by reason of those facts it is just that the employee should be awarded compensation to be paid by the employer.[119]

The amount of compensation in both instances is to be determined in accordance with section 41 of the PA 77 (extracted later in this section). The award is meant to secure for the employee a fair share of the benefit which the employer has derived, or may reasonably be expected to derive from: the invention in question; the patent for the invention; the assignment or grant of the property; or any right in the invention or the property in, or any right in or under, an application for the patent to a person connected with the employer.

Where the invention has always belonged to the employer (pursuant to section 39), the following matters shall be taken into account in determining the award of compensation: the nature of the employee's duties, his remuneration, and other advantages he derives or has derived from his employment (e.g. ex gratia payments); the effort and skill which the employee has applied to making the invention; the effort and skill which any other person has contributed to making the invention jointly with the employee; and the contribution made by the employer to the making, developing, and working of the invention.[120] Where the invention originally belonged to the employee, the following matters shall be taken into account: any licence conditions in respect of the invention or the patent for it; the extent to which the invention was made jointly by the employee with another person; and the contribution made by the employer to the making, developing, and working of the invention.[121] Any order of payment may be for a lump sum or for periodical payment or both.[122] Where any order for compensation is refused, this does not preclude a later application being made.[123]

---

[116] By virtue of PA 77, s. 39. [117] PA 77, s. 40(1).
[118] As a result of Patents Act 2004, s. 10. [119] PA 77, s. 40(2). [120] See PA 77, s. 41(4).
[121] PA 77, s. 41(5). [122] PA 77, s. 41(6). [123] PA 77, s. 41(7).

Thus far, the only applications for statutory compensation have related to the first instance (i.e. section 40(1) of the PA 77).[124] One of the early authoritative decisions on section 41(1) is *Memco-Med Ltd's Patent*.

Memco-Med Ltd's Patent [1992] RPC 403

Mr Trett was a former employee of Memco-Med. Whilst in their employment he invented a new model (the 'R' model) of detector unit for use in lifts. The 'R' model of detector would sense if a person was near the lift doors and prevent the doors from closing on people. Memco-Med had a long-standing business relationship with the Otis Elevator Co. and had been supplying detectors to them for a considerable time. Sales from 1982 to 1989 of the 'R' model of detector to Otis totalled just over £4 million out of a total sales of £11.5 million. Mr Trett brought an application for compensation under section 40(1) of the PA 77. The superintending examiner refused the application and there was an appeal to the Patents Court.

Aldous J (as he then was), **at pp. 412–13:**

Section 40 draws a distinction between the patent and the invention; thus the task of the court is to ascertain whether the patent, not the invention, is of outstanding benefit to the employer, that benefit being a benefit in money or money's worth.

The benefit from the patent may be readily recognisable where the patent is licensed and royalties are paid. However, the task of the court will be more difficult in cases where an employer exploits the patent by manufacturing articles in accordance with the invention of the patent. In such cases, the court will need to differentiate between the benefit from using the inventive advance and that from the patent. It is also possible to imagine a case where the patent is not licensed and the invention is never put into practice, but the patent is of great benefit to the patentee to prevent activities which would compete with those carried on by the patentee.

Aldous J emphasizes that the benefit must be derived by virtue of having a patent and not from the inventive advance and that this may be a difficult distinction to make. However, this distinction has been removed by the amendments to section 40(1) of the PA 77, which now provides that the benefit may derive from the *invention* or the *patent* or *both*.

Aldous J went on to consider the meaning of 'outstanding' benefit. In doing so, he referred to *GEC Avionics Ltd's Patent*[125] in which the superintending examiner held that 'outstanding' connoted 'something out of the ordinary and not such as one would normally expect to arise from the results of the duties that the employee is paid for'.[126] He referred also to the decision in *British Steel Plc's Patent*[127] in which the superintending examiner held that 'outstanding' implies a superlative and considered that the test must be correspondingly stiff. After having considered these decisions, Aldous J concluded:

---

[124] See *GEC Avionics Ltd's Patent* [1992] RPC 107 (Superintending Examiner Mr Vivian); *British Steel Plc's Patent* [1992] RPC 117 (Superintending Examiner Dr Ferdinando); and *Memco-Med Ltd's Patent* [1992] RPC 403 (Aldous J, Patents Court).

[125] [1992] RPC 107.   [126] At 115.   [127] [1992] RPC 117, 122.

I do not disagree with the approaches of those superintending examiners. The word 'outstanding' denotes something special and requires the benefit to be more than substantial or good. I believe that it is unwise to try to redefine the word 'outstanding'. Courts will recognise an outstanding benefit when it occurs.

The section requires the court to assess whether the benefit is outstanding, having regard among other things to the size and nature of the employer's undertaking. Thus the court must look at the employer's undertaking, which may be the whole or a division of the employer's business, and ascertain the benefit to the employer taking into account the size and nature of that business and all the surrounding circumstances.

Aldous J then considered who bears the onus of proof in establishing a claim under section 40 of the PA 77. In *GEC Avionics Ltd's Patent*[128] the superintending examiner held that where the patentee does not license his product or is not paid compensation but is a manufacturer who negotiates contracts for his products which are protected by patent, the initial evidential burden of showing that no benefit is derived from the patent rests with the patentee. Aldous J, however, rejected this approach:

At p. 415:

I cannot agree with that approach. The onus of proof lies upon the person seeking to invoke the provisions of section 40, namely the employee. Thereafter the onus may shift to the employer, but this will depend upon the evidence before the court and will not depend upon any inference of law or presumption. Each case must be decided upon its own facts using the normal standard of proof in civil proceedings, namely the balance of probabilities.

[Finally, Aldous J considered whether an outstanding benefit had been conferred on Memco-Med by virtue of the patent over the 'R' model detector:]

At p. 417:

The fact that a company only sells a patented product to one customer and therefore its existence depends on sales of that product does not mean that the patent is of any benefit.

I suspect that there are companies which depend for their existence upon sales of one product which is not covered by a patent. If so the sales are of vital importance and of great benefit, but they could not be attributable to a non-existing patent. The fact that the sales of the 'R' model were vital is a relevant consideration to decide whether the patent is of outstanding benefit but cannot be determinative. The existence of those sales is consistent with the case of Memco-Med, namely that all the sales were to Otis, that the sales resulted from the price and quality of the product and the good relationship Memco-Med had with Otis, and that the patent played no part in obtaining sales, let alone the profit from those sales.

The superintending examiner first considered whether the benefit to Memco-Med was outstanding on the assumption that the benefit was derived from that patent. He concluded that there were strong pointers to the conclusion that the benefits were not outstanding. Upon the evidence, including the evidence I admitted *de bene esse*, sales of detectors substantially increased when the 'R' model was introduced, but that does not mean the monetary benefit was outstanding. The development to produce the 'R' model was funded by

[128] [1992] RPC 107.

Memco-Med, encouraged by Otis, and therefore it is not surprising that Otis would give increased orders for the new model. No doubt sales of about £4m, between 1982 and 1989, were good but the evidence does not establish that the profit, being the monetary benefit was also good. Discovery would have thrown light on this, but Mr Trett must have had a general idea of the position up to August 1983 and did not give any relevant evidence on this matter. In any case, the important matter to decide is whether the benefit, if any, was obtained from the patent and, if so, was it outstanding.

The superintending examiner decided that Memco-Med had not derived an outstanding benefit from the patent. I agree with his conclusion and reasoning. I have found it helpful when considering the evidence filed by the parties to look for indications as to whether Memco-Med would have sold any fewer detectors if the patent had not been granted. Although Mr Trett did suggest in his reply evidence that the patent had some effect upon other manufacturers and himself, I did not find that evidence convincing. The evidence does not establish that the patent has been of substantial benefit to Memco-Med, let alone of outstanding benefit.

The appeal was dismissed.

The application in *Memco-Med* was unsuccessful, as were the earlier applications in *GEC Avionics* and *British Steel*. It therefore appeared that the right to statutory compensation under UK patent law was more theoretical than real, leading one commentator to describe the provisions on compensation as 'a dead letter'.[129] However, significant awards of employee compensation were made in *Kelly and Chiu v GE Healthcare Ltd*, to which we now turn.

Kelly and Chiu v GE Healthcare Ltd [2009] EWHC 181 (Pat), [2009] RPC 12

Dr Kelly and Dr Chiu had been employed as research scientists at Amersham International Plc, which company was taken over by GE Healthcare Ltd. They were co-inventors of a radioactive imaging agent, which was the subject of two European patents (UK). The patented agent was marketed under the trade mark 'Myoview'. Myoview was a tremendous success, with sales to 2007 exceeding £1.3 billion, and accounted for a large proportion of Amersham's profits. The claimants brought an action under section 40 of the Patents Act 1977 seeking an award of compensation. The law applicable was that prior to the amendment resulting from section 10 of the Patents Act 2004. Thus, the outstanding benefit had to be shown to result from the patent.

Floyd J:

[Floyd J began by considering the existing case law on section 40, including *Memco-Med Ltd's Patent*, and the terms of section 41. He summarized the law as follows:]

60. Drawing this material together:

i) Section 40 is available to an inventor in the sense of the 'actual deviser' of the invention, but not to those who merely contribute to the invention without being joint inventors;

---

[129] P. Grubb, *Patents for Chemicals, Pharmaceuticals and Biotechnology* (4th edn, Oxford: Oxford University Press, 2004), p. 393.

ii) Section 40 is available to an employee who makes an invention (which is subsequently patented by the employer) in the ordinary course of his employment or in the course of duties specifically assigned to him;

iii) Under the section prior to its amendment, it is the patent (as opposed to the invention) which must be of outstanding benefit to the employer, having regard to the size and nature of the employer's undertaking;

iv) 'Outstanding' means 'something special' or 'out of the ordinary' and more than 'substantial', 'significant' or 'good'. The benefit must be something more than one would normally expect to arise from the duties for which the employee is paid;

v) On the other hand it is not necessary to show that the benefit from the patent could not have been exceeded;

vi) Section 40 is not concerned with whether the invention is outstanding, although the nature of the employee's contribution may fall to be considered at the section 41 stage, if it is reached;

vii) It will normally be useful to consider what would have been the position of the company if a patent had not been granted, and compare this with the company's position with the benefit of the patent;

viii) The patent must have been a cause of the benefit, although it does not have to be the only cause. The existence of multiple causes for a benefit does not exclude the benefit from consideration, although the benefit may have to be apportioned to isolate the benefit derived from the patent;

ix) 'Patent' in section 40 does not include regulatory data exclusivity. Thus the scenario without patent protection is one where RDE nevertheless exists;

x) It must be 'just' to make an award: the consideration of what is just is not limited to the facts set out in section 40;

xi) It is not a requirement of obtaining compensation that the employee can prove a loss (for example by reference to inadequate remuneration for his employment) or by the expenditure of effort and skill beyond the call of duty. These are nevertheless factors to take into account under section 41;

xii) The valuation of any benefit is to be performed *ex-post* and in the light of all the available evidence as to benefit derived from the patent: not '*ex-ante*';

xiii) Where the employee shows that the invention has been of outstanding benefit, the amount of compensation is to be determined in the light of all the available evidence in accordance with section 41 so as to secure a just and fair reward to the employee, neither limiting him to compensation for loss or damage, nor placing him in as strong a position as an external patentee or licensor.

[Floyd J went on to consider whether the patents were of outstanding benefit to Amersham:]

148. I have come to the conclusion that the patents were of outstanding benefit to Amersham having regard to all the circumstances, including the size and nature of its undertaking. The benefits went far beyond anything which one could normally expect to arise from the sort of work the employees were doing.

149. The first and most obvious contribution the patents have made to Amersham is in protecting the business against generic competition and reduced profits after the expiry of RDE. The expiry of the patents in about 2008 and the advent of generic competition was one

of the major issues facing the company from 2000 onwards. If the patents had not existed in 2000, and Amersham had been facing the expiry of RDE in 2002, this would not simply have been a major issue, it would have been a crisis for Amersham.

150. The benefit of patent protection is not limited to profits from sales. As I have held, the fact that Amersham had a patented blockbuster radiopharmaceutical has been a major factor in achieving the corporate deals. In this way the patents have helped transform Amersham. Considering the totality of the evidence I had no difficulty in recognising that the patents were of outstanding benefit to Amersham.

Floyd J (as he then was) then concluded that it was just to make an award of compensation in favour of the employees. The defendant argued that it was invidious to single out individual inventors for an award where there had been a truly corporate research effort and much work by others in order to develop Myoview. In response to this argument, Floyd J stated that it was inherent in sections 40 and 41 that employees who have contributed to the invention and its development but who are not joint inventors will not receive an award. Further, Floyd J held that it was immaterial that Dr Kelly and Dr Chiu had waited until the end of 2003 to make a claim because the statute permits the employee to wait until the patent expires before raising any claim.[130]

Having found an outstanding benefit resulting from the patent and that it was just to award compensation to the claimants, Floyd J then considered the value of the benefit of the patents to Amersham. He found as follows:

168. Nevertheless I have held that generic competition would have caused price cutting after the expiry of RDE. A significant part of Amersham's US sales would have been protected to some extent from generic competition, but other parts of their market would not. In my judgment the evidence justifies the conclusion that, at a minimum, generic competition would have caused the price of Myoview to drop by 10% (at least but probably a lot more) on about half of its sales.

…

170. Taking a round figure of £1 billion, a price cut of only 10% on only half of Myoview's sales over that period would have reduced Amersham's revenues by £50 million. I consider that I have been very conservative in arriving at these figures. I think that prices would have fallen by much more than this over the course of the post RDE period.

…

172. I think I am justified in taking a figure of £50 million pounds as the absolute rock bottom figure for the benefit from the patents.

[Floyd J then examined the factors under section 41 relevant to determining the amount of compensation:]

188. In the present case I think the following are important factors favouring the employee:

i)   the overall costs of R&D in the present case are extremely small in relation to the profits generated: some £2.4 million as reported in the Queen's Award document;

ii) neither Dr Kelly nor Dr Chiu were carrying out routine operations: their jobs involved significant thought and creativity.

[130] More specifically, the Patents Rules 2007 (SI 2007/3291), r. 91 stipulates that an employee can make a claim for compensation anytime after the date of grant of the patent and before one year after the patent expires.

189. On the other hand the following factors help the employer:

i) Dr Chiu's and Dr Kelly's work was to a significant degree dependent on the opportunity provided by the employer to make inventions;

ii) the downstream work was well executed, and involved the solution of some problems: Dr Kelly's contribution to this was limited;

iii) the development of the market in the United States was also a major factor of assistance in working the invention;

iv) overall it was the employer who accepted the risk for the project.

Amersham contended that the factors pointed to a nominal award or, alternatively, a bonus by reference to the employee's annual remuneration as at 1989, the year after the patents were granted. Scaled for inflation this would have resulted in a payment of about £100,000 for Dr Kelly and £60,000 for Dr Chiu. The claimants argued that a fair share of the benefit was to be determined by external licensing arrangements in the field, which pointed to 6 per cent of turnover. There was evidence before the judge of a consultancy agreement, whereby the consultant would receive royalties of 0.25–1 per cent for technology involving a 'minimal degree of innovation' and 1–3 per cent for technology involving a 'significant degree of innovation'. There was also evidence that the rate paid by universities to academic inventors was 33 per cent. After considering this evidence, Floyd J concluded:

202. I think, aside from the facts of this case, from the materials I have reviewed, the employee's share of the value of a patent might in principle lie somewhere in the broad range from nil to as much as 33% or beyond. In the present case I think the employee's share lies towards the bottom of the scale, having regard to the factors which I have considered at length above. I have taken a very conservative figure for the valuation of the benefit. Taking the same approach to the share of the benefit, I consider that 3% of the value of the benefit represents a just and fair award to the employee claimants.

203. As between the two inventor claimants, I think Dr Kelly should receive more than Dr Chiu. Dr Kelly should receive 2% and Dr Chiu 1% of the £50 million figure I have taken as the value of the patents. Thus Dr Kelly receives £1 million and Dr Chiu £500,000.

204. These combined figures represent about 0.1% of turnover. I am confident that none of the comparators show this figure to be unreasonable. Whilst it is far from perfect, the closest comparable is the Goldman licence. The lowest figure in the Goldman licence was 0.25% of turnover. Standing back, and looking at these sums in the light of all the evidence I have heard, I consider them to be just and fair. It represents about three days' of the profits from Myoview at current rates.

205. Whilst I have had in mind the fact that the context of the award is employment, I have not thought it right to limit the award by reference to one year's salary. The benefit to Amersham has extended well beyond a single year.

206. Although the Act contemplates that the employee can make more than one application, I was invited to make a once and for all award, which is what I have done.

As mentioned above, *Kelly and Chiu v GE Healthcare Ltd* was a decision concerning section 40 of the PA 1977 before it was amended by the Patents Act 2004 to include reference to the outstanding benefit arising from the invention, and not just the patent. Do you think that if the new section 40 applied, the claimants would have had an easier task of establishing an outstanding benefit?

Floyd J concluded that a fair share of the benefit of the patent received by Amersham was 3 per cent, to be shared between Dr Kelly and Dr Chiu. In your view, was this about the right figure?

Sections 40 and 41 of the PA 77 were the subject of further judicial interpretation in *Shanks v Unilever plc*.[131] While working for Unilever UK Central Resources Ltd (CRL), Professor Shanks had invented a device for precise measurement of fluids that was useful in home diagnostic kits for diabetes. Entitlement to this invention vested in CRL pursuant to section 39(1) of the PA 77. These rights were then assigned to a parent company, Unilever plc, for a nominal sum, which obtained patents based on Professor Shanks's invention. There was a delay in exploiting the invention, but when it eventually was licensed to third parties royalties of approximately £23 million were received over the remaining lifetime of the patent. Professor Shanks applied for compensation under section 40 of the PA 77. There were two issues; first whether the benefit to the employer was the actual or potential benefit; second, the impact of the assignment from CRL to Unilever plc. On first issue, Jacob LJ (with whom Longmore LJ and Kitchin J agreed) held:

> 8. Clearly this, key, subsection [section 40(1)] contemplates the inventor's particular employer, not some notional employer. The fact that it refers to 'the size and nature of the employer's undertaking' makes this clear beyond any argument. It is the real actual benefit to the actual employer which is all that matters. If an invention had been immensely valuable and a patent for it could have been or could be (if still in force) exploited for a vast sum or have fetched vast royalties or a great sum on the open market, that is irrelevant. The inventor's particular employer may not have exploited the invention well or at all. If so, the inventor cannot complain. The employer must be taken as it was, warts and all. The provision is not some kind of 'best endeavours to exploit' requirement.

The second issue turned on an interpretation of section 41(1) and (2), which are set out below:

> (1) An award of compensation to an employee under section 40(1) or (2) above shall be such as will secure for the employee a fair share (having regard to all the circumstances) of the benefit which the employer has derived, or may reasonably be expected to derive, from any of the following—
>
>   (a) the invention in question;
>
>   (b) the patent for the invention;
>
>   (c) the assignment, assignation or grant of—
>
>   (i) the property or any right in the invention, or
>
>   (ii) the property in, or any right in or under, an application for the patent,
>
> to a person connected with the employer.
>
> (2) For the purposes of subsection (1) above the amount of any benefit derived or expected to be derived by an employer from the assignment, assignation or grant of—
>
>   (a) the property in, or any right in or under, a patent for the invention or an application for such a patent; or
>
>   (b) the property or any right in the invention;
>
> to a person connected with him shall be taken to be the amount which could reasonably be expected to be so derived by the employer if that person had not been connected with him.

---

[131] [2010] EWCA Civ 1283, [2011] RPC 12.

The court had to consider whether the assignment from CRL to Unilever plc made a difference by virtue of section 41(2). Jacob LJ held that the 'employer' in that section referred to the actual employer who was the assignor and that the assignee meant the real actual assignee; on the facts, this meant considering the assignment from CRL to Unilever plc. The benefit derived by the assignee was £23 million and thus what CRL would reasonably have expected to derive from the assignment to Unilever plc was £23 million. Jacob LJ expressed the hope that the parties would now be able to agree on what amounted to a 'fair share' for Professor Shanks.

Unfortunately, no such agreement was reached between the parties and Professor Shanks brought a claim before the Comptroller General of Patents (i.e. the Head of the UK Intellectual Property Office). The Hearing Officer concluded that the benefit to Unilever from the Shanks patents had been £24.5 million, but that this was not 'outstanding' within the meaning of section 40(1) of the PA 77 and that, even if it had been 'outstanding', a fair share of that benefit would have been 5 per cent. Professor Shanks appealed the decision of the Hearing Officer to the Patents Court.[132] In dismissing the appeal, Arnold J held that a benefit derived from the patent did not include the time value of the money which Unilever had received and should be considered net of tax. Further, that the Hearing Officer had not been wrong to consider the benefit to the Unilever group as a whole, as opposed to simply CRL. As to whether the benefit was 'outstanding', Arnold J held that the Hearing Officer had undertaken an appropriate multifactorial assessment. Worth noting is that Arnold J found that 'the hearing officer was correct to conclude that the mere fact that the employer received benefit from the patents in a manner which was unusual for that employer [i.e. by licensing and not manufacture], and hence in an amount which the employer did not usually receive in that way, is not in itself an indication that the benefit was outstanding'.[133] Arnold J went on to consider, in *obiter*, what would have constituted a 'fair share' if the benefit had been 'outstanding'. He found that the Hearing Officer had failed to 'take Unilever's ability to extract licence fees due to its size and financial resources into account' and, as such, 3 per cent and not 5 per cent amounted to a 'fair share'.[134]

In your view, what are the differences between *Kelly and Chiu v GE Healthcare Ltd* and *Shanks v Unilever* which account for why employee compensation was awarded in one case and not the other? More generally, is it a good idea to have a compensation scheme in respect of employee-created inventions or should rewards for employees' inventiveness be left to an employer's discretion? If the former, do you think that the provisions in the PA 77 operate effectively?

FURTHER READING

P. W. Grubb and P. R. Thomsen, *Patents for Chemicals, Pharmaceuticals, and Biotechnology: Fundamentals of Global Law, Practice, and Strategy* (5th edn, Oxford: Oxford University Press, 2010), ch. 21.

A. Hobson and T. Shafran, '*Kelly and Chiu v GE Healthcare Ltd*: pharmaceutical companies at risk of successful employer inventor compensation claim following landmark ruling' [2009] EIPR 523.

W. P. Hovell, 'Patent ownership: an employer's rights to his employee's invention' (1983) 58 Notre Dame L. R. 863.

---

[132] *Shanks v Unilever plc* [2014] EWHC 1647 (Ch), [2014] RPC 29.   [133] [75].   [134] [122].

Y. Lee and M. Langley, 'Employees' inventions: statutory compensation schemes in Japan and the UK' [2005] EIPR 250.

R. P. Merges, 'The law and economics of employee inventions' (1999) 13 Harvard Journal of Law & Technology 1.

J. Pila, ' "Sewing the fly buttons on the statute": employee inventions and the employment context' (2012) 32 OJLS 265.

C. G. Stallberg, 'The legal status of academic employees' inventions in Britain and Germany and its consequences for R&D agreements' [2007] IPQ 489.

14

INDUSTRIAL DESIGNS

14.1 INTRODUCTION

Industrial designs may seem like the poor relations of other intellectual property. For the most part, they lack the glamour of a good brand, the creative genius of a best-selling novel, and the outstanding inventiveness of many patents. Nonetheless, it is important not to underestimate the value of industrial designs. Some, like the design of the Apple iPad, might achieve iconic status. Others, such as the design of spare parts for motor vehicles, may have considerable economic value. Perhaps the latter fact explains why the protection for industrial designs after an early life as being purely local in character has been given a makeover by the EU. It is also noteworthy that, for the most part, purely functional industrial designs, in the sense of purely functional features of a product, are afforded much less protection than other sorts of intellectual property. This is not because functional industrial designs are deemed to have any less worth. Indeed, quite the reverse. The short term of protection presently accorded to functional designs stems from a recognition that a monopoly of such designs, for example of motor vehicle spare parts, would run counter to achieving market efficiency through genuine competition between suppliers.

14.1.1 DESIGN PROTECTION IN THE UK AND THE EU

Until the implementation of the Community Designs Directive[1] and the Community Design Regulation,[2] there were two ways in which an industrial design, depending upon its character, might be protected against copying in the UK. These were as a registered design (RD) or by unregistered design right (UDR). The UDR had been introduced by the Copyright, Designs and Patents Act 1988 (CDPA) which removed copyright protection from almost all

---

[1] Designs Directive 98/71/EC of the European Parliament and of the Council of 13 October 1998 on the legal protection of designs.
[2] Council Regulation (EC) No. 6/2002 of 12 December 2001 on Community designs.

industrial designs.[3] The registered design regime was regulated by the Registered Designs Act 1949. Historically, RDs offered protection for industrial designs which had 'eye appeal'. By contrast, the UDR offered protection for functional designs which did not. As we shall see, such a clear distinction has been eroded by the implementation of the Designs Directive and Regulation.

The Designs Directive was intended to approximate national laws relating to the registration of industrial designs as a means of facilitating trade between Member States. Three years later the Design Regulation was introduced. The regulation built on the directive. It introduced a Community registered design (RCD) and a Community unregistered design (CUDR). The introduction of an RCD and a CUDR was intended to unify the protection for industrial designs in the EU. However, it is certainly questionable whether the implementation of the directive and regulation has had a simplifying effect in the protection of industrial designs in the UK. In fact, there are now at least five ways in which an industrial design might be protected in the UK—as opposed to the pre-regulation era when there were only three.

They are:

- as a Community registered design (RCD);
- as a UK registered design (RD);
- as a Community unregistered design (CUDR);
- as a UK unregistered design (UDR);
- by copyright.

14.1.2 THE HISTORY OF INDUSTRIAL DESIGN

The muddled and overlapping protection which in the UK is afforded to industrial designs results in large measure from the piecemeal way in which industrial design protection evolved over the last century. During the 19th and early 20th centuries, the push to protect industrial designs came from the textile industry. The Copyright Act 1911, which was the first to define infringement in its recognisable present form, excluded from copyright protection designs which were reproduced or intended to be reproduced in more than 50 single articles or were to be applied, for example, to carpets and textiles. Instead, the latter were protected by registration under the Patents and Designs Act 1907. This Act evolved into the Registered Designs Act 1949, which has now been amended to accord with the EU Designs Directive and Regulation. Until the implementation of the Designs Directive, only designs with 'eye appeal' could be registered.

The problem, however, remained as to how designs which did not have eye appeal would be protected. This problem was not solved by the Copyright Act 1956 which in effect granted copyright protection to designs which did not have eye appeal, but not to designs which did and so could be registered.[4] The result was that industrial designs that lacked eye appeal received the full term of copyright protection, while the maximum term of protection for registered designs was 25 years. The Design Copyright Act 1968 addressed part of this problem by allowing copyright protection for artistic works which were registrable designs, but only for 15 years. However, the more entrenched problem of what many saw as

---

[3] See 14.4.   [4] *Dorling v Honnor Marine* [1965] Ch 1.

the over-protection of industrial designs lacking eye appeal remained. This issue was finally addressed by the creation of the unregistered design right in the CDPA. The CDPA also restricted the extent to which industrial designs would be protected by copyright.

14.1.3 INDUSTRIAL DESIGNS AND THE MARKET FOR SPARE PARTS

The motive behind granting legal protection to industrial designs in the 19th and early 20th centuries was to protect the flourishing UK textile industry. The industrial design regime introduced by the CDPA 1988 had another agenda fit for an age when free markets were worshipped. It was designed in large measure to open up the UK market to makers of automobile spare parts. As things stood, automobile makers had a virtual monopoly in the provision of spare parts for their cars, because of the lengthy copyright protection afforded to the original designs. The problems inherent in this situation were demonstrated by the House of Lords decision in *British Leyland v Armstrong Patents Co. Ltd.*[5] The claimant, BL, manufactured automobiles and the defendant manufactured spare parts for these automobiles. The claimant sued the defendant for copyright infringement. The House of Lords found that the defendant had infringed copyright in the claimant's design documents. However, it went on to hold that the benefits of having a competitive market in the provision of spare parts overrode the claimant's right to copyright protection.

> **Lord Bridge, at p. 626:**
>
> By selling those same cars BL have also created a large community of car owners who, quite independently of any contractual rights derived from BL, enjoy the inherent right as owners to repair their cars by replacing the exhaust whenever necessary in the most economical way possible. To allow BL to enforce their copyright to maintain a monopoly for themselves and their licensees in the supply and replacement of exhausts is, to a greater or lesser extent, to detract from the owner's rights and, at least potentially, the value of their cars. There is an inconsistency between marketing cars and thereby creating whatever rights attach to their ownership on the one hand and acting to restrain the free exercise of those rights on the other. The law does not countenance such inconsistencies. It may be a novel application of the principle to preclude a plaintiff from enforcing a statutory right to which he is *prima facie* entitled. But, as my noble and learned friend Lord Templeman demonstrates, the application of the principle to the relationship between the mass car manufacturer and those who at any time acquire cars of his manufacture is no more than an extension to a non-contractual relationship of the considerations which underlie the classical doctrine of the law that a grantor may not derogate from his grant.

In effect, the House of Lords decided to introduce a new economic policy, the freeing up of the market for spare parts, in the face of the government's failure to act. Two years later the UDR was introduced, arguably making the decision in *British Leyland* redundant. Indeed, 11 years later the Privy Council decided, in *Canon Kabushiki Kaisha v Green Cartridge*,[6] not to follow the House of Lords' judgment in *British Leyland*. As in *British Leyland*, *Canon* concerned the conflicting interests of the manufacturer of, in this case, printers and

---

[5] [1986] AC 577.   [6] [1997] AC 728.

photocopiers and a defendant who manufactured ink cartridges for the same equipment. It was noted by the court that the claimant, Canon, earned a significant profit from its monopoly over the supply of replacement cartridges for its equipment.

Lord Hoffmann, at pp. 737–8

Their Lordships think the *British Leyland* spare parts exception cannot be regarded as truly founded upon any principle of the law of contract or property. It is instead an expression of what the House perceived as overriding public policy, namely the need to prevent a manufacturer from using copyright (as opposed to patents or design right) in order to control the aftermarket in spare parts. This appears clearly from the emphasis on the need for an 'unrestricted market' as opposed to the right of the manufacturer to 'use his copyright in such a way as to maintain a monopoly in the supply of spare parts' (Lord Bridge at page 625) and the danger of the car owner who 'sells his soul to the company store' being enmeshed in the 'tentacles of copyright' (Lord Templeman at pages 628–629).

It is of course a strong thing (not to say constitutionally questionable) for a judicially-declared head of public policy to be treated as overriding or qualifying an express statutory right. Their Lordships therefore think that the prospect of any extension of the *British Leyland* exception should be treated with some caution. The question of whether it is contrary to the public interest for a manufacturer to be able to exercise monopoly control over his aftermarket cannot usually be answered without some inquiry into the relevant market. For example, if customers are in a position to reckon the lifetime cost of one product (including purchases such as cartridges which will have to be made in the aftermarket) as against the lifetime cost of a competing product, then control of the aftermarket will not be anti-competitive. A manufacturer who charges too much for his cartridges will sell less of his machines. The figures which their Lordships have already quoted for expenditure on the machine itself and on cartridges make it likely that purchasers with any degree of sophistication will be comparing machines on a lifetime cost basis.

Lord Hoffmann went on to differentiate the supply of spare parts for automobiles where, by contrast, the need for repair would be irregular and unpredictable, and was willing to accept that the decision in *British Leyland* could be justified on its facts.

14.1.4 CONCLUSION

Given their importance to the overhaul of the design regime in the UK, it is perhaps ironic that the protection of spare parts was one area of the new EU design regime, where the Member States were unable to reach a consensus. As a result, Article 110(1) of the regulation (known as a transitional provision) reads:

Until such time as amendments to this Regulation enter into force on a proposal from the Commission on this subject, protection as a Community design shall not exist for a design which constitutes a component part of a complex product used within the meaning of Article 19(1) for the purpose of the repair of that complex product so as to restore its original appearance.

In fact, despite a lengthy consultation exercise by the Commission following the entering into force of the directive, which concluded (echoing *British Leyland*) that the most effective way to achieve an internal market was to exclude design protection from the sale of spare parts intended for the repair of so-called complex articles, the transitional provision remains in force. Thus far, its interpretation has been left to individual Member States.[7] This chapter will now go on to examine the law relating to industrial designs following the introduction of the UDR and the new Community industrial designs regime ushered in by the Designs Directive and Regulation.[8]

FURTHER READING

L. Bently, 'The return of industrial copyright' [2012] EIPR 654.

M. C. Howe, J. St Ville, and A. Chantrielle (eds), *Russell-Clarke & Howe on Industrial Designs* (9th edn, London: Sweet & Maxwell, 2016).

J. Rawkins, '*British Leyland* spare part defence: *Canon Kabushiki Kaisha v Green Cartridge Company (Hong Kong) Ltd*' [1998] EIPR 674.

D. Stone, *European Union Design Law: A Practitioner's Guide* (2nd edn, Oxford: Oxford University Press, 2016).

UK IPO, 'UK design as a global industry: International trade and IP' (2012) (www.gov.uk/government/uploads/system/uploads/attachment_data/file/310359/ipresearch-ukdesign-201207.pdf).

14.2 REGISTERED DESIGNS

14.2.1 OBTAINING REGISTRATION

The Registered Design regime in the UK is now regulated by the Registered Designs Act (RDA) 1949, as amended by the CDPA, the Registered Design Regulations 2001,[9] and the Registered Design Regulations 2003.[10] As a result, the law applying to RCDs and RDs is the same. In this respect, the regulation of registered designs mirrors that of registered trade marks. The EU has created a Community right, and the law which applies to this right also applies to a UK registered design.

Applications for an RCD are made to the EU IPO (formerly the OHIM) in Alicante, which also deals with the EUTM (formerly the CTM). The process of registration calls for the applicant to indicate the products into which 'the design is intended to be incorporated'. The applicant may also choose to indicate the class of goods for which the design will be used, by reference to the Locarno Agreement.[11]

It is also possible to register a design in the UK by application to the UK IPO. Both UK registered designs and RCDs will be protected for five years in the first instance and may be renewed thereafter for a total of 25 years. As with patents, the RCD and the RD endow an absolute monopoly. It is not necessary for a registered design to be copied for it to be infringed. Both at the EU IPO and the UK IPO, there will be no substantive examination

---

[7] For the UK approach, see *Bayerische Motoren Werke Aktiengesellschaft v Round and Metal Ltd, Philip David Gross* Case No: HC11C02291 [2012] EWHC 2099 (Pat). See reference in C-435/16 *Acacia et D'Amato*.

[8] The Intellectual Property Act 2014 introduced changes to registered and unregistered design protection which will be looked at in the course of this chapter.

[9] SI 2001/3949.   [10] SI 2003/550.

[11] The Locarno Agreement Establishing an International Classification for Industrial Designs, 1968.

of the design by the registering authority either for novelty or individual character.[12] There will, however, be an examination of the design to see if it falls within the exclusions to registration, for instance if it is functional or offends against public morality.

While the EU IPO is concerned with the process of registering an RCD, domestic courts, designated as Community Design Courts, deal with issues of infringement and counterclaims of invalidity. As regards domestic registered designs, these are governed by the same legal conditions as the RCD. Thus, UK examiners and judges will look to the examiners, the First Board of Appeal in Alicante, and on to the General Court up to the CJEU to see how to interpret the Community Designs Directive and Regulation as they apply to both RCDs and UK RDs.

14.2.2 THE DEFINITION OF A PROTECTABLE DESIGN

This chapter will look first at the Design Regulation itself, before going on to consider the relevant case law which has grown up to interpret it.

14.2.2.1 A registrable design

We have noted that until the implementation of the Designs Directive and Regulation only industrial designs with eye appeal could be registered. This requirement was understood to mean that the appearance of the registered design was a material factor in attracting consumers. In particular, the article's appeal was seen to reside in its shape, pattern, or ornamentation.[13] Under European law, an RD no longer needs to have eye appeal. Instead, a 'design' is defined, more broadly, as:

> the appearance of the whole of the product resulting from the features of, in particular, the lines, contours, colours, shapes, texture of the product or its ornamentation.[14]

It is possible to argue that the requirement that a registered design have eye appeal justified the longer protection it was given in contrast to an unregistered design which did not. The fact that the new law does not make eye appeal a necessary prerequisite for registration represents for some a worrying extension of design protection. The regulation then goes on to define a product as:

> any industrial or handicraft item other than computer programs; and in particular includes packaging, get-up, graphic symbols, typographic type faces and parts intended to be assembled into a complex product.[15]

Here too we might detect an increased measure of protection offered to designs. Under the present law, a registrable design does not have to be applied to a product by an industrial process. A complex product is defined in Article 3(c) of the CDR as 'being composed of multiple components which can be replaced permitting disassembly and re-assembly of the product' and by section 1(3) of the RDA 1949 as amended as 'composed of at least two replaceable

---

[12] For trade marks, see 6.3.1.   [13] *Interlego AG v Tyco Industries Inc.* [1988] AC 217.
[14] Community Design Regulation (CDR), Art. 3(a) (RDA 1949, s. 1(2)).
[15] CDR, Art. 3(b) (RDA 1949, s. 1(3)).

parts permitting disassembly and reassembly of the product'. This definition will, according to the UK IPO, stretch the protection offered by the registration of a design to products which are 'costly, long lasting and complex': an automobile but not a teapot.

The definition of a registrable design is then set out:

> A design shall be protected by a right in a registered design to the extent that the design is new and has individual character.[16]

According to the CDR, a design will be considered novel:[17]

> if no identical design has been made available to the public before the relevant date.

The design must also have individual character. Recital 14 of the regulation states:

> The assessment as to whether a design has individual character should be based on whether the overall impression produced on an informed user viewing the design clearly differs from that produced on him by the existing design corpus, taking into consideration the nature of the product to which the design is applied or in which it is incorporated, and in particular the industrial sector to which it belongs and the degree of freedom of the designer in developing the design.

Within the regulation, individual character is similarly defined as when:[18]

> the overall impression it produces on the informed user differs from the overall impression produced on such a user by any design which has been made available to the public before the relevant date.

The relevant date will most commonly be the date on which the application for the registration of the design was made or is treated as having been made. An exception would be if a design has been substantially modified since an application was first made. In judging the extent to which a design has individual character:

> The degree of freedom of the author in creating the design shall be taken into consideration. Designs shall be deemed to be identical if their features differ only in immaterial details.[19]

Although only novel designs are registrable, it is important to be aware that a design will retain its novelty if disclosure of the design occurred during a 12-month period preceding the date of filing or, if a priority date is claimed, the date of priority.[20] This gives the originator of the design a crucial period in which to decide whether there is sufficient economic justification for registering his design. Such a justification may be absent, for instance, if the design is for a fashion fabric which may only bring economic rewards over a short period.

---

[16] CDR, Art. 4(1) (RDA 1949, s. 1B(1)).
[17] CDR, Art. 5(1). The relevance of immaterial details is at CDR, Art. 5(2).
[18] CDR, Art. 6(1) (RDA 1949, s. 1B(2)).   [19] CDR, Art. 6(2) (RDA 1949, s. 1B(3)).
[20] CDR, Art. 7(2)(b).

14.2.2.2 Exceptions to registration

There are also exceptions to the protection of registered designs set out in the regulation. The most important of these, which also apply to the Community unregistered designs, are:

> A Community design shall not subsist in features of the appearance of a product which are solely dictated by the product's technical function[21]

and

> A right in a registered design shall not subsist in features of the appearance of a product which must necessarily be reproduced in their exact form and dimensions so as to permit the product in which the design is incorporated or to which it is applied to be mechanically connected to, or placed in, around or against, another product so that either product may perform its function.[22]

Otherwise known as the 'must fit' exception, this second exception does not prevent a right in a registered design subsisting in a design serving the purpose of allowing a multiple assembly or connection of mutually interchangeable products within a modular system.

14.2.2.3 Infringement

The regulation defines infringement, by identifying the rights which a registration endows on its proprietor. Most notably, it is:[23]

> the exclusive right to use it [the RD] and to prevent any third party not having his consent from using it.[24]

According to section 7A of the RDA 1949, a registered design would therefore be infringed by a person who, without the consent of the registered proprietor, does anything which by virtue of Article 12 (section 7 of the RDA 1949) is the exclusive right of the registered proprietor.[25] Other rights given to the proprietor include: the making, offering, putting on the market, importing, exporting, or using a product in which the design is incorporated or to which it is applied; or stocking such a product for those purposes. There are, however, defences to an allegation of infringement of a registered design. These are set out at Article 20 (section 7A(2) of the RDA 1949), of which the most notable are that a registered design is not infringed if it is used privately for non-commercial or for experimental purposes. In addition, the right to protect a registered design is exhausted once a product embodying that design has been put on the market in the EEA by the proprietor or with his consent.[26] In *BMW v Round and Metal Ltd*,[27] Mr Justice Arnold held that Article 110(1), the transitional spare parts provision, is not an exclusion to protection but rather an exception to the protection afforded to a design, once it is registered.

---

[21] CDR, Art. 8(1) (RDA 1949, s. 1C(1)).   [22] CDR, Art. 8(2) (RDA 1949, s. 1C(2)).
[23] CDR, Art. 19 (RDA 1949, s. 7A).   [24] CDR, Art. 19(1) (RDA 1949, s. 7A(1)).
[25] There is no equivalent article in the CDR.   [26] CDR, Art. 21 (RDA 1949, s. 7A(2)).
[27] [2012] EWHC 299 (Pat).

14.2.3 REGISTERED DESIGNS: THE CASE LAW

14.2.3.1 The definitions of informed user, design freedom, and a different overall impression

In the case of *PepsiCo v Grupo*, the CJEU interpreted a number of key concepts in the law of registered design which relate to registration, infringement, and invalidity. These are the concepts (set out in Article 14 of the regulation) of the informed user; of design freedom; and when a design will be judged to make a different overall impression of the informed user.

PepsiCo, Inc. v Grupo Promer Mon Graphic SA Case C-281/10 P [2012] FSR 5

The appellant (PepsiCo) was the holder of a Community registered design. The design related to small collectible children's toys, known as pogs, which were often distributed as free gifts with other products. PepsiCo based its priority for a RCD on a design for goods, including promotional items for games, which it had filed in Spain in 2003. The respondent (Grupo Promer) applied for a declaration of invalidity on the basis that the PepsiCo design lacked novelty and individual character (Article 25(1)(b) of the Design Regulation) and on the existence of a prior right (Article 25(1)(d)). The latter claim rested on an earlier registered design, which Grupo had for 'metal plates for games'. The Cancellation Division found for Grupo, and declared PepsiCo's registration to be invalid. PepsiCo successfully appealed to the Board of Appeal and Grupo then appealed, in its turn, to the General Court. The General Court annulled the decision of the Board of Appeal and upheld Grupo's appeal. It found that the differences between the two designs were insufficient to produce a different overall impression on the informed user, whether it be a marketing manager as suggested by the Board of Appeal or a child of between five and ten as suggested by Grupo. In reaching this decision, it confirmed that the concept of conflict between designs, for the purposes of a finding of invalidity, implies that the designs produce the same overall impression of the informed user, and it made no difference whether the informed user was a marketing manager or a child. Furthermore, in ascertaining the design freedom, reference should be made, not to the entire category of promotional items, but to the particular category of 'pogs'. However, it found that even within this more narrowly defined category, it would have been possible for PepsiCo to have produced a design which was distinctive and hence produced a different overall impression on the informed user. PepsiCo then appealed to the CJEU. Among its arguments was that the General Court had applied incorrect criteria when assessing the constraints on design freedom, the concept of the informed user and his level of attention, and whether it was necessary to compare goods rather than the designs at issue.

The CJEU first turned to the question of the constraints on the designer's freedom. It concluded that the General Court's view that the shape of the 'pog' was not the result of constraints on the designer's freedom was a question of fact and could not be overturned by the CJEU. It then turned to the second question relating to the concept of the 'informed user' and his level of attention. It held that the concept of the informed user 'must be understood as lying somewhere between that of the average consumer, applicable in trade mark matters, who need not have any specific knowledge and who, as a rule, makes no direct comparison between the trade marks at issue, and the sectoral expert, who is an expert with detailed technical expertise'.[28] Thus, the concept of the 'informed user' may be understood as referring, not to a user of average attention, but to a particularly observant one, either because of his personal experience or his extensive knowledge of the sector in question. Furthermore, the informed user cannot be assumed to make a direct comparison between the two designs. The CJEU then turned to the informed user's level of attention:

> 59 Thirdly, as regards the informed user's level of attention, it should be noted that, although the informed user is not the well-informed and reasonably observant and circumspect average consumer who normally perceives a design as a whole and does not proceed to analyse its various details (see, by analogy, *Lloyd Schuhfabrik Meyer & Co GmbH v Klijsen Handel BV* (C-342/97) [1999] E.C.R. I-3819; [1999] 2 C.M.L.R. 1343; [2000] F.S.R. 77 at [25] and [26]), he is also not an expert or specialist capable of observing in detail the minimal differences that may exist between the designs in conflict. Thus, the qualifier 'informed' suggests that, without being a designer or a technical expert, the user knows the various designs which exist in the sector concerned, possesses a certain degree of knowledge with regard to the features which those designs normally include, and, as a result of his interest in the products concerned, shows a relatively high degree of attention when he use them.

The CJEU went on to find that the General Court had correctly assessed the informed user's level of attention. As to whether it was the job of the General Court to carry out its own examination of the designs before overruling the Board of Appeal, the CJEU held that it was. It then turned to the next question: did this examination wrongly focus on the goods rather than the designs at issue? Once again, it upheld the approach of the General Court.

> 72 It should be observed that, in [83] of the judgment under appeal, the General Court stated that its assessment of the degree of curvature of the designs at issue is 'borne out by the goods actually marketed, as contained in OHIM's file forwarded to the Court'.
>
> 73 However, since in design matters the person making the comparison is an informed user who—as noted in [53] and [59] above—is different from the ordinary average consumer, it is not mistaken, in the assessment of the overall impression of the designs at issue, to take account of the goods actually marketed which correspond to those designs.
>
> 74 In any event, it follows from the use of the verb 'to bear out' in [83] of the judgment under appeal that the General Court did indeed base its assessments on the designs in conflict as described and reproduced in the respective applications for registration, with the result that the comparison of the actual goods was used only for illustrative purposes in order to confirm the conclusions already drawn and cannot be regarded as forming the basis of the statement of reasons given in the judgment under appeal.
>
> 75 Accordingly, the fourth part of the single ground of appeal must be rejected.

Perhaps one of most interesting aspects of the *PepsiCo* judgment is the differentiation made by the Court of Justice between the informed user in design law and the average

---

[28] [53].

consumer in trade mark law.[29] The definition of the informed user had earlier been examined by Jacob LJ in the Court of Appeal in *Procter & Gamble Co. v Reckitt Benckiser (UK) Ltd.*[30] He too had concluded that the informed user was not the same as the average consumer. Citing a case in the Austrian court, he noted that unlike the average consumer, the informed user would be open to design issues and will be fairly familiar with them.[31] He argued that the contrast between the informed user and the average consumer derived partly from the nature of the different rights which were being protected. Thus the purpose of design registration was:

> 27. … to protect that design *as a design*. So what matters is the overall impression created by it: will the user buy it, consider it or appreciate it *for its individual design*? That involves the user looking at the article, not half-remembering it. The motivation is different from purchasing or otherwise relying on a trade mark as a guarantee of origin.
>
> 28. So the informed user is alert to design issues and is better informed than the average consumer in trade mark law. Things which may infringe a registered trade mark may not infringe a corresponding registered design. I cannot think of any instance where the reverse might be so.

Following the CJEU judgment in *PepsiCo*, it might be worth asking whether the distinction between the informed user and the average consumer remains as clear cut as suggested by Jacob LJ. After all, we have seen that in trade mark law the average consumer is presumed to be the average customer for the particular goods or services at issue. Might it not be difficult to differentiate this individual from the informed user, when the latter category is apparently broad enough to encompass both marketing managers and children aged between five and ten years old?

14.2.3.2 The definition of individual character

In *Senz Technologies v OHIM*, the General Court returned to the issue of the informed user, and also summarized the definition of individual character.[32]

Senz Technologies BV v Office for Harmonisation in the Internal Market (Trade Marks and Designs) (OHIM) (Impliva BV, intervening)
Joined Cases T-22 and 23/13 [2015] ECDR 19

The case concerned an application for invalidity. The applicant, Senz, had two RCDs for umbrellas. The intervener, Impliva BV, sought to have the designs declared invalid because of lack of individual character as the umbrellas would make the same overall impression on the informed user as a number of similar umbrellas which were the subject of patent and design registrations. The Invalidity Division upheld the intervener's application as did the Board of Appeal. But the General Court disagreed. The General

---

[29] For a CJEU decision applying the *PepsiCo* principles, see *Neuman v José Manuel Baena Grupo SA* Case C-101/11 P [2013] ECDR 3.

[30] [2008] ECDR 3.   [31] [26].

[32] See also *Kwang Yang Motor Co. Ltd v OHIM (with intervention from Honda Giken Kogyo Kabushiki Kaisha)* Case T-10/08 [2012] ECDR 2.

Court described the informed user as someone wishing to use an umbrella, who needs to purchase one and who has become informed on the subject. Turning to the degree of design freedom, which is one element in determining whether a design has individual character, the General Court summarized the situation thus:

> 56 According to the case law, the designer's degree of freedom is established by, inter alia, the constraints of the features imposed by the technical function of the product or an element thereof, or by statutory requirements applicable to the product. Those constraints result in a standardisation of certain features, which will thus be common to the designs applied to the product concerned (judgments of 9 September 2011 in *Kwang Yang Motor Co Ltd v Office for Harmonisation in the Internal Market (Trade Marks and Designs) (OHIM)— Honda Giken Kogyo (Internal combustion engine)* (T-11/08), judgment of 9 September 2011, not yet reported, at [32], and of 25 April 2013 in *Bell & Ross BV v Office for Harmonisation in the Internal Market (Trade Marks and Designs) (OHIM)—KIN (Wristwatch case)* (T-80/10) EU:T:2013:214 at [112]).
>
> 57 Therefore, the greater the designer's freedom in developing a design, the less likely it is that minor differences between the designs at issue will be sufficient to produce different overall impressions on an informed user. Conversely, the more restricted the designer's freedom in developing a design, the more likely it is that minor differences between the designs at issue will be sufficient to produce different overall impressions on an informed user. Therefore, if the designer enjoys a high degree of freedom in developing a design, that reinforces the conclusion that designs that do not have significant differences produce the same overall impression on an informed user (judgments in *Internal combustion engine* (T-11/08) at [33], and *Wristwatch case* EU:T:2013:214 at [113]).

The General Court then went on to look at the facts of this particular case. It concluded that the possible variations in the design of an umbrella are quite limited and this was particularly true in this instance where the design was specifically for a wind-resistant umbrella. It continued:

> 59 Accordingly, the conclusion is that the degree of freedom of the designer in the present case is limited, with the result that, in accordance with the case law cited in [57] above, even minor differences between the earlier patent and the contested designs suffice to produce different overall impressions on the informed user.

The General Court then compared the overall impressions produced by the earlier patented umbrella and the RCDs and decided there were some significant differences. Taking into account the limited amount of design freedom of the designer, it was able to conclude that the RCDs did have individual character and that the two registered designs were not invalid.[33] In *Dyson v Vax*,[34] the Court of Appeal held that the correct approach to measuring design freedom was to look at the freedom enjoyed by the later design rather than the design which had been registered.

---

[33] For Community unregistered designs see *Karen Millen Fashions Ltd v Dunnes Stores* Case C-345/13, EU:C:2014:2013 [2014] Bus. L. R. 756; see 14.3.1.
[34] [2011] EWCA Civ 1206.

14.2.3.3 The functionality exception to design registration

Nintendo Co. Ltd v Compatinet SLU et al. R 1772/2012-3 OHIM Third Board of Appeal [2015] ECDR 3

Nintendo had a RCD for 'game cartridges for electronic games and game stations'. Compatinet filed an application for a declaration of invalidity under Article 8(1) of the CDR. It argued that design was solely dictated by its technical function in that it was 'absolutely necessary to reproduce the RCD in its exact shape and size in order for this to perform its function'. The Invalidity Division agreed with the applicant and declared the design invalid. Nintendo appealed. After considering the arguments of both parties, the Board of Appeal looked at the general justification for the functionality exception. In particular, it considered and rejected the 'multiplicity of forms theory' which would allow the registration of a functional shape if another shape could achieve the same purpose.

19 The Board has noted in its case law that if it is accepted that a feature of a product's appearance is not 'solely dictated by its function' simply because an alternative product configuration could achieve the same function, art.8(1) CDR will apply only in highly exceptional circumstances and its very purpose will be in danger of being frustrated. That purpose is to prevent design law from being used to achieve monopolies over technical solutions, the assumption being that such monopolies are only justified if the more restrictive conditions imposed by patent law (and in some countries by the law of utility models) are complied with. If a technical solution can be achieved by two alternative methods, neither solution is, according to the multiplicity-of-forms theory, solely dictated by the function of the product in question. This would mean that both solutions could be the subject of a design registration, possibly held by the same person, which would have the consequence that no one else would be able to manufacture a competing product capable of performing the same technical function. The multiplicity-of-forms theory would, if accepted, deprive art.8(1) CDR of any purpose and content. That provision might just as well be deleted from the regulation since its field of application, at least as a ground of invalidity in conjunction with art.25(1)(b), would be reduced to virtually zero. There are very few features of a product's appearance that have to be exactly the way they are in order for the product to achieve its technical function. A vehicle wheel must be round, a television screen must be rectangular, and there are doubtless other examples of particular features for which there is no alternative design. But it is hard to think of a product of which it can truly be said that all its essential features can have only one form if the product is to perform its function. This leads to the conclusion that the multiplicity-of-forms theory cannot be correct (see decision of 29 April 2010, R 211/2008-3, 'Fluid distribution equipment', para.28).

20 Article 8(1) CDR denies protection to features of a product's appearance that are 'solely dictated by its technical function'. Those words do not, on their natural meaning, imply that the feature in question must be the only means by which the product's technical function can be achieved. On the contrary, they imply that the need to achieve the product's technical function was the only relevant factor when the feature in question was selected. The adverb 'solely' qualifies the phrase 'dictated by its technical function'; thus art.8(1) applies if the feature in question has been dictated by the product's technical function and by no other

consideration, such as the need to design a product that not only works but also looks good. The mere fact that a design alternative exists does not mean that a product's appearance has been dictated by anything other than technical considerations (see decision of 29 April 2010, R 211/2008-3, 'Fluid distribution equipment', paras 29–31). Similarly, as far as concerns trade marks, the Court has found that a sign consisting exclusively of the shape of a product is unregistrable by virtue thereof if it is established that the essential functional features of that shape are attributable only to the technical result. Moreover, the ground for refusal or invalidity of registration imposed by that provision cannot be overcome by establishing that there are other shapes which allow the same technical result to be obtained (see judgment of 18 June 2002, *Koninklijke Philips Electronics NV v Remington Consumer Products Ltd* (C-299/99) [2002] E.C.R. I-5475; [2002] ETMR 81 at [84]).

...

22 The significance of limiting protection to the visual appearance of products is that aesthetic considerations are in principle capable of being relevant only when the designer is developing a product's visual appearance. Most of the time the designer will be concerned with both elements of good design: functionality and eye appeal. In some cases functionality will be the dominant preoccupation of the designer. The need to make a product that works will be uppermost in the designer's mind and will largely determine the appearance of the product. As long as functionality is not the only relevant factor, the design is in principle eligible for protection. It is only when aesthetic considerations are completely irrelevant that the features of the design are solely dictated by the need to achieve a technical solution. This is not, it must be stressed, tantamount to introducing a requirement of aesthetic merit into the legislation. It is simply recognition of the obvious fact that when aesthetics are totally irrelevant, in the sense that no one cares whether the product looks good, bad, ugly or pretty, and all that matters is that the product functions well, there is nothing to protect under the law of designs (see decisions of 22 October 2009, R 690/2007-3, 'Chaff cutters', para.35 and of 29 April 2010, R 211/2008-3, 'Fluid distribution equipment', para.34).

23 It follows from the above that art.8(1) CDR denies protection to those features of a product's appearance that were chosen exclusively for the purpose of designing a product that performs its function, as opposed to features that were chosen, at least to some degree, for the purpose of enhancing the product's visual appearance. It goes without saying that these matters must be assessed objectively: it is not necessary to determine what actually went on in the designer's mind when the design was being developed. The matter must be assessed from the standpoint of a reasonable observer who looks at the design and asks himself/herself whether anything other than purely functional considerations could have been relevant when a specific feature was chosen (see decisions of 22 October 2009, R 690/2007-3, 'Chaff cutters', para.36 and of 29 April 2010, R 211/2008-3, 'Fluid distribution equipment', para.35).

The Board of Appeal then turned to the question of whether the essential features of Nintendo's RCD was dictated by the technical function of the product. It first looked to see what the technical function was. In this case it did so by looking at its US patent application for the same product and it found that the cartridge's appearance on the patent application was almost identical to its appearance on the application for the RCD. Thus, for the Board of Appeal, the question came down to whether the shape of the cartridge as claimed in the contested RCD incorporated elements enhancing the appearance of the product. It concluded that it did not.

> 36 …In the opinion of the Board, a reasonable observer who looks at this contested RCD and asks himself/herself whether anything other than purely functional considerations could have been relevant when the specific feature of the overall body shape was chosen, would not believe that the aesthetic function of the cartridge was a relevant factor and that the purpose of this specific body shape of the product is also to enhance its visual appearance. The reasonable observer does not care whether the product which he/she will not actually even see before having purchased the product and opened it, and he/she will also not see (except for one edge) once the cartridge is put to use inside the game console, looks good, bad, ugly or pretty. All that matters is the content of the cartridge (the game itself) and that the product functions well with the game console.

The Board of Appeal found that the essential features of the cartridge design had been chosen for their functionality, and the registration was invalid. In its judgment, it made clear that even where there are other designs which might achieve the same function as the RCD, this was irrelevant; a similar approach to that taken by the CJEU in the case of trade marks consisting of functional shapes. Clearly, in both cases, the concern has been to prevent registration from creating monopolies. Do you think the position regarding designs and shape marks are synonymous in this way? After all, while the period of protection given by trade mark registration may be open-ended, registration of a design lasts only for a limited period of time.

14.2.3.4 The definition of prior art

In *Green Lane Products*, the Court of Appeal was asked how the Design Regulation views 'prior art' and, in particular, when, under the terms of the regulation, a design would have been made available to the public and hence lack the novelty and individual character which is required both for registration and infringement. The particular article of the regulation for which the parties in the case sought elucidation was Article 7 and the phrase, 'the circles specialised in the sector concerned'. Article 7 reads:

> For the purpose of applying Articles 5 [on novelty] and 6 [on individual character], a design shall be deemed to have been made available to the public if it has been published following registration or otherwise, or exhibited, used in trade or otherwise disclosed … except where these events could not reasonably have become known in the normal course of business to the circles specialised in the sector concerned, operating within the Community.

Green Lane arose as an appeal from a judgment given by Lewison J in the High Court.[35]

Green Lane Products v PMS International Group, PMS International Far East Ltd, Poundland Ltd [2008] FSR 28

Green Lane made and sold spiky plastic balls to be used in tumble driers under the trade mark 'Dryerballs'. In 2004, Green Lane had registered the design of the Dryerballs as a RCD. The application date was 24 August 2004. The purpose of the balls was to soften

---

[35] *Green Lane Products v PMS International Group, PMS International Far East Ltd, Poundland Ltd* [2008] FSR 1.

the fabrics and to separate the laundry in the drier. Some of the balls were pink with rounded nodes; others were green with square nodes. PMS also marketed spiky plastic balls, although these were intended as massage balls not laundry balls. The balls were made in China and had been extensively marketed in the EU since 2002. In 2006, PMS sold its massage balls for other purposes, including as a laundry ball but also as a hand exerciser and a dog trainer. Green Lane alleged that PMS would infringe its RCD unless they sold their product only as massage balls. In return, PMS alleged that Green Lane's RCD was invalid because of the prior sale of their massage balls. The claimant replied that: (1) such prior art is irrelevant as a matter of law; and (2) even if it is relevant, their RCDs are nonetheless valid. In beginning his judgment, Jacob LJ set out the arguments of the parties as to how Article 7 should be construed.

Jacob LJ:

6. Green Lane says that the extent of its rights under its CRDs are defined by Art. 10— *any* article, whatever its intended purpose, will infringe unless it does not produce on the informed user a different overall impression. The only reason why continued sales by PMS of balls for massage purposes do not infringe is that such sales are protected by Art. 22.[36] Even then such sales are protected only to the extent provided by that Article.

7. PMS says the design registrations are not 'new' within the meaning of Art. 5 or do not have 'individual character' within the meaning of Art. 6. They say this is so because of their own prior sales in the EU of what, for all practical purposes is the very design complained of. In short they say the design is old.

8. Now absent Art. 7 one would say that PMS are right: that a design cannot be 'new' or have 'individual character' if it is the same or practically the same as an article previously used in trade. But, say Green Lane, a design may be new or have individual character even if it is fact old: Art. 7 says that a prior design is not taken to be made available to the public, even if it in reality was, where 'these events [i.e. prior use in trade] could not reasonably have become known in the normal course of business to the circles specialised in the sector concerned, operating in the Community'.

9. And, says Green Lane, the 'sector concerned' means the sector for which the design was registered, not the sector of the alleged prior art.

As identified by Jacob LJ, the exact question being asked by the parties was whether when judging the novelty of a registered design, one looks only at the class of goods for which it is registered, as argued by Green Lane. Or, alternatively, one looks at the class of goods of the allegedly infringing party. Or, indeed, does one, as in patent law, look at all 'prior' art. According to Lewison J in his judgment, the sector concerned under Article 7 is the sector which consists of or includes the sector of the alleged prior art. The circles specialized in the sector consist of those individuals who trade in the products in the relevant sector, including those who, inter alia, design, make, and market such products in the EU. Jacob LJ upheld the ruling of Lewison J as 'clearly right'. He pointed to the fact that such a ruling is supported by the language of the regulation, its recitals, and the *travaux préparatoires*. He also compared the language of the regulation with the

---

[36] Art. 22 raises a defence of prior use if use of a design had been undertaken by a third party in good faith before the application for a registered design is filed.

relevant patent law regarding prior art and concluded that the meaning of the prior art is the same for both patents and registered designs.

Jacob LJ:

19. Turning now to the requirements for protection, the basic rule, is that a design must be 'new' and have 'individual character' (Art. 4.1). Art. 5 elaborates on what is meant by 'new' and Art. 6 on what is meant by 'individual character'. In both cases the test involves consideration of an earlier design, that is a design which 'has been made available to the public'.

20. This is a clear incorporation of a key concept and well-known language of patent law defining the prior art which may be used to attack validity of a patent. An invention is 'new' if it is not part of the 'state of the art'. The 'state of the art shall be held to comprise everything made available to the public by means of a written or oral description, by use, or in any other way before [the relevant date]' (see Art. 54 of the European Patent Convention). I shall use the expression conventionally used for this test: 'absolute novelty'....

24. Both sides accept that 'made available to the public' in the conventional patent law sense is also the basic rule for identifying prior art which may be considered for the purpose of attacking the validity of designs...

...

27. It is particularly important to realise that the scope of protection covers any use of the design for an article, whatever its intended purpose. The scope provision, unlike for instance the previous law of the UK (s. 7 of the Registered Designs Act 1949) does not limit infringement to 'articles for which the design is registered' or anything like that. So if you register a design for a car you can stop use of the design for a brooch or a cake or a toy, or if you register a textile design you can stop its use on wallpaper, a shirt or a plate.

Jacob LJ then considered the *travaux préparatoires* in relation to Article 7 which he found as supporting the view that prior art in relation to designs mirrored the meaning of prior art in patent law. He took the view that there would be 'absurd' consequences for the law relating to the RCD if the Green Lane contention was correct, and the relevant prior art was to be found only in the type of products on which the RCD was to be used. To illustrate these 'absurd' consequences, Jacob LJ reproduced some possible scenarios which in the first instance had been described by Lewison J. The following is a fair example:

Jacob LJ:

75. There are a number of potential consequences of Green Lane's interpretation which suggest that it is wrong. First, consider the form of the application. Suppose a designer produces a design of a product which can be used for a multitude of purposes or products, each of which is in a different product class. Call the classes A, B, C and D; and assume that circles specialised in one class do not know about designs in the other classes. The design is both old and well-known in circles specialising in class D. If Dr Lawrence [for Green Lane] is right, then the registration will be invalid if the applicant for registration specifies all four classes (or class D alone); but it will be valid if he only specifies class A. Yet once registered, the registration gives him a monopoly extending across all four classes. So the canny applicant will specify the products to which the design is intended to be applied in the narrowest possible

way, so as to avoid exposing his design to prior art, confident in the expectation that once the design has been registered he will obtain the wide protection given to him by the registration.

...

77. These examples are realistic. Mr Vaughan [for Green Lane] did not really contend otherwise. And he could not find any fault with them. His answer was to suggest that the alternative construction also produced absurd results. First it would involve difficult questions of searching and second that the right holder might find his registration lost by reason of prior art which he could not reasonably learn about because the validity of a design could be challenged on the basis of any prior art in any field unless it was obscure in its own field.

78. I do not accept either point as absurd. As to the practicalities of searching, it has always been the case that design searches are not easy—most prior designs are not registered and so not readily searchable as, for instance, patent literature is. Yet the system has worked well for a long time with absolute novelty in many countries, for instance under the prior UK system.

79. But of even more fundamental significance is this: the right gives a monopoly over any kind of goods according to the design. It makes complete sense that the prior art available for attacking novelty should also extend to all kinds of goods, subject only to the limited exception of prior art obscure even in the sector from which it comes.

In *Green Lane*, the court held that the sector concerned was the sector from which the prior design came not the sector from which the registered design came. In doing so, the court clearly sought to limit the monopoly afforded by registration. It is possible to sympathize with Green Lane's argument that it will be extremely difficult for an applicant to ensure that there is no prior art when seeking to register a design, if that prior art might arise in any sector of goods. But is it not a stronger argument that to limit prior art to the sector concerned would allow for design registrations in one sector which could then be used to stifle designs in other sectors? Certainly, in this case the courts found such an outcome not only logically 'absurd' but also offering too great a penumbra of protection to registered designs.

14.2.3.5 Infringement I: the informed user and the overall impression

In cases of infringement, most of the key aspects of registered design protection which have been examined thus far will inevitably come into play. For example, in *Samsung v Apple*, these included but were not limited to the identification of the informed user and the overall impressions created by the RCD and the allegedly infringing object. After considering *Samsung v Apple*, this chapter will turn to *Magmatic v PMS*, a recent Supreme Court decision, which focuses on arguably the most fundamental question in any infringement action: how to identify the design which is alleged to have been infringed.

Samsung Electronics (UK) Ltd v Apple Inc. [2012] EWHC 1882 (Pat)

The defendant, Apple, had a Community registered design for a tablet computer. The claimant, Samsung, sought a declaration that three of its Galaxy tablet computers did not infringe the Apple RCD. Apple counterclaimed for infringement. In this case, the validity of the registration was not in issue.

Birss J:

3. Samsung contends that its tablets do not infringe. It submits that when the registered design is understood in its proper context, bearing in mind the existing design corpus and the degree of freedom of the designer, the overall impression the Apple design produces on the informed user is a different one from that produced by any of the three Samsung tablets.

4. Apple does not agree. It agrees that the registered design must be understood properly bearing in mind the existing design corpus and the degree of freedom of the designer but contends that when that exercise is carried out, the result is that the overall impression produced on the informed user by each Samsung tablet is not a different one from that produced by the registered design.

[Birss J then considered the Apple and the Samsung designs:]

9. Looking at the Apple design itself, what strikes the eye immediately is its simplicity. The article is unadorned and tile shaped. The large faces are blank with the screen on one side and the back completely blank. Image 0001.3 looks at the article in plan view if it was sitting on a table: the corners are rounded; there is a rim around the whole edge....The side views show that the article is quite thin (images 0001.2, 0001.5, 0001.6, 0001.7) and also show that the edges form a right angle (90°) to the front face but a curve to the back face.

The Samsung Tablets

12. The Samsung Galaxy tablets are at Annex B. They are very thin tile shaped articles. The front face is quite blank. In plan view the corners are rounded, there is a rim around the edge and a border around the screen. The edges of the article are curved, so that they bulge outwards somewhat. The sides have buttons. The back surfaces of the three Samsung tablets differ. (Their backs are different and they differ in size).

Apple had submitted that there were six similarities between their design and the Samsung tablets, among these were that they shared a thin profile and a substantially flat rear surface. Birss J then considered the relevant case law. In particular, he chose to adopt Arnold J's interpretation in *Dyson v Vax* of Article 8(1) CDR regarding the functional aspects of a registered design. He went on to set out what he saw as the correct overall approach to judging whether the two designs created a different overall impression.

53. The exercise must start with identifying the informed user and the existing design corpus. The overall impression is something produced on the informed user.

54. Although the outcome depends on overall impression, as a practical matter the design must be broken down into features. Each feature needs to be considered in order to give it appropriate significance or weight. Each feature needs to be considered in three respects. A feature dictated solely by function is to be disregarded. As long as it is not disregarded, each feature must be considered against the design corpus and it must be considered from the point of view of design freedom.

55. Since this case is concerned with infringement only and not validity, the list of features is a list of similarities said to exist between the design and the alleged infringement. Aside from considering similarities, the differences between the design and the alleged infringement

also need to be addressed and weighted. For all the similarities and differences, the weighting exercise is concerned with assessing the significance of the similarity to the informed user. Things which look the same because all the products in the class look that way do not excite the informed user's interest to the same extent as unusual features.

56. Taking into account the similarities and differences, appropriately weighted, the court can decide whether the alleged infringement produces a different overall impression on the informed user from that produced by the registered design.

57. The point of design protection must be to reward and encourage good product design by protecting the skill, creativity and labour of product designers. This effort is different from the work of artists. The difference between a work of art and a work of design is that design is concerned with both form and function. However design law is not seeking to reward advances in function. That is the sphere of patents. Function imposes constraints on a designer's freedom which do not apply to an artist. Things which look the same because they do the same thing are not examples of infringement of design right.

58. How similar does the alleged infringement have to be to infringe? Community design rights are not simply concerned with anti-counterfeiting. One could imagine a design registration system which was intended only to allow for protection against counterfeits. In that system only identical or nearly identical products would infringe. The test of 'different overall impression' is clearly wider than that. The scope of protection of a Community registered design clearly can include products which can be distinguished to some degree from the registration. On the other hand the fact that the informed user is particularly observant and the fact that designs will often be considered side by side are both clearly intended to narrow the scope of design protection. Although no doubt minute scrutiny by the informed user is not the right approach, attention to detail matters.

Birss J then turned to the specific question of whether the Samsung tablet produced a different overall impression on the informed user than that of the Apple design. He first identified the informed user. He would be a user of tablet computers. He would be interested in the functioning of the products concerned, how they worked, and their performance. In this particular case, the informed user would also be someone interested in the aesthetics. He would consider the products side by side. Birss J then identified the existing design corpus and the design freedom in relation to each of the similarities claimed by Apple. He summarized the overall impression of the Apple design on the informed user and compared it to that made by the Samsung design:

182. The extreme simplicity of the Apple design is striking. Overall it has undecorated flat surfaces with a plate of glass on the front all the way out to a very thin rim and a blank back. There is a crisp edge around the rim and a combination of curves, both at the corners and the sides. The design looks like an object the informed user would want to pick up and hold. It is an understated, smooth and simple product. It is a cool design.

The overall impressions compared

183. I remind myself that the informed user is particularly observant, shows a relatively high degree of attention and in this case conducts a direct comparison between the products.

184. To my eye the most important similarities are as follows:

i) The view from the front is really very striking. The Galaxy tablets are not identical to the Apple design but they are very, very similar in this respect. The Samsung tablets use the very same screen, with a flat glass plate out to a very thin rim and a plain border under the glass.

ii) Also neither Apple nor Samsung have indicator lights or buttons on the front surface or obvious switches or fittings on the other surfaces. There are some subtle buttons on the edges of the Galaxy tablets but they do not contribute to the overall impression. There is an overall simplicity about the Samsung devices albeit not as extreme as the simplicity of the Apple design.

iii) The thinness enhancing effect of the sides creates the same impression. It causes both the Apple design and the Galaxy tablets to appear to float above the surface on which they rest. However the details of the side edges are not the same. The Apple design has a pronounced flat side face which the informed user would see clearly (and feel). It is absent from the Samsung tablets.

Birss J then identified the major differences. The most prominent were that the Samsung tablets were thinner and had different detailing on the backs. With regard to the former, he held that to an informed user, the Galaxy tablets did not merely look like a thin version of the Apple design, they looked like a different, thinner design of product. With regard to the backs, he held that here there was considerable design freedom, and the use of detail on the back of the Samsung tablet would strike the informed user as unusual. He then asked whether these two differences were enough to overcome the similarity of the front and the overall shape of the tablets. He held that they were. He concluded:

190. The informed user's overall impression of each of the Samsung Galaxy Tablets is the following. From the front they belong to the family which includes the Apple design; but the Samsung products are very thin, almost insubstantial members of that family with unusual details on the back. They do not have the same understated and extreme simplicity which is possessed by the Apple design. They are not as cool. The overall impression produced is different.

Conclusion

191. The Samsung tablets do not infringe Apple's registered design No. 000181607-0001.

The decision in *Apple v Samsung* has been criticized by some commentators because it appears to suggest that it is precisely because the iPad design is 'cool' that it produces a different overall impression on the informed user. In other words, had Apple's design been less or Samsung's design more 'cool', would Apple have succeeded in establishing infringement? Apple appealed the decision.[37] When the case came to the Court of Appeal, Jacob LJ endorsed Birss J's judgment in its entirety, agreeing that a publicity order should be granted against Apple, and that for a month it should publicize, on its website, that the British courts had decided that the Samsung products did not infringe the Apple design.

[37] *Samsung Electronics (UK) Ltd v Apple Inc.* [2012] EWCA Civ 1339.

14.2.3.6 Infringement II: the definition of the design

The infringement case of *Magmatic v PMS* had less to do with how the designs at issue would be perceived by users and more to do with what was actually protected by the registration. According to Jacob LJ in *Procter & Gamble*:[38]

> 3. The most important things in a case about registered designs are:
>
> (i) The registered design;
>
> (ii) The accused object;
>
> (iii) The prior art.
>
> And the most important thing about each of these is what they look like.

Magmatic v PMS was concerned precisely with this question: what do the registered design and the accused object look like? Such a question may appear otiose given that to register a design it is necessary to provide a visual image or images of that design. But as *Magmatic* shows, such images may be interpreted in crucially different ways. The recognition of this fact, following *Magmatic*, has important implications for precisely how much protection is accorded to a design through registration.

PMS International Group Plc v Magmatic Ltd [2016] UKSC 12; [2016] RPC 11

The case concerned an alleged infringement of Magmatic's RCD for a ride-on suitcase for children sold under the trade mark, 'Trunki'. The RCD which dates from 2003 consists of six monochrome computer images, from various perspectives, of the suitcase showing grey shading and tonal contrasts between the case, the strap, and the wheels. One of the striking features of the RCD is that the handles and the clasps give the suitcase the appearance of a horned animal. When it was first sold, the Trunki had no ornamentation and this is reflected in the RCDs. Later on the Trunki was sold with coloured ornamentation such as noses and spots. The defendant imported and sold in the UK and Germany a 'Kiddee Case'. The Kiddee Case shares a number of features with the RCD, for instance it is also designed to look like an animal and has a saddle-shaped top for riding. But it has differences. Among these are: its bright colouring, having eyes, spots and circles, stripes, and whiskers; its covered wheels and an unsculptured ridge at the top; two protuberances at the front designed to be ears not horns; and a ridge along the front, centre, and rear but of a different shape to the RCD. Previous to the Trunki, the claimant had sold an earlier version of a child's ride-on suitcase called the 'Rodeo'. The defendant argued that if the RCD was broad enough to cover the Kiddee Case then it was also broad enough to cover the Rodeo and hence would be invalid because of prior art. In the High Court, Arnold J held that the Kiddee Case infringed the claimant's RCD. He held that it was substantially similar to the RCD. He also rejected the argument that if the RCD were infringed then it was similar to the Rodeo and hence invalid. Instead, he held that the RCD and the Rodeo produced different overall impressions and that the Rodeo did not form part of the prior art as its disclosure was too limited. With regard to the infringement, Arnold J identified the informed user as the parent, carer, or relative

---

[38] [2007] EWCA Civ 936.

of a three- to six-year-old child. He held that in comparing the RCD to the infringing design, the surface decorations on the Kiddee Case could be ignored and that the proper comparison was the shape of the Kiddee Case and of the Trunki. Looking simply at the shapes, he held that the Kiddee Case created the same overall impression. The question arose as to whether Arnold J was correct to understand the RCD as representing a shape alone, not taking into account surface decoration, given the tonal contrasts in the photographs; and, second, whether if surface decoration were taken into account, would the Kiddee Case be infringing? The Court of Appeal overturned Arnold J's decision and Magmatic appealed to the Supreme Court. An additional question raised by Magmatic and addressed to the Supreme Court was whether it was necessary to seek an opinion from the CJEU on whether the absence of surface decoration on a registered design should be understood to be a feature of that design and, if so, how should that be made clear. Lord Neuberger began by addressing the central question which is what is meant by a 'design' in the CDR (which he terms the 'Principal Regulation').

The images incorporated in a Community Registered Design

30. Article 3(a) of the Principal Regulation identifies what is meant by 'design', and, unsurprisingly, it refers to the appearance, which is expressed to include a number of different factors, all, some or one of which can be included in a particular registered design. It is, of course, up to an applicant as to what features he includes in his design application. He can make an application based on all or any of 'the lines, contours, colours, shape, texture ... materials ... and/or ... ornamentation' of 'the product' in question. Further, he can make a large number of different applications, particularly as the Principal Regulation itself provides that applications for registration have to be cheap and simple to make. As Lewison J put it in *Procter & Gamble Co v Reckitt Benckiser (UK) Ltd* [2007] FSR 13, para 48, '[t]he registration holder is entitled to choose the level of generality at which his design is to be considered. If he chooses too general a level, his design may be invalidated by prior art. If he chooses too specific a level he may not be protected against similar designs'. So, when it comes to deciding the extent of protection afforded by a particular Community Registered Design, the question must ultimately depend on the proper interpretation of the registration in issue, and in particular of the images included in that registration.

31. Accordingly, it is right to bear in mind that an applicant for a design right is entitled, within very broad limits, to submit any images which he chooses. Further, in the light of article 36(6), an applicant should appreciate that it will almost always be those images which exclusively identify the nature and extent of the monopoly which he is claiming....

Lord Neuberger then turned to the specific criticisms which Lord Justice Kitchin, in the Court of Appeal, had made of Arnold J's judgment. He identified three. The first is that Arnold J failed to give proper weight to the overall impression of the RCD which is as a horned animal and hence a contrast to that given by the Kiddee Case which is either an insect with antennae or an animal with ears. Lord Neuberger agreed with the Court of Appeal that Arnold J was wrong not to have emphasized this contrast. The second criticism made by the Court of Appeal was that Arnold J failed to take into account the effect of the lack of ornamentation on the surface of the RCD. Again Lord Neuberger agreed with the Court of Appeal. He accepted Kitchin LJ's view that the fact that the RCD was unadorned strengthened the impression it gave of its being a horned animal and therefore underlined its contrast with the Kiddee Cases, whose shapes along with their colouring gave a very different impressions of, respectively, a ladybird with antennae and a tiger with ears. Lord Neuberger then looked at how the lack of surface ornamentation had been dealt with in the previous case of *Samsung v Apple*:

47. The notion that absence of ornamentation can be a feature of a registered design, even where the images consist of line drawings, was accepted by His Honour Judge Birss QC and the Court of Appeal (albeit that it was not in dispute between the parties in the case) in *Samsung Electronics (UK) Ltd v Apple Inc* [2013] ECDR 1 and [2013] FSR 9. In that case, the line drawings included one or two small features (an opening catch and a rim around the edge), and the natural implication was that no other ornamentation was intended, a view supported by the fact that the plainness and transparency of the surface was subtly indicated by a few pairs of short lines suggesting the incidence of light on that surface. As Jacob LJ put it at para 18 in that case, 'If an important feature of a design is *no* ornamentation, as Apple contended and was undisputed, the judge was right to say that a departure from no ornamentation would be taken into account by the informed user'.

Lord Neuberger concluded on this second criticism:

50. It is right, however, to address the argument whether absence of ornamentation was a feature of the CRD in the present case. There are powerful practical arguments against such a conclusion, namely the absence of any apparent reason for such a limitation and the inherent unlikelihood of the design of a child's ride-on suitcase positively requiring no ornamentation. On the other hand, there is the elegant uncluttered appearance of the CRD with the play of light on the product's surface as described by Kitchin LJ, the use of a CAD rather than a line drawing, the existence of some specific limited colour differentiation (the strap, strips, wheels and spokes), and (in so far as admissible) the initial unornamented product and the contrast with Magmatic's subsequent registered designs (see para 3 above). Given that the Court of Appeal did not (despite Magmatic's suggestion to the contrary) resolve this issue in the present case and it is unnecessary for us to do so in order to resolve this appeal, I would prefer to leave it open. It is not as if a decision whether the absence of ornamentation in this particular CRD would be of much assistance in other cases; it is, I think, enough that we have decided (albeit on a strictly obiter basis) the point of principle that absence of ornamentation can be a feature of a Community Registered Design.

Lord Neuberger then turned to the Court of Appeal's third criticism of Arnold J:

51. Kitchin LJ's third criticism of Arnold J's judgment was that he failed to take into account the fact that the CRD image, as exemplified in para 1 above, was in two colours, one, shown grey, for the greater part of the body (including the horns), and the other, shown black, for the wheels and spokes, the strap and the strip. As mentioned in para 14 above, Arnold J described the CRD as constituting a claim 'evidently for the shape of the suitcase' and that decorations on the Kiddee Case were therefore to be ignored. On the other hand, Kitchin LJ's view was that the colouring contrasts on the CRD and the allegedly infringing articles represented a potentially significant difference, as the wheels and handles (ie horns) on the CRD rather stood out as features, whereas on the Kiddee Case the wheels were very largely covered, and the handles (at least on the first of the two examples in para 4 above) had the same colour as the body.

52. If, as in the case of the CRD, an applicant for a Community Registered Design elects to submit CADs of an item, whose main body appears as a uniform grey, but which has a black strip, a black strap and black wheels, the natural inference is that the components shown in black are intended to be in a contrasting colour to that of the main body. That conclusion is reinforced by the short passages from Dr Schlötelburg's article cited in paras 31 and 46 above. It is also supported, as Kitchin LJ pointed out, by the fact that other features such as the clasps or the horns are not shown in a contrasting colour. It was argued by Magmatic that the wheels were shown black because they had a specific function, but I find that unconvincing: there is no logical connection between the colour and the function, and it does not explain the black strip.

53. Accordingly, I consider that Kitchin LJ was right in concluding that the CRD claimed not merely a specific shape, but a shape in two contrasting colours—one represented as grey and the other as black on the images, and that Arnold J was correspondingly wrong in holding that the CRD was a claim simply for a shape. Once one concludes that a registered design claims not just a three dimensional shape, but a three dimensional shape in two contrasting colours, one colour for the body and another colour (or possibly other colours) for specified components, then it seems to me that it must follow that, when one compares the allegedly infringing article with that design on a 'like for like' basis, one must take into account the colouring on that article. If the predominant colour of the first example of the Kiddee Case shown in para 4 above was the front part and was coloured red, then one would presumably compare it with the CRD on the basis that the CRD was principally coloured red, but that the wheels and spokes, strap and strips of the CRD were in a contrasting colour, and the Kiddee Case was differently coloured.

54. I therefore consider that Kitchin LJ was right in his third criticism of the judge....

Finally, Lord Neuberger addressed the question of whether there should be a reference to the CJEU regarding how a registered design is understood to lack surface decoration.

60. It is appropriate in this context to refer back to Magmatic's contention that absence of ornamentation cannot be a feature of a Community Registered Design. I accept that that contention raises a point of EU law. However, I would not refer the point for two reasons. First, as explained in para 43 above, it does not arise on this appeal; secondly, as explained in paras 44–48 above, while the Comptroller suggests that the contention may be right, I cannot regard it as arguable. Minimalism can self-evidently be an important aspect of a design just as intensive decoration can be. It would be extraordinary if absence of ornamentation could not be a feature of a design, and, unsurprisingly, no authority has been cited to support such a proposition. On the contrary.

In concluding that the Kiddee Case was not infringing, Lord Neuberger stated that he had not reached this conclusion without regret given the original and clever design of the Trunki and the fact that PMS had been inspired by the Trunki design to create its own. However he also stated that 'this appeal is not concerned with an idea or an invention, but a design'.[39] The decisions both of the Court of Appeal and the Supreme Court have elicited considerable criticism, not least because they appear considerably to erode the certainty of the scope of protection afforded by a design registration. It has been argued that while the RCD

[39] [58].

covered an innovative and original shape, both the Court of Appeal and the Supreme Court held that it was the Kiddee Case's surface decoration which meant that it produced a different overall impression from the RCD. According to critics and to Arnold J in the High Court, the absence of surface decoration on the RCD should have been taken to mean that it was intended to be the shape alone which was protected by registration. Thus, if contrasts between different parts of a design are visible, as in this case, on a computer-generated grey-scale representation which would not be visible on a line drawing, this should not mean courts should understand the design at issue differently. A further point made by critics, although dismissed by both the Court of Appeal and the Supreme Court, is that even allowing for the different understanding in the High Court as to what is represented by the RCD, Arnold J's opinion as to the overall impression it created was justified on the facts and should not have been overturned by an appeal court. Although Lord Neuberger differentiated a design registration from a patent or an idea, we might wonder if it is right, as this decision suggests, that simply by placing surface decoration on a highly original shape a third party can escape a finding of infringement. *Magmatic* also suggests the importance of ensuring that the representation of a RCD is precise and not open to misinterpretation. However, is it not possible to argue that this was exactly what Magmatic sought to do when it submitted its six representations of its design?

> **FURTHER READING**
>
> P. Arrowsmith, 'The relevance of the product in the scope of registered designs' (2013) 8 JIPLP 876.
>
> O. Brancusi, 'Designs determined by the product's technical function: arguments for an autonomous test' [2016] EIPR 23.
>
> P. G. F. A. Geerts, 'The informed user in design law: what should he compare and how should he make the comparison?' [2014] EIPR 181.
>
> M. Marell, 'CJEU defines "informed user" concept in Pepsi registered community design dispute' (2012) 25 WIPR 40.
>
> D. Smyth, 'How is the scope of protection of a registered Community design to be determined?' (2013) 8 JIPLP 270.

14.3 UNREGISTERED DESIGN RIGHT

14.3.1 THE COMMUNITY UNREGISTERED DESIGN RIGHT (CUDR)

The Design Regulation as well as introducing a Community registered design (RCD) also introduced a Community unregistered design right (CUDR). For the most part the regulation treats both the RCD and the CUDR in essentially the same manner. Thus, the meanings of a 'design', 'product', and 'complex product' are the same for both Community designs. So too are the requirements for protection: most notably, the need for novelty (Article 5) and individual character (Article 6). Similarly, the rights endowed on proprietors are the same for both Community designs, so that the scope of protection extends to any design that does not produce on the informed user a different overall impression (Article 10(1)). And, in assessing whether this is so, the designer's degree of freedom will be taken into account

(Article 10(2)). As a result, the CJEU's decision in *PepsiCo* and the Court of Appeal's decision in *Green Lane*, which defined the various terms used in the Design Regulation, for example the informed user in relation to RCDs, should apply equally to CUDRs. Furthermore, the limitations on the rights conferred by an RCD, most notably that there will be no protection for designs dictated by their technical functions or their need to fit with a product which allows the product to function, also applies to both Community designs (Article 8). There are, however, two key differences between the RCD and the CUDR. The first is that a CUDR will only be infringed if infringement results from direct or indirect copying (as is the case in copyright law). Second, a CUDR is only protected for three years from the date on which the design was first made available (or disclosed) to the public within the Community (Article 11). In his article, 'The unregistered community design', Victor Saez identifies the circumstances in which the Community unregistered design may be of use.

V. Saez, 'The unregistered community design' [2002] EIPR 585 at 585

Why an Unregistered Design?

The introduction of a short-term protection system which dispenses with red tape is one of the foundations of this novel form of design protection. In order properly to understand the role played by the unregistered design within the Community system under the Regulation, however, it is necessary to bear in mind that the intention is not to create an alternative system parallel to that of the registered design. Instead, the goal is a system of subsidiary protection which helps to overcome the inevitable shortcomings of the Community registered design.

The main reasons for including this form of protection in the Regulation on Community designs may be summarised as follows:

— Providing industry with prompt design protection, permitting it to market test the products into which the design is incorporated immediately and at no extra cost, while still maintaining the option of more lasting, comprehensive protection by registration. Protection as an unregistered Community design thus complements the 12-month period of grace provided by the Regulation.

— Providing protection for designs which are not intended to remain on the market for very long and for which registration was never contemplated.

At this stage it is not possible to assess in economic terms the real impact that the unregistered design right may have. On the one hand, by the very nature of this right it is not possible to say how many designs will make use of the protection it provides. On the other, this right will provide protection for many designs for which registration has been ruled out from the outset and which, for this reason are not currently protected by any design right.

Saez is of course right to suggest that it will be difficult to measure the value of a CUDR, since by its very nature it subsists in qualifying designs automatically and will only come into play if a proprietor believes his unregistered design has been infringed. It is certainly possible that the existence of the CUDR may act as a deterrent against copying. But it also has to be recognized that such a right might have a chilling effect on the emergence of new designs. The CJEU decision in *Karen Millen v Dunnes Stores* considered the related questions of how to determine whether a CUDR is valid and how to assess its individual character. It is submitted that this decision directly addresses the potential conflict of interest between the design holder and its competitors which is identified above.

Karen Millen Fashions Ltd v Dunnes Stores and another Case C-345/13, EU:C:2014:2013 [2014] Bus. L. R. 756

The case looked at the issues of 'individual character in industrial designs' (Article 6 of the regulation) and also the conditions for the protection of a registered design (Article 11 of the regulation). In doing so it also considered Section 4 of Part II at Article 25 of the TRIPS Agreement in relation to industrial designs which requires that:

> 1. Members shall provide for the protection of independently created industrial designs that are new or original. Members may provide that designs are not new or original if they do not significantly differ from known designs or combinations of known design features. Members may provide that such protection shall not extend to designs dictated essentially by technical or functional considerations...

And it looked at the interpretation of Article 85(2) of the Design Regulation which states that:

> In proceedings in respect of an infringement action or an action for threatened infringement of an unregistered Community design, the Community design court shall treat the Community design as valid if the right holder produces proof that the conditions laid down in article 11 have been met and indicates what constitutes the individual character of his Community design. However, the defendant may contest its validity by way of a plea or with a counterclaim for a declaration of invalidity.

The claimant, KMF, produces and sells women's clothing. The defendant also sells women's clothing. Both have substantial business. KMF is incorporated in England and Wales but has stores in Ireland. Dunnes' stores are located in Ireland. In 2005, KMF designed a striped shirt (in blue and stone brown) and a black knit top, which they placed on the Irish market. Dunnes bought samples of the KMF garments, had copies made, and offered them for sale in their stores. KMF sued Dunnes for infringement in the Irish High Court alleging that the defendant had infringed its unregistered design right in the garments. KMF succeeded in the High Court. Dunnes appealed to the Supreme Court. Dunnes accepted that it had copied the KMF garments but argued that KMF did not have a CUDR in the garments as they do not have individual character within the meaning of the regulation and, further, that it was up to KMF to prove that they did. The Irish court addressed two questions to the CJEU:

> 22 ...'1. In consideration of the individual character of a design which is claimed to be entitled to be protected as an unregistered Community design for the purposes of [Regulation No 6/2002], is the overall impression it produces on the informed user, within the meaning of article 6 of that Regulation, to be considered by reference to whether it differs from the overall impression produced on such a user by: (a) any individual design which has previously been made available to the public, or (b) any combination of known design features from more than one such earlier design?

'2. Is a Community design court obliged to treat an unregistered Community design as valid for the purposes of article 85(2) of [Regulation No 6/2002] where the right holder merely indicates what constitutes the individual character of the design or is the right holder obliged to prove that the design has individual character in accordance with article 6 of that Regulation?'

In answering the first question, the CJEU noted:

24 There is nothing in the wording of article 6 of Regulation No 6/2002 to support the view that the overall impression referred to therein must be produced by such a combination.

25 The reference to the overall impression produced on the informed user by 'any design' which has been made available to the public indicates that article 6 must be interpreted as meaning that the assessment as to whether a design has individual character must be conducted in relation to one or more specific, individualised, defined and identified designs from among all the designs which have been made available to the public previously.

26 As observed by the United Kingdom Government and the Commission of the European Union ('EU'), that interpretation is in keeping with the case law in which it has been held that, when possible, the informed user will make a direct comparison between the designs at issue (see judgment in *PepsiCo Inc v Grupo Promer Mon-Graphic SA* (Case C-281/10P) [2011] ECR I-10153, para 55 and *Neuman v José Manuel Baena Grupo SA* (Joined Cases C-101/11P and C-102/11P) [2013] ECDR 76, para 54), because that type of comparison actually relates to the impression produced on that user by earlier individualised and defined designs, as opposed to an amalgam of specific features or parts of earlier designs.

The CJEU went further to hold, following *PepsiCo*, that there is nothing in the regulation which limits the assessment of potential designs to a direct comparison and it is also possible to base a comparison on 'imperfect' recollections of the overall impressions produced by the designs.[40] It continued:

29 Moreover, and as observed by the Advocate General in points 48 to 50 of his opinion, such an indirect comparison, which is based on an imperfect recollection, is not based on a recollection of specific features from several different earlier designs but of specific designs.

30 The arguments put forward by Dunnes do not cast any doubt on the foregoing considerations.

The CJEU then noted that even though the expressions 'the existing design corpus' and 'comparison with other designs' is to be found in the recital to the regulation, it has no legal force, not least because the former phrase is not to be found in the provisions of the regulation.[41] Furthermore, in Article 25 of TRIPS the phrase 'combination of known design features' is optional. It continued:

34 …[C]onsequently, the parties to that agreement are not required to provide for the novel character or originality of a design to be assessed in comparison with such combinations.

---

[40] [27]–[28].   [41] [31]–[32].

35 In those circumstances, the answer to the first question is that article 6 of Regulation No 6/2002 must be interpreted as meaning that, in order for a design to be considered to have individual character, the overall impression which that design produces on the informed user must be different from that produced on such a user not by a combination of features taken in isolation and drawn from a number of earlier designs, but by one or more earlier designs, taken individually.

The CJEU then turned to the second question, which asks essentially whether it is up to the rightholder of an unregistered design to prove it has individual character. According to the CJEU:

37 It is apparent from the very wording of article 85(2) of Regulation No 6/2002 that, in order for an unregistered Community design to be treated as valid, the right holder of that design is required, first of all, to prove that the conditions laid down in article 11 of that Regulation have been met and, secondly, to indicate what constitutes the individual character of that design.

However, according to the CJEU, Article 85(2) of the regulation should be read as meaning that there is a presumption of validity of an unregistered (and indeed a registered design).[42] To oblige the unregistered design holder to prove that its design has individual character would go against this presumption.

43 In that context, it should be noted that the different procedures provided for in article 85 of Regulation No 6/2002 with regard to a registered Community design and an unregistered Community design arise from the need to determine, with regard to the latter, the date as from which the design at issue is covered by the protection under that Regulation and specifically what is covered, which, as there are no registration formalities, may be more difficult to identify in the case of an unregistered design than for a registered design.

44 Moreover, if article 85(2) of Regulation No 6/2002 were to be interpreted as meaning that an unregistered Community design may be treated as valid only if its holder proves that all of the conditions laid down in section 1 of Title II of that Regulation have been met, the possibility for the defendant to contest the validity of that design by way of a plea or with a counterclaim for a declaration of invalidity, as provided for in the second sentence of article 85(2), would be rendered largely meaningless and nugatory.

But the CJEU held that it is necessary for the design holder to identify what constitutes the individual character of the design. It concluded:

46 Although, given the lack of registration formalities for this category of design, it is necessary for the holder of the design at issue to specify what he wants to have protected under that Regulation, it is sufficient for him to identify the features of his design which give it individual character.

[42] [39]–[42].

> 47 In those circumstances, the answer to the second question is that article 85(2) of Regulation No 6/2002 must be interpreted as meaning that, in order for a Community design court to treat an unregistered Community design as valid, the right holder of that design is not required to prove that it has individual character within the meaning of article 6 of that Regulation, but need only indicate what constitutes the individual character of that design, that is to say, indicates what, in his view, are the element or elements of the design concerned which give it its individual character.

Do you think that the CJEU's decision that, while a CUDR is assumed to have individual character, the design holder must identify where that individual character resides, strikes a fair balance between the rights of the design holder and its competitors? Or does the presumption that a CUDR will have individual character set the bar for protection too low?

14.3.2 THE UK UNREGISTERED DESIGN RIGHT (UDR)

Unlike the situation with registered designs, where UK law has been amended to reflect the Community Designs Directive and Regulation, the same is not true for the UDR in the UK. There has been no harmonization of unregistered designs in the EU. The UDR was introduced by the CDPA 1988 and the courts look to domestic rather than Community legislation when interpreting the relevant law. Nonetheless, the UK UDR does share a number of features with the CUDR. These include the fact that for both the UDR and the CUDR, protection arises automatically without the need for registration. Also, a UDR does not confer a 'monopoly right'. Rather, as with copyright, a UDR—like the CUDR—will be infringed only by copying. There are also major differences between a CUDR and a UDR. Unlike a CUDR which is protected for three years, protection for a UDR will run for 15 years from when it was first recorded or, if the design is marketed within the first five years, ten years from when it was first made available for sale (section 216 of the CDPA). Second, and these are perhaps the key differences between the UDR and the CUDR, the former has a 'must match' exclusion from protection, while the latter does not and the 'must fit' exception is of a different scope.[43] The changes to the UDR introduced by the Intellectual Property Act 2014 were intended both to simplify the UDR regime and to make it more compatible with the CUDR. These changes will be considered where relevant.

14.3.2.1 The statutory definitions

Section 213 of the CDPA[44] defines a UDR:

> (1) Design right is a property right which subsists in accordance with this Part in an original design.

and

> (2) In this Part 'design' means the design of any aspect of the shape or configuration (whether internal or external) of the whole or part of an article.

---

[43] This is discussed at 14.3.3.3.   [44] At Part III.

There are also exceptions to protection which are identified thus:

(3) Design right does not subsist in—

  (a) method or principle of construction,

  (b) features of shape or configuration of an article which—

    (i) enable the article to be connected to, or placed in, around or against, another article so that either article may perform its function, or

    (ii) are dependent upon the appearance of another article of which the article is intended by the designer to form an integral part, or

  (c) surface decoration.

Originality is defined as:

(4) A design is not 'original' for the purposes of this Part if it is commonplace in a qualifying country in the design field in question at the time of its creation; and 'qualifying country' has the meaning given in section 217(3).

The phrase 'qualifying country' was inserted into this provision by the Intellectual Property Act 2014 and includes the UK, the EU, or any country enjoying reciprocal protection.

14.3.2.2 Unregistered design right: authorship, ownership, and duration

The designer is the person who creates the design (section 214 (1) of the CDPA). In a similar approach to copyright, a UDR will not subsist unless or until the design has been recorded in a design document, or an article has been made to that design (section 213(6)). A design document can range from a drawing to data stored in a computer. The designer need not be the same person who records the design.[45]

    The designer is the first owner of a UDR. If the design was produced in the course of employment, ownership will reside with the employer (section 215) or, if the design was commissioned, with the commissionee. The design must be a 'qualifying' design. Whether or not it is qualifying will depend upon a number of factors including the nationality or residence of the designer.[46] A UDR lasts for a total of 15 years from when it is first recorded; or for ten years from when it was made available for sale, if it was marketed within the first five years (section 216). During the final five years of the ten-year period of protection (in other words from the date of first marketing), licences of right may be granted through an application to the UK IPO (section 237).

14.3.2.3 The relationship between the 'design' and the 'article'

According to its definition, a design may include the shape or configuration of the whole or part of the article. Before the changes made by the Intellectual Property Act 2014, design

---

[45] For a computer-generated design, the designer is the individual who makes the arrangements necessary for the creation of the design (s. 214(2)).

[46] CDPA, ss. 217–20.

right could also subsist in 'any aspect' of the shape or configuration of the whole or part of the article. In *Fulton v Totes Isotoner*,[47] a decision which preceded the 2014 Act, Jacob LJ quoted with approval the explanation in *Russell-Clarke & Howe on Industrial Designs* of the relationship between an article and a design.

> unlike a registered design, which protects the design applied to a whole article, unregistered design right subsists in the shape or configuration of part of an article, or indeed in 'any aspect' of the shape or configuration of the whole or part of the article. Thus, a single article (or a design document recording the design of an article) will normally embody not a single design right, but a large bundle of different design rights subsisting in the whole and every part and every aspect of the shape and configuration of the article, provided that the part or aspect concerned is original and is not otherwise excluded from enjoying design right by one of the exceptions considered in the following paragraphs. This concept of a bundle of design rights becomes significant when the question of infringement is considered, because, except in the case of slavish copying of the whole article, the design right proprietor will seek to match a design right which he can contend subsists in a part or aspect of the design of his article with the features of the alleged infringing article which he contends have been copied.

Or, as was put by Laddie J in *Ocular Sciences Ltd v Aspect Vision Care Ltd*:[48]

> If the right is said to reside in the design of a teapot, this can mean that it resides in the design of the whole pot, or in a part such as the spout, the handle or the lid, or, indeed, part of the lid.

However, the idea that a single article might embody a number of UDRs, on the basis that they are an 'aspect' of the whole or part of an article, was widely criticized; some suggesting that until a defendant received a letter before action, it was not possible to know in which parts of an article a UDR was said to subsist. As we have seen, similar concerns were raised regarding the issue of prior art in relation to registered designs. You may recall that in *Green Lane v PMS*, the defendant argued that it was difficult to gauge whether a design was infringing if what constituted the relevant prior art was broadly defined.[49] By removing protection from 'any aspect' of the shape or configuration of an article, the Intellectual Property Act 2014 has sought to address this area of uncertainty in relation to unregistered designs.

The newly amended definition of a design was considered by Hacon HHJ in *DKH Retail Ltd v H. Young (Operations) Ltd*. The case concerned a claim for infringement of a UDR in the claimant's hooded gilet, in particular its hood and collar arrangement. In fact, Hacon HHJ held that the court was not dealing with what might, before the amendment, be understood as an aspect of the shape but he nonetheless considered what changes the amended section 213 might make to cases involving UDRs.

---

[47] *Fulton Co. Ltd v Totes Isotoner (UK) Ltd* [2004] RPC 16, [20].

[48] *Ocular Sciences Ltd v Aspect Vision Care Ltd (No. 2)* [1997] RPC 289. See also Jacob LJ in *Dyson Ltd v Qualtex (UK) Ltd* [2006] RPC 31.

[49] See 14.2.3.4.

DKH Retail Ltd v H. Young (Operations) Ltd [2014] EWHC 4034 (IPEC)

11. The first step in assessing the effect of s.1(1) is to determine what the words taken out used to mean. In *Dyson Ltd v Qualtex (UK) Ltd* [2006] EWCA Civ 166; [2006] R.P.C. 31, Jacob LJ, with whom Lloyd and Tuckey LJJ agreed, said this:

'What is an "aspect of design"'?: the 'visually significant' point

22. So I turn to the individual points argued, of which this was the first. UDR can subsist in the 'design of any aspect of the shape or configuration (whether internal or external) of the whole or part of an article.' This is extremely wide—it means that a particular article may and generally will embody a multitude of 'designs'—as many 'aspects' of the whole or part of the article as can be. What the point was of defining 'design' in this way I do not know. The same approach is not adopted for ordinary copyright where the work is treated as a whole. But even with this wide definition, there is a limit: there must be an 'aspect' of at least a part of the article. What are the limits of that? I put it this way in *A. Fulton Co Ltd v Totes Isotoner (UK) Ltd* [2004] R.P.C. 16; [2003] EWCA Civ 1514 at [31]: 'The notion conveyed by "aspect" in the composite phrase ... is "discernible" or "recognisable" '.

...

12. It would seem that the reason for the extreme width of the definition of 'design', as Jacob LJ saw it, was that the definition of 'design' including the shape or configuration of any part of an article, in contrast with copyright which subsists in the copyright work as a whole. Jacob LJ appears to suggest that 'any aspect of' in s.213(2) has a *limiting* function, that is to say it excludes from the definition of 'design' a feature which is neither discernible nor recognisable. However on that basis the deletion of 'any aspect of' from s.213(2) would extend the scope of what qualifies as a design.

13. Plainly that is not what Parliament intended. Paragraph 10 of the explanatory notes at the end of the 2014 Act says this:

Subsection (1) limits the protection for trivial features of designs, by making sure that protection does not extend to 'any aspect' of the shape or configuration of the whole or part of an article. It is expected that this will reduce the tendency to overstate the breadth of unregistered design right and the uncertainty this creates, particularly in relation to actions before courts.

14. Ms Berkeley submitted that s.1(1) of the 2014 Act has no effect at all since before its entry into force design right could subsist in any part of an article and that is still the case. I do not accept that there has been no change—it would be contrary to the usual principles of statutory construction. I think I must assume that the subsection makes a difference and, guided by the explanatory note, I must further assume that the scope of what can constitute a design under s.213(2) has narrowed. The words 'any aspect of' permitted variations of what a party could claim as a design which are no longer available. Spotting why that might be is not easily done just by looking at the words of s.213(2).

Hacon HHJ goes on to suggest that the new definition of a 'design' brings it closer to the definition of a Community design set out in Article 3 of the Design Regulation, although this was not necessarily what Parliament intended. However, he states:

16 ... [F]or policy reasons of consistency where that can be achieved, there is much to be said for treating 'the design of the shape or configuration (whether internal or external) of the whole or part of an article' as having a meaning as close as possible to 'the appearance of the whole or part of a product' in the Regulation.

It remains to be seen whether the change in wording, reverting to Laddie J's example of the teapot, will allow for the protection of the lid of a teapot but not part of the lid. Indeed, the question arises whether, given the enormous importance of even small details of design for many of today's consumer goods (once again Apple's products spring to mind), and indeed for the discerning consumer, perhaps such an outcome although simplifying the law will not necessarily make it more just.

14.3.2.4 Unregistered design right and originality

A UDR will not subsist unless the design is original. A design is not original if it is 'commonplace in the design field in question at the time of its creation' (section 213(4) of the CDPA). *C. & H. Engineering v Klucznik & Sons*[50] was an early case to consider the meaning of 'original'. In this case, which involved the design of a 'pig fender', Aldous J defined originality:

At p. 421:

The word 'original' in section 213(1) is not defined, but I believe that it should be given the same meaning as the word 'original' in section 1(1)(a) of the Act,[51] namely not copied but the independent work of the designer. It should be contrasted with novelty which is the requirement for registration of a registered design: see section 265(4) of the Act.

Section 213(4) says that the design is not original if it is commonplace in the design field in question. The word 'commonplace' is not defined, but this subsection appears to introduce a consideration akin to novelty. For the design to be original it must be the work of the creator and that work must result in a design which is not commonplace in the relevant field. The designer is the creator and no design right will subsist until the design has been recorded in a document or in an article. Thus the creator is not necessarily the person who records the design but usually will be.

14.3.2.5 The definition of commonplace

The questions of what is meant by 'original' and 'commonplace' and how these concepts are related were looked at again, but this time by the Court of Appeal in *Farmers Build v Carrier Bulk Materials Handling*.

Farmers Build Ltd v Carrier Bulk Materials Handling Ltd [2000] ECDR 42

The claimants owned the intellectual property rights in a slurry separator, a machine which separates manure into solid and liquid parts for use as a fertilizer. The machine, the 'Target', had been designed in 1991 by the defendants, for the claimants. The Target's design was an improvement on the designs of two previous separators. In 1992, the defendants began manufacturing and marketing their own separator, the 'Rotoscreen'. The Rotoscreen was different to the Target in appearance, but the two separators were almost identical inside. The claimants sued the defendants for infringement of their UDRs which they claimed subsisted in various component parts of the

---

[50] *C. & H. Engineering v F. Klucznik & Sons Ltd* [1992] FSR 421.   [51] CDPA.

Target individually and in combination and in the overall design of the machine. The defendants replied that the design of the Target was not original and, indeed, was commonplace in the design field in question at the time of its creation. In the High Court, the judge held, inter alia, that design right subsisted in the Target as a whole and in a number of its component parts and that these had been infringed. The defendants appealed. Among their counter-arguments was the claim that a hopper (a chamber within the slurry) had long existed as a part of agricultural machinery in general and that its design variants were limited. The defendants also maintained that the Target as a whole was commonplace, since its improved performance was simply due to the combining of parts of the two earlier machines. In reply, the claimants maintained that the design of the Target was original, being significantly better than the earlier machines. They also argued that an original machine could be made out of 'trite' ingredients and, in any event, the relevant field for judging originality was not that of agricultural instruments generally but rather the infinitely more restricted field of slurry separators. In his judgment, Mummery LJ considered the meaning of the terms 'original', 'novel', and 'commonplace' (section 213(4) of the CDPA). According to Mummery LJ, it was significant that the UDR had been created to replace copyright protection for functional designs.

Mummery LJ, at pp. 64–6:

The overall purpose of the provision was not to impose a requirement of novelty in order to secure the limited protection enjoyed by unregistered designs, but to guard against situations in which even short term protection for functional designs would create practical difficulties. Substantial similarity of design might well give rise to a suspicion and an allegation of copying in cases where substantial similarity was often not the result of copying but an inevitable consequence of the functional nature of the design. All that is meant by 'original designs' in the context of section 213 is (a) that the design for which protection is claimed must have been originated by the designer in the sense that it is not simply a copy by him of a previous design made by someone else (like a photocopy) and (b) that where it has not been slavishly copied from another design, it must in some respects be different from other designs, so that it can be fairly and reasonably described as not commonplace. The context is important. Design right, like copyright, is informally acquired and affords weaker protection, as only copying is actionable. Copying may be inferred from proof of access to the protected work, coupled with substantial similarity. This may lead to unfounded infringement claims in the case of functional works, which are usually bound to be substantially similar to one another. On the other hand, a registered design, like a patent, is a stronger right, is harder to obtain, but it is vulnerable to challenge on the ground that it is lacking in novelty and it would not be novel if it was well known and used by others. To introduce a requirement of novelty into unregistered designs would effectively remove from the limited new right a large measure of the protection that the right must have been intended to confer on designers to protect their work from plagiarism. It cannot have been the purpose of section 213(4) to take away by one provision all the protection given by another.

Commonplace—conclusion

In the light of the language, context and purpose of section 213(4), what is the proper approach of the court faced with the issue that the design of an article is not original because it is alleged to be 'commonplace'?

(1) It should compare the design of the article in which design right is claimed with the design of other articles in the same field, including the alleged infringing article, as at the time of its creation.

(2) The court must be satisfied that the design for which protection is claimed has not simply been copied (e.g. like a photocopy) from the design of an earlier article. It must not forget that, in the field of designs of functional articles, one design may be very similar to, or even identical with, another design and yet not be a copy: it may be an original and independent shape and configuration coincidentally the same or similar. If, however, the court is satisfied that it has been slavishly copied from an earlier design, it is not an 'original' design in the 'copyright sense' and the 'commonplace' issue does not arise.

(3) If the court is satisfied that the design has not been copied from an earlier design, then it is 'original' in the 'copyright sense'. The court then has to decide whether it is 'commonplace'. For that purpose it is necessary to ascertain how similar that design is to the design of similar articles in the same field of design made by persons other than the parties or persons unconnected with the parties.

(4) This comparative exercise must be conducted objectively and in the light of the evidence, including evidence from experts in the relevant field pointing out the similarities and the differences, and explaining the significance of them. In the end, however, it is for the court and not for the witnesses, expert or otherwise, to decide whether the design is commonplace. That judgment must be one of fact and degree according to the evidence in each particular case. No amount of guidance given in this or in any other judgment can provide the court with the answer to the particular case. The closer the similarity of the various designs to each other, the more likely it is that the designs are commonplace, especially if there is no causal link, such as copying, which accounts for the resemblance of the compared designs. If a number of designers working independently of one another in the same field produce very similar designs by coincidence the most likely explanation of the similarities is that there is only one way of designing that article. In those circumstances the design in question can fairly and reasonably be described as 'commonplace'. It would be a good reason for withholding the exclusive right to prevent the copying in the case of a design that, whether it has been copied or not, it is bound to be substantially similar to other designs in the same field.

(5) If, however, there are aspects of the plaintiff's design of the article which are not to be found in any other design in the field in question, and those aspects are found in the defendant's design, the court would be entitled to conclude that the design in question was not 'commonplace' and that there was good reason for treating it as protected from misappropriation during the limited period laid down in the 1988 Act. That would be so, even though the design in question would not begin to satisfy any requirement of novelty in the registered designs legislation.

[Mummery LJ then went on to apply these concepts to the facts of the case.]

At p. 70:

[He rejected the contention of the defendant that:] there was no design right in the whole of the TARGET machine. It is true that design right may not exist in the whole of the TARGET machine in the sense of the shape or configuration of *each and every part* of the whole machine. For example, in these proceedings Farmers Build have only claimed design right in parts and in combinations of parts which make up a small part of the entire machine. But that does not prevent there being a design right in the overall shape and configuration of the combination of parts which make up the whole. A whole assembly of parts, even if all the individual parts are commonplace, is not itself commonplace if the result is to produce a slurry separator of an over-all design different from the overall design of other slurry separators. The position is that there were detailed design changes in a number of the parts. The combination of those parts, even with other parts in which Farmers Build do not claim any design right, produced a whole which could properly be regarded as an original design of an article which was not commonplace.

Clearly Mummery LJ took the view that functional designs should have less protection than both copyright works and registered designs which at that time had to have eye appeal. In this view, the danger was that too-strong protection for functional designs might inflate their value, especially if the designs were for spare parts, for example for cars. If the UDRs were 'overprotected', there was a danger that the original manufacturers could command monopoly rents on the supply of spare parts. Nonetheless, it still seems fair to ask whether, in terms of their relative social utility, it is obvious that a UDR should have less protection than a registered design.

Another issue also arises in relation to originality and commonplace. What if a design is unique to a particular product, but the product itself becomes widely known and used? It is clear that such a result would not render the design commonplace. As was put by Jacob LJ in *Dyson v Qualtex*:

108. ... There can be no question of a very good design which becomes very well known losing design right by reason of becoming well known. *Ex hypothesi* at the time of its creation such a design would not be commonplace on any view. What happens thereafter could not affect the subsistence of the right. What would be 'lost' would be a protection by way of any further design right in an aspect of a variant of the original design which was only different from the original in a commonplace manner.

In an earlier case, *Lambretta Clothing v Teddy Smith*,[52] Jacob LJ made the same point about the design of the Apple iPod. Surely he is right to hold that really attractive, and therefore popular, designs should not suffer for their popularity by being deemed commonplace?[53]

14.3.2.6 The definition of the 'design field in question'

In *Farmers Build*, Mummery LJ agreed with counsel for the claimant that:

the relevant design field in question was that of slurry separators and that evidence relating to agricultural machinery generally or engineering fields other than slurry separators was irrelevant to the question of what was commonplace within the meaning of section 213(4).

Farmers Build thus gave a relatively narrow interpretation of the 'design field in question' when compared to the broader interpretation of the related concept of prior art in the law of both patents and registered designs.[54] The definition of the 'design field in question' was

---

[52] *Lambretta Clothing Co. Ltd v Teddy Smith (UK) Ltd* [2005] RPC 6.
[53] For a recent case which follows *Farmers Build v Carrier* in relation to commonplace, see *Pendle Metalwares Ltd v Walter Page*, unreported, 31 July 2012.
[54] See 14.2.3.4.

further elaborated in the case of *Scholes Windows v Magnet*. In this case, the Court of Appeal endorsed a more generous definition of the 'design field in question' but still one that falls short of the definition of prior art for design registration.

Scholes Windows Ltd v Magnet [2002] FSR 10

The claimants manufactured UPVC casement windows in which they argued design right subsisted. The designs were adapted from earlier Victorian window designs, in particular by including a 'horn' in their designs, and the windows were sold under the name 'Nostalgia'. The defendants manufactured windows which embodied these same features. At first instance, the judge agreed that the claimant's design was original (in the sense of not copied) but it was commonplace in the design field in question if that was understood to include all windows, whether plastic or wooden, and also to include surviving Victorian windows. The claimants appealed on the basis that the judge had defined the design field in question too broadly and should have confined it to casement windows including UPVC casement windows. In particular, the claimants challenged the inclusion of Victorian windows, which were of course a century old, arguing that only designs 'in use' should be included and not 'historical' designs. In his judgment Mummery LJ approved Underhill J's definition of the design field in question.

Mummery LJ:

The design field point

31. The expression 'design field in question' is not legally defined in the 1988 Act. It must accordingly be understood in its ordinary and natural meaning, bearing in mind that the purpose of the provision in subsection (4) is to withhold legal protection from commonplace designs. The expression is obviously intended to set sensible limits to the inquiry whether a design is 'commonplace'. The making of comparisons with other designs is the essence of that inquiry. The outer bounds of the limits on comparisons with pre-existing designs are matters of fact and degree to be assessed by the tribunal of fact in taking account of all the relevant circumstances of the particular case.

32. Magnet contended that the design field in question is window design simpliciter, regardless of the materials used or the nature and purpose of the design. The initial position of Scholes at the trial was that the design field in question was PVC window design and that the designer is presented with different design problems according to the materials used—wood, steel, aluminium or PVC. By the close of the trial, however, it was the judge's understanding that it had been conceded that the design field extended to mock sash windows in any material, including timber as well as PVC.

33. The deputy judge accordingly posed the relevant question as follows:

was the design of the Nostalgia horn commonplace in the field of window design in July 1994?

34. He held that it was. His conclusion was based on a comparison with the design of window horns in the built environment, using as comparators horns on sash windows made of wood.

35. It was submitted on behalf of Scholes that this approach involved a misdirection or an error of principle. It ignored the fact that there are two primary considerations in ascertaining

what is meant by the term 'the design field in question'. They are: (i) the nature and purpose of the article; and (ii) the material structure of the article.

…

37. In my judgment, there was no misdirection or error of principle in the approach of the deputy judge to the 'design field in question'. It is necessary to examine the submissions of Scholes by reference to the statutory language and by relating it to a correct appreciation of the concept of a design. The definition of 'design' in subsection (2) covers any aspect of the shape or configuration of the whole or part of an article. The definition of design does not incorporate, either expressly or by implication, the nature or purpose of the article itself or the material structure of the article.

38. The submissions advanced on behalf of Scholes confuse the design of the aspect of the shape or configuration of the window horn with (a) the nature of the particular article to which the design is applied and (b) the idea of using horns as a decorative feature on top opening windows with frames made of U-PVC. The property right is in the design of any aspect of the shape or configuration of the horn. It is not a right in the article itself. It is not a right in the idea of a particular construction, use or application of the article itself. Thus the fact that part of the article is made out of U-PVC does not make that material a part of the design of an aspect of the shape or configuration of the Nostalgia horn. The fact that the purpose of the article is to decorate a mock sash casement window, rather than the genuine article, does not make that a design of an aspect of the shape or configuration of the Nostalgia horn. As those matters are not part of the design they are irrelevant to the delineation of the 'design field in question'.

[Mummery LJ also approved Underhill J's approach of including 'historical designs' in the design field in question.]

The time of creation point

44. In my judgment, there is no misdirection or error of principle in the approach of the deputy judge to 'old' designs of horns. The statutory question does not depend on when other designs in the design field with which comparison is to be made were first produced or on when they were in use or whether they have fallen into disuse and become 'historical designs'. The relevant question is 'Is the design in which the right is claimed commonplace?' That question is to be determined by having regard to the 'design field in question at the time of creation'. There is nothing in these provisions which expressly or impliedly excludes from consideration existing designs, which were first produced at an earlier time than the design in suit, if they can be fairly and reasonably regarded as included in the design field in question at the time of the creation of the design in suit. The fact that they could still be seen by designers and interested members of the public as a feature of windows on many houses in July 1994 is a relevant factor in deciding whether or not they were in the design field at the date of creation and were commonplace within the meaning of subsection.

By suggesting that there is no time limit for designs to be included in the design field in question, Mummery LJ could be said to be approaching the patent/registered design definition of prior art. It is possible to question whether such a definition is too broad. UDRs are given only short-lived protection. It may be no bad thing that such protection should be available to those who imaginatively adopt 'historical designs'. After all, UDRs only protect against direct copying. In other words, if a third party were inspired to adopt the same design from the same historical source this would not be infringing—he could do so with impunity. There is also an interesting connection to be drawn between the question of whether a design is commonplace and the ease of proving infringement. In the recent case of *Whitby Specialist Vehicles Ltd v Yorkshire Specialist Vehicles Ltd*,[55] Arnold J noted that the higher the level of abstraction at which a claimant seeks to frame its design, the easier it will be for the claimant to prove infringement.[56] But equally the easier it will be for the defendant to prove the design is commonplace. This observation suggests once again the difficulties, when interpreting unregistered design law, in ensuring there is a correct balance between the interests of the owner of a UDR and the interests of those who might seek to compete in the same design field.

14.3.3 EXCLUSIONS TO UNREGISTERED DESIGN RIGHT PROTECTION

There are four exclusions to UDR protection set out in section 213(3) of the CDPA. Design right does not subsist in:

(1) a method or principle of construction (section 213(3)(a));

(2) the 'must fit' exclusion (section 213(3)(b)(i));

(3) the 'must match' exclusion (section 213(3)(b)(ii));

(4) surface decoration (section 213(3)(c)).

14.3.3.1 Exception 1: a method or principle of construction

This exclusion was considered by the Court of Appeal in *Landor & Hawa v Azure Designs Ltd*.[57]

Landor & Hawa International Ltd v Azure Designs Ltd [2006] EWCA Civ 1285

The dispute was over the design of a type of suitcase which expanded if one panel was unzipped. Suitcases embodying this design, known as the 'Expander', had been sold by the claimants since 2002. The claimants discovered that the defendants were marketing a suitcase made in China which they argued infringed their UDR and their CUDR in the Expander design. The High Court found for the claimant and the defendants appealed arguing, inter alia, that the Expander design constituted a method or principle of construction. In his judgment, Neuberger LJ (as he then was) considered this argument both as a matter of principle and fact.

Neuberger LJ:

9. This contention has given rise to two main arguments, one of principle and one essentially of fact. The argument of principle concerns the meaning and effect of s. 213(3)(a) of CDPA 1998 ('s. 213(3)(a)'). The judge held that the provision should be relatively narrowly

---

[55] [2014] EWHC 4242 (Pat).   [56] [45].

[57] Other earlier cases which considered this exception are *Fulton v Grant Barnett & Co. Ltd* [2001] RPC 257 and *Baby Dan AS v Brevi Srl* [1999] FSR 377.

construed, and that it did not apply merely because a design serves a functional purpose: it would not apply unless it can be shown that that purpose cannot be achieved by any other means. Although this formulation was challenged by Azure at least in its initial skeleton argument, it was not by any means the main focus of the well-sustained submissions of Mr Alastair Wilson QC (who appears with Mr Michael Edenborough) on behalf of Azure.

10. In my opinion, the judge's interpretation of s. 213(3)(a) is correct. First, the section does not, as a matter of ordinary language, preclude a design [from] being protected merely because it has a functional purpose. The language is perhaps a little opaque, but the words 'method or principle' are important, and serve, in my view, to emphasise that mere functionality is quite insufficient to exclude a design from protection. Tempting though it may be to seek to redefine or expand on those words, I think it would normally be unhelpful in practice, and arguably wrong in principle, to do so, save to explain in a particular case why they do or do not apply.

11. Secondly, as Mr Daniel Alexander QC, who appears with Mr David Wilkinson for Landor, says, it would be wrong in principle to conclude that a design is incapable of protection merely because it serves a functional purpose. There is no simply no justification in policy or principle for such a conclusion. It would mean that a design which had only aesthetic features would be favoured over one with both aesthetic and functional features, a curious consequence of legislation one of whose main functions is to reward imagination and inventiveness.

12. As Park J rightly observed in *A Fulton Co Ltd v Grant Barnett & Co Ltd* [2001] RPC 16 at [70]:

> The fact that a special method or principle of construction may have to be used in order to create an article with a particular shape or configuration does not mean that there is no design right in the shape or configuration. The law of design right will not prevent competitors using that method or principle of construction to create competing designs... as long as the competing designs do not have the same shape or configuration as the design right owner's design has.

13. Thirdly, the textbooks support this approach to interpretation. The judge quoted a passage from *Russell-Clarke on Copyright in Industrial Designs* (7th edn), at para. 3-80, which analyses the effect of s. 213(3)(a) in these terms:

> A method or principle of construction is a process or operation by which a shape is produced, as opposed to the shape itself. To say that a shape is to be denied registration because it amounts to a method or principle of construction is meaningless. The real meaning is this: that no design shall be construed so widely as to give to its proprietor a monopoly in a method or principle of construction. What he gets is a monopoly for one particular individual and specific appearance. If it is possible to get several different appearances, which all embody the general features which he claims, then those features are too general and amount to a method or principle of construction. In other words, any conception which is so general as to allow several different specific appearances as being made within it, it is too broad and will be invalid.

14. The judge agreed with that analysis, and so do I. It is a view which is supported by the editors of *Copinger and Skone-James on The Law of Copyright* (15th edn). At para. 13-55, they state that the purpose of the section is 'to ensure that designers cannot create an effective monopoly over articles made in a particular way'. Jacob J appears to have taken the same view in paras. 14 and 15 in *Isaac Oren v Red Box Toy Factory Ltd* [1999] FSR 785. Having decided that 'it is possible to make a device visually very different from Mr Oren's designs but which

works the same way', he went on to hold that '[i]t follows that there is no principle monopolised here—only a visual embodiment of a device constructed in accordance with a principle'.

Essentially, as held by Neuberger LJ, a design would only fall within this exception if it constituted the *only* way of achieving a particular function. Applying this approach to the facts in *Landor & Hawa v Azure*, Neuberger LJ held that, since it was possible to achieve the same design advantage with designs which were different from the Expander design, the claimants did indeed have a valid UDR in the Expander design. The attention of the court then turned to the issue of whether the claimant had a valid CUDR in the Expander design, albeit one that had expired. Interestingly, both parties had sought to argue that the CJEU's interpretation of Article 3(1)(e)(ii) of the Trade Mark Directive, which excludes the registration for functional designs as trade marks,[58] was a model for interpreting Article 8(1) of the Design Regulation.

Neuberger LJ:

35. In my judgment, the judge was right to hold that decisions on the Trademark Directive cannot be safely relied on in a case involving the Designs Directive. Article 3.1(e)(ii) of the Trademark Directive refers to 'signs that consist exclusively of . . . the shape of goods which is necessary to obtain a technical result'. It will be seen at once that the wording is not by any means identical to that of art. 8.1.

36. Indeed, as pointed out by the judge, the opinion of Advocate General Colomer in the *Phillips* case (reported at [2001] RPC 38)[59] contains in [34], an instructive comparison between the two provisions: 'The wording used in the Designs Directive for expressing that ground for refusal does not entirely coincide with that used in the Trade Marks Directive. That discrepancy is not capricious. Whereas the former refuses to recognise external features '"which are solely dictated by its technical function", the latter excludes from its protection "signs which consist exclusively of the shape of goods which is necessary to obtain a technical result". In other words, the level of "functionality" must be greater in order to be able to assess the ground for refusal in the context of designs; the feature concerned must not only be necessary but essential in order to achieve a particular technical result: form follows function. This means that a functional design may, none the less, be eligible for protection if it can be shown that the same technical function could be achieved by another different form.'

37. Nothing in the reasoning of the ECJ in its subsequent decision, which agreed with the ultimate conclusions reached by the Advocate-General, in that case calls into question those observations. Further, as Mr Alexander says, there are real differences between the nature and purpose of trademark protection and design right. Trademarks are badges of origin, and the purpose of (and therefore the regime for) protecting the owner is different from the purpose for protecting designs, which have nothing to do with demonstrating origin.

Neuberger LJ concluded that the High Court was correct in finding that the Expander design was neither at such a level of generality nor was it the only design which would achieve the same technical result. As a result, it was a valid UDR. The judgment in *Landor & Hawa v Azure* once again underlines the fact that a UK UDR and a CUDR, unlike a patent, are not intended to be monopoly rights. As we have seen recently in a number of cases, the

---

[58] For functional designs and trade marks, see 6.3.4.1.
[59] *Koninklijke Philips Electronics NV v Remington Consumer Products Ltd* [2001] RPC 38.

reasoning in *Landor & Hawa* has not been followed as it relates to registered designs. In *Nintendo*, for example, the Board of Appeal held that a design with functional elements may not be registered even if there are other designs which might fulfil the same functions. Yet are not the same public interest considerations, i.e. to avoid a monopoly on a functional design, valid for both registered and unregistered designs?

14.3.3.2 The 'must fit' exclusion

The 'must fit' and 'must match' exclusions have been described as the 'interface' exclusions. The 'must fit' exclusion is defined in section 213(3)(b) of the CDPA as excluding from design right protection:

> features of shape or configuration in an article which enable the article to be connected to, or placed in, around or against, another article so that either article may perform its function.

Again, like the 'must match' exclusion, this exclusion was directly aimed at undermining the monopolies which some manufacturers, such as automobile makers, were able to establish in the field of spare parts. While in the 1980s the prevailing mood was to free up the market for spare parts as much as possible, the decision by the Court of Appeal in *Dyson v Qualtex* suggests that this aim will not be pursued at all costs.

Dyson Ltd v Qualtex (UK) Ltd [2006] RPC 31

The claimant, Dyson, manufactured vacuum cleaners. The defendant manufactured spare parts (or 'pattern parts' as they are known), including for the Dyson vacuum cleaner. Dyson claimed that the defendant's spare parts copied parts of the vacuum cleaner which were protected by UDRs. Among the arguments raised by the defendant was that these parts were covered by both the 'must fit' and 'must match' exclusions, and further that the designs not covered by this exception were commonplace. The claimant succeeded in the High Court and as we shall see also in the Court of Appeal. In the High Court, the claimant alleged that 14 of its UDRs had been infringed. In the Court of Appeal, the number of UDRs at issue had been reduced to six, and the court focused on particular features of the UDRs which both parties claimed illustrated their arguments. In considering *Dyson v Qualtex*, we will focus, in the first instance, on the Court of Appeal's finding with regards to the 'must fit' exception. The arguments relating to the 'must match' exclusion will be considered below. But first it is useful to look at the general points made by Jacob LJ at the start of this judgment. Jacob LJ began by summarizing the conflicting concerns of the claimant and the defendant.

Jacob LJ:

2. The original designers and manufacturers of consumer items, (often known as original equipment manufacturers ('OEMs'), not surprisingly sometimes desire to control the trade in spare parts for their machines. The independent manufacturers or dealers generally wish to imitate the original manufacturer's part as closely as they can—they will sell better than a part which works as well but looks different. The reasons why they will sell better are

complicated. One factor though is self-evident: a consumer is likely to have more confidence in a part which looks exactly the same as the broken one. One can readily imagine the consumer going into a shop with his broken part and saying 'can I have another of these?' If the part looks different there will be sales resistance.

[Jacob LJ then went on to look at the history of the UDR, primarily to ascertain whether the UDR was intended clearly to protect either the interests of the OEMs or the contrasting interests of the makers of pattern parts, as the claimant and defendant claimed respectively. He concluded that it was difficult to approach the 'must fit' exception with, as he put it, 'a clear purpose in mind', and noted:]

14. ... [N]either the language used nor the context of the legislation give any clear idea what was intended. Time and time again one struggles but fails to ascertain a precise meaning, a meaning which men of business can reasonably use to guide their conduct. The amount of textbook writing and conjecture as to the meaning is a testament to its obscurity. We just have to do the best we can, trying to arrive at 'an interpretation which the reasonable reader would give to the statute read against its background' per Lord Hoffmann in *R (Wilkinson) v IRC* [2005] UKHL 30; [2006] 1 All ER 529 at [18]. The absence of any clear policy, as to where the line of compromise was intended to run, means that brightline rules cannot be deduced.

[Having made these general points, Jacob LJ turned to considering the breadth of what he dubbed the 'so-called must fit' exception.]

27. I say this sub-section is 'so-called' because that is the term by which it is known. Mr Arnold [counsel for the defendant] rightly said that its language did not actually say 'must-fit' (just as the next sub-section, so-called 'must-match' does not actually say that). I agree that one must go by the actual language and not by the epithet or even the notion behind the epithet...

[Jacob LJ also reproduced with approval the interpretation of the 'must fit' exception given by Mann J in the High Court.]

20. In his general consideration of the law, the judge used the decisions of Laddie J in *Ultraframe UK Ltd v Fielding* [2003] RPC 23 at [73] and *Ocular Sciences Ltd v Aspect Vision Care Ltd* [1997] RPC 289 at p. 424 to extract three propositions [34]:

(i) It does not matter if there are two ways of achieving the necessary fit or connection between the subject article (the first one referred to in the sub-section) and the article to which it fits or with which it interfaces. If the design chosen by the design right owner is a way of achieving that fit or interface, then it does not attract design right no matter how many alternative ways of achieving the same 'fit' might be available.

(ii) For the purposes of the sub-section, the article with which the subject article is interfacing can be part of the human body. This might have had relevance in the present case because some of the parts (triggers and a catch) are designed to interface with the human finger or thumb. However, Mr Arnold disclaimed reliance on this—he did not rely on the finger or thumb as a must fit item in the context of any article in the present case.

(iii) The sub-section operates to exclude design right even if the relevant part of the design performs some function other than the function described in the sub-section—for example, it is decorative, or has an additional function not falling within the provision. This additional function does not exclude the operation of the provision.

Counsel for the defendant posed a number of questions to the court. The first was whether the 'must fit' exception excludes parts that do not touch each other. It was argued that because the High Court had excluded parts that do not touch from the 'must fit' exception, Mann J had been wrong in law. Indeed, the defence then gave concrete examples of aspects of the design of the cleaner which, while not touching, would be crucial to the overall functioning of other parts of the machine. Jacob LJ approved the approach taken in the High Court:

> 38. Any working part must of course be so located so as not to interfere with the working of other parts—that does mean that any spacing between parts is a feature which enables function.

Second, the defendants argued that Mann J had been wrong to construe the 'must fit' exception as not being satisfied by a feature which merely makes an article function more effectively. Once again the defence gave examples taken from the vacuum cleaner design which it argued should have been included in the 'must fit' exceptions. In this case it identified the 'bleed holes' in the upper knob of the cleaner whose function was to prevent excessive vacuum if the whole end of the tube was blocked. Mann J had held these were not aspects of the design which 'must fit' since they were safety features, not features which had to be touching other aspects of the design (in this case the handle) to function. However, the defence went on to argue that the bleed holes did function to enable the handle to function better as they enabled the handle to be placed against another article (e.g. a stair carpet) in order to vacuum effectively. On this point, Jacob LJ agreed with defence:

> 43. I think Mr Arnold is right here. The judge focussed on the effect on a third object (the motor) but overlooked the function of the wand handle itself. I think the bleed holes fall within the exception: they enable the handle to be placed against a flat surface so as to perform its function as a vacuum cleaner handle.

Third, the defence alleged that the exclusion should apply even where the articles are designed sequentially, for example in this case to allow the vacuum cleaner to function. The defence gave the illustration of the curve of a handle which formed a 'wall' underneath to 'fit' the release catch. The claimant argued that in order to function the handle did not need to be curved. Jacob LJ accepted this contention which meant that the handle 'wall' design did not fall within the UDR exclusions.

Finally, the defence argued that Mann J had failed to 'adopt a practical approach to the "must fit" exclusion'. In other words, it was wrong that the UDR would be understood to cover even 'minor matters' of design such as those adopted by the defendant. Jacob LJ disagreed:

> 48. The trouble with that is that is not what the section says. On the contrary it has gone out of its way to create UDR in any aspect of any part of an article. That is indeed an odd way of going about things but it is what it says. There is no limitation to aspects which have no practical significance. As I have said, the lower limit is where one cannot really say there is an 'aspect' at all.

In *Dyson v Qualtex*, the Court of Appeal looked at a number of issues raised by the 'must fit' exception. On the whole, it sided with the OEMs rather than the spare-parts manufacturers. There is no doubt that by recognizing unregistered design right protection in minor matters of design or parts which are needed for the machine to function but are not touching, the Court of Appeal has made it more difficult for makers of pattern parts to avoid treading on the UDRs of the OEMs. Interestingly, this is not the result we might have expected were we to think back to the original impetus for introducing the UDR, which was to free up the market in spare parts. We shall see, moreover, as we now come to look at the 'must match' exception, that the Court of Appeal is set upon giving OEMs a generous settlement in that area too.

14.3.3.3 The 'must match' exception

Along with the 'must fit' exception, the 'must match' exception is known as an 'interface exception'. The 'must match' exception speaks directly to the concerns which led to the creation of a UDR—that is, the perceived need to free up the competition between OEMs and the suppliers of pattern parts—for the ultimate benefit of the consumer. As we have seen, the 'must match' exception is not part of the CUDR, nor do all other EU countries recognize this exception.

The 'must match' exception is set out at section 213(3)(b)(ii). It states that design right does not subsist in features of the shape or configuration of an article:

> which are dependent upon the appearance of another article of which the article is intended by the design to form an integral part.

An obvious example of a design which would fall under this exclusion would be a replacement of a body panel for a car. What would not be covered would be wing mirrors whose designs can be changed without compromising the integrity of the car's design overall.[60] In the case of *Ultraframe UK Ltd v Clayton (No. 2)*,[61] which concerned components for a conservatory roof, it was held by Laddie J in the High Court, that the fact that certain features of the components helped to achieve a 'consistent theme' for the conservatory as a whole, did not mean that they 'were dependent upon the appearance of another article'. Indeed, the fact that the components had 'little visual impact' meant that they were less likely to be dependent upon similar features on other articles. The 'must match' exception was considered in some detail by the Court of Appeal in *Dyson v Qualtex*. In his judgment, Jacob LJ endorsed the approach taken by Mann J in the High Court in interpreting the 'must match' exception, quoting Mann J's judgment extensively. Like Jacob LJ held in relation to the 'must fit' exception, Mann J had held that the interpretation of the 'must match' exception was not notably aided by a consideration of the legislative context in which it was framed. Nor were there any binding authorities. He suggested that the only case which offered some assistance was *Ford Motor Co. Ltd's Design Application*, which concerned an attempt to register design parts for motor vehicles. From that case came the approach that 'one must ask whether there is a feature of shape of the part which is dependent on the appearance of the whole machine'. He went on to approve the argument put forward by counsel for the claimant as being largely consistent with the approach taken in *Ford Motor Co.* Essentially, this

---

[60] See *Ford Motor Co. Ltd's Design Application* [1993] RPC 399.   [61] [2003] RPC 23.

was a 'radically different in appearance' test. Under this test, if substitutions could be made without radically affecting the appearance or identity of the vehicle then the design would fall outside the exclusion. According to Mann J, as quoted by Jacob LJ, this was 'another way of looking at dependency. If there is, as a practical matter, design freedom for the part, then there is no dependency.' He continued:

> 64. I accept this latter proposition. One has to approach the provision bearing in mind that Parliament did not intend to exclude all spare parts, or even all externally visible portions of spare parts, yet such was the substance of Mr Arnold's submission. 'Dependency' must be viewed practically. In some cases the answer is obvious—the paradigm example being body parts of cars. In others it may be necessary to examine the position more carefully. But unless the spare parts dealer can show that as a practical matter there is a real need to copy a feature of shape or configuration because of some design consideration of the whole article, he is not within the exclusion. It is not enough to assert that the public 'prefers' an exact copy for it will always do so for the reason I gave in [2] above. The more there is design freedom the less is there room for the exclusion. In the end it is a question of degree—the sort of thing where a judge is called upon to make a value judgment. Unless wrong in principle, his evaluation will not be interfered with on appeal.

For example, Mann J considered and rejected the defence argument that changing the design of the handle would undercut the design of the whole, in much the same way as if a car door panel did not match the car design as a whole, because in this case the whole machine would not look 'radically different'. He believed it likely there would be a market for a non-replica handle, where there might not be one for car doors which did not match, since cars were made for public display, whereas vacuum cleaners were not. However, he conceded that a Dyson might be bought, 'at least in part' because of its design. As was noted above, Jacob LJ, in his judgment, approved the 'radically different' test set out by Mann J. He also accepted the claimant's contention that if there were design freedom for the part, it was not dependent on the overall appearance of the product and therefore it fell outside the exclusion. When Jacob LJ applied this interpretation of the exclusion to the facts of this case, notably the handle, he once again endorsed Mann J's finding. Like Mann J, Jacob LJ asked:

> 68. ...[H]ow much does the design of the wand handle really matter to the overall design? Would it matter, for instance, if there were a ribless handle? The more I looked the less I thought it mattered. From the point of view of a consumer, I doubt, as did the judge, whether he/she would care whether his/her Dyson cleaner, if repaired with a ribless wand handle, looked a bit different from as new. There was no evidence of any such concern by a consumer. Such inference as one could get from the sales of the DC02 wand handles suggest otherwise (see above). This is just the sort of area where the judge has made a value judgment, here as to dependency, upon which a court of appeal should not interfere unless there is an error of principle.

Jacob LJ noted, 'That is really all that need be said as regards the "must match" exclusion.' Nor did he find any of the defendant's other examples of designs which fell within the exclusion convincing. In sum, he approved the High Court's decision that none of the pattern spares produced by the defendant were covered by the 'must match' exclusion. As we noted earlier, in the *Dyson v Qualtex* decision, the Court of Appeal threw its weight behind the OEMs to a greater extent than might have been envisaged when the UDR was first introduced. Perhaps it is simply reflecting common sense. We might ourselves ask the question as to whether a consumer, who is willing to pay a premium price for a Dyson vacuum cleaner in part because of its novel and attractive appearance, will really be content with a spare part that alters the overall appearance of the machine, even in minor aspects?

14.3.3.4 The surface decoration exclusion (section 213(3)(c))

Design right will not subsist in surface decoration. Before the Designs Directive, it was this exclusion which set unregistered design right apart from a registered design. Now there is no longer such a clear division. As we have seen, with the implementation of the Designs Directive, it is no longer necessary for a design to possess eye appeal to be registered. This exclusion has been considered in two Court of Appeal decisions, *Lambretta v Teddy Smith* and *Dyson v Qualtex*.

***Lambretta Clothing Co. Ltd v Teddy Smith (UK) Ltd* [2005] RPC 6**

The claimant designed and produced fashion clothes. In particular, it produced a track-top in a striking range of colours. The top itself was of a standard design. The design had been recorded in two documents which included, inter alia, instructions as to the colours to be used and also the fabric. It was successfully marketed in 2002. That same year, the defendants, Teddy Smith and Next plc, marketed track-tops in similar fabric and colour combinations. The claimant alleged that the defendants' tops infringed its design right and also its copyright in the design documents. The defendants argued, relying on section 51 of the CDPA,[62] that the design documentation did not record an artistic work, and therefore it was not an infringement of copyright to copy the design of the tops. The High Court found that no design right subsisted in the tops, as the originality of the design lay in its surface decoration or colourways.[63] The claimant appealed arguing, inter alia, that the colourways were not surface decoration because they were dyed through the garment. The Court of Appeal, Mance LJ dissenting, approved the approach taken by the High Court.

Jacob LJ:

30. ... It is true that the parts of the garment are dyed right through, but any realistic and practical construction of the words 'surface decoration' must cover both the case where a surface is covered with a thin layer and where the decoration, like that in Brighton rock, runs throughout the article. To hold otherwise would mean that whether or not UDR could subsist in two different articles, having exactly the same outward appearance, depended on how deep the colours went. Parliament cannot have intended anything so capricious.

31. I should also deal with an incidental argument arising from the exclusion of surface decoration. It is suggested that 'shape or configuration' would otherwise include surface decoration—that the exclusion is a pointer to the width of those words without it. It is not an argument which could really help Lambretta—for it necessarily concedes that the colourways are surface decoration. But in any event I do not think it right. Surface decoration can be more than essentially flat—you can decorate a thing with three dimensional decoration—for

---

[62] See 14.4.   [63] *Lambretta Clothing Co. Ltd v Teddy Smith (UK) Ltd* [2003] RPC 41.

instance the 'cock beading' considered by Jonathan Parker J in *Mark Wilkinson Furniture Ltd v Woodcraft Designs (Radcliffe) Ltd* [1998] F.S.R. 63. The point of the exclusion is obviously to avoid problems of this sort—three-dimensional embellishments of an article are intended to be excluded. They may have an independent artistic copyright—that depends on the rules for artistic copyright and s. 51.

32. Accordingly I think the judge was right to conclude that UDR cannot subsist in the design of the Lambretta top.

The Court of Appeal also considered the surface decoration exclusion in *Dyson v Qualtex*. In the High Court, the judge had found that the pattern parts produced by the defendant did not fall within the surface decoration exclusion. On appeal, the defence argued that Mann J had wrongly construed surface decoration as limited to decorating a surface that was already there. Instead the defence argued that, 'the exclusion necessarily encompassed, indeed only encompassed, three-dimensional surface decoration'. The defence also argued that a UDR 'is only created in an aspect of the shape or configuration of the whole or part of an article. So it only subsists in 3D shapes. So the exclusion must be dealing with 3D shapes only.' Jacob LJ did not accept this argument for two reasons:

74. First, you can have 2D features of shape or configuration, e.g. one produced by cutting one out from a piece of paper. Secondly, exclusion (a) (to a method or principle of construction) is an exclusion which is probably not necessary—a method or principle of construction can hardly be a mere feature of shape or configuration. Mr Arnold's implied premise that the exclusion does not extend beyond the definition of the right is false—an exclusion can go further than is necessary and clearly does so in the case of (a).

75. Next it seems clear that the exclusion will cover what are essentially 2D designs on a 3D article. A willow-pattern plate, or a painted vase, have what can fairly be described as 2D decoration on a 3D article—and the painting is merely 'surface' even though it has a 3D nature. And you can also clearly have a surface decoration of just a flat part of a 3D article.

Applying these principles, Jacob LJ held that Mann J had not limited surface decoration to a surface which was already there (in other words, 2D decoration) as the defence claimed. Instead, he found on the facts that Mann J was correct to conclude that the ribbing above the handle of the vacuum cleaner would not be viewed by a consumer as surface decoration and thus it fell outside the exclusion. Jacob LJ also considered a further question raised by the defence as to whether the exception would apply if the surface features had a function. He held that surface features which had a significant function and were not merely surface decoration would not fall within the exclusion.[64]

14.3.3.5 The balance between OEMs and pattern parts manufacturers revisited

As we have seen, in *Dyson v Qualtex* Jacob LJ found that the context in which the UDR was created by Parliament did not give an obvious guide to how the law relating to exclusions

---

[64] For a High Court case which considered this issue, see *Hi Tech Autoparts Ltd v Towergate Two Ltd (No. 2)* [2002] FSR 16.

from protection should be interpreted. Instead, he left it up to the 'reasonable man' to interpret the issue of how broadly the boundaries to UDR protection should be drawn. Further, should the balance of interest in interpreting the UDR exclusions fall on the side of the OEMs? After all, it might be argued that, since the UDR was introduced, the design of even functional articles has become much more visually sophisticated. As a result, it might be difficult for spare-part manufacturers to offer competition to OEMs if they cannot market spare parts which fit visually with the original articles.

14.3.3.6 Primary infringement (section 226)

The owner of a UDR has the exclusive right to reproduce the design for commercial purposes (section 226(1)). The design owner also has the right to reproduce the design by making articles to that design exactly or substantially to the design (section 226(2)). Design right is infringed by a person who without the licence of the owner does or authorizes another to do anything which is the exclusive right of the owner. Infringement may consist of direct or indirect copying. The issue of what constitutes infringing use was considered by the High Court in *C. & H. Engineering v Klucznik* which, as we have seen, involved the design of a pig fender.

C. & H. Engineering v Klucznik & Sons Ltd [1992] FSR 421

The claimants manufactured agricultural equipment including 'lamb creep fenders' and pig fenders. A pig fender is a pen outside a pigpen low enough for a sow, but not her piglets, to step over. The claimant sued the defendants for infringing the design of its fenders and the defendants counter-sued, alleging that the claimant had infringed their design in a novel pig fender which, based on suggestions from a customer, had a bar along the top in order to prevent the sow from injuring her teats when she stepped over the fender. The claimant subsequently supplied pig fenders to the same customer, although their design had tubes around the top edge of the fender and was designed to be stackable. A key question for Aldous J to determine was what constitutes an infringing design in the field of UDRs, and in particular whether it was the same test as applied to copyright infringement. He held that it was not.

Aldous J, at p. 428:

Section 226 appears to require the owner of a design right to establish that copying has taken place before infringement can be proved; that is similar to copyright. However the test of infringement is different. Under section 16 copyright will be infringed if the work, or a substantial part of the work, is copied. Under section 226 there will only be infringement if the design is copied so as to produce articles exactly or substantially to the design. Thus the test for infringement requires the alleged infringing article or articles be compared with the document or article embodying the design. Thereafter the court must decide whether copying took place and, if so, whether the alleged infringing article is made exactly to the design or substantially to that design. Whether or not the alleged infringing article is made substantially to the plaintiff's design must be an objective test to be decided through the eyes of the person to whom the design is directed. Pig fenders are purchased by pig farmers and I have no doubt that they purchase them taking into account price and design. In the present case, the plaintiff's alleged infringing pig fenders do not have exactly the same design as shown in the defendant's design document. Thus it is necessary to compare the plaintiff's pig fenders with the defendant's design drawing and, looking at the differences and similarities through the eyes of a person such as a pig farmer, decide whether the design of the plaintiff's pig fender is substantially the same as the design shown in the drawing.

[On the facts, Aldous J held that the claimant's pig fender did not infringe the design document for the defendant's pig fender. He continued:]

At pp. 428–9:

By 1990 pig fenders were commonplace and had been made in metal and wood. In essence Mr Butler wanted a commonplace pig fender with a metal roll bar on the top. He had seen fenders with a wooden roll bar. He gave Mr Jackson the basic measurements needed and the only part of the pig fender shown in the drawing which was not commonplace was the 2 inch tube on the top. Thus the design is the incorporation of the 2 inch pipe into a commonplace pig fender.

…

I have no doubt that the idea of having a tube as the roll bar came from the defendant's pig fender and therefore copying did take place. However, the plaintiff's pig fenders are not made exactly to the defendant's design, and I do not believe that they are made substantially to that design. Metal pig fenders must have an overall similarity due to the function they have to perform, but a person interested in their design would appreciate that the plaintiff's pig fender was of a different design to that of the defendant, although they have in common a tube as the roll bar. In that respect the two designs are substantially the same, but taken as a whole the two designs are not substantially the same. An interested man would be struck by the design features which enable the plaintiff's pig fender to be stacked. Those features not only attract the eye, but would also be seen by an interested person as being functionally significant. They contrast with the overall design features of the defendant's pig fender. The interested man looking at the plaintiff's and the defendant's pig fenders would consider the two designs to be different, but with a similar design feature—namely, the bar around the top. Therefore the defendant's claim for infringement of a design right fails.

The approach to judging infringement taken by Aldous J in *C. & H. Engineering* was approved by the Court of Appeal in *L. Woolley Jewellers Ltd v A. & A. Jewellery Ltd*.[65]

In *C. & H. Engineering*, Aldous J defined the test for infringement as whether the allegedly infringing design had been copied from the earlier UDR and if so whether it was 'not substantially different'. On this basis the claimant's design was not infringing. As summarized by Lewison J in *Virgin*,[66] the test requires a comparison of the alleged infringing article against the article that is said to embody the design relied on and then to ask two questions: has copying occurred and, if so, has the alleged infringement produced exactly or substantially the copied design? Furthermore, as Birss J pointed out in *Albert Packaging Ltd v Nampak Cartons & Healthcare Ltd*,[67] it is important to bear in mind when making the comparison that functional features of two designs may be similar because they are performing the same function, not because of copying.[68] The approach to UDR infringement taken by Aldous J in *C. & H. Engineering* ensures that it will be more difficult to infringe a UDR than to infringe a copyright work, where the test is whether a substantial part has been

---

[65] [2003] FSR 15.   [66] [2009] EWHC 26 (Pat).   [67] [2011] EWPCC 15.
[68] See also *Ifejika v Ifejika* [2012] FSR 6.

taken. Interestingly, the case was decided relatively soon after the introduction of the UDR. If, as we suggested earlier, the introduction of the UDR had been designed to free up the market for spare parts and functional designs generally, this outcome is not surprising. On the other hand, given the relatively favourable treatment which has been given to OEMs in more recent cases involving UDRs, it is worth speculating whether, if the question of what constitutes infringement were to be decided today, the outcome would be quite so sympathetic to the copier of the earlier design.

14.3.3.7 Secondary infringement (sections 227–8)

Design right is infringed by a person who, without the licence of the design right owner, imports or has in his possession for commercial purposes or sells an article which he knows or has reason to believe is infringing.

14.3.3.8 Exceptions to infringement

There are a number of exceptions to the infringement of a UDR which reflect wider public interest concerns. For example, under section 237(1), a person is entitled to a licence of right to use a UDR in its last five years of subsistence even if in principle such use would infringe the UDR. This exception ensures that the protection afforded to a UDR will not be used to prevent the exploitation of a design which might have public benefit. Most notably, the Intellectual Property Act 2014 introduced a series of exceptions which to some extent mirror those offered in relation to patent and copyright works. Section 244A states that a design right is not infringed by:

(a) an act which is done privately and for purposes which are not commercial;

(b) an act which is done for experimental purposes; or

(c) an act of reproduction for teaching purposes or for the purpose of making citations provided that—

    (i) the act of reproduction is compatible with fair trade practice and does not unduly prejudice the normal exploitation of the design, and

    (ii) mention is made of the source.

14.3.3.9 Remedies (sections 277–82)

Like copyright infringement, it is possible to obtain additional damages if an infringement is particularly flagrant. Otherwise the usual remedies are available including damages or an account of profits, delivery up, or destruction of the articles.[69] However, it is worth noting that where a defendant at the time of infringement did not know and had no reason to believe that the design right subsisted in the design to which the action relates, the claimant will not be entitled to damages, although the other remedies identified here will be available. Surely it is correct that innocent infringers should be excluded from having to pay damages given that, as has been noted, it is often difficult to identify a UDR until it becomes the subject of a court action?

---

[69] See Chapter 15 on the Online Resource Centre.

FURTHER READING

S. Clark, 'Design rights all wrapped up: a case comment on *Albert Packaging Ltd. v Nampak Cartons and Healthcare Ltd.*' [2012] EIPR 343.

P. Groves, 'Design protection for spare parts' [2005] Bus. L. R. 291.

D. Stone, 'Justice delayed: in 2015, Karen Millen's 2007 design infringement case comes to an end' [2015] EIPR 617.

M. Ward, 'Has UK design law been given a new lease of life?' [2015] Bus. L. R. 2.

14.4 THE RELATIONSHIP BETWEEN COPYRIGHT AND INDUSTRIAL DESIGNS

The changes in industrial design protection ushered in by the CDPA did not entirely result in the uncoupling of copyright protection from the protection given to industrial designs. According to section 51(1) of the CDPA, it is not an infringement of any copyright in a design document or a model recording or embodying a design for anything other than an artistic work or a typeface to make an article to that design or to copy an article made to that design. In addition, until it was repealed,[70] section 52(1)–(2) held that if an artistic work is exploited by the copyright owner by making and marketing it on an industrial scale (the Act defines this as making 50 or more articles to that design), copyright protection would be reduced to 25 years after it is first marketed. As a result, while full copyright protection would continue to be given to the artistic work which embodied this design (e.g. a painting or a statue) it would not be an infringement to copy the industrial articles embodying that design once the 25-year period had expired.

14.4.1 INDUSTRIAL DESIGNS AND COPYRIGHT: SECTION 51

In brief, section 51 of the CDPA ensures that while the copying of a design document will continue to be a straightforward infringement of copyright, it will not infringe copyright to make an article to the design recorded in the document or to copy an article made to that design. For the purposes of section 51, 'design' means any aspect of shape or configuration other than surface decoration. However, the making of an object to a design recorded in a design document or the copying of an object embodying that design may well be an infringement of any UDR embodied in the finished articles. Two cases which looked at section 51 were *BBC Worldwide v Pally Screen Printing*[71] and *Mackie Designs Inc. v Behringer.*[72] *BBC Worldwide* concerned a company which was making T-shirts carrying unauthorized images of the 'Teletubbies', well-known television characters. The company was sued by the BBC for copyright infringement. The High Court held that there was an arguable defence under section 51 because the images were indirect copies of articles which had been made to original three-dimensional designs, which were not themselves works of artistic craftsmanship. *Mackie Designs* concerned circuit diagrams which

---

[70] See 14.5.   [71] *BBC Worldwide Ltd v Pally Screen Printing Ltd* [1998] FSR 665.
[72] *Mackie Designs Inc. v Behringer Specialised Studio Equipment (UK) Ltd* [2000] ECDR 445.

the claimant alleged had been copied. It was held by Pumfrey J in the High Court that these diagrams were design documents within the meaning of section 51(3) and therefore their copying did not constitute copyright infringement. Instead, they fell to be protected as UDRs.

More recently, the Court of Appeal considered sections 51 and 52 (s. 52 had not yet been repealed) and design right protection in *Lambretta v Teddy Smith*. We have rehearsed the facts of the case when looking at the exceptions to UDR protection, more specifically surface decoration. It is worth noting, however, that the claimant did not argue that the overall design of its track-top was new. Rather, the claimant argued that the design's originality lay in its colourways, which had been recorded in design documents. The claimant alleged that the defendants had not only infringed its UDRs (and as we have seen failed in this claim) but also that the defendants had infringed its artistic copyright in the design documents. The defendants argued, inter alia, that section 51 of the CDPA provided a defence against copyright infringement. In the High Court, Etherton J held that Teddy Smith but not Next had copied the claimant's track-tops, but that design right could not subsist in the design and in any event section 51 offered a defence to infringement. The claimant appealed arguing, inter alia, that Etherton J had wrongly applied section 51. Jacob LJ held, in a majority judgment, that he had not:

Jacob LJ:

34. Section 51 does not apply if the design document is itself for an artistic work. So if it is for, say a sculpture, the defence does not apply. And in relation to certain kinds of artistic works, Parliament has decided that even if s. 51 does not apply, the term of protection (normally 70 years from year of author's death) is reduced if there is industrial production of the work. The details of this are to be found in s. 52 and the statutory instrument made thereunder. The provision broadly carries on the regime formerly existing under s. 10 of the Copyright Act 1956 but only for those artistic works for which s. 51 does not provide a total defence. For present purposes the significance is the period of protection. Even for artistic works identified in the statutory instrument which are reproduced industrially the period is much greater than that for UDR—25 years from first marketing in the case of works within s. 52. For other artistic works the period is 70 years from the year of death of the author.

35. Mr Wyand [for the claimant] submits that if Lambretta do not have UDR, then they must have rights in artistic copyright—that Parliament cannot have intended to leave a 'hole' between UDR and ordinary copyright rights. He relies on what was said by Jonathan Parker J in *Mark Wilkinson*:

s. 51 of the 1988 Act removes copyright protection from designs which are protected by design right. The twin concepts of copyright and design right are thus rendered mutually exclusive.

36. He suggests that Jonathan Parker J was thereby saying you get UDR or ordinary copyright—there are no gaps. Now it is generally the case that that is so—but I do not think Jonathan Parker J was intending to say that it was always and necessarily so. Whether or not there is a 'gap' or 'hole' on the facts of a particular case must in the end depend solely upon the language used to create the rights concerned.

[According to Jacob LJ, to accept the contention that there could never be a 'gap' between copyright protection and protection as a UDR would be to accept the principle that anything worth copying was worth protecting, an axiom he said which 'goes too far' and, in any event, is not unequivocally supported by the case law. He continued:]

38. Accordingly I approach the question of whether s. 51 provides a defence with no pre-conceived bias one way or the other and without regard to the fact that I have concluded that there is no UDR in the colourways as such. All depends on the meaning of s. 51 in context. And as the judge rightly observed s. 51 is obviously not simply saying 'anything protected by UDR is not protected by artistic copyright', as it has the other way round in s. 236.

39. Now, apart from the colourways, there is no doubt that Mr Harmer's drawing is a 'design document'. Does the fact that 'surface decoration' is excluded from the definition of 'design' for the purpose of s. 51 make any difference? I think not. For these colourways are not just colours in the abstract: they are colours applied to shapes. Neither physically nor conceptually can they exist apart from the shapes of the parts of the article. It is not as though this surface decoration could subsist on other substrates in the same way as, for instance, a picture or logo could. If artistic copyright were to be enforced here, it would be enforced in respect of Mr Harmer's whole design drawing. But that is not allowed by s. 51. I think the judge put it elegantly when he said ([74]):

> Such an approach... would appear to give rise... to an impossible task. It would require the Court to consider the existence and infringement of copyright in respect of the juxtaposition of colourways divorced from the shape or configuration of the article in question, even though the shape and configuration of Lambretta's garment provide the borders of the colourways and the means by which the colourways are juxtaposed.

40. Accordingly I think Etherton J was right to hold that s. 51 barred the claim here. I am reinforced in this view by the bizarre oddity that would otherwise arise—that Lambretta would have a much longer period of protection (25 years from first marketing) than if they have a proper UDR, for instance by actually designing a new garment rather than just (for I here ignore the stripes and logos) colouring an old one.

Lucasfilm Ltd v Ainsworth[73] also considered sections 51 and 52. In this case, the director of the *Star Wars* movies alleged, inter alia, copyright infringement in the helmets and armour worn by the Imperial Stormtroopers in the *Star Wars* films. Ainsworth had played a part in their design and manufacture and was now offering replicas for sale to the public. The High Court held that the helmets and the armour were neither sculptures nor works of artistic craftsmanship. It followed that the original drawings on which they were based were not artistic works but design documents. As a result, Ainsworth had a defence under section 51.

14.5 THE FUTURE OF THE INTERFACE BETWEEN DESIGN PROTECTION AND COPYRIGHT

The government put into law the repeal of section 52. This decision stems in large measure from the *Flos SpA v Semeraro* decision at the CJEU. The facts of the case are simple although the law is not.

---

[73] [2008] EWHC 1878 (Ch); [2009] EWCA Civ 1328; [2011] UKSC 39: see Chapter 2 on copyright.

Flos SpA v Semeraro Casa e Famiglia SpA Case C-168/09 [2011] ECDR 8

The case concerns the interpretation of Article 17 of the Community Designs Directive (Directive 98/71). Article 17 provides:

> A design protected by a design right registered in or in respect of a Member State in accordance with this Directive shall also be eligible for protection under the law of copyright of that State as from the date on which the design was created or fixed in any form. The extent to which, and the conditions under which, such a protection is conferred, including the level of originality required, shall be determined by each Member State.

Article 17 was implemented by Italy in April 2001. Flos brought proceedings against Semeraro in the Milan District Court, alleging that it had imported and marketed a lamp, called the 'Fluida', which imitated the aesthetic features of its own, classic 'Arco' lamp. The lamp, which had been created in 1962, had not been registered as a design and hence its design was in the public domain in 2001. Subsequently, in 2007, Italy had introduced a new law (Article 329 of the Industrial Copyright Code), which provided that protection afforded to industrial designs under Italian copyright law would not be enforceable against parties who manufactured products incorporating designs which were in or had entered into the public domain before April 2001. The Italian court in an interim judgment held that the lamp was eligible for copyright protection and had been slavishly imitated by Semararo. The question for the CJEU was whether designs in the public domain before 2001 either because they were never registered as designs (as was the case with the Arco lamp) or because their registration had lapsed, could now be precluded from copyright protection in this way or whether this would offend against Article 17. In relation to designs which had not been registered before 2001, the CJEU held that the relevant law was to be found in the Information Society Directive (Directive 2001/29):

> 34 However, it is conceivable that copyright protection for works which may be unregistered designs could arise under other directives concerning copyright, in particular Directive 2001/19, if the conditions for that directive's application are met, a matter which falls to be determined by the national court.
>
> [Turning to designs which had been registered, but by 2001 had fallen out of protection, the Court held that art. 17 was relevant:]
>
> 35 As regards the second case (that of designs which have entered the public domain because the protection resulting from registration has ceased to be effective), although the first sentence of art. 17 of Directive 98/71 provides that a design protected by a design right registered in or in respect of a Member State is also eligible for protection under the law of copyright of that State as from the date on which the design was created or fixed in any form, the second sentence of art. 17 allows the Member States to determine the extent to which, and the conditions under which, such a protection is conferred, including the level of originality required.
>
> 36 However, the second sentence cannot be interpreted as meaning that Member States have a choice as to whether or not to confer copyright protection for a design protected by a design right registered in or in respect of a Member State if the design meets the conditions under which copyright protection is conferred.

37 Indeed, it is clear from the wording of art. 17 of Directive 98/71 and particularly from the use of the word 'also' in the first sentence thereof, that copyright protection must be conferred on all designs protected by a design right registered in or in respect of the Member State concerned.

...

39 Nor does the fact that the Member States are entitled to determine the extent of copyright protection and the conditions under which it is conferred affect the term of that protection, since the term has already been harmonised at EU level by Directive 93/98.[74]...

43 That reasoning must also hold true in relation to the revival of copyright protection for designs which were previously protected by another intellectual property right. Indeed, in view of recitals 2 and 3[75] in the preamble to Directive 98/71 national law transposing the directive cannot—without undermining both the uniform application of the directive throughout the European Union and the smooth functioning of the internal market for products incorporating designs—preclude copyright protection in the case of designs which, although being in the public domain before the date of entry into force of the national law concerned, at that date meet all the requirements to be eligible for such protection.

44 Accordingly, the answer to the first question is that art. 17 of Directive 98/71 must be interpreted as precluding legislation of a Member State which excludes from copyright protection in that Member State designs which were protected by a design right registered in or in respect of a Member State and which entered the public domain before the date of entry into force of that legislation, although they meet all the requirements to be eligible for such protection.

The CJEU then turned to the second and third questions which, taken together, ask whether Article 17 allows a Member State to exclude from copyright protection designs which, although they meet all the prerequisites for copyright protection, had entered the public domain. The CJEU held that there would be a legitimate concern for the effect of renewed protection on third parties who in good faith had reproduced those designs while they were in the public domain. In Italy, there had been a ten-year moratorium following the introduction of Article 17 during which the protection of the relevant designs was unenforceable against those who had manufactured the designs before 2001. According to the CJEU, it was possible to provide measures which would protect third parties from acts which took place before copyright was revived, and to enforce the law only against future acts where copyright has been revived. However, according to the CJEU this period must be reasonable. For example, it held that a ten-year transitional period did not appear to be justified by the need to safeguard the economic interests of third parties acting in good faith, since it is apparent that a shorter period would also allow the part of their business that was based on earlier use of those designs to be phased out. Ten years would also be a substantial period for the copyright owner to lose copyright protection. In 2007, Italy had abolished the ten-year moratorium and had made copyright unenforceable indefinitely against product manufacture from designs in the public domain before 2001. Not surprisingly, such a broad measure found no favour with the CJEU, especially because it did not specify which third parties would

---

[74] Copyright Term Directive.
[75] These recitals relate to the need for harmonization of design protection to prevent the distortion of competition within the single market.

be protected, nor did it allow copyright enforcement against copying which took place after 2001 in relation to these designs.

The CJEU concluded:

> 65 In view of all the foregoing considerations, the answer to the second and third questions is that, art.17 of Directive 98/71, must be interpreted as precluding legislation of a Member State which—either for a substantial period of 10 years or completely—excludes from copyright protection designs which, although they meet all the requirements to be eligible for copyright protection, entered the public domain before the date of entry into force of that legislation, that being the case with regard to any third party who has manufactured or marketed products based on such designs in that State—irrespective of the date on which those acts were performed.

The decision in *Flos*, although apparently technical in nature, had considerable consequences for the UK design regime and particularly the interrelationship between copyright and designs. In particular, it suggested that Member States would have to protect original designs as copyright works under the same term as under the Information Society Directive (as interpreted in *Infopaq*).[76] Furthermore, it would also appear that the length of protection for such designs must be for 70 years plus life of the creator and this would be true even for designs which had fallen into or were previously in the public domain. Such a reading of the *Flos* decision of course meant that section 52 of the CDPA was no longer tenable. Following *Flos*, the government introduced section 74 of the Enterprise and Regulatory Reform Act 2013 which was intended to remove the exception in section 52. However, section 74 did not commence immediately because of difficulties in agreeing the transitional provisions felt necessary to protect businesses which would need to clear existing stock embodying designs which had relied upon the section 52 exception. In its first attempt at drafting the transitional provisions, the government put the transitional period necessary for the depletion of existing stock at five years. This period was challenged and the government accepted it was too long. The UK IPO subsequently launched a consultation to consider, among other things, the length of the transitional period. The consultation was, according to the UK IPO, directed at creators of works of artistic craftsmanship such as designers, at rightsholders such as licensees, at manufacturers, importers, and retailers of replicas of these works, and at publishers, museums, and educational establishments thus neatly illustrating the wide range of interests which this change in legislation would affect.[77] Following the consultation, repeal of section 52 came into force in July 2016. There was also a transition period until January 2017, to allow for depletion of stocks which were the subject of previous contracts. Lionel Bently considered the question of who would benefit the most from the changes which would be set in train by the *Flos* decision.

L. Bently, 'The return of industrial copyright' [2012] EIPR 654 at 671

In his article, Bently argues that the CJEU made the wrong decision in *Flos* and that the UK is being too hasty in implementing it. His first concern relates to copyright

---

[76] *Infopaq International A/S v Danske Dagblades Forening* Case C-5/08 [2009] ECR I-6569.
[77] UKIP, 'Consultation on transitional arrangements for the repeal of section 52 of the Copyright, Designs and Patent Act 1988', p. 1.

protection. He believes that the *Flos* decision is part of a longer term trend on the part of the CJEU attempting to harmonize copyright law, particularly through its interpretation of the Information Society Directive, and as evidenced in the *Infopaq* decision,[78] in a way that had not necessarily been agreed by Member States. He goes on to suggest that even if such harmonization were justifiable in relation to copyright, there was nothing to suggest that the directive was meant to lead to a similar harmonization of design protection. Indeed, Article 17 of the Designs Directive appears to mandate the reverse: that Member States have the freedom to determine the interface between design protection and copyright protection. He writes:

Thirdly, and most concerning of all, in approaching the question of cumulation of design protection with copyright, neither the ECJ nor the UK IPO appears interested in matters of policy. The Court is focused on harmonisation as an end in itself and the IPO on compliance with its understanding of the *Flos* judgment. Reading between the lines, the UK Government has been threatened by lobbyists and the reform of s.52 is driven by fear of liability. The *Impact Assessment* says that there is no need for consultation, and regards it as 'proportionate' to advocate a policy based on snippets of 'evidence' gleaned from previous submissions to it from lobbyists in the furniture industry and their compatriots. The IPO admits that the reform of s.52 will harm consumer welfare as 'classic designs'—those that are more than 25 years old—will be re-monopolised. Replicas, currently available at 15 per cent the price of the 'original', will no longer be available. But no opportunity has been given for *consumers* to be consulted—though it is not obvious who would represent those interests, as even the Labour spokesman in the Commons supported the change. Moreover, the *Impact Assessment* significantly underestimates the other costs that will arise, partly because of its focus on furniture and three-dimensional design (when s.52's existing role also importantly extends to the exploitation of two-dimensional designs), and because it fails to acknowledge the section's immunising effects on certain secondary uses (which formerly were permissible because subs.(2) added that 'anything may be done in relation to articles so made, without infringing copyright in the work'). In short, the repeal of s.52 will create a whole host of new situations where permissions are required (and right holders are difficult to locate). While these costs are evident, the public benefits from the extension are non-existent or speculative: in terms of incentives, there is no reason to think that design investment decisions are ever based on returns from exploitation more than 25 years into the future; and clearly, there is no benefit from lengthening the copyright protection afforded in relation to designs that already exist. The statements of the Minister that the change would 'encourage innovation and investment in design' are supported by the flimsiest of argument in the *Impact Assessment*. And no 'new evidence' is offered to explain why the balance of interests between designer and owner, and competitors and consumers, should be thought best to be drawn differently today than in 1988 or indeed 1994–5 when the Government successfully negotiated to retain s.52.

This criticism is particularly telling, as the Government, in adopting the *Hargreaves Review, Digital Opportunity: An Independent Review of Intellectual Property and Growth*, purported to approve the *Review*'s recommendation on evidence-based policy-making. Having warned of the dangers of policy-making based on 'lobbynomics', Hargreaves had proposed that:

'Government should ensure that development of the IP System is driven as far as possible by objective evidence. Policy should balance measurable economic objectives against social

[78] The Information Society Directive and *Infopaq International A/S v Danske Dagblades Forening* Case C-5/08 [2009] ECR I-6569 are discussed in Chapter 2 on copyright.

goals and potential benefits for rights holders against impacts on consumers and other interests. These concerns will be of particular importance in assessing future claims to extend rights or in determining desirable limits to rights.'

Unfortunately, in rushing to remove s.52, the Government has not heeded this advice.

14.6 CONCLUSION

At the beginning of this chapter we saw how the reforms to UK design protection in 1988 were motivated in part by an attempt to deny possibly indefinite protection to certain designs which were commercially exploited. According to Bently, the result of the repeal of section 52 may well be the return of this 'industrial copyright'.[79] It remains to be seen if Bently is correct in his prediction. What does seem likely, as has been suggested by the UK IPO, is that since the passage of the Designs Directive, different design protection in Member States may hamper the functioning of the common market. Indeed, the Intellectual Property Act 2014 sought to introduce some relatively uncontroversial elements of harmonization, particularly in the area of UDRs, precisely for this reason,. For example, as we have seen, the Act introduced defences to UDR infringement so that a design right would not be infringed by acts which were done privately and for non-commercial purposes. These defences already apply to the CUDR. However, perhaps the most controversial aspect is that the Act does not have as its aim further harmonization; it is instead the criminalization of registered design infringement where there is deliberate copying. The proponents of this change argued that it would deter widespread piracy and bring the sanctions for RD infringement into line with those which may be applied to copyright infringers. However, it has been argued by others that such a change will hamper innovation especially as, in relation to registered designs, there are no defences either of reverse engineering or that the design was independently created (as with copyright). Nor is the boundary between deliberate copying and simply unintentional infringement clearly defined. Whether or not one supports such a change may also depend on the credence one gives to the idea that criminal sanctions act as a deterrent, especially in relation to an offence which may not be high on the list of the government's law enforcement priorities. As a result, there must always be a danger that introducing criminal sanctions will inevitably privilege those larger enterprises which can afford, and are willing, to bring private prosecutions.

FURTHER READING

D. Beldiman and C. Blanke-Roeser, 'European design law: considerations relating to protection of spare parts for restoring a complex product's original appearance' (2015) 46 IIC 915.

E. Derclaye, *'Flashing Badge Co Ltd v Groves*: a step forward in the clarification of the copyright/design interface' [2008] EIPR 251.

---

[79] The repeal was included in the Enterprise and Regulatory Reform Act 2013.

A. Kingsbury, 'International harmonisation of designs law: the case for diversity' [2010] EIPR 382.

UK IPO, *Consultation on the Reform of the UK Design's Legal Framework* (2012), <http://webarchive.nationalarchives.gov.uk/20140603093549/http://www.ipo.gov.uk/consult-2012-designs.pdf>.

R. Wong, 'Changing the landscape of the intellectual property framework: the Intellectual Property Bill 2013' [2013] CTLR

INDEX